International Encyclopedia of the Social Sciences, 2nd edition

International Encyclopedia of the Social Sciences, 2nd edition

VOLUME 7
RABIN, YITZHAK–SOCIOLOGY, MICRO-

William A. Darity Jr.
EDITOR IN CHIEF

MACMILLAN REFERENCE USA
A part of Gale, Cengage Learning

GALE
CENGAGE Learning

Detroit • New York • San Francisco • New Haven, Conn • Waterville, Maine • London

International Encyclopedia of the Social Sciences, 2nd edition
William A. Darity Jr., Editor in Chief

LIBRARY OF CONGRESS CATALOGING-IN-PUBLICATION DATA

International encyclopedia of the social sciences / William A. Darity, Jr., editor in chief.—2nd ed. v. cm. Rev. ed. of: International encyclopedia of the social sciences / David L. Sills, editor. c1968–c1991.
   Includes bibliographical references and index.
   ISBN 978-0-02-865965-7 (set hardcover : alk. paper)—ISBN 978-0-02-865966-4 (v. 1 hardcover : alk. paper)—ISBN 978-0-02-865967-1 (v. 2 hardcover : alk. paper)—ISBN 978-0-02-865968-8 (v. 3 hardcover : alk. paper)—ISBN 978-0-02-865969-5 (v. 4 hardcover : alk. paper)—ISBN 978-0-02-865970-1 (v. 5 hardcover : alk. paper)—ISBN 978-0-02-865971-8 (v. 6 hardcover : alk. paper)—ISBN 978-0-02-865972-5 (v. 7 hardcover : alk. paper)—ISBN 978-0-02-865973-2 (v. 8 hardcover : alk. paper)—ISBN 978-0-02-866141-4 (v. 9 hardcover : alk. paper)—ISBN 978-0-02-866117-9 (ebook : alk. paper)
   1. Social sciences—Dictionaries. 2. Social sciences—Encyclopedias. I. Darity, William A., 1953– II. Title: Encyclopedia of the social sciences.
   H40.A2I5 2008
   300.3–dc22

2007031829

0-02-865965-1 (set)	0-02-865970-8 (v. 5)
0-02-865966-X (v. 1)	0-02-865971-6 (v. 6)
0-02-865967-8 (v. 2)	0-02-865972-4 (v. 7)
0-02-865968-6 (v. 3)	0-02-865973-2 (v. 8)
0-02-865969-4 (v. 4)	0-02-866141-9 (v. 9)

This title is also available as an e-book.
ISBN 978-0-02-866117-9; 0-02-866117-6
Contact your Gale representative for ordering information.

Printed in the United States of America
3 4 5 6 7 8 14 13 12 11 10 09 08

Editorial Board

Contents

Contents

R

____·____

RABIN, YITZHAK
1922–1995

At a time when Israel's global economic and political prominence was on the rise, the nation's prime minister, Yitzhak Rabin, was tragically gunned down. The three shots fired into Rabin's back on the night of November 4, 1995, also pierced through a newly emerging Israel. As Israel began to forge significant political bonds with its Arab neighbors after years of territorial conflict, an Israeli law student, Yigal Amir, assassinated Rabin out of religious conviction. Rabin's premature death left questions as to whether or not his objectives for a peaceful, economically strong Israel would be fully realized. This article discusses Rabin's political and societal contributions to Israel, his relationship with Palestine, and the impact of his untimely death on Israeli politics and its relations with Palestine.

During Rabin's early years, Israel struggled for national independence. Rabin was born in Jerusalem on March 1, 1922. A little over twenty years later, Rabin fought in the 1948 War of Independence, from which the Jewish population in Palestine could claim Israel as an official state. In 1968, Israel successfully fought against Egypt, Syria, and Jordan during the Six Day War, in which it gained control of the Gaza Strip, the Sinai Peninsula, the West Bank, and the Golan Heights.

Not long after, Rabin entered politics with minimal political experience. In 1974, the incumbent prime minister, Golda Meir of the Israeli Labor Party, stepped down after vociferous public calls for her resignation after Israel's failure in the Yom Kippur War of 1973. Israel suffered a large number of casualties and the loss of limited territory in the Sinai Peninsula to Egypt and Syria during this war. Since Rabin was free from blame, he won the election for prime minister and took the oath of office on June 3, 1974. He faced numerous challenges as a political leader during a tumultuous time in Middle East history.

As prime minister from 1974 to 1977, Rabin contributed greatly to Israel in both the domestic and international arenas. He strategically forged a closer relationship with the White House and the U.S. State Department, a process that began during his tenure as Israeli Ambassador to the United States. This relationship was made evident when Richard Nixon became the first U.S. president to visit Israel. The visit was also a way for Nixon to resurrect his falling public stature during the Watergate trials, according to Rabin's memoirs. This bond became significant as Rabin sought and garnered U.S. support for arms sales to Israel. Rabin also succeeded in finalizing a 1975 interim agreement with Egypt, in which Israel agreed to pull back from the Sinai Peninsula.

Rabin exhibited more skill in his second term as prime minister, from 1992 until his assassination in 1995. Israel and Palestine remained in conflict over the establishment of Israel as a separate state. Yet Rabin and Yasser Arafat, the leader of the Palestinian Liberation Organization (PLO), signed the Declaration of Principles (DOP), which aimed to terminate Israel's occupation of the Gaza Strip and the West Bank. The Jewish and Arab leaders later signed the Oslo II agreement, in which Israel agreed to withdraw from seven West Bank towns and the Palestinians agreed to hold elections. The historically significant cooperation between the two leaders created opportunities for political and economic ties with the rest of the Middle East and nonregional states.

The Arab-Israeli tensions resulted in divisions within Israel itself. Rabin sought to resolve Israel's conflicts with its Arab neighbors, especially Palestine, through political negotiation. However, some Jewish citizens such as Amir felt betrayed by the Oslo II accords. Amir saw the agreement as handing over land given to the Jews by God to Palestine. He felt that what he perceived as betrayal could only be rectified through murdering Rabin.

A focus on the free market contributed to Israel's economic growth. Israel's economic policy shifted away from socialist ideology towards a liberal economic policy, and in the early 1990s Israel experienced an annual growth rate of over 5.5 percent. At the same time, unemployment dropped below 7 percent. Israel's economic stability attracted more foreign investment.

Ultimately, Rabin's premature death had a long-lasting effect on Israel's relationship with the rest of the Middle East. Many years later, Israel still struggles with questions of its identity, democratic order, the future of occupied territories, and the chance for peace with Palestine.

SEE ALSO *Arab-Israeli War of 1967; Arafat, Yasir; Meir, Golda; Nobel Peace Prize*

BIBLIOGRAPHY

Horovitz, David. 1996. *Shalom, Friend: The Life and Legacy of Yitzhak Rabin.* New York: New Market Press.

Kurzman, Dan. 1998. *Soldier of Peace: The Life of Yitzhak Rabin.* New York: HarperCollins.

Peri, Yoram, ed. 2000. *The Assassination of Yitzhak Rabin.* Stanford, CA: Stanford University Press.

Rabin, Yitzhak. 1979. *The Rabin Memoirs.* Boston: Little, Brown.

Sarita D. Jackson

RACE

The concept of race as a categorization system for human beings did not exist formally until the late eighteenth century. Most analysts (e.g., Feagin and Feagin 1999; Allen 1994; Roediger 1991; Omi and Winant 1994) have linked the inception of the biologically based idea of distinct races of human beings to European colonization of the New World. Although prior to this time human beings certainly distinguished between themselves in many ways, these distinctions tended to be based upon tribal, clan, ethnic, or national differences that stemmed from place of residence/territory or shared belief systems rather than on innate, genetic characteristics. However, as capitalist-based exploitation of certain (often darker-skinned) groups began in the form of chattel slavery and other abuses of humanity, those in power began turning to science as a way to rationalize the oppressive conditions to which these groups were consigned. The rush to develop these pseudoscientific claims might have been spawned in part by the need of the colonizers to assuage their guilt and to resolve the cognitive dissonance and contradictions evident in rising new societies that prided themselves on freedom and democracy even as they relegated certain groups in their societies to a nonfree, even subhuman status (Horsman 1997). While the "science" that developed the idea of race is certainly discredited by today's standards, the social ramifications of humans having separated themselves into races still remain firmly intact. As the Thomas theorem once stated, "when men define situations as real, they are real in their consequences" (Thomas and Thomas 1928, p. 572). Thus, although the idea of race as a classification system of human beings is what social scientists call socially constructed rather than biologically based, it still is an enduring category of social analysis. It is so not because of its genetic or biological basis, but because of the power it has wielded as an idea to create dividing lines between different classes of human beings across the globe (Graves 2004).

BEFORE RACE

Prior to the eighteenth century, human beings were recognizing differences between themselves as they crossed national and continental borders in exploration and trade. Sometimes these differences would be reflected upon positively and at others, negatively, especially when groups clashed over territory and power. For example, there are Biblical writings where African kingdoms and Jewish kingdoms are regarded as allies of generally equal worth and status. And in Greek and Roman periods, these two societies expressed a great respect for the learning they gleaned from African cultural developments. Even as occasional negative images of blackness (associated with sin, devil, and non-Christianity) were expressed, "these views were never developed into a broad color consciousness viewing Africans as a greatly inferior species" (Feagin 2000, p. 71). Thus, although human beings reflected upon their own differences as they made contact with each other throughout time, there was generally a mix of negative and positive imagery, and prior to the idea of race, no discussion of an altogether inferior or superior species attached to physical differences yet existed.

From the 1400s to the 1600s, as colonization and enslavement expanded, the Spanish and other Europeans began to use consistently negative language to describe the African human beings they enslaved. This pattern was coupled with positive evaluations of their own group. However, these evaluations still did not amount to explicitly racial designations. The Europeans' negative assessments of Africans at this point were rooted in cultural and religious differences rather than in any biological, unchanging facts of their physical chemistry. For instance, Europeans described themselves as rational and civilized while they described Africans as uncivilized and uncontrolled. Further, the Africans not being Christian resulted in Europeans characterizing them as "heathens," and later in North America, European settlers used the same line of thinking toward the Native Americans (Feagin 2000; Takaki 1993). In fact, in the 1600s, a European named François Bernier (1625–1688) even developed a hierarchy of groups ranking them from the most primitive and civilized to the least, placing Europeans at the top and Africans at the bottom (Feagin and Feagin 1999).

However ethnocentric and biased these claims were, they were based upon the assumption that these were cultural differences emanating from shared, learned beliefs rather than body composition or other unchangeable biological inheritances. Indeed, in the case of the Native Americans, for a brief time, the colonists in power considered the possibility that Native Americans could be civilized and thus considered equal by converting them to Christianity (Takaki 1993). These positions acknowledging a common human *capacity* for acquiring knowledge across all skin color gradations (even as it was perceived as underutilized or underdeveloped for some) still ran counter to later notions of biologically grounded races.

RACE AS IDEOLOGY AND SOCIAL RELATIONSHIP

Several scholars have identified the conception of human races as a key part of the development of a racist ideology (e.g., Feagin 2000; Yetman 2004). An ideology is a belief system intended to rationalize and justify existing social arrangements. In this way the concept of race is a decisively social concept because it is not observed as existing independent of the "racialized social systems" (Bonilla-Silva 1997) that hold it in place. Feagin identifies three dynamics that crystallized by the late 1700s to result in a clearly racist (as opposed to nationalist or cultural) ideology: "(1) an accent on physically and biologically distinctive categories called 'races'; (2) an emphasis on 'race' as the primary determinant of a group's essential personality and cultural traits; and (3) a hierarchy of superior and inferior racial groups" (Feagin 2000, p. 79). Thus, at this point in history, no longer are human differences attributed first and foremost to national, regional, and cultural variations. Instead, they become perceived in a biologically determined (static, unchanging) way, and the differences begin to be encoded into hierarchical categorization schemas that connote superior and inferior species of human beings.

The language of race as a pseudobiological category of humans emerged first in the 1770s with the German philosopher Immanuel Kant (1724–1804). As noted by Emmanuel C. Eze in his 1997 publication, Kant's categorization hierarchy for "races of mankind" was laid out as follows:

Stem genus, white brunette;

First race, very blond (northern Europe), of damp cold;

Second race, copper-red (America), of dry cold;

Third race, black (Senegambia), of dry heat;

Fourth race, olive-yellow (Indians), of dry heat.

Roughly two decades later, another German scholar (of human anatomy) named Johann Blumenbach (1752–1840) ventured into similar territory of racial hierarchies founded on what he viewed as biological premises. Ivan Hannaford noted in his 1996 work that Blumenbach's categories were conceptualized in the following order (top to bottom; superior to inferior):

Caucasians (Europeans)

Mongolians (Asians)

Ethiopians (Africans)

Americans (Native Americans)

Malays (Polynesians)

Blumenbach was the one who coined the term Caucasian simply because he felt the Europeans he observed in the Caucasus mountains were the most beautiful, and he erroneously concluded that the first human remains were found there (Gould 1994). Yet the power of this pseudoscience remains in contemporary consciousness, as some modern-day Americans who view themselves as white, for example, refer to themselves as Caucasian, even when their genealogy hails from nowhere near the Caucasus mountains from which this category got its name. It is work like this that laid the groundwork for the centuries that followed, with human beings across the globe viewing themselves as members of distinct racial groups. These groupings were never just nominal categories; they were always hierarchically arranged and structured by dominance (Hall 1980).

An important point to note about these racial categories is that they did not just come to have meaning simply because a couple of scholars penned these categorizations systems and they attained popularity. They were reified because racialized social systems were structured around them. That is, the social relations of the day mirrored the order that the categories suggested. They would not have acquired such powerful social meaning without the systems that held them in place. Thus, one way to conceptualize race is a way of relating within a particular racial social system. Since its inception in the eighteenth century, the meaning of any particular race changes over time and is culturally specific. A single individual could be deemed one race in one society but move or travel to a different society (or even between states in the same society, as in the case of the United States) and be categorized as a different race. Its basis for meaning resides in a particular society's racialized social system and not within an individual body. Some social scientists use the term reification to describe this process of turning a social relationship into a thing in and of itself. As noted by Margaret Radin, once reified, race "acquires a 'phantom objectivity,' an autonomy that seems so strictly rational and all-embracing as to conceal every trace of its fundamental nature: the relation between people" (Harris 1998, p. 107).

USING BLOOD TO DETERMINE RACE

Although the social distinction of a race of human beings was often based upon physical characteristics, the question of which physical characteristics were used to determine race and in what proportion has varied greatly across cultures and across time. These distinctions are usually set by those in power for a distinctly political purpose. For example, in the United States, the so-called "one-drop rule" predominated for all of the nineteenth and well into the twentieth century. This rule stated that an individual having even a distant ancestor who was categorized as black (conceived as one drop of black blood) also made that individual black as well. It is important to note that this determination was not, of course, made from blood testing but rather from knowledge of the individual's family tree and the racial categorizations (socially) attached to each member. This rule served the political purpose of limiting the numbers of persons who could cross the racial dividing line to become white and enjoy all the perquisites and privileges thereof. In the United States, chattel slavery was officially permitted and governmentally sanctioned until the Emancipation Proclamation of 1865. However, shortly into the nineteenth century, no further importation of slaves from overseas was permitted under the Constitution. Thus, it was convenient for the white patriarchal powers of the country that any offspring resulting from the sexual exploitation of their black female slaves (even though these children were also half white) would still be considered their own property and not eligible for freedom (Graves 2004). However, even after slavery was abolished, individuals who were defined as black by the one drop rule had severely curtailed rights, and many lived in a status that was similar to slavery except in name, due

to sharecropping, the convict lease system, and white terrorism holding all of this in place.

According to court records, in order to escape this awful fate, many individuals attempted to remove their black racial categorizations by way of the law. What fraction of black blood was needed in order to categorize one as black? In Louisiana, for example, it was one-32nd of "black blood" that made someone into "black." The U.S. Census identified the racial categories of Negro, Mulatto (one-half black blood), Quadroon (one-fourth black blood) and Octoroon (one-eighth black blood) as late as 1890 (Lee 1993). When individuals were not able to attain legal freedom from blackness but were somewhat light-skinned, they sometimes participated in passing by portraying themselves as white. It is notable that such passing activities almost always occur when someone categorized as an "inferior" race attempts to pass as a member of the "superior" race and not the other way around. This indicates how race is explicitly hierarchical and designed to keep dividing lines between who does and who does not receive the full rights and privileges of citizenship in any given society.

In the contemporary context in the United States, the pseudoscientific notion of a blood quantum (one-fourth) has to be proven in order for citizens to be able to racially categorize themselves as American Indian. Additionally, this one-fourth fraction of Native American blood must be with a tribe that is officially acknowledged and sanctioned by the federal government (Thornton 2001). In early 2006 there were about 569 such tribes (Taylor 2006). In order to get one's tribe recognized by the government, one goes through a lengthy process of forms and bureaucracy, which is sometimes a challenge for older members of a tribe struggling with the level of literacy in bureaucratic language that these forms require. Thus, there are probably many more U.S. citizens who consider themselves to have Native American ancestry than are officially counted by the federal government, who estimates they are only about 1 percent of the total population. This official count, estimated by the U.S. Census, experienced a sizable increase between the 1960 and 1990 censuses. Researchers pointed out that this "growth" in the American Indian population was not due to increased births, and certainly not to migration, but to the increase in individuals who decided to categorize themselves as Native American (Thornton 2001; Nagel 1995). This finding again underscores the socially constructed basis of race.

RELIGION, ECONOMICS, AND SHARED STIGMA AS RACE

While examining one's family tree and ancestors is one way that societies go about determining who belongs in which race, occasionally, other factors are used. For example, government officials sometimes transform religious groups into races. Adolf Hitler (1889–1945) during Nazi Germany spoke of the Jews as a race and structured gruesome genocidal public policy around this claim. Additionally, the U.S. Census records show that in 1930 and 1940, Hindu was given as a choice for racial categorization (Lee 1993). Besides these cases of religion being racialized, sometimes, one's social class is used as a marker for race. In Brazil there is a saying *o dinheiro embranquece*, which means "money whitens." Because there are many mixtures of skin types in Brazil, skin tone combines with socioeconomic status to create the notion of race. For example, if a person is of a mixed skin tone but is dressed professionally and holds a prestigious position, that person may be considered white while a person with an even lighter skin tone who appears impoverished might be labeled black (Taylor 2006).

In a minority of cases, groups who are not in the majority racially sometimes come together to create a racial group and ask those in power to sanction it as a new race. For example, the pan-ethnic racial category of Asian and Pacific Islander (API) appeared on the U.S. Census for the first time in 1990 (Lee 1993). This race was created by bridging some major differences in terms of national origins, languages, and religions. In fact, the United States had a history of finding favor and disfavor with different ethnic groups that are now in the API category depending on the political and economic climate of the day. When the economy became saturated with Chinese laborers in the nineteenth century, the United States passed the Chinese Exclusion Act. At this time, it was more favorable to be Japanese. However, during World War II (1939–1945) when the federal government placed Japanese Americans (even those who were born and raised in the United States) into internment camps, it was more favorable to be Chinese. Despite these and many other cleavages between the groups that are now united in the API race, the groups came together under a specific political climate in the 1980s when the United States was experiencing an economic recession and some dominant rhetoric blamed a global Asian face for the job loss and downward mobility of those who considered themselves white. Thus, regardless of national origin, many API individuals began to be scapegoats and targets of white hostility and even vicious hate crimes (Espiritu 1992). Perceiving common issues of oppression shared across ethnic lines in the U.S. context was an important motivating factor in the creation of the API race.

Omi and Winant (1994) developed a theory of racial formation that underscores how racial categories such as the API are socially constructed, usually for political ends. Although in the majority of cases of racial formation the state uses its power to control what defines a race and who is allowed to claim membership within it, in a minority of cases (such as the API category), the initiative to construct a racial category comes "from below." These minority individuals still have to find favor with the state in order to make their category official. In the case of the one-drop rule, many people were denied their legal efforts to challenge the state and become recategorized racially. But it is important to note that in the case of the one-drop rule, permission was being asked to join into the dominant group (whites) whereas the API group created a new category that did not upend or challenge the existing racial hierarchy. Similarly, in 2000, a group of individuals who considered themselves multiracial effectively lobbied to change U.S. Census procedure so that for the first time people could check more than one box to define their race. Again, this was a movement from below to create new racial possibilities, and it did not seek to challenge the dominance of the category white. The closer policing of the boundaries of whiteness by the state is indicative of how structured by dominance race is.

DETERMINING WHICH ETHNICITIES GET TO BE WHITE

Unlike ethnicities that are often directly linked to a particular continent, and usually a specific nation, the concept of race is an obviously socially constructed category due to its inability to be traced to any one geographic region. One cannot point to black or white on a map as one can with an ethnicity, such as Chinese, Japanese, Jamaican, Irish, or Mexican. This is particularly evident when studying the dominant category of whiteness. While some might equate the term white with a term such as European American, such terminology conceals how much whiteness has adapted to incorporate various non-European groups over time when it served the purpose of solidifying the material and ideological advantage of the category white in a particular area. For example, although people claiming either Chinese or Japanese ancestry are placed into the API category (usually known as Asian Americans) in the United States, during apartheid in South Africa, individuals with these two ethnicities had very different racial experiences. The Japanese were classified into the white category, enjoying the social privileges of the dominant group, while the Chinese were placed into the "colored" category. Although coloreds were not treated as poorly as those considered Africans, they nonetheless were well below whites on the racial hierarchy (Marger 2006). Thus, when it was crucial and beneficial for South Africa to maintain positive economic relations with Japan, it was not in their best interests to consign Japan's citizens to second-class status. Treating the Japanese as whites meant that South African whites could still cash in on the material advantages that came from trading and doing business with the Japanese in an increasingly globalized marketplace in which China was not yet a key player.

In the U.S. context, the Irish and the Jews are two examples of ethnic groups that, although still predominantly European, were not regarded as white upon arrival into the country and had to "earn" their incorporation into whiteness. In the early nineteenth century, the Irish arrived in a mass migration, escaping famine and British oppression. They had no kind of shared identity with the largely British white majority in the United States since the Irish saw the British as their oppressors. Furthermore, the Irish found themselves still excluded outright from many of the best jobs and were even targets of the exaggerated big-lipped, ruddy-skinned caricatures that students of history would typically associate with African Americans. Yet when the political question of the abolition of slavery reached front and center by the middle of the 1800s, the side that the Irish chose to take en masse would be an important deciding factor in whether they became incorporated into whiteness. To side with the slaves, they perceived, would consign them to the second-class citizenship they had just worked so hard to flee in their native land. In coming out decidedly antiabolition on the slavery question, already speaking the English language, and attaining access to some key positions in civic life (particularly in New York City), the Irish solidified their position into the dominant race, white, by the middle of the nineteenth century (Allen 1994; Roediger 1991; Takaki 1993).

The Jews also faced the kind of in-between racial status upon first arriving to the United States that the Chinese faced by being categorized as colored in South Africa. The immigrant Jews certainly were not as ostracized, disenfranchised, and terrorized as African Americans were, but they were not at first deemed worthy of receiving the full benefits of whiteness. They were excluded from most major universities and were victims of prejudices and ethnic slurs (Takaki 1993). Further illustrating the point that race is a relational category, it was the outright exclusion of blacks from the educational and housing benefits of the post-World War II GI Bill that catapulted Jews into middle-class status. Not unlike the situation of the upper class Brazilians, Jews gained the favor of whiteness by their newly acquired socioeconomic status during an economically prosperous era of U.S. history. This prosperity was generated in part by huge government subsidies for both college scholarships and home mortgages, which could be characterized as the nation's first affirmative action program, giving all those deemed white a leg up over their African American counterparts. Although many blacks technically were eligible for these benefits due to their service in great numbers to the military during World War II, they were often unable to cash in on them when prejudiced southern commanders would give them dishonorable discharges for no particular legitimate reason. Moreover, since the Fair Housing Act was not passed until the late 1960s, it was perfectly legal for African Americans to be excluded from buying any of the quality housing to which those deemed white had full access. The events of this time period have been identified as the major factor contributing to the movement of Jewish Americans from nonwhite to white (Brodkin 1998).

STATE-CREATED CATEGORIES VERSUS PERSONAL IDENTITIES

While one's state-defined race clearly plays a crucial role in whether one can access the full material benefits of a society, due to its explicitly hierarchical basis, it is also the case that individuals are not completely without agency in navigating their relationship to these racial categories. People all over the globe have always resisted their oppression in various ways. For example, a U.S. professional golfer named Tiger Woods resisted the society's one-drop rule categorization of himself as African American and invented the term Cablinasian to encompass his Caucasian, black, Indian, and Asian heritage (Taylor 2006). Furthermore, there is a large group of U.S. citizens who think of themselves racially as Latino or Hispanic even though the nation's census does not allow them the option of identifying this as their race (unless they write it in as "Other," as many do). The census only includes the racial choices of White, Black/African American, Asian Pacific Islander, Native American Indian, and Other but lists various Hispanic national origins under a separate ethnicity question. This structure actually encourages persons of Latino heritage to either identify as a white Hispanic or a black Hispanic (as 50% did in 2000), further reifying the country's dichotomous black–white divide. Nonetheless, as this group of persons with Latino heritage in the United States grew exponentially by the advent of the twenty-first century, national conversations began to occur about the inadequacy of the state categories for race to adequately measure their experiences (Swarns 2004).

Because of the extreme occupational, residential, and social segregation that continues to exist in the United States, distinct cultural and ethnic patterns have come to be associated with these state-identified racial categories. For example, due to their exclusion from white churches, African Americans developed decisively different worship patterns even from those who shared their same denominations as Christians. Additionally, due to the many prohibitions during slavery of African Americans from socializing and congregating with each other, they also developed their own distinct linguistic patterns. Cultural developments and distinctions like these often lead to people talking about feeling (or not feeling) black, white,

Asian, and so on. France Winndance Twine found that some young women of African descent who had mixed parentage and grew up in affluent suburban communities stated that they did not feel black until they came to college campuses where they were not the only token minority and together with others developed a more politicized understanding of racial identity (Twine 1997). Conversely, many whites who subscribe to a colorblind racial ideology state that they do not feel white or see themselves as white at all (McKinney 2005; Bush 2004). Nonetheless, due to the sedimentation of racial inequality (Oliver and Shapiro 1995) where whites collectively transmit their "ill-gotten gains" from slavery and segregation in the form of wealth to succeeding generations (Feagin 2000), these whites still gain a material advantage from being white even if they do not see themselves that way.

Beyond feeling culturally and emotionally linked (or not) to particular racial identities, some individuals may eschew state-created racial categories for other reasons. When perceiving that the dominant culture has a particular disdain for individuals of a certain race, new immigrants may seek to distance themselves from that racial categorization, especially when the dominant culture's tendency is to lump them into that negatively perceived category. For example, some members of immigrant groups who would be classified as blacks in the United States, such as Samoans, West Indians, and Haitians, have been found to distance themselves from the racial category of black due to the pervasive antiblack stereotypes they encounter about such things as work ethic and dedication to education (Waters 1999). Similarly, sensing negative prejudices about Mexicans in the United States, some Cuban Americans and other South American Latinos have chosen to stress their national heritages over a more global racial identity as Hispanic (Fernandez-Kelly and Schauffler 1994). Although it is difficult to escape the systemic benefits or lack thereof of being deemed within a particular racial group (as a pseudoscientific birthright), individuals certainly do participate upon occasion in challenging, at least at the personal identity level, their affiliation with an assumed racial group.

SOCIAL CONSTRUCTION, MATERIAL REALITY

Race is not skin color, nor is it ethnic identity. It is not reducible to genetics. Indeed, there is much more genetic and physiological variation within the members of any given race than between individuals of different races. It has been estimated that the overlap between genetic material of people of any two racial groups is about 99 percent, so less than 1 percent of physiological differences can be explained by race (Lewontin 1996). Moreover, eventually, all genetic material of human beings traces back to Africa,

where the earliest human remains were found (Feagin 2000). It has been established that any separate race (other than the human race) is not an actual scientific category and is, instead, a social construction. The assertion that race is a social construction, though, should not be confused with the notion that race is a complete fabrication only needing deconstruction (or simply ignoring/discrediting) to no longer be relevant. Even if governments decided to stop recording the racial categorizations of their citizens (as many outside of the United States have), race would still continue to be a fundamental organizing principle in society.

As has been demonstrated, the concept of race originated as an ideology meant to justify colonization and exploitation of people who happened to be, usually, darker-skinned than their exploiters. Material conditions between those who were eventually to be considered separate, superior/inferior races were already starkly unequal by the time the pseudoscientific category of race was formalized. Rigid laws enforcing the so-called superior racial group's advantages and the so-called inferior group's disadvantages continued for centuries. These chains have only been lifted, as of early 2006, for a few decades, and the material advantage/disadvantage gap has been so solidified that people's ways of thinking, being, and doing are still very much tied to this way of relating called race. Moreover, the pseudoscientific claims of racial difference in intelligence, athletic/physical ability, and other characteristics are constantly resurging into the present day. People are also finding other ways to further racialized understandings of the world without even mentioning race by using various code words and rhetorical strategies to camouflage what, in the end, has a very similar effect in organizing the social world into superior and inferior beings (Bonilla-Silva 2003).

Thus, regardless of how socially constructed race is, for better or for worse, society is stuck with its legacies. The rigid boundaries it was invented to enforce have created distinct cultures and ways of being. To even expect that these racial categories could eventually remain in society in a more benign way as nominal ways of distinguishing between separate but equally valued cultural groups is to confuse race with ethnicity. Race's raison d'etre was never solely to distinguish between various national and cultural heritages; it was always proposed in a hierarchical order, with attached value judgments of superior/inferior and corresponding material advantages or disadvantages. Until society addresses the material foundations of race and rectifies the resulting imbalances, simply deciding to erase race linguistically from the vocabulary will hardly get rid of it as a fundamental organizing principle of social life.

SEE ALSO *Marriage, Interracial; Miscegenation; Race Mixing; Race Relations; Racialization; Racism*

BIBLIOGRAPHY

Allen, Theodore W. 1994. *The Invention of the White Race Volume 1: Racial Oppression and Social Control.* New York: Verso.

Bonilla-Silva, Eduardo. 1997. Rethinking Racism: Toward a Structural Interpretation. *American Sociological Review* 62 (3): 465–480.

Bonilla-Silva, Eduardo. 2003. *Racism Without Racists: Color-blind Racism and the Persistence of Racial Inequality in the United States.* Lanham, MD: Rowman & Littlefield.

Brodkin, Karen. 1998. *How Jews Became White Folks and What That Says About Race in America.* Rutgers, NJ: Rutgers University Press.

Bush, Melanie E. L. 2004. *Breaking the Code of Good Intentions: Everyday Forms of Whiteness.* Lanham, MD: Rowman & Littlefield.

Espiritu, Yen Le. 1992. *Asian American Panethnicity: Bridging Institutions and Identities.* Philadelphia: Temple University Press.

Eze, Emmanuel C. 1997. Immanuel Kant: On the Different Races of Man. In *Race and the Enlightenment: A Reader*, ed. Emmanuel C. Eze, 38–48. London: Blackwell.

Feagin, Joe R. 2000. *Racist America: Roots, Current Realities, and Future Reparations.* New York: Routledge.

Feagin, Joe R., and Clairece Booher Feagin. 1999. *Racial and Ethnic Relations.* 6th ed. Upper Saddle River, NJ: Prentice Hall.

Fernandez-Kelly, M., Patricia Schauffler, and Richard Schauffler. 1994. Divided Fates: Immigrant Children in a Restructured US Economy. *International Migration Review* 28: 662–689.

Gould, Stephen J. 1994. The Geometer of Race. *Discover* (November): 65–69.

Graves, Joseph L., Jr. 2004. *The Race Myth: Why We Pretend Race Exists in America.* New York: Dutton.

Hall, Stuart. 1980. Race Articulation and Societies Structured in Dominance. In *Sociological Theories: Race and Colonialism*, ed. UNESCO, 305–345. Paris: UNESCO.

Hannaford, Ivan. 1996. *Race: The History of an Idea in the West.* Baltimore: Johns Hopkins University Press.

Harris, Cheryl I. 1993. Whiteness as Property. In *Black on White: Black Writers on What It Means to Be White*, ed. David R. Roediger, 103–118. New York: Schocken Books.

Horsman, Reginald. 1997. Race and Manifest Destiny: The Origins of American Racial Anglo-Saxonism. In *Critical White Studies: Looking Behind the Mirror*, ed. Richard Delgado, and Jean Stefancic, 139–144. Philadelphia: Temple University Press.

Marger, Martin N. 2006. *Race and Ethnic Relations: American and Global Perspectives.* 7th ed. Belmont, CA: Thomson Wadsworth.

McKinney, Karyn D. 2005. *Being White: Stories of Race and Racism.* New York: Routledge.

Lee, Sharon M. 1993. Racial Classifications in the US Census: 1890–1990. *Ethnic and Racial Studies* 16 (1): 75–94.

Lewontin, Richard C. 1995. *Human Diversity.* New York: W. H. Freeman.

Nagel, Joanne. 1995. American Indian Ethnic Renewal: Politics and the Resurgence of Identity. *American Sociological Review* 60: 947–965.

Oliver, Melvin L., and Thomas M. Shapiro. 1995. *Black Wealth/White Wealth: A New Perspective on Racial Inequality.* New York: Routledge.

Omi, Michael, and Howard Winant. 1994. *Racial Formation in the United States: From the 1960s to the 1980s.* New York: Routledge & Kegan Paul.

Roediger, David. 1991. *The Wages of Whiteness: Race and the Making of the American Working Class.* New York: Verso.

Swarns, Rachel L. 2004. Hispanics Resist Racial Grouping by Census. *New York Times*, October 24.

Takaki, Ronald. 1993. *A Different Mirror: A History of Multicultural America.* 1st ed. Boston: Little Brown.

Taylor, Howard F. 2006. Defining Race. In *Race and Ethnicity in Society: The Changing Landscape*, ed. Elizabeth Higginbotham, and Margaret L. Andersen, 47–54. Belmont, CA: Thomson/Wadsworth.

Thomas, William Isaac and Dorothy Swaine Thomas. 1923. *The Child in America: Behavior Problems and Programs.* New York: Alfred A. Knopf.

Thornton, Russell. 2001. Trends among American Indians in the United States. In *America Becoming: Racial Trends and Their Consequences*, ed. Neil J. Smelser, William Julius Wilson, and Faith Mitchell, 135–169, Washington, DC: National Academies Press.

Twine, France Winddance. 1997. Brown-Skinned White Girls: Class, Culture, and the Construction of White Identity in Suburban Communities. In *Displacing Whiteness: Essays in Social and Cultural Criticism*, ed. Ruth Frankenberg, 214–243. Durham, NC: Duke University Press.

Waters, Mary C. 1999. *Black Identities: West Indian Immigrant Dreams and American Realities.* New York: Russell Sage Foundation.

Yetman, Norman. 2004. Prejudice and Discrimination. In *Race, Ethnicity and Gender: Selected Readings*, ed. Joseph F. Healey, and Eileen O'Brien, 8–20. Thousand Oaks, CA: Pine Forge Press.

Eileen O'Brien

RACE AND ANTHROPOLOGY

The history of anthropology has been closely identified with the study of race. In the early twenty-first century the concept of race is highly contested among anthropologists, some of whom claim that it does not exist in either biology or society except as an objectionable, stigmatizing fiction. Its problematic biological status has led some to assume a "no-race" stance that resonates with the color-blind ideology that has gained popularity in some segments of U.S. society. Color blindness denies the extant social significance and the experiential and institutional materiality of race, races, and racial inequalities.

Race is an ideologically charged and invidious social distinction (Berreman 1972). As a social and often legally codified classification, it is applied to populations presumed to share common physical, biological, or natural attributes believed to be heritable. The "naturalizing" effect of many racial discourses translates into claims that the social disparities linked to racial divisions exist naturally rather than having emerged as a result of human practices and inventions. Due to the imprecision of what physical variation, biology, and nature actually mean and the slippage between culture and biology within any cultural context, race is difficult to define in a manner that clearly differentiates it from ethnicity, nationality, or even gender. The permanence and fixity conventionally associated with nature and biology are questionable due to "the human organism's [and nature's] constant state of change"—often in response to human interventions (Wade 2002, p. 6). A cross-cultural approach reveals that in certain parts of the world (e.g., Latin America) racial identification can shift, and the extent to which it is based on appearance, ancestry, or sociocultural status varies. Anthropological inquiry is rethinking and attempting to provide clearer operational definitions for the basic categories around which the social analysis of race has been built. Terms such as *phenotype, nature, biology, blood,* and *heredity* must be scrutinized in view of the unspoken assumptions underpinning them. Rethinking the parameters of race is being done, from different angles, in all of the discipline's subfields: social and cultural anthropology, anthropological linguistics, archaeology (particularly historical archaeology), and biological anthropology (especially the specialty in which a critical biocultural approach is employed).

Although race has long been a gloss for human biological variation, they are not the same. During the eighteenth and nineteenth centuries along with the first half of the twentieth, the race concept was used to make sense of the diversity of human phenotypes, which were assumed to index fundamental biological and sociocultural differences. Biological variation is more complex than the physiognomic diacritics that came to signify race in the broad geographically based taxonomies formulated in 1735 by the Swedish botanist Carolus Linnaeus (1707–1778) and in 1795 by the German professor of medicine Johann Friedrich Blumenbach (1752–1840). Beneath the skin's surface are differences of blood type and strings of DNA. However, genetic variation among human beings is small. Humans are 99.9 percent alike genetically, with most of

the difference "involv[ing] modest degrees of variation in the frequency of shared genes" (IUAES). Most of this is within groups rather than between them. Socially targeted differences ignited the imagination of folk theorists and scientists, who drew on the popular consciousness to construct the formal typologies conferred the legitimacy of science.

Skin color, hair texture, and morphological traits were visible markers used to develop universal taxonomies for classifying human populations during the age of European exploration and colonial expansion. These differences were linked to social and moral characteristics that stereotyped and rank-ordered the world's populations in a global hierarchy (Fluehr-Lobban 2005). These hierarchical classifications naturalized perceived cultural variation and culturalized what was defined as nature. They also justified the colonial expansion that gave rise to a modern world system of culture, power, and political economy in which privileged western Europeans exercised supremacy over the heterogeneous peoples, habitats, and resources of the world. These structures of domination were predicated on the land alienation, coerced labor, and repressive state policies that racialized colonial landscapes, with the transatlantic region playing a central role in the transfers of value that were a catalyst for the Industrial Revolution (Williams 1944; Wolf 1982). This momentous transition in social evolution occurred in the context of the transatlantic slave trade and related forms of enslavement established throughout the Americas.

Although color/phenotype prejudice preexisted the modern world system, race as a worldview (Smedley 2007) and material relation did not emerge until the "post-1400s western European racist order" (Sanjek 1994, p. 8). According to St. Clair Drake (1911–1990), skin-color prejudice and slavery converged for the first time in the New World's colonies of exploitation where the conditions for racial slavery arose (Drake 1987). This transformation laid the foundation for a global racial hierarchy in which sub-Saharan Africans represented the most extreme variant of cultural and racial difference. The primitive savagery attributed to Africa and other peripheralized zones of the world system represented the binary opposite of western Europe's purportedly advanced civilizations.

A chapter in the multinational history of racial typologies is that in which Count Arthur de Gobineau (1816–1882) elaborated the notion of the natural inequality of human races and Aryan supremacy in his *Essai sur l'inégalité des races humaines* (Essay on the Inequality of Human Races, 1851–1855). The part of this history that is usually omitted is that Joseph-Anténor Firmin (1850–1911), a Haitian who belonged to the Anthropology Society of Paris, wrote *De l'égalité des races humaines: Anthropologie positive* (The Equality of the Human Races: Positivist Anthropology, 1885), a robust rebuttal and alternative approach to the study of humankind (Fluehr-Lobban 2005, pp. 110–116). Similar debates occurred in other national and regional contexts, including Latin America, where interpretations of Charles Darwin's (1809–1882) evolutionary theory were informed by cultural orientations significantly different from those of Anglo North America. The Anglo-dominant United States emphasized the permanence and mutual exclusivity of race and that whiteness was constructed along lines of purity. In Brazil and elsewhere in Latin America, whiteness was tied to the idea, goal, and social process of race mixing and its implicit ideal, whitening—becoming white by marrying up the social scale or by acquiring wealth and assimilating socially valued cultural and linguistic characteristics.

Throughout the nineteenth and at least half of the twentieth centuries, scientific racism or racialism (Lieberman 2003) was espoused within theological and secular varieties of monogenesis and polygenesis. At the height of the antislavery movement, polygenists, claiming that a single genesis could not account for the diversity of the world's peoples, honed the technical capacity of phrenology and craniometry to measure differences. They also promulgated their research results through scientific outlets, popular culture, and political debate. Samuel T. Morton (1799–1851), Josiah Clark Nott (1804–1873), and George Gliddon (1809–1857), who constituted the core of the early American school of anthropology, attempted to substantiate the hierarchical ranking of the races, with the Caucasoid at the top, the Mongoloid in the middle, and the Negroid at the bottom. Louis Agassiz (1807–1873), a Harvard professor, supported their polygenetic findings and advised President Abraham Lincoln (1809–1865) that freed blacks were incapable of becoming the equals of whites. Later in the nineteenth and early twentieth centuries, biodeterminism developed along the lines of social Darwinism, couched in Darwinian categories but filtered through Spencerianism. These views underpinned the unilinear evolutionism of Edward B. Tylor (1832–1917) and the physical anthropology of Aleš Hrdlička (1869–1943), leaders in anthropology's professionalization. Anthropology's scientific racism also provided ideological fuel for the eugenics movement. Through sterilization and immigration restrictions, it aimed to limit the growth of poverty, criminality, and intellectual inferiority believed to be concentrated among African Americans, immigrants from southern and eastern Europe, and the poor. Eugenics laws developed in the United States were later used as models for population control policies in Nazi Germany. Also philanthropic support from the United States contributed to the rise of Nazi anthropology (Schafft 2004).

A paradigm shift occurred under the leadership of the Columbia University professor Franz Boas (1858–1942), whose research challenged the dominant perspectives on immigrants and other racialized segments of society. Conceptualizing race, language, and culture as distinct domains (Boas 1911, 1940), he influenced many colleagues and students, including Ruth Benedict (1887–1948), Margaret Mead (1901–1978), Melville Herskovits (1895–1963), Zora Neale Hurston (1891–1960), Ella Deloria (1888–1971, Dakota Sioux), and Ashley Montagu (1905–1999). Montagu (1942) insisted that race was a fallacy and advocated the alternative notions of genogroup and ethnic group. By World War II (1939–1945) Boasianism had become more widely accepted. It cleared the ground for major shifts in the 1960s, when race's biological status was refuted (Livingstone 1962). Many sociocultural anthropologists assumed that race was not useful for understanding social distinctions. This led to a silence concerning structural racism.

The Boasian agenda was not the only antiracist trajectory to influence anthropology. W. E. B. Du Bois (1868–1963) produced critical social analysis that in many respects paralleled Boasian thought (Baker 1998; Harrison 1992). He was part of a tradition of black racial vindication that contested biodeterminist ideas. Early African American anthropologists, trained in leading graduate departments but also influenced by Du Bois's noncanonical public intellectualism, often undertook antiracist scholarship, which entailed negotiating the tensions between mainstream disciplinary approaches and more critical interdisciplinary frameworks. The physical anthropologists Caroline Bond Day (1889–1948) and W. Montague Cobb (1904–1990) along with the social anthropologists W. Allison Davis (1902–1983) and St. Clair Drake exemplify this trend (Harrison and Harrison 1999). Davis and Drake, under W. Lloyd Warner's (1898–1970) supervision, provided important inputs into the collaboratively produced *Deep South: A Social Anthropological Study of Caste and Class* (Davis et al. 1941). Drake and Horace Cayton's (1903–1970) *Black Metropolis* (1945), which became a race relations classic, combined the methods and analytical perspectives of anthropology and sociology. These books' receptions in anthropology were negligible.

After anthropology's "biological revolution," when the discipline was largely silent about social race and racism, Marvin Harris (1927–2001), St. Clair Drake, Eleanor Leacock (1922–1987), Gerald Berreman, and John Ogbu (1939–2003) kept these issues alive, often bringing cross-cultural perspectives and data to bear on them. In the 1980s Virginia Dominguez (1986) and James W. Loewen (1988) explicated the social construction and dynamics of race, including how they related to the social identities of Euro-Americans and Asian Americans. Eric Wolf's (1923–1999) anthropological history of world capitalism (1982) elucidated the differences between ethnicity and race, with race being associated with forced exclusion, stigmatized labor, and other types of dehumanization. Brackette F. Williams (1989) illuminated the ways race and ethnicity operate as distinct yet closely interrelated dimensions of identity formation in projects of imagining, building, and contesting nations.

Since the early 1990s there has been an expanded interest in race (Harrison 1995, 2002). In good part this has arisen because of race's heightened volatility in many parts of the world, especially under the conditions and outcomes of globalization: technologically mediated time-space compression, widening disparities in subsistence security and wealth, new migrations, transnational cultural citizenries, and diasporic identities. Sociocultural anthropologists have investigated the multiple histories and cultural dynamics of race, the persistence of its social significance, the shifts in its meanings, and its overt and covert modalities (Smedley 2007; Baker 1998). Neoracisms without races, the social censorship of talk about race and racism, and race's intersections with gender and class have also captured anthropologists' scrutiny and ethnographic gaze. Research is being undertaken in many parts of the world, from eastern Europe, where postcommunist restructuring has exacerbated discrimination against the region's Roma ("Gypsies"), to the more paradigmatic settings of the United States, South Africa, and Brazil, which have long been a focus of debates over the varieties of racial formation (Scheffel 2005; Sheriff 2001; Wilson 2001).

A great deal of attention has been given to the social life of discourses that biologize or culturalize difference—that is, use notions of culture to produce racializing effects. Linguistic anthropologists have examined language practices that contribute to or resist the dynamics of racialization. Their approach to the racial politics of language may lead them from explicit hate language to covert language whose efficacy is affected by indirect indexes or widely understood but never directly articulated nonreferential meanings (Hill 1998). Critical biocultural anthropologists explore the embodied experiences that affect human exposure to stress and susceptibility to diseases. In their view, race affects the internal and external workings of the body, which is always situated in a nexus of power. These dynamics have health-related outcomes. Racism has concrete consequences for human biology, which is socialized in historically specific contexts of culture, power, and political ecology (Goodman and Leatherman 1998). Historical archaeology is also unburying new layers of understanding about past landscapes of race and racism. Studies of the material cultural remnants of plantation slavery, maroons (runaways), free and freed communities,

and the cultural life of other racialized or subracialized groups (e.g., Irish immigrants) fill in some of the gaps that historiographical research cannot (Orser 1998; Singleton 2006).

Other trends are studies of whiteness, which shift from the traditional focus on racial subordinates (Brodkin 1998; Buck 2001). Critical studies of race and racism are also examining indigeneity, especially in contexts in which the concept of ethnicity has provided the conventional analytical lens (Cowlishaw 1999; Wade 1997). Analyses of nontraditional Indians and African descendants with a history of contact with or even citizenship in Indian nations are disrupting conventional boundaries of classification and identity (Sturm 2002; Warren 2001). There are also studies of racism as a site of human rights violation and of antiracism's place within the international context of human rights struggle (Banton 1996; Harrison 2005).

Finally, anthropologists have been vigilant in challenging the latest revival of biological determinism (e.g., Herrnstein and Murray 1994; *Current Anthropology* 1996) and in detecting the potential dangers of reifying race in the Human Genome Project. The intellectual and ideological heterogeneity of anthropology precludes a consensus. In light of this, it should be of no surprise that the bell curve thesis made sense to Vincent Sarich (1995) or that Glenn Custred coauthored Proposition 209, the 1996 California civil rights initiative that aimed to dismantle affirmative action. Race has figured prominently in anthropology's history of ideas and public engagement. That relationship is likely to persist.

SEE ALSO *Anthropology; Anthropology, Biological; Anthropology, Linguistic; Boas, Franz; Colorism; Determinism, Biological; Drake, St. Clair; Du Bois, W. E. B.; Heredity; Hurston, Zora Neale; Mead, Margaret; Montagu, Ashley; Nature vs. Nurture; Other, The; Race; Racial Classification; Racialization; Racism; Social Constructionism; Social Constructs; White Supremacy; Whiteness*

BIBLIOGRAPHY

Baker, Lee D. 1998. *From Savage to Negro: Anthropology and the Construction of Race, 1896–1954*. Berkeley: University of California Press.

Banton, Michael. 1996. *International Action against Racial Discrimination*. Oxford: Clarendon.

Berreman, Gerald D. 1972. Race, Caste, and Other Invidious Distinctions in Social Stratification. *Race* 13 (4): 385–414.

Blumenbach, Johann Friedrich [1795] 1895. *On the Natural Variety of Mankind*. 3rd ed. In *The Anthropological Treatises of Johann Friedrich Blumenbach*, trans. and ed. Thomas Bendyshe. London: Longman, Green.

Boas, Franz. [1911] 1963. *The Mind of Primitive Man*. Rev. ed. New York: Collier.

Boas, Franz. 1940. *Race, Language, and Culture*. New York: Macmillan.

Brodkin, Karen. 1998. *How Jews Became White Folks and What That Says about Race in America*. New Brunswick, NJ: Rutgers University Press.

Buck, Pem Davidson. 2001. *Worked to the Bone: Race, Class, Power, and Privilege in Kentucky*. New York: Monthly Review.

Cowlishaw, Gillian. 1999. *Rednecks, Eggheads, and Blackfellas: A Study of Racial Power and Intimacy in Australia*. Ann Arbor: University of Michigan Press.

Current Anthropology. 1996. The Eternal Triangle: Race, Class, and IQ. Reviews on *The Bell Curve: Intelligence and Class Structure in American Life* 37 (February supp.): S181.

Davis, Allison, Burleigh B. Gardner, and Mary R. Gardner. [1941] 1988. *Deep South: A Social Anthropological Study of Caste and Class*. Los Angeles: Center for Afro-American Studies, University of California, Los Angeles.

De Gobineau, Arthur. [1851–1855] 1967. *The Inequality of Human Races*. Trans. Adrian Collins. New York: Fertig.

Dominguez, Virginia R. 1986. *White by Definition: Social Classification in Creole Louisiana*. New Brunswick, NJ: Rutgers University Press.

Drake, St. Clair 1987. *Black Folk Here and There: An Essay in History and Anthropology*. Los Angeles: Center for Afro-American Studies, University of California, Los Angeles.

Drake, St. Clair, and Horace Cayton. [1945] 1993. *Black Metropolis: A Study of Negro Life in a Northern City*. Chicago: University of Chicago Press.

Firmin, Joseph-Anténor. [1885] 2000. *The Equality of the Human Races: Positivist Anthropology*. Trans. Asselin Charles. New York: Garland.

Fluehr-Lobban, Carolyn. 2005. *Race and Racism: An Introduction*. Lanham, MD: AltaMira.

Goodman, Alan, and Thomas Leatherman, eds. 1998. *Building a New Biocultural Synthesis: Political-Economic Perspectives on Human Biology*. Ann Arbor: University of Michigan Press.

Harrison, Faye V. 1992. The Du Boisian Legacy in Anthropology. *Critique of Anthropology* 12 (3): 239–260.

Harrison, Faye V. 1995. The Persistent Power of "Race" in the Cultural and Political Economy of Racism. *Annual Review of Anthropology* 24: 47–74.

Harrison, Faye V. 2002. Unraveling "Race" for the Twenty-First Century. In *Exotic No More: Anthropology on the Front Lines*, ed. Jeremy MacClancy, 145–166. Chicago: University of Chicago Press.

Harrison, Faye V., ed. 2005. *Resisting Racism and Xenophobia: Global Perspectives on Race, Gender, and Human Rights*. Walnut Creek, CA: AltaMira.

Harrison, Ira E., and Faye V. Harrison. 1999. *African-American Pioneers in Anthropology*. Urbana: University of Illinois Press.

Herrnstein, Richard J., and Charles Murray. 1994. *The Bell Curve: Intelligence and Class Structure in American Life*. New York: Free Press.

Hill, Joan H. 1998. Language, Race, and White Public Space. *American Anthropologist* 100 (3): 680–689.

IUAES (International Union of Anthropological and Ethnological Sciences). n.d. Proposed Replacement Statement for the UNESCO Documents on Biological Aspects of Race. http://www.leidenuniv.nl/fsw/iuaes/08-race.htm.

Lieberman, Leonard. 2003. A History of "Scientific" Liberalism. In *Race and Ethnicity: An Anthropological Focus on the United States and the World*, ed. Raymond Scupin, 36–66. Upper Saddle River, NJ: Prentice Hall.

Linnaeus, Carolus. [1735] 1806. *A General System of Nature*. London: Lackington, Allen.

Livingstone, Frank B. 1962. On the Non-Existence of Human Races. *Current Anthropology* 3: 279–281.

Loewen, James W. 1988. *The Mississippi Chinese: Between Black and White*. 2nd ed. Prospect Heights, IL: Waveland.

Montagu, Ashley. [1942] 1975. *Man's Most Dangerous Myth: The Fallacy of Race*. 5th ed. New York: Oxford University Press.

Orser, Charles E., Jr. 1998. The Challenge of Race to American Historical Archaeology. *American Anthropologist* 100 (3): 661–668.

Sanjek, Roger. 1994. The Enduring Inequalities of Race. In *Race*, eds. Steven Gregory and Roger Sanjek, 1–17. New Brunswick, NJ: Rutgers University Press.

Sarich, Vincent. 1995. In Defense of *The Bell Curve*: The Reality of Race and the Importance of Human Difference. *Skeptic* 3 (3): 84–93.

Schafft, Gretchen E. 2004. *From Racism to Genocide: Anthropology in the Third Reich*. Urbana: University of Illinois Press.

Scheffel, David Z. 2005. *Svinia in Black and White: Slovak Roma and Their Neighbors*. Toronto: Broadview.

Sheriff, Robin E. 2001. *Dreaming Equality: Color, Race, and Racism in Urban Brazil*. New Brunswick, NJ: Rutgers University Press.

Singleton, Theresa. 2006. African Diaspora Archaeology in Dialogue. In *Afro-Atlantic Dialogues: Anthropology in the Diaspora*, ed. Kevin A. Yelvington, 249–287. Santa Fe, NM: School of American Research Press.

Smedley, Audrey. 2007. *Race in North America: Origin and Evolution of a Worldview*. 3rd ed. Boulder, CO: Westview.

Sturm, Circe. 2002. *Blood Politics: Race, Culture, and Identity in the Cherokee Nation of Oklahoma*. Berkeley: University of California Press.

Wade, Peter. 1997. *Race and Ethnicity in Latin America*. London: Pluto.

Wade, Peter. 2002. *Race, Nature, and Culture: An Anthropological Perspective*. London: Pluto.

Warren, Jonathan W. 2001. *Racial Revolutions: Antiracism and Indian Resurgence in Brazil*. Durham, NC: Duke University Press.

Williams, Brackette F. 1989. A Class Act: Anthropology and the Race to Nation across Ethnic Terrain. *Annual Review of Anthropology* 18: 401–444.

Williams, Eric. [1944] 1994. *Capitalism and Slavery*. Chapel Hill: University of North Carolina Press.

Wilson, Richard A. 2001. *The Politics of Truth and Reconciliation in South Africa: Legitimizing the Post-Apartheid State*. Cambridge, U.K.: Cambridge University Press.

Wolf, Eric. 1982. *Europe and the People without History.* Berkeley: University of California Press.

Faye V. Harrison

RACE AND ECONOMICS

Commentaries by political economists about the concepts of race and ethnicity and the implications of those categories for economic behavior and outcomes date back to the eighteenth century. Classical political economists generally maintained that all groups have comparable abilities to make rational economic decisions. Variations in observed outcomes among groups were explained in terms of history, luck, and incentives. Incentives and markets were seen as especially powerful forces capable of generating convergence in observed outcomes. In contrast, most postclassical economists believed that permanent and semipermanent group differences in desirable wealth-generating characteristics are primarily responsible for differences in levels of development.

Although the Irish were often a principal subject of discussion, the colonization of the Americas and the massive expansion of African enslavement ensured that attention would shift to Native Americans and blacks. Much of that discourse consisted of thinly veiled rationalizations for policies of discrimination, exploitation, and oppression through assertions that the victims were less than fully human. The expropriation of Native American land was justified by a "natural law" argument by which so-called civilized communities were divinely mandated to master and transform that environment.

EARLY THEORIES

Philosophers' theories of Caucasian, Aryan, and Anglo-Saxon racial superiority provided a rubric for distinguishing between the civilized and the uncivilized. The philosopher David Hume (1711–1776) insisted, for example, on the universality of human nature in 1748, but by 1753 he had become a staunch proponent of racial hierarchies. Hume wrote, "I am apt to suspect the negroes and in general all the other species of men … to be naturally inferior to the whites. There never was a civilized nation of any other complexion than white, nor even any individual eminent either in action or speculation." (Morton 2002, p. 3).

Such contrived claims about black inferiority served to justify enslavement. As was noted by Eric Williams, "Slavery in no way implied, in any scientific sense, the inferiority of the Negro" (Williams 1994, p. 29). Supporters of slavery predicted disastrous consequences if blacks were emancipated. The inaccuracy of those predic-

tions did not deter mid-nineteenth-century postclassical economists who were influenced by the writings of anthropologists from fully endorsing notions of differences among racial groups in the capacity to exercise economic rationality. Nonwhites and the Irish were characterized as "lower races," and the category "Africanoid Celt" and an "Index of Nigrescence" were introduced in 1870 to measure how close the Irish were to blacks (Levy and Peart 2002).

DARWIN AND MARX

Charles Darwin's 1859 book *On the Origin of Species by Means of Natural Selection, or, The Preservation of Favoured Races in the Struggle for Life* provided additional fuel for speculations about racial hierarchies, although Darwin and some of his supporters were dubious about the extent to which the dictum "survival of the fittest" could be applied appropriately to human beings. Alfred Russel Wallace, for example, insisted in 1864 that natural selection does not apply to humans because of ethical issues deriving from the phenomenon of human sympathy. However, prominent social Darwinists, including Herbert Spencer (1820–1903) and William Graham Sumner (1840–1910), argued that human progress depends on unbridled competition in all areas of economic life. As individuals sought to improve their circumstances, continuous movement toward the perfection of the human race inevitably would occur.

Karl Marx (1818–1883) was fascinated by Darwin's work, although his views about race were more nuanced than those of most of his contemporaries. Although Marx and Friedrich Engels (1820–1895) envisioned the eventual disappearance of national and ethnic identities through the expansion of global capitalism, Marx recognized that in the interim a variety of social formations were sustainable and that economic progress "does not prevent the same economic basis … from displaying endless variations and gradations in its appearance, as the result of innumerable different empirical circumstances, natural conditions, racial relations, historical influences acting from outside, etc." (Marx 1991 *Capital,* vol. 3, p. 927).

Marx's sensitivity to issues of race and culture is evident in his discussion of Native American societies, in which he expressed special admiration for the Iroquois, highlighting their "sense of independence" and "personal dignity." In addition, his writings are generally devoid of many of the prevailing stereotypes about non-Western traditional societies, including India and pre-Columbian Mexico (Anderson 2002). Nevertheless, the influence of Darwin is suggested by Marx's comments about the dependency of barbaric and semibarbaric countries on civilized ones, indicating that he, like most thinkers of that period, failed to recognize white supremacy as an overarching global phenomenon (Robinson 1983). However, unlike most postclassical economists, Marx believed that differences in levels of social development among groups could be mediated through social interventions rather than reflecting a permanent pattern enshrined by innate genetically or culturally based variations in development potential. He argued that "all this crippling under existing social relations has arisen historically, and in the same way can be abolished again in the course of historical development" (Marx and Engels 1976, p. 425). That view resonated with those of classical political economists who insisted on the efficacy of incentives and markets to produce convergence in economic behavior and outcomes.

RACIAL HIERARCHIES IN POSTCLASSICAL ECONOMICS

Pseudoscientific notions of racial hierarchies can be found in the writings of several prominent postclassical economists, including William Stanley Jevons, Alfred Marshall, Arthur Pigou (1907), John R. Commons, and Irving Fisher (1930). In 1871 Jevons stated: "A man of lower race, a negro, for instance, enjoys possession less, and loathes labour more; his exertions, therefore, soon stop. A poor savage would be content to gather the almost gratuitous fruits of nature, if they were sufficient to give sustenance; it is only physical work which drives him to exertion" (Jevons 1871, p. 183). Those postclassical economists explored a variety of areas in which racial variations in economic rationality were hypothesized to exist, including labor supply, family size, consumption, and savings decisions. Marshall wrote about savage life ruled by custom and impulse in which there was no conception of future planning and rational economic decision-making and people were incapable of steady work. Individuals belonging to the "lower races" were deemed to be especially prone to the consumption of luxury goods and alcoholic beverages (Marshall 1891).

Large-scale migration from southern and eastern Europe to the United States beginning in the last decade of the nineteenth century led to the extension of notions of racial inferiority to those population groups. In 1907 Commons warned, for example, that the new immigrants were genetically inferior and would reduce the genetic quality of the nation. Various postclassical economists characterized those immigrants as "untaxed imports" and advocated eugenics policies to improve the genetic pool of the nation, including measures to encourage fertility among the "superior" genetic stock and reduce fertility among those with "inferior" natural abilities, including permanent segregation, sterilization, and selective restrictions on immigration (Levy and Peart 2002).

As described by William Darity, several researchers who were actively involved with the American Economic Association during its formative years subscribed to the view that African Americans eventually would face extinction as a result of a combination of genetic deficiencies and social maladjustment. Proponents of that view refused to discard the underlying assumptions of black inferiority even after demographic trends contradicted the predictions associated with the "Black Disappearance Hypothesis" (Darity 1994).

REVIVAL OF THE CLASSICAL VIEW

Beginning in the 1930s, the Chicago School played a pivotal role in reviving the classical tradition of treating individuals as possessing equal competence to engage in rational economic decision-making and reestablishing the critical role of incentives and markets in conditioning human behavior. Frank Knight's 1931 critique of the presumed correlation between time preference and race in a 1931 review of Irving Fisher's *Theory of Interest* was a major turning point.

George Stigler and Gary Becker also helped undermine postclassical views about racially distinct time preferences. Becker's well-known "taste" or preference theory of discrimination has determined the contours of discussions about race for most contemporary neoclassical economists (Becker 1957). His analysis was conceived as a response to the failure of economists to examine the phenomenon of racial economic discrimination systematically. Two exceptions to the pattern of neglect of this topic noted by Becker include a 1952 study of black workers in southern industry by Donald Dewey and a 1955 analysis of occupational racial wage differentials by Morton Zeman. In Becker's model social identities are treated as economically nonproductive individual characteristics that may, however, have significant economic consequences. A racial group thus can be treated simply as the aggregation of those individuals identified by a particular classifying parameter, allowing neoclassical economists to ignore the economic implications of individuals' decisions for the intensity of group identification. The key theoretical conclusion flowing from Becker's model is that the competitive forces of the market inevitably undermine the economic impact of racial prejudices, which are presumably irrational. However, the persistence of inequality in outcomes across groups has been documented, and this finding poses a formidable challenge to the efficacy of Becker's model. Among others, Patrick Mason (1999) has suggested that racial discrimination may be consistent with the competitive process.

LATER RECONCEPTUALIZATIONS

Efforts to explain persistent racial differentials have generated two markedly different approaches to reconceptualizing the relationship between race and economic outcomes. One approach reintroduces the postclassical notion of racial hierarchies. Monographs by George Gilder and Charles Murray in the early 1980s assert that differentials in economic outcomes between blacks and whites stem primarily from dysfunctional behaviors endemic to black culture, including willful refusal to adhere to the traditional American values of hard work, self-reliance, future orientation, thriftiness, a strong emphasis on education, and individualism. Economists such as Thomas Sowell and Walter Williams readily integrated aspects of this discourse into their writings in the 1980s, and subsequently the number of subscribers to those views increased significantly (Akerlof and Kranton 2000; Loury 2002). Although claims about black genetic inferiority that were prominent during the postclassical period have been resurrected, few economists have been willing to endorse those claims openly (Herrnstein and Murray 1994).

The second approach to reconceptualizing the ways in which race affects economic behavior and outcomes revives the classical tradition of focusing on the role of incentives and institutions in reducing disparities and is associated with the emergent subdiscipline of stratification economics. Stratification economists conceptualize race as a produced form of personal identity that is responsive to changes in incentives for altruistic versus antagonistic behavior in social interactions. Collective identity is deemed to have economic value even as there are also costs to identity formation. As a consequence, reductions in intergroup wealth differentials are a necessary but not sufficient condition for eroding traditional patterns of collective identification. This conclusion is consistent with Marx's views on the value of culture and institutions. Stratification economists believe that racial disparities and racial discrimination are endemic features of the U.S. economy and social systems that are reproduced by a myriad of institutional practices that require transformation to produce outcomes characterized by sustainable reductions in racial differentials. Like Marx, stratification economists recognize that historical inertia is a powerful barrier to change, leading to caution in making predictions about short-term reductions in racial differentials.

SEE ALSO *Akerlof, George A.; American Economic Association; Culture; Darwin, Charles; Discrimination; Economics; Economics, Classical; Economics, Neoclassical; Economics, Stratification; Fisher, Irving; Hume, David; Immigration; Inequality, Racial; Marshall, Alfred; Marx, Karl; Race; Race and Religion; Racism; Stratification; Williams, Eric*

BIBLIOGRAPHY

Akerlof, George D., and Rachel E. Kranton. 2000. Economics and Identity. *Quarterly Journal of Economics* 115 (3): 715–733.

Anderson, Kevin. 2002. Marx's Late Writings on Non-Western and Pre-Capitalist Societies and Gender. *Rethinking Marxism* 14 (4): 84–96.

Becker, Gary Stanley. 1957. *The Economics of Discrimination.* Chicago: University of Chicago Press.

Bigelow, Gordon. 2003. *Fiction, Famine, and the Rise of Economics in Victorian Britain and Ireland.* Cambridge, U.K., and New York: Cambridge University Press.

Commons, John Rogers. 1907. *Races and Immigrants in America.* New York and London: Macmillan.

Darity, William, Jr. 1994. Many Roads to Extinction: Early AEA Economists and the Black Disappearance Hypothesis. *History of Economics Review* 21: 47–64.

Darity, William, Jr. 2005. Stratification Economics: The Role of Intergroup Inequality. *Journal of Economics and Finance* 29 (2): 144–153.

Darity, William, Jr., Patrick Mason, and James Stewart. 2006. The Economics of Identity: The Origin and Persistence of Racial Identity Norms. *Journal of Economic and Behavioral Organization* 60 (3): 283–305.

Darwin, Charles. 1859. *On the Origin of Species by Means of Natural Selection, or, The Preservation of Favoured Races in the Struggle for Life.* London: J. Murray.

Dewey, Donald. 1952. Negro Employment in Southern Industry. *Journal of Political Economy* 60 (4): 279–293.

Fisher, Irving. 1930. *Theory of Interest as Determined by Impatience to Spend Income and Opportunity to Invest It.* New York: Macmillan.

Gilder, George. 1981. *Wealth and Poverty.* New York: Basic Books.

Herrnstein, Richard J., and Charles Murray. 1994. *The Bell Curve: Intelligence and Class Structure in American Life.* New York: Free Press.

Jevons, W. Stanley. 1871. *Theory of Political Economy.* London: Macmillan.

Knight, Frank H. 1931. Professor Fisher's Interest Theory: A Case in Point. *Journal of Political Economy* 39: 176–212.

Krader, Lawrence. 1975. *The Asiatic Mode of Production: Sources, Development and Critique in the Writings of Karl Marx.* Assen, Germany: Van Gorcum.

Levy, David, and Sandra Peart. 2002. *The Secret History of the Dismal Science: Eugenics and the Amoralization of Economics.* Library of Economics and Liberty. http:www.econlib.org/Library/Columns/LevyPeartdismal6.html.

Loury, Glenn C. 2002. *The Anatomy of Racial Inequality.* Cambridge, MA: Harvard University Press.

Marshall, Alfred. 1891. *Principles of Economics.* London and New York: Macmillan.

Marx, Karl. 1991. *Capital: A Critique of Political Economy.* Vol. 3. Intro. Ernest Mandel. Trans. David Fernbach. London and New York: Penguin Books.

Marx, Karl, and Frederick Engels. 1976. The German Ideology. In *The Collected Works of Karl Marx and Frederick Engels.* Vol. 5, *April 1845–April 1847.* New York: International Publishers; London: Lawrence & Wishart.

Mason, Patrick Leon. 1999. Male Interracial Wage Differentials: Competing Explanations. *Cambridge Journal of Economics* 23: 1–39.

Morton, Eric. 2002. Race and Racism in the Works of David Hume. *Journal on African Philosophy* 1 (1). http://www.africanphilosophy.com/vol1.1/morton.html.

Munro, John. 2004. Roots of Whiteness. *Labour/Le Travail* (54). http://www.historycooperative.org/journals/llt/54/munro.html.

Murray, Charles. 1984. *Losing Ground, American Social Policy, 1950–1980*. New York: Basic Books.

Pigou, Arthur. 1907. Social Improvement and Modern Biology. *Economic Journal* 17 (3): 358–369.

Robinson, Cedric J. 1983. *Black Marxism: The Making of the Black Radical Tradition*. London: Zed Press.

Sowell, Thomas. 1981. *Markets and Minorities*. New York: Basic Books.

Stewart, James. 1997. NEA Presidential Address, 1994: Toward Broader Involvement of Black Economists in Discussions of Race and Public Policy: A Plea for a Reconceptualization of Race and Power in Economic Theory. In *African Americans and Post-Industrial Labor Markets*, ed. James Stewart, 15–38. New Brunswick, NJ: Transactions.

Stewart, James, and Major Coleman. 2005. The Black Political Economy Paradigm and the Dynamics of Racial Economic Inequality. In *African Americans in the U.S. Economy*, eds. Cecilia Conrad, John Whitehead, Patrick Mason, and James Stewart, 118–129. Lanham, MD: Rowman & Littlefield.

Wallace, A. R. 1864. The Origin of Human Races and the Antiquity of Man Deduced from the Theory of Natural Selection. *Journal of the Anthropological Society of London* 2: 158–170.

Williams, Eric. 1994. *Capitalism & Slavery*. Chapel Hill: University of North Carolina Press. (Orig. pub. 1944).

Williams, Walter E. 1982. *The State against Blacks*. New York: New Press.

Zeman, Morton. 1955. A Quantitative Analysis of White-Non-White Income Differentials in the United States in 1939. Unpublished PhD diss., Department of Economics, University of Chicago.

James B. Stewart

RACE AND EDUCATION

Race and education becomes a social issue when educational opportunities are differentially available to members of diverse racial groups within a society.

Educational discrimination has a variety of effects that often lead to interracial conflict. Because education is a major means of social mobility, discrimination in this domain forces less-favored racial groups to occupy lower-status jobs and receive less income. Such results form a vital component in a wider system of racial oppression—as in the former apartheid policies of South Africa and state-mandated segregation in the U.S. South. But educational segregation by race also operates to limit the life chances of discriminated racial groups in nations without such formal systems of oppression, such as Brazil. And in countries where social class and race are highly intercorrelated, as throughout Latin America, racial segregation in schools results directly from intense patterns of residential segregation by class.

Racially segregated schools are the hallmark of racial discrimination in education. Separate schools allow for vastly fewer resources to be provided for the oppressed race. Indeed, racially separate schools are so central to systems of racial oppression that they are tenaciously maintained in the face of efforts to end them. The protracted and only partially successful efforts to end segregated schools in the United States provide a striking illustration.

Public schools did not emerge in the U.S. South until late in the nineteenth century, and these early schools were for whites only. Black schools came later, after formal state laws for racial segregation had been sanctioned in 1896 by the U.S. Supreme Court in *Plessy v. Ferguson*. Although the case involved segregated railroad seating, its decision establishing the formula of "separate but equal" was promptly applied by the white South to schools, which became extremely separate and unequal.

It was fifty-eight years before the High Court overturned *Plessy*. By 1950, in two graduate education cases, the meaning of "equal" went beyond mere parity in brick-and-mortar terms to include such intangibles as faculty reputation and general prestige. The decisions prepared the ground for *Brown v. Board of Education* four years later to hold separate facilities to be inherently unequal. But implementing this unpopular decision has proven difficult.

Critical to the acceptance of mandated social change that runs counter to dominant public opinion is the perception of inevitability. The responses of the white South to the varying firmness of the High Court's rulings illustrate the point. With an uncompromising, nine-to-zero decision in *Brown*, the Court in 1954 generated a strong sense of inevitability. But in 1955 the Supreme Court retreated in its implementation order to a vague "all deliberate speed" formula (*Brown II*). This formula returned the enforcement of desegregation back to southern federal district courts without guidelines. Only when this weak order undermined the sense of inevitability did southern politicians become uniformly defiant and prosegregationist organizations gain momentum. Then the opposition believed *Brown* could be effectively opposed. *Brown II* is not solely responsible for the violent opposition that followed, but its vagueness contributed to the resistance by eroding the strong sense of inevitability that had prevailed.

Consequently, the region's school desegregation did not take hold until the federal courts lost patience between 1968 and 1973 (Orfield and Eaton 1996). This brief period saw court orders achieve sweeping gains—especially in the recalcitrant South but also in the cities of the North and West. By the 1970s the South had more racial desegregation in its public schools than any other region. But this process ended abruptly in 1974 when the Supreme Court reversed direction. In *Milliken v. Bradley* the Court by five to four struck down a metropolitan solution ordered by a district court to remedy the intense racial segregation of Detroit's public schools. What made this decision so regressive is that such remedies were the *only* means available to desegregate the public schools of many of the nation's largest cities (Orfield and Eaton 1996; Pettigrew 1981). Moreover, segregation between city and suburban districts is now by far the major component today in metropolitan school segregation (Clotfelter 2004). Decisions of the High Court from 1974 into the twenty-first century continued this trend, and allowed racial segregation of the public schools to return not only in the South but also throughout much of the United States.

Thus, *Brown* was largely reversed without the High Court ever stating that it was overturning the famous decision. By 2000 black children were more likely to be attending majority-black schools than at any time since the 1960s; 70 percent went to predominantly black schools and 37 percent to schools with 90 percent or more black students. The greatest retrogression during the 1990s occurred in the South, the region that had previously witnessed the greatest gains (Orfield 2001). And Latino school children became more educationally segregated from white children than African American children (Orfield and Eaton 1996).

Supporting this retreat from desegregated schools, the sociologist James Coleman (1926–1995) claimed in a highly publicized speech that urban interracial schools were impossible to achieve because desegregation causes massive "white flight." Desegregation led, he claimed, to whites fleeing to the suburbs and leaving minority concentrations in central city cores. This research had serious weaknesses, and its policy recommendations ignored metropolitan solutions (Pettigrew 1981).

The "white flight" thesis is far more complex than Coleman claimed (Pettigrew and Green 1976). Some whites did move from large cities when school desegregation began, but this movement was neither universal nor permanently damaging. Some cities without any school desegregation also experienced widespread white suburbanization. Other cities experienced little such movement at the time of desegregation. And where so-called "white flight" to the suburbs did occur, it constituted a "hasten-ing up" process; within a few years the loss was what would have been expected without desegregation (Farley, Richards, and Wurdock 1980).

But does school desegregation improve the life chances of African Americans? From the 1970s to the 1990s, black high school completion rates rose sharply. Although less than half finished high school at midcentury, by 2000 the figure approached that of white Americans. During these same years, the mean difference between black and white achievement test scores steadily narrowed (Neisser 1998). White scores were improving, but blacks who entered school during the late 1960s showed especially strong gains—when extensive school desegregation began. Mean racial differences in achievement tests were not eliminated, but they began to close. However, these positive trends stalled and were even reversed by the late 1990s once the federal courts allowed resegregation. Yet these trends are only suggestive, because other factors were also influential—notably, rising black incomes and such effective national educational programs as Head Start.

More to the point, did school desegregation expand opportunities for African Americans in the long term? An array of sociological studies tracked the products of desegregated schools in later life to find answers (Pettigrew 2004). With social class controlled, black children from desegregated schools, when compared with black children from segregated schools, are later more likely:

1. to attend and finish majority-white colleges;
2. to work with white coworkers and have better jobs;
3. to live in interracial neighborhoods;
4. to have somewhat higher incomes;
5. to have more white friends and contacts and more positive attitudes toward whites.

Similarly, white products of desegregation have more positive attitudes toward blacks than comparable whites from segregated schools. In short, desegregated education prepares black and white Americans for an interracial world.

These positive lifetime effects of desegregation are not limited to test score gains—more important is the fact that desegregation enables African Americans to break through the monopoly that white Americans have traditionally had on informational flows and institutional access. Sociologists have identified several interrelated processes underlying this phenomenon (Pettigrew 2004). These processes mirror the harsh fact that life chances in America flow through white-dominated institutions.

Desegregation involves interracial contact. Intergroup contact is one of social psychology's best-established theories. A comprehensive meta-analysis found that 95 percent of 714 independent samples with 250,000 subjects show that intergroup contact reduces prejudice (Pettigrew and Tropp 2006).

Desegregation teaches interracial interaction skills. Given the nation's racist past, neither black nor white Americans are skilled in interracial interaction. The products of desegregated schools have the opportunity to learn these skills. Their anxiety about such interaction is reduced. This is highly useful for both blacks and whites, for it contributes to their willingness to enter biracial environments and their acceptance in these situations.

Desegregation erodes avoidance learning. After long facing discriminatory treatment, some black Americans learn to avoid whites. But this reaction has negative consequences. It closes off for ghetto dwellers the better opportunities that exist in the wider society. And, like all avoidance learning, it keeps one from knowing when the situation has changed. Desegregated schooling overcomes such avoidance.

Desegregated blacks gain access to formerly all-white social networks, such as those that share information about colleges and jobs. This process does not require personal friendships: Weak interpersonal ties are the most informative, because close friends are likely to possess the same information (Granovetter 1983). Interracial schools allow black students to gain access to these networks.

Thus, although it is not a popularly recognized fact, the racial desegregation of America's public schools has led to positive outcomes. But the resegregation of the nation's schools in the twenty-first century threatens to reverse these beneficial processes.

Although the racial scene in the United States has many unique features, social research in other nations suggests that similar intergroup processes operate in schools throughout the world. Additional research is needed, but the separation of groups in schools and other societal institutions, whether the groups are racial or not, appears to have comparably negative effects. Indeed, in some interracial nations such as Brazil, the deleterious effects of separate education may be even greater than in the United States. Educational differences between Brazilians of different skin colors explains much of the nation's variation in racial occupational inequality and its racial gap in white-nonwhite mobility (Telles 2004).

In addition to thwarting beneficial intergroup contact, intergroup separation triggers a series of interlocking processes that make group conflict more likely. Negative stereotypes do not just persist but are magnified; distrust cumulates; and misperceptions and awkwardness typify the limited intergroup interaction that does take place. The powerful majority comes in time to believe that segregated housing, low-skilled jobs, and constrained educational opportunities are justified, even "appropriate," for

the minority. In short, racially segregated schools reproduce racial inequality. Intergroup schools have proven one of the needed antidotes for combating these negative processes—from Northern Ireland to South Africa.

SEE ALSO *Colorism; Cox, Oliver C.; Park, Robert E.; Park School, The; Race; Race Relations; Racism; Sociology*

BIBLIOGRAPHY

Clotfelter, Charles T. 2004. *After* Brown: *The Rise and Retreat of School Desegregation.* Princeton, NJ: Princeton University Press.

Farley, Reynolds, Toni Richards, and Clarence Werdock. 1980. School Desegregation and White Flight: An Investigation of Competing Models and Their Discrepant Findings. *Sociology of Education* 53: 123–139.

Granovetter, Mark S. 1983. The Strength of Weak Ties: A Network Theory Revisited. *Sociological Theory* 1: 201–233.

Neisser, Ulric, ed. 1998. *The Rising Curve: Long-term Gains in I.Q. and Related Measures.* Washington, DC: American Psychological Association.

Orfield, Gary. 2001. *Schools More Separate: Consequences of a Decade of Resegregation.* Cambridge, MA: Harvard University Civil Rights Project.

Orfield, Gary, and Susan E. Eaton. 1996. *Dismantling Desegregation: The Quiet Reversal of* Brown v. Board of Education. New York: New Press.

Pettigrew, Thomas F. 1981. The Case for Metropolitan Approaches to Public School Desegregation. In *Race and Schooling in the City,* ed. Adam Yarmolinsky, Lance Liebman, and Corinne S. Schelling, 163–181. Cambridge, MA: Harvard University Press.

Pettigrew, Thomas F. 2004. Justice Deferred: A Half Century after *Brown v. Board of Education. American Psychologist* 59 (6): 521–529.

Pettigrew, Thomas F., and Robert L. Green. 1976. School Desegregation in Large Cities: A Critique of the Coleman "White Flight" Thesis. *Harvard Educational Review* 46: 1–53.

Pettigrew, Thomas F., and Linda Tropp. 2006. A Meta-Analytic Test of Intergroup Contact Theory. *Journal of Personality and Social Psychology* 90 (5): 751–783.

Telles, Edward E. 2004. *Race in Another America: The Significance of Skin Color in Brazil.* Princeton, NJ: Princeton University Press.

Thomas F. Pettigrew

RACE AND POLITICAL SCIENCE

Although controversies surrounding race have arisen in a variety of nations since at least the sixteenth century, it has only been since the mid-twentieth century that these issues have generated serious attention in the discipline of political science. Beginning primarily in the aftermath of such watershed events as the civil rights movement in the United States, the rise of Fidel Castro in Cuba, and the demise of the apartheid system in South Africa, political scientists have slowly begun to focus on the impact of race in politics. In particular, scholars have examined issues such as the impact of racial group membership and racial attitudes on public opinion and voting behavior, partisanship, and political incorporation.

The literature on race and politics is perhaps most developed in the United States, where race plays a role in the level of support garnered by black candidates. There is little doubt that African Americans represent a small percentage of elected officials nationwide and that self-identified black candidates are rarely elected in majority-white political jurisdictions. It is not at all clear, however, that blacks fare poorly among white voters because of their race. Scholars have sought to get a better grasp on this question by relying upon experimental designs as a way of isolating the effects of candidate race. When white voters are randomly assigned to experimental conditions wherein otherwise identical candidates differ only in their racial background, some studies have found that black candidates are evaluated less favorably relative to white candidates.

Racial considerations do not just figure prominently in biracial contests. Some political scientists argue that the contemporary American party system is primarily based on racial cleavages. According to this view, after the 1964 presidential contest pitting racial liberal Lyndon Johnson (1908–1973) against racial conservative Barry Goldwater (1909–1998), voters began to view the political parties as primarily distinctive on matters of race. This view became solidified with the War on Poverty, which seemed to link the Democratic Party with the aspirations of racial minorities. There is some support for this controversial claim. Although African Americans have been part of the Democratic coalition since Franklin D. Roosevelt's (1882–1945) second term, blacks have supported Democratic presidential candidates—and identified with the party—by increasingly lopsided margins since the mid-1960s. Many whites, on the other hand, are now firmly attached to the Republican Party, and since the late 1960s have consistently supported Republican presidential candidates over their Democratic opponents.

Much of this "realignment" of partisan loyalties has occurred in the American South. Although solidly Democratic since the end of Reconstruction, the South began to abandon the Democratic Party in the 1970s and 1980s. The political science literature has not reached consensus as to whether this is primarily due to racial considerations. For example, some scholars would argue that

social issues such as abortion, gay rights, and prayer in the schools are more important as explanations for the contemporary embrace of the Republican Party among white southerners. However this debate is resolved, there is no doubt that the South remains the most racially conservative region in the United States. Whether the issue is school integration, enforcement of antidiscrimination laws, or increased spending on race-targeted programs, national surveys conducted as recently as the 1990s have consistently shown that white southerners are more conservative than their northern counterparts.

Regional differences have not only emerged from standard survey data but also using experimental methods. James Kuklinski, Michael Cobb, and Martin Gilens (1997), for example, developed an unobtrusive method for gauging racial attitudes. In short, they provide a nationally representative group of respondents with an opportunity to indicate how angry they are at a list of four items, one of which (the experimental condition) includes a specific reference to African Americans, as well as three topics not related to race. A randomly selected half of the sample is asked only about the three nonracial topics (the control condition), and all respondents are assured that no one will be able to determine which specific item makes them angry. However, because of random assignment, if levels of racial resentment are higher in the experimental condition relative to the control, then the differences can only be attributed to racial concerns. With this technique, Kuklinski and his colleagues show that white southerners are far more racially resentful toward blacks than their northern counterparts. This difference is also much greater than the results from traditional surveys.

RACIAL ATTITUDES

Racial schisms and the influence of racial attitudes do not just occur in the United States. Although some scholars have argued that Latin America and the Spanish Caribbean are mostly free from the racial strife associated with the United States, more recent work has called this Latin American exceptionalism thesis into question. For example, Mark Sawyer, Yesilernis Peña, and Jim Sidanius (2004) fielded surveys in Cuba, the Dominican Republican, and Puerto Rico and found that respondents perceived racial hierarchies in their respective countries that were very similar to those in the United States. Whites were consistently perceived as having greater social status, followed by "mulattos" and finally blacks. Similarly, in follow-up work, Sawyer has found that Cubans who identify as white are much more likely than their darker-skinned counterparts to perceive other races as less intelligent and moral.

Another area where scholars are beginning to examine the impact of racial identity and attitudes on public opinion is South Africa. This country has, of course, been wracked with racial divisions since its founding and has only been a multiracial democracy since 1994. James Gibson conducted the first systematic nationwide survey of attitudes on racial identity, national identity, and the Truth and Reconciliation Commission. His 2001 survey included a large number of whites, blacks, "colored," and South Africans of Asian ancestry. Gibson finds that race relations in South Africa are far more complicated than many often assume, with considerable variation on public opinion within racial groups. Nevertheless, whites are far more likely to *not* identify with blacks than are blacks to reject identification with whites. On a more optimistic note, he finds that white South Africans who have greater contact with other races are also more likely to embrace the results from the Truth and Reconciliation Commission.

In the United States, the empirical study of the impact of racial attitudes on policy opinion can be traced to David Sears and Donald Kinder, and their subsequent development of the theory of *symbolic racism* (also sometimes referred to as *modern racism* or *racial resentment*). According to this theory, a new form of racial attitude emerged in the waning days of the civil rights movement. Support for the biological inferiority of African Americans was discredited, but antipathy directed at blacks remained a powerful force among whites. This anti-black affect would, in the aftermath of the urban riots in the late 1960s, merge with the widespread perception that blacks were making unfair demands on the system and not working hard enough to get ahead. According to Sears and Kinder, it is this new form of racism—which blends negative attitudes about blacks with the perception that they violate cherished values such as hard work—that accounts for white opposition to various policies designed to achieve racial equality.

The theory of symbolic racism has sparked a spirited and longstanding debate in the literature as to the manner and the extent to which racial attitudes influence whites' policy preferences. None of the critics insist that racism is nonexistent, or that it has no influence on the policy preferences of white Americans. Instead, controversy has arisen with regard to the ambiguity in the conceptual definition and the measurement of the theory. These criticisms have on occasion hit their mark, as the symbolic racism theorists have modified their measures and sought to specify their model more carefully. Some of the more recent work in this literature has, however, generally supported the theory (see, for example, Sears and Henry 2003).

An emerging literature on the influence of race-based campaign communications also highlights the enduring linkage between race and politics. This work suggests that these communications can be effective, provided they do not rely on overtly racist messages. Specifically, Tali

Mendelberg (2001) has shown that subtle racial cues, such as pairing pictures of African Americans with a standard conservative narrative condemning welfare, increased the role of racial considerations in candidate evaluations. Although this literature is both provocative and promising, scholars have yet to explore the frequency or impact of candidate appeals that invoke race explicitly but in a way that could not be interpreted as "racist."

RACE AND RACIAL MINORITIES

Although most of the racial attitudes literature focuses on the United States and white attitudes about African Americans, an emerging literature has begun to examine the role that race-based political perceptions have on black public opinion. Much of this research can be traced back to the pioneering work of Patricia Gurin, Shirley Hatchett, and James Jackson's 1989 book, *Hope and Independence*. These authors argued that black attitudes about prominent political figures, such as Jesse Jackson and Ronald Reagan (1911–2004), are influenced strongly by race-based perceptions of group solidarity and group consciousness. This work, and much of the literature inspired by it, finds that African Americans' racial attitudes and policy preferences seem to be driven more by their in-group bias rather than out-group animus. Additionally, high levels of in-group identity appear to account for the unprecedented levels of black political unity.

Unlike the study of African American political behavior, there has been comparatively little attention devoted to other racial and ethnic minorities in the United States, such as Latinos, Asian Americans, and Native Americans. This has begun to change, however, as these groups have become an increasingly large share of the American population. Of these groups, the most attention has been devoted to Latino politics. One of the central questions in this emerging field is whether theoretical models designed to explain the broader electorate, or subgroups such as African Americans, can also be applied to Latinos (de la Garza 2004). This comparison with blacks is a common one since both groups are socially and economically disadvantaged relative to whites and both groups tend to support the Democratic Party. One question researchers have asked is: Are Latinos more likely to participate in politics when Latinos seek or have already achieved elective office in the local jurisdiction? This pattern holds for blacks, and some research finds similar effects among Latinos in California. It remains to be seen whether this applies elsewhere in the country. Another issue that arises frequently in this literature is whether Latinos should be treated as a single ethnic group or if national origin is the more salient identity. There is not yet a consensus on this question, although it is clear that Mexican Americans and Puerto

Ricans tend to have different partisan and political preferences compared to Cuban Americans.

With the 2000–2001 Pilot National Asian American Political Study (PNAAPS), scholars have taken their first steps toward understanding the political views of this rapidly growing demographic group. Relying on this groundbreaking dataset, *The Politics of Asian Americans* (Lien et al. 2004) provides a wealth of descriptive information on this diverse population. For example, it reports that most Asian Americans identify with their country of origin rather than with pan-ethnic labels. Additionally, more Asian Americans identify with the Democratic Party than with the Republicans, although about half do not identify with either major party. Although this work is largely descriptive, it represents an important first step in mapping the contours and variations present among this largely foreign-born population. At a minimum, it is clear from the PNAAPS that many of the political theories and hypotheses developed for the larger electorate must be modified when applied to Asian Americans.

SEE ALSO *Affirmative Action; African Americans; Apartheid; Attitudes, Racial; Blackness; Civil Rights Movement, U.S.; Democratic Party, U.S.; Identification, Racial; Japanese Americans; Latinos; Native Americans; Political Science; Politics, Asian American; Politics, Black; Politics, Latino; Race; Racial Classification; Racism; Reagan, Ronald; Reconstruction Era (U.S.); Reparations; Republican Party; Segregation; Southern Strategy; Terror; Truth and Reconciliation Commissions; Violence; Voting Patterns; Whiteness*

BIBLIOGRAPHY

de la Garza, Rudolpho O. 2004. Latino Politics. *Annual Review of Political Science* 7: 91–123.

Gibson, James L. 2004. *Overcoming Apartheid: Can Truth Reconcile a Divided Nation?* New York: Sage Foundation.

Gurin Patricia, Shirley Hatchett, and James J. Jackson. 1989. *Hope and Independence: Blacks' Response to Electoral and Party Politics.* New York: Sage Foundation.

Kinder, Donald R., and David O. Sears. 1981. Prejudice and Politics: Symbolic Racism Versus Racial Threats to the Good Life. *Journal of Personality and Social Psychology* 40: 414–431.

Kuklinski, James H., Michael D. Cobb, and Martin Gilens. 1997. Racial Attitudes and the "New South." *Journal of Politics* 59 (2): 323–349.

Lien, Pei-Te, M. Margaret Conway, and Janelle Wong. 2004. *The Politics of Asian Americans: Diversity and Community.* New York and London: Routledge.

Mendelberg, Tali. 2001. *The Race Card: Campaign Strategy, Implicit Messages, and the Norm of Equality.* Princeton, NJ: Princeton University Press.

Sawyer, Mark Q., Yesilernis Peña, and Jim Sidanius. 2004. Cuban Exceptionalism: Group-based Hierarchy and the Dynamics of Patriotism in Puerto Rico, the Dominican-Republic, and Cuba. *Du Bois Review* 1 (1): 93–114.

Sears, David O., and P. J. Henry. 2003. The Origins of Symbolic Racism. *Journal of Personality and Social Psychology* 85 (2): 259–275.

Vincent L. Hutchings

RACE AND PSYCHOLOGY

Before the formal institutionalization of psychology in the nineteenth century, academics attributed psychological qualities to specific ethnic groups (such attributions can even be found in Aristotle's writings). However, the systematic combination of psychological characteristics with race occurred in the eighteenth century when Carolus Linnaeus (1707–1778) linked varieties of humans ("races") with psychological and social characteristics in his taxonomy. Johann Friedrich Blumenbach (1752–1840) advanced the concept of the *Caucasian* based on his idea that European culture originated in the Caucasus. The term *Caucasian*, still used in empirical psychological studies, has no scientific validity.

In the second half of the nineteenth century, some European scholars suggested that the Caucasian variety divided into two branches, identified as Semites and Aryans. Both were associated with different psychological characteristics and formed the theoretical basis for Hitler's ideology. In the 1860s John Langdon H. Down (1829–1896) studied the structure and function of various organs in "idiots" and "imbeciles." He observed a group of individuals that he characterized as having round faces, flattened skulls, extra folds of skin over their eyelids, protruding tongues, short limbs, and retardation of motor and mental abilities. Down classified this group on the basis of their resemblance to racial groups. He suggested that the physical features and behavioral attributes of these individuals represented typical Mongols—hence the term *Mongolism* for what is now called *Down syndrome*.

Pioneers of social psychology such as Gustave Le Bon (1841–1931) incorporated an ideology of race into their studies of intellectual ability, emotion, and volition. Le Bon understood races as physiologically and psychologically distinct entities that each possessed an immutable race soul. Paul Broca (1824–1880) was convinced that non-European races were inferior and used a variety of scientific studies to prove his preconceived conviction. Francis Galton (1822–1911) argued that Europeans were by nature more intelligent than "primitive races" and suggested the quantification of levels of racial intelligence. In the United States, pioneers of psychology such as

Granville Stanley Hall (1844–1924), the first president of the American Psychological Association (APA), argued that "lower races" were in a state of adolescence, a claim that provided a justification for segregation.

Empirical race psychology was prominent and influential during the first half of the twentieth century. Race psychologists used the accepted methods of the discipline and applied them to the empirical comparison of various groups. An early example is the research emerging from the Cambridge Torres Straits Expedition, which produced psychophysiological data on racial differences. Many race-psychological studies were used to demonstrate the inferiority of certain races and thus were part of the program of *scientific racism*. American race psychologists performed empirical studies on immigrants and were motivated by fears that the "national stock" was declining. They participated in empirically "evidencing" the inferiority of southern and eastern Europeans and African Americans.

Based on the results of the Army Mental Tests, administered to 1.75 million American recruits during World War I, it was concluded that there were inborn racial differences between whites and blacks, and among various European "races." Psychological studies played a role in the Immigration Restriction Act of 1924, which imposed quotas on the allegedly less intelligent European nations. Leading American psychologists participated in race psychology, including two APA presidents: Robert M. Yerkes (1876–1956), who played a decisive role in the army testing, and Lewis Terman (1877–1956), who supported segregated education. Also popular in race psychology was the study of the *mulatto hypothesis*, which suggested that a greater proportion of white "blood" in a black person's ancestry would lead to higher intelligence.

Most of the empirical studies on race carried out in North America and Europe during this period were unable to overcome prejudicial ideas. Research found differences and these differences were frequently interpreted in racist terms. These studies were also unable to challenge the cultural meaning of psychological instruments, concepts, theories, and methods. After World War II and the international recognition that racism was an integral component of the atrocities committed in the name of racial superiority in Europe and Asia, empirical race psychology, which could not overcome its racist connotations, declined significantly. However, contemporary studies on differences among races on intelligence tests continue a racist legacy when these differences are interpreted as representing essential racial divisions in mental life or when ideas of inferiority or superiority are invoked.

Social psychologists began, as early as the 1930s, to shift away from studying race differences to researching prejudice. Some racial studies took on a different perspective and were performed in the context of challenging

racism, especially in the United States, where racial conflict, injustice, and discrimination were still endemic. Kenneth Clark (1914–1995) and Mamie Clark (1917–1983) performed a variety of studies in order to demonstrate the negative impact of prejudice, racism, and discrimination on African American identity. The best-known studies included a "doll test" that assessed whether African American children preferred to play with a brown or white doll and which color they considered nice. Many of the children preferred the white doll and considered it nice. The Clarks interpreted the results as showing that black children had low self-worth, an argument that played a role in court cases concerning desegregation and also in the 1954 *Brown v. Board of Education of Topeka* case, in which the U.S. Supreme Court judged segregation to be unconstitutional.

In the wake of the civil rights movement, Lyndon B. Johnson's War on Poverty, and early educational compensatory programs such as Head Start, a dedicated and high-profile group of researchers personally and ideologically committed to a naturalistic concept of race emerged in Great Britain and North America. In 1969 Arthur Jensen published an article in the *Harvard Educational Review* that challenged the idea of the value of compensatory education. He also suggested that because intelligence had a heritable component, it seemed reasonable to hypothesize that genetic factors might play a role in producing racial differences in IQ. His argument was speculative but had an enormous impact on the field of psychology and on society in general.

From a methodological point of view it is important to understand that even if intelligence has a heritable component, mostly estimated through twin studies, this does not mean that differences *between* groups can be explained through heredity. For example, a heritability estimate of .50 for IQ means that 50 percent of the variability of IQ that one finds within a given population can be attributed to heredity. Hypothetically assume that a researcher finds a heritability of 55 percent in a "white group," 50 percent in a "black sample," and 45 percent in a sample that contains various ethnicities (heritability estimates do not have a single true value and change with environment). These results mean that 55 percent of the differences that can be found *within* the "white group," 50 percent of the differences *within* the "black group," and 45 percent of the differences *within* the "mixed group" can be attributed to heredity. They say nothing about the differences *between* the groups.

In 1994 Richard Herrnstein and Charles Murray suggested in their book *The Bell Curve* that genetic differences might be involved in producing racial differences in IQ. Again, they provided no evidence for this speculation. Beginning in the 1990s J. Philippe Rushton promoted his ideas of a racial hierarchy. He presupposed the existence of three major races (Orientals, whites, and blacks) and has argued that there is a three-way pattern of differences in brain size, IQ, and behavior. For Rushton, whites and Asian developed larger brains and are more intelligent than blacks because gathering food, providing shelter, making clothes, and raising children during long winters was more mentally demanding than accomplishing the same tasks in permanently warm climates. Rushton has not provided any genetic evidence for his interpretations that genes cause racial IQ differences.

The genetic speculations of contemporary race researchers in psychology take place in the context of anthropological and biological research that posits *race* as a sociohistorical and not a natural-biological category. Empirical differences are not interpreted as inborn and as reflecting a natural hierarchy, but as variations that must be understood as the product of cultural difference. Advancements in genetic analyses have shown that the variation within traditionally conceptualized races is much larger than between them. Instead of three or five races one should assume several thousand *populations* that are in the process of changing. Empirical studies that include race as a variable are now often motivated by the idea that a socio-historical concept of "race" should be taken into account when making generalizations in psychology.

Social psychologists have provided alternative and more complex explanations for ethnic group differences than have traditional race psychologists. Experimental *stereotype threat* research conducted by Claude Steele (1997) is of particular significance. It is based on the empirically validated finding that the threat of being negatively stereotyped leads to underperformance in accordance with that stereotype. A negative stereotype is threatening when it provides an explanation for one's actions or experiences, or aligns with one's self-definition. For example, when a test is presented as assessing intellectual ability, black participants underperform in comparison to white participants. When the same test is presented as assessing problem solving unrelated to intellectual ability (and therefore unrelated to stereotypes about black intellectual ability) both groups achieve the same level of performance.

Effects of stereotypes can also be found in other areas. A study examining the stereotype that Asians perform well at numerical tasks has shown that Asian American women performed better than a control group on a mathematics test when ethnic identity was focused on, but worse when their gender identity was highlighted (Shih, Pittinsky, and Ambady 1999). In addition, social psychologists have studied attitudes associated with minority life that increase successful psychological functioning. Robert Sellers has investigated the meaning that African Americans attribute to race in their self-definitions (e.g., Sellers and Shelton 2003). He has developed a conceptual framework as well as instruments to provide a comprehensive assessment of African American racial identity. Instead of focusing on the negative impact of prejudice and discrimination, he has studied the protective role of identity. He has analyzed how African Americans are able to live normal lives in a context of discrimination. This has allowed him to provide a more precise picture of African American realities.

Other researchers have looked at interethnic interaction and its consequences from the standpoint of both minorities and majorities. Nicole Shelton, Jennifer Richeson, and Jessica Salvatore (2005) have demonstrated that the expectation of being the target of prejudice has complex implications for the dynamics of interethnic interaction. For example, the more ethnic minorities expected whites to be prejudiced, the more they had negative experiences during interethnic interactions. Yet, for whites, the more ethnic minorities expected them to be prejudiced, the more positive experiences they had during interethnic interactions. Richeson and Shelton (2003) have also examined the influence of interracial interaction on the cognitive functioning of members of a dominant racial group. Racial attitudes were predictive of impaired cognitive performance for individuals who participated in interracial interactions. This means that the activation of racist beliefs on the part of "whites" actually reduces their own cognitive functioning.

Despite the human genome project and advancements in human population genetics, ideological struggles over the concept of race continue. In the genome era, psychologists have been publishing increasingly on race and psychology. Although many psychologists suggest that the results from genomic research demonstrate that a biological concept of race is not tenable in psychology, others disagree. What is evident from the history of race psychology is that scientific methods are not sufficient to prevent bias, prejudice, and racism. In fact, empirical research has been used to support racism. Finally, it must be emphasized that much of race psychology has participated in *epistemological violence*—meaning that psychologists have produced and distributed interpretations, presented as knowledge, that have negatively shaped the life, health, and opportunities of minorities.

SEE ALSO *American Psychological Association; Aryans; Bigotry;* Brown v. Board of Education, *1954; Clark, Kenneth B.; Cognition; Determinism, Genetic; Discrimination; Galton, Francis; Genomics; Head Start; Heredity; Hitler, Adolf; Immigrants to North America; Immigration; Intelligence; IQ Controversy; Nature vs. Nurture; Psychology; Race; Racism; Stereotypes; Twin Studies; War on Poverty*

BIBLIOGRAPHY

Gould, Stephen Jay. 1996. *The Mismeasure of Man*. Rev. ed. New York: Norton.

Jackson, John P., Jr., and Nadine M. Weidman. 2004. *Race, Racism, and Science: Social Impact and Interaction*. Santa Barbara, CA: ABC-CLIO.

Richards, Graham. 1997. *"Race," Racism, and Psychology: Towards a Reflexive History*. London: Routledge.

Richeson, Jennifer A., and J. Nicole Shelton. 2003. When Prejudice Does Not Pay: Effects of Interracial Contact on Executive Function. *Psychological Science* 14 (3): 287–290.

Rushton, J. Philippe. 1995. *Race, Evolution, and Behavior: A Life History Perspective*. New Brunswick, NJ: Transaction.

Sellers, Robert M., and J. Nicole Shelton. 2003. The Role of Racial Identity in Perceived Racial Discrimination. *Journal of Personality and Social Psychology* 84 (5): 1079–1092.

Shelton, J. Nicole, Jennifer A. Richeson, and Jessica Salvatore. 2005. Expecting to Be the Target of Prejudice: Implications for Interethnic Interactions. *Personality and Social Psychology Bulletin* 31 (9): 1189–1202.

Shih, Margaret, Todd L. Pittinsky, and Nalini Ambady. 1999. Stereotype Susceptibility: Identity Salience and Shifts in Quantitative Performance. *Psychological Science* 10 (13): 80–83.

Steele, Claude M. 1997. A Threat in the Air: How Stereotypes Shape Intellectual Identity and Performance. *American Psychologist* 52 (6): 613–629.

Tucker, William H. 1994. *The Science and Politics of Racial Research*. Urbana: University of Illinois Press.

Winston, Andrew S., ed. 2004. *Defining Difference: Race and Racism in the History of Psychology*. Washington, DC: American Psychological Association.

Thomas Teo

RACE AND RELIGION

Although both *race* and *religion* are enormously difficult to define, almost all human beings in almost all societies recognize, shape themselves, and are shaped by representations, influences, effects of the phenomena and dynamics to which each term generally refers. Bringing these two freighted and problematic terms together in critical analysis may force consideration of certain issues that may otherwise not be addressed at all, or at least not addressed in the manner befitting their complexity. Notwithstanding evidence of phenomena associated with both terms going back to the beginning of social ordering among human beings—for example, language and behaviors—the understandings, usages, and representations most often associated with both race and religion among contemporaries in the English-speaking world were determined by interests at the beginning of the modern era.

RELIGION AND MODERNITY

The modern and contemporary English term *religion* is taken from Middle English (*religioun*) and the Latin of ancient Rome (*religio*, "piety"; *re-ligare*, "to tie," "to bind back"). Although different connotations and uses of the term have developed over the centuries in different cultures and settings, the baseline assumption that has persisted in the English-speaking world has to do with different understandings about the operations, officers, ideologies, rhetorics, and symbolic objects facilitating orientation to—that is, communication with and reverence of—what is understood to be the supernatural, the Other. This supernatural or Other is a social-psychological projection that can be experienced as a form of transcendence or as a special aspect of inward presence.

Those human beings for whom a certain set of the operations, ideologies, rhetorics, and symbolic objects come to mean generally the same things, through whatever means, are thereby bound together into a type of society. This society may be large-scale and international, nationalist, or local and on the fringes of the dominant host society. It may have its beginning as an alternate, oppositional, unpopular, and illicit society, but over a period of time, with growth, complexity of organization, and social power, it may develop into a dominant force such that its boundaries overlap with the boundaries and interests of the dominant society. The binding effect of that large-scale "society" inspired by or reflective of "religion" then comes to be represented in recognizable external forms—in canonical practices, structures, societies, offices, officers, ideologies, and operations. Such forms generally have fairly serious ramifications—social-cultural, political, economic—for the larger host societies; and they are what distinguish "religion" in strict terms from some of the ongoing experiences, practices, and sentiments of single individuals often understood and claimed to be comparable.

What has come to be called "religion," then, can be considered ways of orienting individuals to certain types of societies. Given this general function, religion has some specific complex purposes and effects—that of binding persons into a new alternate society or order. It simultaneously and to different degrees and in different respects separates such bound persons from all or some other societies that do not recognize and respond to the same forms. It leads to a binding with larger-scale pressure and challenge for the purpose of institutionalizing the new society's ideologies within or across a larger expanse of society or territory.

RACE AND MODERNITY

The origins of the modern and contemporary English term *race* are not at all clear. The term has multiple origins and valences from different cultural settings and discursive domains. It comes from Middle and Old English (*rase[e]*) and (*raes*) and from Old Norse (*ras*), meaning "a running," "rush," "swift movement," "attack." These meanings may have had an Indo-European base (*-eras*), carrying the meaning "to flow," "to move rapidly." The term has for centuries if not millennia been used most basically to refer to particular types of athletic competition. From this specific usage the term has been widely borrowed and pressed into service to reflect a rather wide range of provocative meanings in domains far from the original. Uses have come to be more figurative in order to reference different types of competition and differentiation.

Included among such figurative uses is the poignant usage whereby different groups of human beings are differentiated, classified, and hierarchialized. That at the onset of modernity the term *race* came to be accepted by almost everyone—from scientists and learned scholars of many types within and beyond the academy to politicians in their chambers to the haranguers on the streets—as a way to refer to and classify human beings was consequential. That the term came to be used to refer to and classify human beings not on the basis of their activities, accomplishments, or exploits but in terms of external physical features, especially color of skin, was decisive. This change facilitated a type of freezing of categories to the point that, notwithstanding more recent scientific (especially biological) and postmodernist arguments about the problematics, even nonexistence, of "race" (in strict physiological terms) as applied to human beings, many observers and critics would consider the contemporary world to be obsessed with it and many persons—especially "racial" and "ethnic" minorities—radically (over-) determined by it.

RELIGION AND RACE AND MODERNITY

No responsible critical grasp or engagement of "religion" and "race" in our times is possible without attention to the specifically modern-era determination of the concepts and phenomena associated with the terms. The modern-era understandings and uses begin with the European encounters—through the exploits of their commissioned merchants, military seamen, explorers, and missionaries—with other peoples in the lands mistakenly and unfortunately called "new." Beginning in the fifteenth century these contacts challenged and inspired Europeans to name and conceptualize themselves in relationship to the newly "discovered" peoples and their lands. This naming and conceptualization led to a type of hierarchy of human classification that squared with and justified the eventual domination of many of the newly discovered peoples. Notwithstanding the emergence of modern nation-states and their nationalist ideologies and fierce competition, in

this period of "discovery" Europeans began to think of themselves more consistently and collectively as "European" in culture and orientation over against the several newly discovered other worlds and their ways, and they began to think of themselves as "white" over against the others who were "black," "red," "yellow," and "brown." The recognition of the differences between European and North American "white Christian European" ways (in all their variety) and the ways of the others came to be exploited. This exploitation came to include a conceptualization of power on terms that determined some of the others as inferior, befitting the roles of natural perennial servants and slaves. The "discovery" of other peoples by Europeans made for Europeans the "race"-ing of all peoples compelling and strategic.

In such circumstances "religion" became along with "race" a marker of associations and identities shaped in relationship to modern imperial forces. Throughout the nineteenth century and into the early twentieth century, the critical study of the "science" of religion, the history of religions and comparative religions, was invented, and the concept of "world religions" evolved in conjunction with the first convocation of the World Parliament of Religions. These developments reflected the heightened awareness of the complexity of the world, its many different peoples, traditions, varied global developments, challenges, and crises, including the beginning of global wars and their resultant power reformations and arrangements. Religion increasingly came to be seen as one of the reflectors of social-cultural differences, with a presumed hierarchy that established the "world religions"—those religions built around literacy and sacred books—as the superior formations. Within this larger period and set of developments, there could be found alongside the large transnational boundaries and formations—for example, the "Christian" West, the "Islamic" Near East, the "Hinduism" of South Asia; and the "Buddhist" Far East—modern nationalist religious formations—for example, French Catholics, German Lutherans, and Chinese Buddhists.

In relationship to these large-scale global formations, one can further distinguish the religions of the formerly colonized, enslaved, and otherwise dominated, who were through various more or less violent means heavily missionized—for example, African American Baptists and Methodists, East African Anglicans, Korean Presbyterians, Mexican Catholics, Brazilian Pentecostals, Nigerian Muslims, and so forth. As religion was used to integrate persons into and to hold together large social-political formations, it also provided minorities and the subaltern within the large-scale formations media and means by which to register resistance and criticism. The symbols, offices, officers, operations, and ideologies that constituted local traditions, on the one hand, and the "religions" of dominants, on the other, have in certain situations been critically engaged by the subaltern as part of efforts to undermine the social-cultural and political-economic effects of dominance as well as to help restructure identity and reorient themselves to the world.

The historical and ongoing consequences of the imbrication of the two categories are at best mixed. The enslavement and disenfranchisement of black peoples in Europe and in the Americas, the Holocaust and pogroms against Jews in Europe, the violence of apartheid in South Africa, ethnic conflicts and wars among black Africans, hate crimes in the United States and Europe, denominational splits, the Israeli-Palestinian-Arab world conflicts, the genocidal crisis in Darfur—these are just a few examples of religion-inflected conflicts in the modern world. Yet not to be forgotten are the biblically inspired songs and artistry as well as insurrections of the slaves and the religious piety and formations of the soldiers of the civil rights movement, of the modern-day Palestinian movement, and of the Irish Republican Army. These examples suggest that the confusion of "religion" and "race" set forth at the beginning of modernity is likely to obtain with mixed consequences for the futures that can be imagined.

SEE ALSO *Black Nationalism; Blackness; Christianity; Culture; Discrimination; Islam, Shia and Sunni; Liberation Theology; Modernism; Modernity; Nation of Islam; Natives; Palestinians; Postmodernism; Protestantism; Race; Race and Economics; Racism; Religion; Segregation; Whiteness*

BIBLIOGRAPHY

Bhabha, Homi K. 1994. *The Location of Culture.* New York: Routledge.

Chidester, David. 1996. *Savage Systems: Colonialism and Comparative Religion in Southern Africa.* Charlottesville: University of Virginia Press.

Goldschmidt, Henry, and Elizabeth A. McAlister, eds. 2004. *Race, Nation, and Religion in the Americas.* New York: Oxford University Press.

Kidd, Colin. 2006. *The Forging of Races: Race and Scripture in the Protestant Atlantic World, 1600–2000.* New York: Cambridge University Press.

Long, Charles H. 1999. *Significations: Signs, Symbols, and Images in the Interpretation of Religion.* 2nd ed. Aurora, CO: Davies Group Publishers.

Masuzawa, Tomoko. 2005. *Invention of World Religions: Or, How European Universalism Was Preserved in the Language of Pluralism.* Chicago: University of Chicago Press.

Prentiss, Craig, ed. 2003. *Religion and the Creation of Race and Ethnicity.* New York: New York University Press.

Reid, Jennifer I. M., ed. 2004. *Religion and Global Culture: New Terrain in the Study of Religion and the Work of Charles H. Long.* Lanham, MD: Rowman and Littlefield.

Vincent L. Wimbush

RACE MIXING

Shortly after Europeans first arrived in America in the mid-1600s to colonize the region that would become the United States, the issue of race mixing arose. The concept of race itself was then just emerging in its modern form, but European thinkers drawing from firsthand accounts of encounters with Native Americans and Africans began debating the meaning and scope of the physiological and cultural differences among people from different regions of the world. The conception that eventually won out understood racial difference to be real, intrinsic to individuals, and linked to hierarchies of status and capability.

In addition to the well-known case of Pocahontas, the Powhatan woman who entered into a formal European marriage in 1614 with an English settler and traveled to England before her untimely death, there are many documented instances of intermarriage and other sexual connections between Native Americans and European settlers. Although unions between Native American women and European men were more likely to be acknowledged and accepted, occasionally European women partnered with assimilated Native American men or joined Native American tribes. As time passed partnerings between Native American men and white women became less acceptable culturally, and by the late 1700s these types of partnerings gave rise to a stock story that a variety of Native American tribes readily kidnapped and assimilated white women forcibly. (James Fenimore Cooper's 1826 novel *The Last of the Mohicans* provides an example of this type of narrative.) Still, even as late as the twentieth century, descendants of prominent families in southeastern states such as Virginia and Alabama related family stories of their descent from early male European settlers and "Indian princesses."

Race mixing between Africans and Europeans in the colonial era was also initially a matter of debate and confusion rather than censure. Records dating back to the mid-1600s suggest that colonial officials struggled to sort out whether sexual relations between slaves and white indentured servants were legally problematic. By the late 1600s several colonies had begun to regulate against relationships between white women and slave men by rendering them as crimes, shifting the status of white women involved with black men to that of slaves rather than free or indentured persons or by fixing the status of children produced in such relationships as slaves. By the dawn of the 1700s the legal status of slavery had been more firmly fixed, and the descendants of slaves were understood by most people in the southern colonies to be slaves themselves, absent formal emancipation by their owners.

Despite the centrality of slavery and its increasing connection to blackness, European conceptualization of race mixing in the Caribbean and Latin American colonies did not initially rest upon a rigid bifurcation between white and black. As early as the seventeenth century white Spaniards and their descendants living in Mexico developed the concept of *casta*, a classificatory scheme for race mixing that categorized individuals by descent. In addition to introducing the categories of "quadroon" and "octoroon," designating individuals with three white and one black grandparents and seven white and one black great-grandparents respectively, such schemes provided means of taxonomizing by name various degrees of native and black ancestry. These categories had real legal consequences for the status and rights of individuals placed in them—in but one example, the required amount of tribute paid to the Spanish Crown varied on the basis of one's racial classification, and that variance marked individuals as belonging to particular classes and holding particular statuses.

At this point the cultural and legal differences between relationships involving white men and black women versus black men and white women became more distinct. Although both types of relationships had the capacity to produce children, intimate connections between white women and black men gradually became perceived as more worthy of censure, based on culturally embedded beliefs about the threat of black masculinity and the need to protect white femininity. Interracial intimacy between slave women and white men became defined as undesirable and occasionally scandalous conduct on the part of the white men, but the legal system did not define it as a crime even if the relationship was overtly coercive or violent; the children born from such relationships were universally understood to be slaves. (Same-sex interracial intimacy was not formally recognized or regulated other than under the general rubric of same-sex sexual intimacy, which was often culturally and legally effaced when between women and punished as sodomy when between men.)

In the Revolutionary era in the United States, blacks experienced a brief taste of a more egalitarian ideology as several northern states abolished slavery or set it on a course for extinction after the freedom of the United States had been won. Some states experimented with extending the franchise to blacks and women as well. By the 1820s, however, this openness had dissipated completely as the franchise was withdrawn in state after state and southern pressures to protect and defend the institution of slavery increasingly led to harsh application of fugitive slave laws. Nonetheless, by the 1820s a substantial and growing mixed-race population was established in the United States. Descendants of blacks and whites were called mulattoes, although some scientists who studied race in the United States, the Caribbean, and Latin America persisted with intricate classification schemes for various combinations of black, native, and white ancestry.

Mulattoes were at the time understood to be a distinct race but one more closely related to the African race than the white race. In some circles in the South, mulattoes were particularly prized as house servants or concubines.

At the same time, although some descendants of Native Americans and whites assimilated into white communities and gradually forgot their mixed-race heritage over the generations, some tribes actively embraced mixed-race individuals and defined them as wholly Indian. In some regions of the South small communities composed of the descendants of free blacks and Native Americans who had resisted removal began to establish themselves. The Seminole Indians of Florida, Georgia, and Alabama are an example. Eventually the United States became frustrated with the Seminoles' refusal to cede their land and move west, and the government entered into a long and vicious war to remove them forcibly, which was won only through the U.S. Army's betrayal and capture of the Seminoles' leader under a false truce.

As sectional conflict worsened, understandings of race and racial difference shifted toward a harder line based in emerging scientific theories about the superiority of the white race and the inferiority of other races. As scientists began to argue for a rigid hierarchy of physical, emotional, and intellectual fitness among the races, they also began to warn of the dangers of race mixing. In the 1840s and 1850s *Debow's Review*, a southern agricultural and social journal, began to publicize much of this work, including various versions of the theory that the mixed-race descendants of white and black parents were inferior. As scientific debates hardened racial categories and separated them more broadly, new theories emerged about the dangers of racial mixing.

This scientific anxiety reflected and reinforced social and cultural anxieties about race mixing, which became increasingly disfavored. Although some black men accused of engaging in intercourse with white women were able to avoid severe punishment even in the South, such connections increasingly were framed as rape. And although white men continued to have the legal authority to exercise sexual control over slave women, many southern states passed laws limiting white slave owners' ability to free their slaves and give them substantial property, actions that white men occasionally took to benefit their enslaved sexual partners and children. By the time of the Civil War many southern states had adopted rules that allowed property to pass to enslaved individuals by will only if they were first freed and then sent out of the state or the country.

Anxieties about race mixing ran high among whites as slavery was abolished and the possibility for a new, more egalitarian, political order arose. Two Democratic newspaper editors sought to capitalize on these anxieties by secretly publishing a pamphlet extolling the virtues and benefits of race mixing, coining the word *miscegenation* to refer to the practice; they sent copies of the pamphlet to prominent Republicans in the hopes that some would endorse it. Although the plot failed, the term quickly became part of the public lexicon, and despite an intense constitutional struggle in the early postbellum years, bans on interracial marriage were passed and upheld across the South. Through the remainder of the nineteenth century and into the twentieth century, these bans spread into the western states as well.

Bans on interracial intimacy took different forms. Some states, such as Alabama, broadly criminalized attempts at intermarriage, interracial adultery, and interracial fornication between blacks and whites as felonies, and the courts interpreted these bans to bar sexual relationships that paralleled legitimate same-race marital relationships. Other southern states such as Florida made intermarriage between blacks and whites a serious crime but left interracial fornication at the level of a misdemeanor offense. Western states often incorporated a bewildering array of racial groups in their injunctions against interracial intimacy between whites and people of color; Native Americans were prohibited from marrying whites in many states, but the western coastal states also barred marriages between whites and Asians, whites and Hawaiians, and whites and Filipinos.

Through the first three decades of the twentieth century, cultural and legal definitions of race increasingly moved toward eliminating the broad array of terms for mixed-race individuals in favor of a limited range of rigid categories. The category of mulatto gradually disappeared in favor of a strict separation between black and white, with those formerly considered to be mulattoes reclassified as black. Although communities of racially ambiguous individuals with Native American, white, and black ancestors persisted in southern rural areas, they increasingly had to operate under difficult conditions of fitting into the legal regime of segregation, which presupposed a black-white binary universe.

The bans on interracial marriage fell to judicial attack, first in California's 1948 state court ruling in *Perez v. Sharp* that such bans violated the Fourteenth Amendment and then nationally in 1967 when the U.S. Supreme Court decided in *Loving v. Virginia* that Virginia's antimiscegenation statute was unconstituional. In conjunction with this, however, state legislatures in the West had been removing bans in the 1950s; by the time *Loving* was announced, only the Old South retained statutory bans. Although further judicial action was necessary to enforce the rule of *Loving* in a few southern states, by 1970 the legal struggle was essentially over regarding marriage. Social acceptability of interracial relationships required more time, and even in the early twenty-first century marriages between blacks and whites comprise only a small percentage of marriages in the United States.

Controversy over race mixing arose again over proposals to add a mixed-race category to the 2000 census, which allowed individuals to select more than one race as an identifier. Nearly seven million Americans identified themselves as mixed race or multiracial.

SEE ALSO *Miscegenation; Sex, Interracial*

BIBLIOGRAPHY

Bynum, Victoria. 1998. "'White Negroes" in Segregated Mississippi: Miscegenation, Racial Identity, and the Law. *Journal of Southern History* 44: 247–275.

Jacobson, Matthew Frye. 1998. *Whiteness of a Different Color: European Immigrants and the Alchemy of Race.* Cambridge, MA: Harvard University Press.

Klinkner, Philip, and Rogers Smith. 1999. *The Unsteady March: The Rise and Decline of Racial Equality in America.* Chicago: University of Chicago Press.

Milton, Cynthia, and Ben Vinson III. 2002. Counting Heads: Race and Non-Native Tribute Policy in Colonial Spanish America. *Journal of Colonialism and Colonial History* 3: 1–18.

Novkov, Julie. 2002. Racial Constructions: The Legal Regulation of Miscegenation in Alabama, 1890–1934. *Law and History Review* 20: 225–277.

Robinson, Charles F. 2003. *Dangerous Liaisons: Sex and Love in the Segregated South.* Fayetteville: University of Arkansas Press.

Romano, Renee. 2003. *Race Mixing: Black-White Marriage in Postwar America.* Cambridge, MA: Harvard University Press.

Root, Maria P. P. 2001. *Love's Revolution: Interracial Marriage.* Philadelphia: Temple University Press.

Saxton, Alexander. 1990. *The Rise and Fall of the White Republic: Class Politics and Mass Culture in Nineteenth-Century America.* London: Verso.

Vinson, Ben, III. 2001. *Bearing Arms for His Majesty: The Free-Colored Militia in Colonial Mexico.* Stanford, CA: Stanford University Press.

Wallenstein, Peter. 2002. *Tell the Court I Love My Wife: Race, Marriage, and Law; An American History.* New York: Palgrave.

Julie Novkov

RACE RELATIONS

The term *race relations* entered the sociological lexicon through Robert Ezra Park (1864–1944), who pioneered the study of race at the University of Chicago. Before becoming a professor in 1914 at the age of forty-nine, Park did a stint as a reporter and then worked for eight years as publicist and ghostwriter for Booker T. Washington (1856–1915), the founder of Tuskegee Institute in Alabama, whose mission was to provide blacks with "industrial education." Washington, of course, is famous as the apostle of self-help and racial accommodation. He was catapulted to national prominence in 1895 with his speech at the Atlanta Exposition exhorting blacks to forego politics and to pursue education and manual labor. His core assumption was that once blacks demonstrated that they were deserving of full rights of citizenship, better race relations would ensue. This raises the tantalizing question: To what extent was Park, as he entered the nascent field of sociology, the purveyor of ideological tenets associated with Washington's uplift ideology?

Park was also heavily influenced by the evolutionary theories prevalent at the turn of the century when he studied social philosophy at Harvard and in Germany. Herbert Spencer (1820–1903), the English philosopher and political theorist, applied Charles Darwin's (1809–1882) theory of evolution to the social order, arguing that history progressed through a series of stages from lower to higher levels of development. Park, in turn, applied Spencer's theory to the domain of race, and expounded a theory that "in the relations of races there is a cycle of events which tends everywhere to repeat itself" (1950, p.150).

According to Park's famous formulation, the race relations cycle has four distinct phases. It begins with *contact* when different races come together through migration or conquest. This leads to *conflict* as the rival groups compete for supremacy. During the third stage, *accommodation*, the weaker group resigns itself to its subordination, and a *racial etiquette* is established that maintains *social distance* between the races. The final stage of the race relations cycle is *assimilation*, which involves the gradual but inexorable absorption of the subordinate group into the dominant group, culturally and biologically. Thus, according to Park, new races are formed out of "the broken fragments" of different racial groups, and the race relations cycle provides the impetus of human evolution.

Park applied the race relations cycle both to people of color and to "the races" of Europe who were flocking to Chicago and other American cities at the time he wrote. Park's race relations model had a sanguine political subtext: it rebuffed the nativist claim that the new immigrants were "unassimilable," and provided reassurance that the intermingling of the peoples of the world was the stuff of human evolution. As Park wrote in *Race and Culture*: "Every society, every nation, and every civilization has been a kind of melting pot and has thus contributed to the intermingling of races by which new races and new cultures eventually emerge" (1950, p.192).

Park acknowledged that the race relations model did not proceed as rapidly or completely when it came to people of color. Even so, he clung to his evolutionary optimism that the assimilation process eventually would run its course, and like Washington, he emphasized the great progress that blacks had made during the half-century after slavery. Park also shared Spencer's view that attempts to influence the flux of history were in vain. He was contemptuous of social reformers, and exhorted social scientists to observe an Olympian distance from the world of politics. Thus, Park's race relations model gave theoretical exposition and scientific legitimacy to Booker T. Washington's politics of accommodation. As Charles U. Smith and Lewis Killian observed, Park "constructed a theory of assimilation which paralleled Washington's program in its major premises of accommodation and assimilation, realism and optimism" (1974, p. 200).

Park's race relations model emerged as the reigning paradigm in the social sciences, both in the United States and Britain (Banton 1967; Rex 1983). The hallmark of this paradigm was to normalize and naturalize race and racial inequality, and to remove them from the political realm. Even black demands for full civil rights remained off the radar screen of mainstream social science. In a trenchant analysis of the social science literature on race, Stanford Lyman shows how leading sociological theorists from Park to Gunnar Myrdal (1898–1987) to Talcott Parsons (1902–1979) avoided the issue of civil rights. Instead, they advanced teleological models that projected racial improvement as part of an evolutionary process of societal change. "Since the time for teleological redemption is ever long," Lyman writes sardonically, "blacks might consign their civil and equalitarian future to faith in the ultimate fulfillment of the inclusion cycle's promise" (1993, p. 394). Lyman concludes with an indictment of the entire discipline: "Sociology, in this respect, has been part of the problem and not part of the solution" (1993, p. 397).

The race relations paradigm had enormous implications for praxis as well as for theory. Social scientists of all disciplinary stripes were cast into the role of managers of the troubled and fractured "relations" between the races (Steinberg 2001). The root cause of racial conflict was seen as prejudice: the distorted, derogatory, and often malicious beliefs that placed a stigma of inferiority onto blacks and led to their discriminatory treatment. Sociologists over many decades have charted historical trends in the prevalence and distribution of prejudiced beliefs. Other practitioners in "the race relations industry," as it came to be called, engaged in projects of education and social work, designed to bridge the racial chasm and to forge better, more tolerant and harmonious "relations" between the races (Killian 1979; McKee 1993). According to critics, the fatal problem with this otherwise innocuous approach was that it elided those structures of oppression that enforced black subordination: Jim Crow laws in the South, racial apartheid in jobs and housing in the North, and structured inequalities along racial lines that pervaded all major societal institutions.

Nor was criticism of the University of Chicago's race relations model only a matter of hindsight. There were some contemporaneous critics, though they were mostly black or Marxist, and therefore could be easily marginalized. Throughout his long career as both scholar and activist, W. E. B. Du Bois (1868–1963) treated racism not as an individual anomaly but as a feature of major political and economic institutions. In 1909 Du Bois was a principal founder of the National Association for the Advancement of Colored People (NAACP), whose main purpose was to secure full rights of citizenship for blacks. Oliver Cox (1901–1974), another black Marxist, directly challenged Park's "new orthodoxy" on race relations, arguing that Park's "teleological approach has diverted him from an examination of specific causal events in the development of modern race antagonism" (1948, p. 476). For Cox, race prejudice was merely "the social-attitudinal concomitant of the racial-exploitative practice of a ruling class in a capitalist society" (1948, p. 476). That both Du Bois and Cox were beleaguered and ostracized within the sociological profession, and their work dismissed as "propaganda," underscores the intellectual hegemony of the Chicago School of race relations (Deegan 2000, p. 284).

Just as the Chicago School studiously ignored power "from above," it was oblivious to the possibility of revolt "from below." All of this changed with the eruption of black insurgency, beginning with the Birmingham, Alabama, boycott in 1955 and culminating with the passage of landmark civil rights legislation in 1964 and 1965. The ensuing societal crisis threw into question the prevailing paradigm on race. A pivotal moment occurred at the 1963 Annual Meeting of the American Sociological Association when Everett Hughes (1897–1983), a student of Robert Park, delivered his presidential address in which he pondered the reasons that sociology had failed to anticipate the civil rights revolution (McKee 1993, p. 9). Here was a rare admission of intellectual failure and an unmistakable sign of paradigm crisis. Indeed, with the intensification of racial conflict beginning with the Watts revolt in Los Angeles in 1965 and the escalating black militancy during the 1970s, events demonstrated the utter failure of the race relations paradigm to shed light on the forces that were tearing American society apart. The time was ripe for paradigm change.

TOWARD A NEW PARADIGM

The civil rights revolution engendered a "scholarship of confrontation" that emphasized the centrality of race and racism, and incorporated minority and radical voices that had long been relegated to the fringes (Steinberg 1995).

The most important revision to the race relations paradigm came from a book that was a collaboration between Stokely Carmichael (1941–1998), a frontline activist, and Charles V. Hamilton, a political scientist at Lincoln University. In *Black Power* (1967), Carmichael and Hamilton posited a distinction between "individual racism" and "institutional racism," the latter referring to the ways in which racism is not necessarily predicated on racist motives but rather embedded in routine institutional practices that reproduce racial inequalities. The concept of institutionalized racism provided a crucial theoretical underpinning for affirmative action policy, which succeeded in integrating significant numbers of blacks into blue-collar industries, corporate management, and the professions (Collins 1983; Darity and Myers 1998).

In another landmark study, *Racial Oppression in America* (1972), Bob Blauner gave theoretical exposition to ideas that emanated from the anticolonial movements in the third world. Even his title, *Racial Oppression*, implicitly challenged the obfuscating terminology of the "race relations" model. Blauner also drew a sharp distinction between "immigrant" and "colonized" minorities— the latter referring to people of color who did not arrive as voluntary immigrants seeking a better life, but who entered American society en masse, as the result of conquest or slavery. These "colonized minorities" were not only exposed to more virulent prejudice, but were also denied the rights and opportunities that delivered immigrants from poverty.

Recent scholarship is marked by two opposing schools of thought. On the one hand, there has been a "scholarship of backlash" that contends that racism is of declining significance, and restores the victim-blaming discourses that anteceded the civil rights revolution (Wilson 1978; D'Souza 1995; Thernstrom and Thernstrom 1997). In the tradition of Washington and Park, these theorists see racial progress as contingent upon blacks acquiring the education and skills that explain the relative success of the black middle class. The flip side of this proposition is that the sources of persistent inequalities are located not in societal structures but in putative defects of black families, communities, and culture. Institutionalized racism is either ignored or defined out of existence.

On the other hand, there is a rival discourse that builds on "the scholarship of confrontation" associated with the civil rights movement, and posits "colorblind racism" as the central concept for both theory and praxis (Bonilla-Silva 2006; Brown et al. 2003; Feagin 2006). According to these writers, despite progress on some fronts, we are far from the colorblind society that Martin Luther King (1929–1968) envisioned in his 1963 "I Have a Dream" oration. Indeed, the claim of colorblindness has been used as a smokescreen to conceal the retreat from the affirmative action and other antiracist policies that account for much of the success during the post–civil rights era.

This intellectual contestation is indicative of an ongoing struggle for intellectual hegemony between rival paradigms. The outcome may well determine whether sociology will continue to be part of the problem, as Stanford Lyman has alleged, or whether it will be part of the solution.

SEE ALSO *Park School, The; Park, Robert E.; Race; Race and Education; Race Relations Cycle; Racism*

BIBLIOGRAPHY

Banton, Michael. 1967. *Race Relations*. London: Tavistock.

Blauner, Bob. 1972. *Racial Oppression in America*. New York: Harper. 2nd ed., 2001, with the revised title *Still the Big News: Racial Oppression in America*. Philadelphia: Temple University Press.

Bonilla-Silva, Eduardo. 2006. *Racism Without Racists: Color-Blind Racism and the Persistence of Racial Inequality in the United States*. 2nd ed. Lanham, MD: Rowman & Littlefield.

Brown, Michael K., et al. 2003. *Whitewashing Race: The Myth of a Color-Blind Society*. Berkeley: University of California Press.

Carmichael, Stokely, and Charles V. Hamilton. 1967. *Black Power: The Politics of Liberation*. 2nd ed. 1992. New York: Vintage.

Collins, Sharon M. 1983. The Making of the Black Middle Class. *Social Problems* 30: 369–382.

Cox, Oliver Cromwell. 1948. *Caste, Class, and Race: A Study in Social Dynamics*. Garden City, NY: Doubleday.

Darity, William A., and Samuel L. Myers Jr. 1998. *Persistent Disparity: Race and Economic Inequality in the United States Since 1945*. Northampton, MA: E. Elgar.

Deegan, Mary Jo. 2000. Oliver C. Cox and the Chicago School of Race Relations, 1892–1960. *Research in Race and Ethnic Relations* 2: 271–288.

D'Souza, Dinesh. 1995. *The End of Racism*. New York: Free Press.

Feagin, Joe R. 2006. *Systemic Racism: A Theory of Oppression*. New York: Routledge.

Killian, Lewis M. 1979. "The Race Relations Industry" as a Sensitizing Concept. *Research in Social Problems and Public Policy* 1: 113–137.

Lyman, Stanford M. 1972. *The Black American in Sociological Thought: A Failure of Perspective*. New York: Putnam.

Lyman, Stanford M. 1993. Race Relations as Social Process: Sociology's Resistance to a Civil Rights Orientation. In *Race in America: The Struggle for Equality*, eds. Herbert Hill and James E. Jones, 370–401. Madison: University of Wisconsin Press.

McKee, James B. 1993. *Sociology and the Race Problem: The Failure of a Perspective*. Urbana: University of Illinois Press.

Park, Robert Ezra. 1950. *Race and Culture*. Eds. Everett C. Hughes et al. Glencoe, IL: Free Press.

Rex, John. 1983. *Race Relations in Sociological Theory*. 2nd ed. London: Routledge.

Smith, Charles U., and Lewis M. Killian. 1974. Black Sociologists and Social Protest. In *Black Sociologists: Historical and Contemporary Perspectives*, eds. James E. Blackwell and Morris Janowitz, 191–230. Chicago: University of Chicago Press.

Steinberg, Stephen. 1995. *Turning Back: The Retreat from Racial Justice in American Thought and Policy*. Boston: Beacon.

Steinberg, Stephen. 2001. "Race Relations": The Problem with the Wrong Name. *New Politics* 8 (2) (new series), whole no. 30. http://www.wpunj.edu/newpol/issue30/steinb30.htm.

Thernstrom, Stephen, and Abigail Thernstrom. 1997. *America in Black and White*. New York: Simon and Schuster.

Wilson, William Julius. 1978. *The Declining Significance of Race: Blacks and Changing American Institutions*. Chicago: University of Chicago Press.

Stephen Steinberg

RACE RELATIONS ACT OF 1968

SEE *Integration*.

RACE RELATIONS ACT OF 1976

SEE *Integration*.

RACE RELATIONS AMENDMENT 2000

SEE *Integration*.

RACE RELATIONS CYCLE

Robert Ezra Park (1864–1944) was a member of the Chicago school of sociology and had a major hand in establishing the discipline of sociology in the United States. One of his many contributions was his "race relations cycle," the first systematic attempt to account for the origins and evolution of group relationships. Park posited four stages in the development of group relations: competition, conflict, accommodation, and assimilation.

When groups first come into contact (through immigration, conquest, and so forth), relations tend to be competitive and conflictual. Park (1969) saw competition between individuals and groups as fundamental and universal. In a world of finite resources, all living things compete to satisfy their needs and survive. Competition is impersonal and unconscious and does not require contact or face-to-face interaction. Competition becomes conflict when competitors become aware of each other. "Competition … is continuous and impersonal, conflict is intermittent and personal" (p. 574). Group conflict requires some form of ethnocentric awareness of group differences—some sense of "we" versus "they"—and is a struggle for control of the other group—for resources, status, or other scarce commodities.

Conflict between groups is disruptive and costly and will tend to move toward an accommodation or an institutionalized, stable relationship. Accommodations can take a variety of forms, including slavery and other forms of institutionalized discrimination. An accommodation organizes social relations and encourages social attitudes and norms that permit groups to coexist and conduct their daily activities.

Accommodations may persist for long periods of time, may be disrupted and dissolve into further periods of conflict, or they may evolve into assimilation, which is "a process of interpenetration and fusion in which persons and groups acquire the memories, sentiments, and attitudes of other persons or groups, and, by sharing their experience and history, are incorporated with them into a common cultural life" (Park 1969, p. 735). Thus, assimilation merges two or more cultures into a single, shared set of traditions and memories.

Assimilation does not produce uniformity or sameness but rather a "unity of experience and orientation, out of which may develop a community of purpose and action" (Park 1969, p. 737). Competition and episodes of conflict continue after assimilation but are organized along lines other than those of ethnicity, culture, or race, such as class, for example.

Although his ideas have been extremely influential, they are not without their limitations. Park's theory has been criticized for its lack of specificity in the time frame required for assimilation and, more importantly perhaps, in its lack of detail with regard to the process of assimilation. On the other hand, Park's work initiated a tradition of theory and research that has guided the American sociology of immigration and assimilation for the past eight decades.

The cycle can be illustrated in the history of black–white relations in the United States. The earliest period of competition and conflict in colonial days was followed by the institutionalization of slavery, an accommodation that began to emerge in the 1660s and ended in 1865 at the end of the American Civil War. After a brief period of renewed conflict (Reconstruction), black–white relations were stabilized in a second accommodation: de jure segregation, which ended in the 1960s. Since that time, black–white relations have returned to conflict and struggle. There are some signs of assimilation (e.g., rates of intermarriage are increasing, even though they remain a tiny percentage of all marriages), but continuing sharp distinctions in group identity and cultural traditions persist, reinforced by continuing racial exclusion and persistent racial inequalities of income and wealth.

While black–white relations have not (yet?) evolved to assimilation, examples of the completed cycle can be found in the histories of other American groups. European immigrants who arrived between the 1820s and 1920s competed for jobs, housing, and status and faced intense rejection, prejudice, and discrimination. Accommodations gradually emerged, and the descendents of the immigrants eventually assimilated and achieved parity with national norms in terms of occupations, income, and other measures of equality. Various researchers (e.g., Alba 1990; Gallagher 2001) have found that white ethnic identity is currently in its "twilight" and that descendents of European immigrants currently share identity, memories, and traditions with other white Americans.

Since the 1960s, the United States has received a second great wave of immigration. These immigrants are extremely diverse and compete for jobs and position in every niche of American society from high (e.g., scientists and surgeons) to low (e.g., day laborers and nannies), including work in the irregular economy (e.g., piecework in garment industry "sweatshops" and sex workers). Some analysts (e.g., Portes and Rumbaut, 2001) argue that some contemporary immigrant groups will not assimilate into the dominant culture but into the marginalized urban underclass, where they will learn cultures, values, and traditions that invert or challenge the dominant culture. Evidence for this assertion includes the high rates of unemployment and poverty and low levels of education for some groups, even those with substantially large third generations. For example, some recent immigrant groups, such as Mexicans and Haitians, bring low levels of education and job skills and take jobs marginal to the mainstream economy. In an era of hardening social mobility and increasing inequality, these immigrant groups and their descendents may find themselves permanently excluded from the mainstream job market.

Other analysts believe that this viewpoint amounts to little more than "blaming the victim" and present evidence (e.g., Bean and Stevens 2003) that suggests that the descendents of current immigrants will acquire the values and traditions of the larger society and, much like the descendents of the first mass immigration, gradually assimilate. For example, Alba et al. (2002) report that the tendency to speak English rather than the "mother tongue" at home increases by generation for recent immigrant groups. They found that the percentage of second-generation group members who reported that they spoke only English at home ranged from a low of 8 percent for Dominicans to a high of almost 80 percent for Filipinos. For the third generation, the percentage speaking only English at home rose for every group and ranged from a low of 50 percent for Dominicans to a high of almost 100 percent for Japanese and Filipinos. This pattern of language assimilation is quite consistent with the experiences of the descendants of the great wave of European immigrants who arrived between the 1820s and 1920s and may denote a movement of these groups toward higher levels of inclusion and assimilation. The ultimate fate of these groups—whether they will move toward assimilation or be caught up in a constant cycle of conflict and accommodation—will not be known for some time. As Park himself noted, immigration can be very fast but assimilation is by nature slow.

SEE ALSO *Assimilation; Competition; Conflict; Culture of Poverty; Ethnic Conflict; Identity; Immigration; Intergroup Relations; Park School, The; Park, Robert E.; Race; Race Relations; Reconstruction Era (U.S.); Sociology; U.S. Civil War*

BIBLIOGRAPHY

Alba, Richard. 1990. *Ethnic Identity: The Transformation of White America.* New Haven, CT: Yale University Press.

Alba, Richard, John Logan, Amy Lutz, and Brian Stults. 2002. Only English by the Third Generation? Loss and Preservation of the Mother Tongue among the Grandchildren of Contemporary Immigrants. *Demography* 39 (3): 467–484.

Bean, Frank, and Gillian Stevens. 2003. *America's Newcomers and the Dynamics of Diversity.* New York: Russell Sage Foundation.

Gallagher, Charles. 2001. "Playing the Ethnic Card: How Ethnic Narratives Maintain Racial Privilege." Paper presented at the annual meeting of the Southern Sociological Society, Atlanta, GA.

Portes, Alejandro, and Rubén Rumbaut. 2001. *Legacies: The Story of the Immigrant Second Generation.* Berkeley: University of California Press.

Park, Robert E., and Ernest W. Burgess. 1969. *Introduction to the Science of Sociology*, 3rd ed. Chicago: University of Chicago Press.

Joseph F. Healey

RACE RIOTS, UNITED STATES

Scholarly concern with riots and crowd behavior dates back to some of the earliest theorists who can be called social scientists. Gustave Le Bon (1841–1931), often credited as the most important early writer on crowd behavior, published *The Crowd* at the end of the nineteenth century, a book that influenced thinking about temporary assemblies of people for decades after. Le Bon and other important crowd theorists, such as Sigmund Freud (1856–1939), viewed crowds as crazed, criminal, unanimous masses of anonymous individuals who had ceded psychological control of themselves to the group mind and whose behavior was being directly controlled by the mob. Although this view of the crowd has been almost completely debunked in later empirical work, it is important not only because it had a decisive influence on the development of social psychology and sociology, but because the notion of mob psychology still lives on in the popular mind and the media. In particular, when serious rioting occurs, it is inevitable that commentators will draw on LeBonian notions to characterize both what happened and those who participated. But, in fact, riots in general, and race riots even more so, are expressive incidents in which actors have a large variety of motives for participating. They also make purposeful choices about their own behavior, and although some coordination of activity occurs, crowd members actually engage in very heterogeneous behaviors.

WHAT IS A RACE RIOT?

Defining race riots is a two-step process. First, we must come to an understanding of what constitutes a riot and then, among those events that qualify, decide which are fundamentally racial in character. One can easily imagine an event that would qualify as a race riot: hundreds of people in a pitched battle on the streets of a large city, where one racial group hurls rocks, bottles, and epithets at the other, and then receives an in-kind response. Such prototypical visions of race riots are straightforward. The edges of the concept, however, are more difficult to establish.

One tricky issue is the number of people involved. Rioting is undoubtedly a collective phenomenon—a single person cannot riot. But how many people are necessary before we can call the event a *riot*? Indeed social scientists have often faced this issue, and lacking a reason to use a particular threshold, have instead decided to call the events in question *collective violence* or *civil disorders*—and, in fact, many of the events analyzed in such studies would not be recognized as riots by most social scientists. Most social scientific studies of phenomena that are called riots appear to involve a minimum of thirty to fifty people, even if the popular conception of a riot is something of a much grander scale.

A second defining characteristic of a riot is violence. Protest marches, confrontations between two racial groups, or even face-offs between citizens and police cannot be called riots unless some kind of physical violence transpires. Definitions of riots and of the broader category of collective violence almost always include the requirement that someone is injured or significant property damage occurs before the event can be counted. Sometimes, however, it is only necessary that such damage or injury be attempted, rather than accomplished. If a large crowd of protestors pelts the police with stones and refuse, but the police are adequately protected with riot gear so as to prevent any injury, scholars would still judge that a riot has occurred.

Third, riots must have a significant period of duration. A clash of only a few moments that is immediately broken up by authorities is rarely considered a riot. And finally, riots involve a temporary breaking away from the participants' normal routines in a way that is not typically sanctioned by authorities or prevailing social norms. Rioting is not everyday behavior and also must be distinguished from sanctioned violence like an American football game or the running of the bulls in Pamplona, Spain.

Even having drawn a boundary about what social scientists have considered to be riots, it is still important to recognize the diversity within the category. Consider the differences among these subtypes of riots, all of which meet the demands of the core definition: sports celebration riots that often occur after championship games; genocidal ethnic purges such as those that occurred in Rwanda in the 1990s; food riots in Latin America; machine-breaking raids in nineteenth-century Britain; brawls among soccer fans throughout Europe in the 1980s and 1990s; lynch mobs in the southern United States in the late nineteenth and early twentieth century; immigrant protests of French police brutality that resulted in thousands of torched automobiles; and the urban riots of the 1960s that occurred throughout the United States.

Among these many forms of rioting, a *race* riot occurs when a racial grievance is expressed or is apparent through the behavior of the rioters. For example, if African American riot participants selectively loot white-owned stores, then a racial riot has occurred. If white Klansmen attack a peaceful African American civil rights rally, if an African American crowd burns down a government building in reaction to reports of white police brutality, or if Mexican Americans and African Americans clash on the border of their neighborhoods, causing deaths among one or both groups, then a racial riot has occurred. All of these scenarios were repeated throughout the 1960s in the United States.

WHAT CAUSES RACE RIOTS?

Although the U.S. urban riots of the 1960s dominate both the popular vision of race rioting and the scholarly literature on the subject, it is far from the only race rioting in the history of the United States. U.S. race riots can be thought of as belonging to one of two categories. The first are those typified by the Watts riot of 1965 (in Los Angeles, California); the Newark, New Jersey, riot of 1967; the Detroit, Michigan, riot of 1967; and the Washington, D.C., riot of 1968. These riots were most typically sparked by a confrontation between local police and African American residents of poor inner-city neighborhoods. In the most severe of these riots, the action lasted for several days and millions of dollars of property damage occurred before the authorities reasserted control of the riot areas. The activity of rioters was most often directed at damaging stores and government property, rather than attacking members of another racial group. Injuries and a few deaths did occur, but these were mainly the result of police attempts to contain and extinguish the riot. Imitative events followed in the wake of large riots and spread unrest across the region and the nation. And although there was a major concentration of these events during the 1960s, similar riots have since occurred throughout the United States and in urban environments in other countries.

Before the 1960s, the dominant kind of racial collective violence did not involve minority attacks on symbols of economic and political exploitation. Rather, they involved majority group members attacking minorities who had made gains in competition over occupational and residential turf. Here the dominant character of the conflict was white groups physically attacking members of minority groups, and destroying their property as well. For example, thousands of whites gathered in the "five points" area of downtown Atlanta in September of 1906 and ended up murdering dozens of blacks. Other such riots occurred throughout the United States, including both southern and northern cities. In the "Red Summer" of 1919, a devastating string of riots crossed the United States, killing many whites and blacks in cities such as Washington, D.C., Chicago, and Omaha. Although in extreme cases the authorities had to step in to quell the violence, more often than not, the attacks were carried out with the approval, if not the active participation, of the police.

For both of these types of race riots, economic conditions have been at the center of theorizing about their causes. In the case of the 1960s, sociologists hypothesized that unemployment and poverty were root causes of the dissatisfaction that African Americans seemed to be expressing through the riots. In this view, African Americans were not receiving their fair share of the American dream, and in many cases, they were struggling to even survive. Lacking the political access to address their problems through institutional means, they turned to the streets in order to draw needed attention to their problems. Although this argument seemed more than plausible, the research has been considerably less than definitive. Studies attempting to explain why riots broke out in some cities but not others, and why riots in some locations were more severe than others, have had a hard time connecting rioting to poor economic conditions. Closely related ideas about insufficient social services, population changes, and political access to the city government have not been any more robust than the core economic indicators.

Competition notions, however, have had more success in predicting both kinds of rioting. Here, the idea is that competition over scarce resources (jobs and coveted residential areas) produce conflict—especially when one group begins to make gains perceived to be at the expense of another. The group that is losing ground is therefore motivated to fight back and to punish those who seem to be threatening its position. In the end though, economic conditions are not strong predictors of racial rioting. Economic hardship may very well be a prerequisite for rioting, but it is not sufficient to ignite the flames of rioting itself. Other conditions, such as poor relations between the police and the community, must provide a catalyst in areas where economic conditions have created fertile ground for unrest.

SEE ALSO *Riots; Tulsa Riot; Urban Riots*

BIBLIOGRAPHY

Feagin, Joe R., and Harlan Hahn. 1973. *Ghetto Revolts: The Politics of Violence in American Cities.* New York: Macmillan.

Le Bon, Gustave. [1896] 1952. *The Crowd: A Study of the Popular Mind.* London: Ernest Benn.

McPhail, Clark. 1991. *The Myth of the Madding Crowd.* New York: de Gruyter.

McPhail, Clark. 1994. Presidential Address—The Dark Side of Purpose: Individual and Collective Violence in Riots. *The Sociological Quarterly* 35: 1–32.

National Advisory Commission on Civil Disorders. 1968. *Report of the National Advisory Commission on Civil Disorders.* New York: Bantam.

Olzak, Susan. 1992. *The Dynamics of Ethnic Competition and Conflict.* Stanford, CA: Stanford University Press.

Daniel J. Myers

RACE-BLIND POLICIES

In a race-blind (or synonymously color-blind) society, persons of all ethnic backgrounds are supposedly viewed as equal and have access to the entitlements of a meritoc-racy. It is a theoretical position that gradually emerged in the post-1960s civil rights era and has become a contentious topic in both academic and social policy circles. Many advocates of race-blind policies, but not all, tend to be from the conservative-right school of thought. They adhere to the view that "racelessness" will help bring about equal opportunity for all and is ultimately good for society. Moreover, they view overt racism as an issue from the past that does not figure in the imagination of the majority of Americans. Hence, there is no longer a need for affirmative action policies (or positive discrimination) that were designed socially to engineer greater equality for minority cultural groups—in the United States, primarily African Americans, American Indians, and Hispanics—that had historically been underrepresented in key institutions such as education, law, the media, and politics. However, one could argue that any group considered as a "people of color" could come under an affirmative action mandate.

Race should not be viewed as the only criterion for affirmative action policies. The main beneficiaries of such policy initiatives have been white women. However, race is arguably the key factor in determining the push for race-blind policies. Those who are most vociferous in advocating race-blind policies tend to focus on race being *the* salient factor in creating what is often deemed reverse discrimination. Arguably, one of the key personalities in race-blind policies is Ward Connerly, who made his name after being appointed to the University of California Board of Regents by Republican governor Pete Wilson in 1993. Connerly is largely acknowledged as responsible for Proposition 209, which outlawed racial preferences in the California university system in November 1996. Ironically, Connerly professes to be of one-fourth African ancestry, and his opposition to racial preferences in admission to universities or to employment, which gained widespread support in the 1990s, shows no sign of diminishing in the 2000s. Indeed, writers of all hues such as Shelby Steele, Ann Coulter, David Horowitz, Dinesh D'Souza, and Thomas Sowell, to name a few, have provided ideological support for Connerly's position as probably the preeminent anti-affirmative action proponent.

Interestingly, some conservatives employ Dr. Martin Luther King Jr.'s perspective on race to argue for race-blind policies, arguing that King wanted his children to be judged by the content of their character and not by the color of their skin. However, it could be contended that race-blind advocates have taken King's perspective out of context. It would be wrong to suggest, for example, that he envisioned a society devoid of color or that his children would not be seen as African American. Rather, he wanted a society that did not discriminate on the grounds of race, as had been the case for centuries through the African American experience of enslavement, segregation, and second-class citizenship. To suggest that King did not favor affirmative action to provide a fairer playing field is tantamount to not comprehending the civil rights movement. In this sense, there had to be some form of institutionalized redress for centuries of systemic exclusion based on one's racialized identity.

Contemporary advocates for race-blind policies contend that institutions that favor race-based preferences actually do harm to the person of color by stigmatizing the person with the "affirmative action" label. The argument is that the person has gained his or her place in the university or employment sphere on unmeritocratic principles. For commentators like Shelby Steele, race-preferential treatment actually does more harm than good. Moreover, Steele argues that racism is no longer a relevant factor in the experience of African Americans. For him it is a matter of applying one's individual talent to the task of achievement in society. Race should not enter the equation when it comes to getting ahead in life.

Criticism of the race-blind school of thought has been constant and ever-present. One of the key opponents of the color-blind approach is sociologist Eduardo Bonilla-Silva. He argues forcefully that it is simply another form of ideological racism on behalf of those who benefit from the practice of racialized discrimination. To be sure, individuals such as Steele and Connerly, from historically disadvantaged racial groups, are personally benefiting greatly from their anti-affirmative action points of view. What they oppose, it could be said, is what they most benefit from. Some critics see race-blind advocates as persons wanting to shed every vestige of their ancestral past that identifies them as a "person of color" or as an African American. Others claim that the Katrina hurricane tragedy in Louisiana in 2006 all but confirms the reality of race in North America and continues to be a salient factor in the life chances of many millions born into a cycle of essentially racialized poverty. When millions viewed the tragedy on television screens across the world it was obvious that the Katrina hurricane exposed both race and class in relation to the African American experience. Moreover, if one considers the criminal justice system and how defendants and prisoners continue to be grossly overrepresented by African American males, there is certainly food for thought in considering race as a major factor in the life chances of many.

In short, critics of the race-blind perspective contend that there is still too much social significance in the determining factor of race for North America to suddenly become color-blind in finding methods that ensure equality of opportunity. One only has to read King's books carefully to realize that his vision of a "beloved community" meant, in relation to the reality of race, being aware of the past while carefully monitoring the future via affirmative action policies. There is a strong case for a color-conscious affirmative action initiative that offers equal opportunity without relinquishing fairness in the process. To put it another way, some would suggest that not to consider race as a factor in determining life chances is to suggest cancer will go away if we simply ignore it. Although Proposition 209 has gained momentum, most universities still employ affirmative action, but now it has become based more on one's overall socioeconomic standing rather than one factor such as race or gender. In the latter part of the 2000s, a more nuanced approach to equality of opportunity is being thought through by university administrations.

SEE ALSO *Affirmative Action; African Americans; Civil Rights Movement, U.S.; Diversity; Equal Opportunity; King, Martin Luther, Jr.; Race-Conscious Policies; Stigma; University, The; Whites*

BIBLIOGRAPHY

Bonilla-Silva, Eduardo. 2003. *Racism without Racists: Color-Blind Racism and the Persistence of Racial Inequality in the United States.* New York: Rowman and Littlefield.

Christian, Mark. 2000. *Multiracial Identity: An International Perspective.* New York: St. Martin's.

King, Martin Luther, Jr. 1967. *Where Do We Go from Here: Chaos or Community?* Boston: Beacon.

Pincus, Fred L. 2003. *Reverse Discrimination: Dismantling the Myth.* Boulder, CO: Lynne Rienner.

Steele, Shelby. 2006. *White Guilt: How Blacks and Whites Together Destroyed the Promise of the Civil Rights Era.* New York: HarperCollins.

Mark Christian

RACE-CONSCIOUS POLICIES

Race-conscious policies are usually defined as those explicitly and directly intended to affect the life conditions of racial minorities, whether it be to promote racial equality or preserve the racial status quo. Race-conscious policies in the contemporary United States have been targeted predominantly at African Americans.

Race has been entangled with public policy throughout the history of European settlement in North America. Slavery was introduced early in the seventeenth century, and lasted until the Civil War (1861–1865), more than two centuries later. It was soon replaced by the two-caste racial system known as "Jim Crow," which was most formally organized in the American South. That system was passionately supported by most southern whites, and it was, by common agreement, essentially ignored in both local and national political debates for many years.

The 1930s brought renewed political attention to race. The peremptory lynching of blacks for real or imagined offenses was then a common, though extreme, technique for enforcing the two-caste racial system. Federal anti-lynching legislation was proposed in Congress, but President Roosevelt refused to support it, fearing the loss of his critical political base in the white South. Roosevelt's centerpiece economic legislation, however, which created the Social Security system, was intended to provide support to all older and disabled Americans, regardless of race. But at the behest of white congressmen from the South, agricultural workers and domestic servants were excluded from coverage, leaving those predominantly black segments of the southern work force dependent on the low wages normally paid by white farmers, businessmen, and families. Race was central to congressional debates on both of these issues. Unlike lynching, however, social security was not an explicitly race-conscious issue.

At the end of World War II (1939–1945), formal racial segregation and discrimination remained the cornerstones of southern society, and they were only somewhat less common elsewhere. Civil rights advocates soon began to propose a wide variety of race-conscious policies, all designed to eliminate the elaborate machinery of law, institutional practice, personal behavior, and public opinion that sustained racial inequality. These proposals were almost always greeted with overwhelming opposition in the white South, and they were often initially opposed by whites elsewhere as well. Nevertheless, a number of civil rights successes followed, including the 1950 desegregation of the armed services; the 1954 Supreme Court order to end school segregation; the Civil Rights Act of 1964, which mandated the desegregation of public schools and public accommodations and banned discrimination in employment; the Voting Rights Act of 1965, which outlawed discrimination in the voting process; the 1967 Supreme Court order invalidating laws against racial intermarriage; and the Civil Rights Act of 1968, which banned discrimination in housing. By the 1970s, these paradigmatic race-conscious policies had largely eliminated both the legal foundations and public support for formalized racial segregation and discrimination.

Still, major racial gaps persisted in most areas of life, including educational attainment, income, wealth, health, crime, and mortality. These racial gaps were national problems, but outside of the South they often were perpetuated by custom rather than law, making them more difficult to address directly. Moreover, many of the new civil rights policies had initially been accompanied by weak enforcement provisions. For example, the 1964 Civil Rights Act mandated equal opportunity for all individuals, but lawmakers explicitly rejected proposals that would have required racial equality in outcomes, such as quotas for hiring or college admissions.

In the 1970s, a variety of new race-conscious policies were proposed that were more results-oriented. That is, they were designed to produce actual racial equality in outcomes, not just opportunities, with less concern about the reasons for inequality. The end of de jure segregation, originally created by the legally mandated separation of the races in the public schools, had not ended extensive de facto segregation, created by the largely voluntary residential separation of the races. In 1971 the Supreme Court first ordered the use of busing to redistribute children across school systems. Court-ordered busing soon spread throughout the nation as a solution to racial segregation. This race-conscious policy was vastly unpopular among whites, and racial prejudice was apparently the strongest factor in generating that white opposition.

"Affirmative action" became a blanket term applied to results-oriented policies in several domains, including preferences for minorities in hiring and promotion, "set-asides" of government contracts for minorities, and preferences for underrepresented, minorities in higher education. Such policies soon attracted opposition from many, if not most, whites, again often driven by racial prejudice. A series of closely divided court cases followed. The Supreme Court narrowly upheld preferences in higher education in the 1978 Bakke case, but in 2003 it rejected one University of Michigan plan while narrowly accepting another.

A second category of race-conscious policies is somewhat different. Like de jure segregation, explicit racial policies directly target blacks. Like de facto segregation, implicit racial policies may disproportionately affect blacks, although they are designed to be universalistic and apply equally to people of all races. Implicit racial policies are marked by advocacy that usually includes racial overtones in its visual aids and stereotyped anecdotes, by the polarization of the attitudes of whites and blacks (both among advocates and the mass public), and by the role of racial attitudes in motivating policy preferences, both pro and con.

"Welfare" is a prominent implicit racial-policy domain. In the late 1960s, "the poor" came to be increasingly identified by many Americans as being urban and African American (Gilens 1999), and the opposition to "welfare" among whites became rooted more strongly in racial animosity. A second implicit racial domain is that of "law and order." A number of tough crime policies have been tainted by their association with racial inequality, such as the death penalty, "three strikes" laws, mandatory sentencing laws, the opposition to "permissive" judges, and the especially harsh penalties for the sale and use of crack cocaine, which is used extensively by African Americans. A celebrated political case focused on Willie Horton, a black murderer who, while on a weekend furlough from prison, brutally assaulted a white couple in their home. This case was used successfully by the 1988 Republican presidential campaign to attract racially conservative whites.

A third category of potentially race-conscious policies has been generated by the expanding waves of immigration to the United States and western Europe. Immigration policies concerning border control, citizenship requirements, and public services for the undocumented are all relevant here, as are language policies, such as bilingual education, multi-language ballots, and the drive for an "official" language. These political issues do not comfortably fit within the category of explicit race-conscious issues, because most of the new immigration to the United States has come from Latin America and Asia, rather than involving people of African descent. However, they often are framed as explicitly targeting other stigmatized groups, such as Mexican Americans.

By the turn of the twenty-first century, white support for the old system of legalized segregation and discrimination had virtually disappeared. However, there was still much white opposition to policies intended to remedy racial inequality, and new theories explaining this opposition began to develop. Social psychologists described new forms of racism—such as "symbolic racism"—that had replaced the old, discredited Jim Crow racism (Sears & Henry 2005). Sociologists, meanwhile, focused more on whites' feelings that black gains threatened their real resources and superior group position (Bobo and Tuan 2006).

The gradual movement of American society to formal racial equality and the expanding numbers of non-European immigrants have converged to produce new political debates on multiculturalism and identity politics. "Multiculturalism" has several meanings, variously describing a society with peoples of many cultures, tolerance and equal treatment for people differing in values and customs, or the privileging of group identities as bases for resource allocation, political alliances, and even self-concepts (Citrin et al. 2001). Although multiculturalism has been influenced by the long intellectual history of black nationalism, it has spread far beyond race and ethnicity as group categories, and therefore well beyond race-conscious policies as well.

SEE ALSO *Affirmative Action; Attitudes, Racial;* Brown v. Board of Education, *1954; Civil Rights Movement, U.S.; Desegregation; Desegregation, School; Jim Crow; Lynchings; Racism; Welfare*

BIBLIOGRAPHY

Bobo, Lawrence, and Mia Tuan. 2006. *Prejudice in Politics: Group Position, Public Opinion, and the Wisconsin Treaty Rights Dispute.* Cambridge, MA: Harvard University Press.

Citrin, Jack, David O. Sears, Christopher Muste, and Cara Wong. 2001. Multiculturalism in American Public Opinion. *British Journal of Political Science* 31 (2): 247–275.

Gilens, Martin. 1999. *Why Americans Hate Welfare: Race, Media, and the Politics of Antipoverty Policy.* Chicago: University of Chicago Press.

Mendelberg, Tali. 2001. *The Race Card: Campaign Strategy, Implicit Messages, and the Norm of Equality.* Princeton, NJ: Princeton University Press.

Schuman, Howard, Charlotte Steeh, Lawrence Bobo, and Maria Krysan. 1997. *Racial Attitudes in America: Trends and Interpretations.* Rev. ed. Cambridge, MA: Harvard University Press.

Sears, David O., and P. J. Henry. 2005. Over Thirty Years Later: A Contemporary Look at Symbolic Racism. In *Advances in Experimental Social Psychology*, ed. Mark Zanna, Vol. 37, 95–150. San Diego, CA: Elsevier/Academic Press.

Sears, David O., Carl P. Hensler, and Leslie K. Speer. 1979. Whites' Opposition to "Busing": Self-interest or Symbolic Politics? *American Political Science Review* 73: 369–384.

David O. Sears

RACIAL CLASSIFICATION

Modern racial classification schemes emerged in the eighteenth century during a period of European colonization and empire building. Racial classifications have been central to state formation, nation building, and the establishment of hierarchies that determine access to power in the form of material, social, cultural, and natural resources. The racial classifications schemes employed in the English-speaking, French-speaking, Spanish-speaking, and Portuguese-speaking worlds were established during European colonialism, when indigenous peoples were conquered, enslaved, and forcefully incorporated into European nation-states as colonial subjects. These classification schemes are not simple reflections of "biological" or natural differences in physical appearance, but power relations that were established during the seventeenth and eighteenth centuries as colonial expansion brought people in diverse regions under the control of Europeans.

HISTORICAL BACKGROUND

The scientists who produced classifications of human groups were Europeans. Carolus Linnaeus (1707–1778), a Swedish botanist, produced the first modern classification of human populations in 1735. Linnaeus, the founder of scientific taxonomy, divided the genus *Homo* into four racial types: Eurapaeus, Americanus, Asiaticus, and Africanus. During this period the dominant view was monogenesis—the view that all humans were the descendants of a common original ancestor. Johann Blumenbach (1752–1840), a German professor of medicine, became the most influential of the scientists who classified human populations. Between 1770 and 1781 Blumenbach proposed the division of humans into four and later five "varieties" that represented the world's major regions: Caucasian, Mongolian, Ethiopian, American, and Malay. Blumenbach considered women from the Caucasus region in Russia to be the most beautiful of all Europeans, so he chose them to represent the European ideal type, and all other human groups were a departure and degeneration from this ideal. These racial typologies were ranked and were not considered equal in aesthetic beauty, intelligence, temperament, or morality. The racial typologies created by Blumenbach reflected a belief in European supremacy, legitimated racialized slavery, and the subordination of groups of people based upon their physical and cultural differences. These racial classification schemes linked physical traits such as eye color, skin color, hair texture, nose shape, and mouth size to intellectual capacities, cultural traits, and moral temperaments. To formulate these classification schemes Blumenbach and other scientists relied primarily on the written observations and descriptions of "ordinary" men who earned their living as slave traders, slave owners, merchants, or others in dominant positions over peoples whom they considered "savages."

By the end of the eighteenth century the economic interests and political goals of European colonizers had firmly established racial classification systems as tools employed by nation-states to subordinate the people whom they had colonized and conquered. Three hundred years after the establishment of modern racial classification systems, patterns of social and economic inequalities remain between racial and ethnic groups in multiracial nations throughout the world. The racial typologies established by European men during the eighteenth century are used as "legal" and political identities, and they continue to inform "scientific" thinking today. Many of these typologies' terms remain in use today. For example, the term *Caucasian* continues to be used as a reference to white people of known and visible European ancestry, and is a term of self-identification in North America. In some countries such as the United States it is common to classify children by race when they are born in hospitals. Race, like gender, has become part of people's "legal" identities, which follows them through their lives as they move from various institutions such as schools, hospitals, and prisons. Their "racial" and ethnic identity may change as they move across nation-state boundaries where the criteria for inclusion or exclusion in a racial category

changes. In other cases, individuals may be "reclassified" as adults upon their request. For example, prior to the dismantling of apartheid in South Africa, special legal courts were established to handle racial reclassification cases.

POLITICS OF RACIAL CLASSIFICATION

In nations that were structured by state-sponsored racial segregation (and white supremacy) such as the United States and South Africa, one's racial classification determined where one could live, purchase a home, and attend school, whom one could marry, and what occupation was suitable. In other words, all aspects of one's economic, intimate, social, and political life were structured along racial lines. In the late twentieth century as state-sanctioned racial inequality such as Jim Crow segregation in the United States and apartheid in South Africa were dismantled, nations established a range of public policies designed to remedy past group-based discrimination. These policies have taken various forms, such as affirmative action in the United States and positive discrimination in the United Kingdom. Although nation-states have dismantled *de jure* (legal) racial segregation and formally criminalized discrimination against members of racial and ethnic minorities, one's racial status continues to overdetermine an individual's life chances and access to resources in multiracial societies.

Social scientists have documented patterns of social inequality that demonstrate that belonging to a racially dominant or racially subordinate group is correlated with infant mortality rates, educational achievements, access to healthcare, housing, and wealth, and freedom from routinized violence. In other words, resources and privileges are unequally distributed along racial and ethnic lines. Public-policy initiatives by nation-states and local governments depend on racial classifications to remedy and counter group-based inequalities. Governments employ census data that classifies individuals by race and "ethnicity" in order to redistribute resources such as education, health care, housing, public assistance, and other resources in an effort to eliminate and minimize racialized inequality that continue to determine life chances. For example, in the United States, the direct descendants of American Indians and the descendants of enslaved Africans are more likely to endure intense poverty, lower life expectancies, residential segregation, social isolation, higher suicide rates, and higher infant mortality rates, and are more likely to be victims of hate crimes when compared to European and Asian Americans in the same age cohort and/or class position. One's racial classification is strongly associated with one's location in economically impoverished regions and communities where access to valued resources is minimal.

CHANGES IN THE U.S. CENSUS CATEGORIES

Racial classification schemes reflect power relations and political constituencies and thus are not stable. For example, in the United States, racial categories have been added, removed, revised, and altered during the past 300 years in response to demographic changes, immigration, political mobilization, technologies, cultural shifts, and economic interests. The United States is unique in its historical enforcement of what has become known as the "one-drop rule," in which a person of multiracial ancestry, who had known or visible African ancestry, is legally classified as "black," regardless of appearance, cultural training, and self-identification. The one-drop rule has been consistently upheld by state and federal courts. In states such as Louisiana there were so many people of African ancestry socially classified and living as "whites" that "race clerks" were hired to strictly enforce the one-drop rule. A number of significant changes have occurred in the census during the past 100 years including changes in census categories, instructions to the census enumerator, and the ability of individuals to self-report their race and ancestry.

In 1918, the U.S. Census Bureau estimated at least three-fourths of all native blacks were racially mixed, and it predicted that pure blacks would disappear (see Davis 1991, p. 57). Consequently after 1920 the mulatto category was removed from the census and no further attempt was made by the U.S. government to systematically count the number of visible mulattos in the United States, partly because there were so many persons with some black ancestry who appeared white.

Social scientists have documented the inconsistencies in the logic employed by the U.S. census and the disparity between social-cultural and scientific definitions of race. By 1960 the practice of self-identification by race replaced the earlier practice in which the census taker assigned race. Beginning in 1960 the head of household indicated the "race" of all of its members. Surprisingly this did not introduce any noticeable changes in the numbers of blacks in the population. In 1970 the Hispanic category was added to the U.S. census for the first time. While in 1980, for the first time, a question on ancestry was included in the census. In response to increased political mobilization by members of interracial or multiracial families, the United States added the category "multiracial" to the 2000 census. In the following year the United Kingdom also added a "mixed race" category to their 2001 census. These changes in the official census reflect political struggles over the boundaries between and within racial groups, as well as how resources will be distributed and who will be counted and included in racial and ethnic minority categories. Racial classification schemes are socially produced, yet they have real material, social, and economic consequences for members of racialized groups.

SEE ALSO Discrimination; Economics, Stratification; Hierarchy; Identification, Racial; Identity; Identity, Social; Policing, Biased; Race; Racism; Self-Classification; Social Categorization

BIBLIOGRAPHY

Anderson, Warwick. 2003. *The Cultivation of Whiteness: Science, Health, and Racial Destiny in Australia.* New York: Basic Books.

Davis, Floyd James. 1991. *Who Is Black? One Nation's Definition.* University Park: Pennsylvania State University Press.

Dubow, Saul. 1995. *Scientific Racism in Modern South Africa.* New York: Cambridge University Press.

Fredrickson, George. 1981. *White Supremacy: A Comparative Study of American and South African History.* New York: Oxford University Press.

Nesiah, Devanesan. 1997. *Discrimination with Reason?: The Policy of Reservations in the United States, India, and Malaysia.* New York: Oxford University Press.

Perlmann, Joel, and Mary Waters, eds. 2002. *The New Race Question: How the Census Counts Multiracial Individuals.* New York: Russell Sage Foundation.

Smedley, Audrey. 1993. *Race in North America: Origin and Evolution of a Worldview.* Boulder, CO: Westview Press.

France Winddance Twine

RACIAL EPITHETS

SEE *Racial Slurs.*

RACIAL IDENTIFICATION

SEE *Identification, Racial.*

RACIAL INEQUALITY

SEE *Inequality, Racial.*

RACIAL PROFILING

SEE *Policing, Biased.*

RACIAL SLURS

Racial slurs, often called *racial epithets*, are words or phrases that refer to members of racial and ethnic groups in a derogatory manner. Slurs and all other forms of racial defamation dehumanize targeted groups and justify racial oppression by suggesting that targeted populations are unworthy of equality (Clark 1995, p. 6). Racial slurs take myriad forms and are often adapted by users to fit a variety of contexts. They may mention a racial category explicitly (e.g., *Japs* for Japanese people, *Chinks* for Chinese people, and *spics* for Hispanics) or indirectly allude to the targeted racial group by referencing common derogatory stereotypes (e.g., *porch monkeys* and *spearchuckers* for African Americans). Other racial slurs refer to historical encounters (e.g., *redskins* for Native Americans). In some cases, racial epithets targeting one group are derived from slurs targeting a different group (e.g., *sand niggers* for Middle Eastern people). Other examples of racial slurs commonly used in the United States include *nigger, wetback, coolie, kike,* and *dago*.

Racial slurs are usually created and used primarily by the dominant racial group in society. A variety of sociopolitical circumstances govern the creation and duration of racial slurs. Initial contact between racial groups in the form of militaristic exploration (colonialism) or migration frequently leads to racial conflict. This, in turn, often generates racial imaging and racial slurs, when one racial group considers itself distinct from and better than another. During conquests, European conquistadors and colonists invented numerous racial slurs (for example, *Indian savages*) to denigrate and rationalize the oppression of Native Americans. Subsequent generations of European Americans coined other slurs to disparage and rationalize the subordination of African Americans and various populations of immigrants of color.

After their creation during initial contact, racial slurs persist in two contexts, which Leslie Picca and Joe Feagin (2007) have termed the social *frontstage* and *backstage*. Frontstage refers to multiracial environments where racist acts are performed. These environments range from relatively private gatherings to major public events. Members of dominant groups use racial slurs in public spaces to intimidate members of other groups and to prevent challenges to the dominant group's status and privileges. Racial slurs are extremely common when the economic and political privileges of dominant groups are threatened by resistance from oppressed groups. In 1994 six African American employees were embattled in a racial discrimination lawsuit against the Texaco company. Threatened by their act of resistance, some angry Texaco executives were tape-recorded referring to the employees as "black jelly-beans."

Explicit public uses of racial slurs range from their appearance on signs during white supremacist demonstrations to their use by whites during lynchings and other incidents of racial violence. In the absence of a sufficiently powerful formal or informal social structure, dominant groups may use racial slurs as the primary colloquial term for discussing racial others. In contemporary times, some have resorted to referring to African Americans with derogatory "coded" racial slurs. In 2006 the Equal Employment Opportunity Commission filed a lawsuit against a medical clinic that was referring to a black employee as a "reggin," the N-word spelled backwards. There has been a rise in the use of "coded" racial slurs such as "boy," "drug dealer," "you people," and "thug." These coded racial slurs carry a contemporary message of hate.

Despite the attention such public usage receives, racial slurs are now most commonly used *backstage*, in settings where only members of the dominant racial group are present. In this environment, slurs insult the relevant racial others and build solidarity among those present. Formal and informal sanctions against the public use of racial slurs have created a climate of political correctness in which most people refrain from the use of terms and symbols that may be viewed by other populations as offensive. Ever since the moral climate of the civil rights movement there have been changes in the United States that have curbed the public use of racist epithets; however, in private, members of the dominant racial group may continue to use them with impunity.

Because race is a social construction and not a biological reality, over time a minority group may be redefined as part of the dominant racial group. As this process occurs, these redefined groups are less often the targets of racial slurs. For example, in the United States, white Anglo-Saxon Protestant Americans originally classified Irish Catholic immigrants as nonwhite and racially inferior. During the mid-nineteenth century, established European Americans targeted the Irish with racialized slurs, such as *paddy* and *mick*. As generations of Irish Catholic families assimilated to the Anglo-Saxon core culture, the established white groups were unable to distinguish Irish people from other European Americans, and the use of anti-Irish slurs decreased. The use of slurs against racial groups who cannot pass as white does not decline as sharply, regardless of their degree of cultural assimilation.

Arguably, no racial slur has been as prominent and damaging as *nigger*, which remains a potent epithet used against people of African descent. Use of *nigger* is so hurtful to African Americans that most people publicly reference it as "the N-word." Possibly derived from *niger*, the Latin word meaning black, *nigger* has been decidedly derogatory since the eighteenth century. The term has primarily been used by white Americans to derogate blacks as unworthy of equality due to their alleged intellectual, moral, and cultural inferiority. Although generations of white Americans used *nigger* as their primary term for referring to African Americans, whites would often use the slur during explicitly violent racist actions, such as lynchings, adding an implicit threat of violence to any use of the word. Despite contemporary use in popular media, sometimes by black musicians attempting to defang its potency, *nigger* retains its power to insult, intimidate, and threaten African Americans.

In the United States, many citizens have looked to the political and judicial systems for relief from hateful terms. In a landmark case, *Chaplinsky v. New Hampshire* (1942), the U.S. Supreme Court ruled that " 'fighting' words—those which by their very utterance inflict injury or tend to incite an immediate breach of the peace," are not protected by the First Amendment to the U.S. Constitution. The court ruled that restricting fighting words is permissible because hate speech is not valuable for contributing to greater understandings and because the state has a legitimate interest in limiting disruptions of the peace. Under *Chaplinsky*, state laws proscribing the public use of racial slurs were deemed constitutional. Since *Chaplinsky*, however, the Court has limited the scope of the doctrine to incidents in which provocative words are "directed at the person of the hearer" and there is an immediate threat of retaliatory violence (*UWM Post, Incorporated v. Board of Regents of the University of Wisconsin System*, 1991). In so doing, the court has largely disregarded the first half of the fighting words doctrine, which recognized the injury that racial slurs and other hate speech inflict on hearers.

The Supreme Court has generally struck down laws limiting free speech on the grounds that they are either "overbroad," meaning they restrict speech beyond that which falls under the fighting words doctrine, or are attempts to regulate ideas and content. Speaking to attempts to regulate content, in *R.A.V. v. St Paul, Minnesota* (1992), the Supreme Court declared that the purpose of the First Amendment is to prevent the majority from expressing its preferences by silencing the minority. Consequently, the high court provided protection for racially hostile speech in public spaces by deeming unconstitutional laws precluding speech simply because that speech is racially hostile.

Academics and legal scholars have responded to the courts by emphasizing the right of individuals to move in public spaces without the fear of racial hostility. These scholars take seriously the harmful effects that racial slurs and closely related actions have on their targets. Many victims of hostile and intense racial slurs suffer physiological and psychological injuries, including high blood pressure, breathing difficulty, nightmares, and thoughts of suicide

(McKinney and Feagin 2003; Matsuda 1995). To avoid subjection to recurring racist slurs, people of color often must leave their homes or jobs, which limits their socioeconomic opportunities. Scholars also criticize the Court's insistence on limiting only words directed at individuals. Because racial slurs dehumanize members of the targeted group, they lay the groundwork for both individual and state-sponsored violence against that group (Fergenson 1995). To take a major example, the German Nazis' hostile slurs against Jews as *vermin* and *parasites* were directly connected to the "final solution" that Jews must be "exterminated."

Prompted by the effects of German Nazi propaganda during World War II (1939–1945), international efforts to regulate hate speech have given far more consideration than have U.S. policymakers to the rights of the targets of such speech. Consequently, the international community has outlawed most racist hate speech (Matsuda 1995, pp. 92, 96). Article 4 of the International Convention on the Elimination of All Forms of Racial Discrimination (1965) declares illegal all propaganda based on ideas of the superiority of one race over another or that promote racial hatred and discrimination. Other human rights treaties, including the European Convention for the Protection of Human Rights and Fundamental Freedoms (1950) and the Inter-American Declaration of the Rights and Duties of Man, (1948) protect people against recurring racist slurs and other hate speech. Similarly, many national governments have outlawed racist speech.

SEE ALSO *Anti-Semitism; Civil Rights Movement, U.S.; Colonialism; Feagin, Joseph; Harassment; Humiliation; Immigration; Nativism; Obscenity; Other, The; Political Correctness; Race Relations; Racism; Supreme Court, U.S.*

BIBLIOGRAPHY

Clark, Kenneth. 1995. Group Defamation and the Oppression of Black Americans. In *Group Defamation and Freedom of Speech: The Relationship between Language and Violence*, eds. Monroe H. Freedman and Eric M. Freedman, 3–8. Westport, CT: Greenwood.

Fergenson, Laraine R. 1995. Group Defamation: From Language to Thought to Action. In *Group Defamation and Freedom of Speech: The Relationship between Language and Violence*, eds. Monroe H. Freedman and Eric M. Freedman, 71–86. Westport, CT: Greenwood.

Matsuda, Mari J. 1995. Outsider Jurisprudence: Toward a Victim's Analysis of Racial Hate Messages. In *Group Defamation and Freedom of Speech: The Relationship between Language and Violence*, eds. Monroe H. Freedman and Eric M. Freedman, 87–120. Westport, CT: Greenwood.

McKinney, Karyn D., and Joe R. Feagin. 2003. *The Many Costs of Racism*. New York: Rowman and Littlefield.

Picca, Leslie, and Joe R. Feagin. 2007. *Two-Faced Racism: Whites in the Backstage and Frontstage.* New York: Routledge.

Joe R. Feagin
Glenn E. Bracey II

RACIALIZATION

The concept of racialization has developed over time. In his 1989 book *Racism*, sociologist Robert Miles described racialization as "a dialectical process by which meaning is attributed to particular biological features of human beings, as a result of which individuals may be assigned to a general category of persons which reproduces itself biologically.... The process of racialization of human beings entails the racialization of the processes in which they participate and the structures and institutions that result" (Miles 1989, p. 76). Earlier, in *The Wretched of the Earth*, the political theorist Frantz Fanon (1925–1961) had described the "racialization of thought" in reference to the failure of early Europeans to recognize that Africans had a distinct culture that was unique to them. Instead Europeans, "set up white culture to fill the gap left by [what they believed was] the absence of other cultures" (Fanon 2001, p. 171). Sociologist Yehudi Webster later defined the concept of racialization as "a systemic accentuation of certain physical attributes to allocate persons to races that are projected as real and thereby become the basis for analyzing all social relations" (Webster 1992, p. 3). Webster goes on to argue that "the second foundations of racialization are provided by social scientific research on race relations, in which the disciplines of history and sociology play an eminent role" (p. 4).

Culture is a key aspect in both Miles's and Fanon's definitions of racialization. Historically, there have been intense debates over the issue of race as a social construction versus race based on biology. Omi and Winant addressed the debate and articulated the concept of racialization that many scholars use today. They defined racial formation as "the sociohistorical process by which racial categories are created, inhabited, transformed, and destroyed.... Race is a matter of both social structure and cultural representation" (Omi and Winant 1994, pp. 55–56). This view revolutionized the conception of race as a process and as a social construction.

CRITIQUING "RACIALIZATION"

Some scholars have critiqued current definitions of racialization. Karim Murji and John Solomos, for example, argue that the idea of racialization "has become a core concept in the analysis of racial phenomena, particularly to signal the processes by which ideas about race are con-structed, come to be regarded as meaningful, and are acted upon.... Racialization is applied to whole institutions such as the police, educational or legal systems, or entire religions, nations, and countries" (Solomos 2005, p. 1).

Sociologist Joe Feagin argues that "Omi and Winant view the past of North American slavery and legal segregation as not weighing 'like a nightmare on the brain of the living,' but rather as lingering on 'like a hangover' that is gradually going away" (Feagin 2006, p. 7). Feagin adds that what is "missing in both the mainstream race-ethnic relations approach and much of the racial formation approach is a full recognition of the big picture—the reality of this whole society being founded on, and firmly grounded in, oppression targeting African Americans (and other people of color) now for several centuries. Given that deep underlying reality of this society, all racial-ethnic relationships and events, past and present, must be placed within that racial oppression context in order to be well-understood" (p. 7).

Sociologist Eduardo Bonilla-Silva notes that although the perspective of Omi and Winant "represents a breakthrough, it still gives undue attention to ideological/cultural processes, does not regard races as truly social collectivities, and overemphasizes the racial projects ... of certain actors (neoconservatives, members of the far right, liberals), thus obscuring the social and general character of racialized societies" (Bonilla-Silva 1997, p. 466). Bonilla-Silva further states:

> Although all racialized systems are hierarchical, the particular character of the hierarchy, and thus the racial structure, is variable.... The racial practices and mechanisms that have kept Blacks subordinated changed from overt to eminently racist to covert and indirectly racist. The unchanging element throughout these stages is that Blacks' life chances are significantly lower than those of Whites, and ultimately a racialized social order is distinguished by this difference in life chances.... The historical struggle against chattel slavery led not to the development of race-free societies but to the establishment of social system with a different kind of racialization. (Bonilla-Silva 1997, p. 470)

In their 2005 book *Racialization*, Murji and Solomos summarize the arguments that suggest that the conception of racialization introduced by Omi and Winant may not have represented a breakthrough:

> Barot and Bird feel that Omi and Winant "use the concept of racial formation as a perspective that is not fundamentally different from the concept of racialization as deployed in British literature in the 1980's.... Miles himself has argued that Omi and

Winant's conception of racialization is underdeveloped and not used systematically.... Miles and Torres state, 'Omi and Winant's defence of the race concept is a classic example of the way in which the academy in the US continues to racialize the world.' " (Murji and Solomos 2005, p. 22–23)

RETHINKING RACIALIZATION

Bonilla-Silva proposes use of "the more general concept of racialized social systems as the starting point for an alternative framework. This term refers to societies in which economic, political, social and ideological levels are partially structured by the placement of actors in racial categories or races" (Bonilla-Silva 1997, p. 469). In rethinking a theory of racial oppression, Feagin suggests three elements: "It should indicate clearly the major features—both the structures and the counterforces—of the social phenomenon being studied; it should show the relationships between the important structures and forces; and it should assist in understanding both the patterns of social change and the lack of social change" (Feagin 2006, p. 7). As the critiques of these scholars suggest, the concept of racialization has changed over time and continues to change.

SEE ALSO *Discrimination; Preference, Color; Race; Race Relations; Racism; Whiteness; Whitening*

BIBLIOGRAPHY

Barot, Rohit, and John Bird. 2001. Racialization: The Genealogy and Critique of a Concept. *Ethnic and Racial Studies* 24 (4): 601–618.

Bonilla-Silva, Eduardo. 1997. Rethinking Racism: Toward a Structural Interpretation. *American Sociological Review* 62 (3): 465–480.

Fanon, Frantz. 2001. *The Wretched of the Earth*. Trans. Constance Farrington. New York: Penguin.

Feagin, Joe R. 2006. *Systemic Racism: A Theory of Oppression*. New York: Routledge.

Miles, Robert. 1989. *Racism*. London: Routledge. 2nd ed., 2003.

Miles, Robert, and Rodolfo D. Torres. 1999. Does Race Matter? In *Race, Identity, and Citizenship: A Reader*, eds. Rodolfo Torres, Louis Mirón, and Jonathan Xavier Inda, 3–38. Malden, MA: Blackwell.

Murji, Karim, and John Solomos. 2005. *Racialization: Studies in Theory and Practice*. New York: Oxford University Press.

Omi, Michael, and Howard Winant. 1994. *Racial Formation in the United States: From the 1960s to the 1990s*. 2nd ed. New York: Routledge.

Webster, Yehudi O. 1992. *The Racialization of America*. New York: St. Martin's Press.

Ruth Thompson-Miller

RACISM

Racism is intertwined with discrimination in two dimensions. On the one hand, discrimination is a specific practice that can arise from racism. On the other hand, racism is a specific form of discrimination directed against a social group that is constructed with regard to physical attributes, for example the color of the skin or the hair type. To these physical attributes specific social features such as behaviors and values are ascribed, thus naturalizing social attributes. Privileges and disadvantages of groups are therefore grounded in nature and gain their legitimacy through this naturalization. The identity of a person is always dependent on the marking, the ascription, and the perception of others. Self and other are defined in a reciprocal relationship: Racism is a specific process of producing self and other (see Darity, Mason, and Stewart 2006). It is the praxis of a dominant group classifying and characterizing an inferior group. Thus some scholars argue that racism transforms political or economical interests into apparently natural facts. Because racism affects social relations, class and race should be examined together (see Hall 1980).

Racism is produced on different levels of societies. On the macro level, racism comes into being through institutional rules, guidelines, and processes of exclusion that are based on and justified by racist discourse. Examples are the Jim Crow laws in the United States, the Nazi regime in Germany, and the apartheid system in South Africa. On the micro level, individual racism comes into being through generalizations, stereotypes, and discrimination against the other's everyday activities.

The phenomenon of racism existed long before social scientists defined the term. In the 1930s the term *racism* was first used by the German physician Magnus Hirschfeld (1868–1935) to describe the ideology upon which the Nazis based their identification of the Jews as members of an alien, subordinate, and dangerous race, providing an ideological foundation for the Holocaust (for a wider analysis see Horkheimer and Adorno 1947).

THE DEVELOPMENT OF IDEOLOGICAL RACISM

Ideological racism developed from the processes of construing the human races as apparently homogenous and then building a hierarchy of these races on the basis of ascribed features. These concepts were developed in Europe in the eighteenth century in the context of the Enlightenment and the increased trust in scientific knowledge. Laws of nature were presented as the foundation for differences between social groups, and scientists tried to classify human beings according to categorizations developed in the natural sciences.

Some argue that these classifications based on nature replaced former classifications based on religion, following a trend to secularization. In contrast, Robert Miles and Malcolm Brown argued in *Racism* (2003) that the clash between the idea of biologically constituted different races and the religious belief that all human species descend from Adam and Eve and are therefore homogenous was harmonized by the claim that in response to human sin God damned the sinners and their descendents by distinctive features, such as black skin.

The main impulse to formulate racism as a theory came from French aristocrats striving to get back the privileges they lost in the French Revolution. According to them, the French aristocrats were descendants of the Franconian conqueror, so any restriction of their privileges was a violation of their inherited rights; this idea was formulated as "the legend of the Franconia" by the French historian Henri de Boulainvilliers (1658–1722). Socially different estates in France became referred to as different "races." In consequence, the privileges of the aristocracy became legitimized not only by the legal system, but also by what were presented as hereditary, physical traits. Charles Darwin's theory of natural selection and evolution (1863) provided further justification for this theory of the naturally grounded inequality of human beings. The adaptation of Darwin's theory of evolution to society is called *social Darwinism* (see Hawkins 1997, Dickens 2000). Following this theory, disadvantaged races have their social positions because of their inferior qualities, and those inferior qualities are translated to inevitably lower social status in the common struggle for existence. The idea of a racial hierarchy based on nature became important during the colonization period beginning at the end of the fifteenth century when in the process of oppressing and exploiting Africans, Asians, and Native Americans the supposed racial superiority of whites was established (for a discussion of whiteness, see Bonnett 2000 and Allen 1994).

Racial inequality is a matter of scholarly debate. Some academics argue, with the help of recent genetic research, that there are more genetic variations *within* races than between them. In this view, races do not naturally exist, but instead are powerful social constructions of racist people (see Miles and Brown 2003). Adherents to this theory argue that there are no clear *natural* borders between the races; racism itself constitutes these borders and tries to maintain them by ignoring any exceptions. Two crucial aspects of the impact of racism emerge: On the one hand, there is the practice of defining an apparently homogenous group of human beings as a race by negating differences between the individual members of the group; on the other hand, it is essential that the differences between the social groups that are constructed as races are emphasized.

Other scholars argue that the reason for racism is not that there are different races. According to them, racism is caused by the ascription of specific attributes to the races, and they hold that by identifying races as an ideological effect the racial solidarity of the disadvantaged race is undermined.

PSYCHOLOGICAL EFFECTS OF RACISM AND REFLECTIONS OF RACISM IN THE PSYCHE

Racism gets its full power by infiltrating people's own specific perceptions. In the minds of both victims and perpetrators, racism is produced and reproduced with prejudices and stereotypes from the other and the own. It has been widely demonstrated that from the perspective of whites, blacks are seen as violent and criminal. Studies in psychology illustrate that the same behavior pattern is interpreted differently depending on the race of the actor (see, for example, Eberhardt, Goff, Purdie, et al. 2004). From the point of view of whites, a positive action by a black person, like being smart and helpful, often is seen as an atypical event explained by special circumstances, whereas a negative action by a black, like committing a crime or an aggressive behavior, is seen as typical of the genuine personal characteristics of black people. For the actions of whites, the relation is reversed. Claude Steele and Joshua Aronson illustrated the harmful effects of stereotypes when they demonstrated that the mere presence of a question asking the race of those taking an academic test led to a distinct decrease in the scores of participating African American college students: The race question activated negative stereotypes and self-confirming mental representations of poor academic performance. In consequence, the test participants confirmed unwittingly the stereotype that African Americans are intellectually inferior. Different tests showed that the simple activation of race stereotypes had different effects on test performances, depending on the kind of stereotypes (Shih, Ambady, Richeson, et al. 2002).

RACISM IN THE UNITED STATES

Because racism depends on economic and political factors, it is important to point out that racism came into being in different forms depending on the historic epoch and geographical region in which it appeared.

Slavery Slavery came into existence in China, imperial Rome, and West Africa without relying on racist concepts. However, in the colonial period the ideology of racism was useful in circumventing any of the conquerors' religious or moral considerations that would make all human beings equal before God and thus require that they be treated equally by man. Using racist arguments, white conquerors could justify slavery, the use of slaves as property, the destruction of their social and cultural identities (Patterson 1982), and their exploitation. This was possible because the conceived hierarchy of races presented the whites as superior to other races; from a racist perspective, human beings are not equal and therefore they can be treated unequally.

The main reasons for the growth of slavery were economic. Slaves were used as a cheap labor force and as a profitable trade good. In the United States the profits acquired through slavery were an important factor in the growth of the shipping industry and a source of surplus wealth for early industrialism. Slaves worked in households, in mines, and on sugar and cotton plantations in the southern states of North America, in Brazil, and in the Caribbean. Most of the 4 million slaves in 1860 were the property of a small upper class in the U.S. southern states, and for this elite, their own economic power was bound directly to their property of slaves. They justified slavery by identifying blacks as a weak race that had to be protected by the slave owners, who knew how to treat them according to their natural status.

Before the end of the slave trade in the mid-nineteenth century, between 11 and 15 million Africans were enslaved and transported to Europe and South, Central, and North America. Most of them were enslaved during the eighteenth century, and most came from the West African coast and from central Africa.

After the Civil War After the U.S. Civil War (1861–1865) slavery was legally banned in 1870 by the Fifteenth Amendment to the Constitution. Because there was no land reform most African Americans were solidly concentrated in the southeastern states, nominally free but economically tied to the same cotton lands and the same employers as before the war. Former slaves were still stigmatized and pressed into economic poverty. From the perspective of racist whites in the northern and southern states, African Americans were an inferior race without the right to participate equally in political and social life. After the end of slavery in the United States racism took shape in the oppression of the African American population and in defining them as a subordinated race.

Discriminatory practices continued in the United States; the Jim Crow laws (1890–1912) banned African Americans from public places, curtailed their educational rights, and allowed widespread violence against people of color, including the lynching of more than 3,000 African Americans in the southern states between 1882 and 1936. Clandestine organizations such as the Ku Klux Klan murdered and harassed African Americans.

The Twenty-First Century The civil rights movement in the United States led to the passage of the Civil Rights Act of 1964, ending institutionalized racism in the United States. However, racism is still alive; the durability of ideological racism and the idea of naturally based inequality between races still is present in the attribution of social traits to racial groups. In consequence, economic and educational opportunities are still unequal between the races. African Americans are still put into a position of inferiority in the hierarchy of races; an expression of this is segregation in urban ghettos (see Massey and Denton 1993 and Wilson 1987). Racist discourse still exists and reproduces itself in the stereotypes; it is part of everyday discrimination, and it leads to different chances for access and participation in the contemporary United States and elsewhere.

SEE ALSO *Discrimination; Economics, Stratification; Hierarchy; IQ Controversy; Prejudice; Race; Stigma; Stratification; White Supremacy; Whiteness; Whites*

BIBLIOGRAPHY

Allen, Theodore. 1994. *The Invention of White Race: Racial Oppression and Social Control.* London: Verso.

Bonnett, Alastair. 2000. *White Identities: Historical and International Perspectives.* Harlow, U.K.: Prentice Hall.

Darity, William A. Jr., Patrick L. Mason, and James Stewart. 2006. The Economics of Identity: The Origin and Persistence of Racial Identity Norms. *Journal of Economic Behavior and Organizations* 60 (3): 283–305.

Dickens, Peter. 2000. *Social Darwinism: Linking Evolutionary Thought to Social Theory.* Philadelphia: Open University Press.

Eberhardt, Jennifer L., Phillip Atiba Goff, Valerie J. Purdie, and Paul G. Davies. 2004. Seeing Black: Race, Crime, and Visual Processing. *Journal of Personality and Social Psychology* 87 (6): 876–893.

Fredrickson, George M. 2002. *Racism: A Short History.* Princeton, NJ: Princeton University Press.

Hall, Stuart. 1980. Race, Articulation, and Societies Structured in Dominance. In *Sociological Theories: Race and Colonialism*, 305–345. Paris: UNESCO.

Hawkins, Mike. 1997. *Social Darwinism in European and American Thought, 1860–1945: Nature and Model and Nature as Threat.* London: Cambridge University Press.

Horkheimer, Max, and Theodor W. Adorno. [1947] 2002. *Dialectic of Enlightenment.* Stanford, CA: Stanford University Press.

Massey, Douglas, and Nancy Denton. 1993. *American Apartheid: Segregation and the Making of the Underclass.* Cambridge, MA: Harvard University Press.

Miles, Robert, and Malcolm Brown. 2003. *Racism.* 2nd ed. London and New York: Routledge.

Patterson, Orlando. 1982. *Slavery and Social Death: A Comparative Study.* Cambridge, MA: Harvard University Press.

Shih, Margaret, Nalini Ambady, Jennifer A. Richeson, et al. 2002. Stereotype Performance Boosts: The Impact of Self-Relevance and the Manner of Stereotype Activation. *Journal of Personality and Social Psychology* 83 (3): 638–647.

Steele, Claude M., and Joshua Aronson. 1995. Stereotype Threat and the Intellectual Test Performance of African Americans. *Journal of Personality and Social Psychology* 69: 797–811.

Wilson, William J. 1987. *The Truly Disadvantaged: The Inner City, the Underclass, and Public Policy*. Chicago: University of Chicago Press.

Lars Meier

RADCLIFFE-BROWN, A. R.
1881–1955

Alfred Reginald Radcliffe-Brown was a British anthropologist closely associated with the development of structural-functionalism. His firm theoretical framework and his administrative skills helped to consolidate social anthropology as an academic discipline across the British Commonwealth.

Defying his impoverished lower-middle-class beginnings, Radcliffe-Brown enjoyed an elite academic education at Cambridge University, where A. C. Haddon (1855–1940) and W. H. R. Rivers (1864–1922) were his mentors. He first wanted to study natural sciences, but was directed toward "moral sciences" (comprising philosophy, psychology, and economics). Yet his leanings toward the natural sciences remained with him throughout his career, and the use of analogies between social structures and structures occurring in nature are emblematic of his style of thought. At the same time, he was able to combine his insistence on "structure" with a flamboyant way of dressing and a fascination with Peter Kropotkin's (1842–1921) anarchism, earning Radcliffe-Brown the nickname "Anarchy Brown."

Most of Radcliffe-Brown's adult life was spent outside England. He conducted ethnographic fieldwork in the Andaman Islands (1906–1908) and Western Australia (1910–1912), but never achieved the kind of in-depth familiarity with local settings that would soon become typical of social anthropology. Radcliffe-Brown's influential academic career began in 1920, when he became the founding professor of social anthropology at the University of Cape Town in South Africa. He went on to become founding professor at the University of Sydney (1926–1931), professor at the University of Chicago (1931–1937), and chair of social anthropology at the University of Oxford (1937–1946). He continued lecturing at universities in Brazil, Egypt, England, and South Africa, and served as president of the Association of Social Anthropologists until shortly before his death.

Even by his own account, Radcliffe-Brown was a slow writer. His only monograph is *The Andaman Islanders* (1922); the rest of his publications are articles and lecture transcriptions. Although his academic career spanned half a century, Radcliffe-Brown's theory remained more or less unchanged throughout. He constantly systematized the idea that social anthropology should become a "natural science of human society" through empirical investigations of social structures. Comparisons between different societies should enable anthropologists to discover universal and essential relations; apparent diversity should be reduced to clear classifications. Anthropology should focus on directly observable networks between persons, and distill "general structural forms." Rejecting diffusionism, evolutionism, and any kind of "conjectural history," Radcliffe-Brown was also critical of the concept of "culture," which for him was a foggy abstraction and subordinate to social structure.

Assessments of Radcliffe-Brown's contribution to anthropology tend to be polarized. He was a charismatic lecturer, able to impress upon others a habitus of scientific rigor. Even some streams of American anthropology, with its longstanding emphasis on culture and historical particularity, were influenced by him. But just as much as he united scholars during his lifetime, his name soon became synonymous with an overly rigid and intellectually unsatisfying approach that no one wanted to follow anymore. From the 1950s onward, all major figures in British social anthropology, notably E. E. Evans-Pritchard (1902–1973), Raymond Firth (1901–2002), and Edmund Leach (1910–1989), denounced Radcliffe-Brown's theory as unable to grasp history, social change, and unequal relations of power. That he wanted anthropology to become a "natural science" attracted particular scorn (e.g., Leach 1976). Even if Radcliffe-Brown's importance for the discipline is now widely seen as historical, his emphasis on observable social networks, as opposed to cultural values, retains a certain influence, especially in Britain.

BIBLIOGRAPHY

Leach, Edmund. 1976. *Social Anthropology: A Natural Science of Society*. London: British Academy.

Radcliffe-Brown, A. R. 1922. *The Andaman Islanders: A Study in Social Anthropology*. Cambridge, U.K.: Cambridge University Press.

Radcliffe-Brown, A. R. 1940. Preface. In *African Political Systems*. eds. Meyer Fortes and E. E. Evans-Pritchard, xi-xxii. London: Oxford University Press.

Radcliffe-Brown, A. R. 1952. *Structure and Function in Primitive Society: Essays and Addresses*. London: Cohen & West.

Radcliffe-Brown, A. R. 1958. *Method in Social Anthropology: Selected Essays.* Ed. M. N. Srinivas. Chicago: University of Chicago Press.

Stefan Ecks

RADICALISM

The word *radical* has a number of meanings, one of which involves "getting to the root of the matter." This analogy is helpful in focusing attention on the key characteristics of the term, and on its various usages within social science. When people talk about "radicals," they mean those who take ideas and concepts back to first principles. They are those who are unafraid of laying bare what is hidden, subterranean, or uncomfortable to discuss. Radicals do not mind upsetting the status quo, received wisdom, or "common sense" conceptions of any kind. To talk about radicalism is therefore to talk about the belief systems of radicals. Yet what is it that characterizes radicalism, and how does this impact our understanding of knowledge generally?

As is clear from the above, radicalism is not a concept that denotes a particular set of ideas or a particular approach, in the manner of many other terms in the lexicon of social science. When one discusses Marxism, it is clear that this relates to the word and ideas of Karl Marx and his many followers. The same cannot be said of radicalism, which is a concept that is positional or contextual. Whether a given ideology or stance can be regarded as radical depends on where it stands in relation to dominant or "accepted" ideas. Thus a "radical conservative" (if this is not an oxymoron) is someone whose radicalism is defined in relation to dominant conservative ideas. He or she wishes to get to the "root" of conservatism, or of the problems discussed by conservatives. Radical conservatism is therefore not inherently radical, it is only radical in relation to other conservative ideas. Likewise, radicalism only exists insofar as there are ideas that are mainstream, orthodox, and widely accepted.

Radicalism can also be regarded as contextually dependent. In other words, whether a set of ideas is radical depends on the context in which these ideas are being offered or pursued. Many ideas that were once perceived to be radical have, over the course of time, come to be regarded as mainstream. Thus, radicalism should be understood less as a description of a core orientation of the kind associated with labels such as "Marxist," "liberal," or "conservative," and more as a set of ideas that is inclined to query orthodoxy, whether it be secular, religious, social, or scientific. A starting point of this article is thus the contention that radicalism does not denote a par-

ticular set of ideas or arguments, but rather any ideology or position that takes issue (or appears to take issue) with settled, accepted or otherwise mainstream views. Some examples will help to clarify the above.

RADICALISM AS POSITIONAL AND CONTEXTUAL

As mentioned above, radicalism does not denote a particular set of ideas or arguments, but any argument that takes issue with accepted positions, however defined. In this positional sense, radicalism can be mapped in terms of certain well-known debates. To take an obvious starting point, Darwin's account of evolution was once regarded as radical (as well as absurd and despicable) by mainstream commentary. However, from the late nineteenth century onward, more and more scientists in the West began to hold Darwinian views. A great deal of the evidence, from a wide variety of scientific and social scientific investigations, seemed to support the view that evolution takes place over very long periods of time and can be adduced to random genetic mutations. Darwinism, therefore, once a radical and heretical doctrine, became mainstream science. Likewise, those who opposed Darwinism, such as Christians and other religious groups, were once in the majority, but over the course of a century or so they became "minoritarian" in relation to issues in basic science. One might ask whether Darwinism or intelligent design should now be regarded as the more radical position. This is a moot point, however. In areas or communities that are deeply committed to a deist view of the universe, Darwinism remains a radical doctrine to be combated wherever possible. To Darwinists, the claims of creationists are radically conservative.

It is often held that radicalism is necessary because progress is impossible without challenges to orthodoxy. Thus, philosophers of science frequently reserve a special place for radical ideas as necessary, and indeed desirable. This usually comes with the caveat that radicals submit to the norms of falsification and experimentation. Radicalism can be good if it is seen to be in tune with the general tenor of scientific understanding, but it is less so when it appears to take issue with a certain set of expectations. Albert Einstein's radicalism is useful on these terms, for example, but Sigmund Freud's is less so, at least according to figures such as the philosopher Karl Popper (1902–1994). Those who oppose such a conventional view of scientific progress, such as Jean-François Lyotard (1924–1998) and Paul Feyerabend (1924–1998), are themselves regarded as radicals by philosophers of science and social science because of their insistence on the relativism of knowledge claims. This kind of radicalism equates to the view that science does not deserve the special status many accord it, for it is merely one kind of "narrative" to set alongside other narratives—such as "Creationism"—that claim to offer privileged access to the true nature of things.

FROM SCIENCE TO IDEOLOGY

More generally, there have always been radical views that have challenged or undermined the mainstream. The twentieth century, for example, is often noted for the variety and impact of unorthodox, extreme, and nonmainstream views that surfaced during this period. To illustrate the way in which radicalism is context-dependent, the century can be divided up into four periods: the interwar years; the postwar era up to the oil crisis of the mid-1970s; the period of conservative preeminence to the fall of the Berlin Wall; and finally the period of the "Post–Cold War Order," which carried over into the twenty-first century. Traversing a century of radicalisms will illustrate the changes in the nature and form of radicalism from modernity to what is often termed "postmodernity" or a "second" modernity.

In the interwar years (1918–1939), the world witnessed an astonishing burst of radicalism, radical parties, and radical politics. This was due to a number of factors, principally the impact of war, the rise of capitalism, and the perceived shortcomings of individualism. The radicalism of the Russian Revolution came out of a deep discontent with the inherited monarchic order. Bolshevism promised a world without hunger, hierarchy, or war, and a world without capitalism, individualism, or imperialism. The rise of Hitler owed a great deal to similar sentiments, although it translated into a different set of demands. Nevertheless, radicalism in this period meant collectivism, as opposed to individualism; state control, as opposed to the free market; and universalist claims, in the name of "proletarian internationalism" or Aryan superiority. The individual counted for little when compared with the needs of the class or the race. This common set of characteristics offered commentators such as Hannah Arendt, Karl Popper and Carl J. Friedrich license to roll up these otherwise diverse radicalisms into one overarching phenomenon: "totalitarianism." This was a radicalism that threatened the annihilation of prevailing orthodoxy, whether characterized as liberal or conservative.

In the postwar period (1945–1975) the dominant or mainstream ideology in most Western states was that associated with the work of the British economist John Maynard Keynes. The "postwar consensus" insisted on the growth of the public sector or welfare state, the extension of basic rights and liberties (as announced in the UN Charter), and the pursuit of policies of growth through the management of demand. Social-democratic or welfare-state thinking became dominant across the developed world.

In terms of political ideas and positions, "radicalism" at this point referred to two main tendencies: those who were opposed to Keynesian because it was too statist, and those who argued that it was not statist enough. With regard to the former, the period is noted for the emergence of neoliberal ideas associated with figures such as Friedrich von Hayek, Milton Friedman and, later, Robert Nozick. Their radicalism consisted in the suggestion that the welfare state was despotic and heralded the end of choice, the end of the individual's control over his or her fate, and the elimination of the entrepreneurial and risk-taking characteristics upon which economic growth depended. The state should give way to the market, they believed, not the other way around. At the same time, considerable interest developed in models of socialism that radicalized the terms of the postwar consensus while also seeking to avoid the perils of communist dictatorship. Multiple left-wing radicalisms emerged and flourished (e.g., The Frankfurt School, situationism, Maoism, "humanist Marxism"), reflecting the "postmaterialist" discontent with both Western and Eastern society that was to be such a feature of the late 1960s.

Other kinds of radicalism arose in this period out of the desire for "liberation," particularly liberation from racism, colonialism and, "patriarchy." Antiracism became a powerful current and gave birth to a number of radical groups and figures across the developing and developed world, including the Black Panthers, Malcolm X, and various figures in the civil rights movement, such as Martin Luther King Jr. Anticolonial or postcolonial demands were articulated in the work of writers such as Paolo Freire, Frantz Fanon, and Jean-Paul Sartre, while radical anticolonial movements swept the globe, led by figures such as Che Guevara and Ho Chi Minh. For feminists, the problem was the "patriarchal" assumptions of mainstream political theories and practices. "Radical feminism" spared little in its critique of the exclusionary and demeaning character of patriarchal practices. Women had to assert not equality, but their difference from men. This entailed developing novel and inclusive strategies in relation to oppressive discourses wherever they were found.

The oil crisis of 1973 and 1974 was followed by a period of conservative preeminence, which put into relief what was at stake in these ideological battles and allowed advocates of what had been regarded as a deeply radical position to win support in the mainstream. In a matter of a decade, neoliberalism moved from being a deeply heterodox and radical position to being "common sense"—as described by prominent advocates such as Margaret Thatcher and Ronald Reagan. Orthodoxy now shifted away from being protective of public services and demand-fuelled economic growth, moving toward a position hostile to the welfare state, "dependency culture," and public spending. This, in turn, encouraged a new set of radicalisms highlighting the perceived shortcomings of the prevailing political orthodoxy. Chief among these was the emergence of environmentalism. Associated with figures such as James Lovelock, who developed the "Gaia hypothesis," E. F. Schumacher and Ivan Illich, environmentalism was a response to the oil crisis and the perception that there were structural "limits to growth." The problem was not too little market, as advocated by the neoliberals, but too much. In particular, there was too much unfettered market activity in relation to scarce natural resources.

There was also a change in the morphology of radical activism during this period, coinciding with the decline of the mass party in the wake of the emergence of so-called new social movements. These movements were much more diffuse than mass parties, less ideological, and often very radical. This radicalism expressed itself in terms of a rejection of mainstream political processes in favor of "direct action" or DIY (do-it-yourself) practices.

The era of the "Post–Cold War Order," which began with the fall of the Berlin Wall in 1989, has witnessed an explosion of radicalisms in response to widespread discontent with several new orthodoxies, particularly the "Washington Consensus," associated with the extension of neoliberal policies to many different areas of economic and social activity; the idea of the "clash of civilizations," positing an inevitable conflict between cultures; and the continuing dominance of individualism and consumerism.

In the 1990s an "antiglobalization movement" emerged in response to the neoliberal ideology that had come to prominence. This involved a panoply of radicalisms—some old, some new—all responding to the perceived shortcomings of the free-market policies pursued by global institutions such as the International Monetary Fund (IMF), the World Trade Organization (WTO), and the World Bank. The antiglobalization movement gives witness to one of the more remarked-upon features of the contemporary period, namely the proliferation of radical currents and energies, as opposed to their crystallization within mass parties united by a single ideology. This is not to be mistaken for the "end of ideology," as long lamented by cultural commentators such as Daniel Bell, Herbert Marcuse, and Francis Fukuyama, but rather the proliferation of ideologies, some of which are radical, while others are much less so.

Samuel Huntington's "clash of civilization" thesis is perhaps both a result and a cause of the profusion of cultural and political radicalisms across the world. This is paradoxical in the same sense that globalization is, for while globalization seems to be drawing people closer together, it also renders "local" resistance more intense and radical. Thus, key radicalisms that emerged at the start of the twenty-first century include neoconservatism

and Islamic fundamentalism. Both are responses to perceived isolation and cultural embattlement: the former in defense of values associated with the imperiled Greco-Roman civilization; the latter in defense of an ever more literal reading of the Qu'ran. Each faces the other as a defensive response against incorporation into what are perceived to be homogenizing global forces beyond the control of distinct nations and cultures.

More generally, any set of ideas that challenges the supremacy of the free market, of dominant interpretations of ideals such as equality and freedom, or of the idea of the individual as preeminently a consumer will be perceived by the mainstream as "radical." In this sense, there are many sources of radicalism, including religion (and not just Islam). There has also been a rise in the influence of all manner of fundamentalisms, New Age ideas, alternative therapies and perspectives, and postmaterial ideas and ways of living that stress the need to escape from the dominant ethic and values.

FROM MODERN TO POSTMODERN RADICALISM?

In the political sense, radicalism has ceased to express itself on the same terms that marked the radical currents of the twentieth century. Radicalism had one goal during that period: the transformation of the existing world into a world that would, so it was claimed, be markedly better than the one displaced. Today's radicalisms are rarely built from such certainties. Nor are they, in the main, built on the kinds of universalist ambitions that characterized earlier radicalisms. Instead, they are partial, sectional, particularistic, local, and fragmented. Where commentators once lamented the prospect of being engulfed by a singular countervailing radicalism ("totalitarianism"), there are now many radical currents and tendencies—some benign, and others much less so. Orthodoxy, however defined, does not have one rival but many, and radical ideas are often resolutely minoritarian. Ideas, positions, philosophies, and therapies no longer seem to harbor the ambition, once shared by the world-transforming ideologies of modernity, to transform the world itself. What they demand is a space of "difference," a space in which heterodoxy, otherness, and particular identities and positions can stand apart and flourish.

These "postmodern" radicalisms are modest, even parsimonious, in relation to the claims they make for themselves. With the "end of grand narratives," as Lyotard put it, many radical groups and movements have evidently lost or abandoned that sense of certainty that was such a hallmark of the ideologies and movements of the twentieth century. In a world of skeptics, radicalism (as expressed in the ideas of the leftist Zapatistas in Mexico, for example) can only be sustained by thin or partial affinities and affiliations, by appeals to shared "intuitions" and the desire for "dignity." This is hardly the basis for the kind of mass mobilization hoped for by yesterday's radicals, but it seems to be enough to sustain the radicals and radicalisms of today.

In sum, radicalism is not on the wane or in danger of being made redundant by an overarching conformity to ideas and values, no matter how expressed (as per Fukuyama's "end of history" thesis). Any such view reveals a certain naivety about the role of ideas in history. As this brief overview suggests, mainstream and conventional ideas are always faced by ideas that challenge or undermine them. Indeed it makes little sense to talk about "the mainstream" or "the conventional" without reference to ideas or positions that lie outside them. Radicalism is, in simple terms, the name given to whatever is different, challenging, or otherwise difficult to digest. As such, radicalism is just as much a feature of contemporary life as is the status quo, however defined.

BIBLIOGRAPHY

Bell, Daniel. 1960. *The End of Ideology.* Glencoe, IL: Free Press.

Festenstein, Mathew, and Michael Kenny, eds. 2005. *Political Ideologies: A Reader and Guide.* Oxford: Oxford University Press.

Fukuyama, Francis. 1992. *The End of History and the Last Man.* London: Penguin.

Gleason, Abbott. 1995. *Totalitarianism: The Inner History of the Cold War.* New York: Oxford University Press.

Hobsbawm, Eric. 1994. *Age of Extremes: The Short Twentieth Century, 1914–1991.* London: Abacus.

Huntington, Samuel P. 1996. *The Clash of Civilizations and the Remaking of World Order.* New York: Simon & Schuster.

Lyotard, Jean-François. 1984. *The Postmodern Condition: A Report on Knowledge.* Trans. Geoff Bennington and Brian Massumi. Minneapolis: University of Minnesota Press.

Marcuse, Herbert. 1964. *One-Dimensional Man: Studies in the Ideology of Advanced Industrial Society.* Boston: Beacon Press.

Popper, Karl. 1959. *The Logic of Scientific Discovery.* New York: Basic Books.

Tormey, Simon. 2004. *Anti-Capitalism: A Beginner's Guide.* Oxford: Oneworld.

Simon Tormey

RADIO TALK SHOWS

Radio talk shows can be defined as radio broadcasts centered primarily on conversational speech. They encompass numerous discourse genres and formats, ranging from political diatribes to highly interactive exchanges with members of the listening audience. Many talk shows have hybrid formats featuring music, sound effects, and news interspersed with interviews, debates, social and political commentary, religious exegesis, medical advice, therapeutic discourse, question-and-answer sessions, sports-fan exchanges, and storytelling.

Talk shows are typically hosted by a single radio personality, usually positioned as an expert in some area. Many also feature occasional guests who are interviewed, as well as one or two regular interlocutors who assist the host. Audience participation is usually a major feature of talk radio shows worldwide, with opportunities for listeners to telephone or write to the program host with questions, comments, or music requests, which are then relayed on air. The place of talk radio in non-Western nations parallels the role of talk radio in Western nations, yet it is a relatively new area of exploration that merits more in-depth research.

The social consequences of talk radio are extensive. Three major types of impact can be identified. First, talk radio has far-reaching implications for the nature of the public sphere in modern societies as it creates forums for participatory democracy and the development of public opinion. Second, talk radio influences both everyday discourse and political discourse by providing models of talk and by setting agendas through talk. And third, talk radio has become a major part of everyday life for countless people around the globe as they structure their days around favorite programs and as they develop affective ties to radio personalities.

HISTORY

Talk shows have been a prominent feature of radio since the inception of broadcasting in Western nations in the 1920s and in non-Western contexts from the 1940s onward. Early examples include Alexander Woolcott's (1887–1943) urbane commentary on New York's WOR in the 1920s and Walter Winchell's (1897–1972) political gossip program on NBC in the 1930s. More interactive formats emerged in the 1930s, first with *vox populi* "man on the street" interviews being taped and then later relayed on air, and then with radio "town hall meetings," which featured live broadcasts of studio audiences discussing current events. Such formats were also introduced in colonial broadcasting in Africa as early as the late 1940s. In the United States, radio call-in programs began in the mid-1940s. Precursors of talk radio formats and functions include public traditions such as town hall meetings, and gathering places such as literary circles, coffee houses, village squares, and beer gardens, as well as mass entertainment forms, such as vaudeville and circus sideshows.

Between the early 1980s and the mid-1990s, the number of radio stations in the United States featuring talk radio quadrupled. By the mid-1990s, talk radio ranked as the second most popular radio format in the United States, with country music being the first. The dramatic rise of talk radio during this period is attributed to several factors, including a general collapse of public life in the United States, coupled with an increased predictability and absence of personality in FM radio programming. Some scholars have argued that Americans found themselves increasingly isolated and thus turned to talk radio as a way to be connected to community and to others. Similar arguments have been made about talk radio in other parts of the world, such as England and Israel.

During the 1980s, certain AM stations as well as National Public Radio (NPR) strategized to "reactivate attentive listening" (Douglas 1999, p. 286) through less predictable formats, more chatty ad-libbing, and greater emphasis on sound effects and voice qualities. Further contributing factors to the prevalence and popularity of talk radio at the end of the twentieth century include the increased facility of national broadcasting afforded by satellite technology and the increased facility of audience interactivity afforded by cell phones. A final factor relatively unnoticed by scholarship is the fact that countless radio listeners are engaged in lengthy commutes to and from work. Morning "drive time" talk radio formats as well as evening news magazines fit into these lifestyle patterns and relieve the boredom and isolation of commuting for long periods every day.

CONTEMPORARY TRENDS

Approximately 80 percent of all U.S. radio stations include some form of talk radio in their programming. Many stations, such as NBC's Talknet, ABC's Talkradio Network, and Air America Radio, are exclusively devoted to round-the-clock live talk programming. NPR also features a substantial number of entertaining and informative talk programs, such as *All Things Considered, Talk of the Nation, Car Talk*, and *A Prairie Home Companion.*

While the genre of talk radio might be best known for its strong language, irreverence, and polarizing discourse, encapsulated in the persona of the *shock jock*, the majority of talk radio programs worldwide do not adhere to this model. Examples of the former in the United States include broadcasters Howard Stern, Rush Limbaugh, and Don Imus. As with many shock jocks, these individuals and their stations have been subject to investigations by the Federal Communications Commission (FCC), a governmental regulatory body, and some have received fines and suspensions for pushing the limits of respectability on the airwaves.

By contrast, most of the world's talk show hosts, including those in the United States, are models of respectability. They work to build community, air common concerns, solve problems, and develop better futures for their listeners. In many African nations, for example, talk radio programs play a significant role in informing people about electoral processes, debating political issues, and allowing citizens to air their views. One dramatic case of talk radio in the service of democracy in Africa is exemplified by the *Talk Mogadishu* program on Somalia's station, HornAfrik. On this program, listeners from different parts of the city call in to update each other on events across the chaotic, war-torn city landscape. In addition, they pose pointed questions to rival warlords who appear as program guests. Other examples include the popular talk shows on Zambia's national radio station. Two Bemba-language programs, *Baanacimbuusa* (Women Advisors) and *Kabuusha Takolelwe Boowa* (a proverb meaning "the inquirer was not poisoned by a mushroom"), are inspired directly by indigenous modes of advising. In the former, the host introduces a topic concerning family and marriage, which a panel of elder women then discusses. In some cases, the topic is developed from a listener's letter. In the *Kabuusha* program, an expert advisor answers listeners' letters on a variety of subjects, including corrupt politicians, adulterous spouses, in-laws who demand more marriage payments, and employers who exploit their workers.

In their capacity as important avenues for influencing public opinion and voting behavior, talk radio programs have attracted the attention of politicians in numerous contexts worldwide. In the United States, for example, talk radio contributed to a coordinated popular protest against a proposed congressional pay raise in 1989. It continues to be a vital influence on the tenor of presidential campaigns, cabinet and Supreme Court nomination hearings, and the reception of government policies in general. In contexts where there is less media freedom, political radio talk show hosts often risk charges of sedition, physical threat, or forced exile, as recent cases from Uganda and Haiti attest.

CRITICISMS, CONCERNS, AND PROSPECTS

Critics of talk radio describe it as a debased form of journalism and public discourse. Their concern is that personal opinions and private experiences are emphasized over relevant facts and information. Listeners are thus not enlightened in ways that allow them to develop informed opinions. In this analysis, talk radio is not about citizenship or participatory democracy, but about sensationalism and ratings. Other criticisms include an assessment that hosts with call-in programs simulate a model of authentic dialogue, but in reality are engaged in a complex form of social control and norm making. These criticisms are well founded when applied to certain forms of talk radio, particularly the shock jock genres, but detract from the fact that a multiplicity of talk radio genres also work to foster positive social change, personal growth, and enjoyable listening experiences among audiences.

Talk radio will continue to be a vibrant and multifaceted hybrid genre well into the future. The recent emergence of Internet radio and Internet telephoning is already yielding many more possibilities for talk radio formats and talk radio communities, including global talk radio. Coupled with the rise of other participatory and audience-produced media such as blogs and wikis, talk radio will continue to be a media form that allows audiences to "be the media" and thus have an impact on the tenor of political life and communication environments more generally. From ice hockey fan exchanges to dialogues on compassion in Zen Buddhism, talk radio provides an important area of scholarly inquiry as it touches on virtually every field of the social sciences, including media studies, cultural studies, anthropology, sociolinguistics, social psychology, and political science.

BIBLIOGRAPHY

Barker, David C. 2002. *Rushed to Judgment: Talk Radio, Persuasion, and American Political Behavior.* New York: Colombia University Press.

Douglas, Susan J. 1999. *Listening In: Radio and the American Imagination.* New York: Times Books.

Horton, Donald, and R. Richard Wohl. 1956. Mass Communication and Para-Social Interaction: Observations on Intimacy and Distance. *Psychiatry* 19: 215–229.

Hutchby, Ian. 1996. *Confrontation Talk: Arguments, Asymmetries, and Power on Talk Radio.* Mahwah, NJ: Erlbaum.

Katriel, Tamar. 2004. *Dialogic Moments: From Soul Talks to Talk Radio in Israeli Culture.* Detroit, MI: Wayne State University Press.

Munson, Wayne. 1993. *All Talk: The Talkshow in Media Culture.* Philadelphia: Temple University Press.

Tacchi, Jo. 1998. Radio Texture: Between Self and Others. In *Material Cultures: Why Some Things Matter*, ed. Daniel Miller, 25–45. Chicago: University of Chicago Press.

Debra Spitulnik

RAILWAY INDUSTRY

A railway industry is a group of companies that transport goods (freight) or individuals (passengers) by railcars from one place to another. Locomotives pull or push railcars (containing freight or passengers) over rail tracks. Railways enhance the access consumer and resource markets have to goods and individuals, which in turn contributes to economic development and rising land values, and influences industry locations.

Even before the advent of locomotives, horse-drawn railcars (or tramways) were an improvement over other means of land transportation—the resistance encountered by a wheeled vehicle traveling over smooth rails is less than with non-smooth roadways. By the late eighteenth century, tramways were commonly used in the United Kingdom for transporting coal. The first tramway in the United States appeared in Boston in 1807. Experiments with steam-driven rail locomotives began in the 1820s. By the middle of the nineteenth century, steam locomotives had made the railway industry the world's dominant provider of land transportation. Steam locomotives, in turn, were subsequently replaced by diesel locomotives.

Freight railway companies are primarily transporters of bulk commodities (such as coal, chemicals, and grain) over relatively long distances. By comparison, trucking companies are transporters of manufactured commodities over relatively short distances. In the United States, railway companies generally incur less cost than trucking companies in transporting goods at a distance of five hundred or more miles. Passenger railway companies provide intercity transportation service, moving individuals from one city to another. Rail service for passengers traveling within a city or to and from a city and its suburbs is provided by urban transit companies.

Governments in many countries have assisted in the early expansion of the railway industry. Forms of government assistance include government ownership, outright donations, tax exemptions, and loans. This assistance stimulated railway construction and, in turn, economic development. At the same time, many projects were undertaken that were not economically justified, resulting in an overexpansion of the railway network.

Cheap labor also stimulated the early growth of the railway industry. Chinese laborers were hired by the Central Pacific Railroad Company in 1863 to build a section of the U.S. transcontinental railroad over the Sierras and into the interior plains. They worked for meager wages through harsh winters and under dangerous working conditions. Convicts and slaves also built railways in the United States and in other countries.

Eric Williams (1944) has argued that, because the African slave trade was instrumental in U.S. and British economic development, it indirectly stimulated the expansion of railway networks in the United States and Britain. This claim was countered by Stanley L. Engerman (1972) through what is called the "small ratios" argument, which maintains that slave-trade profits were too small to stimulate British industrialization. In response to Engerman, William Darity Jr. (1990) argues that there are several growth and trade theories supporting a prominent role for the African slave trade in British industrialization that cannot be dismissed or disproven by the small ratios argument.

An earlier application of the small ratios argument by Robert Fogel (1964) focused on the economic history of the railway sector itself. As part of his development of an overarching hypothetical picture of American economic growth without a transport revolution, Fogel sought to demonstrate that the revenues generated by the railway system as a percentage of gross domestic product were too low to have been decisively important. But Fogel's argument is subject to the same response that has been given to Engerman's attempted refutation of the Williams hypothesis: While it is true that the revenues or profits of any single sector as a percentage of total national income generally will look "small," the critical consideration is the full impact of the sector via its linkages with numerous other productive sectors forming the economy.

To protect the public against monopoly-related abuses, railway companies were often economically regulated by government. In the United States, for example, the 1887 Interstate Commerce Act established the Interstate Commerce Commission (ICC) to economically regulate interstate railway transportation service. Economic regulation of railways may include rate/fare regulation, entry regulation, service regulation, and financial regulation. Rates (prices for freight service) and fares (prices for passenger service) charged and entry into the industry are subject to approval by the regulatory commission. Freight and passengers are to be delivered in the same physical condition as received. Various financial aspects of the railway industry, such as mergers and accounting systems, are also regulated.

Government assistance and regulation aimed at economic development and protection of the public interest may also restrict competition. In the United States, restrictions on "intermodal" competition (i.e., between two modes of transportation, such as railways and trucking) have contributed to a decline in the U.S. railway industry, exhibited by a decrease in industry market share and return on investment. In 1945, 67.2 percent of the U.S. domestic intercity freight traffic (in ton-miles) was transported by railways and 6.5 percent by truck; by 1975, 36.7 percent was transported by rail and 22 percent by truck. The rate of return on net investment for U.S. Class I (the largest) railroads was 4.7 percent in 1944, but declined to 1.2 percent in 1975. Regulation suppressed intermodal price competition and the abandonment of excess track capacity.

In the 1970s the U.S. Congress responded to the decline in the railway industry by creating Amtrak (the National Railroad Passenger Corporation) to take over all rail passenger-service lines over seventy-five miles in length, and Conrail (a government corporation), to operate the freight service of seven major Northeast railways in bankruptcy. The Staggers Act of 1980 partially deregulated the industry by providing railway companies with greater opportunities to compete and thus reverse the industry's decline. Specifically, the Act provided greater pricing freedom and reduced the time permitted for the ICC to make merger and track-abandonment decisions.

The U.S. railway industry, its shareholders, and most shippers have benefited from deregulation—the industry's share of intercity freight traffic (in ton-miles) increased to 41.7 percent by 2001, the rate of return on net investment for Class I railroads increased to 6.1 percent by 2004, and real railway prices (adjusted for inflation) have declined. On the other hand, labor has been harmed. In 1975 the industry had 548,000 (488,000 Class I) employees; by 2004 the number had declined to 226,000 (158,000 Class I) employees. These job losses are attributed to industry restructuring and the increased use of technology.

The United Kingdom has sought to promote competition in its railway industry by privatizing the government-owned British Railways (BR) through passage of the Railways Act of 1993. The ownership and control of infrastructure were separated from train operation. Infrastructure was placed under the control of a new government company, Railtrack, in 1994, but in 1996 BR's freight-train operations (including rolling stock) were split into six companies and sold to the private sector. Passenger train operations were not sold, but were franchised to twenty-five private-sector train-operating companies. Under privatization, however, government subsidization of the railway industry has more than tripled, due to subsidies to passenger franchises and to Network Rail, the company that replaced the collapsed Railtrack. The numerous private freight-operators that have entered the market have resulted in more competitive freight operations. The four remaining freight-operators are profitable.

The European Commission (EC) is seeking to liberalize the national railways of its European Union member-states by creating a single market for rail transport through the removal of barriers to cross-border freight and passenger rail traffic. Specifically, the EC is seeking to separate the control of rail infrastructure from operations, to eliminate physical differences among national railways (e.g., with respect to signaling, electrification, and operating rules), and to open the market up to competition. The entry of numerous private freight operators into the market has forced the national railways to become competitive.

An important challenge facing railways in many countries is to provide enough capacity to keep pace with the growth in world trade. The volume of ocean-container shipments is growing worldwide at the rate of 9 percent per year, thereby overburdening the infrastructure of railways that transport containerized cargo to and from ports (i.e., railways engaged in intermodal traffic). Today, the largest share of the cargo mix for U.S. railroads is intermodal cargo. In Canada, a shortage of intermodal rail cars has resulted in congestion (or traffic delays) at a number of its ports. Intermodal rail service in China has numerous problems, such as lateness and cargo damage.

SEE ALSO *Immigrants, Asian; Industry; Servitude; Slavery; Transportation Industry*

BIBLIOGRAPHY

Darity, William, Jr. 1990. British Industry and the West Indies Plantations. *Social Science History* 14 (1): 117–149.

Engerman, Stanley L. 1972. The Slave Trade and British Capital Formation in the Eighteenth Century: A Comment on the Williams Thesis. *Business History Review* 46 (4): 430–443.

Fogel, Robert William. 1964. *Railroads and American Economic Growth: Essays in Econometric History.* Baltimore: Johns Hopkins Press.

Keeler, Theodore E. 1983. *Railroads, Freight, and Public Policy.* Washington, DC: Brookings Institution.

Schwarz-Miller, Ann V., and Wayne K. Talley. 1998. Railroad Deregulation and Union Labor Earnings. In *Regulatory Reform and Labor Markets*, ed. James Peoples, 125–153. Boston: Kluwer Academic Publishers.

Schwarz-Miller, Ann V., and Wayne K. Talley. 2002. Technology and Labor Relations: Railroads and Ports. In *Technological Change and Employment Conditions in Traditionally Heavily Unionized Industries.* Vol. 23 of *Journal of Labor Research*, ed. James T. Bennett and Daphne G. Taras, 513–533.

Williams, Eric. 1944. *Capitalism and Slavery.* Chapel Hill: University of North Carolina Press.

Wayne K. Talley

RAINBOW/PUSH COALITION

SEE *Coalition.*

RAJ, THE

The *Raj*, a Hindi word meaning "rule," is the epithet most closely associated with British rule of the Indian subcontinent. While the English East India Company (EIC) had been present in South Asia from the early seventeenth century, formal British rule began in 1757. The British finally left the subcontinent in 1947, ceding independence to the new states of India and Pakistan on August

14/15. The latter included Bangladesh as East Pakistan, which gained independence in 1971. The period of the Raj covers two hundred years of South Asian history and is one of the most important episodes of colonialism in modern history.

THE EAST INDIA COMPANY
(1757–1858)

The origins of British rule of South Asia lay in the founding of the English East India Company (EIC) in 1600. The company's participation in the lucrative spice trade led it to establish trading posts first at Surat on the Gujarati coast and later at Bombay, Madras, and Calcutta. By the mid-eighteenth century, competition with the French drew the British into the South Asian political scene through alliances with local powers. Political instability following the disintegration of Mughal authority enabled the EIC to transform from a mere trading interest to a territorial ruler. The company exercised power indirectly through local allies and rulers, setting a precedent followed up to 1947.

The indirect exercise of control contributed to the hybridity of EIC governance. An English trading company driven by European ideas of economy as well as European norms and practices of political authority, the EIC was also a participant in the South Asian political universe, asserting its credentials as a successor state to the Mughal empire. It continued to transact the business of government through local allies, according to local custom and in local languages. The company made an extensive effort to codify indigenous law and practice. Yet this effort to preserve and participate in Indian "traditions" fundamentally transformed them. The EIC became the ultimate arbiter of what constituted tradition, and its codification turned previously fluid arrangements of social interaction into rigid systems of social classification. Throughout its reign, the debate as to whether the company's role was to transform Indian society or to preserve Indian tradition continued unabated.

THE GOVERNMENT OF INDIA
(1858–1947)

Company rule ended with the abolition of the East India Company in 1858 in the wake of the Indian rebellion, more commonly known as the Indian Mutiny. The revolt convinced the British that their efforts at reform of Indian society had been dangerously miscalculated. Consequently the Government of India (GoI) understood its role in an extremely conservative light. India was to be governed for the benefit of the British metropole as cheaply as possible. The GoI's mission was thus to preserve stability and control, largely through a strategy of "divide and rule." Government was to be exercised through a collaborative elite responsible for the implementation of government policy in the locality.

The emergence of a national political discourse in the late 1800s came about against the wishes of the GoI, but on a stage prepared by it. Only in a society penetrated by contemporary European ideas of nationalism and tied together by modern communication and transportation technologies could the conceptualization of an "Indian" political community emerge. That conceptualization was dominated by the all-India Congress, initially a vehicle for the collaborative elite to advocate their interests. By the turn of the century however, Congress began to transform itself from a party of collaborators to a party advocating home rule (*swaraj*) and eventually independence. During the First World War, Indian nationalists promised their support in exchange for guarantees of postwar political movement. They were bitterly disappointed as the expected peace dividends dissolved in the face of a reassertion of imperial control. The 1920s witnessed the transformation of the Congress and Indian nationalism into a mass political movement. This change was largely engineered by Mohandas Gandhi (1869–1948), who organized mass campaigns of civil disobedience built upon a cross-communal political platform of Indian nationalism. Gandhi's efforts redefined the bounds of India's public political space, including parts of society, such as women and so-called untouchables (*dalits*), previously excluded from political participation. Yet local elites proved wary of the perceived peasantization of politics and the erosion of their autonomy by the nationalist cause.

The preeminence of Indian nationalist discourse was threatened by communalist politics, progressively more prominent from the late nineteenth century. India's formerly plural religious traditions became increasingly standardized, hardening the boundaries between them. The Anglo-Indian judiciary arguably played the primary role in the standardization of the diverse traditions of India's various communities, in turn leading to the solidification of communal borders. As the colonial state became more involved in civic disputes through the course of the nineteenth century, it increasingly usurped the spaces formerly regulated by communal "tradition" and "custom." Faced with an array of competing and often contradictory customs, the judiciary established the parameters of what constituted judicially recognized, and therefore state-sanctioned, "tradition." The judicial establishment of tradition was followed by its codification by the colonial executive, such as in the Hindu and Muslim law code bills, which created corpuses of standard communal private law. These traditions thus transformed into central tenets of exclusivist communal identities, which in turn became politicized through their patronage by the colonial state. Rather than the state enforcement of uniformity, so often central to the construction of the modern state, colonial authorities codified and enforced difference.

The Raj reinforced this difference through the categorization of its subjects in the decennial census, where it denominated people into religiously based communities to which it then dispensed entitlements. The most important manifestation of this communally centered politics in the formal, state-regulated arena was the creation and extension of separate electorates. Muslims, Christians, and Anglo-Indians were granted separate electoral lists in which candidates and eligible voters were restricted to members of these denominated communities. The Morley-Minto reforms of 1909 first made widespread use of separate electorates, which were significantly extended by the Montague-Chelmsford reforms of 1919 and the 1935 Act on the basis of the 1932 Communal Award. GoI leaders' official rationale for the use of separate electorates was twofold. First, they sought to deny Indian nationalists an outright majority in the formal structures of government, which they feared open elections would ensure them. Second, the Government believed that by granting Muslims separate electorates where they would be electoral minorities in all but two of the provinces of British India (Bengal and the Punjab) they would be forced to look to the Raj as their protector, thus more firmly tying Muslim fortunes to those of the British. The British believed that because separate electorates would fracture the formal spaces of governance they surrendered to Indians, native politicians would be forced to work on the basis of cross-communal alliances. This course would therefore have a moderating influence on communal politics, which would reward the collaborative, conservative elites on whom British authority largely depended.

The colonial state's enumeration of people along confessional lines was only one of the ways in which it categorized people. It also enumerated people according to their caste affiliation, specifying their *varna* as well as *jati*. The colonial state used these categories to create communal rights and entitlements as well as to facilitate communal punishments. Untouchables, also known as "backward" or "scheduled caste," mainly suffered social discrimination widespread throughout the subcontinent, while the "criminal tribes" were the objects of penal state regulation. Whereas the separate enumeration of the former by the Raj was partly an attempt to ameliorate their low social position through special state dispensation, the latter was purely a punitive construction of the colonial state creating categories of "group" criminality. Yet the consequences of categorization varied widely throughout India, with members of the "same" community experiencing differential treatment in the various regions of British India as well as in the princely states. The legal positions of both the untouchables and tribals were transformed with the advent of independence, when these groups were granted comparatively extensive political entitlements and reservations. The use of communal patronage and punishment as a strategy of governance imprinted a lasting legacy on Indian politics.

By the end of the First World War, British governing circles reached a consensus that India would eventually have to be granted independence. However, no time line for such a move was agreed upon. Their actions during the interwar period were designed to more firmly embed British rule. The Raj endeavored to undermine the appeal of all-Indian nationalists through the inclusion of Indian elites in local elected assemblies. Yet as the GoI invested localities with governmental responsibilities, it tightened its grip on key areas of governance it considered essential to its paramountcy—defense, communications, and foreign affairs. The British sought to fracture Indian political opinion further through the use and extension of separate electorates for "minorities" within the newly elected assemblies. By channeling state-recognized political power through communal identity, separate electorates had dire consequences for the Indian body politic.

By 1945 the once far-off potentiality of Indian independence had become an imminent reality. The cost of the Second World War, Britain's early defeats by the Japanese, and the force of Indian nationalism combined to shatter the myth of the Raj's invincibility. The most extreme anti-British nationalists found expression during the war under the leadership of Subhas Chandra Bose, former president of the Congress, in his Indian National Army (INA) set up under the tutelage and ultimate control of the Japanese. The campaigns against the Japanese and their INA auxiliaries in Burma from 1942 onward had a lasting psychological effect on the Raj. More powerfully however, the activities of mainstream Indian nationalists, culminating in the Quit India movement of 1942, underlined the Raj's moral and political bankruptcy and also laid bare the costs and limits of what force could achieve. The memory of the wartime experiences of Indian nationalism weighed heavily on the minds of British policy makers as they looked to their future in the subcontinent, forcing an acknowledgment that the local collaborationist politics that had been the foundation of authority during the interwar period no longer served the realities of a postwar world. Opting for a quick exit, the British negotiated the transfer of power with India's nationalist politicians, represented by Congress and the All-India Muslim League. Congress, proponent of a strong center, jockeyed with the League, which claimed to exclusively represent India's Muslims and advocated a federal outcome, to author India's independent future. Under pressure to leave and recognizing the League's weakness, the British decided on Congress. Their withdrawal led to the independence and partition of the Indian subconti-

nent into the successor states of Pakistan and India. Partition was accompanied by horrendous communal violence and resulted in the largest forced migration in recorded history. After nearly two hundred years, the Raj succumbed to a bloody and ignominious end.

In the early twenty-first century the memory of the Raj remains contested. In the immediate aftermath of independence, nationalists attempted to minimize the legacy of the Raj and largely expunge it as a historical aberration in the Subcontinent's history. A nationalist tradition of historiography buttressed popular perceptions of the Raj as an episode of exploitation that was eventually defeated by the strength of the Indian freedom struggle. This image remains firmly fixed in the public imaginations not only of India and Pakistan but also to a significant extent of Britain as well. Nostalgia for the Raj, however, has continued to be a subtle but powerful countercurrent. The belief in the ultimate munificence of the Raj, held by a few intransigent imperialists and their collaborators, has morphed into a more muted romantic reminiscence. The experience of rule is projected through the memory of those who wielded authority, such as the families of imperial administrators, as days of order, innocence, and benevolence. The juxtaposition of "Raj nostalgia" with a narrative nationalist "freedom struggle" underlines the depth of the experience linking South Asia and Britain. Just as the experience of the Raj had a diverse array of expressions, so too does its memory.

SEE ALSO *Colonialism*

BIBLIOGRAPHY

Bayly, C. A. 1988. *Indian Society and the Making of the British Empire.* Cambridge, U.K.: Cambridge University Press.

Bayly, C. A., and T. N. Harper. 2005. *Forgotten Armies: Britain's Asian Empire and the War with Japan.* London: Penguin.

Bose, Sugata, and Ayesha Jalal. 2004. *Modern South Asia: History, Culture, Political Economy.* 2nd ed. New York: Routledge.

Chatterji, Joya. 1994. *Bengal Divided: Hindu Communalism and Partition, 1932–1947.* Cambridge, U.K.: Cambridge University Press.

Jalal, Ayesha. 1994. *The Sole Spokesman: Jinnah, the Muslim League, and the Demand for Pakistan.* Cambridge, U.K.: Cambridge University Press.

Metcalf, Barbara D., and Thomas R. Metcalf. 2002. *A Concise History of India.* Cambridge, U.K.: Cambridge University Press.

Metcalf, Thomas R. 1995. *Ideologies of the Raj.* Cambridge, U.K.: Cambridge University Press.

B. D. Hopkins

RAND, AYN

SEE *Objectivism.*

RANDOLPH, A. PHILIP

SEE *Pullman Porters.*

RANDOM EFFECTS

SEE *General Linear Model.*

RANDOM EFFECTS REGRESSION

The random effects estimator is applicable in the context of panel data—that is, data comprising observations on two or more "units" or "groups" (e.g., persons, firms, countries) in two or more time periods. The simplest regression model for such data is pooled Ordinary Least Squares (OLS), the specification for which may be written as

$$y_{it} = X_{it}\beta + u_{it} \qquad (1)$$

where y_{it} is the observation on the dependent variable for cross-sectional unit i in period t, X_{it} is a $1 \times k$ vector of independent variables observed for unit i in period t, β is a $k \times 1$ vector of parameters, and u_{it} is an error or disturbance term specific to unit i in period t.

One of the assumptions required in order that OLS is optimal is that the error term is independently and identically distributed (IID). In the panel context, the IID assumption means that $E(u_{it}^2)$, in relation to equation (1), equals a constant, σ_u^2, for all i and t, whereas the covariance $E(u_{is}u_{it})$ equals zero for all $s \neq t$, and the covariance $E(u_{jt}u_{it})$ equals zero for all $j \neq i$.

This may be inappropriate in a panel data context, because it amounts to saying that y_{it} is no more different from y_{jt} than it is from y_{is}. That is, observations from the same individual at a different time are just as independent from y_{it} as those coming from different individuals. Because this assumption is hard to maintain in many situations, the probabilistic model is often taken to be

$$y_{it} = X_{it}\beta + v_i + \varepsilon_{it}, \qquad (2)$$

where we decompose u_{it} into a unit-specific and time-invariant component, v_i, and an observation-specific error, $\varepsilon_{it}.$

The fixed-effects and random-effects models differ in their interpretations of the v_i term: In the fixed-effects model, the v_is are treated as fixed parameters (unit-specific y-intercepts); in the random-effects model, in contrast, they are treated as random drawings from a given probability distribution.

In the fixed-effects approach, we merely acknowledge that differences between individuals exist. Therefore, the parameter β can be estimated by including a dummy variable for each cross-sectional unit and suppressing the global constant. If, however, we are willing to go the extra step of modeling the v_i, greater efficiency may be attained by using Generalized Least Squares (GLS), taking into account the structure of the error term. This is the random effects approach (for an early and influential example of this, see Balestra and Nerlove 1966).

Consider observations on a given unit i at two times s and t. From the hypotheses above, it follows that $\mathrm{Var}(u_{is}) = \mathrm{Var}(u_{it}) = \sigma_v^2 + \sigma_\varepsilon^2$, whereas between u_{is} and u_{it} is $E(u_{is}u_{it}) = \sigma_v^2$. In matrix notation, we may group the T_i observations for unit i into the vector y_i and write

$$y_i = X_i\beta + u_i \qquad (3)$$

The vector u_i, which includes all the disturbances for i, has covariance matrix

$$\mathrm{Var}(u_i) = \sum_i = \sigma_\varepsilon^2 I + \sigma_v^2 J \qquad (4)$$

where J is a square matrix with all elements equal to 1. It can be shown that the matrix

$$K_i = I - \frac{\theta}{T_i} J,$$

where $\theta = 1 - \sqrt{\dfrac{\sigma_\varepsilon^2}{\sigma_\varepsilon^2 + T_i\sigma_v^2}}$ has the property

$$K_i \sum_i K_i' = \sigma_\varepsilon^2 I$$

It follows that the transformed system

$$K_i y_i = K_i X_i \beta_i + K_i u_i \qquad (5)$$

satisfies the Gauss-Markov conditions, and OLS estimation of (5) provides efficient inference. But because

$$K_i y_i = y_i - \theta \bar{y}_i$$

GLS estimation is equivalent to OLS using "quasi-demeaned" data—that is, variables from which we subtract a fraction θ of their average. Notice that for $\sigma_\varepsilon^2 \to 0$, $\theta \to 1$, whereas for $\sigma_v^2 \to 0$, $\theta \to 0$. If all the variance is attributable to the individual effects, the fixed-effects estimator is optimal; if, instead, individual effects are negligible, then pooled OLS is optimal.

To implement GLS we need to calculate θ, which in turn requires estimates of the variances σ_ε^2 and σ_v^2. (These are often referred to as the "within" and "between" variances, respectively, because the former refers to variation within each cross-sectional unit and the latter to variation between the units). Several means of estimating these magnitudes have been suggested in the literature (see Baltagi 2005).

The above derivation presupposes that the ε_{it} term is IID. Departures from this assumption (e.g., heteroskedasticity) have been analyzed, leading to a sizable body of literature (see, for example, Baltagi 2005 and Arellano 2003).

When is the random effects estimator preferable to fixed effects? If the panel comprises observations on a fixed and relatively small set of units of interest (for example, the member states of the European Union), there is a presumption in favor of fixed effects, because it makes little sense to consider the v_i terms as sampled from an underlying population: In the case of the European Union states, the sample and the population coincide, and even a thought experiment in which the units are different would be audacious. If, instead, the sample comprises observations on a large number of randomly selected individuals (as in many epidemiological and other longitudinal studies), there is a presumption in favor of random effects. Besides this general heuristic, however, certain statistical issues must be taken into account.

First, some panel data sets contain variables whose values are specific to the cross-sectional unit but which do not vary over time (for example, the gender of an individual). If such variables are to be included in the model, the fixed-effects option is simply not available. (When the fixed-effects model is implemented using the dummy variables approach, the trouble is that any time-invariant variables are perfectly collinear with the unit dummies.) Second, the random-effects estimator can be shown to be a matrix-weighted average of pooled OLS and the "between" estimator (a regression using the group means, and hence ignoring the intragroup variation). Suppose we have observations on m units and there are k independent variables of interest. If $k > m$, the "between" estimator is undefined—we have only m effective observations—and hence so is the random-effects estimator.

If one does not fall foul of one or other of these issues, the choice between fixed effects and random effects may be expressed as a tradeoff between robustness and efficiency.

The robustness of the fixed-effects approach stems from the fact that it makes no hypotheses regarding the differences in mean across the units, except that such differences exist. This estimator "always works," but at the cost of not being able to estimate the effect of time-invariant regressors.

The richer hypothesis set of the random-effects estimator allows for estimation of the parameters for time-invariant regressors, and ensures that estimation of the parameters for time-varying regressors is performed more efficiently. But these advantages are tied to the validity of the additional hypotheses. If the individual effects are correlated with some of the explanatory variables, then the random-effects estimator is inconsistent, whereas fixed-effects estimates are still valid. It is on this principle that the "Hausman test" (Hausman 1978) is built: If the fixed- and random-effects estimates agree, to within the usual statistical margin of error, then there is no reason to believe the additional hypotheses are invalid, and as a consequence, no reason *not* to use the more efficient random-effects estimator.

SEE ALSO *Regression*

BIBLIOGRAPHY

Arellano, Manuel. 2003. *Panel Data Econometrics*. Oxford: Oxford University Press.

Balestra, Pietro, and Marc Nerlove. 1966. Pooling Cross-Section and Time Series Data in the Estimation of a Dynamic Model: The Demand for Natural Gas. *Econometrica* 34 (3): 585–612.

Baltagi, Badi H. 2005. *Econometric Analysis of Panel Data*. 3rd ed. New York: Wiley.

Hausman, James A. 1978. Specification Tests in Econometrics. *Econometrica* 46: 1251–1271.

Allin Cottrell
Riccardo "Jack" Lucchetti

RANDOM SAMPLES

A teacher has four students who have done well in their homework, and she wants to reward them by assigning them a special task that they enjoy. The problem is that the task requires only two students. What is a "fair" way to choose the two students who receive the reward? When this question is posed to the students themselves, they are quite likely to say something like, "Put the four names on individual slips of paper in a box, mix them up, and have someone draw out two names, sight unseen."

The students are describing a *random sample* of two names from the four. Labeling the names as *A, B, C,* and *D,* the six possible samples of size two are (A,B), (A,C), (A,D), (B,C), (B,D), and (C,D). Because there is no reason to suspect that one sample is any more likely than another, the appropriate probability model for this random sampling assigns each of the six a probability of 1/6. This leads to a definition of a *simple random sample* for the general case in which *n* names are selected from the *N* names in the box, generally called the *population*. A simple random sample of *n* objects selected from a population of *N* distinct objects is a sample chosen so that all possible samples of size *n* have an equal chance of being selected.

It follows from basic rules of probability that the probability that person *A* gets selected, written *P(A)*, is given by *P(A)* = 1/2; because three of the six equally likely samples have *A* in them. For the general case, the probability of any one object ending up in the sample is *n/N*. Thus the definition implies that, in simple random sampling, each individual has the same chance of being selected as any other individual. The reverse statement is not true, however. A method of sampling that gives each individual the same chance of being selected is not necessarily a simple random sample. For example, suppose *A* and *B* are male and *C* and *D* are female. Then selecting one male at random and one female at random gives each person the same chance (1/2) of being selected, but no sample would ever contain two boys or two girls.

If *N* and *n* were large, the process of physically drawing names from a box would be impractical if not impossible. Most often simple random samples are selected by a process that essentially numbers each of the *N* objects and then generates *n* random numbers between 1 and *N* by means of a calculator or computer, selecting as the sample those objects whose numbers were so generated.

SAMPLING WITHOUT AND WITH REPLACEMENT

The sampling scheme described above is referred to as *sampling without replacement*. Drawing the two names is mathematically the same as drawing one name at random and then drawing a second name from those that remain in the box. Using basic rules of probability, it follows that

P (selecting *A* and then selecting *B*)

= *P* (*A* on first draw) · *P* (*B* on second draw given that *A* is already selected)

= (1/4)(1/3) = 1/12.

To get the probability of the sample (*A,B*) this has to be doubled, because *B* could have been selected first and *A* second. Thus *P(A,B)* = 1/6, as shown above.

Suppose, however, that the two students receiving the reward could perform the task separately and at different times, so the same person could be selected twice. This could be accomplished by selecting one name at random, placing that name back in the box, and selecting the sec-

ond name at random from the same set of four names. Under this scheme of *sampling with replacement*,

P (selecting *A* and then selecting *B*)

= *P* (*A* on first draw) · *P* (*B* on second draw given that *A* is already selected)

= (1/4)(1/4) = 1/16.

Because the probability of selecting *B* after *A* is the same as the probability of selecting *B* on the fist draw, the events "select *A*" and "select *B*" are said to be *independent*. Under independence (sampling with replacement), the probability of selecting two specific students changed from that of sampling without replacement. Suppose, however, that *N* were 40,000 instead of 4. Then removing one object would not appreciably change the probability on the second draw, and the counterparts of the two probabilities displayed above would be practically equal.

This fact leads to a second definition of a random sample, one based on independence. A random sample of size *n* is a set of n objects selected independently and at random from the same set of *N* objects.

If *N* is large compared to *n*, the second definition results in a probability structure for the sample that is approximately the same as that of the first definition. Moreover the second definition makes the statistical theory of sampling much easier to work out. That fact, coupled with the fact that the most common uses of random sampling, sample surveys and opinion polls generally involve large populations, makes the second definition more useful in practice.

Populations have been discussed thus far as if they were well-defined entities that the sampler could actually see or list. Consider a classical die toss using a balanced die. The population of possible outcomes of die tosses is infinite and conceptual, but it can readily be modeled as if the possible outcomes, 1 through 6, were represented in equal numbers because it seems logical to think of each possible outcome as having probability 1/6. Using the second definition then, a set of n outcomes generated from independent tosses of a balanced die can be considered as a random sample, each outcome being randomly (through the tossing) and independently (assuming the second toss is not influenced by the first) selected from this large, conceptual population.

RANDOM SAMPLING AND STATISTICAL INFERENCE

Random sampling forms the probabilistic basis for statistical inference. Consider the common opinion poll in which *n* people are randomly sampled from a large population of *N* people. Because *N* is usually large, the inde-

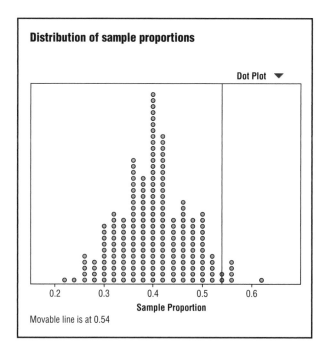

Distribution of sample proportions

Dot Plot ▼

Sample Proportion

Movable line is at 0.54

Figure 1.

pendence model provides a good approximation, even though the samples are selected without replacement. The goal of such a poll is to estimate a population proportion, p, such as the proportion of voters that favor a certain candidate. The estimate of p is the corresponding sample proportion, often designated by $\hat{p}$, of voters in the sample who favor the candidate. Due to the random sampling and the mathematics of probability, many facts can be established with regard to $\hat{p}$. If n is large, $\hat{p}$ has a small chance of being "far" from the true p it is estimating. In fact $\hat{p}$ will be within a distance of approximately $1/\sqrt{n}$ from p about 95 percent of the time in repeated sampling. (This is why a poll of 1,000 persons is said to have a *margin of error* of about 3 percent.) If a poll is done many times, it will give results close to p most of the time but can miss by a large amount on occasion (about 5 percent of the time).

The facts stated above are related the result that the values of $\hat{p}$ will have an approximately normal distribution (mound-shaped symmetric distribution) when random samples of the same size are taken repeatedly from the same population. The figure below shows a simulated distribution of 200 $\hat{p}$ values for samples of size 50 taken for a population with $p = 0.40$. The theoretical margin of error is approximately $1/\sqrt{50} = 0.14$, indicating that a $\hat{p}$ of 0.54 or more would be an extremely rare occurrence. Such an outcome occurred only 7 times out of 200 in this simulation (see figure 1).

THEORY VERSUS PRACTICE

All of the above presents a neat theory of random sampling, but obtaining a truly random sample in practice is nearly impossible for most sampling situations. Consider the relatively simple situation of selecting a sample of students from a college. First, the population to be sampled needs a clear definition (but what constitutes a student?). Second, a list of students will be needed (but this changes almost every day). Third, even with a good definition and a good list, the sampled students may not be able to be found or, if found, may not be willing to respond (or respond correctly) to a survey. These three concerns, population definition, population dynamics, and nonresponse, cover many of the practical difficulties that occur in nearly all sampling problems. They are compounded with others in surveys of subjects who are hard to find anyway, such as victims of war atrocities. In many situations the difficulties can be mitigated by a more complex sampling design, the most common features of which involve stratification (divide the population into nonoverlapping but relatively large groups and take a random sample from each) and clustering (divide the population into many relatively small nonoverlapping groups and take a random sample of the groups). A national survey that selects respondents by state is an example of stratification. A city survey that samples city blocks, rather than households, and then interviews someone in each household in every sampled block is an example of clustering.

SEE ALSO *Central Limit Theorem; Probability; Research, Survey; Sample Attrition; Sampling; Survey*

BIBLIOGRAPHY

Levy, Paul S., and Stanley Lemeshow. 1999. *Sampling of Populations.* New York: Wiley.

Lohr, Sharon L. 1999. *Sampling: Design and Analysis.* Pacific Grove, CA: Duxbury.

Scheaffer, Richard L., William Mendenhall III, and R. Lyman Ott. 2006. *Elementary Survey Sampling.* Belmont, CA: Thomson Brooks/Cole.

Richard L. Scheaffer

RANDOM WALK

A *random walk* is one in which future steps or directions cannot be predicted on the basis of past actions. When the term is applied to the stock market, it means that short-run changes in stock prices cannot be predicted: Investment advisory services, earnings predictions, and complicated chart patterns are useless to the investor.

ORIGINS AND RATIONALES

The application of the random walk hypothesis to stock prices usually is associated with Samuelson (1965), although the general idea that security prices change randomly goes back at least to the time of Bachelier (1900). The basic rationale for the hypothesis is that securities markets are very efficient at digesting information. When information arises about a particular security or about the market in general, the news spreads quickly and is incorporated into the price of that security without delay. Armies of investment managers pounce on any news that could affect the value of a security. By their trading, they ensure that security prices fully reflect all available information. As a result it is not possible to make profitable trades on the basis of that information because any potential profit will have been realized already. Changes in the prices of securities will be random and unpredictable.

The random walk hypothesis does not imply that movements in security prices are erratic or capricious. However, tomorrow's price change in securities markets will reflect only tomorrow's "news" and will be independent of the price change today. True news by definition is unpredictable, and thus the resulting price change also must be unpredictable and random.

The term *random walk* usually is used loosely in the finance literature to characterize a price series in which all subsequent price changes represent random departures from previous prices. Thus, changes in price essentially are not related to past price changes. It is believed that the term was used first in an exchange of correspondence in *Nature* in 1905. The subject was the optimal search procedure for finding a drunk who had been left in the middle of a field. The solution was simply to start where the drunk had been left. That point provides the best unbiased estimate of the drunk's future position because presumably he will have staggered along in an unpredictable and random fashion.

If stock price movements approximate those of a random walk, technical analysis (the making and interpretation of stock charts to divine the future) is unlikely to offer investors a guide to making above-average profits. Moreover, trading strategies that seek to buy and sell stocks on the basis of charting signals will not help investors outperform a simple buy-and-hold strategy.

Considerable statistical work has supported the random walk hypothesis. Changes in stock prices from day to day are essentially uncorrelated, and news seems to be reflected in the prices of securities without delay. Although markets sometimes overreact to news, they underreact at other times. Several technical trading systems have been tested, and they do not produce greater profits after transactions costs than does a simple buy-and-hold strategy.

The stock market does not fully meet all the conditions for a random walk, however. Some slight dependencies have been found, and there is a small degree of momentum in stock prices. Some seasonal patterns have been discovered. However, the dependencies that have been found are very small relative to the transactions costs that would be required to exploit them, and they are not dependable from period to period.

Logic suggests that any patterns that might have existed in the past are likely to self-destruct in the future. Suppose, for example, there was a dependable Christmas rally; that is, the stock market consistently rose in the trading days between Christmas and New Year's Day. Traders attempting to profit from that pattern would plan to buy the day before Christmas and sell the day before New Year's Day. However, pre-Christmas buying would make stock prices rise the day before Christmas and fall the day before New Year's as traders unloaded their positions to realize profits. Hence, to beat the gun, traders would have to buy two days before Christmas and sell two days before New Year's Day. Before long all the buying would take place before Christmas and the selling would occur after Christmas, and the year-end rally would disappear. Any dependable pattern that could be exploited for profit would self-destruct. This is the logical reason why dependable patterns in stock prices are unlikely to persist.

IMPLICATIONS FOR INVESTORS

The random walk hypothesis has important implications for investors in the stock market. Visually, charts of stock prices appear to display some obvious patterns, but those patterns are simply a manifestation of a statistical illusion. The "cycles" in stock charts are no more true cycles than are the runs of luck or misfortunes of the ordinary gambler. History tends to repeat itself best in an infinitely surprising variety of ways that confound any attempts to profit from knowledge of past price patterns. Although the market does not meet the statistician's ideal of a perfect random walk, any systematic relationships that exist are so small and undependable that they are not useful for an investor. The history of stock price movements contains no useful information that will enable an investor consistently to outperform a buy-and-hold strategy in managing a portfolio.

Attempting to use past patterns of stock prices to ascertain the times when investors should be out of the market is especially dangerous. Because there is a long-term uptrend in the stock market, it can be very risky to be in cash. An investor who frequently carries a large cash position to avoid periods of market decline is very likely to be out of the market during some periods when it rallies smartly. Market timers risk missing the infrequent big gains that are the main contributors to performance, and they also pay more in taxes and transactions costs than does an investor who simply buys and holds a diversified portfolio.

SEE ALSO *Efficient Market Hypothesis; Expectations, Implicit; Expectations, Rational; Financial Markets; Information, Economics of; Stocks*

BIBLIOGRAPHY

Bachalier, Louis. 1900. Theory of Speculation. *Ann Sci. École Norm. Sup.* (5) No. 1018. Paris: Gauthier-Villars.

Lo, Andrew W., and A. Craig MacKinlay. 1999. *A Non-Random Walk Down Wall Street.* Princeton, NJ: Princeton University Press.

Malkiel, Burton G. 2007. *A Random Walk Down Wall Street: The Time-Tested Strategy for Successful Investing.* New York: W. W. Norton.

Samuelson, Paul A. 1965. Proof That Properly Anticipated Prices Fluctuate Randomly. *Industrial Management Review* 6, No. 1 (Spring): pp. 321–351.

Burton G. Malkiel

RANDOMNESS

Randomness is a term used in the social sciences and mathematics to refer to chance factors occurring in a manner that the individual events in a series of events or outcomes do not exhibit a connection to each other in their occurrence. Events are independent of each other, and thus the occurrence of one event is not linked to the occurrence of other events in a series in any systematic manner.

Randomness as a quality of a series of events is believed to be the result of numerous minor causes producing small effects as an outcome that results in no systematic predictability for a given event in the series. The result of the many small causes, some canceling each other, is the independence of each event from the others. It is notable that the operation of causation is not denied in the universe of events and experiences. Rather, the causal background to a series of random events is interpreted as a multiplicity of small influences, some almost infinitesimal in impact, with some causes canceling or partially canceling the influence of other causes. The outcome is a series of events with independent occurrence in relation to each other. The word *chance* is used in popular speech to refer to this condition wherein events are generated independently of each other.

RANDOMNESS AND RANDOM DISTRIBUTIONS

Of great interest to social scientists is the demonstrable fact that some random distributions follow broadly pre-

dictable patterns when a series of events occurs in large numbers. Individual outcomes or instances cannot be predicted with any certainty, but a random pattern may be demonstrated to follow a broad configuration in such a manner that larger areas in the distribution of random events may be assigned a broad likelihood or probability of occurrence. Examples include various known or empirical distributions of random events that follow the bilaterally symmetrical distribution that forms a curve known as the normal curve. Another related known probability distribution is the binomial distribution, where only two possible outcomes can occur in a random series of events, such as tossing an unweighted coin a large or an even infinite number of times. The binomial distribution approximates the normal curve of probability with a large series of discrete, independent trials of two possible outcomes. Yet another known distribution of random events is the chi-square distribution when the X^2 statistic is calculated on a number of randomly drawn samples if the samples themselves are drawn from a larger universe of randomly distributed frequencies for a number of categories of observations. The tables that summarize the patterns of these known distributions of statistics are available in any book on statistical method.

STATISTICS AND RANDOMNESS

The field of statistics as it is applied in research in the social sciences can be broken into two broad divisions: descriptive statistics and inferential statistics. The purpose of the first division, descriptive statistics, is the summary of data. Data are ordinarily summarized by measures of central tendency, such as means, medians, and the mode. Variation or dispersion of data can be summarized with measures of variance and standard deviations. If there are two or more variables measured, a researcher may search for association through measures of correlation.

The second broad division in statistics is inferential statistics. This is the division used to deal with randomness and the use of known random distributions to compare for departures from randomness in empirical distributions. Departures from randomness in the latter situation can be assessed probabilistically and can be of great value in the assessment of causation. The search for causation begins with the determination by an observer of correlation or association between observations. Departures from randomness are of great importance because there is an initial indication of a pattern of association or correlation.

This second broad area of inferential statistics is itself broken into two large divisions. The first division involves estimation of parameters or universe values. This is attempted when a smaller sample must be drawn from a larger population or universe. The value calculated on a sample is referred to as a *statistic*. A mean calculated for a sample is a statistic. If the mean were calculated for an entire population, it would be referred to as the *parameter*. Researchers are often required to estimate parameters based on sample statistics due to limitations in time, personnel, and particularly the cost of conducting research on an entire population. Randomness is an important consideration for estimation of parameters because a sample must be drawn through a random process if an inference is to be made as a probability statement for the parameter value.

This requirement exists because the estimation of the parameter, or population mean, is based on knowledge of the pattern of a series of randomly sampled means, or a *sampling distribution* of means. This known sampling distribution approximates a normal curve, with the latter's known probabilities for areas under the curve. Random sampling matches the assumptions of randomness for the pattern of means in the sampling distribution and thus enables a researcher to calculate the probability of being in error while using a sample mean to estimate the parameter of the population.

A second division of inferential statistics involves prescribed procedures used in hypotheses testing. Hypotheses testing is used in research as a search for the existence of relationships in a population or larger universe of possible observations. Again, random samples must be used if exact statements of probability are to be made in regard to the hypotheses being tested. Research scholars vary in style of work, but a typical model utilizing randomness is one that searches for non-randomness or hypothesized correlated variables by generating research hypotheses of correlation between categories of empirical observations or variables and then tests for these correlations through statistical procedures, such as a difference of means test, chi-square, or tests of significance for randomly sampled measures that yield the sampled correlation coefficients.

In this manner of conducting research, the hypothesis of randomness, or no relationship, which is referred to as the null hypothesis, is cast against a set of empirical frequencies drawn from a random sample. If the test of differences between means, or the X^2 statistic, or the sampled correlation coefficients yield a value or values that are so large that they are unlikely to occur by chance in repeated random samples from random distributions with their known statistical patterns, inferences can be made regarding the likelihood of a correlation or relationship between the hypothesized variables in the larger universe from which the samples have been randomly selected. This family of tests is known as significance tests. Thus the observation and understanding of random events enables one to become knowledgeable about random patterns. This knowledge of random patterns is useful for social sci-

entists as it enables them to make inferences about causes in the social world, which is largely a non-random world, and thereby to build theoretical explanations based on empirical research to reach a better understanding of the complex social world in its many structured variations.

SEE ALSO *Butterfly Effect; Chaos Theory; Regression Analysis; Residuals*

BIBLIOGRAPHY

Blalock, Hubert M., Jr. 1972. *Social Statistics.* 2nd ed. New York: McGraw-Hill.

Bowerman, Bruce L., and Richard T. O'Connell. 2007. *Business Statistics in Practice.* 4th ed. Boston: McGraw-Hill/Irwin.

Lindgren, Bernard W. 1968. *Statistical Theory.* 2nd ed. New York: Macmillan.

Mueller, John H., Karl F. Schuessler, and Herbert L. Costner. 1977. *Statistical Reasoning in Sociology.* 3rd ed. Boston: Houghton Mifflin.

Spatz, Chris. 1997. *Basic Statistics: Tales of Distributions.* Pacific Grove, CA: Brooks/Cole.

Walker, Helen M., and Joseph Lev. 1953. *Statistical Inference.* New York: Holt.

Kenneth N. Eslinger

RAPE

Rape is a crime of sexual coercion that can cause acute physical and psychological trauma. Its victims are mostly female, although males may be rape victims as well. Nearly all rape perpetrators are male.

PREVALENCE AND EFFECTS

Research conducted in the United States provides a window on the prevalence of rape. Approximately 20 percent of American women report that at some point in their lives they have been forced to have sexual intercourse against their will. Approximately 8 percent of American females indicate that their first experience of sexual intercourse was coerced. Although legal and cultural climates surrounding the crime of rape vary greatly around the globe, research suggests that rape is a widespread phenomenon and that most rapes go undetected. Mass rape has also been used as a weapon of warfare, torture, and genocide—notorious in the 1990s and early 2000s in Bosnia, Rwanda, and Darfur—and has been classified under international law as a crime against humanity. Rape in U.S. prisons is a significant problem that remains largely unaddressed.

Victims of rape report an experience of degradation, often with immediate effects of physical paralysis and mental dissociation. Studies indicate that victims of acquaintance rape can suffer as much or more psychological harm than victims of stranger rape, in part because they experience more intense feelings of guilt and self-blame. Almost one-third of rape victims experience fragmented memory, traumatic amnesia, or other long-term effects, similar to those associated with posttraumatic stress disorder. These common symptoms of sexual trauma can compromise the victim's ability to report the crime in a coherent narrative and to demonstrate nonconsent for a legal proceeding.

DEFINITION AND PUNISHMENT

Historically, the law defined rape as a man having sexual intercourse with a woman through the use of force and without her consent. In his leading legal treatise of the eighteenth century, *Commentaries on the Laws of England* (1765), William Blackstone (1723–1780) described rape as "carnal knowledge of a woman forcibly and against her will" (p. 209). This definition remained remarkably static for generations.

In contemporary law, force and consent became irrelevant in *statutory rape*, which presumes involuntary any sexual relations with a person under an age specified by statute. First enacted into law in England in 1275, statutory rape laws are common in the United States but rarely enforced against consensual sexual relationships between adolescents. The rare statutory rape prosecution is likely to involve an older man and an underage woman, and some jurisdictions have statutes that require the perpetrator to be over twenty-one or significantly older than the victim. Originally the age of consent for statutory rape was twelve, later reduced to ten. Although the nineteenth-century women's movement successfully lobbied to raise the age limit for statutory rape, in some states the age limit remains as low as thirteen. Other states consider sixteen or eighteen to be the appropriate age of consent.

In early England, rape was classified as a misdemeanor to be punished by a fine or imprisonment. By virtue of a statute enacted in 1285, rape became a capital felony, a classification imported to colonial America. During the twentieth century, however, imprisonment became the most common punishment for rape convictions.

PROPERTY AND RACE

From the seventeenth through the nineteenth century, notions of property shaped the understanding of rape. Female slaves, deemed the property of their owners, could not be raped under law and therefore received no protection from rape law. In situations where rape law applied, rape was understood as a crime of trespass committed by a male stranger against the property of another man, the husband or father of the woman who was raped. Hence,

rape within marriage was considered legally impossible. Even after America's formal abandonment of the notion of women as property, its influence reached into the twentieth century through the marital exemption from rape laws that continued to presume a wife's consent to all intercourse with her husband, even when it was coerced. Although all states have abolished the full marital rape exemption, some still retain it in partial forms.

From the eighteenth through the mid-twentieth century, rape indictments and conviction rates in America were low, except when defendants were nonwhite. African American men alleged to have raped white women were zealously prosecuted, even in cases where there was reason to doubt the allegation's reliability. About 90 percent of the men executed for rape in the twentieth century in the United States were African Americans. This racialized pattern of punishment was noted by the U.S. Supreme Court in the 1977 case of *Coker v. Georgia*, which held the death penalty for rape to be unconstitutional.

In marked contrast, when victims were African American women, rape laws were largely unenforced, especially during the slavery era. Rape of female slaves, which could reproduce more slave labor for the owner's service, was a commonplace occurrence. Studies suggest that African American women who report being raped continue to have disproportionate difficulties obtaining redress through the legal system, as their reports are especially likely to be regarded with suspicion.

REFORM EFFORTS

For centuries a culture of skepticism surrounded all women's accusations of rape. Such skepticism is revealed in the language of the seventeenth-century English jurist Matthew Hale (1609–1676) in his *History of the Pleas of the Crown* (1847): "It must be remembered, that [rape] is an accusation easily to be made and hard to be proved, and harder to be defended by the party accused, tho never so innocent" (p. 635). Such an attitude is also apparent in the law's traditional requirements that proof of rape entailed not only evidence of the use or threatened use of force but also evidence of resistance—resistance to the utmost of the victim's physical capacities in some states—as a proxy for nonconsent. Additionally, some jurisdictions required corroboration of a victim's testimony and cautioned jurors to give it extra scrutiny. Most of these procedural hurdles have formally disappeared in the United States, although some, such as corroboration requirements, remain in other legal systems around the world.

The first twentieth-century effort to modernize rape law in the United States came with the 1950s revision of the Model Penal Code (MPC), an influential model statute written by recognized legal experts. According to the MPC, rape victims no longer needed to resist "to the utmost" to demonstrate nonconsent. This revision led many states to abolish resistance requirements. The MPC also proposed three grades of sexual assault. Violent stranger rape was felony rape in the first degree. Violent acquaintance rape was a second-degree felony. Other kinds of sexual coercion established the third-degree felony of "gross sexual imposition." Adapting this approach, many states adopted statutory schemes that graded rape offenses by severity.

Rape law reform continued in the 1970s and 1980s when feminist reformers raised awareness of the extent of the incidence and harm of rape and the law's failure, despite harsh potential penalties, to hold most perpetrators accountable. In her book *Real Rape: How the Legal System Victimizes Women Who Say No* (1987), law professor Susan Estrich observed that date rapes or acquaintance rapes are the most common kinds of rape, yet the criminal justice system is less likely to treat these cases as crimes and may even blame the victims for the incidents. Victims experience dehumanization from all of these rapes, all of them violate a victim's bodily integrity and sexual autonomy, but only victims of violent stranger rape are likely to have recourse to the legal system.

Some proposed reforms have received widespread acceptance. For example, along with the broad elimination of resistance and corroboration requirements, rape shield laws that, with some exceptions, prohibit admission of the victim's prior sexual conduct have been widely adopted. Studies, however, are inconclusive as to whether these reforms have made a measurable difference in victim behavior or case outcomes.

Other proposed reforms remain controversial, such as whether sex obtained through fraud or extortion can constitute rape. Another area of controversy concerns whether and under what circumstances to allow mistakes about consent to establish a defense to rape. Estrich's book sparked a "no-means-no" movement, advocating verbal resistance as sufficient to establish nonconsent. Others have suggested that the absence of affirmative assent or of a verbal discussion about desired acts should undermine consent as a defense in rape cases. Strong arguments have been made to abandon force as an element of rape, because the use of force is inherent in unwanted sex. New Jersey did so in the case of *In re M.T.S.* (1992), and some state statutes classify nonconsensual penetration without force as a sexual offense, although typically one less serious than rape.

While reform efforts have been influential in drawing attention to a variety of problems in social and legal responses to rape, popular attitudes are harder to modify than written laws. Solving many of these problems will require deeper cultural change.

BIBLIOGRAPHY

Allison, Julie A., and Lawrence S. Wrightsman. 1993. *Rape: The Misunderstood Crime*. Newbury Park, CA: Sage.

Anderson, Michelle J. Negotiating Sex. 2005. *Southern California Law Review* 78: 1401–1438.

Blackstone, William. 1765. *Commentaries on the Laws of England*. Vol. 2. Chicago: University of Chicago Press.

Dripps, Donald A. Beyond Rape: An Essay on the Difference Between the Presence of Force and the Absence of Consent. 1992. *Columbia Law Review* 92 (7): 1780–1809.

Estrich, Susan. 1987. *Real Rape: How the Legal System Victimizes Women Who Say No*. Cambridge, MA: Harvard University Press.

Greenfield, Lawrence A. 1997. *Sex Offenses and Offenders: An Analysis of Data on Rape and Sexual Assault*. Washington, DC: Bureau of Justice Statistics, U.S. Department of Justice. http://www.ojp.usdoj.gov/bjs/pub/pdf/soo.pdf.

Hale, Matthew. 1847. *The History of the Pleas of the Crown*. Vol. 1. Ed. Sollom Emlyn. Philadelphia: R. H. Small.

LaFree, Gary D. 1989. *Rape and Criminal Justice: The Social Construction of Sexual Assault*. Belmont, CA: Wadsworth.

Larson, Jane E. 1997. "Even a Worm Will Turn at Last": Rape Reform in Late Nineteenth-Century America. *Yale Journal of Law and Humanities* 9 (1): 1–71.

MacKinnon, Catharine A. 2001. *Sex Equality: Rape Law*. New York: Foundation Press.

Parrot, Andrea, and Laurie Bechhofer, eds. 1991. *Acquaintance Rape: The Hidden Crime*. New York: Wiley.

Schulhofer, Stephen J. 1998. *Unwanted Sex: The Culture of Intimidation and the Failure of Law*. Cambridge, MA: Harvard University Press.

Spohn, Cassia, and Julie Horney. 1992. *Rape Law Reform: A Grassroots Revolution and Its Impact*. New York: Plenum.

Wriggins, Jennifer. 1983. Rape, Racism, and the Law. *Harvard Women's Law Journal* 6: 103–141.

Phyllis Goldfarb

RAPE OF NANKING

SEE *Chinese Revolution*.

RASTAFARI

Following the 1930 crowning of Ras Tafari (1892–1975) as Haile Selassie ("Power of the Trinity"), Emperor of Ethiopia, several street-corner preachers in Jamaica (among them, Joseph Hibbert, Leonard P. Howell, Robert Hinds, Archibald Dunkley, and Paul Earlington) began asserting that Selassie was a divine personage or the reincarnated Christ. For these Jamaicans, Selassie embodied Marcus Garvey's vision of black pride, self-reliance, and repatriation to Africa; signaled the restoration of Ethiopia's ancient glory; and fulfilled the Bible's prophecies of a messianic deliverer. In proclaiming Selassie a messianic figure, they pinned on him their longing for liberation from the legacy of slavery and colonialism.

From the activities of these founding personalities there emerged a set of religious, social, and political beliefs known as *Rastafari* (or *Rastafarianism*), the adherents of which are termed *Rastas* (or *Rastafarians*). From its beginning, Rastafari represented a fundamental critique of the values and institutions of Jamaican society. Rastas' declaration of adherence to a black messiah indicated their rejection of both European religion and the authority of the colonial state. By referring to Jamaica as *Babylon*—land of exile, oppression, and exploitation—they expressed their conviction that this was a society with no redeemable values or institutions, and declared their intention to repatriate to their African homeland, from which they had been "stolen." The Rastas' explicit promulgation of black superiority—admittedly, an overcompensation for centuries of denigration—signaled not just a rejection of the ideology of white supremacy, but even more a reclamation of blackness and of Africa.

From the 1930s to the 1960s, conflict characterized the relationship between Rastafari and Jamaican civil authorities. The charismatic Rastafarian leader Leonard P. Howell exemplified this conflict in the early decades. For inveighing against the British colonial government, he was repeatedly arrested and imprisoned. Law enforcement also repeatedly raided Pinnacle—the commune he established—and eventually demolished it in 1954. The authorities concluded that Howell was demented and committed him to a metal institution. After his release, Howell lived in relative obscurity until his death in the mid-1980s.

By the late 1940s or early 1950s, the House of Youth Black Faith (HYBF) had emerged as the avant-garde of the Rastafari movement. These young Rastas were even more radical than their elders. They elevated the smoking of *ganja* (marijuana) to a personal and communal ritual, which they believed aided them in the discovery of their spiritual and cultural identity by breaking through the mental confines imposed by Babylon. They adopted the dreadlocks hairstyle to accentuate their Africanness and to symbolize their rejection of European standards of beauty (favoring fine, straight hair). They are also credited with the development of *dreadtalk*, an argot that made their speech often unintelligible to outsiders. Furthermore, HYBF projected an aura of militancy through marches and street meetings, vitriolic language calling down "blood and fire" on Babylon and its agents, and the flaunting of laws against ganja possession and use.

For their marijuana use, dreadlocks hairstyle, and general insubordination, Rastas became subjected to the ire of the agents of social control and public opinion: They suffered frequent arrests on drug charges, scapegoating that saw them blamed for a range of criminal activities, and characterizations in the media as lazy, demented, and disposed to violence. When a few weapons were found in the compound of Claudius Henry, a Rastafarian elder, and when his son was implicated in an alleged plot against the Jamaican government, the repression escalated into indiscriminate harassment, arrests, and forced cutting of the locks of Rastas.

Though a 1960 study of Rastafari by University of the West Indies professors M. G. Smith, Roy Augier, and Rex Nettleford effectively debunked myths about the mental deficiency, laziness, and criminality of Rastas, negative views of Rastafari persisted. These prejudices reached a boiling point in 1963, when an attempt to keep Rastas out of the area surrounding the Rose Hall Great House (a tourist attraction) escalated into a virtual riot in which several people were killed. When the government found "evidence" of the endemic criminality of a West Kingston slum in the mid-1960s, Rastas again took the rap. In an attempt to deal with what it considered entrenched Rastafarian criminality, the government bulldozed the entire shantytown where Rastas and others had constructed shacks on an urban dump.

Though a negative perception of Rastafari persisted among many in Jamaican society after 1960, the Smith, Augier, and Nettleford study helped to influence Jamaica's political leadership to adopt a less confrontational approach to the Rastafarian phenomenon. In 1961 Norman Manley's People National Party (PNP) government sent a delegation of civic leaders and Rastas to West Africa and Ethiopia to determine which African countries would be willing to receive Jamaicans desiring to return to the continent of their ancestors. The official report indicated that these countries were only willing to welcome educated and skilled workers. The Rastas of the delegation issued their own report, however, painting a picture of African countries waiting to receive their diasporic children with open arms. Jamaica gained its independence in 1962 under a new Jamaican Labor Party (JLP) government that was less disposed to pursue repatriation for Rastas. Though some Rastas formed their own delegation to make another trip to Africa in 1963, no official repatriation ever took place.

Another measure growing out of the 1960 study was a concerted effort by the Jamaican government to establish cultural and political ties with African countries. This included an invitation to the Ethiopian Orthodox Church to establish itself in Jamaica, and an exchange of visits by Jamaican and African dignitaries. The Ethiopian

Orthodox Church eventually established a congregation in Kingston in 1970, and has established further congregations in several other towns since then. Many Rastas identify with or have become members of this church, but they have often come into conflict with its orthodox teachings. The visitor exchange culminated with Haile Selassie's three-day visit to Jamaica in April 1966. From his arrival until his departure, he was greeted at every public appearance by throngs of Jamaicans, including a multitude of Rastas decked out in their symbolic colors of red, green, and gold. Rastas were among the invited guests at the Vale Royal residence of the prime minister and at fancy hotels where events were held in honor of Selassie. According to reports, some members of the movement were even granted a private audience with the emperor. While Selassie publicly declared that he was not a divine personage, Rastas reported that he confirmed his divinity to them in private, and requested that they work for the liberation of Jamaica before repatriating. After Selassie's visit, the phrase *liberation before repatriation* gained currency among Rastas, and the fervor for repatriation seems to have diminished accordingly. Despite the new emphasis on the need for liberation, the visibility and civility of Rastas at public and private functions conferred a measure of legitimacy on the Rastafarian movement.

By the late 1960s, signs of the changing perception and fortunes of Rastafari were becoming evident. One sign was the diffusion of Rastafarian perspectives and symbolism throughout society and particularly among young people and radical intellectuals. Young people, including many from middle-class families, assumed the Rastafarian mode of dress (knitted caps and the colors red, green, and gold), mode of speech, and ideological stance vis-à-vis the oppressive nature of Jamaican society. Many black intellectuals, who had adopted the black nationalism of the Black Power movement in the United States, found a vernacular expression of such nationalism in Rastafari and established dialogue with the movement. This is best exemplified by the Black Power radical Walter Rodney, a history professor at the University of the West Indies, Mona.

Another sign was the growing influence of Rastafari on local popular music. In the 1950s, Rastafari adopted an African drumming style that had been preserved in Jamaica by a cultural group called the Burru. Rastas made this style into their ritual music and regarded it as having mystical power for use in the fight against oppression. In the early 1960s, Count Ossie, a Rastafarian drummer, arranged and accompanied "O Carolina," which became a hugely popular song in Jamaica. For the first time, Rastafarian rhythms were incorporated into popular music. After the recording of "O Carolina," Ossie's compound in East Kingston became a gathering place where local musicians congregated and participated in lengthy jam sessions, thus fostering the exchange of musical ideas.

These and other musicians began to incorporate Rastafarian rhythms into reggae music, and they eventually reproduced the whole range of Rastafarian rhythms on modern instruments.

The incorporation of Rastafarian rhythms into Jamaican popular music was followed by the insertion of Rastafarian spirituality and social criticism into the lyrics of popular songs. Lyricists, whether they were Rastas or not, tended to aim their barbs at the establishment, employing the verbal tools and the critical perspective of Rastafari. No one did this with more clarity and consistency than Bob Marley. His growing social consciousness and his proximity to his Rastafarian neighbors eventually led him to embrace Rastafari. In a short time, Marley made himself the public persona and international ambassador of Rastafari and reggae. Through his considerable repertoire, from "Concrete Jungle" to "Redemption Song," Marley became the voice of the marginalized, expressing their critical assessment of the values and institutions of the West, their resolve and resilience in the struggle against extreme odds, and their determination to resist and rebel against their oppression.

Despite their activism around issues relating to poverty, the importance of African heritage, repatriation of blacks to Africa, and the legalization of ganja, Rastas have traditionally despised politics, calling it *politricks*, to indicate their belief that it was marked by deception and trickery. However, some members of the movement have made forays into Jamaica's electoral politics. Most notable are the candidacies of Ras Sam Brown in 1961, Ras Astor Black of the Jamaica Alliance Movement in 2002 and after, and members of Imperial Ethiopian World Federation Party in 2003. In all instances, Rastafarian candidates received minimal support at the polls. Nevertheless, Rastafarian ideas, symbols, and lingo and Rastafari-inspired songs have been tools of political electioneering in Jamaica, as was particularly evident in the 1970s.

During the lead-up to the 1972 Jamaican general election, the PNP leader, Michael Manley, presented himself as the champion of the poor masses. In doing so, he co-opted many of the ideas and much of the language used by Rastas in their criticism of Jamaica's sociopolitical establishment. Specifically, he painted the members of the ruling Jamaica Labor Party as agents of Babylon, and presented himself as Joshua (of Biblical fame), presumably appointed by God to "beat down Babylon" and establish justice for all. A central symbol in this political drama was a walking stick continuously brandished by Michael Manley. Manley claimed to have received the stick from Haile Selassie during a visit to Addis Abba. It was dubbed the *Rod of Correction* and portrayed as symbolic of Manley's authority, bestowed by Jah (God) or Selassie, to right the wrongs of Jamaican society.

Probably the most effective electioneering tool in Jamaica in the 1970s was reggae music, with its Rastafari-inspired lyrics. Manley and the PNP adopted such songs as "Better Must Come," "Beat Down Babylon," and "Dem Ha Fi Get a Beatin" to convey to the masses that they intended to change fundamentally social conditions in Jamaica. Such Rastafarian terms as "One Love," "Peace and Love," and "Hail De Man" flowed from the lips of PNP politicians in a streetwise and populist attempt to woo the young and poor who made up the majority of the voting public. While the PNP referenced elements of Rastafari more extensively and managed to win the 1972 and 1976 elections, the JLP was also quick to invoke the vernacular culture deeply influenced by Rastafari. Its campaigners made liberal use of reggae songs, and its leaders, such as Hugh Shearer and Edward Seaga, gave speeches that were laced with Rastafari-inspired street lingo. By the 1980 election, which was won by the JLP, the overt use of Rastafarian references and language was clearly on the wane in political campaigning. Manley had become steeped in Marxist/socialist rhetoric, whereas Seaga, who had become the leader of the JLP, appealed more to the folk-Christian sensibilities of followers of Revivalism and Pentecostalism, religious movements that are even more pervasive in Jamaican society than Rastafari. Seaga had been a promoter of Jamaican folk culture since the 1960s, had done ethnographic research on Revivalism, and had been rumored to be a secret practitioner of its healing arts.

Though politicians may have been self-serving when they co-opted Rastafarian lingo and symbolism as electioneering tools, they unwittingly bestowed legitimacy on both. At the same time, reggae's status was on the rise. Artists such as Desmond Decker, Toots and the Maytals, and Jimmy Cliff gained international success, while Bob Marley and the Wailers achieved superstardom, making them the epitome of reggae's cultural ascendancy. Despite earlier misgivings, Jamaicans of all walks of life came to embrace reggae as Jamaica's cultural gift to the world. Marley was eventually awarded Jamaica's second-highest honor, the Order of Merit, and at his passing he received a state funeral. Since then, reggae and Rastafari have become a source of inspiration for artistic and cultural production in Jamaica, the Caribbean, and beyond.

From its inauspicious beginnings among the marginalized in Jamaica, Rastafari has blossomed into a global religious and cultural movement. Today Rastafari claims followers throughout the Caribbean, including Cuba; in West and Southern Africa; throughout North America and Europe; in Central and South America, especially Brazil; in New Zealand and Australia; and even in Japan. The spread of Rastafari has been facilitated by international travel and migration and by the worldwide distribution of reggae via the global music industry and communication technology.

The post–World War II era saw the immigration of numerous Jamaicans, including Rastas, to England and North America. When many of the children of these immigrants looked to Jamaica in the 1960s and 1970s for something to counter the alienation they felt in their parents' adopted homelands, it was Rastafari that provided them with both a critique of alienating Western culture and a sense of self that celebrated their African heritage. Students from other Caribbean islands studying in Jamaica, and Jamaicans traveling to and studying in other parts of the Caribbean, were the main agents of the spread of Rastafarian ideas and practices throughout the Caribbean, especially to Barbados, Cuba, Dominica, and Trinidad and Tobago. Over the years, Rastas have traveled far and wide throughout the world, taking their message with them, and visitors to Jamaica from around the world have also contributed to the dispersal of the Rastafarian message.

Probably even more important than travel and migration has been the spreading of the Rastafarian message through reggae music. Through the global marketing of reggae and the ubiquity of modern communication technology, even people who have never seen a Rasta in the flesh have come in contact with the message of Rastafari and have found resonances with their own experiences and aspirations in the music. Thus, we find reggae and Rastafari inspiring the struggles of people around the world: the Maoris of New Zealand, the Aborigines of Australia, the Punjabis in India, Native Americans, and the Palestinians.

The earliest studies on Rastafari tended to focus on its rejection of Jamaica, its call for repatriation, and its deification of Haile Selassie. Using a label commonly applied to new religious movements in colonial or former colonial societies, these studies identified Rastafari as an example of messianic millennialism (Simpson 1955; Barrett 1977; Kitzinger 1969). The next wave of studies tended to highlight the political dimensions and revolutionary potential of Rastafari and hence saw Rastafari as a call for social change in Jamaica (Nettleford 1970; Owens 1976). The third wave was more serious about taking an ethnographic approach and about exploring the character of the Rastafari movement. These scholars described the contours of the movement, highlighting its cultural, social, and spiritual beliefs and practices (Chevannes 1994; Yawney 1978). Into the twenty-first century, the output is almost too varied for categorization. The spread of Rastafari and its growing globalization have led to mutations and transformations. Most academic studies have built upon the second and third waves mentioned above. In addition, many Rastas have written accounts and interpretations of their experiences; numerous studies of reggae and its relationship to Rastafari have been published; biographies of Rastafarian reggae artists, chiefly Marley, abound; and various studies of Rastafari in a range of locations (Britain, West Africa, South Africa, Brazil, Trinidad, Dominica, Cuba) are now available.

SEE ALSO *Garvey, Marcus; Reggae; Religion; Selassie, Haile*

BIBLIOGRAPHY

Barrett, Leonard E. 1977. *The Rastafarians.* Boston: Beacon Press.

Bradley, Lloyd. 2000. *This Is Reggae Music: The Story of Jamaica's Music.* New York: Grove Press.

Campbell, Horace. 1987. *Rasta and Resistance: From Marcus Garvey to Walter Rodney.* Trenton, NJ: Africa World Press.

Chevannes, Barry. 1994. *Rastafari: Roots and Ideology.* Syracuse, NY: Syracuse University Press.

Dawes, Kwame. 2002. *Bob Marley: Lyrical Genius.* London: Sanctuary.

Edmonds, Ennis. 2003. *Rastafari: From Outcasts to Culture Bearers.* New York: Oxford University Press.

Forsythe, Dennis. 1999. *Rastafari: For the Healing of the Nation.* New York: One Drop Books.

Kitzinger, Sheila. 1969. Protest and Mysticism: The Ras Tafari Cult in Jamaica. *Journal for the Scientific Study of Religion* 8: 240–262.

Mack, Douglas R. A. 1999. *From Babylon to Rastafari: Origin and History of the Rastafarian Movement.* Chicago: Research Associates School Times Publications.

Nettleford, Rex M. 1970. *Mirror, Mirror: Identity, Race, and Protest in Jamaica.* Kingston, Jamaica: W. Collins/Sangster.

Owens, Joseph. 1976. *Dread: The Rastafarians of Jamaica.* Kingston, Jamaica: Sangster.

Simpson, George Eaton. 1955. Political Cultism in West Kingston, Jamaica. *Social and Economic Studies* 4 (2): 133–149.

Smith, M. G., Roy Augier, and Rex Nettleford. 1960. *The Rastafari Movement in Kingston, Jamaica.* Kingston, Jamaica: Institute of Social and Economic Research, University College of the West Indies.

Yawney, Carole D. 1978. Dread Wasteland: Rastafarian Ritual in West Kingston, Jamaica. In *Ritual Symbolism and Ceremonialism in the Americas: Studies in Symbolic Anthropology*, ed. N. Ross Crumrine, 154–178. Greely, CO: Museum of Anthropology, University of Northern Colorado.

Ennis B. Edmonds

RATE OF EXPLOITATION

According to Karl Marx, exploitation takes place under capitalism through the extraction of *surplus value*. In the capitalist mode of production, the surplus takes the form of profits appropriated by the capitalist, and exploitation results from the working class producing a net product that can be sold for more than they receive as wages. Marx made a distinction between *labor* and *labor power* that is important for understanding the source of profits. Labor power is the sum total of abilities (spiritual and physical) a worker uses to produce use-values. It is a commodity owned by a laborer but sold in the labor market, and its value—as with any other commodity purchased by the entrepreneur—equals the socially necessary labor time required for the production of goods and services consumed by a laborer for the reproduction of himself and his family. *Labor*, on the other hand, is the use of labor power—that is, the amount of useful labor provided by a worker in a given period of time (an hour or a day). According to Marx, the amount of labor spent in producing a commodity determines that commodity's value.

In the capitalist mode of production, the labor time required for the production of the means of subsistence for the laborer is smaller than the labor time actually provided by him to his employer during a labor day. Hence, for any given time period, the laborer produces more value than the equivalent of his or her remuneration (wage). This difference Marx calls *unpaid labor* or *surplus labor*. The net product produced by the worker during the labor time that is above and beyond the time needed for the reproduction of the labor class is called *surplus value* and is the foundation on which the Marxian theory of profit rests. Hence, the amount of surplus value (s) a worker produces is the difference between the value he or she produces and the value of his or her labor power (v). The value produced by a worker during a labor day is determined by the conditions of the labor process, whereas the value of his or her labor power is determined by the conditions of the labor market and the value of the goods a worker must consume. The ratio s/v represents the rate of surplus value (sometimes called the *rate of exploitation*), because it indicates how much value has been produced during a labor day beyond the value that laborers actually receive as remuneration. This surplus product is appropriated by the employers, who are the owners of the means of production.

In a capitalist mode of production, the driving force of the system is the self-expansion of capital that can be attained with the creation of more surplus value. This is because profits are realized as surplus value (through the selling of commodities in the market), and the more surplus value there is, the higher are the profits and profit rates, and by extension, the easier is the process of accumulation and concentration of capital. If π stands for profits and approximates the surplus value and w stands for wages and approximates the *variable capital* (that is, the wage proportional to labor hours spent for the reproduction of the laborer and his family), then the rate of surplus value or exploitation can be approximated in a real economy by the ratio π/w, which gives us a good idea of the income distribution in the economy. The higher the profit-wage ratio, the higher the distribution of income in favor of profits and, eventually, the higher the investment.

Several economists (right-wing and left-wing) have argued that the constant decline in the above ratio in most economies since the end of World War II indicates an increase in the wage bill relative to profit share, the redistribution of income toward labor, and the lessening of the exploitation rate. One of the reasons claimed for this rise in the wage bill is the unionization of the labor force and the concomitant "malfunctioning" of the labor market (that is, wages do not fall to the level necessary to clear the markets). The same economists argue that the slowdown in growth rates observed after the 1970s is also due to the rise in the wage bill, because that rise deprives capital of the profits needed for investment. Hence, policymakers, based on this evidence, promote the liberalization of the labor market in an attempt to increase profit share.

The counterargument to these suggestions comes from Marxist economists who claim that before the profit-wage ratio can be accurately measured, a distinction must be made between productive and nonproductive labor, to ensure that the correct surplus value (s/v) is computed. Relevant studies have shown that the rate of surplus value has increased, indicating an increase in labor exploitation. This increase in the rate of surplus value is absolutely consistent with the falling rate of profit (r) during the same time period. In fact, by definition the rate of profit is $r = s/(c + v)$—that is, surplus value over capital invested (circulating and variable)—or $r = (s/v) / [1 + (c/v)]$. The term c/v represents the organic composition of capital, an index of capital intensity whose rate of increase is higher than that of the rate of surplus value, giving rise to a falling rate of profit.

SEE ALSO *Accumulation of Capital; Marx, Karl; Primitive Accumulation; Rate of Profit; Social Surplus; Surplus Value; Work Day*

BIBLIOGRAPHY

Marx, Karl. [1857] 1973. *Grundrisse: Foundations of the Critique of Political Economy.* Trans. Martin Nicolaus. New York: Vintage Books.

Marx, Karl. [1867] 1967. *The Process of Capitalist Production.* Vol. 1 of *Capital*. Ed. Frederick Engels. New York: International Publishers.

Shaikh, Anwar M., and E. Ahmat Tonak. 1994. *Measuring the Wealth of Nations: The Political Economy of National Accounts.* New York: Cambridge University Press.

Persefoni V. Tsaliki

RATE OF PROFIT

The *rate of profit* is defined as ratio of profits, the difference between total revenues and total costs, to the capital advanced for production. Theories differ in terms of how both profits and capital are defined. The profit rate is also defined on the aggregate or economy-wide level, the industry level, and the firm level. In most theories with competitive markets, capital will flow to higher-profit firms, and there will be a tendency for the rate of profit to be equalized among firms in the long run.

The rate of profit is a category not generally modeled in standard neoclassical economics. Indeed, in general equilibrium models with competitive markets, the rate of profit will tend toward zero. Instead, neoclassical economists focus on the existence of *rent*—that is, returns to factors of production such as mineral resources or special talents that are not generally reproducible—rather than profits. In contrast, the rate of profit is the central category in Marxian economics. The rate of profit is also an important category in Keynesian, neo-Keynesian, and post-Keynesian economics. As a result, most of the theoretical work on this subject comes out of these fields, particularly Marxian economics.

This article examines trends since the end of World War II in the rate of profit in the United States and reviews some of the theoretical literature on the rate of profit in the Marxian tradition.

TRENDS IN THE RATE OF PROFIT IN THE UNITED STATES SINCE WORLD WAR II

It is helpful to begin by considering the relation between productivity and earnings. In the case of an economy characterized by competitive input markets and constant returns to scale, it follows from a standard neoclassical aggregate production function that wages and labor productivity should grow at exactly the same rate. (In this case, $w = \partial X/\partial L = \varepsilon_L \, X/L$ where w is the wage rate, X is total output, L is total employment, and ε_L is output elasticity of labor, which equals the wage share in this special case.) The wage is thus a fixed percentage of overall labor productivity, and the wage share is also constant (the wage share $wL/X = \varepsilon_L$).

Basic data are from the U.S. Bureau of Economic Analysis National Income and Product Accounts, as well as its series on net capital stock (data are all available on the Web site supported by the U.S. Bureau of Economic Analysis). From 1947 to 1973 real wages in the United States grew almost in tandem with overall labor productivity growth (see Figure 1). While the latter averaged 2.4 percent per year, the former ran at 2.6 percent per year. Labor productivity growth plummeted after 1973. Between 1947 and 1973, it averaged 2.4 percent per year

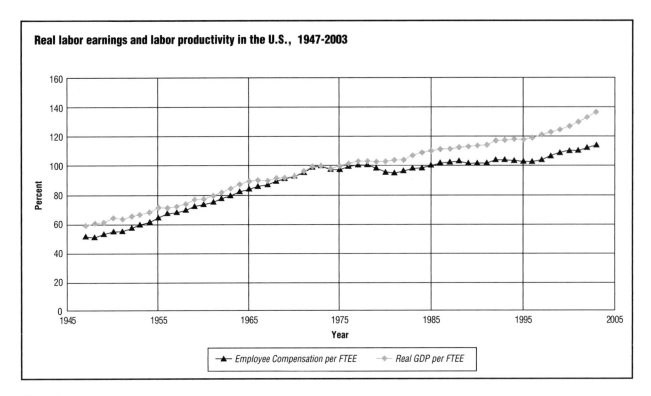

Real labor earnings and labor productivity in the U.S., 1947-2003

Figure 1

whereas from 1973 to 2003 it averaged only 1.0 percent per year. The period from 1973 to 1979, in particular, witnessed the slowest growth in labor productivity during the postwar period, 0.5 percent per year, and the growth in real employee compensation per full time equivalent employee (FTEE) actually turned negative during this period. Since 1979, the U.S. economy experienced a modest reversal in labor productivity growth, which averaged 1.2 percent per year from 1979 to 2003, whereas real wage growth was 0.6 percent per year. In particular, the historical connection between labor productivity growth and real wage growth appears to have broken down after 1973.

If productivity rose faster than earnings after 1973, where did the excess go? The answer is increased profitability in the United States. The Bureau of Economic Analysis defines profits as total gross property-type income, including corporate profits, interest, rent, and half of proprietors' income. The definition excludes the capital consumption allowance (CCA). The net rate of profit is defined as the ratio of total net property income to total private net fixed capital. The net profit rate declined by 7.5 percentage points between 1947 and its nadir, 13.1 percent, in 1982 (see Figure 2). It then climbed by 6.0 percentage points from 1982 to 1997 but fell off by 1.1 percentage points between 1997 and 2001. However, after 2001, it surged upward, reaching 20.5 percent in 2003, fairly close to its postwar high of 22.7 percent in 1948.

Figure 2 also shows trends in the net profit share in national income. It rose by 2.4 percentage points between 1947 and its peak value of 32.0 percent in 1950 and then fell by 7.2 percentage points between 1950 and its low point of 24.8 percent in 1970. It then generally drifted upward, rising by 4.2 percentage points between 1970 and its next high point of 29.1 percent in 1997. It then fell off by 1.7 percentage points between 1997 and 2000 but once again climbed upward to reach 29.4 percent by 2003. The results show a remarkable recovery in both the overall rate of profit and the profit share since the early 1980s in the United States.

A number of studies have documented these trends. Earlier ones such as the 1986 study by Edward Wolff and the 1994 study by Anwar Shaikh and Ahmet Tonak looked into the factors responsible for what seemed to be a secular decline in the profit rate in the United States from the late 1940s to the early 1980s. The rise in profitability since the early 1980s has been discussed by Gérard Duménil and Dominique Lévy (2002) and Wolff (2001). Duménil and Lévy (2002) also provide time trends on the profit rate for Germany, the United Kingdom, and particularly, France. All three countries, as with the United States, showed declines in profitability from 1960 to the early 1980s and a sharp reversal through the late 1990s. Both Lewis Corey in 1934 and Duménil and Lévy in 1993 presented data on movements in the

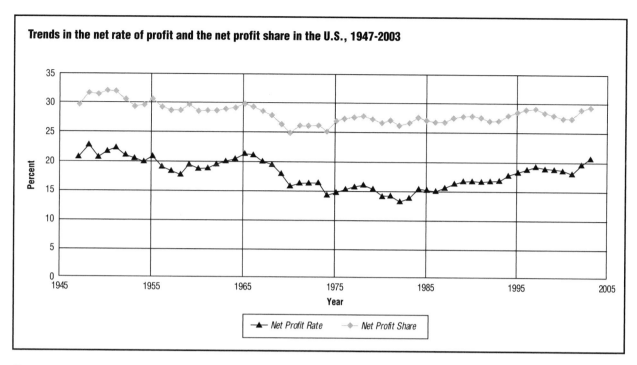

Trends in the net rate of profit and the net profit share in the U.S., 1947-2003

Figure 2

rate of profit in the United States from the early part of the twentieth century. These authors make the case that the onset of the Great Depression beginning in 1929 coincided with a sharp decline in the rate of profit in the United States.

THEORIES OF THE RATE OF PROFIT

As noted above, movements in the rate of profit have long occupied Marxian economists. Marx himself argued that the rate of profit would tend to decline over the long run. His "law of the tendency of the rate of profit to fall" states that over time, the organic composition of capital (the ratio of capital valued in nominal terms to the wage bill) would rise, thereby causing the general rate of profit to fall (Marx 1894). This law has been subject to criticism on theoretical grounds as discussed, for example, by Paul Samuelson in his 1971 article, though more recent literature has reversed some of these theoretical criticisms, as developed by Duncan Foley in his 1986 work.

Despite the theoretical disagreements, Marx's theory does provide a useful framework in which to analyze factors that affect movements in the rate of profit, and many papers have done this. Marx's law can be formalized as follows (where variables in current prices are specified instead of labor values): The ratio of total profits to total worker compensation (the *rate of surplus value*) is defined as: $e = \pi/wL$, where π is total profits, w is the wage rate,

and L is total employment. The economy-wide *organic composition of capital* s is given by: $s = p_k K/wL$, where p_k is the price of capital and K is total capital. The *standard capital–labor ratio* (the *technical composition of capital*) is given by: $t = K/L$. The relation between the organic and technical composition of capital can be derived as: $s = t (p_k /w)$. The rate of profit r is defined as: $r = \pi/p_k K$. Here it should be noted that the rate of profit is defined as the ratio of profits to the current dollar value of capital. Finally, it can be shown that the rate of profit $r = e/s$, the ratio of the rate of surplus value to the organic composition of capital.

Marx believed that the rate of surplus value, or the *rate of exploitation* as he also termed it, was relatively fixed over time because it reflected the *social relations of production*, which were relatively stable over time. He also argued that the organic composition would rise over time because of the increasing capital intensity of production and that this would lead to a falling rate of profit in the long term. The problem in this line of reasoning is that while it was true that the capital–labor ratio did tend to rise over time because of the rising capital intensity of production, the price of capital relative to labor also tended to fall over time, offsetting the increase in the capital–labor ratio. Empirically, the organic composition also tends to remain relatively stable over time. Marx did discuss many mitigating factors to his "law" and, indeed, referred to it as a "tendency" rather than in absolute terms.

Two other very important contributions to the theoretical literature come out of the Keynesian tradition. The first, by Michał Kalecki (1971), develops a model in which national income is directly determined by autonomous investment and profits, in turn, are determined as a fixed share of national income. This model led to an extensive literature tracking the profit share in national income. The second, by Piero Sraffa (1972), develops the concept of the maximum rate of profit. He shows analytically that the maximum rate of profit depends exclusively on the technology of production and is independent of the wage (and therefore profit) share.

SEE ALSO *Markup Pricing; Profits; Returns to a Fixed Factor*

BIBLIOGRAPHY

Corey, Lewis. 1934. *The Decline of American Capitalism.* New York: Arno Press.

Duménil, Gérard, and Dominique Lévy. 1993. *The Economics of the Profit Rate: Competition, Crises, and Historical Tendencies in Capitalism.* Aldershot, Hants, U.K.: Edward Elgar.

Duménil, Gérard, and Dominique Lévy. 2002. The Profit Rate: Where and How Much Did It Fall? Did It Recover? (USA 1948–2000). *Review of Radical Political Economics* 34: 437–461.

Foley, Duncan K. 1986. *Understanding Capital: Marx's Economic Theory.* Cambridge, MA: Harvard University Press.

Kalecki, Michał. 1971. *Selected Essays on the Dynamics of the Capitalist Economy 1933–1970.* Cambridge, U.K.: Cambridge University Press.

Laibman, David. 1996. Technical Change, Accumulation, and the Rate of Profit Revisited. *Review of Radical Political Economics* 28 (2): 33–53.

Marx, Karl. 1894. *Capital.* Vol. 3. New York: International Publishers.

Samuelson, Paul A. 1971. Understanding the Marxian Notion of Exploitation. *Journal of Economic Literature* 9: 399–431.

Shaikh, Anwar M., and E. Ahmet Tonak. 1994. *Measuring the Wealth of Nations: The Political Economy of National Accounts.* New York: Cambridge University Press.

Sraffa, Piero. 1972. *The Production of Commodities by Means of Commodities.* Cambridge, U.K.: Cambridge University Press.

U.S. Bureau of Economic Analysis National Income and Product Accounts. http://www.bea.gov/bea/.

Weisskopf, Thomas E. 1979. Marxian Crisis Theory and the Rate of Profit in the Postwar U.S. Economy. *Cambridge Journal of Economics* 3 (4): 341–378.

Wolff, Edward N. 1979. The Rate of Surplus Value, the Organic Composition, and the General Rate of Profit in the U.S. Economy, 1947–67. *American Economic Review* 69 (3): 329–341.

Wolff, Edward N. 1986. The Productivity Slowdown and the Fall in the U.S. Rate of Profit, 1947–76. *Review of Radical Political Economy* 18 (1&2): 87–109.

Wolff, Edward N. 2001. The Recent Rise of Profits in the United States. *Review of Radical Political Economics* 33 (3): 315–324.

Edward N. Wolff

RATE OF SURPLUS VALUE

SEE *Rate of Exploitation.*

RATIONAL CHOICE THEORY

Rational choice theory (RCT) in sociology draws on the tradition of utilitarian philosophy, and insights from the field of economics. While the central elements of RCT found expression in some earlier sociological accounts (most notably exchange theory), the formal development of RCT in sociology came only recently. Sociologists tend to explain human behavior as patterned outcomes of macro-level causes (culture and social structure) that have an impact on individual and groups. In contrast, RCT focuses on the intentional, goal-oriented behavior of individual actors. Social interaction, and the development of cultural systems and social structure, reflect the outcome of the purposive pursuit of individual self-interest.

The methodological individualism of RCT clearly sets it apart from traditional sociological accounts. Rational choice theorists maintain that the starting point for explanations of macro-level structures and group behavior is determined by the behavior of the core element of such systems, the individual actor. Individuals, including the corporate actor, are characterized as rational actors who choose actions designed to maximize their own individual interests—the satisfaction of their needs and wants:

1. Actors calculate the benefits (utility) of expected outcomes resulting from particular activities and interactions.

2. Actors take into account the expected costs of particular behaviors and include in these calculations the variable utility related to alternative courses of action (opportunity costs).

3. Actors engage in actions they expect to maximize their own interests.

Recognizing that other factors (cultural norms and values as well as the structure of the existing social context) also influence decision-making, RCT stipulates that individuals nonetheless employ a utilitarian strategy designed to insure their access to and control over desired resources (material and nonmaterial). RCT offers an explanation of how macro-level structures emerge from the micro-level, purposive activity of individuals.

Social exchange theory (Homans 1961) represents an early approach that incorporated this image of the rational actor. Whereas George Homans's approach rests on a behaviorist conception of the individual actor motivated by rewards and punishments, contemporary RCT (Coleman 1990) simply argues that individuals act *as if* they are rational, and that human rationality needs no further explanation. RCT is not concerned with how actors define utility, or what particular objectives they seek to acquire; rather, the focus is simply on the fact that actions are chosen to achieve such ends efficiently.

RCT characterizes social interaction as social exchange. Individuals enter into interaction with others when the potential rewards (tangible and intangible) outweigh the calculated costs. Although it is not always possible for individuals to satisfy all their needs, they will choose alternatives they think lead to the greatest maximization of their individual interests within the constraints of particular situations. Sustained interaction, and the emergence of social structure, depends on the recognition, from the perspective of each individual involved, of the ongoing effort to achieve fulfillment of individual self-interest (Homans 1961).

Within a social context, a variety of factors affect the calculation of individual utility. The scarcity of available resources and differential access to those resources can limit opportunities for specific actors. Individuals who possess scarce resources can use them to further their own interests. Differential control of available resources produces differentials in power, allows for control over the exchange process, and opens up the potential for exploitation. Individual actors also vary in their relative dependence on the utility associated with expected outcomes, and the costs involved in pursuing particular actions versus others (opportunity costs) require consideration as well. The rational actor does not choose one goal over another because of its overall value, but due to the distribution of resources related to achieving that goal, the feasibility of success in obtaining the goal, the relative costs of any exchange involved in pursuit of the goal, and the variable value (objective and subjective) assigned to alternative strategies and their related rewards (Ritzer and Goodman 2004).

The development of sustained interaction and the emergence of a social system present certain problems for RCT:

1. If all actions are based on self-interest, why do individuals cooperate? (The so-called *free-rider problem*.)

2. What are the roles of institutionalized norms and sanctions, as well as values, that may both limit particular courses of action and encourage others (and how do these elements develop)?

Two types of collective interaction are involved—structured and unstructured. For organized, structured groups and organizations, participation by the rational actor is based on the costs involved in participation versus *relative* benefits accrued. The structuring of the context is important, with "selective incentives" altering the rewards/cost equation (Olson 1965; Hechter 1987). An actor may calculate that the relative costs of an exchange are outweighed by the potential benefits of sustained cooperation; however, such calculations are oftentimes based on unequal distribution of desired resources. Control of desired resources provides an individual or corporate actor the power to force (or legitimate) the surrendering of individual control and decision-making from one actor to others. Whether voluntary or not, the surrendering of authority and rights possessed by one individual to another produces a relatively stable, independent social structure and a redirection of purposive behavior based on both reciprocity and restraint (Scott 2000). Unstructured (collective) behavior emerges when individual maximization of utility becomes defined in terms of unilateral (nonreciprocal) transfer of control to the collective. As the individual cedes authority to a collective based on the recognition that individual success is *only* served through collective action, a dynamic character to social action ensues, resulting in the potential for disorder or change (Coleman 1990; Ritzer and Goodman 2004).

As collective interaction persists, a normative system is established, supporting the interests of actors with control over scarce resources, and the mutual interests of actors who recognize the utility of cooperative engagement. James Coleman (1990) maintains that norms are created and enforced by people who see benefits resulting from obedience, and harm or costs associated with violation. Norms allow the individual to transfer partial control within a shared system of rules, and relative maximization of utility is achieved by gaining partial control over the behavior of others. Normative structures legitimate the authority of particular collective actors based on their control over desired resources, or represent actors' trust or anticipated long-term reciprocity (Blau 1964; Scott 2000).

Although criticized for its reductionist approach, for ignoring the role of cultural values and subjective meaning in individual and group behavior, and for an overreliance on the idea of the rationality of the human actor,

RCT retains support among sociologists. Advocates claim that RCT provides an integrated theoretical analysis that bridges the differences across disciplines in the social sciences.

SEE ALSO *Choice in Economics; Choice in Psychology; Collective Action; Economics, Neoclassical; Free Rider; Individualism; Maximization; Microeconomics; Microfoundations; Minimization; Public Goods; Rationality; Reductionism; Satisficing Behavior; Utility Function; Utility, Objective; Utility, Subjective*

BIBLIOGRAPHY

Blau, Peter M. 1964. *Exchange and Power in Social Life.* New York: John Wiley.

Coleman, James S. 1990. *Foundations of Social Theory.* Cambridge, MA: Belknap.

Hechter, Michael. 1987. *Principles of Group Solidarity.* Berkeley: University of California Press.

Homans, George Caspar. 1961. *Social Behavior: Its Elementary Forms.* London: Routledge & Kegan Paul.

Olson, Mancur, Jr. 1965. *The Logic of Collective Action: Public Goods and the Theory of Groups.* Cambridge, MA: Harvard University Press.

Ritzer, George, and Douglas Goodman. 2004. *Sociological Theory.* 6th ed. St. Louis, MO: McGraw-Hill. (See pp. 401–404 and 427–435.)

Scott, John. 2000. Rational Choice Theory. In *Understanding Contemporary Society: Theories of the Present,* eds. Gary Browning, Abigail Halcli, and Frank Webster, 126–138. Thousand Oaks, CA: Sage Publications.

Robert O. Keel

RATIONAL CHOICE THEORY (ECONOMICS)

SEE *Choice in Economics; Constrained Choice; Rationality.*

RATIONAL EMOTIVE THERAPY

SEE *Psychotherapy.*

RATIONALISM

Rationalism comes in various versions and makes wider or narrower claims. The idea underlying most versions is that reason is the most characteristic faculty of *Homo sapiens*.

Appeal to reason is part of traditional wisdom, yet traditional (ancient Greek) rationalism includes an out of hand dismissal of traditional wisdom. The modern version of this dismissal is the radical demand for starting afresh (Enlightenment radicalism) and admitting only ideas that are proven, absolutely certain, and fully justified by rigorous proof. Science begins with rejecting all doubtful ideas. Francis Bacon initiated the idea that traditional unfounded views are the causes of all error; René Descartes tried to ignore all doubtful ideas and start afresh from nothing. David Hume began his investigations in efforts to delineate all that is certain while ignoring all else; he and many others, from Denis Diderot to Pierre-Simon de Laplace, took it for granted that Isaac Newton's success was due to his adherence to Bacon's advice. Auguste Comte and T. H. Huxley took it for granted that other fields will be as successful if they only jettison tradition more fully; Ludwig Wittgenstein went further and said only scientific assertions are grammatical (positivism, scientism).

ENLIGHTENMENT RADICALISM AND THE ROMANTIC REACTION

Yet what proof is no one knew. Mathematics was the paradigm of proof, and the success of physics was largely ascribed to its use of mathematical methods, a practice for all to emulate. What is that method, and how can it be applied to the social domain? How does the relinquishing of tradition help word theories mathematically? This was unclear even after the discipline of statistics was developed enough to become applicable to some social studies (as in the work of Adolphe Quételet, 1796–1874). Yet clearly as usefulness gives rational thought its initial (even if not final) worth, at least the rationality of action is obvious: its goal-directedness. Hence the study of rationality is vital for the study of the rational action that is the heart of the study of humanity. Whereas students of nature seldom pay attention to the rationality and the scientific character of their studies, students of humanities are engrossed in them. And whatever their views on this rationality, at least they openly center on it. Thus in the opening of his classic *An Inquiry into the Nature and Causes of the Wealth of Nations* (1776), Adam Smith declares his intent to ignore irrationality, no matter how widespread it is. Slavery is widespread, yet everyone knows that putting a worker in chains is no incentive, he observed.

The Enlightenment movement deemed Smith's argument obvious; this led to its dismissal of human history as the sad story of needless pain caused by ignorance and superstition. This was an error. The advocacy of the abolition of slavery came in total disregard for its immediate impact on the lot of slave owners. Smith spoke of rationality in the abstract. Because high productivity depends on the division of labor and because this division leads to trade, freedom is efficient. Selfish conduct is rational as long as it is scientific, that is, undogmatic. Life in the light of reason is egalitarian, simple, and happy. This abstract reasoning led to concrete results, including the French Revolution and its terror and wars. Edmund Burke and Georg Wilhelm Friedrich Hegel blamed the radicalism of the revolution for its deterioration into terror. The reaction to the French Revolution was aggressively hostile to radicalism, to egalitarianism, and even to reason (Hegel).

MARX AND AFTER

Karl Marx wedded the two great modern movements, the radical Enlightenment movement and the Romantic reaction to it. The former had the right vision, and the latter had the historically right view of the obstacle to its realization. Smith-style harmony between individual and society has no place in traditional society. Hence the institution of enlightened equality is an essential precondition for it. The realization of the radical dream of harmony requires civil war. But it is certainly realizable, he insisted.

Marx's critique of radicalism from within is as popular as ever. We are chained to our social conditions, and rationalism cannot break them. Max Weber, the author of the most popular alternative to Marx's ideas, stressed this; so do all the popular radical critics of the ills of modern ("bourgeois") society, chiefly imperialism, racism, and sexism, perhaps also alienation from work. These critics puzzle the uninitiated, as they seem to belabor condemnations of obviously indefensible aspects of modern society. But they do something else; they advance a thesis. Social evils will not go away by sheer mental exercises. Are there any reasonable people who disagree with this thesis? It is hard to say. Perhaps some thinkers still follow the central thesis of the Enlightenment movement. If such people do exist (as seems true but not obviously so), then they are the neoliberals, the Chicago school of economics, which is not confined to economics, as it preaches the idea that a world with free markets still is the best of all possible worlds, even though it is far from ideal (Friedrich A. von Hayek).

VARIANTS OF RATIONALISM

What then is rationalism? Of the alternative views on reason, which can count as variants of rationalism? Consider pragmatism, the view of the useful as the true (Hegel, William James, John Dewey). It is unsatisfactory, because assessments of usefulness may be true or not; but is it a version of rationalism? Consider the traditionalist reliance on the test of time (ordinary-language philosophy; neo-Thomism). The assessment of the relative worth of traditions may be cultural (Martin Buber, Amitai Ezioni; communitarianism) or intellectual (Michael Polanyi,

Thomas S. Kuhn; postcriticalism). It is unsatisfactory, as these assessments may be true or not; but is it a version of rationalism? There is no telling. The same holds for appeals to other criteria for truth. These are common sense (Hume, Smith, Thomas Reid, Adam Ferguson, George Edward Moore), the intuitions of Great Men (Johann Gottlieb Fichte, Hegel, Martin Heidegger), higher religious sentiments (Friedrich Schleiermacher, Fyodor Dostoevsky, Leo Tolstoy), and superior tastes (Richard Rorty). Are these variants of rationalism? Do they lead to more reasonable human conduct? The standard claim is that their asset is in their ability to maintain social stability. But in the early twenty-first century stability is unattainable and even deemed inferior to democratic controls (Karl R. Popper).

There is no consensus about whether the counsel to limit reason and admit religion is rationalism proper (Moses Maimonides, Saint Thomas Aquinas, Robert Boyle, Moses Mendelssohn, Polanyi) or not (Immanuel Kant, David Strauss, Ludwig Feuerbach, Sigmund Freud, Bertrand Russell, Adolf Grünbaum). The only consensus is about the defiance of reason (Søren Kierkegaard, Max Stirner, Joseph Arthur Comte de Gobineau, Georges Sorel, Friedrich Nietzsche, D. H. Lawrence, Heidegger, perhaps also Paul Feyerabend). The only generally admitted necessary condition for rationalism is the demand to side with reason. Therefore it is fashionable to limit rationalism by allowing the taking of a single axiom on faith while otherwise swearing allegiance to reason (Polanyi, Richard H. Popkin, Pope John Paul II; fideism). The default view should then be that this allegiance suffices. Add to this the consensus around a necessary condition for this allegiance. It is the critical attitude, openness to criticism, the readiness to admit the success of the criticism of any given view. Consider the view that the critical attitude is sufficient as the default option (Popper) and seek valid criticism of it that may lead to its modification, to the admission of some unavoidable limitations on reason, whether in the spirit of Marx or in that of his critics. The need for this limitation comes from purely philosophical considerations. Hume said that we need induction for knowledge and for practice, yet it is not rational (it has no basis in logic); instead, we rely on it out of habit and necessity and this is the best we can do. A popular variant of this is that because induction is necessary, it is in no need of justification (Kant, Russell). Another variant takes it on faith (Polanyi, Popkin; fideism). Is induction really necessary?

This question is welcome. Since finding alternative answers to a worthy question improves their assessment, they are all worthy. Hence all versions of limited rationalism are welcome—as hypotheses to investigate (Salomon Maimon, Popper). This is the power of the method of always trying out the minimal solution as the default.

CRITICAL RATIONALISM

Critical rationalism is revolutionary because it replaces proof with test; it replaces radical, wholesale dismissal of ideas with the readiness to test piecemeal (Albert Einstein, Popper; reformism). The demand to prove thus yields to the critical attitude (William Warren Bartley III, Willard Van Orman Quine; non-justificationism), recognizing that theories possess graded merit (Einstein, Leonard Nelson, Popper; critical rationalism)—by whatever rule we happen to follow, no matter how tentative. Rules are then hopefully improvable (Charles Sanders Peirce, Russell, Popper; fallibilism). Hence diverse rules may serve as competing criteria or as complementary. Being minimalist, critical rationalism invites considering some older theologians as allies, although not their contemporary followers. Unlike radical rationalism, critical rationalism is historically oriented. (It is the view of rationality as relative to contexts and of truth as absolute, as a guiding principle à la Kant.)

This invites critical rationalism to enlist rational thought as a category of rational action (Ian C. Jarvie and Joseph Agassi). And this in turn invites the study of rationalism as an aspect of extant scientific research. It also invites comparison of the various versions of rationalism as to the degree of their adequacy to this task: take scientific research as it is, warts and all, and examine its merits and defects according to the diverse alternatives. This attitude is new and expressed in various studies of the sociology of science, so-called, that often spread over diverse disciplines, including political science and even criminology no less. This renders a part of the project of rationalism the assessments of the intellectual value of the outcome of research, theoretical, practical, or cultural—or even aesthetic. The only intellectual justification of a scientific theory, said Einstein, is its ability to explain; its best reward is its successor's admission of it as approximate. In this way he stressed that the aim of research is to explain in the hope of approximating the truth. This is open to debate. Social science as a whole may serve as a test case, with the sociology of science at the center of the debate on this matter.

Historically, rationalism doggedly accompanied studies of nature, not social studies. What in these should rationalism approve of? Discussion of this question allowed rationalism to inform the social sciences. A conspicuous example is the vagueness in social studies of the boundaries between philosophy, science, and practice that still invites open discussion. Anything less is below the minimal criterion of the critical attitude.

Critics of minimal rationalism find criticism insufficient, since positive criteria of choice need justification. If so, then rationalism is back to square one. If not, then positive criteria must be tentative, and the issue must shift from their justification to efforts at their improvement. Some do not like this, as it rests on their initial choice that was too arbitrary. They prefer to return to the initial criterion and replace it with the least arbitrary one. They are radicals. The clash is thus between the radical and the critical version of rationalism—as well as between them and fideism.

The agenda of rationalism—in philosophy, in science, or in practice—is the same: heightening the critical attitude, seeking improvement through criticism everywhere. Where is the starting point? How are we to decide on our agenda? Parliamentary steering committees decide on agendas. The commonwealth of learning, however, is its own steering committee. Those concerned to promote rationalism should do their best to put discussions of it high on the public agenda.

BIBLIOGRAPHY

Agassi, Joseph. 1996. The Philosophy of Science Today. In *Philosophy of Science, Logic, and Mathematics in the Twentieth Century.* Vol. 9 of *Routledge History of Philosophy*, ed. Stuart G. Shanker, 235–265. London: Routledge.

Agassi, Joseph, and Ian C. Jarvie, eds. 1987. *Rationality: The Critical View.* The Hague: Nijhoff.

Baumgardt, Carola. 1952. *Johannes Kepler: Life and Letters.* Introduction by Albert Einstein. London: Golancz.

Burtt, E. A. 1926. *The Metaphysical Foundations of Modern Physical Science.* London: Routledge.

Churchman, C. West. 1968. *Challenge to Reason.* New York: McGraw-Hill.

Einstein, Albert. 1954. *Ideas and Opinions.* New York: Bonanza Books.

Festinger, Leon. 1957. *Theory of Cognitive Dissonance.* Stanford, CA: Stanford University Press.

Feyerabend, Paul. 1987. *Farewell to Reason.* London: New Left Books.

Haakonssen, Knud, ed. 2006. *The Cambridge History of Eighteenth-Century Philosophy.* 2 vols. Cambridge, U.K.: Cambridge University Press.

Hayek, Friedrich August von. 1952. *The Counter-Revolution of Science: Studies on the Abuse of Reason.* Glencoe, IL: Free Press.

Hayek, Friedrich August von. 1960. *The Constitution of Liberty.* Chicago: Chicago University Press.

Jarvie, Ian C. 1964. *The Revolution in Anthropology.* London: Routledge.

Jarvie, Ian C., and Joseph Agassi. 1987. The Rationality of Magic. In *Rationality: The Critical View*, ed. Joseph Agassi and Ian C. Jarvie, 363–383. The Hague: Nijhoff.

John Paul II, Pope. 1998. *Fides et Ratio.* Washington, DC: United States Catholic Conference.

Koyré, Alexandre, 1968. *Metaphysics and Measurement.* London: Chapman and Hall.

Kuhn, Thomas S. 1970. *The Structure of Scientific Revolutions.* 2nd ed. Chicago: University of Chicago Press.

Lakatos, Imre, and Alan Musgrave. 1970. *Criticism and the Growth of Knowledge.* Cambridge, U.K.: Cambridge University Press.

Mill, John Stuart. 1843. *A System of Logic.* London: J. W. Parker.

Naess, Arne. 1968. *Scepticism.* London: Routledge and K. Paul; New York: Humanities.

Nelson, Leonard. 1949. *Socratic Method and Critical Philosophy: Selected Essays.* New Haven, CT: Yale University Press; repr. New York: Dover, 1965.

Nisbet, Robert A. 1966. *The Sociological Tradition.* New York: Basic Books.

Osler, Margaret J., ed. 2000. *Rethinking the Scientific Revolution.* Cambridge, U.K.: Cambridge University Press.

Parkinson, G. H. R., ed. 1993. *The Renaissance and Seventeenth-Century Rationalism.* Vol. 4 of *Routledge History of Philosophy.* London: Routledge.

Phillips, Derek L. 1973. *Abandoning Method.* London: Jossey-Bass.

Pitte, Frederick P. van de. 1971. *Kant as Philosophical Anthropologist.* The Hague: Nijhoff.

Polanyi, Michael. 1958. *Personal Knowledge: Towards a Post-Critical Philosophy.* London: Routledge.

Polanyi, Michael. 1962. The Republic of Science. In *Criteria for Scientific Development*, ed. Edward Shils, 1–20. Cambridge, MA: MIT Press.

Popper, Karl R. 1945. *The Open Society and Its Enemies.* 2 vols. London: Routledge.

Rees, Graham, and Maria Wakely. 2004. Introduction. In *The Instauratio Magna.* Part 2, *"Novum Organum" and Associated Texts.* Vol. 11 of *The Oxford Francis Bacon.* Oxford: Oxford University Press.

Russell, Bertrand. 1912. *The Problems of Philosophy.* London: Williams and Norgate; New York: Henry Holt.

Russell, Bertrand. 1945. *A History of Western Philosophy.* New York: Simon and Schuster.

Simon, Robert L., ed. 2002. *The Blackwell Guide to Social and Political Philosophy.* Oxford: Blackwell.

Solomon, Robert C. 1988. *Continental Philosophy since 1750: The Rise and Fall of the Self.* Oxford: Oxford University Press.

Wettersten, John R. 1992. *The Roots of Critical Rationalism.* Amsterdam: Rodopi.

Joseph Agassi

RATIONALITY

Rationality in its ordinary sense is reasonableness. It requires justified beliefs and sensible goals as well as judicious decisions. Scholars study rationality in many ways and adopt diverse views about it.

Some theorists adopt a technical definition of rationality, according to which it is just maximization of utility. This definition is too narrow. It considers only adoption of means to reach ends, that is, instrumental rationality. It also evades a major normative question, namely, whether rationality requires maximization of utility. The definition simply stipulates an affirmative answer.

A traditional theory of the mind takes reason as a mental faculty. It characterizes humans as rational animals because they have the faculty of reason, whereas other animals lack that faculty. According to this tradition, any behavior resulting from reasoning is rational. This account of rationality sets the bar low. Most accounts hold that the products of reasoning must meet certain standards before they qualify as rational. A conclusion, for example, must fit the evidence to be rational. It is not rational simply because it results from an inference. Reasoning must be good to yield rational beliefs reliably.

For simplicity, some theorists take being rational to be the same as being self-interested. Being rational differs from being self-interested, however. Promoting self-interest means doing what is good for oneself. Doing what is good for others promotes their interests, not one's own. Rationality may require some measure of self-interestedness but does not require exclusive attention to self-interest. It permits altruism, as Amartya Sen (1977) and Howard Rachlin (2002) explain.

Epistemologists treat justified belief. Under one interpretation, a justified belief is just a rational belief. However, other interpretations of justification are common because a conventional view takes knowledge to be true, justified belief. Making justification fit into that view of knowledge motivates taking justified belief to differ from rational belief. Children rationally believe many true propositions without having knowledge of them because the grounds for their beliefs do not amount to justification.

Rationality is a normative concept. Principles of rationality state how people should behave rather than how they behave. However, some fields assume that people are rational by and large and then use principles of rationality to describe and explain behavior. For instance, some economic theories assert that consumers make purchases that express their preferences. They take this as a fact about consumers' behavior rather than as a norm for it. Psychologists seeking to infer a person's beliefs and desires from the person's behavior may assume that behavior maximizes utility. The assumption simplifies inference of beliefs and desires. Several prominent representation theorems show that if a person's preferences concerning acts meet certain axioms, such as transitivity, then one may infer the person's probability and utility assignments (given a choice of scale) from the person's preferences, under the assumption that preferences concerning acts agree with their expected utilities. Richard Jeffrey ([1965] 1983) presents a theorem of this sort.

PHILOSOPHY AND RATIONALITY

Philosophy treats rationality because it is the most important normative concept besides morality. Understanding how a person should conduct her or his life requires a thorough understanding of rationality. Being a rational person requires being sufficiently rational in the various aspects of one's life. Common principles of rationality attend to beliefs and desires and to the decisions they yield. Some principles evaluate character traits and emotions. They judge, for example, that some fears are rational and that others are irrational. Principles of rationality extend from individuals to groups. Committees may pass rational or irrational resolutions. Political philosophy evaluates social contracts for rationality. Mancur Olson (1965) investigates rational collective action and the conditions that foster it.

A traditional metaphysical question asks for the grounds of principles of rationality. What makes consistency a requirement of rationality? Are the principle's grounds conventions or something more universal? A common answer claims that natural properties realize normative properties. Consistency increases prospects for true beliefs.

A traditional practical question asks for reasons to be rational. A common answer is that being rational yields the best prospects (with respect to one's evidence) for meeting one's goals and so achieving a type of success. Decisions that maximize expected utility are more likely to be successful than decisions that do not maximize expected utility.

Some philosophers hope to derive principles of morality from principles of rationality. Kantians, for example, hold that a rational person acts in accord with moral principles. Hobbesians hold that the legitimacy of a government derives from the rationality of the social contract that creates it. Rawlsians hold that principles of justice emerge from a hypothetical social contract rational to adopt given ignorance of one's position in society.

BELIEF AND INFERENCE

A general principle states that rationality is attainable. Its attainability follows from the familiar principle that "ought" implies "can." Well-established principles of rationality also treat formation of belief and inference. Consistency is a noncontroversial requirement. Holding inconsistent beliefs is irrational unless some extenuating factor, such as the difficulty of spotting the inconsistency, provides an excuse. Perceptual beliefs are rational when the processes producing them are reliable. Vision in good light yields reliable judgments about the colors of objects. Logic describes in meticulous detail patterns of inference that are rational. For example, if one believes a conditional and believes its antecedent, then believing its consequent

is a rational conclusion. Repeated application of rules of inference to prove theorems in logic requires sophistication that ordinary rationality does not demand. Rationality requires an ideal agent to believe each and every logical consequence of her or his beliefs. Its requirements for real people are less demanding. (For a sample of principles of rationality concerning belief, see Foley 1993; Halpern 2003; and Levi 2004.)

Rationality governs both deductive and inductive inference. Principles of statistical reasoning express principles of rational inductive inference. If one knows that an urn has exactly eighty red balls and twenty black balls, then it is rational to conclude that 80 percent is the probability that a random draw will yield a red ball. Given a statistical sample drawn from a population, principles of statistical inference attending to the size of the sample and other factors state reasonable conclusions about the whole population.

PREFERENCES

Preferences may arise from partial or complete consideration of relevant reasons. Common principles of rational preference apply to preferences held all things considered.

The principle of transitivity requires preferring *A* to *C* given that one prefers *A* to *B* and also prefers *B* to *C*. The principle of coherence requires having preferences among acts that may be represented as maximizing expected utility. The definition of preference affects the force of such principles. The ordinary sense of preference acknowledges the possibility of weakness of will and acting contrary to preferences. However, some theorists for technical reasons define preferences so that a person acts according to preferences, so telling a person to pick an option from the top of her or his preference ranking of options has no normative force—she or he does that by stipulation.

The principle of consumer sovereignty puts basic preferences beyond criticism. Some basic preferences are irrational, however. Forming preferences among ice cream flavors one has not tasted may be irrational. Having a pure time preference may be irrational. That is, it may be irrational to prefer the smaller of two goods just because it will arrive sooner than the larger good. Certainty of having the larger good if one waits for it is a strong reason for waiting.

The chief principle of rational decision making is to pick an option from the top of one's preference ranking of options. If some options are gambles, a supplementary principle says to prefer one option to another option just in case its expected utility is higher than the expected utility of the other option. J. Howard Sobel (1994) and Paul Weirich (2001) analyze such principles of rational choice.

DECISION MAKING

Rationality evaluates free acts that an agent fully controls. Decisions are in this category; so are acts such as taking a walk. Rationality evaluates acts an agent controls directly by comparing them with rivals and evaluates acts an agent controls indirectly by evaluating their components. An agent directly controls a decision, and so rationality evaluates it by comparing it with its rivals. An agent indirectly controls taking a walk, and so rationality evaluates it by evaluating its directly controlled components. The rationality of a series of acts, such as having dinner and going to a movie, depends on the rationality of its temporal components.

Game theory, expounded in classic texts by John von Neumann and Oskar Morgenstern (1944) and R. Duncan Luce and Howard Raiffa (1957), addresses decisions people make in contexts where the outcome of one person's decision depends on the decisions that other people make. Strategic reasoning looks for combinations of decisions that form an equilibrium in the sense that each decision is rational given the other decisions. A common principle for such strategic situations recommends making a decision that is part of an equilibrium combination of decisions. Edward McClennen (1990), Robert Stalnaker (1998, 1999), Weirich (1998), Andrew Colman (2003), and Michael Bacharach (2006) conduct critical appraisals of principles of rationality widespread in game theory.

A principle of rationality may be controversial. A common pattern for controversy begins with a claim that in some cases thoughtful people fail to comply with the principle. Some respond that in those cases people are rational and the principle is faulty. Others respond that the principle is fine and people are irrational. Still others hold that people in the problem cases actually comply with the principle, contrary to the initial claim.

For example, Amos Tversky and Daniel Kahneman (Tversky and Kahneman 1982) present cases in which people form judgments that fail to comply with the probability axioms. In their study a story describes a young woman as a political activist and a college graduate with a philosophy major. People asked to speculate about the woman's current activities may put the probability of her being a feminist and a bank teller higher than the probability of her being a bank teller only. This ignores the law that the probability of a conjunction cannot be higher than the probability of a conjunct. Some theorists may conclude that people are irrational in their probability judgments, others that people have in mind the probability that the woman is a feminist given that she is a bank teller rather than the probability of the conjunction that she is a feminist and is a bank teller. In this particular example, few dispute the law of probability concerning conjunctions.

Kahneman and Tversky (Kahneman and Tversky 1979) also present cases in which it seems that people fail to comply with the principle to maximize expected utility. A person may prefer a gamble that pays a guaranteed \$3,000 to a gamble that pays \$4,000 with probability 80 percent and \$0 with probability 20 percent. The same person may prefer a gamble that pays \$4,000 with probability 20 percent and \$0 with probability 80 percent to a gamble that pays \$3,000 with probability 25 percent and \$0 with probability 75 percent. Let U stand for utility. If the first preference agrees with expected utilities, it seems that $U(\$3,000) > 0.80\,U(\$4,000)$. If the second preference agrees with expected utilities, it seems that $0.20\,U(\$4,000) > 0.25\,U(\$3,000)$ and hence, multiplying both sides by 4, that $0.80\,U(\$4,000) > U(\$3,000)$. Because the inequalities for the two preferences are inconsistent, it seems impossible that both preferences agree with expected utilities.

One response is to reject the principle of expected utility maximization. Another response denies the rationality of having the pair of preferences. A third response claims that people care about factors besides monetary outcomes. They may, for instance, value certainty and the elimination of risk. Then the pair of preferences may agree with broadly based expected utilities without implying inconsistent inequalities.

RATIONAL CHOICE THEORY

Rational choice theory uses principles of rationality to explain behavior. The social and behavioral sciences and even literary interpretation employ it. Proponents claim that rational choice theory yields insightful analyses using simple principles of rational behavior. Critics claim that those simple principles are too austere to adequately characterize human behavior. This debate turns on the principles of rationality at issue. Some rational choice theorists may use only principles of instrumental rationality. In that case, evaluation of basic goals is missing. Other rational choice theorists use more comprehensive principles of rationality to extend the theory's scope. They provide for principles that evaluate basic goals.

Various applications of rationality yield distinct types of rationality, such as bounded, procedural, and substantive rationality. Herbert Simon (1982) is famous for treating these types of rationality. Principles of bounded rationality set standards for people and other nonideal agents with limited cognitive power. Contrasting principles set high standards for ideal agents with unlimited cognitive power. Rationality may require ideal agents to maximize utility, whereas it requires real people to satisfice, that is, to adopt the first satisfactory option discovered. The principle to satisfice is a principle of procedural rationality because it recommends a procedure for making a decision and does not characterize the content of the decision it recommends. A substantive principle may recommend making a decision that maximizes utility. Whether a decision maximizes utility depends on its content. It depends on the prospects of acting according to the decision. Compliance with a substantive principle of rationality, such as utility maximization, may require a procedure that is more trouble than its outcome justifies. Spending hours to make a move in a chess game may sap the game's fun. Sometimes thorough calculation is too costly, and one should make a quick decision. It may be sensible to adopt the first satisfactory course of action that comes to light instead of running through all options, calculating and comparing their utilities.

An evaluator may apply a substantive principle to an act already performed. The principle judges the act without regard for the process that produced it. The principle of utility maximization gives an optimal option high marks whether it arose from a thorough or a hasty review of options. The principle evaluates the option adopted and not the method of its adoption. In contrast, an agent applies a procedural principle to discover an act to perform. A rational procedure may culminate in an act that is not optimal. Rationality does not require calculating in all cases. In many cases, weighing pros and cons, computing utilities, and comparing all options is not a rational way to make a decision—spontaneity may be appropriate. A rational decision procedure takes account of circumstances. Brian Skyrms (1990), Ariel Rubinstein (1998), Gerd Gigerenzer (2000), Gigerenzer and Reinhard Selten (2000), Weirich (2004), and John Pollock (2006) pursue these themes.

Principles of rationality vary in the scope of their evaluations of acts. Some principles evaluate a decision for instrumental rationality, taking for granted the beliefs and desires that generate it. Others evaluate the beliefs and desires along with the decision. Principles of rationality also adopt conditions. A principle may evaluate a decision, assuming unlimited time and cognitive resources for reaching it. Idealizations play a crucial role by generating an initial theory with simplified principles of rationality. Relaxing idealizations later leads to more general principles and to a more realistic theory.

Principles of conditional rational also provide a way of putting aside mistakes. A person's act may be rational given his or her beliefs, though his or her beliefs are mistaken and if corrected would support a different act. Evaluating his or her act for nonconditional rationality requires a complex assessment of the significance of the mistaken beliefs. Conditional rationality has an interesting structure resembling the structure of conditional probability. The rationality of an act given a background feature is not the rationality of the conditional that if the background feature holds then the act is performed. Nor

is it the truth of the conditional that if the background feature holds then the act is rational.

Theoretical rationality treats belief formation, and practical rationality treats action. A theory of practical reasoning formulates rules of inference, leading to a conclusion that an act should be performed. It classifies reasons for acts and assesses their force. (For a survey, see Parfit 1984; Bratman 1987; Broome 2001; and Bittner 2001.)

Some arguments that degrees of belief should conform with the probability axioms point out that failure to comply leaves one open to a series of bets that guarantees a loss, that is, a Dutch book. This observation yields pragmatic reasons for compliance with the axioms. Some theorists hold that the probability axioms require a purely epistemic justification.

The principle to maximize expected utility uses probability, and so there are grounds for holding that probability is not purely epistemic and that its axioms do not need a purely epistemic justification. In contrast, probability's role in assessing an option's prospects requires that it represent only the strength of evidence. If it is sensitive to an agent's goals, even cognitive goals, then using it to calculate an option's expected utility counts the agent's goals twice: one time in calculating the utilities of the option's possible outcomes and a second time in calculating the probabilities of the possible outcomes. A purely epistemic justification of the probability axioms may be required given probability's role in the calculation of an option's expected utility. It may be required because of probability's role as a guide to action.

Studies of rationality are multidisciplinary because several fields have a stake in their outcomes. Progress with theories of rationality is broadly rewarding, and many scholars are contributing.

SEE ALSO *Altruism; Behavior, Self-Constrained; Collective Action; Economics, Experimental; Epistemology; Expected Utility Theory; Game Theory; Information, Economics of; Kant, Immanuel; Logic; Maximization; Minimization; Morality; Optimizing Behavior; Philosophy; Probability Theory; Psychology; Random Samples; Rawls, John; Risk; Sen, Amartya Kumar; Simon, Herbert A.; Social Contract; Theory of Mind; Utility, Von Neumann-Morgenstern*

BIBLIOGRAPHY

Bacharach, Michael. 2006. *Beyond Individual Choice: Teams and Frames in Game Theory*. Eds. Natalie Gold and Robert Sugden. Princeton, NJ: Princeton University Press.

Bittner, Rüdiger. 2001. *Doing Things for Reasons*. Oxford: Oxford University Press.

Bratman, Michael. 1987. *Intention, Plans, and Practical Reason*. Cambridge, MA: Harvard University Press.

Broome, John. 2001. Normative Practical Reasoning. *Proceedings of the Aristotelian Society* 75 (supp.): 175–193.

Colman, Andrew. 2003. Cooperation, Psychological Game Theory, and Limitations of Rationality in Social Interaction. *Behavioral and Brain Sciences* 26: 139–198.

Foley, Richard. 1993. *Working without a Net*. New York: Oxford University Press.

Gigerenzer, Gerd. 2000. *Adaptive Thinking: Rationality in the Real World*. New York: Oxford University Press.

Gigerenzer, Gerd, and Reinhard Selten. 2000. Rethinking Rationality. In *Bounded Rationality: The Adaptive Toolbox*, eds. Gerd Gigerenzer and Reinhard Selten, 1–12. Cambridge, MA: MIT Press.

Halpern, Joseph. 2003. *Reasoning about Uncertainty*. Cambridge, MA: MIT Press.

Jeffrey, Richard. [1965] 1983. *The Logic of Decision*. 2nd ed. Chicago: Chicago University Press.

Kahneman, Daniel, and Amos Tversky. 1979. Prospect Theory: An Analysis of Decision under Risk. *Econometrica* 47: 263–291.

Levi, Isaac. 2004. *Mild Contraction: Evaluating Loss of Information due to Loss of Belief*. Oxford: Clarendon.

Luce, R. Duncan, and Howard Raiffa. 1957. *Games and Decisions: Introduction and Critical Survey*. New York: Wiley.

McClennen, Edward. 1990. *Rationality and Dynamic Choice: Foundational Explorations*. Cambridge, U.K.: Cambridge University Press.

Mele, Alfred, and Piers Rawling, eds. 2004. *The Oxford Handbook of Rationality*. New York: Oxford University Press.

Olson, Mancur. 1965. *The Logic of Collective Action: Public Goods and the Theory of Groups*. Cambridge, MA: Harvard University Press.

Parfit, Derek. 1984. *Reasons and Persons*. Oxford: Clarendon.

Pollock, John. 2006. *Thinking about Acting: Logical Foundations for Rational Decision Making*. New York: Oxford University Press.

Rachlin, Howard. 2002. Altruism and Selfishness. *Behavioral and Brain Sciences* 25: 239–296.

Rescher, Nicholas. 1988. *Rationality: A Philosophical Inquiry into the Nature and the Rationale of Reason*. Oxford: Clarendon.

Resnik, Michael. 1987. *Choices*. Minneapolis: University of Minnesota Press.

Rubinstein, Ariel. 1998. *Modeling Bounded Rationality*. Cambridge, MA: MIT Press.

Sen, Amartya. 1977. Rational Fools. *Philosophy and Public Affairs* 6: 317–344.

Simon, Herbert. 1982. *Behavioral Economics and Business Organization*. Vol. 2 of *Models of Bounded Rationality*. Cambridge, MA: MIT Press.

Skyrms, Brian. 1990. *The Dynamics of Rational Deliberation*. Cambridge, MA: Harvard University Press.

Sobel, J. Howard. 1994. *Taking Chances: Essays on Rational Choice*. Cambridge, U.K.: Cambridge University Press.

Stalnaker, Robert. 1998. Belief Revision in Games: Forward and Backward Induction. *Mathematical Social Sciences* 36: 31–56.

Stalnaker, Robert. 1999. Knowledge, Belief, and Counterfactual Reasoning in Games. In *The Logic of Strategy*, eds. Cristina Bicchieri, Richard Jeffrey, and Brian Skyrms, 3–38. New York: Oxford University Press.

Tversky, Amos, and Daniel Kahneman. 1982. Judgments of and by Representativeness. In *Judgment under Uncertainty: Heuristics and Biases*, eds. Daniel Kahneman, Paul Slovic, and Amos Tversky, 84–98. Cambridge, U.K.: Cambridge University Press.

Von Neumann, John, and Oskar Morgenstern. 1944. *Theory of Games and Economic Behavior*. Princeton, NJ: Princeton University Press.

Weirich, Paul. 1998. *Equilibrium and Rationality: Game Theory Revised by Decision Rules*. Cambridge, U.K.: Cambridge University Press.

Weirich, Paul. 2001. *Decision Space: Multidimensional Utility Analysis*. Cambridge, U.K.: Cambridge University Press.

Weirich, Paul. 2004. *Realistic Decision Theory: Rules for Nonideal Agents in Nonideal Circumstances*. New York: Oxford University Press.

Paul Weirich

RATIONALITY, BOUNDED

SEE *Rationality.*

RATIONALITY, PROCEDURAL

SEE *Rationality.*

RATIONALITY, SUBSTANTIVE

SEE *Rationality.*

RATIONING

SEE *Wage and Price Controls.*

RATIONING MODELS

SEE *Barro-Grossman Model.*

RAWLS, JOHN
1921–2002

John Rawls was one of the leading political philosophers of the twentieth century. His magisterial work, *A Theory of Justice,* was published in 1971. That book was deeply influenced by philosophers in the social contract tradition, including John Locke, Jean-Jacques Rousseau, and especially Immanuel Kant. *A Theory of Justice* stands with Thomas Hobbes's *Leviathan* and Locke's *Second Treatise* as a classic statement of the contract view. In Rawls's later work, epitomized in his book *Political Liberalism*, he rethought and clarified some of his earlier positions and made explicit a highly original philosophical methodology. In his last book, *The Law of Peoples*, Rawls used the social contract to approach problems of international justice.

John Rawls was born in Baltimore, Maryland, in 1921. He received his BA in philosophy from Princeton in January 1943. He entered the army shortly after graduating from college and saw combat in the Pacific theater during World War II. After his discharge from the military, Rawls returned to Princeton, where he received his doctorate in philosophy in 1949. In that year, he also married Margaret Fox, to whom he remained married until his death. Rawls spent 1950–1952 as an instructor at Princeton and 1952–1953 on a Fulbright Fellowship at Oxford. Upon his return to the United States, Rawls joined the philosophy department at Cornell. He moved to the Massachusetts Institute of Technology in 1960 and to Harvard in 1962. Rawls remained a member of the Harvard faculty until he retired in 1991. He taught and published in retirement until ill health made it impossible for him to continue working. He died on November 24, 2002.

Rawls took the central problem of contemporary political philosophy to be that of framing a conception of justice that would be appropriate for liberal democracies existing under modern conditions. At the heart of a conception of justice, Rawls thought, are norms for distributing the "primary goods" generated by social cooperation and distributed by society's "basic structure." These goods are rights, liberties, income, wealth, opportunity, and the social bases of self-respect. The basic structure is the set of a society's most important economic, legal, and political institutions. In *A Theory of Justice*, Rawls defended two principles of justice governing the basic structure's distribution of these goods: (1) Each person is to have an equal right to the most extensive total system of equal basic liberties compatible with a similar system of liberty for all. (2) Social and economic inequalities are to be arranged so that they are both (a) to the greatest expected benefit of the least advantaged and (b) attached to offices and positions open to all under conditions of fair equality of opportunity.

Rawls defended these principles by arguing that they are the solution to an important choice problem. More specifically, he argued that they would be adopted in a version of the social contract that he called "the original position." In the social contract theories of Hobbes and Locke, the contract is arrived at in "the state of nature." Both Hobbes and Locke imagine this state to be one in which there is no government and in which human beings have God-given authority over themselves, but in which they also know that living under a common human authority would be advantageous. The choice problem confronting parties in the state of nature, according to Hobbes and Locke, is that of determining what form that authority should assume. Hobbes famously argued that parties faced with this problem would choose to delegate their powers to an absolute sovereign, while Locke defended limited sovereignty. In the original position, parties do not choose a form of government. Instead, they choose principles of justice to regulate their society. They choose from a menu of principles by asking which ones would guarantee them the greatest stock of primary goods if basic institutions conformed to them.

In the states of nature described by Hobbes and Locke, parties are free and are roughly equal in power. Despite their equality, they have information about themselves and their situation that they could, in principle, use to their advantage. In Locke's theory, for example, parties could know the extent of their property holdings, since Locke held that property rights are established before agreement on the terms of the social contract is reached. Differences in the parties' holdings could give some an advantage over others, and so parties' knowledge of differences in their holdings could affect the outcome of the contract.

According to Rawls's description of the original position, parties in it are deprived of all information about themselves and of all but the most general information about society. Given these restrictions on information, Rawls argued that it would be rational for parties in the original position to decide on principles using the maximin rule of rational choice. This rule enjoins choosers to select the option that guarantees the best worst outcome. Applied to the original position, maximin enjoins parties to maximize the stock of primary goods they would enjoy if they were in the worst-off social position. Rawls argued that parties choosing in the original position, using maximin, would adopt his two principles. The first principle guarantees equal liberty. The second clearly imposes a strong restriction on economic inequality and requires that all have equal opportunities to secure positions of advantage. Equality of opportunity, in turn, requires far more than the absence of legal barriers to such positions. Rawls believed that social and economic class of origin should not affect life prospects. Fair equality of opportunity therefore requires systems of education and training sufficient to ensure that developed talents are widely dispersed. Equal liberty has long been a part of the liberal tradition. Part of Rawls's own pioneering contribution was to show the resources of the social contract tradition could be deployed to defend equality of opportunity and highly economic egalitarianism as well.

The lack of information available in the original position, effected by what Rawls called "the veil of ignorance," struck many rational choice theorists as an implausible stipulation. Rawls defended the informational constraints by arguing that the veil of ignorance merely makes vivid a condition we intuitively recognize as a plausible one to impose on our own reasoning about justice: Our thinking about what is right should not, we think, be distorted by information about what is to our own advantage. The veil of ignorance guarantees that the parties' reasoning about justice will not be distorted in this way. Because parties in the original position are free, equal, and unbiased, Rawls argued, they are situated fairly. Because they are situated fairly, he concluded, the principles they would choose are fair. Rawls therefore called his conception of justice "justice as fairness."

Modern liberal democracies exist under conditions of religious and philosophical pluralism. In *Political Liberalism* and other later work, Rawls argued that justice as fairness could secure agreement about basic justice among citizens of democracies in these conditions. It could do so because justice as fairness does not begin with metaphysical theses about the human person or the human good that are drawn from any one religious or philosophical view. Rather, it begins with ideas about the person, about political argument, and about social cooperation that are implicit in the public culture of democratic societies. For example, Rawls argued that the conditions of the original position "represent" fundamental elements of human moral personality. Rawls's argument that political philosophy should begin with ideas latent in public culture seemed to some philosophers to introduce a highly questionable method into political theorizing. But, Rawls countered, liberal thinkers in the early modern period sought a basis for political agreement that could be shared by citizens of diverse religions. To claim that political philosophy should not presuppose the truth of a contentious metaphysical theory is to do no more, he maintained, than to extend their principle of toleration from religion to philosophy itself. Because the principle of religious toleration is so much a part of the liberal tradition, Rawls's imaginative extension of the principle of toleration—like his defense of economic egalitarianism and

fair equality of opportunity—counts as an important part of his enduring bequest to that tradition.

SEE ALSO *Democracy; Hobbes, Thomas; Justice; Justice, Distributive; Locke, John; Maximin Principle; Rousseau, Jean-Jacques; Social Contract; State of Nature*

BIBLIOGRAPHY

Freeman, Samuel, ed. 2003. *The Cambridge Companion to Rawls.* Cambridge, U.K.: Cambridge University Press.

Rawls, John. 1971. *A Theory of Justice.* Cambridge, MA: Harvard University Press, 1999.

Rawls, John. 1993. *Political Liberalism.* New York: Columbia University Press.

Rawls, John. 1999. *The Law of Peoples.* Cambridge, MA: Harvard University Press.

Paul Weithman

REACTANCE THEORY

Research in social influence demonstrates that individuals often move in the direction demanded by a leader (obedience) or modeled by a majority (conformity), and cognitive dissonance theory suggests that individuals will depreciate the items and activities that are denied them ("sour grapes"). However, despite the allure of cognitive consistency and the power of the leader and majority, there are many cases in which people resist influence and even move in the opposite direction ("boomerang"). American psychologist Jack Brehm's (1966; Brehm and Brehm 1981) theory of psychological reactance offers an explanation for this obstinate behavior and identifies the conditions under which individuals will be motivated to resist compliance.

Brehm argues that individuals have a set of "free behaviors" that they believe they can engage in at present or some time in the future. Behavioral freedoms vary in importance, with some being highly important because they deal with critical survival. Stephen Worchel (2004) suggested that these freedoms help define the individual's self-identity, and many are based on the positions one holds in groups. Jack Brehm and Sharon Brehm (1981) argued that these freedoms help establish the individual's sense of control over his or her environment. Events that threaten or eliminate behavioral freedom create a motivational state (reactance) aimed at restoring the freedom(s) in question. The degree of reactance is determined by the importance of the threatened/eliminated freedom(s) and the degree of threat. A threat or elimination of freedom results in an increase of attractiveness of the forbidden act and the motivation to engage in that behavior. Hence, pressure to engage in a specific act may arouse reactance because this pressure threatens the individual's freedom to adopt other positions or engage in other behaviors. The result will be an increase in the motivation to embrace the forbidden alternative.

For example, Thomas Hammock and Brehm (1966) led children to believe that they could choose between a number of candy bars. When the experimenter threatened the freedom to choose candy bar X by stating that candy bar X should not be chosen, children reacted by choosing the item. In another situation, the importance of the freedom to play with a toy was varied by pairing it with a similar type of toy (low importance) or a different type of toy (high importance). The degree of threat to play with a specific toy was manipulated by placing it behind either a high barrier (high threat) or low barrier (low threat). The combination of high importance and high threat increased the likelihood of children choosing the toy behind the barrier (Brehm and Weinraub 1977). And Worchel and Brehm (1970) found that a target audience was more likely to adopt a forbidden position (boomerang) when the communicator threatened their freedom by explicitly telling them that they could not adopt this position.

Reactance theory has also been applied to explicate findings in a variety of other areas. For example, the empirical foundation of cognitive dissonance theory was research demonstrating that after choosing between two relatively attractive items, individuals enhanced the attractiveness of the chosen item and depreciated the rejected item (Brehm 1956). However, closer inspection of the behaviors in this free-choice paradigm reveals that prior to the decision individuals often pay closer attention to the item they eventually reject, and immediately after the choice the rejected alternative increases in attractiveness and the chosen alternative's attractiveness decreases (regret). These effects have been explained by suggesting that choosing an alternative eliminates the freedom of the individual to have the rejected alternative, thereby creating reactance.

In another realm, research has demonstrated that an item (a commodity or individual) becomes more attractive when it becomes more scarce, distant, or difficult to obtain. Each of these conditions can be viewed as threatening the individual's freedom to possess the item and as arousing a state of reactance. Similar reasoning has been applied to explain why censored material is often more desired and influential than material readily available to the individual. Other research has shown that an individual's freedom may be threatened when he or she observes the freedom of a closely related group member being threatened (implied threat), and freedom may be restored (implied restoration) when the individual observes a group member regaining his or her freedom (Worchel and Brehm 1971). In a unique twist, reactance theory has been applied to explain why desired behavior change in therapy settings may be achieved by discouraging the desired behavior (paradoxical intervention), and to caution health communicators about overly strenuous efforts to dissuade an audience from engaging in risky behaviors (e.g., the use of drugs, unprotected sex) that audience members view as being important options.

Overall, reactance theory points out that for every force pushing in one direction, there will be a counterforce moving people away from this position. The counterforce will be strongest when a negated position (or behavior) is perceived as important and as comprising a free behavior.

SEE ALSO *American Psychological Association; Behaviorism; Censorship; Cognitive Dissonance; Developmental Psychology; Evolutionary Psychology; Happiness; Optimism/Pessimism; Resistance; Social Cognition*

BIBLIOGRAPHY

Brehm, Jack W. 1956. Postdecision Changes in the Desirability of Alternatives. *Journal of Abnormal and Social Psychology* 52: 384–389.

Brehm, Jack W. 1966. *A Theory of Psychological Reactance.* New York: Academic Press.

Brehm, Jack W., and Sharon Brehm. 1981. *Psychological Reactance: A Theory of Freedom and Control.* Mahwah, NJ: Erlbaum.

Brehm, Jack W., and Marcia Weinraub. 1977. Physical Barriers and Psychological Reactance: 2-Year-Olds' Responses to Threats to Freedom. *Journal of Personality and Social Psychology* 35: 830–836.

Hammock, Thomas, and Jack W. Brehm. 1966. The Attractiveness of Choice Alternatives when Freedom to Choose Is Eliminated by a Social Agent. *Journal of Personality* 34: 546–554.

Worchel, Stephen. 2004. The Diamond in the Stone: Exploring the Place of Free Behavior in the Study of Human Rights and Culture. In *Motivational Analyses of Social Behavior: Building on Jack Brehm's Contributions to Psychology*, eds. Rex A. Wright, Jeff Greenberg, and Sharon Brehm, 107–128. Mahwah, NJ: Erlbaum.

Worchel, Stephen, and Jack W. Brehm. 1970. Effect of Threat to Attitudinal Freedom as a Function of Agreement with the Communicator. *Journal of Personality and Social Psychology* 14: 18–22.

Worchel, Stephen, and Jack W. Brehm. 1971. Direct and Implied Social Restoration of Freedom. *Journal of Personality and Social Psychology* 18: 294–304.

Stephen Worchel

READINESS, SCHOOL

There are two universal principles regarding the readiness of children for formal education. They are (1) that children will learn most effectively if they have certain personal characteristics, and (2) that teachers must adjust their instruction to accommodate those features. Many lists of the specific factors that constitute children's readiness for conventional instruction have been drafted. These tallies include, among other things, children's interest in books and reading, their fondness for conversation, curiosity about the world, and the quality of their oral language, including the extent of their knowledge of the meanings of words.

Also included on these lists are youngsters' emotional, psychological, and physiological characteristics, how well they function socially, and the economic status of their families. The last factor is considered to be especially important: Children in low-income families frequently suffer not only from a lack of the necessities of daily life, but also from inattention from their parents. Aggravating this situation is the fact that parents of such children often are not married. It is found at all socioeconomic levels that children raised in married, two-parent families display greater readiness for formal education than do youngsters brought up by single parents.

In the United States an educational program called Head Start was established in 1965 to benefit four-year-old children from low-income families. A major assumption of Head Start is that many children have handicaps to learning due to deficits in the culture of poverty, which encompasses issues such as substance abuse by parents, homeless families, little if any family health care, lack of prenatal care for mothers, neighborhood crime, and the relatively large number of children in foster care. Head Start programs have not always succeeded in one of their main goals: to raise children's later standardized academic test scores. However, there are indications that children's attendance in Head Start classes produces other favorable results such as greater social maturity, a higher rate of high school graduation, fewer absences from school, greater self-esteem, and more positive aspirations for life. As a consequence, Head Start has not lost any significant financial support from the U.S. federal government.

There also is widespread recognition that all children need to be ready to perform adequately in grades one through high school. Students who display significant difficulties in learning at these grade levels usually are enrolled in small-sized "special education" classes, which acknowledge that some students are not able to take advantage of regular school offerings, and that teachers must be prepared to help them overcome specific handicaps to learning that they have either inherited or developed. There is disagreement about the most time- and cost-effective methods for teaching these students. The two most prevalent special-education teaching methods are the academic skills and knowledge approach and the child-centered method.

Advocates of the former insist that students' acquisition of discrete academic knowledge and skills must be the paramount goal of schools. Hence, they argue for "direct, systematic, intensive, early, and comprehensive" (DISEC) instruction of a prearranged hierarchy of discrete scholastic skills and knowledge. This view assumes that some students enter schools without having mastered the standard English grammar that is considered to be necessary for them to become effective learners. Under the DISEC method, children's knowledge about basic academic subject matter and skills, sometimes called "cultural literacy," is developed in as interesting a manner as possible. This itself is not a controversial position, but the kind of learning assessment favored by DISEC teachers of children's learning has been disputed. Most DISEC teachers strongly defend standardized tests designed to measure students' subject matter knowledge and their mastery of standard English grammar.

Teachers who oppose DISEC instruction conduct their classes in a very different way. Their first action is to determine what children are interested in learning. If a given subject matter is found to be meaningful to children, it will be selected for their further attention. In addition, individual children are allowed to pursue queries that excite their particular fancies. A goal of the non-DISEC teacher is to develop children's abilities to explain and find solutions for everyday dilemmas. In these classes the conventional skills of reading, spelling, handwriting, written composition, speaking, and listening are taught only when they are needed to aid a student's process of solving problems. The traditional subjects science, history, geography, mathematics, literature, art, and drama also are only engaged by students when and if they are deemed useful to finding solutions to questions that they themselves have decided to resolve. Also, non-DISEC teachers usually honor nonstandard-English spoken dialects as valid and legitimate idioms.

Non-DISEC teachers generally are strongly opposed to the administration of standardized tests of students' academic skills and knowledge because these tests do not measure the kinds of skills and knowledge their pupils acquire from problem-solving activities. Thus, whereas DISEC teachers view standardized tests as allies in their instructional endeavors, non-DISEC teachers declare them to be unacceptable because they hold all students to uniform standards of learning.

Teachers opposed to DISEC instruction also often deplore what they consider to be unnecessary stress on children to regulate their mental behavior at earlier and earlier ages. In this respect, they voice doubts as to the merits of the conventional homework that younger students ordinarily are required to complete. Traditional homework exercises are deemed an unsatisfactory substitute for children's free play, the exercise of their creative imaginations outside of school, and intimate interactions with their parents. Both positive and negative findings about the merits of homework have been reported.

Children's readiness for schooling is a complex matter, and educators still hold strikingly contradictory viewpoints on the subject. Confounding the issue is the fact that empirical as opposed to subjective evidence about it often has been contradictory.

SEE ALSO *Achievement Gap, Racial; Children; Education, USA; Head Start; Head Start Experiments; Schooling; Schooling in the USA; Self-Esteem; Standardized Tests*

BIBLIOGRAPHY

Ashenfelter, Orley, and Cecila Rouse. 2000. *Meritocracy and Economic Inequality.* Princeton, NJ: Princeton University Press.

Delpit, Lisa, and Joanne K. Dowdy. 2002. *The Skin that We Speak.* New York: New Press.

McLanahan, Sara, and Gary Sandefur. 1994. *Growing Up with a Single Parent.* Cambridge, MA: Harvard University Press.

Resnick, Lauren B. 1987. *Education and Learning to Think.* Washington, DC: National Academy Press.

Patrick Groff

REAGAN, RONALD
1911–2004

Ronald Wilson Reagan, the fortieth president of the United States, held office from 1981 to 1989. Reagan was born in Tampico, Illinois, on February 6, 1911. In 1937 he started a thirty-year career in film and television, and his time in Hollywood engendered his interest in politics. Upon leaving military service at the end of World War II (1939–1945), Reagan was an active member of the Democratic Party and had been a supporter of U.S. presidents Franklin Roosevelt (1882–1945) and Harry Truman (1884–1972). Newly out of uniform, he engaged in union activity with the Screen Actors Guild and was its president for six years. Reagan's experiences of the postwar red scare in the movie industry during the heyday of McCarthyism worked to solidify his staunch anti-Communist orientation. In 1952, owing to the new trajectory of his career and accompanying events, Reagan publicly renounced his Democratic Party affiliation and became a conservative Republican. His extensive acting experience, his service as president of the Screen Actors Guild, and his tenure as public spokesman for General Electric all prepared Reagan well for his entrance into California politics as state governor, and then beyond onto the national stage. Reagan's political style is noted for his ability as a highly effective public speaker and his successful use of the presidential pulpit to advance his policy agenda, skills that earned him the moniker of "the great communicator."

At the age of fifty-five, Reagan defeated the Democratic incumbent and was sworn in as California governor in 1967. He was reelected in 1970. His tenure as governor was marked by his sensitivity to the need to compromise his conservatively driven policies so as to allow enactment of legislation, as well as his management style of delegation and decentralization. Reagan's aides exercised great authority and served as important formulators of policy, a management orientation that later marked his presidency and would be criticized subsequently as excessive abdication by Reagan of his presidential responsibilities. In the late 1960s, he took a firm and aggressive stance against student protesters at colleges, most notably at the University of California at Berkeley in 1969, by calling in the national guard and state police to deal with demonstrators.

Reagan secured the Republican presidential nomination in 1980 and chose George H. W. Bush as his vice-presidential running mate. Reagan's campaign stressed the economy, governmental growth, the budget deficit, declining U.S. prestige abroad, and the threat of the Soviet Union. Winning the presidency with 51 percent of the popular vote and 489 electoral college votes, Reagan took office with a new Republican majority in the Senate but with a House of Representatives controlled by Democrats. In 1984 Reagan won reelection with a landslide victory over Democratic opponent Walter Mondale, obtaining a record 525 electoral votes and 59 percent of the popular vote.

The first year of Reagan's presidency is regarded as his most significant domestically. After recovering quickly from an assassination attempt in early 1981, Reagan advanced his supply-side economic policies through Congress. Showing political skill, he was able to get congressional enactment of sweeping tax reductions that were designed to induce economic growth. Congress passed most of the president's proposals, including a cut in income-tax rates, a substantial increase in defense spending, and a drastic shrinking of nondefense, social-welfare expenditures. The purpose of these policies was to drive economic growth, and the resulting increase in governmental revenue via taxes was expected to offset the deficit and produce a balanced federal budget. The actual results were not as envisioned: Tax cuts and defense spending pushed the United States into becoming the world's biggest debtor nation, and the federal budget deficit and national debt exploded. Reagan did, however, preside over the longest peacetime economic expansion in American history.

With a Republican-controlled Senate, Reagan effectively and efficiently used his judicial appointment power to advance his conservative social agenda at all levels of the federal judiciary by nominating only "the ideologically faithful." By the time of his departure from the White House in 1989, Reagan had appointed over 60 percent of all federal judges and four U.S. Supreme Court justices, a highly significant legacy.

In foreign affairs, Reagan's stern anti-Communist posture in his first term evolved into one of relative conciliation and rapprochement in his second term. His building of a line of communications with the new Soviet leader Mikhail Gorbachev through several summit meetings was pivotal in the reduction of tension between the two superpowers. This development ostensibly ushered in a new era of U.S.-Soviet relations. In addition, Reagan successfully enhanced American power in the international arena through a military buildup and the use of force in selected regional conflicts.

Reagan will be particularly remembered for bringing forth a new tide of conservatism to American politics. Domestically, Reagan changed the face of campaigning and governing with effective imagery, symbols, and video. He emphasized personal warmth and charisma, and forged success through economic growth, tax cuts, and tax reform. His legacy has been tempered by his administration's long-term budget deficits and national debt concerns, and by the Iran-Contra scandal, in which presidential aides violated federal law in an effort to advance foreign policy endeavors that Congress had prohibited. Many of the tenets of Reagan's 1980 campaign, including reducing the size and scope of government and balancing the federal budget, were not achieved.

Reagan left office in 1989. He was diagnosed in 1994 with Alzheimer's disease, a condition typically associated with the elderly in which the mental capacity and intellectual functions decline due to deterioration of brain cells. Some analysts assert that early signs of this illness (such as memory troubles) could be observed while Reagan was still in office, but this is a point of contention and speculation. Ronald Reagan passed away at his home in Los Angeles, California, on June 5, 2004. He remains a revered figure in the Republican Party and among adherents of conservative ideology.

SEE ALSO *Berlin Wall; Bush, George H. W.; Gorbachev, Mikhail; Iran-Contra Affair; McCarthyism; Neoconservatism; Presidency, The*

BIBLIOGRAPHY

Berman, Larry, ed. 1990. *Looking Back on the Reagan Presidency.* Baltimore, MD: Johns Hopkins University Press.

Greenstein, Fred. 2000. *The Presidential Difference: Leadership Style from FDR to Clinton.* Princeton, NJ: Princeton University Press.

Jones, Charles. 1988. *The Reagan Legacy: Promise and Performance.* Chatham, NJ: Chatham House.

Stephen R. Routh

REAL INCOME

Many societies strive to improve the well-being of their members by increasing their incomes. But an increase in one's income (wage, pension, and so forth) does not necessarily mean that he or she is better off unless inflation is appropriately factored in. This is because inflation reduces purchasing power, the amount of goods or services that one can afford with a given amount of income, thus eroding some or all of one's nominal income gains. In order to make an accurate assessment of the effect of an income change on well-being, it is important to consider *real income* (income in constant dollars), which takes inflation into account, instead of *nominal income* (income in current dollars), which does not.

MEANING AND ORIGIN OF THE CONCEPT

Real income of a particular individual or household is the income that is adjusted for the effects of inflation on purchasing power. To see the rationale for inflation adjustments, suppose that your nominal income increases by 50 percent (from $200 to $300) this year over last year, but the price per bottle of your favorite drink increases by 25 percent (from $2.00 to $2.50) over the same period. With last year's lower income ($200) you could afford $200 / $2.00 = 100 bottles of the drink at that year's price ($2.00). With this year's higher income ($300), you can afford $300 / $2.50 = 120 bottles of the drink, which is more than the 100 bottles you could afford with last year's income, indicating that you are better off (i.e., your real income has increased). However, if the price of a bottle of the drink increases by 100 percent (from $2.00 to $4.00), you can afford $300 / $4.00 = 75 bottles of the drink with this year's higher income ($300) at this year's higher price ($4.00), which is less than the 100 bottles you could afford with last year's lower income ($200) at last year's lower price ($2.00). Hence you are worse off this year relative to last year, even though your income has increased, because your real income has decreased. You are better (worse) off if the percentage increase in your nominal income is greater (less) than the percentage inflation rate because the percentage growth in your real income (i.e., the percentage growth in your nominal income minus the percentage inflation rate) is positive (negative). A fall in your nominal income does not necessarily imply that you are worse off as long as the percentage decrease in the price level is higher than the percentage decrease in your nominal income, because the percentage change in your real income is positive. In summary, you are better off as a result of an increase or decrease in your nominal income provided that the percentage change in your real income is positive. If the inflation rate is positive, doubling nominal income this year over last year will less than double the corresponding real income. If the inflation rate is zero, however, doubling nominal income also doubles the corresponding real income.

Real income could be viewed in two equivalent ways. Again suppose that your nominal income rises by 50 percent (from $200 to $300) this year over last year but the price per bottle of your favorite drink rises by 25 percent (from $2.00 to $2.50) over the same period. First, with the $200 you could afford $200 / $2.00 = 100 bottles of the drink at last year's price ($2.00). However, to buy the same 100 bottles of the drink at this year's price ($2.50), you require $250. Because your income has increased from $200 to $300, your real income has increased by only $300 − $250 = $50, a 25 percent increase from your original income of $200 last year (i.e., less than the 50 percent increase in your nominal income). Second, because your nominal income increases by 50 percent (from $200 to $300) and the price of the drink increases by 25 percent (from $2.00 to $2.50), your real income increases by 50 − 25 = 25 percent, which also amounts to $50.

Real income is relevant in wage contract negotiations. An important goal of unions is to protect the real wages of their members. Achieving this goal involves determining the appropriate amount of nominal income adjustment that would protect union members' real incomes in inflationary situations. To demonstrate the adjustment process, suppose that your nominal wage increases from $50,000 to $52,000 this year over last year, but the price of a given basket of goods and services that you buy increases by 10 percent. With the 10 percent price increase, you would require $50,000 × 1.10 = $55,000 this year to afford the same basket as last year. Because your new nominal income is only $52,000, your real income will have decreased by $55,000 − $52,000 = $3,000, which is 6 percent lower than your nominal wage of $50,000 last year. This can also be confirmed by noting that the percentage increase in your nominal wage from $50,000 to $52,000 is 4; the percentage increase in the price level is 10; hence the percentage increase in your real wage is 4 − 10 = −6, indicating a 6 percent decrease in

your real wage. To maintain the same real income, your nominal income has to be increased (or indexed) by 10 percent, the same as the inflation rate (i.e., from $50,000 to $50,000 × 1.1 = $55,000). The same principle is used to index pensions, welfare allowances, and other incomes in order to maintain desired real income levels. In general, if real income decreases by, say, 5 percent, nominal incomes must be increased by 5 percent in order to maintain the same real income as before.

As noted above, adjusting nominal income to maintain some desired level of real income requires information about the inflation rate. However, practical difficulties arise in the measurement of inflation. In practice, the inflation rate is computed from a price (or cost-of-living) index, a summary measure describing relative price changes between some reference (base) period and another (current) period. For purposes of indexing wages, pensions, and so on, the inflation rates are commonly derived from a Consumer Price Index (CPI). The CPI is based on the prices of a representative "basket of goods and services" purchased by households. The economists M. C. McCracken and E. Ruddick (1980) provide a simple exposition of the nature and practical difficulties associated with CPI as an inflation measure. The economic statistician Roy Allen (1975) describes some applications of price index numbers in the measurement and international comparisons of real incomes. Given the aforementioned connection among real income, prices, and purchasing power, the origin of the real income concept can be linked to that of price index numbers, which the economic statistician Wesley Mitchell (1938) traced as far back as the 1700s.

The concept of real income is used in national income accounting to refer to real gross domestic product (GDP), the real value of all final goods and services produced in a country during a specific time period. In evaluating real GDP, the output for different years is evaluated using a common set of prices, thus eliminating the contamination of the value of actual output by inflation. Real GDP is obtained by deflating nominal GDP by a special price index called the *GDP deflator*, which measures changes in the average price of a broader "basket of goods and services" than does CPI. The usage of real income to mean real GDP is commonplace in the literature on economic growth and the measurement of human well-being, among others.

REAL INCOME AS A MEASURE OF WELL-BEING

Because real income takes into account the actual physical quantity of goods and services that can be consumed with the income, it is a better measure of human well-being than its nominal counterpart. It is therefore not surprising that real income has been incorporated into several measures of human well-being developed by the United Nations Development Program (UNDP) in its annual issues of the Human Development Report. UNDP (2006) describes these measures, including the Human Development Index (HDI), the Gender-Related Development Index (GDI), and two human poverty measures (HPI–1 and HPI–2).

Amartya Sen, winner of the 1998 Nobel Prize in Economics, has raised some philosophical issues surrounding the appropriateness of real (or nominal) income as a measure of well-being. Sen (1985) argues that functional capabilities (i.e., what a person can do or can be) are more important than income improvements. This view, which has come to be known as the "capabilities approach," emphasizes the removal of obstacles to what a person can be or can do. Such obstacles include illiteracy, poor health, lack of access to resources, and lack of civil or political freedom, among others. The ideas underlying the capabilities approach have been incorporated in UNDP's human development and poverty measures.

The link between real (or nominal) income and happiness has been the subject of empirical investigations by economists and sociologists. There is evidence that higher incomes may not necessarily translate to greater happiness. The economist Mathias Binswanger (2006) has reviewed several explanations for the failure of (real) income growth to increase happiness.

SEE ALSO *Economic Growth; Happiness; Inflation; Mitchell, Wesley Clair; Money Illusion; Nominal Wages; Price Indices; Sen, Amartya Kumar; Welfare Economics*

BIBLIOGRAPHY

Allen, Roy G. D. 1975. *Index Numbers in Theory and Practice.* London: Macmillan.

Binswanger, Mathias. 2006. Why Does Income Growth Fail to Make Us Happier? Searching for the Treadmill behind the Paradox of Happiness. *Journal of Socio-Economics* 35 (2): 366–381.

McCracken, M. C., and E. Ruddick. 1980. *Towards a Better Understanding of the Consumer Price Index.* Hull, Canada: Minister of Supply and Services Canada.

Mitchell, Wesley C. 1938. *The Making and Using of Index Numbers.* New York: Sentry.

Sen, Amartya. 1985. *Commodities and Capabilities.* Amsterdam and New York: North-Holland.

United Nations Development Program. 2006. *Human Development Report 2006: Beyond Scarcity: Power, Poverty, and the Global Water Crisis.* New York: United Nations Development Program. http://hdr.undp.org/.

Tomson Ogwang

REAL RATE OF INTEREST

SEE *Interest, Real Rate of.*

REALIGNMENT

SEE *Dealignment.*

REALISM

Realism as a nameable phenomenon in Western thought and culture emerged in France during the mid-nineteenth century. Primarily a movement in art and literature, it claimed to represent common people and their everyday circumstances based on accurate observation. Realism challenged centuries of tradition, when the highest art aspired to idealized pictorial forms and heroic subjects. Supporters of realist art considered its veracity to be an indication of an artist's "sincerity," a moral judgment. It acquired a democratic political dimension from its inclusiveness and from the accessibility of its imagery to ordinary people unversed in the classics but capable of recognizing "truth." These appeals were informed by progressive attitudes and an empirical concept of knowledge, as in the social theories of Pierre-Joseph Proudhon (1809–1865) and the scientific epistemology and the positivist philosophy of Auguste Comte (1798–1857). The leader of artistic realism was the French painter Gustave Courbet (1819–1877). Its advent revolutionized the history of art, leading to impressionism. In literature, various writers represented realism, from Gustave Flaubert (1821–1880) to Henry James (1843–1916). Unlike in art, literary realism was rarely self-conscious or polemical.

The movement realism must be distinguished from the generic term *realism*—the latter an aspect of much art and literature throughout time. In its general meaning, the word can refer to an optical or descriptive realism, in which forms or details appear to be drawn from life or produce an illusion of reality. In art, this type of realism is an ingredient in the high classicism of the Greek age of the Parthenon, in Roman portraiture, in certain Renaissance and Baroque styles, in Pre-Raphaelitism, and in photorealism, among many others. In literature, it is an aspect in certain passages of Homer's *Iliad*, in the early novel generally, and in the provincial settings of Honoré de Balzac (1799–1850) or the urban settings of James. Indeed, in literature, prose generally developed as a realist genre, as opposed to epic or lyric poetry. In theater, realism was associated primarily with comedy, whereas tragedy was considered more ideal. Following a related hierarchy, realism in art developed in opposition to academic classicism, which looked back to antiquity and the conventions of the French classical theater of Pierre Corneille (1606–1684) and Jean Racine (1639–1699) for its idealist forms.

The realism movement was a response to two interrelated factors. On the one hand, there was an increasing demand for rational and eventually scientific empiricism, which since the Enlightenment had been regarded as intellectually and socially progressive. The invention of photography in 1839, which introduced a new standard for optical realism, can be considered in the light of the same spirit, for there would otherwise have been no incentive or use for it. Second, the same rationalism encouraged the rights of the individual against both coercive political regimes and their art academies. Realism represented a rebellion, said to be grounded in "truth," against academic recipes and conventions. When Courbet's paintings of 1849 to 1855 made such attitudes militant, he adopted the term *realism*, which was being used by both his critics and supporters. A later term, *naturalism*, was developed as a more scientific-sounding, less-politicized alternative by the French novelist Émile Zola (1840–1902) and the art critic Jules Castagnary (1830–1888).

Realism's most coherent artistic manifestation occurred in mid-nineteenth-century France. It followed romanticism, which was already encouraging artistic freedom and self-expression, with artists looking to nature as their source. In his *Realist Manifesto* (1955), Courbet stated his aim as: "to translate the customs, the ideas, the appearance of my epoch according to my own appreciation" (Rubin 1997, pp. 157-158). Linking a faithful portrayal of his times with artistic independence (from teachings based on imitations of classical art), he made both elements the basis for the movement of which he became the undisputed leader. In the 1840s, Courbet's generation drew on two related artistic trends. First was the Barbizon school of landscape painters, who studied people and places from a recognizable countryside, usually near Paris. Second was the recent popularity in literature and art of rural and provincial life. As a contrast to urban materialism and its inequities, the virtues and innocence of country folk were extolled in novels by George Sand (1804–1876) and stories by Courbet's friend Champfleury (Jules Husson, 1821–1889). Painters like the Leleux brothers and Jean-François Millet (1814–1875) embodied this ethos in their representations of peasants. In addition, simple, often crude folk art and poetry were admired as naive expressions of popular culture and the working class.

The difference between Courbet and these artists was that, beginning with his *Stonebreakers* (1849, destroyed during World War II), the people, places, and activities in Courbet's paintings appeared specifically contemporary,

devoid of antimodern nostalgia, whereas his predecessors evoked a timelessness associated with romantic innocence and virtue. Courbet's workers alluded to the harsh conditions of the 1840s, when failing harvests drove many off the land into day-wage labor, providing raw materials for modern roads, railroads, housing, and industry. *A Burial at Ornans*, painted in 1850, showed a ceremony outside Courbet's hometown in the region of Franche-Comté near Switzerland. Against their rugged landscape, some thirty odd friends and neighbors gathered at the open grave of a respected citizen. Courbet portrays death as a prosaic, literally "down-to-earth" event whose meaning goes no further than laying the body in the ground. The huge canvas with life-sized figures flaunted Courbet's challenge to assumptions about what was worthy of large-scale artistic representation, and his ostensibly coarse technique evoked a worker's handicraft. Combined with their ostensible politics, the lower-class content and unrefined surfaces of his paintings caused a scandal. In 1855 Courbet challenged authority in a solo exhibition outside the grounds of the Universal Exposition. The central painting in his "Realist Pavilion" was *The Studio of the Painter*, in which he showed himself at the easel, supported by friends on the right and facing on the left a mix of figures embodying various ideas he considered outdated. The purpose of this much-interpreted painting was a declaration of both artistic freedom and solidarity with his own community.

Similar scandals shook the realm of literature. Earlier in the nineteenth century, Stendhal (Henri Beyle, 1783–1842) began the study of contemporary manners as a way to expose hypocrisy. In 1856 and 1857 respectively, Flaubert and the poet Charles Baudelaire (1821–1867) were brought to trial for offending public morality. Flaubert's novel *Madame Bovary* (1856) was about an adulterous housewife bored by her conventional husband. Poems from Baudelaire's *Les Fleurs du Mal* (1857) were often set in contemporary Paris and sometimes described erotic experience in a highly suggestive manner. A decade later, Zola considered his own novels analytic. In a preface to his notorious murder story *Thérèse Racquin* (1867), he compared his way of representing subjects—an adulterous woman and her lover plotting to murder her husband—to the scientific analysis performed by surgeons in medical dissections. In his art criticism, Zola's interpretation of the painting of Édouard Manet (1832–1883) was similar. Calling Manet a child of his times, in which the direction was toward positivism, Zola praised the artist's *Olympia* (1863–1864), a painting of a naked prostitute that was obviously meant to shock. Zola wrote that this picture, drawn from modern life, was sincerely observed by a dispassionate artist whose sole interest was to observe forms, colors, light, and shade.

Realism was associated with impressionism when the latter first appeared, since impressionism took up the commitment to modern life and contemporary manners flaunted by Manet and the contemporary novel. The young Claude Monet (1840–1926) was friendly with and drew upon Courbet and his technique, as did several other impressionists. Their imagery ranged from sailboats, promenades, and other forms of modern leisure to representations of industrial riverbanks, railroads, and factories. But the greater legacy of realism was to free artists to paint "sincerely"—that is, from their personal vision, which they indicated by a highly individualized style, often loosely handled as if the performance of representation were as important as the subject matter being painted. Hence, impressionism, praised by many for capturing the reality of a fleeting moment, contained the seeds of the demise of realism. The artifice of its execution was in constant tension with its illusion of the real. Yet realism successfully undermined doctrinal academicism once and for all by legitimizing images of modern life, heroic or anecdotal, rural or urban, and painted in whatever way the artist chose. It even entered sculpture, though as a more literal medium sculpture was far less challenging to traditional modes of representation than was painting, until the liberties with form taken by the "impressionist" sculptor Auguste Rodin (1840–1917).

Russian linguist Roman Jakobson (1896–1982) theorized that at the core of realism in art and literature is metonymy, a mode of figuration in which the part stands for the physical whole. The metonym is opposed to metaphor, in which an object stands for an idea; it is, in other words, a wholly concrete means of expression. Roland Barthes (1915–1980), in his famous short essay "The Reality Effect" (1968), pointed out that a profusion of observed detail in the realist novel slows the narrative, making it seem to advance almost unnoticeably, as if in real time, and making it appear to be the result of the concrete context established by such extensive description. In realist and impressionist painting, a sense of materiality and a dispersion of interest were achieved by a profusion of detail and a fragmentation of form across the entire image, along with subject matter from everyday modernity. Such painting was often compared to photography, the latter considered no more than a mechanical exercise, devoid of imagination and creativity. Painting was expected to emphasize certain truths in order to uplift and educate its audience, whereas photography's lack of selectivity made the edges of a composition as interesting as the center and seemed to negate the possibility of moral content.

The response to realism by establishment artists was to employ their labor toward a finished optical realism, as in the work of Léon Bonnat (1833–1922), or to incorporate occasional free paint handling, as did Jules Bastien-Lepage (1848–1884). In other countries, realism reinforced existing trends in genre painting, as occurred in Holland (e.g., Jozef Israëls [1824–1911]) and England. The *macchiaioli* movement in Italy paralleled realism and impressionism, especially in outdoor scenes. *Verismo* in opera followed later, near the turn of the century. In Germany, where Courbet was popular, realist images acquired a grander scale and avant-garde technique, as seen in the work of Wilhelm Leibl (1844–1900) and Max Liebermann (1847–1935). Artists in the United States adopted realism, as exemplified by Thomas Eakins (1844–1916), then impressionism, as national styles, although usually without the avant-garde connotations. Later realisms, such as in Richard Estes's displays of photograph-like technique or Eric Fischl's suburban psychorealism, were often ostentatious. Even in politics, first with Klemens von Metternich (1773–1859) in Austria, then with Willy Brandt (1913–1992) in Germany, there emerged a so-called realpolitik that looked to facts on the ground rather than ideology for its goals. Whatever its manifestations, then, realism continues to have a grip on consciousness thanks to its claim to represent "reality" truthfully, compared to forms of thought that defy material verification.

SEE ALSO *Naturalism*

BIBLIOGRAPHY

Auerbach, Erich. 1953. *Mimesis: The Representation of Reality in Western Literature.* Trans. Willard R. Trask. Princeton, NJ: Princeton University Press.

Becker, George J., ed. 1963. *Documents of Modern Literary Realism.* Princeton, NJ: Princeton University Press.

Nochlin, Linda. 1971. *Realism.* Harmondsworth, U.K.: Penguin.

Rubin, James H. 1997. *Courbet.* London: Phaidon.

Rubin, James H. 1999. *Impressionism.* London: Phaidon.

Weisberg, Gabriel P., ed. 1981. *The Realist Tradition: French Paintings and Drawings, 1830–1900.* Exhibition catalog. Cleveland, OH: Cleveland Museum of Art.

James H. Rubin

REALISM, EXPERIMENTAL

Experimental realism refers to the extent to which an experimental manipulation actively involves the participants in the research. If the manipulations are realistic, the phenomenology of the participant will be like that of a person in the social circumstance being indexed by the manipulation even if the lab circumstance is quite different than the naturalistic one. Thus, the goal of developing realistic experimental manipulations is to have participants really experience whatever psychological states the experimenters are interested in studying in the context of the conditional variations that might instantiate those states. To the extent that the participant is made to take the experiment seriously they will be more likely to be influenced by the manipulations.

The general logic of the experimental method in research is based on the detection of causal relationships. An independent variable is manipulated in a controlled environment, with the intention of assessing how the changes in the independent variable influence the dependent variable. Therefore, by controlling for other possible influences, an experiment can help determine whether changes in the independent variable cause changes in the dependent variable. It is important for the manipulation of the independent variable to be strong enough to have the desired effect on the participants. If the experimental manipulation does not actively involve the participants, the resultant experiment is not an accurate test of the causal relationship between the independent and dependent variables.

ISSUES OF VALIDITY

If an experiment lacks experimental realism, the participants are not affected by the manipulation of the independent variable. Thus, researchers' efforts to maximize a study's experimental realism are important in ensuring the construct validity of an experiment. Construct validity refers to the effectiveness of experimental manipulation. A study is high in construct validity when the manipulation produces the intended changes in the conceptual variable. When the variables in an experiment truly represent the abstract, hypothetical variables of which the researcher is interested, the study is said to possess a high level of construct validity.

The issue of validity is often used to critique experimental designs. It is sometimes difficult for researchers to defend their experiment and show that their study was high in experimental realism. One way to measure the extent to which participants were actively involved in the psychological processes engaged by the research is to use manipulation checks. A manipulation check involves measuring whether the participants actually experienced different levels of the independent variable. This serves to provide a test of whether the study had adequate experimental realism. That is, did the participants believe the manipulation?

RESEARCH PROCEDURES

It is difficult to specify exactly what makes a study high in experimental realism. The experimental design typically involves the use of some deception. This is because the

researcher needs to create a convincing illusion in order to have participants become engaged in the manipulation of the independent variable. It is generally advised that a researcher create a manipulation that is as strong as possible, within the confines of ethical and practical concerns. This ensures that the manipulation is maximally effective, thereby increasing the experimental realism of the study.

Even if explicit deception is not used in the experimental design, the researcher will often misinform the participants about the true purpose of the experiment. This involves what is referred to as a "cover story," where the researcher describes the purpose of the study to the participant using a believable but fake explanation. This serves to get participants into the right frame of mind for the purposes of the experiment, while ensuring that participants will not know the true purpose of the study and behave in a certain manner simply because it is what the experimenter expects.

One famous psychological experiment, conducted by Stanley Milgram in 1974, relied on deception to achieve experimental realism. In this experiment of obedience, participants were led to believe that they were taking part in a study of the effects of punishment on learning and were asked to deliver strong electric shocks to a fellow participant whenever he failed to learn an association between two words. As the intensity of the shock the participant ostensibly delivered to the learner increased, and the learner began to complain of a heart condition, participants often questioned the method or protested the use of such strong shocks. The researcher would always respond in the same manner, assuring the participant that the learner would not suffer any permanent damage and that the integrity of the experiment required that he continue with the shocks. The true purpose of the experiment was to determine whether participants would obey the instructions of the researcher and continue to injure the learner even when they personally felt that it was wrong to do so. If participants had known the true purpose of the experiment, one can assume that they would not have continued to obey the experimenter. However, the deception used in this experiment allowed researchers to investigate the conditions under which participants will obey an authority figure that orders them to harm another person.

This strategy of using deception to minimize reactivity and response bias on the part of participants is a matter of ethical debate, since participants agree to take part in the research based on a fabricated explanation of the purpose of the experiment. However, the use of this deceptive practice is justified by researchers explaining that many questions cannot be meaningfully addressed in the context of an experiment without the use of deception, and that this practice results in minimal risk or harm to the participant. Indeed, after researchers explained the true purpose of the experiment to participants in Milgram's experiment (in a process known as debriefing), most participants said that they understood why deception needed to be used in explaining the purpose of the study and that they did not regret participating.

Experimental realism is often discussed in contrast to mundane realism (also known as ecological validity). Mundane realism refers to the extent to which the research is conducted in situations that are highly similar to everyday life experiences. Experimental research designs often don't have high levels of mundane realism, since they are typically conducted in artificially created situations. However, even if the research situation doesn't look the same as an everyday situation, it can still feel like a real experience. That is the goal of maximizing experimental realism: to get an artificial experimental manipulation to feel like a real experience.

SEE ALSO *Experiments, Controlled; Experiments, Human; Validation*

BIBLIOGRAPHY

Pelham, Brett W., and Hart Blanton. 2002. *Conducting Experiments in Psychology: Measuring the Weight of Smoke.* 2nd ed. Belmont, CA: Wadsworth/Thompson Learning.

Charlene Christie

REALISM, MORAL

Moral realism is the doctrine that some moral claims are true in a way that is independent of their being endorsed, or regarded as true, by any human being. Consider, for instance, the claim that torturing babies for the sole purpose of deriving sadistic pleasure is immoral. Moral realists would regard this claim as true. But that itself does not distinguish the moral realist from many other moral theorists. What is distinctive about the moral realist is that the truth of this claim in no way depends on the attitudes that people take toward the claim itself. It is not true because one believes it or because society endorses it. For the moral realist, the standards that determine whether moral claims are true or false are as objective as those that determine the accuracy of claims in logic or the natural sciences.

All moral realists will accept that an action's rightness depends to some extent on the circumstances in which one is situated. That is because, for the realist, the correct standards of morality may well dictate different actions, depending on the circumstances. In some cases, for instance, it is morally acceptable to cut into the flesh of human beings—for instance, during surgery. But in other cases, such action is impermissible, because it is being done in the name of coercion or humiliation. What is centrally important for the moral realist is that attitudes about what is right and wrong do not determine what really qualifies as such. Even the most cherished moral beliefs might be mistaken, because their authority does not depend on an endorsement of them.

Moral realists qualify as cognitivists. Cognitivists are theorists who conceive of moral judgments in terms of their cognitive content and function. Cognitivists regard moral claims as capable of truth or falsity, and conceive of the function of moral discourse to be that of attempting to describe the nature of moral reality. This differs from noncognitivists, who consider moral judgments to be primarily expressions of emotions or commitments, and, thus, incapable of being either true or false.

Error theorists, like moral realists, accept cognitivism. But error theorists deny that there is any moral reality awaiting discovery. In rendering sincere moral judgments, one is indeed trying to state the truth about what is moral and immoral. But there is, according to error theorists, no such truth. Therefore, all fall into error when issuing moral judgments. Perhaps the most illuminating analogy here is that of the atheist, who regards theistic discourse as intended to describe an objective, divinely ordered reality. But, from the atheist's perspective, there is no such reality, and so all theistic discourse is riddled with error.

Moral realism should also be distinguished from ethical relativism. The relativist is also a cognitivist, and so believes that moral judgments are capable of truth and falsity. Unlike the error theorist, the relativist thinks that some moral claims are true. But they are true only because they accurately capture the implications of different social agreements. The realist and the relativist differ, in other words, on the ultimate source of correct moral standards. For the relativist, moral standards are correct because they are endorsed by various groups of human beings. For the moral realist, human endorsement is not the ultimate authority in morality.

In psychological circles, moral realism is often associated with the work of the Swiss psychologist Jean Piaget (1896–1980), who attributed a belief in it to very young children. In Piaget's hands, moral realism stands for the idea that there are objectively correct moral rules that are never permissibly broken, such that failure to adhere to them is always morally blameworthy. Neither of these latter implications is essential to the doctrine as it is currently discussed within the philosophical community.

SEE ALSO *Morality; Objectivism; Relativism*

BIBLIOGRAPHY

Brink, David. 1989. *Moral Realism and the Foundations of Ethics.* Cambridge, U.K.: Cambridge University Press.

Piaget, Jean, and Bärbel Inhelder. 1969. *The Psychology of the Child.* Trans. Helen Weaver. New York: Basic Books.

Sayre-McCord, Geoffrey, ed. 1988. *Essays on Moral Realism.* Ithaca, NY: Cornell University Press.

Shafer-Landau, Russ. 2003. *Moral Realism: A Defence.* Oxford: Oxford University Press.

Smith, Michael. 1995. *The Moral Problem.* Oxford: Blackwell.

Russ Shafer-Landau

REALISM, POLITICAL

Political realism is a view of politics that centers on power and conflict. The term goes back to the British historian E. H. Carr, who argued in 1939 that fact-driven "realism" needed to replace "utopian" trust in legal arrangements to preserve peace among nations. Unfamiliar to the liberal elites of America at the time, this view had a long tradition in European statecraft. Since the nineteenth-century, Germans had spoken of *Realpolitik* (realistic policy) and *Machtpolitik* (whose translation gave us "power politics") in reference to a foreign policy that recognizes self-interest and power as the driving forces of international reality. Even older is the doctrine of "reason of state" (It. *ragione dello stato*, Fr. *raison d'état*, Germ. *Staatsräson*), which asserts that the state has principles of action of its own, allowing it to do what law and morality forbid to its subjects. (Since it acquired this meaning under the influence of Niccolò Machiavelli, the Florentine political thinker of the early sixteenth century, it is also known as "Machiavellism.")

This type of intellectual reflection on power and politics goes back to the beginnings of political thought in the great civilizations of antiquity. In ancient Greece, for example, itinerant teachers of rhetoric and politics (known as sophists) argued during the fifth century BCE that morality is merely a convention (*nomos*) that stands in contrast to real human nature (*phusis*), which commands a ruthless struggle for advantage and the rule of the strong. This point was famously rendered by Thucydides in his *History of the Peloponnesian War.* In China, the legalist school (*fa chia*)—whose principal texts are the *Book of Lord Shang* and the *Han Fei Tzu* (written by the philosopher of the same name)—argued from the third century BCE onward that order required strict laws aimed at maximizing the power of the state and backed up by harsh punishments. In India, the tradition of *arthaśāstra* (science of material gain), especially the text attributed to Kautilya, who lived in the fourth century BCE, maintained that only the king's "rod of punishment" prevented people from devouring each other in accordance with the "law of the fishes."

Realpolitik, reason of state, Chinese legalism, and *arthaśāstra* are largely limited to providing practitioners of politics with maxims of action, such as punishing small infractions harshly so that big ones will not arise, or dividing one's enemies to defeat them one by one. Political realism contains these maxims, but it also relates them in theoretical fashion to assumptions about human nature, morality, and the world at large. Its generative logic was stated most cogently by Machiavelli and the seventeenth-century English philosopher Thomas Hobbes. Human beings, by nature, fear each other on account of their capacity to inflict harm and their uncertainty of each other's intentions. To secure themselves, they acquire enough power to deter or, even better, subdue the others.

From this nature arises a general struggle for power, which is aggravated by the fact that people want not only security, but also glory, power, and wealth. In addition, they will readily commit acts of aggression to attain these things. As the weak are forced to submit to the rule of the strong, political units (e.g., tribal chiefdoms, ancient city-states, feudal kingdoms) arise, providing a measure of protection and prosperity in exchange for obedience. But they cannot maintain order without repeatedly injuring innocents, which is morally warranted by the good consequences that order has for the others. Moreover, force and fraud continue unabated in the relations between units (that is, in their foreign affairs). Hence, the world is not a coherent ethical order, as the classical and Christian traditions maintain, but a chaos of conflicting ends and calamitous accidents.

Political realism became one of the major approaches in the field of international relations—where it is simply called "realism"—around World War II (1939–1945), when Reinhold Niebuhr, E. H. Carr, Hans Morgenthau, and John Herz combined the logic of Machiavelli and Hobbes with the lessons of European statecraft in order to explain why international law and the collective security arrangement of the League of Nations had failed to prevent Japanese and German aggression, and to advise American leaders on dealing with the newly threatening Soviet Union. They argued that nothing but countervailing power can check an expansionist state, because the foreign realm lacks both the central authority and sense of community that hold domestic societies together. At root, the liberal effort to subordinate politics to the rule of reason—by enlightening people about their harmony of interests and the absolute respect owed to persons—must founder on the dark side of human nature. A realistic foreign policy consists of the firm and prudent use of power in pursuit of the national interest, which is primarily to provide security. Power consists most readily of military capabilities, followed by industrial capacity, natural resources, quality of leadership, and the size and morale of the population.

Whereas the first generation of realists in international relations relied on philosophical insight and historical experience to address particular foreign policy problems—an approach now called "classical realism"—the second generation embraced the methods of social science to explain state behavior in general. In the 1980s, this effort led to the ascendancy of Kenneth Waltz's "neorealism," which ignores the particular characteristics of states (e.g., their ideologies, economic systems, ties of friendship, and the personalities of leaders) in order to explain their behavior solely from the constraint exercised by the "anarchic structure." This structure consists of the absence of central authority among states, and of the distribution of capabilities (i.e., power) across them. Neorealism predicts that states balance each other's power either by their own efforts or in alliance with others, and that balances of power form recurrently in the international system.

Since the mid-1990s, the (intentional) inability of neorealism to account for variations in the behavior of states caused by their characteristics has prompted the rise of "neoclassical realism." Its proponents insert the particular characteristics of a state—especially its perception of other states and its incentives arising from domestic politics—as a secondary cause, placing it between its structural position in the distribution of capabilities (the primary cause) and its foreign policy (the effect). It is hoped that this approach will yield a synthesis between the empirical richness of the case-study method and the analytical rigor of Waltz's structuralism.

SEE ALSO *Deterrence, Mutual; Hobbes, Thomas; Machiavelli, Niccolò; Morgenthau, Hans; United Nations; Waltz, Kenneth*

BIBLIOGRAPHY

Boesche, Roger. 2003. *The First Great Political Realist: Kautilya and His Arthashastra.* Lanham, MD: Lexington Books.

Carr, Edward Hallett. 1939. *The Twenty Years' Crisis, 1919–1939: An Introduction to the Study of International Relations.* Basingstoke, U.K.: Palgrave Macmillan, 2001.

Donnelly, Jack. 2000. *Realism and International Relations.* Cambridge, U.K.: Cambridge University Press.

Guthrie, W. K. C. 1971. *The Sophists.* Cambridge, U.K.: Cambridge University Press.

Han Fei Tzu. 1964. *Han Fei Tzu: Basic Writings.* Trans. Burton Watson. New York: Columbia University Press.

Herz, John H. 1951. *Political Realism and Political Idealism: A Study in Theories and Realities.* Midway Reprint. Chicago: The University of Chicago Press, 1973.

Hobbes, Thomas. 1651. *Leviathan.* New York: Penguin Classics, 1982.

Machiavelli, Niccolò. 1513. *The Prince.* 2nd ed. Trans. Harvey C. Mansfield. Chicago: University of Chicago Press, 1998.

Meinecke, Friedrich. 1925. *Machiavellism: The Doctrine of Raison d'Etat and Its Place in Modern History.* Piscataway, NJ: Transaction Publishers, 1997.

Morgenthau, Hans J. 1946. *Scientific Man vs. Power Politics.* Midway Reprint. Chicago: University of Chicago Press, 1974.

Morgenthau, Hans J. 1948. *Politics among Nations: The Struggle for Power and Peace.* 6th ed. Rev. Kenneth W. Thompson. New York: McGraw-Hill, 1993.

Niebuhr, Reinhold. 1932. *Moral Man and Immoral Society: A Study of Ethics and Politics.* Louisville, KY: Westminster John Knox Press, 2002.

Scharfstein, Ben-Ami. 1995. *Amoral Politics: The Persistent Truth of Machiavellism.* Albany: State University of New York Press.

Schweller, Randall L. 2003. The Progressiveness of Neoclassical Realism. In *Progress in International Relations Theory*, ed. Colin Elman and Miriam Fendius Elman, 311–346. Cambridge, MA: MIT Press.

Shang, Yang. 2003. *The Book of Lord Shang: A Classic of the Chinese School of Law.* Trans. J. J. L. Duyvendak. Union, NJ: Lawbook Exchange.

Smith, Michael Joseph. 1986. *Realist Thought from Weber to Kissinger.* Baton Rouge: Louisiana State University Press.

Thucydides. 1972. *History of the Peloponnesian War.* Trans. Rex Warner. Oxford: Penguin Classics.

Waltz, Kenneth N. 1979. *Theory of International Politics.* Boston: McGraw-Hill.

Markus Fischer

REALIST THEORY

Theoretical schools and trends represent more than abstract, free-floating ideas. They are socially moored, and need to be seen in relation to other intellectual and social trends. "Realism" has been present in philosophical thought at least since Aristotle, but the return of realism in recent years can be best understood as a reaction against the dominance of "postmodernism" in the academy, especially in the humanities and humanistic social sciences. What we have now come to call postmodernism (even when some of its adherents disavow the label) is a theoretical position that relies on a definable epistemic stance—what the philosopher Bernard Williams has called the stance of the "denier." At the most general level, what is being denied is the value of such intellectual (and social) ideals as *truth* and *objectivity*.

The current version of realism in literary and cultural disciplines emerged as a response to postmodernism as an epistemological position. Drawing on sources in realist philosophy of science (e.g., the work of Putnam and Boyd; see Antony [1993] for a good exposition), and in solidarity with the progressive goals of postmodernist thinkers, recent versions of realist theory, identified as "critical realism" or "postpositivist realism," attempt to go beyond both idealism and positivism without relying on the relativist and skeptical stance that characterizes postmodernist thought of various stripes (see Steinmetz 1998 on "critical realism," inspired by Bhaskar's work; on postpositivist realism, see Boyd 1988; Livingston 1988; S. Mohanty 1997, 2001, 2004; Moya and Hames-García 2000). In the social sciences, where postmodernism has had at best marginal influence, some critics of positivism invoke postmodernist theses about the social and discursive construction of social phenomena to move beyond narrow empiricism, but other theorists of social science, suspicious of postmodernism, are more robustly realist (see Calhoun 1995; Gilbert 2001). (Postmodernists and contemporary antipositivist realists share a commitment to one version or another of the social construction idea, but much depends on how that idea is specified and developed.)

Key postmodernist figures such as Jacques Derrida saw themselves as deconstructing the idealist substructure of "Western thought," the idealism that sometimes permeates even some self-avowed materialist approaches. Contemporary realists share the anti-idealist perspective of deconstruction and other strands of postmodernism but also develop a nonpositivist account of the very concepts postmodernists wanted to deny—concepts such as truth and objectivity most centrally, but also reference (Boyd 1988; S. Mohanty 2004), causation (Miller 1987; also see Somers 1998, a sociologist who draws on an alternative tradition of realism), identity, and experience (Alcoff 2000; S. Mohanty 1993; Moya and Hames-García 2000; Siebers 2004).

A serious debate between the postmodernist position and the contemporary realist one has barely begun, and narrowly partisan rhetoric, mistaking intellectual disagreement for political hostility, has prevented a genuine engagement. But the implications of the questions that are being scrutinized are large—and these questions could, for the first time in recent years, gather practitioners of the humanities and the social sciences together on common intellectual ground.

BEYOND POSITIVISM

Often, key theoretical slogans become more useful when their underlying claims are questioned and clarified. The postmodernist movement relies, for instance, on a critique of illegitimate and overly general historical accounts— what Jean-Francois Lyotard (1984) and many others following his lead called "grand narratives." On one level the rejection of grand narratives is a rejection of ethnocentric (Hegelian) accounts of entire cultures and civilizations. But on another level the critique extends more generally

to all explanations—historical or social (see Spivak 1990 for one typical example). The danger with this approach is that it is too extreme, conflating as it does all kinds of idealization, legitimate and illegitimate. After all, all explanation (in the natural and the social sciences) requires idealization, the tracing of a perspicuous pattern through the vast mass of available data, and an indiscriminate skepticism toward all grand narratives and all explanations prevents us from distinguishing good, productive use of idealization from overly general and distorting ideal accounts.

A more useful critical approach would examine the ways in which both Hegelian idealizations of history and positivist methodologies, despite their differences, demand (as Richard Miller [1987] puts it about the latter) a debilitating "worship of generality." As Miller argues, the positivist "covering law" model of explanation relies on an overly abstract understanding of phenomena, given its primary commitment to "subsumption under general laws," scientific or historical. Realist philosophers of science such as Miller thus typically emphasize an approach that is more hermeneutical, reflexive, and dialectical.

The crucial antipositivist point made by realist philosophers of science and social science is this: Background or auxiliary theories, which are ineliminable, have epistemic significance; there are no theory-independent "methods" and there is no unmediated knowledge. This is a hermeneutical point on which they agree with such forebears of postmodernism as Martin Heidegger, who urged that we acknowledge the theoretical "forestructures" of understanding. Realists such as Hilary Putnam and Richard Boyd would differ sharply from Heidegger's postmodernist descendants, however, by insisting that a nonpositivist objective knowledge is possible and that it is gained by taking the epistemic import of our background theories seriously. Putnam's antipositivist insights lead him and others not toward relativism or skepticism but to a sophisticated notion of objectivity as theory dependent and situated. On this view, objectivity is not neutrality; rather, it is the product of active engagement with the content and implications of our theoretical and ideological presuppositions. For Putnam and others, the postmodernist denial of objectivity rests, ironically, on an essentially positivist framework: The postmodernist thinks that the only possible form of objectivity is a positivist one, based on the ideal of a completely atheoretical and aperspectival knower. And when the postmodernist (rightly) sees that such a knower is a dangerous fiction, a false myth, he or she (wrongly) concludes that objectivity *as such* is impossible to achieve. That conclusion follows only if one agrees with the postmodernist that the positivist conception of objectivity is the only candidate available. The nonpositivist account of theory-mediated (or theory-dependent) objectivity is an attempt to sketch an alternative notion of objective knowledge that is dialectical, hermeneutical, and situated.

SCIENTIFIC KNOWLEDGE AND MORAL KNOWLEDGE

Richard Boyd (1988) makes the important argument that after recent developments in realist philosophy it is possible to see how the justification of moral claims is not altogether different from justification procedures in natural science. Both rely on a holistic process of achieving "reflective equilibrium" (Rawls's phrase) among our various beliefs, theories, and rational conjectures. The sharp positivist distinction between the "hard" sciences and the softer areas of human knowledge is untenable on this view. Boyd proposes a materialist account of the human good as based on our best scientific understanding of human nature—our deepest needs and capacities, for instance—*and* on our best conjectures about how these needs can be met and these capacities realized. Realist thinkers argue that even the most "objective" moral—and aesthetic—theory be seen as corrigible, since it is the product of social inquiry. Even when such inquiry is based in everyday practice, it is rational—in the broadest sense of the word—and purposive, and hence not all that different from inquiry in the natural sciences (Babbitt 1996; Boyd 1988; Gilbert 2001; S. Mohanty 1997, 2001; Railton 2003).

REHABILITATING IDENTITY AND EXPERIENCE

In literary and cultural theory, where postmodernist ideas have been immensely popular, realist theorists have outlined a series of proposals about such key concepts as experience and identity (and, more recently, values). Extending the nonpositivist view of moral objectivity to these social-theoretical domains, realists have argued since the mid-1990s against a purely constructivist view of experience and identity, showing how both can be not only "constructed" but also "real" (see Alcoff 2000, 2006; S. Mohanty 1993; Moya 2002; Moya and Hames-García 2000; Siebers 2004; Wilkerson 2000). The key thesis here is that claims about our subjective experiences and social identities are mediated by ideology and social context, and by theoretical presuppositions, but are nonetheless evaluable claims. They are explanations, and can be evaluated by comparing them with other relevant and competing explanations—since they refer not to mysterious inner essences but "outward," to key features of the social world and to the individual's location in that world. This theoretical proposal counters the postmodernist argument that experiences and identities are purely constructed and hence epistemically unreliable (Culler 1982; Scott 1991).

Realists about identity argue, moreover, that the future of progressive social struggles depends on greater clarity about the ways in which identity claims are justified, clarity about where and why such claims are valid, and where and why they are specious. Realists propose that we take the epistemic content of experiences and identities of minoritized groups seriously, since they contain alternative (buried or explicit) accounts of the world we all share. The development of objective knowledge about society grows out of an engagement with such alternative perspectives (see the ongoing work of the Future of Minority Studies Project).

One important consequence of this rehabilitation of identity is we can see how the best kind of moral universalism (the kind that underwrites our conceptions of human rights, for instance) is compatible with those particularist moral claims that require us to take minority identities seriously. Instead of railing against all aspects of Enlightenment thought, realists suggest how the best strands of Enlightenment universalism can accommodate—and indeed complement—the identity-based struggles of minoritized groups (e.g., women, racialized populations, gays and lesbians, the disabled) in a modern, diverse society (S. Mohanty 1997; C. Mohanty 2003; Teuton 2006).

SEE ALSO *Civilization; Culture; Derrida, Jacques; Empiricism; Epistemology; Hermeneutics; Human Rights; Idealism; Identity; Identity, Social; Minorities; Narratives; Objectivity; Philosophy; Philosophy of Science; Politics, Identity; Positivism; Postmodernism; Relativism; Social Science; Subjectivity: Overview; Universalism*

BIBLIOGRAPHY

Alcoff, Linda Martín. 2000. Who's Afraid of Identity Politics? In *Reclaiming Identity: Realist Theory and the Predicament of Postmodernism*, eds. Paula Moya and Michael Hames-García, 312–344. Berkeley: University of California Press.

Alcoff, Linda Martín. 2006. *Visible Identities: Race, Gender, and the Self.* New York: Oxford University Press.

Alcoff, Linda Martín, Michael Hames-García, Satya P. Mohanty, and Paula Moya, eds. 2006. *Identity Politics Reconsidered.* New York: Palgrave Macmillan.

Antony, Louise M. 1993. Quine as Feminist: The Radical Import of Naturalized Epistemology. In *A Mind of One's Own: Feminist Essays on Reason and Objectivity*, eds. Louise M. Antony and Charlotte Witt, 183–225. Boulder, CO: Westview Press.

Babbitt, Susan. 1996. *Impossible Dreams: Rationality, Integrity, and Moral Imagination.* Boulder, CO: Westview Press.

Boyd, Richard N. 1988. How to Be a Moral Realist. In *Essays on Moral Realism*, ed. Geoffrey Sayre-McCord, 181–228. Ithaca, NY: Cornell University Press.

Calhoun, Craig. 1995. *Critical Social Theory: Culture, History and the Challenge of Difference.* Cambridge, MA: Blackwell.

Culler, Jonathan. 1982. *On Deconstruction: Theory and Criticism After Structuralism.* Ithaca, NY: Cornell University Press.

Derrida, Jacques. 1981. *Positions.* Trans. Alan Bass. Chicago: University of Chicago Press.

Future of Minority Studies Project. www.fmsproject.cornell.edu.

Gilbert, Alan. 2001. *Democratic Individuality.* New York: Cambridge University Press.

Hames-García, Michael. 2004. *Fugitive Thought: Prison Movements, Race, and the Meaning of Justice.* Minneapolis: University of Minnesota Press.

Heidegger, Martin. 1962. *Being and Time.* Trans. John Macquarrie and Edward Robinson. New York: Harper.

Livingston, Paisley. 1988. *Literary Knowledge: Humanistic Inquiry and the Philosophy of Science.* Ithaca, NY: Cornell University Press.

Lyotard, Jean-Francois. 1984. *The Postmodern Condition: A Report on Knowledge.* Trans. Geoff Bennington and Brian Massumi. Minneapolis: University of Minnesota Press.

Miller, Richard. 1987. *Fact and Method: Explanation, Confirmation and Reality in the Natural and the Social Sciences.* Princeton, NJ: Princeton University Press.

Mohanty, Chandra Talpade. 2003. "Under Western Eyes" Revisited: Feminist Solidarity through Anticapitalist Struggles. In *Feminism Without Borders: Decolonizing Theory, Practicing Solidarity,* 221–251; 270–273. Durham, NC: Duke University Press.

Mohanty, Satya P. 1993. The Epistemic Status of Cultural Identity: On Beloved and the Postcolonial Condition. *Cultural Critique* 24: 41–80.

Mohanty, Satya P. 1997. *Literary Theory and the Claims of History: Postmodernism, Objectivity, Multicultural Politics.* Ithaca, NY: Cornell University Press.

Mohanty, Satya P. 2001. Can Our Values Be Objective? On Ethics, Aesthetics, and Progressive Politics. *New Literary History* 32 (4): 803–833.

Mohanty, Satya P. 2004. The Dynamics of Literary Reference: Narrative Discourse and Social Ideology in Two 19th-Century Indian Novels. In *Thematology: Literary Studies in India,* ed. Sibaji Bandyopadhyay, 230–248. Calcutta: Jadavpur University.

Moya, Paula. 2002. *Learning from Experience: Minority Identities, Multicultural Struggles.* Berkeley: University of California Press.

Moya, Paula, and Michael Hames-García, eds. 2000. *Reclaiming Identity: Realist Theory and the Predicament of Postmodernism.* Berkeley: University of California Press.

Putnam, Hilary. 1992. *Realism with a Human Face.* Cambridge, MA: Harvard University Press.

Putnam, Hilary. 1993. *Philosophical Papers.* Vol. 2, *Mind, Language, and Reality.* Cambridge, U.K.: Cambridge University Press.

Railton, Peter. 2003. Aesthetic Value, Moral Value, and the Ambitions of Naturalism. In *Facts, Values, and Norms: Essays toward a Morality of Consequence,* 85–130. Cambridge, U.K.: Cambridge University Press.

Scott, Joan. 1991. The Evidence of Experience. *Critical Inquiry* 17 (4): 773–797.

Siebers, Tobin. 2004. Disability as Masquerade. *Literature and Medicine* 23 (1): 1–22.

Somers, Margaret R. 1998. "We're No Angels": Realism, Rational Choice, and Relationality in Social Science. *American Journal of Sociology* 104 (3): 722–784.

Spivak, Gayatri Chakravorty. 1990. *The Post-colonial Critic: Interviews, Strategies, Dialogues.* New York: Routledge.

Steinmetz, George. 1998. Critical Realism and Historical Sociology. A Review Article. *Comparative Studies in Society and History* 40 (1): 170–186.

Teuton, Sean. 2006. Internationalism and the American Indian Scholar. In *Identity Politics Reconsidered,* eds. Linda Martín Alcoff, Michael Hames-García, Satya P. Mohanty, and Paula Moya, 264–284. New York: Palgrave Macmillan.

Wilkerson, William. 2000. Is There Something You Need to Tell Me? Coming Out and the Ambiguity of Experience. In *Reclaiming Identity: Realist Theory and the Predicament of Postmodernism,* eds. Paula Moya and Michael Hames-García, 251–278. Berkeley: University of California Press.

Williams, Bernard. 2002. *Truth and Truthfulness: An Essay in Genealogy.* Princeton, NJ: Princeton University Press.

Satya P. Mohanty

REALITY

In everyday usage, *reality* refers to the universe that exists independent of our thoughts. Dreams or delusions, which we experience when we are asleep or are otherwise not in full possession of our senses, are examples of the *nonreal.*

In philosophy, this commonsense view is known as *realism.* The opposing view in which only our thoughts are real is called *idealism.* An intermediate view is *dualism,* in which reality is composed of both the concrete objects of experience, which we call *matter,* and some other non-material element usually associated with mind and perhaps some external supernatural substance called *spirit.* While dualism is a common belief within most of the world's religions, it is nonparsimonious in the sense that no evidence requires the complication of dual realities. Spirit can be incorporated into either realism or idealism, although it is explicitly excluded in a form of realism called *materialism.* In the materialist view, matter and perhaps space and time are all that exist.

Associated with many thinkers since ancient times in both the East and the West, idealism asserts that our only knowledge of the outside world comes from perceptions, which are developed in the mind. So, it is reasoned but not proved that these are the only entities that can be real. The implication of idealism is that our thoughts are somehow more perfect, more truthful than the raw data that impinges our senses. Furthermore, perceptions that may be formed independent of the senses are equally real. Plato (c. 427–347 BCE) told the allegory of the cave, in which the cave's inhabitants are constrained to view only shadows on the wall and cannot observe the sources of the shadows. He introduced the notion that reality is composed of perfect *Forms* such as the *Form of the Good*, which some interpret as Plato's notion of God. In an example of Plato's view, the planets travel in perfect circles around Earth, and their observed zigzag motion across the sky is a distortion, much as the images of our bodies are distorted when viewed in a funhouse mirror.

In modern times, many mathematicians and theoretical physicists have adopted an updated Platonic view of reality. Mathematical truths seem to exist independent of individual opinions and cultures. Some are not only unproved but also provably unprovable, yet they are known by other means to be correct (Gödel's theorem). Furthermore, mathematical models in the physical sciences have the remarkable ability to predict future observations with exquisite precision. Surely, the argument goes, mathematics and mathematical physics must carry some aspect of reality. Yet they are still inventions of the human mind. Carried to its extreme, idealism implies that we should be able to make our own reality simply by thinking about it. Clearly this is not the case, despite the claims of some New Age gurus. Try as they might, none have been able to think themselves younger.

Each of us has an intuitive feeling that the concrete objects we confront during our waking experience constitute some aspect of reality. Samuel Johnson (1709–1784) expressed this common view when he heard of the idealistic philosophy espoused by Bishop George Berkeley (1685–1753). As described in James Boswell's *Life of Johnson*:

> We stood talking for some time together of Bishop Berkeley's ingenious sophistry to prove the nonexistence of matter, and that every thing in the universe is merely ideal. I observed, that though we are satisfied his doctrine is not true, it is impossible to refute it. I shall never forget the alacrity with which Johnson answered, striking his foot with mighty force against a large stone, till he rebounded from it, "I refute it thus." ([1791] 1934, Vol. I, p. 471)

When we kick an object and it kicks back, we are pretty certain that we have interacted with some aspect of a world outside our heads (and feet). In simple terms, this describes the processes of everyday observations as well as the most sophisticated scientific experiments. According to physics, when we look at an object with our naked eyes, particles of light called *photons* bounce off the object into our eyes. This process generates electrical signals that are analyzed by our brains. Essentially the same process takes place with scientific observations, where various particles besides photons and instruments more sensitive than the eye are used.

From the available data, scientists form mathematical models, or theories, to describe their observations and predict future observations. In the twentieth century, physicists developed the remarkably successful theories of *relativity* and *quantum mechanics*, leading to the *standard model of particles and forces* that accurately describes the nature of matter as we observe it. An equally successful *standard model of cosmology* has resulted from the application of the above theories to astronomical observations of increasing precision. With these theories, we can now describe the basic physics and cosmology of our universe from one trillionth of a second after it came into existence until the present. Surely the quarks and quasars of these models constitute some element of reality.

More than two thousand years ago, the Greek philosophers Leucippus (480–420 BCE) and Democritus (460–370 BCE) proposed that reality is composed of *atoms* and the *void*, where atoms were defined as particles that could not be divided further and the void was the empty space between atoms. This became the working model of Newtonian physics (Sir Isaac Newton, 1642–1727), although it seemed necessary to also include some kind of continuous, smooth background of fields to account for gravity and electromagnetism. In the nineteenth century, atoms came to be associated with the chemical elements, and that term is still used in that context. However, we have now cut the elements into smaller pieces in nuclear reactions.

In the twentieth century, it was found that theoretical quantum fields exist in one-to-one correspondence with particles, the so-called quanta of the fields. The quantum of an electromagnetic field is the particle of light, called the *photon*. The fields associated with forces that appear at the nuclear level have quanta called *weak bosons* and *gluons*. While a quantum theory of gravity has not yet been developed, it is speculated that the gravitational field will be associated with a quantum particle called the *graviton*.

Thus it remains possible, though not provable, that ultimate reality is composed of only atoms and the void, where the atoms are localized bits of matter, whatever the ultimate uncuttable objects may turn out to be. Einstein's theory of general relativity, which led him and others to attribute a reality to space and time, suggests a connection between geometry and matter. The currently fashionable *string theory* supports that connection.

SEE ALSO *Idealism; Materialism; Realism*

BIBLIOGRAPHY

Boswell, James. [1791] 1934. *Life of Johnson*. Ed. G. Birkbeek Hill. Oxford: Clarendon Press.

Penrose, Roger. 2004. *The Road to Reality: A Complete Guide to the Laws of the Universe.* New York: Knopf.

Stenger, Victor J. 2000. *Timeless Reality: Symmetry, Simplicity, and Multiple Universes.* Amherst, NY: Prometheus.

Stenger, Victor J. 2006. *The Comprehensible Cosmos: Where Do the Laws of Physics Come From?* Amherst, NY: Prometheus.

Susskind, Leonard. 2006. *The Cosmic Landscape: String Theory and the Illusion of Intelligent Design.* New York: Little, Brown.

Victor J. Stenger

REALPOLITIK

SEE *Kissinger, Henry; Realism, Political.*

REASON OF STATE

SEE *Realism, Political.*

RECALL

Recall is an electoral procedure that allows citizens to vote on whether or not a public official should be removed from office. It is distinct from an impeachment, which involves a formal trial. A recall is simply a special election open to all voters in the area represented by the official in question. Similar types of procedures date back to ancient Athens, where politicians could be banished from the city by a vote of the citizens. The idea of citizens taking the initiative to remove public officials exists in many but by no means all local, state, and national jurisdictions. Depending on the political unit, the recall may apply to administrators, executives, judges, or legislators. Moreover the grounds for recall, such as incompetence, malfeasance, neglect, and so on, may vary from jurisdiction to jurisdiction. In many cases no rationale is even necessary.

All recall procedures are typically initiated by a petition. The required number of signatories may be a percentage of citizens in the political unit or of voters in a preceding election. If the appropriate number of signatories is secured, then the official is recalled and an election is scheduled. There are at least four types of recall elections. In one type, a special election requires that the incumbent run in an election against all other contenders, with the winner assuming office. In another, a simultaneous recall and replacement election decides the fate of the incumbent separately but simultaneously with the choice of a successor. Voters cast ballots on the worthiness of the incumbent and the preferred replacement candidate. If the incumbent loses the recall, then the winner of the replacement election takes office. If the incumbent wins, then the outcome of the replacement election is moot. In a third type, a sequential recall and replacement election first decides the fate of the incumbent. Given that the incumbent is successfully recalled, then a replacement election is scheduled at a later date, with the vacant office filled by the winner. Finally, in the fourth type, a sequential recall and appointment procedure begins with a recall election. If the incumbent is voted out of office, then he or she is replaced by an appointee selected according to some constitutional provision.

In the early twenty-first century eighteen U.S. states allowed for the recall of public officials on the state level, and thirty-six states permitted the recall in local jurisdictions. The best-known contemporary example of this procedure is the 2003 recall of California governor Gray Davis. The governor was recalled in large part because of the state's economic downturn and large budget deficit. In a contentious race, Davis lost the recall election and the Hollywood actor Arnold Schwarzenegger won the simultaneous replacement election. The event attracted much public attention because of Schwarzenegger's celebrity, but it was also notable because state recall elections are rare and there had only been one other successful recall of a governor. In contrast, recalls at the local levels of government are used much more often.

Because the recall gives citizens the power to remove public officials before their terms expire, it serves the aims of direct democracy within a representative political system. It is consistent with an understanding of representatives as delegates for their constituents, as opposed to trustees. Proponents of the recall procedure contend that it advances democracy by increasing the accountability of public officials, giving them a reason to remain responsive to the general public. It also offers citizens the opportunity to more quickly remove incompetent, irresponsible, or unethical officials from office, instead of waiting for the end of their terms.

Opponents of recall procedures cite at least two basic problems. First, the recall is contrary to the principles of republican government because it undermines the independence of public officials. It encourages public officials to cater to the desires of citizens at the expense of the community, and it gives them an incentive to promote the satisfaction of short-term interests over long-term benefits. Second, recall elections are disruptive and costly. Recalled officials usually devote time to winning their elections so they can remain in office. More time spent campaigning means less time spent on serving the public. The recall is also expensive because it requires the government to conduct unscheduled elections.

When used judiciously, the recall can be an important tool for citizens to protect the integrity of their political systems. However, it can also be a destructive weapon when abused by an impetuous constituency or an opportunistic demagogue. Consequently, whether or not the recall is a good idea may depend on one's confidence, or lack thereof, in the intelligence and savvy of the electorate.

SEE ALSO *Accountability*

BIBLIOGRAPHY

Cronin, Thomas E. 1989. *Direct Democracy: The Politics of Initiative, Referendum, and Recall.* Cambridge, MA: Harvard University Press.

Zimmerman, Joseph. 1997. *The Recall: Tribunal of the People.* Westport, CT: Praeger.

Johnny Goldfinger

RECESSION

A recession is the declining phase of a business cycle, when seasonally adjusted output falls significantly and unemployment increases, though by no means in every industry. A recession should not be confused with periods of low output and high unemployment. Early in a recession output, though falling, is still above its trend value. Similarly, shortly after the recession ends, output is still below its pre-recession level. Recessions should not be confused with depressions. While economic historians sometimes use this term to refer to conditions in the early 1890s, most American economists use it only in connection with the Great Depression, which started in August 1929 and encompassed one catastrophic recession until March 1933. This was followed by a recovery that was succeeded by another sharp recession from May 1937 to June 1938.

DETERMINING THE TIMING OF RECESSIONS

There are three major ways of determining when a recession has occurred. A popular one is two or more successive quarters of declining GDP (gross domestic product). This is simplistic. Suppose quarterly GDP grows at the following rates: –2.0 percent, 0.1 percent, –2.5 percent. Under this definition that would not be a recession. Moreover, since official GDP figures are issued only quarterly in the United States, it cannot provide the months of turning points, without relying on unofficial estimates. And looking only at a single variable, GDP, is risky because the U.S. Department of Commerce revises, sometimes substantially, its initial GDP estimates.

Economists therefore use more complex procedures. By far the most widely accepted is that of the National Bureau of Economic Research (NBER), a private research organization. As it explained in an October 21, 2003, press release titled "The NBER's Business-Cycle Dating Procedure" it defines a recession as "a significant decline in economic activity spread across the economy, lasting more than a few months, normally visible in real GDP, real income, employment, industrial production, and whole-sale-retail sales." It determines when a recession started or ended by looking primarily at four statistical series, the most important of which is quarterly real GDP, supplemented by data that allow it to gauge monthly GDP. The other series it uses are real personal income minus transfer payments, employment, industrial production, and real wholesale and retail sales. Primarily because the initially issued data are subject to substantial revisions, it identifies the cyclical peaks and troughs only with substantial lags; for example it did not identify the November 2001 trough until July 2002. The NBER has also identified peaks and troughs back to 1857. To do so it had to rely on a large number of less comprehensive series, and on contemporaneous descriptions of business conditions. The table shows the NBER's turning points.

The NBER's contraction dates

Peak	Trough	Duration (months)
1857, June	1858, Dec.	18
1860, Oct.	1861, June	8
1865, April	1867, Dec.	32
1869, June	1870, Dec.	18
1873, Oct.	1879, Mar.	65
1882, Mar.	1885, May	38
1887, Mar.	1888, Apr.	13
1890, July	1891, May	10
1893, Jan.	1894, June	17
1895, Dec.	1897, June	18
1899, June	1990, Dec.	18
1902, Sept.	1904, Aug.	23
1907, May	1908, June	13
1910, Jan.	1912, Jan.	24
1913, Jan.	1914, Dec.	23
1918, Aug.	1919, Mar.	7
1920, Jan.	1921, July	18
1923, May	1924, July	14
1926, Oct.	1927, Nov.	13
1929, Aug.	1933, Mar.	43
1937, May	1938, June	13
1945, Feb.	1945, Oct.	8
1948, Nov.	1949, Oct.	11
1953, July	1954, May	10
1957, Aug.	1958, Apr.	8
1960, April	1961, Feb.	10
1969, Dec.	1970, Nov.	11
1973, Nov.	1975, Mar.	16
1980, Jan.	1980, July	6
1981, July	1982, Nov.	16
1990, July	1991, Mar.	8
2001, Mar.	2001, Nov.	8

Average, all 32 cycles: 37

SOURCE: National Bureau of Economic Research, "Business Cycle Expansions and Contractions," 2006 (www.nber.org).

Table 1

Although widely used, the NBER's estimation of turning points has been criticized for being subjective or based on arbitrary rules. Take for example the following hypothetical growth rates –0.1, 0.1, –2.0, –1.8, –0.9. Did the recession start with the 0.1 percent decline, or only with the 2.0 decline? Thus, Christina Romer estimated alternative turning points in her 1999 article "Changes in Business Cycles: Evidence and Explanations." The largest discrepancy between the NBER and Romer's estimates, five months, occurred in the 1982 trough. Another problem is the NBER's delay in announcing turning points. Hence some economists developed methods that, using the growth rate of GDP in successive quarters, allow them to quickly determine in an objective way the likelihood that the NBER will subsequently declare that a turning point has occurred.

Following the NBER's lead turning point chronologies have also been developed for other countries. There is some tendency for recessions to be synchronized in various countries since a recession in one country lowers its demand for the products of other countries, thus "exporting" part of its recession.

CHANGES IN THE SEVERITY OF RECESSIONS

There is much debate about whether U.S. recessions have been milder in the post–World War II era. What is clear is that recessions have become substantially shorter since 1983–1984, a phenomenon called "the great moderation." The reasons for this are controversial. One hypothesis is that computerization has reduced inventory investment. That matters because about half of business-cycle fluctuations consist of fluctuating in inventories. However, the timing does not fit: Computerization has been a steady process, while the great moderation started abruptly. Another hypothesis points to other institutional changes: the larger role of government with its automatic stabilizers; the greater availability of consumer credit, which allows the unemployed to maintain consumption; and the shift from manufacturing to the more stable service sector. But these changes are not large enough to explain the great moderation. A third hypothesis points to the greatly increased efficiency of monetary policy. Finally, some economists attribute the moderation to good luck; that is, to the shocks to the economy being smaller since 1983. Several of these explanations may well be part of the story. In any case, unlike the fluctuations that the NBER measures, fluctuations in the unemployment rate have not become shorter. This is possible because the peaks and troughs in unemployment lag those of GDP.

Given that recent U.S. recessions have been moderate, how damaging are they? Some economists argue that relative to changes in the trend rate of growth they are unimportant. Imagine that the trend rate of growth falls from 3 percent to 2.75 percent. After thirty years income has grown by only 86 percent, instead of by 126 percent as it would have at the 3 percent growth rate, a 40 percent difference. Compare that to a recession that lowers GDP by 5 percent for a year. However, happiness studies have shown that above a certain threshold long-run per capita income has little effect on happiness, while temporary unemployment has a substantial effect. Moreover, recessions could reduce the trend rate of growth.

WHAT CAUSES RECESSIONS?

Explaining why initial declines in income are followed by subsequent declines is relatively easy. As their incomes fall consumers spend less, and falling sales also lower the incentive to invest. Moreover, if prices fall (or rise less than expected) the real interest rate exceeds the rate borrowers expected, and that may drive them into bankruptcy; a more salient danger in the nineteenth century when prices declined much more in recessions than they do now.

There is much less consensus on what causes the initial downturn. One should distinguish two types of explanations. The first considers recessions as endogenous (related to) to capitalism, with expansions generating forces that terminate them. The other considers recessions to be due to exogenous, or outside, shocks. An old-fashioned example of the former is underconsumption theory. A more modern version is that expansions generate overconfidence that leads to excessive borrowing, risky lending, and lax financial practices that make firms vulnerable to failure.

Modern theories stress exogenous shocks. Monetarist theory, which for major U.S. recessions has much empirical support, focuses on declines in the growth rate of money due mainly to bank failures (until 1934) and since 1921 to inept monetary policy. It faces the problem that the growth rate of money may be endogenous rather than causal. Another theory argues that recessions are due to negative shocks to productivity that lower equilibrium real wage, which workers, who do not know this, refuse to accept. Still another theory claims that the government adopts expansionary policies prior to elections, and subsequently offsets them with restrictive policies.

More than one theory may be correct, because recessions differ. The 1914 recession was not preceded by a monetary shock, the 1921 recession was. The 1945 recession was due to end of wartime pressures for high output, while the 1973–1975 recession followed a doubling of oil prices to which the U.S. Federal Reserve Board initially responded with a restrictive policy, and the 1981 recession probably resulted from a major shift in monetary policy. The 1929 stock market crash may perhaps have played a significant role in the severity of the 1929–1933 recession, while subsequent crashes did much less damage.

SEE ALSO *Business Cycles, Political; Business Cycles, Real; Depression, Economic; Economic Crises; Great Depression; Stagflation; Stagnation; Underconsumption*

BIBLIOGRAPHY

Friedman, Milton, and Anna Schwartz.1963. *A Monetary History of the United States, 1867–1960.* Princeton, NJ: Princeton University Press.

Hall, Robert, et al. 2003. The NBER's Business-Cycle Dating Procedure. *The National Bureau of Economic Research,* October 21.

McAdams, Peter. 2003. *US, Japan and the Euro-Area: Comparing Business-Cycle Features,* European Central Bank Working Paper 283.

Romer, Christina. 1999. Changes in Business Cycles: Evidence and Explanations. *Journal of Economic Perspectives* 13 (2): 23–44.

Sill, Keith. 2004. What Accounts for the Postwar Decline in Economic Volatility? *Business Review* (Q1): 23–31.

Thomas Mayer

RECIPROCITY

Reciprocity is mutual exchange. It is the back-and-forth movement of goods and services between people. Reciprocity is the defining characteristic of nearly every nonmarket exchange system, and it shapes formal market economics as well. Dynamic social and political aspects of mutual exchange significantly influence the production, distribution, and consumption of goods and services in all societies. Nuances in reciprocity also influence how various items and labor are imbued with culturally specific values.

Marshall Sahlins (1972), drawing on the work of Bronislaw Malinowski (1922) and Marcel Mauss (1925), pinpoints three overarching categories of reciprocal exchange among different past and present peoples: (1) generalized reciprocity, (2) balanced reciprocity, and (3) negative reciprocity. These distinct forms of mutual exchange often correspond with differing degrees of closeness in society. Whereas intensely social groups employ generalized reciprocity, moderately engaged communities practice balanced reciprocity, and distant networks of individuals commonly use negative reciprocity. Within a given culture, the different kinds of reciprocal exchange are not exclusive; multiple forms can coexist and be used for interaction with various groups.

Generalized reciprocity is driven by generosity and magnanimity. The exchange consists of pure something-for-nothing gifts. However, since the giver enjoys giving and gains satisfaction from the apparently one-sided transaction, the exchange is, in fact, reciprocal. Although givers engaging in generalized reciprocity may seem disinterested because they do not actively seek compensation for their altruistic actions, they are nonetheless rewarded with contentment for their good deeds. Westerners often only engage in generalized reciprocity when dealing with close family members and friends, but many non-Western societies employ generalized reciprocity on a much wider scale. Successful generalized reciprocity relies overwhelmingly on trust and interpersonal bonds.

Balanced reciprocity consists of giving that is later requited and balanced by return offerings. The original giver must trust the recipient enough to know that the gift will ultimately be fairly and adequately requited. Since there is always a danger that the initial gift will not be properly reciprocated, these offerings are often made publicly. The presence of an audience helps to ensure that gifts are properly repaid in two respects. First, they serve as a public record for exactly what was offered and accepted. Second, the local community can punish those who accept gifts without reciprocating by spreading word of the exchange transgression, thus socially humiliating ungracious recipients and discouraging others from making future gifts to them.

The timing of balanced reciprocity is essential to the success of this informal exchange system. Jacques Derrida (1992) asserts that the only thing the gift truly offers is time—"time to forget, time to return, time for delayed reciprocation that is no longer a return" (Schrift 1997, p. 10). Since an immediate countergift diminishes the necessary display of trust, the initial offering creates a temporal buffer. When discussing the time that a gift offers, Derrida identified a meaningful cross-cultural linguistic similarity between the term *present* as (1) a description of time and (2) a reference to an offering. All in one, the word *present* captures the duality of Derrida's argument. A present—a material gift—provides the recipient with the present, the here and now. The offering requires future reciprocation yet frees the recipient from doing anything in the present; it provides the recipient with time. In a single word, the present presents the present (Mallios 2005).

Mauss notes an important link between perceptions of generalized and balanced reciprocity. He poetically writes, "Society always pays itself in the counterfeit coin of its dream" (Bourdieu 1997, p. 231). Mauss's metaphor captures two distinct aspects of the gift. "Society paying itself" is a reference to obligatory reciprocation, the mandatory return offerings made by individuals engaging in balanced reciprocity. Yet, the exchange is made "in the counterfeit coin of its dream," an offering that maintains the superficial form of pure something-for-nothing generosity. It appears to be a selfless act of altruism. Although these transactions are indeed mandatory, they are physically indistinguishable from blissful magnanimity. The dream is generosity; the hidden reality is the obligation to give (Mallios 2005).

Negative reciprocity is trade. It is the simultaneous and immediate exchange of one good or service for another. Trade can be characterized by antagonistic haggling or complete anonymity. The transaction is in no way dependent on trust or the closeness of the individuals involved in the exchange. The only relationship of significance is the equation of exchange values between the goods or services being traded.

Chris Gregory (1982) summarizes the differences between balanced reciprocity and negative reciprocity. Calling the former a gift-exchange system and the latter a commodity-exchange system, Gregory explains that, "Commodities are *alienable* objects transacted by aliens; gifts are *inalienable* objects transacted by non-aliens" (1982, p. 42). One is a sale between strangers; the other is a loan between friends. There is also an important exchange-form distinction that adds to Gregory's dichotomy: commodities are alienable objects *traded*—something for something—by aliens; gifts are inalienable objects given—something for nothing—by non-aliens (Mallios 2006). Although the initial gift in balanced reciprocity mandates a return gift and is ultimately an exchange of something for something, it nevertheless takes the meaningful form of something for nothing. Gregory presents these two models as opposites, with the giving of inalienable goods between permanently allied and perpetually interdependent transactors on one side and the trading of alienable goods between momentarily allied and perpetually independent transactors on the other.

Distinct differences exist between the world's many economic systems that are based primarily on balanced reciprocity. Anthropologists often use the terms *limited* and *unlimited* exchange to describe an important difference within these economic systems. Limited exchange confines the interaction between a set of partners. It is symmetrically dyadic, meaning that one person gives an item to someone else and that recipient makes a return offering back to the original benefactor. The most common form of reciprocal interaction, limited exchange includes only two people—that is its inherent limitation—and only two sets of offerings. Unlimited exchange, to the contrary, is open-ended. Different people pass gifts on asymmetrically in a series of exchanges. In this case, a person gives a present to another individual, who then regales a third person. Unlimited gift exchange spirals outward to include multiple parties, one of whom will ultimately make an offering to the original gift giver. This final present completes the circular exchange system. Ideally, blood donation in the United States follows a process of unlimited gift exchange. People who give blood pass their offering onto anonymous others, who then feel obliged by these magnanimous gifts to repeat the action at some point later in time. In the long run, donors participating in a successful system of unlimited balanced reciprocity are able to depend on the available blood donations of equally anonymous others should they find themselves or their loved ones deficient. The driving force behind seemingly random acts of kindness, unlimited reciprocity establishes a favorable gift karma that its participants expect to produce far-reaching benefits for all.

A similar distinction concerns *even* and *incremental* exchange. Even gift giving results when an offering completely cancels out a previous debt. A present that both eliminates debt and creates a new obligation contributes to incremental gift giving. Repeated incremental gifts further connect exchange partners as they continue to seesaw back and forth in terms of debt owed and debt accrued. This type of gift exchange is more common than even gift giving for the simple fact that evenness is not a primary goal or concern in the gift economy. Social reciprocity hinges on creating and enhancing mutually beneficial relationships, not canceling them out.

Undermining reciprocity is more than a simple economic transgression. Mauss explains that, "To refuse to give, just as to refuse to accept is tantamount to declaring war; it is to reject the bond of alliance and commonality" (1925, p. 13). Failure to perpetuate reciprocal exchanges and relationships that draw individuals closer together, in fact, pushes intended exchange partners away from each other. This denial frequently leads to conflict. Claude Lévi-Strauss (1969) identified a link between exchange and hostility. He writes in specific reference to native Nambikwaras of western Brazil and in general of societies that engage in balanced reciprocity, "Exchanges are peacefully resolved wars, and wars are the result of unsuccessful transactions" (Lévi-Strauss 1969, p. 62).

One of the most pronounced examples of a reciprocity-based culture clash occurred in 1607 at Jamestown Island, the first permanent English settlement in the Americas. Historical records and analogous ethnographic accounts reveal how profit-minded English colonists and their emphasis on negative reciprocity collided with the Powhatan's indigenous expectations of balanced reciprocity (Mallios 2006). The English failed to reciprocate the Paspaheghs—geographically the closest tribe in the Powhatan chiefdom to the new European outpost—on four separate occasions during the first weeks of colonization. Wowinchopunk, the local leader of the Paspaheghs, gave the settlers food, the land on which the colonists would build James Fort, and other goods, but the English made no return offerings. The natives grew frustrated, at one point even attempting unsuccessfully to steal reciprocal items. A Paspahegh warrior took an iron hatchet from the English camp following the series of unrequited native offerings, but a colonist snatched it back in a confrontation that nearly erupted into violence. Immediately following English trade with indigenous social rivals and enemies of the Paspaheghs, Wowinchopunk and his followers spearheaded a multitribal attack on the colonists at James Fort. Overall, exchange transgressions by the English—be they failures to give, accept, or reciprocate property—immediately preceded nearly every intercultural assault at Jamestown during the colony's first five years.

SEE ALSO *Trade*

BIBLIOGRAPHY

Bourdieu, Pierre. 1997. Marginalia—Some Additional Notes on the Gift. In *The Logic of the Gift: Toward an Ethic of Generosity*, ed. Alan Schrift, 231–241. London: Routledge.

Derrida, Jacques. 1992. *Given Time, I: Counterfeit Money*. Trans. Peggy Kamuf. Chicago: University of Chicago Press.

Gregory, Christopher. 1982. *Gifts and Commodities*. London: Academic Press.

Lévi-Strauss, Claude. 1969. *The Elementary Structures of Kinship*. Boston: Beacon.

Malinowski, Bronislaw. 1922. *Argonauts of the Western Pacific*. London: Routledge and Kegan Paul.

Mallios, Seth. 2005. Homo Regalos: A Call for Applied Gift Exchange in a Time of Global Commodification, Symbolic Violence, and Bloodshed. *International Journal of the Humanities* 1: 1485–1490.

Mallios, Seth. 2006. *The Deadly Politics of Giving: Exchange and Violence at Ajacan, Roanoke, and Jamestown*. Tuscaloosa: University of Alabama Press.

Mauss, Marcel. 1925. *Essai sur le don: Forme et raison de l'echange dans les sociétés archaiques*. Paris: Alcan.

Sahlins, Marshall. 1972. *Stone Age Economics*. New York: de Gruyter.

Schrift, Alan. 1997. Introduction: Why Gift? In *The Logic of the Gift: Toward an Ethic of Generosity*, ed. Alan Schrift, 1–22. London: Routledge.

Seth W. Mallios

RECIPROCITY, NORM OF

Social norms refer to the rules and expectations about how people should behave in a group or culture, and pertain to generally accepted ways of thinking, feeling, and behaving that people agree on and endorse as right or proper.

Various norms can be distinguished: among others, the *norm of social responsibility*, prescribing that people should help others who are dependent on them; the *norm of social justice* or fairness, which relates to the just distribution of resources; and the *norm of social commitment*, which concerns the shared view that people should honor their agreements and obligations.

American sociologist Alvin Gouldner (1960) was the first to propose the existence of a universal, generalized *norm of reciprocity*. He argued that almost all societies endorse some form of the reciprocity norm, and that only a few members were exempt from it—the very young, the sick, and the old. The norm regulates the exchanges of goods and services between people in ongoing group or individual relationships, dictating that people should help those who have helped them, that people should not injure those who have helped them, and that legitimate penalties may be imposed on those who fail to reciprocate. Reciprocity thus calls for positive reactions to favorable treatment and for negative reactions to unfavorable treatment. The things exchanged may be heteromorphic; that is, the goods or services may be concretely different but equal in value, as perceived as such by the exchange partners. Or the things may be homomorphic; that is, the goods or services may be roughly equivalent, or identical. Recent developments indicate support for Gouldner's general statement concerning the universality of the norm (Cosmides and Tooby 1992; Ridley 1997; Sober and Wilson 1998; for primates, see De Waal, 1982, 1996).

The norm has important social functions in ongoing relationships. It increases social stability in social groups or systems, and it structures and maintains the social relationships. Additionally, reciprocity may function as a positive, facilitating starting mechanism for the development of stable and enduring social relations in newly formed relationships. If a future time perspective is imposed in the social exchange relationship, the norm hinders the pursuit of nonreciprocal, selfish, and/or exploitative moves on the part of the exchange partners, thereby fostering mutual cooperation between them. As such, the time variable increases stability in the social system through reciprocity (Axelrod 1984).

Reciprocity is an evolutionary factor that can favor, among others, altruism among kin (*kin selection*; Hamilton 1964), and nonkin (*reciprocal altruism*, Trivers 1971; Axelrod and Hamilton 1981). As such it is an important factor in the social exchanges of many species, including humans, influencing such diverse behavior as helping (Lorenz 1966), cooperation (Axelrod 1984), compliance with requests in economic exchanges (Cialdini 1993), dealing with conflict and associated health impairment in organizational settings (Buunk and Schaufeli

1999), and bargaining and negotiations in conflicts in international settings (Lindskold 1978).

To indicate its relevance in social relationships, mechanisms have evolved to detect *cheaters* (that is, nonreciprocators, or exploiters; see Cosmides and Tooby 1992; Wright 1994). Furthermore, research on negative reciprocity has shown a strong relationship between the violation of the reciprocity norm by cheaters and norm-enforcing, punitive, aggressive actions, exemplifying the *lex talionis*, or the "eye-for an-eye" tendency. This research involved computer simulations by Axelrod (1986: *punitive meta-norm*) and Boyd and Richerson (1992: *moralistic strategies*); research among primates by Brosnan and De Waal (2003; *equity aversion*); and neuropsychological studies among human subjects (e.g., De Quervain et al. 2004: *altruistic punishment*). The findings of all these studies generally revealed that (a) parallel to the norm of reciprocity in social exchange relationships, secondary, punitive norms have evolved that dictate the legitimate, aggressive enforcement of the former one in different species, and (b) that effective retaliation against transgressors or cheaters may be more satisfactory than ineffective retaliation.

A pervasive phenomenon in intergroup relations is *in-group favoritism*, or *in-group bias*. Individuals evaluate their own group (or in-group) and its members more favorably than an out-group and its members on relevant dimensions, or they allocate more of a valued resource (money) to in-group members than to out-group members. Many social-psychological theories, such as social identity theory (Tajfel and Turner 1986) and self-categorization theory (e.g., Hogg 1992), serve as the main explanations for this phenomenon. However, recent developments indicate that in-group reciprocity can also at least partially account for this pervasive intergroup behavior (Gaertner and Insko 2000; Rabbie and Lodewijkx 1994; Stroebe, Lodewijkx, and Spears 2005).

SEE ALSO *Altruism; Collective Action; Communitarianism; Culture; Evolutionary Psychology; Exchangeability; Identity, Social; Norms; Punishment; Shame; Social Exchange Theory; Social Psychology; Trust*

BIBLIOGRAPHY

Axelrod, Robert. 1984. *The Evolution of Cooperation.* New York: Basic Books.

Axelrod, Robert. 1986. An Evolutionary Approach to the Norms. *American Political Science Review* 80 (4): 1095–1111.

Axelrod, Robert, and William D. Hamilton. 1981. The Evolution of Cooperation. *Science* 211: 1390–1396.

Boyd, Robert, and Peter J. Richerson. 1992. Punishment Allows the Evolution of Cooperation (or Anything Else) in Sizable Groups. *Ethology and Sociobiology* 13 (3): 171–195.

Brosnan, Sarah F., and Frans B. M. De Waal. 2003. Monkeys Reject Unequal Pay. *Nature* 425: 297–299.

Buunk, Bram P., and Wilmar B. Schaufeli. 1999. Reciprocity in Interpersonal Relationships: An Evolutionary Perspective on Its Importance for Health and Well-being. In *European Review of Social Psychology,* vol. 10, ed. Wolfgang Stroebe and Miles Hewstone, 259–291. New York: Wiley.

Cialdini, Robert B. 1993. *Influence: Science and Practice.* 3rd ed. New York: HarperCollins.

Cosmides, Leda, and John Tooby. 1992. Cognitive Adaptations for Social Exchange. In *The Adapted Mind,* ed. Jerome H. Barkow, Leda Cosmides, and John Tooby, 163–228. New York: Oxford University Press.

De Quervain, Dominique, J-F., Urs Fischbacher, Valerie Treyer, et al. 2004. The Neural Basis of Altruistic Punishment. *Science* 305: 1254–1258.

De Waal, Frans B. M. 1982. *Chimpanzee Politics: Power and Sex among Apes.* London: Jonathan Cape.

De Waal, Frans B. M. 1996. *Good Natured: The Origins of Right and Wrong in Humans and Other Animals.* Cambridge, MA: Harvard University Press.

Gaertner, Lowell, and Chester A. Insko. 2000. Intergroup Discrimination in the Minimal Group Paradigm: Categorization, Reciprocation or Fear? *Journal of Personality and Social Psychology* 79: 77–94.

Gouldner, Alvin W. 1960. The Norm of Reciprocity: A Preliminary Statement. *American Sociological Review* 25: 161–178.

Hamilton, William. D. 1964. The Genetical Evolution of Social Behavior, Parts 1 and 2. *Journal of Theoretical Biology* 7: 1–52.

Hogg, Michael. 1992. *The Social Psychology of Group Cohesiveness: From Attraction to Social Identity.* London: Harvester-Wheatsheaf.

Lindskold, Svenn. 1978. Trust Development, the GRIT Proposal, and the Effects of Conciliatory Acts on Conflict and Cooperation. *Psychological Bulletin* 85 (4): 772–793.

Lorenz, Konrad. 1966. *On Aggression.* Trans. Marjorie Kerr Wilson. New York: Harcourt, Brace and World.

Rabbie, Jaap M., and Hein F. M. Lodewijkx. 1994. Conflict and Aggression: An Individual-Group Continuum. In *Advances in Group Processes,* vol. 11, ed. Barry Markovsky, Karen Heimer, Jodi O'Brien, and Edward L. Lawler, 139–174. Greenwich, CT: JAI Press.

Ridley, Matt. 1997. *The Origins of Virtue.* London: Penguin.

Sober, Elliott, and David S. Wilson. 1998. *Unto Others: The Evolution and Psychology of Unselfish Behavior.* Cambridge, MA: Harvard University Press.

Stroebe, Katherine E., Hein F. M. Lodewijkx, and Russell Spears. 2005. Do Unto Others as They Do Unto You: Reciprocity and Social Identification as Determinants of Ingroup Favoritism. *Personality and Social Psychology Bulletin* 31 (6): 831–845.

Tajfel, Henri, and John C. Turner. 1986. The Social Identity Theory of Intergroup Behavior. In *The Social Psychology of Intergroup Relations,* 2nd ed., ed. Stephen Worchel and William G. Austin, 7–24. Chicago: Nelson-Hall.

Trivers, Robert. 1971. The Evolution of Reciprocal Altruism. *Quarterly Review of Biology* 46: 35–57.

Wright, Robert. 1994. *The Moral Animal: Why We Are the Way We Are: The New Science of Evolutionary Psychology.* New York: Vintage.

Hein F. M. Lodewijkx

RECOGNITION

Recognition is a term that has been increasingly employed in the social sciences. In psychology, the term usually refers to identifying external objects or to other mental processes. In other disciplines within the social sciences, *recognition* has been used rather freely to denote an act of or motivation for acknowledgment of certain demands, goals, values, and identities. It is this latter social and political meaning of recognition that has increasingly become a matter of importance, moral concern, and focus of scholarship.

At the level of the individual, the importance of recognition can be observed when, for example, one person assaults another person due to what is perceived as a lack of respect or recognition. The "code of the streets" emphasizes recognition and "saving-face" as issues of the highest importance. At the collective level, people strive for recognition of group values, identities, and reparations for past wrongs. To recognize, in this sense, means to behave in a manner that satisfies expectations of respect and contributes to a sense of positive self-esteem in those who are recognized.

The psychological motivation for recognition is defined in social psychology as the pursuit, defense, and maintenance of positive self-esteem. In fact, recognition and self-esteem are often used interchangeably because positive self-esteem is intertwined with, and affected by, attitudes of others, such as the granting or withholding of social acknowledgement. Social psychologists assert that positive self-esteem contributes to optimal functioning, higher efficacy, development (self-enhancement), happiness, satisfaction with life, better performance, persistence at tasks, and reduced anxieties. In contrast, low self-esteem is strongly associated with mental disorders, malfunctioning, antisocial behavior, aggression, delinquency, and opposite traits and effects of positive self-esteem. Because recognition enhances positive self-esteem and the lack of recognition tends to produce low self-esteem, it is understandable that people are highly motivated to pursue recognition and may act aggressively if denied recognition.

The notion of recognition has also been examined in philosophy. Plato identified recognition with the *thymos*, the enthusiastic part of the soul that seeks honor and pride. Thomas Hobbes argued that people are led by a natural human passion for fame and honor, which is a desire to be recognized by others. Many other political philosophers discuss recognition as *esteem*. G. W. F Hegel, however, was the first to discuss recognition in the context of the relationship between a master and a slave, and to suggest that equal recognition is the key for the development of human freedom over the course of history. Several political philosophers were influenced by Hegel's conception of recognition, such as Karl Marx, Alexandre Kojève (1902–1968), and Francis Fukuyama (1952–).

Later in the twentieth century, the notion of recognition was discussed in new contexts. John Rawls argued that to acknowledge the moral duty of fair play is to recognize others as human beings with equal aspirations and interests. According to Rawls, this recognition is a necessary element of just societies. Charles Taylor introduced the idea of recognition in the debate on multiculturalism and differential treatment of minority groups. In the opening of his treatise "The Politics of Recognition" (1992), Taylor argues that contemporary politics had become significantly shaped by needs and demands for recognition. Because identity and self-respect are affected by recognition or the lack thereof, and because nonrecognition or misrecognition can inflict real harm and serve as a form of oppression, Taylor argues that recognition is not only a matter of a moral obligation to others, it is a vital human need.

The transition from the normative to the descriptive aspect of recognition also characterizes Francis Fukuyama's *The End of History and the Last Man* (1992). Following Hegel, Fukuyama argues that the pursuit of recognition is part and parcel of human nature. Fukuyama discusses the moral aspects of recognition and the necessary acceptance of equal recognition as the foundation for liberal democracy, but he continues to suggest that recognition is also the causal engine of democratization. Nondemocratic regimes tend to inflict a sense of low self-esteem in the population, and hence the oppressed become motivated to regain a sense of recognition and human dignity. They can achieve this only through the establishment of a democratic order that entails equal recognition to all citizens.

Given the importance of recognition to self-esteem, and the growing awareness that demands for recognition are often voiced in politics, the pursuit of recognition may become the new frontier of research as an explanatory factor to various social and political phenomena. An array of social change phenomena seems to be associated with the pursuit of recognition, at least as members of social change movements express their ultimate goals. This has been the case for slaves and other oppressed groups, feminist groups, and minority groups. Democratization also appears to be affected by struggles for recognition, as demands for political and civil rights are often demands for recognition. Struggles for recognition are usually expressed as struggles for human dignity and against humiliation, and for restoration of self-esteem and similar concepts that are associated with self-respect and self-esteem. As such, the pursuit of recognition appears to lie at the heart of political life. Recognition, thus, has become not only an important normative concept, but also an overarching explanatory concept.

SEE ALSO *Black Power; Civil Rights; Democratization; Feminism; Hegel, Georg Wilhelm Friedrich; Hobbes, Thomas; Human Rights; Public Rights; Reparations; Self-Esteem; Subaltern*

BIBLIOGRAPHY

Crocker, Jennifer, and Wayne Bylsma. 1995. Self-Esteem. In *The Blackwell Encyclopedia of Social Psychology*, ed. A. S. R. Manstead, Miles Hewstone, and Susan T. Fiske, 505-509. Oxford: Blackwell.

Fukuyama, Francis. 1992. *The End of History and the Last Man*. New York: Free Press.

Hegel, G. W. F. [1807] 2003. *Phenomenology of Mind*. New York: Dover.

Taylor, Charles. 1992. The Politics of Recognition. In *Multiculturalism and "The Politics of Recognition": An Essay*, ed. Amy Gutmann, 25–73. Princeton, NJ: Princeton University Press.

Doron Shultziner

RECONCILIATION

Reconciliation, the overcoming of differences, the healing of broken relations, is initially a religious concept addressed in the Hebrew Bible and especially in the New Testament. It has acquired wider meaning in the context of the wars and violence of the twentieth century.

In the Hebrew Bible, the term *kiffer* (from the verb *kaffar*: covering over, atonement, propitiation, reconciliation) was used in the context of animal ritual sacrifice. Propitiation of God was the objective. Saint Paul, especially in 2 *Corinthians* 5:18–20 and in *Romans* 5:10, raises this concept to the level of a restoration to the favor of God for sinners who repent and put their trust in the expiatory death of Christ. But the term refers not only to such reconciliation with God but also to the task of reconciliation with other persons as a primary requirement for the followers of Christ. In *Matthew* 5:23–24: "If therefore you are presenting your offering at the altar, and there remember that your brother has something against you, leave your offering there before the altar, and go your way; first be reconciled to your brother, and then come and present your offering."

In the Gospels, as in much later discussion, reconciliation came to be paired with the concept of forgiveness, the forgiveness freely given by God and to be imitated by all. In this, the New Testament's reconciliation with God and with others took on the full character of the Hebrew Bible's *shalom*: completeness, soundness, welfare, peace. Yet in practice, the concept long tended to be confined to the private sphere, the individual's forgiveness by God, as in the Catholic practice of confession to a priest and the absolution of sins, now called the *sacrament of reconciliation* rather than, as in the past, *of penance*.

But the wars of the twentieth century and the many situations of *transitional justice* (the restoration of civil relations after periods of oppression) brought the wider social-political concept of reconciliation back into prominence in Christian thinking and made it the property of all the world. Thus, in South Africa, the effort to heal the society after the ills of apartheid gave rise to the Truth and Reconciliation Commission. Its grant of amnesty to offenders, on condition that they admit their guilt, was seen as far more satisfactory than the more vengeful process of the Nuremberg Trials after the collapse of Nazism. We can observe an outgrowth of this development in the growing interest in *restorative justice*, a legal concept that defines the objective of a justice system as the restoration of relations rather than simply the determination of guilt and the punishment of the offender—*retributive justice*.

Christian proponents of reconciliation, such as Archbishop Desmond Tutu of South Africa or the Croatian theologian Miroslav Volf, have consequently held prominence in this movement, although it has also been taken up as a managed and secular technical process conducted by professional mediators. Realization of the benefits that can be derived from this kind of process has brought about the rise of *Track II diplomacy*, the work of nongovernmental peace-building professionals who can often help the citizenry of conflicted societies reach reconciliation in ways that the official diplomatic representatives of governments cannot, or who can be the catalysts of solutions to conflict that governments could not generate themselves.

Distinguishing between the concepts of forgiveness and reconciliation has troubled many. We may see forgiveness as the personalized action of individuals and reconciliation as the effect of the healing of relations in the broader society.

Welcome as all this has been in its humanity and generosity, it carries its dangers. Most obvious is that a demand for instant forgiveness and reconciliation, and a blaming of victims who cannot bring themselves simply to forget the evils done to them, can lead to the hasty covering up of severe trauma in a society, leaving the underlying ills unaddressed. Connected with this is the tendency, sometimes, of churches and religious actors, as well as those who most benefit from systems of exploitation, to treat reconciliation as an alternative to the liberation of victims of oppression, imposing a sense of guilt on them if they persist in their quest for justice rather than reconciling themselves to an unjust status quo. In an atmosphere in which reconciliation is seen as a virtuous action, superior (more religiously acceptable) to the pursuit of justice, this can take on the character of blackmail. And in this context the professionalization of the mediator's task in managing conflict can easily become an unwelcome form of coercion.

Warning indications hang, therefore, over this valuable practice and concept of reconciliation. An understanding is required that unfair disparities of power between victims and controllers of society may not be tolerated. The third-party reconciler must realize that forgiveness is not an instant process, and that those who feel themselves victimized, often from both or all sides of a conflict, must have time to mourn, to lament the harm that has come to them. They must have an opportunity to learn, through what may be a difficult and time-consuming process, the common humanity of those who have hurt them. They and their victimizers need to unlearn the stereotypes by which they have perceived one another. And all the participants need to understand that it may not be possible to resolve all problems and contentions among them, but that the more promising course is a conflict transformation by which the relations among them are seen in a different light.

Setting the objective of reconciliation, however, rather than simply a cessation of violence or the stifling of protest, as in a military process of "pacification," holds promise to bring about more humane relations among peoples, possibilities of addressing their inevitable differences of interest or aspiration nonviolently, and the healing of past traumas in ways that do not call for visiting retributive trauma on those who have harmed us. The development, as rather a new discipline, of peace studies has been a result of the renewed social and political interest in the concept of reconciliation.

SEE ALSO *Truth and Reconciliation Commissions*

BIBLIOGRAPHY

Helmick, Raymond G., and Rodney L. Petersen, eds. 2001. *Forgiveness and Reconciliation: Religion, Public Policy, and Conflict Transformation.* Philadelphia: Templeton Foundation Press.

Kritz, Neil J., ed. 1995. *Transitional Justice: How Emerging Democracies Reckon with Former Regimes.* 3 vols. Washington, DC: U.S. Institute of Peace Press.

Minow, Martha. 1998. *Between Vengeance and Forgiveness: Facing History After Genocide and Mass Violence.* Boston: Beacon.

Schreiter, Robert J. 1992. *Reconciliation: Mission and Ministry in a Changing Social Order.* Maryknoll, NY: Orbis.

Tutu, Desmond. 1999. *No Future Without Forgiveness.* New York: Doubleday.

Volf, Miroslav. 1996. *Exclusion and Embrace: A Theological Exploration of Identity, Otherness, and Reconciliation.* Nashville, TN: Abingdon.

Raymond G. Helmick

RECONSTRUCTION ERA (U.S.)

The Reconstruction Era refers to the period following the Civil War from 1865 to 1877, during which the victorious North reorganized, or reconstructed, the Southern states that had formed the Confederacy. This reorganization was carried out under the requirements of the Military Reconstruction Act passed by the U.S. Congress on March 2, 1867, hence the term *Reconstruction.* But the attempt to reorganize the South's political system in order to move the region in a new direction, away from the priorities and practices of the slavery regime, ran into difficulties. By the early 1870s, governments formed under the provisions of the Reconstruction Act were encountering such opposition and hostility from the former Confederates that they were unable to stay in power. After the contested presidential election of 1876, the federal government withdrew its political support and its troops from the South, bringing the Reconstruction experiment to an end.

THE VICTOR'S BURDEN, 1865

The Civil War was precipitated by the decision of the Southern states to secede from the Union in 1860–1861, but it was caused by the Southerners' long-term fear that their valuable and profitable institution of slavery was endangered by a hostile majority in the North. This fear came to a head with the election of a Republican, Abraham Lincoln, to the presidency and his Northern party's capture of Congress. As a result of the war, secession was defeated and slavery abolished. Alarmingly, however, the successful resolution of the long-term cause of the war (slavery) and of the short-term cause (secession) did not end the matter. Rather, it gave rise to new problems. First, what was to be the future status of the emancipated slaves? How free would they be and did freedom involve equality of some kind? Would they obtain land, as several Union government actions during the war had hinted? Second, what was to be the future status of the rebels who had been defeated on the battlefield? Would they be allowed to return to the Union they had broken up four years earlier and, if so, under what terms? Terminating slavery and Southern independence had solved one set of problems, but emancipation and reunion immediately presented another, as massive and vexing as the first. Even more was at stake, however, because failure to handle emancipation and reunion satisfactorily would raise doubts about how much the Union's victory had ultimately achieved. The North had won the war, but it might lose the peace.

PRESIDENTIAL RECONSTRUCTION, 1865

After the war, the federal government was embroiled in a struggle over the terms for readmitting the South to the Union. Instead of collaborating, the president and Congress found themselves dangerously at odds over the appropriate course to pursue. The conflict centered on the fundamental issues of what policy would be adopted and which branch of government would prevail. But it was exacerbated by the personality of Andrew Johnson who had succeeded to the presidency when Lincoln was assassinated just a few days after the Confederacy's surrender on April 9, 1865. A stubborn and combative man, Johnson was a Southern Democrat who had stayed with the Union after his state had seceded in 1861 and who had practiced politics in Tennessee as the art of confrontation, rather than compromise.

Promulgated in May 1865, Johnson's plan for the South required that new governments be formed in each state, elected by voters who had sworn an oath of loyalty to the United States. But Johnson's conciliatory scheme soon encountered difficulties because even its minimal requirements were questioned and sometimes rejected by the Southern states, and the voters sent prominent Confederates to Congress, among them the former vice-president, Alexander H. Stephens. Simultaneously, reports of mistreatment and violence toward the freed slaves (the freedmen) were pouring into Washington and began appearing in the newspapers. Not surprisingly, the Republican majority in Congress rejected the South's congressmen-elect.

Rather than adapting to the emerging realities in the South and changing course, as Lincoln would almost certainly have done, Johnson stood his ground. He proceeded to thwart the efforts of the Republicans to formulate alternative proposals for the South, resorting to his veto power on every possible occasion. This extremely dangerous confrontation continued until 1868 when,

after several attempts had been defeated by a veto-wielding president, Congress managed to enact and implement a reconstruction policy that readmitted the South to Congress and established a Republican-controlled government in each of the ex-Confederate states.

CONGRESSIONAL RECONSTRUCTION, 1866–1867

After taking the initiative in December 1865, Congress proposed three different approaches for dealing with the South. The first took the form of two measures, introduced in early 1866, to protect the freedmen who, although no longer slaves, were still vulnerable and in need of physical and legal protection. One measure extended the life of the Freedmen's Bureau, a wartime agency created to supervise the transition from slavery to freedom and provide relief for the destitute of both races in the war-torn South. The other was a civil rights bill that defined citizenship as a national, not state, matter, and therefore extended citizenship to 4.5 million African Americans, all but 500,000 of whom had been slaves. The statute also provided federal protection for the civil rights of all citizens, that is, equality before the law, ensuring equal access to the courts and prohibiting legal discrimination. Although the Civil Rights Act marked a major expansion of federal jurisdiction, it was still limited in scope because it did not ban private discrimination, and the federal government could only intervene when a state failed to provide formal legal protection. Nevertheless, to most Republicans' surprise, the president rejected both bills, accompanying his vetoes with hostile messages that pronounced them unconstitutional. Although the vetoes were soon overridden, Johnson clearly intended to oppose Congress. Furthermore, by vetoing the Republicans' proposals and declaring them unconstitutional, he was obviously provoking a fight.

Congress's second initiative was a set of terms for readmission in the form of a constitutional amendment to be submitted to the Southern legislatures elected in 1865 under Johnson's plan. The Fourteenth Amendment, as it became known after its ratification in 1868, consisted of three basic propositions. First, a federal guarantee of citizenship and civil rights, incorporating the provisions of the Civil Rights Act into the Constitution. Second, a reduced representation in Congress for the South if African Americans were denied the vote. And third, the disqualification of leading Confederates from holding office. The civil rights clause became the enduring contribution of this amendment, especially its equal protection feature, but it was the third clause—keeping former Confederates out of power—that made the proposal unacceptable to the South in 1866. Accordingly, the Southern legislatures rejected the amendment decisively, following the president's earlier and predictable veto. In the congressional elections of 1866, Johnson's determination to defeat his former Republican allies and their proposed amendment had led him to create a party of his own called the National Union party, with the Northern Democrats as its primary source of support. But it had been defeated overwhelmingly, allowing the Republicans to increase their majority.

With the president still defiant and the South emboldened, the Republicans moved quickly to produce yet another plan before the Thirty-ninth Congress expired in March 1867. The outcome was a law, the Military Reconstruction Act, the terms of which would be mandatory, unlike an amendment that needed to be ratified by the states. As first introduced by Thaddeus Stevens of Pennsylvania, the leading radical Republican in the House, the bill was conceived as a program for keeping the South under federal military supervision, for several years perhaps, until loyalty returned and changes were under way democratizing the region's political system and modernizing its economy. The radical wing of the party saw the postwar moment as a critical opportunity to move the South in a new direction, but Republican moderates amended Stevens's bill so thoroughly that it became instead a formula for immediate readmission.

Under the terms of the law, the eleven Southern states were divided into five military districts, each of them under the command of a U.S. general. The troops stationed in each district were to supervise the creation and registration of a new electorate that was to include all adult male African Americans. Black suffrage was a radical innovation never even contemplated by other slave societies in the Americas, although none of them had been forced to end slavery after defeat in a massive civil war. The new electorate included just under a million African Americans, but not the leading Confederates who were now disfranchised by the Act. These former Confederates were also barred from holding office under the Fourteenth Amendment, which the reconstructed states were required to ratify.

The Reconstruction Act became law—over Johnson's veto, of course. Immediately, the process of reconstructing the South began and it required that new governments be created and Congressmen elected. As a result, a Republican party was formed in the South and the Republicans proceeded to gain control of every Southern state and its Congressional delegation. This outcome was achieved, despite constant opposition from President Johnson who used his authority as chief executive and commander in chief to obstruct the implementation of the complicated political process laid down by the Reconstruction Act. Also presenting a problem was the South's political class whose members opposed, not only

the idea of enfranchising their ex-slaves, but also the creation of a new political order from which they were to be excluded. As the South was being reconstructed, Johnson was impeached for his persistent obstruction, although the Senate failed to produce the two-thirds majority needed to convict and remove him from office. Meanwhile, the former Confederates, who were now out of office but actively organizing an opposition party, lived to fight another day.

RECONSTRUCTION IN THE SOUTH, 1868–1877

The newly created Republican party managed to win control of every Southern state between 1868 and 1870. The success of Reconstruction now depended on how well the party governed and how long it could stay in power. This task was enormously difficult, not only because the party was new to the region and most of its elected officials were inexperienced, but also because it was faced by a relentless foe determined to see it fail. In the eyes of the conservative opposition that consisted of former Confederate officeholders and most of the region's political class, the Republican-controlled state governments were unworthy of their support, and therefore they were deemed illegitimate. The federal government had created the party, and the state governments that the party controlled had been imposed upon the South. Moreover, the party's constituency and leadership were drawn from elements that were alien and unacceptable, namely, Northerners whom they called derisively carpetbaggers, Southern whites dismissed as scalawags and, of course, blacks, most of them ex-slaves.

Besides ridiculing and vilifying these Republican governments, the opposition employed every means possible for attacking, destabilizing, and ultimately overthrowing them, one by one, during the early 1870s. They resorted to electoral fraud and intimidation. They frustrated the operation of these state governments by withholding taxes. They broke up the Republican coalition by encouraging dissidence among the racial and sectional groups within it and then offering to give electoral support to any faction prepared to leave and run an independent campaign. And when the masked and secret Ku Klux Klan emerged in 1868, intimidating Republican supporters and assassinating some of the party's leaders, the conservatives did nothing to discourage this insurgency until the federal government intervened in 1871–1872. By 1872, many of the states with white majorities had slipped from Republican control, a result of favorable electoral conditions for the opposition, supplemented by pressure, fraud, and violence.

Although the Klan was subsequently dispersed, the violence soon assumed a different and more deadly form as the paramilitary White Leagues appeared in Louisiana in 1873 and various other overtly violent organizations arose in the Deep South that was still under rather precarious Republican control. The Republicans' opponents, who were at that time aligning with the Democrats and determined to regain control of their states, officially sanctioned these forces that styled themselves Rifle Clubs or Red Shirts. Accordingly, they unleashed virulent and violent race-based campaigns aimed at rousing white voters and discouraging blacks and carrying elections "peaceably if we can, forcibly if we must." Faced by this onslaught, the last remaining Republican governments located in the heavily black states of Alabama, Mississippi, South Carolina, and Louisiana were overthrown between 1874 and 1876. A few months later, federal troops were withdrawn, allowing the Democrats to take over throughout the region.

Painfully aware at the outset that the opposition was going to be fierce, the Republican state governments were caught in a dilemma. They had to provide for and protect their supporters who were, for the most part, former slaves and less advantaged whites. Simultaneously, the governments they controlled had to govern for the state as a whole, while defusing the criticism of the conservatives and fending off their attacks. Pulled in these two different directions and under constant attack, the party began to collapse. Nevertheless, the Republicans began well. In 1868, they drew up a new constitution for each state, as required by the Reconstruction Act. Liberal and democratic in thrust, these constitutions reduced privilege and increased political participation, and also provided government services previously lacking in most Southern states. They made adult male suffrage a constitutional right, lowered or removed age- and property-qualifications for holding office, and ensured that most offices were elective rather than appointive. Government assumed responsibility for creating and funding institutions to care for orphans, the insane, and the deaf and dumb, as well as for building penitentiaries and systems of public schools. Because government was to be more active than before, the powers of the executive branch were increased.

But the Republican framers of these constitutions proved unwilling to push much further. They did not provide for any redistribution of land to the landless, in particular the freed slaves who felt they deserved a portion of the land that had gained value from their unpaid labor (the possibility of making land available to the former slaves was all but eliminated by earlier developments at the national level, first, by Johnson's executive proclamation of August 1865 allowing the rebels to regain their lands and, then by the Republican party's general lack of enthusiasm for pursuing such a policy). The public schools were to be racially separate, a decision actually favored by black delegates because they feared losing the entire system if white parents refused to send their chil-

dren to schools attended by blacks. And the constitutions usually removed the ban on former Confederates holding office, because the Republicans who wrote them favored equal rights, even though this liberality would allow the South's political class to reenter politics.

Cautious and moderate rather than extreme, these new constitutions provided the framework for Republican rule. Although the party leaders hoped that this constitutional foundation would satisfy their supporters and reassure their opponents, they knew that successful programs were needed if the party was to consolidate its power and acquire legitimacy. To this end, the Republicans promoted three initiatives in particular: the creation of a viable school system, the protection of civil rights, and the development of the region's railroad system. Of these three, the railroads were considered critical in the Republicans' attempt to prove that they could govern efficiently and effectively. Accordingly, the Republican legislatures moved forcefully to encourage economic development by offering state aid to builders of railroads in the hope that they would create vital infrastructure and develop the localities that their roads penetrated and opened up. Had these ventures succeeded, the Republicans expected to gain considerable political capital. But, for a variety of reasons, they failed. The states were left holding the debt of these enterprises and, somewhat unfairly, the Republicans were accused of mismanagement and fiscal irresponsibility, but not the railroad companies that had actually failed to build the lines.

This serious setback was compounded by the party's inability to raise the necessary revenue to fund the public schools adequately, a direct result of the taxpayers' unwillingness to pay and of the precipitous decline in the value of the land on which the school tax was levied. Also disappointing was the party's record on race relations. Despite legislation to end racial discrimination on transportation and in other public places, the patterns of separation established under slavery remained the norm. Whites were unwilling to break with the past, and blacks themselves were hesitant to challenge these customs, believing it was safer and more constructive to develop their own institutions, a calculation similar to the one they had made earlier over mixed schooling. Nevertheless, most black and many white children attended school during and after Reconstruction, and a significant cadre of African Americans were trained as teachers. In addition, hundreds of African Americans held office under the Republicans. Two hundred sixty-seven were delegates to the constitutional conventions in 1868; nearly 800 served in the state legislatures during Reconstruction; and 18 held national office as members of Congress. Meanwhile, hundreds more served in lower-level positions, such as sheriff, county commissioner, justice of the peace, and even an occasional mayor. Although inexperienced, these officials were usually literate and their visible presence in public life was evidence that race relations were improving, somewhat dramatically in fact.

Unfortunately, African Americans, and most of the white population who also stood to gain from the Republicans' new initiatives, depended upon the Republican party's ability to remain in power. But the Democrats relentlessly opposed the Republicans. They subverted and attacked the Republicans and were quick to exploit their mistakes and aggravate their difficulties. By the mid-1870s, less than a decade after the South had been politically reconstructed, the Republican party had lost control, either through its inability to hold its diverse coalition together or by losing elections because of force or fraud.

SEE ALSO *Confederate States of America; Lincoln, Abraham; Slavery; U.S. Civil War*

BIBLIOGRAPHY

Anderson, Eric, and Alfred A. Moss Jr. 1991. *The Facts of Reconstruction: Essays in Honor of John Hope Franklin.* Baton Rouge: Louisiana State University Press.

Benedict, Michael Les. 2006. *Preserving the Constitution: Essays on Politics and the Constitution in the Reconstruction Era.* New York: Fordham University Press.

Foner, Eric. 1983. *Nothing but Freedom: Emancipation and Its Legacy.* Baton Rouge: Louisiana State University Press.

Foner, Eric. 1988. *Reconstruction: America's Unfinished Revolution, 1863–1877.* New York: Harper and Row.

Perman, Michael. 1984. *The Road to Redemption: Southern Politics, 1869–1879.* Chapel Hill: University of North Carolina Press.

Perman, Michael. 2003. *Emancipation and Reconstruction.* 2nd ed. Wheeling, IL: Harlan Davidson.

Rable, George C. 1984. *But There Was No Peace: The Role of Violence in the Politics of Reconstruction.* Athens: University of Georgia Press.

Schwalm, Leslie A. 1997. *A Hard Fight for We: Women's Transition from Slavery to Freedom in South Carolina.* Urbana: University of Illinois Press.

Stanley, Amy Dru. 1998. *From Bondage to Contract: Wage Labor, Marriage, and the Market in the Age of Slave Emancipation.* New York: Cambridge University Press.

Summers, Mark W. 1984. *Railroads, Reconstruction and the Gospel of Prosperity: Aid under the Radical Republicans, 1865–1877.* Princeton, NJ: Princeton University Press.

Michael Perman

RECORDING INDUSTRY

The growth of the global recording industry represents a post–World War II (1939–1945) phenomenon. Despite the inventions of the radio and the phonograph, record sales remained relatively low in the first half of the twentieth century. It was not until 1948, when Columbia Records introduced the 12-inch vinylite long-playing (LP) record onto the market in the United States, that the industry enjoyed its first significant stimulus to growth. The emergence of new low-cost recording equipment followed in the 1950s and allowed many independent record labels, known as *indies*, to compete with the major record labels, or *majors*, namely, Columbia, RCA, and Decca. This provided an opportunity for a greater variety of artists to release music and increased demand as consumers exploited the wider choice of music available.

The 1960s was a creative decade in which many of the old formulas and structures changed. Hi-fi stereo recordings were first introduced, and the development of tape formats that would eventually transform the industry picked up pace in the mid-1960s with the appearance of *four-track* and *eight-track* tapes. The eight-track achieved a dominant position over the four-track until the cassette tape, introduced by the Philips Company in 1963, eventually took over in the 1970s. Cassette tapes were smaller, more convenient, reasonably cheap to produce, and, in combination with the development of accompanying compatible software, transformed the production and consumption of music.

Growth of the industry continued until the recession of the early 1980s when the demand for music fell. Many in the industry at this time believed that the availability of home cassette recorders was responsible for much of the loss in sales and there were attempts to tax blank recording cassette tapes. Yet, some analysts suggest that the decline was predominantly related to the poor quality of the recordings, inferior software, the global recession, and a shortage of creative work.

The downturn only proved temporary, however, and a period of high growth followed, largely due to recording improvements and the expanded use of digital formats, such as the compact disc (CD). Because of the low cost of production and strong market demand for high-quality recordings, record companies focused on low-risk opportunities for profit. This took the form of issuing CDs of back catalogues and compilations of works by established artists. At the same time, the development and growth of global satellite television channels catering to music lovers only, such as MTV, also contributed to an increased demand for music.

By the late 1990s, a culture of "free" music was emerging as use of the Internet expanded. In 1999, Shawn Fanning, then an eighteen-year-old student at Northeastern University in Boston, created a computer program called Napster that allowed Internet users to search for songs in MP3 format ("near" CD-quality sound) on the hard drives of other users, and then download this music to their own hard drives at no cost. However, within only a few months of its existence, Napster was sued by the Recording Industry Association of America on behalf of the major record labels for copyright infringement. Napster lost the case, and in July 2001 was forced to shut down.

By 2004 global sales of physical recorded music (audio and video) were estimated to be $33.6 billion, representing a fall of 10 percent in real terms since 1999. Total global unit sales in 2004 were 2.8 billion, 77 percent of which were accounted for by sales of CDs. In the same year, the United Kingdom had the world's highest per capita sales of recorded music in both volume and value terms, at 3.2 units and $58.20 respectively. The figures for the United States were 2.8 and $41.50 respectively. However, the recording industry also helps drive a much broader music sector, from subscription radio stations to mobile ringtone sales, that was estimated to be worth more than $100 billion globally in 2005. Music has an economic importance that extends well beyond the scope of record sales.

In terms of its organization, the recording industry has a highly concentrated, oligopolistic structure dominated by four majors: Sony-BMG, EMI, Universal, and Warner. In 2004 these four companies enjoyed a combined global market share of 75 percent. The remainder was accounted for by numerous indies whose continued presence reflects two factors: (1) an ability to expand markets and specialize in market niches; and (2) a reliance upon the majors to bring their music to market. One consequence of this symbiotic relationship between the majors and indies has been the reduction of potential competition. However, digital technologies and the Internet are reducing costs and barriers to entry and represent an opportunity for the indies to loosen the majors' stranglehold on the distribution of music.

As noted earlier, the growth of Internet technology that allows consumers to download music without paying the producers represents a major challenge to the recording industry. In theory, the main concern is that the activity may reduce legitimate demand for albums as potential consumers turn to pirated versions, though it can be argued that illegal downloading may stimulate legitimate demand. For example, online "sampling" of individual songs may increase demand for full album recordings.

Most empirical work by economists on this issue suggests that the negative effects of online piracy outweigh the positive effects, that is, piracy is associated with a fall in legitimate music sales. However, history shows that technology has been responsible for the growth of the mass consumption of music and has allowed today's superstars to earn huge sums of money compared to musicians of two hundred years ago. Like the invention of recording tape and the compact disc, therefore, the

Internet is likely to ultimately result in an increase in demand for music once new business models are in place. Indeed, the success of Apple's iTunes music store has demonstrated that consumers are willing to pay for music downloads from the Internet. Industries that do not innovate in a market economy, or ineffectively compete with producers of other similar products, will decline, a rule that applies to the recording industry.

SEE ALSO *Entertainment Industry*

BIBLIOGRAPHY

Bowmaker, Simon W., Ronnie J. Phillips, and Richard L. Johnson. 2005. The Economics of Rock 'n' Roll. In *Economics Uncut: A Complete Guide to Life, Death, and Misadventure*, ed. Simon W. Bowmaker, 389–421. Cheltenham, U.K., and Northampton, MA: Edward Elgar.

International Federation of the Phonographic Industry. 2005. *Recording Industry in Numbers 2005*. London: IFPI.

Strobl, Eric A., and Clive Tucker. 2000. The Dynamics of Chart Success in the U.K. Pre-recorded Popular Music Industry. *Journal of Cultural Economics* 24: 113–134.

Simon W. Bowmaker

RECTANGULAR DISTRIBUTION
SEE *Distribution, Normal.*

RECURSIVE MODELS

A system of equations is recursive rather than simultaneous if there is unidirectional dependency among the endogenous variables such that, for given values of exogenous variables, values for the endogenous variables can be determined sequentially rather than jointly. Due to the ease with which they can often be estimated and the temptation to interpret them in terms of causal chains, recursive systems were the earliest equation systems to be used in empirical work in the social sciences.

In any equation system there will be a number of exogenous variables and as many endogenous variables as there are equations in the system. Exogenous variables are those whose values are determined outside the system and that affect the endogenous variables without being affected by them. Variables that can depend on each other and on the exogenous variables are called "endogenous variables." These are the variables whose values are explained by the equation system. (Some endogenous variables enter with a lag and are called "lagged endogenous variables.") An endogenous variable that appears on the left-hand side of one equation will typically appear on the right-hand side of some or all of the other equations in the system.

A recursive model is a special case of an equation system where the endogenous variables are determined one at a time in sequence. Thus the right-hand side of the equation for the first endogenous variable includes no endogenous variables, only exogenous variables. The right-hand side of the equation for the second endogenous variable includes exogenous variables and only the first endogenous variable. The right-hand side of the equation for the third endogenous variable includes exogenous variables and only the first and second endogenous variables, and so on. Another way to put this is to say that a system is recursive if the solution for the gth endogenous variable involves only the first g equations.

A simple example involving three endogenous variables (y_1, y_2, and y_3) and only one exogenous variable (x) would be the following system—the εs represent the stochastic disturbances (if the system was a purely deterministic, mathematical one, all of the εs would be zero).

$$y_1 = \beta_1 x + \varepsilon_1$$
$$y_2 = \beta_2 x + \gamma_{21} y_1 + \varepsilon_2$$
$$y_3 = \beta_3 x + \gamma_{31} y_1 + \gamma_{32} y_2 + \varepsilon_3$$

From the structure of this system, it is clear that there is a sequential (one-way) rather than a simultaneous (two-way) relationship between the endogenous variables. Thus y_1 affects y_2, but y_2 does not affect y_1 either directly or indirectly. Similarly y_1 and y_2 influence y_3 without in turn being influenced by y_3. Systems of equations of this kind are called "recursive" or "triangular models." If in addition there is no correlation between the stochastic disturbances, then we refer to the system as "diagonally recursive." Ordinary Least Squares (OLS) is an appropriate estimator for each single equation in a diagonally recursive system because it can be shown that for such a system OLS yields consistent and (asymptotically) efficient estimates. This is because in a diagonally recursive system there is no correlation between the explanatory variables in any one equation and that equation's stochastic disturbances.

More formally, in matrix notation a system of structural equations may be written as

$$\Gamma y = \mathrm{B} x + \varepsilon$$

where y is a vector of the g endogenous variables, x is a vector of the k exogenous variables (these might also include any lagged endogenous variables), ε is a vector of the g stochastic disturbances, Γ is a $g \times g$ matrix of the coefficients on the g endogenous variables, and B is a $g \times k$ matrix of the coefficients on the k exogenous variables.

If Γ is a triangular matrix (that is, it has zeroes in all of the cells above the principal diagonal) we refer to the

system as "recursive." This is why recursive models are also called "triangular models."

In the case of the three equations system given above, we would write Γ as

$$\Gamma = \begin{bmatrix} 1 & 0 & 0 \\ -\gamma_{21} & 1 & 0 \\ -\gamma_{31} & -\gamma_{32} & 1 \end{bmatrix}$$

This is a triangular matrix, indicating that the system is recursive.

Define Σ to be a matrix of the variances and covariance's of the stochastic disturbance terms. In the case of the three equations system given above, we would write Σ as

$$\Sigma = \begin{bmatrix} \mathrm{var}\,(\varepsilon_1) & \mathrm{cov}\,(\varepsilon_1\varepsilon_2) & \mathrm{cov}\,(\varepsilon_1\varepsilon_3) \\ \mathrm{cov}\,(\varepsilon_2\varepsilon_1) & \mathrm{var}\,(\varepsilon_2) & \mathrm{cov}\,(\varepsilon_2\varepsilon_3) \\ \mathrm{cov}\,(\varepsilon_3\varepsilon_1) & \mathrm{cov}\,(\varepsilon_3\varepsilon_2) & \mathrm{var}\,(\varepsilon_3) \end{bmatrix}$$

If Γ is a triangular matrix and in addition Σ is a diagonal matrix (so that all the covariance terms are zero), the system is diagonally recursive, and OLS is an appropriate estimator. Now Σ will be a diagonal matrix only if the disturbances across the different equations are (contemporaneously) uncorrelated—in other words, the disturbance terms are independent of each other. If a system is recursive but not diagonally recursive, in other words if Γ is a triangular matrix whereas Σ is not a diagonal matrix, we describe the system as "seemingly unrelated," and the Seemingly Unrelated Regressions (SUR) method of estimation is more appropriate (more efficient) than OLS (Zellner 1962). One reason why the stochastic disturbances might be correlated across equations is if the equations have in common omitted variables, sometimes even variables that by their nature cannot be observed. This is not an unusual situation in the social sciences.

Some equation systems are said to be "block recursive," meaning that the recursive or triangular property applies only to blocks made up of subsets of the equations in the model. If the system can be characterized as block recursive, then the endogenous variables listed in each block of equations may be jointly determined, but the blocks of equations can be ordered such that they (the blocks) form a triangular structure (see Bodkin, Klein, and Marwah 1991 for examples).

Computer packages exist that will take a list of equations and order them in such a way that any recursive structure including recursive blocks are identified. Statistical tests to ascertain whether or not the variance-covariance matrix is diagonal are also available (see Breusch and Pagan 1980 for an example).

The technique of path analysis that features in psychology and other disciplines often utilizes a recursive system, following on the ideas of Sewall Wright (1921). However, while recursive models are easier to interpret than models that are simultaneous, there is no mathematical or statistical reason why path analysis has to be limited to recursive models (see Seneta 2006 and the references cited therein).

SEE ALSO *Multiple Equilibria; Regression; Simultaneous Equation Bias*

BIBLIOGRAPHY

Bodkin, Ronald G., Lawrence R. Klein, and Kanta Marwah. 1991. *A History of Macroeconometric Model-Building.* Aldershot, U.K.: Edward Elgar.

Breusch, Trevor, and Adrian Pagan. 1980. The Lagrange Multiplier Test and Its Applications to Model Specification in Econometrics. *Review of Economic Studies* 47 (1): 239–253.

Intriligator, Michael. 1983. Economic and Econometric Models. In *Handbook of Econometrics*, vol. 1, eds. Zvi Griliches and Michael Intriligator, 181–221. Amsterdam: North-Holland.

Seneta, Eugene. 2006. Path Analysis. In *Encyclopedia of Statistical Sciences*, vol. 9, eds. Samuel Kotz, N. Balakrishnan, Campbell Read, and Brandi Vidakovic, 6016–6018. Hoboken, NJ: Wiley-Interscience.

Wright, Sewall. 1921. Correlation and Causation. *Journal of Agricultural Research* 20 (7): 557–585.

Zellner, Arnold. 1962. An Efficient Method of Estimating Seemingly Unrelated Regressions and Tests for Aggregation Bias. *Journal of the American Statistical Association* 57 (June): 348–368.

Robert Dixon

RED ARMY

SEE *Chinese Revolution.*

RED BOOK (CHINA)

SEE *Little Red Book.*

REDUCED FORM EQUATION

SEE *Variables, Predetermined.*

REDUCTIONISM

Reductionism is the hypothesis that science is unified by chains of intertheoretic reductions across disciplines, with theories from basic physics providing the ultimate ground. The classic work on intertheoretic reduction in the philosophy of science is chapter 11 of Ernest Nagel's *The Structure of Science.* For Nagel, reduction is logical deduction (derivation) of the statements of the reduced theory T_R from those of the reducing theory T_B. In interesting cases from science's history, the T_Rs contain terms that do not occur within the descriptive vocabulary of T_B (e.g., equilibrium thermodynamics contains "pressure" and "temperature," which do not occur in statistical mechanics and the kinetic/corpuscular theory of matter). Such cases are especially prominent in the psychological and social sciences because their theories developed mostly independently of one another. To derive such T_Rs from T_Bs in something other than a trivial fashion, Nagel insisted that the premises of the derivation require bridge principles connecting terms across the theories (e.g., "temperature in a gas is mean kinetic energy of molecular constituents"). Furthermore, most historical scientific reductions are corrective—they indicate where the T_R is false. Thus Nagel insisted that the premises of the deduction must contain not only the T_B and the necessary bridge principles but also various limiting assumptions and boundary conditions on T_B's application, some of which are contrary to fact. These elements circumscribe the falsity in the premises of the valid derivation of a false conclusion (T_R) away from the (presumed true) T_B. Challenges to Nagel's account were quickly raised by philosophers of science, but virtually every alternative account of intertheoretic reduction—for example those by Kenneth F. Schaffner in 1967 and Clifford Hooker in 1981—emerged as a direct response to Nagel's details.

With physics providing the ultimate reducing theories, reductionism is allied with physicalism about mental and social phenomena. As an explicit program, it has focused primarily on cases from biology and psychology rather than the social sciences. The rationale is straightforward: Claims about accomplished reductions in the former remain controversial, and if these controversies cannot be resolved, then the plausibility of the program for the latter seems remote. However, social phenomena do make an explicit appearance in one of the classic papers on reductionism in the philosophy of science. Paul Oppenheim and Hilary Putnam (1958, p. 7) illustrate the "working hypothesis" of the unity of science as follows:

6......... Social groups

5......... (Multicellular) living things

4......... Cells

3......... Molecules

2......... Atoms

1......... Elementary particles

Each level is related as parts (below) to wholes (immediately above), with "micro-reductions" hypothesized to obtain between theories explaining phenomena at a lower and an immediately higher level. And while Oppenheim and Putnam admit that accomplished micro-reductions from levels 6 to 5 have not advanced very far, they cite individual choice theories in economics and the "principal theoretical approaches" in sociology (Marxist, Veblenian, Weberian, Mannheimian) as examples of attempted micro-reductions to individualist psychology.

One popular general criticism of reductionism focuses on the *multiple realizability* of given higher-level kinds on lower-level mechanisms. (Bickle's 2006 article "Multiple Realizability" provides a survey of these arguments and many reductionist responses, with an extensive bibliography.) An example from the social sciences often appealed to is Gresham's law (colloquially stated, that "bad money drives out good," and more precisely stated in terms of what happens in monetary exchanges under specific exchange conditions). Monetary exchange is realized by a wide variety of physical phenomena—exchanging paper bills or minted coins or strings of wampum, signing checks, or depressing the "Enter" button on one's desktop computer, to name just a few. It seems a safe empirical bet that no single physical kind, described and studied by some lower-level physical science, obtains in all these cases (not to mention in the myriad possible realizations of monetary exchange). One could disjoin all the lower-level realizers of such a high-level kind, but it seems an even safer bet that the resulting disjunctive kind does not occur in the explanatory laws of any physical science from which the laws of the higher-level science can be derived.

From the mid-1970s until the mid-1990s this argument held sway against reductionism. A few replies emerged during this time. Some reductionists advocated domain-specific reductions, limited to classes of realizers that shared lower-level mechanisms. Others pointed out examples of accomplished reductions from science's history that included multiply realized kinds in the reduced theories, showing that multiple realizability is not sufficient by itself to block intertheoretic reduction. Since the late 1990s some critics have appealed to different "grains" in the characterizations of higher- and lower-level kinds. Advocates of multiple realizability tend to tolerate a wide variety of functional differences in their specification of higher-level kinds shared across distinct realizers, but they insist that a single (minute) physical difference indicates distinct lower-level kinds. When grains are matched across higher- and lower-level theories, multiple realizability vanishes. Others have noticed a dilemma for advocates of multiple realizability. The more that the physical mechanisms across distinct realizers are similar, the less likely is *multiple* realization of the same higher-level kind. The more that the physical mechanisms are dissimilar, the easier it is to find functional differences across realizers at the higher level and hence the less likely is multiple realization

of *the same* higher-level kind. At the time of this writing, anti-reductionists appealing to multiple realizability owe responses to these challenges.

A more diffuse anti-reductionist argument focuses on the *complexity* of social phenomena. Most likely it is this intuition that lies behind critiques of reductionist approaches by critics of neoclassical economics: Reducing social phenomena to the dynamics of individual decision makers will fail to explain some crucial economic or social features. (Reductionism to individuals is often characterized as "doctrinaire" or "simplistic" in the social sciences.) But turning this intuition into rational argument is not easy. One recent attempt applies the sophisticated mathematics of *complexity theory* to social sciences—dynamical systems, chaotic nonlinearity, trajectories through high-dimensional state spaces, and the like. Explanations in the form of differential equations are proposed to account for the behavior of *systems*, but not in terms of the mechanical outputs of its components. (Timothy van Gelder's application of complexity theory to cognitive psychology is a detailed attempt of this sort.) The principal worry is whether the "reductionism" targeted here is a straw man. If the behavior of systems requires these explanatory resources, then so will the lower-level sciences that appeal not only to the structure but also the dynamics and organization of the systems' components. The philosopher William Bechtel (2001), for example, replies that complexity is compatible with reduction, in the form of decomposition and localization explanatory strategies. He argues not just on conceptual grounds but also by appealing to empirical work by cognitive neuroscientists studying memory.

SEE ALSO *Choice in Economics; Choice in Psychology; Determinism; Economics; Economics, Neoclassical; Individualism; Marginalism; Materialism; Microeconomics; Objectivism; Psychology; Rational Choice Theory; Sociology; Sociology, Micro-*

BIBLIOGRAPHY

Bechtel, William. 2001. The Compatibility of Complex Systems and Reduction: A Case Analysis of Memory Research. *Minds and Machines* 11: 483–502.

Bickle, John. 2006. Multiple Realizability. In *Stanford Encyclopedia of Philosophy*, ed. Edward N. Zalta. http://plato.stanford.edu/archives/fall2006/entries/multiple-realizability.

Hooker, Clifford. 1981. Towards a General Theory of Reduction. Part 1, Historical and Scientific Setting. Part 2, Identity in Reduction. Part 3, Cross-Categorial Reductions. *Dialogue* 20: 38–59, 201–236, 496–529.

Nagel, Ernest. 1961. *The Structure of Science: Problems in the Logic of Scientific Explanation.* New York: Harcourt, Brace and World.

Oppenheim, Paul, and Hilary Putnam. 1958. Unity of Science as a Working Hypothesis. In *Concepts, Theories, and the Mind-Body Problem*, Vol. 2 of *Minnesota Studies in the Philosophy of Science*, ed. Herbert Feigl, Michael Scriven, and Grover Maxwell, 3–36. Minneapolis: University of Minnesota Press.

Schaffner, Kenneth F. 1967. Approaches to Reduction. *Philosophy of Science* 34 (2): 137–147.

Van Gelder, Timothy. 1998. The Dynamical Hypothesis in Cognitive Science. *Behavioral and Brain Sciences* 21: 615–628.

John Bickle

REFERENDUM

A referendum is a form of direct democracy in which the entire electorate votes to accept or reject a policy proposal. Nearly all democracies in the international community provide for national referendums. Yet there is no provision in the U.S. Constitution for one. The Tenth Amendment implies that referendums are left up to the states. Because of this, states decide individually whether to allow referendums and how they are to proceed.

In the United States a *legislative referendum* is an election in which the state legislature passes a bill for consideration by a state's voters for final adoption. Not all states have a legislative referendum provision for nonconstitutional issues, even though all states except Delaware allow or require constitutional amendments to be approved through referendums. Some states allow for voters to overrule legislation by referendum, so long as supporters gather a requisite number of signatures. This is known as the *popular referendum*. Twenty-four states (mostly in the American West) and myriad local governments provide for legislative and popular referendums. Referendums are similar to but conceptually distinct from *initiatives*. Although similar in that the people have the final say to support or oppose a policy and citizens groups may be required to gather signatures for both referendums and initiatives, referendums are a direct response to action by the legislature. Conversely, citizens, citizens groups, or other interest groups initiate the policy proposal to be placed on an election ballot.

REFERENDUMS AS PROGRESSIVE REFORMS

The history and initiation of referendums in the United States is a product of the progressive reforms. In response to the political corruption of party machines in urban areas throughout the United States, the Progressives pushed numerous reforms to depoliticize politics.

Progressive reforms began with the creation of the federal civil service system with the Pendleton Act of 1883. They also included state-printed secret ballots, direct primary elections, nonpartisan elections, and initiatives, recalls, and referendums. The goal of these reforms was to wrest political control away from centralized and strong political parties and return democracy to the people. Although they had their intended effect of weakening political parties, they also contributed to a significant decline in voter participation over time. Even directly deciding policy through referendums is typically not sufficient to mobilize high voter turnout.

States vary in their use of referendum. For legislative, nonconstitutional referendums, California requires that the measure, with valid signatures equal in number to 5 percent of all votes cast in the previous gubernatorial contest, be presented to the secretary of state within ninety days after its enactment by the state legislature. The secretary of state then submits the referendum for placement on the ballot in the next general or special election, or the governor may request a special election. California's procedure for legislative referendum is fairly typical of most other states. California used the legislative referendum process in 2000 to pass Proposition 22, which held that only heterosexual marriages were legally valid in the state. Citizens in the state of South Dakota relied on a popular referendum to overturn, or veto, a 2006 state law that would have banned abortion except to protect the life of the mother. Citizens were required to gather over 18,000 valid signatures (or 5 percent of votes cast in the previous gubernatorial race) to place this popular referendum on the November 2006 ballot. Texas state law requires that any amendment to the Texas Constitution be approved by two-thirds of both houses of the state legislature and then placed on an election ballot for final adoption by the voters. In November 2005 Texas amended its constitution in this manner by defining marriage as a union between a man and a woman. All states may place advisory or nonbinding referendums on an election ballot. These referendums have no binding policy effect but instead are consultative referendums initiated by the government, perhaps, to poll the electorate as to their general belief on an issue. It is ultimately up to the state legislature whether to embrace or ignore these results.

CONSEQUENCES OF REFERENDUMS

Although the goal of referendums and other forms of direct democracy is to allow people to decide policy, there may be unintended consequences for some of the people as a result of these popular initiatives. James Madison (1751–1836), fourth president of the United States, warned about the deleterious effects of factions, that majority will—if left unchecked—could actually punish the minority, creating a "tyranny of the majority." For these and other reasons, the framers of the U.S. Constitution adopted a document that was exceedingly thin on direct democratic provisions but instead provided for representative democracy.

With the institution and proliferation of forms of direct democracy as a policy tool in the late twentieth century, scholars began to explore the consequences of direct democracy and whether or not referendums or initiatives actually harm minorities. Barbara Gamble found in her 1997 article "Putting Civil Rights to a Popular Vote," for instance, that local and state ballot measures (referendum included) typically harm minorities, and she concluded that representative democracy protects minorities better than direct democracy does. Todd Donovan and Shaun Bowler showed in their 1998 article "Direct Democracy and Minority Rights: An Extension," on the other hand, that direct democracy is not necessarily harmful to minorities. Instead, largely populated areas with well-educated citizens tend to adopt ballot measures that actually protect homosexuals. Donovan and Bowler concluded that both direct and representative democracies have comparable limitations in protecting specific minority groups.

The claim that referendums reflect the popular will of the majority or that they provide for direct democracy in the truest sense is open to question for several reasons. First, as with most other elections, only a small and self-selected percentage of the voting public participates in referendum elections. Constitutional amendments that must be approved of through referendum may be placed on the ballot during special elections, not associated with either statewide or nationally elected office. The skew in voter participation for these referendums is likely to be especially pronounced. Moreover many of these referendums may pertain to mundane matters, such as issuing bonds for economic development or pollution control, which are not of interest to many voters. Second, large states, like California and Texas, may have too many referendums on an election ballot, which may cause voters to *roll off*, or not finish the ballot, actually reducing the proportion of voters who participate. Indeed the 2006 midterm election ballot used in several California counties was over 120 pages long. Third, referendums may be worded in a confusing fashion, with a "yes" vote supporting change in one referendum and a "no" vote supporting change in another. Fourth, voters may make policy based on a whim, not careful research, leading to ineffective or countereffective policies. Finally, government accountability may be reduced if citizens—not their elected representatives—are responsible for making public policy.

Unlike the United States, referendums are more central to governance in many other democracies, with numerous states relying extensively on national referendums for policy making. Switzerland's referendum process is central to policy making, whether for constitutional amendments, legislative enactments, or according to Lawrence LeDuc in his 2003 book *The Politics of Direct Democracy: Referendums in a Global Perspective*, "rejective" referendums. It does not have a nonbinding or advisory referendum provision. Although Sweden provides for both binding and nonbinding referendums, most of its late-twentieth-century referendums were advisory to the legislature. Other countries use the referendum process to approve constitutional amendments (France), vote on independence (Puerto Rico), recall politicians from office (Venezuela), determine public policy directly (Brazil), or decide European Union membership (United Kingdom).

SEE ALSO *Accountability; California Civil Rights Initiative; Democracy, Representative and Participatory; Government; Initiative; Representation; Voting*

BIBLIOGRAPHY

Braunstein, Richard. 2004. *Initiatives and Referendum: Governing through Direct Democracy in the United States.* New York: LFB Scholarly Publishing.

Donovan, Todd, and Shaun Bowler. 1998. Direct Democracy and Minority Rights: An Extension. *American Journal of Political Science* 42 (3): 1020–1024.

Gamble, Barbara. 1997. Putting Civil Rights to a Popular Vote. *American Journal of Political Science* 41 (1): 245–269.

LeDuc, Lawrence. 2003. *The Politics of Direct Democracy: Referendums in a Global Perspective.* Toronto: Broadview.

Matthew Eshbaugh-Soha

REFLECTION PROBLEM

In his extension of the identification problem to the social sciences, Charles Manski, in his book *Identification Problems in the Social Sciences* (1995), poses the reflection problem. The problem surfaces when one tries to predict the behavior of an individual by the behavior of the group of which the individual is a member. The problem is likened to the image of a person reflected in a mirror. The mirror can be said to reflect the image of the person's motion or to reflect the image and the person moving together consequent to an external stimulus.

The reflection problem is further explained through the variables used in a statistical model. Standard identification problems in economics use observations of prices and quantities, two endogenous variables, to reveal consumers' and producers' behavior. The economist would add predetermined variables to identify the demand and supply curves. The reflection problem, however, looks at other endogenous effects that are overlooked or ignored in the standard order-and-rank identification process in economics. These additional variables are used mostly by sociologists who are concerned with how problems are reflected from society to the individual, while economists usually use social effects as constraints of individual opportunities.

Modern researchers are unable to solve the reflection problem through the modeling of output data, which cannot capture the reflection problem. One of their hypotheses might be that individuals belonging to a group tend to behave similarly. The researchers probe their models for endogenous, contextual, and correlated effects. Models with endogenous effects explain variations in individual behavior by the prevalence of the behavior in a group. Individuals behave similarly because they may experience pressure to conform to certain norms. Models of contextual effects explain individual behavior with the variation of background characteristics of the group, such as the influence of the neighborhood environment. Models of correlated effects assess whether individuals facing a similar environment or sharing similar individual characteristics will behave the same way. For example, people may associate with each other because they share similar characteristics.

Manski provides an intuitive example to explain the problem of separating these effects. A measure of the mean behavior of the group will contain the individual behavior. A measure of the outcome of a group behavior might simply be an aggregation of individual behaviors. One cannot be sure, therefore, that it reveals the individual behavior. By using the mean behavior of a group, the mean value of exogenous attributes of a group, or similar characteristics of members of a group to explain individual behavior, one captures exogenous, contextual, and correlated effects, respectively. To infer individual behavior from a measure of group behavior would require prior information that explains the composition of the group. To distinguish among these effects, it is necessary to know something more about how the groups are formed and how the members interact.

One can solve the reflection problem if one knows that the group mean influences individual behavior with a specific lag structure. Analogous assertions can be made if the researchers know a nonlinear specification, specific group features, or some instrument that conveys influences from the group to the individual. Generally, such information is not available.

SEE ALSO *Behaviorism; General Linear Model; Identification Problem; Least Squares, Ordinary; Nonlinear Regression; Structural Equation Models*

BIBLIOGRAPHY

Manski, Charles F. 1993. Identification of Endogenous Social Effects: The Reflection Problem. *Review of Economic Studies* 60 (3): 531–542.

Manski, Charles F. 1995. *Identification Problems in the Social Sciences.* Cambridge, MA: Harvard University Press.

Manski, Charles F. 2003. Identification Problems in the Social Sciences and Everyday Life. *Southern Economic Journal* 70 (1): 11–21.

Lall Ramrattan
Michael Szenberg

REFLEXIVE COUNSCIOUSNESS

SEE *Consciousness.*

REFLEXIVITY

Individuals, institutions, and societies are reflexive: They "turn back" upon themselves to observe, reference, describe, predict, assess and explain their own ways and workings. *Reflexive turns* are not mere adjuncts to social life: They make it possible and increasingly comprise its very fabric. Selfhood, mind, and agency are constituted through the human capacity to reflexively make an object of oneself. Individuals interact with one another in light of their reflexive understanding of the contexts and consequences of their actions. Innumerable professionals—social scientists among them—audit, analyze, and forecast the functioning of organizations, institutions, and the society itself. Reflexive turns, then, are implicated in the very construction of social actors, social actions, and the disciplines and professions that study and monitor them.

Reflexive turns are complexly related to the circumstances from which they emerge. First, rather than mirror a preexistent domain, reflexive turns are constitutively *entwined* with the form, dynamics, and even existence of what is observed or described. Self-fulfilling prophecies illustrate one way reflexive "knowledge" about circumstances affects their development. In the classic example of self-fulfilling prophecies provided by R. K. Merton in 1948, rumors of insolvency precipitate a run on a financially sound bank culminating in actual insolvency. Second, while reflexive turns may claim an objective vantage point from which to observe, analyze, and explain, they are *embedded* in and informed by the embodied, interactional, organizational, and cultural contexts from which they emerge. A perspicuous example of the embeddedness of reflexive explanations is provided by E. E. Evans-Pritchard's 1937 study of Azande beliefs regarding magic, witchcraft, and oracles. Azande explanations of the occasional failure of oracles to correctly predict future events were predicated on the cultural assumptions that contributed to belief in the efficacy of oracles in the first place. Finally, reflexive turns efface their own embeddedness and entwining. Forgetful of both their origins and contributions to what they "discover," reflexive turns (including this description of reflexive turns) treat the phenomena they discern as preexistent independent objects and themselves as (mere) observation, revelation, or representation.

INQUIRY INTO REFLEXIVITY AND REFLEXIVE INQUIRY

The embedded and entwined features of reflexive turns are topics of social scientific inquiry. Studies of social interaction, for example, highlight how discourse and background knowledge "about" a social setting contributes to its collaborative construction. Studies in economic sociology and kindred fields identify how lay and professional economic reasoning shapes financial markets and even the reasoners themselves. In examining how economic theories are appropriated by the society, Fabrizio Ferraro, Jeffrey Pfeffer, and Robert I. Sutton in 2005 suggested that as the model of *homo economicus* of classical economics infiltrates the discourse, norms, and circumstances of society, individuals increasingly invoke, conform to and thereby "validate" the model intended to explain their behavior. Analysts of major sociohistorical developments suggest that "late-modern" social life is marked by unprecedented levels of institutional and individual reflexive monitoring. Modern life requires, as Anthony Giddens observed in 1991, that "the question, 'How shall I live?' has to be answered in day-to-day decisions about how to behave, what to wear and what to eat" (Giddens 1991, p. 14).

In addition to being a topic for social science, reflexive turns are also challenges to social science. Nourished by the sociology of knowledge and amplified by the heightened reflexivity of late modernity, a panoply of voices asserts that the social (and natural) sciences have yet to recognize the full extent of their own embedding in and entwining with the processes they study. Calls for reflexive inquiry (in contrast to inquiry into reflexivity) challenge social scientists to explicate how they themselves and their projects, perspectives, operations, and findings are embedded in a nexus of enabling and constraining relationships, presuppositions, interests, and practices whose operation and effects escape the delimited self-reflection of conventional inquiry.

Reflexive inquiry bids researchers to address themselves, their inquiries, and the inquiries' products in terms of the processes found elsewhere in social life. On the micro level, reflexive inquiry focuses on tacit practices of categorization, interpretation, interaction, and textualization through which research is conducted. On the institutional level, reflexive inquiry examines how various contexts or fields foster intellectual dispositions and prejudgments that form what Pierre Bourdieu in 1992 referred to as "the collective scientific unconscious" (Bourdieu and Wacquant 1992). On the structural level, reflexive inquiry invites self-examination in terms of how the process and products of inquiry are shaped by the researcher's social location in political, economic, ethnic, or gender hierarchies.

PROBLEMS AND PROMISES OF REFLEXIVE INQUIRY

Promising to deepen and even improve research, reflexive inquiry may give rise to unsettling problems. Reflexive inquiry tends to blur the very distinctions between observer and observed and between representation and reality upon which conventional inquiry is predicated. Further, explication of the embedded and entwined features of social scientific inquiry threatens to initiate an infinite regress in which each successive reflexive turn calls forth yet another to explicate its predecessor. Moreover, reflexive inquiry may so divest itself of analytic concepts (treating them as phenomena to be reflexively explicated) that it threatens to devolve into a vacuous exercise. Finally, the extent to which reflexive inquiry can access and explicate the effaced background of research is uncertain. Unsurprisingly, social scientists vary in their enthusiasm for taking the reflexive turn and exposing themselves to these (and other) problems.

The ways persons, institutions, and societies take account of themselves are constitutive processes of social life. The social sciences are themselves reflexive turns and thus are charged not only with inquiry into reflexivity but also with reflexive inquiry, that is, with explicating their own embeddedness in and entwining with the affairs they purport to illuminate. The dividends of reflexive inquiry include insight into the constitutive role of observation, description, and analysis and the practices and prejudgments implicated in such activities. As daunting as they may be, the unsettling problems of reflexive inquiry, in the very ways they unsettle, are potent resources for discerning fundamental assumptions, practices, and limits of social science.

SEE ALSO *Anthropology; Ethnography; Ethnology and Folklore; Observation, Participant; Primitivism*

BIBLIOGRAPHY

Ashmore, Malcolm. 1989. *The Reflexive Thesis: Wrighting Sociology of Scientific Knowledge.* Chicago: Chicago University Press.

Bourdieu, Pierre. 2004. *Science of Science and Reflexivity.* Trans. Richard Nice. Chicago: University of Chicago Press.

Bourdieu, Pierre, and Loic J. D. Wacquant. 1992. *An Invitation to Reflexive Sociology.* Cambridge, U.K.: Polity.

Evans-Pritchard, E. E. 1937. *Witchcraft, Oracles, and Magic among the Azande.* London: Oxford University Press.

Ferraro, Fabrizio, Jeffrey Pfeffer, and Robert I. Sutton. 2005. Economics, Language, and Assumptions: How Theories Can Become Self-Fulfilling. *Academy of Management Review* 30 (1): 8–24.

Garfinkel, Harold. 1967. *Studies in Ethnomethodology.* Englewood Cliffs, NJ: Prentice-Hall.

Giddens, Anthony. 1991. *Modernity and Self-Identity: Self and Society in the Late Modern Age.* Stanford, CA: Stanford University Press.

Lynch, Michael. 2000. Against Reflexivity as an Academic Virtue and Source of Privileged Knowledge. *Theory, Culture, and Society* 17 (3): 26–54.

Mannheim, Karl. 1968. *Ideology and Utopia: An Introduction to the Sociology of Knowledge.* Trans. Louis Wirth and Edward Shils. New York: Harcourt, Brace, and World.

Mead, George H. 1934. *Mind, Self, and Society: From the Standpoint of a Social Behaviorist,* ed. Charles W. Morris. Chicago: University of Chicago Press.

Merton, R. K. 1948. The Self-Fulfilling Prophecy. *Antioch Review* 8: 193–210.

Pollner, Melvin. 1987. *Mundane Reason: Reality in Everyday and Sociological Discourse.* Cambridge, U.K.: Cambridge University Press.

Woolgar, Steve, ed. 1988. *Knowledge and Reflexivity: New Frontiers in the Sociology of Knowledge.* London: Sage.

Melvin Pollner

REFUGEE CAMPS

Refugee camp refers to a place where temporary housing is provided by governments or nongovernmental organizations (NGOs) for persons displaced from their homes due to war, political oppression, and/or religious persecution. The displaced person, referred to as a refugee, is someone with a well-founded fear of persecution on the basis of his or her race, religion, nationality, membership in a particular social group, or political opinion, who is outside of his or her country of nationality and unable or unwilling to return. A broader definition might include internally displaced persons (IDPs), those who had been uprooted within their own countries.

The basic infrastructure for refugee camps normally includes sleeping accommodations, hygiene facilities (bathrooms and showers), medical supplies, and communication equipment but the quality of infrastructure varies within and across geographic locations. The camp sites might be composed of tents, huts, or boxcar living structures. The development of refugee camps, however, is not always the result of government or NGO initiatives. Often makeshift refugee camps emerge because of massive numbers of people fleeing conflictual situations gathering in spaces that offer some greater level of personal security. At this point governments and organizations providing humanitarian assistance intervene to provide relief that might include latrines, food, medical assistance, and sleeping accommodations.

HISTORICAL DEVELOPMENT

Refugee camps are not solely a contemporary world phenomenon. One of the earliest recorded refugee camps is described in the biblical account of the Israelites' flight from Egypt in Exodus. Moreover, throughout human history there have always existed clashes of interests that had profound implications for human suffering, forced removal from homelands, and caused displacement. The development of refugee camps, however, is associated most often with conflicts transpiring in the contemporary world. In the aftermath of World War I significant numbers of people could be categorized as refugees, but the existence of refugee camps took on global significance after World War II and has become increasingly more common since the end of the cold war.

At the end of both world wars, individuals who feared for their lives or otherwise felt threatened were likely to seek refuge by fleeing to another country. The United Nations (UN) Charter included provisions that established the UN High Commissioner for Refugees (UNHCR) in 1951. The UNHCR had a mandate to seek durable solutions for affected refugee populations through repatriation programs, integration into host communities of the country of first asylum, or resettlement in a third country. This indicates that refugee camps as they have come to be known in the early-twenty-first century were not as widely dispersed globally as they were in the late 1990s. However, one of the oldest known camps, which was created in 1948, still exists in Palestine. Internal conflicts that can be traced back to the end of colonialism have contributed to the proliferation of refugee camps in modern times. The end of the cold war also revived historic animosities and ethnic tensions leading to increased numbers of complex emergencies, increased numbers of people affected by them, and a change in the nature of population displacements that contributed to a proliferation of refugee camps. Such conflicts coupled with natural catastrophes have created a global challenge and make clear the need to ensure that people worldwide enjoy security and freedom.

TWENTY-FIRST CENTURY PERSPECTIVES

According to the 2005 World Refugee Survey, there were more than 11 million refugees worldwide and more than 21 million IDPs as of December 2004. Not all refugees live in camps, and it is difficult to obtain reliable data pertaining to the actual number who do. In some cases, refugees permanently settle in the host country and integrate into the communities in which they live. In other cases, it is difficult to distinguish between what constitutes the refugee camp, camps for IDPs, and normal housing for a given area. Even so, providing basic accommodations for refugees, as well as IDPs, is a problem that demands global attention. The number of refugees and IDPs associated with ethnic conflicts—such as those in Rwanda in 1994; the Sudan from the 1980s to 2006; East Timor; Kosovo in the 1990s; Afghanistan; and other Third World countries—led to the establishment of refugee camps such as those in Musasa in Northern Burundi; Mboki in Central Africa Republic; Darfur, Sudan; Karama in the Democratic Republic of Congo; Kupang in Indonesia; and Kelli Fazo in Pakistan, which are some of the most populated sites.

Despite enormous efforts by the UN, host governments, and NGOs to render these and other refugee camps livable, conditions have ranged from bearable to horrendous. Some lack very basic supplies such as potable drinking water, latrines, medical supplies, and ample food. Diseases are widespread; many of the children lack access to medical care of any kind and schooling can be unavailable or inadequate; and some refugees live under the threat of forced removal from camps. Although refugee camps tend to be set up near border areas, away from conflicts, many are subject to violence inflicted upon the inhabitants by government forces and/or insurgents on both sides of the border.

One of the greatest threats to peace and security in the twenty-first century is the large-scale movement of refugees and other forced migrants stemming mostly from internal conflicts and natural catastrophes. Failure to address the problem may lead to greater ethnic conflict within countries and across borders, the uncontrollable spread of disease, and greater environmental degradation. Given that Third World nations hosting refugees have challenges in terms of meeting the needs and demands of their own citizens, industrialized nations must step up their efforts to address the problem. In addition to providing financial and humanitarian support, these nations must pressure governments to observe human rights; demonstrate a stronger commitment to timely diplomatic intervention, as a first step, to avert conflicts that are likely to increase the refugee population; and revisit restrictive asylum policies that came to fruition during the 1980s.

SEE ALSO *Disease; Genocide; Nongovernmental Organizations (NGOs); Palestinian Diaspora; Palestinians; Refugees; War; World War I; World War II*

BIBLIOGRAPHY

Homer-Dixon, Thomas. 1994. Environmental Scarcity and Intergroup Conflict. In *World Security: Challenges for a New Century*, 2nd ed., eds. Michael T. Klare and Daniel C. Thomas, 290–313. New York: St. Martin's.

Tessitore, John, and Susan Woolfson, eds. 1995. *A Global Agenda: Issues before the 50th General Assembly of the United Nations.* New York: University Press of America.

United Nations High Commissioner for Refugees. 1995. *The State of the World's Refugees.* New York: Oxford University Press.

United States Committee for Refugees and Immigrants. 2005. *World Refugee Survey 2005.* Washington, DC: Author.

Kathie Stromile Golden

REFUGEES

Refugees are a subset of immigrants often termed *political migrants*. They are pushed out of their homelands, typically by war or government persecution due to religion, ethnicity, or political activism. For example, Albert Einstein (1879–1955), often considered the most influential scientist of the twentieth century, was among the Jews who left Germany during the 1930s due to Nazi anti-Semitism. The Buddhist monk His Holiness the Dalai Lama is an internationally recognized advocate of human rights for Tibetans; he fled Tibet in 1959 following the brutal crackdown by China against Tibetans opposing Chinese rule.

In contrast to refugees, most immigrants are pulled from their homes by the prospects of better jobs in other countries, or to join family members who already reside abroad. These economic and social forms of international migration allow time for a considerable amount of planning and preparation. Such immigrants often believe they will return to their homelands at some point in the future. Refugee migrations, however, are unanticipated and forced, and will keep the émigrés away from home for a very long time, possibly for the rest of their lives.

Since the mid-1990s the world has averaged between 11 million and 15 million refugees per year. The majority are women and children. The United Nations (UN) first defined a refugee in 1951 as a person who "owing to a well founded fear of persecution for reasons of race, religion, nationality, membership of a particular social group or political opinion, is outside the country of his nationality and is unable or, owing to such fear, is unwilling to avail himself of that country." This definition is contained in the 1951 Convention Relating to the Status of Refugees, which was developed in the aftermath of World War II (1939–1945) and only pertained to people in Europe. The 1967 Protocol Relating to the Status of Refugees broadened the policy to include people in the rest of the world. Today there are five refugee populations numbering 500,000 people or more: those from the former Palestine, Afghanistan, Iraq, Myanmar (Burma), and Sudan.

The 1951 convention and the 1967 protocol establish the rights of refugees in exile, including the rights to protection, movement, and work. They specifically prohibit *refoulement*—the forced return of refugees to a country where they would be persecuted. One hundred forty-five countries have signed the convention and/or the protocol, but forty-four countries, including India, Pakistan, and Indonesia, have not. Some governments use the UN definition of *refugee* in their national laws, as the United States did when it passed the landmark Refugee Act of 1980. Nonetheless, foreign-policy interests often determine to what degree signatories of the convention and protocol actually abide by them. The U.S. government historically has given a very favorable reception to political migrants from Cuba, but uses the U.S. Coast Guard to interdict those leaving Haiti.

There have been several global trends in refugee migrations since World War II. European decolonization produced intense ethnic conflict in newly independent states in Africa and Asia (e.g., the 1947 partition of India), and it was a major cause of refugee crises from the late 1940s through the 1960s. The cold war between the United States, the former Soviet Union, and the client states of each superpower was the main cause of refugee crises from the 1960s through the 1980s. In the United States the best known cold-war refugees are the Cubans and the Vietnamese.

Since the 1990s a new cause of refugees has been the total collapse of national institutions in some countries (termed *failed states*), leading to perpetual social conflict and disorder. This occurred in Somalia during the early 1990s, and other countries in Africa have followed this same pattern. In the western hemisphere, Haiti shows many signs of being a failed state and Colombia has some symptoms as well. Two catastrophic ethnic conflicts occurred almost simultaneously in the mid-1990s: More than 1 million Bosnian refugees fled Serbian ethnic cleansing in Bosnia, and about 2 million Hutus fled Rwanda when Tutsi forces regained power following the genocide of some 800,000 Tutsis at the hands of Hutu militias.

The UN High Commissioner for Refugees, created in 1950, is the primary international body charged with advocating for refugees and providing them with assistance. Many nongovernmental organizations (NGOs) also assist refugees, such as the U.S. Committee for Refugees, U.S. Catholic Conference, and Médecins Sans Frontières (Doctors Without Borders). NGOs lobby states for more favorable policies, provide services in refugee camps, and facilitate adaptation when refugees resettle in host countries or repatriate to their homelands. But refugees often endure years of waiting in impoverished, segregated camps, a situation termed *warehousing*. If the root political problems remain unresolved for a long time, warehousing creates multigenerational refugee populations. Nearly 2 million Afghani refugees reside in Iran and Pakistan, a legacy of the Soviet invasion in 1979 and subsequent wars. About 2.5 million Palestinians throughout the Middle East receive assistance from the UN Relief and Works Administration for Palestine Refugees. The Palestinians were originally displaced by the wars that followed the creation of Israel in 1948.

An important legal distinction for political migrants is whether they seek refugee status before or after arriving in a host country where they hope to permanently reside. The United States, Canada, Australia, and the countries of the European Union allow people with a well-founded fear of persecution to apply for entry while still living in their homelands or in adjacent countries to which they have fled. Since passage of the Refugee Act of 1980 the United States has accepted more than 2.5 million refugees in this way. Congress and the president establish an annual refugee admissions quota, and refugees who arrive are eligible for social welfare programs operated by the federal government, state governments, and NGOs. Since 2000 the former Soviet Union, Somalia, and Iran have been the leading source countries of refugee admissions to the United States.

Actual or imminent persecution can be so dire that people flee without waiting for permission to resettle in a host country. When political migrants cross into another country without legal authorization and then apply for refugee status they are called *asylum seekers*. China, Haiti, El Salvador, and Guatemala are the sources of about 45 percent of all asylum seekers who have entered the United States since 1989. In western Europe most asylum seekers come from Turkey, Africa, and the Middle East. The United States and other western countries use legal proceedings, which often are hasty and haphazard, to determine whether asylum seekers have credible reasons to fear persecution if deported to their homelands. U.S. asylum officers approve fewer than half of all asylum requests. U.S. immigration judges adjudicate claims initially denied, but the success rate of these appeals is even lower.

People who flee persecution but stay within their native country rather than crossing an international border share many of the same experiences as refugees. They are termed *internally displaced persons* (IDPs). The term *displaced persons* gained prominence in Europe after World War II, when it was used to describe Poles, Germans, and other people who were outside their homelands due to the war; in some cases they did not wish to return home. IDPs now is used to refer to people who have fled persecution or war but who cannot avail themselves of the 1951 convention or the 1967 protocol because they are still within the jurisdiction of the state which regulates their citizenship.

There are more IDPs in the world than refugees: about 25 million compared to 11.5 million. Five countries have more than 1 million IDPs: Sudan, Colombia, Uganda, Congo-Kinshasa, and Iraq. International protection and aid for IDPs conflicts with national sovereignty and requires asserting that a state is unwilling or incapable of protecting its own citizens. For a brief period during the 1990s the UN undertook such humanitarian intervention in northern Iraq, Bosnia, and Somalia. Unfortunately, the humanitarian crisis that began in 2003 in the Darfur region of Sudan did not produce a similar response from the international community. In 2005 the UN adopted guidelines for assisting internally displaced persons by creating a division of labor among its various agencies. Social scientists are divided over whether or not to extend the concept of IDPs to the survivors of catastrophic natural disasters, such as the South Asian tsunami in 2004 and Hurricane Katrina on the U.S. Gulf Coast in 2005. Many of the people displaced by Hurricane Katrina were offended when the media described them as "refugees," believing that the label equated them with "foreigners" who did not merit the protections granted to "citizens." Whether to use the term *environmental refugees* to describe people who flee the environmental problems caused by deforestation and global warming is also a matter of debate.

There are two solutions to a refugee crisis. Voluntary repatriation occurs when homeland conditions have improved and the refugees return from abroad. They require economic development assistance similar to that provided for other projects in the developing world. Resettlement in the United States, Canada, Australia, and the European Union is a second though less frequent outcome for refugees. Resettled refugees share with other immigrants many of the same adaptation challenges, such as acculturation and finding employment. But refugees have some distinct adaptation concerns, including mental health problems and often a particularly intense interest in homeland politics. Given the trauma of forced migration, it is not surprising that refugees carry lifelong vestiges of their experiences.

SEE ALSO *Refugee Camps*

BIBLIOGRAPHY

Hein, Jeremy. 1993. Refugees, Immigrants, and the State. *Annual Review of Sociology* 19: 43–59.

Immigration and Refugee Services of America. 2004. 2004 Statistical Issue. *Refugee Reports* 25 (9): 1–13.

Massey, Douglas S., Joaquín Arango, Graeme Hugo, et al. 1998. *Worlds in Motion: Understanding International Migration at the End of the Millennium.* Oxford: Clarendon Press.

United Nations High Commissioner for Refugees. 2000. *The State of the World's Refugees: Fifty Years of Humanitarian Action.* Oxford: Oxford University Press.

U.S. Committee for Refugees. 2006. *World Refugee Survey 2006.* Washington, DC: Author.

Yin, Sandra. 2005. The Plight of Internally Displaced Persons. Population Reference Bureau Web site. http://www.prb.org/ Template.cfm?Section=PRB&template=/ ContentManagement/ContentDisplay.cfm&ContentID= 13240.

Zolberg, Aristide R., Astri Suhrke, and Sergio Aguayo. 1989. *Escape from Violence: Conflict and the Refugee Crisis in the Developing World.* New York: Oxford University Press.

Jeremy Hein

REGGAE

Reggae is a complex Afro-Jamaican twentieth-century musical phenomenon that has profoundly influenced global popular musical culture. As a genre of modern black cultural production, reggae music dates from the 1970s, when it emerged from the musical confluence of ska and rock steady, two forms born in early postcolonial Jamaica. As a cultural practice in Jamaican postcolonial society, reggae was closely tied to subaltern representations of slavery, colonialism, history, and Africa. As a consequence in many instances reggae became a counter-hegemonic practice critiquing the formal Jamaican Creole nationalist project of political independence.

Ska was a 1960s musical synthesis that ruptured the Jamaican musical form known as *mento*, which emerged from the encounter between European colonialism, racial plantation slavery, and the slave African population. Mento adapted and morphed the harmonic structures, instrumentation, and melodies of European musical styles into indigenous sounds. It added other instruments, in particular rhumba scrapers and drums, and wove melodic structures within the sound of the rhumba scraper to produce a unique rhythm to which many rural Jamaicans enjoyed dancing.

Profoundly influenced by African American jazz and big band swing music, ska broke with mento in two ways. It used different instrumentation, and it became an urban-based rather than a rural-based musical form. Ska was driven in part by two migratory patterns: the external migration to the American Eastern Seaboard and the internal migration between the island's rural areas and the capital city Kingston, where impoverished young men and women not only wanted to carve out a future but also brought with them the culture of the rural folk. Particularly in Kingston's western sections—Jones Town, Trench Town, and Denham Town—postcolonial popular Jamaican music found its moorings. This rural-to-urban shift in Jamaican society is visually captured by the opening moments of the film *The Harder They Come* and Jimmy Cliff's driving lyrics of the song: "You can get it if you really want."

In addition to ska, the cauldron of west Kingston gave birth to the sound system, the early recording industry, rock steady, and eventually to reggae. The Folkes Brothers' 1961 record *Oh Carolina* marks a watershed in Jamaican recorded music. With the Rastafarian nyabinghi-style drumming of Count Ossie forming the spine of the track, the song is now a classic of Jamaican music. Although ska incorporated big band horn-blowing elements, it differed from jazz and swing in the way Jamaican musicians sped up the second beat while slowing down the fourth, so that the music seemed offbeat with loose skips. One of the most important ska instrumentalists was the trombonist Don Drummond, who played with the Skatalites, perhaps Jamaica's most accomplished musicians at the time. This group produced such titles as "Freedom Sounds," "Far East," "Addis Ababa," and "Man in the Street," indicating the tight relationship between urban poor communities in Jamaica and Africa and certainly the cultural importance of Rastafari. The music of the Skatalites remains a rich archive of early Jamaican music.

Jamaican music is organically tied to dance and the body. There is no popular music without dance steps. In the history of Jamaican music, with its reliance on the local sound system as the conduit of its popularity, the participation of both audience and dancers in giving the music its form is critical. When the audience comprises primarily urban dwellers alienated from official society, then the relationship among the music, musicians, form, and audience becomes especially intimate and can become a practice of counter-signification. This practice is clearly illustrated by the morphing of ska into the musical form of rock steady. If ska began as the music of hope, it quickly came to express a growing alienation and despair, as "Simmer Down," the single most important ska hit of the Wailers, illustrates. In the song the Wailers ask the "rude bwoy" to "simmer down." The "rude bwoy" was the iconic young black male of the city, a figure of rebellion who began to confront notions of Jamaican citizenship and respectability. Prince Buster, the Nation of Islam producer and singer, also sang in "Judge Dread" of the confronta-

tion between the Jamaican justice system and the "rude bwoy." These songs were not reflective of but rather an integral part of Jamaican social and political discourse of the period.

In rock steady, the transitional music between ska and reggae, the music slowed down, lost its skip, became languid. The dance movements were transformed, with the shoulders and hands operating in different time from the motions of the pelvis. Singing groups were central to this style; the Wailers, Heptones, Ethiopians, Paragons, Melodians, and Mighty Diamonds were popular. Singers like Jimmy Cliff, Alton Ellis, Delroy Wilson, and Ken Boothe also emerged, and along with the centrality of the sound systems of Sir Coxsone and Duke Reid and Prince Buster, Jamaican popular music consolidated itself locally. The singers and instrumental creativity of ska and rock steady combined with the creative musical drives of the urban dispossessed population to lay the ground for reggae.

In reggae the drum and bass became pronounced and the individual singer was given more scope; the horns surround the bridge segments of the music, and the dancer skips and moves with feet free from the thralldom of postcolonial oppression, while the body retraces the memory of the Middle Passage. Reggae music relies heavily on the message it delivers—from Marley's "Trench Town Rock" to Junior Byles's "Fade Away" and perhaps that most reproduced of all reggae riddims, the rhythm of the Abyssinians, "Satta Massagana." Reggae music operates in the languages of black struggle and redemption and is shaped by the language—what Velma Pollard calls "dread talk"—and religious and political doctrines of Rastafari. Dread talk undertakes the lexical reorganization of Jamaican language in an effort to linguistically reorder society. The themes of reggae music are history, slavery, Africa, and exile alongside the machinations of record producers. These themes are lyrically enunciated in the idioms of proverbs, rereadings of biblical passages, Jamaican folksongs, and children's songs. The lyrical rhetorical strategies of many reggae songs are embedded within the social and linguistic complexities of Afro-Jamaican life. One only has to listen to the vast musical archives of the Black Ark studio of Lee Scratch Perry, of Channel One Studio operated by the Hoo-Kim brothers, and of Gussie Clarke to understand how reggae presented alternative narratives of Jamaica's history and postcolonial society. As the reggae producer Rupie Edwards put it, "The music was a way of life, the whole thing is not just a music being made … it's a people … a culture … it's an attitude, it's a way of life coming out of the people" (Bradley 2000, p. 1). Marley put this well another way in the song "Trench Town":

Whoa my head
In desolate places we'll find our bread

And everyone see what's taking place …
We come from Trench Town
Lord, we free the people with music. Sweet
   Music.

For many reggae musicians, Jamaican postcolonial society was, in the words of the Rastafari and reggae singer Johnny Clark, a "Babylon system" that the Jamaican people had to move out of. History was a "stench" that consisted of "old pirates," and freedom was possible only through some sort of revolution or redemption. Reggae music became the voice of black prophetic criticism in postcolonial Jamaican society. At the international level reggae has produced many iconic figures, with Marley being the most popular. Many factors shaped both Marley's Jamaican and international appeal: the rise in Jamaican radical nationalist politics driven by conceptions of black power, the anticolonial struggles in Africa, the civil rights movement in the United States, and the failures of the immediate Caribbean postcolonial state to deliver on the hopes and aspirations of political independence. In the last stage of Marley's life, his concert for the guerrillas of the Zimbabwean anticolonial struggle illustrated the deep connections between reggae as a popular antihegemonic musical form and aspects of international black struggles. This dimension of reggae is now being practiced by reggae poets like Mutabaruka.

Reggae continues to develop in the twenty-first century. One genre, roots reggae, popularized by the singer Luciano, distinguishes itself by its message of openness, its rebellious quality, its firm affirmation of Rastafari, and a central preoccupation with social and political issues. Other genres are dub and dance hall. In the 1970s many children of Jamaican immigrants to the United Kingdom, often called "black British," deployed reggae as a cultural form not only of identity but of protest. Bands such as Steel Pulse and Aswad played a role in the black cultural politics of the United Kingdom. Thematically these bands reflected on the concerns of the black British experience as part of an international black experience. It was from this experience that one of the most important reggae poets, Linton Kwesi Johnson, emerged. Johnson's poetry, as Fred D'Aguiar put it, is "an epicure of this familiar metre and rhyme served up into a reggae rhythm" (Johnson 2002, p. xi). Reggae has come to constitute an aesthetic form for many Caribbean poets.

Reggae still shapes black popular music around the globe, with reggae bands in Africa, Europe, and Latin America. In addition the philosophy of Rastafari, which traveled with reggae, remains an important cultural and social movement in many parts of the world. Perhaps the best summary of the importance of the historic achievement of reggae is that given by Count Ossie, the drummer and Rastafarian personality, who remarked that both reggae and rasta were "fighting colonialism and oppression but not with guns and bayonet, but wordically, culturally" (Bogues 2003, p. 192). Reggae as a black cultural achievement is an integral element of late-twentieth-century efforts of former colonized people to achieve full decolonization.

SEE ALSO *Black Power; Blackness; Caribbean, The; Culture, Low and High; Migration, Rural to Urban; Music; Music, Psychology of; Pan-Africanism; Popular Culture; Protest; Rastafari; Slavery; Social Movements; Urbanization; World Music*

BIBLIOGRAPHY

Bogues, Anthony. 2003. *Black Heretic, Black Prophets: Radical Political Intellectuals.* New York: Routledge.

Bordowitz, Hank, ed. 2004. *Every Little Thing Gonna Be Alright: The Bob Marley Reader.* Cambridge, MA: Da Capo.

Bradley, Lloyd. 2000. *Bass Culture.* London: Viking.

Johnson, Linton Kwesi. 2002. *Mi Revolutionary Fren: Selected Poems.* London: Penguin.

Katz, David. 2003. *Solid Foundation: An Oral History of Reggae.* New York: Bloomsbury.

Manuel, Peter. 2006. *Caribbean Currents: Caribbean Music from Rumba to Reggae.* Rev. ed. Philadelphia: Temple University Press.

Pollard Velma. 1994. *Dread Talk: The Language of Rastafari.* Kinsgton, Jamaica: Canoe.

Potash, Chris. 1997. *Reggae, Rasta, Revolution.* New York: Schirmer Books.

Prahlad, Sw. Anand. 2001. *Reggae Wisdom.* Jackson: University Press of Mississippi.

Special Issue on Reggae Studies. 1998. *Social and Economic Studies* 47 (1). Kingston: Arthur Lewis Institutue of Social and Economic Studies.

Veal, Michael E. 2007. *Soundscapes and Shattered Songs in Jamaican Reggae.* Middletown: Wesleyan University Press.

Anthony Bogues

REGIME THEORY
SEE *Politics, Urban.*

REGIMES, MILITARY
SEE *Military Regimes.*

REGIONAL SCIENCE
SEE *Geography.*

REGIONS

Social scientists looking for an organizing principle with which to understand a large area of social life have long employed broad concepts aimed at integrating complex observations and categories of social behavior. One such concept that has demonstrated broad utility is that of *regions*. Its application has been great in sociology, history, political analysis, economics, geography, and anthropology. In turn, each of these disciplines has contributed something to the understanding of regions.

During the first half of the twentieth century the study of urban sociology grew strongly, and a major center of this research and theorizing was the sociology department at the University of Chicago. Scholars such as Robert Park, Ernest Burgess, Louis Wirth, and Roderick D. McKenzie developed innovative research projects and interpretations of the human community. Their emphasis overall was on the urban community, and a significant aspect of their work elaborated an ecological conception of the region as an extension of the study of the community.

The ecological approach studies human beings as organisms adapting to a physical environment. Using concepts originally developed in plant and animal ecology, these sociologists focused on the spatial patterns and social organization of the community that resulted from competition for space and available resources in a geographical locale. The approach became distinctively sociological through its focus on social organization, role specialization, population concentration and centralization, and interdependence resulting from differing economic activities. Age and sex distributions are affected by ecological interactions, as is the distribution of various groupings by ethnicity and race. These stratified orders are a salient aspect of the social organization of the human community, and a significant source of these patterns lies in the realm of ecological relationships.

This approach has significant ties with *demography*, or the statistical study of human population aggregates, and *human geography*, particularly *economic geography*, with its attention to the physical factors that determine strategic points of location for commerce and industry. Human ecologists devote great attention to *concentration*, or increasing density of a population in an area, which often becomes regional concentration. Thus, regional development has its origins in population growth and movement and the tendency of people to concentrate.

TYPES OF REGIONS

The classic conception of the region as taking one of four forms was developed by Louis Wirth, a prominent member of the Chicago school of sociology. His scholarship approached the region as an area distinguished by physical characteristics, such as the type of soil, annual and seasonal amounts and patterns of rainfall, length of growing season, crops grown, and border contours. Here the region is a recognizable physical area in relation to human activities carried on within, or limited by, the contours of the place inhabited or utilized. Wirth continues his analysis of the region by giving attention to areal variations in cultural features of the people who make the region their home. Cultural attributes such as language or local dialects, distinctive religious beliefs and practices, customs in dress, architectural patterns, and unique customs and forms of social organization are considered here. He concludes that either natural areas or cultural areas comprise regions, due to the homogeneity of specific features.

Wirth distinguishes a second form of region set off from other areas by physical features that serve as barriers to migration. These barriers may be mountain ranges, deserts, lakes, rivers, and oceans, or large protected valleys. He also viewed barriers created by human beings as equally powerful. These can include state and national boundaries as well as trade and custom regulations that inhibit or prevent contact between geographical locales and operate to limit the activities of an area and isolate it from surrounding areas.

The third form of region analyzed by Wirth emphasized the interdependence of activities in an area. Activities and units of organization are not homogeneous or necessarily similar, but are integrated as a way of life. This third pattern is likely to involve a trade area with a network of economic linkages with multiple radii of influence extending from a trade center outward. Examples of this third variation of the region are political capitals, cultural centers, colonial primate cities, and in the modern era, the metropolitan region with its urban center. These forms of centered regions frequently have fewer discernible boundaries, with the periphery gradually shading into a vast hinterland, or in some instances, a borderland receiving influence from a competing center or area of dominance. This third form of the region is likely to be less bound by local traditions and is likely to be dynamic, with the life activities of the region's inhabitants in flux.

The fourth type of region is referred to by Wirth as an *administrative region* or *ad hoc* region. It often develops in an attempt to control some human problem such as crime, traffic, slum life, or contagious disease. Units of administration are created in order to ameliorate or, at minimum, set limits to the growth of one or more problems of a community. The planning region is likely to take form in a manner that does not coincide with a "natural" or physically bounded area. The New York Port Authority and Tennessee Valley Authority serve as illustrations of this fourth form of the region.

It should be noted that each of these types of region involves an areal and a spatial dimension in relation to the distribution of people and social behavior. The organized social behavior of human beings is analyzed in terms of location and position in some form of physical, cultural, or social utilization of space. Wirth cautions that none of the conceptions of the regions implies a form of geographical or physical determinism. Soil and atmosphere do not determine culture and social organization. In contrast, some of the previous writings on regionalism took physical determinism for granted and might have reflected earlier viewpoints asserting a close connection between habitat and economic and political activity.

REGIONAL RIVALRY AND CONFLICT

The concept of the region should be clearly separated from *sectionalism*, which implies organization and political consciousness based on the economic and political interests of a geographical area in a nation. In the United States, and during periods in the history of some European nations, sectional interests have been based on the natural resources of a geographical region. Historical interpretations of sectionalism incline toward a form of economic determinism. The presence of sectional interests and consciousness do point to the manner in which regional organization, and the similarity of a region's qualities, can lead to conflict between regions. The American Civil War was an extreme example of sectional conflict based in part on regional conflict and differing economic interests, along with differing culture and way of life. Regional differences in ethnicity and racial identification, industrial development, types of agriculture, interests in tariff and trade policy, and military traditions were involved in a regional conflict of catastrophic proportions in the War between the States. A result was long-term domination by the North over the South in political and economic relations that followed the conflict.

There is no shortage of conflicts in the world at large in which regional differences play a large role. The domination of Tibet by China is a striking example in Asia. Through centuries the strategic location of Tibet between East, South, and Central Asia made it a focus of contention between more powerful rival empires. Nonetheless, its extreme difficulty of access enabled Tibet to live in isolation through most of its history. It was governed by a series of aristocratic families and became the religious center of Lamaistic Buddhism.

After the victory of the Chinese Communists over the Nationalists in 1949, the victors announced plans to "liberate" Tibet and secure China's "traditional boundaries." The Peking government acted on its threat in 1950, attacking in Eastern Tibet. After appeals for support that were ignored or rebuffed, Chinese terms were accepted in 1951. Chinese sovereignty was recognized, in exchange for assurances of broad Tibetan autonomy. The Chinese soon widened their administrative control and in response Tibet's people rose up in revolt in 1956, and again in 1959. After the Dalai Lama was forced to flee to India, the Chinese crushed the rebellion. In 1965 Tibet became an "Autonomous Region of the People's Republic of China." This sequence of events represents an example of a more powerful nation exerting domination over a smaller, less powerful region near its border.

Governance in Spain represents another illustration of strains between regions within a nation containing historical regional-based divisions in language and culture. A part of the basis for representation is regional variation in interest. At the beginning of the twenty-first century, Spain's senate, composed of 256 members, includes 46 members chosen by regional governments. Earlier, during the 1980s, Catalonia and the Basque Provinces had begun asking for greater autonomy, as well as the official use of Catalan and the Basque languages in their respective provinces. The Basque separatists were defeated politically in 1994. When the major Catalonian terrorist group renounced violence in 1991, Catalonia's president was given an influential position in the Spanish government.

Italy represents another example of a nation with major regional divisions based on natural resources, economic development, local custom, and dialects, as well as other regional subcultural differences. In this case, the northern region of Italy is largely dominant over the south.

Northern Italy includes the Italian Alps, a northern plain, and the region of Liguria, on the steep and narrow coastline of the Ligurian Sea. The northern plain of Italy, south of the Alps, is an extended lowland that benefits from an abundant water supply from rainfall and the region's rivers. Summers are long, farmlands are fertile, and there is a heavy concentration of industry. The large city of Genoa provides services to the industries of Lombardy, as well as hosting local enterprises that include chemical firms, shipbuilders, and oil refineries. Genoa's oil pipelines penetrate into Switzerland and Germany.

Central Italy includes the regions of Tuscany, Umbria, Latium, and Marche. This area has contributed very strongly to Western civilization. The peninsula is highly urbanized, with centers such as Rome, though industry is not highly developed. Farther south, the islands of Sicily and Sardinia have no notable resources; their terrain is rugged, and droughts as well as floods are frequent. These islands are also physically more isolated, and despite attempts at development following World War II, industrial growth has been slow. These conditions have meant that economically, the north of Italy has been dominant, with population migration more frequently directed at the northern cities. Social mobility has increased in recent years with population movement from villages into cities, and particularly from the south to the more industrialized north.

World development can also be seen from the perspective of large regional variations in industrial development and political influence. Colonialism has had an overarching influence on large world areas. European influence in North America, New Zealand, and Australia resulted in the domination of small groupings of traditional hunters and gatherers, or in some instances, pastoral societies. European settlements became dominant, and long-term colonial administrative relations were established. In large areas in southern portions of the globe—in Africa, Asia, and South America—the autochthonous, or native, populations remained numerically predominant, but under colonial rule.

These latter areas have experienced much slower industrial development than North America, the Western and Northern European capitalist centers, or Australia and New Zealand. In recent years, conditions in some of the impoverished regions of the South have actually deteriorated. Poverty is extremely widespread in the former colonial areas: In the year 2000, an estimated 1.5 billion people, nearly a quarter of the world's population, lived in poverty in developing countries around the world. An estimated half of the global poor live in Asia, and around one-third live in Africa, with many of the remaining portion of the world's impoverished people living in Central and South America. These statistics are now frequently seen as reflecting a worldwide division between North and South—a division that is perhaps world history's greatest regional variation, with the largest human consequences.

SEE ALSO *Development in Sociology; Geography; Globalization, Social and Economic Aspects of; Nationalism and Nationality*

BIBLIOGRAPHY

Caudill, Harry M. 1963. *Night Comes to the Cumberlands: A Biography of a Depressed Area.* Boston: Little, Brown.

Giddens, Anthony, Mitchell Duneier, and Richard P. Applebaum. 2005. *Introduction to Sociology.* 5th ed. New York: Norton.

Hawley, Amos H. 1950. *Human Ecology: A Theory of Community Structure.* New York: Ronald Press.

Hawley, Amos H. 1981. *Urban Society: An Ecological Approach.* 2nd ed. New York: Wiley.

Macionis, John J., and Vincent N. Parrillo. 2007. *Cities and Urban Life.* 4th ed. Upper Saddle River, NJ: Pearson Prentice-Hall.

McKenzie, Roderick D. 1968. The Scope of Human Ecology. In *Roderick D. McKenzie on Human Ecology,* ed. Amos H. Hawley, 19–32. Chicago: University of Chicago Press.

Odum, Howard W., and Harry Estill Moore. 1938. *American Regionalism: A Cultural-Historical Approach to National Integration.* New York: Holt.

Palen, J. John. 2005. *The Urban World.* 7th ed. New York: McGraw-Hill.

Pious, Richard M. 1998. *India–Seychelles.* Vol. 2 of *Governments of the World: A Student Companion.* New York: Oxford University Press.

Saunders, William S., ed. 2005. *Sprawl and Suburbia: A* Harvard Design Magazine *Reader.* Minneapolis: University of Minnesota Press.

Wirth, Louis. 1964. *On Cities and Social Life,* ed. Albert J. Reiss Jr. Chicago: University of Chicago Press.

Kenneth N. Eslinger

REGIONS, METROPOLITAN

At the beginning of the twentieth century it was widely recognized that the frontier in the United States had passed and that the new growth in population was in and around cities. As rural counties lost population and cities became centers of nonfarm employment, students of social behavior in North America saw a trend toward the development of larger cities. What was not immediately apparent was that the trend toward urbanization and larger cities would continue within another significant trend. This other trend was the centrifugal movement of population around large cities as the urban population, including both older urban dwellers and newcomers, would begin to move outward around larger urban places. This new trend was one of metropolitan development in contrast to merely urban growth, and it carried with it strong changes in population distribution first toward the periphery, then well beyond the boundaries of central cities.

The growth of the metropolitan region was a major social pattern during the entire twentieth century and has continued into the twenty-first century. Roderick D. McKenzie was the first urban sociologist to recognize and call attention to the national trend of metropolitan regional growth in his 1933 book, *The Metropolitan Community.* This growth pattern involves the ecological process of concentration of population in cities, combined with locally significant deconcentration into nearby areas around cities and their outlying areas. Associated with these demographic and ecological tendencies is an accompanying centralization of administrative control in urban areas, which results in a large-scale regional integration of occupational opportunities. Business decisions, employment, governmental services, shopping and consumer behavior, and a range of recreational and other quotidian activities spread in interlinked fashion over an enlarged regional area.

The major source of the expansion of urban influences into outlying spaces, creating a region of metropolitan impact, is the reduction of the "friction" of space by reducing the limiting effects of time and distance. The enhanced speed and flexibility of motor-vehicle travel has now enlarged the radius of one hour of travel time to thirty miles or so. In the nineteenth century with horseback travel and horse-drawn wagons, this distance was closer to six miles. On foot, an hour's walking is around three miles. Few people will commute distances that require more than an hour in travel time. The effect has been to expand the square miles of space with urban influence from travel, including shopping, from around thirty-six square miles to two thousand to three thousand square miles or even more. This much greater separation of residence from work, and of errands and shopping areas from residences, has greatly expanded the metropolitan influence into a larger area. Railroad travel between cities in the latter half of the nineteenth century, followed by motor truck transport after the 1920s, have expanded the metropolitan impact to entire regions.

For purposes of clarification and definition, the terms *metropolitan community* or *metropolitan areas* are used to refer to the city and the immediately surrounding countryside, usually within a radius of twenty-five to thirty miles. *Metropolitan region* is the term used to refer to the much broader area, which includes a multiplicity of scattered activities that have come under administrative influences and even supervision of the large central city, or metropolis.

THE GROWTH OF METROPOLITAN REGIONS

The widely observed trend in modern societies toward large-scale social organization and greater economic reach is a fundamental source of the growth of regions and the great expansion of the metropolitan community. This pattern of growth has developed over about the last hundred years and has been documented for that length of time in the U.S. Census. These changes follow the great redirections in time and cost of movement that motorized vehicles traveling on hard-surfaced roads provide. The telephone, radio, and television followed improvements in transmitting electrical power and made possible the expansion of urban community boundaries. More recently, the computer has facilitated instant communication of information and speeded economic transactions in a manner that reduces the importance of traditionally recognized community boundaries.

The growth of a metropolitan region occurs through ecological processes that involve transportation and con-

tact and exchange, typically in connection with distributive functions arising from various sustenance activities. A center with specialized functions and an involuted administrative organization may be the coordinating base for a hierarchy of socially connected but dispersed activities. The boundaries of a region may be set by the points of intersection of interregional routes. The size of the metropolitan center and spacing of coordinated service functions influence the emerging regional pattern. Interregional nodes of transportation may determine the early development of regional boundaries. It should be added that extractive industries as well as manufacturing exert an eccentric or decentralizing influence on large metropolitan urban locations. Continued expansion of population along with a widened range of administrative organizations extends economic activities over a larger territory.

The U.S. Census Bureau began recognizing metropolitan areas with impact on a nearby region as early as 1910. At that time approximately one-third of the population lived in these newly recognized urban "metropolitan districts," as they were known. Before midcentury they were named Standard Metropolitan Statistical Areas. Today these metropolitan areas are known as MSAs, or Metropolitan Statistical Areas, the change in designation having been made in 1983. Approximately four out of five people in the United States now live in these metropolitan areas.

A review of population data on metropolitan areas in the United States shows a long-term but massive shift outward from central cities in metropolitan areas as population moves in a large-scale pattern of decentralization into suburbs and adjacent regions. This movement of people and industry was one of the great social trends of the twentieth century, comparable to the decline of small farms and self-employment during the first half of the twentieth century, with the consequent migration to larger towns and cities. A third major social pattern, that of married women entering the labor force and remaining in the workplace after the birth of children, began to develop strongly after World War II and remains a vigorous trend. A visible effect of this tendency toward metropolitan decentralization is the high proportion of Americans who maintain suburban and exurban residences, and in moving even farther outward, contribute to the large-scale growth of urban sprawl as population continues to spread into more distant areas of metropolitan regions and beyond.

Currently, urban life in the United States, viewed demographically and ecologically, has become a metropolitan way of life, with day-to-day activities and living arrangements occurring in a continually growing multicentered region. The metropolitan center is actually replacing the city itself as the most significant urban unit.

Whereas the first half of the twentieth century had seen a little heralded emergence of a larger metropolitan unit dominated by a central city, the later twentieth and early twenty-first centuries have seen the growth of deconcentrated populations with a multicentered pattern of growth over entire regions. These major changes have been fueled by the spread of the private automobile and the use of motor truck transport in combination with the national interstate highway systems begun in the late 1950s. Quite influential at the level of individual consumers and families have been federal tax laws that provide for mortgage interest income-tax deductions. The effect has been to subsidize middle-income families in the purchase of affordable single-family dwellings. The dearth of city lots in central cities combined with lower-cost land in rural and developing suburban areas created a potential for large-scale suburban growth and even rapid, leapfrog-style exurban development.

Scholarship in human ecology has assumed consumer demand and improvements in transportation technology as vital in reducing the critical time and distance factors prominent in urban location theory. More recent scholarship in urban sociology and urban ecology has pointed to the strong role of real estate development promotions as well as the interactions of business and local government elites in facilitating the growth of the suburbs and a continuation of the sprawl pattern around urban areas. Thus, a newer trend in urban research and scholarship emphasizes supply-side activities and real estate developers, in cooperation with banks and lending organizations, combined with government subsidies of various kinds in producing the spatial patterns of suburbs around Metropolitan Statistical Areas. All the while, continued belief in seemingly endless supplies of cheap fossil fuel for motor vehicle transportation and maintenance have contributed an ideational support for the continued growth of suburban housing and shopping malls.

METROPOLITAN CHANGES IN EMPLOYMENT AND CONSUMPTION

In metropolitan areas of the United States, there are more than three suburban residents for every two residents of the area's central city. This trend has been growing for nearly a generation as industrial cities have lost manufacturing jobs that were often unionized with high pay and benefits, along with other lower-paying entry-level jobs that might have been filled by younger workers and poorer urbanites. As early as the 1980s, nearly twice as many people were employed in manufacturing in the suburbs than in the cities. Interestingly, since the 1980s, the typical commuter's trip to work has been from suburb to suburb rather than the more traditional suburb to city, or

earlier, urban neighborhood to city factory by foot, bicycle, or streetcar, or automobile.

Retail sales of various types, including major department stores, were concentrated in downtown locations until the 1970s. A decline in this concentration had started as much as a decade or so earlier as urban-based manufacturing and businesses as well as retail activity moved from central city locations to outlying areas, typically following highway arteries and suburban housing development. These changes in retail location and activity are seen most clearly in the growth of shopping malls. Only a few malls existed in the 1950s. Today there are more than forty-five thousand shopping malls of various sizes in the United States.

SOME CONSEQUENCES OF POPULATION CHANGES IN METROPOLITAN REGIONS

In the United States in the early twenty-first century, over half of the population lives in suburban areas. In the metropolitan areas of the nation, more than 60 percent of the population lives in the suburbs. Not surprisingly, the suburban areas have increasingly taken on an urban character in the social and cultural attributes of their populations. This is seen structurally and demographically in changes in social-class composition and increased numbers of minority group members in the suburbs of metropolitan areas. Working-class and industrial suburbs are a strong presence around larger cities in metropolitan areas. Major segments of middle-status white-collar employees find themselves pressured financially to maintain what is viewed as a middle-class and suburban level of living. This is seen in widespread credit abuse and second mortgages on houses purchased on installments. People in manual occupations are very likely to be dependent on two incomes.

Poverty is also a stronger presence in the suburban portions of metropolitan regions. The federal standard for the measurement of poverty is based on the ability of an individual or family to purchase food. Under the official methods of determining poverty levels, around one person in eight in the United States is in poverty. One-third of the people classified as poor under that standard live in a suburban location.

RESIDENTIAL PATTERNS OF MINORITY GROUPS IN METROPOLITAN AREAS

Impressions from the middle to the third quarter of the twentieth century linger in mass media and public imagery of the suburbs. Some of these stereotypical perceptions of suburbs as dwelling places for a white population have their source in the development of the early suburbs around large cities in the late nineteenth and early twentieth centuries. As with much stereotyped imagery, they have some basis, historically, in fact. Also, at present some of the oldest and most established traditional incorporated suburbs in outlying areas of the largest North American cities exemplify what sociologists refer to as "suburban persistence," meaning that they retain a significant degree of their original exclusiveness and Anglo-American characteristics.

In looking at metropolitan areas nationally, a different picture emerges. Almost 40 percent of black Americans live in a suburban location, and a growing proportion of this population continues to move to the suburbs. Half of the people from a Latino background are suburban dwellers. For the last two decades or so, Latino people have accounted for around one-quarter of all suburban growth in the United States. Finally, although a small proportion of the total population, 55 percent of all Asian Americans live in suburbs, often in suburbs that are predominantly Asian but contain a significant proportion of Anglo-American residents.

METROPOLITAN REGIONS, THE SUBURBS, AND CHANGES IN POLITICAL BEHAVIOR

The deconcentration of population around large urban areas in the United States is associated with changes in politics, political alignments, and election outcomes in public life. First is the large number of political jurisdictions in the multicentered urban region. This has many implications, but the most direct impact is on the region and its frequent inability to regulate urban sprawl and its connected problems of leapfrog growth, traffic congestion, and pollution as well as maintaining clean water resources. There is also a growth in the number of local public officials, and as regional-level problems develop, these officials are often unable to operate in a coordinated manner to resolve them and ameliorate the social problems that arise from the organizational features of the metropolitan region. At the national level, the changes reviewed above are reflected in new areas of influence with altered political alignments. Central-city areas have declined in political influence, and an urban, union-influenced vote has determined fewer outcomes than in past decades. The suburban vote is not easy to characterize as it is not nearly as uniformly conservative as it was in past generations. Recent elections have seen a shift toward independent voters in the suburbs, who are issues-oriented and often concerned about lifestyle, with weakened ties to traditional social-class-based political involvement.

In conclusion, central cities are no longer the dominant locations in political decisions and economic activity in metropolitan regions. The newer territorial organization is multicentered, with edge cities and specialized nodes developing along major interstate highways and with services used by a more affluent suburban population. Ethnic variation is commonplace in suburban areas, as is manufacturing activity with suburban commuting working-class populations. Shopping malls are the predominant medium for retail business, and most jobs are in the services sector. Typical commuting occurs from one suburb to another. The longer term effect on politics is not clear, but regional problems are far from experiencing resolution at the local, regional, or national level.

SEE ALSO *Anthropology, Urban; Borders; Cities; Economics, Urban; Ethnicity; Human Ecology; Metropolis; Migration; Migration, Rural to Urban; Poverty; Public Goods; Race; Regions; Sociology, Urban; Spatial Theory; Suburban Sprawl; Suburbs; Transportation Industry; Urban Renewal; Urban Sprawl; Urban Studies; Urbanization*

BIBLIOGRAPHY

Gottdiener, Mark, and Ray Hutchison. 2006. *The New Urban Sociology*, 3rd ed. Boulder, CO: Westview Press.

Hawley, Amos H. 1981. *Urban Society: An Ecological Approach*, 2nd ed. New York: Wiley.

Hutter, Mark. 2007. *Experiencing Cities*. Boston: Pearson/Allyn and Bacon.

Macionis, John, and Vincent N. Parrillo. 2007. *Cities and Urban Life*, 4th ed. Upper Saddle River, NJ: Pearson Prentice Hall.

Mark, Harold, and Kent P. Schwirian. 1967. Ecological Position, Urban Central Place Function, and Community Population Growth. *American Journal of Sociology* 73: 30–41.

McKenzie, Roderick D. 1933. *The Metropolitan Community*. New York: McGraw-Hill.

McKenzie, Roderick D. 1968. The Scope of Human Ecology. In *Roderick D. McKenzie on Human Ecology: Selected Writings*, ed. Amos H. Hawley, 19–32. Chicago: University of Chicago Press.

Palen, J. John. 2005. *The Urban World*, 7th ed. Boston: McGraw-Hill.

Pious, Richard M. 1998. *Governments of the World: A Student Companion*. Vol. 2. New York: Oxford University Press.

Saunders, William S., ed. 2005. *Sprawl and Suburbia: A Harvard Design Magazine Reader*. Minneapolis: University of Minnesota Press.

Wirth, Louis. 1964. *Louis Wirth on Cities and Social Life: Selected Papers*, ed. Albert J. Reiss Jr. Chicago: University of Chicago Press.

Kenneth N. Eslinger

REGRESSION

Regression is a broad class of statistical models that is the foundation of data analysis and inference in the social sciences. Moreover, many contemporary statistical methods derive from the linear regression model. At its heart, regression describes systematic relationships between one or more predictor variables with (typically) one outcome. The flexibility of regression and its many extensions make it the primary statistical tool that social scientists use to model their substantive hypotheses with empirical data.

HISTORY AND DEFINITION

The original application of regression was Sir Francis Galton's study of the heights of parents and children in the late 1800s. Galton noted that tall parents tended to have somewhat shorter children, and vice versa. He described the relationship between parents' and children's heights using a type of regression line and termed the phenomenon *regression to mediocrity*. Thus, the term *regression* described a specific finding (i.e., relationship between parents' and children's heights) but quickly became attached to the statistical method.

The foundation of regression is the regression equation; for Galton's study of height, the equation might be: $Child_i = \beta_0 + \beta_1 (Parent_i) + \varepsilon_i$. Each family provides values for child's height (i.e., $Child_i$) and parent's height (i.e., $Parent_i$). The simple regression equation above is identical with the mathematical equation for a straight line, often expressed as $y = mx + b$. The two regression coefficients (i.e., β_0 and β_1) represent the y-intercept and slope. The y-intercept estimates the average value of children's height when parent's height equals 0, and the slope coefficient estimates the increase in average children's height for a 1-inch increase in parent's height, assuming height is measured in inches. The intercept and slope define the regression line, which describes a linear relationship between children's and parents' heights. Most data points (i.e., child and parent height pairs) will not lie directly on the simple regression line; the scatter of the data points around the regression line is captured by the residual error term ε_i, which is the vertical displacement of each datum point from the regression line.

The regression line describes the conditional mean of the outcome at specific values of the predictor. As such, it is a summary of the relationship between the two variables, which leads directly to a definition of regression: "[to understand] as far as possible with the available data how the conditional distribution of the response … varies across subpopulations determined by the possible values of the predictor or predictors" (Cook and Weisberg 1999, p. 27). This definition makes no reference to estimation (i.e., how are the regression coefficients determined?) or statistical inference (i.e., how well do the sample coeffi-

cients reflect the population from which they were selected?). Historically, regression has used least-squares estimation (i.e., coefficient values are found that minimize the squared errors ε_i) and frequentist inference (i.e., variability of sample regression coefficients are examined within theoretical sampling distributions and summarized by p-values or confidence intervals). Although least-squares regression estimates and p-values based on frequentist inference are the most common default settings within statistical packages, they are not the only methods of estimation and inference available, nor are they inherently aspects of regression.

EXTENSIONS OF THE BASIC REGRESSION MODEL

If regression only summarized associations between two continuous variables, it would be a very limited tool for social scientists. However, regression has been extended in numerous ways. An initial and important expansion of the model allowed for multiple predictors and multiple types of predictors, including continuous, binary, and categorical. With the inclusion of categorical predictors, statisticians noted that analysis of variance models with a single error term and similar models are special cases of regression, and the two methods (i.e., regression and analysis of variance) are seen as different facets of a general linear model.

A second important expansion of regression allowed for different types of outcome variables such as binary, ordinal, nominal, and count variables. The basic linear regression model uses the normal distribution as its probability model. The generalized linear model, which includes non-normal outcomes, increases the flexibility of regression by allowing different probability models (e.g., binomial distribution for binary outcomes and Poisson distribution for count outcomes), and predictors are connected to the outcome through a link function (e.g., logit transformation for binary outcomes and natural logarithm for count outcomes).

Beyond the general and generalized linear models, numerous other extensions have been made to the basic regression model that allow for greater complexity, including multivariate outcomes, path models that allow for multiple predictors and outcomes with complex associations, structural equation models that nest measurement models for latent constructs within path models, multilevel models that allow for correlated data due to nested designs (e.g., students within classrooms), and nonlinear regression models that use regression to fit complex mathematical models in which the coefficients are not additively related to the outcome. Although each of the preceding methods has unique qualities, they all derive from the basic linear regression model.

REGRESSION AS A TOOL IN SOCIAL SCIENCE RESEARCH

Research is a marriage of three components: Theory-driven research questions dictate the study design, which in turn dictates the statistical methods. Thus, statistical methods map the research questions onto the empirical data, and the statistical results yield answers to those questions in a well-designed study. Within the context of scientific inquiry, regression is primarily an applied tool for theory testing with empirical data. This symbiosis between theoretical models and statistical models has been the driving force behind many of the advances and extensions of regression discussed above.

Although regression can be applied to either observational or experimental data, regression has played an especially important role in observational data. With observational data there is no randomization or intervention, and there may be a variety of potential causes and explanations for the phenomenon under study. Regression methods allow researchers to statistically control for additional variables that may influence the outcome. For example, in an observational study of infidelity that focuses on age as a predictor, it might be important to control for relationship satisfaction, as previous research has suggested it is related to both the likelihood of infidelity and age. Because regression coefficients in multiple regression models are estimated simultaneously, they control for the presence of the other predictors, often described as partialing out the effects of other predictors.

Regression can also play a practical role in conveying research results. Regression coefficients as well as regression summaries (e.g., percentage of the outcome variability explained by the predictors) quantitatively convey the importance of a regression model and consequently the underlying theoretical model. In addition, regression models are prediction equations (i.e., regression coefficients are scaling factors for predicting the outcome based on the predictors), and regression models can provide estimates of the outcome based on predictors, allowing the researcher to consider how the outcome varies across combinations of specific predictor values.

LIMITATIONS

Even though regression is an extremely flexible tool for social science research, it is not without limitations. Not all research questions are well described by regression models, particularly questions that do not specify outcome variables. As an example, cluster analysis is a statistical tool used to reveal whether there are coherent groups or clusters within data; because there is no outcome or target variable, regression is not appropriate. At the same time, because regression focuses on an outcome variable, users of regression may believe that fitting a regression

model connotes causality (i.e., predictors cause the outcome). This is patently false, and outcomes in some analyses may be predictors in others. Proving causality requires much more than the use of regression.

Another criticism of regression focuses on its use for statistical inference. To provide valid inference (e.g., p-values or confidence intervals), the data must be a random sample from a population, or involve randomization to a treatment condition in experimental studies. Most samples in the social sciences are samples of convenience (e.g., undergraduate students taking introductory psychology). Of course, this is not a criticism of regression per se, but of study design and the limitations of statistical inference with nonrandom sampling. Limitations notwithstanding, regression and its extensions continue to be an incredibly useful tool for social scientists.

SEE ALSO *Vector Autoregression*

BIBLIOGRAPHY

Berk, Richard A. 2004. *Regression Analysis: A Constructive Critique.* Thousand Oaks, CA: Sage.

Cohen, Jacob, Patricia Cohen, Stephen G. West, and Leona S. Aiken. 2003. *Applied Multiple Regression/Correlation Analysis for the Behavioral Sciences.* Mahwah, NJ: Lawrence Erlbaum Associates.

Cook, Dennis R., and Sanford Weisberg. 1999. *Applied Regression Including Computing and Graphics.* New York: John Wiley.

Fox, John. 1997. *Applied Regression Analysis, Linear Models, and Related Methods.* Thousand Oaks, CA: Sage.

David C. Atkins

REGRESSION, LOGISTICAL

SEE *Logistic Regression.*

REGRESSION, PROBABILISTIC

SEE *Probabilistic Regression.*

REGRESSION, RANDOM COEFFICIENTS

SEE *Random Effects Regression.*

REGRESSION ANALYSIS

The term *regression* was initially conceptualized by Francis Galton (1822–1911) within the framework of inheritance characteristics of fathers and sons. In his famous 1886 paper, Galton examined the average regression relationship between the height of fathers and the height of their sons. A more formal treatment of multiple regression modeling and correlation was introduced in 1903 by Galton's friend Karl Pearson (1857–1936). Regression analysis is the statistical methodology of estimating a relationship between a single dependent variable (Y) and a set of predictor (explanatory/independent) variables (X_2, X_3, … X_k) based on a theoretical or empirical concept. In some natural science or engineering applications, this relationship is exactly described, but in most social science applications, these relationships are not exact. These nonexact models are probabilistic in nature and capture only approximate features of the relationship. For example, an energy analyst may want to model how the demand for heating oil varies with the price of oil and the average daily temperature. The problem is that energy demand may be determined by other factors, and the nature of the relationship between energy demand and explanatory variables is unknown. Thus, only an approximate relation can be modeled.

The simplest relationship between Y and X is a linear regression model, which is typically written as,

$$Y_i = \beta_1 + \beta_2 X_{2i} + \beta_3 X_{3i} + \ldots + \beta_k X_{ki} + U_i \qquad (1)$$

where the index i represents the i-th observation and U_i is the random error term. The β coefficients measure the net effect of each explanatory variable on the dependent variable, and the random disturbance term captures the net effect of all the factors that affect Y_i except the influence of the predictor variables. In other words, U_i is the difference between the actual and mean value ($E(Y_i/X_i, i = 1, 2, \ldots, k) = \beta_1 + \beta_2 X_{2i} + \beta_3 X_{3i} + \ldots + \beta_k X_{ki}$) of the dependent variable. It is customary to assume that $U_i s (i = 1, \ldots, n)$ are independently normally distributed with zero mean and constant variance (σ^2). The parameters are estimated from a random sample of $n(n > k)$ observations. The explanatory variables are assumed to be nonstochastic and uncorrelated with the error term. The meaning of the β coefficient varies with the functional form of the regression model. For example, if the variables are in linear form, the net effect represents the rate of change, and if the variables are in log form, the net effect represents elasticity, which can be interpreted as a percentage change in the dependent variable with respect to a 1 percent change in the independent variable.

The parameters βs are estimated by minimizing the residual sum of squares $\sum_{i=1}^{n} U_i^2 = \sum_{i=1}^{n} (Y_i - \beta_1 - \beta_2 X_{2i} - \beta_3 X_{3i} - \ldots - \beta_k X_{ki})^2$, which is known as the *ordinary least squares* (OLS) method. The minimization problem results in k equations in k unknowns, which gives a unique estimate as long as the explanatory variables are not collinear. An unbiased estimate of σ^2 is obtained from the residual sum of squares. When the random error term satisfies the standard assumptions, the OLS method gives the best linear unbiased estimates (BLUE). The statistical significance of the coefficients is tested with the usual t-statistic ($t = \hat{\beta}_j/\text{s.e.}(\hat{\beta}_j)$), which follows a t-distribution with $n - k$ degrees of freedom. In fact, some researchers use this t-statistic as a criterion in a stepwise process to add or delete variables from the preliminary model.

The fit of the regression equation is evaluated by the statistic R^2, which measures the extent of the variation in Y explained by the regression equation. The value of R^2 ranges from 0 to 1, where 0 means no fit and 1 means a perfect fit. The adjusted R^2 ($\bar{R}^2 = 1 - (1 - R^2)(n - 1)/(n - k)$), which compensates for n and k, is more suitable than R^2 in comparing models with different subsets of explanatory variables. Sometimes researchers choose the model with the highest R^2, but the purpose of the regression analysis is to obtain the best model based on a theoretical concept or an empirically observed phenomena. Therefore, in formulating models, researchers should consider the logical, theoretical, and prior knowledge between the dependent and explanatory variables. Nevertheless, it is not unusual to get high R^2 with the signs of the coefficients inconsistent with prior knowledge or expectations. Note that R^2s of two different models are comparable only if the dependent variables and the number of observations are the same, because R^2 measures the fraction of the total variation in the dependent variable explained by the regression equation. In addition to $\bar{R}^2$, there are other measures, such as Mallows's C_p statistic and information criteria AIC (Akaike) and BIC (Bayesean), to choose between different combinations of regressors. Francis Diebold (1998) showed that there is no obvious advantage between AIC or BIC, and they are routinely calculated in many statistical programs.

Regression models are often plagued with data problems, such as multicollinearity, heteroskedasticity, and autocorrelation, that violate standard OLS assumptions. Multicollinearity occurs when two or more (or a combination of) regressors are highly correlated. Multicollinearity is suspected when inconsistencies in the estimates, such as high R^2 and low t-values or high pairwise correlation among regressors, are observed. Remedial measures of multicollinearity include dropping a variable that causes multicollinearity, using a priori information to combine coefficients, pooling time series and cross-section data, adding new observations, transforming variables, and ridge and Stein-rule estimates. It is worthwhile to note that transforming variables and dropping variables may cause specification errors, and Stein-rule and ridge estimates produce biased and inefficient estimates.

The assumption of constant variance of the error term is somewhat unreasonable in empirical research. For example, expenditure on food is steady for low-income households, while it varies substantially for high-income households. Furthermore, heteroskedasticity is more common in cross-sectional data (e.g., sample surveys) than in time series data, because in time series data, changes in all variables are in more or less the same magnitude. Plotting OLS residuals against the predicted Y values provides a visual picture of the heteroskedasticity problem. Formal tests for heteroskedasticity are based on regressing the OLS residuals on various functional forms of the regressors. Halbert White's (1980) general procedure is widely used among practitioners in detecting and correcting heteroskedasticity. Often, regression models with variables observed over time conflict with the classical assumption of uncorrelated errors. For example, in modeling the impact of public expenditures on economic growth, the OLS model would not be appropriate because the level of public expenditures are correlated over time. OLS estimates of βs in the presence of autocorrelated errors are unbiased, but there is a tendency for σ^2 to be underestimated, leading to overestimated R^2 and invalid t- and F-tests. First-order autocorrelation is detected by the Durbin-Watson test and is corrected by estimating difference equations or by the Cochrane-Orcutt iterative procedure.

SPECIFICATION ERRORS

The OLS method gives the best linear unbiased estimates contingent upon the standard assumptions of the model and the sample data. Any errors in the model and the data may produce misleading results. For example, the true model may have variables in log form, but the estimated model is linear. Even though in social sciences, the true nature of the model is almost always unknown, the researchers' understanding of the variables and the topic may help to formulate a reasonable functional form for the model. In a situation where the functional form is unknown, possible choices include transforming variables into log form, polynomial regression, a translog model, and Box-Cox transformation. Parameters of the Box-Cox model are estimated by the maximum likelihood method because the variable transformation and the parameter estimation of the model are inseparable.

Specification errors also occur either when relevant explanatory variables are missing from the model or when irrelevant variables are added to the model. For example, let the true regression model be $Y_i = \beta_1 + \beta_2 X_{2i} + \beta_3 X_{3i} + U_i$ and the estimated model be $Y_i = \beta_1 + \beta_2 X_{2i} + U_i$. If the omitted variable X_3 is correlated with the included variable X_2, then the estimates of β_1 and β_2 are biased and inconsistent. The extent and the direction of the bias depends on the true parameter β_3 and the correlation between the variables X_2 and X_3. In addition, incorrect estimation of σ^2 may lead to misleading significance tests. Researchers do not commit these specification errors willingly; often the errors are due to unavailability of data or lack of understanding of the topic. Researchers sometimes include all conceivable variables without paying much attention to the underlying theoretical framework, which leads to unbiased but inefficient estimates, which is less serious than omitting a relevant variable.

Instead of dropping an unobserved variable, it is common practice to use proxy variables. For example, most researchers use general aptitude test scores as proxies for individual abilities. When a proxy variable is substituted for a dependent variable, OLS gives unbiased estimates of the coefficients with a larger variance than in the model with no measurement error. However, when an independent variable is measured with an error, OLS gives biased and inconsistent estimates of the parameters. In general, there is no satisfactory way to handle measurement error problems. A real question that arises is whether to omit a variable altogether or instead use a proxy variable. B. T. McCallum (1972) and Michael Wickens (1972) showed that omitting a variable is more severe than using a proxy variable, even if the proxy variable is a poor one.

CATEGORICAL VARIABLES

In regression analysis, researchers frequently encounter qualitative variables, especially in survey data. A person's decision to join a labor union or a homemaker's decision to join the workforce are examples of *dichotomous* dependent variables. Dichotomous variables also appear in models due to nonobservance of the variable. In general, a dichotomous variable model can be defined as,

$$Y_i^* = X_i \beta + U_i$$

where $X_i \beta = \beta_1 + \sum_{j=1}^{k} \beta_j X_{ji}$ and Y^* is an unobservable variable. An observable binary outcome variable Y_i is defined as,

$$Y_i = \begin{cases} 1 & \text{if } Y_i^* \text{ exceeds zero and} \\ 0 & \text{if otherwise.} \end{cases}$$

Substituting Y_i for Y_i^* and estimating the model by OLS is unsuitable primarily because $X_i \beta$ represents the probability $Y = 1$ and it could lie outside the range 0 to 1. In the probit and logit formulations of the above model, the probability that Y_i is equal to 1 is defined as a probability distribution function,

$$\begin{aligned} Pr(Y_i = 1) &= Pr(Y_i^* > 0) \\ &= Pr(U_i > -X_i \beta) \\ &= 1 - F(-X_i \beta) \end{aligned}$$

where F is the cumulative distribution function of U. The choice of the distribution function F translates the regression function $X_i\beta$ into a number between 0 and 1. Parameters of the model are estimated by maximizing the likelihood function,

$$L(\beta_1, b_2) = \Pi \mid_{Y_i = 0} F(-X_i\beta) \Pi_{Y_i = 1}[1 - F(-X_i\beta)]$$

Choosing the normal probability distribution for F yields the probit model, and choosing the logistic distribution for F gives the logit model where $P(Y_i = 1)$ is given by,

$$Pr(Y = 1) = \Phi\left(\frac{X_i\beta}{\sigma}\right) \quad \text{for the probit model, and}$$

$$Pr(Y = 1) = \frac{\exp(X_i\beta)}{1 + \exp(X_i\beta)} \quad \text{for the logic art model}$$

where $\Phi(.)$ is the cumulative normal distribution function. Many statistical packages have standard routines to estimate both probit and logit models. In the probit model, the β parameters and σ appear as a ratio, and therefore cannot be estimated separately. Hence, in the probit model, σ is set to 1 without any loss of generality. The cumulative distributions of logit and normal are close to each other, except in the tails, and therefore, the estimates from both models will not be much different from each other. Since the variance of the normal distribution is set to one, and the logistic distribution has a variance of $\pi^2/3$, it is necessary to divide the logit estimates by $\pi^2/3$ to make the estimates comparable. In practical applications, it is useful to compare the effect of each explanatory variable on the probability. A change in probabilities in the probit and logit models for a unit change in the k-th variable are given by $\pi(X_i\beta)\beta_k$ and $\exp(X_i\beta)\beta_k/(1 + \exp(X_i\beta))^2$, respectively, where $\varphi(.)$ is the standard normal probability density function.

In the multivariate probit models, dichotomous variables are jointly distributed with appropriate multivariate distributions. Likelihood functions are based on the possible combinations of the binary choice variable (Y_i) values. A practical difficulty in multivariate models is the presence of multiple integrals in the likelihood function. Some authors have proposed methods for simulating the multivariate probabilities; details were published in the November 1994 issue of the *Review of Economics and Statistics*. This problem of multiple integration does not arise in the multinomial logit model because the cumulative logistic distribution has a closed form.

TOBIT MODEL

The Tobit model can be considered as an extension of the probit and logit models where the dependent variable Y_i^* is observed in the positive range and is unobserved or unavailable in the negative range. Consider the model described in equation (2), where

$$Y_i = \begin{cases} Y_i^* & \text{if } Y_i^* > 0 \text{ and} \\ 0 & \text{if } Y_i^* \leq 0. \end{cases}$$

This a censored regression model where Y^* observations below zero are censored or not available, but the X observations are available. On the other hand, in the truncated regression model, both Y^* and X observations are unavailable for Y^* values below zero. Estimation of parameters are carried out by the maximum likelihood method, where the likelihood function of the model is based on $Pr(Y^* > 0)$ and $Pr(Y^* \leq 0)$. When U_i is normally distributed, the likelihood function is given by,

$$L = \Pi_{Y_i < 0}\left[1 - \Phi\left(\frac{X_i\beta}{\sigma}\right)\right] \Pi_{Y_i > 0} \frac{1}{\sqrt{2\pi\sigma^2}} \exp\left[-\frac{(Y_i - X_i\beta)^2}{2\sigma^2}\right].$$

Unlike the probit model, where σ was arbitrarily set to 1, the Tobit model estimates the parameters. In the probit model, only the effect on the probabilities for changes in X values are meaningful to a practitioner. However, in the Tobit model, a practitioner may be interested in how the predicted values of Y_i^* change due to a unit change in one X variable in three possible scenarios of the model, linear functional form, unconditional mean and conditional mean (i.e., $E(Y^*) = X\beta$, $E(Y^*)$ and $E(Y^*/Y^* > 0)$). The impacts of the variable X_j on the above three expressions are given by the β_j, $\Phi(Z).\beta_j$ and $\beta_j[1 - Z\varphi(Z)/\Phi(Z) - (\varphi(Z)/\Phi(Z))^2]$, respectively, where $Z = X_i\beta/\sigma$, and $\varphi()$ and $\Phi()$ are standard normal density and distribution functions. An extension of the Tobit model with the presence of heteroskedasticity has been proposed by James Powell (1984).

CAUSALITY BETWEEN TIME SERIES VARIABLES

The concept of causality in time series variables was introduced by Norbert Wiener (1956) and Clive W. J. Granger (1969), and refers to the predictability of one variable X_t from its past behavior, another variable Y_t, and a set of auxiliary variables Z_t. In other words, causality refers to a certain type of statistical feedback between the variables. Some variables have a tendency to move together—for example, average household income and level of education. The question is: Does improvement in education level cause the income to increase or vice versa? It is also worthwhile to note that even with a strong statistical relation between variables, causation between the variables may not exist. The idea of causation must come from a plausible theory rather than from statistical methodology. Causality can be tested by regressing each variable on its own and other variables' lagged values.

A closely related concept in time series variables, as well as in cross-sectional data to a lesser degree, is simultaneity, where the behavior of $g (g > 1)$ stochastic variables are characterized by g structural regression equations. Some of the regressors of these regression equations contain stochastic variables that are directly correlated with the random error term. OLS estimates of such a model produce biased estimates, and the extent of the bias is called *simultaneity bias*. The implications of simultaneity were recognized long before the estimation methods were devised. Within the regression analysis context, the identification problem has another dimension—that is, whether the difficulty in determining a variable is truly random or not. Moreover, a more serious fundamental question that arises is whether the parameters of a model are estimable.

SEE ALSO *Causality; Censoring, Left and Right; Censoring, Sample; Frequency Distributions; Galton, Francis; Identification Problem; Linear Regression; Logistic Regression; Multicollinearity; Ordinary Least Squares Regression; Pearson, Karl; Probabilistic Regression; Probability; Regression; Regression Towards the Mean; Serial Correlation; Specification Error; Specification Tests; Student's T-Statistic; Test Statistics; Tobit*

BIBLIOGRAPHY

Aigner, Dennis. 1974. MSE Dominance of Least Squares with Errors-of-Observation. *Journal of Econometrics* 2 (4): 365–372.

Angrist, Joshua D., and Alan B. Krueger. 2001. Instrumental Variables and the Search for Identification: From Supply and Demand to Natural Experiments. *Journal of Economic Perspectives* 15 (4): 69–85.

Box, G. E. P., and D. R. Cox. 1964. An Analysis of Transformations. *Journal of the Royal Statistical Society, Series B* 26 (2): 211–252.

Chamberlin, Gary. 1982. The General Equivalence of Granger and Sims Causality. *Econometrica* 50 (3): 569–582.

Diebold, Francis X. 1998. *Elements of Forecasting*. 3rd ed. Cincinnati, OH: South-Western.

Draper, Norman, and Harry Smith. 1998. *Applied Regression Analysis*. 3rd ed. New York: Wiley.

Dufour, Jean-Marie, Denis Pelletier, and Éric Renault. 2006. Short Run and Long Run Causality in Time Series: Inference. *Journal of Econometrics* 132 (2): 337–362.

Galton, Francis. 1886. Regression Towards Mediocrity in Hereditary Stature. *Journal of the Anthropological Institute* 15: 246–263.

Granger, C. W. J. 1969. Investigating Casual Relationships by Econometric Models and Cross-Spectral Methods. *Econometrica* 37 (3): 424–238.

Greene, William H. 2003. *Econometric Analysis*. Upper Saddle River, NJ: Prentice Hall.

Gujarati, Damodar M. 2003. *Basic Econometrics*. 4th ed. Boston: McGraw-Hill.

Hocking, R. R. 1976. The Analysis and Selection of Variables in Linear Regression. *Biometrics* 32 (1): 1–49.

Madalla, G. S. 1983. *Limited Dependent and Qualitative Variables in Econometrics*. Cambridge, U.K.: Cambridge University Press.

McCallum, B. T. 1972. Relative Asymptotic Bias from Errors of Omission and Measurement. *Econometrica* 40 (4): 757–758.

Pearson, Karl, and Alice Lee. 1903. On the Laws of Inheritance in Man. *Biometrika* 11 (4): 357–462.

Powell, James L. 1984. Least Absolute Deviations Estimation for the Censored Regression Model. *Journal of Econometrics* 25 (3): 303–325.

Powell, James L. 1986. Symmetrically Trimmed Least Squares Estimation for Tobit Models. *Econometrica* 54 (6): 1435–1460.

Sims, Christopher A. 1972. Money, Income, and Causality. *American Economic Review* 62 (4): 540–552.

Tobin, James. 1958. Estimation of Relationships for Limited Dependent Variables. *Econometrica* 26 (1): 24–36.

Vinod, Hrishikesh D. 1978. A Survey of Ridge Regression and Related Techniques for Improvements over Ordinary Least Squares. *Review of Economics and Statistics* 60 (1): 121–131.

White, Halbert. 1980. A HeterosKedasticity-consistent Covariance Matrix Estimator and Direct Test for HeterosKedasticity. *Econometrica* 48 (4): 817–838.

Wickens, Michael. 1972. A Note on the Use of Proxy Variables. *Econometrica* 40 (4): 759–760.

Wiener, Norbert. 1956. The Theory of Prediction, in *Modern Mathematics for the Engineer, Series 1*, chapter 8, ed. Edwin F. Beckenback. New York: McGraw Hill.

Zellner, Arnold. 1979. Causality and Econometrics. In *Three Aspects of Policy and Policymaking: Knowledge, Data, and Institutions*, eds. Karl Brunner and Allan H. Meltzer, 9–50. Amsterdam, NY: North Holland.

Gaminie Meepagala
Haydar Kurban

REGRESSION TOWARDS THE MEAN

Regression towards the mean is a fundamental yet at first sight puzzling statistical phenomenon occurring between data from two variables, and it is a natural and inherent consequence of correlation being generally imperfect.

The effect of regression towards the mean was recognized in the late nineteenth century by Francis Galton (1822–1911) when investigating the relationship of the heights of parents and their adult children (see Bland and Altman 1994, Stigler 1986). Such height data are positively correlated; tall parents tend to produce tall adult children.

The diagram shows an ellipse that represents a cloud of correlated data points. The X and Y values are assumed for simplicity here to have equal mean and equal standard deviation. The X and Y values for Galton would be parent's height and adult offspring's height, but they could be any correlated variables, for example a measure of crime

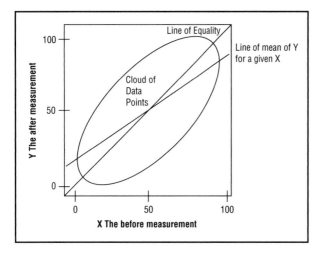

on some scale, for a sample of areas at one time, *X*, and at a later time, *Y*. The tilt of the ellipse shows that high values earlier are associated with high values later and vice versa; that is, positive correlation exists. Also on the diagram is the line of equality going diagonally bottom left to top right along the major axis of the ellipse. (Equality means that its slope = 1). Any point below this line indicates that the value of *Y* is smaller than that of *X*, whereas a point above indicates that it is greater. If correlation was perfect, the ellipse would narrow and become identical with the line of equality.

Also on the diagram is a line of shallower slope that gives the mean of *Y* for a given *X*. This is the *conditional mean* of *Y*. One can see that the conditional mean of *Y* given *X* is not the line of equality, because taking a vertical slice through the ellipse shows that the bulk of the distribution lies above the line of equality for an *X*-value below the mean of *X*, whereas it is below the line for an *X*-value above the mean of *X*. In fact, the line of the conditional mean for the situation described, that is, with standard deviations of *X* and *Y* equal, has a slope equal to the (Pearson) *correlation coefficient.* Therefore, the expected *Y*-value for a given *X*-value, in other words the conditional mean, is above the line of equality for *X* below the mean of *X*, and below the line of equality for *X* above its mean. Therefore, there is a tendency for values to be closer to the overall *Y*-mean, the effect being greater the weaker the correlation is.

This is precisely what Galton found: that the heights of adult children tended to be closer to the mean of the population than their parents' heights were; that is, they regressed towards the mean. Note that this does not make every one the same height in the end—the distribution can remain stable generation after generation.

A similar situation applies in a more general case than that described when neither the means nor the standard deviations of *X* and *Y* variables are equal to each other, such

as when successive generations are getting taller on average and becoming more variable in absolute terms, that is, in centimeters. In a more general case such as this the elliptical cloud of data points will be shifted up and will have greater vertical extension due to the greater standard deviation of the *Y* variable. The major axis of the elliptical cloud will no longer be the line of equality, but will still represent the line that the ellipse shrinks towards as the correlation becomes perfect. As in the earlier case, the line of conditional mean is still at a shallower slope than the major axis, and so the same effect occurs, that there is regression towards the mean such that the expected *Y*-value will be fewer *Y*-standard deviations from the *Y*-mean than the *X*-value is *X*-standard deviations from the *X*-mean. In fact, for an *X*-value Z_x standard deviations from the *X*-mean the expected *Y*-value will be "(1-correlation coefficient) multiplied by Z_x" standard deviations in *Y* from the major axis line, and equivalently only "correlation coefficient multiplied by Z_x" standard deviations in *Y* from the *Y*-mean. So, for example, if the *X* value is 1.5 standard deviations above its mean and the correlation coefficient between *X* and *Y* is 0.2, then the expected *Y*-value is only 0.3 standard deviations above its mean, that is, 1.2 below the original number of standard deviations.

The statistical method of *regression* owes its name to the discovery by Galton of this effect. Indeed, the *regression line* is simply the line of the conditional mean, exactly as discussed above. It is a surprise to some that the regression line does not run along the major axis of the cloud of data points. The equation for the line of conditional mean can be determined mathematically (see, for example, Freund 2004, which treats the more general case).

A consequence of the effect of regression towards the mean is if an intervention is applied to a group with high values before, for example a bad state before, and the control is another with lower values, a better state before, one is likely to find that the intervention appears to work even if it really has no superior effect. This is because the expectation is that the higher measurements will become lower. It is therefore vital that comparison is made like with like.

While it is possible to envisage situations that are more complex than those described above, so that the conditional mean is consequently no longer a simple straight line, one should never assume that the effect described is nonexistent.

BIBLIOGRAPHY

Bland, J. Martin, and Douglas G. Altman. 1994. Regression Towards the Mean. *British Medical Journal* 308 (June 4): 1499. http://bmj.bmjjournals.com/cgi/content/full/308/6942/1499.

Miller, Irwin, and Marylees Miller. 2004. *John E. Freund's Mathematical Statistics with Applications.* 7th ed. London: Prentice Hall.

Stigler, Stephen M. 1986 *The History of Statistics: The Measurement of Uncertainty Before 1900.* Cambridge, MA: Belknap.

Paul R. Marchant

REGRESSIVE TAXES

SEE *Taxes, Regressive.*

REGRET

SEE *Farsightedness.*

REGULATION

Regulation involves attempts by the government to monitor and correct any disorders in the workings of free markets. Formally, economic regulation refers to all types of taxes and subsidies as well as to governmental controls over prices, market entry, and other aspects of economic activity. Some regulation might directly impose monetary costs (e.g., taxes or fines on noncompliers), while other types of regulation might impose costs indirectly by mandating standards that might be costly to adhere to. Examples of regulation include limits on emissions from vehicles, fire-retardant materials used in children's bedding, airline safety standards, smoking bans, food safety, and consumer protection laws.

While the extent of government intervention in economic activity remains a matter of heated debate, few individuals would argue for a complete absence of regulation. Two widely accepted issues deserving of regulation might be related to a country's monetary system (smooth working of the banking system and the money supply) and national defense. These attempts might be focused on both buyers and sellers, or might be directed at one of the parties. Banking laws are examples of laws that affect both buyers and sellers, while regulations by the Occupational Safety and Health Administration (OSHA) can be viewed as aimed directly at sellers. The disorders or imperfections that regulation seeks to rectify might be related to prices (too high prices), quantity or service (not all customers being served), reliability (failure to adhere to schedules), and fairness, among other issues. In practice, common instances of regulation include promotion of competition, safeguarding the interests of buyers or sellers (or both), protecting the environment, and defending national interests. For instance, the Clayton Act and the Sherman Act

are two primary laws in the United States that deal with provision of fair market competition.

HISTORICAL PERSPECTIVE

Historically speaking, regulations have changed over time with new technologies, new concerns, and new revelations (e.g., harmful environmental effects of certain known substances). Sometimes, however, certain unexpected events bring about a flurry of regulations (or deregulations) in a rather short period of time. Examples of such events include the Great Depression, the 1973 oil embargo, and certain natural calamities. The Great Depression prompted governments to better regulate their economies so they could prevent wide and sudden variations in the unemployment and inflation rates. In the United States, the Federal Reserve System, which governs the money supply and oversees the banking system, was a direct offshoot of the Great Depression. The oil embargo led to various regulations regarding oil conservation including provisions for minimum fuel efficiency on automobiles. Further, natural disasters such as hurricanes and earthquakes can lead to tougher building codes in vulnerable areas.

Governments generally set up regulatory agencies to impose and monitor regulations. These agencies usually have semi-autonomous status to keep them relatively free of political pressures, although in a number of instances the regulated agencies end up enforcing the regulations passed by the executive branch. These agencies might be national (Federal Communications Commission), or they may be sub-national (Illinois Commerce Commission). In some instances, cross-national organizations such as the World Bank and United Nations impose codes of conduct across nations. However, such regulations generally are difficult to enforce and are usually less effective.

THEORETICAL UNDERPINNINGS

The theoretical underpinnings of regulation may be understood in the context of the three widely cited theories of regulation: (1) public interest theory; (2) capture theory; and (3) economic theory of regulation. According to the public interest theory, regulation is supplied or enacted by governments to correct inefficient and/or unfair market practices or outcomes. However, this theory implicitly assumes that regulators have the capacity and the willpower to determine what is fair and efficient. Since the late twentieth century, the public interest theory has been somewhat revised to recognize that regulatory agencies themselves might be inefficient. It is also unclear from this theory how public interest matters take the form of legislation. The capture theory of regulation can be seen as drawing from both economics and political science. According to this theory, regulatory agencies over time tend to be dominated or influenced by the industries they regulate. In other words, the integrity of the regulatory agencies tends to be compromised by their clientele. This theory, however, ignores special interest groups other than the regulated industries (e.g., consumers). The economic theory of regulation is primarily due to the work of the scholar George Stigler. This theory suggests that the economic laws of demand and supply can be employed to understand regulation. Alternately stated, the optimal amount of regulation would balance the demand and supply of government intervention. The demanders of regulation may be viewed as special interest groups (consumers) or parties being harmed by the current state of affairs (businesses unable to compete in protected markets). The suppliers of regulation are the regulatory agencies. This theory also recognizes that in the real world enactment of rules and regulations is not based purely on economic considerations. Rather, they are enacted in a political-economic context. The use of the laws of demand and supply enables efficiency in the provision of regulation. However, the economic theory of regulation has not been refined to the point where it enables us to predict specific industries in which regulation will be found.

IMPLEMENTATION AND BENEFITS

In imposing various types of regulation, regulators should be mindful of equity or fairness aspects on the one hand and efficiency or wastage considerations on the other hand. Generally, there is a tradeoff between the two criteria. For instance, some regulatory intervention that is relatively equitable (e.g., minimum wage laws providing a "fair" wage to unskilled or less-skilled workers) is usually not efficient (i.e., minimum wage laws do not allow the markets to work efficiently and impose undue hardships on some businesses). Thus, regulators have to weigh relative pros and cons of intervention and impose the socially optimal level of regulation. The socially optimal level would generally be less than total regulation (e.g., there should be a socially desirable level of pollution; getting rid of all pollution would impose undue costs on the society in terms of sacrifices to be made, such as no electricity generated via nuclear or thermal power plants and no polluting vehicles).

The main benefit of regulation is that it corrects shortcomings in the workings of markets. Some benefits of regulation, however, might be diffused over time, while the costs might be upfront. In such cases, it becomes difficult for regulators to convince the affected parties of the desirability of regulation. An example of this may be environmental regulation. Regulations mandating the cleanup of toxic waste dumps impose costs up front but their benefits in terms of improvement in the environment and related health benefits would only be realized over time.

The costs of regulation include the costs of compliance and the costs of monitoring. Sometimes the monitoring costs can turn out to be very high with the result that in certain instances products might either not be regulated or not be regulated effectively. Other times there are unexpected consequences of regulation when markets are connected or are interdependent. For instance, tougher regulation ensuring the purity of the milk supply would affect the milk industry directly, but also related industries that make use of dairy products (restaurants, cheese, coffee, and ice cream, for example).

Price regulation might impose direct price controls on products (price cap regulation), or it might control prices indirectly (via rate of return regulation where regulated firms are free to set prices, provided they do not earn above a specified rate of return on capital). Price cap regulation can affect the regulated firm's investments in research and development, while it has been shown that the rate of return regulation leads to overcapitalization (i.e., regulated firms would use more capital than they would in the absence of such regulation). Thus, one type of regulation does not seem suitable for all cases.

Sometimes regulation is uncertain and not all types of intervention are predictable. Such uncertainty might plague both suppliers of regulation (i.e., government) and the parties affected by regulation. Governments might not know a priori whether they would have to regulate a new technology (new supersonic airplane) because of some future undesirable side effects (new airplane too noisy for residential areas). The public is uncertain whether and when current or future products might face additional regulations. A case in point is the impending threat of restrictions on cell phone usage while driving.

In practice, even after regulators have determined that certain products or industries need to be regulated, there is generally a time delay (called a regulatory lag) between the realization of the need for intervention, the enactment of relevant laws and their implementation. This reduces the effectiveness of regulatory intervention as it affords the affected parties time to find ways to circumvent the regulations. In certain cases, the regulatory lag might be long enough to make rules unnecessary when they are finally put into place.

In conclusion, regulation seems essential in many instances. One could differ in one's perceptions about the scope of regulation, but its desirability in many instances seems real. Over time government intervention needs to be dynamic to be efficient and effective. Certain industries might not need regulations over time, while new regulatory instruments might have to be developed in other instances, such as in the regulation of the Internet.

SEE ALSO *Antitrust; Antitrust Regulation; Deregulation; Privatization*

BIBLIOGRAPHY

Kahn, Alfred E. 1971. *The Economics of Regulation: Principles and Institutions.* 2 vols. New York: Wiley.

Peltzman, Sam. 1967. Toward a More General Theory of Regulation. *Journal of Law and Economics* 19: 211–240.

Posner, Richard. 1974. Theories of Economic Regulation. *Bell Journal of Economics* 5: 335–358.

Stigler, George J. 1971. The Theory of Economic Regulation. *Bell Journal of Economics* 2: 3–21.

Rajeev K. Goel

REHABILITATION

SEE *Prisons.*

REIGN OF TERROR

SEE *French Revolution.*

REINCARNATION

Reincarnation is the cultural belief that human beings can be born and reborn in endless cycles of births and rebirths. Forms of reincarnation are found in a wide range of human societies, ranging from small scale or "tribal" groups to the ancient Greeks and most conspicuously, those religions that developed in India during and after 6 BCE, if not earlier. Nevertheless, there has been a surprising lack of ethnographic documentation of the cross-cultural spread of these religions. The reasons are many: Perhaps most significant was the impact of Christian missions generally hostile to indigenous religions, especially reincarnation theories that were declared "anathema" by the Church in 553 CE.

Until recent times ethnographers were unfamiliar with such doctrines and tended to subsume them under the better known class of "ancestor cults," easy enough to do because reincarnation is often associated with the world of ancestors. Additionally, there was the widespread prejudice that reincarnation is uniquely associated with Indic religions like that of Buddhism and Hinduism, tending scholars to neglect its presence elsewhere. The historical evidence is clear that reincarnation doctrines known as metempsychosis, metacosmesis, or metensomatosis existed in ancient Greece even prior to the Buddha in the cosmology of Pythagoras. These doctrines continued outside of the dominant or mainline Greek traditions of cosmology between 7 BCE to about 3 CE

through such figures as Empedocles, Pindar, Plato and the neo-Platonic traditions, especially Plotinus. Greek reincarnation doctrines influenced some Middle Eastern societies, most notably the Druze of Israel and Lebanon from around 1017 CE; the Shiite Nusayriyah of Western Syria belonging to the Ismā'ilī tradition around the same time; and the Alevis of Central Turkey, perhaps during the same time period although no clear historical evidence is available. All these societies had reincarnation theories that for the most part posited immediate reincarnation after death followed by rebirth in the larger religious community, if not a specific social group or clan.

Studies by ethnographers found that the presence of reincarnation doctrines among Northwest Coast Indians was the basis of the Indians' eschatological and cosmic beliefs. These studies culminated in a 1994 pioneer work, *Amerindian Rebirth: Reincarnation Beliefs among North American Indians and Inuit*, which described a wide range of Amerindian groups believing in reincarnation. For Melanesia, the only detailed study is the classic work of anthropologist Bronislaw Malinowski (1884–1942). Malinowski documented in great detail the reincarnation theories of the Trobriand Islanders, most notably in his 1916 essay "Baloma: the Spirits of the Dead in the Trobriand Islands," based on his fieldwork in New Guinea during World War I. A similar ethnographic lacuna exists for West Africa where scattered references indicate that reincarnation theories were widely prevalent before colonial contact. Fortunately, there are detailed ethnographic accounts for at least one large group, the Ibo of southeastern Nigeria, now highly Christianized but still retaining some of their traditional reincarnation beliefs. What the cross-cultural evidence reveals is that reincarnation doctrines are found in various parts of the world, many of whom were unaffected by Indic civilization.

In order to bring some order into widely dispersed reincarnation doctrines it is necessary to deal with their simplest manifestation among small-scale societies, and then the more complex Greek and Indic representatives. Propitiation of ancestors ("ancestor cults") is a widespread form of religious life. After death, the spirit goes into a realm of the ancestors and ancestral spirits continue to interact with living persons, who in turn have to propitiate them. Only one structural feature is required for an ancestor cult to develop into a reincarnation doctrine. The spirit at death goes into the world of the ancestors and then, after a temporary stay in that realm, returns to the human world by being reborn among former kin. Then, after death, the spirit goes back to the ancestral world and the rebirth cycle continues. More complex systems are constructed upon this "elementary form" of a reincarnation doctrine.

Among small-scale societies there are two trajectories of rebirth: The Northwest Coast Indians and the Inuit share a widespread circumpolar complex (spreading into Central Asia) in affirming that after death one could be reborn as an animal. In West Africa and Melanesia one cannot be reborn except as a human being. When there is a belief in rebirth as an animal or when humans and animals have their own reincarnation cycles there develops a concomitant respect for animal life. Thus, while killing animals is necessary for existence, the Inuit hunter thanks the animal for its sacrificial gift and implores it to return to another rebirth, human or animal. Within the two broad complexes of being reborn as animal or human, there is considerable variation as to whether cross-sex reincarnation is possible or not.

The striking feature of reincarnation in small-scale societies is the absence of other-worldly rewards and punishments imposed on the departing soul at death, even though such societies have highly developed secular moral codes. Once the appropriate funeral rites have been performed, anyone can enter the temporary world of ancestors. By contrast, owing to Indian and Greek philosophical preoccupation with social morality and ethics, the entry into the other world is conditional on the good and bad done in this world. Thus, in Indian thought there developed the doctrine of "karma," the idea that the good and bad humans do on earth will result in punishments or rewards in the other world, followed by similar rewards and punishments in the next reincarnation. By contrast, the Greek tradition does not have this uniformity although considerable emphasis is placed on otherworld compensations rather than rewards in the next rebirth.

Greek reincarnation can be illustrated with an example from Plato in the final chapter of *The Republic*. Plato mentions the case of a warrior named Er whose spirit escaped after ten days while his hitherto undecomposed corpse was being cremated. Er then went on a long underground journey followed by a sojourn in a strange place where he confronted judges sitting beside two chasms. These judges order the righteous to take a right road of the heavenly chasms whereas the bad must take the left that went downward into places of punishment. Er was instructed to watch and remember the proceedings so that he could relay his experiences to fellow mortals when he returned to Earth. Er mentions specific punishments and rewards offered to people right then and there by the judges, the bad undergoing cruel but just punishment and the good enjoying the rewards of heaven.

Having expiated their past in this manner, people are now free beings who will eventually assemble in a meadow awaiting their rebirth in the human world. One of the Fates, the goddess Lachesis, gives the people a choice of "packages" containing their future life projections on Earth. Unhappily, people do not choose wisely. Enticed by power and wealth they pick the wrong life choices, often replicating the habits of their former lives on Earth. They come back to Lachesis who allocates each a guardian spirit; the other Fates seal these compacts making them irreversible. People then come to a land of dreadful thirst and reach Lethe, the river of forgetfulness. All drink the waters of Lethe except Er, who must remember to tell his tale to mortals when his spirit eventually returns to his corpse and revives it. The Platonic myth culminates in people going to sleep but when midnight comes there is an earthquake and thunder. Suddenly, the people are all swept up and away like shooting stars, here and there, propelled to another rebirth in the human world.

SEE ALSO *Anthropology; Buddha; Buddhism; Ethnography; Hinduism; Malinowski, Bronislaw; Religion*

BIBLIOGRAPHY

De Laguna, Frederica. 1972. *Under Mount Saint Elias: The History and Culture of Yukutat Tlingit.* Washington D.C.: Smithsonian, 1972.

Henderson, Richard N. 1972. *The King in Every Man.* New Haven, CT: Yale University Press.

Malinowski, Bronislaw. 1948. Baloma: The Spirits of the Dead in the Trobriand Islands. In *Magic, Science, and Religion and Other Essays.* Boston: Beacon Press.

Mills, Antonia, and Richard Slobodin, eds. 1994. *Amerindian Rebirth: Reincarnation Beliefs among North American Indians and Inuit.* Toronto: University of Toronto Press.

Obeyesekere, Gananath. 2002. *Imagining Karma: Ethical Transformation in Amerindian, Buddhist and Greek Rebirth.* Berkeley: University of California Press.

Uchendu, Victor. 1965. *The Igbo of Southeast Nigeria.* New York: Holt, Rinehart and Winston.

Walens, Stanley. 1981. *Feasting with Cannibals: An Essay on Kwakiutl Cosmology.* Princeton, NJ: Princeton University Press.

Gananath Obeyesekere

REINFORCEMENT THEORIES

For more than a century, the term *reinforcement* has referred to the emergence of a reliable, learned change in behavior produced when a response or stimulus is differentially followed by a rewarding or punishing event (a reinforcer). Early examples of instrumental reinforcement included: Edward Lee Thorndike's (1874–1949) experiments with cats learning to escape (what he called) a puzzle box by manipulating a release mechanism for the door,

B. F. Skinner's (1904–1990) training of rats to press a lever for food, and the work of Willard Stanton Small (1870–1943) and Edward Chace Tolman (1886–1959) showing that rats could learn a maze path with, or without, food in the goal box. The dominant example of early Pavlovian reinforcement—from the work of the Russian physiologist Ivan Petrovich Pavlov (1849–1936)—showed that a dog could be conditioned to salivate to a signal predicting the imminent arrival of either meat powder or a weak acid solution in its mouth.

THEORY WARS

Each of the above examples provided an answer to a critical conceptual and practical question, "What conditions must be added to the simple repetition of a stimulus and/or a response to produce learning?" However, each answer also left notable theoretical questions unresolved. As a result, more than half of the twentieth century was spent on attempts to develop a general theory of learning. These theories differed in: (1) how learning was represented (for example, as stimulus-response or stimulus-stimulus associations, as cognitive maps, memories, or transmitted information; (2) the necessary and sufficient qualities of a reinforcer (for example, a drive reducer vs. a drive inducer); and (3) the necessary temporal and spatial relations between the response and/or stimulus and the reinforcer (for example, contiguity vs. contingency). For additional differences see the analyses in William K. Estes's *Modern Learning Theory: A Critical Analysis of Five Examples* (1954) of Thorndike's concept of the strengthening of neural connections, Edwin Ray Guthrie's (1886–1959) emphasis on temporal contiguity and repetition, Tolman's cognitive maps and expectancies, and Clark L. Hull's (1884–1952) multiple learning variables and performance equations relating them to each other and behavior.

The theory wars were both exciting and frustrating. Excitement came from the development of extensive frameworks like Hull's hypothetico-deductive system, which was applied to behaviors ranging from approach-withdrawal reactions (Neal E. Miller, 1944), to curiosity (Harry Fowler, 1967), and personality and psychotherapy (John Dollard and Neal E. Miller, 1950). Difficulties arose from the inability of researchers to agree on critical tests to distinguish alternative theories and concepts, and from the continued failure of general theories to account for important empirical phenomena like partial reinforcement, and incentive contrast. For example, Abram Amsel (1922–2006; 1992) and E. J. Capaldi (1967) showed that relatively unpredictable reinforcers produced greater resistance to extinction than more frequent but predictable reinforcers. Similarly, Charles F. Flaherty (c. 1937–2004; 1966) showed that the effects of presenting

two different reinforcers depended on their order. The absence of a satisfying general theoretical account of diverse phenomena led many researchers to abandon the search for a general theory and focus on the empirical effectiveness and applications of specific reinforcement procedures.

EFFECTIVE REINFORCEMENT PROCEDURES AND APPLICATIONS

Thorndike claimed that all organisms were susceptible to the effects of reinforcement. Skinner supported the empirical generality of this claim by showing how reinforcement could be used to readily control the laboratory behavior of rats and pigeons. Marian Breland Bailey and Keller Breland, early students of Skinner, handily extended his reinforcement approach to the training of animals in shows and zoos by using "bridge stimuli" (secondary reinforcers). During his lengthy career, Skinner focused increasingly on the control of human behaviors by reinforcers, at first by using reinforcement schedules to produce human-like behaviors in pigeons, including "superstitions" and "assembly-line" response patterns. In a recent continuation of this kind of comparative approach, Brian Lau and Paul W. Glimcher used brain scanning to identify specific areas involved in the well-known operant behavior of matching response rates to reinforcer frequency in rhesus monkeys.

Skinner also added a specific human focus, emphasizing the potential effects of operant conditioning on everyday human behavior in his writing of a utopian novel, *Walden Two* (1948), followed by several books of essays: *Science and Human Behavior* (1953), *Beyond Freedom and Dignity* (1971), and *About Behaviorism* (1974). Further, Skinner helped develop specific reinforcement applications in the form of programmed learning in education, and token economies for treating the mentally ill and deficient. Many examples of such procedures are described in an extensive applied literature, e.g., the *Journal of Applied Behavior Analysis*, and in edited volumes (such as William O'Donohue's *Learning and Behavior Therapy*, 1998; see also work of Leonard Krasner).

MOTIVATIONAL AND OPTIMALITY MODELS OF REINFORCEMENT

Reinforcers, in terms of their ability to produce learning and behavior, were first limited largely to incentives that reduced physiological imbalances of the body; but reinforcers also can be novel stimuli, social or sexual cues, or simply access to a higher probability response. For example, William Timberlake and James W. Allison showed that reinforcement depends on the use of operant schedules that restrict access to a response or reinforcer relative to its free (unconstrained) baseline level. William

Timberlake and Valerie Farmer-Dougan reviewed how such a general regulatory framework could be translated to applied settings, and James W. Allison showed the relevance of regulatory work-income trade-offs to economic models (see *Behavioral Economics* 1983). J. E. R. Staddon (see *Adaptive Dynamics: The Theoretical Analysis of Behavior,* 2001) linked operant behavior to general optimization models, and J. C. David (see MacKay in *Information Theory, Inference, and Learning Algorithms,* 2003) and other scientists used computer modeling to produce optimizing algorithms leading to adaptive learning in machines.

PAVLOVIAN MODELS OF REINFORCEMENT

Beginning with work on information processing and interaction among predictive cues in the 1960s, Pavlovian conditioning became an important focus of reinforcement research and theory. Psychologists Robert A. Rescorla and Allan R. Wagner modeled the interaction of cues in Pavlovian conditioning using a variant of a linear operator model in which stimuli predicting a reinforcer compete for its incremental strengthening effect. Their model appropriately predicts that when two predictive stimuli are trained together, the more salient stimulus typically overshadows learning about the less salient stimulus, and a stimulus learned first most often interferes with (blocks) learning about a stimulus added later (although both facilitation and configural learning can occur in similar circumstances).

Subsequent researchers, like Ralph Miller and Mark E. Bouton, added a role for context conditioning, especially in application-related phenomena like the reinstatement of extinguished fear. Similar models of reinforcement have focused either on aspects of the interaction of Pavlovian and instrumental contingencies (see Geoffery Hall, 2002), or on the scalar effect on acquisition speed and performance of the length of the CS relative to the length of inter-reinforcer interval (see a summary by Russell M. Church, 2002). Finally, Modelers such as Nestor A. Schmajuk (1977) have turned to the use of multilayer connectionist models, based on error-correction algorithms, to simulate interactions among multiple predictive cues.

To complete the picture, current investigators interested in neurophysiological substrates of learning often use Pavlovian and Operant reinforcement procedures to clarify the effects of brain stimulation, lesions, drugs (see Shepherd Siegel), neural transmitters and trans-gene manipulations (see Louis D. Matzel). Finally, considerable progress has been made in deciphering the contribution of simple sensory, motor, and Pavlovian mechanisms to learning related to species typical behavior. See the admirable book by Thomas J. Carew, 2000, in which he includes accounts of the neurophysiological work by Richard W. Thompson (see also Thompson, 2005) on conditioning of the nictitating membrane in rabbits, and by Eric Kandel (see also Frank Krasne, 1985) on gill withdrawal in Aplysia (sea slugs).

EVOLUTIONARY AND ECOLOGICAL APPROACHES TO REINFORCEMENT

A final approach to reinforcement began with twentieth-century researchers interested in evolution and learning. For example, T. C. Schneirla and M. E. Bitterman examined similarities and differences among species in reinforcement learning (see accounts in *Comparative Psychology: A Handbook* edited by Gary Greenberg and Martin Haraway). More recent investigators have explored the extent to which phenomena of human cognition can be produced by selective reinforcement of the perceptual choices of nonhuman animals. See Edward A. Wasserman and Thomas R. Zentall's edited book on categorization and short-term memory mechanisms in animals, and edited book of Cecilia M. Heyes and Bennet G. Galef focused on imitation and social learning (*Social Learning in Animals: The Roots of Culture*).

More ecologically oriented researchers like John Garcia, Alan Kamil, David Sherry, and Charles R. Gallistel have clarified how ecologically specialized perceptual-motor learning mechanisms evolved to meet requirements for survival (summarized in Sara J. Shettleworth, 1998 *Cognition, Evolution, and Behavior*). The relevance of such mechanisms to all laboratory research was pointed out by William Timberlake (2002) in examples of how ecologically-based abilities of common laboratory species have affected the design and results of common laboratory apparatus and procedures. Finally, work on human information-processing abilities, like that of John Tooby and Leda Cosmides on causal reasoning, and Paul Rozin and Carol Nemeroff on contamination and disgust reactions to foodstuffs, apply a similar ecological and evolutionary logic in the study of humans.

In short, given the diversity of reinforcement phenomena, mechanisms, and results, it appears that further increases in the effectiveness and generality of Reinforcement Theories and Models will depend on considering the effects of evolutionary, functional, applied, and neurophysiological contexts, rather than depending solely on general learning principles and theories.

SEE ALSO *Classical Conditioning; Cognition; Economics, Behavioral; Hull, Clark; Learned Helplessness; Neuroscience; Operant Conditioning; Pavlov, Ivan; Skinner, B. F.; Thorndike, Edward; Tolman, Edward*

BIBLIOGRAPHY

Allison, James W. 1983. *Behavioral Economics*. New York: Praeger.

Amsel, Abram. 1992. *Frustration Theory: An Analysis of Dispositional Learning and Memory*. New York: Cambridge University Press.

Capaldi, E. J. 1966. Partial Reinforcement: A Hypothesis of Sequential Effects. *Psychological Review* 73: 459–477.

Church, Russel M. 2002. Temporal Learning. In *Stevens' Handbook of Experimental Psychology*, vol. 3, eds. Hal Pashler and Randy Gallistel, 365–394. 3rd ed. New York: John Wiley and Sons.

Dollard, John, and Neal E. Miller. 1950. *Personality and Psychotherapy: An Analysis in Terms of Learning, Thinking, and Culture*. New York: McGraw-Hill.

Domjan, Michael. 2006. *The Principles of Learning and Behavior*. 5th ed. Belmont, CA: Thomson/Wadsworth.

Estes, William K. 1954. *Modern Learning Theory: A Critical Analysis of Five Examples*. New York: Appleton-Century-Crofts.

Flaherty, Charles F. 1996. *Incentive Relativity*. New York: Cambridge University Press.

Fowler, Harry. 1965. *Curiosity and Exploratory Behavior*. New York: Macmillan.

Gallistel, Charles R. 1990. *The Organization of Learning*. Cambridge, MA: MIT Press.

Garcia, John, and Rodrigo Garcia y Robertson. 1985. Evolution of Learning Mechanisms. In *Psychology and Learning*, ed. Barbara L. Hammonds, 187–243. Washington, DC: American Psychological Association.

Greenberg, Gary, and Maury M. Haraway. 1998. *Comparative Psychology: A Handbook*. New York: Garland.

Heyes, Cecilia M., and Bennet G. Galef Jr., eds. 1996. *Social Learning in Animals: The Roots of Culture*. San Diego, CA: Academic Press.

Hull, Clark L. 1943. *Principles of Behavior: An Introduction to Behavior Theory*. New York: Appleton-Century.

Krasne, Frank. 2002. Neural Analysis of Learning in Simple Systems. In *Stevens' Handbook of Experimental Psychology*, vol. 3, eds. Hal Pashler and Randy Gallistel, 131–200. 3rd ed. New York: John Wiley and Sons.

Krasner, Leonard. 1985. Applications of Learning Theory in the Environment. In *Psychology and Learning*, ed. Barbara L. Hammonds, 49–94. Washington, DC: American Psychological Association.

Lau, Brian, and Paul W. Glimcher. 2005. Dynamic Response-by-Response Models of Matching Behavior in Rhesus Monkeys. *Journal of the Experimental Analysis of Behavior* 84 (3): 555–579.

MacKay, David J.C. 2003. *Information Theory, Inference, and Learning Algorithms*. Cambridge, U.K.: Cambridge University Press.

Mackintosh, Nicholas John. 1983. *Conditioning and Associative Learning*. Oxford: Clarendon Press.

Matzel, Louis D. 2002. Learning Mutants. In *Stevens' Handbook of Experimental Psychology*, Vol. 3, eds. Hal Pashler and Randy Gallistel, 201–238. 3rd eds. New York: John Wiley and Sons.

Miller, Neal E. 1944. Experimental Studies of Conflict. In *Personality and the Behavior Disorders*, ed. J. McV. Hunt, 1044. New York: Ronald.

Miller, Ralph, and Martha Escobar. 2002. Learning: Laws and Models of Basic Conditioning. In *Stevens' Handbook of Experimental Psychology*, vol. 3, eds. Hal Pashler and Randy Gallistel, 47–102. 3rd ed. New York: John Wiley and Sons.

O'Donohue, William. 1998. *Learning and Behavior Therapy*. Boston: Allyn and Bacon.

Rozin, Paul, and Carol Nemeroff. 2002. Sympathetic Magical Thinking: The Contagion and Similarity "Heuristics." In *Heuristics and Biases: The Psychology of Intuitive Judgement*, eds. Thomas Gilovich, Dale Griffin, and Daniel Kahneman, 201–216. Cambridge, U.K.: Cambridge University Press.

Schmajuk, Nestor A. 1997. *Animal Learning and Cognition: A Neural Network Approach*. Cambridge, U.K.: Cambridge University Press.

Shettleworth, Sara J. 1998. *Cognition, Evolution, and Behavior*. New York: Oxford University Press.

Siegel, Shepherd. 2005. Drug Tolerance, Drug Addiction, and Drug Anticipation. *Current Directions in Psychological Science* 14 (6): 296–300.

Staddon, J. E. R. 2001. *Adaptive Dynamics: The Theoretical Analysis of Behavior*. Cambridge, MA: MIT Press.

Thompson, Richard F. 2005. In Search of Memory Traces. *Annual Review of Psychology* 56: 1–23.

Timberlake, William D. 2002. Niche-related Learning in Laboratory Paradigms: The Case of Maze Behavior in Norway Rats. *Behavioural Brain Research* 134 (1): 355–374.

Timberlake, William D., and Valeri A. Farmer-Dougan. 1991. Reinforcement in Applied Settings: Figuring Out ahead of Time What Will Work. *Psychological Bulletin* 110 (3): 379–391.

Tooby, John, and Leda Cosmides. 2005. Conceptual Foundations of Evolutionary Psychology. In *The Handbook of Evolutionary Psychology*, ed. David M. Buss, 5–67. Hoboken, NJ: John Wiley and Sons.

Wasserman, Edward A., and Thomas R. Zentall, eds. 2006. *Comparative Cognition: Experimental Explorations of Animal Intelligence*. Oxford: Oxford University Press.

William Timberlake

REJECTION/ ACCEPTANCE

Whether people perceive that they are socially rejected or accepted plays a role in determining how individuals evaluate themselves and the world around them. People who generally feel accepted or included by important others may fare better emotionally and interpersonally than people who generally feel rejected or excluded. In fact, research has demonstrated that people may possess a fundamental need to belong that closely ties their feelings of self-worth, or self-esteem, with their yearnings for social acceptance (Baumeister and Leary 1995). Because of the apparent pervasiveness of people's quest for social inclusion, systematic investigation of experiences and consequences of social rejection has enjoyed considerable popularity. Social psychologists, for example, may be interested in examining how people's perceptions of inclusion or exclusion during a given situation may influence their self-esteem. Clinical psychologists, on the other hand, may be more interested in investigating the long-term consequences of people's perceptions of inclusion or exclusion (e.g., marital satisfaction).

One theory of self-esteem, *sociometer theory*, states that people's self-esteem and mood may function as a gauge, much like a fuel gauge, alerting them when they are experiencing feelings of rejection or exclusion (Leary, Tambor, Terdal, and Downs 1995). People experience increases in state self-esteem (momentary feelings of self-worth) and positive mood in response to inclusion experiences and decreases in state self-esteem and positive mood in response to exclusion experiences. In fact, people may be attuned more to decreases in perceived social acceptance than to increases in social acceptance (Leary, Haupt, Strausser, and Chokel 1998). This is because feelings of social rejection provide a signal for the rejected person to behave in ways that will increase their likelihood of social inclusion at the current time or in the future. For example, if a man perceives that he is being socially excluded, he may make a greater effort to increase his interaction partner's liking for him. Alternately, he may be aggressive toward his rejector, temporarily sacrificing his need for acceptance but, perhaps, influencing the rejector and others to reconsider excluding him in the future.

Because people respond to experiences of social rejection in different fashions, researchers have investigated the influence of certain individual difference, or personality, variables on their reactions to instances of social inclusion, including, for example the influence of trait, or overall self-esteem, and *rejection sensitivity* (Downey and Feldman 1996) on people's responses to exclusion feedback. Although trait self-esteem does not differentially influence people's responses to exclusion, rejection sensitivity, a tendency to anxiously perceive and interpret social interactions as exclusion experiences, may do so. More specifically, people who are highly sensitive to rejection may respond to perceived exclusion experiences in ways that ultimately lead to continued negative social interactions. In contrast, people who are less sensitive to rejection may be both more likely to accurately identify rejection experiences and more adept at restoring positive interpersonal interactions.

SEE ALSO *Self-Awareness Theory; Self-Esteem; Sociometry*

BIBLIOGRAPHY

Baumeister, Roy F., and Mark R. Leary. 1995. The Need to Belong: Desire for Interpersonal Attachments as a Fundamental Human Motivation. *Psychological Bulletin* 117: 497–529.

Downey, Geraldine, and Scott I. Feldman. 1996. Implications of Rejection Sensitivity for Intimate Relationships. *Journal of Personality and Social Psychology* 70: 1327–1343.

Leary, Mark R., Alison L. Haupt, Kristine S. Strausser, and Jason T. Chokel. 1998. Calibrating the Sociometer: The Relationship between Interpersonal Relationships and State Self-Esteem. *Journal of Personality and Social Psychology* 74: 1290–1299.

Leary, Mark R., Ellen S. Tambor, Sonja K. Terdal, and Deborah L. Downs. 1995. Self-Esteem as an Interpersonal Monitor: The Sociometer Hypothesis. *Journal of Personality and Social Psychology* 68: 518–530.

Jorgianne Civey Robinson

RELATIONS, INTERGROUP

SEE *Intergroup Relations.*

RELATIONS, INTERNATIONAL

SEE *International Relations.*

RELATIONS, RACE

SEE *Race Relations.*

RELATIONS, SOCIAL

SEE *Social Relations.*

RELATIONS, WORKPLACE

SEE *Workplace Relations.*

RELATIONSHIP SATISFACTION

Satisfaction in close relationships is defined as the subjective attitude (satisfaction) and affective experience (happiness) in the evaluation of one's relationship. Most of the existing research on this topic focuses on the correlates and predictors of satisfaction in married couples. The subjective perception of satisfaction is an important indicator of relationship quality and has consequences for the longevity of the relationship, as less satisfied relationships are more likely to end. Multidimensional analyses indicate that the structure of satisfaction is different for men and women. Men's marital satisfaction usually can be determined by one factor that taps into overall happiness in the marriage (e.g., lack of regret over marrying, the amount of disagreement with their spouses on affection and sex). Women's marital satisfaction, in contrast, appears to be two-dimensional. The first factor is overall happiness in the marriage, as with men, and the second dimension concerns the ways in which the couple relates to other people, including proper behavior with family members and friends.

In terms of stability, research by Carolyn Pape Cowan and Philip A. Cowan on the patterns of change in marital satisfaction (2000) shows that satisfaction is highest during the premarital and early years of marriage, then declines later. This decline holds true for both men and women, but appears to level off after several years. Despite this drop, couples that stay together often still report that they are happily married.

Research on predictors of relationship satisfaction has centered on intrapersonal, interpersonal/interactional, and environmental determinants of marital satisfaction. Researchers examining the intrapersonal determinants of relationship satisfaction investigate the ways personality characteristics of the members influence happiness in the context of the marriage. Analyses of differences and similarities between members of a couple reveal that "homogamy," or partner similarity on different dimensions such as personality, emotionality, and values, predicts greater relationship stability and satisfaction. There is also evidence that specific personality characteristics of one or both of the members of the couple predict relationship satisfaction. Individuals who score high on the scale for emotional instability and those with negative views about themselves tend to have less satisfied partners. Similarly, Lilah Raynor Koski and Phillip R. Shaver in *Satisfaction in Close Relationships* (1997) note that in general, people with an insecure attachment style (i.e., those who doubt their own worthiness for love, as well as the dependability and availability of their partners) tend to have less satisfied spouses. It has also been shown, however, that attachment styles in men and women relate to relationship satisfaction somewhat differently. Women with an anxious attachment style (i.e., being preoccupied with relationships, and wanting extreme closeness and being afraid of being in love) experience lower levels of self- and partner satisfaction. Among men, in contrast, it is an avoidant attachment style (i.e., being uncomfortable with closeness, and dependency on other people) that predicts lower levels of self- and partner satisfaction. These personality differences relate to differences in communication and emotions. Securely attached men and women, who believe in their self-worth and have a trust in the availability of significant others for love and safety, appear to be more comfortable with self-disclosure, trust, and commitment, and report higher levels of positive emotions that are characteristic of satisfied relationships.

Researchers who focus on interpersonal and interactional correlates of marital satisfaction have observed that certain emotional and communication patterns are more prevalent among dissatisfied couples. One main finding is that it is the communication style between the partners, and not the number of conflicts per se, that predicts enduring relationship satisfaction. For example, Mari Clements, Allan Cordova, Howard Markman, and Jean-Philippe Laurenceau identified a pattern of "escalation-withdrawal-invalidation" in communication as detrimental to relationship satisfaction (1997). In this pattern, the couple allows negative interactions to spiral out of control and reach increasing levels of negativity. John Gottman in *What Predicts Divorce?* (1994) refers to a similar processes of "negative reciprocity" that prevents the couple from snapping out of the negative mood state the conflict has put them in. Such escalation and negative reciprocity is then followed by one or both members of the couple becoming less communicative (withdrawal). In the next phase, the couple usually engages in invalidation, whereby partners angrily assail each other's character. Gottman's research shows that a communication style characterized by a "demand-withdrawal" pattern is similarly maladaptive. The repetition of this pattern, in which one partner's criticism, demands, or complaints produces defensiveness and passive inaction (stonewalling) in the other partner, erodes relationship satisfaction and ultimately leads to the dissolution of the relationship.

There is very little research on relationship satisfaction outside of heterosexual married couples. Based on the limited evidence available on same-sex partners, Gottman and his colleagues reported that there are many commonalities in the correlates of relationship satisfaction in homosexual and heterosexual relationships (Gottman, Levenson, Gross, et al. 2003). Consistent with findings on heterosexual couples, behavioral expressions of contempt, disgust, and defensiveness are related to lower levels of relationship satisfaction, whereas positive expressions, such as humor and affection, are related to higher levels of relationship satisfaction in gay and lesbian couples.

In addition to the intrapersonal and interpersonal factors reviewed, environmental factors also affect relationship satisfaction. Life events such as the loss of a job or illness, as well as chronic stressors such as unemployment, can contribute to decreased levels of satisfaction. The effects of environmental factors can best be explained through their interaction with intrapersonal and interpersonal vulnerabilities, however. For example, although Cowan and Cowan reported significant drops in satisfaction around the time couples have their first child, couples who communicate better appear to be less vulnerable to erosion of marital satisfaction around this stressful time (2000).

Interventions aimed at increasing relationship satisfaction target maladaptive communication styles and/or negative emotions. For instance, therapeutic approaches try to change negative expectations about the partner and the relationship in order to enhance constructive discussion. Likewise, emotion-focused interventions attempt to enhance the understanding and down-regulation of negative emotions such as anger that hinder more constructive styles of coping with problems in the relationship.

BIBLIOGRAPHY

Clements, Mari L., Allan D. Cordova, Howard J. Markman, and Jean-Philippe Laurenceau. 1997. The Erosion of Marital Satisfaction Over Time and How To Prevent It. In *Satisfaction in Close Relationships*, eds. Robert J. Sternberg and Mahzad Hojjat, 335–355. New York: Guilford Press.

Cowan, Carolyn Pape, and Philip A. Cowan. 2000. *When Partners Become Parents: The Big Life Change for Couples.* Mahwah, NJ: Lawrence Erlbaum Associates.

Gottman, John Mordechai. 1994. *What Predicts Divorce? The Relationship Between Marital Processes and Marital Outcomes.* Hillsdale, NJ: Lawrence Erlbaum Associates.

Gottman, John Mordechai, Robert W. Levenson, James Gross, et al. 2003. Correlates of Gay and Lesbian Couples' Relationship Satisfaction and Relationship Dissolution. *Journal of Homosexuality* 45 (1): 23–43.

Koski, Lilah Raynor, and Phillip R. Shaver. 1997. Attachment and Relationship Satisfaction Across the Lifespan. In *Satisfaction in Close Relationships*, eds. Robert J. Sternberg and Mahzad Hojjat, 26–55. New York: Guilford Press.

Ozlem Ayduk
Anett Gyurak

RELATIONSHIPS, PARENT-CHILD

SEE *Parent-Child Relationships.*

RELATIONSHIPS, SIBLING

SEE *Sibling Relationships.*

RELATIONSHIPS, TEACHER-CHILD

SEE *Teacher-Child Relationships.*

RELATIVE DEPRIVATION

Nearly all theorists of social movements identify *relative deprivation*, rather than absolute deprivation, as the leading cause of revolution and rebellion. This accounts for the counterintuitive but persistent finding that typically such revolts are launched by groups that enjoy rising, not falling, socioeconomic conditions. However, two underlying questions remain the subject of academic inquiry. First is the specific definition of relative deprivation—namely, deprivation of what and relative to whom or what? The second is which factors mediate the connection between deprivation and rebellion—that is, when will relative deprivation actually lead to rebellion?

Aristotle wrote that people will rebel "if they think that they have too little although they are the equals of those who have more" (Davies 1971, p. 86). Marx typically focused narrowly on the relative material inequality between classes, predicting that workers would rebel even in the face of improving living standards if they perceived capitalist living standards to be rising even faster. Alexis de Tocqueville crucially observed that relative deprivation alone was insufficient; also necessary was an expectation that rebellion would improve the situation: "Evils which are patiently endured when they seem inevitable become intolerable when once the idea of escape from them is suggested" (Davies 1971, p. 135). This, he said, explained his empirical observation that revolution tended to occur when states were relaxing, not heightening, oppression.

In the early 1960s James C. Davies posited that the decisive relative deprivation was not between groups but rather between the expected satisfaction and actual satisfaction of one group. Rebellion was caused by "an intolerable gap between what people want and what they get," so that it was "most likely to occur when a prolonged period of objective economic and social development is followed by a short period of sharp reversal" (Davies 1971, pp. 135–136). Like Tocqueville, he identified the key mediating factor between deprivation and rebellion as the expectation of success. "It is when the chains have been loosened somewhat, so that they can be cast off without a high probability of losing life, that people are put in a condition of rebelliousness" (Davies 1971, pp. 135–136).

Subsequently theorists such as Doug McAdam and Sidney Tarrow have emphasized the mediating role of "political opportunity structures" in determining when relative deprivation and mobilization actually will lead to actions such as rebellions (McAdam, Tarrow, and Tilly 2001). This work clearly echoes Tocqueville.

For more than three decades Ted Robert Gurr integrated these and other emergent findings of the literature into his repeatedly revised and expanded general theory of ethnocultural rebellion and political action. His primary causal variable continues to be relative deprivation, although he defines it broadly like Davies as the difference between perceived entitlement and actual welfare, so that even relatively privileged groups may be motivated to rebel by perceived disadvantage. Gurr (2000) says three mediating variables determine whether deprivation actually will lead a group to take action—salience of ethnocultural identity, group capacity for mobilization (based partly on geography), and political opportunities for success. A domestic political variable—whether state institutions and resources favor repression or accommodation of group demands—determines whether ethnopolitical action will take the form of peaceful protest or violent rebellion. Prominent economists and political scientists, including Paul Collier, Anke Hoeffler, David Laitin, and Jim Fearon, have disputed the primary role of relative deprivation in motivating rebellion, which they say is driven less by grievance than by greed.

SEE ALSO *Aristotle; Coup d'Etat; Ethnic Conflict; Ethnocentrism; Marx, Karl; Poverty; Resistance; Revolution; Social Movements; Tocqueville, Alexis de; Wages*

BIBLIOGRAPHY

Davies, James C., ed. 1971. *When Men Revolt and Why: A Reader in Political Violence and Revolution.* New York: Free Press.

Gurr, Ted Robert. 2000. *Peoples versus States.* Washington, DC: U.S. Institute of Peace.

Hoeffler, Anke, and Paul Collier. 2004. Greed and Grievance in Civil War. *Oxford Economic Papers* 56 (4): 563–595.

McAdam, Doug, Sidney Tarrow, and Charles Tilly. 2001. *Dynamics of Contention.* New York: Cambridge University Press.

Alan J. Kuperman

RELATIVE INCOME HYPOTHESIS

Relative income hypothesis states that the satisfaction (or utility) an individual derives from a given consumption level depends on its relative magnitude in the society (e.g., relative to the average consumption) rather than its absolute level. It is based on a postulate that has long been acknowledged by psychologists and sociologists, namely that individuals care about status. In economics, relative income hypothesis is attributed to James Duesenberry, who investigated the implications of this idea for consumption behavior in his 1949 book titled *Income, Saving and the Theory of Consumer Behavior.*

At the time when Duesenberry wrote his book the dominant theory of consumption was the one developed by the English economist John Maynard Keynes, which was based on the hypothesis that individuals consume a decreasing, and save an increasing, percentage of their income as their income increases. This was indeed the pattern observed in cross-sectional consumption data: At a given point in time the rich in the population saved a higher fraction of their income than the poor did. However, Keynesian theory was contradicted by another empirical regularity: Aggregate saving rate did not grow over time as aggregate income grew. Duesenberry argued that relative income hypothesis could account for both the cross-sectional and time series evidence.

Duesenberry claimed that an individual's utility index depended on the ratio of his or her consumption to a weighted average of the consumption of the others. From this he drew two conclusions: (1) aggregate saving rate is independent of aggregate income, which is consistent with the time series evidence; and (2) the propensity to save of an individual is an increasing function of his or her percentile position in the income distribution, which is consistent with the cross-sectional evidence.

Despite its intuitive and empirical appeal Duesenberry's theory has not found wide acceptance and has been dominated by the life-cycle/permanent-income hypothesis of Franco Modigliani and Richard Brumberg (published in 1954) and Milton Friedman (1957). These closely related theories implied that consumption is an increasing function of the expected lifetime resources of an individual and could account for both the cross-sectional and time series evidence previously mentioned. However, starting with the 1970s, inability of these theories to explain some other puzzling empirical observations as well as the increasing evidence that people indeed seem to care about relative income have generated renewed interest in relative income hypothesis.

The first piece of evidence was presented in 1974 by Richard Easterlin, who found that self-reported happiness of individuals (i.e., subjective well-being) varies directly with income at a given point in time but average well-being tends to be highly stable over time despite tremendous income growth. Easterlin argued that these patterns are consistent with the claim that an individual's well-being depends mostly on relative income rather than absolute income. Subsequent research, such as that published by Andrew Oswald in 1997, has accumulated abundant evidence in support of this claim.

Relative income hypothesis has also found some corroboration from indirect macroeconomic evidence. One of these is the observation that higher growth rates lead to higher saving rates, which is inconsistent with the life-cycle/permanent-income theory since the lifetime resources of an individual increases as growth rate increases. The work of Christopher Carroll, Jody Overland, and David N. Weil explains this observation with a growth model in which preferences depend negatively on the past consumption of the individual or on the past average consumption in the economy that is under the relative income hypothesis.

Another empirical observation that has been problematic for the life-cycle/permanent-income theory is the equity premium puzzle, which states that the observed difference between the return on equity and the return on riskless assets is too large to be explained by a plausible specification of the theory. Introducing past average consumption into the preferences accounts for this observation much better.

Relative income hypothesis has other important economic implications. Perhaps the most obvious implication is that consumption creates negative externalities in the society, which are not taken into account in individual decision-making. If individuals consume, and therefore work, to increase their status, then they will tend to work too much relative to the socially optimal level and hence income taxation could improve the social welfare.

Relative income hypothesis is a special case of negatively interdependent preferences according to which individuals care about both their absolute and relative material payoffs. In 2000 Levent Koçkesen, Efe Ok, and Rajiv Sethi showed that negatively interdependent preferences yield a higher material payoff than do selfish preferences in many strategic environments, which implies that evolution will tend to favor the emergence of negatively interdependent preferences. This could be regarded as one explanation for the empirical support behind relative income hypothesis.

SEE ALSO *Absolute Income Hypothesis; Consumption; Life-Cycle Hypothesis; Microfoundations; Modigliani-Miller Theorems; Permanent Income Hypothesis*

BIBLIOGRAPHY

Abel, Andrew B. 1990. Asset Prices under Habit Formation and Catching Up with the Joneses. *American Economic Review* 80 (2): 38–42.

Boskin, Michael J., and Eytan Sheshinski. 1978. Optimal Redistributive Taxation when Individual Welfare Depends upon Relative Income. *Quarterly Journal of Economics* 92 (4): 589–601.

Campbell, John Y., and John H. Cochrane. 1999. By Force of Habit: A Consumption-Based Explanation of Aggregate Stock Market Behavior. *Journal of Political Economy* 107 (2): 205–251.

Carroll, Christopher D., Jody Overland, and David N. Weil. 1997. Comparison Utility in a Growth Model. *Journal of Economic Growth* 2 (4): 339–367.

Carroll, Christopher D., Jody Overland, and David N. Weil. 2000. Saving and Growth with Habit Formation. *American Economic Review* 90 (3): 341–355.

Duesenberry, James S. 1949. *Income, Saving and the Theory of Consumer Behavior*. Cambridge, MA: Harvard University Press.

Easterlin, Richard. 1974. Does Economic Growth Improve the Human Lot? Some Empirical Evidence. In *Nations and Households in Economic Growth*, ed. Paul A. David and Melvin W. Reder. New York: Academic Press.

Friedman, Milton. 1957. *A Theory of the Consumption Function*. Princeton, NJ: Princeton University Press.

Koçkesen, Levent, Efe A. Ok, and Rajiv Sethi. 2000. The Strategic Advantage of Negatively Interdependent Preferences. *Journal of Economic Theory* 92 (2): 274–299.

Modigliani, Franco, and Richard Brumberg. 1954. Utility Analysis and the Consumption Function: An Interpretation of Cross-Section Data. In *Post-Keynesian Economics*, ed. Kenneth K. Kurihara. New Brunswick, NJ: Rutgers University Press.

Oswald, Andrew J. 1997. Happiness and Economic Performance. *Economic Journal* 107 (November): 1815–1831.

Levent Koçkesen

RELATIVE SURPLUS VALUE

Relative surplus value is a concept introduced by Karl Marx in chapter 12 of the first volume of his book *Capital* (1867). One of the key objectives of this book was to explain the origins of capitalist profit. Marx argued that profits could not arise simply from trading between commodity owners because such trade was what von Neumann (1944) would later call a zero sum game. Instead, the source of profit had to be sought outside the sphere of circulation in the process of capitalist production. Here, labor power that had been purchased by the capitalist was set to work to make things. The amount of value created by the laborers would be proportional to the number of hours worked whereas the sum advanced by the capitalist to purchase labor power would be proportional to the value of that labor power itself as a commodity. Laboring power was the ability to perform work, a concept analogous to Watt's rating of the cotton mill engine's ability to perform work in terms of normalized horsepower. Because the ability to perform work and the work actually done by employees are distinct, the zero sum game is avoided.

Marx argued that there were systematic processes in a capitalist economy that caused the value of labor power to be less than the value created during the working day. The first of these was the prolongation of working hours beyond preindustrial levels to twelve or fourteen hours a day. This lengthening of the day, which he termed *absolute surplus value*, was the principle source of profit during the early encroachments of capitalist production on an economic sector. During this phase the technology of production would be comparatively static, still depending on hand-operated tools.

The real revolution in production came with mechanization, which enabled the production of relative surplus value. Individual capitalists had an incentive to introduce new machinery because it gave them a competitive advantage. When power looms, for example, were first introduced, the mills using them could produce cloth using less labor than the competing hand-loom weavers. Because the market value of cloth was still regulated by the dominant hand looms, the powered mills earned higher profits. The hand-loom weavers were squeezed and eventually ruined by the process.

The surplus profit accruing to innovators was transitory, vanishing once the new technology was generally adopted, but it drove a process of continuous technical change. It was this change, operating at the level of the whole economy, that produced relative surplus value. Commodities entering into the consumption of the laboring classes—bread, coal, cotton clothing—were being constantly cheapened by innovation. This tended to reduce the value of labor power across the whole economy. The industrial revolution in textiles, mining, and mechanized agriculture had thus increased profits in all other sectors of the economy because labor power could now be purchased more cheaply. The constant efflux of impoverished handicraft producers onto the labor market also acted to force down wages. Accumulation of wealth by the new factory owners went hand in hand with an absolute immiserization of the mass of the population.

The possibility of innovator profit was always there, so the drive to produce relative surplus value was an invariant structural feature of capitalism. Unlike all previous exploiting classes, capitalists were forced to constantly transform the conditions of production. Constant revolutionizing of production, uninterrupted disturbance of all social conditions, everlasting uncertainty, and agitation distinguished the bourgeois epoch from all earlier ones.

The basic mechanism set out by Marx seems to accurately describe the broad economic transformation of the world economy over the nineteenth and twentieth centuries. Indeed, it seems more credible than ever in the epoch of globalization. However, taken at its face value, it would predict a constantly rising rate of surplus value over the period of capitalist history, and whether this has actually occurred is questionable. Evidence shows that the rise of surplus value due to mechanization has at times been offset by increased real wages. The production of relative surplus value may be seen as a process that interacts with other forces, including demographic ones, to regulate the overall level of profits. In countries with a stagnant or declining working population, shortages of labor power allow some of the gains of technological change to be transferred to the working classes. These factors were probably important in developed countries during the mid-twentieth century. The extent to which these offsetting tendencies will operate in the period of globalization is still an open question.

SEE ALSO *Labor Theory of Value; Profitability; Profits; Rate of Profit; Surplus Value; Value*

BIBLIOGRAPHY

Marx, Karl. 1867. *Capital: A Critique of Political Economy*. Vol. 1. Trans. Ben Fowkes. London: Penguin, 1976.

von Neumann, John, and Oskar Morgenstern. 1944. *Theory of Games and Economic Behavior*. Princeton, NJ: Princeton University Press.

W. Paul Cockshott

RELATIVES

SEE *Family; Kinship.*

RELATIVISM

Relativism, put very generally, states that a particular feature varies (or at least can vary) relative to certain phenomena. Prime candidates for the varying feature have been meaning, truth, rationality, justification, knowledge, value, and morality. Relativism thus arises in many areas of inquiry, and it has numerous variations within each area.

TRUTH AND REALITY

Relativism about truth states that truth varies relative to, for example, the concepts, the beliefs, the purposes, or the reasons possessed by an individual or a group. Relativists about truth thus suggest that truth is, in a sense, always truth for an individual or a group with certain concepts, beliefs, purposes, or reasons. Cultural relativism about truth, for instance, implies that truths are true for a culture (perhaps in virtue of that culture's system of concepts, or conceptual scheme) but need not therefore be true for a different culture (say, with a different conceptual scheme). Relativism about truth, then, denies that truths obtain in virtue of reality independently of an individual's or a group's concepts, beliefs, purposes, or reasons. It thus opposes certain kinds of realism, or objectivism, about truth. Relativists must be cautious, however, not to suggest that their relativism about truth is true *absolutely*, or nonrelatively. If, however, relativism is true relatively, and not absolutely, opponents will find room for their absolutism about truth.

Concepts, truth-bearers, and statements are perhaps relative, regarding their existence, to a natural language or some other person-dependent phenomenon. This position seems coherent at least. Even so, we cannot thereby infer that what concepts, truth-bearers, or statements are about is similarly relative to person-dependent phenomena. Referring, describing, and explaining are perhaps relative to a natural language or some other person-dependent phenomenon, but it does not follow that the things about which one says something are similarly relative. Relativists and antirealists sometimes overlook this important lesson. It calls for a plausible distinction between human semantical activity and what such activity is about (e.g., objects, properties, states, or relations).

MORAL RELATIVISM

Morality has long been a prime candidate for relativism. Moral relativism, put very broadly, states that certain moral features vary relative to certain phenomena. Such moral features can include the basic moral beliefs accepted by an individual or a group, the basic moral requirements pertaining to an individual or a group, and the correctness of moral judgments or standards. Relativism corresponding to such moral features encompasses *moral-belief* relativism, *moral-requirement* relativism, and *moral-correctness* relativism. Moral-belief relativism can be assessed by empirical investigation, and is much less controversial than the other two versions.

Moral-requirement relativism entails that the moral requirements binding on a person depend on, and are relative to, the person's intentions, desires, or beliefs (or those of certain people in the person's society). Moral-requirement relativism has two common forms. *Individual* moral-requirement relativism states that an action is morally obligatory for a person if and only if that action is prescribed by the basic moral principles accepted by that person. *Social* moral-requirement relativism states that an action is morally obligatory for a person if and only if that action is prescribed by the basic moral principles accepted by that person's society.

Moral-correctness relativism states that moral judgments are not objectively correct or incorrect and thus that different people or societies can hold contradictory moral judgments without any incorrectness. In other words, what is morally correct for one person or group need not be correct for another person or group. Moral-correctness relativism can be developed with various accounts of "relative correctness," some of which do not imply that whatever moral judgments a person accepts are correct for that person.

Proponents of moral-correctness and moral-requirement relativism have based their case on various considerations, including moral *tolerance*. They sometimes stress that people should tolerate diverse moral views by allowing those views to be freely expressed. Even so, opponents of moral relativism need not disagree; they can hold that views conflicting with their own should be treated with full tolerance in terms of expression. In contrast, moral-correctness relativists cannot consistently hold that it is *objectively* correct that "a person morally ought to be tolerant of the views of others." Such relativists, then, may face a problem of tolerance in morality.

Some moral-requirement relativists hold that a moral requirement applies to a person only if that person accepts (perhaps implicitly) the requirement as reasonable for himself or herself. This view upholds a connection between (1) what is morally required of a person and (2) what that person approves of and has a convincing reason to do. Many relativists hold that a person's moral reasons (and thus moral requirements) have their basis in that person's own psychological attitudes, such as that person's desires, intentions, or beliefs. Gilbert Harman thus proposes that "for Hitler there might have been no [moral] reasons at all not to order the extermination of the Jews" (1975, p. 9). The underlying relativist position is inspired by David Hume (1711–1776); it claims that desire-independent objective principles of morality are inadequate as a source of moral reasons and that certain psychological attitudes (e.g., intentions) of a person are central to any source of moral reasons for that person. The opposite view is inspired by Immanuel Kant (1724–1804); it implies that desire-independent moral principles themselves can supply compelling moral reasons and requirements.

MOTIVATION AND RIGHTNESS

Is a person subject to a moral requirement only if that person has a psychological attitude, such as an intention, that recommends the satisfaction of that requirement? We can evidently "be subject" to a moral requirement in two ways: (1) as a motivating principle and (2) as a rightness-determining principle. A moral requirement is a motivating principle for me if and only if I have, on the basis of my psychological attitudes, an inclination to satisfy that principle. In contrast, a moral requirement is a rightness-determining principle for me if and only if that principle determines whether an action I might perform is morally right. The first concerns motivation for a person; the second concerns moral rightness of an action for a person.

Relativism about the *motivational* efficacy of moral requirements does not entail relativism about the *rightness-determining* relevance of moral requirements. A person's motivating psychological attitudes are not automatically morally obligatory or even morally permissible. For instance, Adolf Hitler's psychological attitudes motivated him to wipe out millions of innocent Jewish people. Obviously, however, Hitler morally should have renounced those evil attitudes, given their role in bringing unjust harm to others.

According to a plausible nonrelativist view, the moral rightness of an action is determined by the action's consistency with what is prescribed by the set of correct moral principles. Of course, we cannot quickly or easily specify the exact conditions for a moral principle's belonging to the set of correct moral principles. The task is difficult. Even so, we need not finish that demanding task to recognize that a rightness-determining moral principle for a person does not depend on that person's intending to satisfy that principle. A moral principle can be rightness-determining for me even if I intend not to act in accordance with it. Morality, as ordinarily understood, is intention-independent in this respect.

Some relativists will reply that there is no such thing as a "correct" moral principle in the sense suggested. These relativists, however, will need to identify the defect in the view that moral principles are correct in the sense suggested. In particular, they will need to show why we should not hold on to a robust notion of moral correctness. They must also specify, in this connection, the sense of "should" in the previous sentence in a way that fits with relativism. In response, nonrelativists will then be able to consider whether the resulting relativism is "true for them." If it is not, they may proceed with their nonrelativism.

A general lesson emerges. Relativists must avoid a self-referential problem in their needed relativist notion of correctness: the problem that their notion of correctness either assumes nonrelativism about correctness or fails to challenge nonrelativism about correctness in virtue of allowing for absolutism about correctness. This is no easy task for relativists about correctness.

SEE ALSO *Cultural Relativism; Fundamentalism*

BIBLIOGRAPHY

Harman, Gilbert. 1975. Moral Relativism Defended. *Philosophical Review* 84: 3–22.

Krausz, Michael, ed. 1989. *Relativism: Interpretation and Confrontation.* Notre Dame, IN: University of Notre Dame Press.

Moser, Paul K. 1993. *Philosophy after Objectivity: Making Sense in Perspective.* New York: Oxford University Press.

Moser, Paul K., and Thomas L. Carson, eds. 2001. *Moral Relativism: A Reader.* New York: Oxford University Press.

Paul K. Moser

RELATIVISM, CULTURAL

SEE *Cultural Relativism.*

RELIABILITY, STATISTICAL

Statistical reliability refers to the consistency of measurement. According to Jum C. Nunnally and Ira H. Bernstein in their 1994 publication *Psychometric Theory,* in classical test theory reliability is defined mathematically as the ratio of true-score variance to total variance. A true score can be thought of as the score an individual would receive if the construct of interest were measured without error. If a researcher developed a perfect way to measure shyness, then each individual's shyness score would be a true score. In the social sciences, constructs are virtually always measured with error, and as such true scores are unknowns that must be estimated by observed scores.

The expected standard deviation of scores for an individual taking a test many times is known as the standard error of measurement (SEM). The SEM of a score is estimated by

$$SEM = s_x\sqrt{1 - r_{xx}}$$

where s_x is the between-groups standard deviation of scores on the test and r_{xx} is the estimate of score reliability. The expectation is that if an individual takes a test many times, 68 percent of scores will fall within one and 95 percent of scores will fall within two SEM's of the observed score. Assume that Jamie scored 1,000 on a test with an observed standard deviation of 100 and a score reliability estimate of .84. The SEM for Jamie would be

$$SEM = 100\sqrt{1 - .84} = 40$$

If Jamie took the achievement test many times, one would expect approximately 68 percent of the resulting scores to fall between 960 and 1,040, and approximately 95 percent of the scores to fall between 920 and 1,080.

RELIABILITY AND ESTIMATES OF CONSISTENCY

Reliability can refer to several different types of estimates of consistency. *Alternative form* reliability refers to the degree of consistency between two equivalent forms of a measure. *Split-half* reliability refers to the consistency between two randomly-created sections of a single test. The internal consistency statistics coefficient α (also referred to as Cronbach's α) and the related Kuder-Richardson 20 (or "KR-20") can be thought of as the mean of all possible split-half estimates. *Test-retest* reliability is the consistency of scores on separate administrations of the same test. Determining an appropriate delay between the initial and follow-up administrations can be difficult. As examples, if the chosen delay is too long, expected changes (e.g., learning) in the respondents may contribute to a low test-retest correlation, which may be mistaken for evidence of invalidity. If the delay is too short respondents' remembering and repeating their responses from the first test may contribute to a high test-retest correlation, which may be mistaken as evidence of validity. Ideally in this context, respondents would receive the exact same score on the test and the retest. If scores tend to go up or down from the test to the retest, the correlation between the test and the retest will be reduced unless all scores rise or fall by the same amount.

Inter-rater reliability refers to the extent to which judges or raters agree with one another. As an example, assume two judges rate teachers on the extent to which they promote a mastery orientation among students. The consistency of the judges can be estimated by correlating the scores of both judges. A 1965 study by John E. Overall found that the effective reliability of the judging process (i.e., of both judges together) can also be estimated; effective reliability will generally be better than the reliability of either judge in isolation. One problem in estimating inter-rater reliability is that the judges' scores may reflect both random error and systematic differences in responding. This problem reflects a fundamental concern about the representativeness of judges, and, according to Richard J. Shavelson and Noreen M. Webb in their 1991 publication *Generalizability Theory: A Primer*, it is addressed in an extension of classical test theory known as generalizability theory.

SAMPLE AND CONTEXT DEPENDENT

The assertion "this measure is reliable" reflects a common misunderstanding about the nature of reliability. Reliability is a property of scores, not of measures, and it is therefore sample and context dependent. A test yielding good reliability estimates with one sample might yield poor reliability estimates with a sample from a different population, or even with the same sample under different testing conditions. The decision about whether to adopt an existing measure should therefore be based on more than a simple examination of score reliability in a few studies. Further, score reliability should be examined on each administration regardless of the measure's empirical history (Thompson, 2002).

RELIABILITY AND VALIDITY

Reliability and validity are not necessarily related. Validity concerns the extent to which a measure actually measures what it is supposed to. While reliability does set a maximum limit on the correlation that can be observed between two measures, it is possible for scores to be perfectly reliable on a measure that has no validity or for scores to have no reliability on a measure that is perfectly valid. As an example of the latter, suppose that students in a pharmacology class are given a test of content knowledge at the beginning of the semester and at the end of the semester. Assume that on the pretest the students know nothing and therefore respond randomly, while on the post-test they all receive As. Estimating reliability via the split-half method or coefficient α on the pre-test would suggest very little consistency, as would the test-retest method. The test itself, however, would seem to be measuring content taught during the course (indicating good validity).

BIBLIOGRAPHY

Nunnally, Jum C., and Ira H. Bernstein. 1994. *Psychometric Theory*. 3rd ed. New York: McGraw-Hill.

Overall, John E. 1965. Reliability of Composite Ratings. *Educational and Psychological Measurement* 25: 1011–1022.

Shavelson, Richard J., and Noreen M. Webb. 1991. *Generalizability Theory: A Primer*. Newbury Park, CA: Sage Publications.

Thompson, Bruce, ed. 2002. *Score Reliability: Contemporary Thinking on Reliability Issues*. Newbury Park, CA: Sage Publications.

Jeffrey C. Valentine

RELIEF TAX

SEE *Tax Relief.*

RELIGION

Though difficult to define from an intercultural perspective, religion informs the lives of virtually every society as a complex system involving beliefs, behavior, organizational structures, and symbols. Problems in satisfactorily defining the term emerge from the manifold ways in which religion expresses itself, the varied roles that it performs both for individuals and for social groups, and the plethora of academic disciplines that study it.

DEFINITION AND SCOPE

Beliefs that may be deemed "religious" range from precisely articulated perceptions of a complex array of anthropomorphic deities, such as the myriad levels of divinity recognized in Hinduism, to vague notions of impersonal, overarching power—for example, the concept of *mana* recognized in many Polynesian societies. Behaviors include a variety of practices, such as the silent meditation practiced on a personal level by mystics from a diversity of religious traditions, including Buddhism and Christianity, and complicated ritual scenarios involving scores of people such as the annual Sun Dance that has provided the central corporate religious experience for many American Indian groups on the Great Plains. Religion's organizational structure may be simple groupings of individuals brought together temporarily for specific religious purposes, such as the *big meetings* held by some Aborigines in the Western Australian desert, as well as multileveled hierarchies that have endured over millennia (for instance, the Roman Catholic Church). Symbolic representations with religious dimensions can be discrete metaphors that stand for a single concept (e.g., a shaman's characterization of his or her mystical experience as a death and rebirth) as well as variegated iconographic vocabularies of interrelated images, such as that which characterized medieval and Renaissance Christianity and which continues to afford ways for Christians to communicate about their faith.

Social scientists and others have noted that religion plays varied roles in society, including validating other features of a society, such as its political or economic system, and compensating individuals for the limitations that their humanity imposes on them and for the prohibitions dictated by specific societal norms. Religion also has an integrative function as it provides a focus for cultural identity, endorses those values and norms that ensure that a person will truly be a respectable member of the society, and discourages behavior that undermines social cohesion. Religion also offers answers to some of life's persistent problems, especially the meaning of death and the possibility of an afterlife.

The study of religion is genuinely multidisciplinary, and different fields stress different emphases in their approaches to the concept. Sociologists, for example, usually highlight the organizational structures and patterns of behavior as central to their concerns, whereas practitioners of philosophy, theology, and comparative religious studies focus their attention on beliefs. Literature and art history are most likely to foreground religious symbolism. Priding itself on its holistic approach to society and culture, anthropology is more apt than other disciplines to pay more or less equal attention to all four components of religion.

The problem of defining religion is further complicated when one attempts to differentiate it from other systems of belief, behavior, organization, and symbolism. These attempts often rely on terms that themselves need definition and clarification: *sacred, transcendent, supernatural, spiritual,* and *ultimate.* Most of these terms suggest that religion focuses on nonroutine phenomena that are set apart in some way from nonreligious experience (the *secular* or the *profane*). But exactly what sets them apart and the degree to which they differ from the rest of life have not been consistently articulated. What may be perceived as sacred phenomena in some systems of belief may be regarded as secular elsewhere. Mysterious lights, for example, may signal the presence of a supernatural entity, or they may be explained as the product of gases emitted by decaying vegetation. One may base the decision whether to eat meat on religious proscriptions, or the decision may be simply a nutritional issue.

Another contributor to the difficulty in defining religion is that although religion is apparently universal—that is, found in all societies—the concept of a system of beliefs, behavior, organizational structures, and symbolism distinct from other social systems is largely a Western construct. Many languages have no equivalent for the English word *religion,* though the societies that speak those languages evince much that would be considered religious in Western terms.

RESEARCH CONCERNS

Theoretical and methodological approaches to the study of religion generally reflect different emphases in how the concept is defined. Whereas social scientists, for example, usually focus on how religion operates within specific cultural contexts, theologians and comparative religion scholars may examine the nuances of religious beliefs. But one area of concern that has transcended a range of academic disciplines is the issue of origins. For example, a historian may be interested in how Mormonism emerged from the ferment of religious enthusiasm that characterized the burned-over district of western New York in the early nineteenth century, or in tracing the origins of Christian apocalypticism of the twenty-first century to

Zoroastrian beliefs in Persia from perhaps as early as the tenth century BCE.

More fundamentally, interest in origins has often addressed how religion as a system originated in the human individual and collective psyche: as a response to dream experiences (the view of the nineteenth-century anthropologist E. B. Tylor), out of fear and guilt regarding a primordial father figure (one of the ideas articulated by Sigmund Freud), as a product of the human tendency to personify incomprehensible natural forces (articulated by the eighteenth-century philosopher and historian Giambattista Vico, among others), as a method for suppressing social discontent and for promoting adherence to a society's power structure (advocated by philosophers from Plato to Marx), and even as the product of revelation from a god or other spiritual being or force (the stance assumed by many religious adherents—at least in regard to their own religions). Of course, many other explanations of religion's origin have been and continue to be proposed, and many of them lack the criterion of testability upon which many academic fields insist in order for an idea to be more than hypothesis. Consequently, many other issues in religion have received more scholarly attention.

Many sociologists, in particular, look to the pioneering concepts of Émile Durkheim, a late-nineteenth-century social scientist who argued that religion is principally a social phenomenon. Drawing upon data from the religions of Australian Aboriginal groups, he proposed that the object of religious belief and behavior was, in fact, the society itself, and that religion operated to maintain social stability through the devotion of its adherents. Whereas many of his contemporaries were more attracted by the issue of religion's origins, Durkheim concentrated on how religion operated. This concern anticipated the functional emphases of anthropologists Bronislaw Malinowski and A. R. Radcliffe-Brown, who early in the twentieth century examined how religion operated as a support for other social institutions and—in Malinowski's case—how it might assist believers in their everyday lives by providing ways of dealing with issues that lay beyond their scientific knowledge. Malinowski studied the culture of the Trobriand Islanders, Melanesians who inhabited an archipelago to the east of New Guinea and who relied on seafaring for much of their livelihoods. He noted that Trobriand sailors did not evoke religion when they were operating within the peaceful lagoons just offshore from their island homes, but when they faced the potentially uncontrollable forces of the open seas, they turned to religious beliefs and behavior to complement their knowledge of ocean currents, the weather, and other variables.

Though they might reject the designation "functionalist" as too simplistic for how they approach the study of religion, many social scientists nevertheless continue to deal principally with how religion operates in social life collectively and in the lives of individuals. Durkheim's belief that the object of religious interest symbolizes the society finds echoes in the more recent ideas about *civil religion.* Sociologist Robert Bellah has suggested that in many societies—the United States, in particular—patriotism has developed beliefs, behaviors, organizational structures, and symbolism tantamount to a religious system (1967).

Many social scientists have been especially interested in the nature of religious participation: who finds given religious systems amenable to meeting their particular needs and who performs what roles in religious behavior and organization. In heterogeneous, stratified societies such as those in the West, research has attempted to correlate membership in a particular class or caste with participation in a particular religious system or subset thereof. For instance, the wealthy and highly educated populations in the United States are more likely to affiliate with branches of Christianity that stress the importance of formal liturgy, whereas middle- and lower-class individuals prefer Christian groups that stress less organization and underscore instead the importance of personal religious experience. Ethnicity also has been a frequently identified variable in determining religious affiliation. In fact, some ethnic groups in the United Kingdom and France use religion, particularly Islam, to reinforce and signal their ethnic cultural identity. In the latter half of the twentieth century, researchers became more and more interested in ways in which gender might affect not so much a person's specific affiliation but the nature of that person's involvement in religion. While the women's movement was encouraging a more visible, active role for women in many Christian denominations in the West, researchers looking at religions in other parts of the world often found that women traditionally had been central in local religious belief and polity.

Another focus of social scientific interest in religion has been the way in which it interacts with other systems of ideology in a society. Max Weber is an important early figure in this interest because of his demonstration of the way in which Protestant Christianity, especially Calvinism in western Europe, created a milieu conducive to the emergence of capitalism by emphasizing individualism and hard work, among other values. Of particular interest in the late-twentieth and twenty-first centuries has been the association between religion and nationalism. Islamic-based governments, primarily in the Middle East, have become among the most important participants in global politics, and competition between different branches of Islam (Sunni and Shia, in particular) has characterized their internal politics. Christianity has assumed a similar role in some Western nation-states such as the United States, where fundamentalist groups have become powerful elements on the political landscape. Sociologists and political scientists have shown particular interest in measuring the ways in which religious affiliation has affected the voting patterns of the U.S. electorate and in shaping the programs of the politicians they support.

An important and very fundamental development in social scientific interest in religion concerns the way in which scholars position themselves in regard to their subject. Conventionally, social scientists have been urged to develop a stance of methodological agnosticism in which they eschew their own religious beliefs at least temporarily and adopt a perspective of cultural relativism that is not concerned with whether a religious belief is true or whether a ritual actually produces the results that its practitioners desire. Instead, researchers have attended to the internal consistency of belief systems, the social and cultural functions of ritual, and the extent to which adherents lend credence to beliefs and rituals. Recently, however, some social scientists have begun to recognize that this perspective brings with it certain assumptions that color what researchers observe, how they report what they encounter, and the directions taken by their analyses. Influenced by the set of ideas loosely known as "postmodernism," researchers have become more aware of the role of their own religious ideas in their work and have become more forthcoming about those ideas. The cultural anthropologist Victor Turner, for example, was usually very open about his own Roman Catholicism in his work focusing on the symbolic dimension of religious systems. In addition to this move toward reflexivity on the part of religious researchers, some social scientists have begun to accept that religious beliefs may often stem from actual wondrous events that an individual has experienced and which the social group interprets in terms of the events' relation to indigenous ideas about the sacred, the supernatural, the spiritual, or the ultimate.

New tools have allowed social scientists to explore traditional areas of religious study more fully and accurately. The availability of computer programs, for instance, allows demographic studies to be done more quickly and with a larger number of variables than was feasible before the computer age. Meanwhile, technology has taken religious studies into some new, still controversial, and largely unexplored areas such as the possibility of a genetic basis for the need for religion. Interestingly—and perhaps counterintuitively—the growth of technology during the latter half of the twentieth century did not parallel a decline in religious adherence; instead, many religions have witnessed significant growth as technology has blossomed.

DEMOGRAPHICS

Literally thousands of religious systems flourish throughout today's world. Although many of these appeal only to small groups (and have consequently been labeled "tribal" or "primal-indigenous" religions), even these may exert international influence through the globalized mass media and through such phenomena as cultural tourism. Other religious systems are truly world religions whose practitioners believe that they can and should promulgate their beliefs to everyone. Despite their purported international scope, though, these world religions are often focused on specific territories. For example, the largest religious system, Christianity (with more than two billion adherents), developed in the eastern basin of the Mediterranean Sea and then spread primarily through Europe and then to those parts of the world that were subjects of European colonialism. Most branches of Christianity retain primary geographical ties with Europe or with the United States, but some are flourishing most luxuriantly in other parts of the world—Roman Catholicism in Central and South America and in Africa, for example.

Meanwhile, Islam—second in number of adherents to Christianity with perhaps a billion and a half followers—maintains its primary geographical association with southwestern Asia and southeastern Europe. But it has spread throughout the world, and, in fact, the country with the most Muslims is Indonesia. Hinduism, with close to a billion practitioners, remains principally associated with the Indian subcontinent, and Buddhism, with maybe half a billion adherents, also has an Asian focus. Nevertheless, both these religions have had enormous influence elsewhere, especially as replacements for or supplements to Christianity. The diaspora of the Jewish population has made Judaism a world religion with a symbolic attachment to the nation of Israel.

As contact between societies becomes more efficient, these world religions as well as more local systems of belief, behavior, organizational structures, and symbolism will spread more widely. Meanwhile, they will continue to influence one another to create syncretistic systems such as the Native American Church, which blends Christianity, various North American Indian religions, and ritual behavior that apparently originated in Mexico; and Vodoun, the principal religion of Haiti, which merges Roman Catholic Christianity and several West African religious systems, with influences from native Caribbean religions. The endurance of religions whose roots lie in the distant past, as well as the emergence of new religions, often the result of syncretism and other processes of cultural exchange, ensures that social scientists and other scholars who specialize in the study of religion will not lack for subject matter any time soon.

SEE ALSO *Animism; Anthropology; Buddhism; Christianity; Church and State; Church, The; Coptic Christian Church; Cults; Durkheim, Émile; Ethnicity; Heaven; Hell; Hinduism; Islam, Shia and Sunni;*

Jainism; Judaism; Malinowski, Bronislaw; Monotheism; Polytheism; Protestant Ethic; Protestantism; Radcliffe-Brown, A. R.; Rastafari; Religiosity; Roman Catholic Church; Santería; Shinto; Sociology; Weber, Max

BIBLIOGRAPHY

Bellah, Robert N. 1967. "Civil Religion in America." *Daedalus* 96 (Winter): 1–21.

Berger, Peter. 1967. *The Sacred Canopy: Elements of a Sociological Theory of Religion.* Garden City, NY: Doubleday.

Carmody, Denise. 1979. *Women and World Religions.* Nashville, TN: Abingdon Press.

Eliade, Mircea, ed. 1987. *The Encyclopedia of Religion.* 16 vols. New York: Macmillan.

Guthrie, Stewart Elliott. 1993. *Faces in the Clouds: A New Theory of Religion.* New York: Oxford University Press.

Lessa, William A., and Evon Z. Vogt, eds. 1979. *Reader in Comparative Religion: An Anthropological Approach.* 4th ed. New York: Harper and Row.

Major Religions of the World Ranked by Number of Adherents. Adherents.com.

McClenon, John. 1994. *Wondrous Events: Foundations of Religious Belief.* Philadelphia: University of Pennsylvania Press.

Smith, Huston. 1991. *The World's Religions: Our Great Wisdom Traditions.* San Francisco: Harper.

Wilson, Brian. 1990. *The Social Dimensions of Sectarianism: Sects and New Religious Movements in Contemporary Society.* Oxford: Clarendon Press.

Yinger, J. Milton. 1970. *The Scientific Study of Religion.* New York: Macmillan.

William M. Clements

RELIGIOSITY

Religiosity is a term used by social scientists to refer to religious behavior. Social scientists generally view religion as a cultural system of shared beliefs and rituals that offers a sense of transcendent meaning and purpose. Religion is often constrained within the natural and material categories. Religiosity therefore refers to the way people and communities are influenced by religious ideas and shape social reality accordingly.

From its inception, religiosity has been a central issue for social scientists. The German political philosopher Karl Marx viewed religion as an ideology of capitalist oppression. For Marx, religion compensated for the needs denied under capitalism, and the elimination of religion was indispensable to human emancipation. The German sociologist Max Weber (1864–1920) viewed religion as a meaning-making system that determined human behavior and shaped societies. Weber predicted that with the increase of rationalization there would be a "disenchantment of the world" that would lead to the decline of religious beliefs. The French sociologist Émile Durkheim viewed religion as the very essence of society that constrained individuals from egocentric behavior while simultaneously enabling them to adjust and function in social settings.

In the 1950s and the 1960s social scholars, most notably Peter L. Berger, proposed the secularization theory. The secularization theory claims that modernization necessarily leads to the decline of religion, both in society and in the minds of individuals. This in turn leads to the privatization of religion that marginalizes religion from the public sphere. Therefore as modernity ushered in plurality, subjectivity, and different authorities for legitimation, religion, unable to deal with these challenges, eventually withdrew from the public realm. According to the theory, the future of religion is a private one, eventually existing mainly in the private lives of individuals.

Decades after the secularization theory was popularized, Berger and its other champions revised and reconsidered the theory in light of an unsecularized modern world. Modernity not only did not secularize society but it created a counter-secularization movement that resulted in the increasing influence of religiosity in the modern world. In *Public Religions in the Modern World* (1994) Jose Casanova argued against the assumption that the increasing differentiation between religious and public institutions automatically leads to the decline of religion. Casanova claimed that public religions do not necessarily challenge the foundation of modern liberal society. In fact Casanova suggested that public religions can help advance modern agendas such as those of human rights and democracy.

FUNDAMENTALISM

One public form of religiosity is the religious phenomenon known as fundamentalism. Fundamentalism is characterized by a strict adherence to religious doctrines in their original form in order to restore a previous social order in the present world. The sociologist James Davison Hunter argued that fundamentalism is a direct product of modernity. Hunter characterized fundamentalists as those who believe that something has gone wrong in human history. Religious fundamentalists believe that their sacred order for human life has been disturbed and they must correct it to the best of their abilities. Hence religious fundamentalists are religious adherents who believe that they must restore the sacred order that their deity intended for this world. Though the term *fundamentalist* is ambiguously used to characterize both peaceful devout Muslims and extremist terrorists, it is important to note that religious fundamentalism does not always involve acts of violence. As the scholar Nancy T. Ammerman noted, one characteristic of many fundamentalist sects is that they are separatists. They seek to restore what they believe to be a sacred order only for their religious community. Many of these fundamentalists retreat from the secular world in order to construct the social reality of their liking. For example, the fastest growing Christian denominations in the United States are religious groups with fundamentalist beliefs.

One of the most notable branches of Christian fundamentalism is Pentecostalism. This form of Christianity emphasizes the experience of the Holy Spirit. Adherents are highly expressive and emotional, and their religious rituals often involve spiritual healings and the act of speaking in tongues, which is the utterance of what appears to be an unknown foreign language or simply nonsense syllables. In less than one hundred years Pentecostalism, along with its offshoot the charismatic movement, has become the largest segment of Protestant Christianity and the second largest Christian tradition after the Roman Catholic Church. In the early twenty-first century one out of every four Christians in the world is Pentecostal or charismatic. Pentecostal Christians use mass media to carry their message around the world and are arguably the most visible form of Christianity in the world.

The resurgence of religiosity in social sciences is especially clear at the beginning of the twenty-first century. The clear relationship between church and state in the United States was apparent to the great French observer Alexis de Tocqueville in the 1830s when he noted that churches and other voluntary organizations were the cradle of American democracy. The interconnectedness of religion and politics should not be confused with the conflict between church and state, though the clash of both are increasing in modern times. The conflict between church and state is institutional, while the conflict of religiosity and politics is within individuals. All religious citizens must negotiate between personal sacred beliefs and secular laws designed to appease a plurality of religions. This creates a cognitive dissonance that often leads to public confrontations between religion and politics. In *The Clash of Civilizations and the Remaking of World Order* (1997) Samuel Huntington traced the shifting focus of global conflict toward the end of the twentieth century. He noted that international conflict has shifted from ideological differences to religious and cultural conflict. Gone are the days when the United States allied with Islamic fundamentalists to repel the then communist Soviet Union out of Afghanistan. Under Huntington's new order, religiosity determines enemies and allies.

SEE ALSO *Fundamentalism; Religion*

BIBLIOGRAPHY

Anderson, Allan. 2004. *An Introduction to Pentecostalism: Global Charismatic Christianity.* Cambridge, U.K.: Cambridge University Press.

Berger, Peter. 1967. *The Sacred Canopy.* New York: Anchor Books.

Casanova, Jose. 1994. *Public Religions in the Modern World.* Chicago: University of Chicago Press.

Davidman, Lynn. 1991. *Tradition in a Rootless World: Women Turn to Orthodox Judaism.* Berkeley: University of California Press.

Huntington. Samuel P. 1997. *The Clash of Civilizations and the Remaking of World Order.* New York: Touchstone.

Marty, Martin E., and R. Scott Appleby, eds. 1991. *Fundamentalism Observed.* Chicago: University of Chicago Press.

Tony Tian-Ren Lin

REMEDIAL TRACKS
SEE *Tracking in Schools.*

RENEWAL, URBAN
SEE *Urban Renewal.*

RENT

The term rent has two meanings in economics and one taken from everyday usage. When a person leases an apartment or house from its owner, the lease provides for a payment to the owner. Although commonly called rent, it is very different in both orientation and calculation from the two uses in economics, namely, economic (or Ricardian) rent and rent-seeking, which are themselves very different from each other.

ECONOMIC RENT

The rent paid to an owner of leased property is a composite payment. It covers or includes the following items: the cost of the land, the cost of improvements, interest on the combined costs, the amount of appreciation of the land and improvement values, taxes, the cost of any services provided along with the leased property, and, given the overall workings of demand and supply, any further profit; all of which are calculated on a per-period basis. Should the owner have a mortgage, the owner's receipt of rent enables the owner to accumulate equity in the property. Should the renter arrange with the present owner to purchase the property, it is the former renter, now owner, who accumulates equity in the property by paying off the mortgage, if any. The principal connection with economics, or economic theory, of such rent is that the rent paid for the leasing of the property must be worth its expenditure to the renter (including consideration of alternative leasing) and must be suitable, relative to the owner's costs and alternative leasing), to warrant for both of them to enter into the rental contract, or lease.

The concept of economic rent stems from the English economists David Ricardo and Thomas Robert Malthus in the early nineteenth century. Ricardian, or economic, rent is the return to the owner of land (or any factor of production) that is fixed in supply and whose level is governed by the pressure of population growth. With trivial exceptions, such as filling in shallow bodies of water for one reason or another, the amount of land does not change with a change in the demand for it. The demand for land is driven by the need for land on which to grow crops and to erect homes. This need increases with population increase and is due solely to the growth of society. The increment in the price of land thus generated is widely considered unearned compared to situations in which investment in improving land and its appurtenances takes place.

Several additional features stemmed from early-nineteenth-century study. One feature is that land rent is differential with regard to location and to fertility. Increments or decrements of property value will reflect relative location and fertility, and likely will not be constant in either amount or percentage change. The second feature is a specific form of the first, namely, that as increasing levels of labor and capital are applied to the same amount of land, output per unit of input will fall. This is called diminishing returns. The third feature is due to the fact that not all land is equally fertile or located equidistant to a given point. This means that as the price of food increases due to the population-driven demand for food and thereby land, the increments of price (rent) of the more fertile or better situated land will increase more rapidly than those of less fertile or worse situated land. The fourth feature is that rent is a residual category such that any tax on land rent will have no disincentive effect on the level of food production on the land.

Given both that the increased price of pure, unimproved land is due to the growth of society and that any tax on the rent will have no adverse effects on income-maximizing owner calculations and farming, it has followed for many economists that a tax on unimproved land would have no negative effects and would be a fit subject of taxation. Objection to this reasoning arose from those who felt that acquisition of the increased value was one of the rights of property. The rejoinder to that objection was this: Land-value increments being due to the growth of society and not the activities of the owner, not taxing land rent but maintaining the same governmental budget, meant that tax revenues would have to come from taxes levied on productive activities. Nevertheless, a tax on land-value increments conflicted with the principle of conservatism, that appropriation of the increase of value was a right of property. However, for the American economist Henry George (1839–1897), for example, whose reasoning was initially based on Ricardo's, nothing was more conservative than promoting income in accordance with productivity rather than unearned increments.

The theory of Ricardian rent must be supplemented by consideration of the competition over pieces of land by people who had different, and conflicting, uses for the land. The idea of quasi-rent was developed by the English economist Alfred Marshall to identify the return to owners of factors of production, such as one's own labor or pieces of capital, that are in temporary inelastic supply.

RENT-SEEKING

The second notion of rent in economic theory is that of rent-seeking. The idea is that rent is the difference between two sets of rights, that people could invest money in efforts, through lobbying, legislation, and/or litigation, even bribery and extortion, to change the law in their favor, thereby increasing their incomes. Rent-seeking would engender counter-measures by those threatened with loss. The result would be wasted resources deployed in such activities. The objection to rent-seeking theory is that prohibition of such activity, were it actually possible, would remove the opportunity to address grievances, perpetuate the law in existence at the time of prohibition, and deny people their legal and constitutional rights, including their right to a lawyer, and their right to participate in government as well as limit competition. The perpetuation criticism is particularly objectionable, inasmuch as modern urban industrial society and political democracy would never have been feasible had the beneficiaries of the old post-feudal order had a veto, as it were, on legal, political, and social change. Anne Krueger's more limited model, centering on bribery and extortion, is much less amenable to criticism along these lines than several other broader and less discriminating versions of rent-seeking.

Both theories, Ricardian rent and rent-seeking, are greatly affected by the situation that, under post-feudal structures, land ownership conveyed important rights of governance and therefore control of social evolution.

SEE ALSO *Returns, Diminishing; Ricardo, David*

BIBLIOGRAPHY

Colander, David C., ed. 1984. *Neoclassical Political Economy.* Cambridge, MA: Ballinger.

George, Henry. [1884] 1982. *The Land Question.* New York: Schalkenbach Foundation.

Krueger, Anne O. 1974. The Political Economy of the Rent-Seeking Society. *American Economic Review* 64: 291–303.

Laurent, John, ed. 2003. *Henry George's Legacy in Economic Thought.* Northampton, MA: Edward Elgar.

Ricardo, David. [1817] 1948. *The Principles of Political Economy and Taxation.* New York: E. P. Dutton.

Tullock, Gordon. 1989. *The Economics of Special Privilege and Rent Seeking.* Norwell, MA: Kluwer Academic Publishers.

Warren J. Samuels

RENT CONTROL

Rent controls can be broadly defined as governmental regulations that limit landlords' ability to set and increase rents freely on residential properties. Rent controls often coincide with a host of other regulations concerning landlords' responsibilities and tenants' rights in a rental arrangement. Most rent controls are one of two types: rent ceilings, which place hard limits on the amount of money a landlord can charge for a rental unit that is based on the unit itself; and tenancy rent control, which is a set of regulations that limit the actions a landlord can take during the tenure of a sitting tenant, including limitations on landlords' ability to increase rents.

Rent ceilings (or first-generation rent controls) are the most commonly studied type of rent control, but have become quite uncommon in practice. Most rental ceilings came into being at the end of World War II (1939–1945) to help mitigate expected disruptions in the rental housing market due to the demand shock of veterans returning from overseas service in the war. The most well-known example is in New York City, where a number of rental properties are still controlled under a rent ceiling. Tenancy rent controls (also known as second-generation rent controls) are much more common in the contemporary world. Most tenancy rent control laws were enacted in the wake of the global economic downturn of the mid-1970s that brought high inflation, and many were then abolished in the 1980s and 1990s. Tenancy rent controls are still relatively common in North America and Europe and elsewhere. Tenancy rent controls are typically one component of a host of policies that strengthen tenants' rights in the rental housing market. In addition to limiting the amount of rent increases a landlord can impose on a sitting tenant, they often regulate or prohibit the practice of collecting nonrefundable deposits, limit the ability of landlords to evict sitting tenants, and restrict the use of fixed-term contracts.

One particular aspect of tenancy rent controls that differs considerably from rent ceilings is the "vacancy decontrol" provision most employ. This provision frees landlords to set rents freely once a rental unit becomes vacant. The common justification for tenancy rent control is the shift to the landlord in the balance of power once a tenant has taken up occupancy in a rental unit due to the expense to the tenant (both financial and emotional) of vacating the unit and moving elsewhere. As arbitrary evictions are generally prohibited, it is necessary to limit the landlords' ability to increase rents on sitting tenants so that they are not deliberately priced out of the unit to affect the same result as an eviction.

Rent ceilings are fairly straightforward to analyze and have thus secured a place in almost every basic textbook on economics. The artificially low rents created by these laws create excess demand for apartments. This excess demand would normally drive prices up, but the regulation prevents this, leaving a group of potential tenants unable to find housing. Those who do secure housing are better off as they are paying less than they would in the absence of the policy. Landlords receive less than they would in the free market, which serves to limit the supply of apartments. So there are fewer units available under rent control than without, and there are winners and losers among those who want housing at the rent ceiling price: the winners are those that are able to find a rental unit and who pay the depressed rent, and the losers are those that cannot find housing.

Tenancy rent controls are less straightforward to analyze. Since initial rents are generally set to market clearing rates, the problem of excess demand is not realized. However, as rental increases on sitting tenants are limited, it creates a situation where apartments are more valuable for those that are able to remain in them for a long time as they get the benefit of diminishing real rents, and these types will therefore bid up initial rents. Those that are more peripatetic are likely to find initial rents too high as they will not be able to realize the full benefit of decreasing real rents. The result in this situation is a different type of winner and loser. The winners under tenancy rent control are those that can remain in an apartment for a long time (perhaps older, more established individuals) and the losers are those that need to move more frequently (perhaps younger, less established individuals). In the end, landlords are able, through the setting of high initial rents, to do just as well under tenancy rent control as in an unregulated market and therefore supply is not affected.

SEE ALSO *Regulation; Wage and Price Controls*

BIBLIOGRAPHY

Arnott, Richard. 1995. Time for Revisionism on Rent Control? *Journal of Economic Perspectives* 9 (1): 99–120.

Basu, Kaushik, and Patrick M. Emerson. 2000. The Economics of Tenancy Rent Control. *The Economic Journal* 110 (466): 939–962.

Niebanck, Paul L., ed. 1985. *The Rent Control Debate*. Chapel Hill: University of North Carolina Press.

Patrick M. Emerson

RENT-SEEKING

SEE *Rent*.

REPARATIONS

The term *reparations* refers to a concept and tool for providing monetary payments to members of aggrieved groups based on past wrongful actions against them or their ancestors. Reparations are used for addressing injuries and damages in relations among nations, ethnic groups, and other victims of sustained economic and sociopolitical injustice or military or police aggression. Examples include reparations paid to victims of the German Holocaust in Europe from 1930 to 1945 and Japanese Americans who were partially compensated for their internment and loss of property in the United States during World War II (1939–1945). Earlier reparations were paid by Germany to the Allies after World War I (1914–1918), but in a manner and intensity that probably contributed to reopened hostilities later in the century. The reparations concept is being thought of by some as a potentially useful tool for helping to resolve chronic ancestral grievances in many situations worldwide, including in Northern Ireland, the Balkans, the Middle East, South Asia, and elsewhere.

In the United States, the idea of reparations has gained strength as a way to remedy injustices against African Americans as a group, as well as Native American Indians and Native Hispanic American Indians. This latter debate over what many call *reparations* has often been a catchall for discussion of a wider range of concerns in social policy and the expression of other agendas. In that sense, some reparation advocates seek monetary damages for their ancestors' pain and suffering, for their loss of language and African identity, and for the slave trade itself. The debate has also been characterized by imprecision, and the parties to the argument often mischaracterize, disregard, or distort opponents' actual positions and beliefs. This was the case, for example, in the article "Ten Reasons

Why Reparations for Slavery Is a Bad Idea for Blacks—and Racist Too" (2001) by the conservative activist and media personality David Horowitz.

After Horowitz's article was published, a sharp encounter ensued between Horowitz and several others involving the definition of "reparations for slavery" and whether it was justified or fair to white Americans currently living and paying taxes. None of the parties to the discussion, on either side, had carefully reviewed the literature or provided any original opposing or clarifying analysis. Thus, the entire episode primarily illustrated the tendency toward carelessness in thought and discussion on racial redistributive justice, even by most proponents. This encounter also underscored the highly emotional quality of much discussion of the subject of reparations, which brings to the surface fundamental, and long-buried and unarticulated, core racial concerns on all sides. The debate also raises questions about the political feasibility of reparations, whatever the term means. Is there broad support for a practical policy and program of explicitly redistributive and compensatory justice in the United States?

There is a growing scholarly analytical literature on the subject of reparations. Among the earliest articles was one by Robert Browne, published in 1972 in a special issue of the *Review of Black Political Economy*. This issue featured the first attempts to quantify the present value of the stream of benefits to whites from past wrongful takings under slavery, segregation, and discrimination. Much of that analysis was based on work done by the economist Lester Thurow in his 1969 book *Poverty and Discrimination*. Thurow developed a model, and using census data he established that white Americans gained approximately $15 billion in one year, 1960, from racial discrimination in the labor market.

From 1985 to 1990, the National Economic Association, an organization of African American economists and policy analysts, conducted sessions on reparations at their annual meetings. The papers presented at these sessions were published in *The Wealth of Races: The Present Value of the Benefits of Past Injustices* (1990), edited by Richard F. America. This volume included the work of William Darity, Roger Ransom and Richard Sutch, Warren Whatley and Gavin Wright, Larry Neal and Robert Browne, and other established economists, and carried quantitative and historically based analysis several steps forward. In a 1993 monograph Richard America continued to refine and develop the concept of reparations, focusing on unjust enrichment and the income and wealth-transfer effects of slavery and discrimination. In 2003 Darity and Dania Frank published a short but comprehensive summary of research to date. This volume refines the analysis and points to a new framework that can produce an even more robust analytical basis.

A common question raised about reparations is that if they are suitable for African Americans, are they not also appropriate for other aggrieved groups? Reponses vary widely. But the emerging approach with the deepest analytical grounding involves an analysis of wrongful taking and unjust enrichment, and findings of magnitudes of compensation based on historical auditing. This approach can be used for other groups with similar historical backgrounds, wherever appropriate.

What about popular opinion and support for or opposition to reparations for African Americans? Michael Dawson and Rovana Popoff (2004) found that 79 percent of blacks and 30 percent of whites in the United States favored an apology for slavery, but 66 percent of blacks and only 4 percent of whites favored monetary reparations to blacks "for slavery." This finding may or may not reflect actual views on reparations when defined differently as "recapture of unjust enrichment" rather than reparations "for slavery." That distinction is crucial. The question of reparations, in various forms, has become a serious public policy issue since it first emerged in the late stages of the civil rights movement of the 1960s. Of course, as early as the American Revolution, some advocates of abolition were framing remedies that included some form of compensatory justice for freedmen and freedwomen.

The concept of reparations varies according to the worldview of those in the debate. There are three broad views. For some, reparations primarily mean compensation for the slave trade. A second view is that reparations are owed to current generations for the pain and suffering of their collective ancestors—for crimes against humanity. A third view of reparations is narrower and seeks to recapture, recover, and reclaim unjust enrichment that resulted from wrongful takings under slavery, segregation, and many forms of discrimination from 1619 through the present. The focus in this entry is on this third definition.

The idea of unjust enrichment is key, and functions as a useful framework for understanding chronic poverty, poor educational performance, substandard housing, high unemployment, and low income and wealth accumulation among African Americans, as well as persistent black-white disparities in health care, business investment, and competitiveness. These conditions all derive, significantly, from the processes of wrongful taking and unjust enrichment. In addition, these conditions can be measured because they all include a measurable, historically based component. The processes of slavery, Jim Crow segregation, and discrimination were all mechanisms that transferred or diverted income and wealth from blacks as a class to whites as a class, producing unjust enrichment. Reparations, in this view, constitute the proper basis for a well-founded

program for rational compensatory public policy. Unjust enrichment and reparations are ways to understand chronic social distress in a long-term historical context. Slavery and discrimination operated in many forms, in every aspect of American life, for 350 years, and this explains much of the current dysfunction. Social problems derive largely from the extraction or confiscation of black property and income by white decision-makers, for white benefit, in millions of daily microdecisions.

The cumulative effect of those wrongful takings produces current unjust enrichment and a range of conditions referred to as affluence and poverty. This situation helps explain the problems we objectively see on the ground, but this fact has been absent from policy discussions. The reparations concept inserts these ideas into the heart of policy analysis, and changes the way problems are viewed and the way policy and programs are created.

There has been widespread and consistent white discrimination against blacks. This behavior has been outlawed in the United States since 1965, but policy analysts and social scientists have not failed to note the full long-term consequences, especially the unjust enrichment. Explicitly accounting for the ways in which black and white ancestors behaved puts a spotlight on the transferred income and wealth. The concept of reparations, and the associated framework of wrongful taking and unjust enrichment, provides a public policy framework for examining objective reality by quantifying and taking into full account historical context. In this way, it is a new or, at least, improved paradigm—a new or improved way of viewing the world. There has been massive, systematic exploitation and confiscation. And those practices—slavery and discrimination—produced wrongful benefits that have been passed on, transferred intergenerationally, to the present.

This analysis points to redistributive justice—recovering monies wrongfully taken through restitution—as the general remedy. That is what reparations mean in public policy terms. Other analysts emphasize payment for pain and suffering or for crimes against humanity. And still others have focused on a form of reparations as a means of laying the groundwork for atonement and reconciliation; they emphasize healing.

But reparations of the kind described here focus on improved public policy analysis, in which national tax and budget priorities are informed by the concept of unjust enrichment, and, by implication, reparations. Thus, social spending becomes a tool for explicitly making restitution.

The amount of reparations owed would equal the net present value of the sum of the deviations from "fair" standards in prices, wages, rents, employment, interest, and investment in education, plus all other affected transactions between whites and blacks. This is an overly simple but illustrative form of the model that leads to a grasp of the dimensions of the wrongful taking and unjust enrichment that produced the need for reparations. We can audit the actual patterns of labor, trade, and investment relations long after the fact. We can also posit a set of "fair" wages, occupational distributions, employment levels, prices, rents, interest rates, educational expenditures, taxes, profits, and returns on investment. We can then estimate the deviations from those "fair" standards. And we find that those deviations resulted, in part, from force, manipulation, and coercion. Then we aggregate, compound, and adjust for price changes over time. That produces a "bill" that represents the financial basis for redistributive justice. We can then negotiate the bill, and reach rational, feasible, make-whole settlement agreements that will restore African Americans as a class to their rightful place. These actions are reparations. Clarifying that will help clarify policy choices in education, housing, employment, and every other controversial sector. The remedy is income and wealth redistribution in capital injections, or grants, in housing equity, quality education, and business equity, targeted to rectify the injustice.

Reparations are a way of looking at complex policy issues that can be rationally applied to understanding, defining, and solving chronic social problems in housing, health, education, employment, and business and community development. Without this historical framework, public policy cannot effectively address these problems.

BIBLIOGRAPHY

America, Richard F., ed. 1990. *The Wealth of Races: The Present Value of Benefits from Past Injustices.* New York: Greenwood.

America, Richard F. 1993. *Paying the Social Debt: What White America Owes Black America.* Westport, CT: Praeger.

Browne, Robert, ed. 1972. *Review of Black Political Economy.* Special Issue on reparations.

Darity, William A., and Dania Frank. 2003. The Political Economy of Ending Racism and the WCAR: The Economics of Reparations. *American Economic Review* 93 (2): 326–329.

Dawson, Michael, and Rovana Popoff. 2004. Justice and Greed: Black and White Support for Reparations. *Du Bois Review* 1 (1).

Horowitz, David. 2001. Ten Reasons Why Reparations for Blacks Is a Bad Idea for Blacks—and Racist Too. *Front Page Magazine* (January 3). http://www.frontpagemag.com/Articles/ReadArticle.asp?ID=1153.

Thurow, Lester. 1969. *Poverty and Discrimination.* Washington, DC: Brookings Institution.

Richard F. America

REPATRIATION

From the Latin for "fatherland" (*patria*), *repatriation* literally means to return, voluntarily or involuntarily, to one's homeland. The term now has two distinct meanings: either the return of people to their homeland, or the return of cultural objects to their place of origin. The repatriation of people, for example after a war, has a long history, whereas the repatriation of cultural objects, typically the cultural artifacts of aboriginal communities, is associated with postcolonialism, the social movements of native peoples, and the changing function of museums in modern societies.

The repatriation of peoples is closely associated with the growth of national citizenship, the involvement of civilians as victims of modern warfare, and the development of human rights legislation. After World War II (1939–1945), there were over one million displaced persons in Europe, and in 1950 the post of United Nations High Commissioner for Refugees (UNHCR) was established, a year before the 1951 Refugee Convention. In the first fifty years of its existence, the UNHCR gave assistance to at least fifty million people who have been displaced, both internally and externally, as a result of warfare and civil conflict. With the apparently unstoppable growth in the numbers of refugees in the second half of the twentieth century, the humanitarian protection of refugees led to greater concern by the UNHCR in a right to "return in safety and dignity," as expressed in a 1989 policy document (Coles 1989). *Safety* refers to physical security and the entitlement to protection from a forced return. *Dignity* is to be measured by the quality of life in the location to which displaced persons return voluntarily. In practice, achieving a consensus over safety and dignity between states, refugees, and UN agencies is extremely difficult, often because there is little reliable information about the security of war zones that have been subject to a long period of conflict. The protracted arrangements between five separate organizations and a commission in the 1990s to return Guatemalans to Mexico or the case of 200,000 Tigrayans walking home to Ethiopia against the wishes of UNHCR and the government of Sudan are typical of such political uncertainty.

Any account of the repatriation of cultural artifacts needs to consider the historical development of museums as institutions for collecting the material cultures of aboriginal communities and the ancient world. The expansion of museums in the Victorian period was in part a function of the growth of European colonization and the colonial sense of superiority. Britain's acquisition of the Elgin Marbles from classical Greece was a notorious illustration of the acquisitiveness of Western classicism and archaeology. Thomas Bruce (1766–1841), the seventh Earl of Elgin, obtained a *firman* (legal document) from the Ottoman sultan to remove sculptures from the Parthenon in Athens in 1801. Attempts by the Greek government with the support of the United Nations Educational, Scientific, and Cultural Organization (UNESCO) to repatriate the Elgin Marbles have so far been rejected by the British government.

In addition to plundering the classical world, museum curators were especially interested in the primitive and the exotic as collectable items. This was also the period in which the native peoples of the Western Hemisphere were at their lowest cultural ebb. War and disease had produced a demographic catastrophe, and the cultural heritage of native peoples was removed to museums in policies that amounted to deculturalization. In addition to cultural artifacts, human remains from battlefields entered the medical collections of the U.S. Army and physical anthropologists.

The federal Antiquities Act (1906) prevented the destruction of antiquities on public land in the United States, but allowed free import and export of Native American artifacts. It was not until the repatriation movement of the 1980s and 1990s that there was a fundamental change in the relationships between museums and Native American communities, resulting in the National Museum of the American Indian Act (1989) and the Native American Graves Protection and Repatriation Act (1990). Although this legislation is significant, the demand for sacred and ceremonial materials on the international art market is such that looting from archaeological sites continues to be a serious problem.

SEE ALSO *Burial Grounds, Native American; Migration*

BIBLIOGRAPHY

Coles, G. 1989. Solutions to the Problem of Refugees and the Protection of Refugees: A Background Paper. Geneva: International Institute of Humanitarian Law/UNHCR.

West, W. Richard, Jr. 1996. Repatriation. In *Encyclopedia of North American Indians*, ed. Frederick E. Hoxie, 543–546. Boston: Houghton Mifflin.

Bryan S. Turner

REPLICATOR DYNAMICS

The replicator dynamics are part of evolutionary game theory and are especially prominent in models of cultural evolution. Evolutionary game theory uses principles of interactive behavior to explain the emergence of behavioral regularities in organisms forming a population. The results of organisms' interactions affect their fitness, meas-

ured as their ability to reproduce. If one organism is fitter than another, then it is more likely to reproduce than the other. An organism's offspring inherit its traits. The offspring may differ from the parent in fitness, however, because the offspring's fitness depends on their success in interactions with their contemporaries. As the population changes, the traits that confer fitness may change, too.

The replicator dynamics explain changes in fitness that arise from changes in a population's composition. Applications divide a population according to organisms' behavioral traits, in particular strategies for interacting with others. For instance, in a dispute over food, one strategy may be to fight. Another strategy may be to retreat. A strategy's consequences are assessed in terms of fitness, or average number of offspring.

A mathematical equation characterizes the replicator dynamics. It applies to a population given simplifying assumptions. They specify four conditions: (1) The population is infinite. Assuming an infinite population makes the relative frequency of an outcome match its probability. (2) An individual in the population has the same probability of interacting with any other member of the population. Pairs of interacting individuals form as if individuals were matched at random. (3) Strategies breed true. That is, if an organism has offspring, its offspring adopt the same strategy it follows. An organism's fitness equals the average number of offspring following its strategy. (4) Reproduction is asexual. An organism has a single parent and so inherits the parent's strategy. This condition puts aside the possibility that an organism's strategy differs from a parent's strategy because it has two parents with differing strategies. The proportion of individuals following a strategy changes only if some organisms with that strategy are more or less fit than their parents and so reproduce more or less frequently than their parents did.

Brian Skyrms's (1996, pp. 51–53) notation is used here to present the replicator equation. First, assume that a population evolves in steps from one generation to the next. Using the proportion of individuals following a strategy in one generation, and the strategy's consequences for their fitness, one may compute the proportion of individuals following the strategy in the next generation. Let $U(A)$ be the average fitness of a strategy A, and let U be the average fitness of all strategies. Then the proportion of the population using A in the next generation equals the proportion of the population using A in the current generation times the ratio $U(A)/U$. That is, if $p(A)$ is the proportion using strategy A in the current generation and $p'(A)$ is the proportion using A in the next generation, then $p'(A) = p(A) U(A)/U$. If A has greater than average fitness, its proportion increases. A little algebra yields the following equation specifying the change from one generation to the next in the proportion of the population using strategy *A*.

$$p'(A) - p(A) = p(A)[U(A) - U]/U$$

Next, suppose that evolution is continuous with respect to time. Then the population evolves according to this differential equation.

$$dp(A)/dt = p(A)[U(A) - U]/U$$

The equation gives the rate of change in the proportion of the population using strategy *A*. Given that the average fitness of the population is positive, the following simpler differential equation describes the structural features of the population's evolution.

$$dp(A)/dt = p(A)[U(A) - U]$$

This equation characterizes the replicator dynamics. Peter Taylor and Leo Jonker (1978) were the first theorists to formulate the equation (using different notation). Peter Schuster and Karl Sigmund (1983) called it the replicator equation and the pattern of change it describes the replicator dynamics.

Social scientists use the replicator dynamics to construct models of human behavior, for example, models of the emergence of cultural norms. When applying the dynamics to cultural evolution, imitation may replace reproduction as the mechanism responsible for replication of strategies. Because human populations do not satisfy exactly the idealizations of the replicator dynamics, the models the dynamics yield are simplifications. However, in some cases the dynamics may approximate the course of evolution.

Applications of the replicator dynamics look for the emergences of stable behavior. Consider, for example, food sharing in a hunter-gatherer society. This strategy may enhance fitness, propagate within a population, and drive out rival strategies. It may be evolutionarily stable in the sense that once a population adopts it, even if a few organisms with different strategies arrive, those new strategies do not propagate within the population. The stable strategy resists invasion by mutants. A strategy that is evolutionarily stable with respect to the replicator dynamics corresponds to a stable Nash equilibrium in a game representing individuals' interactions.

SEE ALSO *Game Theory; Nash Equilibrium; Strategy*

BIBLIOGRAPHY

Hofbauer, Joseph, and Karl Sigmund. 1998. *Evolutionary Games and Population Dynamics.* Cambridge, U.K.: Cambridge University Press.

Schuster, Peter, and Karl Sigmund. 1983. Replicator Dynamics. *Journal of Theoretical Biology* 100: 533–538.

Skyrms, Brian. 1996. *Evolution of the Social Contract.* Cambridge, U.K.: Cambridge University Press.

Taylor, Peter, and Leo Jonker. 1978. Evolutionarily Stable Strategies and Game Dynamics. *Mathematical Biosciences* 40: 145–156.

Paul Weirich

REPORT OF THE WARREN COMMISSION

SEE *Warren Report.*

REPRESENTATION

Any major dictionary offers numerous definitions of the term *representation*. This indicates that the concept comprises a range of meanings and usages, depending on the type of discourse in which it emerges, the variety of cultural phenomena to which it may refer, and the philosophical programs and ideological perspectives it is intended to serve. Within the realm of sociocultural studies, two clusters of meanings of the term—defined as the "act or action of representing: the state of being represented" (*Merriam-Webster's Collegiate Dictionary* 2003, p. 1057)—have acquired critical importance:

1. To bring clearly before the mind (a book that *represents* the character of America); to serve as a sign or symbol of (the flag *represents* a country); to portray or exhibit in art; to serve as the counterpart or image of (a movie hero who *represents* the character of a culture); to describe or depict in language.

2. To take the place of in some respect; to act in the place of or for usually by legal right; to serve especially in a legislative body by delegated authority usually resulting from election. (*Merriam-Webster's Collegiate Dictionary* 2003, p. 1057)

Both clusters of meaning suggest that representations essentially stand in for something or someone else, and, as such, present something or someone a second time—they literally re-present. Although it is fair to say that representation functions through reproduction (for example, most people in the Western world are familiar with the image of Rembrandt's 1642 painting *The Night Watch*, without ever having seen the original painting, through reproductions), or by processing the likeness of an object, this is not the sense in which the issue of representation has come to prevail in recent theoretical discussions. In the simplest terms, representation in contemporary sociocultural theory is the production of meaning through language. As Stuart Hall points out in *Representation: Cultural Representations and Signifying Practices* (1997, p. 17), representation constitutes the link between concepts and language that allows us to refer to objects, people, and events in the "real" world, or to imaginary worlds of fictional objects, people, and events (as in films or literary texts). In this line of thought, representations do not so much stand for some underlying "real," or re-represent some original or preexisting object, as they call into being, in fact quite literally *produce*, that to which they supposedly refer, or re-present.

The philosophical concern with representation dates back to ancient times, with Plato (427–347 BCE) and Aristotle (384–322 BCE) acting as key figures. Plato considered representations—whether musical, literary, or visual—as potentially dangerous, creating illusory worlds that would lead one away from "real things." Aristotle, in contrast, regarded the ability to re-create, through *mimesis* (the imitative representation of nature and human behavior in art and literature), as that which distinguishes human beings from animals, and thus as necessary for people's learning and being in the world. In his influential book *The Mirror and the Lamp* (1953), literary scholar M. H. Abrams argues that the Aristotelian notion of representation in terms of *mimesis* (the supposition that the mind, and its products, reflect the external world) dominated Western attitudes toward representation up to the eighteenth century. The antimimetic approach that emerged with the advent of romanticism subsequently came to substitute the idea of the mind as an essentially passive, reproductive apparatus with the notion of the mind as an active and creative power. Since reality is only accessible through representation—through texts, discourses, and images—there is no unmediated access to reality. The products of the mind, in the form of representations, consequently came to be regarded as so many different and, indeed, active attempts to make sense of the world, as historically and culturally shifting constructions of equally shifting realities, rather than as accurate reflections of preexisting objects, people, and events in the world. Moreover, since reality is always more complicated and therefore necessarily exceeds the ways in which it can be signified by any culturally and historically prevailing means of representation, it remains always necessary to construct new ways of seeing reality, to produce new (modes of) representation.

The productive notion of representation suggests that there is no inherent meaning in any picture or sentence or sound; rather, as Dani Cavallaro posits in *Critical and Cultural Theory*, a representation "only represents by virtue of being interpreted and ultimately represents anything it is capable of suggesting" (2001, p. 39). This entails that, rather than acting individually and exclusively on their own terms, any representation is part of a *system of representation*. First, as Hall argues, there is the system that allows us to sort all kinds of objects, people, and events, in correlation with a set of concepts and ideas that "we carry around in our heads" (1997, p. 17). This system does not so much consist of individual concepts or ideas, but rather of different ways of organizing, arranging, and classifying concepts on the basis of similarity and difference. Representations, therefore, always require interpretation within a specific set of interpretive conventions that make up the dominant way of looking at reality within a culture at a certain time in history. Second, there is the system of language. The conceptual map of reality that is shared by individual people within a given society, and which enables them to make sense of reality, is necessarily mediated by a shared system of signs, a common language of words, images, and sounds. Signs—in the broadest sense, so as to include not only spoken and written languages proper, but also visual images, facial expressions, and body language, as well fashion, music, or any other body of signs that carries and expresses meaning—jointly make up the system of signification and representation, that is, the sociohistorically specific system of organizing reality that helps us to make sense of the otherwise incoherent mass of our everyday experience. Since systems of representation mediate our access to the world, representations are never immediately and unequivocally connected with an underlying reality: We only experience reality through the mediation of texts, discourses, and images. The real as such is unattainable, and may only be grasped according to the codes and conventions of interpretation and signification of any specific society.

Understanding representational practices as the medium or channel through which meaning production happens, most contemporary theorists infer that objects, people, and events in the world do not have fixed or stable meanings, but only acquire meaning within a specific culture, and are defined by human beings, participants in a culture, who speak with a certain authority to make things mean or signify something. At this point, the first and the second cluster of meanings of the term *representation* begin to converge, as well as to show up its ideological and political aspects. Since those who speak with authority about the ways in which (certain aspects of) reality make sense, or signify, and since no representational account of reality can ever fully grasp the complexities of such realities, systems of representation cannot but offer partial and, indeed, interested ways of viewing the world and the people, objects, and events within it. As W. J. T. Mitchell points out in *Picture Theory*, representation not only works to mediate our "knowledge (of slavery and of many other things), but obstructs, fragments, and negates that knowledge" (1994, p. 188). Instead of seeing representations as only particular kinds of objects representing something or someone else, this perspective asks us to approach representation as an active process and product of power (relations), in which certain kinds of representations are produced, valued, and exchanged on the basis of underlying interests and investments, while alternative ways and conventions of representation are either disavowed or simply negated so as to affect, fragment, or deny other forms of knowledge about the world, and the objects, people, and events within it. As such, particular modes of representation can be seen to offer clues to a given culture's (dominant) belief systems, its interpretations of reality, and its translations of factual and fictional situations into words and images. Representations, on this view, embody certain kinds of social relations, the interpretations and evaluation of which are necessarily partial, more imaginary than "real," and always already endowed with specific interests and investments. Rather than objectively reflecting the world as it is, representation thus constructs shifting realities as they are perceived through various, ideologically informed filters and channels.

SEE ALSO *Aristotle; Critical Theory; Culture; Hall, Stuart; History, Social; Nonverbal Communication; Plato; Representation in Postcolonial Analysis; Society; Symbols*

BIBLIOGRAPHY

Abrams, M. H. 1953. *The Mirror and the Lamp: Romantic Theory and the Critical Tradition.* Oxford: Oxford University Press.

Cavallaro, Dani. 2001. *Critical and Cultural Theory: Thematic Variations.* London and New Brunswick, NJ: Athlone.

Hall, Stuart, ed. 1997. *Representation: Cultural Representations and Signifying Practices.* London: Open University Press.

Merriam-Webster's Collegiate Dictionary. 2003. 11th ed. Springfield, MA: Merriam-Webster.

Mitchell, W. J. T. 1994. *Picture Theory: Essays on Verbal and Visual Representation.* Chicago: University of Chicago Press.

renée c. hoogland

REPRESENTATION, MIRROR

SEE *Constituency.*

REPRESENTATION, POLITICAL

SEE *Constituency; Democracy.*

REPRESENTATION IN POSTCOLONIAL ANALYSIS

People know and comprehend the complex world in which we live through the act of naming it; thus through language and representations. The term *representation* embodies a range of meanings and interpretations. Etymologically, *representation* can be understood as a presentation drawn up not by depicting the object as it is but by re-presenting it or constructing it in a new form and/or environment. In ancient times representation played a central role in studying and understanding literature, aesthetics, and semiotics. The construct has since evolved into a significant component to analyze the contemporary world's creation of audio visual as well as textual arts, such as films, museum exhibitions, television programs, photographs, paintings, advertisements, and literature. None of these representational forms are neutral because it is impossible to divorce them from the culture and society that produces them. R-rated films are an example of cultural restrictions, highlighting society's attempt to control and modify representations to promote a certain set of ideologies and values. Despite these restrictions, representations have the ability to take on a life of their own once in the public sphere. The term *representation* cannot be given a definitive meaning because there will always be a gap between intention and realization, original and copy.

In a 1997 essay entitled *The Work of Representation*, the sociologist Stuart Hall discusses the relationship between politics and representation and the systems representing both. He approaches representation as the medium or process through which meaning, associations, and values are socially constructed and reified by people in a shared culture. Representation involves understanding how language and systems of knowledge production work together to produce and circulate meanings. According to Hall, we give things meaning by how we represent them. Cultural representations help form the images people have of others; if assimilated by those others, they help form the images people have of themselves as well; cultural representations get embodied in institutions and inform policies and practices. The politics of representation, then, revolve around issues of power and control over one's own self and its representations and reproduction by others.

In sociocultural representations it is often difference that signifies by creating binary oppositions. Within this dichotomized relationship, one pole always tends to dominate (e.g., male over female, us over them, high over low), bringing issues of dissimilarity and power to the fore within a representation. The act of unreflexively representing the other has significant resonances with long-standing practices of domination within the context of colonization. A heightened awareness that asymmetries of representation enacted and reproduced the asymmetries of power in the colonial world has enhanced the significance of cultural politics in the academic field of postcolonial studies. The focus on culture and representation is not necessarily a diversion from the political realities of postcolonial struggle; culture and representation can even be used to inform the understanding of those colonial processes.

Much postcolonial scholarship is informed, in one way or another, by theories that elucidate the politics of representations. The single most influential scholar demystifying the process of constructing "the Other" is Edward Said (1935–2003). Employing a Foucaultian conception of the power/knowledge nexus and the politics of representation, Said's seminal book *Orientalism* established how the "West" (especially Britain, France, and the United States), through an academic, literary, and philosophical endeavor executed by Western intellectuals, was able to manage—and even produce—the Orient politically, sociologically, militarily, ideologically, scientifically, and imaginatively during the post-Enlightenment period (an era initiated by colonial conquest). This linear and uninterrupted construction of the Orient as "Other" over many centuries became the basis and rationale for colonial oppression and served to strengthen the identity of Western culture. In Said's words, "Orientalism is—and does not simply represent—a considerable dimension of modern political-intellectual culture, and as such has less to do with the Orient than it does with 'our' world" (Said 1994, p. 12).

Said eloquently demonstrated how the representations of Orientalism pervade the writings of European and North American literature icons such as Charles Dickens, Jane Austen, Henry James, and Thomas Hardy as well as modern-day media reports about the developing world, particularly the Islamic world. Although Said's arguments have been challenged and extended, his work is still the governing voice that leads scholars in anthropology, literature, mass communication, and postcolonial studies to critically analyze representations that demarcate "us" versus "them." Said's insights provide a handy toolbox with which one can easily demystify how the global media exacerbated the stereotyped conflict between the West and the Islamic world in the post 9/11 era.

The postcolonial scholar Gayatri Spivak made an important contribution to theories of representation by insisting that the concept in a literary or semiotic sense must be reconsidered in connection with representation in politics, representation in the sense of any capacity for a person to be the agent of, to stand for, the will of other people. In her provocative essay *Can the Subaltern Speak?* Spivak underlined how representations, especially of marginalized groups from developing countries, are intimately linked to positioning: socioeconomic, gendered, cultural, geographic, historical, and institutional. The crux of Spivak's argument is that the representations of the developing world conflate two related but discontinuous meanings of representation (Spivak 1988, pp. 275–276). One meaning is "speaking for," in the sense of political representation, and the second is "speaking about" or "re-presenting," in the sense of making a portrait. While Spivak recognizes that representations cannot escape "othering," Spivak argues for us to be scrupulous in so doing, especially in the case of unequal power relationships, when representing the West's Other (the developing world) and the developing world's Other (the subaltern).

Awareness of the constructed nature of sociocultural representations does not mean that people can do without them. A way to bypass the dilemma of representation of and for others is to acknowledge and articulate how power enters into the process of cultural translation. In the end, the crisis of cross-cultural representation can be resolved only through cross-cultural communications that are actually, rather than virtually, decentered and multivocal, that is, through the empowerment of others to participate as equal partners in the conversation of humankind.

SEE ALSO *Colonialism; Cultural Studies; Culture; Foucault, Michel; Hall, Stuart; Islam, Shia and Sunni; Orientalism; Other, The; Popular Culture; Postcolonialism; Representation; Said, Edward; Social Constructs; Subaltern; Visual Arts*

BIBLIOGRAPHY

Hall, Stuart. 1997. The Work of Representation. In *Representation: Cultural Representations and Signifying Practices*, ed. Stuart Hall, 13–74. London, Sage Publishing.

Said, Edward W. [1978] 1994. *Orientalism*. Rev. ed. New York: Vintage Books.

Spivak, Gayatri C. 1988. Can the Subaltern Speak? In *Marxism and the Interpretation of Culture*, ed. Cary Nelson and Larry Grossberg, 271–313. Basingstoke, U.K.: Macmillan Education.

Noel B. Salazar

REPRESENTATIVE AGENT

The representative agent is a device used by economists to model the macroeconomy. The general idea is to solve a well-specified microeconomic problem, and then use the relationships between the variables in that model as a description of the macroeconomy. For example, we can model the decisions that would be made by a person who would like to consume goods and enjoy leisure, but can only purchase goods after earning wages through working. Additionally, we can posit a specific production technology that determines how many goods are produced when the person works. From this problem, we can solve for the relationship between the state of the economy and the person's decision on how much to work and consume. A representative agent model would then take these relationships, which were derived for an individual, and use them as an exact specification of the macroeconomy. Thus, if the representative agent would increase consumption by 10 percent in response to a 5 percent increase in the level of technology, it is assumed that aggregate consumption will also rise by 10 percent in response to the same change.

The earliest form of a representative agent was in Alfred Marshall's *Principles of Economics* (1890). Marshall constructed a representative firm as a means of specifying an industry supply curve. This representative firm was vigorously criticized by economists at the time, and the notion vanished from economics.

Representative agent models were resurrected by macroeconomists in the 1970s and became the predominant means of studying the macroeconomy in the 1980s. Surprisingly, nobody has ever written an explicit defense of this technique. The underlying rationale seems to be a desire to provide microfoundations for macroeconomic research. If we acknowledge that macroeconomic relationships are the result of a vast number of decisions made by individuals, then it might be desirable to have our macroeconomic models derived from relationships found in microeconomic problems. Because it is impossible to model the decisions of every individual in an economy separately, some shortcut is needed. Hence the representative agent is a stand-in for an average person, and the macroeconomy is assumed to behave, on average, like the average person.

Representative agent models have been roundly criticized as being an improper means of studying the macroeconomy for several reasons. It is simply not the case, even in very simple economies, that the aggregate of many decisions is exactly the same as the decision made by the representative agent. Representative agent models are incapable of capturing the effects of heterogeneity and interaction among agents, nor can they capture the effects of problems related to asymmetric information or strategic interactions. Fundamentally, representative agent models suffer from the fallacy of composition (that what is true of the part is true of the whole). The extensive criticisms demonstrating that representative agent models are neither good nor useful means of studying the macroeconomy have never been addressed by those who use such models. Yet, the use of the representative agent model continues apace.

SEE ALSO *Macroeconomics; Marshall, Alfred; Microfoundations*

BIBLIOGRAPHY

Hartley, James E. 1997. *The Representative Agent in Macroeconomics.* London: Routledge.

Kirman, Alan P. 1992. Whom or What Does the Representative Individual Represent? *Journal of Economic Perspectives* 6 (2): 117–136.

Marshall, Alfred. [1890] 1997. *Principles of Economics.* Amherst, NY: Prometheus.

James E. Hartley

REPRESSION

Repression is the use or threat of actions taken by state "authorities, or their supporters, against opponents or potential opponents to prevent, weaken, or eliminate their capacity to oppose policies" (Stohl and Lopez 1984, p. 7). Authorities include security forces and paramilitaries that target groups or individuals because of "their perceived political beliefs" (Goldstein 1978, p. xvi). Repression is associated with the related but distinct phenomena of terror, violence, and oppression.

Terror and violence describe actions by authorities against political opponents or by insurgent groups in their own campaigns against the incumbent government. The distinguishing characteristic is the perpetrator. State terror is a strategy of repression to instill fear and quiescence in the entire population. Violence by the state is also repression.

Oppression and repression are distinct but may occur together, such as with the policies of the white apartheid government in South Africa from 1948 until 1990. The apartheid system denied civil and political rights and economic and social privileges to the black South African majority as a matter of government policy (oppression). Nelson Mandela, a political prisoner for almost thirty years and leader of South Africa's black-majority African National Congress, was also the target of repression, including torture during his imprisonment.

Common examples of repression are media censorship, surveillance of political meetings, the suspension of habeas corpus, the banning of political parties, and the violation of due process rights (e.g., illegal searches and arbitrary arrests). Some restrictions may be ostensibly nonviolent, like censorship. Violent repression is sometimes called a *personal integrity violation* because it violates bodily and personal autonomy. Examples are torture, disappearances, and extrajudicial killings by security forces and paramilitaries associated with military governments

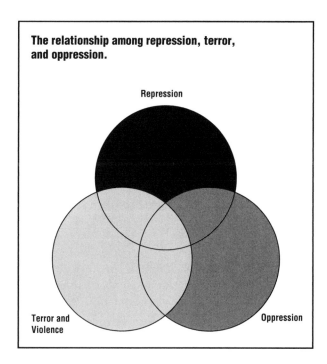

The relationship among repression, terror, and oppression.

Repression

Terror and Violence

Oppression

Figure 1

where civilian rule is suspended or abolished. This type of repression occurred under the Argentine military junta during the "Dirty War" (1976–1983) against Peronists, labor leaders, and other civilians.

Well-known examples of violent repression include the genocide of six million Jews, along with dissidents, Catholics, and countless others, by the German Nazi government (1930s to 1940s); forced collectivization under Joseph Stalin (1879–1953) in Soviet Russia in the 1940s; and the Cultural Revolution (1966–1976) in China under Mao Zedong (1893–1976). The 1980s were marked by extensive disappearances and killings by military regimes in Guatemala and El Salvador that targeted indigenous groups, whether or not they were politically mobilized.

Constitutional or emergency provisions may provide a legal character to such actions as detaining people (without charge) suspected of political violence, conducting surveillance on radical groups, or banning political parties accused of threatening political stability. Legal prohibitions may be codified into statutes to restrict political behavior or reconstitute political quiescence. For example, in the 1980s the Polish Communist government imposed martial law and banned the politically mobilized labor organization Solidarity to avert a Soviet intervention. In Germany, *Mein Kampf* (My Struggle, 1925–1926), an anti-Semitic political manifesto by Adolf Hitler (1889–1945), has been banned to prevent the expression of fascist ideology. Legal repression, especially in democ-

racies, is not necessarily legitimate behavior and is often admonished by citizens, world leaders, and human rights organizations.

Repression in the form of repressive tolerance puts pressure on unpopular political minorities to conform to majoritarian views. This may occur under democratic governments along with surveillance of political groups. For example, the U.S. House of Representative's Un-American Activities Committee (HUAC), active from 1945 to 1975, targeted the American Communist Party and its supporters during the tenure of Senator Joseph McCarthy (1908–1957). Similarly, J. Edgar Hoover (1895–1972), director of the Federal Bureau of Investigation (FBI), established the covert COINTELPRO (counterintelligence program) in 1956 using the FBI to monitor communists, civil rights leaders, and political activists like Martin Luther King Jr. (1929–1968), Malcolm X (1925–1965), and Huey P. Newton (1942–1989) of the Black Panther Party. COINTELPRO operations lasted until 1971, when Hoover officially disbanded the program in anticipation of congressional investigations.

No ideological system evinces exclusive association with repression, although healthy debate exists over this issue. Different patterns are identified within certain political historical contexts. Some scholars argue that in the United States and historically, groups representing leftist ideas, such as labor, student movements, and the more radical Black Panther Party, were targeted much more than violent groups on the extreme right, such as the Ku Klux Klan. News media and other scholars have produced equally extensive documentation on Soviet and Chinese Communist repression against their own populations. For example, the secret police in the Soviet Union imprisoned political dissidents and used surveillance and propaganda for the duration of the twentieth century. The Chinese government killed many prodemocracy demonstrators in the Tiananmen Square massacre in 1989.

Claims are advanced on each side of this ideological debate, backed by historical evidence in books, reports, and other material. A more tenable position is that no clear affinity exists between repression and the ideological orientation of government. Repression has been used against internal political opponents by communist (leftist), fascist (rightist), and even democratic governments.

SEE ALSO *Civil-Military Relation; Repressive Tolerance; Violence*

BIBLIOGRAPHY

Davenport, Christian, ed. 2000. *Paths to State Repression: Human Rights Violations and Contentious Politics.* Lanham, MD: Rowman and Littlefield.

Goldstein, Robert J. 1978. *Political Repression in Modern America from 1870 to the Present.* Cambridge, MA: Schenkman.

Poe, Steve, and Neal Tate. 1994. Repression of Human Rights to Personal Integrity in the 1980s: A Global Analysis. *American Political Science Review* 88 (4): 853–872.

Rummel, Rudolph. 1994. *Death by Government.* New Brunswick, NJ: Transaction.

Stohl, Michael, and George Lopez, eds. 1984. *The State as Terrorist: The Dynamics of Governmental Violence and Repression.* Westport, CT: Greenwood.

Claudia Dahlerus

REPRESSIVE TOLERANCE

In the essay "Repressive Tolerance" (1965), the German-born American critical theorist Herbert Marcuse (1898–1979) of the Franklin School of political theorists argued that, under the conditions of advanced industrial capitalism, the only hope for realizing the original objectives of "liberalist" or "pure" toleration (as articulated by the British philosopher John Stuart Mill [1806–1873])— freeing the mind to rationally pursue the truth—was to practice a deliberately selective "liberating tolerance" that both targeted and enacted the repression alluded to in the essay's paradoxical title (Marcuse 1965, pp. 81, 85, 90). This "liberating tolerance" would involve "the withdrawal of toleration of speech and assembly from groups and movements" on the Right, and the aggressively partisan promotion of speech, groups, and progressive movements on the Left (pp. 81, 100).

Marcuse professed to share liberalism's belief in human rationality and objective truth, and a commitment to its core mechanisms, including toleration. Following G. W. F. Hegel (1770–1831), however, Marcuse insisted that the meaning and logic of ideas, concepts, and principles cannot be determined abstractly, but instead are dialectically conditioned by the totality of the historical epoch in which they are practiced. Following Karl Marx (1818–1883), Marcuse insisted that domination was the central social fact and the most importance moral and political problem, and that a humane society of genuinely free and equal individuals living "without fear and misery" is history's telos (Marcuse 1965, p. 82). And, following Sigmund Freud (1856–1939), Marcuse conceded that, in any civilized society, intractable conflicts would necessitate the suppression of important human desires. Nevertheless, Marcuse argued that developments in the political and cultural economies of the affluent, post–World War II (1939–1945) liberal capitalist societies

had ushered in new forms of domination—"surplus repression"—that placed intolerable fetters on human freedom (Marcuse 1955). In the process, they had undermined the basis of both economic and political liberalism and "the liberal function of tolerance" (Marcuse 1965, p. 115). The practice of a liberating tolerance was the only hope for its restoration.

"The function and value of tolerance," Marcuse explained, "depend on the equality prevalent in the society in which tolerance is practiced" (Marcuse 1965, p. 84). Driven as they are by the engines of advertising, propaganda, and militarism in the service of ever-increasing affluence, advanced liberal capitalist societies are defined by their inequality. Moreover, their dominant social institutions, including the "monopolistic media," use new and dystopian forms of "technological and mental coordination" to administer what has become a "totalitarian," self-perpetuating system (pp. 94, 95, 97). In these societies, where "the economic and political process is subjected to an ubiquitous and effective administration in accordance with the predominant interests," individuals have been systematically divested of their capacity to think as rational, autonomous individuals (p. 115). As such, they have lost their capacity to pursue truth through the free exercise of their individual reason, and, in turn, to create a just and humane society.

In a "democracy with totalitarian organization," the administration is so permeating that it comes to define consciousness itself (Marcuse 1965, p. 97). Far from serving as a neutral medium for rational reflection, the language, its very concepts and categories, is transformed into a neutralizing instrument of repression. Through the operation of language, "mental attitude[s]" are formed that tend to "obliterate the difference between true and false, information and indoctrination, right and wrong" (p. 97). People "are indoctrinated by the conditions under which they live and think and which they do not transcend" (p. 98). We observe "the systematic moronization of children and adults alike by publicity and propaganda" (p. 83). The populace is incorporated into "a system which fosters tolerance as a means of perpetuating the struggle for existence and suppressing the alternatives" in significant part by "testifying to the existence of democratic liberties" (pp. 83, 84). The society's ceaseless congratulation of itself for its commitment to "the marketplace of ideas" acts as an opiate on the mass consciousness, turning individuals away from radical possibilities and reconciling them to the status quo (p. 110). While the toleration of ostensible dissent is celebrated, truly "effective dissent" becomes impossible (p. 95). Under these historical conditions, the purportedly neutral "liberalist" tolerance becomes repressive (p. 90). To weigh truth and falsity rationally and accurately, to be in practice the rational and autonomous beings that Mill envisioned, individuals first need to be "freed from the prevailing indoctrination" (p. 99). For this reason, affirmative, partisan steps slanted to the Left are needed to liberate individuals and to restore their ability to reason.

"The efforts to counteract this dehumanization," Marcuse explained, "must begin at the place of entrance, there where the false consciousness takes form (or rather: is systematically formed—it must begin with stopping the words and images which feed this consciousness)" (Marcuse 1965, p. 111). To be liberated, individuals "would have to get information slanted in the opposite direction" (p. 99). The withdrawal of tolerance would have to be aimed at ideas, groups, and movements "which promote aggressive policies, armament, chauvinism, discrimination on the grounds of race and religion, or which oppose the extension of public services, social security, medical care, etc." (p. 99).

Marcuse's call for "the restoration of freedom" through the practice of liberating tolerance raised the question of "who is to decide on the distinction between liberating and repressive, human and inhuman teachings and practices" (Marcuse 1965, p. 101). Rejecting relativism, he maintained that these distinctions "can be made rationally on empirical grounds" by "everyone who has learned to think rationally and autonomously" (pp. 105, 106). Who would these clear-sighted leaders be, and how many could we expect to find? "Where society has entered the phase of total administration and indoctrination," he noted, "this would be a small number indeed, and not necessarily that of the elected representatives of the people" (p. 106).

Marcuse was often pessimistic about the prospects of a widespread liberation from "the false consciousness [that] has become the general consciousness" (Marcuse 1965, p. 110). But in "Repressive Tolerance," he appealed hopefully to engaged intellectuals whose "task and duty … [is] to recall and preserve historical possibilities which seem to have become utopian possibilities," and "to break the concreteness of oppression in order to open the mental space in which this society can be recognized as what it is and does" (pp. 81–82).

Marcuse insisted that, unlike in the spheres of business, advertising, and the broader culture, "the trend in the educational enterprise … could conceivably be enforced by the students and teachers themselves, and thus be self-imposed" (Marcuse 1965, p. 101). "The restoration of freedom of thought," of course,

> may necessitate new and rigid restrictions on teachings and practices in the educational institutions which, by their very methods and concepts, serve to enclose the mind within the established universe of discourse and behavior—thereby precluding a priori a rational evaluation of the alternatives.… Restoration of such freedom would

also imply intolerance toward scientific research in the interest of deadly "deterrents," of abnormal human endurance under inhuman conditions, etc. (pp. 100–101)

"Unless the student learns to think in the opposite direction," Marcuse insisted, "he will be inclined to place facts into the predominant framework of values" (p. 113). Under these historical conditions, all genuine education is "counter-education" (p. 112).

Marcuse's call for a liberating tolerance was adopted enthusiastically by the radical student movements of the late 1960s in both Europe and the United States, and was particularly influential on the American New Left. His argument that a vanguard of students, teachers, and intellectuals had a special role to play, especially within educational institutions, of "break[ing] the concreteness of oppression" by suppressing ideas and actions (and language) objectively determined to be "regressive" and "inhumane" with the object of freeing students from "the prevailing indoctrination" and reestablishing the conditions of equality conducive to true freedom, played a major role in reshaping the mission and practices of the contemporary "politically correct" multiculturalist college and university (Marcuse 1965, pp. 81, 101, 99).

As liberalism and leftism made common cause in the historical crucible of the late 1960s and the 1970s, the Marcusian approach to tolerance insinuated itself—if not always self-evidently in theory, then more transparently in practice—into even ostensibly mainstream or "pure" liberal thinking (the thought of libertarians excepted), as well as into the governing rules and practices of institutions, such as universities, under liberal-left control. Whether this marks a departure from liberal principles, or (as Marcuse maintained) a return to liberalism's traditional historical function, is a question of considerable interest and complexity.

SEE ALSO *Liberalism; Marxism; Repression*

BIBLIOGRAPHY

Eidelberg, Paul. 1969. The Temptation of Herbert Marcuse. *The Review of Politics* 31: 442–458.

Marcuse, Herbert. 1955. *Eros and Civilization: A Philosophical Inquiry into Freud.* Boston: Beacon Press.

Marcuse, Herbert. 1964. *One Dimensional Man: Studies in the Ideology of Advanced Industrial Society.* Boston: Beacon Press.

Marcuse, Herbert. 1965. Repressive Tolerance. In *A Critique of Pure Tolerance*, Robert Paul Wolff, Barrington Moore Jr., and Herbert Marcuse. Boston: Beacon Press.

Spitz, David. 1966. Pure Tolerance: A Critique of Criticisms. *Dissent* (September-October): 511–525.

Wolff, Robert Paul. 1974. Marcuse's Theory of Toleration. *Polity* 6: 469–479.

Ken I. Kersch

REPRODUCTION

"Reproduction" in anthropology refers to the processes by which new social members are produced—specifically, the physiological processes of conception, pregnancy, birth, and child-raising. In its larger sense, reproduction encompasses the processes by which societies are reproduced for the future. The term is thus fraught with biological, cultural, and political meanings; power is a central focus in reproductive studies, as those who have the power to influence the process of reproduction can control both individual and large populations for better or for worse.

The maturation of the field of the anthropology of reproduction was marked by the publication of *Conceiving the New World Order: The Global Politics of Reproduction* (1995), edited by Faye Ginsburg and Rayna Rapp. This collection expanded the meaning of reproduction into the political arena and generated the interface of reproductive studies with wider issues in the politics of women's health care. From a study of anti-abortion policies in Romania, to China's one-child policy, to the displacement of thousands of women in India and Pakistan to "purify the national bodies" of both countries, the chapters in this volume called attention to the impact of national and global processes on everyday reproductive experience, most especially through the notion of "stratified reproduction," which points to transnational reproductive inequalities based on gender, race, and class. In addition, Rapp's long-term fieldwork on amniocentesis illustrates racial, class, and religious differences in how women make choices about this technology, and demonstrates the linguistic power of genetic counselors to influence these choices in favor of the culturally approved choice of abortion for genetically defective babies.

Since the 1990s, most anthropological studies of reproduction have focused on what have come to be called "the new reproductive technologies" (NRTs)—technologies designed to intervene in human reproduction. From the birth of the world's first test-tube baby in 1978 to the cloning of a higher vertebrate from an adult cell in 1997, the rapid expansion of the NRTs in the latter half of the twentieth century dramatically redefined the parameters of biological reproduction. The NRTs include, among many others: birth control technologies such as intrauterine devices (IUDs) and the birth control pill; assisted conception technologies such as artificial insemination and in-vitro fertilization (IVF); screening technologies such as ultrasound, amniocentesis, and blood testing; reparative technologies such as fetal surgeries performed in utero; labor and birth technologies such as electronic fetal monitoring, synthetic hormones for labor induction and augmentation, and multiple types of anesthesia; and postnatal technologies such as infant surgeries and high-tech treatment of babies in neonatal intensive care units. All of these technologies are increasingly affected by developments in biotechnology, such as genetic engineering, which have major implications for the control and management of human fertility.

Like the obstetrical forceps developed by the Chamberlen brothers in the sixteenth century, the NRTs have double-edged implications for women and their offspring. While those early forceps did save the lives of babies who otherwise might have died, their overzealous and ill-informed application during childbirth by male midwives and obstetricians often left the mother and baby severely damaged. The NRTs have been equally problematic, often creating as many problems as they solve and causing as much damage as they repair. For example, maternal mortality as a result of ovarian hyperstimulation, and increased congenital abnormality because of multiple births, are but two examples of the downside of in-vitro fertilization (IVF).

Reproductive technology has affected every facet of the reproductive process, from preconception onward. To an extent, these developments respond to specific impediments to fertility: IVF, for example, was originally used to assist women with blocked ovarian tubes. Feminist critics, however, have rightly pointed to other, less woman-centered influences shaping the development of these technologies. For example, Robert Edwards, the research scientist who helped to develop IVF, was trained in embryology and foresaw tremendous research potential from the ability to manipulate the human embryo *ex vivo*. This potential was extensively exploited in the rapid expansion of human embryo experimentation in the 1980s and the 1990s.

The encounter between a largely male medical and scientific establishment and women's reproductive capacity is very pointed in the context of IVF, which is often represented as being a response to the "desperate" desires of infertile women but can as readily be interpreted as a response to the irresistible scientific urge to "unveil" and indeed to redesign "the facts of life." The tremendous value of early embryonic cells—both commercially and in terms of research—has made IVF an important source of human embryonic stem cells. This fact exists in uneasy tension with women's demands for improved reproductive services. As in other historical periods, the neglect of women's reproductive needs is most evident in terms of which kinds of services will be developed and prioritized.

While new embryo therapies are used to detect, and even to eliminate, genetic disease, other reproductive priorities remain devalued and underfunded. For example, while ever more sophisticated technologies are developed to deal with the complications of labor and birth, the normal physiological needs of laboring women remain understudied and unfulfilled. The scientific evidence that does exist supports simple technologies like eating and drinking during labor, woman-centered, supportive care, and upright positions for delivery as being of far more help to birthing women than high-tech machines. Nevertheless, the hegemonic global influence of what Davis-Floyd (2004) calls "the technocratic model of birth" has resulted in rapidly rising cesarean rates in many countries and has simultaneously precluded adoption of more humanistic and physiologic techniques for supporting normal birth. A growing body of anthropological literature reveals the systematic deconstruction of traditional birthing systems around the world. These systems are being replaced by biomedical care that disregards women's individual needs in favor of standardized approaches (DeVries et al. 2001), and that, in the developing world, often suffers from such drastic underfunding that basic supplies, clean facilities, and sufficient numbers of trained caregivers are regularly unavailable (Allen 2002; Davis-Floyd and Sargent 1997; Feldman-Savelsberg 1999; Hunt 1999; Luckere and Jolly 2002; Ram and Jolly 1998; Van Hollen 2003).

Two major influences continue to shape the development of reproductive technology in ways that are not in women's interests. One is the continuing, and indeed worsening, effects of global inequality that are borne most heavily by women and young children, especially infants. Adequate, or indeed any, access to basic contraceptive technology remains out of reach of the majority of the world's female population (despite concerns about population growth, and largely as a result of U.S. anti-abortion policy). Consequently, resource-intensive and largely private fertility care is provided to a predominantly wealthy world elite. Meanwhile, enduring tragedies of high maternal and infant mortality from preventable causes such as malnutrition and lack of a clean water supply, inadequate access to safe abortion and contraceptives, and limited, nonexistent, or ineffective reproductive health care are the main issues affecting the majority of the world's women. In sum, proper sanitation, adequate nutrition, improved vaccination programs, access to culturally appropriate forms of birth control, access to community midwives backed by adequate transport systems, and above all increased literacy and education rates among women remain the most important and lifesaving "reproductive technologies."

At the other end of the spectrum, at the cutting edge of twenty-first-century medical science, is the resurgence of a new genetic essentialism. Reproductive technology is shifting its focus in the direction of germline gene therapies (therapies that can be genetically transmitted because they modify reproductive cells). Annexed to the project of mapping the human genome, reproductive science and medicine are increasingly aimed at both the elimination of genetic pathology and the effort to reengineer the genomes of humans and other life-forms. In addition to

existing means of technologically assisting conception, the effort to alter human genealogy is the single most important influence on contemporary reproductive technologies. This effort is driven by enormously competitive economic forces and by an "if we can do it, we must do it" technocratic mentality, resulting in rapidly escalating and largely unregulated technological innovation.

While some commentators argue that reproductive technologies such as the freezing of eggs, cloning by nuclear transfer, germline gene therapy, and embryo biopsy will have a radical effect on gender roles and kinship definitions, the majority of evidence demonstrates a reverse effect: the restabilization of traditional and conservative family ideologies in the face of their potential disruption. At the same time, other influences, such as the lesbian and gay movement, the increase in transnational adoption, rising divorce rates, and greater economic independence for women, have proven more influential in the redefinition of family and parenthood. Consequently, although some uses of reproductive technology have created more parenting options, such as the use of artificial insemination by lesbians, the overwhelming pattern of access to NRTs is defined by the goal of enhancing conventional parenting arrangements by married, heterosexual, and middle-class couples.

Feminist concern about reproductive technologies in the twenty-first century will increasingly overlap with the criticisms of biotechnology and genetic engineering raised by environmentalists and the general public. Concern about genetically modified organisms in the food chain and in medical applications will increase, particularly as the human-animal border becomes ever more permeable. The extensive feminist literature on NRTs anticipates with great precision many of the profound social, ethical, and political concerns surrounding new forms of genetic and biological determinism arising out of the attempt to alter the human genome. In addition to the effort to redefine medical and scientific priorities in relation to women's reproductive health worldwide, feminist anthropological scholarship will continue to insist upon the primacy of fully informed reproductive decision making, in its widest sense, as a fundamental component of human rights.

SEE ALSO *Abortion; Abortion Rights; Anthropology; Birth Control; Childlessness; Demography; Fertility, Human; Genetic Testing; Limits of Growth; Malthusian Trap; Marriage; Multiple Births; Population Growth; Reproductive Rights; Sexual Orientation, Social and Economic Consequences; Women's Movement*

BIBLIOGRAPHY

Allen, Denise Roth. 2002. *Managing Motherhood, Managing Risk: Fertility and Danger in West Central Tanzania.* Ann Arbor: University of Michigan Press.

Davis-Floyd, Robbie. 2004. *Birth as an American Rite of Passage*, 2nd ed. Berkeley: University of California Press.

Davis-Floyd, Robbie, and Carolyn Sargent. 1997. *Childbirth and Authoritative Knowledge: Cross-Cultural Perspectives*. Berkeley: University of California Press.

Davis-Floyd, Robbie, and Joseph Dumit. 1998. *Cyborg Babies: From Techno-Sex to Techno-Tots*. New York: Routledge.

DeVries, Raymond, Edwin van Teijlingen, Sirpa Wrede, and Cecilia Benoit, eds. 2001. *Birth by Design: Pregnancy, Maternity Care and Midwifery in North America and Europe*. New York: Routledge.

Feldman-Savelsberg, Pamela. 1999. *Plundered Kitchens, Empty Wombs: Threatened Reproduction and Identity in the Cameroon Grassfields*. Ann Arbor: University of Michigan Press.

Franklin, Sarah, and Helene Ragoné. 1997. *Reproducing Reproduction: Kinship, Power, and Technological Innovation*. Philadelphia: University of Pennsylvania Press.

Ginsburg, Faye, and Rayna Rapp, eds. 1995. *Conceiving the New World Order: The Global Politics of Reproduction*. Berkeley: University of California Press.

Hunt, Nancy Rose. 1999. *A Colonial Lexicon of Birth Ritual, Medicalization, and Mobility in the Congo*. Durham, NC: Duke University Press.

Luckere, Vicki, and Margaret Jolly, eds. 2002. *Birthing in the Pacific: Beyond Tradition and Modernity*. Honolulu: University of Hawaii Press.

Ram, Kalpana, and Margaret Jolly. 1998. *Maternities and Modernities: Colonial and Postcolonial Experiences in Asia and the Pacific*. Cambridge, U.K., and New York: Cambridge University Press.

Taylor, Janelle, Linda Layne, and Danielle Wozniak, eds. 2004. *Consuming Motherhood*. New Brunswick, NJ: Rutgers University Press.

Van Hollen, Cecilia. 2003. *Birth on the Threshold: Childbirth and Modernity in South India*. Berkeley: University of California Press.

Robbie Davis-Floyd
Sarah Franklin

REPRODUCTIVE FITNESS

SEE *Eugenics; Sociobiology.*

REPRODUCTIVE POLITICS

Reproductive politics address fundamental values relating to highly personal topics, such as sexuality, marriage, bodily integrity, and the definition of life. Specific topics addressed are drawn from the steps in human reproduc-tion (sexual intercourse, conception, gestation, and parturition) as well as the major interventions in fertility control (abstinence, contraception, and induced abortion). Because only women become pregnant and bear children, reproductive politics necessarily reflect attitudes and social mores about the role of women. While reproductive politics in the United States became particularly fierce after the 1973 *Roe v. Wade* decision, the state's role in reproductive behavior has been debated for considerably longer.

At the beginning of the nineteenth century, reproductive matters were largely outside of American politics, but contraception and induced abortion were legal. Puritan disapproval of birth control as well as other social conventions kept these subjects out of the realm of politics. By the end of the century, both contraceptive practice and induced abortion had been outlawed in every state. Physicians led the way in passing state anti-abortion legislation, but opposed contraceptive restrictions. In 1873, Congress passed the *Act for the Suppression of Trade in and Circulation of, Obscene Literature and Articles of Immoral Use*. Known as the Comstock law, the act prohibited interstate trading in any article that prevented conception or caused abortion. Twenty-two states followed with even more contraceptive restrictions, called the "little Comstock laws."

Removing nineteenth-century prohibitions was a major part of reproductive politics during much of the twentieth century. The most influential birth control crusader was Margaret Sanger, founder of the American Birth Control League, which eventually became Planned Parenthood Federation of America. By 1937, the birth control movement had orchestrated and won the *U.S. v. One Package* case, which largely invalidated the federal Comstock law. It was 1965, however, before the U.S. Supreme Court overturned Connecticut's Comstock law prohibiting the use of birth control by even married couples (*Griswold v. Connecticut*) and 1972 before the Court invalidated the Massachusetts law specifically prohibiting unmarried persons from obtaining contraceptives (*Eisenstadt v. Baird*). In the 1973 *Roe v. Wade* decision, the Court legalized abortion.

Roe v. Wade ignited interest group activity in reproductive politics. There are many advocacy groups in this arena, including the NARAL Pro Choice America (pro-choice or favoring the legal status of abortion) and National Right to Life (pro-life or opposing the legal status of abortion). Their debates have expanded far beyond the legal status of abortion and now focus on policies toward welfare, scientific research, custody of offspring, international humanitarian assistance, and a variety of other subjects. These topics are best framed within steps in reproduction.

STEPS IN REPRODUCTION

Except for artificial insemination and in vitro fertilization, the first step in human reproduction is sexual intercourse. Within reproductive politics, who should be sexually active and with whom are active debates. Religious conservatives believe that heterosexual marriage is the only suitable context for sexual activity; their growing political involvement has spawned significant federal support for abstinence-only education and the ABC (Abstain, Be faithful, or use Condoms if you cannot follow A or B) policy in HIV/AIDS prevention. Opposing groups argue for accurate, comprehensive sex education that includes contraceptive information, pointing out that the effectiveness of abstinence-only education has not been demonstrated and that most people are sexually active years before marriage.

Conception is the second step in human reproduction. The politics regarding it include both contraception and fertilization. Here there are differing viewpoints concerning who should have access to birth control, what methods are appropriate, and how to pay for contraceptives. The provision of contraception to minors is hotly debated, particularly whether there should be mandated parental involvement (e.g., permission or notification). The politics around available methods includes the U.S. Food and Drug Administration (such as delays in the approval of over-the-counter emergency contraception) and product liability laws, which have limited contraceptive options in the United States. Political issues around fertilization include who should have access to assisted fertility technology (such as single women, married heterosexual couples, persons under a certain age) and how fertilized eggs can be used (for example, stem cell research and embryo adoption).

The third step in human reproduction is gestation and parturition. The dominant issue here is induced abortion or pregnancy termination. Abortion brings up a number of policy issues such as parental involvement, mandatory waiting periods, informed consent, funding, allowable procedures (such as partial birth abortion, which is a political term from the Christian Coalition, not a specific medical procedure) pharmaceutical abortifacients, and gestational limits. Many of these policies vary widely among the states.

Other political issues related to gestation include violence against pregnant women; the Mexico City policy, also known as the Global Gag Rule; surrogate maternity; and drug use and pregnancy. For example, the Unborn Victims of Violence Act, enacted in 2004, known as the "Laci and Conner Law," establishes the same penalty for killing a fetus in utero as for killing a pregnant woman. Both sides in the abortion debate have seen this legislation as a step toward criminalizing abortion. The Mexico City policy forbids foreign nongovernmental organizations that are recipients of American population assistance from referring their patients for abortions or from engaging in political activity to legalize abortion in their countries.

Advances in technology have brought many new questions, including who should pay for in vitro fertilization, who is able to benefit from this technology, whether children conceived with donated sperm or ova have the right to know their biological origins, and whether embryos can be created for research purposes. In human reproduction, science has raced far ahead of policy. All of these issues and many more will be decided within the rubric of reproductive politics.

Since *Roe v. Wade*, the coalitions in this policy arena have been fairly consistent, and they have become more partisan. Pro-choice groups tend to line up with other groups supporting access to contraception and comprehensive sex education. Pro-life groups tend to support abstinence-only education as well as legally mandated parental involvement in both contraceptive and abortion decisions. Several prominent scholars think that these divisions are based on beliefs about the role of women. Although there are individual exceptions, the Democratic Party generally reflects the pro-choice positions, and the Republican Party espouses the pro-life position. Advances in reproductive technology, however, sometimes alter these coalitions; the stem cell controversy within the Republican Party is an example of such a development.

REPRODUCTIVE POLICIES OUTSIDE THE UNITED STATES

Although American reproductive politics are particularly contentious, public debates about reproductive issues are certainly not confined to the United States. Issues that achieve prominence vary by region and culture. In western Europe, for example, adolescent sexual activity is generally a subject for public debate. Public health policies support widespread contraceptive availability. Consequently, western European abortion rates are a small fraction of those in the United States. Moreover, abortion politics are not as nearly as vociferous.

Low fertility is a concern in much of Europe and Japan. Public policies to increase childbearing have had mixed results. Generous French maternity leave and childcare policies, however, have apparently achieved their pronatalist objectives, and recently the Japanese birth rate has increased slightly.

In much of the world, reducing fertility rates is still on the public agenda. China retains its one-child policy, instituted in 1979, although the impact of that measure on fertility has been debated. Moreover, the one-child policy has skewed the ratio of males to females in that nation. As birth rates decrease in Latin America, politics in that region are focusing more upon maternal health measures such as legal access to emergency contraception and safe abortion.

As a continent, Africa has the highest fertility rates in the world as well as some of the highest maternal mortality ratios due to the unavailability of contraception, female genital mutilation, and unsafe abortion. Because of the low status of women in many African countries, these issues have not been salient until the mid-2000s. The HIV/AIDS epidemic has put reproductive politics on the public agenda in several African nations.

SEE ALSO Roe v. Wade; *Abortion; Birth Control; Fertility, Human; Infertility Drugs, Psychosocial Issues; Politics: Gay, Lesbian, Transgender, and Bisexual; Politics, Gender; Pro-Choice/Pro-Life*

BIBLIOGRAPHY

Hesketh, Therese, Li Lu, and Zhu Wei Xing. 2005. The Effect of China's One Child Family After 25 Years. *New England Journal of Medicine* 353 (11): 1171–1176.

Kulczycki, Andrzej. 1999. *The Abortion Debate in the World Arena.* New York: Routledge.

McFarlane, Deborah R. 2006. Reproductive Health Policies in President Bush's Second Term: Old Battles and New Fronts in the United States and Internationally. *Journal of Public Health Policy* 27 (4): 405–426.

Population Reference Bureau. 2004. *Transitions in World Population (Population Bulletin 59:1).* Washington, DC: Population Reference Bureau. http://www.prb.org/Template.cfm?Section=Population_Bulletin1&Template=/PopulationBulletin2.cfm.

Deborah R. McFarlane

REPRODUCTIVE RIGHTS

Reproductive rights is a term used to describe the rights of individuals as it relates to sexual reproduction, including the right to have or not have children; to have information about all aspects of sex, sexuality, and reproduction; to have the highest attainable level of reproductive health; and to be free from harassment, coercion, and violence with respect to sex and sexual expression. Reproductive rights encompasses concepts of both privacy (the right to decide on matters related to reproduction and sexuality without intervention by other individuals, institutions, or governments) and human rights, which are founded on principles of dignity and equality for all people. Because women are uniquely affected by matters relating to reproduction (including pregnancy, childbearing, and in most

societies, childrearing), many people view women's rights as inextricably tied to reproductive rights. As a result, women have historically led and been the focus of many of the struggles for reproductive rights around the world. These movements have included efforts to gain access to contraception; legalize abortion; reduce maternal mortality; give birth without unnecessary medical intervention; have sexual pleasure and health; and eliminate rape and sexual harassment, to name just some.

EXAMPLES OF DENIAL OF REPRODUCTIVE RIGHTS

There are many examples of the denial of reproductive rights in the United States and around the world. One example is the experience that many women have had with forced sterilization. In the United States, permanent sterilization of women who were deemed socially "unfit" to have children either because of their race, socio-economic status, intelligence or mental stability (or some combination of the above) became a common practice as early as 1907 in many states. The United States also carried out similar policies in Puerto Rico beginning as early as 1898 when it took over governance of that country. Thus, many women, particularly those who were poor, of color, uneducated, or mentally retarded were sterilized either without their consent or against their will. This form of abuse went on into the 1970s when a movement to end sterilization abuse eventually led to laws and regulations that ended this practice.

Other examples of reproductive rights abuses (both historic and current) include rape as a weapon of war; forced childbearing (as evidenced by laws restricting access to contraception and abortion); female genital circumcision; and a lack of control over childbirth practices (as evidenced by high rates of cesarean section or conversely lack of access to emergency obstetric care). Many other examples of reproductive rights abuse exist.

HISTORY OF REPRODUCTIVE RIGHTS MOVEMENTS

Although humans have attempted to control their reproductive destinies for many thousands of years, the notion of "reproductive rights" is a relatively recent phenomenon. The term was first articulated on a global level in 1984 at the International Meeting on Women and Health in Amsterdam. However, in individual societies and countries around the world, movements to gain rights related to reproduction had emerged prior to this time. Nonetheless, these movements were discrete and in many cases, such as with the struggles to legalize contraception and abortion in the United States, the focus was primarily on rights as they related to an individual's right to privacy. It was not until the meeting in Amsterdam that the emerging concept of human rights was applied to reproductive concerns, marking the beginning of what would become a global "reproductive rights" movement.

Following the 1984 meeting, the next significant international gathering in which reproductive rights became a major focus was at the World Conference on Human Rights, held in Vienna in 1993. At the Vienna meeting, participating countries agreed that any violation of the specific rights of women would be regarded as a human rights violation. Furthermore, an important shift in human rights theory took place at that meeting with the groundbreaking recognition that human rights exist in both private and public realms and as such, can be violated in either sphere. This shift brought the notions of privacy and human rights together, a critical joining of two previously separate ideas at an international level, which further spurred the global reproductive rights movement.

Since 1993 there have been a number of other significant international meetings that have built upon the foundations that were established in Amsterdam and Vienna to promote an international reproductive rights agenda and movement. In 1994 the United Nations International Conference on Population and Development (ICPD) in Cairo codified and furthered these ideas through its consensus document, the ICPD Programme of Action which states:

> Reproductive rights embrace certain human rights that are already recognized in national laws, international human rights documents and other consensus documents. The rights rest on the basic right of all couples and individuals to decide freely and responsibly the number, spacing and timing of their children and to have the information and means to do so, and the right to attain the highest standard of sexual and reproductive health. It also includes the right to make decisions concerning reproduction free of discrimination, coercion and violence, as expressed in human rights documents. (ICPD 1994, paragraph 7.3)

Similarly, the United Nations Fourth World Conference on Women held in Beijing in 1995 advanced a broad agenda that linked women's advancement and empowerment globally to human rights, and recognized reproductive rights as a critical element to achieving the goals it laid out as part of its future agenda.

Since those seminal meetings, there have been numerous follow up gatherings at international and regional levels where reproductive rights advocates from both government agencies and non-governmental organizations have come together to assess progress and further implementation efforts related to these goals, formidable challenges unto themselves. These efforts have been further complicated by the influences of a growing, world-

wide movement to restrict reproductive rights—in particular abortion, but also contraception and freedom of sexual expression. This movement is based in conservative beliefs and/or religious fundamentalism. The United States has been extremely influential in this regard, using its significant power to block the passage of consensus documents that aim to promote a broad reproductive rights agenda from these meetings and refusing to provide funding to reproductive health organizations in other countries that have any connection to abortion procedures. These actions have had a chilling effect on efforts to advance reproductive rights around the world.

At the same time that these anti-abortion and anti-sexuality movements have emerged in the United States and other parts of the world, reproductive rights advocates have also expressed concern about practices that lead to the selective termination of fetuses and coercive abortions. For example, in India the use of ultrasound or amniocentesis to determine the sex of a fetus has been a growing practice that has led to an increase in the rate of abortion of females. In China, the government mandated one-child policy has led to a high rate of abortion which may often not coincide with a woman's choice. Both of these examples represent reproductive rights violations from another angle.

In the early twenty-first century a dialogue emerged within reproductive rights movements in the United States (and elsewhere) about the need to expand to a broader concept of "reproductive justice" in order for women and girls to truly achieve "complete physical, mental, spiritual, political, economic, and social well-being" (ACRJ 2005, p. 1). Critical of the traditionally narrow focus on individual women's rights and the reliance on primarily legal or public policy strategies that many reproductive rights groups have relied on, those who advocate a reproductive justice framework emphasize the need to promote "a model grounded in organizing women and girls to change structural power inequalities" (ACRJ 2005, p. 2).

With the advent of new reproductive technologies (such as assisted reproductive technologies, cloning, and genetic screening), a growing global population, and widening health disparities in the United States and around the world, struggles for reproductive rights will undoubtedly continue to be a dynamic and compelling aspect of human society into the foreseeable future.

SEE ALSO *Abortion Rights; Human Rights; Pro-Choice/Pro-Life; Reproduction; Sterilization, Human; Women's Liberation; Women's Movement*

BIBLIOGRAPHY

Asian Communities for Reproductive Justice. 2005. *A New Vision for Advancing Our Movement for Reproductive Health,*

Reproductive Rights and Reproductive Justice.
http://www.reproductivejustice.org/reproductive.html.

Krase, Katherine. 2005. Sterilization Abuse. In *Our Bodies Ourselves.* New York: Touchstone.

Programme of Action of the International Conference on Population and Development, Cairo, Egypt, Sept. 5–13, 1994, U.N. Doc A/Conf.171/13/Rev. 1 (1994). http://www.unfpa.org/icpd/icpd_poa.htm.

Katherine Simmonds

REPUBLIC

The origin of the term *republic* lies in the Latin phrase *res publica,* or "public thing." The term implies the development of the public, distinct from the private, in both degree and manner. First, a republic must be developed socially and economically to a degree that sets it apart from a mere collection of private households. Second, a republic must be developed politically in a manner that distinguishes its rule from despotism, wherein the ruler regards all land and people as his or her private property. Over time, as noted in Paul Rahe's definitive work, *Republics Ancient and Modern,* republics have taken on different characteristics. Some have been authoritarian, using the power of the regime to establish a fixed way of life for all citizens, while others have been liberal, allowing citizens to pursue happiness as each individual defines it. Some republics have been highly democratic, others less so. Consequently, republics have featured different kinds of institutions, from presidential to parliamentary systems and constitutional monarchies. This diversity has developed largely in response to the changing relationship between public and private.

Early republics, such as the Greek *polis,* or "city-state," tended to be small and homogeneous. Aristotle argued that the *polis* came into existence for the sake of security, but once formed it assumed the higher purpose of providing a venue for self-perfection or virtue. In order to promote virtue, the classical republic assigned not only politics, but also religion, the arts, and the economy, to the public sphere. Politics were generally democratic, but they were also inegalitarian and illiberal. The regime expected citizens to conform to the public understanding of the best way of life, and it rewarded those who did with rule over those who did not. The nineteenth-century historian Fustel de Coulanges notes that public control of the economy was not intended to equalize wealth so much as it was used to make sure people found a vocation and engaged in production and exchange in a manner consistent with the moral vision of the regime. In sum, the ancient republics left little other than matters exclusive to the household to the private sphere. Yet the ancient republic is also the birthplace of philosophy—a pursuit that entails questioning public ideas. This was considered hostile to the regime, so ancient republics tended to protect themselves by exiling or, in the case of Socrates, executing those who questioned the city's beliefs.

Changing public ideas about the household, economy, and religion brought to light a new conception of the republic. The English philosopher John Locke argued that people had a natural right to appropriate the goods of the earth to satisfy their personal self-interest. This required an economy in which people took up a vocation and engaged in the production and exchange of goods based on personal appetites and desires. At the same time, the idea of religious toleration left decisions about faith to individuals, prompting the secularization of the modern republic. With greater emphasis on the household, there was less justification for the use of law to establish a common way of life. This did not, however, constitute an unqualified preference for the private, or any disregard for the public. Rather, the expanded private sphere was intended to serve a public purpose by mediating and channeling behavior driven by self-interest to raise the standard of living for all.

Thus, the modern republic is, by definition, liberal in character, existing not for virtue but for security. Consequently, modern republics feature institutional safeguards to prevent the abuse of power, particularly the separation of the legislative, executive, and judicial branches, as recommended by the French philosopher Montesquieu. Most scholars, including Thomas Pangle, credit Montesquieu and Locke with having a considerable influence on the founding of the United States. Others, however, such as J. G. A. Pocock, dispute the degree of this influence.

James Madison took a special interest in the development of republics, noting the problem of instability that had plagued both classical and modern regimes. In *Federalist No. 10,* Madison argued that instability was the result of factions, or organized groups motivated by a common goal adverse to the rights of others. Factions arose because republics permitted citizens to formulate individual opinions, gave them the freedom to associate, and offered groups the ability to influence policy to reflect their narrow interests. Madison's solution was the extensive commercial republic, which was a break with earlier thinkers who believed republics had to be small and homogeneous.

Madison used the idea of representation to distinguish the republic from a pure democracy. A representative government, he argued, could take in greater territory and population. People would put the land to use differently, and the different types and amounts of property would lead to diverse opinions. This would result in a multiplicity of factions, such that no single interest could dominate political decisions—a condition Robert Dahl famously termed *pluralism*. However, James W. Ceaser, among others, has disputed the fidelity of Dahl's logic to Madison's argument. Madison's strategy intended the political arena to be a public place where people of differing passions and interests would engage one another, allowing the experience to refine and enlarge their views. This would produce decisions that did not benefit some at the expense of others, but that were conducive to a common good. Ultimately, Madison's plan would have a centralizing effect on public opinion, but it would still offer freedom for those who desired to pursue more unconventional ideas.

Pressure from those exercising the right to explore the margins continues to redefine the center. This has made the modern republic the site of important rights movements, particularly the women's liberation movement and the civil rights movement. This has intensified as globalization has prompted yet another reconsideration of the place of the market, religion, and the household. Economically, some want the market to be more purely private, seeking to reduce regulatory controls on land use, production, and exchange. Others advocate greater public control over the marketplace in the name of safety, fairness, and increased public assistance to the poor. At the same time, some desire a greater separation between religion and the public sphere, while others would prefer to see an increased public role for religion, allowing church groups to replace government agencies in the provision of social services. Finally, there is a debate over the nature of the household itself. Many republics, for example, are considering public recognition of same-sex marriages. Some see these changes as the next logical step in the evolution of the republic. Others consider them a radical departure and a threat to the very existence of the republic. Thus, the persistent redefinition of the relationship between public and private, especially with regard to the economy, religion, and the household, continues to shape the nature of the republic.

SEE ALSO *City-State; Democracy; Federalism; Locke, John; Monarchy, Constitutional; Pluralism; Republicanism; State, The*

BIBLIOGRAPHY

Aristotle. 1986. *The Politics*. Trans. Carnes Lord. New York: Prometheus Books.

Ceaser, James W. 1986. In Defense of Republican Constitutionalism: A Reply to Dahl. In *The Moral Foundations of the American Republic*, 3rd ed., ed. Robert H. Horwitz et al., 253–281. Charlottesville: University Press of Virginia.

Dahl, Robert A. 1956. *A Preface to Democratic Theory*. Chicago: The University of Chicago Press.

Fustel de Coulanges, Numa Denis. 1864. *The Ancient City: A Study on the Religion, Laws, and Institutions of Greece and Rome*. Baltimore, MD: Johns Hopkins University Press, 1980.

Locke, John. 1689. *Two Treatises of Government*. Ed. Peter Laslett. Cambridge, U.K.: Cambridge University Press, 1988.

Madison, James. 1788. *The Federalist Papers*. Ed. Charles R. Kesler. New York: Signet Classics, 2003.

Montesquieu, Charles de Secondat, Baron de. 1748. *The Spirit of the Laws*. Trans. and ed. Anne Cohler, Basia Miller, and Harold Stone. Cambridge, U.K.: Cambridge University Press, 1989.

Pangle, Thomas L. 1988. *The Spirit of Modern Republicanism: The Moral Vision of the American Founders and the Philosophy of Locke*. Chicago: The University of Chicago Press.

Pocock, J. G. A. 1975. *The Machiavellian Moment: Florentine Political Thought and the Atlantic Republican Tradition*. Princeton, NJ: Princeton University Press.

Rahe, Paul A. 1992. *Republics Ancient and Modern: Classical Republicanism and the American Revolution*. Chapel Hill: University of North Carolina Press.

B. Jeffrey Reno

REPUBLICAN PARTY

The Republican Party is one of the two major parties in American politics and government. Like the Democratic Party, the Republican Party's organization reflects federalism and the separation of powers. Each state has a Republican state committee and most American cities, towns, and counties also have Republican committees. Usually, Republican voters choose members, officers, and chairs of these state and local committees. Through primaries and caucuses, they also choose delegates to represent them at Republican national conventions.

Republicans in the states and territories also choose members of the Republican National Committee (RNC). In addition to representing their states and territories in the RNC, RNC members also elect RNC officials, such as chairs and treasurers, choose the city that will host the next Republican national convention, and determine party rules and procedures, relating to such matters as the apportionment and selection of delegates from the states and territories and platform-making processes. At Republican national conventions, held during the summers of presidential election years, the major responsibilities of Republican delegates are to ratify or reject national platforms and to nominate presidential and vice presidential candidates.

Besides federalism, the separation of powers also divides and distributes the Republican Party's organization, authority, and functions. The National Republican Congressional Committee (NRCC) and the National Republican Senatorial Committee (NRSC) respectively serve the campaign needs of Republican candidates who run for election or reelection to the U.S. House of Representatives and Senate. Like the RNC, the NRCC and NRSC receive and distribute campaign funds and provide research, information, and literature on Republican policy positions, media and mailing services, and coordination among Republican candidates. The campaign finance role of the RNC, NRCC, and NRSC has diminished as Republican presidential and congressional candidates have become more dependent on individuals, state and local party committees, and interest groups, such as the National Rifle Association (NRA) and Christian Coalition, for campaign spending and the delivery of campaign services, such as advertising, direct mail, and voter mobilization.

The Republican Party was established in 1854. Most of its founders were disaffected Democrats and former Whigs. The Republican Party's major, initial policy position was its opposition to the extension of slavery into new states and territories. It adopted this policy position from the Free Soil Party, which it soon absorbed. Like the Whig and Federalist parties that preceded it in the two-party system, the Republican Party supported high, protective tariffs, a national bank, federal supremacy over the states, and a flexible interpretation of the federal government's powers in the Constitution. With the Democratic Party divided over the slavery issue, Abraham Lincoln was elected as the first Republican president in 1860.

During the period of closely contested presidential elections from 1876 until 1896, Thomas Nast, a political cartoonist, popularized the use of the elephant as the unofficial symbol of the Republican Party, which was also nicknamed the "Grand Old Party," or the GOP, because of the party's close association with the Grand Army of the Republic, an organization of Union army veterans of the Civil War. In 1896 the Democratic Party nominated William Jennings Bryan for president. Bryan was a Nebraska congressman affiliated with both the Democratic and Populist parties. His rousing campaign speeches zealously denounced the GOP's positions on high tariffs and the gold standard for enriching big business and impoverishing farmers and laborers.

Orchestrated by Marcus Hanna, an Ohio businessman, the Republican presidential campaign portrayed Bryan as a dangerous economic radical and rural demagogue with an anti-urban, anti-immigrant bias and contended that high tariffs and the gold standard promoted a broad, national prosperity. The Republican landslide in the 1896 national elections established a long-term Republican realignment of voters that enabled the GOP to usually control the presidency and Congress from 1896 until 1932. Growing intra-party conflicts between the Old Guard, i.e., the conservative wing, and the Progressives, i.e., the GOP's liberal wing, helped Woodrow Wilson, a Democrat, to win the 1912 and 1916 presidential elections.

The Great Depression that began in 1929 during the Republican presidency of Herbert Hoover discredited the Republican Party's reputation among many Americans for competent economic leadership and ended their association with national prosperity. Democratic president Franklin D. Roosevelt's attractive leadership style and the popularity of New Deal economic policies broadened and diversified the coalition of the Democratic Party, thereby transforming it into the new majority party among voters. In particular, African Americans, who recently were the most loyal Republican voters, became the most loyal Democratic voters during the 1930s because of Roosevelt and the New Deal, despite the continuing association of the Democratic Party with Southern whites and segregation.

The Democratic realignment of the 1930s helped the Democratic Party to dominate American politics and government until the election of Republican president Richard M. Nixon in 1968. During those years, Republicans disagreed about how to defeat Democrats in elections and what ideological and policy alternatives they should offer American voters. Moderate and liberal Republicans, such as President Dwight D. Eisenhower (1953–1961), accepted most of the New Deal's policy legacy and an internationalistic, bipartisan foreign policy in the cold war. These Republicans emphasized that the GOP could manage liberal Democratic policies with greater efficiency and fiscal responsibility and could achieve civil rights for African Americans more sincerely and effectively than the Democratic Party, with its powerful anti-civil rights Southern wing in Congress. Meanwhile, conservative Republicans, such as Senators Robert A. Taft of Ohio and Barry Goldwater of Arizona, criticized the moderate-liberal wing of the GOP for "me too-ism" and argued that the GOP would perform better in federal elections if it offered voters a distinctly conservative ideological and policy alternative to liberal Democratic policies and candidates. This conservatism included an emphasis on less domestic spending, greater protection of states' rights and property rights through opposition to new civil rights bills, and a more nationalistic, aggressive, and partisan American foreign policy in the Cold War. Nonetheless, except for the 1964 presidential election, moderate and liberal Republicans dominated the GOP's presidential nominations and major platform planks at Republican national conventions from 1940 until 1980.

Despite the Democratic realignment of the 1930s, a substantial minority of African Americans remained Republicans because they perceived the Republican Party, with its "Lincoln legacy," to be more sincere and effective on civil rights. To black Republicans, the noisy defection of some Southern Democrats to Strom Thurmond's "Dixiecrat" presidential candidacy in 1948, because of their opposition to Truman's doomed civil rights legislation, proved that the Democratic Party would also be sharply divided between its Northern and Southern wings on civil rights. In the 1964 presidential election, however, Barry Goldwater, one of the few Republican senators to vote against the Civil Rights Act of 1964, received most of the Southern white vote and only around 6 percent of the black vote. As the presence and influence of conservative Southern whites steadily increased within the Republican Party, fewer white Republican politicians supported liberal policies on race, such as affirmative action, court-ordered busing, and antipoverty programs.

During the 1970s, conservative Republicans, such as Ronald W. Reagan, often disagreed with the moderate policies of Republican presidents Richard M. Nixon and Gerald R. Ford, especially regarding détente with the Soviet Union and China. After nearly defeating Ford for the GOP's 1976 presidential nomination, Reagan was nominated and elected president in 1980. Reagan's policy goals prioritized the conservative agenda of major tax cuts, defense spending increases, reduced federal regulation of the economy, less domestic spending, a return of more domestic policy responsibilities to the states, and a more aggressive foreign policy. Aided by Republican control of the Senate from 1981 to 1987, Reagan increased the number of conservative federal judges, especially those with conservative judicial positions on abortion, crime control, school prayer, and other social issues. The conservative domination of the GOP by the end of Reagan's presidency (1981–1989) was also a consequence of the growing political influence of the religious right, especially in the South.

Although William J. Clinton, the Democratic presidential nominee, won the 1992 presidential election against Republican incumbent George H. W. Bush, the Republicans won control of both houses of Congress in 1994. For the first time since the Reconstruction Era (1865–1877), most members of Congress from the South were Republicans. When Republicans in Congress impeached Clinton and tried unsuccessfully to convict him during 1998 and 1999, polls indicated that many Americans perceived the Republican leadership of Congress, especially Speaker of the House Newt Gingrich, to be harsh, extreme, and unreasonable in its relationship with the president.

Realizing the need for the GOP to express a more inclusive and less divisive type of conservatism, George W. Bush, the Republican presidential nominee in 2000, promised an ideology and domestic policy agenda based on "compassionate conservatism" during his successful presidential campaign. Bush's "compassionate conservatism" included cultivation of minority voters, especially Latinos, and his proposal to use "faith-based initiatives" to provide some federally funded social services. Following the terrorist attacks of September 11, 2001, Bush's perspectives, actions, and objectives in foreign and defense policy were influenced by neoconservative positions. Neoconservatism advocates and justifies the use of American military force, including preemptive attacks and invasions, to protect the security of the United States and its allies, especially Israel, and to promote freedom and democracy in the Middle East. Neoconservatives are willing to engage in these actions, including "nation-building" efforts in American-occupied Afghanistan and Iraq, without the support and participation of most U.S. allies.

After Bush was reelected in 2004 with 44 percent of the Latino vote and a victory margin of over three million popular votes, Karl Rove, Bush's top political strategist, hoped that Bush's presidency would stimulate a Republican realignment of voters similar to that of 1896. As Bush's second term progressed, however, the president experienced low public approval ratings, and more Republicans in Congress openly disagreed with each other and Bush over the Iraq war, deficit spending, and immigration. The Democrats won control of Congress in the 2006 elections with net gains of twenty-nine House seats and six Senate seats. Polls and media analyses indicated that voters were reacting against lobbying scandals, the Iraq war, inadequate health care, and Republican control of both the presidency and Congress.

SEE ALSO *Bush, George H. W.; Bush, George W.; Left and Right; Multiparty Systems; Nixon, Richard M.; Political Parties; Reagan, Ronald; Republic*

BIBLIOGRAPHY

Phillips, Kevin P. 1969. *The Emerging Republican Majority.* New Rochelle, NY: Arlington House.

Rae, Nicol C. 1989. *The Decline and Fall of the Liberal Republicans: From 1952 to the Present.* New York: Oxford University Press.

Sean J. Savage

REPUBLICANISM

In rudimentary form, the origins of republicanism can be traced to Aristotle (384–322 BCE). However, this political form finds its first institutional embodiment in the republic of Rome (510–23 BCE), and its most comprehensive expression is in the writings of Marcus Tullius Cicero (106–43 BCE) and Titus Livius (59 BCE –17 CE). Both Cicero and Livius argued that Rome's failure resulted from internal corruption and conflict, which disrupted the checks and balances between the senate, the magistrates, and the people. The tradition was amended and revived during the Middle Ages and the Renaissance by Italian city-states and thinkers such as Niccolò Machiavelli (1469–1527) and Francesco Guicciardini (1483–1540). It underwent further developments in England and the United States in the seventeenth and eighteenth centuries, when individuals such as James Harrington (1611–1677), Thomas Jefferson (1743–1826), and James Madison (1751–1836) attempted to restrain or remove monarchical power.

Republicanism is a political doctrine principally concerned with freedom and its realization through self-governance. For republicans, the people are the source of sovereignty. Freedom thus consists in not being subject to another's will, and by having the power to raise claims for or against the laws under which one is governed. The primary danger to freedom, republicans argue, comes in the form of internal corruption and conflict that, if left unchecked, threaten to run roughshod over the common good. In its classical form, it emphasizes the importance of a mixed constitution that provides an institutional balance between the diverging interests of the many (the plebeian or democratic element), the few (the patrician or aristocratic dimension), and the one (the monarchical aspect) in society. The classical model is reflected in the Roman system, which included tribunes of the people, the aristocratic Senate, and consuls, usually two elected annually.

Classical republicanism, however, has undergone an important transformation in modern times, centering on the weight different thinkers attach to self-governance. Robert Dahl refers to this as a shift in emphasis from the older aristocratic republicanism to a radical view that places a greater emphasis on the democratic character of the constitution. The older aristocratic position is articulated by thinkers such as Aristotle and Guicciardini, while the second radical character is embodied in the works of Machiavelli, Paine, and Jefferson.

While both forms worry about the consolidation of power and the extent to which it will become a form of domination, they disagree over how this danger will be realized, and from what sectors of society. In the older view, the people have an institutional place in the constitutional structure, but because they lack the reflective capacity to curb their desires, the constitution needs to limit their power to selecting leaders that will govern on their behalf. Aristocratic republicans argue that these individuals are guided by an interest in the public good and have an ability to engage in impartial and careful reflection, making them uniquely situated to govern on the people's behalf and for their long-term interests.

In contrast, egalitarian republicans believe that modern societies no longer reflect these distinct social classes. The presence of a hereditary aristocracy, for example, becomes increasingly difficult to distinguish, especially in the earlier American context. Egalitarian republicans further argue that those trying to balance the aristocratic and democratic elements of society fail to see that the only legitimate good is the public good. The hallmark of modern radical republicanism, then, consists in dividing powers among separate institutions more carefully than reflected in the mixed constitution, with each serving as a check on the other. Modern examples include the British parliamentary system, and the United States Constitution, with its executive branch, bicameral legislative branch (the House and Senate), and judicial branch. The significant improvement to note is that these different branches of government do not reflect diverging but natural political cleavages in society vying for supremacy. Rather, they are constructed institutional appendages in which each element is but a part, with each designed to realize and protect the public good. As such, the public good is no longer a by-product of an institutional arrangement, as was often the case in the older view, but rather the end to which those institutions aim.

Another important transformation relates to political representation. Classical republics were unable to effectively incorporate growing populations into their institutional structure to ensure that the people remained sufficiently involved. In the case of Rome, for example, a population expansion did not result in a further development of sites for political participation. The problem of participation in large republics seemingly pointed to a limitation of the political doctrine—namely, that it was inappropriate in the modern expansive nation-states of the seventeenth and eighteenth centuries.

In modern times the answer comes in the form of representative democracy. As John Locke (1632–1704), Baron de Montesquieu (1689–1755), and Madison argue, a modern republic can connect the otherwise antidemocratic practice of representation with the sovereignty of the people. Indeed, as Madison explains in *Federalist No. 39*, the people never give up their power because they always hold in reserve the right to change their representatives. Representation is based upon a revocable trust precisely because it is merely a proxy for direct participation and not a replacement of popular sovereignty. The result allows power to extend over vast territories in response to various problems of collective organization.

SEE ALSO *Aristotle; Dahl, Robert Alan; Democracy; Freedom; Locke, John; Machiavelli, Niccolò; Pluralism; Republic; Separation of Powers*

BIBLIOGRAPHY

Dahl, Robert A. 1989. *Democracy and Its Critics.* New Haven, CT: Yale University Press.

Guicciardini, Francesco. 1520. *Dialogue on the Government of Florence.* Trans. Alison Brown. New York: Cambridge University Press, 1994.

Hamilton, Alexander, James Madison, and John Jay. 1788. *The Federalist.* Ed. Jacob E. Cooke. Middletown, CT: Wesleyan University Press, 1961.

Machiavelli, Niccolò. 1517. *Discourses on Livy.* Trans. Harvey C. Mansfield and Nathan Tarcov. Chicago: University of Chicago Press, 1996.

Pocock, J. G. A. 1975. *The Machiavellian Moment: Florentine Political Thought and the Atlantic Republican Tradition.* Princeton, NJ: Princeton University Press.

Wood, Gordon S. 1969. *The Creation of the American Republic: 1776–1787.* Chapel Hill: University of North Carolina Press.

Melvin L. Rogers

REPULSION

SEE *Similarity/Attraction Theory.*

RESEARCH, CROSS-SECTIONAL

A cross-sectional study is a type of research study widely used in economic, social, health, and marketing research. A cross-sectional study provides a snapshot of the distribution of factors and outcomes in a population at a specified period of time. In this type of study the prevalence of specific factors and outcomes can be calculated for a given population (community, state) and levels of exposure to factors and outcome status can be compared. In contrast to other study designs, cross-sectional studies sample individuals not based on their outcome status or the presence of a particular risk factor; rather, the presence of factors and outcomes are determined simultaneously.

Cross-sectional studies are very useful from the policy and public health point of view because, for example, they can provide a picture of the burden of a particular disease in a population and measure the prevalence of risk factors, such as smoking, in the population. However, this type of study is limited in its ability to give rise to inferences about causality. Cross-sectional studies are also very useful in monitoring conditions in a population, such as the surveillance of specific diseases (e.g., diabetes) or important risk factors (e.g., obesity), or in monitoring socioeconomic characteristics of the population (e.g., unemployment).

Cross-sectional studies offer several advantages over other types of research design. Compared to longitudinal cohort studies, which are studies that follow individuals with and without a specific risk factor over time to observe the occurrence of outcomes, cross-sectional studies are cheaper and can be carried out faster. Cross-sectional studies also allow for examining multiple factors and multiple outcomes in one single study. Generally, cohort studies can evaluate only one risk factor at a time, and case-control studies, a type of study that selects participants based on their outcome status, can evaluate only one outcome at a time. Another strength of cross-sectional studies is that when they are based on a representative sample of the population, their results can be generalized to the overall population from which the sample came. Analyses of surveys using representative samples require special analytic techniques to account for the sampling probability—the probability of being selected as a participant in the study—since this type of survey may oversample segments of the population (e.g., minority groups) to make sure they are adequately represented in the survey.

A major limitation of cross-sectional studies is called temporality bias. Since risk factors and outcomes are measured simultaneously, it is not possible to know whether the factor preceded the occurrence of the outcome, which is a criterion for determining causality. For example, in a cross-sectional study relating unemployment to heart disease, we cannot determine whether being unemployed contributed to the development of disease, or whether heart disease caused people to lose their jobs, perhaps by making them too sick to continue working. Another limitation that is particularly important in medical research is that in cross-sectional studies, diseases with longer duration are overrepresented because people who have the disease for a longer period are more likely to be included in the sample compared to people who quickly recovered or died from it. Thus, the association observed between risk factors and the disease may reflect survival rather than etiology. This limitation is often referred to as length bias or prevalent case bias.

Opinion polls are cross-sectional studies. They are commonly used in political research to determine voters' preferences for candidates in an election, people's perceptions of government policies, and the distribution of these preferences and perceptions by segments of the population such as gender, race/ethnicity, and age group. In market research, cross-sectional surveys are conducted to examine consumer preferences for certain products, shopping patterns, and the impact of advertisements. Social scientists use cross-sectional surveys to examine societal factors, such as the association of social capital, a measure of neighborhood cohesion, collective efficacy, and social trust with adolescent pregnancy and domestic violence. Such studies have found, for example, that neighborhoods with higher social capital have lower prevalence of teen pregnancy and family violence.

In the education field cross-sectional studies are used to examine factors associated with academic achievement. For example, Gwen Glew conducted a survey of elementary schools across the United Stated that reported a high prevalence of bullying and found that bully victims have low academic achievement and feel unsafe at school. Cross-sectional studies are widely used in medical research to identify risk factors associated with disease and explore associations among risk factors, as well as factors associated with health care. These studies have helped to identify the risk factors for heart disease (smoking, hypertension, cholesterol), determine the association of psychosocial factors (e.g., self-efficacy) and dietary behaviors or physical activity, and examine ethnic and gender inequalities in access to health care (e.g., access to cardiovascular procedures).

An example of the use of cross-sectional studies in surveillance is the National Health and Nutrition Examination Survey (NHANES). In this national survey a representative sample of the population living in the United States has a comprehensive examination and completes questionnaires about their lifestyle behaviors. Such a survey reports on access to health care, the prevalence of overweight and obesity, dietary patterns and physical activity levels across U.S. states, and other health-related factors. The NHANES is repeated periodically and allows researchers to compare trends in health behaviors and conditions over time. The Youth Risk Behavior Survey (YRBS) is another example of a national cross-sectional survey. The YRBS, a school-based survey of adolescents living in the United States, reports on the prevalence of lifestyle behaviors such as smoking, drug use, sexual behavior, fruit and vegetable intake, and physical activity levels.

SEE ALSO *Causality; Demography; Demography, Social; Polls, Opinion; Public Health; Public Policy; Research, Longitudinal; Risk; Social Science; Survey; Surveys, Sample*

BIBLIOGRAPHY

Glew, Gwen M., Ming-Yu Fan, Wayne Katon, Frederick P. Rivara, and Mary A. Kernic. 2005. Bullying, Psychosocial Adjustment, and Academic Performance in Elementary School. *Archives of Pediatrics and Adolescent Medicine* 159: 1026–1031.

Kelsey, Jennifer L., Alice S. Whittemore, Alfred S. Evans, and W. Douglas Thompson. 1996. *Methods in Observational Epidemiology.* 2nd ed. New York: Oxford University Press.

Rothman, Kenneth, and Sander Greenland. 1998. *Modern Epidemiology.* Philadelphia: Lippincott-Raven.

Way, Sandra, Brian K. Finch, and Deborah Cohen. 2006. Hispanic Concentration and the Conditional Influence of Collective Efficacy on Adolescent Childbearing. *Archives of Pediatrics & Adolescent Medicine* 160: 925–930.

Zolotor, Adam J., and Desmond K. Runyan. 2006. Social Capital, Family Violence, and Neglect. *Pediatrics* 117: 1124–1131.

Carmen R. Isasi

RESEARCH, DEMOCRACY

Research into democratization is as old as the democratic idea. Aristotle studied, with some prejudice, the democracy of Athens. Much later, James Madison tried to design a "republican remedy" for the "disease" of too much democratization. For most of western history, democracy was mistrusted by most of those most famous for having studied it.

Democracy as a positive ideal had a rebirth in the nineteenth century, eventually attaining hegemony after World War II as the political ideal appropriate for all nations (even Communist nations such as East Germany—the German Democratic Republic—claimed to be democratic). Research into democratization therefore is perceived by many today to be research into the best possible form of political society.

DEMOCRATIZATION RESEARCH TODAY

What, however, are we researching when we research democratization? Most western political scientists have defined *democracy* in ways that mirror the political and legal institutions and political culture of western liberal states, including ideas about citizenship, constitutions and rights, market economy, and separation of the public and private spheres. In this, political scientists have moved the ideal of popular rule in a decidedly liberal, republican, and market-oriented direction.

This predilection was reinforced by a mid-twentieth-century turn in the study of politics away from political science, broadly conceived, toward a social science presumed to be modeled on the natural sciences. Many students believed that "operationalizable" standards with which to measure democratic performance could only be "scientifically" derived from existing democracies—that is, from the west. Although this model is open to the charge of being culturally and ideologically biased, it contains important democratic features, and it is the one that has been most often used as the standard for democratization research.

In the 1960s modernization theory, premised on the developmental path of western industrial societies, took hold among western political scientists studying newly (re)emerging nations. Similarly, in the 1960s and 1970s some scholars sought to discover prerequisites for establishing stable democracies, mirroring modernization theory. As authoritarian regimes fell in the mid-1970s, democratization studies grew rapidly. By the 1980s, instead of developing a general theory of democratization, scholarship moved to trying to understand strategic interactions between elites, downplaying the importance of masses in democratic transitions, and to categorizing the forces at work in democratic transitions, the type of democratic political system being created, and the requirements for democratic consolidation. In the 1990s studies shifted to also trying to study democratic development over time. Scholars popularized the metaphor of three democratization "waves": the first from 1826 to 1926; a shorter post–World War II wave; and the famous "third wave," beginning around 1974. It is this third wave, encompassing developments in Latin America, Eastern Europe, and East Asia, that most democratization research explores.

Overall, the literature recognizes four stages in the transition to democracy: decay of authoritarianism, transition, consolidation, and maturation. Democratization is facilitated by a decline in legitimacy of authoritarian rule due to either an inability to solve problems or a shift in values. It is supported by the development of civil society, increasing education and income levels, external democratic pressures and/or support, the "snowball" effect of being within a democratizing region, and citizens valuing it as an intrinsic good rather than for economic or social performance. Many scholars now believe the reasons for democracy's emergence are not the same as those for its consolidation or maturation, and they see ebb and flow and sideways movement rather than linear progress.

In addition to regime type and patterns of transition and consolidation, scholars devote attention to the impact of democratization on regime performance; the need for a "mature state" for democratization; the importance of external actors, whether they be states or nongovernmental organizations (NGOs), in trying to promote internal democratization; and the effect of democratization on citizen well-being. Some who see strategic interaction among elites as decisive argue that third-wave democracies are fragile because democratic elites are forced to bargain with nondemocratic elites, and are further constrained by undemocratic constitutions that protect privilege. Some fear that fragile democracies can be overloaded with citizen demands, making the development of competitive economies problematic, thereby undermining the regime. Others think robust citizen participation is essential in democracy, and see international constraints on domestic democracy emanating from the "world market" and its key institutions.

Although analysts empirically find democratic features within "third-wave" regimes, such as free elections, other critical features of these regimes are found by some to be problematic, especially inadequate civil rights and concentration of power in the executive. They use a variety of terms to define these problematic regimes, such as "illiberal," "delegative," "imperfect," and "immature" democracies. Scholars have begun to rethink whether some of these "hybrid" regimes should be called democratic at all, and have coined terms such as "electoral," "competitive," or "contested authoritarianism" to indicate a notion of "enhanced authoritarianism" rather than "qualified democracy." Some "third-wave" scholarship indicates that democracy emerges through a complex process that varies from country to country with few preconditions or causing factors. Scholars often emphasize elite interaction as decisive in the foundation and consolidation of democracy, but some also still point to the importance of mass mobilization for both.

CRITICISM OF DEMOCRACY RESEARCH

Democratization research has been criticized in a number of ways that are relevant for future twenty-first-century researchers. Some criticism points to the need to further refine concepts and measurements, or to the need to be more selective in developing new concepts, or to how the "wave" metaphor can be misleading; others point to biases in the research itself and the inadequacy of past approaches to a more rapidly "globalizing" world.

An important line of criticism is that the overall emphasis on terminology is confusing and occludes the fact that although third-wave democracies may be less effective, the kind of problems they face—such as inequalities of rights, institutional power imbalances, and failures of accountability—were, and to a degree still are, faced by first-wave democracies. Favoring "minimalist" procedural definitions rather than robust ones that stipulate deeper notions of political equality and social justice, therefore, runs the risks of repressing the history of conflict and struggle in western democracy and of evaluating newer democracies by a sanitized and static metric.

Some caution researchers against trying to implicate other states or NGOs into the process of democratization, recalling the difficulty of efforts to "transplant" democracy, including through war, for example, in Vietnam and Iraq. Others temper this by suggesting that research into efforts to aid democratization can be successful if they are culturally sensitive and invoke a broader standard than western liberalism.

DEMOCRACY AND GLOBALIZATION

Internationalization of the world economy brings both economic development and new ideas, which can aid democratization. However, it can also promote greater inequality and/or foster constraints on the choices open to democratically elected officials, which generally impede it. Research shows that lessening inequality and insulating politics from inequalities do advance democratization and make de-democratization less likely. The sources of inequality, however, are shifting to include not just domestic, coercive control characteristic of industrial and agricultural production, but also transnational niches of elite control of finance, science, technology, information, and media, characteristic of postindustrialism and global neoliberalism. These international forces of economics, business, politics, culture, communication, migration, and ideas such as democracy bring religions, cultures, and subcultures into closer contact, possibly stirring popular movements of political action and resistance. The democratic idea may even take on unfamiliar forms. Although procedural definitions and certainly constitutional protections remain very important benchmarks in the study of democratization, in this context, how are we to judge what should count as critical democratic supplements to them?

Researchers should also ask: Have elected representatives within western liberal democracies ceded significant new power to unaccountable international markets, administrators, and elites, thereby diminishing the real impact of the voting power—the democracy—of their citizens? Does research therefore need to evaluate global as well as national, regional, religious, and cultural obstacles to democratization, obstacles applicable to all societies, including those in the west? If so, the freedom and ability of citizens to organize across borders and to engage in international political participation and agenda setting become important measures of democratization for all societies.

As economic and political integration, and resistance to it, proceed toward an uncertain future, as new groups emerge and define their rights, democratization research faces another powerful challenge. Just as democratic theory has needed to—and continues to need to—address the harms done to those left out in the consolidation of liberal institutions, systems of representation, and even concepts of normal citizenship, whether of race, gender, ethnicity, or economic standing, so too, does democratiza-

tion research need to open itself even more to the unfamiliar on all these registers. None of this obliges researchers to cede valuable standards—quite the contrary. It asks them to go back to the root and engage the primary but difficult question: In today's world, what advances popular rule and what stands against it?

SEE ALSO *Aristotle; Citizenship; Democracy; Democracy, Indices of; Democratization; Globalization, Social and Economic Aspects of; Politics; Sociology, Political; Strategic Behavior*

BIBLIOGRAPHY

Armony, Ariel C., and Hector E. Schamis. 2005. Babel in Democratization Studies. *Journal of Democracy* 16 (4): 113–128.

Bunce, Valerie. 2003. Rethinking Recent Democratization: Lessons from the Postcommunist Experience. *World Politics* 55 (2): 167–192.

Doorenspleet, Renske. 2000. Research Note: Reassessing the Three Waves of Democratization. *World Politics* 52 (April): 384–406.

McKinlay, Patrick F. 1998. Postmodernism and Democracy: Learning from Lyotard and Lefort. *The Journal of Politics* 60 (2): 481–502.

Muller, Edward N. 1995. Economic Determinants of Democracy. *American Sociological Review* 60 (December): 966–982.

Pateman, Carole. 1996. Democracy and Democratization. *International Political Science Review* 17 (1): 5–12.

Rose, Richard, and Doh Chull Shin. 2001. Democratization Backwards: The Problem of Third-Wave Democracies. *British Journal of Political Science* 31 (2): 331–354.

Shin, Doh Chull. 1994. Review: On the Third Wave of Democratization: A Synthesis and Evaluation of Recent Theory and Research. *World Politics* 47 (1): 135–170.

Tilly, Charles. 2003. Inequality, Democratization, and De-Democratization. *Sociological Theory* 21 (1): 37–43.

Tom De Luca

RESEARCH, ETHNOGRAPHIC

The discipline variously called *social anthropology, cultural anthropology, ethnology,* or *ethnography* seeks to describe the entire range of distinctive cultures in the world, past and present, and to arrive at a general understanding of human society through systematic comparison between them. This vast research undertaking uses a wide range of methods, both quantitative and qualitative, and is buttressed by related disciplines, principally archeology, human paleontology, biological anthropology, sociology, demography, history, and psychology. Although anthropologists, like other social scientists, commonly use and even collect censuses, surveys, written documents, and other sources of data, and analyze them with the help of statistical methods, their main claim to methodological distinctiveness is fieldwork.

Ethnographic fieldwork consists of spending extended periods of time, ideally a year or longer, in intensive observation of, and interaction with, a study population. Such observations and interactions are recorded in the form of daily field notes, transcriptions of texts, construction of genealogies, and household surveys, often with the help of such mechanical devices as tape recorders, cameras, and camcorders.

Much of that methodology is shared with students of the behavior of other animals, namely ethologists or animal behaviorists, with, however, two crucial distinctions. Anthropologists and their study animal belong to the same species, and they communicate through symbolic language. This means that ethnographic fieldwork requires additional skills besides keen observation and recording. Though anthropologists sometimes work through interpreters, or use a common second language (such as Spanish in Latin America or French in Africa), being fluent in the language of a study population is considered important if not crucial to good ethnography.

The heart of fieldwork consists of the twin methods of "depth interviewing" and "participant observation." Depth interviewing generally involves a small number of informants (five to twenty is a typical range), who are interviewed repeatedly and at length, preferably in their own language and over a period of months or even years. These informants are carefully chosen for their knowledge and understanding of their culture, and often become real partners in inquiry to the anthropologist. Participant observation consists of participation by ethnographers in the events they record and a general immersion in a culture, as opposed to simply observing and recording interaction from the outside. Ethnographers strive to be accepted, as much as possible, as one of those studied. In practice, however, total acceptance is rare, and total participation is not necessarily desirable. Ethnographers must be wary, for instance, of sexual involvement, of entanglement in local politics and factions, and of activities that may be illegal.

In the first half of the twentieth century, when it was first established, field ethnography was applied mostly to non-Western, non-literate societies, often colonial dependencies of the imperial countries to which anthropologists belonged. This led to the more recent criticism of anthropology as the handmaiden of colonialism, exemplified by Edward Said's *Orientalism* (1979), and various articles in collections edited by James Clifford and George

Marcus, and by Dell Hymes. If you studied whites, it was said, you called your work *sociology*; if blacks, *anthropology*. Partly in response to this criticism (and partly as a result of decolonization during the second half of the twentieth century), anthropologists increasingly applied their field methods to the entire range of human societies, including their own. We now have a thriving urban anthropology of Western societies, which was indeed prefigured by the "Chicago school" of sociology in the 1920s.

Related to the charge of colonialism leveled at anthropology is the question of who "owns" a culture, and who can legitimately interpret it and present it to the world. Some critics argue that only native members can and may do so. Clearly, there are advantages to belonging to the culture under study (familiarity, access, linguistic fluency, depth of understanding), and many ethnographic "informants" no doubt deserve more recognition as coauthors than some anthropologists are willing to grant them. However, the advantages of being an insider are counterbalanced by drawbacks (lack of objectivity and distance, taking too much for granted, being captive of one's position within the culture). Ideally, perhaps, fieldwork should be done by a team consisting of insiders and outsiders.

Participant observation also raises several problems, which potentially affect the validity and reliability of ethnography. The first is the effect of the observer on the observed. Animal behaviorists speak of "habituating" their subjects, that is, of accustoming them to their presence, to the point that they are ignored. This is easy enough if one studies, say, ants, but much less so with chimpanzees. Between humans, true habituation is simply impossible, except in highly impersonal urban situations, where fieldwork can be done surreptitiously. But, then, fieldwork without the informed consent of those observed is generally considered unethical by most anthropologists.

Informants almost invariably alter or manage their "presentation of self" to the anthropologist. Their account of themselves and their people is contaminated by their personal interests, their likes and dislikes, their attempt to manipulate the fieldworker, and their perception of what the anthropologist likes or wants to hear. Not uncommonly, key informants become quasi-anthropologists, and adopt the approach of the fieldworker. Some are not above telling tall tales and pulling the anthropologist's leg.

Another serious problem in participant observation is the inevitable tension between objectivity and subjectivity, between trying to be both an insider and an outsider. On the one hand, anthropologists seek a deep understanding of what an event, a ritual, a text, a conflict, a folktale means to their subjects. Ethnography involves telling the story from the native perspective, as an insider sees it. But it is not simply a matter of accepting at face value, then repeating, what informants have said. Understanding social reality involves analysis, and that, in turn, implies detachment, seeing things as an outsider. The anthropologist is, thus, constantly involved in alternating between immersion in, and detachment from, the studied "reality."

Few anthropologists are naive enough to claim Olympian detachment from "their people." Indeed, most claim warm affection for them. But quite a few clearly disliked them. For instance, the great pioneer of fieldwork, the Polish-British anthropologist Bronislaw Malinowski, referred to the Trobrianders he made famous as "niggers" in his intimate diary. Others, like Colin Turnbull, make no effort to hide their likes (of the Mbuti) and dislikes (of the Ik). It is considered good form to address the problem of objectivity in ethnographic fieldwork through an explicit statement of one's position and an account of one's field experiences. Often such matters are relegated to a methodological appendix, but sometimes their explication results in book-length autobiographies, such as those written by Claude Lévi-Strauss and Elenore Smith Bowen.

Finally, there is the issue of self-censorship. Many anthropologists refrain, for a variety of reasons, from telling all. They have a responsibility as scientists to share their findings, but they must also do their best to protect the anonymity of their hosts, to respect the secrets they pledged to keep, and to shield their hosts from condemnation, exploitation, or persecution by hostile outside forces.

In the 2000s, ethnographic research came under fire from academics of "postmodernist" persuasion, who have argued that objectivity is a delusion, that no human experience can truly be communicated, and that any attempt to do so is but one "discourse," usually self-serving, among many. Such a position is one of intellectual nihilism: It negates the possibility of any social science. Understanding across cultural, gender, age, and class divides—indeed, between two persons of any kind—becomes impossible if everyone is enclosed within the self.

Others draw a different conclusion about ethnography, namely that from it emerges a vision of a common humanity, transcending the wide range of cultural differences and the diversity of anthropological approaches. From this perspective, the ultimate mission of anthropology is to make human diversity communicable, and, by doing so, to reveal our unity as a species.

SEE ALSO *Anthropology; Ethnography; Ethnomethodology; Observation, Participant; Race and Anthropology*

BIBLIOGRAPHY

Bowen, Elenore Smith. 1954. *Return to Laughter*. New York: Harper.

Clifford, James, and George E. Marcus, eds. 1986. *Writing Culture: The Poetics and Politics of Ethnography*. Berkeley: University of California Press.

Grills, Scott, ed. 1998. *Doing Ethnographic Research: Fieldwork Settings*. Thousand Oaks, CA: Sage Publications.

Hume, Lynne, and Jane Mulcock, eds. 2004. *Anthropologists in the Field: Cases in Participant Observation*. New York: Columbia University Press.

Hymes, Dell H., ed. 1999. *Reinventing Anthropology*. Ann Arbor: University of Michigan Press. (With a new introduction; orig. pub. 1972.)

Lévi-Strauss, Claude. [1955] 1970. *Tristes Tropiques*. Trans. John Russell. New York: Atheneum.

Said, Edward W. 1979. *Orientalism*. New York: Vintage.

Pierre L. van den Berghe

RESEARCH, LONGITUDINAL

Longitudinal studies are investigations that study the same units (individual, households, communities, etc.) over time, with repeated waves of data gathering. They may be small-scale studies of a particular group, large-scale surveys of samples of national populations, or large-scale social experiments.

DISTINCTIONS FROM OTHER TYPES OF STUDIES

In contrast to longitudinal studies, cross-sectional studies collect data at one point in time; repeated cross-sectional studies collect data from comparable units at successive time points. This distinction, however, depends on the unit of inference. For example, in the 1970s the researchers Howard M. Bahr, Theodore Caplow, and Bruce A. Chadwick replicated the 1924 Middletown study in the form of a repeated cross-section, meaning they asked the same questions as in 1924 of a new random sample of the town's inhabitants. But inferences about the social structure and prevailing attitudes of the community were longitudinal.

Both panel studies and cohort studies trace units through time, with the distinction that a cohort study chooses units experiencing an event in the same time period (e.g., a birth or age cohort as in the National Longitudinal Survey of Youth [NLSY]), whereas a panel study uses a sample, random or otherwise, chosen without respect to a defining event (e.g., the Panel Study of Income Dynamics [PSID]).

Collecting data longitudinally confers several advantages. Such data are necessary for studying individual processes, such as of aging, of labor force transitions, of family formation and change. Longitudinal data are especially crucial when the research attempts to establish causality. Only with longitudinal data can the criterion of temporal priority be established unambiguously. In cross-sectional data one can sometimes infer temporality, but often one must trust memory, which is very unreliable. (This criticism applies equally to what are sometimes called longitudinal designs but which collect data retrospectively. The recall of attitudes and opinions is so influenced by the current state of those variables as to make recall an exercise in creative imagination.) In addition, if the research purpose is to study "flows" (e.g., the number of people who move into or out of unemployment during a month) rather than "stocks" (e.g., the number of people unemployed on a given date), then longitudinal data are absolutely required. The study of flows employs a turnover table, as illustrated by Bernard Levenson's 1978 article.

Although temporal priority can be established via a longitudinal study, without a true experiment involving randomization and manipulation of an independent variable, causality cannot be proved. Large-scale social experiments, however, such as the negative income tax experiments of the 1960s and 1970s, involve longitudinal data collection and hence partake of all the advantages and disadvantages of longitudinal studies.

SPECIAL ISSUES IN LONGITUDINAL STUDIES

When investigators analyze data from longitudinal studies in the aggregate, they seek to separate age effects (caused, for example, by physical aging or moving to different age-related roles) from period effects (caused, for example, by changing social environments) and from cohort effects (caused, for example, by different social environments at critical stages in individuals' development). Work by Erdman Palmore, as presented in his 1978 article, points out that longitudinal differences (between measurements of the same cohort taken at two time periods) are the sum of age and period effects; cross-sectional differences (between measurements of different cohorts taken at the same time period) are the sum of age and cohort effects; and time lag differences (between measurements of an older cohort taken at time one and those on a younger cohort taken at time two, when they have achieved the same age the older cohort was at time one) are the difference between period and cohort effects. Disentangling these effects requires careful thought and analysis, especially if only a single cohort is being followed over time.

Because measurements on the same unit at different time points are correlated, longitudinal data rely on special statistical techniques that take such correlation into account. Analogous to analysis of variance models appropriate for repeated measures designs, these techniques employ certain forms of generalized linear models.

Dorothy D. Dunlop's work from 1994 and that of James H. Ware from 1985 are explications of these statistical techniques.

The problem of attrition haunts longitudinal data collection. Researchers lose the opportunity to conduct follow-up when people move out of the study area, refuse to continue, or die. Investigators do their utmost to prevent attrition; for example, the PSID sends postcards to its respondents yearly to determine their whereabouts. Attrition degrades data from a longitudinal study to the extent that data from those not participating in later rounds differ from the data of those participating. Imputation of missing data is, in theory at least, easier for a longitudinal study than for a cross-sectional one, as data from earlier rounds of the study can aid in the effort; Roderick Little's 1988 work offers examples of such techniques.

To avoid missing data, some longitudinal studies (e.g., NLSY) use a life-history method, asking respondents to report not only their current status on such variables as employment and marital status, but also to report and date any changes in these statuses since the previous interview. Thus if a respondent misses one or more interviews, longitudinal data for that respondent are nevertheless available from these retrospective reports, although possibly at some cost in accuracy if respondents' memories are faulty.

When a longitudinal study is concerned with units other than individuals, additional complications arise. For example, PSID, which studies income dynamics for families, sampled approximately 4,800 families in 1968. Because PSID follows all members of these original families as they leave (children marrying, original couples divorcing, etc.), by 1996 the study encompassed about 8,500 families. To keep the sample representative of the general population, about 440 immigrant families were added in 1996 and almost 1,500 families had to be dropped.

When data are collected repeatedly from the same unit, those data present an increasingly detailed and thus increasingly identifiable picture of the study subjects. Thus issues of confidentiality and data security become increasingly important and increasingly difficult.

In addition to studies designed longitudinally to study change, several large-scale government surveys (e.g., the Current Population Survey [CPS] and the National Crime Victimization Survey [NCVS]) use rotating panel designs in which a unit participates in the survey for several reference periods. This design makes contacting respondents easier than if a new sample were drawn for every wave and increases the efficiency of statistical estimation. It is difficult for the government agencies collecting these data to link respondents across waves in order to study them longitudinally; nevertheless, such linked files have been produced and used fruitfully in both methodological and substantive research.

BIBLIOGRAPHY

Bahr, Howard M., Theodore Caplow, and Bruce A. Chadwick. 1983. Middletown III: Problems of Replication, Longitudinal Measurement, and Triangulation. *Annual Review of Sociology* 9: 243–264.

Dunlop, Dorothy D. 1994. Regression for Longitudinal Data: A Bridge from Least Squares Regression. *American Statistician* 48 (4): 299–303.

Fienberg, Stephen E., and Judith M. Tanur. 1986. The Design and Analysis of Longitudinal Surveys: Controversies and Issues of Cost and Continuity. In *Survey Research Designs: Towards a Better Understanding of Their Costs and Benefits*, eds. Robert W. Pearson and Robert F. Boruch, 60–93. New York: Springer-Verlag.

Levenson, Bernard. 1978. Panel Studies. In *International Encyclopedia of Statistics*, eds. William H. Kruskal and Judith M. Tanur, 683–691. New York: Macmillan and Free Press.

Little, Roderick J. A. 1988. Missing-Data Adjustments in Large Surveys. *Journal of Business and Economic Statistics* 6 (3): 287–296.

Lynd, Robert S., and Helen Merrell Lynd. 1929. *Middletown: A Study in Contemporary American Culture*. New York: Harcourt, Brace.

Palmore, Erdman. 1978. When Can Age, Period, and Cohort Be Separated? *Social Forces* 57 (1): 282–295.

Ware, James H. 1985. Linear Models for the Analysis of Longitudinal Studies. *American Statistician* 39 (2): 95–101.

Judith M. Tanur

RESEARCH, QUALITATIVE

SEE *Methods, Qualitative.*

RESEARCH, QUANTITATIVE

SEE *Methods, Quantitative.*

RESEARCH, SURVEY

Survey research is a methodological process by which social scientists convert theoretical concepts into numbers. The quantification of theoretical concepts via the survey instrument allows for the modeling of relationships between variables such as education and socioeconomic status. Surveys are used by researchers across all of the social sciences as one of the primary means of data collection. For example, in order to measure a theoretical concept such as religiosity, the social scientist can use an indicator or set of indicators of religiosity, and the aggregate responses can then be coded numerically. A common example of such an indicator is the question "How important is religion in your life?" The subjects being surveyed would typically select one of the following responses: "Very Important," "Pretty Important," or "Not Too Important." The three response categories are then coded as follows: 1= "Very Important," 2= "Pretty Important," and 3= "Not Too Important." In this way, social scientists are able to quantify theoretical concepts.

EPISTEMOLOGICAL FOUNDATIONS

The philosophical underpinnings of survey research rest squarely on the side of positivism, as opposed to interpretivism. Positivist social scientists seek to emulate the level of quantification that is characteristic of the natural sciences, particularly physics. The aim of survey research, from a purely positivist viewpoint, is to discover the universal laws operating in society. It is thought that such laws are best uncovered through a deductive, scientific method, whereby data is collected through a survey instrument in order to test a theory. Interpretive theorists, with a more qualitative focus on issues such as meaning and historicity, are critical of positivist assumptions and tend to prefer a more inductive, theory-building approach to data collection.

QUESTIONNAIRE CONSTRUCTION

The successful execution of survey research depends in great measure on the proper construction of the questionnaire. Good questionnaires provide measures of theoretical concepts, also referred to as variables, that are concomitantly reliable (i.e., able to be reproduced) and valid (i.e., accurate). The questionnaire should be clear and concise in presentation and wording. The researcher can choose between single items or multiple items in order to measure a variable. For example, another question that measures religiosity might be: "How often do you attend religious services?" Possible response categories could include: 1= "Often," 2= "Not Too Often," and 3= "Never." This is an example of a closed-ended question, in which response categories are predetermined by the researcher. Such categories should be exhaustive (i.e., they should cover all possible responses) and mutually exclusive (i.e., there should be no overlap among the responses).

One of the most common sets of response categories is the Likert scale, which measures how strongly a person agrees or disagrees with a statement. One way to measure happiness, for example, is with a four-point Likert scale in which the response categories range from "Strongly Agree" to "Strongly Disagree." Consider the following indicator of happiness: "On the whole, I am happy with my life." A standard Likert scale would code the responses as: 1= "Strongly Agree," 2= "Agree," 3= "Disagree," and 4= "Strongly Disagree."

When multiple items are used to measure a single concept like happiness, it is sometimes useful to invert some items, such as: "On the whole, I am unhappy with my life." The inversion of items can disrupt potential patterns in which the respondent "Strongly Agrees" or "Agrees" with all of the items.

In addition to closed-ended questions, which tend to be comparatively high on reliability, survey instruments can also be constructed with open-ended questions, which tend to be comparatively high on validity. Open-ended items probe the respondent's knowledge on a given issue, but they do not offer a predetermined set of response categories. For example, a social scientist interested in studying the nature and determinants of trust might include the following item in a questionnaire: "What are the most important factors in your decision to extend trust?" The obvious advantage of such open-ended items is that the researcher does not need to be concerned with the development of exhaustive and mutually exclusive response categories. The major disadvantage is that open-ended responses, as a result of their variability, are difficult to code, leading to reduced reliability.

ADMINISTRATION AND INTERVIEWING

The three most common methods of administering questionnaires are by mail, by telephone, and in face-to-face interviews. Since the 1990s, there has also been an interest in the use of the Internet to administer electronic surveys. The principal advantage of administration via post and the Internet is the comparatively low cost of the research vis-à-vis telephone and personal interviews. The disadvantages of survey research conducted via post and the Internet are the comparatively lower response rates and the overall length of the research process.

Telephone interviews have the obvious advantage of being cheaper to conduct than face-to-face interviews. In terms of the length of the research process, a second clear advantage is that questionnaires can be administered and data collected more quickly than with face-to-face interviews. The third advantage of telephone interviews is that a random sample can be readily selected using random digit dialing (RDD), whereby a computer generates random telephone numbers. However, the fact that not every household has a telephone can bias the sample. Furthermore, telephone interviews are generally not suitable for long questionnaires.

The consensus is that face-to-face interviews yield the highest quality data. In general, there are three main advantages of face-to-face interviews. First, the instrument can be longer than if it were administered by telephone, post, or the Internet. Second, interviewers can use visual aids to assist respondents. Third, it is easier for interviewers to clarify questions and items that are unclear, although it is possible that clarification on the part of the interviewer can bias the results. The main disadvantage of personal interviews is the high cost involved in the research.

STRENGTHS AND WEAKNESSES

In short, survey research has several strengths vis-à-vis the more qualitative methodological approaches. First, the results of survey research are, on balance, more generalizable than the results of qualitative research. In other words, because of the greater number of respondents, survey research typically yields findings that are more representative of the population being studied. Second, survey instruments yield more reliable results than qualitative interviews. Third, questionnaires are useful in terms of both testing theories and establishing correlations between variables.

There are four main weaknesses of survey research. First, it can be potentially very expensive to conduct. Second, it is rigid and inflexible, especially in the absence of open-ended items. Third, it is open to the criticism of having a top-down bias; that is, it seldom allows for theory construction from the bottom-up. Fourth, although it is strong in terms of establishing statistical correlations, it is weak in terms of proving causality between two variables. In spite of these weaknesses, survey research is one of the most widely used methodological approaches.

SEE ALSO *Methods, Research; Surveys, Sample*

BIBLIOGRAPHY

Babbie, Earl. 1999. *The Basics of Social Research*. Belmont, CA: Wadsworth Publishing.

Dillman, Don A. 2000. *Mail and Internet Surveys: The Tailored Design Method*. 2nd ed. New York: Wiley.

Judd, Charles M., Eliot R. Smith, and Louise H. Kidder. 1991. *Research Methods in Social Relations*. 6th ed. Fort Worth, TX: Holt, Rinehart, and Winston.

Andrew R. Timming

RESEARCH, TRANS-DISCIPLINARY

The complexity of defining trans-disciplinary research lies in its roots. While maintaining its own niche in research disciplines, trans-disciplinary research owes much of its identity to the related structures of inquiry of multidisciplinary and interdisciplinary research.

The Transdisciplinary Prevention Research Centers defines trans-disciplinary research as "A cooperative effort by a team of investigators from diverse disciplines including meaningful representation of basic sciences as well as clinical or applied sciences. Normally, a trans-disciplinary team of investigators will include persons from different departments but the key issue is that the team will include members who bring markedly diverse methods and concepts to bear on the scientific theme" (Transdisciplinary Prevention Research Centers Request for Application, 2002).

To better understand trans-disciplinary research, one needs to distinguish its approach from other models. Multi-disciplinary and inter-disciplinary research are the two models that trans-disciplinary research broadens.

In his 2004 article "Transdisciplinarity and Its Challenges: The Case of Urban Studies" Thierry Ramadier distinguished the models this way: "Interdisciplinarity differs from multidisciplinarity in that it constructs a common model for the disciplines involved, based on a process of dialogue between disciplines" (Ramadier 2004, p. 433). In other words an inter-discipline is often a discipline of its own. Examples of this synthesis of disciplines are numerous and include such fields as biochemistry, social psychology, and biological anthropology. However a second important aspect of inter-disciplinary research lies in the practice of transferring models or tools from one discipline to another. For example, scholars might apply the mathematics of topography to the study of group dynamics. In this case, according to Ramadier, the concepts of one discipline are appropriated by the other disciplines. Ramadier maintained that interdisciplinarity, like multidisciplinarity, avoids paradoxes and having to solve them, resulting in fragmented approaches in each model.

He further argued that transdisciplinarity breaks away with this type of thinking in a significant way, since the objective is to preserve the different realities and to confront paradoxes between them. Transdisciplinarity is based on a controlled conflict generated by these paradoxes, and the goal is the search for more advanced articulation rather than consensus among the disciplines involved. Ultimately, through simultaneously combining multidisciplinary and interdisciplinary, transdisciplinarity transcends and incorporates these forms of thought. Ramadier argued that transdisciplinarity emerges from the confluence of the three scientific approaches of disciplinarity, multidisciplinarity, and interdisciplinarity.

In his 2004 article Roderick J. Lawrence describes multi-disciplinary research as:

Research in which each specialist remains within her/his discipline and contributes using disciplinary concepts and methods. Multidisciplinary contributions can be interpreted as the bringing together of disciplines which retain their own concepts and methods that are applied to a mutually agreed subject. In these studies one contributor will usually co-ordinate the research process and seek integration. Interdisciplinarity can be considered as the mixing together of disciplines, whereas transdisciplinarity implies a fusion of disciplinary knowledge with the know-how of lay-people that creates a new hybrid which is different from any specific constituent part. (Lawrence 2004, p. 488)

It is this "fusion" that distinguishes trans-disciplinary research from other research models. As with other models, team building is essential to success. Trans-disciplinary research, however, requires that traditional boundaries and responsibilities be set aside so that team members can fully embrace new skills and knowledge. It requires that team members be willing to step away from the prejudices of their individual disciplines and open themselves up to the perspectives of others, including laypeople, and embrace the learning that takes place when distinct ideas are threaded together. In their 1981 article Frederick Rossini and Alan Porter liken the trans-disciplinary process to a "seamless woven garment" in contrast to the "patch-work quilt" of multi-disciplinary research.

It is this holistic approach that proponents of trans-disciplinary research find so rewarding. A trans-disciplinary research model accepts that complex problems are best understood by acknowledging, from the outset, that effective solutions are more than the sum of critical perspectives from a range of disciplines. It embraces a more modern approach that calls for true collaboration, a dynamic collaboration that crosses turf boundaries and insists that team members be responsible not only for their own success, but for the success of the team as a whole.

Trans-disciplinary research has found proponents in a wide range of research environments. The trans-disciplinary approach has been used successfully in areas as diverse as disability prevention, infectious diseases, drug misuse, and physical therapy. By examining these and other complex problems from a unique vantage point, trans-disciplinary research programs may offer a new perspective on solutions to serious problems, both old and new.

While it owes its origins to interdisciplinary and multidisciplinary research, the trans-disciplinary model has established itself as a distinct and modern research method. Basarab Nicolescu clarifies both the approach and goals of transdisciplinarity: "As the prefix 'trans' indicates, transdisciplinarity concerns that which is at once between the disciplines, across the different disciplines, and beyond all discipline. Its goal is the understanding of the present world, of which one of the imperatives is the unity of knowledge" (Nicolescu 2002, p. 44).

SEE ALSO *Methodology; Social Science; University, The*

BIBLIOGRAPHY

Lawrence, Roderick J. 2004. Housing and Health: From Interdisciplinary Principles to Trans-disciplinary Research and Practice. *Futures* 36 (16): 487–500.

Nicolescu, Basarab. 2002. *Manifesto of Transdisciplinarity*. Trans. Karen-Claire Voss. Albany: State University of New York Press.

Ramadier, Thierry. 2004. Transdisciplinarity and its Challenges: The Case of Urban Studies. *Futures* 36: 423–439.

Rossini, Frederick A., and Alan L. Porter. 1981. Interdisciplinary Research: Performance and Policy Issues. *Journal of the Society of Research Administrators* 13 (2): 8–25.

Transdisciplinary Prevention Research Centers Request for Application. 2002. National Institute of Heath, Office of Intramural Research. http://grants.nih.gov/grants/guide/rfa-files/RFA-DA-03-008.html.

Susan G. Alexander

RESEARCH AND DEVELOPMENT

Research and development (R&D) is the term commonly used to describe the activities undertaken by firms and other entities such as individual entrepreneurs to create new or improved products and processes. The broadest meaning of the term covers activities from basic scientific research performed in universities and laboratories all the way to testing and refining products before commercial sale or use. The performance of, the incentives for, and the contributions of R&D are topics that are widely studied in management, economics, and other social science disciplines. Total spending on R&D activities is also one of the most widely used indicators of the innovative performance of firms, industries, and countries.

Informal R&D has existed at least since the first person experimented with methods of knapping flint to make Stone Age tools. In a formalized sense, it became part of the arsenal of the modern corporation beginning with the creation of industrial labs in the late nineteenth century, and in the early twenty-first century it comprises about 2 to 3 percent of the gross domestic product (GDP) in advanced economies. (For a history of the rise of organized R&D in the United States, see Mowery and Rosenberg 1989.) Spending on and outcomes of R&D investments have become important enough to be the subject of a satellite account in the U.S. System of National Income Accounts that was introduced in 2006 and 2007 (U.S. Department of Commerce 2006) and to be considered for inclusion in the international standard

for systems of national income accounts (United Nations Statistics Division 2006).

The *Frascati Manual* of the Organisation for Economic Co-operation and Development (OECD), first published in 1963, created an international standard for surveys of spending on R&D. This manual defines R&D as "creative work undertaken on a systematic basis in order to increase the stock of knowledge, including knowledge of man, culture, and society, and the use of this stock of knowledge to devise new applications" (Organisation for Economic Co-operation and Development 2002, p. 30). R&D is generally thought to consist of three main activities: basic research, applied research, and development. Basic research is research undertaken primarily to acquire new knowledge without a view to its application. Applied research is research directed toward a specific objective, and development is work drawing on existing research results and is directed specifically toward the creation of new and improved products and processes. In general more than two-thirds of R&D spending by firms or countries is directed toward development rather than research. The 2003 *OECD Science, Technology, and Industry Scoreboard* reports that in developed countries with high R&D intensities, basic research is less than one-fifth of total R&D spending.

ECONOMIC ANALYSIS OF R&D

In the theoretical economics literature, the term *R&D* is commonly used to describe the conscious choice of firms and individuals to invest in the invention and commercialization of new products and processes. Although the activity described is seldom made precise in these models, in practice this kind of investment is assumed to correspond roughly to the spending on R&D that is reported in firm accounts and to various governmental surveys. Important insights into the motives underlying investments in R&D were first developed in seminal papers by Richard Nelson in 1959 and Kenneth Arrow in 1962. These two authors clearly argued the economic policy case for subsidies to R&D investment that arise from the nature of its output.

Briefly stated, the argument is that because most inventions (processes and products) can be imitated once they are made and at a cost lower than the original cost of making them, the incentives for undertaking R&D directed toward the creation of such inventions are inevitably weaker than society would like. The performance of R&D therefore generates positive externalities, or "spillovers," that benefit others. Nelson distinguished between basic research with wide applications (which is most likely to be insufficiently provided) and development expenditures targeted to particular products or processes (which are more easily protected by patenting and other means). Arrow made the case for underinvestment in R&D more broadly by setting it in the context of the then newly invented Arrow-Debreu general equilibrium model. He argued that the allocation of resources for invention (that is, R&D spending) was likely to be nonoptimal because the production of information about new products and processes failed all three of the assumptions required for perfect competition to achieve a Pareto optimum: that the good (information) be infinitely divisible, that it be tradable on the market (that is, that its returns are fully appropriable by the owner), and that there be no associated uncertainty.

All three of these characteristics (indivisibility, inappropriability, and uncertainty) have proved to be important in the case of R&D. Indivisibility implies returns to scale because information about new products and processes can be spread over many units at increasingly lower cost per unit, leading to monopolistic competition in R&D-intensive industries. As Arrow and subsequent economic theorists have shown (see, for example, Reinganum 1989), this can lead to either over- or underinvestment in R&D from a social perspective. In contrast, lack of full appropriability suggests that there will be underinvestment in R&D. In a 1992 article, Zvi Griliches surveyed the evidence on the existence of R&D spillovers, and based on the evidence on measured private and social returns to R&D from a wide number of empirical studies, he concluded that overall R&D spillovers were both "prevalent and important." This result suggests that underinvestment dominates overinvestment, at least in the majority of sectors.

Finally, uncertainty about the nature of the information to be produced by R&D makes it a risky undertaking and sometimes implies that there will be an asymmetric information problem between its producers and those who might finance its production, again leading to potential underinvestment. Empirical evidence for the existence of difficulties in financing R&D investment is surveyed by Bronwyn H. Hall (2002).

R&D AS INVESTMENT

The term *R&D* is often followed by *investment*, which hints at one of its most important attributes. Research and development continues to benefit both those who undertake it and society at large into the uncertain future. Another attribute of R&D that has been emphasized in the modern economic growth literature is its cumulative nature, which can lead to increasing returns, both in the aggregate and also for individuals and firms. The idea is that the stock of knowledge created by doing R&D makes one more productive in acquiring additional knowledge. At the economy-wide level, this idea is the basis of the modern endogenous growth literature that is discussed in

Philippe Aghion and Peter Howitt's *Endogenous Growth Theory* (1998).

These attributes create some interesting problems for measurement and analysis. In general applied researchers have dealt with the intertemporal nature of R&D investment by treating it in the same way as ordinary investment in tangible assets, adding up expenditures to create an R&D stock and using a suitable depreciation rate to capture the fact that older research may become less useful over time. However, the aforementioned spillover effects make this exercise somewhat more speculative than in the case of ordinary assets, because R&D that has ceased to be useful for the production of private profit may still be useful to others in the production of new knowledge. The process that renders some R&D output obsolete is the same one that was termed "creative destruction" long ago by Joseph Schumpeter (1942). For a survey of the R&D depreciation problem and its implications for measuring the returns to R&D, see Hall (2006).

SEE ALSO *Arrow, Kenneth J.; Investment; Schumpeter, Joseph Alois; Technological Progress, Economic Growth; Technology*

BIBLIOGRAPHY

Aghion, Philippe, and Peter Howitt. 1998. *Endogenous Growth Theory.* Cambridge, MA, and London: MIT Press.

Arrow, Kenneth. 1962. Economic Welfare and the Allocation of Resources for Invention. In *The Rate and Direction of Inventive Activity,* ed. Richard R. Nelson, 609–625. Princeton, NJ: Princeton University Press.

Bush, Vannevar. 1945. *Science: The Endless Frontier.* Washington, DC: U.S. Government Printing Office.

Cohen, Wesley M., and Richard C. Levin. 1989. Empirical Studies of Innovation and Market Structure. In *The Handbook of Industrial Organization,* ed. Richard Schmalensee and Robert D. Willig, 1059–1107. Amsterdam: North-Holland.

Griliches, Zvi. 1979. Issues in Assessing the Contribution of R&D to Productivity Growth. *Bell Journal of Economics* 10: 92–116.

Griliches, Zvi. 1992. The Search for R&D Spillovers. *Scandinavian Journal of Economics* 94: S29–S47.

Hall, Bronwyn H. 2002. The Financing of Research and Development. *Oxford Review of Economic Policy* 18 (1): 35–51.

Hall, Bronwyn H. 2006. R&D, Productivity, and Market Value. http://www.econ.berkeley.edu/~bhhall/bhpapers.html.

Mowery, David C., and Nathan Rosenberg. 1989. *Technology and the Pursuit of Economic Growth.* Cambridge, U.K.: Cambridge University Press.

Nelson, Richard R. 1959. The Simple Economics of Basic Scientific Research. *Journal of Political Economy* 77: 297–306.

Organisation for Economic Co-operation and Development. 2002. *Frascati Manual: Proposed Standard Practice for Surveys on Research and Experimental Development.* Paris: Author.

Organisation for Economic Co-operation and Development. 2003. *Science, Technology, and Industry Scoreboard.* Paris: Author.

Reinganum, Jennifer F. 1989. The Timing of Innovation: Research, Development, and Diffusion. In *The Handbook of Industrial Organization,* ed. Richard Schmalensee and Robert D. Willig, 850–908. Amsterdam: North-Holland.

Schumpeter, Joseph. [1942] 1976. *Capitalism, Socialism, and Democracy.* New York: Harper and Row.

United Nations Statistics Division. 2006. National Accounts: Research and Development. http://unstats.un.org/unsd/nationalaccount/nadefault.htm.

U.S. Department of Commerce. 2006. R&D Satellite Account. News release, September 28. http://bea.gov/bea/newsrel/rdspendnewsrelease.htm.

Bronwyn H. Hall

RESEARCH ETHICS

SEE *Ethics in Experimentation; Experiments, Shock; Informed Consent; Institutional Review Board.*

RESEGREGATION OF SCHOOLS

In *Brown v. Board of Education* (1954), the Supreme Court declared separate schools to be "inherently unequal" and outlawed segregation in schools. Desegregation efforts were slow, but succeeded in reducing the number of students in racially isolated schools. Despite problems—most prominently the phenomenon of within-school segregation, which led to minority students frequently being concentrated in the lower academic tracks—desegregation helped to narrow the achievement gap.

Since 1988, however, there has been a growing trend toward resegregation. The number of black students in the South attending predominantly white schools grew from 0.001 percent in 1954 to 43.5 percent in 1988, to again drop to 32.7 percent by 1998. Nationwide, the number of African American students attending schools with more than 90 percent African American students has grown from 62.9 percent in 1986 to 70.2 percent in 1998–1999. A new phenomenon is the increasing segregation of Latinos, who by 1998 experienced a higher degree of segregation than in 1968. This trend toward increasing segregation of Latinos and African Americans is concentrated in large cities, but also occurs in some smaller cities and in suburbs of large metropolitan areas.

Three reasons have been proposed to explain this trend. First, a growing Latino immigration, particularly in the West, has led to Latinos now making up the largest population in many major cities and older suburbs; second, residential segregation remains and thus contributes to the perpetuation of segregated schools. Residential segregation had become deeply entrenched in the first half of the twentieth century through public policy that disproportionately benefited whites and created predominantly white suburbs. Fair housing laws since the 1970s have had limited success in curbing ongoing discrimination in housing and mortgage markets.

"White flight," or the tendency of whites to leave neighborhoods with growing numbers of black residents, has also been cited as a cause for a growing isolation of African Americans and Latinos in metropolitan centers. Charles T. Clotfelter's study (2004) shows a trend toward integration in all areas of the United States, except in the Northeast. However, Clotfelter also identifies a series of "contrary forces" that have hampered or limited desegregation, several of which support the idea of a "white flight." These include, first, whites avoiding mixed schools with high percentages of minority students; second, whites having options available to escape from desegregation (private schools, suburban schools, academic tracking, segregated school activities), while still appearing to support desegregation in principle; and third, white parents' ability to exert pressure on track assignments, assuring their children attend predominantly white schools or classes.

One of the most far-reaching causes hindering further desegregation and preventing resegregation, however, is the alarming trend in Supreme Court decisions toward turning away from a commitment to integration. In *Milliken v. Bradley* (1974), the Supreme Court adopted a position of "suburban innocence." Declaring that suburbs could not be held accountable for residential segregation, it decided against interdistrict busing, thus making it impossible to achieve integration in highly segregated school districts in Detroit. In *Riddick v. School Board of the City of Norfolk* (1986), the Supreme Court allowed districts to dismantle their desegregation efforts once they were integrated, or had achieved "unitary status," even if such practices would lead to resegregation.

Two new large-scale and controversial educational reforms emerged in the 1990s: first, school vouchers, and later, the No Child Left Behind (NCLB) policy. Both moved the debate on school reform away from the goal of integration. The idea of school vouchers (1994) was to provide federal funding to parents who wanted to send their children to private schools, giving parents the right to "choose," irrespective of their financial status. Critics argued that only a fraction of students would have been able to be offered these funds, which typically would not cover the entire tuition. Poor students would likely be left behind in schools with declining student enrollment and public funds. While vouchers now only exist in a few metropolitan districts, the NCLB initiative became a nationally adopted reform in 2002, promising to overcome "the soft bigotry of low expectations" through rigorous high-stakes testing. Proponents argue that NCLB has increased achievement, but its critics counter that while it adds little to already well-achieving schools, it is damaging to the poorest ones with the most disadvantaged student populations. With NCLB forcing schools to produce significant and sustained improvement, but often without being granted adequate funding, many urban schools face the likelihood of failure or closure.

As of 2006, many Latino and African American students are attending schools with more than 90 percent Latino and black enrollment. While there is considerable debate about whether the resegregation of schools is due to public policy or to natural demographic changes across region and by race, few question that integrated schools, despite the problem of within-school segregation, tend to provide better conditions for students of color than segregated schools.

SEE ALSO *Segregation, Residential; Segregation, School*

BIBLIOGRAPHY

Clotfelter, Charles T. 2004. *After Brown: The Rise and Retreat of School Desegregation.* Princeton, NJ: Princeton University Press.

Kozol, Jonathan. 2005. *The Shame of the Nation: The Restoration of Apartheid Schooling in America.* New York: Crown Publishers.

Logan, John. 2004. Resegregation in American Public Schools? Not in the 1990s. Lewis Mumford Center for Comparative Urban and Regional Research, University at Albany, State University of New York. http://mumford.albany.edu/census/noresegregation/noresegregation01.htm.

Orfield, Gary, Susan E. Eaton, and the Harvard Project on School Desegregation.1996. *Dismantling Desegregation: The Quiet Reversal of* Brown v. Board of Education. New York: New Press.

Annegret Staiger

RESERVATIONS

SEE *Affirmative Action.*

RESERVES, FOREIGN

In economics, the concept of foreign reserves describes the holdings of gold and foreign assets, such as foreign government bonds and foreign currency, by a country's central bank or monetary authority. The amount of foreign reserves a central bank holds is largely determined by the macroeconomic policy and foreign transactions of the country. In balance-of-payments accounts, which record all the cross-border flows of foreign currency, central bank foreign reserves equilibrate inflows and outflows. If a country is running a trade surplus, more foreign currency is coming into the country through trade in goods and services than is leaving the country through this channel. This excess foreign currency could be used to lend to other countries (positive net foreign investment) through the banking industry or other financial institutions. If the country does not spend all the excess currency on foreign lending, the remainder will accumulate as central bank foreign reserves, also known as the *official settlement balance* or *balance of payments* (the narrow definition). For example, in the early 2000s the Chinese central bank accumulated a very large amount of U.S. Treasury bonds largely due to many years of a substantial trade surplus in China.

FOREIGN RESERVES AND EXCHANGE RATE

The foreign reserves of the central bank play a central role in the exchange rate policy. If a country's monetary authority is following a regime of *dirty float*, it might want to intervene in the foreign exchange market to prevent large changes in the exchange rate. Frequently, such interventions are *sterilized*, in order not to affect the total amount of domestic currency in circulation. For example, if the U.S. Federal Reserve (Fed) wanted to keep the dollar from rising in value relative to the euro (that is, to keep the dollar from appreciating), the Fed would use dollars to purchase euros. The supply of dollars in circulation in the United States would increase because of this transaction. The Fed may sterilize this foreign exchange effect on the money supply by selling more U.S. bonds to the public in exchange for dollars, thereby reducing the money supply to its original level.

So, to prevent currency appreciation, the monetary authority would sell domestic currency and purchase foreign currency, thus accumulating foreign reserves. This is another reason, in addition to its trade surplus, that China had such large foreign reserve holdings: the Chinese monetary authority kept the Chinese currency, the *renminbi*, from appreciating with respect to the U.S. dollar.

To prevent currency depreciation, the monetary authority would sell some of its foreign reserves in exchange for domestic currency. In order to do that the monetary authority has to have sufficient holdings of foreign reserves to sell. For this reason, the central banks of many countries like to hold a substantial amount of foreign reserves to protect themselves from external shocks that could cause sharp depreciation of their currency, such as a sudden outflow of foreign investment from the country or a sudden drop in export revenues.

The amount of foreign reserves is particularly important for countries that follow a *fixed* exchange rate regime—that is, they commit to maintaining the value of their currency at a preannounced level. In many cases, such policies were adopted in order to anchor inflationary expectations and lower the level of inflation. In these cases, inflationary pressure in a flexible exchange rate regime would lead to currency depreciation. When the exchange rate is fixed, the monetary authority has to keep spending its foreign reserves to maintain the promised level of the exchange rate. Most of such fixed exchange rate regimes ended in *currency crises*, also known as *balance-of-payments crises*, because monetary authorities ran out of foreign reserves. Sometimes the currency crisis in such a situation can be delayed through currency devaluation, when the fixed exchange rate is reset to a new level. The most commonly used model that links foreign reserves to currency crises was developed in Paul Krugman's 1979 article "A Model of Balance-of-Payments Crises," modified later by Robert Flood and Peter Garber in their 1984 article "Collapsing Exchange Rate Regimes: Some Linear Examples."

CURRENCIES USED FOR FOREIGN RESERVES

Historically, the currencies used for foreign reserves were largely dictated by the exchange rate policies in the economies that used paper money. Initially, when paper money was introduced, in order to make people believe in its value, many countries tied the value of the paper money to gold or silver—each banknote could be redeemed at the central bank in exchange for the amount of gold or silver indicated on that banknote. Such an arrangement required the central bank to hold sufficient reserves of gold or silver to exchange all of the banknotes it printed for precious metal. If the central bank did not have sufficient reserves, it would devalue the paper currency by lowering the amount of precious metal the holder of the banknote could obtain.

Under the Bretton Woods arrangement (1944–1971), participating countries' currency values were tied to the U.S. dollar, while the value of the U.S. dollar was tied to gold. Thus, the Federal Reserve System, the central bank of the United States, would hold foreign reserves primarily in gold while other countries held their foreign reserves primarily in U.S. dollars. As a rule, countries that

adopt fixed exchange rates tend to hold their foreign reserves in the foreign currency to which they tie the value of their national currency.

Most countries, regardless of their exchange rate regime, hold their foreign reserves in *hard currencies*, currencies that are known to have low inflation: the U.S. dollar, the euro (before the existence of the euro, the German mark), or the Japanese yen. As of 2004, as much as 75 percent of total world foreign reserves were held in U.S. dollars. This U.S. dollar dominance is due mainly to the fact that many countries held the U.S. dollar as their foreign reserves during the Bretton Woods period. In addition, as Cedric Tille and Linda Goldberg argue in "Vehicle Currency Use in International Trade" (2005), much of this dollar dominance today is due to the fact that most international trade is invoiced in U.S. dollars. Nevertheless, this need not be the case in the future—as Menzie Chinn and Jeffrey Frankel show in "Will the Euro Eventually Surpass the Dollar as Leading International Reserve Currency?" (2005), the euro may surpass the U.S. dollar in the role of major currency as early as 2020, mostly due to a substantial depreciation of the U.S. dollar from 2001 to 2005.

SEE ALSO *Banking Industry; Currency; Currency Appreciation and Depreciation; Currency Devaluation and Revaluation; Dirty Float; Exchange Rates; Greenspan, Alan; Hedging; Money; Mundell-Fleming Model; Purchasing Power Parity; Trade Surplus*

BIBLIOGRAPHY

Chinn, Menzie, and Jeffrey A. Frankel. 2005. Will the Euro Eventually Surpass the Dollar as Leading International Reserve Currency? KSG Faculty Research Working Paper Series RWP05-064. Also NBER Working Paper 11508.

Flood, Robert P., and Peter Garber. 1984. Collapsing Exchange Rate Regimes: Some Linear Examples. *Journal of International Economics* 17 (1): 1–13.

Goldberg, Linda S., and Cedric Tille. 2005. Vehicle Currency Use in International Trade. Staff Reports 200, Federal Reserve Bank of New York. Also NBER Working Paper 11127.

Krugman, Paul R. 1979. A Model of Balance-of-Payments Crises. *Journal of Money, Credit, and Banking* 11 (3): 311–325.

Galina Hale

RESIDUALS

To define the notion of residuals, let us introduce a linear model describing the relationship between $K + 1$ independent variables x_j with $j = 0, 1, 2, \ldots, K$ and a dependent variable y:

$$y = \beta_0 + \beta_1 x_1 + \beta_2 x_2 + \ldots + \beta_K x_K + u$$

with u being the stochastic error representing all factors affecting y not included in the x_j's.

Assuming $E(u|x) = E(u) = 0$, the population regression function is:

$$E(y|x) = \beta_0 + \beta_1 x_1 + \beta_2 x_2 + \ldots + \beta_K x_K$$

This is estimated by the sample regression function:

$$\hat{y} = \hat{\beta}_0 + \hat{\beta}_1 x_1 + \hat{\beta}_2 x_2 + \ldots + \hat{\beta}_K x_K$$

where $\hat{\beta}_0, \hat{\beta}_1, \ldots, \hat{\beta}_K$ identify a set of estimated parameters calculated using the estimation rule $\hat{\beta}$.

Assuming a sample of N observations, the residual for observation i, with $i = 0, 1, 2, \ldots, N$, is the difference between the actual value of y_i and the fitted value of the estimated regression, that is:

$$\hat{u}_i = y_i - \hat{y}_i = y_i - \hat{\beta}_0 - \hat{\beta}_1 x_{i1} - \hat{\beta}_2 x_{i2} - \ldots - \hat{\beta}_K x_{iK}$$

If the residual is positive, the estimated regression underpredicts y_i and vice versa if the residual is negative. Each residual $\hat{u}_i$ can be interpreted as an estimate of the unobservable error u_i and as such can be employed in constructing a number of statistical tests assessing the properties of the estimated model and a set of indicators determining the goodness of fit.

Ideally, a good model is characterized by small residuals, that is, by fitted values $\hat{y}_i$ that are close to the actual values y_i. The ordinary least squares (OLS) estimator of the parameters β_j is calculated by fitting the regression line that best approximates the data through the minimization of the sum of squared residuals. The resulting first-order conditions for the OLS estimator are $\sum_{i=1}^{N} \hat{u}_i = 0$ and $\sum_{i=1}^{N} x_{ij} \hat{u}_i = 0$, with $j = 1, 2, \ldots, K$.

As regards the goodness of fit, defining the total sum of squares $SST = \sum_{i=1}^{N} (y_i - \bar{y})^2$, the explained sum of squares $SSE = \sum_{i=1}^{N} (\hat{y}_i - \bar{y})^2$, and the residual sum of squares $SSR = \sum_{i=1}^{N} \hat{u}_i^2$, the part of variation in y that is explained by the regressors, is given by the coefficient $R^2 = 1 - SSR/SST$. R^2 is between 0 and 1, with the fit of the regression improving as R^2 approaches 1. A consistent estimator of the variance of the stochastic error is given by $\hat{\sigma}^2 = (N - K - 1)^{-1} \sum_{i=1}^{N} \hat{u}_i^2$. Its square root $\hat{\sigma}$ is then an estimator of the standard deviation of the unobservable factors affecting the dependent variable y. It indicates how well the model predicts y given the information set represented by the observables x_j's. The estimate $\hat{\sigma}$ is used to construct the standard error of the OLS estimator, equal to $se(\hat{\beta}_j) = \hat{\sigma}/[SST_j(1 - R_j^2)]^{\frac{1}{2}}$ where SST_j is the total sum of squares of x_{ij} and R_j^2 is the R^2 of the regression of x_j on all other regressors. The standard error $se(\hat{\beta}_j)$ is then employed to test for statistical significance of each estimated parameter through the t-statistic.

If the errors were homoskedastic, we would have that $Var(u|x_1, x_2, \ldots, x_K) = E(u^2|x_1, x_2, \ldots, x_K) = E(u^2) = \sigma^2$. On the contrary, in the presence of heteroskedasticity the expected value of u^2 can be assumed to depend on some function of the explanatory variables. Following this logic, Breusch and Pagan suggest a test for heteroskedasticity that consists of an F-test on the regression of the squared residuals on the explanatory variables. The White test for heteroskedasticity simply consists of a similar regression including nonlinearities, that is, the squares and cross-products of the explanatory variables.

White suggests using the residuals $\hat{u}_i$ to calculate a heteroskedasticity-robust standard error for $\hat{\beta}_j$. This is given by $se_{robust}(\hat{\beta}_j) = \sum_{i=1}^{N} [\hat{r}_{ij}^2 \hat{u}_i^2 / SSR_j^2]^{\frac{1}{2}}$, where $\hat{r}_{ij}$ is the i-th residual of the regression of x_j on all other regressors and SSR_j is the residual sum of squares of this regression.

SEE ALSO *Hausman Tests; Least Squares, Ordinary; Least Squares, Three-Stage; Least Squares, Two-Stage; Ordinary Least Squares Regression; Regression; Test Statistics; White Noise*

BIBLIOGRAPHY

Breusch, T. S., and A. R. Pagan. 1979. A Simple Test for Heteroskedasticity and Random Coefficient Variation. *Econometrica* 50: 987–1007.

Greene, William H. 1997. *Econometric Analysis.* 3rd ed. Upper Saddle River, NJ: Prentice Hall.

White, H. 1980. A Heteroskedasticity-Consistent Covariance Matrix Estimator and a Direct Test for Heteroskedasticity. *Econometrica* 48: 817–838.

Wooldridge, J. M. 2003. *Introductory Econometrics: A Modern Approach.* 2nd ed. Cincinnati, OH: South-Western.

Luca Nunziata

RESILIENCY

Resilience is an increasingly common term used in concept in various branches of psychology, in particular developmental psychology, severe mental illness (SMI), trauma studies, disaster response, social psychology, and "positive" psychology. Across all of these areas of psychological investigation, resilience refers to the human ability to have withstood, or to be able to withstand, challenge, crisis, stress, or trauma of differing types.

In their 1998 work, researchers Ann Masten and J. Douglas Coatsworth conceptualize resilience as "manifested competence in the context of significant challenges to adaptation or development" (p. 206). Thus they believe, as Nancy Davis noted in 1999, that there needs to have been a considerable menace to a person or an actual traumatic experience and, in spite of this, the individual's quality of adjustment or development is nevertheless good.

According to Masten and Coatsworth in 1998, in the area of clinical psychology and psychopathology, Norman Garmezy is considered to be a "peerless pioneer in the study of competence and resilience." This accolade is the result of his groundbreaking work examining adults with schizophrenia and their functioning that is adaptive as well as dysfunctional and the children of parents with schizophrenia. In investigating the risk factors for these children, vis-à-vis their developing schizophrenia, Garmezy and his colleagues found that while having a parent with schizophrenia does indeed increase an offspring's likelihood for subsequently developing schizophrenia, they were amazed that their investigation indicated that ninety percent of those they surveyed did not develop the illness. He noted that their subjects upset predictions and, in fact, displayed many qualities that arise from good peer relations, including academic achievement and purposeful goals. Garmezy stated in 1971, "Were we to study the forces that move such children to survival and to adaptation, the long range benefits to our society might be far more significant than our many efforts to construct models of primary prevention designed to curtail the incidence of vulnerability" (p.114). He went on to explore what it was that seemed to protect these offspring and, as a parallel result, the scientific investigation of resilience began.

Subsequently, developmental researchers have conducted studies that are not just within psychopathological areas, but other stressful environments such as neglectful or abusive parents, war zones and environments of high poverty, or children who have physical illness. One of the leading authorities in the field, Michael Rutter, noted concerns with early conceptualizations of resilience, with individuals being referred to as "invulnerable" or "invincible." Davis reports in 1999 that Rutter's point is that vulnerability to stress is a continuum, not all-or-none, and some people may display better resilience in response to some stressors, but this may not be uniform across all stressful situations or at all times. Thus, someone is not very likely to be invincible in the face of all adversities. Rutter notes in 1991 that the features that contribute to resiliency will vary in response to risk mechanisms and that resiliency may be contingent as much on social context as on the individual. As a result, rather than being a static characteristic, resiliency is affected by developmental changes (pp. 1–2).

What may seem a rather straightforward concept or construct may indeed not be. In fact, Suniya Luthar notes in 1993 that "overt social competence among high risk individuals is not necessarily paralleled by superior adjustment on covert mental health indices" (p. 441). This may seem surprising or even counter-intuitive. For example, in her study of adolescents who appeared socially competent and who were in stressful situations, Luthar found that they actually self-reported experiencing high levels of mood problems such as anxiety and depression.

Marian Radke-Yarrow and Elisa Brown conducted a 10-year longitudinal study of children with parents who were diagnosed with mood disorders, which they reported in 1993. When they compared resilient offspring to control offspring, they discovered that 56 percent suffered from somatic complaints, versus only 21 percent of the cohorts. This raises the question asked by George Vaillant: "Does resilience merely mean survival in the face of vulnerability and multiple risk factors, or should we think of resilience only when it also permits happiness? Is it enough that the vulnerable patient survives the operation and that the orphan survives the concentration camp, or, in addition, should they be able to run and laugh and feel joy as well?" (1993, p. 285).

Resiliency is much less focused on an individual's deficits or psychopathology in the face of trauma or adverse conditions. For example, Emmy Werner and Ruth Smith consider resiliency to be a "self-righting capacity" involving not only the individual but including the support that comes from loved ones, schools, or even communities that all conspire to aid in one's healthy responses or healing. Thus, when adversity strikes, the individual is able to compensate or "self-right." They believe that all people have some innate self-righting capacity (Werner and Smith 1992, p. 202).

CHARACTERISTICS OF RESILIENT INDIVIDUALS

The Ego-Resiliency (ER) construct views individuals as being able to demonstrate "resourceful adaptation to changing circumstances and environmental contingencies, (ability to) analy(ize) the 'goodness of fit' between situational demands and behavioral possibility, and (have an) … available repertoire of problem-solving strategies," as reported by Jeanne H. Block and Jack Block in 1980 (p. 48). In 1996 Eva Klohnen summarized characteristics of resilient individuals as including the ability to be happy and contented, with a sense of direction and purpose; the capacity for productive work and a sense of competence and environmental mastery; emotional security; self-acceptance; self-knowledge; a realistic and undistorted perception of oneself, others, and one's surroundings; interpersonal adequacy and the capacity for warm and caring relating to others and for intimacy and respect; confident optimism; autonomous and productive activity; interpersonal insight and warmth; and skilled expressiveness.

Resilience, as conceptualized as Ego-Resiliency, has been measured using the California Adult Q-Set (CAQ), as Jack Block noted in 1978. The Q-set is a number of atheoretical, descriptive personality items used in the CAQ. This instrument used a Q-sort methodology and is thus fairly time consuming. A Q-sort is a sorting task made up of descriptive personality characteristics on cards that require a subject to sort or rank order the cards from high to low relevance to the subject's self-perceived personality characteristics (Stephenson, 1936). In 1996 Klohnen developed an empirically derived, 29-item self-report scale that has good internal consistency, good reliability, substantial convergent validity with the CAQ-based observer measure, and solid external criterion validity with another index of psychological adjustment.

RISK FACTORS

Risk factors in resilience research are defined by Jon Rolf and Jeannette Johnson in 1990 as "those variables that have proven or presumed effects that can directly increase the likelihood of a maladaptive outcome" (p. 387). Various studies issued by Peter Fonagy, Miriam Steele, Howard Steele, Anna Higgitt, and Mary Target in 1994, by Masten and Coatsworth in 1998, Lois Barclay Murphy and Alice Moriarty in 1976, and Werner in 1996 have discovered an almost limitless number of risk and stress factors. These factors include but are not limited to genetic abnormalities, developmental delays or irregularities, lack of education, poverty, parents with chronic or mental illness, death of a close family member, familial violence, and war, as well as constitutional vulnerabilities such as sensory-motor deficits and insufficient impulse control.

PROTECTIVE OR PROMOTIONAL FACTORS

Masten and Coatsworth noted in 1998 that resilience studies are "remarkably consistent in pointing to qualities of child and environment that are associated with competence or better psychosocial functioning during or following adverse experiences" (p. 212). For the individual these include good intellectual functioning; an easygoing disposition; self-efficacy; self-confidence; high self-esteem; talents; and faith. Familial qualities include a child having a close relationship with a caring parent figure; authoritative parenting that provides warmth, structure, and high expectations; socioeconomic advantages; and connections to extended supportive family networks. Outside the family, bonds to pro-social adults, connections to social organizations, and attendance at effective schools also contribute to an individual's resiliency.

Naimah Weinberg, Elizabeth Rahdert, James Colliver, and Meyer Glantz's 1998 meta-analysis suggests that "while there is no single 'resilience' trait," such qualities as those noted above seem to hold some protective ability. Edith Grotberg, through her works in 1995 and 1998, offers a different conceptualization from her international work, suggesting that to overcome adversities, people draw upon as many as fifteen sources of resilience. They include such factors as having people around that are trusted and loving, being a person that people like and love, and being able to find someone to help when needed, for example.

PREDICTORS OF RESILIENCY

A review of the literature compiled by Davis in 1999 resulted in a list of predictors structured within areas of competency. These issues should be interpreted with the caveat that "all of these characteristics are only known to correlate with resilience; they are not necessarily causes. In fact, Davis says they could just as well be consequences of success rather than causes of it" (1999). Having more is better, but absence is not catastrophic.

- Physical Competence: Good health, easy temperament, and good prenatal care.

- Social and Relational Competence: Secure parental attachment and basic trust, ability to reflect upon the mental states of oneself and others, ability and opportunity to recruit actively people who can help, strong ability to make and keep a few good friends, positive peer relationships, interpersonal awareness or role-taking abilities, and empathy.

- Cognitive Competence: Average to above average intelligence quotient and emotional (intelligence) quotient, good language acquisition and reading ability, capacity to plan/have foresight, good problem-solving abilities, positive future expectations, internal locus of control, assertiveness, and optimism.

- Emotional Competence: Emotional regulation, ability to delay gratification, realistically high self-esteem, sense of autonomy, ability to think and work creativity, and a sense of humor.

- Moral Competence: The ability and opportunity to contribute.

- Spiritual Competence: Having faith that one's own life matters, and conviction that there is a meaning to what one does.

RESILIENCY TRAINING

A number of social support and stress inoculation programs were developed in the 1990s. These programs used methods of outdoor education, classroom simulations, and other methods in community intervention efforts. Davis noted in 1999 that these programs include family skills training, strengthening families program, Focus On Families, Families and Schools Together, Family Effectiveness Training, behavioral family therapy, structural family therapy, functional family therapy, Parenting Adolescents Wisely, Kempe Prevention Research Center for Family and Child Health, Dare to Be You, Be A Star, Learn and Service America, Say It Straight, Big Brothers/ Big Sisters of America, Adventure Education, and Outward Bound.

In 2002 the American Psychological Association developed a program that is publicly available titled *The Road to Resilience*. It involves a combination of media (television such as the Discovery Health Channel, Web sites, printed materials) through which psychologists could gain training and provide lectures in communities.

SEE ALSO *Child Development; Family Functioning; Parenting Styles; Personality; Psychotherapy; Schooling; Self-Concept; Self-Efficacy; Self-Esteem; Temperament*

BIBLIOGRAPHY

American Psychological Association. 2002. *The Road to Resilience*. http://helping.apa.org/featuredtopics/feature.php?id=6.

Block, Jack. 1978. *The Q-sort Method in Personality Assessment and Psychiatric Research*. Palo Alto, CA: Consulting Psychologists Press. (Orig. pub. 1961).

Block, Jeanne H., and Jack Block. 1980. The Role of Ego-control and Ego-resiliency in the Organization of Behavior. In *Minnesota Symposium on Child Psychology*, vol. 12, ed. W. A. Collins, 39–101. Hillsdale, NJ: Erlbaum.

Davis, Nancy J. 1999. *Resilience Working Paper: Status of the Research and Research-based Programs*. http://mentalhealth.samhsa.gov/schoolviolence/5-28Resilience.asp.

Fonagy, Peter, Miriam Steele, Howard Steele, Anna Higgitt, and Mary Target. 1994. The Emanuel Miller Memorial Lecture 1992: The Theory and Practice of Resilience. *Journal of Child Psychology and Psychiatry* 34 (2): 231–257.

Garmezy, Norman. 1971. Vulnerability Research and the Issue of Primary Prevention. *American Journal of Orthopsychiatry* 41: 101–116.

Grotberg, Edith H. 1995. *A Guide to Promoting Resilience in Children: Strengthening the Human Spirit*. The Hague, Netherlands: Bernard Van Leer Foundation. http://resilnet.uiuc.edu/library/grotb95b.html.

Grotberg, Edith H. 1998. I Am, I Have, I Can: What Families Worldwide Taught Us about Resilience. *Reaching Today's Youth* (Spring): 36–39.

Klohnen, Eva C. 1996. Conceptual Analysis and Measurement of the Construct of Ego-resiliency. *Journal of Personality and Social Psychology* 70 (5): 1067–1079.

Luthar, Suniya S. 1993. Annotation: Methodological and Conceptual Issues in Research on Childhood Resilience. *Journal of Child Psychology and Psychiatry* 34: 441–454.

Masten, Ann S., and J. Douglas Coatsworth. 1998. The Development of Competence in Favorable and Unfavorable Environments: Lessons from Research on Successful Children. *American Psychologist* 53 (2): 205–220.

Murphy, Lois Barclay, and Alice Moriarty. 1976. *Vulnerability, Coping and Growth: From Infancy to Adolescence*. New Haven, CT: Yale University Press.

Radke-Yarrow, Marian, and Elisa Brown. 1993. Resilience and Vulnerability in Children of Multiple-risk Families. *Development and Psychopathology* 5: 581–592.

Rolf, Jon, and Jeannette Johnson. 1990. Protected or Vulnerable: The Challenges of AIDS to Developmental Psychopathology. In *Risk and Protective Factors in the Development of Psychopathology*, eds. Jon Rolf, Ann S. Masten, Dante Nicchetti, Keith H. Nuechterlein, and Sheldon Weintraub, 384–404. Cambridge, U.K.: Cambridge University Press.

Rutter, Michael. 1991. *Resilience: Some Conceptual Considerations*. Institute of Mental Health Initiatives Conference on Fostering Resilience. Washington, DC, December 5–6.

Stephenson, W. 1936. Introduction to Inverted Factor Analysis, with Some Applications to Studies in Orexis. *Journal of Educational Psychology* 27: 353–367.

Vaillant, George E. 1993. *The Wisdom of the Ego*. Cambridge, MA: Harvard University Press.

Weinberg, Naimah Z., Elizabeth Rahdert, James Colliver, and Meyer Glantz. 1998. Adolescent Substance Abuse: A Review of the Past 10 Years. *Journal of the American Academy of Child and Adolescent Psychiatry* 37 (3): 252–261.

Werner, Emmy E. 1996. *Fostering Resiliency in Kids: Overcoming Adversity*. Transcript of proceedings of a congressional breakfast seminar, March 29, 1996, sponsored by the Consortium of Social Science Associations, Washington, DC.

Werner, Emmy E., and Ruth S. Smith. 1992. *Overcoming the Odds*. Ithaca, NY: Cornell University Press.

Chris E. Stout

RESISTANCE

The concept of *resistance*, meaning literally to stand against, entered the social sciences primarily from politics and culture. While there is a clinical psychoanalytic definition of the term, and a technical one used by the physical sciences, it is really resistance in a critical politico-cultural sense that has had the greatest impact in the field.

Resistance in a political context is often thought of as the property of the left. The famed French (and often communist-led) *Résistance* against the Nazi occupation immediately comes to mind. But the concept was first introduced into the modern political lexicon from the right, by Edmund Burke, who argued for the necessity of resisting revolutionary "progress" in his *Reflections on the Revolution in France* (1790). Burke was incensed at the French overthrow of birthright authority and the leveling of classes (he was particularly horrified by the thought of the hairdresser who thinks himself the equal of his betters). These, and other such revolutionary abuses, fly in the face of time-tested tradition and threaten to upset the natural order of things. As such, it is the "best wisdom and the first duty" of every Englishman to stand against such radical change, with "jealous, ever-waking vigilance" (p. 54).

The conservative call for a resistance against change was taken up by Burke's countryman Matthew Arnold. By the mid-nineteenth century the republican ideals of the French revolution had the lead over Burke's beloved tradition, and nature, after Darwin, was harnessed to progress. A new principle of resistance was needed—and for Arnold, it was culture. As "the best that has ever been thought and said" (as he defines it in *Culture and Anarchy*, 1869), culture offered a means with which to rise above the politics, commerce, and industry of the day and supply a universal standard upon which to base authority and order.

Karl Marx, exiled in England when Arnold was writing, also thought *resistance* a conservative ideal. In their 1848 *Communist Manifesto* Marx and Engels paint a heady portrait of dynamic change: traditions overthrown, nature transformed, nations dissolved, people uprooted; a world where "all that is solid melts into air" (p. 38). For Marx, resistance is *not* the answer—it's the problem. It is capitalism's bourgeois caretakers who are resisting the system's own logic. Capitalism has socialized the means of production, yet ownership is kept in the hands of the few. The revolutionary solution is to tear asunder this final resistance and herald in the new world.

Resistance moved leftward with the anticolonial struggles of the twentieth century. Mohandas K. Gandhi, waging a battle against British rule in India, advocated a political philosophy of *satyagraha*. In Sanskrit this word means "insistence on the truth," but Gandhi also used it to denote "civil resistance." This conflation of meanings makes a certain sense, as for Gandhi it was the untruths of colonial rule—that power must rest upon violence, that English culture comprised the "best that has ever been thought and said"—that needed to be resisted more fiercely than even the British themselves. To be free of European bodies on Indian soil was one thing; to be free of their ideas, their prejudices, and their technology was another. Drawing upon both Burke and Arnold, but turning these ideas on their head, Gandhi advised the practice of civil disobedience, not merely in the streets, but through a political and spiritual return to traditional Indian culture and practices like *khaddar*, the hand-looming of cloth.

Radical resistance, defined in part as the rejection of foreign cultures and the celebration of indigenous traditions, spread across the globe as European colonies in Africa and Asia were overturned by struggles of national liberation. Gandhi's strategy of nonviolent civil disobedience was not adopted by all. The Caribbean psychiatrist-cum-rebel Frantz Fanon made the case for bloody resistance in his influential *The Wretched of the Earth* (1963). Indeed, for Fanon it is the very violence of the resistance that will clear the way to a new society. But for all their differences, Gandhi and Fanon agreed on one thing: that the enemy that one had to resist the most virulently was the enemy one had internalized—what the Tunisian writer and activist Albert Memmi referred to in his 1957 book *The Colonizer and the Colonized* as "the colonizer within."

The concept of *resistance* returned to the West via concerns with identity and identity-construction. In the early 1960s the American sociologist Erving Goffman argued that the job of total institutions like prisons, hospitals, and armies is to create—or recreate—their charge's identity in order to integrate them into the system. However, Goffman observes, the patients in the mental institution he studied actually formed their identities by eliding institutional demands and creating "underlives" within the institution. In brief, it is in resisting the definitions pressed upon them that inmates of institutions develop their own sense of identity: "It is *against something* that the self can emerge" (p. 320). Goffman's book, *Asylums* (1961), was not merely a critique of total institutions, but a critical assessment of the postwar "Free World" of big business and the welfare state, mass media, and compulsory education—a mostly benign, but nonetheless totalizing system.

It was in resistance to this benign totality—the ticky-tacky little boxes where everyone comes out all the same, as Pete Seeger sang in 1962—that a youth counterculture emerged in the 1960s, as young people created "underlives" by defining themselves against The System. Some of this resistance was political—opposition to the American war in Vietnam, for instance—but it was also a stylistic confrontation: new styles of clothes, forms of music, and types of intoxicants. In other words, it was *cultural resistance*.

The idea, and ideal, of cultural resistance, while first championed by Matthew Arnold, takes its radical articulation from the Italian Marxist Antonio Gramsci. Gramsci held that hegemony is both a political and cultural process and thus part of the revolutionary project is to create a counterhegemonic culture. But if this culture is to have real power, and radical integrity, it cannot—contra Arnold—be imposed from above; it must come out of the experiences and consciousness of "the people." Thus, the job of the revolutionary is to discover the progressive potentialities that reside within popular consciousness and from this material fashion a culture of resistance.

It was this implicit politico-cultural mission that guided the Centre for Contemporary Cultural Studies (CCCS) at the University of Birmingham in the 1970s. The CCCS is best known for its study of subcultures, and it was within mainly working class subcultures—punks, mods, skinheads, and Rastafarians—that researchers found an inchoate culture of resistance. For Stuart Hall and his CCCS colleagues, however, cultural resistance was politically ambiguous. Subcultures opened up spaces where dominant ideology was contested and counter-hegemonic culture was created; at the same time, these contestations and symbolic victories often remained purely cultural, leaving the political and economic systems untouched. Cultural resistance, unless translated into political action, becomes what Hall and others referred to as "imaginary" solutions to real-world problems (Hall 1976).

This raises a nagging question that dogs the whole project of politico-cultural *resistance*: Is this resistance really resistance at all? The efficacy of cultural resistance has been questioned since at least 1934, when Malcolm Cowley, reminiscing about his Greenwich Village life in *Exile's Return*, pointed out that while bohemians may have flouted Victorian values of thrift and savings, their libertinism and emphasis on style and innovation mesh quite nicely with the needs of consumer capitalism. As the Frankfurt School theorist Theodor Adorno snidely remarked about the jazz fan of the era, "he pictures himself as the individualist who whistles at the world. But what he whistles is its melody" (Adorno 1938, p. 298). Resistance as a political strategy also has its critics. Resistance only exists in relation to the dominant power—"bonds of rejection" is what Richard Sennett calls this relationship in his discussion of *Authority* (1985)—and without that dominant power, resistance has no coherence or purpose. What, then, is the point of resistance if it rests on the maintenance of the very thing being resisted?

Michel Foucault, like his contemporary Erving Goffman, studied total institutions—prisons, asylums, and schools—but the French intellectual was interested in institutions of the mind as well: disciplinary boundaries and classification systems. The failures of radical political resistance in 1968 confirmed what Foucault had already known: that power was not something "out there"—easy to identify and overthrow. Instead, it was everywhere, continuous, anonymous, intimate, and even pleasurable: "the disciplinary grid of society" (p. 111), as he names it

in *Power/Knowledge* (1980). For most critics, the individual subject/self is the hero of resistance against totalizing control; Foucault countered that the subject itself was problematic. The Enlightenment's focus on the subject allowed for new ideals of personal freedom, but it also opened up new sites of oppression: the individual's mind, body, and spirit. Because power is impressed upon and internalized in the subject, it raises a vexing problem: Who is it that resists and what exactly are they resisting? Can one resist the very subject doing the resisting? Resistance remains a stated goal for Foucault, but one that must be reconceptualized. The ideal of developing the pure subject in opposition to the corrupting object of society must be rejected. "Maybe the target nowadays," he suggests in "The Subject and Power" (1984), "is not to discover what we are, but to refuse what we are" (p. 208).

This idea of resistance is played out to its—perhaps illogical—conclusion by the playful postmodernist Jean Baudrillard. In his 1985 essay "The Masses: The Implosion of the Social in the Media," Baudrillard argues that strategies of resistance always change to reflect strategies of control. Against a system that excludes or represses the individual, the natural demand is one of inclusion: to become a subject. Today, however, people are bombarded with appeals for their participation—and yet they still feel that their choice or vote matters little. Against a system that justifies and sustains its existence by the political consent (or consumer purchases) of those it governs, the masses have devised a new strategy of resistance: apathy, "a massive desisting from will" (p. 109). A resistance to resistance.

Another path taken has been to move beyond resistance—to reimagine identities and politics not tied to the negation of the other. Michael Hardt and Antonio Negri sketch a bleak portrait of an all-pervasive, omnipotent system of control: *Empire* (2000). They acknowledge that within such a system, political and cultural resistance is usually expressed in a generalized "being-against"—a negative resistance. Yet they also see the chance for something different. They argue, like Marxists before them, that the system itself is generating the very tools and social conditions that make transcendence possible. The system of Empire relies upon new communication flows, new forms of organization, and new subjectivities—all of which might give rise to radical identities, ideals, and collective actions not mired in the negation of being-against, thereby offering the subjectivity necessary for proactive social change, that is: a "being-for." The boldest, and perhaps most outrageous, proposal to move beyond resistance comes from the Slovenian philosopher Slavoj Žižek who, drawing upon ideas of Jacques Lacan in *The Ticklish Subject* (1999), proposes something he calls "the Act"—a radical act that jumps outside the coordinates of the dominant system, including any opposition tied to these coordinates. This act transcends resistance and its attendant disobedient obedience—but one might also legitimately ask: Where does an act like this lead?

SEE ALSO *Colonialism; Cultural Studies; Fanon, Frantz; Foucault, Michel; Gandhi, Mohandas K.; Goffman, Erving; Gramsci, Antonio; Hall, Stuart; Marx, Karl; Marxism*

BIBLIOGRAPHY

Adorno, Theodor. 1938. "On the Fetish-Character in Music and the Regression of Listening." In *Cultural Resistance Reader*, ed. Stephen Duncombe, 275–303. New York and London: Verso, 2002.

Arnold, Matthew. 1869. *Culture and Anarchy*. Ed. J. Dover Wilson. Cambridge, UK: Cambridge University Press, 1990.

Baudrillard, Jean. 1985. "The Masses: The Implosion of the Social in the Media." In *Cultural Resistance Reader*, Ed. Stephen Duncombe, 100–113. New York and London: Verso, 2002.

Burke, Edmund. 1790. *Reflections on the Revolution in France*. Ed. L. G. Mitchell. Oxford: Oxford University Press, 1993.

Cowley, Malcolm. 1934. *Exile's Return: A Literary Odyssey of the 1920s*. London: Penguin, 1976.

Duncombe, Stephen, ed. 2002. *Cultural Resistance Reader*. New York and London: Verso.

Fanon, Frantz. 1963. *The Wretched of the Earth*. Trans. Richard Philcox. New York: Grove Press.

Foucault, Michel. 1980. *Power/Knowledge: Selected Interviews and Other Writings, 1972–1977*. Ed. Colin Gordon; trans. Colin Gordon et al. New York: Pantheon.

Foucault, Michel. 1982. "The Subject and Power." In *Michel Foucault: Beyond Structuralism and Hermeneutics*, ed. Hubert L. Dreyfus and Paul Rabinow, 208–226. Chicago: University of Chicago Press.

Gandhi, M. K. 1919. *Hind Swaraj; or, Indian Home Rule*. Madras, India: Ganesh/Nationalist Press.

Goffman, Erving. 1961. *Asylums: Essays on the Social Situation of Mental Patients and Other Inmates*. New York: Anchor.

Gramsci, Antonio. 1929–1935. *Prison Notebooks*. Ed. Quinton Hoare and Geoffrey Nowell-Smith. New York: International Publishers, 1971.

Hall, Stuart, and Tony Jefferson, eds. 1976. *Resistance through Rituals: Youth Cultures in Post-War Britain*. London: Unwin Hyman.

Hardt, Michael, and Antonio Negri. 2000. *Empire*. Cambridge, MA: Harvard University Press.

Marx, Karl, and Frederick Engels. 1848. *The Communist Manifesto*. Trans. Samuel Moore. New York and London: Verso, 1998.

Memmi, Albert. 1957. *The Colonizer and the Colonized*. Trans. Howard Greenfield. New York: Beacon Press, 1991.

Sennett, Richard. 1980. *Authority*. New York: Norton.

Žižek, Slavoj. 1999. *The Ticklish Subject: The Absent Centre of Political Ontology*. London and New York: Verso.

Stephen Duncombe

RESOURCE ECONOMICS

As a subfield of economics, resource economics examines the allocation of natural resources between uses and over time. Natural resources have enjoyed a prominent role in the history of economic thought. French physiocrats Francois Quesnay (1694–1774) and Anne Robert Jacques Turgot (1721–1781) considered in the mid-eighteenth century that agriculture (land) creates all value and supports manufacturing and service sectors in the economy. Land had a central role also in classical political economy, particularly in the works of English political economists Thomas Malthus and David Ricardo. Later in the late-nineteenth century, English economist Stanley Jevons (1835–1882) devoted attention to coal as the crucial natural resource for industrialization and growth in Great Britain.

Land economics emerged in the United States in the early decades of the twentieth century as the immediate predecessor of natural resource economics; this body of theory addressed economic issues related to agriculture and agricultural land in particular. Economists have developed major theories in resource economics since the 1930s. Harold Hotelling (1895–1973) suggested that reserves of nonrenewable resources such as ores, coal, and oil could be considered capital assets. They can either be extracted now or left for the future to appreciate in value. The decision to extract the reserve depends on the relative returns of the two alternatives. Hotelling argued that the optimal extraction rate of a resource equates the change in its net price (price net of extraction costs) with the interest rate or the rate of return from other capital assets. This is known as the *Hotelling Rule*. Its significance lies in underlining the role of interest rate in extraction decisions.

Economist H. Scott Gordon (b. 1924) and fisheries scientist Milner B. Schaefer (1912–1970) produced the key insights into renewable natural resources when they combined biological and economic models of fisheries. The biological model postulates a bell-shaped relationship between a fish population (stock) and its growth. Key aspects of the model also include a minimum viable stock level and the natural equilibrium (or natural maximum stock level), and the maximum sustainable yield at some intermediary level of stock. This biological model can be transformed into an economic one by assuming constant prices for the fish and a direct relationship between the fishing effort and the size of stock, and by recognizing that harvesting involves cost. The bell-shaped relationship now depicts the revenue from fishing, while total costs of harvesting increase monotonously with fishing effort. The efficient level of catch is achieved at a level of harvesting below maximum sustainable yield when the net benefits as the difference between revenue and cost are maximized. However, in the case of open access fisheries, it is profitable for fishermen to increase their catch until their marginal revenue equals their marginal costs. While individually rational, this results in excessive and economically inefficient harvesting, and suggests controlling of harvesting levels by regulating gear or imposing catch quotas. More recent work in resource economics, such as that of economist V. Kerry Smith, frequently focuses on the monetary valuation of non-market environmental harms, risks, and benefits.

Other contributions to understanding natural resource use and problems associated with it have come, for example, from environmentalist Garrett Hardin (1915–2003). His application of game-theoretic ideas to the use of pastures and other natural resources, in 1968, popularized the notion of the *Tragedy of the Commons* as an explanation for the degradation and depletion of renewable natural resources. While Hardin erred in attributing the destructive competition for resources to the commons (instead of open access to a resource), his game theoretic analysis of natural resource use problems shifted attention away from the conditions of optimal inter-temporal allocation to factors which engender nonoptimal outcomes and institutional arrangements that can assist in avoiding them. New institutional scholars such as Elinor Ostrom have popularized this approach in research on the use and management of renewable natural resources since the early 1990s.

SEE ALSO *Externality; Malthus, Thomas Robert; Natural Resources, Nonrenewable; Overfishing; Pollution; Resources; Tragedy of the Commons*

BIBLIOGRAPHY

Gordon, H. Scott. 1953. An Economic Approach to the Optimum Utilization of Fishery Resources. *Journal of the Fisheries Research Board of Canada* 10: 442–457.

Hardin, Garrett. 1968. The Tragedy of the Commons. *Science* 162 (3859): 1243–1248.

Hotelling, Harold. 1931. The Economics of Exhaustible Resources. *Journal of Political Economy* 39 (2): 137–175.

Kula, Erhun. 1998. *History of Environmental Economic Thought.* London: Routledge.

Ostrom, Elinor. 1990. *Governing the Commons: The Evolution of Institutions for Collective Action.* Cambridge, UK: Cambridge University Press.

Schaefer, Milner B. 1957. Some Considerations of Population Dynamics and Economics in Relation to the Management of the Commercial Marine Fisheries. *Journal of the Fisheries Research Board of Canada* 14: 669–681.

Smith, V. Kerry, William H. Desvousges, and Ann Fisher. 1987. A Comparison of Direct and Indirect Methods for Estimating Environmental Benefits. *American Journal of Agricultural Economics* 68 (2): 280–290.

Jouni Paavola

RESOURCES

A resource is anything of value as an input in production. Classical political economy identified land, labor, and capital as the three factors of production, and in this way it distinguished between natural resources, human resources, and financial resources. Capital could be understood merely as physical instruments of production, but, for example, William Stanley Jevons (1871) considered a sum of money or financial resources a transitory form or capital that could be transformed into physical instruments of production. Whereas human resources and financial resources are terms that are still in common usage, the term *resources* can also be used more narrowly to refer to natural resources only. This is the sense in which resources are discussed in this article.

Natural resources are conventionally divided into three categories: indestructible or nondepletable, renewable or depletable, and exhaustible or nonrenewable resources. Examples of nondepletable resources include wind and solar energy, whereas fisheries, pastures, forest resources, and soils are examples of renewable resources. Minerals, ores, coal, and oil are exhaustible resources. Sometimes the term *exhaustible resources* is also used to refer to both renewable and nonrenewable resources. A broader definition of environmental resources would include newly discovered or defined resources such as biodiversity, the ozone layer, and atmospheric and other sinks, in addition to conventional natural resources. Most of these resources are best understood as renewable or depletable resources.

Exhaustible resources are categorized further by the U.S. Bureau of Mines and the U.S. Geological Survey (1976) on the basis of the economic feasibility of their extraction and the state of knowledge on their quantity and quality: Resources are identified or undiscovered, and economic or subeconomic. Identified and economic resources constitute reserves. Reserves, such as those of oil, increase when technology changes and reduces extraction costs, making it economically feasible to extract previously identified but subeconomic resources. New discoveries can also increase reserves if it is economically feasible to extract them.

The 1972 book *The Limits to Growth: A Report for the Club of Rome's Project on the Predicament of Mankind* (Meadows, Meadows, Randers, and Behrens 1972) raised concerns upon its publication regarding the future availability of key resources. Its computer simulations, which were based on the postwar experiences of high population and economic growth and the prevailing technological performance of the time, suggested that a continuation of resource use as it was happening would result in the exhaustion of many important resources such as oil, coal, and metals in a few decades. However, the standard economic argument is that when resources become scarcer, new stocks are called into reserves by increasing prices. Price increases also give incentives for technological development and new discoveries that harness new resources to replace the ones that are exhausted. The exhaustion of resources is not a problem from an economic point of view if the proceeds from resource use can be invested in a way that compensates for the loss of economic returns from the resource use.

While the predictions of the report have not become literally true, some general trends have played out: Population growth, increasing income levels, and globalization have put pressure on renewable resources, in particular, to such an extent that physical scarcity and absolute limits have to be taken seriously. In their article "Human Appropriation of the Products of Photosynthesis" (1986), Peter M. Vitousek and his coauthors estimate that humans consume 40 percent of total terrestrial net primary production. Boris Worm and his coauthors in "Impacts of Biodiversity Loss on Ocean Ecosystem Services" (2006) find that global fish landings have diminished since 1994 despite significantly increased fishing efforts, and that the main commercial fisheries are likely to collapse in the coming decades if marine biodiversity is not protected effectively. In their article "Tracking the Ecological Overshoot of the Human Economy" (2002), Mathis Wackernagel and his coauthors estimate that the global mean ecological footprint is 2.3 hectares per person, but it is twice that figure in Europe and four times higher in the United States. This means that many developed countries have to import carrying capacity, often from the developing world, as described by Marc L. Imhoff and his coauthors in "Global Patterns in Human Consumption of Net Primary Production" (2004). The global ecological footprint, the area needed to produce the goods and resources that humanity uses, currently amounts to 1.3 Earths. According to the authors, we currently overshoot the carrying capacity of the earth by a large margin.

SEE ALSO *Natural Resources, Nonrenewable*

BIBLIOGRAPHY

Imhoff, Marc L., Lahouari Bounoua, Taylor Ricketts, et al. 2004. Global Patterns in Human Consumption of Net Primary Production. *Nature* 429 (6994): 870–873.

Jevons, W. Stanley. 1871. *The Theory of Political Economy.* London and New York: Macmillan.

Meadows, Donella H., Dennis L. Meadows, Jørgen Randers, and William W. Behrens III. 1972. *The Limits to Growth: A Report for the Club of Rome's Project on the Predicament of Mankind.* New York: Universe Books.

U.S. Bureau of Mines and the U.S. Geological Survey. 1976. Coal Resource Classification System of the U.S. Bureau of Mines and U.S. Geological Survey. *Geological Survey Bulletin* 1450-B.

Vitousek, Peter M., Paul R. Erlich, Anne H. Erlich, and Pamela A. Matson. 1986. Human Appropriation of the Products of Photosynthesis. *BioScience* 36 (6): 368–373.

Wackernagel, Mathis, Niels B. Schulz, Diana Deumling, et al. 2002. Tracking the Ecological Overshoot of the Human Economy. *Proceedings of the National Academy of Sciences of the United States of America* 99 (14): 9266–9271.

Worm, Boris, Edward B. Barbier, Nicola J. Beaumont, et al. 2006. Impacts of Biodiversity Loss on Ocean Ecosystem Services. *Science* 314 (5800): 787–790.

Jouni Paavola

RESOURCES, EXHAUSTIBLE

SEE *Natural Resources, Nonrenewable.*

RESOURCES, NATURAL

SEE *Natural Resources, Nonrenewable.*

RESPONSE, CONDITIONED

SEE *Classical Conditioning.*

RESPONSE, UNCONDITIONED

SEE *Classical Conditioning.*

RESPONSE BIAS

SEE *Survey.*

RESPONSE RATE

SEE *Survey.*

RESTITUTION PRINCIPLE

The theory of restitution is a neglected aspect of international and national income accounting. The concept addresses the problem of how to measure, and account for, the costs and benefits of systemic economic injustice. What are the economic consequences of longstanding, historically grounded, systemic exploitation, wrongful taking, unjust enrichment, unequal exchange, immoral accumulation, and excessive profiteering based on racial, ethnic, religious, or language-cultural domination and control? Restitution theory provides a basis for understanding and analyzing problems of chronic poverty and inequality, and developing rational public policy remedies.

A related concept is the restitution principle. It is a moral concept that says that if a society democratically decides that certain practices, such as slavery, segregation, and discrimination, are wrong and makes them illegal, then it is not morally acceptable to retain class pecuniary benefits that were produced by those past practices. These benefits must be returned to the class from which they were taken. Whenever there are chronic grievances—between nations, races, or other large social groups—a fundamental issue is invariably the sense that one party has systematically perpetrated unremedied economic injustices.

The theory of restitution is based on the intuition that it is possible to:

- Reconstruct historic economic relations.

- Specify "fair" standards for prices, wages, terms of trade, and interest rates.

- Specify fair rates of return on investments that were violated, usually by force.

- Audit the historic pattern of transactions between the groups in question.

- Compare the actual with the "fair" standard, then estimate the deviation from "fairness."

- Designate that result as unjust enrichment, and estimate its present value and distribution.

- Draw policy implications that will usually lead to remedies in the form of lump sum or other redistributive income and wealth transfers, in-kind subsidies, or investments in real and human capital.

In the case of African Americans, for example, for four hundred years, income and wealth have been coercively diverted from Africans and African Americans to the benefit of Europeans and European Americans. This was primarily done through slavery, then Jim Crow segregation, and then discrimination in education, housing, and labor and capital markets. It is possible now to reconstruct that history in detail, develop national income accounting tools to regularly measure the magnitude of income and wealth transfers, then estimate their present value and distribution.

These unjust enrichments were not dissipated. They were transferred intergenerationally and are currently held by whites in the top 30 percent of the income and wealth distribution. The processes that produced the benefits are now widely regarded as wrong, illegal, and illegitimate. They violate current standards of fairness; therefore, the benefits these processes produced are unjust, and should be returned to those who were harmed or to their descendants collectively.

This becomes a matter of restitution. And the restitution owed—by some estimates, $5 to 10 trillion—can be paid through adjustments in tax and budget policies over approximately forty years. The restitution could also be paid primarily through investments in human capital, housing, and business formation.

U.S. national income accounts do not help much in managing social dysfunction. They overlook unjust enrichment. Similarly, U.S. international income accounts overlook systemic unequal exchange—overcharges and underpayments between trade and investment partners who have asymmetric power and bargaining strength. Without proper accounting, policymakers produce weak concepts and weak policies and programs that fail to remedy problems of poverty and underdevelopment. Scholars and policymakers do recognize disparities and inequalities, and the basic reasons for continuing chronic economic distress, among many African Americans, have been thoroughly documented. But the descriptions and analyses do not produce policies sufficient to manage or solve the phenomenon of gross disparities in income and wealth by race. Economists and other social scientists and policy analysts have focused on the costs of racial exclusion and discrimination. But that is an incomplete approach, and one reason that relatively little progress has been made against intransigent, chronic economic underperformance and persistent poverty.

The concept of restitution is based on the understanding that justice and morality are fundamental to sound public policy. And retaining unjust enrichment is inconsistent and incompatible with holding in perpetuity benefits derived from past immoral and wrongful systemic transactions and processes. Americans, for example, can acknowledge that much wealth has been built in the past by methods that cannot stand scrutiny by today's standards, even though such methods may have been acceptable at the time. But morality according to the restitution principle makes it impossible to accept the fruits of wrongful actions that were committed on one's behalf—as posterity—by one's collective if not direct biological ancestors.

Boris Bittker's *The Case for Black Reparations* (1973) examined these questions thoroughly and successfully. He dealt with all the common objections—that raising these issues now, so late in the game, is ex post facto, and that justice is not meted out that way under the American system. In response, Bittker argued that there is ample precedent for finding retroactive responsibility and culpability, and correcting it, if practicable. As part of national and international accounting, government and nongovernmental agencies can perform the statistical and analytical work in the process of managing national economic life.

In the U.S. case, slavery, primarily agricultural slavery, produced benefits for over two hundred years. But many Americans only think of slavery in terms of agricultural commodity production. In fact, slavery generated great benefits in other ways as well. Slaves were used in manufacturing, services, and activities that today would be called municipal or state government, running transportation, utility, and emergency services. Enslaved people also cleared land and built infrastructure—roads, dams, levees, canals, railroads, and bridges. Without this labor, it can be argued, the United States would not have expanded west as it did. Indeed, it is possible, and perhaps probable, that the United States would never have become a continental nation. It likely would not have been able to complete the Louisiana Purchase, nor gain the territories that became the Southwest and West Coast states, so vital to twentieth-century growth. Without the labor of enslaved people, the United States could well have ended, territorially, at about the Mississippi River, and never emerged as a world power. The point is not to speculate on counterfactual history, but the crucial role of slave labor in creating the basis for expansion and total continental development is worth underlining.

Slave-produced goods and services benefited most white Americans indirectly and passively through the process of human capital formation. Slaves made it possible for many whites to go into more rewarding occupations, gain increased skills, and generate greater lifetime earnings for themselves and their descendants. In these indirect and passive ways, slavery produced enormous benefits beyond those usually considered that flowed directly from production. Similarly, after the slavery era, exclusion and discrimination allowed millions of Americans and immigrants to enter occupations with greater prospects. In these ways, racism generated income and wealth that flow to present-day recipients. That is an important reality, and its consequences can be measured.

Historian Theodore Hershberg studied immigration and found that successful, accomplished black tradespeople and skilled operators were displaced by immigrants. So it is not simply a matter of black entrance being blocked. Black earnings were established, then forcibly discontinued by private practice and by conscious, active, wrongful interventionist public policy.

Discrimination continued through the mid-twentieth century. During the twentieth century, discrimination produced far greater benefits than those piled up during the preceding 270 years because of the greater population and size of the economy. The most significant sources of unjust enrichments have fairly recent origins, notwithstanding the dramatic effects of compound interest on the earlier, longer stream of coercively, interracially diverted income.

Exploitation, exclusion, and discrimination were mechanisms that produced unjust enrichment. *Exploitation* is a loaded term that carries great emotional baggage with the general public even when used in a technical sense. In restitution analysis, exploitation refers to super benefits over and above "normal" returns on investment, or above a unit of labor's marginal productivity. *Exclusion* refers to what is usually known as *occupational discrimination*, in which whites occupied jobs that otherwise, in a freely competitive market, would have been occupied by blacks of equal ability and training, exerting equal effort. *Discrimination* refers to three other phenomena in addition to occupational discrimination. First, employment discrimination is commonly seen in the "last-hired, first-fired" practice, whereby blacks and whites of equal endowments experience different lengths of employment in similar economic cycles. Second, wage discrimination refers to situations in which whites and blacks, equally endowed, receive different wages for the same occupational and skill contribution. Third, there are other forms of discrimination, as outlined by economist Lester Thurow in *Generating Inequality* (1975). These include discrimination in capital, housing, medical and health care, and other subtle twentieth-century practices.

All these differential practices produce a diversion of income and wealth in the United States from blacks to whites. All of them made whites better off relative to blacks, in the aggregate, than they otherwise would have been in a society, and in markets, using free and openly competitive selection processes.

The total consequence of these direct and indirect, active and passive methods of diverting income and wealth interracially resulted in unjust enrichment that can be measured. The information will be salutary for all concerned, and it will focus policy discussion on constructive remedies. That leads to the "so what?" question: What difference will this information make? What practical value will restitution theory have? Managing overall national economic performance requires that policymakers understand the concept of unjust enrichment and the restitution theory. Economic underperformance is caused in part by the alienation of millions of people who believe they are victims of injustice, and withhold their best efforts in response.

Systemic economic arrangements often are imposed by dominant social groups on less powerful ones. Invariably, these patterns of transactions produce costs for the latter and benefits for the former. Economic injustices, sustained over time, produce cumulative benefits—that is, unjust enrichment. This can be measured. When such cumulative benefits are measured, the results can then be introduced into public policy discussions for the purpose of acknowledging the transgressions, admitting the consequences, and accepting the fact that remedies are proper, feasible, and just.

Restitution theory offers a basis for correcting the lopsided results of distortions in markets characterized by coercion, exclusion, and discrimination. It raises the prospect that the simple fact of illuminating economic relationships this way will, in and of itself, tend to reduce the offending behavior. That is because a major reason the injustices occurred in the first place, and then perpetuated, was that a veil of ignorance rested over the phenomena. Restitution theory lifts that veil, and will make it harder in the future for economic injustices to become systemic. Such injustices rely on the fact that their magnitude is not understood. Once their magnitude is discovered, political and social forces will mobilize to stop the practices and to retrieve the unjust enrichments that have been produced.

SEE ALSO *Discrimination; Discrimination, Racial; Discrimination, Wage, by Race; Genocide; Immigration; Jim Crow; Justice; Reparations; Slavery*

BIBLIOGRAPHY

Bittker, Boris. 1973. *The Case for Black Reparations.* New York: Random House.

Hershberg, Theodore. 1981. *Philadelphia: Work, Space, Family, and Group Experience in the 19th Century: Essays Toward an Interdisciplinary History of the City.* New York: Oxford University Press.

Thurow, Lester. 1975. *Generating Inequality: Mechanisms of Distribution in the U.S. Economy.* New York: Basic Books.

Richard F. America

RESTRAINT THEORY
SEE *Weight.*

RESTRICTED STOCKS
SEE *Stocks, Restricted and Unrestricted.*

RETALIATION

Retaliation historically refers to a legal provision that punishes the perpetrator of physical injury, whether committed as a deliberate act or through negligence, in exact conformity to the type and amount of damage that was inflicted. In a broader sense, retaliation refers to a system of justice in which the measure of payback for harms done (not just physical harms) is stated in law and recognized as equivalent punishment or compensation. In some modern contexts, retaliation for inflicting injury, quite broadly conceived, continues in use but with an extended application.

First attested in the laws of Hammurabi from ancient Babylonia c. 1750 BCE, the law of retaliation is undoubtedly best known in the form of the biblical injunction "an eye for an eye, a tooth for a tooth" (Exod. 21:23–25; similarly, Lev. 24:17–21). This provision is also known in Roman legal terminology as *lex talionis* (Latin *talion* is at the root of English "retaliation"), although Roman law (Table VIII. 2, c. 450 BCE) permitted pecuniary compensation in the place of literal retaliation. It has been argued that compensation as an alternative means of satisfaction reflects an evolution of customary practices that dealt with the inadequacy of literal retaliation, namely, the potential to increase the number of physically maimed persons in society. Although compensation became the explicit norm in Roman, Jewish and medieval law, there also is evidence for it in the laws of Hammurabi (for example, laws ¶¶ 203–204), and it dominates the relevant sections of the laws of Eshnunna (laws ¶¶ 42–48, 55–57), Babylonian laws only slightly earlier than Hammurabi. It is likely that compensation, either set by law or negotiated between the relevant parties, was always an option available to the injured party.

The purpose of laws of retaliation originally may have been to curtail excessive vengeance by or on behalf of a wronged party that would have provoked a spiral of retaliatory attacks. These laws set a just balance: an eye for an eye, or compensation determined to be equivalent. Additionally, the law may have been meant to deter prospective perpetrators by drawing attention to the personal cost of actions that cause injury. Literal retaliation prompts you to value my eye (or other body part, or life, or child, or whatever) as much as you value your own. If you would not deliberately remove your own eye, then do not deliberately remove mine, else I demand yours of you; and as you would guard against negligently losing your own eye, so you should equally guard against negligently losing mine, else I demand yours of you.

In ancient and medieval societies justice was usually not impartial; it graded punishments and compensation according to the social statuses of the perpetrator and the victim. So, for example, in the laws of Hammurabi, if an *awīlu* (a high-status person) blinded the eye of a fellow *awīlu*, then the penalty was the blinding of his own eye. However, if he blinded the eye of a commoner, then fixed monetary compensation was paid. Should an *awīlu* blind the eye of a slave, a lesser fixed monetary compensation was due, apparently to the slave owner (laws ¶¶ 196, 198–199; compare Exod. 21:26, where the blinded slave is allowed to go free, thus compensating the slave, but in common with Hammurabi, the higher-status perpetrator is not blinded). Laws of retaliation reflected and served to reinforce status distinctions in society, and thus protected the honor of high-status individuals. Certain individuals, their family members, their body parts, and their pain, were simply worth more than lower-status individuals under the law.

The developing polity, as a law-making body, assumed the role earlier performed by the extended kin group to regulate retaliatory punishments and to maintain the social status–honor regime. In modern western law, tort law regulated by the state-appointed courts has replaced retaliation, and covers a myriad of "injuries" for which one can seek redress, although the determination of just pecuniary compensation that dominates tort law obviously has roots in its ancient and medieval counterpart. "Retaliation" still features in current U.S. law in respect to employment. "Unlawful retaliation" pertains to actions taken by an employer that discriminate against an employee under the provisions of Title VII of the Civil Rights Act of 1964. If, for example, an employee makes a claim or supports the claim of a fellow worker in respect to discrimination or harassment in the workplace based on the Civil Rights Act, the employer cannot retaliate against the employee to materially adversely affect the employee in terms or conditions of employment (section 704(a) of Title VII). The Supreme Court's 2006 decision in *Burlington Northern and Santa Fe Railway v. White* has significantly lowered the standard claimants must prove to win a retaliation claim. If proven to have retaliated, the employer is liable to pay a court-determined amount in compensation to the harmed employee.

Although laws of retaliation, and tort law generally, focus on individuals, the concept of retaliation has found a distinctively communal application in certain modern contexts. In international relations, for example, the nuclear arms race between the United States and the Soviet Union during the cold war moved the superpowers toward mutually assured destruction. Each developed the capability to destroy the other by launching a retaliatory strike after absorbing a first strike. Nuclear deterrence theory was predicated on the notion that the credible prospect of retaliation should act as a deterrent to a prospective perpetrator.

A second area featuring a communal conception of retaliation is international trade. In this context, trade protection by one nation can issue in trade retaliation by a trading partner, sanctioned by an international body such as the World Trade Organization (WTO). The retaliation might be of a literal kind: a tariff imposed on some good(s) to counteract a tariff imposed by the trading partner, and according to the WTO Dispute Settlement Understanding, the countermeasures should be "equivalent to the level of nullification and impairment" (Article 22.4). That is, the penalty should justly balance the infringement. The point of the retaliation is only partly to obtain compensation for the financial harm caused by protectionist policies of a trading partner. It actually seeks to pressure the protectionist trader to abandon its practices and comply with its WTO commitments. Here retaliation serves mainly as a mechanism to get a party to modify its behavior, but it also serves to warn potential perpetrators because there is a sanctioned retaliatory response.

SEE ALSO *Cold War; Deterrence, Mutual; Policy, Fiscal; Public Policy; Punishment; Restitution Principle; Tariffs; War; World Trade Organization*

BIBLIOGRAPHY

Jürgensen, Thomas. 2005. Crime and Punishment: Retaliation under the World Trade Organization Dispute Settlement System. *Journal of World Trade* 39 (2): 327–340.

LaPointe, Martin K. 2006. The Supreme Court Sets the Standard for Title VII Retaliation Claims: *Burlington Northern & Santa Fe Railway v. White. Labor Law Journal* 57 (4): 205–215.

Miller, William Ian. 2006. *Eye for an Eye.* New York: Cambridge University Press.

Parisi, Francesco. 2001. The Genesis of Liability in Ancient Law. *American Law and Economics Review* 3 (1): 82–124.

Peter R. Bedford

RETALIATION, TARIFF
SEE *Tariffs.*

RETARDATION, MENTAL
SEE *Mental Retardation.*

RETARDATION, PROGRAMMED
SEE *Programmed Retardation.*

RETRIBUTION

SEE *Punishment.*

RETURNS

The idea of returns has a long history in economics. This is not surprising because the concept of a "return" is just the flip side of the concept of cost. Accordingly we may define a return as a change in output (or the cost of producing an additional unit of output) resulting from a change in the quantity of quality of inputs. Adam Smith's famous pin factory discussion of the division of labor in the opening pages of *An Inquiry into the Nature and Causes of the Wealth of Nations* (1776) regards the declining costs associated with productivity-enhancing technical change. David Ricardo, in both the *Essay on Profits* (1815) and *Of the Principles of Political Economy and Taxation* (1817), described the diminishing returns associated with economic growth. Capital accumulation would lead to higher population, increasing the demand for food and thus the need to intensify and extend agricultural production. Intensification of production and the extending of production on to lands of inferior quality or further from the central markets (and thus associated with higher transportation costs) would lead to higher rents and wages, squeezing profits and choking off accumulation.

In economics the distinction must be made between returns to scale and returns to substitution. Returns to scale regards the changes in output resulting from increases in all factors of production (land, labor, and capital). For example, when all inputs are doubled: If output more than doubles, there are increasing returns to scale; if output exactly doubles, there are constant returns to scale; and if output less than doubles, there are decreasing returns to scale. Returns to substitution regards the impact of changing the quantity of one factor of production when one or more other factors are fixed in quantity. For example, when there is an increase in one input, holding the quantity of all other inputs constant: If the cost of producing an additional unit of output falls, there are increasing returns; if the cost of producing an additional unit of output stays constant, there are constant returns; if the cost of producing an additional unit of output rises, there are diminishing returns. There is no such thing as "decreasing returns to scale." If all factors are variable, then they can be combined in the proportions that produce the highest productivity and lowest costs and then replicated. There is no such thing as "increasing returns to substitution," as producers will always use the proportions that give them the lowest cost and highest productivity, even if that means not using the entire quantity of some of a resource.

Piero Sraffa (1925, 1926) showed that the neoclassical versions of nonproportional returns embodied in the U-shaped average cost curve—a necessary component of determining the equilibrium size of the firm in a perfectly competitive market—are indeed problematic. First, the two kinds of nonproportional returns—increasing and diminishing—refer to different parts of economic theory. Increasing returns is part of the theory of general economic progress and so the theory of production, while diminishing returns is part of the theory of rent and so the theory of distribution. Second, in Alfred Marshall's framework, these must be compatible with the ceteris paribus conditions of the partial equilibrium framework while still not violating the assumptions of perfect competition (Marshall 1961). Sraffa shows this to be either terribly unrealistic or logically impossible.

In the case of diminishing returns, unless we find an industry where all firms use a scarce factor, variations in average cost associated with increased production in the industry under consideration will be of the same order of magnitude as variations in costs experienced by other industries using the same scarce factor. This violates the ceteris paribus assumption of partial equilibrium analysis. As for increasing returns, these cannot be present at the same time in both an industry and the firms within it, because otherwise firms will keep on expanding until they reach a size incompatible with perfect competition. Nor can they be found in various industries at the same time, or ceteris paribus conditions will be breached again. Marshall, aware of this, developed a category of economies of production external to the individual firm but internal to the industry. This may be proper in terms of perfect competition and partial equilibrium but wholly unrealistic.

Sraffa's conclusion that we may find some use in the "old classical" conception of constant costs may help in theoretical models, but this does not mean that he did not acknowledge the importance of economies of scale and increasing returns in the real economy. Allyn Young (1928) just a few years later went back to Smith's discussion of the division of labor and drew out its contemporary relevance for economic growth. One of Young's students at the London School of Economics, Nicholas Kaldor, combined the Smith-Young insight into the mutually reinforcing relation between economic growth and technical progress and wed it to a dynamic version of John Maynard Keynes's principle of effective demand in his notion of cumulative causation (Kaldor 1972). This analysis resulted in Kaldor's "polarization thesis" regarding the division of the global economy into rich, industrialized nations and poor, developing national economies, which has links to the Prebisch-Singer hypothesis of declining terms of trade between the two sets of countries (Prebisch 1950; Singer 1950). Even in Smith there is the asymmetric analysis of manufactures and agriculture, the former characterized by increasing returns and the latter by diminishing returns. This was abandoned by Marshall, whose model portrays all factors of production symmetrically, experiencing increasing returns as production begins and diminishing returns as production continues (as in the U-shaped average cost curve). Marshall also abandoned the qualitative aspects of returns, limiting the causes to quantitative differences only. Thus the important distinction between the classical and neoclassical notions of returns.

SEE ALSO *Average and Marginal Cost; Competition; Competition, Perfect; General Equilibrium; Marshall, Alfred; North-South Models; Partial Equilibrium; Returns to a Fixed Factor; Returns to Scale; Returns to Scale, Asymmetric; Returns, Diminishing; Returns, Increasing; Risk-Return Tradeoff; Sraffa, Piero*

BIBLIOGRAPHY

Kaldor, Nicholas. 1972. The Irrelevance of Equilibrium Economics. *Economic Journal* 82 (328): 1237–1255.

Marshall, Alfred. 1961. *Principles of Economics.* 9th ed. London: Macmillan.

Prebisch, Raul. 1950. *The Economic Development of Latin America and Its Principal Problems.* New York: United Nations.

Ricardo, David. [1815] 1951–1973. An Essay on the Influence of a Low Price of Corn on the Profits of Stock. In *The Works and Correspondence of David Ricardo*, vol. 4, ed. Piero Sraffa, 1–48. Cambridge, U.K.: Cambridge University Press.

Ricardo, David. [1817] 1951–1973. *Of the Principles of Political Economy and Taxation.* In *The Works and Correspondence of David Ricardo*, vol. 1, ed. Piero Sraffa. Cambridge, U.K.: Cambridge University Press.

Singer, Hans W. 1950. The Distribution of Gains between Investing and Borrowing Countries. *American Economic Review Papers and Proceedings* 11: 473–485.

Smith, Adam. [1776] 1937. *An Inquiry into the Nature and Causes of the Wealth of Nations*, ed. Edwin Cannan. New York: Modern Library.

Sraffa, Piero. 1925. Sulle relazione fra costa e quantita prodotta. *Annali di economia* 2: 227–328.

Sraffa, Piero. 1926. The Laws of Returns under Competitive Conditions. *Economic Journal* 36 (144): 535–550.

Young, Allyn. 1928. Increasing Returns and Economic Progress. *Economic Journal* 38 (152): 527–542.

Mathew Forstater

RETURNS, DIMINISHING

The French economist Anne-Robert-Jacques Turgot (1727–1781) is credited with introducing the concept of diminishing returns into economics. In production the-

ory, it refers to the changes in output associated with changes in some inputs, called variable factors, while other inputs, called fixed factors, are held constant. The relation is stated as a law: *with given production techniques, the increment to output associated with each additional unit of a variable factor applied to a given amount of a fixed factor will* eventually *diminish*, which is why it is more properly called the Law of Eventually Diminishing Returns.

The short-run concept of diminishing returns is not to be confused with the long-run concept of returns to scale. The latter refers to changes in output when all inputs are altered in equal proportion. Diminishing returns caused by a hidden fixed factor has, however, been offered as one explanation of the observation of what appears to be diminishing returns to scale.

Diminishing returns provides a possible explanation of the eventual positive slope of cost curves in the short run (defined as a situation in which at least one key input is fixed). However, its most famous application was made in 1798 by the English economist Thomas Robert Malthus, who argued that increased population (and capital) applied to the given amount of a nation's land would eventually encounter diminishing returns. Each new person added to the labor force would then add less and less to total production, until living standards are reduced to the subsistence level. It is non-controversial that, if techniques of production remain constant, increases in population (and all other inputs) with land held constant, must encounter diminishing returns to agricultural output and, hence, cause falling living standards. Malthus also noted that, if unchecked, populations tend to grow at a geometric progression. He then added the arbitrary assumption that the growth of productivity, due to the development of new technologies, would follow an arithmetic progression, which researchers today know to be incorrect. This theory produced two famous predictions. First, the growth of population and capital would eventually lead to continually falling living standards until bare subsistence is reached. Second, the growth of capital alone could raise living standards but at a falling rate (due to diminishing returns) until the arrival of the "stationary state" in which per capita income could not be raised further. These predictions led the Scottish historian Thomas Carlyle (1795–1881) to label economics "the dismal science."

A related concept, called diminishing returns to income, is used in the economic theory of consumption. It holds that successive increments of income give decreasing amounts of satisfaction (what economists call utility) since people's most pressing needs will be satisfied first and then as income rises further, along with the consumption that it permits, successively less and less pressing needs will be met. The concept was long regarded as an untested although plausible hypothesis. Research summarized by Richard Layard in 2005 has, however, succeeded in measuring satisfaction and has largely confirmed the hypothesis of diminishing returns to consumption—although not necessarily that of diminishing returns to income, since income may serve other purposes than permitting consumption, such as conferring power and prestige.

Physical diminishing returns is often appealed to by those who believe that sustained growth is impossible. They argue that when variable amounts of human capital and effort are applied to the world's fixed amount of resources, diminishing returns must sooner or later be encountered, slowing and eventually halting growth. Modern students of the accumulation of knowledge, and the technological change that it allows, argue otherwise. They make two points. First, unlike most economic entities that are rivalrous—if one person uses a machine, another person cannot simultaneously use it—knowledge is nonrivalrous—if one invents a new technology, everyone can use that knowledge simultaneously. Second, there is no reason to believe that the accumulation of knowledge will encounter diminishing returns when acting through the new technologies that it enables. New knowledge occasionally generates new general purpose technologies (GPTs) such as the steam engine, electricity, and the computer. These in turn make possible a massive set of derivate technological applications. There is no law in physics or economics that suggests that the power of successive GPTs to generate derivative innovations will lessen over time. Indeed, it is clear that the dynamo brought with it a much richer implied research program than did the steam engine.

Knowledge accumulation is the historical process that has allowed humanity to overcome diminishing returns through the invention of new technologies, which have enabled bursts of economic growth throughout history. The accelerating creation of new technological knowledge since the first industrial revolution may well permit the circumvention of diminishing returns by being the source of sustainable improvements in living standards in the foreseeable future.

SEE ALSO *Returns; Returns to a Fixed Factor; Returns to Scale; Returns to Scale, Asymmetric; Returns, Increasing*

BIBLIOGRAPHY

Appleman, Philip, ed. 2004. *An Essay on the Principle of Population: Influences on Malthus' Work Nineteenth-Century Comment, Malthus in the Twenty-first Century.* 2nd ed. New York: Norton.

Layard, Richard. 2005. *Happiness: Lessons from a New Science.* London: Penguin Books.

Lipsey, Richard G., Kenneth Carlaw, and Clifford Bekar. 2005. *Economic Transformations: General Purpose Technologies and Long-Term Economic Growth.* New York: Oxford University Press.

Malthus, Thomas Robert. 1798. *An Essay on the Principle of Population, as It Affects the Future Improvement of Society with Remarks on the Speculations of Mr. Godwin, M. Condorcet, and Other Writers.* London: J. Johnson.

Romer, Paul. 1993. Idea Gaps and Object Gaps in Economic Development. *Journal of Monetary Economics* 32: 543–573.

Kenneth I. Carlaw
Richard G. Lipsey

RETURNS, INCREASING

A firm or an industry, having a given technology, exhibits increasing returns to scale if an increase in the inputs it uses to produce a particular product increases its output more than proportionately. This effect is evidenced in a decreasing long-run average cost curve. While the increasing returns concept has relevance for both microeconomics and contemporary growth theory, historically it dates from Adam Smith's *Wealth of Nations* (1776), which links the cost experiences of manufacturing firms to the division of labor (Smith 1776, Book I, Chapter 3). The practice leads to specialization and therefore the capability among those who specialize to trade their surpluses, which has the effect of expanding the market. Under perfect competition, declining cost has the effect of reducing selling prices. Although it reduces profits, it increases the real incomes of all classes.

Antoine Augustin Cournot, a French mathematician, was the first among several thinkers to note that increasing returns to scale are incompatible with price-taking behavior by competitive firms (Cournot 1838, pp. 59–60). A decade later, John Stuart Mill also became cognizant that economies of scale could compromise competitive markets. This possibility was, however, categorically negated by Alfred Marshall, who rejected the idea that increasing returns to scale characteristically cause industries to become monopolized. He invented external economies in the form of "general improvements," which are equally available to all firms in the industrial environment and were believed to account for the already observable tendency in the England of his day to explain declining commodity prices. Economies that are internal to firms are self-limiting, Marshall believed, partly because the full effects of economies of scale are likely to be impeded because over time "the guidance of business falls into the hands of people with less energy and less creative genius" (Marshall 1890, p. 316). Thus, Marshall maintained that monopolistic tendencies would be curbed, and competition would continue to prevail, rendering unfounded Mill's fear that increasing returns to scale would compromise pure competition; that is, firms and industries invariably produce under conditions of increasing supply price, which explains the upward slope of the industry supply curve.

The definitive theoretical challenge to Marshall's conclusion that increasing returns to scale are compatible with ongoing pure competition was articulated by Piero Sraffa, who maintained that the economies needed to satisfy Marshall's logic "were nowhere to be found" (1926, p. 540). Marshall's particular equilibrium analysis was designed to explain price determination in a competitive industry that is identifiable in terms of the cost curves of its "representative firm." These cost curves must be independent of those of all other firms in the industry and the industry's factor suppliers. Thus, economies that are external to the representative firm but internal to the industry of which it is a part, which is a requirement of the particular equilibrium method, are incompatible with Marshall's methodology. If these economies exist at all, they are "in the middle where nothing or almost nothing is to be found" because Marshall's explanation of increasing returns is methodologically inconsistent (Sraffa 1926, p. 542). Sraffa recommended that economists give up trying to explain competitive prices and turn their attention instead to explaining prices under imperfect competition. Shortly afterward this became the objective of Joan Robinson (1933) and Edward Chamberlin (1933).

More recently, Marshall's concept of increasing returns to scale has been "rediscovered" by contemporary "new growth" theorists (Romer 1986, 1987), who have taken the "internal-external economies" construct out of its original particular equilibrium setting in which it was intended to explain competitive price determination. They have placed it into a Walrasian general equilibrium context in which the prices of all commodity and factor markets are interdependent. The premise of the model is that the external effects of knowledge and capital accumulation can amend the Cobb-Douglas productions function by a multiplicative factor to generate endogenous growth in the affected economies. It is ironic that the theoretical problem that Sraffa identified as being associated with Alfred Marshall's concept of external economies to explain the compatibility of increasing returns and competitive equilibrium has been revived within a general equilibrium framework that is clearly incompatible with the cost-independence requirement of Marshall's particular equilibrium analysis.

By the mid-1920s, with the assembly-line production of automobiles and other industrial products already a fact of life, a trend toward oligopoly—that is, competition among the few—was already apparent. Shortly afterward, the advent of the theories of "imperfect" and "monopolis-tic" competition (Robinson 1933; Chamberlin 1933) challenged the predominance of pure competition on the premise that product demand curves had come to exhibit a downward slope because firms engaged in differentiating their output had become able to charge prices in excess of the competitive "law of one price." While they were not monopolists of their own commodities, they were able to establish demand curves for their particular brands that were less price elastic than would be the case in competitive markets in which product homogeneity assured that buyers had no basis for preferring one seller's product over another. More recently, despite the institutional and theoretical relevance of the theory of imperfect and monopolistic competition, many thinkers maintained that economies of scale could be theoretically reconciled with perfect competition. A case in point is the interpretation by contemporary trade theorists. Helpman and Krugman (1985) argue that increasing returns might prevail as an external effect that can generate economic growth as an endogenous phenomenon and thus preserve Marshallian perfect competition.

The most forward-looking post-Marshallian interpretation about the relationship between increasing returns and market competition came from Allyn Young's return to Smith's theme of division of labor. In his presidential address to the British Association for the Advancement of Science, "Increasing Returns and Economic Progress," Young noted that "the most important single factor in determining the effectiveness of its industry appears to be the size of its market" (1928, p. 122) and whether it is sufficiently large to generate increasing returns. Except for the impetus that comes from new knowledge, economic progress is principally generated by division of labor to realize more fully the economies of capitalistic or roundabout methods of production. Thus, Young's "Increasing Returns" paper specifically separated Marshall's increasing returns concept from its particular (i.e., microeconomic) industry setting and, following Smith, extended increasing returns to the economy as a whole. Thus, Young anticipated the role of Keynes's emphasis on aggregate demand and Nicholas Kaldor's theory of increasing returns in the process of economic growth. Yet it is only comparatively recently that Young's special insight into the process of growth as "self perpetuating, rather than self-exhausting" has been recognized (Blitch 1983; Sandilands 2000; Rima 2004).

SEE ALSO *Returns; Returns to a Fixed Factor; Returns to Scale; Returns to Scale, Asymmetric; Returns, Diminishing*

BIBLIOGRAPHY

Blitch, C. 1983. Allyn Young on Increasing Returns. *Journal of Post-Keynesian Economics.* Spring 5(3), 59–372.

Chamberlin, E. [1933] 1948. *The Theory of Monopolistic Competition.* Cambridge MA: Harvard University Press.

Cournot, A. 1939. *Recherches sur les principes mathématiques de la théories des recheses.* Paris: M. Riviére.

Helpman, E., and P. Krugman. 1985. *Market Structure and Foreign Trade.* Cambridge MA: MIT Press.

Kaldor, N. 1966. *Causes of the Slow Rate of Economic Growth in the United Kingdom.* Cambridge, U.K.: Cambridge University Press.

Marshall, A. 1890. *Principles of Economics.* London: Macmillan.

Mill, J. S. 1848. *Principles of Political Economy, with Some of Their Applications to Social Philosophy.* London: J. W. Parker.

Rima, I. H. 2004. Increasing Returns, New Growth Theory and the Classicals. *Journal of Post-Keynesian Economics* 27 (1): 171–184.

Robinson, J. 1969. *The Economics of Imperfect Competition.* 2nd ed. London: Macmillan.

Romer, Paul. 1986. Increasing Returns and Long-Run Growth. *Journal of Political Economy* 94 (5): 1002–1037.

Romer, Paul. 1987. Growth Based on Increasing Returns Due to Specialization. *American Economic Review* 77 (2): 56–62.

Sandilands, R. J. 2000. Perspectives on Allyn Young in Theories of Endogenous Growth. *Journal of the History of Economic Thought* 22 (3): 310–328.

Smith, A. 1776. *An Inquiry into the Nature and the Courses of the Wealth of Nations.* New York: Modern Library, 1937.

Sraffa, P. 1926. The Laws of Return under Competitive Conditions. *Economic Journal* 36 (December): 535–550.

Symposium on Increasing Returns and Unemployment Theory. 1985. *Journal of Post-Keynesian Economics* 7 (3): 350–409.

Young, A. 1928. Increasing Returns and Economic Progress. *Economic Journal* 38 (December): 527–542.

Ingrid H. Rima

RETURNS TO A FIXED FACTOR

A *factor of production* is any input that contributes in a positive way to a production process. For example, to grow wheat a farmer requires inputs such as seed, farm machinery, land, and labor. Economists aggregate factors into three categories: (1) *land* or *natural capital* (such as soil, the air individuals breathe, or the fish in the sea); (2) *labor* (the skills people have and their education, the hours they work and how they cooperate and interact with each other); and (3) *capital* (machinery and tools that can be used to produce other goods).

An input that can only be changed in a production process in the long run is called a *fixed factor*. A factor may be fixed because: (1) the input might take a long time to build or replace; (2) it has few substitutes and is required in fixed proportion to other inputs; or (3) more cannot be purchased because its supply is fixed in the short run.

The return to a fixed factor is the payment to owners of fixed inputs. This return is related to the concept of economic rent, described by the English economist David Ricardo (1772–1823) in *Principles of Political Economy and Taxation* (1817) and defined as the payment in excess of the minimum required to elicit the supply of an input in the long run. Rent is like a windfall gain and can arise because of a factor's overall scarcity, but may also be due to differential quality, location, or other desirable characteristics of particular units of the input, as shown by R. Quentin Grafton et al. in *The Economics of the Environment and Natural Resources* (2004, pp. 215–216).

If demand exceeds current supply at the existing price, an input's price will be bid up, thereby attracting a greater supply in the future. The larger the excess demand and the slower the supply response to a price increase, the greater will be the amount a firm has to pay for an input. Thus a factor fixed in supply, all else equal, will accrue greater returns per unit than if its supply were highly responsive to price changes. Similarly, if a factor is fixed because of inflexibilities in the production process, then any price increase imposes a greater cost burden than if the short-run use of the input could be varied.

Returns to fixed factors have a major influence on the world economy. For example, due to excess demand, the price of crude oil more than doubled over the period 2002 to 2005, despite an increase in supply. Because oil is an essential input into many production processes, firms have, in the short run, little choice but to pay the higher prices in order to maintain their production. The beneficiaries of these price hikes are oil producers. By providing a factor that has few substitutes in many production processes and is also, more or less, globally fixed in supply in the short run, petroleum suppliers receive a windfall gain. These surpluses are worth hundreds of billions of dollars each year and affect the standards of living of millions of people. High oil prices, in turn, encourage oil exploration that should increase supply in the future and also provide incentives for firms to modify their input mix and become less reliant on oil.

SEE ALSO *Rent; Returns; Returns to Scale; Returns to Scale, Asymmetric; Returns, Diminishing; Returns, Increasing*

BIBLIOGRAPHY

Grafton, R. Quentin, Wiktor Adamowicz, Diane Dupont, et al. 2004. *The Economics of the Environment and Natural Resources.* Malden, MA: Blackwell.

Ricardo, David. [1817] 1891. *Principles of Political Economy and Taxation.* Ed. E. C. K. Gonner. London: George Bell.

R. Quentin Grafton

RETURNS TO SCALE

Returns to scale are defined as the relation between an equi-proportionate change in all the inputs used in a commodity's production and the resulting proportionate change in the output of that commodity. The three possibilities are labeled "decreasing," "constant," or "increasing returns," depending on whether a given proportionate change in all inputs causes a less than proportionate, a proportionate, or a more than proportionate change in output. Although economists debate what generates these effects, all three types are used in microeconomic theory. The common assumption in neoclassical macroeconomics is that gross domestic product (GDP) behaves as if it were generated by an aggregate production function obeying constant returns to scale.

While commonly used in economics, the concept is also used in many of the social and physical sciences. For example, in 1986 Nathan Rosenberg and L. E. Birdzell noted that the invention of the three masted sailing ship allowed Europeans to build larger ships exploiting increasing returns to scale, such as carrying capacity increasing more than in proportion to the increase in materials for construction. In 1991 Leonard Dudley analyzed military returns to scale. Some technologies, such as stone-age weapons, entailed constant returns (a larger army could expect casualties equal to those of a smaller opponent), while others, such as bronze weapons, entailed increasing returns (a larger army could expect fewer casualties than a smaller opponent). Other applications of the concept include the analysis of networks, social organization, governance, and technological change.

Mainstream micro-economists typically argue that constant returns to scale, and hence horizontal long run average cost curves, are ubiquitous given complete divisibility of all inputs. The argument is in two parts. First, decreasing returns are ruled out because it is assumed that all production activities can be replicated, for example, by building a series of identical factories, identically run and managed. Second, increasing returns are ruled out by the proportionality postulate, which states that in the absence of indivisible inputs or hidden fixed factors, any activity can be subdivided so that an equi-proportionate reduction in all inputs yield the same percentage reduction in output. Thus, if there were increasing returns to scale, the larger scale of activities could be achieved and then subdivided, leaving inputs per unit of output unchanged.

The commonly assumed U-shaped long run average cost curve for a firm, with its single most efficient scale of output, is then explained in two parts. First, the falling part (increasing returns to scale) is due to such things as indivisibilities (or "lumpiness") in some inputs so that too much must be used at small scales of output. The rising portion (decreasing returns) is usually explained rather weakly by

such things as diseconomies of management in coordinating the activities of many separate production units.

An alternative view, implicit in the work of the nineteenth-century Austrian capital theorists such as Eugene von Böhm-Bawerk and Knut Wicksell, is that returns to scale are latent in the superior productive power of indirect or intermediate production processes that create capital goods. In the twentieth century, scholars B. Curtis Eaton and Richard G. Lipsey examined this theme, providing a proof by contradiction of the existence of latent returns to scale. Lipsey, Kenneth Carlaw, and Clifford Bekar develop this further in 2005. In their research, they maintained that the standard abstract argument for constant returns to scale based on replication and the proportionality postulate is scholastic in purporting to deduce empirical relations from a priori considerations. They argued that checking the hypothesis of the ubiquitous possibility of replication requires an appeal to empirical evidence. For example, replication may not be possible if more output is required at a point in space, such as building a larger bridge over a narrows or applying more pumping power at the pit head of a coal mine. They observed that "… if the list of possible missing inputs is defined as anything that might cause the neoclassical production function to display decreasing returns, such as climate, spatial conditions of production … and a host of other unspecified influences, the proposition becomes tautological and hence uninteresting empirically" (Lipsey et al., p. 399).

Lipsey and colleagues argued similarly with respect to the proportionality postulate. If, for example, one wishes to halve the horsepower of some automobile, a smaller engine is needed. But neither "subdividing" by halving the engine's dimensions, nor by halving all the inputs that make it, will halve the engine's power output. Physics shows that halving its dimensions alters its cost of production, the power delivered, and running costs in different proportions, while halving all the inputs is technically inefficient because of the different dimensionality of the various components. They further argued, " '[h]istorical increasing returns' [to scale] arise because the scale effects are permanently embedded in the geometry and physical nature of the world in which we live, but our ability to exploit them is dependent on the existing state of technology" (Lipsey et al., p. 397).

Increasing returns to scale also arise from complementarity among components of capital and the risk of breakdown, and decreasing returns from the time cost associated with waiting to extract the service flow from durable capital goods. In all of these cases, the relationship between indivisibilities and returns to scale is the reverse of the mainstream view. Indivisibilities—building capital goods with more capacity than the minimum possible—

are the consequence of endogenous decisions to exploit naturally occurring scale effects, whereas in the mainstream view, exogenous indivisibilities are the cause of scale effects.

SEE ALSO *Returns; Returns to a Fixed Factor; Returns to Scale, Asymmetric; Returns, Diminishing; Returns, Increasing*

BIBLIOGRAPHY

Böhm-Bawerk. 1889. *Positive Theory of Capital.* Trans. W. Smart. New York: Scechert.

Carlaw, Kenneth I. 2004. Uncertainty and Complementarity Lead to Increasing Returns to Durability. *Journal of Economic Behaviour and Organization* 53 (2): 261–282.

Dudley, Leonard. 1991. *The Word and the Sword: How Techniques of Information and Violence Have Shaped Our World.* Cambridge, U.K.: Cambridge University Press.

Eaton, B. Curtis, and Richard G. Lipsey. 1997. Increasing Returns, Indivisibility and All That. In *On the Foundations of Monopolistic Competition and Economic Geography: The Selected Essays of B. Curtis Eaton and Richard G. Lipsey.* Cheltenham, U.K.: Edward Elgar Publishing.

Koopmans, Tjalling C. 1957. *Three Essays on the State of Economic Science.* New York: McGraw-Hill.

Lipsey, Richard G., Kenneth Carlaw, and Clifford Bekar. 2005. *Economic Transformations: General Purpose Technologies and Long-Term Economic Growth.* New York: Oxford University Press.

Rosenberg, Nathan, and L. E. Birdzell. 1986. *How the West Grew Rich.* New York: Basic Books.

Wicksell, Knut. [1893] 1954. *Value, Capital and Rent.* London: Allen and Unwin.

Kenneth I. Carlaw
Richard G. Lipsey

RETURNS TO SCALE, ASYMMETRIC

The forces which make for Increasing Return are not of the same order as those that make for Diminishing Return: and there are undoubtedly cases in which it is better to emphasize this difference by describing causes rather than results. (Marshall 1890, p. 266)

Asymmetric returns to scale are defined in three ways in economics. The first is the one referred to in the above quote, which is an asymmetry among increasing, constant, and decreasing returns to scale that may exist because decreasing returns to scale are thought by many to be implausible if the theoretical exercise concerning returns to scale is conducted properly. Therefore, there may be no symmetric counterpart to the increasing returns portion of production so that long run average cost curves are not symmetrically U-shaped. (Notice that the existence of decreasing returns does not necessarily imply exact symmetry in the shape of the cost curve and so this concept defined in this way is perhaps inappropriately labeled.) The a priori argument for the lack of decreasing returns is that observed apparent decreasing returns to scale actually depends on the existence of a hidden or fixed factor such as managerial or entrepreneurial capacity so that the required scaling of all factors is not actually occurring.

One counterargument to the existence of asymmetry under the first definition was provided in 2004 by Kenneth Carlaw. In his work Carlaw showed that scale effects result from the complementarities among components that make up capital goods and the risk associated with how long each component will last. The cost minimizing agent will create more durability of components than is needed for one period's final production in order to exploit the scale effects inherent in the nature of multiple component systems and environmental uncertainty. However, at some point decreasing returns to scale set in for the durability of the capital good that is obtained from the scaling up of the durability of its components. Thus in such cases returns to scale are symmetric in the sense that increasing and then decreasing returns to scale are encountered as production with multicomponent capital goods is scaled up.

In 2005 Richard Lipsey, Kenneth Carlaw, and Clifford Bekar introduced another argument justifying the existence of diminishing returns to scale: Because real world production takes place in spatial contexts duplication may not always be possible. When and where it is possible must then be determined on empirical not a priori grounds.

A second definition of asymmetric returns to scale is that they are encountered when new technologies are applied in varying contexts. The same technology may be applied in a variety of different production, market, and institutional contexts as it emerges and is diffused across different economies. For example, lean or "just-in-time" production applied in North America is generating lower returns than in China. One suggested reason is that China has no pre-existing manufacturing infrastructure and managerial orthodoxy, whereas North American manufacturing has a solidified structure that has evolved out of the technology of mass production. It is therefore not a good fit for lean production techniques and is generating lower returns.

A third definition of asymmetric returns to scale is found in the arguments of Nicholas Kaldor. His view is that asymmetry in the returns to scale encountered in developed and developing economies arise because of differences in the goods they produce. The comparative advantage of developing economies leads them to specialize in production technologies that have decreasing returns to scale (e.g., agriculture) while developed economies specialize in technologies that have increasing returns to scale (e.g., manufacturing).

SEE ALSO *Production Function; Returns; Returns to a Fixed Factor; Returns to Scale; Returns, Diminishing; Returns, Increasing*

BIBLIOGRAPHY

Conway, P., and William Darity Jr. 1991. Growth and Trade with Asymmetric Returns to Scale: A Model for Nicholas Kaldor. *Southern Economic Journal* 57 (3): 745–759. http://cepa.newschool.edu/het/essays/product/returns.htm.

Kaldor, Nicholas. 1978. *Further Essays on Economic Theory.* London: Duckworth.

Lipsey, Richard G., Kenneth I. Carlaw, and Clifford T. Bekar. 2005. *Economic Transformations.* Oxford: Oxford University Press.

Marshall, Alfred. 1890. *Principles of Economics.* London: Macmillan and Co. Ltd.

Kenneth I. Carlaw
Richard G. Lipsey

REVEALED PREFERENCE

The theory of revealed preference was originally developed by Paul Samuelson using choice as a primitive to derive some fundamental principles of demand theory. In contrast, in the traditional framework of utility theory approach, the weak preference ordering of a chooser is the primitive. The motivation was that an observer does not know or observe a chooser's preferences, but a bundle of goods a consumer buys is observable. Put differently, Samuelson's objective was to derive the laws of demand from assumptions regarding price-quantity data without getting into any traces of preferences. The basic approach is based on the notion that in a given price-income situation, a chooser has an affordable set of consumption bundles, the *budget set*, and if a consumer chooses a particular bundle over all alternative bundles in the budget set, then this choice is revealed to be the chooser's underlying preference.

This revealed preference is not necessarily the true preference of the chooser. Rather, it is the chooser's "as if" preference. Suppose for a price-income situation (p,M), $B(p,M)$ is the budget set. A demand function is a rule that specifies exactly one element of $B(p,M)$ for every budget set $B(p,M)$. If both x and y are in $B(p,M)$, and x is chosen, then x is said to be (directly) strictly *revealed preferred* to y. It is *directly* revealed preferred because both x and y are compared in a budget set $B(p,M)$; it is *strictly* revealed preferred since x is chosen from a budget set while y is rejected, since demand function is single-valued.

Samuelson introduces a condition, known as the *weak axiom of revealed preference* (WARP), which says that if x is (directly) strictly revealed preferred to y, then there is no other price-income situation (i.e., budget set) in which y will be chosen while x is available. In other words, WARP requires that if x is (directly) strictly revealed preferred to y, then y cannot be (directly) strictly revealed preferred to x. It can be viewed as a two-term consistency. If the demand function satisfies the WARP, then it must satisfy the property that a demand function is homogeneous of degree zero in income and prices; it exhibits the nonpositivity of the own compensated price effect (i.e., the substitution effect); and for every normal good, the price effect must be nonpositive. There are additional implications of the utility theory approach to consumer behavior (namely, symmetry of the cross-substitution term) that are not implied by the WARP.

The rationalizability of the demand function in terms of weak preference orderings implies that the consumer behaves as if he or she has a weak preference ordering and, given the budget set, he or she optimizes on the basis of a realized preference ordering. Rationalizability in terms of weak preference orderings implies, but is not implied by, the WARP. So the WARP needs to be strengthened. Suppose x and z are two alternatives that never appear together in any budget set. In addition, suppose x is (directly) strictly revealed preferred to y, y is (directly) strictly revealed preferred to u, u is (directly) strictly revealed preferred to w, and w is (directly) strictly revealed preferred to z. Then we say x is *indirectly strictly revealed preferred* to z. Strengthening the WARP from a two-term consistency requirement to a multiterm consistency—known as the *strong axiom of revealed preference* (SARP), which says that if x is (directly) strictly revealed preferred to y, then y cannot be directly or indirectly strictly revealed preferred to x—it can be demonstrated that this stronger requirement is a necessary and sufficient condition for the rationalizability of a demand function in terms of weak preference orderings (Houthakker). Furthermore, the SARP, together with a continuity condition, implies the existence of a utility function that rationalizes the consumer's revealed preferences. This establishes the logical equivalence of the revealed preference approach and the utility theory approach.

Following Samuelson's pioneering work, the revealed preference approach was developed further in an abstract choice theoretic framework. For any given universal set of alternatives X, consider all possible nonempty subsets [X] of X, which is the power set of the universal set minus the empty set. Consider a well-specified family S of nonempty subsets of X; i.e., S is a subset of [X]. A choice function is a rule, $C(\cdot)$, which for any element A of S specifies a nonempty subset of A, that is, $C(A)$ is a subset of A. Note that $C(A)$ is not necessarily single-valued. Clearly, demand function is a special case of a choice function. Now for any A in S, if x is in $C(A)$ and y is in A, then x is said to be (directly) revealed preferred to y. If x and z together are not in any S, and if x is (directly) revealed preferred to y, y is (directly) revealed preferred to u, u is (directly) revealed preferred to w, and w is (directly) revealed preferred to z, then x is said to be indirectly revealed preferred to z.

For Samuelson, a choice function must be single-valued, and the domain S must be the convex polyhedra (or the budget triangles in a two-commodity world) since the objective is to derive the laws of demand of a competitive consumer (i.e., a price taker) from observed data. For the domain $S = [X]$, the multiterm consistency requirement of the SARP is collapsed into a two-term consistency. Consequently, the WARP becomes equivalent to the SARP (Arrow).

Suppose a multivalued choice function is defined over any arbitrary domain S, a subset of [X]. Marcel Richter (1966) introduces a condition, called *congruence axiom*, which says that if x is (directly) revealed preferred to y, then y cannot be directly or indirectly revealed preferred to x. This condition is necessary and sufficient for transitive rationalization of a multivalued choice function in a general domain framework. Clearly, using this general approach, the demand theory results can be derived as a special case. This generalized framework helps to analyze rational choice in a wider context, such as social choice theory, voting theory, and production analysis.

The revealed preference approach developed in two directions. Following the requirement of the preference-based approach that a weak preference relation is transitive, the revealed preference literature originally developed to focus on transitive rationalization of a choice function. For the existence of a maximum, transitivity is indeed very restrictive. A less restrictive requirement could be transitivity of strict preference relation (known as *quasi-transitivity*) and the least restrictive requirement could be acyclicity of strict preference relation. The WARP requires that no revealed inferior alternative of a set A can be chosen in any other set in the presence of *any* revealed preferred alternative in A. This consistency condition can be weakened by simply requiring that no revealed inferior alternative of a set A can be chosen in any other set in the presence of *some* revealed preferred alternative in A. This

weaker requirement turns out to be a necessary and sufficient condition for quasi-transitive rationalization of a choice function. Furthermore, if one requires that no revealed inferior alternative of a set A can be chosen in any other set in the presence of *some* alternative in A, then this condition turns out to be necessary and sufficient for (acyclic) rationalization of a choice function. These results are obtained for the domain $S = [X]$ using Samuelsonian revealed preference approach (Bandyopadhyay and Sengupta). Following Arrow's approach, there is a large literature on alternative characterization of various weak rationalization for the domain $S = [X]$. The results for the domain $S = [X]$ can also be obtained for the domain that consists with all pairs and triples in [X]. However, there is no complete characterization of weaker rationalization result for any arbitrary S that is a subset of [X].

The other line of development is in the context of stochastic demand theory. For every price-income situation (p,M), a stochastic demand function (SDF) is a rule d, which, for a given budget set $B(p,M)$, specifies exactly one probability measure q over the class of all subsets of $B(p,M)$. Let $q = d(p,M)$, where d is an SDF, and let A be a subset of $B(p,M)$. Then $q(A)$ is the probability that the bundle chosen by the consumer from $B(p,M)$ will lie in the set A. Let $B(p,M)$ and $B(p^*,M^*)$ be the budget sets for two price-income situations. A stochastic demand function, d, satisfies the *weak axiom of stochastic revealed preference* (WASRP) whenever for all pairs of price-income situations, and for all subsets of the intersection of the two budget sets, A, $q^*(A) - q(A) \leq q(B(p,M) - B(p^*,M^*))$, where $q = d(p,M)$ and $q^* = d(p^*,M^*)$. WASRP generalizes laws of demand from its deterministic environment to a stochastic environment (Bandyopadhyay, Dasgupta and Pattanaik, 1999). The rationalizability of a stochastic demand function in terms of stochastic orderings has also been established. Recently, these results are generalized further by considering a stochastic demand correspondence.

The revealed preference theory has been applied largely in the evaluation of economic index numbers and in empirical tests of consistency in consumer behavior. The WARP can be used to evaluate directly a given index number.

SEE ALSO *Demand; Preferences; Samuelson, Paul A.; Tastes; Utility Function*

BIBLIOGRAPHY

Arrow, Kenneth J. 1959. Rational Choice Functions and Orderings. *Economica* 26: 121–127.

Bandyopadhyay, Taradas, and Kunal Sengupta. 1993. Characterization of Generalized Weak Orders and Revealed Preference. *Economic Theory* 3: 571–576.

Bandyopadhyay, Taradas, Indraneel Dasgupta, and Prasanta K. Pattanaik. 1999. Stochastic Revealed Preference and the Theory of Demand. *Journal of Economic Theory* 84: 95–110.

Houthakker, H. S. 1950. Revealed Preference and the Utility Function. *Economica* (N.S.) 17: 159–174.

Richter, Marcel K. 1966. Revealed Preference Theory. *Econometrica* 34: 635–645.

Samuelson, Paul. A. 1948. Consumption Theory in Terms of Revealed Preference. *Economica* 15: 243–253.

Taradas Bandyopadhyay

REVENUE

A firm's revenue is distinguished from its profit: Revenue is the total money received by the firm ("total revenue"), whereas profit is total revenue less total cost. *Revenue* and *total revenue* are usually synonyms, but the latter term is used especially to delineate total money received, as distinct from the "marginal revenue" of each unit and the "average revenue" received for all units.

Marginal revenue is a central concept in microeconomic theory (Marshall [1890] 1961). It is the change in total revenue created by a one-unit increase in the quantity sold. As long as marginal revenue is positive, increasing output will cause total revenues to increase. Mathematically, marginal revenue is the derivative of total revenue with respect to quantity. Average revenue is the money collected per unit, or total revenue divided by quantity. When all units of a firm's output (q) are sold for the same price (p), total revenue is price multiplied by quantity, pq, and both marginal and average revenue are equal to price.

A perfectly competitive firm's marginal revenue is determined solely by price because a single firm's chosen quantity of production has a negligible effect on the market price. When one firm in a perfectly competitive market decides to produce and sell one more unit of output, the market price does not change, and so the increase in the firm's revenues is exactly equal to the number of dollars brought in by that extra unit: its price. The mathematics behind this intuition recognizes that in this case, the derivative of total revenue is $d(pq)/dq = p$ because price (p) does not change as the firm's output (q) changes.

A firm with market power wields a double-edged sword. The firm can set the price for its output, but it still must contend with a downward-sloping demand curve: Selling more output requires a decrease in price, by the "law of demand." Because of these two effects (increasing quantity while decreasing price), marginal revenue is made up of two components. When the firm decides to produce and sell one more unit of output, (1) selling more of the good increases revenue, while (2) lowering price means that less revenue is collected on each of the units that could have been sold at the higher price. Thus marginal revenue must be less than price for a firm with market power (rather than equal to price, as in the case of perfect competition, above). The two components of revenue are, respectively, the output effect and the price effect. A mathematical analysis recognizes that price now changes as the firm's quantity changes: The derivative dp/dq is nonzero. The derivative of total revenue is thus $d(pq)/dq = p + (dp/dq)q$. The first term is the output effect and the second term is the price effect. The price effect is negative because price falls when quantity rises, and this means that the marginal revenue of producing and selling one more unit of output is less than the price for which each unit can now be sold.

Marginal revenue is also closely related to the own-price elasticity of demand, or the responsiveness of quantity demanded to a change in price. A decrease in price when demand is "elastic" causes a greater percentage increase in quantity demanded than the percentage decrease in price—thus revenues must increase. A decrease in price when demand is "inelastic," in contrast, causes a smaller reaction in quantity demanded, and so revenues will fall. This is especially relevant when a firm is choosing the optimal quantity to sell and costs are fixed as the quantity sold changes: Maximizing total revenue is equivalent to maximizing profits in this case. For example, a toll-road operator should decrease price as long as the resulting increase in drivers (quantity) compensates for the loss in revenue per unit. In other words, price should be decreased as long as demand is still elastic. Total revenue (and in this case, profits) will be maximized when demand is neither elastic nor inelastic. This is also the quantity at which marginal revenue is zero.

The firm with market power thus far has been assumed to sell all units of its output for the same price; that is, it does not "price discriminate." When the firm does price discriminate it can do so either by setting separate prices for each customer or setting separate prices for different customer groups, or by adjusting price according to each customer's quantity purchased. Average revenue will vary as quantity changes, depending on the method of price discrimination, and so total revenue may not be simply price multiplied by total quantity. One example is a quantity discount: In this case, larger quantities will have lower average revenue than smaller quantities. Another example is when the customer must pay a fee for the right to purchase each unit (a "cover charge" or "membership fee"): Total revenue includes both this fee and the revenues collected on each unit's sale, so average revenue (per unit sold) decreases as quantity increases.

In fact, the ability to price discriminate allows the firm with market power to reduce the negative effect that the law of demand has on marginal revenue. The firm can set a higher price for those units of output for which customers have a higher willingness to pay, and set a lower price only for those units of output for which there is a lower willingness to pay. As output increases, charging separate prices for each unit or group of units purchased mitigates the price effect. The price effect may even fall to zero. Thus, when the firm price discriminates, it can be true that marginal revenue approaches price and the economic outcome may approach that of perfect competition, except that the economic value created is reallocated toward the price discriminating firm and away from the customer. This means that a firm with market power may produce more output if it can price discriminate than if it cannot. The firm will benefit from this practice, and this advantage to society may more than outweigh the loss to the consumer.

SEE ALSO *Revenue, Average; Revenue, Marginal*

BIBLIOGRAPHY

Marshall, Alfred. [1890] 1961. *Principles of Economics.* 8th ed. New York: Macmillan.

Christopher S. Ruebeck

REVENUE, MARGINAL

Marginal revenue is a concept introduced into economics by neoclassical economists, especially Alfred Marshall in his *Principles of Economics* (1890). It became a central concept in discussion of market structure with the publication of Joan Robinson's *The Economics of Imperfect Competition* and Edward Chamberlin's *The Theory of Monopolistic Competition*, both published in 1933. Since then it has been taught in all courses in microeconomics as part of the theory of the firm.

Marginal revenue refers to the change in total revenue arising from a change in output, where the change in output can denote a rise or fall and is usually thought of as a one-unit change. More formally,

$$MR = \frac{\text{Change in total revenue}}{\text{Change in output}} = \frac{\Delta TR}{\Delta Q}$$

where *MR* denotes marginal revenue, *TR* denotes total revenue, and *Q* the level of output. Δ is the symbol to denote "a change in."

When used in terms of market structure, marginal revenue is related to the demand curve. The demand curve is also the average revenue curve, because it denotes the price people are willing to pay for each particular quantity. In perfect competition the demand curve is horizontal at a particular price, whereas for the typical demand curve, it is downward sloping, indicating that the quantity rises when the price falls. The relationship between marginal revenue and demand is obtained by considering the change in total revenue (ΔTR). Because total revenue is price times quantity, then $TR = P.Q$ and $\Delta TR = P.\Delta Q + Q.\Delta P$. Hence, marginal revenue can be expressed as

$$MR = \frac{\Delta TR}{\Delta Q} = P + Q.\frac{\Delta P}{\Delta Q}.$$

Under perfect competition, the price does not change whatever the level of output, so $\Delta P/\Delta Q = 0$ and hence marginal revenue is equal to price, which in turn is equal to average revenue. In market structures other than perfect competition, the demand curve is downward sloping, in which case $\Delta P/\Delta Q < 0$, and so marginal revenue is less than price and the marginal revenue curve lies below the average revenue curve—the curve that denotes the price for any level of output.

The concept of marginal revenue is useful when it is combined with other marginal concepts, especially *marginal cost*, which refers to the change in total cost when output changes. More specifically, because profit is the difference between total revenue and total cost, then if marginal revenue exceeds marginal cost, profit must be increasing. Profits are falling when the reverse inequality holds. This means maximum profits can be identified when marginal revenue is equal to marginal cost. In the case of perfect competition, this also means that at the profit-maximizing output level, price is equal to marginal cost. However, under imperfect competition, monopolistic competition, and other market structures such as oligopoly, at the profit-maximizing output level, marginal revenue is below average revenue, which means price is above marginal cost (which is equal to marginal revenue). Both these results have social implications.

If price is equal to marginal cost (equal to marginal revenue), then society is paying at the margin just what it costs society to produce that final extra unit. This is the condition that holds under perfect competition. In contrast, in market structures where the demand curve is downward sloping, price is above marginal cost (which is equal to marginal revenue) at the profit-maximizing output level. Socially, this means that society is paying at the margin more than it is costing society to produce that last unit. In the case of monopoly, this leads to monopoly profits. This is not the case under monopolistic competition, where in the long run such profits can be eliminated as firms enter the industry. What can be observed from this analysis therefore is that it is the combination of marginal concepts that is important, and marginal revenue is just one of these.

Although marginal revenue, along with other marginal concepts, is taught in most courses in microeconomics, the concept is limited. The market structures referred to above in which the concept of marginal revenue played such an important part applies only to a single product firm. In fact almost all neoclassical analysis applies to single-product firms, which are abstract entities: not only do the firms produce only one product, but there is no internal organization. It would be difficult to apply the concept of marginal revenue to a modern multiproduct multinational company. Even so, as a logical concept it can eliminate muddled thinking.

SEE ALSO *Average and Marginal Cost; Competition; Competition, Imperfect; Competition, Monopolistic; Competition, Perfect; Economics, Neoclassical; Economics, Neo-Ricardian; Marginalism; Maximization; Profits; Revenue; Revenue, Average*

BIBLIOGRAPHY

Chamberlin, Edward H. 1933. *The Theory of Monopolistic Competition.* Cambridge, MA: Harvard University Press.

Pindyck, Robert S., and Daniel L. Rubinfeld. 2004. *Microeconomics.* 6th ed. New York: Prentice Hall.

Robinson, Joan. 1933. *The Economics of Imperfect Competition.* London: Macmillan.

Ronald Shone

REVOLUTION

Revolution as applied to social change originally referred to the overturning of a government but not to changes that ushered in a new age. From the fourteenth through the seventeenth centuries, Europeans spoke of "revolutions" when one form of government gave way to another, as when a monarchy was overthrown or restored or a city-state's government shifted between republican and aristocratic rule.

The notion of political revolutions as overturning tradition, creating a new era, and thereby bringing about progress was first used toward the end of the eighteenth century to describe the overthrow of monarchies and the founding of national republics in the United States in 1776 and France in 1789. Inspired by the intellectual movement of the Enlightenment, which aimed to make reason the arbiter of governing and social institutions, opponents of traditional authority saw these events as breaking the shackles of tradition and ushering in a new

era of freedom under rationally conceived political institutions. Thomas Paine, in *The Rights of Man* (1791), referred to both the "American Revolution" and "The French Revolution" in this manner.

Since the eighteenth century, the notion of revolution as marking a major break with the past, destroying old ways, and bringing progress has been applied to numerous historical and intellectual events. Archaeologists call the prehistoric onset of agriculture the Neolithic Revolution. In economics, the shift from agricultural to industrial economies is called the Industrial Revolution. In science, major shifts in leading theories are commonly labeled scientific revolutions, such as the Darwinian Revolution or the Copernican Revolution, while the term "Scientific Revolution" is used to denote the shift from traditional natural philosophy to experimental science that occurred from the sixteenth to the eighteenth centuries. More recently, agronomists have used the term "Green Revolution" to describe the widespread adoption of high-yield grains and artificial fertilizers in East Asia. In military tactics, the introduction of stealth, satellite, and laser technologies has been labeled "the revolution in military affairs." Almost every area of human endeavor thus has come to use the term "revolution" to mark relatively sudden, progressive change.

SOCIAL AND POLITICAL REVOLUTIONS: HISTORICAL PATTERNS

The most common use of the term *revolution* in the social sciences is to designate major, sudden changes in political regimes, especially when carried forward through mass demonstrations or popular revolts and accompanied by attacks on government officials or elites, on public or private property, or on symbols of elite status or political authority. Such events are called "political revolutions" when they alter government institutions but leave much of the economic and social structure of society intact; they are called "social revolutions" (or "great revolutions") when they alter not only government structures but also the organization of the economy, the social hierarchy, the role of religion, and major symbols and beliefs regarding authority and national identity.

Revolutions are a form of internal political conflict, related to popular rebellions, civil wars, or coups d'état. Revolutions usually include one or more of these events; but these events, by themselves or in combination, do not constitute a revolution (or attempted revolution). What defines revolution is not merely challenges to political authority or contests for power but efforts to change a society's major political or economic or religious institutions.

Although the term is relatively new, revolutions can be identified in history as far back as ancient Egypt, where the Old Dynasty was overthrown amid popular revolts and the pharaoh was replaced by committees of notables. In classical Greece and Rome, and in medieval European city-states, political conflicts often led to a monarchy being overturned and replaced by a republic, or a republic being overthrown and replaced by a monarch or tyrant. Another form of revolutionary movement that arose in many parts of Europe, Asia, and Africa—from the early days of Christianity to the White Lotus rebellions in eighteenth-century China—were religiously inspired movements that sought to replace secular authorities with rule by a charismatic savior or a community of "saints."

The distinctively modern idea of revolution that developed in the eighteenth century was to see revolutions as permanent and progressive changes in the entire social order, changes that replaced outmoded and unjust political, economic, religious, and social institutions with a new social organization based on reason. This kind of revolution has since taken several forms.

Constitutional revolutions sought to replace traditional monarchies or empires with republics bound by newly written rules that would limit state power, end the privileges of hereditary elites, and confer rights and responsibilities on citizens. Major examples include the American Revolution (1776); the French Revolution (1789); the Revolutions of 1848 in France, Germany, and Austria; the Turkish Revolution of 1919; the Iranian Revolution of 1905; and the Chinese Republican Revolution (1911).

Anticolonial revolutions aimed to end rule by foreign countries, drawing on nationalist identities to inspire resistance and the foundation of new institutions of local self-rule. In many cases, nationalist traditions were in fact newly developed by elites, and in some cases self-rule became rule by local elites rather than citizen-based democracy. Major examples include the Latin American revolutions (1808–1828), the Vietnamese (1954) and Algerian (1962) revolutions, the Indian independence movement (1949), and the Mozambique and Angolan revolutions (1974).

Fascist revolutions also drew on nationalist traditions but used them to mobilize mass support for the replacement of weak monarchies or republics with authoritarian regimes. Major examples include Italy (1921) and Germany (1933).

Communist revolutions, inspired by the historical theories of Karl Marx, aimed to overturn existing regimes and replace them with one-party states that abolished private property. They created dictatorships that destroyed economic elites "in the name of the people." Major examples include Russia (1917), China (1949), and Cuba (1959).

Antidictatorial revolutions, provoked by the excessive corruption or depredations of modernizing dictatorships, aimed to create new regimes based on constitutions or one-party states. Major examples include Mexico (1911), Nicaragua (1979), and the Philippines (1976).

Some revolutions combined these features; for example, the Vietnamese revolution was anticolonial and Communist. Other revolutions were distinctive and fit none of these categories; examples include the South African anti-apartheid revolution (1994), which replaced a racially exclusive regime with a multiracial democracy, or the Iranian Islamic Revolution (1979), which replaced a modernizing dictatorship with an elected government that was overseen by nonelected religious leaders.

The last several decades have seen the emergence of yet another kind of revolution, the "people power" or "color" revolutions—so termed because popular demonstrations toppled dictators, not by mass violence, but instead by rallying huge crowds around symbols of national unity and popular opposition, which were mainly colored symbols such as yellow or orange ribbons, roses, or tulips. Examples include the Philippines (1976), Ukraine (2004), Georgia (2003), and Kyrgyzstan (2005). Other examples include the Velvet Revolution in Czechoslovakia (1989) and the Cedar Revolution in Lebanon (2005).

SOCIAL AND POLITICAL REVOLUTIONS: CAUSES, PROCESSES, OUTCOMES

Despite their varied nature, social and political revolutions have been generally rooted in a similar set of causes. These are: (1) a crisis of state authority, often rooted in fiscal problems, military pressures, a succession crisis, or severe corruption, though it can also reflect the rise of religious or nationalist grievances against the ruling regime; (2) major divisions among and defections by the official, military, economic, and/or religious elites of the state, weakening the state and providing leadership to the opposition; (3) economic conditions that are perceived as unjustly imposing hardships on workers or peasants, and that the state is held responsible for causing or failing to ameliorate; and (4) a broad culture of opposition, which unites different social and political groups around a set of ideologies and symbols that produce antistate coalitions among diverse groups and that justifies and encourages efforts to oppose the regime. Such a culture of opposition generally draws on both historical memories of resistance and modern ideologies that depict the injustices of the current regime. In some cases, a fifth condition is important: international conditions, alliances, or conflicts that weaken the power of the ruling regime and offer opportunity or support to opposition movements seeking to challenge state power.

The presence of these conditions is rarely, if ever, created simply by the efforts of revolutionary movements. Rather, such movements create some conditions, exacerbate some conditions once they begin, and take advantage of others. In many cases, the ruling regime itself creates the conditions for revolution by blundering into military or fiscal crises, alienating elites, and forging a culture of opposition by engaging in repression of opponents that is widely seen as unjustified or excessive. Revolutions thus often arise unexpectedly, as neither states nor revolutionaries expect to create all these conditions; rather, a combination of actions by state leaders, elites, and revolutionary movements, plus shifting international or economic conditions, creates the necessary conjunction.

Once a revolution begins, the process of revolution can be long drawn out. Even where the central government collapses quickly, the conflicts that ensue among moderate and radical groups contesting for power, or between the new revolutionary state and recalcitrant regions or groups, can lead to civil war, as in France, Russia, and Mexico. It thus may be a decade or more before a stable revolutionary government is established.

Alternatively, revolutionary movements may gradually establish themselves in remote regions of the countryside, patiently winning allies and extending their zones of control, and waiting for weakness and defections from the ruling regime. In such cases, although the revolutionary regime may take years or even decades to come to power, once the central government has fallen the new regime is often battle-hardened and ready to suppress its remaining foes and quickly take control of the country. This was the pattern in the Chinese and Cuban Communist revolutions.

Where the process of revolution involves drawn-out struggles for power, such processes generally favor the rise of more extreme, radical groups. These groups are often more ruthless in attacking their enemies and better able to rouse popular support by claiming more truly to embody new national identities and to be more devoted to popular demands for rapid change. Revolutions thus typically begin with a mix of moderate and radical groups in opposition to the regime; yet in the course of struggles for control of the new revolutionary state, more extremist groups tend to win out and banish or destroy the moderate opposition. Eventually, however, the regime becomes more stable and conservative, seeking mainly to conserve its power and privileges.

In some cases, the conflict between moderates and radicals persists, leading to a "second phase" of radicalism. In this phase, radicals come to worry that the original revolutionary impetus has been lost and that current officials in the revolutionary regime have become conservative; they therefore launch a renewed set of radicalizing policy initiatives. This often takes place one or two decades or more after the onset of the revolution. Examples include the Jacksonian Revolution in the new United States, the Proletarian Revolution launched by Mao Zedong in China, the radical and nationalizing policies undertaken by Lazaro Cardenas in Mexico, and the radical foreign and nuclear policies backed by Mahmoud Ahmadinejad in modern Iran.

The process of revolutionary conflicts can thus stretch over many decades. In France one can argue that the conflicts among republicans and monarchists were not settled until the defeat of Napoleon III by Prussia in 1870, almost a century after the French Revolution had begun. In China, the conflicts among republicans, warlords, Maoist radicals, and economic moderates lasted from 1911 to at least 1989.

While the causes of political and social revolutions are basically similar, the outcomes of revolutions vary greatly. In some cases, revolutionaries start with, and maintain, relatively moderate and focused goals of political change. Examples include the American Revolution (1776), the Latin American Revolutions (1808–1826), and the Philippines Revolution (1996). In other cases, whether through internal or external struggles in defending their revolutionary program or through ideological inspiration, revolutionaries come to embrace a more radical program of economic and social transformation, as occurred in Russia, China, Cambodia, and Cuba.

The political nature of revolutionary regimes also varies. In some cases, revolutionary leaders have been genuinely committed to achieving democracy and guided their new regimes to that goal. Examples include the United States, South Africa, Poland, Hungary, the Czech Republic, and the Philippines. In other cases, revolutionary leaders placed a higher value on staying in power or maintaining the revolutionary regime in the face of powerful threats; in these cases revolutionary regimes swiftly moved toward one-party or personal dictatorships. Examples include France, the Soviet Union, China, Cuba, Mexico, and Algeria. In some cases, the revolutionary outcomes remained mixed and unclear for some time, as with Russia's anti-Communist revolution of 1981 (first moving toward, then away from democracy), or Nicaragua's Sandinista Revolution of 1979 (first moving away, then toward, democracy).

In sum, once begun, revolutions have a wide variety of lengthy trajectories and varied outcomes. It is rarely possible to be certain in advance what those outcomes will be; instead, domestic and international struggles to defend the revolutionary regime almost inevitably reshape it, so that eventual outcomes are more a result of continuing processes and struggles than of a prior plan or the conditions of the former regime.

REVOLUTIONS OF IDEAS AND RELATIONSHIPS: GLOBALIZATION, MODERNIZATION, EXPECTATIONS

Although there were many national and anticolonial revolutions in the twentieth century, these events occurred against a backdrop of general, globalizing change. Some of these changes include substantial gains in life expectancies around the world, huge rises in living standards in developed countries, and vast increases in the flow of people, goods, capital, and information across and within national boundaries.

One result of these changes has been a "revolution of rising expectations." This refers to a major shift in how people in poor regions consider their own circumstances. In earlier times, most poor people considered how they lived in comparison to that of their parents, grandparents, and immediate neighbors. How wealthy landowners, nobles, or businessmen lived was of little concern. However, rapidly rising material wealth in developed countries, plus the flow of information and communications in the form of television, movies, CDs, and travel, have made poorer regions cognizant of the much higher living standards and the progress of democracy elsewhere in the world. This has led to a revolution of "rising expectations," such that even poor people in developing countries now expect their governments to bring material improvements to their locale and provide access for participation.

This revolution of rising expectations can, in some circumstances, feed into political movements of rebellion and revolution as well. Where governments are perceived as actively blocking improvement, as unjustly repressing political expression or social or economic opportunities, then oppositions may mobilize for rebellion. When such states are weakened, elite defections occur, and international conditions are favorable, revolutions in ideas can fuel revolutions in politics. Thus, the age of revolutions is likely far from over.

SEE ALSO *American Revolution;* Battle of Algiers, The; *Coup d'Etat; Cuban Revolution; French Revolution; Guerrilla Warfare; Haitian Revolution; Hungarian Revolution; Internet; Media; Political System; Protest; Resistance; Revolution of Rising Expectations; Revolutions, Latin American; Russian Revolution; Sandinistas; Violence*

BIBLIOGRAPHY

Foran, John. 2005. *Taking Power: On the Origins of Third World Revolutions.* New York: Cambridge University Press.

Goldstone, Jack A. 1991. *Revolution and Rebellion in the Early Modern World.* Berkeley: University of California Press.

Goodwin, Jeffrey. 2001. *No Other Way Out: States and Revolutionary Movements, 1945–1991.* New York: Cambridge University Press.

Selbin, Eric. 1999. *Modern Latin American Revolutions.* 2nd ed. Boulder, CO: Westview.

Skocpol, Theda. 1979. *States and Social Revolutions: A Comparative Analysis of France, Russia, and China.* New York: Cambridge University Press.

Jack A. Goldstone

REVOLUTION, ALGERIAN

SEE Battle of Algiers, The.

REVOLUTION OF RISING EXPECTATIONS

The idea that unfulfilled, rising expectations create unstable political situations has a long tradition in political and social analysis. As far back as the early nineteenth century Alexis de Tocqueville suggested that it explained why the strongholds of the French Revolution were in regions where standards of living had been improving. Throughout the second half of the twentieth century the concept was associated with explanations of revolutions, insurgencies, and civil unrest throughout the world and the urban riots of the 1960s in the United States.

THEORY AND APPLICATIONS

The term *revolution of rising expectations* was popularized during the 1950s in discussions of the foreign and developmental aid policies of the United States. It was used to describe the hope of the poorest counties for a better future in the wake of postwar decolonialization. It was said that rising expectations embodied the twentieth century's "real" revolution insofar as it represented for the vast majority of the world's population a break from centuries of stagnation, fatalism, and exploitation. During the immediate postwar years, regions of Asia, Africa, and the Middle East successfully mobilized national liberation movements against British, French, and Dutch rule to create newly independent countries. Nationalist leaders had fueled their followers' aspirations during struggles for independence and subsequently used promises of industrial development, improved education, and health care to sustain their legitimacy. In India, Indonesia, Malaya,

Burma, Laos, the partitioned Vietnam, and several Middle Eastern countries industrial development based on a Soviet-style planned economy held great attraction, especially in light of the Chinese revolution—a non-Western, nonwhite, and proximate model. In the cold war context the key question was whether a developmental model based on communism or one based on capitalism best satisfied the rising expectations in those countries.

In the 1960s researchers in sociology and political science applied the concept of the revolution of rising expectations to explain not only the attractiveness of communism in many third world countries but also revolutions in general, for example, the French, American, Russian, and Mexican revolutions. In 1969 James C. Davies used those cases to illustrate his J-curve hypothesis, a formal model of the relationships among rising expectations, their level of satisfaction, and revolutionary upheavals. He proposed that revolution is likely when, after a long period of rising expectations accompanied by a parallel increase in their satisfaction, a downturn occurs. When perceptions of need satisfaction decrease but expectations continue to rise, a widening gap is created between expectations and reality. That gap eventually becomes intolerable and sets the stage for rebellion against a social system that fails to fulfill its promises.

The Cuban revolution, the communist insurgency in the Dominican Republic, and several leftist movements in Latin America were attributed to unfulfilled expectations, as was the electoral success of leftist parties such as the election of Jacobo Arbenz in Guatemala (1950) and Salvador Allende in Chile (1970). At the heart of this reasoning was the assumption that the frustration of unfulfilled expectations leads to aggressive behavior, which can be manifested in political rebellion or electoral change.

RELATIVE DEPRIVATION

The idea that unfulfilled expectations create unstable social and political situations is closely related to the variable of relative deprivation as an explanation of civil unrest. Relative deprivation is the perceived discrepancy in what people think they should achieve and what they do achieve. It was the animating concept for a large body of research (Gurr 1970) that attempted to explain both domestic and international civil unrest. The early successes of the civil rights movement in the 1950s had been characterized as a revolution in rising expectations among American blacks, and their perceptions of the slow pace of change during the 1960s were seen as a cause of urban riots in the United States (Geschwender 1964; Runciman 1966). Several studies showed that the most intense rioting occurred in cities where improvement of conditions for blacks had been the greatest.

Most research along these lines on both urban riots and comparative revolution or insurgencies used objective macroeconomic measures to infer deprivation, for example, rising gross national product and regional occupational patterns. However, because relative deprivation is an individual judgment, conclusive proof of its determining role requires survey or interview data to gauge respondents' perceptions directly. Studies that did collect survey data often found that the relationship was weaker than expected (Abeles 1976; McPhail 1971) or that people were much more pragmatic about future expectations than aggregate economic data might indicate (Obershall 1968), suggesting that other variables may cause civil unrest. Also, because perceptions of relative deprivation are individual phenomena, research studies often failed to explain how individual states were translated into collective action, a key process that often was left implicit or assumed.

LATER MODELS

Because of inconclusive empirical proof, methodological constraints, and conceptual criticisms of this body of research, more recent social science models of civil unrest and revolutionary violence have deemphasized the idea of rising expectations, their frustration by state policies, and feelings of relative deprivation. Since the 1990s the focus has been on the structure and strength of state institutions, the mobilization capacity of aggrieved populations, and the cultural processes that channel perceptions of deprivation or injustice into collective action.

SEE ALSO *Anticolonial Movements; Civil Rights; Coup d'Etat; French Revolution; Left and Right; Liberation Movements; Political Science; Political System; Relative Deprivation; Revolution; Social Movements; Stability, Political; Tocqueville, Alexis de; Violence*

BIBLIOGRAPHY

Abeles, Ronald P. 1976. Relative Deprivation, Rising Expectations and Black Militancy. *Journal of Social Issues* 32: 119–137.

Davies, J. C. 1969. The J-Curve of Rising and Declining Satisfactions as a Cause of Some Great Revolutions and a Contained Rebellion. In *Violence in America: The History of Violence in America: Historical and Comparative Perspectives*, ed. Hugh Davis Graham and Ted Robert Gurr, 690–730. New York: Praeger.

Geschwender, James A. 1964. Social Structure and the Negro Revolt: An Examination of Some Hypotheses. *Social Forces* 43: 248–256.

Gurr, Ted Robert. 1970 *Why Men Rebel*. Princeton, NJ: Princeton University Press.

McPhail, Clark. 1971. Civil Disorder and Participation: A Critical Examination of Recent Research. *American Sociological Review* 36 (6): 1058–1073.

Obershall, Anthony. 1968. Rising Expectations and Political Turmoil. *Journal of Development Studies* 6: 5–23.

Runciman, W. G. 1966. *Relative Deprivation and Social Justice: A Study of Attitudes to Social Inequality in Twentieth-Century England.* London: Routledge and Kegan Paul.

Tocqueville, Alexis de. 1955. *The Old Regime and the French Revolution.* Trans. Stuart Gilbert. Garden City, NY: Doubleday.

Hank Johnston

REVOLUTIONS, LATIN AMERICAN

Revolutions are a relatively rare but commonly studied and vaguely understood historical phenomenon. The word *revolution* comes from the physical world and generally refers to a political rotation that replaces those in power with a previously dispossessed class of people. The term is sometimes used so loosely to refer to any palace coup or change of power that it loses all meaning. Alternatively, some historians will restrict usage to highly exceptional events, such as the 1640 English Revolution, the 1789 French Revolution, and the 1917 Bolshevik Revolution. Others contend that even those changes were not profound or permanent enough to warrant use of the term. Some assert that social changes, such as those that accompanied the Industrial Revolution, were more significant than those in the political realm where the term is commonly applied.

Likewise, Latin America scholars have not reached consensus on which events to characterize as revolutionary. Previously the term was commonly applied to early nineteenth-century anticolonial movements. Many scholars now view these as elite movements that, while resulting in political independence from European powers, also entrenched preexisting social, political, and economic structures. The one exception is the 1791 Haitian slave revolt. After ten years of sustained warfare, plantation slaves in this French colony overthrew the planter class, destroyed the sugar-based export economic system, and created a new government led largely by ex-slaves. Although rarely considered as one of the classic examples of a revolutionary movement, it was one of the deepest and most profound revolutionary changes in the history of the modern world. Some have taken its levels of brutal violence and the resulting impoverished state as a caution against attempting revolutionary changes.

Interpretations of what causes revolutionary changes, how to understand them, and how they have uniquely developed in Latin America tend to revolve around numerous themes, including the question of who is most likely to revolt. Writing in a European context, Karl Marx (1818–1883) contended that an urban proletariat would lead revolutionary changes. He considered Latin America, with its lack of an advanced industrial economy, to be not ready for a revolution. In the twentieth century, however, Latin America has perhaps experienced more revolutionary movements than any other area of the world, and these have mostly been led by the peasant classes. Revolutionaries also debated how quickly changes could be implemented, and whether violence was necessary to achieve change.

Revolutions are commonly assumed to emerge out of oppression, but Russian revolutionary Leon Trotsky (1879–1940) famously observed that if exploitation alone caused an insurrection, the masses would constantly be in revolt. Rather, as historian Crane Brinton (1898–1968) argued in *The Anatomy of Revolution* (1965), revolutions emerge out of rising expectations. Latin American events seem to underscore the need for a charismatic leader (such as Fidel Castro in Cuba) who can appeal to a coherent (and often nationalist) ideology that gains broad appeal. Anti-imperialist rhetoric and actions usually trigger strong responses from the United States. A successful revolution required the mobilization of significant organizational and material resources, both to overcome U.S. support for the previous government and to overcome opposition to the new regime. It would also appear that revolutions only succeed with the collapse of a weakened and discredited *ancien régime*. While revolution is often seen as synonymous with violence, notable examples (Chile in 1970, Venezuela in 1989) point to the potential for deep structural changes through peaceful and institutional means.

MEXICAN REVOLUTION

The 1910 Mexican Revolution is often seen as a standard bearer through which other subsequent Latin American revolutions are interpreted. Historians debate whether it was truly a social revolution, a rebellion, a civil war, or a mindless blood-letting. It began in 1910 with Francisco Madero's (1873–1913) liberal Plan of San Luis Potosí that called for free elections in the face of Porfirio Díaz's (1830–1915) seemingly entrenched thirty-five-year dictatorship. A popular uprising led Díaz to resign and leave for exile in Europe the following year, but this led to ten years of often chaotic warfare that left one million people dead. On Madero's left, Emiliano Zapata (1879–1919) and Francisco (Pancho) Villa (1878–1923) demanded deeper social and political changes. Zapata's Plan of Ayala called for agrarian reform and introduced one of the revolution's most noted slogans, "Land and Liberty." These peasant demands, together with a wide-reaching labor code and liberal anticlerical reforms that curtailed the power of the Catholic Church, were institutionalized into a progressive 1917 constitution. Many of these promised reforms were not realized until the 1930s under the Lázaro Cárdenas (1895–1970) government, which is best known for nationalizing the country's petroleum reserves.

GUATEMALA

Similar to Díaz in Mexico, Guatemala's strongly pro–United States dictator, Jorge Ubico (1878–1946), appeared to be deeply entrenched in power (1931–1944) but quickly fell when the population withdrew support. An urban middle class called for liberal reforms similar to those that Madero had championed. Educator Juan José Arévalo (1904–1990) won elections and served for five years (1945–1950), during which time he implemented moderate labor, social security, and agrarian reforms. Jacobo Arbenz (1913–1971) won the 1950 presidential elections and dramatically increased the speed of reforms. Most notably, a 1952 land reform program known as Decree 900 expropriated unused United Fruit Company (UFCO) land. In response, U.S. Secretary of State John Foster Dulles (1888–1959) and CIA director Allen Dulles (1893–1969), who both sat on the UFCO board of directors, authorized a 1954 coup that overthrew Arbenz and implemented a long and bloody military dictatorship.

MOVIMIENTO NACIONALISTA REVOLUCIONARIO (MNR)

A short insurrection on April 9 to 11, 1952, brought the Nationalist Revolutionary Movement (MNR) to power in Bolivia after leader Víctor Paz Estenssoro (1907–2001) had won the 1951 elections but the military prevented him from taking power. As in Guatemala, the MNR's base of support was in the urban middle classes. Workers and peasants quickly exploited this political opening, and demanded more radical structural changes, including nationalization of tin mines, agrarian reform that broke up large landed estates (haciendas), and universal suffrage that eliminated literacy restrictions. This led to some of the most militant labor and peasant unions in Latin America. Notably, the MNR's radical reforms did not trigger U.S. intervention as did Arbenz's in Guatemala. Historians have debated these contrasting responses, with explanatory factors including Bolivia's greater distance from the U.S. sphere of influence, domestic rather than foreign ownership of the nationalized commodities, and the MNR's willingness to accommodate U.S. demands.

CUBAN REVOLUTION

The 1959 Cuban Revolution was the most successful, long lasting, and far-reaching of the twentieth-century revolutions. On July 26, 1953, Fidel Castro led a failed attack on the Moncada Barracks in Santiago in eastern Cuba that he hoped would spark a popular uprising against the corrupt Fulgencio Batista (1901–1973) dictatorship (1934–1959). Timed to correspond with the centennial of the birth of the independence hero José Martí (1853–1895), Castro appealed to his nationalist legacy. Castro went into exile in Mexico, where he met the Argentine Ernesto "Che" Guevara (1928–1967), who had just witnessed the coup against Arbenz in Guatemala. Guevara, who subsequently became the Americas' most renowned guerrilla leader and theoretician, argued that revolutionaries should arm the masses and not hesitate to execute their opponents. His policies assured Cuba's survival even as the new revolutionary government's extensive land reform program and expropriation of foreign industries led to the failed U.S.-backed Bay of Pigs invasion in 1961.

As revolutionary leaders consolidated their control over the island, they radicalized and extended reforms, often with dramatic results. Gains in education and health care led to socioeconomic indicators that rivaled those of the industrial world, sometimes surpassing those in the United States. Critics complained, however, that this was done at the cost of individual liberties. Although strong by developing world standards, Cuba failed to reach the goal of an industrialized economy.

Meanwhile, Guevara left Cuba to continue revolutionary struggles elsewhere in Latin America and Africa. He was most noted for his *foco* theory of guerrilla warfare that challenged traditional Marxist doctrines of waiting for proper objective conditions for a revolutionary struggle. Rather, Guevara believed that the triumph of the Cuban Revolution demonstrated that a small insurrectionary guerrilla force (the *foco*) could create the conditions for a revolution. A subsequent attempt to implement this theory in Bolivia in 1967 failed spectacularly and led to Guevara's death. As a martyr, Guevara became renowned for his selfless dedication to a revolutionary struggle.

CHILEAN ROAD TO SOCIALISM

With Guevara's defeat in Bolivia and the 1970 election of Marxist Salvador Allende (1908–1973) to the presidency in Chile, leftist sentiments swung away from searching for revolutionary changes through guerrilla struggles and toward using constitutional and institutional means. Similar to Arbenz in Guatemala, Allende came to power through constitutional means, dramatically accelerated reforms begun under his predecessor, and quickly alienated the U.S. government. His goal to transform Chile from a capitalist and dependent society into a socialist and independent one within a democratic and constitutional framework realized significant gains for the lower classes at a cost to the wealthy elite. Nationalization of U.S.-owned copper mines led, as in Guatemala, to U.S. support for Augusto Pinochet's brutal September 11, 1973, military coup.

SANDINISTAS

With the collapse of Allende's government, leftist sentiments swung away from the possibilities for electoral means to social revolutionary changes. Led by the Frente Sandinista para la Liberación Nacional (FSLN, Sandinista Front for National Liberation), on July 19, 1979, a guerrilla army defeated U.S.-backed dictator Anastasio Somoza (1925–1980) and took power in Nicaragua. The Somoza family dynasty had ruled the small Central American country since the 1930s. Similar to Castro's use of Martí in Cuba, revolutionary leader Carlos Fonseca (1936–1976) appealed to the nationalist image of Augusto César Sandino (1895–1934), who had fought the U.S. Marines to a standstill in the 1930s.

In power, the Sandinistas implemented goals of a mixed economy, plural political system, and a nonaligned foreign policy. As one of the poorest countries in Latin America, Nicaragua lacked the economic significance of Chile, Cuba, or Guatemala. Nevertheless, the United States feared its independent example and helped train and arm a counter-revolutionary force (called the *contras*) that drug the country down and halted agrarian and social reforms. Ironically, the one lasting legacy of the Sandinistas was implementation for the first time of a functioning electoral system that opponents used to remove the revolutionaries from power in 1990. The defeat of the Sandinistas brought to an end in the minds of many proponents the possibilities for an armed path toward a socialist revolution.

ZAPATISTAS

Four years after the electoral defeat of the Sandinistas, the launch of a guerrilla war in the impoverished southern Mexican state of Chiapas caught the world by surprise. Led by a charismatic masked Subcomandante Marcos, the Ejército Zapatista de Liberación Nacional (EZLN, Zapatista Army of National Liberation) occupied five towns on January 1, 1994. They announced their opposition to neoliberal economic policies that favored the elite at a cost to the impoverished indigenous masses. The EZLN conceptualized the struggle as a continuation of that which their namesake, Emiliano Zapata, had launched at the beginning of the twentieth century. Despite sparking the imagination of leftists around the world, they made few concrete gains.

BOLIVARIAN REVOLUTION

Since elected president in 1998, Hugo Chávez has brought his uniquely styled Bolivarian Revolution to Venezuela. Chávez embodied many of the debates concerning revolutionary movements from throughout the twentieth century. After a failed 1992 coup, Chávez turned toward an electoral apparatus to gain power.

Rather than contradictory or ironic, it indicates that these are simply different and not necessarily contradictory strategies in a common revolutionary struggle. As with previous revolutionaries, Chávez is a charismatic leader who provided the inspiration that drove his movement. Similar to how Castro appealed to Martí, and Fonseca to Sandino, Chávez held up Latin American independence leader Simón Bolívar (1783–1830) as his symbolic nationalist hero. Even though Venezuela is primarily an urban country, Chávez continued to emphasize and draw support from peasant and indigenous peoples. His fervent anti-imperialist rhetoric led to strong opposition from the United States, but unlike Allende he weathered an April 11, 2002, coup attempt and consolidated his hold on power. Meanwhile, Chávez's social programs brought education and health care to the lower classes, significantly raising their standard of living. Chávez seemed not only to have learned the lessons of a century of revolutionary movements, but also to embody a synthesis of their gains.

SEE ALSO *Colonialism; Cuban Revolution; Decolonization; Indigenous Rights; Nationalism and Nationality*

BIBLIOGRAPHY

Allende Gossens, Salvador. 2000. *Salvador Allende Reader: Chile's Voice of Democracy.* Melbourne, Australia, and New York: Ocean Press.

Gott, Richard. 2005. *Hugo Chávez and the Bolivarian Revolution.* London: Verso.

Guevara, Ernesto. 2006. *Reminiscences of the Cuban Revolutionary War.* Melbourne: Ocean Press.

James, C. L. R. 1963. *The Black Jacobins: Toussaint L'Ouverture and the San Domingo Revolution*, 2nd ed. New York: Vintage.

Liss, Sheldon B. 1984. *Marxist Thought in Latin America.* Berkeley: University of California Press.

Wolf, Eric R. 1969. *Peasant Wars of the Twentieth Century.* New York: Harper.

Womack, John, Jr. 1968. *Zapata and the Mexican Revolution.* New York: Vintage.

Zimmermann, Matilde. 2001. *Sandinista: Carlos Fonseca and the Nicaraguan Revolution.* Durham, NC: Duke University Press.

Marc Becker

REVOLUTIONS, SCIENTIFIC

Although the expression *scientific revolution* is perhaps most closely associated with Thomas Kuhn (1922–1996), who embedded the phrase in a general theory of scientific change, it also names a specific time and place—western

Europe of the seventeenth century—from which descend the modern institutions, methods, theories, and attitudes of science, as epitomized in the achievements of such figures as Galileo (1564–1642), Francis Bacon (1561–1626), René Descartes (1596–1650), and most of all, Isaac Newton (1642–1727). That sense was only coined in the 1940s by Herbert Butterfield (1900–1979) and Kuhn's historiographical inspiration, Alexandre Koyré (1892–1964), an émigré Russo-French philosopher influenced in equal measures by Plato (c. 427–347 BCE) and G. W. F. Hegel (1770–1831).

The use of the same phrase, *scientific revolution*, in its general and specific senses is only partly justified. The specific coinage was intended as provocative. It served to consign the Renaissance to a premodern past in which the scientific imagination (which Koyré understood as purely theory-driven) had been held back by the demands of secular governance and everyday life. Thus, Koyré contrasted two Italians who had been previously seen in much the same light: Galileo's single-minded pursuit of a unified truth marked him as a scientist, whereas Leonardo da Vinci's (1452–1519) jack-of-all-trades empiricism did not. The rhetorical force of this distinction was not lost in the postwar period. In the aftermath of two world wars that implicated science in the manufacture of weapons of mass destruction, the future of science required that it be seen as having revolted not only from religion but perhaps more importantly, technology.

A deeper point became more apparent with another postwar project: Joseph Needham's (1900–1995) multivolume comparative study of "science and civilization" in China. China was Europe's economic superior until the early nineteenth century, though it had never passed through a scientific revolution. Science required the belief that humans enjoy a privileged cognitive position in nature, a status associated with the great monotheistic religions descended from Judaism but not those of Asia, where humans were seen more as one with the natural world. The idea that humans might transcend—rather than simply adapt to—their natural condition so as to adopt a "god's eye point of view," especially one that would enable the "reverse engineering" of nature, was profoundly alien to the Chinese way of knowing. In this respect, the scientific revolution marked a revolt against nature itself, which was seen as not fully formed, an unrealized potential. Francis Bacon's account of experimentation famously expressed this sensibility as forcing nature to reveal her secrets, namely, possibilities that would not be encountered in the normal course of experience.

This deeper point had become widespread in the West by the late eighteenth century, especially after Newton's achievement inspired philosophers—not least those behind the American and French revolutions—to envisage society as something designed *ex nihilo* on the basis of a few mutually agreeable principles, what continues today as *social contract theory*. In this context, the precontractarian "natural" state of humanity appears unruly because its wilder animal tendencies have yet to be subject to a higher intelligence, secularly known as *rationality*.

The joining of political and scientific revolutions in this radical sense is due to the Marquis de Condorcet (1743–1794), who specifically connected the successful American Revolution and the ongoing French Revolution via the rhetoric of the first self-declared scientific revolutionary, Antoine Lavoisier (1743–1794). Lavoisier had recently reorganized chemistry from its traditional alchemical practices to a science founded on the systematic interrelation of elements. However, he himself was not an enthusiastic supporter of revolutionary politics, unlike his great English scientific rival, Joseph Priestley (1733–1804). Lavoisier believed that a scientific revolution could stabilize (rather than dynamize, as Priestley thought) the political order. Here Lavoisier fell back on the classical conception of *revolution*, suggested in the Latin etymology, as a restoration of equilibrium after some crime or societal disorder. Specifically, Lavoisier opposed Priestley's continued support for the practically useful, but logically confused, concept of *phlogiston*, the modern remnant of the ancient idea that fire is an ultimate constituent of nature.

Kuhn's relevance emerges at this point—and not only because his own most carefully worked out case of a scientific revolution was the dispute between Priestley and Lavoisier over the nature of oxygen. Kuhn too thought that revolutions restored stability to a science fraught with long unsolved problems. But more generally, Kuhn portrays scientists as the final arbiters of when their knowledge has sufficiently matured to be applied in society without destabilizing it. This doubly conservative conception of revolutions reflects Kuhn's definition of science as dominated by only one paradigm at any given moment. Consequently, despite Kuhn's broad cross-disciplinary appeal, especially among social scientists, he consistently maintained that only the physical sciences satisfy his strict definition because only in these fields (and arguably only until about the 1920s) are scientists in sufficient control of the research agenda to determine when and how a revolution begins and ends, and its results spread more widely.

Kuhn's conception of scientific revolutions appeared radical in the late 1960s because it was conflated with the prevalent Marxist idea of revolution as an irreversible break with the past, something closer in spirit to Condorcet's original conception. This conflation was facilitated by Kuhn's portrayal of scientists in the vanguard vis-à-vis the direction of their own work and its larger societal import. This image was in marked contrast with the perceived captivity of scientists to what C. Wright Mills (1916–1962) called the "military-industrial complex." However, Kuhn's own reluctance to engage with his radical admirers suggests that his model was proposed more in the spirit of nostalgia than criticism and reform. This interpretation is supported by the original Harvard context for the restorative conception of revolution, the so-called Pareto Circle, a reading group named after the Italian political economist whose "circulation of elites" model was seen in the middle third of the twentieth century as the strongest rival to Karl Marx's (1818–1883) theory of proletarian revolution. This group was convened in the 1930s by the biochemist Lawrence Henderson (1878–1942), who taught the first history of science courses at Harvard, and who was instrumental in the appointment of chemistry department head, James Bryant Conant (1893–1978), as university president. As president, Conant hired Kuhn and coauthored the case history on the chemical revolution that launched the latter's more generally influential thinking about scientific revolutions.

SEE ALSO *Kuhn, Thomas; Philosophy of Science*

BIBLIOGRAPHY

Cohen, H. Floris. 1994. *The Scientific Revolution: A Historiographical Inquiry.* Chicago: University of Chicago Press.

Cohen, I. Bernard. 1985. *Revolution in Science.* Cambridge, MA: Harvard University Press.

Fuller, Steve. 2000. *Thomas Kuhn: A Philosophical History for Our Times.* Chicago: University of Chicago Press.

Kuhn, Thomas. 1962. *The Structure of Scientific Revolutions.* Chicago: University of Chicago Press. 2nd ed., 1970.

Steve Fuller

RHETORIC

Rhetoric is employed in both act and perception, in private thought and public communication. It is a means of communication as well as a theory for understanding and criticizing itself and the alternative means of communication. Wedded by the motives of both author and audience, the rhetoric of the social sciences is, like other rhetorics, simultaneously a guide for persuasive writing and a framework for intelligent reading. Centrally speaking, the rhetoric of the social sciences is the study and practice of argumentation and proof making, constrained only by the available means of persuasion. As such, rhetoric judges and is judged, it moves and is moved. Rhetoric is our ways and means of scientific deliberation. Following the models of

Aristotle (c. 384–322 BCE) and of Cicero (106–43 BCE), the Roman statesman and philosopher, rhetoric is also importantly about the *ethos* or *character* of the author; to some theorists, such as Quintilian (35–96 CE), it is nothing less than "the good person speaking well."

Rarely claimed after Aristotle to be a science unto itself, rhetoric as a discipline has profoundly shaped the sciences, and each of the sciences, including the social sciences, have returned the sometimes painful favor by reshaping and redefining the theories and vocabularies of rhetoric; (cf. Socrates, in Plato's *Phaedrus*: "The method of the science of medicine is, I suppose, the same as the science of rhetoric. . . . In both sciences it is necessary to determine the nature of something" [2005, p. 56]).

An ancient discipline of Greek and Latin origins established originally for pleadings in law, politics, and international commerce, the rhetorical theories of Cicero, Quintilian, St. Augustine (354–430 CE), and especially Aristotle proved to be of central importance to all of human communication, including scientific communication, and became the foundation for liberal education in Europe for more than twenty centuries. The influence of rhetoric was particularly strong in the medieval university *trivium*, of which St. Thomas Aquinas (c. 1225–1274) is a product. The trivium was organized around three basic subjects: grammar (that is, words, word order, phonics, sentence structure, and the like), logic (syllogism, cause and effect, quality versus quantity, and so forth), and rhetoric—with rhetoric presiding as queen and lord. Rhetoric was not a mere synthesis of grammar and logic, though partly it was; rhetoric provided fundamental training in strategic theories of persuasion. It gave students practice in the arts of persuasion and good citizenship that would be necessary for success in later pursuits, such as immediately in the *quadrivium* (the study of mathematics, science, and music) and followed by (at least for some students) investigations in philosophy, theology, and public service. Compared to today's four- or five-step handbooks on "valid" scientific method, the handbooks of rhetoric appear, like scientific argument itself, copious. In Aristotle's *On Rhetoric* alone, one can identify several scores of distinct strategies for argument and proof, and literally thousands more of unique "commonplaces" (or *topoi*)—that is, general and particular sites of knowledge and belief—for use in designing arguments (Aristotle [c. 350 BCE] 1991). The sum of the permutations, a subset of all the available means of persuasion, is immense.

In the sixteenth century a Frenchman named Peter Ramus (1515–1572) was deeply inspired by his surface reading of Plato (c. 427–347 BCE), the sophists, and other classical rhetoricians. A persuasive and powerful (but not, it seems, a highly original or ethical thinker), Ramus commenced to reduce the very word *rhetoric* to mere "style," "emotion," "ornament," or, in the foulest of moods, "manipulation"—a project that was encouraged by the so-called scientific revolution, of which Ramus was a part. In the century before René Descartes, Ramus thought a new language and taxonomy of thought were necessary to suit the scientific and mathematical ideas of the Renaissance, and Aristotelian rhetoric and logic, which students had been learning for centuries, was eclipsing, he said, the full reception of those ideas (Ong 1958; Olmsted 2006). That Ramus himself adapted ancient principles of rhetoric (such as the pairing of opposites) to enact his, as Ong puts it, "superficial" revolution was to Ramus and his followers apparently beside the point. The fleeting success of antirhetoric rhetoric—such as, to repeat, Ramus's own reduction of the very word to mean "mere" style—had been observed in previous epochs, however, and would periodically recur.

In educated circles of the late eighteenth century, rhetoric reappeared in a form closer to its ancient, philosophical stature (Adam Smith and Jeremy Bentham each wrote a book on rhetoric, Smith emphasizing the rhetoric of *belles lettres* and Bentham the fallacies of political pundits). In the second half of the nineteenth century a notable addition to rhetoric and religion was supplied by Cardinal Newman in *Essay in Aid of a Grammar of Assent* (c. 1870). Rhetoric was then shoved far under the rug by neopositivists of the late nineteenth and early twentieth century (the neopositivists were a diverse group that included, among others, the scientist-philosophers Karl Pearson, Ernst Mach, and the so-called "scientific socialists"). But the logical positivists, the members and philosophical allies of the Vienna Circle, went even further and tried with some success to bury rhetoric along with other "cognitively meaningless" subjects such as, they said, metaphysics, theology, and poetry. In retrospect, the positivists said, their goal was not to kill off rhetoric and other humanistic disciplines but simply to banish them from scientific deliberation.

In the 1940s and 1950s the study of rhetoric was again revived to respectability, this time by the writings of I. A. Richards, Kenneth Burke, Richard McKeon, Chaim Perelman, Wayne Booth, Richard Weaver, and some others. A tiny postwar boom came to rhetoric by way of a delayed interest in the philosophy of Friedrich Nietzsche (1844–1900) and American philosophical pragmatism (represented by C. S. Peirce, William James, and John Dewey), both of which, like Aristotle and his followers, saw symbols and human action as inextricably entwined, even in science. A larger boost came from specific economic and cultural change. Demand for workers in the fields of technology, such as in for example the increasingly important radio and broadcast journalism industries, gave new value to the skills of the rhetorician. And in the 1970s and 1980s the philosophical and cultural

movements generally referred to as "postmodernism" gave new purpose to theories and arts of communication, that is, to rhetoric.

Nowadays the larger universities maintain a department of rhetoric. If lacking a full department of their own, academic rhetoricians find employment with journalists and others in a department of communication studies, with political scientists and others in a school of public affairs, or with scientists, historians, and philosophers in the departments of classics and science and technology studies.

Rhetoric is among the oldest of subjects and also the most fluid. The fluidity of rhetoric—its ability to adapt to radically changing social, economic, and political conditions—is essential to and descriptive of its fitness. Rhetoric is constantly under attack, often by highly skilled writers. To them—the Platonists, the Ramists, the Cartesians, the logical positivists, the scientific socialists, and the media journalists—the University of Chicago philosopher Richard McKeon (1900–1985) never tired of pointing out that because rhetorical choices are always being made—from the arid symbols of first-order predicate logic to the manifestos of scientists and philosophers who would deny the force of rhetoric—rhetorical training is always relevant to the human condition.

Contemporary social scientists are formally speaking innocent of their own rhetoric. That is not to say they do not grasp the words, facts, models, theories, experimental methods, and institutional environments with which and in which they operate; rather, with a few exceptions, professional societies and the modern university do not require more than an imitative capacity to work with other than highly specific, state-of-the-art rhetorical forms to gain in-group authority (Latour and Woolgar 1979; McCloskey 1985; Nelson, Megill, McCloskey 1987; Brown 1989; Klamer 2007). A mathematical article purporting to prove with utility theory the goodness of market economies, for example, is not likely to refer to the decline of "character" talk in nineteenth-century economic psychology. Nor is the positive social scientist likely to know or even care about the purposive erasure of "ethics" and "narrative" from twentieth-century economic thought. Today's social scientist is trained to believe with the *Publication Manual of the American Psychological Association* that there is only one scientific style—today's style, exemplified by articles published in the top-ranked journals. Her neatly separated section titles—introduction, theory, model, data, hypothesis test, policy implications, conclusion—are said by her teachers to represent distinct and nonrhetorical epistemic objects (Bazerman 1988). She is trained to "let the facts speak for themselves" and to keep her values out of sight (Burke 1950; Booth 1974; Fish 1990). Likewise, the empirical economist does not bother to learn the rhetorical history of "statistical significance testing," even though significance testing is his lifeblood, and does not achieve the crucial "test" of "economic" or "social scientific significance" his handbook on method imagines (McCloskey and Ziliak 1996; Ziliak and McCloskey 2007). The loss of rhetoric in social science training is more than a simple academic farewell to reason.

Some observers argue that without a basic training in rhetoric, a social scientist cannot know the difference between knowledge and belief, and why the difference matters. Quite a few others think that the reason to bring rhetoric back to the center of education—including graduate education—is that highly specialized scientists would become better equipped to speak with other specialists, and, perhaps more importantly, with policy makers and the general public. Specialization, Adam Smith observed, is on balance good for society; but he added that it is only through mutually beneficial exchange that the gains from specialization can be realized ([1762–1763] 1963). Rhetoric, some say, enables both the means and the ends.

BIBLIOGRAPHY

Aristotle. [c. 350 BCE] 1991. *On Rhetoric: A Theory of Civic Discourse.* Trans. George A. Kennedy. New York: Oxford University Press.

Bazerman, Charles. 1988. *Shaping Written Knowledge: The Genre and Activity of the Experimental Article in Science.* Madison: University of Wisconsin Press.

Bentham, Jeremy. [1824] 1962. *The Handbook of Political Fallacies.* Intro. Crane Brinton. New York: Harper.

Booth, Wayne C. 1974. *Modern Dogma and the Rhetoric of Assent.* Chicago: University of Chicago Press.

Brown, Richard Harvey. 1989. *Social Science as Civic Discourse.* Chicago: University of Chicago Press.

Burke, Kenneth. 1945. *A Grammar of Motives.* Berkeley and Los Angeles: University of California Press.

Burke, Kenneth. 1950. *A Rhetoric of Motives.* Berkeley and Los Angeles: University of California Press.

Fish, Stanley. 1990. Rhetoric. In *Critical Terms for Literary Study*, ed. Frank Lentricchia and Thomas McLaughlin, 203–222. Chicago: University of Chicago Press.

Klamer, Arjo. 2007. *Speaking of Economics: How to Be in the Conversation.* London: Routledge.

Klamer, Arjo, Robert M. Solow, and Donald N. McCloskey, eds. 1989. *The Consequences of Economic Rhetoric.* Cambridge, U.K.: Cambridge University Press.

Lanham, Richard A. 1991. *A Handlist of Rhetorical Terms.* Chicago: University of Chicago Press.

Latour, Bruno, and Steve Woolgar. 1979. *Laboratory Life: The Social Construction of Scientific Facts.* New York: Sage.

McCloskey, Deirdre N. [1985] 1998. *The Rhetoric of Economics.* Madison: University of Wisconsin Press.

McCloskey, Deirdre N., and Stephen T. Ziliak. 1996. The Standard Error of Regressions. *Journal of Economic Literature* 34 (March): 97–114.

McKeon, Richard. 1987. *Rhetoric: Essays in Invention and Discovery.* Ed. and intro. Mark Backman. Woodbridge, CT: Ox Bow Press.

McKeon, Richard. 1990. *Freedom and History, and Other Essays: An Introduction to the Thought of Richard McKeon.* Ed. Zahava K. McKeon. Chicago: University of Chicago Press.

Nelson, John S., Allan Megill, and Donald N. McCloskey. 1987. *The Rhetoric of the Human Sciences.* Madison: University of Wisconsin Press.

Olmsted, Wendy. 2006. *Rhetoric: An Historical Introduction.* Malden, MA: Blackwell.

Ong, Walter J. [1958] 1983. *Ramus, Method, and the Decay of Dialogue.* Chicago: University of Chicago Press.

Pearson, Karl. 1892. *The Grammar of Science.* London: J. M. Dent and Sons.

Perelman, Chaim. 1979. *The New Rhetoric and the Humanities.* Dordrecht, Netherlands: D. Reidel.

Plato. [c. 380s–370s BCE] 2005. *Phaedrus.* Trans. Christopher Rowe. London: Penguin.

Rorty, Richard. 1982. *Consequences of Pragmatism.* Minneapolis: University of Minnesota Press.

Smith, Adam. [1762–1763] 1963. *Lectures on Rhetoric and "Belle Lettres".* Ed. John C. Bryce. Oxford: Clarendon Press.

Ziliak, Stephen T., and Deirdre N. McCloskey. 2007. *The Standard Error: How Some Sciences Lost Interest in Magnitude, and What to Do About It.* Ann Arbor: University of Michigan Press.

Stephen Ziliak

RHODES, CECIL
1853–1902

Cecil John Rhodes, a British immigrant to southern Africa, founded the De Beers diamond monopoly, served as prime minister of Britain's Cape Colony, and colonized Southern and Northern Rhodesia (later Zimbabwe and Zambia). Rhodes was the embodiment of late nineteenth-century rapacious capitalism and imperialism. His activities did much to shape important objects of social scientific study with respect to southern Africa: monopoly capitalism, migrant labor, and colonialism.

Rhodes was born to an English parson of modest circumstances. At the age of seventeen, he emigrated to southern Africa. Rhodes arrived in 1870, three years after a diamond-mining rush had begun in an area soon to be annexed by Britain and incorporated into the Cape Colony. The following year, Rhodes left for the diamond fields, where the town of Kimberley emerged to support the mines. Diamonds quickly transformed the region's political economy, becoming the Cape Colony's largest export by 1875 and leading to calls for confederation of the region's colonies and settler states.

In 1880 Rhodes and Charles Dunnell Rudd (1844–1916) formed the De Beers Mining Company to pursue amalgamation of claims, by then considered essential to continued profitability of the mines. By the end of the decade, De Beers completely controlled the diamond mines; more than a century later, De Beers remains the world's largest miner and seller of diamonds and controls the world market in these gems. Amalgamation was intended to remedy major problems of production and marketing. First, as the mines went deeper, enormous amounts of machinery and technical expertise were needed to shore up walls and to cart ore to the surface. Though operations were capital-intensive, they were also labor-intensive, requiring increasing numbers of African men who came to the mines as migrant workers. Second, the huge volume of diamonds being produced from the Kimberley mines meant that it was necessary to limit the numbers reaching the market in order for sales to be profitable. Amalgamation enabled De Beers to solve these problems through centrally organizing flows of capital and labor into the mines and the flow of diamonds out of them. Key innovations, introduced in 1882, were closed compounds to house African workers and legislation to control illicit diamond buying. Closed compounds enabled mining concerns to closely supervise workers, bringing about tighter labor discipline and providing a model for later mining enterprises in southern Africa.

In the late-1880s, prospectors discovered the world's largest gold deposit on the Witwatersrand (Rand) in the Boer-ruled Transvaal. The city of Johannesburg grew up above the mines, becoming the subcontinent's largest city. Kimberley capitalists invested heavily in the Rand, but Rhodes was late to do so, securing poor claims. As a result, his interest was drawn in two directions: toward politics and toward possible mineral discoveries in areas then beyond colonial control north of the Limpopo River.

At the end of the 1880s, Rhodes's agents fraudulently secured from Ndebele king Lobengula (c. 1836–1894) a concession (the Rudd Concession) to exploit all the minerals in his domain. On the strength of this concession, Rhodes obtained a royal charter for his British South Africa Company (BSAC) and sold shares for an enterprise to settle and mine what became Northern and Southern Rhodesia. When the areas the BSAC first exploited failed to produce a "second Rand," the BSAC provoked war with and swiftly defeated the Ndebele. The politics of the Cape, the Transvaal, and BSAC-occupied territories to the north now became deeply entwined. Rhodes, then the Cape's prime minister, conspired with others to topple the Transvaal government in order to install a government more conducive to mining and British imperialism. An armed force under Rhodes's aide, Leander Starr Jameson (1853–1917), launched a hapless invasion from the north in late 1895; its failure forced Rhodes's resignation as prime minister. Tensions over the Jameson raid helped precipitate war between Britain and the Boer republics (the Transvaal and Orange Free State). The Boer War, later known as the South African War, led to uniting South Africa as a white settler state within the British Empire. Meanwhile, oppressive BSAC policies toward Africans in Rhodesia led to a widespread uprising in 1896 to 1897 that was put down at great cost in African lives.

As he gained wealth and power, Rhodes promoted a broad imperialist vision, summed up in his scheme for a transportation network that would span Africa from the Cape to Cairo and parodied in a contemporary political cartoon that showed Rhodes astride the African continent as the "Colossus of Rhodes." As the Cape's prime minister, in 1894 he secured passage of the Glen Grey Act, designed to limit African access to land, force Africans onto the labor market, and reduce African voting strength. His rhetoric and actions thus place him as one of a handful of white power brokers in late nineteenth-century southern Africa who shaped the regimes of alienation of land, exploitation of minerals, and racist regimentation of labor that were to define white-ruled southern Africa for most of the twentieth century. Not yet fifty when he died, Rhodes's will founded the Rhodes Scholarship program for anglo-saxon men from settler societies to study at Oxford University, where he had taken a degree in 1881. He is buried on a hilltop in the Matopos hills of southwestern Zimbabwe, a site sacred to indigenous peoples. His grave thus is a continual reminder of colonial conquest and insensitivity, while its broad vistas give expression to imperial desires to be master of all one surveys.

SEE ALSO *Diamond Industry*

BIBLIOGRAPHY

Davenport, T. R. H., and Christopher Saunders. 2000. *South Africa: A Modern History*. 5th ed. Houndmills, U.K.: Macmillan.

Rotberg, Robert I., with Miles F. Shore. 1988. *The Founder: Cecil Rhodes and the Pursuit of Power*. New York: Oxford University Press.

Worger, William H. 1987. *South Africa's City of Diamonds: Mine Workers and Monopoly Capitalism in Kimberley, 1867–1895*. New Haven, CT: Yale University Press.

Thomas McClendon

RICARDIAN EQUIVALENCE

The term *Ricardian equivalence* was coined by the American economist Robert Barro in the 1970s and subsequently became a standard topic in public finance and macroeconomic theory. The Ricardian equivalence theorem ascribes to David Ricardo (1772–1823), the English economist, the view that taxation and public borrowing constitute equivalent forms of financing public expenditure. The rationale behind this view is that the government is expected at some future time to redeem its debt. If one now supposes a closed economy, the repayment of debt will take place via increased future taxation, which means that, on the basis of the rational expectations hypothesis, individuals increase their savings through buying the bonds that have been issued by the government. The amount of savings, in other words, matches the size of the public deficit and therefore the interest-rate remains the same. This means that there is no crowding-out effect of private investment from public expenditure and the overall demand remains the same together with the other real variables of the economy.

A similar mechanism operates in the case of an open economy, where the redemption of public debt takes place via the sale of assets to international institutional agents. Such a possibility raises, once again, the question of limited future government income, hence the inevitable future increase of taxation. Consequently, Robert Barro in the early 1970s and the new classical economists argued that either method of financing public expenditure, that is, through taxation or borrowing, leads to the same final results. The theorem has been used to argue against government intervention in the economy through fiscal policy because it suggests that the government cannot achieve anything quite different from the free operation of market forces. Monetary policy has similar effects; for example, if government expands the money supply, the public does not increase its expenditures but rather its savings in order to meet the future tax obligations. In short, Ricardian equivalence became a necessary weapon in the armory of the new classical economics in their defense of "free market."

The truth, however, is that Ricardo, to whom this theorem is attributed, repudiated the notion of equivalence between the two ways of financing government expenditure. He reasoned that taxation falls on current incomes and primarily reduces current consumption and only secondarily saving. By contrast, borrowing falls entirely on savings, which for Ricardo and classical economists are identical to investment. As a consequence, public borrowing diminishes the investable product and has detrimental effects on the economy's capacity to accumulate capital.

The empirical evidence from various countries does not lend support to the Ricardian equivalence in its pure form, although there is some evidence that saving rates follow government spending—that is, it has been observed that the personal saving rate increases in the case of deficit spending and decreases in the case of government surpluses. It is very hard, however, to show a direct one-to-one relationship here. A usual criticism of the Ricardian equivalence theorem is that real-life situations are characterized by uncertainty regarding future income and also tax liability, which prevents individuals from behaving in accordance to rational expectations. Furthermore, Ricardian equivalence does not hold in cases where the growth rate of the economy exceeds the rate of interest.

SEE ALSO *Policy, Fiscal; Policy, Monetary*

BIBLIOGRAPHY

Buchanan, James M. 1976. Barro on the Ricardian Equivalence Theorem. *Journal of Political Economy* 84 (2): 337–342.

Tsoulfidis, Lefteris. 2006. Classical Economists and Public Debt: J. S. Mill's Conjecture. http://econlab.uom.gr/~lnt/images/stories/pdf/classics_and_debt.doc.

Lefteris Tsoulfidis

RICARDIAN VICE

The term *Ricardian vice*, which refers to the English economist David Ricardo (1772–1823), was coined by Joseph A. Schumpeter in his *History of Economic Analysis* (1954). It was intended to highlight Ricardo's alleged habit of introducing utterly bold assumptions into an already oversimplified representation of the economy and treating these as givens when in fact they are unknowns. In Schumpeter's words, Ricardo's "fundamental problem" was that he "wanted to solve in terms of an equation between four variables: net output equals rent plus profits plus wages" (Schumpeter 1954, p. 569). Operating with this perspective, Ricardo was bound to treat three of the variables as constants. Schumpeter also deplored Ricardo's alleged habit of "piling a heavy load of practical conclusions upon a tenuous groundwork" (Schumpeter 1954, p. 1171). Two examples serve to illustrate what Schumpeter considered to be Ricardo's inadmissible way of reasoning. The first is Ricardo's famous suggestion, made in 1819, that the whole of the British national debt accumulated during the Napoleonic Wars could be repaid in a few years by means of a tax on property (Ricardo 1951–1973, vol. 5, pp. 38, 271). Such a tax, Ricardo argued, would not diminish total wealth and would also not unduly hurt the propertied classes, because the capital value of the current taxes levied on them to cover interest charges and amortization was equal to the lump-sum property tax suggested.

This proposal became known as *Ricardo's equivalence theorem*. The second example is Ricardo's view that the burden of a tax on wages or on goods consumed by workers will not be borne by workers (e.g., Ricardo 1951–1973, vol. 1, p. 203). Both conclusions are the logical consequence of the underlying premise that workers are paid a subsistence wage that cannot be changed. As Schumpeter opined, Ricardo's theory of wages amounted to taking wages as fixed at the "subsistence" level (Schumpeter 1954, p. 665).

These criticisms elicit two remarks. The first concerns the way Ricardo reasoned. Apparently his critics have not taken seriously his statement that "in all these calculations I have been desirous only to elucidate the principle, and it is scarcely necessary to observe, that my whole basis is assumed at random, and merely for the purpose of exemplification. The results though different in degree, would have been the same in principle. … My object has been to simplify the subject" (Ricardo 1951–1973, vol. 1, pp. 121–122). Hence, while it is true that Ricardo frequently employed bold cases to "elucidate" the principle at hand and draw attention to what he considered the most important aspects of the problem under consideration, he certainly did not seek to prevent his readers from trying out less restrictive assumptions and investigating their implications, nor did he himself abstain from doing so. Some later commentators rightly praised him for having heralded an approach in economics that requires a clear statement of the assumptions on the basis of which certain propositions are taken to be valid within a given analytical context. This is now considered an indispensable prerequisite of scientific communication. Therefore what Schumpeter considered a vice, others took to be a virtue.

As regards the analytical core of Ricardo's argument, it would be wrong to take Ricardo to have been a strict follower of the Malthusian concept of a subsistence wage. While he used this concept in some contexts for the sake of simplicity, in others he explicitly stressed the historical and social dimensions of the "natural wage" and warned that it must not be mistaken for a minimum required for physiological subsistence (see, e.g., Ricardo 1951–1973, vol. 1, pp. 96–97). He took into account the possibility that workers might receive a share of the social surplus product and maintained that the rate of profits is inversely related to "the proportion of the annual labour of the country devoted to the support of the labourers" (Ricardo 1951–1973, vol. 4, p. 49).

This brings us to the second observation, which concerns the fact that the "standpoint … of the old classical economists from Adam Smith to Ricardo has been submerged and forgotten since the advent of the 'marginal' method," as Piero Sraffa remarked perceptively (Sraffa 1960, p. v). By the turn of the nineteenth century it was no longer understood that the classical economists had advocated a theory of income distribution that was fundamentally different from the marginalist one. The marginalist approach sought to determine the rate of profits and the wage rate in terms of the relative "scarcities" of the respective factors of production, *capital*, and labor and thus on the basis of the economy's given initial endowment of the factors. (With heterogeneous capital goods the amount of *capital* in given supply can be expressed only as a sum of value, which spoils the symmetry between the factors with [homogeneous] labor given in terms of its own natural unit.) The classical economists, on the contrary, determined the rate of profits for the system of production in use in terms of the "social surplus" left over after all used-up means of production and wage goods consumed by workers at a given wage rate have been deducted from gross output levels. Hence, whereas the marginalist authors treated profits and wages symmetrically, the classicals treated them asymmetrically. This asymmetric treatment was unimaginable to the marginalist authors, who therefore felt entitled to accuse the classical authors of treating as a constant what is a variable—that is, the wage rate. Schumpeter's incomprehension was in fact anticipated by major marginalist authors, such as William Stanley Jevons and Léon Walras (see Kurz and Salvadori 2002, pp. 390–395). However, to treat wages as a given in one part of classical theory is a priori no less admissible than to treat the capital endowment as a given in one part of marginalist theory. As Sraffa (1960) has shown, the classical approach to the theory of value and distribution can be formulated in a coherent way that allows one to determine the unknowns (one of the distributive variables and relative prices) in terms of the givens, without depending on bold assumptions, such as the existence of a subsistence wage.

In light of these considerations and granting the fact that Ricardo based some of his arguments on highly simplified analytical constructions, it appears to be somewhat problematic to speak of "Ricardian vice." One can only wonder whether it would be more appropriate to speak of "Schumpeterian incomprehension."

SEE ALSO *Economics; Economics, Neo-Ricardian; Long Period Analysis; Marginalism; Napoleonic Wars; Ricardo, David; Schumpeter, Joseph Alois; Sraffa, Piero; Surplus; Taxation; Wages; Walras, Léon*

BIBLIOGRAPHY

Kurz, Heinz D., and Neri Salvadori. 2002. One Theory or Two? Walras's Critique of Ricardo. *History of Political Economy* 42 (2): 365–398. Reprinted in Heinz D. Kurz and Neri Salvadori, *Interpreting Classical Economics: Studies in Long-Period Analysis* (London: Routledge, 2007).

Ricardo, David. 1951–1973. *The Works and Correspondence of David Ricardo.* 11 vols. Ed. Piero Sraffa, with the collaboration of Maurice H. Dobb. Cambridge, U.K.: Cambridge University Press.

Schumpeter, Joseph A. 1954. *History of Economic Analysis.* Ed. Elizabeth Boody Schumpeter. London: Allen and Unwin.

Sraffa, Piero. 1960. *Production of Commodities by Means of Commodities: Prelude to a Critique of Economic Theory.* Cambridge, U.K.: Cambridge University Press.

Heinz D. Kurz

RICARDO, DAVID
1772–1823

David Ricardo was born into a prolific Sephardic Jewish family in London on April 18, 1772. His father was a well-to-do stockbroker. David, already "when young, showed a taste for abstract and general reasoning" (Ricardo 1951–1973, *Works*, vol. 10, p. 4). At the age of fourteen he joined the business of his father. When at the age of twenty-one he married Priscilla Ann Wilkinson, a Quaker, his parents broke with him. Ricardo then began a highly successful career as a stockjobber. He made a fortune on the occasion of the Battle of Waterloo (June 18, 1815) by betting on a defeat of the Napoleonic troops.

CAREER AND WRITINGS

Ricardo's interest in political economy was ignited by Adam Smith's *Wealth of Nations* (1776), and it was amplified by economic events at the time, especially the Bank of England's suspension of the convertibility of bank notes into gold in February 1797 and inflationary tendencies during the Napoleonic Wars. In 1809 Ricardo anonymously published his first article, "The Price of Gold," in the *Morning Chronicle*. One year later he published the pamphlet *The High Price of Bullion, a Proof of the Depreciation of Bank-Notes*, which swiftly made him known in learned and political circles. The famous Bullion Report to the British House of Commons reflects his influence, and Ricardo became a major contributor in the Bullion controversy. (The controversy unrolled after the Bank of England in 1797 had suspended convertibility of its notes into gold. The Bullionists, including Ricardo, argued that the ensuing increase in money supply would lead to rising prices, whereas the Anti-Bullionists maintained that the money supply was driven by the "needs of trade" reflected by the real bills presented to the Bank for discount. The Bullion Report was strongly influenced by the monetary theorist Robert Thornton, a Bullionist.) In several letters to the *Morning Chronicle* and in a pamphlet titled *Reply to Mr. Bosanquet's "Practical*

Observations on the Report of the Bullion Committee" (1811), he defended the Bullion Report. In his hands, the quantity theory of money became a powerful weapon against the Bank of England's inflationary expansion of money circulation, which, while beneficial to a few, was detrimental to the interests of the nation at large.

Eventually, Ricardo came to know James Mill (1773–1836) and Thomas Robert Malthus (1766–1834). Mill incessantly urged Ricardo to write down his ideas and publish them. With Malthus, Ricardo engaged in many controversial discussions until the end of his life. It was Malthus's relentless criticism that forced Ricardo to rethink his positions and develop what he considered "a very consistent theory" (*Works*, vol. 7, p. 246).

Probably prompted by a move before Parliament to restrict the corn trade in early 1813, Ricardo started to investigate the impact of the accumulation of capital on the rate of profits. This resulted in March 1814 in some "papers on the profits of Capital," which unfortunately have never been found, and in February 1815 in the publication of his *Essay on the Influence of a Low Price of Corn on the Profits of Stock; Shewing the Inexpediency of Restrictions on Importation*. The *Essay* was eventually to grow into his magnum opus, *On the Principles of Political Economy and Taxation*, published in April 1817. The book sold out in a few months. A second, substantially revised edition came out in 1819, and a third, carrying the new chapter "On Machinery," in 1821. Ricardo's "principal problem" in this work was to determine the "laws" that regulate the distribution of the product between the three classes of society—landowners, capitalists, and workers (*Works*, vol. 1, p. 5).

By late 1815 Ricardo had decided to withdraw from the Stock Exchange and invest his money in landed estates—a move supported by his theory of rent, according to which, in an "improving society," ever larger parts of the soil of a country would become scarce and rise in price. In February 1816 Ricardo published some *Proposals for an Economical and Secure Currency*, in which he put forward anew his "ingot plan." The plan suggested a return to the gold standard by making bank notes convertible into gold ingots rather than coins. This practice would allow Britain to continue to use paper as the actual means of payment and it would curb the huge profits of the Bank of England (a private institution until 1946), which in Ricardo's view ought to accrue to the public rather than to the bank's directors. In 1821, with the resumption of cash payments by the Bank of England, Ricardo's plan was implemented.

In 1819 Ricardo became a member of Parliament by buying the seat of Portarlington, Ireland. He participated in many debates, mostly on monetary and financial matters. He became famous for his suggestion in 1819 to repay the whole of the national debt in a few years by means of a tax on property. Ricardo argued that such a tax would not diminish total wealth and would also not unduly hit the propertied classes because the capital value of the current taxes levied on them to cover interest charges and amortization of the national debt was equal to the lump-sum property tax suggested. This proposal became known as "Ricardo's equivalence theorem."

After the publication of the first edition of the *Principles*, Ricardo was predominantly concerned with the problems of value and distribution, the measure of value, and the machinery question. The second edition brought substantial changes in the chapter "On Value." In the third edition, he withdrew his earlier optimistic view on the swift compensation of labor displacement due to the introduction of improved machinery.

Ricardo died at his country seat, Gatcomb Park in Gloucestershire, on September 11, 1823, from an "infection of the ear, which ultimately extended itself to the internal part of the head" (*Works*, vol. 10, p. 12).

RICARDO ON VALUE, DISTRIBUTION, AND CAPITAL ACCUMULATION

In this entry, emphasis will be placed on Ricardo's contributions to the theory of value, distribution, and capital accumulation. For his views on money, taxation, public debt, and politics, see Giancarlo de Vivo (1987), Samuel Hollander (1979), and Murray Milgate and Shannon Stimson (1991).

Ricardo, a man with considerable practical sense and experience, always defended economic theory against the "vulgar charge" of those who are "all for fact and nothing for theory. Such men can hardly ever sift their facts. They are credulous, and necessarily so, because they have no standard of reference" (*Works*, vol. 3, pp. 160, 181).

Ricardo adopted Smith's *long-period method*, which focuses attention on "natural" as opposed to "market" prices and thus on the persistent and systematic as opposed to the temporary and accidental factors at work in the economic system. However, Ricardo gave greater emphasis to the members of the "monied class" in bringing about, in conditions of free competition, a tendency toward a uniform rate of profits (see *Works*, vol. 1, p. 88).

Ricardo offered clear statements of the principles of *extensive* and *intensive diminishing returns* in agriculture due to the scarcity of land. While Ricardo was not the first to discover these principles, he deserves credit for their incorporation into a system of political economy whose main aim was the determination of the general rate of profits. With extensive diminishing returns, different plots of land can be brought into a ranking of natural "fertility" that corresponds to the ranking of unit costs of the

agricultural product, say corn. With very low levels of production of corn, only land of the highest fertility will be cultivated and there will be no rent, for essentially the same reason that nothing is given for "the gifts of nature which exist in boundless quantity" (*Works*, vol. 1, p. 69). It is only as capital accumulates and population grows that land of second and third quality, and so forth, will have to be cultivated in order to satisfy a growing social demand. As a consequence, the price of corn will have to rise relative to that of other commodities. The price is determined on no-rent-bearing (i.e., marginal) land and equals unit costs (including profits at the normal rate) on it; the owners of intramarginal lands obtain differential rents reflecting lower unit costs. From this Ricardo concluded against Smith that rent "cannot enter in the least degree as a component part of its price" (see *Works*, vol. 1, p. 77). In addition, rent was not an expression of the generosity of nature, but of its "niggardliness": it was not the cause of the high price of corn, but its effect.

Setting aside "improvements" in agriculture and assuming a given and constant real wage rate, an extension of cultivation while increasing the surplus product involves an ever larger part of it being appropriated as rent. It follows that the "natural tendency of [the rate of] profits then is to fall" (*Works*, vol. 1, p. 120). The fall is not due to an intensified "competition of capitals," as Smith had maintained, but to diminishing returns in agriculture (and mining).

Profits in turn depend on wages. As is the case with all commodities, Ricardo distinguished with regard to labor between its "natural" and its "market" price. The former is defined in conjunction with the rate of capital accumulation: in an "improving society," natural wages are typically higher than in a stagnant one because, via the wage rate, the growth of population is attuned to the requirements of accumulation. Ricardo also stressed the historical and social dimensions of the natural wage and warned that it must not be mistaken for a purely physiological minimum of subsistence (*Works*, vol. 1, pp. 96–97). He even contemplated the possibility that the "population may be so little stimulated by ample wages as to increase at the slowest rate—or it may even go in a retrograde direction" (*Works*, vol. 8, p. 169). Therefore, Ricardo can hardly be called a strict adherent to Malthus's "law of population." He also discussed the possibility of workers participating in the sharing out of the surplus product. In this case, he felt the need to replace the concept of a given real (i.e., commodity) wage rate by a share concept, or "proportional wages" (Sraffa 1951, p. lii), that is, "the proportion of the annual labour of the country … devoted to the support of the labourers" (*Works*, vol. 1, p. 49). It was on the basis of the new wage concept (and on the premise that the social capital consisted only of, or could be reduced to, wages) that Ricardo then asserted what was called his "fundamental proposition on distribution": that the rate of profits depends on *proportional wages*, and on nothing else.

One element of Ricardo's theory of profits has particularly puzzled his interpreters. In a letter written in March 1814 he stated: "It is the profits of the farmer which regulate the profits of all other trades, and as the profits of the farmer must necessarily decrease with every augmentation of Capital employed on the land, provided no improvements be at the same time made in husbandry, all other profits must diminish and therefore the rate of interest must fall" (*Works*, vol. 6, p. 104). According to the Italian economist Piero Sraffa (1898–1983), the "rational foundation" of the "basic principle" of the determining role of the profits of agriculture was that "in agriculture the same commodity, namely corn, forms both the capital (conceived as composed of the subsistence necessary for workers) and the product," so that "the determination of the ratio of this profit to the capital, is done directly between quantities of corn without any question of valuation" (Sraffa 1951, p. xxxi). In order for other trades to earn the same competitive rate of profits, their prices have to adjust relative to corn. Sraffa was careful to stress that this model was "never stated by Ricardo in any of his extant letters and papers." Yet although direct evidence is missing, Sraffa saw enough indirect evidence to support this view (Sraffa 1951, p. xxxi). It is interesting to note that the "basic principle" that Sraffa ascribes to Ricardo was clearly spelled out by Robert Torrens (1780–1864), who called it a "general principle" and acknowledged his indebtedness to Ricardo (1820, p. 361).

Malthus's insistence that capital never really consists of a single commodity that is identical with the product obviously required a deeper analysis. This forced Ricardo in the *Principles* to abandon his corn-ratio theory in favor of the labor-embodiment principle of value. Whereas in his early theory the rate of profits was conceived as the ratio between two quantities of *corn*, it was now conceived as the ratio between two quantities of *labor*: the amount of labor "embodied" in the *surplus* product (exclusive of the rents of land) and the amount embodied in the social capital (where Ricardo frequently identified capital with wages). This change was possible by introducing the hypothesis that commodities exchange according to the direct and indirect labor necessary in their production. In this way, bundles of heterogeneous commodities are made commensurable. The new theory replicated the important finding that the *rate* of "profits would be high or low in proportion as wages were low or high" (*Works*, vol. 1, p. 111). The labor theory of value enabled Ricardo to dispel the idea deriving from Adam Smith's "adding-up theory" of prices (Sraffa 1951) that wages and the rate of profits could move independently of one another and to establish the constraint binding changes in the two distributive

variables, given the system of production. It was an ingenious move that allowed him, or so he thought, to free the simple inverse relationship between wages and the rate of profits from "a labyrinth of difficulties" (*Works*, vol. 6, p. 214) caused by price movements.

However, Ricardo was aware of the fact that his "general rule" of value was "not rigidly true" (*Works*, vol. 7, p. 279) and was "considerably modified by the employment of machinery and other fixed and durable capital" (vol. 7, p. 30). Different proportions of means of production and direct labor, along with different durabilities of capital goods employed in their production, would make the relative prices of commodities depend on income distribution: the higher the rate of profits (and, correspondingly, the lower the wages), the relatively more expensive will be commodities produced with a high proportion of means of production to labor and means of production that are long-lived. The fact that "profits [are] increasing at a compound rate … makes a great part of the difficulty" (*Works*, vol. 9, p. 387).

This fact threatened to undermine Ricardo's novel solution to the theory of profits. The task of finding a way out of the impasse occupied him until the end of his life. Apparently, to play down the modifications to the labor theory of value as unimportant was not good enough (see *Works*, vol. 9, p. 178). He sought to cope with this problem in terms of his concept of an "invariable measure of value" (see Kurz and Salvadori 1993). Originally, that concept was designed by Ricardo for the purpose of carrying out interspatial and intertemporal comparisons, that is, comparisons relating to *different* technical environments. An invariable standard of value would consist of a commodity produced with an unvarying quantity of total labor. Hence, if another commodity varied in value relative to the standard, it would be clear that this was due to a change in the quantity of labor bestowed on the production of that commodity.

Ricardo now had to face the entirely different problem that even in a given technical environment two commodities may vary in relative value consequent upon a change in income distribution. This was due to the "variety of circumstances" under which commodities are produced (*Works*, vol. 4, p. 368). Ricardo tried to tackle the problem in terms of searching for a standard of value that would have to be a "medium between the extremes" (vol. 4, p. 372). While Ricardo's discussion of this problem is layered with different meanings, and is not always very clear, there can be no doubt that the main purpose of his investigation was to elaborate a consistent theory of value and distribution. This necessitated first and foremost unraveling the properties of a given system of social production as regards the set of alternative constellations of distribution and relative prices compatible with it.

However, since he did not fully master the subject, Ricardo, for lack of a more satisfactory theory, clung to a doctrine that, he felt, offered a sufficiently solid ground to stand on: the labor theory of value. Embodied labor was seen by him to be the main determinant of value and somehow, he thought, both "invariability" requirements could be formulated in terms of a standard that fared well on both counts. The standard had to be produced by a constant amount of labor and by medium circumstances. As regards the second requirement, by expressing bundles of commodities such as the surplus product distributed as profits on the one hand and social capital on the other in terms of such a standard, the positive and negative deviations of prices from labor values could, in each aggregate, be expected to balance. This would allow one to continue to envisage the rate of profits as a ratio of two quantities of labor and thus depend on "the proportion of the annual labour of the country devoted to the support of the labourers" (*Works*, vol. 4, p. 49). The measure was designed to corroborate Ricardo's dictum that the laws of distribution "are not essentially connected with the doctrine of value" (*Works*, vol. 8, p. 194).

While there is no general theoretical solution to Ricardo's first problem, Sraffa (1960), in terms of the concept of "standard commodity," provided a solution to a somewhat reformulated version of Ricardo's second problem. It goes without saying that Ricardo was wrong in assuming that two birds can be killed with one stone (see Kurz and Salvadori 1993).

The theory of value and distribution formed the analytical centerpiece of Ricardo's political economy. It was designed to lay the foundation of all other economic analysis, including the investigation of capital accumulation and technical progress, of development and growth, of trade, and of taxation and public debt.

Like Adam Smith, Ricardo advocated free trade, but he felt that an explanation of the pattern of trade in terms of absolute cost advantages was unsatisfactory. He elaborated the principle of comparative cost and illustrated it in terms of a famous numerical example involving two countries, Portugal and England, and two commodities, cloth and wine. He showed that even if Portugal were to have an absolute advantage in the production of both commodities, there would be room for mutually beneficial trade provided Portugal specialized in the production (and export) of that commodity where its absolute advantage was relatively larger, wine, while England specialized in the production (and export) of the commodity where its absolute disadvantage was relatively smaller, cloth. The effect of foreign trade could be an augmentation of the riches of both trading countries. Ricardo's principle of comparative cost was called the "deepest and most beautiful result in all of economics" (Findlay 1987, p. 514).

In the *Principles*, a great deal of attention is devoted to taxes, the problem of tax incidence, and the impact of taxes on capital accumulation. Ricardo stressed that "there are no taxes which have not a tendency to lessen the power to accumulate. All taxes must either fall on capital or revenue." However, he added: "Taxes are not necessarily taxes on capital, because they are laid on capital; nor on income, because they are laid on income." (*Works*, vol. 1, p. 152). The problem of tax incidence is then illustrated in a number of cases. For example, on the premise that workers are paid a subsistence wage, a tax on wages could not be borne by workers: nominal wages would have to rise, leaving real wages constant, and the tax would accordingly be borne by capitalists. (This premise also underlies Ricardo's tax proposal to repay the national debt.) The situation is similar when a tax is laid on a wage good. In accordance with his doctrine that rent does not enter price, Ricardo concluded that "a tax on rent would affect rent only; it would fall wholly on landlords, and could not be shifted to any class of consumers" (vol. 1, p. 171). A tax on profits would raise the prices of products: "if a tax in proportion to profits were laid on all trades, every commodity would be raised in price" (vol. 1, p. 205). Depending on the consumption patterns of the different classes of society, this would affect their members differently. A rise in the price of wage goods would again entail a corresponding adjustment of nominal wages: "whatever raises the wages of labour, lowers the profits of stock; therefore every tax on any commodity consumed by the labourer, has a tendency to lower the rate of profits" (vol. 1, p. 203).

Ricardo's treatment of taxes, while containing many interesting ideas and suggestions, is generally not considered to be the strongest part of his book and is said to suffer from a poor arrangement of the material and an argument that is frequently tied to excessively restrictive assumptions, such as constant real wages.

BIBLIOGRAPHY

de Vivo, Giancarlo. 1987. Ricardo, David, 1772–1823. In *The New Palgrave: A Dictionary of Economics*, eds. John Eatwell, Murray Milgate, and Peter Newman, Vol. 4, 183–198. London: Macmillan.

Findlay, Ronald. 1987. Comparative Advantage. In *The New Palgrave: A Dictionary of Economics*, eds. John Eatwell, Murray Milgate, and Peter Newman, Vol. 1, 514-517. London: Macmillan.

Hollander, Samuel. 1979. *The Economics of David Ricardo.* Toronto, Ontario: University of Toronto Press.

Kurz, Heinz D., and Neri Salvadori. 1993. The "Standard Commodity" and Ricardo's Search for an "Invariable Measure of Value." In *The Dynamics of the Wealth of Nations: Growth, Distribution, and Structural Change: Essays in Honour of Luigi*

Pasinetti, eds. Mauro Baranzini and G. C. Harcourt, 95–123. New York: St. Martin's Press.

Milgate, Murray, and Shannon Stimson. 1991. *Ricardian Politics.* Princeton, NJ: Princeton University Press.

Ricardo, David. 1951–1973. *The Works and Correspondence of David Ricardo*, ed. Piero Sraffa with Maurice H. Dobb. 11 vols. Cambridge, U.K.: Cambridge University Press.

Schumpeter, Joseph A. 1954. *History of Economic Analysis.* New York: Oxford University Press.

Sraffa, Piero. 1951. Introduction. In *The Works and Correspondence of David Ricardo*, ed. Piero Sraffa with Maurice H. Dobb, Vol. 1, xiii–lxii. Cambridge, U.K.: Cambridge University Press.

Sraffa, Piero. 1960. *Production of Commodities by Means of Commodities: Prelude to a Critique of Economic Theory.* Cambridge, U.K.: Cambridge University Press.

Torrens, Robert. 1820. *An Essay on the External Corn Trade.* London: Longman.

Heinz D. Kurz

RIGHT TO WORK LAWS

SEE *Labor Law.*

RIGHT WING

The term *right wing* originated with the seating arrangement of the French National Assembly of 1791. The royalists sat on the right side of the chamber while their opponents were seated to their left on an elevated section called the Mountain. Between them sat a mass of deputies, known as the Plain, who did not belong to any particular faction.

OPPOSITION TO THE FRENCH REVOLUTION

The Right, representing aristocratic, royalist and clerical interests, supported the monarchy. The Left called for a limited monarchy and a unicameral legislature. But these labels took on new meanings during the course of the French Revolution. Although originally advocates for moderate reform, the powerful Jacobin clubs became increasingly radicalized as popular figures such as Maximilien Robespierre, Louis St. Just, and Jean-Paul Marat, whose inflammatory rhetoric led to the execution of King Louis XVI and the Reign of Terror, gained influence. Eventually, anyone who defended the monarchy was regarded as a member of the Right.

Since the beginning of the French Revolution, right-wingers typically have resisted calls for revolutionary change. The earliest and perhaps the most famous and influential of them, English statesman Edmund Burke (1729–1797), furiously denounced the *armed doctrines* of the revolutionaries in his *Reflections on the Revolution in France* (1790). He appealed to custom, tradition, religion, prescriptive rights, and social hierarchy. Many subsequent critics of the Revolution acknowledged their intellectual debt to Burke. They believed that the Revolution threatened not only traditional institutions and arrangements but the very foundations of European civilization itself.

CHANGING MEANINGS

What it meant to be a right winger would vary depending on the country, culture, and the particular issue. English conservatives, for example, opposed the Utilitarians, or Classical Liberals, who favored free market economics and minimal government. But by the end of the nineteenth century, the positions were reversed. As the Left embraced socialism, the Right became defenders of the free market.

For nearly two centuries, these competing groups battled each other mostly over questions of economics and class. The Right defended the propertied interests of the privileged classes while the Left sought to equalize wealth and property. For the most part, they debated the extent to which wealth should be redistributed through government intervention. In the early-twenty-first century, cultural and social issues, such as abortion, same-sex marriage, secularism, and multiculturalism, have come to play a more dominant role in Left-Right political struggles.

THE RIGHT WING IN THE TWENTY-FIRST CENTURY

Although there is little consensus over what is meant by right wing, most persons of the Right would subscribe to a basic set of beliefs. The Right gives greater primacy to liberty than equality. Social hierarchy is not only the natural order of things, but desirable. Human nature is fixed and cannot be perfected. Original sin or inherent defects of character explain our proclivity toward violence and evil. Members of the Right generally value religion (usually Christian) as a civilizing force. Culture matters more than either politics or economics. With the exception of the authoritarian Right and radical libertarians, right-wingers detest both collectivist and extreme individualist ideologies. Believing that humans are social creatures, right-wingers hold that people find meaning and purpose in their existence through membership in strong, viable groups such as family, voluntary associations, church, and local community. They equally condemn all efforts to either collectivize or atomize society. Because of the importance right-wingers place on cultural, ethnic, and national particularity, they oppose globalist and multicultural ideologies as inimical to rooted communities. Aware of the limited capacity of human beings for reason, right-wingers believe that traditions and prescriptive institutions are more reliable guides to general happiness and harmony than most proposals for change. They would agree with Samuel Johnson's famous observation that "most schemes of political improvement are very laughable things" (Boswell 1980).

The Right can be divided into three basic categories: reactionary, moderate, and radical or extreme. The reactionary Right longs nostalgically for the ancien régime. They are aristocratic, authoritarian, and often pre-Reformation Catholics. Such views are rarely heard in the early-twenty-first century.

Most members of the moderate, democratic Right can trace their intellectual lineage to Burke, the father of modern conservatism. They reject the Jacobin philosophy of universal rights and the extreme individualism of the Utilitarians, and stress the importance of family, tradition, and religion as indispensable mainstays of civilized existence. Moderates favor limited constitutional government. In U.S. politics, the democratic Right can be broken down further into paleoconservative, neoconservative, and libertarian camps. The paleoconservatives are a group of traditionalists or Old Rightists who support minimal government, traditional institutions, and an isolationist foreign policy. They oppose liberal immigration policies. The neoconservatives are mostly Jewish intellectuals who moved to the Right in response to the excesses of the Left during the 1970s. They propose *big-government* conservatism with a welfare-state component, foreign policy crusades to spread democracy and human rights, and liberal immigration policies. Although defined as right-wingers by the popular media, the libertarians do not share many of the philosophical principles of the Right. They place a greater faith in human rationality and tend to be extreme individualists. Most problems, they believe, can be resolved through the free workings of an unregulated marketplace. Minimal taxes, small government, and laissez-faire economics are the hallmark positions of the libertarians.

Included as well under the rubric of right-wing is the Religious Right, a collection of Christian groups that share a common concern with the decline of moral values in U.S. society and crusade against abortion, same-sex marriage, and the secularization of public school instruction. Also affiliated with the Right are a variety of single-issue groups such as anti–gun-control advocates and tax protestors.

The radical Right groups share few opinions other than extreme nationalism, nativism, and a tendency to spin conspiratorial theories. The John Birch Society, the Ku Klux Klan, neo-fascists, and militia groups are a few representative examples. Most oppose immigration and are racialists such as Jean-Marie Le Pen's Front National movement in France. Others, such as the Ku Klux Klan, White Peoples Party, and neo-Nazis, are overtly racist.

Like those on the Left, who prefer to be called progressive, people on the Right generally do not apply the label right-winger to themselves. More frequently, the Left labels its opponents as right-wingers to distinguish themselves and to define those on the Right as outside of the political mainstream.

SEE ALSO *Capitalism; Cleavages; Conservatism; French Revolution; Hierarchy; Inequality, Political; Jacobinism; Ku Klux Klan; Left and Right; Liberalism; Liberty; Monarchy; Neoconservatism; Political Parties; Property; Religion; Sin; Socialism; Tradition*

BIBLIOGRAPHY

Boswell, James. 1980. *Life of Samuel Johnson,* ed. R. W. Chapman. New York: Oxford University Press.

Diamond, Sara. 1995. *Roads to Dominion: Right-Wing Movements and Political Power in the United States.* New York: Guilford.

Eatwell, Roger, and Noël O'Sullivan, eds. 1990. *The Nature of the Right: American and European Politics and Political Thought since 1789.* Boston: Twayne.

Kirk, Russell. 1986. *The Conservative Mind: From Burke to Eliot.* 7th ed. Washington, DC: Regnery.

W. Wesley McDonald

RIGHT-WING AUTHORITARIANISM

SEE *Personality, Authoritarian.*

RIGHTS, ABORIGINAL

SEE *Indigenous Rights.*

RIGHTS, CIVIL

SEE *Civil Rights.*

RIGHTS, HUMAN

SEE *Human Rights.*

RIGHTS, INDIGENOUS

SEE *Indigenous Rights.*

RIKER, WILLIAM
1920–1993

William Harrison Riker pioneered the use of mathematical reasoning in the study of politics, an approach he termed "positive political theory." The method was positive because of the aspiration to explain observed behavior rather than to make normative prescriptions for how people should behave. It was "theoretical" in the same sense as neoclassical microeconomics in that it used axiomatic methods, especially game theory, to derive a coherent set of propositions that comport with observed behavior.

Riker's early work focused on the development of theories of legislative behavior. Of particular import was *The Theory of Political Coalitions* (1962), which used mathematical methods to identify the optimal size of a voting coalition. Previous work suggested that legislators or candidates in election campaigns should work to maximize the number of votes for preferred measures (Downs 1957). Riker's argument was that this behavior would not be rational in settings, such as the distribution of pork-barrel spending, where resources allocated to the benefit of one actor do not benefit others. Instead, he argued that legislators would prefer to belong to a minimum winning coalition that restricted the number of individuals with a claim to the benefits of a particular program.

Another influential work by Riker, written with the political scientist Peter Ordeshook, was "A Theory of the Calculus of Voting" (1968), which elaborated a rational choice model of voter turnout. They argued that rational citizens should not participate if their goal is to influence election outcomes because the probability that their vote would be decisive is essentially zero. Instead, they argue that the factor motivating participation is the sense of satisfaction people get from performing their civic duty. Critics suggest that Riker and Ordeshook's model of political participation is evidence of the nonfalsifiability of microeconomic models because the effect of civic duty has the flavor of a post hoc rationalization for why rational citizens participate when they get no benefit in expectation from the activity (Green and Shapiro 1994).

Riker's later work turned to fundamental questions about the effects of political institutions. In *Liberalism against Populism* (1982), Riker builds on the intuition from Arrow's Theorem that democracies are no better than other political systems at achieving socially desirable (*pareto optimal*) outcomes. He argues that the real value of democratic political systems is not their ability to make good decisions, especially given the possibility of social

choice problems, but is instead the public's ability to punish leaders. In *The Art of Political Manipulation* (1986), Riker considers how politicians can strategically manipulate the issues they bring to the fore for political advantage.

Riker's contributions as an institution builder may be even more influential and long lasting than his scholarship. At the University of Rochester in New York, he was given wide latitude to construct a political science department whose faculty and students shared his interest in developing a positive political theory. His success in this endeavor is highlighted by the fact that the Rochester School came to be associated with the body of knowledge derived from the methodological and theoretical orientation Riker advanced, with adherents at almost every major American university. Not wanting to limit the advancement of social science to the study of politics, Riker was instrumental in the formation of the Public Choice Society, which helped positive political theorists form connections with sister disciplines in economics, sociology, public finance, and even philosophy.

SEE ALSO *Positivism; Public Choice Theory*

BIBLIOGRAPHY

Amadae, S. M., and Bruce Bueno de Mesquite. 1999. The Rochester School: The Origins of Positive Political Theory. *Annual Review of Political Science* 2: 269–296.

Downs, Anthony. 1957. *An Economic Theory of Democracy.* New York: Harper.

Green, Donald P., and Ian Shapiro. 1994. *Pathologies of Rational Choice Theory: A Critique of Applications in Political Science.* New Haven, CT: Yale University Press.

Riker, William H. 1962. *The Theory of Political Coalitions.* New Haven, CT: Yale University Press.

Riker, William H. 1982. *Liberalism against Populism: A Confrontation between the Theory of Democracy and the Theory of Social Choice.* San Francisco: Freeman.

Riker, William H. 1986. *The Art of Political Manipulation.* New Haven, CT: Yale University Press.

Riker, William H., and Peter Ordeshook. 1968. A Theory of the Calculus of Voting. *American Political Science Review* 62: 25–42.

Jeffrey Grynaviski

RIOT ACT, THE

SEE *Riots.*

RIOTS

A riot is a social occasion involving relatively spontaneous collective violence directed at property, persons, or authority. Five main concepts characterize a riot. First, riots are *socially constructed* in that those participating in them define or redefine their social environment through a negotiation or renegotiation of symbols and meanings. For example, if looting occurs during a riot, what is conventionally defined as stealing private property may come to be redefined as "taking" or "receiving" items that are now collectively considered within the domain of public property. Second, riots are not singular events or moments in time, but *occasions*, in that there is a "before," "during," and "after." Although a riot may have an immediate precipitating incident, this moment is only one among many in the processional history of a riot. For example, the Watts Riot (August 1965) began with a relatively routine traffic stop of an African American motorist and quickly escalated into six days of arson, rock throwing, looting, and sniping that resulted in thirty-four dead and $45 million in damages. Though the traffic stop was the precipitating event, it would not be correct to consider it the *cause* of the riot; rather, the cause was the cumulative effect of many events and circumstances. Third, a riot is *relatively spontaneous* in that it does not involve a significant amount of planning and coordination. Although a small number of individuals may instigate a riot and serve as emergent leaders by providing examples of "appropriate" behavior, these individuals are generally unable to plan and coordinate action in a meaningful way once a riot has begun. The relative spontaneity of riots led some of the earliest researchers to conclude that once in crowds, individuals became irrational, highly suggestible, and without social control. More recent research, however, has found these claims to be largely unsubstantiated, noting that during most riots, collective violence is purposive and targeted. Fourth, a riot involves *collective violence*, meaning that groups or communities engage in the infliction of harm or destruction for the purpose of producing social change. Although individual violence may produce social change and even rioting—as in the case of the assassination of Martin Luther King (April 4, 1968)—to be considered a riot, both collective action and violence for the purpose of social change must be present. Finally, a riot involves collective violence directed at *property, persons, or authority*. It is important to note that in many instances, collective violence is directed not solely at property, persons, or authority but at some combination, such as state-controlled property or persons in authority. For example, in reaction to Italian Reform Minister Roberto Calderoli wearing a shirt decorated with cartoons satirizing the Muslim prophet Muhammad, hundreds of Libyans rioted by throwing stones and burning the Italian embassy, killing ten (on February 17, 2006).

TYPES OF RIOTS

Just as actors participate in a variety of actions during a riot, so too are there different types of riot. There are four main categories of riot, though these distinctions are not mutually exclusive. A *communal riot* is characterized by collective violence directed at persons of an opposing group, and may involve racial, ethnic, or religious groupings. Although police or agents of social control may engage in violence to keep the groups apart, the vast majority of collective violence occurs between groups. A *commodity riot* is characterized by collective violence directed primarily at property, but may involve people of different groups. Next, a *protest riot* involves spontaneous collective violence directed against a specific policy. In contrast to the communal riot, during a protest riot most of the collective violence occurs between the police or other agents of social control and the rioters. The final, and perhaps most frequent, form of rioting is the *revelry* or *celebration riot*. As with a commodity riot, collective violence is directed primarily at property, but may involve persons. However, in contrast to all other riots, a celebration riot does not necessitate grievance and often occurs after a victory over a traditional rival or the winning of a championship.

A riot is distinct from a variety of concepts that are often employed interchangeably in popular usage. The term most frequently used as an equivalent is *demonstration*. However, a demonstration is distinct from a riot in three fundamental ways. First, a demonstration is often planned and thus lacks the relative spontaneity of a riot. Second, unlike a riot, collective violence does not need to occur for something to be considered a demonstration. Finally, during a demonstration, leaders often have enough control to coordinate and direct the actions of others, which rarely, if ever, happens during a riot. Another term often used interchangeably with *riot* is *protest*, which is the act of expressing grievance in hopes of achieving amelioration or to draw attention to a cause. A key feature of protest is the condition of grievance, which although sometimes present is not always necessary for a riot.

A riot is also distinct from a *revolt*, which is an action aimed at the overthrow of an established social order, which may involve a transfer of power and the radical restructuring of social relations. Although riots have the potential to produce some social change, they are perhaps better understood as "proto-political" movements that rarely, if ever, result in a transfer of power from one social group to another.

HISTORY OF THE RIOT

The current understanding of the term *riot* dates back to the fourteenth century, when it began to connote violence, strife, or disorder on behalf of a particular portion of the populace. By the early eighteenth century, violence and strife was on the rise in England, which resulted in Parliament passing the Riot Act of 1715. The Riot Act stated that if twelve or more persons unlawfully or riotously assembled and refused to disperse within an hour after being read a specified portion of the act by proper authority, those persons would be considered felons and authorities would have the right to use lethal force against them. The Act provided broad powers to institutional authority during riots and despite some notable riots over the next two centuries, resulted in a general decline in the number and severity of riots in England. Although repealed in 1973, the Riot Act was influential in providing a legal framework for similar legislation in many other nations, including Australia, Belize, Canada, and the United States. From 1965 to 1973 the United States experienced a significant increase in the number of domestic riots, particularly in large urban areas with high concentrations of poverty and racially based residential segregation. Some community members from these areas objected to the term *riot*, as they believed it called to mind the image of an unruly ghetto. Consequently, many scholars and politicians began to refer to riots as *civil disorders*. Although *riot* no longer appears to have this same negative connation and again appears in popular and social science terminology, the term *civil disorder* is still often used interchangeably.

Recent research by social scientists has again sparked interest in the study of riots. In a comprehensive review and reanalysis of riots in the United States during the 1960s and 1970s, Clark McPhail (1994) found that a lack of resources, grievance, and aggression did not play as large a role in riots as originally claimed. In addition, McPhail found that actors in a riot are far more purposive in their actions than previously supposed. However, McPhail's findings regarding the causes of riots may be limited in generalizability, as research by Ashutosh Varshney (2002) found urban, caste, and community factors to be predictors of riots in India. This renewed interest in riots highlights the need for a better understanding of where and why they are likely to occur.

SEE ALSO *Communalism; Ethnocentrism; Kerner Commission Report; Protest; Quotas; Race Riots, United States; Resistance; Tulsa Riot; Urban Riots; Violence; Wilmington Riot of 1898*

BIBLIOGRAPHY

Anderson, William A. 1973. The Reorganization of Protest: Civil Disturbances and Social Change in the Black Community. *American Behavioral Scientist* 16 (3): 426–439.

Dynes, Russell R., and Enrico L. Quarantelli. 1968. Redefinitions of Property Norms in Community Emergencies. *International Journal of Legal Research* 3 (December): 100–112.

LeBon, Gustave. [1895] 1960. *The Crowd: A Study of the Popular-Mind.* New York: Viking Press.

Mackay, Charles. [1841] 1980. *Extraordinary Popular Delusions and the Madness of Crowds.* New York: Harmony Books.

McPhail, Clark. 1991. *The Myth of the Madding Crowd.* New York: Aldine de Gruyter.

McPhail, Clark. 1994. Presidential Address—The Dark Side of Purpose: Individual and Collective Violence in Riots. *Sociological Quarterly* 35 (1): 1–32.

Simpson, John, and Edmund Weiner. Riot. In *Oxford English Dictionary*, 2nd ed., Vol. 13, 966–968. Oxford: Oxford University Press.

U.S. National Advisory Commission on Civil Disorders. 1968. *Report of the National Advisory Commission on Civil Disorders.* New York: Dutton/New York Times.

John Barnshaw

RIOTS, URBAN

SEE *Urban Riots.*

RISK

The concept of risk is fundamental in the social sciences. Risk appears in numerous guises, from theoretical modeling of financial decisions to determining the social consequences of expanded nuclear power usage. Despite this importance, the precise definition of risk depends on the context and application. Common usage is derived from insurance applications where risk represents the possibility of loss, injury, or peril. This definition is reflected in various risk assessment and management applications, ranging from social and psychological risk to environmental and biohazard risk, where units of measurement for risk vary with context. In contrast, financial economics associates risk with the possibility that the actual return for a security will differ from the expected return. This financial risk is typically measured using the variance or standard deviation of historical return from the mean return, a definition of risk that includes both positive and negative outcomes. Key theoretical notions such as risk aversion and the risk-return tradeoff employ this definition. Where only the possibility of financial loss is of concern, as in value-at-risk applications, measurements are evaluated using the left tail of the relevant probability distribution.

RISK, UNCERTAINTY, AND PERCEPTION

The evolution of methods for the identification, assessment, and management of risk have played a central role in the progress of civilization. In ancient times, religious beliefs were important in reconciling the risks confronting a society. Appeals to the gods by the priesthood, prophecies from the oracle, and chanting by the shaman were all methods of passively dealing with risks encountered. The development of scientific, mathematical, and probabilistic methods during the Enlightenment permitted risk to be more actively identified and assessed. This advancement encountered a philosophical quandary concerning subjective and objective interpretations of probability. More precisely, the objective interpretation views probability as inherent in nature. Logic, scientific investigation, and statistical analysis can be used to discover objective probabilities. In contrast, subjective probabilities quantify an individual's belief in the truth of a proposition or the occurrence of an event and are revealed in an individual's choice behavior. Such probabilities can vary among individuals due, for instance, to differing degrees of ignorance about the event of interest.

Debate over subjective versus objective probability reached a peak around the time that Frank Knight (1885–1972) introduced a distinction between risk—where the objective probability of an event is at least measurable—and uncertainty, where the probability is not knowable and has to be determined subjectively. This terminological distinction between risk and uncertainty has now faded from common usage as the subjectivist approach has gained prominence, supported by seminal contributions from Frank Ramsey (1903–1930), Bruno di Finetti (1906–1985), and Leonard Savage (1917–1971). Attention has shifted to whether subjective beliefs derive from intuition or are realized only in choice behavior. The intuitive approach leads to a focus on the perception of risk, a concept often employed in psychometric and sociological research. Development of the choice-theoretic approach to subjective probability was facilitated by the expected utility function introduced by John von Neumann (1903–1957) and Oskar Morgenstern (1902–1976) in a classic work of social science, *The Theory of Games and Economic Behavior* (1944). The choice-theoretic approach has sustained the modeling of decision-making under uncertainty that is a central component of modern economic theory.

RISK IN ECONOMICS

Prior to von Neumann and Morgenstern, mathematically formal neoclassical economic theory was based on certainty or perfect foresight. Consideration of risk in decision-making could be found in the less formal approaches of Frank Knight, John Maynard Keynes (1883–1946), and Irving Fisher (1867–1947) that have contributed to a range of future contributions and perspectives on the impacts of risk in economics. Knight's recognition that uncertainty could be handled by the insurance principle led to contributions on the importance of moral hazard and adverse selection in decision-making under uncertainty. By explicitly recognizing what he termed the "caution coefficient," which measures the difference between the mathematical expectation and the price that will be paid for a gamble, Fisher laid the foundation for later contributions in mean-variance portfolio theory. The numerous contributions by Keynes on risk and uncertainty range from the *Treatise on Probability* (1921) to the *General Theory of Employment, Interest and Money* (1936). Disciples of Keynes, such as George L. S. Shackle (1903–1992) argue against the use of probability theory to model decision-making under uncertainty. Similarly, the failings of the ergodicity assumption are an important post-Keynesian critique of mathematically formal economic theory.

In addition to the diverse approaches to risk generated by Knight, Keynes, and Fisher, the application of mathematical formalism in economic theory has also produced impressive progress. Using preference orderings over state contingent commodities, Kenneth Arrow (born 1921) and Gerard Debreu (1921–2004) were able to extend the neoclassical economics of Stanley Jevons (1835–1882), Léon Walras (1843–1910) and Alfred Marshall (1842–1924) to include decision-making under uncertainty. This development follows naturally from using the choice-theoretic approach to subjective probability developed by von Neumann and Morgenstern. The utility of a certain outcome is replaced by the expected utility, calculated using known probabilities and the utilities for a set of random outcomes. The known probabilities are notionally determined by direct observation of previous choice behavior. Using this approach, while there is no formal distinction between risk and uncertainty, risk is usually associated with the variability of random outcomes and uncertainty with randomness. Sensitivity to risk is measured by comparing a certain outcome to a random outcome with the same expected value. Risky outcomes are measured in income, dollars, or returns, and can take both positive and negative values.

In financial economics, the expected utility framework has been applied to the problem of determining how to optimally combine individual securities into a portfolio of securities. Using an expected utility function specified over the expected portfolio return and variance of portfolio return, Harry Markowitz (born 1927) and William Sharpe (born 1934) were able to demonstrate that the variability or risk of a portfolio can be further divided into two components: firm specific risk, which is diversifiable and non-systematic; and market related risk, which is systematic and not diversifiable. Applying this to the tradeoff between risk and return, it is demonstrated that only increases in the systematic risk of an individual security will be rewarded with higher expected return. Hence, it is only that portion of the total variability of a security's return that cannot be diversified away that warrants higher expected return. A measure of systematic risk—the beta of a security—is provided. Beta can be calculated as the slope coefficient in a least squares regression of individual security return on market return: the ratio of the covariance between the individual security return and the market return divided by the variance of the market return. More recently, a variety of risk measures have been developed to deal with limitations of variance of return and beta. These new measures include expected regret, conditional value at risk, and expected shortfall.

RISK IN OTHER SOCIAL SCIENCES

In social sciences other than economics, risk is usually identified with only negative outcomes. Units of measurement vary and can include the annual death toll, deaths or injuries per hour of exposure, loss of life expectancy, loss of working hours, accidents per mile driven, and crop loss per storm. A wide range of risk definitions and risk models are employed, including the classical approach based on objective probabilities, adapted from engineering and medicine; the choice-theoretic expected utility approach employed in economics; and the risk perception approach popular in sociology and psychometrics, where it is explicitly recognized that risk depends on cultural and individual perceptions that can differ from expert or objectively specified risk estimates. Because a variety of different negative outcomes can be of interest, measures of risk vary with the consequences involved. For example, in the classical approach, risk is defined as the loss or hazard if the event occurs times the probability the event will occur. In other words, risk is a combination of exposure and uncertainty. However, when risk involves an event such as death, then risk relates only to the probability of the event occurring.

In many situations in the social sciences, the application of objective probabilities to determine risk is problematic. Though it is possible to specify the relative frequency of a negative outcome from past data, the data is often limited and the estimated risk can be less than objective. In addition, because risk depends on the context, there is room for disagreement over the selection and measurement of relevant consequences. This poses problems in studies of perceived risk where individual perceptions are compared with calculated risk obtained from expert or objective estimates. Early studies on risk perception were concerned with determining whether there were

significant deviations between individual risk perceptions and expert estimates. If such deviations were present, this provided support for the presence of heuristics and other sources of probability judgment bias. Further research has revealed that risk perception is a more complicated phenomenon. For example, risk perception depends on the target selected. This is manifested in risk denial, where individuals perceive risk to the general public from, say, alcohol or nuclear waste, to be greater than perceived risk to the individual or the individual's family.

SEE ALSO *Economics, Post Keynesian; Expected Utility Theory; Insurance; Keynes, John Maynard; Markowitz, Harry M.; Risk Neutrality; Risk Takers; Risk-Return Tradeoff; Utility, Von Neumann-Morgenstern; Von Neumann, John*

BIBLIOGRAPHY

Arrow, Kenneth J. 1965. *Aspects in the Theory of Risk Bearing.* Helsinki: Yrjö Jahnssonin Säätiö.

Bernstein, Peter L. 1996. *Against the Gods: The Remarkable Story of Risk.* New York: John Wiley.

Fischhoff, Baruch, Stephen R. Watson and Chris Hope. 1984. Defining Risk. *Policy Sciences* 17 (2): 123–139.

Holton, Glyn A. 2004. Defining Risk. *Financial Analysts Journal* 60 (6): 19–25.

Karni, Edi. 1996. Probabilities and Beliefs. *Journal of Risk and Uncertainty* 13 (3): 249–262.

Poitras, Geoffrey. 2002. *Risk Management, Speculation and Derivative Securities.* Boston: Academic Press.

Slovic, Paul. 1987. Perception of Risk. *Science* 236 (April): 280–285.

Szegö, Giorgio. 2005. Measures of Risk. *European Journal of Operational Research* 163 (1): 5–19.

Geoffrey Poitras

RISK AVERSION

SEE *Maximin Principle; Risk; Risk Neutrality.*

RISK NEUTRALITY

Risk neutrality is an economic term that describes individuals' indifference between various levels of risk. When confronted with a choice among different investment opportunities, risk-neutral decision makers only take into account the expected value of the alternative and not the associated level of risk. For example, a risk-neutral investor will be indifferent between receiving $100 for sure, or playing a lottery that gives her a 50 percent chance of winning $200 and a 50 percent chance of getting nothing. Both alternatives have the same expected value; the lottery, however, is riskier.

In economic theory it is generally accepted that most individuals are not risk-neutral. People tend to prefer safer choices to riskier ones, meaning they are risk-averse. In the above example, a risk-averse person would prefer getting the expected value of the lottery for sure rather than choose the gamble. In other words, a risk-averse person would require a premium above the expected value in order to play this lottery. Risk-neutral individuals would neither pay nor require a payment for the risk incurred.

In terms of utility theory, a risk-neutral individual's utility of expected wealth from a lottery is always equal to his or her expected utility of wealth provided by the same lottery. This implies a linear utility function, or relationship between the wealth and the utility of wealth. A simple example of such utility function is $U(W) = W$, where W is wealth and $U(W)$ is utility of wealth. In this case, a one-dollar increase in wealth will always result in the same increase in utility for any starting wealth level.

In finance, modern portfolio theory states that an investor needs to be compensated for the risk that she takes by receiving extra expected return. Such compensation is referred to as risk premium. The fact that historical returns for riskier asset classes, such as equities, consistently outperform returns for less risky assets (such as Treasury bills) confirms the existence of a considerable risk premium. For example, John Campbell, Andrew Lo, and A. Craig MacKinley reported in 1997 that in the period from 1889 to 1994 U.S. stock market returns were on average 4.18 percent higher than the returns on commercial paper. Risk neutrality, on the contrary, implies that investors do not require any risk premium since they are indifferent to the level of risk (p. 308). Therefore, in a world consisting of risk-neutral investors the difference between stock and commercial paper returns would be expected to be zero.

While risk neutrality is uncommon in the real world, the concept of risk neutrality plays an important role in option pricing. Risk-neutral valuation of options was first introduced by John Cox and Stephen Ross in 1976, and further developed by Cox, Ross, and Mark Rubinstein in 1979. This method is based on an observation that prices of derivatives are the same in the real as in the risk-neutral world. The risk preferences of individuals and the shape of their utility function do not affect the option prices as long as the agents prefer more wealth to less (the so-called nonsatiation condition). The fact that option prices are not affected by the risk preferences and utility functions of individuals allows us to price the options by calculating their expected values in the risk-neutral world and to use the risk-free discount rate to find their present value. The

risk-neutral valuation principle is widely used in practice to calculate values of different financial derivatives.

SEE ALSO *Risk; Risk Takers; Risk-Return Tradeoff*

BIBLIOGRAPHY

Campbell, John Y., Andrew W. Lo, and A. Craig MacKinlay. 1997. *The Econometrics of Financial Markets.* Princeton, NJ: Princeton University Press.

Cox, John C. and Stephen A. Ross. 1976. The Valuation of Options for Alternative Stochastic Processes. *Journal of Financial Economics* 3: 145–166.

Cox, John C., Stephen A. Ross, and Mark Rubinstein. 1979. Option Pricing: A Simplified Approach. *Journal of Financial Economics* 7: 229–263.

Yulia Veld-Merkoulova

RISK TAKERS

To take risks is to make decisions for which the favorability of outcomes is uncertain. Therefore, every individual and business entity is a *risk taker* at some level. However, the existence of risk takers who are prepared to put their capital and/or reputation at risk in the hope of a financial reward is a necessary precondition for a capitalist model of society. In the discipline of financial economics, risk takers are subcategorized into *risk lover, risk neutral,* and *risk averse* (Blake 2000). Traditional finance theory, applying assumptions of rational behavior, argues that the majority of people are risk averters, and hence "risk averse." Given a choice of two investment opportunities with identical expected returns and uncertain but symmetrical probability distributions with different degrees of dispersion, i.e. risk, the less risky option is always selected by risk averters. Risk averters are said to have a declining *marginal utility* of wealth. A risk-neutral investor, in contrast, would be indifferent between the two options presented above, because the potential for a less favorable outcome than expected is exactly offset by the equal probability of a more favorable outcome. Finally, a risk lover would prefer the riskier choice because the utility conferred by a *financial* gain more than offsets the utility destroyed by a financial loss of equal magnitude. Under the above distribution assumption risk lovers, unlike risk averters, always have an increasing marginal utility of wealth (Tobin 1958).

According to traditional finance theory based on rational risk-averse behavior, a professional risk taker such as a firm manager or an entrepreneur differs from an individual investor or portfolio manager who is concerned with the preservation of wealth (capital) in real terms.

Professional risk takers apply their knowledge and expertise to gain exposure to a specific category, or categories, of largely nonsystematic business risk in which they believe themselves to have a competitive advantage. Such risk averters resemble the "plungers" described by James Tobin (1958) who have indifference curves that, although always upward sloping, may be either linear or upwardly convex. In contrast, wealth-preserving investors seek to diversify away nonsystematic risk exposure to retain only systematic risk that can then be managed according to their risk preferences. They achieve this by allocating their capital between many specialist professional risk takers—that is, by investing the capital in many firms and risky assets—hence delegating their nonsystematic risk decisions to firm managers. Tobin (1958) describes the second category of risk averters as "diversifiers," and explains how the existence of plungers and the shape of utility functions are dependent upon the restrictions applied to the assumed probability distribution.

Frank H. Knight (1921) refers to risk as the quantifiable component of uncertainty in economic decision-making. However, John Maynard Keynes (1936) refers to "animal spirits" when he questions the foundations of neoclassical economics on the grounds that the risk-return trade-off implied by rational models of decision-making are difficult to implement in practice because risk is largely unquantifiable beforehand; furthermore, he argues that it is not possible to distinguish quantifiable risk from unquantifiable risk when making long-term investment decisions. Milton Friedman and Leonard J. Savage (1948) examine the implications for investors' utility functions of the apparently contradictory behavior of individuals who purchase insurance contracts, accepting a certain small loss in exchange for avoiding the low probability of a big loss (risk-avoiding behavior), while at the same time purchasing lottery tickets with a negative expected return in exchange for the very low probability of a big gain (risk-seeking behavior). Subsequent work in behavioral finance, such as that reviewed by David Hirshleifer (2001) and Meir Statman (1999), argues that rather than the cold calculating behavior implied by neoclassical economics and traditional finance theory, many risk takers exhibit an optimistic bias, referred to as "overconfidence," that may lead to risk-seeking behavior when faced with certain losses. Eddie Dekel and Suzanne Scotchmer (1999) discuss evolutionary explanations for risk-seeking behavior, citing the arguments of psychologists and evolutionary biologists to the effect that optimistic risk-seeking behavior exhibited by some individuals has allowed humans, as a species, to survive environmental shocks in which the expected value, and outcome, for the risk-averse majority would have been negative, and fatal.

SEE ALSO *Friedman, Milton; Risk; Risk Neutrality; Risk-Return Tradeoff; Tobin, James*

BIBLIOGRAPHY

Blake, David. 2000. *Financial Market Analysis.* Chichester, U.K.: Wiley.

Dekel, Eddie, and Suzanne Scotchmer. 1999. On the Evolution of Attitudes Towards Risk in Winner-Take-All Games. *Journal of Economic Theory* 87 (1): 125–143.

Friedman, Milton, and Leonard J. Savage. 1948. The Utility Analysis of Choices Involving Risk. *Journal of Political Economy* 56 (4): 279–304.

Hirshleifer, David. 2001. Investor Psychology and Asset Pricing. *Journal of Finance* 56 (4): 1533–1597.

Keynes, John Maynard. 1936. *The General Theory of Employment, Interest, and Money.* London: Macmillan.

Knight, Frank H. [1921] 1933. *Risk, Uncertainty, and Profit.* London: London School of Economics and Political Sciences.

Statman, Meir. 1999. Behavioural Finance: Past Battles and Future Engagements. *Financial Analysts Journal* 55 (6): 18–27.

Tobin, James. 1958. Liquidity Preference as Behaviour Towards Risk. *Review of Economic Studies* 25 (2): 65–86.

Isaac T. Tabner

RISK-RETURN TRADEOFF

The tradeoff between risk and return is one of the cornerstones of financial economics. When capital markets are in equilibrium, they determine a tradeoff between expected return and risk. The only way for investors to achieve a higher expected return is by taking on extra risk. This relationship between return and risk was first formalized by Harry Markowitz in 1952. In what later came to be known as the *modern portfolio theory*, he examined the tradeoff between risk and return in the context of the optimal selection problem for a portfolio of securities. In this theory investors aim to achieve the highest expected return for a certain level of risk; alternatively, they aim for the lowest level of risk for a certain expected return. An interesting graphical treatment of the risk-return tradeoff and variations in tastes for risk is given by James Tobin (1958).

Risk is measured as the standard deviation of the portfolio returns. This relationship is generally confirmed in total annual risk and return series. For example, over the period 1926 to 2002 stocks of small U.S. companies showed a mean return of 16.9 percent, stocks of large U.S. companies had a mean return of 12.2 percent, long-term government bonds had a mean return of 6.2 percent, and short-term government bonds had a mean return of 3.8 percent. The standard deviations of the returns are in line with the realized returns, as they are 33.2 percent for the small stocks, 20.5 percent for the large stocks, 9.4 percent for long-term government bonds, and 3.2 percent for short-term government bonds (Ross, Westerfield, and Jaffe 2005).

The difference in returns between stocks and short-term government securities is generally referred to as the equity premium. In their 1985 work Rajnish Mehra and Edward Prescott questioned the high level of the equity premium. Their argument is that the size of the equity premium implies an unrealistically high degree of risk aversion on the part of the investors. Stephen Ross, Randolph Westerfield, and Jeffrey Jaffe, in their 2005 study, present an average equity premium of 8.4 percent over the period from 1926 to 2002. They also show that the premium was much lower between 1802 and 1870 (2.9 percent) and between 1871 and 1925 (4.6 percent). Ross, Westerfield, and Jaffe (2005) state that, because of the low-risk premiums in the historical data from 1802 to 1925, caution is needed in making assumptions about the current equity premium.

An important lesson from the theory of Markowitz is that, on the level of individual securities, the covariance between different securities is a more important risk measure than the variance of the individual securities. Securities that have a negative covariance with each other tend to absorb each other's risk. If the price of one of the securities goes down, the other goes up and vice versa. In the 1960s the portfolio theory of Markowitz was further developed into the *capital asset pricing model* (CAPM). According to this model, the contribution of a security to the risk of a large well-diversified portfolio is proportional to the covariance of the security's return with the market's return. The standardized contribution is the beta, which can be interpreted as the responsiveness of the security's return to that of the market. According to this model investors divide their wealth between the market portfolio of assets and the risk-free asset. They are allowed to hold short positions in either the market portfolio or the risk-free asset. The market portfolio consists of all risky investments in the economy. Therefore it does not only include shares of common stock, but also corporate bonds, real estate and more exotic investments such as wine and stamp collections. From a theoretical point of view, the CAPM has been criticized because it assumes a market portfolio the contents of which are not observable, thus making it impossible to test this model. Empirical research by Eugene Fama and Kenneth French in 1993 has shown that the responsiveness to the market is not the only determinant of the expected return of a security. Besides the earlier mentioned beta, their three-factor model includes two additional explanatory variables for

security returns. These are the ratio of the market value of stock to the book value and the size of the company.

An important disadvantage of the use of the portfolio variance as the risk measure is that the variance is symmetrical. This means that it assigns the same weight to positive and negative deviations from the expected value. In other words, variance does not capture the common notion of risk as negative and undesired. The 2006 study by Chris Veld and Yulia Veld-Merkoulova of risk preferences of individual investors found that most investors use more than one risk measure. For those investors who systematically choose one risk measure, semivariance is most popular. This is also the case for stock investors, whereas bond investors favor the probability of loss as the most important risk measure.

SEE ALSO *Expected Utility Theory; Insurance; Risk; Risk Neutrality; Risk Takers*

BIBLIOGRAPHY

Fama, Eugene, and Kenneth French. 1993. Common Risk Factors in the Returns on Stocks and Bonds. *Journal of Financial Economics* 33 (1): 3–56.

Markowitz, Harry. 1952. Portfolio Selection. *The Journal of Finance* 7: 77–91.

Mehra, Rajnish, and Edward C. Prescott. 1985. The Equity Premium: A Puzzle. *Journal of Monetary Economics* 15 (2): 145–161.

Ross, Stephen A., Randolph W. Westerfield, and Jeffrey Jaffe. 2005. *Corporate Finance*. 7th ed. Boston: McGraw-Hill/Irwin.

Tobin, James. 1958. Liquidity Preference as Behavior towards Risk. *The Review of Economic Studies* 25 (2): 65–86.

Veld, Chris, and Yulia V. Veld-Merkoulova. 2006. The Risk Preferences of Individual Investors. Working Paper Series. Social Science Research Network. http://ssrn.com/abstract=821412.

Chris Veld

RITES OF PASSAGE

A rite of passage is a series of rituals that conveys an individual from one social state or status to another—for example, from adolescence to adulthood, from single to married, from student to graduate, from apprentice to a full member of a profession, from life to death—thereby transforming both society's definition of the individual and the individual's self-perception. Such rituals of social transition mark culturally recognized stages of life and assist the individual and social group in adjusting to an individual's new status and its implications for behavior and social relations. Transition rituals—rites of passage—

reduce the ambiguity associated with change, protecting individual psyches during the vulnerable period by reducing uncertainty and stress. Transition rituals are often directed toward the relationships between social conditions and physiological conditions (e.g., birth, puberty, marriage, pregnancy, death), demarcating certain points of the life cycle as especially significant. Ritual association of symbols and physiological processes provides a means of shaping and controlling human emotions and biological drives and then explaining them within wider cosmological frameworks.

Key social scientists who have studied rites of passage include Arnold van Gennep (1873–1957), who was the first to name and analyze them in 1908 in *Rites de Passage*; Bronislaw Malinowski (1884–1942), one of the first anthropologists to conduct on-site ethnography, who studied the functions of ritual on the Trobriand Islands off the coast of Australia; Victor Turner (1920–1983), who analyzed the roles of ritual and symbol among the Ndembu of Africa (1967, 1969); Mary Douglas (1921–2007), whose work on symbols provided a profound understanding of their uses and effectiveness in ritual (1966, 1973); Clifford Geertz (1926–2006), whose *The Interpretation of Cultures* (1973) offers deep analysis of ritual's roles in cultural preservation and revitalization; the biogenetic structuralists Charles Laughlin, John McManus, and Eugene d'Aquili (1979), who offer a neurologically based understanding of the effects of ritual and rites of passage; and Ronald Grimes, who explores first-person experiences of birth, initiation, marriage, and death (2000).

STRUCTURE AND ROLES OF RITES OF PASSAGE

Robbie Davis-Floyd defines ritual as "a patterned, repetitive, and symbolic enactment of a cultural belief or value" (2004, p. 8). Rituals usually work to enhance social cohesion, as their primary purpose in most cases is to align the belief system of the individual with that of the group. Ritual's role in rites of passage is fourfold:

1. to give humans a sense of control over natural processes that may be beyond their control, by making it appear that natural transformations (e.g., birth, puberty, death) are actually effected by society and serve society's ends (Malinowski 1954);

2. to "fence in" the dangers perceived cross-culturally to be present in transitional periods (when individuals are in-between social categories and therefore call the conceptual reality of those categories into question), while at the same time allowing controlled access to their energizing and revitalizing power (Douglas 1966);

3. to convey, through the emotions and the body, a series of repetitive and unforgettable messages to the initiate concerning the core values of the society into which he or she is being initiated through the carefully structured manipulation of appropriately representative symbols, and thereby to integrate those values, as well as the basic premises of the belief system on which they are based, into the inmost being of the initiate (Turner 1967, 1969; d'Aquili, Laughlin, and McManus 1979); and

4. to renew and revitalize these values for those conducting, as well as for those participating in or merely watching, the rituals through which these transformations are effected, so that both the perpetuation and the vitality of the belief and value system of the society in question can be assured (Turner 1967, 1969; Geertz 1973).

Rites of passage generally consist of three principal stages, outlined by van Gennep as: (1) separation of the individuals involved from their preceding social state; (2) a period of transition in which they are neither one thing nor the other; (3) a reintegration phase in which through various rites of incorporation they are absorbed into their new social state (van Gennep [1908] 1966). Van Gennep states that these three stages may be of varying degrees of importance, with rites of separation generally emphasized at funerals, and rites of incorporation at weddings. Yet, the most salient feature of all rites of passage is their transitional nature, the fact that they always involve what Victor Turner (1967, 1979) has called *liminality*, the stage of being betwixt and between, neither here nor there—no longer part of the old and not yet part of the new. In the liminal phase of initiatory rites of passage, "the ritual subject passes through a realm that has few or none of the attributes of the past or coming state" (Turner 1979, p. 237). Of this liminal phase, Turner writes:

> The passivity of neophytes to their instructors, their malleability, which is increased by submission to ordeal, their reduction to a uniform condition, are signs of the process whereby they are ground down to be fashioned anew and endowed with additional powers to cope with their new station in life…. It is the ritual and the esoteric teaching which grows girls and makes men…. The arcane knowledge, or "gnosis" obtained in the liminal period is felt to change the inmost nature of the neophyte, impressing him, as a seal impresses wax, with the characteristics of his new state. It is not a mere acquisition of knowledge, but a change in being. (1979, pp. 238–239)

One of the chief characteristics of this liminal period of any rite of passage is the gradual psychological "opening" of the initiates to profound interior change. In many initiation rites involving major transitions into new social roles, this openness is achieved through rituals designed to break down the initiates' belief system—the internal mental structure of concepts and categories through which they perceive and interpret the world and their relationship to it. Ritual techniques that facilitate this process include hazing—the imposition of physical and mental hardships (familiar to participants in fraternity initiation rites), and strange-making—making the commonplace strange by juxtaposing it with the unfamiliar. In *The Reversible World* (1978) Barbara Babcock describes a third such device, symbolic inversion, which works by metaphorically turning specific elements of this belief system upside-down or inside-out, so that the high is brought low, the low is raised high, and the world in general is thrown into confusion. The end result of this inversion, however, is usually that core cultural elements—values, practices, hierarchies—are in the end firmly returned to their positions of centrality, reverence, and weight. Yet, rites of passage can be used to completely overturn these core cultural elements, creating new societies and new religions.

For example, in studying the Moonies (followers of the Korean evangelist Reverend Sun Myung Moon), the sociologist Marc Galanter (1989) found that many of those who attended one of the five-day workshops ostensibly offered to explain the religion to interested newcomers ended up converting—even if their original reason for going was to learn enough about the religion to talk a loved one into getting out. How could this happen? Participants sat through many hours of lecture, during which they were bombarded with an overload of confusing information, resulting in a narrowing of their cognitive abilities. Interspersed between lectures were periods of playful fun—volleyball, dancing—during which the newcomers were made to feel wholly important, wholly wanted, wholly loved. Allusions were made to Moon in connection with the Second Coming of Christ, and it was suggested that if newcomers were truly blessed, they might see visions of Moon himself during their regularly scheduled meditation periods. Not surprisingly, many did. Neuropsychologist John McManus explains:

> As this process is continued over time, the cognitive reality model begins to disintegrate. Learned versions of reality and previously instrumental responses repeatedly fail the initiate. Confusion and disorganization ensue.... at this point the individual should be searching for a way to structure or make sense out of reality, and in terms of the initiation, his search constitutes the launching point for the transformation of identity. (1979, p. 239)

The breakdown of their belief systems leaves initiates profoundly open to new learning and to the construction of new categories. Any symbolic messages conveyed to an initiate during this opening process can thus be imprinted on his or her psyche as deeply "as a seal impresses wax" (Turner 1979, p. 239).

TYPES OF RITES OF PASSAGE

Military initiation rites constitute a classic example of hazing, strange-making, and symbolic inversion. In the rite of passage of Marine basic training, the initiate's normal patterns of action and thought are turned topsy-turvy. He is made strange to himself: His head is shaved, so that he does not even recognize himself in the mirror. He must give up his clothes, those expressions of individual identity and personality, and put on a uniform indistinguishable from that of other initiates. Constant and apparently meaningless hazing (e.g., orders to dig ditches and then fill them up) break down his cognitive structure. Then through repetitive and highly symbolic rituals (such as sleeping with his rifle), his physical habits and patterns of thought are literally reorganized into alignment with the basic values, beliefs, and practices of the Marines.

Cross-culturally, the most prominent types of rites of passage are those dealing with life crises. They accompany what Lloyd Warner has called

> the movement of a man [sic] through his lifetime, from a fixed placental placement within his mother's womb to his death and ultimate fixed point of his tombstone ... punctuated by a number of critical moments of transition which all societies ritualize and publicly mark with suitable observances to impress the significance of the individual and the group on living members of the community. These are the important times of birth, puberty, marriage and death. (1959, p. 303)

The sequence of these life-crisis events that Warner uses refers to the baby's birth and not to the woman's giving birth, nor to her transition into motherhood. Thus, this sequence reveals a strong male bias that for many years influenced a general neglect within anthropological research and theory regarding the significance of women's rites across cultures. Arranged from a non–gender-biased perspective, the sequence would have to read: birth, puberty and coming of age, marriage, childbearing, menopause, death. (By now, female life transitions have been studied intensively by female anthropologists.) Additionally, for some cultures, we would have to add first haircuts, adolescent circumcision, debutante balls or quinceaneras, ritual scarring or tattooing, and other such to this list.

For example, in *Birth as an American Rite of Passage* (2004), Davis-Floyd analyzed obstetric procedures as rituals that convey the core values of the U.S. technocracy—a society organized around an ideology of technological progress—to birthing women. These core values center around science, technology, and institutions. The IV is the symbolic umbilical cord to the hospital, communicating to the laboring woman the powerful message that she is now dependent on the institution for her life. Likewise, the electronic fetal monitor (to which nowadays nearly all laboring women in developed countries are attached by means of two giant belts around their stomachs) serves as a powerful symbol of the cultural supremacy of science and technology—it makes the laboring woman dependent on a machine to help her produce her baby. The ability of symbols to imprint their messages onto an individual's psyche is clearly expressed in the words of an interviewee, who said, "As soon as I got hooked up to the monitor, all everyone did was stare at it. Pretty soon I got the feeling that it was having the baby, not me" (Davis-Floyd 2004, p. 107). As this example shows, as an individual experiences the messages conveyed by a powerful symbol, her cognitive system can be partially or completely realigned around those messages. Whether the individual is giving birth, becoming an adult in the eyes of her society, undergoing a religious indoctrination, or being initiated into the army or a secret society, the ritual processes that constitute rites of passage are very much the same.

SEE ALSO *Church, The; Conformity; Culture; Ethnography; Geertz, Clifford; Hitler, Adolf; Malinowski, Bronislaw; Maturation; Military; Performance; Religion; Rituals; Self-Perception Theory; Shamans; Stages of Development; Symbols; Technocracy; Turner, Victor; Values*

BIBLIOGRAPHY

Babcock, Barbara, ed. 1978. *The Reversible World: Symbolic Inversion in Art and Society*. Ithaca, NY: Cornell University Press.

d'Aquili, Eugene G., Charles D. Laughlin, and John McManus. 1979. *The Spectrum of Ritual: A Biogenetic Structural Analysis*. New York: Columbia University Press.

Davis-Floyd, Robbie. [1992] 2004. *Birth as an American Rite of Passage*. 2nd ed. Berkeley: University of California Press.

Douglas, Mary. 1966. *Purity and Danger*. London: Routledge and Kegan Paul.

Douglas, Mary. 1973. *Natural Symbols: Explorations in Cosmology*. New York: Vintage Books.

Galanter, Marc. 1989. *Cults: Faith, Healing, and Coercion*. New York: Oxford University Press.

Grimes, Ronald. 2000. *Deeply into the Bone: Re-Inventing Rites of Passage*. Berkeley: University of California Press.

Laughlin, Charles D., Eugene d'Aquili, and John McManus. 1993. *Brain, Symbol, and Experience: Toward a Neurophenomenology of Human Consciousness*. New York: Columbia University Press.

Malinowski, Bronislaw. [1925] 1954. Magic, Science, and Religion. In *Magic, Science, and Religion and Other Essays*, 17–87. New York: Doubleday/Anchor.

McManus, John. 1979. Ritual and Human Social Cognition. In *The Spectrum of Ritual: A Biogenetic Structural Analysis*, eds. Eugene d'Aquili, Charles D. Laughlin, and John McManus, 216–248. New York: Columbia University Press.

Turner, Victor W. 1967. *The Forest of Symbols*. Ithaca, NY and London: Cornell University Press.

Turner, Victor W. 1969. *The Ritual Process: Structure and Anti-Structure*. Chicago: Aldine.

Van Gennep, Arnold. [1908] 1966. *The Rites of Passage*. Chicago: University of Chicago Press.

Robbie Davis-Floyd

RITUALS

A ritual is a patterned, repetitive, and symbolic enactment of a cultural belief or value. Rituals usually work to enhance social cohesion, because their primary purpose in most cases is to align the belief system of the individual with that of the group. The more a belief system is enacted through ritual, the stronger it becomes; the less it is enacted, the weaker it becomes. For this reason, religious leaders often exhort their members to participate regularly—for example, to come to church every Sunday and to prayer group every Wednesday night. If people stop going, that is, if they cease to enact the religion's rituals, over time that religion will have less and less meaning for them. Rituals are most commonly thought of as religious, but they can enact secular beliefs and values as effectively as religious ones.

A common misconception holds that ritual is something that goes on only in "primitive" cultures, whereas in so-called modern, developed societies, citizens benefiting from scientific enlightenment lead rational, de-ritualized lives. But the facts suggest otherwise. Across cultures and throughout history, all human cultures use ritual as the physical and psychological means for dealing with the mystery and unpredictability of the natural, social, and cosmic realms. Ritual's cultural roles are myriad; they include engendering belief, maintaining religious vitality, stimulating economic exchange, enhancing courage, effecting healing, and transforming individual consciousness, often in order to bring it into alignment with group values as well as to intensify individual and group investment in social structure.

CHARACTERISTICS OF RITUAL

Nine characteristics are integral to ritual's myriad roles in human cultural life and constitute a sort of anatomy of ritual. They include:

1. the symbolic nature of ritual's messages;

2. its embeddedness in a cognitive matrix (belief system);

3. ritual drivers—rhythmic repetition and redundancy;

4. the use of specific tools, technologies, and clothing;

5. the framing of ritual performances—their set-apartness from everyday life;

6. order and formality;

7. the sense of inviolability and inevitability that is established during ritual performances;

8. the acting, stylization, and staging that often give ritual its elements of high drama, and the fact that it is performed; and

9. often, a ludic dimension—the inclusion of play within the ritual frame.

Symbolism Ritual sends its messages through symbols. A symbol, most simply, is an object, idea, or action loaded with cultural meaning. Symbols are multivocal—that is, many meanings can be brought together and expressed in one symbol (e.g., a cross, a U.S. flag, a swastika). Unlike symbols, straightforward verbal messages are intellectually analyzed by the left hemisphere of the human brain, enabling the recipient to accept or reject their content. Symbols, in contrast, are received through the right hemisphere of the brain as a gestalt—that is, they are felt in the body and the emotions; their meanings are often internalized without conscious awareness. Objects or procedures can function powerfully as symbols even if the conscious intent of their performers is instrumental, not symbolic. For example, a blood-pressure cuff both records blood pressure and symbolizes western technocratic medicine, specifically the value it places on objective information; the stethoscope a physician wears around her neck both enables her to listen to a patient's breathing and symbolizes her authoritative status. When a Marine basic trainee is required to sleep with his rifle, he "in-corporates" its symbolic meanings—they become part of his psyche through his body.

Because ritual works through symbols, the ritual process is fundamentally experiential, and the learning that takes place through ritual is experiential. Anthropological research on the difference between the experiential and didactic (explicit teaching) modes of learning has shown that experiential learning is by far the most powerful kind. Didactic learning can be intellectually rejected or easily forgotten, but experiential learning habituates the individual to specific patterns of behavior and response, and is much longer-lasting. It is no cultural accident that in contemporary society, as in the evolutionary past, skills, trades, and crafts, from tool-carving to eye surgery, have been taught experientially, through the process of apprenticeship.

A Cognitive Matrix A matrix (from the Latin *mater*, meaning "mother"), like a womb, is something from within which something else emerges. Rituals are not arbitrary; they come from within the belief system of a group. Each symbolic message that a given ritual sends manifests an underlying cultural belief or value embedded in that cognitive matrix. Sometimes these are made explicit in ritual, but quite often these deep beliefs that the ritual expresses are held unconsciously, rather than consciously. Ritual's primary purpose is to symbolically enact and thereby to transmit a group's belief system into the psyches of its participants, aligning their individual beliefs and values with those of the group.

Because the belief system of a culture is enacted through ritual, analysis of ritual can lead directly to a profound understanding of that belief system. For this reason, anthropologists studying various cultures often have focused on interpreting the rituals of that culture as a primary way to gain a deep understanding of it. In "Baseball Magic" (2000) George Gmelch decodes the rituals of baseball players to reveal their tensions, anxieties, and value system. Likewise, W. Lloyd Warner's (1959) analysis of Memorial Day, "An American Sacred Ceremony," shows how Americans use the rituals of this day to celebrate the unity of the nation in the face of its diversity, providing important insights into American life.

Ritual Drivers: Repetition and Redundancy For maximum effectiveness, a ritual will concentrate on sending one basic set of messages, which it will rhythmically repeat over and over again in different forms. What is repeated in ritual can include: (1) the occasion for its performance (as in a ceremony that happens every year at the same time); (2) its content (as in a chant); (3) the form into which this content is structured (as in a church ceremony); or any combination of these. This redundancy enhances ritual's efficiency in communicating whatever messages it is designed to send; the Mayan farmer who hears the shaman chant the names of the gods twenty times in one hour, several times a day, is not likely to forget them.

Rhythmicity has long been recognized by anthropologists as a key feature of ritual. Rhythmic, repetitive stimuli affect the human central nervous system, generating (especially in safe, relaxed settings) a high degree of limbic arousal, coordinating emotional, cognitive, and motor processes within an individual, and synchronizing these processes among the various ritual participants. This process of entrainment may be experienced as a loss of self-consciousness, a feeling of flow. Ritual entrainment can lead to transpersonal bonding, a sense of the unity and oneness of the group. This is a common experience at rock concerts—as the audience begins to entrain with the rhythms of the music, the huge auditorium suddenly seems to shrink and be suffused with shared energy; individuals feel like organic parts of a pulsating whole. Mickey Hart, the drummer for the rock group the Grateful Dead, said of this process, "Sometimes I felt that we were becoming a big noisy animal that made music when it breathed" (Hart, Stevens, and Lieberman 1990, p. 144).

Use of Tools, Technologies, and Clothing All rituals employ specific tools and technologies to achieve their purposes: altars and candles, the shaman's drum and rattle, the priest's robes and communion cup, the diviner's tea leaves and tarot cards, the wrapped Christmas gift. From the Navajo hogan to the Internet, ritual technologies both construct the spaces within which ritual happens, and assist in effecting the external and internal transformations it achieves. As noted above, the technologies of ritual often fulfill both utilitarian and symbolic functions. The candle both sheds light and opens the doorway between dimensions; the communion cup both holds liquid and evokes the Last Supper. In healing rituals, the healer often perceives the patient through the medium of the technology (herbs, smudging, rattling, sandpainting in traditional cultures; x-rays, EEG printouts, vital-sign monitors in modern hospitals). As with much of everyday social life, humans mediate their experience through the technologies they create. This technological mediation influences our perceptions of reality in myriad ways. The technologies employed in ritual play a particularly significant role in altering and mediating perception and experience because their uses in the heightened, set-apart, and formalized structures of ritual make them especially effective at achieving the neural entrainment of the participants, en face or at a distance, with the rhythms of the ritual and with the symbolic messages it sends. The production, sale, and exchange of ritual artifacts serve as major economic drivers in all societies (Malinowski 1948).

Framing Rituals are framed, set apart from everyday life, often in spaces reserved solely for their performance such as churches, temples, theaters, sports stadiums, or simply the space in front of a home altar. This ritual framing works to ensure that participants will keep their attention focused on a limited stimulus field, facilitating their entrainment with the ritual's symbolic messages.

Order and Formality In ritual events, things are no longer casual, but precise. Order matters, and the feeling is formal. Participants must pay special attention to body movements to be sure they are behaving appropriately, as in church or at a formal dinner. Order and formality—the careful sequencing of ritual performances—enhance the strength of this stimulus field and further work to set rituals apart from other modes of social interaction.

Inviolability and Inevitability Rituals establish an atmosphere that feels both inevitable and inviolate—the ritual must proceed to its conclusion through a pre-established sequence of events. Americans would find it hard to imagine, for example, stopping a graduation ceremony, interrupting the Pledge of Allegiance, or standing up in the middle of a church service to argue with the minister. Precise performance of ritual gives humans the feeling of setting into motion cosmic gears—an inviolable process that will inevitably propel the individual through danger to safety. Thus, ritual enhances courage. The anthropologists Sally Falk Moore and Barbara Myerhoff (1977) suggested that ritual's insistence on repetition and order evokes the perpetual processes of the cosmos, thereby metaphorically implying that the belief system being enacted has the same permanence and legitimacy as the cosmos itself.

Performance: Acting, Stylization, and Staging Like a play, ritual is performed, often giving it an element of high drama. The more dramatic ritual is, the more effectively it engages the emotions. These qualities enable ritual to command the attention of participants and audience, while at the same time serving to deflect questioning and the presentation of alternative points of view. A major part of ritual's job is to imbue participants with a strong sense of the value, validity, and importance of the belief system being enacted; in so doing, ritual must also work to preclude challenges to that belief system. Those who manipulate and control ritual are powerful performers, from traditional shamans to Jerry Falwell and Adolf Hitler. Ritual experts have both total command of the belief system being enacted, and dramatic, often charismatic, flair. Their effectiveness rests on their ability to entrain groups, to reorder divergent individual cognition around the symbolic matrix they represent. Hitler's ability to accomplish this through ritual was so profound that within a few years he was able to restructure the cognitive system of an entire nation around the symbolic matrix of German dominance and Aryan supremacy, represented by one powerful symbol, the swastika. On a smaller scale, the continued survival of many indigenous cultures often depends in large part on the ability of their shamans to dramatically and inspirationally perform the rituals that enact and thus perpetuate their unique cultural values, beliefs, and sense of connectedness to place. When the shamans die without transmitting this cultural lore to apprentices who can carry on, the culture is well on its way to extinction, or at least profound alteration.

A Ludic Dimension In spite of its serious formality, ritual often has an intensely ludic (playful) dimension. In some cultures, such as the Mescalero Apache of New Mexico described by anthropologist Claire R. Farrer (1991), during their most sacred ceremonies a clown mimics and mocks the singers as they perform the ritual acts in the required sequence, while the watching participants laugh uproariously at his antics. The Mescalero do not feel that their laughter decreases the sacredness of the event; on the contrary, it increases it through the revitalizing energy that laughter brings to the culture's most deeply held beliefs. A parallel can be found in the rodeo clown. Rodeo bull riders ritually display the manly heroic virtues that their subculture holds dear; the clowns, whose task it is to divert the bulls while entertaining the audience, mock those manly traits even as they themselves exemplify them.

THE EFFECTS OF RITUAL

The primary effects of ritual include:

1. the cognitive transformation of its participants that is ritual's primary purpose;

2. the cognitive simplification that ritual works to engender in its participants by rendering complex ideas more straightforward or unitary, which can generate habituation;

3. the cognitive stabilization that ritual can achieve for individuals under stress, which can include the enhancement of courage;

4. the preservation of the status quo in a given society; and

5. ritual's paradoxical effectiveness at facilitating social change.

Although not every ritual achieves each of these purposes, these are all part of the capacity of ritual as a symbolic form. Ritual is a powerful didactic and socializing tool. To grasp its inner workings is to have a choice in our response to the rituals that permeate our daily lives, and of which we are often unaware.

Cognitive Transformation Belief follows emotion. In general, people are far more likely to remember events, and to absorb lessons from those events, if they carry an emotional charge. Ritual generates that charge—it focuses the emotions on the symbolic messages it presents. This focusing process is enhanced by the rhythmic repetition of

the ritual's messages, which will often intensify toward a climax. If the ritual is successful, belief will be generated through the mapping-on process. And because of the emotions associated with that belief, neither the experience nor the belief will be forgotten.

For example, in *Juan the Chamula* (Pozas 1962), a Chamula Indian from highland Chiapas in southern Mexico describes a healing ceremony in which the shaman attempts to cure him of "soul-loss" through a long and elaborate ceremony. At the climax, the shaman twists the neck of a rooster and kills it, and Juan exclaims, "suddenly I felt free!" (p. 90). This experience of ritual healing constituted for Juan an important step in his cognitive reintegration into the cultural system he had left years ago, and to which he was now returning. As this example demonstrates, healers can use ritual's ability to generate belief to map their interpretation of the illness into the mind-body of the patient. When these fuse, healing can be achieved, as the body responds to what the mind now believes.

The emotional affect generated by ritual can do much more than generate belief. Humans have two nervous subsystems, the excitation and the relaxation systems. Usually, when one is discharging, the other is quiescent. But their repeated stimulation may cause both to simultaneously discharge. Under conditions of stress, the sensations so produced are more likely to be those of calm, reassurance, and a sense of control. Under stable social and environmental conditions, this simultaneous discharge of both nervous systems produces an intensely pleasurable, almost orgasmic sensation—indeed, both subsystems do simultaneously discharge during orgasm. This ecstatic state occurs in ritual when physical, emotional, and intellectual experiences of the symbolic messages become one. It may be very brief, experienced only as, for example, goose bumps popping out as the banner-bearing choir marches down the aisle on Easter Sunday, or a shiver down the back as you salute your national flag during a parade. It may happen only once during the ritual, or may be repeated at numerous focal points. Or this ecstatic state may be prolonged, as in meditation and religious trance or dance. In any case, these ecstatic sensations become experientially associated by ritual participants with the belief system enacted in the ritual. Charismatic Christian groups are filled with the Holy Spirit; !Kung bushmen trance-dancers with the boiling energy they call *n/um*. Biological research has established that during this state, high levels of endorphins—natural pain-relieving, pleasure-producing chemicals—flood the central nervous system. This ritually induced experience of ecstasy is one of the most powerfully emotion-filled experiences available to humans. Once they experience this state (especially the prolonged version) during a ritual, they are likely to want more. This desire can be a powerful incentive to begin regular attendance at the ritual events that can induce and consistently reproduce these feelings.

Through the ritual drivers of rhythmic repetition, evocative style, and precise manipulation of symbols and sensory stimuli, collective rituals focus the emotions of participants on the calculated intensification of their messages. Ritual generates intense emotion, even ecstasy, in humans, and intense emotion, in turn, generates belief (d'Aquili, Laughlin, and McManus 1979).

Transformation for ritual participants can be both mental and physical. It can be external in the eyes of society, and/or internal in the psyche of the participant. Some kind of transformation can be said to occur in all types of ritual—even a simple ritual greeting opens a previously nonexistent channel of communication between two individuals, resulting in almost immediate entrainment of their bodily rhythms. Deep transformation for ritual participants occurs when the symbolic messages of ritual fuse with individual emotion and belief, and the individual's entire cognitive structure reorganizes around the newly internalized symbolic complex. Although this process may sound final, as if it could happen only once, it is not. Human neural structures are not made of cement; they are relatively fluid. As most religious adherents know from experience, belief waxes and wanes, and must be continually reinforced through ritual if it is to retain a significant role in shaping individual cognition and behavior. Each time a person attends a religious service or a political rally, he or she can experience this process anew, diving deeper and deeper into the symbolic constellations of belief of the religious or political system.

The most profoundly transformative of all rituals are initiatory rites of passage and religious indoctrinations. These break down the belief system of the initiate, then rebuild it around the beliefs and values of the group—a conversion experience. Whether the individual is converted to Islam or Christianity, or initiated into the army or a fraternity, the ritual process is very much the same.

Cognitive Simplification In any culture, ritual participants will differ from each other both in intellectual ability and in cognitive structure. Straightforward didactic communications must take these differences into account if their messages are to be understood. But ritual must work collectively, for the masses. Ritual overcomes this problem by working to reduce its participants, at least temporarily, to the same cognitive level, at which they will all see the world from within the confines of one cognitive matrix. An individual thinking at this level will tend to see the world in terms of black and white, interpreting others as either with her or against her (as do religious fundamentalists, for example). This sort of either/or thinking does not allow for the consideration of options or alternative views. The advantage of this reduction of ritual participants to univariate thinking is that a single ritual structure is now sufficient to communicate social norms and values to a wide variety of individuals. This process is most clearly visible in the performance of religious rituals such as the Catholic Mass, which can be deeply and equally convincing to individuals of all levels of cognitive complexity, or in the political rallies of totalitarian regimes such as Nazi Germany. Such cognitive simplification must precede the conceptual reorganization that accompanies true psychological transformation. The most common technique employed in ritual to accomplish this end is the rhythmically repetitive bombardment of participants with ritual's symbolic messages.

The order and precision of ritual, combined with its repetitious nature, can be highly effective at habituating individuals to doing things one way only. Physicians have described how their learning process was channeled into a "narrow riverbank" in which the water can only flow one way; one said, "You do it, and you do it, and you do it some more" (Davis-Floyd and St. John 1998, p. 54). Habituation to this one way can be efficient; it can also preclude openness to new and perhaps better ways.

Cognitive Stabilization When humans are subjected to extremes of stress, they are likely, at least temporarily, to retrogress cognitively into a dysfunctional condition in which they become panic-stricken, unreasonable, or simply out of touch with reality. Whenever the danger of such retrogression is present, ritual plays a critical role, because it stabilizes individuals under stress by giving them a conceptual handle-hold to keep them from losing it. When the airplane starts to falter, even those who do not go to church are likely to pray! The simple act of rhythmically repeating, "Dear Lord, please save us," can enable terrified passengers to avoid the panic behavior that might increase the likelihood of disaster.

Ritual stands as a barrier between cognition and chaos by making reality appear to fit accepted cognitive categories—that is, by making the world look the way it ought to. In other words, to perform a ritual in the face of chaos is to restore conceptual order. Even a small semblance of order can enable individuals to function under the most chaotic of conditions. The earthquake victim sweeps off her front steps when the entire house lies in ruins around her. This behavior is not as irrational as it seems at first glance. Those steps represent one ordered cognitive category, and for the householder, to make them clean is to ground herself in a little piece of the known and the familiar. From that cognitive anchor, she can then begin to deal, a little at a time, with the surrounding chaos.

To perform a series of rituals is to seek to induce a particular outcome, often involved with creating a sense of safety in the presence of danger. The Trobriand sea fisherman who makes elaborate offerings and incantations in precise order before embarking into perilous waters believes that, if he does his part correctly, so must the gods of the sea do their part to bring him safely home. For the same reasons, the batter turns his cap backwards and clutches his rabbit's foot before he steps up to the plate. And the Bolivian tin miner, before descending into the hot and dangerous mines that he thinks of as the devil's territory, makes an offering of candy or tobacco to the devil so that the devil will be obliged to reciprocate by protecting him. In such cases, the rituals provide a sense of control that gives individuals the courage to act in the face of the challenge and caprice of nature. But the inevitability of ritual can be a double-edged sword: Rituals do not always work, and the sense of confidence they generate can be a false one. Nevertheless, that sense of confidence does facilitate action in the face of fear.

Rituals—from prayer, to carefully setting the table, to lighting candles for loved ones in danger—provide their participants with many such cognitive anchors. Ritual thus has high evolutionary value; it was a powerful adaptive technique our hominid ancestors most likely utilized to help them continue to function at a survival level whenever they faced conditions of environmental or social stress. Groups that believe together can act together to meet and overcome crises and danger. When belief is not shared, joint action is much more difficult to achieve. Even warring armies often rely on a number of shared beliefs, symbols, and rituals—the Red Cross or Red Crescent of medical facilities, the white flag of truce, the process of formal surrender. These are rituals of stabilization that can work even in the face of the mayhem of war.

Preserving the Status Quo Through explicit enactment of a culture's belief system, ritual works both to preserve and to transmit that belief system, and so becomes an important force in the preservation of the status quo in any society. Thus one usually finds that those in power in a given social group strive to maintain control over ritual performances. They utilize ritual's tremendous power to reinforce both their own importance and the importance of the belief and value system that sustains them in their positions.

Effecting Social Change Paradoxically, ritual, with all of its insistence on continuity and order, can be an important factor not only in individual transformation but also in social change. New belief and value systems are most effectively spread through new rituals designed to enact and transmit them. Even if a ritual is being performed for the very first time, its stylistic similarities with other rituals make it feel tradition-like, thus giving entirely new belief systems the feel and flavor of being strongly entrenched and sanctioned by ancient practice. Moreover, entrenched belief and value systems are most effectively altered through changes in the rituals that enact them. Indeed, ritual represents one of society's greatest potentials for the kind of revitalization that comes from internal growth and change in response to changing circumstances.

BIBLIOGRAPHY

Bell, Catherine. 1997. *Ritual: Perspectives and Dimensions.* New York: Oxford University Press.

Bloch, Maurice. 1992. *Prey into Hunter: The Politics of Religious Experience.* Cambridge, U.K.: Cambridge University Press.

d'Aquili, Eugene G., Charles D. Laughlin, and John McManus. 1979. *The Spectrum of Ritual: A Biogenetic Structural Analysis.* New York: Columbia University Press.

Davis-Floyd, Robbie. 2004. *Birth as an American Rite of Passage.* 2nd ed. Berkeley: University of California Press.

Davis-Floyd, Robbie, and Gloria St. John. 1998. *From Doctor to Healer: The Transformative Journey.* New Brunswick, NJ: Rutgers University Press.

Douglas, Mary. 1966. *Purity and Danger: An Analysis of Concepts of Pollution and Taboo.* London: Routledge.

Farrer, Claire R. 1991. *Living Life's Circle: Mescalero Apache Cosmovision.* Albuquerque: University of New Mexico Press.

Gmelch, George. 2000. Baseball Magic. http://sa.ncsu.edu/S&A/people/lecturers/terry_i/class_materials/252/baseball_magic.pdf.

Grimes, Ronald L. 1994. *The Beginnings of Ritual Studies.* Columbia: University of South Carolina Press.

Hart, Mickey, Jay Stevens, and Frederic Lieberman. 1990. *Drumming at the Edge of Magic: A Journey into the Spirit of Percussion.* San Francisco, CA: HarperSanFrancisco.

Malinowski, Bronislaw. 1948. *Magic, Science, and Religion.* Boston: Beacon Press.

Moore, Sally Falk, and Barbara Myerhoff, eds. 1977. *Secular Ritual.* Assen, Netherlands: Van Gorcum.

Pozas, Ricardo. 1962. *Juan the Chamula: An Ethnological Recreation of the Life of a Mexican Indian.* Berkeley: University of California Press.

Rappaport, Roy A. 1999. *Ritual and Religion in the Making of Humanity.* Cambridge, U.K.: Cambridge University Press.

Smith, Jonathan Z. 1987. *To Take Place: Toward Theory in Ritual.* Chicago: University of Chicago Press.

Turner, Victor W. 1969. *The Ritual Process: Structure and Anti-Structure.* Chicago: Aldine.

Warner, W. Lloyd. 1959. *The Living and the Dead: A Study of the Symbolic Life of Americans.* New Haven, CT: Yale University Press.

Robbie Davis-Floyd

RITUAL DRIVER

SEE *Rituals.*

RIVALRY, SIBLING

SEE *Sibling Relationships.*

ROBBER CAVE EXPERIMENT

SEE *Superordinate Goals; Sherif, Muzafer.*

ROBESON, PAUL
1898–1976

Paul Robeson, an African American actor, singer, and social activist, was born on April 9, 1898, in Princeton, New Jersey, and died on January 23, 1976, in Philadelphia, Pennsylvania. During the 1930s and 1940s, Robeson gained international renown as a concert singer and stage actor. His embrace of the Soviet Union and communism, however, especially during the formative years of the Cold War and the backlash against left-wing causes during the 1950s, effectively ended his artistic career and contributed to his physical decline.

Robeson was the youngest of five children. His father, William Drew Robeson, was born a slave in North Carolina, but he escaped and went on to become a Presbyterian minister in New Jersey, until he was forced to leave his congregation over a major dispute. Robeson's mother, Maria Louisa Bustill, hailed from a prominent Philadelphia family and became a schoolteacher. She burned to death tragically in a house fire when Robeson was only six years old, an experience that undoubtedly affected the youngster.

Between 1916 and 1919, Robeson attended Rutgers College in New Jersey as the only African American student. While there, he gained both academic and athletic distinction, being elected to Phi Beta Kappa and twice named an all-American football player. Between 1920 and 1923, he attended Columbia Law School in New York City, playing professional football on weekends and acting to pay the bills.

It was at Columbia University that Robeson met chemistry student Eslanda Cardoza Goode (1896–1965). Her grandfather, Francis L. Cardozo (1837–1903), was trained as a teacher, minister, and carpenter, and served between 1868 and 1872 as the first black person elected to state office in the history of South Carolina. Robeson and Eslanda married in 1921 and had their only child, Paul Robeson Jr., in 1927. Eslanda went on to become an anthropologist and journalist, as well as her husband's manager and life-long partner until her death.

After graduating from law school, Robeson turned his back on a legal career because of the limited opportunities afforded qualified African Americans. This decision was to prove momentous because it resulted in the launching of one of the most gifted and committed artistic lives of the twentieth century. Robeson's career embraced theater, music, and film. During the early 1920s, he worked with the Provincetown Players based in Greenwich Village and earned praise for his roles in playwright Eugene O'Neill's *The Emperor Jones* (1920) and *All God's Chillun Got Wings* (1924). In 1930 he appeared opposite renowned British actress Peggy Ashcroft (1907–1991) in a London production of Shakespeare's *Othello* and in 1932 a Broadway version of Jerome Kern's musical *Show Boat* (1927). Despite his glittering stage success, not everyone was impressed. The Trinidadian writer and activist C. L. R. James (1901–1989) saw Robeson play Othello on Broadway in 1943 and declared: "Robeson was rotten. He is a magnificent figure, a superb voice, and, as usual with him, at moments he is overwhelming. But in between his lack of training, his lack of imagination, were awful" (1996, p. 90).

Robeson also gained fame as a concert singer and recording artist. Both Robeson and his longtime pianist and arranger Lawrence Brown (1893–1972) played an important role in performing and disseminating African American spirituals and folk songs throughout the United States and Europe. As such, the duo belongs to a black Atlantic musical tradition stretching back to the Fisk Jubilee Singers of the 1870s. It is important to note, however, that their recorded spirituals revolutionized such music by allowing the voice to be free from the performer.

Robeson's third artistic arena was film. During the 1930s, the film industry embarked upon a major transformation with the advent of sound and mass audiences. Robeson appeared in about a dozen American and British films between 1933 and 1942, including *The Emperor Jones* (1933), *Sanders of the River* (1935), *Show Boat* (1936), and *The Proud Valley* (1941). Although his characters often challenged existing racial stereotypes portrayed on the silver screen, these films also reinforced stereotypes about subservient and comedic black people and the benefits of Western colonialism. Robeson later expressed regret over some of these films, a regret the modern viewer can appreciate.

Between 1927 and 1939, Robeson and Eslanda sojourned in Europe. These were important years for Robeson's development as a black artist because they exposed him to the international communist movement, as well as Pan-African and anticolonial politics. While living in London, Robeson and his wife undertook the study of African history, politics, and languages. At the same time, Robeson participated in the West African Student's Union and became acquainted with a younger generation of Caribbean and African leaders, such as C. L. R. James and George Padmore (1903–1959) of Trinidad, Jomo Kenyatta (1890?–1978) of Kenya, and Nnamdi Azikiwe (1904–1996) of Nigeria. It was this milieu that encouraged Robeson's "return" to Africa. This spiritual rather than physical return encouraged Robeson to espouse a set of universal values that included, rather than derided, the importance of African culture to world historical development. It was a position familiar to many black abolitionists of the nineteenth century and recognizable in some of the more sober statements of modern Afrocentrists.

The other important component of Robeson's political development concerned international socialism. The Great Depression had destroyed many people's lives and corroded their faith in capitalist democracies. In contrast, the new Union of Soviet Socialist Republics (USSR) promised a more equitable distribution of resources, constitutional guarantees of the equality of all people regardless of nationality or race, and international solidarity. In 1934 Robeson made the first of numerous visits to the USSR, eventually learning Russian and schooling his son there for several years. At the same time, Robeson became involved in socialist and pacifist causes, including performing benefit concerts for Republican troops fighting against the fascist takeover in Spain. Although some black radicals, such as Padmore and Richard Wright (1908–1960), saw irreconcilable differences between communism and Pan-Africanism, others like C. L. R. James and Robeson envisioned new connections between the two ideologies.

On his return to the United States, Robeson continued his artistic endeavors, as well as his commitment to numerous left-wing and antiracist causes. In the gathering hysteria of the cold war, however, Robeson was to experience serious state and civil obstacles. Although never a member of the Communist Party, officials in both Sacramento and Washington, D.C., accused Robeson of being a communist. In 1950 the U.S. State Department revoked his passport, keeping it until 1958. An invitation for him to appear at a musical festival in Peekskill, New York, sparked white vigilante violence and resulted in scores of injured people, while both Broadway and Hollywood blacklisted him. Despite this, Robeson continued performing at black churches and small functions sponsored by radical groups. He also continued his radical politics. In 1951 Robeson, on behalf of the Civil Rights Congress, submitted a petition to the United Nations titled "We Charge Genocide," detailing 153 killings, 344 crimes of violence, and numerous other human rights abuses against black citizens in the United States during the previous six years. This tactic of exerting international pressure on the United States stretched back to the proposed building of an antislavery wall, a project advocated by Frederick Douglass (1818–1895) and others during the mid-nineteenth century.

After regaining his passport, Robeson and his family moved to Europe. The persecution and blacklisting, however, began to take its toll. Robeson moved in and out of hospitals in the Soviet Union and Europe, and in 1961 he had a nervous breakdown and attempted suicide. In 1963 the Robeson family returned to the United States. After Eslanda's death in 1965, Robeson moved to Philadelphia to live with his sister. A year later he made his final public appearance at a benefit dinner for the Student Nonviolent Coordinating Committee. During a seventy-fifth birthday tribute at New York's Carnegie Hall, which he could not attend because of ill health, Robeson sent a message declaring that he was as "dedicated as ever to the worldwide cause of humanity for freedom, peace, and brotherhood."

Scholars have debated Robeson's historical significance. Was he an idealist whose adherence to the Communist Party made him, in the words of critic Harold Cruse, "a great potential spokesman with a misdirected and ineffective political line" (1967, p. 297)? Or was he an important radical social democrat who played a critical role in propagating popular front culture from the 1930s through 1950s as argued by Michael Denning (1996)? Or was he, as Sterling Stuckey (1987) claims, primarily a black cultural nationalist who brilliantly fused African and black American cultural activities? Interested readers, especially young artists, should read, hear, and see more about Robeson's remarkable life and make up their own minds. Paul Robeson's true significance concerns his obvious artistic talent; his consistent support for antiracist, anticolonial, and international liberation struggles; and his commitment to a radical political and cultural tradition. In today's world, we can imagine Robeson challenging the iniquities of globalization, demanding peace in the Middle-East, and insisting on racial justice for all.

SEE ALSO *Civil Rights; Cold War; Communism; James, C. L. R.; Pan-Africanism; Racism; Slavery; Theater*

BIBLIOGRAPHY

Cruse, Harold. 1967. *The Crisis of the Negro Intellectual.* New York: Morrow.

Denning, Michael. 1996. *The Cultural Front: The Laboring of American Culture in the Twentieth Century.* London and New York: Verso.

Duberman, Martin. 1988. *Paul Robeson.* New York: Knopf.

Grimshaw, Anna, ed. 1996. *Special Delivery: The Letters of C. L. R. James to Constance Webb, 1939–1948.* Oxford, U.K. and Cambridge, MA: Blackwell.

Robeson, Paul. 1958. *Here I Stand.* New York: Othello Associates.

Robeson, Paul, Jr. 2001. *The Undiscovered Paul Robeson: An Artist's Journey, 1898–1938.* New York: Wiley.

Stuckey, Sterling. 1987. *Slave Culture: Nationalist Theory and the Foundations of Black America.* New York: Oxford University Press.

J. R. Kerr-Ritchie

ROBINSON, JOAN
1903–1983

Among the great scholars who made significant contributions to economics in the twentieth century, one could say that there were scores of men but only one woman who really stood out. Of course there were well-respected female economists of the time, such as Mary Marshall (1850–1944) and Ursula Hicks (1896–1985), but for bravado none of them trumped Joan Violet Morris Robinson. She was swift, sharp, and influential. To her friends, admirers, and students, she was gentle, caring, and encouraging. To those who saw in her a menacing adversary and detractor, she was rude, ruthless, and inconsiderate. While she was at home or abroad, whether lecturing or listening, her presence was noticed.

Joan Robinson was born in Surrey, England, and was first educated in London. She then entered the University of Cambridge for economics, where she graduated in 1925. She married the economist Austin Robinson in 1926. Although she traveled extensively throughout the world, her heart remained in Cambridge, site of her home and her university position and where she died in 1983.

As an economist, Joan Robinson was not only a theorist and pragmatist but her knowledge and interest in history, a subject she had studied before economics, afforded her a good grasp of politics and world affairs. She was truly a complete social scientist who believed that knowledge and theory should be the handmaidens of policymaking. Two words could encapsulate the driving motivation for her research and leftist political persuasion: *economic justice.* Whether in her preoccupation with unemployment in the making of John Maynard Keynes's *General Theory of Employment, Interest, and Money* (1936), with the disparities of classes in her version of Marxian economics, or with economic development in her writings on China and India, she was compassionately engaged by all aspects of income distribution.

In her sixty-three-year academic career, Joan Robinson published 378 books, articles, and other writings, all noted in a bibliography compiled by Maria Cristina Marcuzzo (1991). There are numerous writings about Joan Robinson, the most notable being the enormous two volumes edited by George R. Feiwel and published in 1989. The collection's essays, some critical, some laudatory, are of particular interest because their contents highlight reactions from economic theorists across the whole spectrum in relation to Joan Robinson's philosophy, methodology, macroeconomics, and economic theory and specifically the notions of equilibrium, time, capital and growth, and unemployment and the theories of general equilibrium, trade, imperfect competition, games, credit markets, and finance. On reading the various essays, one could not conclude that Joan Robinson had an answer to every theoretical issue, but she touched a sensitive chord for many foundational premises of economics.

For economic-theory purists, *The Economics of Imperfect Competition* (1933, 1969) places Joan Robinson in the pantheon of economists. For economists in general, her work on employment and interest and especially *The Accumulation of Capital* (1956, 1969) was the catalyst to the highly charged Cambridge Capital Controversy, which pitted Joan Robinson and Pierro Sraffa of Cambridge, England, against Robert Solow and Paul Samuelson of Cambridge, Massachusetts, among others. Joan Robinson voiced opposition to the claims of the dominant neoclassical economics for the universality of its theory of production. Her critique, which targeted the "circularity" of the neoclassical interrelationship of capital value and interest rate, pushed economists of every stripe to ponder the relevance and logic of the production function, disembodied technical change, labor-capital substitution, relative prices, and capital accumulation, among other concepts, and led to a fruitful period of intense debate. Put simply, proponents of the Capital Controversy claimed to have shown that the neoclassical explanation of factor payments and substitution and to some extent growth is restrictive, only valid in a world of constant capital-labor ratio. For die-hard Robinsonians, a subgroup of post-Keynesians, for whom she was in battle with the foundations of neoclassical economics, Joan Robinson will forever remain a Joan of Arc.

BIBLIOGRAPHY

PRIMARY WORKS

Robinson, Joan. [1933] 1969. *The Economics of Imperfect Competition.* London: Macmillan.

Robinson, Joan. [1956] 1969. *The Accumulation of Capital.* 3rd ed. London: Macmillan.

Robinson, Joan. 1966. *An Essay on Marxian Economics.* 2nd ed. London: Macmillan. (Orig. pub. 1942.)

Robinson, Joan. 1978. *Contributions to Modern Economics*. Oxford: Blackwell.

Robinson, Joan. 1980. *Further Contributions to Modern Economics*. Oxford: Blackwell.

SECONDARY WORKS

Feiwel, George R., ed. 1989. *Joan Robinson and Modern Economy Theory*. Houndsmills, U.K.: Macmillan.

Feiwel, George R., ed. 1989. *"The Economics of Imperfect Competition" and Employment: Joan Robinson and Beyond*. Houndsmills, U.K.: Macmillan.

Marcuzzo, Maria Cristina. 1991. Bibliography: The Writings of Joan Robinson. In *The Joan Robinson Legacy*, ed. Ingrid H. Rima, 250–275. Armonk, NY: Sharpe.

Rima, Ingrid H., ed. 1991. *The Joan Robinson Legacy*. Armonk, NY: Sharpe.

Omar Hamouda

ROCK 'N' ROLL

Rock 'n' roll, a hybrid popular musical form that emerged in the United States in the early 1950s, became one of the most important cultural forces around the world. Rock 'n' roll began when musicians mixed black rhythm and blues with Southern white country and gospel musics, helping to spark a cultural revolution in the 1950s and 1960s. The first exhilarating blasts of rock 'n' roll defied the Eisenhower era's puritanical emphasis on social and political conformity. This interracial music, edgy and rebellious, broke down social barriers by challenging sexual, racial, and, later, political taboos. The music made a powerful statement that young Americans were less divided by race than their parents.

During the 1950s white musicians such as Bill Haley, Elvis Presley, Buddy Holly, and Jerry Lee Lewis and black musicians such as Chuck Berry, Little Richard, and Fats Domino created rock 'n' roll; often fast and highly danceable, it posed a challenge to urban pop music from Tin Pan Alley and rural-oriented country music. Haley took rhythm and blues songs and reconfigured them for a white teen audience. Influenced by the electric blues, Berry created the distinctive rock 'n' roll guitar style. Presley, known as "Elvis the Pelvis" because of his suggestive, hip-swinging performances, became the first rock superstar, aided by skillful marketing. American rock 'n' rollers also developed a large following in Britain and Europe.

Rock 'n' roll evolved into rock in the early 1960s and became the heart of that decade's youth movement. American society in the 1960s grew to be deeply divided over the war in Vietnam, protest movements against racism and sexism, and "countercultural" youth who flouted social norms. In 1963 the Beatles began a "British Invasion"—a wave of U.K. rock groups, such as the Rolling Stones and the Kinks—that electrified American audiences and energized rock. "Beatlemania" reached around the world, spawning local imitators and spreading new fashions. The Beatles revolutionized recording technology and matured from top-selling pop stars to musical philosophers; many of their later albums, such as *Sgt. Pepper's Lonely Hearts Club Band* (1967), are infused with deep meaning. Bob Dylan, once a folk singer, wrote poetic songs exploring the human experience, including politics. The probing music of Dylan, the Beatles, and the musicians they influenced played a major role in protest and social movements. New rock styles also emerged. Hence, the Byrds and Crosby, Stills, and Nash created country rock and folk rock, while the Beach Boys expanded the boundaries of Southern California–based surf music. Often inspired by drug experiences, San Francisco musicians like the Jefferson Airplane and the bluesy Janis Joplin created psychedelic rock. The innovative guitarist Jimi Hendrix laid the foundation for heavy metal and hard rock. The merging of rock music, political protest, and the counterculture of disaffected youth led to the Summer of Love in 1967, when thousands congregated in San Francisco, and culminated in the Woodstock Music Festival of 1969, when 300,000 rock fans crowded a New York farm.

By the early 1970s several rock icons (including Hendrix and Joplin) had died, the war in Vietnam had wound down, protest movements had faded, and a more conservative social and political environment had emerged in the United States. New rock-derived styles developed over the next four decades. In the United States and especially Britain, punk music—loud, fast, and anarchic—appealed to alienated working-class youth with its frontal assault on prevailing social and political values. Heavy metal, with its deafening guitars, was angry and often obsessed with sex and violence. In contrast, dance musics such as disco, techno, and rave were escapist. But some rock musicians directly addressed social and political issues. The superstar Bruce Springsteen, mixing rock and folk, criticized U.S. foreign policies and the neglect of the working class and poor. In the 1990s punk and heavy metal were combined into a new style, grunge, most prominently represented by the Seattle group Nirvana. By the twenty-first century rock had fragmented into diverse styles with niche audiences.

African Americans created popular musics influenced by rock. The soul music of the 1960s, from artists like James Brown and Aretha Franklin, conveyed a message of black self-respect and unity parallel to the civil rights movements. The slickly produced Motown sound appealed to both blacks and whites. Beginning in the

1980s rap, an eclectic urban mix of African American and Caribbean traditions, became the most cutting-edge, politicized music, sometimes called the CNN of the black ghetto. The boastful, angry lyrics highlighted conflict between black and white, rich and poor, male and female. Like rock, rap was adopted by alienated groups around the world, but in the United States its radical message was watered down by the twenty-first century. Whether rock and its kindred musics were empowering or diversionary, promoting social and political change or helping maintain the status quo, remained subject to debate. Whatever the case may be, these debates reflected the enduring appeal of musics rooted, despite five decades of changes, in the black-white fusion of early rock 'n' roll.

SEE ALSO *Blues; Eisenhower, Dwight D.; Jazz; Music; Music, Psychology of; Reggae; World Music; Youth Culture*

BIBLIOGRAPHY

Garofalo, Reebee. 2005. *Rockin' Out: Popular Music in the U.S.A.* 3rd ed. Upper Saddle River, N.J.: Prentice Hall.

Szatmary, David P. 2007. *Rockin' in Time: A Social History of Rock-and-Roll.* 6th ed. Upper Saddle River, N.J.: Prentice Hall.

Wicke, Peter. 1987. *Rock Music: Culture, Aesthetics, and Sociology.* Trans. Rachel Fogg. New York: Cambridge University Press.

Craig A. Lockard

RODNEY, WALTER
1942–1980

Walter Rodney was born on March 23 in the colony of British Guiana and educated at Queen's College in the capital, Georgetown, and the University of the West Indies in Jamaica where he gained a First Class Honors BA degree in history. Rodney grew up during the country's anticolonial movement; his father was a member of the Marxist-oriented People's Progressive Party, which led the struggle for freedom from British rule. Rodney went on to complete his doctoral dissertation, titled "A History of the Upper Guinea Coast, 1545–1800," at the University of London in 1966. He taught at the University of Dar es Salaam in Tanzania during the period of radical political and agrarian reform led by Julius Nyerere.

TEACHING CAREER

Tanzania was the headquarters of the Organization of African Unity's Liberation Committee, and Dar es Salaam became the base for many of the exiled liberation move-ments of Southern Africa. Among these organizations were the African National Congress of South Africa, Frente da Libertaçao de Moçambique (FRELIMO) of Mozambique, and Movimento Popular da Libertação de Angola (MPLA) of Angola. In this atmosphere Rodney developed his Pan-African perspectives along Marxist lines and sided with Southern Africa's left-wing activists.

He returned to Jamaica to teach at the University of the West Indies in 1968. His radical views and association with Rastafarians and the Black Power movement in Jamaica led to Rodney being banned from reentering Jamaica by the government after he attended a Black Power conference in Canada in October 1968. The demonstration of university students together with Kingston's urban youth against the ban marked a watershed in Jamaica's political development; the scale of mass action in support of Rodney surprised the regime. There were protests throughout the Caribbean, and in Tanzania, Canada, and London. Rodney's reputation as a scholar-activist with a relevant critique of the Jamaican and Caribbean post-colonial elites was firmly established. In the nearly ten months in 1968 that Walter Rodney spent in Jamaica he not only taught but also spoke to groups in the slums of Kingston and in the rural areas. He had an extraordinary ability to speak with and listen to working people and unemployed youth. He explained the significance of Africa to Caribbean history and the importance of the struggles against the racial and social legacies of slavery and colonialism. His articles and speeches embodying these positions were published in the book *The Groundings with My Brothers* (1969).

HOW EUROPE UNDERDEVELOPED AFRICA

Rodney returned to lecture at the University of Dar es Salaam from 1969 to 1974. In 1972 he published his best-known work *How Europe Underdeveloped Africa.* This work brings together historical scholarship and development theory to argue that the transatlantic slave trade and European and North American capitalist slavery did serious damage to Africa in depriving it of millions of its young people from the sixteenth to nineteenth centuries. Rodney was also critical of the impact of colonialism in retarding the development of the continent. The book is more than protest literature in that it advances a revolutionary humanist view of development and decolonization at a time when many countries on the continent were achieving political independence, a process that was also under way in the English-speaking Caribbean whose territories were populated largely by descendants of African slaves.

Some scholars argue that Rodney relies too heavily on the dependency theory of the 1960s and *How Europe*

Underdeveloped Africa has been criticized for not looking sufficiently at the internal factors in Africa that accounted for the slave trade and African underdevelopment. Ironically, however, much of his early work had focused on internal factors that retarded Africa's development and Rodney's analysis of Africa's traditional elites was caustic. So in a sense *How Europe Underdeveloped Africa* was a departure and the emphasis on European involvement in the hugely profitable trade completed his treatment of the relationship between European slave traders and plantation owners on the one hand and on the other hand Africa's elites who facilitated the slave trade. Also in 1972, Oxford University published Rodney's doctoral thesis *A History of the Upper Guinea Coast 1545–1800*. In 1975 two chapters titled "The Guinea Coast" and "Africa in Europe and the Americas" were published in the *Cambridge History of Africa*. The latter essay was a pioneering study of the African Diaspora.

A HISTORY OF THE GUYANESE WORKING PEOPLE, 1881–1905

Walter Rodney returned to his native country, now called Guyana, in 1974 and was denied a job at the University of Guyana by President Forbes Burnham. Burnham saw the young scholar-activist as a political opponent and hoped to keep him out of Guyana. Rodney was associated with the Working People's Alliance, a political organization that sought to offer a nonracial approach to Guyanese politics in a country where party politics had been divided between Cheddi Jagan's East Indian–based People's Progressive Party and Forbes Burnham's African-based People's National Congress. Between 1974 and 1980, when he was murdered at age thirty-eight by a booby-trapped walkie-talkie given to him by a member of Guyana's Defense Force, Rodney lectured in the United States and Europe for short periods in order to ensure an income. He continued his research and completed working on *A History of the Guyanese Working People, 1881–1905*, which was published posthumously in 1981. This work embodies his philosophy on the creative role of ordinary people in the making of history and introduces the contribution of African slaves "to the humanization of the Guyanese coastal environment" in creating "an elaborate system of canals … to provide drainage, irrigation, and transportation" (Rodney 1981, pp. 2–3) in a remarkable transfer of Dutch technology to a coastal landscape that was below sea level. It was the first book on the Guyanese working people written in the twentieth century. In 1982, the book won the American Historical Association's Albert J. Beveridge Prize and in 1983 the Association of Caribbean Historians gave Rodney a posthumous award.

Rodney's reputation as a historian of the Caribbean was duly recognized. He harnessed history in the service of African and Caribbean decolonization with a view to giving his readers a sense of their creative capacity to build postcolonial societies. The Barbadian novelist George Lamming, in his foreword to *A History of the Guyanese Working People, 1881–1905*, described Rodney's approach to history as "a way of ordering knowledge which could become an active part of the consciousness of an uncertified mass of ordinary people and which could be used by all as an instrument of social change. He taught from that assumption. He wrote out of that conviction" (Rodney 1981, p. xvii).

Rodney was also a gifted and compelling speaker whose arguments were backed up by a mastery of contemporary data. He possessed a capacity to communicate complex ideas to small study groups and large audiences with great clarity drawing on his solidly rooted knowledge of African and Caribbean history.

SEE ALSO *Black Power; Caribbean, The; Colonialism; Decolonization; Ethnic Fractionalization; Exploitation; Imperialism; James, C. L. R.; James, William; Marxism; Pan-Africanism; Rastafari; Underdevelopment; Williams, Eric*

BIBLIOGRAPHY

Lewis, Rupert. 1998. *Walter Rodney's Intellectual and Political Thought*. Detroit, MI: Wayne State University Press.

Rodney, Walter. 1969. *The Groundings with My Brothers*. London: Bogle–L'Ouverture Publications.

Rodney, Walter. 1972. *How Europe Underdeveloped Africa*. London: Bogle L'Ouverture Publications.

Rodney, Walter. 1981. *A History of the Guyanese Working People, 1881–1905*. London: Heinemann Educational Books.

Rupert Lewis

ROE V. WADE

Few U.S. Supreme Court rulings have been as contentious as the Court's 1973 decision in *Roe v. Wade*. This landmark decision not only invalidated a number of state abortion laws, it also served to further divide public opinion with respect to "discretionary" abortion decisions (Franklin and Kosaki 1989, p. 759).

A number of states reformed their abortion statutes to broaden access to legal abortions in the late 1960s. Some of these laws, for example, permitted abortion when a woman's health was in danger as opposed to only her life. Some reforms, moreover, provided for legal abortions if a woman had been a victim of rape or incest, as well as in situations in which a fetal defect was present (Tribe 1991, p. 42). Of course, prior to *Roe*, a number of states, including Texas, prohibited abortions except when a woman's life was in danger.

In addition to a perceived need for further abortion law reform, developments in the Supreme Court's privacy doctrine with respect to the use and distribution of contraceptives provided constitutional arguments that could potentially be applied to the expansion of abortion rights (Nossiff 2001, p. 41). In *Griswold v. Connecticut* (1965), the Supreme Court held that a Connecticut statute prohibiting the use of contraceptives violated a married couple's constitutional right to privacy. In *Eisenstadt v. Baird* (1972), the Court recognized that single persons also enjoy a right to privacy with respect to reproductive decisions when it struck down a Massachusetts law banning the provision of contraceptives to unmarried persons in order to prevent pregnancy.

The legal question as to whether a woman's privacy right could extend to her decision to terminate a pregnancy was presented to the Supreme Court in *Roe v. Wade.* Jane Roe, who would later reveal her identity as Norma McCorvey, was pregnant and wanted to obtain an abortion in Texas, her state of residence. Texas law, however, prohibited abortions except when necessary to preserve the mother's life. McCorvey's pregnancy did not threaten her life, nor did she have the finances to travel to a state in which abortion was legal. A Dallas attorney referred McCorvey to Sarah Weddington and Linda Coffee, two attorneys who were preparing a legal challenge to the Texas abortion laws. The case, which eventually became a class-action lawsuit, also involved a married couple dubbed John and Mary Doe. They argued that the law interfered with their marital relationship since Mary's physician had cautioned her about becoming pregnant but directed her to refrain from using birth control pills because of a medical condition. Under Texas law, however, abortion would be a foreclosed option for the couple in the event of an unintended pregnancy. James Hallford, a physician who was charged with violating the Texas abortion laws, also participated in the lawsuit. The plaintiffs sought a declaration that the Texas laws were unconstitutional, as well as an injunction to prevent their enforcement (Weddington 1992, pp. 50–62).

Jay Floyd, representing the Texas Office of the Attorney General, raised important challenges concerning the plaintiffs' standing to sue and the timing of the lawsuit. With respect to the merits, he argued that there was no constitutional right to an abortion and that the state had a "compelling interest in protecting the fetus" (Weddington 1992, p. 66). The representative for the district attorney's office argued further that abortion was an appropriate area for state regulation and also suggested that the privacy interests of women seeking abortions

must give way to the protection of the unborn (Weddington 1992, pp. 65–66).

Although the three-judge trial court agreed with Floyd's argument that John and Mary Doe did not have standing to sue, the court held that Roe and Hallford could pursue their claims. On the merits, the court found that the laws violated the constitutional right of individuals to determine whether they wanted children; however, it refused to issue the plaintiffs' request for an injunction. Dallas County district attorney Henry Wade's assertion that he would continue to enforce the contested law assisted Weddington's efforts in obtaining a Supreme Court review of the decision (Weddington 1992, pp. 67–69).

The Supreme Court first heard oral arguments in *Roe* in 1971. However, the justices agreed that the case should be reargued to allow newly appointed justices William Rehnquist (1924–2005) and Lewis Powell (1907–1998) to take part in the decision. Accordingly, the Court issued its landmark decision in 1973. Writing for a seven-member majority, Justice Harry Blackmun (1908–1999) argued that a constitutional "right of privacy … is broad enough to encompass a woman's decision whether or not to terminate her pregnancy." (410 U.S. 113, 153). However, the majority also recognized that the state has legitimate interests with respect to "health," "medical standards," and "potential life" that might justify regulating abortion at certain points (410 U.S. 113, 154).

Specifically, Blackmun articulated a trimester framework to evaluate when these state interests could justify regulation of a woman's decision to have an abortion. During the first trimester of a woman's pregnancy, when the risk of mortality from an abortion is low relative to the risk of childbirth, the Court held that "the abortion decision … must be left to the medical judgment" of a woman's doctor (410 U.S. 113, 164). However, by the second trimester, the state could regulate abortions in order to protect maternal health (410 U.S. 113, 163). Finally, the state's interest in protecting "potential life" could justify regulation when the fetus reaches the stage of "viability," defined as the point at which it has "the capability of meaningful life outside the mother's womb." At this stage, Blackmun held that the state could prohibit abortion so long as exceptions were made "to preserve the life or health of the mother" (410 U.S. 113, 154).

While many individuals and groups defended the Supreme Court's decision in *Roe*, others criticized the ruling in the hope of seeing it limited or overruled. At the state level, for example, attempts to restrict access to abortion have been made through laws requiring parental or spousal notification or consent, informed consent, waiting periods, and tests to determine fetal viability, as well as through laws prohibiting public financing or assistance for abortion procedures (Nossiff 2001, p. 148; Tribe 1991, p. 144). McCorvey herself later backed away from her affiliation with the *Roe* decision and the pro-choice movement. In 1995 McCorvey was baptized by the national director of Operation Rescue, a well-known organization opposing abortion rights in the United States (*New York Times* 1995, p. A12), and in 2003 she unsuccessfully petitioned a federal court to reconsider the result announced in *Roe* (*New York Sun* 2003, p. 6).

The battle over abortion rights and the *Roe* decision has also colored the Supreme Court judicial selection process. Nominees to the Court after *Roe* have been scrutinized concerning their positions on privacy rights generally and their opinion of *Roe* specifically. Although John Roberts was tapped to replace Chief Justice Rehnquist in 2005, particular concern was raised that Justice Sandra Day O'Connor's replacement in 2006, Samuel Alito, might provide the Court with the votes needed to overrule this controversial decision. However, as legal analyst Jeffrey Toobin (2005, p. 81) noted, a number of Republican-appointed justices have joined the Court since *Roe*, and, although the Court has revisited the topic of abortion rights in a number of cases, it has yet to overrule the decision.

SEE ALSO *Abortion; Supreme Court, U.S.; Women's Movement*

BIBLIOGRAPHY

Eisenstadt v. Baird, 405 U.S. 438 (1972).

Franklin, Charles H., and Liane C. Kosaki. 1989. Republican Schoolmaster: The U.S. Supreme Court, Public Opinion, and Abortion. *American Political Science Review* 83 (3): 751–771.

Griswold v. Connecticut, 381 U.S. 479 (1965).

New York Sun. 2003. Roe's Regrets. June 23: 6.

New York Times. 1995. "Jane Roe" Joins Anti-Abortion Group. August 11: A12.

Nossiff, Rosemary. 2001. *Before Roe: Abortion Policy in the States*. Philadelphia: Temple University Press.

O'Brien, David M. 1993. A Struggle for Power. In *Storm Center: The Supreme Court in American Politics*, 3rd ed., 23–64. New York: Norton.

Roe v. Wade, 410 U.S. 113 (1973).

Toobin, Jeffrey. 2005. Still Standing: The Resilience of *Roe v. Wade*. *New Yorker*. November 28: 70–81.

Tribe, Laurence H. 1991. *Abortion: The Clash of Absolutes*. New York: Norton.

Weddington, Sarah. 1992. *A Question of Choice*. New York: Putnam's.

Erin B. Kaheny

ROGERS, CARL

SEE *Psychotherapy.*

ROLE CONFLICT

The term *role conflict* refers to a clash between two or more of a person's roles or incompatible features within the same role. These incompatibilities can consist of differing expectations, requirements, beliefs, and/or attitudes. The term *role* relies on the theatrical metaphor of an actor performing his or her part in a staged play. Although stage actors generally play only one character per play, the same actor will go on to play multiple characters throughout his or her career, and different actors often play the same role in different ways. Unlike theatrical actors, people in everyday life enact multiple roles simultaneously. For example, Jane might be a boss, an employee, a daughter, a mother, and so on. Often, these roles are activated concurrently and harmoniously. Jane's role as the primary wage earner for her family is not likely to be in conflict with her role as a supervisor at work. Different roles are sometime incompatible, however, and the requirements of one role can clash with those of another. In addition, contradictory requirements within the same role can produce role conflict.

There are two types of role conflict: *intrarole* conflict, referring to incompatible requirements within the same role, and *interrole* conflict, referring to clashing expectations from separate roles within the same person. Intrarole conflict can arise in two ways. First, different people sometimes have inconsistent conceptions concerning the requirements and expectations that constitute a particular role. Jane's conception of being a good mother might consist of having a job outside of the home. She might also believe that providing socioemotional support to her family is a necessary ingredient in her role as a mother. However, Jane's mother-in-law might think that to be a good mother Jane would need to relinquish her job to provide around-the-clock care for her children. Because of these differing conceptions concerning the role of a mother, Jane is likely to experience intrarole conflict.

Intrarole conflict can also occur when the role itself has contradictory expectations or requirements. Jane might feel that her role as a mother requires her to provide emotional warmth to her children. The same role might also require her to discipline her children following misbehavior. Because being sensitive and supportive is at odds with enacting discipline, Jane is likely to experience intrarole conflict in situations where her children misbehave. To resolve intrarole conflict, the role can be compartmentalized. In her role as mother, Jane might justify her job outside the home by noting that it allows her to care for her children financially. Working outside the home provides them with groceries, housing, heat, schooling, medical care, and so on. As such, it fits with Jane's conception of the motherhood role. An additional way to resolve intrarole conflicts is to avoid those who define a role differently. As such, Jane might avoid her mother-in-law because of their clashing conceptions concerning the motherhood role.

Interrole conflict arises when the requirements and expectations of one role interfere or conflict with those of another role. Jane's role as mother is likely to conflict occasionally with her role as a worker employed outside the home. When one of her children becomes ill, Jane may find that the demands of her job (e.g., staying at work) are in conflict with the demands of motherhood (e.g., taking her child to the doctor). There are a number of ways to resolve interrole conflicts. Often, people will prioritize their roles. In some situations, such as when an important deadline looms at work, it may be more important for Jane to stay late at work. In this situation, her role as a worker will take priority over her role as a mother. At other times, such as when her children are ill and in need of care, her role as mother will take priority. We can also compartmentalize different roles. For example, Jane may find that she interacts with others very differently at work and home. By compartmentalizing her roles, she can be task-oriented in her role as a boss, but socioemotionally oriented in her role as wife and mother. Roles can also be specialized. If children need to be disciplined, Jane and her husband can develop a system in which her husband is in charge of discipline while Jane is in charge of providing warmth and comfort.

The experience of role conflict has been associated with negative health, psychological, social, and work-related outcomes. Role conflict is positively correlated with experienced stress level and depression and negatively correlated with self-esteem. In the workplace, role conflict is negatively correlated with job commitment, job involvement, participation in decision-making, and satisfaction with compensation, coworkers, and supervision and, as Mary Van Sell, Arthur Brief, and Randall Schuler (1981) observed, positively associated with job dissatisfaction, on-the-job tension, and intentions to leave an organization.

SEE ALSO *Conflict; Family; Happiness; Identity; Mental Health; Motherhood; Performance; Role Theory; Self-Concept; Self-Esteem; Work*

BIBLIOGRAPHY

Goffman, Erving. 1961. *Encounters: Two Studies in the Sociology of Interaction.* Indianapolis, IN: Bobbs-Merrill.

Van Snell, Mary, Arthur P. Brief, and Randall S. Schuler. 1981. Role Conflict and Role Ambiguity: Integration of the Literature and Directions for Future Research. *Human Relations* 34 (1): 43–71.

Scott T. Wolf

ROLE MODELS

A *role model* is an individual who is perceived as exemplary or worthy of identification or imitation. It is a conscious or unconscious emotional attachment *not* necessarily involving direct personal contact; for example, identification with sports or entertainment figures is common. *Mentors*, a subset of role models, deliberately support, guide, and shape younger or less experienced individuals as they weather difficult periods, enter new arenas, or undertake challenging tasks. Mentoring may include elements that are instrumental (e.g., career advice, networking contacts, financial assistance) and psychosocial (e.g., emotional support, companionship). Having a role model or mentor is a commonly identified protective factor contributing to resilience—that is, successfully responding to challenges or overcoming adversity—and mitigating risk, particularly in ethnic minority adolescents experiencing poverty or familial dysfunction.

Role model selection reflects critical elements of psychosocial functioning and self-perception, particularly ethnic identity. Individuals generally identify sociodemographically similar role models, and socioeconomic status (SES) is associated with having a role model. In a study of a representative sample of Los Angeles adolescents, African American teens almost exclusively chose African American role models (96%), whereas two thirds (64%) of Latinos chose an ethnically congruent model. Overall, 75 percent of Latinos chose a role model of color, with 11 percent having chosen African Americans. Four in five whites identified a white role model. About one in five teens chose relatives as role models, the most common choice. Whites were more likely than African Americans or Latinos to have known extrafamilial role models. Lower SES and being male were associated with selecting a *figure* role model available primarily through the media, as opposed to a known individual. Consistent with these findings, a qualitative study found that the type of role model (family member or figure) most often identified by low-income African American males differed in high school and college samples: Identified role models for the college students were primarily, though not exclusively, family members (Taylor, 1989). Extrafamilial models tended to be ethnically similar to the young men. Enduring and substantive role models were less frequently identified in the high school sample than in the college sample. Still, even as subjects of fleeting interest, African

Americans—mainly entertainers and political or religious figures—were most often chosen. Regarding the other primary sociodemographic characteristic, gender, boys are more likely than girls to choose a gender-congruent role model. This difference is only found for the figure category of models. For known role models, boys and girls choose same-sex or opposite-sex persons at about the same rate. The greater availability of powerful male figures in the popular media and in sports, in particular, and the greater status that our society affords to men may explain this finding.

That learning occurs through observation and imitation or *modeling of revered others* has been well established by social learning theorists. For example, a parenting study demonstrated that teen fathers often come from families in which there were role models for teen parenthood; for example, first-time teen fathers were three times as likely to have older brothers who were themselves teenaged parents. Certainly, the effectiveness of role models in encouraging the adoption of commercially desirable but risky behavior (e.g., cigarette smoking and alcohol consumption) is well known to the advertising industry. Commercial marketing utilizes *inspirational* and *aspirational* role models in product "branding" and sales promotion. Inspirational role models are quite similar to the target audience ("people like us"); social distance is minimal and "cultural" values and traditions are shared, thereby increasing motivation and enhancing self-efficacy. Peer modeling, in which youth or adult lay health advisers (*promotoras*) are used in outreach, embodies this construct. In contrast, aspirational role models have culturally valued attributes that are coveted by but less prevalent in the targeted population, for example, a higher position within a work hierarchy, extraordinary athletic or musical talent, or physical attractiveness.

The evidence for the utility of role modeling is growing. Evidence that suggests the positive influence of ethnically matched role models may be seen in the educational persistence of graduates of historically black colleges and universities. Although only one in five African American undergraduate students are enrolled in these institutions, one in three black college graduates hail from these institutions, as do more than half of those earning doctorates and more than two thirds of all black professionals. Several recent empirical studies also support the positive influence of role models on certain measures of resilience in ethnically diverse and, particularly, high-risk adolescent populations. This influence may operate largely by enhancing ethnic identity among African American, Latino, and Native American youths. Having a role model, particularly one known to the adolescent, has been linked to higher self-esteem and academic performance, decreased substance use, fewer behavioral problems in school, higher levels of physical activity, and lower levels of engagement in early or high-risk sexual activity. Extrafamilial known role models were just as positively influential as family members. Even a figure role model is associated with some lowered risk, though they exert less influence than known role models. Ethnic congruence of role models does not seem to affect outcomes, but because it is apparent that adolescents for whom ethnicity is most salient strongly gravitate to role models of the same ethnicity, sufficient variability to test this hypothesis is unlikely to be found.

Many young people do not have role models or mentors. Exposure of low SES ethnic minority youngsters, in particular, to positive role models and adult images of their own ethnicity—a task previously performed by racially segregated but socioeconomically heterogeneous churches, neighborhoods, and schools—is increasingly recognized as critical to their development of a stable identity. Social service programs of many varieties have been developed to address this gap through, for example, faith-based organizations, schools, government programs, and unaffiliated community-based efforts. One-to-one mentoring (e.g., Big Brother/Big Sister, center-based programs at YMCAs/YWCAs and Girls'/Boys' Clubs) is a common programmatic approach to providing this resource. However, these programs place tremendous time and energy demands on mentors, who also face their own family demands and often professional struggles with discrimination. Thus, there is limited availability of appropriate one-to-one mentors, given the scarcity of volunteers and increasing socioeconomic homogeneity of ethnic minority neighborhoods. School-based "career day" programs, another common approach, present useful opportunities for role modeling. They do not, however, provide the continuity and personalization of contact necessary for a sustaining influence. Small-scale self-image–enhancement approaches that directly or indirectly utilize role models have been used with measurable success with high-risk African American and Latino youth, and are integral parts of many community institutions. Such emerging "hybrid" role-modeling or mentoring interventions (e.g., many culturally grounded "rites-of-passage" programs) are less taxing to volunteers than one-to-one involvement, but offer more consistent and personal contact than "career days."

Positive images and examples of ethnically diverse individuals of both genders are needed. Attention should be directed to developing and systematically evaluating innovative and cost-effective approaches, both stand-alone programs and programs in conjunction with the provision of other services, via media or in person. Feasible and effective interventions to expose youth to appropriate role models are early in their development, and the process by which youths identify role models is not well understood. Because the process of selecting and emulating a role model provides critical—and potentially socially constructive—access to the self-images of young people, progress in this area is central to advancing the field of adolescent health promotion.

SEE ALSO *Attachment Theory; Resiliency*

BIBLIOGRAPHY

Barnes, Edward J. 2004. The Black Community as the Source of Positive Self-Concept for Black Children: A Theoretical Perspective. In *Black Psychology*, ed. Reginald Lanier Jones, 106–130. Hampton, VA: Cobb and Henry.

Beier, Sharon R., Walter D. Rosenfeld, Kenneth C. Spitalny, et al. 2000. The Potential Role of an Adult Mentor in Influencing High-Risk Behaviors in Adolescents. *Archives of Pediatric Adolescent Medicine* 154 (4): 327–331.

LaFromboise, Teresa D., and Dolores S. Bigfoot. 1988. Cultural and Cognitive Considerations in the Prevention of American Indian Adolescent Suicide. *Journal of Adolescence* 11 (2): 139–153.

Malgady, Robert G., Lloyd H. Rogler, and Giuseppe Costantino. 1990. Hero/Heroine Modeling for Puerto Rican Adolescents: A Preventive Mental Health Intervention. *Journal of Consulting and Clinical Psychology* 58 (4): 469–474.

Salazar, Laura F., Ralph J. DiClemente, Gina M. Wingood, et al. Self-Concept and Adolescents' Refusal of Unprotected Sex: A Test of Mediating Mechanisms among African American Girls. *Prevention Science* 5 (3): 137–149.

Taylor, Ronald L. 1989. Black Youth, Role Models and the Social Construction of Identity. In *Black Adolescents*, ed. Reginald Lanier Jones, 155–174. Berkeley, CA: Cobb and Henry.

Watts, Roderick J. 1993. Community Action through Manhood Development: A Look at Concepts and Concerns from the Frontline. *American Journal of Community Psychology* 21: 333–359.

Werner, Emmy E., and Jeanette L. Johnson. 2004. The Role of Caring Adults in the Lives of Children of Alcoholics. *Substance Use and Misuse* 39 (5): 699–720.

Yancey, Antronette K. 1998. Building Positive Self-Image in Adolescents in Foster Care: The Use of Role Models in an Interactive Group Approach. *Adolescence* 33 (130): 253–267.

Yancey, Antronette K., Judith M. Siegel, and Kimberly L. McDaniel. 2002. Role Models, Ethnic Identity, and Health-Risk Behaviors in Urban Adolescents. *Archives of Pediatric and Adolescent Medicine* 156 (1): 55–61.

Antronette (Toni) Yancey

ROLE OVERLOAD

SEE *Role Theory.*

ROLE THEORY

Role theory is generally concerned with explaining the relationship between the individual and society. It has guided empirical research on a range of topics, including the structure of interaction in small groups, the maintenance of gender differences, the development of commitment to deviant behavior, the genesis and resolution of conflict in organizations, and the construction of personal identity. Although the development of role theory has occurred primarily within sociology, it originated in several different social science disciplines. The first significant contributions were published in the 1930s with independent work by the anthropologist Ralph Linton (1893–1953), the psychotherapist Jacob Moreno (1889–1974), and the social philosopher George Herbert Mead (1863–1931). Of these three, Mead's contributions have been the most significant as he was an important influence on the emerging new discipline of sociology. Within sociology, there have been two distinct traditions of role theory; these have been nominally categorized as the structural and interactionist schools.

THE STRUCTURAL SCHOOL

Starting in the 1950s and continuing through the 1960s, role theory was associated mostly with the work of the American sociologist Talcott Parsons (1902–1979). During this period, Parsons and his associates were developing a comprehensive theory of society that came to be known as structural functionalism. Under structural functionalism, society is viewed as a complex system of structures and processes with layers of interconnected subsystems, institutions, values, positions, and roles. In Parsons's scheme, the role concept is used to explain how individual desires and motivations are reconciled with the collective needs of society. This occurs in part through the process of socialization, where kinship, educational, and religious institutions transmit societal values. When individuals are properly socialized, they fulfill the expectations and needs of an orderly social system by playing the roles associated with their position in society. Parsons argued, for example, that the preponderance of men in the occupational system of the 1940s was functional in that it eliminated competition for status between husband and wife. While the husband achieved status through his role as provider in a high-prestige job, the wife achieved a functionally equivalent status in her role as homemaker where prestige could be achieved through superiority in personal appearance, house furnishings, and other artistic pursuits.

In the structural tradition, roles are typically defined as the socially shared expectations and behaviors associated with a position in society. Because individuals have multiple positions in society, however, there are times when role expectations pull in competing directions so that fulfilling one role may mean failing to fulfill another. This dilemma has been called role conflict, and it can take several different forms. One of these is role overload, which occurs when there is not enough time or energy to play all the roles in one's role set. Related structural interpretations of role theory have been concerned with differentiating among the different types of roles, describing changes in roles, and explaining why people often deviate from role expectations.

THE INTERACTIONIST SCHOOL

By the middle of the 1960s a competing version of role theory was in development. The so-called interactionist school emerged initially as a critique of the dominant structural perspective. The interactionist critics argued that the structural approach to role theory put too much emphasis on societal consensus, relied naively on the existence of widespread conformity with social norms, and held an overly mechanical and deterministic view of social behavior.

The American sociologist Ralph H. Turner spearheaded the development of the interactionist approach by introducing the idea of role making. According to Turner, in everyday situations there is always a degree of uncertainty and discretion. Since roles can only suggest general patterns of action, individuals must cooperate to create and modify roles in particular settings. Research has shown this to be true even in strict, hierarchical organizations such as the military and correctional institutions, where positions are rigidly defined and rules are enforced within a clear authority structure. From the interactionist perspective, understanding the process by which individuals learn to coordinate their actions and construct role-related behavior is crucial.

The central idea in the coordination of joint action is a process called role taking, a concept developed in the seminal work of Mead. Role taking, sometimes called *taking the role of other*, occurs when an actor anticipates the behavior of others in specific situations and adjusts his or her action accordingly. This uniquely human ability develops along with language and other basic skills of symbolic interaction. Once in place, a capacity for role taking enables mutual understanding, coordinated action, and the development of common plans. It is also fundamental to the more complex process of building and maintaining large social institutions. Thus, in contrast to the top-down structural approach to role behavior that focuses on role playing, the interactionists present a bottom-up approach that stresses the creative aspects of role making.

INTEGRATION

After the 1980s, differences between structuralists and interactionists gave way to more synthetic approaches where ideas from both theoretical traditions were integrated. Thus, there developed a general acknowledgment that social roles can profoundly limit and structure patterns of social behavior while at the same time they can serve as resources for enabling and facilitating other actions. Rather than emphasizing role playing or role making, it became more productive to see roles as social resources that are deployed by institutions and persons in different ways; in short, the emphasis was now on role using.

Although role theory is no longer central to most comprehensive theories of society, as it was for Parsons and Mead, it does continue to generate a stream of work at different levels of analysis. At the social psychological level, for example, scholars have found that social roles are central components of one's overall identity, and evidence shows that roles have profound influence on people's behavior in social settings, on how they organize and process information, and on their political, economic, and moral priorities. At the macro and institutional level, research has documented the increasing proliferation of new, more specialized roles in modern society as well as the changing nature of traditional roles resulting from economic and cultural globalization.

SEE ALSO *Conformity; Functionalism; Norms; Role Conflict; Role Models; Self-Concept; Social Psychology; Socialization; Structuralism*

BIBLIOGRAPHY

Callero, Peter L. 1994. From Role-Playing to Role-Using: Understanding Role as Resource. *Social Psychology Quarterly* 57 (3): 228–243.

Joas, Hans. 1993. *Pragmatism and Social Theory*. Chicago: University of Chicago Press.

Mead, George H. 1934. *Mind, Self, and Society from the Standpoint of a Social Behaviorist*. Chicago: University of Chicago Press.

Parsons, Talcott. 1951. *The Social System*. Glencoe, IL: The Free Press.

Turner, Ralph H. 2001. Role Theory. In *Handbook of Sociological Theory*, ed. Jonathan H. Turner, 233–254. New York: Kluwer Academic/Plenum.

Peter L. Callero

ROLE USING

SEE *Role Theory.*

ROLL CALLS

Roll calls are votes taken by a legislative chamber in which the names of legislators are recorded along with their votes on a question. Rules and practices surrounding roll call votes vary across legislatures because of differences in constitutions, chambers rules, actions of legislative leaders, political cultures, legislature sizes, and the technologies used to record votes. Because they are highly visible, roll call votes are useful to social scientists who research legislative behavior. Techniques used to study roll call votes range from simple descriptions to sophisticated scaling techniques adapted from psychometrics and econometrics.

The most thoroughly studied roll call record is that of the U.S. Congress. Article I, section 5 of the U.S. Constitution requires that "the Yeas and Nays of the members of either House on any question" shall be entered in the journal upon the demand of one-fifth of those present. Through the end of the 109th Congress (2006), the U.S. House of Representatives and Senate together had recorded nearly 94,000 roll call votes.

The first social scientific use of roll call votes is attributed to A. Lawrence Lowell's 1902 essay "The Influence of Party upon Legislation in England and America." Lowell introduced the idea of the "party vote," defined as a vote in which at least 90 percent of one party in a legislature voted against at least 90 percent of the other party. An important extension of Lowell's idea was suggested by Stuart Rice in 1928 through his "index of cohesion" and "index of likeness."

Efforts by the liberal interest group Americans for Democratic Action (ADA) in the 1940s encouraged the use of roll call votes to summarize the voting tendencies of individual legislators. The ADA began publishing an annual list of "key votes" in Congress, reporting how often each member of Congress (MC) supported the ADA position. These reports allowed one to array MCs along a continuum, ranging from the most liberal, with a "liberal quotient" of 100 percent, to the most conservative, at a quotient of 0 percent. Ever since the ADA pioneered this technique, dozens of groups have developed "support scores" that reflect their own agendas.

Interest-group support scores are easy to calculate and intuitive to understand, but they have serious shortcomings. Interest-group ratings tend to be based on a small number of roll call votes, thus discarding the rich information that the omitted roll call votes can provide. The roll call votes chosen are typically unusually divisive, which causes the resulting ratings to be too extreme. These techniques also require a priori agreement about which votes best reveal the underlying ideological dimension being described.

Beginning in the 1980s social scientists started exploring ways to overcome these deficiencies, taking advantage of advances in measurement theory and computational capabilities. A frequently used example of this is a class of techniques pioneered by Keith Poole and Howard Rosenthal, called NOMINATE (for *Nominal Three-step Estimation*). NOMINATE scores can be constructed from a large number of roll call votes analyzed simultaneously across a long period of time. Ratings from such techniques as NOMINATE show that a single left-right ideological dimension underlies most roll call behavior across American history, that a second dimension of choice sometimes emerges that corresponds to race-related issues, and that individual legislative voting behavior is highly stable over time.

SEE ALSO *Congress, U.S.; Conservatism; Constitutions; Interest Groups and Interests; Left and Right; Liberalism; Political Science; Voting*

BIBLIOGRAPHY

Lowell, A. Lawrence. The Influence of Party upon Legislation in England and America. *Annual Report of the American Historical Association for 1901* 1 (1902): 321–542.

Oleszek, Walter J. 2007. *Congressional Procedures and the Policy Process*. 7th ed. Washington, DC: CQ.

Poole, Keith T., and Howard Rosenthal. 1997. *Congress: A Political-Economic History of Roll Call Voting*. New York: Oxford University Press.

Charles Stewart III

ROMA, THE

The term *Roma* has come into common parlance to refer to all the populations in Europe (and indeed the rest of the world) that used to be referred to in their host societies as Gypsies, Cigány, Tsigani, and other terms. It thus covers a number of populations with particular histories but also certain distinctive commonalities. This article focuses on those who have a historical link to populations that have spoken Romani, an Indic language now in use on all the continents of the world. Speakers of an ancestral form of Romani were in all likelihood among a number of populations of service nomads who circulated in the southern ranges of the Eurasian landmass between northern India and the Middle East over the past thousand years or more. Other related ethnic-linguistic groups include the Dom (speakers of Domari), found across the Middle East, and the Lom (speakers of Lomavren, spoken in Armenia, Georgia, and eastern Turkey).

The reconstruction of the early history of Romani-speaking populations is fraught with difficulties as archival records are scant. Moreover the procedure by which earlier historians attempted to reconstruct early modern Romani social life from philological materials is now widely discredited. Genetic evidence (mitochondrial and Y-chromosome DNA) unsurprisingly supports the linguistic link to North India, but founder effects and other sampling uncertainties mean detailed and datable population histories cannot as yet be reconstructed.

While all Romani speakers can be called Gypsy, not all Gypsies are Romani speakers. Nevertheless, there are some signs of a broader Roma ethnic awareness developing in some circles, at least across Europe, including people whose ancestors may never have spoken any Indic language.

On the basis of dialect differentiation it is possible to distinguish four large segments of the European Romani population. The four branches of Romani are Balkan, Vlax (centered in Romania but spreading westward), Central, and Northern. British or Welsh and Iberian Romani once constituted independent branches but survive only as special lexicons used as part of English or Spanish.

These linguistically determined regions of diffusion indicate zones of greater and more intense interaction among Romani speakers but cannot be used to determine the movements or settlement history of all Roma. Since the dialect groupings mentioned here are more or less territorially based (even if the boundaries between them are loose and alterable), dialect corresponds to some extent to history. It thus makes heuristic sense to talk, for instance, of Sinte (in Germany), of Gitanos (in Spain), or Vlax (in various parts of Europe and beyond) as loosely defined cultural groups within the Roma.

Roma speak Romani (often spelled Romany) or Romanes. This is an Indic language, probably originating in central India over one thousand years ago. Yaron Matras has estimated that in the early Romani inherited lexicon, of 1,000 lexical roots, 200 to 250 are from Greek, around 70 from Iranian, and 40 from Armenian, leaving about 650 to 700 roots of Indic origin. There are no monolingual speakers of Romani, and the language as spoken by Roma in different parts of Europe incorporates loan words reflecting the history of local contact with other languages. The fact that the term *Gypsy* and other exonyms such as the Hungarian *Cigány* or the German *Zigeuner* are found from the late Middle Ages in Europe indicates a likely time of arrival for Romani speakers. These exogenous terms are more or less abusive and have strongly negative connotations of deceit and laziness.

Roma make up approximately 3 to 5 percent of the population of most eastern European countries as well as of Spain. Exceptional cases (Poland and the Baltic States, for example, where Roma represent tiny minorities) are areas where Nazi-led persecution and killings were particularly intense. In the early industrialized west of the Continent, Roma or Gypsies constitute around .1 percent of the total population.

Scholarly dispute rages as to the reasons for the persistence and success of the Roma way of life. For some, this is simply a matter of the fall of the cultural dice. The ability of Roma groups to retain a distinctive set of values and then to remain relatively unnoticed and unknown has been stressed by one school of anthropologists. Another focuses on the particular ways Roma have resisted assimilation into sedentary societies and the ways they have constructed cultural values in an oppositional strategy to peasant and farming communities.

The traditional Roma economic orientation was strikingly differentiated from that of the surrounding agricultural population, known by Roma as *gaže* or "farmers." Though there are communities of Roma who own land, most tend not to rely directly on the natural environment for their livelihood. Rather, they depend on human environments. Thus Roma are found wherever the non-Roma environment provides them with the human resources they need to carry out their economic activities.

In early modern Europe, Roma were known as blacksmiths and musicians, both "infamous" professions that were construed as either polluting or socially dangerous. For much of the twentieth century successful Roma engaged, if possible, in various forms of trade, especially with antiques, horses or other animals, and (more recently) secondhand cars. Poorer Roma are often engaged in various forms of scavenging of industrial waste goods that are then sold back to the *gažos* (non-Roma).

For most Roma, trade provides an insufficient income to support a family, and so wage labor in factories became the norm after World War II, at least in Spain and Eastern Europe. Under communist rule all citizens were obliged to have a registered workplace. The collapse of the planned economies and with them the heavily subsidized and profoundly inefficient and unmodernized industries of the region led to mass unemployment among Roma families across the region, especially elder Roma. Rates of unemployment are estimated at between 30 and 70 percent in many of the former communist countries.

Relations between Roma and the authorities do not always reflect directly the state of Roma's economic position. The relationship between Roma and majority populations has by no means always been conflictual, though issues around sedentarization and resistance to proletarianization have recurrently led to periods of persecution.

Eighteenth- and nineteenth-century policy toward Gypsies was largely driven by police concerns that they represented a hard-to-identify, unsettled population, and the origin of extraterritorial police (such as Interpol) procedures in Europe lies in part in police work dealing with Roma in Germany and other areas of central Europe. The history of Roma in the principalities of Wallachia and Moldavia is of particular note, as many were enslaved to feudal lords and monasteries until the mid-nineteenth century. Slavery here refers to a form of unbreakable personal and domestic bond rather than the more familiar plantation slavery characteristic of the Americas in the eighteenth and nineteenth centuries.

During the 1930s persecution of Roma across central and eastern Europe intensified, in particular inside the German Third Reich. Using anthropological and, more importantly, police procedures for identifying "the unsettled," the Third Reich registered the entire German Romani population before deporting two-thirds to camps in the occupied east. Although the Nazis never formulated an explicit "final solution" for the Roma, the cumulative effect of sterilization programs in the Third Reich, mass deportations to Auschwitz, and systematic massacres on the eastern and southeastern fronts constituted a genocidal campaign in which well over 100,000 Roma died.

For forty years after the war the democratic German successor state failed to fully acknowledge the nature and extent of the Nazi persecution, and thousands of Roma died without receiving proper reparation or compensation for their suffering. This remains a potent symbol to young activists of the marginalization of Roma in European political and civic society.

Historical work has demonstrated the existence of a sharp sense of persecution and discrimination among Roma as early as the eighteenth century. But it was not until the second and third decades of the twentieth century that any serious attempts at local and international self-organization began. Communist nationality policy tended to blow alternately hot and cold on Romani self-organization, but the legacy in Bulgaria and Hungary of political movements in the 1950s can still be felt. The formation of the International Romany Union in 1971 counts as a formal landmark in the process of Romany self-organization, but perhaps more important has been the emergence of a broadly based Romani intelligentsia across eastern Europe since the early 1970s. In the early twenty-first century scores of young Romani intellectuals are shaping a new, Europe-wide Romani movement. The presence, in 2007, in the European Parliament of two young Romani members, Livia Jároka and Viktória Mohácsi (both from Hungary), is indicative of the dynamism of this new generation.

Government policies toward Roma vary widely across Europe. In the former communist countries a certain policy schizophrenia may be observed: encouraging an ethnicization of public policy (with programs targeted not at social problems but ethnic groups) and at the same time a tendency to represent the so-called Roma question as one of national security, playing on fears of demographic explo-

sion among Roma and demographic collapse of the majority population. In reality Romani demographic trends mirror the decline in fertility witnessed across Europe.

Mass mobilization of Roma has been hampered by a number of factors. In most Romani communities social organization is kinship based, with no formal political structures existing over and above loose networks of related families. Romani communities tend to be extremely egalitarian in values, despite economic inequalities among households being marked. This militates against the emergence of stable political leadership. Occasionally "kings" or other forms of traditional leaders arise when non-Gypsy authorities collaborate with prominent Roma to control access to some limitable resource, but the authority of such people is largely contingent on their ability to "serve up" the non-Gypsies.

In the last two decades of the twentieth century the importation of a human and civic rights discourse through mainly U.S.-based nongovernmental organizations (NGOs) has provided an oppositional language of self-representation to activists. With most of the former communist countries now inside the European Union (EU), the U.S.-backed NGOs tend to be withdrawing. At the same time EU structures tend to encourage a demand for participation and collaboration at a local level with community representatives. It remains to be seen whether the imported oppositional stance of civic rights can be adapted to the needs and opportunities of the new situation. It is in this complex context that the new, highly educated young Romani elite are trying to create a politics of Romani identity fit for the twenty-first century.

SEE ALSO *Discrimination; Ethnicity; Holocaust, The; Identity; Kinship; Racism*

BIBLIOGRAPHY

Budrala, Dumitru. 2005. *The Curse of the Hedgehog.* Sibiu, Romania: Foundation for Visual Anthropology. Film.

Margalit, Gilad. 2002. *Germany and Its Gypsies: A Post-Auschwitz Ordeal.* Madison: University of Wisconsin Press.

Matras, Yaron. 2002. *Romani: A Linguistic Introduction.* Cambridge, U.K.: Cambridge University Press.

Stewart, Michael. 2002. Deprivation, the Roma and "the Underclass." In *Postsocialism: Ideals, Ideologies, and Practices in Eurasia,* ed. Chris Hann, 133–155. London: Routledge.

Vermeersch, Peter. 2006. *The Romani Movement: Minority Politics and Ethnic Mobilization in Contemporary Central Europe.* New York: Berghahn Books.

Michael Stewart

ROMAN CATHOLIC CHURCH

The Roman Catholic Church refers to the worldwide assembly of Christians who are in full communion with the pope, the bishop of Rome, who is regarded as the sign and instrument of Catholic unity among bishops and faithful alike. Statistically, Roman Catholics form the largest single Christian body, with close to 1.1 billion members worldwide. The rise of Christian culture in western Europe is virtually synonymous with the history of the Roman Catholic Church.

Although other Christians sometimes refer to themselves as *catholic* (from the Greek word meaning universal or complete), Roman Catholics believe communion with the See of Rome is required for full membership in the Catholic Church. In addition to the Western or Latin Rite Catholics, there are some 20 million Eastern Christians in full communion with Rome (better identified as Eastern Catholics than Roman Catholics).

Roman Catholics believe the pope is the successor of Peter, appointed by Jesus Christ as the chief apostle and head of the Church. By the late second century, Irenaeus, the bishop of Lyon (c.130–200), saw agreement with the Church of Rome as necessary for all Christian churches.

Following persecutions by various Roman emperors, the Church received legal recognition from Constantine in 313. The move of the imperial capital from Rome to Byzantium (Constantinople) in 330 set the stage for the later split (schism) of the Byzantine Church from the Church of Rome in 1054.

The monasteries of the Church preserved learning after the collapse of the Roman Empire. The rise of Islam in the seventh century and the Muslim invasions of Spain and Gaul prompted the pope to form an alliance with Charlemagne and the Franks. The Crusades (1095–1291) failed to maintain Christian control over Jerusalem and stem the eventual spread of Muslim power into Asia Minor (Turkey).

During the Middle Ages (c. 800–1400), the Church inspired cultural achievements in art (e.g., Gothic architecture), poetry (e.g., Dante), philosophy (e.g., Thomas Aquinas), and learning (e.g., the universities of Oxford, Paris, Salamanca, and Bologna). During the Renaissance (c.1400–1550), the Church continued its patronage of the arts, but many areas of Europe (e.g., England, Holland, northern Germany, and Scandinavia) broke with papal authority in the sixteenth century following the Protestant Reformation. In the 1500s and 1600s, missionaries and colonial rulers spread Roman Catholicism into the Americas and Asia.

Although the Roman Catholic Church contributed much to the cultural achievements of the medieval and Renaissance eras, religious minorities, such as the Jews, often suffered persecutions in countries under Roman Catholic control. Theological ideas were enforced by various inquisitions (Church tribunals) that conducted trials for those accused of heresies (false teachings). Technically, the inquisition only had jurisdiction over the baptized, but after the Jews and Muslims were expelled from Iberia in 1492, the Spanish Inquisition would often target *Los Conversos*, the Jews and Muslims who had accepted baptism rather than leave the country of their birth.

In the 1700s and 1800s, the influence of the Roman Catholic Church over European culture began to fade. The French Revolution (1789–1799) placed the Church in France under virtual state control. In 1870, the Papal States of central Italy were seized from the Church, leaving control only over Vatican City State (according to the Lateran Agreement of 1929).

Deprived of secular power, the Roman Catholic Church in the twentieth century tried to exert moral authority. Pope Pius XI (1857–1939), who was pope from 1922 to his death, issued encyclical letters protesting Italian Fascism (1931), German Nazism (1937), and atheistic Communism (1937). His successor, Pius XII (pope from 1939–1958), led the Church through the difficult years of World War II (1939–1945). His policies during this time—especially with regard to helping the Jews—have been praised by some and criticized by others.

The Second Vatican Council (1962–1965) urged dialogue with other Christians and non-Christians (most notably Jews and Muslims). In his 1994 apostolic letter, *Tertio Millennio Adveniente*, John Paul II (pope from 1978–2005) called Catholics to a "spirit of repentance" for practices of past centuries that involved "intolerance and even the use of violence in the service of truth." Pope Benedict XVI, who succeeded John Paul in 2005, has continued this spirit into the early-twenty-first century, while at the same time condemning secularization and moral relativism.

SEE ALSO *Christianity; Church, The; Enlightenment; French Revolution; Greek Orthodox Church; Islam, Shia and Sunni; Jesus Christ; Missionaries; Protestantism; Religion; Rituals; Secular, Secularism, Secularization; Vatican, The*

BIBLIOGRAPHY

Bunson, Matthew, ed. 2006. *Our Sunday Visitor's 2007 Catholic Almanac.* Huntington, IN: Our Sunday Visitor.

O'Collins, Gerald, and Mario Farrugia. 2003. *Catholicism: The Story of Catholic Christianity.* Oxford: Oxford University Press.

Woods, Thomas E., Jr. 2005. *How the Catholic Church Built Western Civilization.* Washington, D.C.: Regnery.

Robert Fastiggi

ROMANCE

Social psychologists have defined "romance" in a variety of ways. These include: (1) Tales of idealized romantic love between two lovers; (2) A dreamy, imaginative, cognitive state in which people imagine a perfect love relationship; (3) A *feeling* of passionate love. In the early 1950s social psychologists focused on romantic love, attempting to discover if couples' attitudes toward romantic love had an impact on marital happiness and stability. A popular scale at that time was Charles Hobart's "Romantic Love Scale" (1958). It contained such items as: "When one is in love … one lives almost solely for the other." Later, in 1973, Zick Rubin developed a more modern scale to measure romantic love versus friendship. Rubin argued that romantic love was made up of three elements: attachment, caring, and intimacy.

DEFINITIONS

By the end of the twentieth century, however, scientists' attention had shifted to passionate love. *Passionate love* (sometimes called "obsessive love," "infatuation," "lovesickness," "romantic love," or "being-in-love") is a powerful emotional state. It has been defined by Elaine Hatfield and Richard Rapson as "A state of intense longing for union with another. Passionate love is a complex functional whole including appraisals or appreciations, subjective feelings, expressions, patterned physiological processes, action tendencies, and instrumental behaviors. Reciprocated love (union with the other) is associated with fulfillment and ecstasy. Unrequited love (separation) is associated with feelings of emptiness, anxiety, and despair" (1993, p. 5). The Passionate Love Scale is designed to tap into the cognitive, emotional, and behavioral indicants of such longings, as reported by Hatfield and Susan Sprecher in 1986.

GENETIC AND BIOLOGICAL BASES OF LOVE, LUST, AND ATTACHMENT

In the 1990s social psychologists, neuroscientists, and physiologists began to explore the links between romantic and passionate love, sexual desire, and sexual behavior. The first neuroscientists to study romantic and passionate love were Niels Birbaumer and his colleagues in 1993. They concluded that passionate love was "mental chaos." In 2000 Andreas Bartels and Semir Zeki studied the neural bases of passionate love using fMRI (brain imaging) techniques. They interviewed young men and women from eleven countries who claimed to be "truly, deeply, and madly" in love and who scored high on the Passionate Love Scale. They discovered that passionate love produced increased activity in the brain areas associated with euphoria and reward, and decreased levels of activity in the areas associated with distress and depression. Passionate love

and sexual arousal appeared to be tightly linked. Other psychologists who have studied the links between passionate love and sexual desire (using fMRI techniques), such as those reported by Helen Fisher in 2004, have found similar results.

Scientists interested in the chemistry of passionate love, sexual desire, and mating, detailed by C. Sue Carter in 1998 and Donatella Marazziti and Domenico Canale in 2004, have found that a variety of neurochemicals shape romantic love, passionate love, sexual desire, and sexual mating. One theorist, Helen Fisher, argued in 2004 that passionate love, lust, and attachment are associated with slightly different chemical reactions—although generally coming together in a single package. According to Fisher, passionate love is associated with the natural stimulant dopamine (and perhaps norepinephrine and serotonin.) Lust is associated primarily with the hormone testosterone. Attachment (a commitment to another) is produced primarily by the hormones oxytocin and vasopressin.

Psychologists may differ on whether romantic and passionate love are or are not emotions and whether passionate love, sexual desire, and sexual motivation are closely related constructs (both neurobiologically and physiologically) or very different in their natures. Nonetheless, this path-breaking research has the potential to answer age-old questions as to the nature of culture, love, and human sexuality.

CULTURAL DIFFERENCES IN ROMANTIC ATTITUDES, FEELINGS, AND BEHAVIOR

Passionate love is as old as humankind. (The Sumerian love fable of Inanna and Dumuzi was spun by tribal storytellers in 2,000 BCE.) People in all cultures also recognize the power of romantic love. In south Indian Tamil families, for example, a person who falls head-over-heels in love with another is said to be suffering from *mayakkam*—dizziness, confusion, intoxication, and delusion. The wild hopes and despairs of love are, as Margaret Trawick noted in 1990, thought to "mix you up."

At one time, however, social commentators contended that the idealization of romantic and passionate love was a peculiarly Western institution. Thus, cultural researchers began to investigate the impact of culture on people's definitions of love, what they desired in romantic partners, their likelihood of falling in love, the intensity of their passion, and their willingness to acquiesce in arranged marriages *versus* insisting on marrying for love. When social psychologists explored folk conceptions of love in a variety of cultures—including the People's Republic of China, Indonesia, Micronesia, Palau, and Turkey—they were surprised to find that men and women in all of these cultures possessed surprisingly similar views of romantic love and other "feelings of the heart" (Jankowiak 1995; Shaver, Murdaya, and Fraley 2001). Subsequent research by cultural and evolutionary psychologists discovered that there appear to be cultural universals in what men and women desire in mates (Buss 1994), and according to Hatfield and Rapson's 1996 work, in their likelihood of being in love, in how intensely they love, and whether or not they would be willing to marry someone they did not love. One impact of globalization (and the ubiquitous MTV, Hollywood and Bollywood movies, chat rooms, and foreign travel) may be to ensure that young people are becoming increasingly similar in their definitions of love and their romantic aspirations and behavior (Hatfield and Rapson 1996; Hatfield, et al. 2007).

HOW LONG DOES LOVE LAST?

Like any intense emotion, passionate love does tend to erode with time. Jane Traupmann and Elaine Hatfield in 1981, for example, interviewed a random sample of dating couples, newlyweds, and older women (who had been married an average of thirty-three years) in Madison, Wisconsin. (The longest marriage was fifty-nine years.) The authors assumed that passionate love would decline precipitously with time; they expected companionate love to last far longer. They were wrong. Over time, passionate love did plummet. Couples began loving their partners intensely. Both steady daters and newlyweds expressed "a great deal of passionate love" for their mates. After many years of marriage, however, women reported that they and their husbands now felt only "some" passionate love for one another. And what of the fate of companionate love? The authors found that over time, both passionate and companionate love tended to decline at approximately the same rate. This finding was especially surprising since the authors were only interviewing couples whose marriages had survived for ten, twenty, or fifty years. Couples whose relationships were the most dismal may well have divorced and thus been lost from the sample.

SEE ALSO *Similarity/Attraction Theory*

BIBLIOGRAPHY

Bartels, Andreas, and Semir Zeki. November 27, 2000. The Neural Basis of Romantic Love. *Neuroreport* 11: 3829–3834.

Birbaumer, Niels, Werner Lutzenberger, Thomas Elbert, et al. 1993. Imagery and Brain Processes. In *The Structure of Emotion: Psychophysiological, Cognitive, and Clinical Aspects*, eds. Niels Birbaumer and Arne Öhman, 132–134. Seattle, WA: Hogrefe and Huber.

Buss, David M. 1994. *The Evolution of Desire: Strategies of Human Mating*. New York: Basic Books.

Carter, C. Sue. 1998. Neuroendocrine Perspectives on Social Attachment and Love. *Psychoneuroendocrinology* 23: 779–818.

Fisher, Helen E. 2004. *Why We Love: The Nature and Chemistry of Romantic Love*. New York: Henry Holt and Company.

Hatfield, Elaine, and Richard L. Rapson. 1993. *Love, Sex, and Intimacy: Their Psychology, Biology, and History*. New York: HarperCollins.

Hatfield, Elaine, and Richard L. Rapson. 1996. *Love and Sex: Cross-cultural Perspectives*. Boston, MA: Allyn & Bacon.

Hatfield, Elaine, Richard L. Rapson, and Lise D. Martel. 2007. Passionate Love. In *Handbook of Cultural Psychology*, eds. Shinobu Kitayama and Dov Cohen. New York: Guilford Press.

Hatfield, Elaine, and Susan Sprecher. 1986. Measuring Passionate Love in Intimate Relations. *Journal of Adolescence* 9: 383–410.

Hobart, Charles W. 1958. The Incidence of Romanticism during Courtship. *Social Forces* 36: 362–367.

Jankowiak, William R., and Edward F. Fischer. 1992. A Cross-cultural Perspective on Romantic Love. *Ethology* 31: 149–155.

Marazziti, Donatella, and Domenico Canale. 2004. Hormonal Changes When Falling in Love. *Psychoneuroendocrinology* 29 (7): 931–936.

Rubin, Zick. 1970. Measurement of Romantic Love. *Journal of Personality and Social Psychology* 16: 265–273.

Shaver, Phillip R., Upekkha Murdaya, and R. Chris Fraley. 2001. Structure of the Indonesian Emotion Lexicon. *Asian Journal of Social Psychology* 4: 201–224.

Traupmann, Jane, and Elaine Hatfield. 1981. Love and Its Effect on Mental and Physical Health. In *Aging: Stability and Change in the Family*, eds. R. Fogel, E. Hatfield, S. Kiesler, and E. Shanas, 253–274. New York: Academic Press.

Trawick, Margaret. 1990. *Notes on Love in a Tamil Family*. Berkeley: University of California Press.

Elaine Hatfield
Richard L. Rapson

ROOSEVELT, FRANKLIN D.
1882–1945

Franklin Delano Roosevelt was the thirty-second president of the United States of America. He served as president from March 4, 1933, until his death on April 12, 1945. He was elected president four times, more than any other American president.

Franklin D. Roosevelt was born on January 30, 1882, in Hyde Park, New York. He was the only child of James and Sara (Delano) Roosevelt. A graduate of the Groton School and Harvard University, he also attended the law school of Columbia University before becoming an attorney in 1907.

Like his father, Franklin D. Roosevelt was a Democrat, but he wanted to follow the career path of his Republican cousin, President Theodore Roosevelt (1901–1909). As a young attorney, Roosevelt became active in the progressive wing of the Democratic Party. In 1910 he was elected to the New York state senate. An admirer and supporter of Democratic president Woodrow Wilson (1913–1921), Roosevelt was appointed assistant secretary of the navy in 1913. Like Wilson, Roosevelt supported an active, leading role for the United States in the League of Nations after World War I.

After the Democratic national convention nominated James Cox for president and Roosevelt for vice president in 1920, the Democratic Party decisively lost the 1920 presidential election. In 1921 Roosevelt was stricken by polio, which permanently paralyzed his legs. After resuming his political activism, Roosevelt became closely allied with Democratic governor Alfred E. Smith of New York; he also relied on his wife, Eleanor Roosevelt, who served as a political operative. After Smith was nominated for president in 1928, Roosevelt, at Smith's request, ran for governor. While Smith lost the 1928 presidential election by a landslide, Roosevelt was narrowly elected governor of New York.

For a Democratic governor, Roosevelt was unusually popular in heavily Republican rural areas of upstate New York. He advocated such policies as state-sponsored rural electrification, property tax relief for farmers, and the state construction of paved farm-to-market roads. He directly communicated to New Yorkers through radio broadcasts, and increased public works and relief spending when the economy worsened after 1929. Reelected in 1930, Roosevelt emerged as the leading candidate for the 1932 Democratic presidential nomination.

Citing his rural-oriented policies as governor, Roosevelt emphasized agricultural and rural economic issues as he gained greater political support in the South and West while the Great Depression worsened. Competing against Smith, Speaker of the House John N. Garner, and several minor candidates, Roosevelt was nominated for president at the 1932 Democratic national convention. He chose Garner as his running mate.

The Great Depression helped Roosevelt to easily defeat Republican president Herbert Hoover in 1932. In his campaign speeches and 1933 inaugural address, Roosevelt promised bold, innovative presidential leadership to combat economic suffering and reform the economy. Roosevelt's domestic policies, collectively known as the New Deal, included public works programs, the Social Security Act of 1935, stricter federal regulation of banks and the stock market, agricultural subsidies, legal powers for labor unions, and a national minimum wage. Roosevelt's landslide reelection in 1936 solidified changes in American voting behavior that caused a Democratic realignment which lasted until 1968.

During his second term (1937–1941), Roosevelt was less successful in realizing his domestic policy agenda. The rejection of his "court-packing bill" in 1937 and Republican gains in the 1938 elections increased opposition in Congress to further New Deal legislation. After the outbreak of World War II in Europe in 1939, Roosevelt concentrated on foreign and defense policies. Before the United States entered World War II following the Japanese attack on Pearl Harbor on December 7, 1941, Roosevelt assisted Great Britain against Nazi Germany through military and economic aid, despite strong isolationist opinion in the United States.

In his treatment of African Americans, Roosevelt generally deferred to the pro-segregation beliefs and policies of white Southern Democrats who dominated Congress and the Democratic Party. He never submitted a civil rights bill to Congress and only reluctantly created a Fair Employment Practices Committee (FEPC) after black civil rights leaders threatened a march on Washington. New Deal programs, especially the Works Progress Administration and Civilian Conservation Corps, were often racially segregated and discriminatory. Roosevelt did not publicly support federal anti-lynching legislation and the American military remained racially segregated during World War II.

Roosevelt was reelected president in 1940 and 1944 by narrower margins. During the period of American participation in World War II (1941–1945), Roosevelt converted the U.S. economy's productive capacity for military and foreign aid purposes and developed military and political alliances with Great Britain and the Soviet Union to defeat Germany and Japan. He also secretly authorized the development of atomic bombs and promoted the creation of the United Nations and the establishment of the concept and practice of international human rights.

SEE ALSO *Democratic Party, U.S.; Great Depression; New Deal, The; Pearl Harbor; Truman, Harry S.; World War II*

BIBLIOGRAPHY

Burns, James MacGregor. 1970. *Roosevelt: The Soldier of Freedom.* New York: Konecky and Konecky.

Leuchtenburg, William E. 1963. *Franklin D. Roosevelt and the New Deal, 1932–1940.* New York: Harper and Row.

Savage, Sean J. 1991. *Roosevelt: The Party Leader, 1932–1945.* Lexington: University Press of Kentucky.

Sean J. Savage

ROPER POLL

SEE *Pollsters.*

RORSCHACH, HERMAN

SEE *Rorschach Test.*

RORSCHACH TEST

The Rorschach inkblot test is one of several inkblot-based personality assessment instruments, though it is by far the most well known, commonly used, and frequently researched. Its name is derived from its developer, Hermann Rorschach (1884–1922), a Swiss physician and artist. Rorschach experimented with forty or more inkblots between 1917 and 1920, largely with the goal of understanding the syndrome of schizophrenia (dementia praecox) that had recently been identified and described by his mentor, the Swiss psychiatrist Eugen Bleuler (1857–1939). Contrary to popular perception, these were not simply blots of ink placed on a piece of paper that was folded in half and opened again. Instead, Rorschach used his artistic skills to refine and enhance his final inkblots so that each contained some contours that would suggest objects or images to most people. His interests were in the perceptual operations that contributed to what people saw more than in the content of those perceptions. Ultimately he selected twelve inkblots as most optimal for eliciting and identifying personality characteristics. However, reproducing them was expensive, and Rorschach had to omit two in order to publish the final set of ten in 1921.

Each inkblot appears on a white background. Five are black and gray; two are black, gray, and red; and three are various pastel colors without any black. As the inkblots were prepared for publication, imperfections in the printing process accentuated gradations in saturation that were not obvious before. Rorschach initially was concerned about this but ultimately realized the shading gradations provided another set of perceptual processes that could influence how people perceived the stimuli.

HISTORY

Rorschach died in 1922, less than a year after his work was published. In the late 1920s his test was introduced in the United States, and by the late 1960s five distinct approaches to its use had been developed by the psychologists Samuel Beck, Marguerite Hertz, Bruno Klopfer, Zygmunt Piotrowski, and David Rapaport. Each practitioner had a different approach to administration, scoring, and interpretation of the Rorschach test, which created

disorganization in the research literature because there was no single "test" per se. In the late 1960s the American psychologist John Exner (1928–2006) reviewed the similarities and differences between these systems and then in 1974 published the first edition of what he called the Comprehensive System, which synthesized the most logically and empirically defensible elements of the earlier approaches. Fairly quickly the Comprehensive System became the dominant approach to administering, scoring, and interpreting the test in the United States and in other parts of the world. Although not specific to the Comprehensive System, the International Rorschach Society promotes research and clinical practice with the instrument and has twenty-seven member organizations worldwide.

TERMINOLOGY

In the late 1930s the Rorschach was classified as a "projective" test. This term was applied to a range of different kinds of tasks that could be used for personality assessment, such as having people tell imaginative stories that go along with certain pictures or generate pencil drawings of people. The idea was that these tasks required people to project or put forward distinctive aspects of their personality when spontaneously completing an activity without much external guidance. Projective tests were also contrasted with "objective" personality tests, which referred to self-rating questionnaires, where people indicate whether verbal descriptions are characteristic of them, using a fixed set of response options, such as true or false. Although the terms *projective* and *objective* are still used, they have misleading connotations and do not do a good job of describing the methods that psychologists can use to assess personality; so increasingly the Rorschach is called a performance task or implicit measure of personality.

ADMINISTRATION, SCORING, AND INTERPRETATION

Regardless of the label, the Rorschach provides a standard set of inkblot stimuli that are used with children, adolescents, and adults in a wide range of settings where questions of personality and problem solving are relevant, including psychiatric, medical, criminal, or legal settings, as well as when assessing normal personality functioning. Using the Comprehensive System's guidelines for standardized administration and scoring, normative reference data are available for children, adolescents, and adults. On average it takes about an hour and a half to administer and score the test. During administration the examiner sits next to the test taker, presents the cards sequentially, saying, "What might this be?" and then records all responses verbatim. On average people give about twenty-two or twenty-three responses, and a minimum of fourteen is required. To facilitate accurate scoring, the examiner reviews each response a second time and strives to see it through the test taker's eyes by clarifying the content of what is seen, where it is located in the inkblot, and the perceptual features of the ink that contribute to the response. Each response is then coded on dimensions that include location (e.g., the whole inkblot versus an unusual detail), developmental quality (e.g., vague versus defined object), determinants (e.g., movement, color, shading), form quality (e.g., how typical it is to see an object in a particular location based on an extensive table derived from more than 200,000 responses), content (e.g., human, landscape), organizational synthesis, and a series of special coding categories, many of which indicate disruptions in logic and thought processes. The codes are then summed across all responses to form what is known as the structural summary, which contains about seventy ratios, percentages, and derived scores that are considered important for interpretation. In addition to formal scores, Rorschach interpretation is also based on behaviors expressed during the testing, patterns of scores across responses, unique or consistent themes in the responses, and unique or idiosyncratic perceptions.

Unlike interview-based measures or self-report questionnaires, the Rorschach does not have people describe what they are like but has them show what they are like via the sample of behavior provided in each response. By relying on an actual sample of behavior collected under standardized conditions rather than a self-description, the Rorschach can provide information about personality that may reside outside of a person's conscious awareness.

ISSUES AND EVIDENCE CONCERNING THE RORSCHACH

The Rorschach has frequently been criticized for lacking reliability and validity. Like most personality inventories, it needs more systematically organized data evaluating the focused validity for each of its scales. In addition, based on emerging findings from around the world, the normative expectations for certain scores probably will need to be adjusted, particularly for children. Nonetheless systematically gathered statistical summaries of the research evidence show that its scores can be reliably coded and they are reasonably stable over time. Globally, across all scores that have been researched, the Rorschach is as valid as other commonly used and widely regarded personality tests. Even the most ardent contemporary critics acknowledge that its scores can validly evaluate disorders of thinking, the accuracy and conventionality of perceptions, psychotic disturbances (such as schizophrenia), dependent personality traits, cognitive complexity, anxiousness, hostility, and the ability to predict who will benefit from psychotherapy. Replicated evidence also shows that the Rorschach can quantify improvement from therapy as validly as other tests, assess the maturity with which other people are perceived, and predict suicidal self-harming behavior.

SEE ALSO *Personality; Psychoanalytic Theory; Psychometrics; Psychotherapy; Reliability, Statistical; Validity, Statistical*

BIBLIOGRAPHY

Bornstein, Robert F., and Joseph M. Masling, eds. 2005. *Scoring the Rorschach: Seven Validated Systems.* Mahwah, NJ: Erlbaum.

Exner, John E. 2003. *The Rorschach: A Comprehensive System.* 4th ed., vol. 1. New York: Wiley.

Lilienfeld, Scott O., James M. Wood, and Howard N. Garb. 2000. The Scientific Status of Projective Techniques. *Psychological Science in the Public Interest* 1: 27–66.

Meyer, Gregory J., ed. 2001. Special Section II: The Utility of the Rorschach for Clinical Assessment. *Psychological Assessment* 13: 419–502.

Meyer, Gregory J., and R. P. Archer. 2001. The Hard Science of Rorschach Research: What Do We Know and Where Do We Go? *Psychological Assessment* 13: 486–502.

Society for Personality Assessment. 2005. The Status of the Rorschach in Clinical and Forensic Practice: An Official Statement by the Board of Trustees of the Society for Personality Assessment. *Journal of Personality Assessment* 85: 219–237.

Gregory J. Meyer
Joni L. Mihura
James B. Hoelzle

RORTY, RICHARD
1931–2007

Richard Rorty was at his death a professor of comparative literature and philosophy at Stanford University and one of the most influential and controversial American philosophers of the twentieth century. He crafted a unique version of pragmatism from a blend of Anglo-American analytic philosophy with the Continental tradition, and his impact was felt across a broad range of the humanities and social sciences, including philosophy, literature, political science, and the fine arts.

Rorty was the grandson of Walter Rauschenbusch (1861–1918), a founder of the Social Gospel movement. Though he began his career in academic philosophy, Rorty later emerged as a social critic and political theorist of the first rank, connecting his earlier interest in epistemology with a critique of the foundations of twentieth-century liberalism. His early work in philosophy was limited to the Anglo-American tradition, but in *Philosophy and the Mirror of Nature* (1979) he connected the radical implications of the doctrines of Wilfrid Sellars (1912–1989), W. V. O. Quine (1908–2000), and Donald Davidson (1917–2003) with the insights of Ludwig Wittgenstein (1889–1951), John Dewey (1859–1952), and Martin Heidegger (1889–1976).

Rorty's main target, in both epistemology and political philosophy, was the hegemony of the paradigm of "representation" that had been in ascendance since the time of Immanuel Kant (1724–1804). According to Rorty, this tradition privileged a conception of truth that sought to bring the objects "out there" in the world into correspondence with the representations "inside" our heads. This led philosophers into a misguided search for ways of purifying representations (hence the analytic tradition's emphasis on clarifying linguistic propositions); however, instead of searching for a "final vocabulary" that could somehow bring the world and our representations into complete correspondence, philosophers should have taken up the more mundane tasks issuing from the pragmatism of John Dewey. Since philosophy and language are tools, not objective measuring sticks for determining truth, philosophers should avoid questions of validity, opt for an ironic detachment toward their own pronouncements, and reorient their discipline as therapeutic storytelling rather than rational adjudication.

Rorty's pragmatism and antifoundationalism were disturbing to both sides of the political spectrum. To the Right he represented the worst of liberal relativism, and to the Left his "liberal ironist" pose seemed to justify political quiescence. From Rorty's standpoint both sides mistake the issue—we need neither ontological foundations to justify our political stances, nor a fixed vocabulary to inspire us to political action. In any event, Rorty argued, rationality and foundationalist claims to knowledge are never the effective agents in history, since contending ontological positions (say between a Thomist and a Kantian liberal) are not themselves capable of rational resolution—it is in the "sad, sentimental" stories that we tell to one another that ultimate hope for the elimination of cruelty is to be found. This shift in the self-understanding of philosophy is Rorty's most lasting contribution to the Anglo-American philosophic tradition, and while his idea of philosophy is not universally accepted, it is almost always the one proffered by his opponents as the relevant position to be refuted.

SEE ALSO *Critical Theory; Epistemology; Linguistic Turn; Philosophy; Political Science; Pragmatism; Representation; Storytelling*

BIBLIOGRAPHY

Rorty, Richard, ed. [1967] 1992. *The Linguistic Turn: Recent Essays in Philosophical Method.* 2nd enlarged ed. Chicago: University of Chicago Press.

Rorty, Richard. 1979. *Philosophy and the Mirror of Nature.* Princeton, NJ: Princeton University Press.

Rorty, Richard. 1982. *Consequences of Pragmatism: Essays, 1972–1980.* Minneapolis: University of Minnesota Press.

Rorty, Richard. 1987. Thugs and Theorists: A Reply to Bernstein's "One Step Forward, Two Steps Backward." *Political Theory* 15 (4): 564–580.

Rorty, Richard. 1989. *Contingency, Irony, and Solidarity.* Cambridge, U.K.: Cambridge University Press.

Rorty, Richard. 1991. *Objectivity, Relativism, and Truth: Philosophical Papers I.* Cambridge, U.K.: Cambridge University Press.

Rorty, Richard. 1993. Human Rights, Rationality, and Sentimentality. In *On Human Rights: The Oxford Amnesty Lectures*, ed. Susan Hurley and Stephen Shute, 112–134. New York: Basic Books.

Stefan Dolgert

ROSCAs

Rotating savings and credit associations (ROSCAs) constitute one of the most commonly found informal financial institutions in the developing world. ROSCAs are known by many different names, such as *susu* in Ghana, *tontines* in franchophone Africa, *gamias* in Egypt, *njangis* in Cameroon, *upatu* in Tanzania, *ekub* in Ethiopia, *chilemba* in parts of East Africa, *hagbad* in Somalia, *chit* funds in India, *cheetu* in Sri Lanka, *pasanakus* in Bolivia, *cundina* in Mexico, *kye* in Korea, *arisan* in Indonesia, *pia huey* in Thailand, *kou* in Japan, *hui* in China, and *altin gunu* in Cyprus. The origins of ROSCAs are unclear, but records show that they have existed since premodern times in China, the ninth century in Japan, the seventeenth century in Korea, and the early nineteenth century in many parts of Africa. ROSCAs are particularly prolific in Africa, where they have exceptionally high membership rates (between 50% and 95% of the adult population in many countries). In many rural areas, these associations are the sole saving and credit institution. It has been estimated that the annual sums mobilized in these associations amount to more than 25 percent of national credit for countries of Africa, South Asia, and East Asia. Although ROSCAs are most common in very poor areas of the world, there are places where they exist alongside more formal financial institutions, and where they are sometimes preferred. ROSCAs are also popular among immigrant groups in developed countries.

In these associations, a group of individuals gather for a series of regular meetings, at which each person contributes a predetermined amount into a collective "pot," which is then given to a single member. This person is subsequently excluded from receiving the pot in future meetings, while still being obliged to contribute to the pot. The meeting process repeats itself until all members have had a turn at receiving the pot. The frequency of the meetings, the amount of the contribution, and the number of members determine the total group savings for each ROSCA cycle. Essentially, members take turns in benefiting from collected savings. Members who receive the pot early in the cycle are in debt to other members until the last contribution, while the last member to receive the pot is a creditor to all other members throughout the ROSCA cycle. As a result, the order of turns is an important component of ROSCAs, and there is substantial variation in its determination. At the start of the scheme, the order of such turns is decided either by a lottery draw, a bidding process, or according to a predetermined pattern.

ROSCAs are usually viewed as a way for individuals with little or no access to formal credit markets to save up for the purchase of indivisible durable goods. There is no interest to be gained by saving in a ROSCA since, over the ROSCA cycle, individual participants contribute the total funds that they, in turn, withdraw from the association. The question, therefore, is why do individuals choose to save through a ROSCA instead of individually accumulating savings? Several rationales for ROSCA formation have been put forth. Timothy Besley and colleagues point to the gains from reduced delay: the participants, on average, expect to enjoy the benefits of savings sooner than if they had saved on their own. Other rationales point to the insurance role of ROSCAs. Stefan Klonner notes that when ROSCA funds are allocated by a bidding process, the participants can use ROSCAs to insure themselves against idiosyncratic risks. Other explanations refer to the savings commitment role of ROSCAs. According to Mary Kay Gugerty, if individuals face self-control problems and are unable to credibly commit themselves to future behavior, then ROSCAs can serve as a collective savings commitment mechanism. A related explanation is that, in many cases, ROSCA participants are predominantly women. In a 2002 article, Siwan Anderson and Jean-Marie Baland pointed out that when men have a greater preference for present consumption, relative to women, then women can use ROSCAs as a forced savings device to hide money from their husbands in order to accumulate savings.

In spite of their organizational simplicity, ROSCAs do suffer from incentive problems. Because of the rotational structure of ROSCAs, the incentive for members who receive the pot earlier in the cycle to default on their later contributions is high. A ROSCA cannot function unless all members continue to maintain their obligations throughout the cycle. Since ROSCAs are typically formed by a relatively small group of individuals who live in the same area, it is generally assumed that the threat of social sanctions by the other members of the group are sufficient to deter opportunistic defection. Therefore, social collateral and trust among members seem crucial to the success of these organizations. To this end, as Ngina Chiteji points out in "Promises Kept" (2002), ROSCAs typically organize along ethnic lines or bring together friends and neighbors, for whom existing social capital circumvents inherent problems of enforcement.

SEE ALSO *Finance; Informal Economy; Loans; Trust*

BIBLIOGRAPHY

Anderson, Siwan, and Jean-Marie Baland. 2002. The Economics of Roscas and Intra-household Resource Allocation. *Quarterly Journal of Economics* 117 (3): 963–995.

Besley, Timothy, Stephen Coate, and Glenn Loury. 1993. The Economics of Rotating Savings and Credit Associations. *American Economic Review* 83 (4): 792–810.

Chiteji, Ngina. S. 2002. Promises Kept: Enforcement and the Role of Rotating Savings and Credit Associations in an Economy. *Journal of International Development* 14: 393–411.

Gugerty, Mary Kay. 2006. You Can't Save Alone: Commitment in Rotating Savings and Credit Associations in Kenya. Evans School Working Paper 2006–08. Seattle: Evans School of Public Affairs, University of Washington. http://evans.washington.edu/webtools/working_papers/.

Klonner, Stefan. 2003. Rotating Savings and Credit Associations When Participants Are Risk Averse. *International Economic Review* 44 (3): 979–1005.

Siwan Anderson

ROSCH, ELEANOR

SEE *Prototypes.*

ROSENBERG'S SELF-ESTEEM SCALE

Morris Rosenberg's (1965) Self-Esteem Scale (RSES) is perhaps the most widely used instrument for the assessment of *trait self-esteem*, defined as relatively stable feelings of overall self-worth. The importance of self-esteem in the prediction of other self-attitudes and behavior in conjunction with the ease of administration and scoring of the RSES make the instrument useful for social scientists in many different settings.

Rosenberg originally designed the RSES as a face-valid, unidimensional measure of self-esteem designed to assess adolescent self-worth. Example items from the RSES include "I feel that I am a person of worth, at least on an equal basis with others" and "At times I think I am no good at all." Negatively worded items are reverse-scored to create an overall score. The underlying view of self-esteem on which the scale was founded defines self-esteem as a positive or negative attitude about the self. People with high self-esteem respect and consider themselves worthy. Rosenberg noted that high-self-esteem people do not necessarily feel that they are better than others, but they do not consider themselves to be worse than others. People with low self-esteem express "self-rejection, self-dissatisfaction," and "self-contempt" (Rosenberg 1965, p. 31). According to Rosenberg, low-self-esteem people do not respect themselves and wish that they could evaluate themselves more favorably.

Though Rosenberg fashioned the RSES as a ten-item Guttman scale, researchers most commonly adopt five- or seven-point Likert-style response formats anchored by, for example, 1 = *not at all like me* to 7 = *very much like me.* (Blascovich and Tomaka 1991). Internal consistency estimates for the scale typically fall in a range from .77 to .88, indicating acceptable internal reliability. Additionally, test-retest estimates for the RSES range from .85 to .82, revealing that the RSES demonstrates excellent test-retest reliability.

In addition to being reliable, the RSES surfaces as a valid measure of self-worth as well. RSES scores are positively related to an abundance of conceptually related constructs such as confidence and social acceptance, as well as to other self-esteem scales (Blascovich and Tomaka 1991). Moreover, RSES scores are negatively associated with constructs that are typically symptomatic of low self-worth, including anxiety, depression, and feelings of rejection.

Researchers have adapted the RSES for use with different populations (i.e., younger children; Rosenberg and Simmons 1972) and for different purposes. By modifying instructions for the RSES, asking that respondents answer according to how they feel about themselves *right now, at the present moment,* researchers may assess *state self-esteem,* an evaluation of self-worth that is more variable than trait self-esteem using the RSES (Kernis, Grannemann, and Barclay 1992).

Although the RSES is a conceptually and psychometrically sound measure of unidimensional self-esteem, it does not assess all facets of self-worth. Researchers who are interested in assessing domain-specific elements of self-esteem (e.g., appearance self-esteem, school competence, moral self-worth) should include domain-specific measures in addition to or instead of the RSES, depending on their research questions. Additionally, the RSES is transparent, or face valid, making it easy for the respondent to surmise that they are completing a measure of self-esteem. Such obvious face validity might result in artificially inflated self-esteem scores. Researchers who are more interested in people's automatic or uncontrolled ratings of self-worth should make use of available implicit measures of self-worth.

SEE ALSO *Anxiety; Depression, Psychological; Guttman Scale; Likert Scale; Psychology; Psychometrics; Reliability, Statistical; Scales; Self-Concept; Self-Esteem; Self-Perception Theory; Self-Presentation; Self-Representation; Social Psychology; Validation; Validity, Statistical*

BIBLIOGRAPHY

Blascovich, Jim Robert, and Joseph Tomaka. 1991. Measures of Self-Esteem. In *Measures of Personality and Social Psychological Attitudes,* ed. John P. Robinson, Phillip R. Shaver, and Lawrence S. Wrightsman, 115–160. San Diego, CA: Academic Press.

Kernis, Michael H., Bruce D. Grannemann, and Lynda C. Barclay. 1992. Stability of Self-Esteem: Assessment, Correlates, and Excuse Making. *Journal of Personality* 60 (3): 621–644.

Rosenberg, Morris. 1965. *Society and the Adolescent Self-Image.* Princeton, NJ: Princeton University Press.

Rosenberg, Morris, and R. G. Simmons. 1972. *Black and White Self-Esteem: The Urban School Child.* Washington, DC: American Sociological Association.

Jorgianne Civey Robinson

ROSSI, PELLEGRINO

SEE *Public Rights.*

ROTATING SAVINGS AND CREDIT ASSOCIATIONS

SEE *ROSCAs.*

ROTHBARD, MURRAY

SEE *Anarchism.*

ROTHSCHILDS, THE

The Rothschild family, the most influential banking and finance dynasty of modern Europe, began with Mayer Amschel Rothschild (1743–1812) in Frankfurt am Main, Germany, and expanded across Europe under his five sons: Amschel Mayer Rothschild (1773–1855) in Frankfurt; Salomon Rothschild (1774–1855) in Vienna, Austria; Nathan Mayer Rothschild (1777–1836) in London, England; Karl Rothschild (1788–1855) in Naples, Italy; and James Rothschild (1792–1868) in Paris, France. Throughout its history, the family has used its unparalleled, networked financial and political assets to support large-scale government borrowing, industrial development, health, education, art collecting, scientific discovery, and Jewish rights.

After moving from Frankfurt to Manchester in 1799, Nathan used the expanding British cotton industry to accelerate the process of wealth accumulation started by his father. He consolidated large quantities of fabric for export from many of the smaller British cloth manufacturers, and supplied these producers with dyes and other raw materials. Using the profits that he earned, Nathan moved to London and refocused on the bullion market. Buoyed by his father's and brothers' continental connections, Nathan smuggled gold through Napoléon Bonaparte's continental blockade, funded the Duke of Wellington's Peninsular and Waterloo campaigns, propped up the Bank of England during the liquidity crisis of 1834, and created a new European state bond market based on easily tradable notes. Benefiting from carefully cultivated friendships with royal and political leaders, Nathan's brothers worked with the governments of France, Austria, and Belgium to finance the reconstruction of Europe, devastated by two decades of war. Beginning in the 1840s they established much of the continental railway network. Through their railways, as well as their development of mining and oil exploration, the Rothschilds powered nineteenth-century industrial growth from Spain to Russia. The Rothschilds also played an instrumental role in late nineteenth-century British imperial expansion, financing the Suez Canal Company and the South African diamond trade.

Like its banking concerns, the family's philanthropic activities have been global, including the building and support of hospitals, schools, and art collections. As a result of intense family pursuit of the natural sciences, more than 150 insect species, 81 animal species, and 14 plant species bear the Rothschild name. Beginning with the Rothschild's early years in the Jewish ghetto, however, anti-Semites viciously attacked the family for its adherence to Judaism, its high-profile wealth, and its Zionist support. Throughout, the Rothschilds remained proud of their faith, and actively supported Jewish personal and legal rights around the world. Nathan's son, Lionel Nathan Rothschild (1808–1879) successfully fought to become Britain's first Jewish member of Parliament in 1847. During World War II (1939–1945), the family suffered substantial loss and hardship in Nazi-occupied Europe. After the war, the Rothschilds expanded into North America, most prominently through the Brinco resource and hydroelectric development scheme in Newfoundland. In the 1980s the French government nationalized the original Paris branch, while the British government depended on the London branch to privatize several major public corporations. Signaling their new emphasis on corporate finance, in 2004 the Rothschilds withdrew from the bullion market that had been critical to their early success.

BIBLIOGRAPHY

Ferguson, Niall. 1998. *The House of Rothschild.* 2 vols. New York: Viking.

Wilson, Derek. 1988. *Rothschild: A Story of Wealth and Power.* London: André Deutsch.

Jonathan Eacott

ROTTEN KID THEOREM

SEE *Bequests.*

ROTTER, JULIAN

SEE *Locus of Control.*

ROTTER'S INTERNAL-EXTERNAL LOCUS OF CONTROL SCALE

In an effort to explain how personal characteristics interact with the environment to predict behavior, the psychologist Julian Rotter (b. 1916) proposed a social learning theory in 1954. Although Rotter emphasized both personal and environmental factors in behavioral prediction, much of the research generated by his theory focused on the role of people's expectancies or their subjective estimates of how likely it is that a given behavior will lead to a desired outcome.

According to Rotter, there are two types of expectancies. Specific expectancies apply to single situations, such as whether a student expects to do well on an exam. Over time people learn to apply their expectancies to a variety of related experiences, resulting in generalized expectancies. A generalized expectancy might refer to how well a student expects to do on exams in all of his or her courses. Rotter proposed that one of the most important generalized expectancies is a person's locus of control (LOC).

LOC refers to the perceived location of reinforcement sources for a person—that is, who or what is responsible to the things that happen to a person. As such, it is similar to other control-related constructs, such as attributions, learned helplessness, and self-efficacy. Those with an internal LOC expect the important things in their lives to occur because of their own effort, skills, or abilities. People with an external LOC expect these things to occur because of outside forces (such as luck, fate, chance, or powerful others).

In 1966 Rotter published the Internal-External Locus of Control Scale. Respondents were asked to choose between pairs of internal and external items relating to everyday situations. For example, on one item respondents must choose whether people's misfortunes are due to their own mistakes (internal) or to bad luck (external). Since its formulation, LOC has been one of the most frequently researched personality variables in the social sciences. Scores on the LOC Scale have been correlated with scores on nearly every social and personality characteristic imaginable. Among the areas that most commonly have used the LOC Scale are personality and social, educational, political, clinical, and health psychology. For example, research shows that whereas high externality scores are associated with high depression scores, internality is associated with more positive adjustment to a physical disability. In addition discrimination based on race or sex has been associated with differences in LOC. Researchers have shown that such group-level internality-externality differences have implications for mental and physical health outcomes.

Researchers have focused a great deal of attention on the psychometric properties and factor structure of the LOC Scale. In Rotter's original conception, LOC was a unitary construct along the internality-externality dimension. However, researchers soon began uncovering several other dimensions related to LOC. Initial analyses revealed a personal control factor and a system (or political) control factor. Other researchers proposed independent dimensions of internality, chance, and powerful others. Based in part on dissatisfaction with the properties of the original scale, researchers have developed new content-specific, multidimensional LOC measures. One of the most popular is a measure of health LOC (Wallston, Wallston, and DeVellis 1978). Although interest in Rotter's original LOC scale has waned, the development of new measures ensures that LOC will continue to be a topic of interest to social scientists for years to come.

SEE ALSO *Attribution; Likert Scale; Locus of Control; Mental Health; Psychological Capital; Psychology; Psychometrics; Scales; Self-Efficacy*

BIBLIOGRAPHY

Rotter, Julian B. 1966. Generalized Expectancies for Internal versus External Control of Reinforcement. *Psychological Monographs* 80 (1): 1–28.

Wallston, Kenneth A., Barbara S. Wallston, and Robert DeVellis. 1978. Development of the Multidimensional Health Locus of Control (MHLC) Scales. *Health Education Monographs* 6: 160–170.

Thomas M. Brinthaupt

ROUSSEAU, JEAN-JACQUES
1712–1778

Born in Geneva, Switzerland, Jean-Jacques Rousseau spent much of his life in and around Paris acting as the gadfly of the *philosophes*, leaders of the French Enlightenment. He championed equality and popular sovereignty on the eve of the French Revolution, encouraged the birth of nationalism, historicism, and romanticism, and provided prescient critiques of the "bourgeois," the quintessential figure of the democratic age he helped launch.

In *On the Social Contract* (1762), Rousseau denied the existence of any natural hierarchy or divine right that could legitimize political inequality, arguing that natural inequalities between human beings were politically irrelevant. The social contract substituted "a moral and legitimate equality for whatever inequality nature may have placed between men, and … while they may be unequal in force or genius, they all become equal by convention and right" (*On the Social Contract*, I.ix). While he believed every legitimate government was republican, he understood by this only that the executive power should be beholden to the sovereign people (II.vi). His preferred regime was an aristocratic government, or executive, responsible to the people (III.vi). Ironically, while he was one of the first political thinkers to champion popular sovereignty, he maintained that a democratic government was suited only to a people of gods (Iii.iv).

Central to his political thought was the general will: the will of the political community as a whole, manifest in laws to which all citizens had consented and by which all were bound (II.iv). Rousseau held that "what generalizes the will is not so much the number of votes, as it is the common interest which unites them" (II.iv), and he wrote extensively, in *Considerations on the Government of Poland* (1772) and the *Letter to M. d'Alembert on the Theatre* (1758), on the need to encourage community spirit through civic education and the promotion of virtue. His emphasis on the particular character of political communities inspired the rise of nationalism, influencing the German philosophers Johann Gottfried Herder (1744–1803) and Johann Gottlieb Fichte (1762–1814).

The argument of *The Discourse on the Origins of Inequality* (1754) helped give birth to historicism: the idea that human ideas and actions are better explained by history rather than by nature or divine will. History, not nature, nor God, was responsible for the great paradox that: "Man is born free, and everywhere he is in chains" (*On the Social Contract*, I.i). Free, contented, but asocial by nature, humans could hope only to legitimate rather than remove the chains brought by political life.

Rousseau's autobiographical work, especially *The Confessions* (1782), his praise of nature, particularly in *The Reveries of the Solitary Walker* (1782), and his argument in the *Discourse on the Sciences ands Arts* (1751) that the popularization of science diverted people from the practice of moral duties, all contributed to the romantic movement.

Rousseau also offered one of the first critiques of the "bourgeois." Alienated from nature, without being committed to political life, the bourgeois were torn between private interests and public duties. Materialistic and inauthentic, they were enslaved by the opinions of others and strangers to themselves.

SEE ALSO *Enlightenment; Hobbes, Thomas; Locke, John; Naturalism; Social Contract; State of Nature*

BIBLIOGRAPHY

O'Hagan, Timothy. 1999. *Rousseau*. London and New York: Routledge.

Wokler, Robert. 1995. *Rousseau*. Oxford: Oxford University Press.

Fiona Miller

ROYAL ANTHROPOLOGICAL INSTITUTE

SEE *Anthropology, Public.*

ROYAL COMMISSIONS

In Britain and in some of its former colonies such as Australia, Canada, and New Zealand, Royal Commissions of Inquiry have been an ad hoc, flexible, adaptive, and adaptable mode of inquiry established by centralized authority to investigate nominated issues. These topics are specified within a Royal Commission's Terms of Reference and approved under the royal prerogative in its Letters Patent. The first recorded Royal Commission in England is better known as the Domesday Book, ordered by the Norman conqueror William I and compiled between 1080 and 1086. It was an information-gathering exercise for taxation purposes that also sought to cement the authority of a foreign king over his newly conquered population. That Royal Commissions have survived for almost a thousand years since the Domesday Book inquiry is testimony to their flexibility. Royal Commissions, like many other mechanisms of official inquiry, have continued to perform one or both of two broad functions for the state: (1) a pragmatic and/or legal function to investigate an issue for a government, collect information, submit a report, and make recommendations; and (2) a broader political, or ideological, function as a technique of governance, in particular a capability for crisis management of an issue or a range of issues.

In carrying out either, or both, of these broad functions as an information gatherer or a mechanism that provides breathing space for governments, Royal Commissions can be investigatory, inquisitorial, or a combination of both. Their capacity for coercive powers of investigation varies between jurisdictions, but in Australia, for example, they include the ability to compel the attendance of witnesses and/or the production of documents, and to examine witnesses under oath or affirmation. Australia, like the United States, is a federal jurisdiction, so the statutes underpinning the legality of a Royal Commission, can operate at a federal level, such as the Royal Commissions Act 1902, or at a state level, such as the Commission of Inquiry Statute 1854 in the state of Victoria. In Britain, Royal Commissions are established under the Tribunal of Inquiry Act 1921. There is little doubt that political considerations can be a major influence upon the establishment of Royal Commissions. Once governments have decided to establish a Royal Commission they are faced with a range of decisions regarding the form, direction, and timescale of the inquiry. They are not merely the decisions of a minister, but also reflect the opinion of a permanent civil bureaucracy. Generally, civil bureaucrats provide government ministers with advice and draft the actual terms of reference for a Royal Commission. They also provide the secretary and often a short list of appropriate potential commissioners. There has been a traditional tendency in most jurisdictions that operate Royal Commissions to appoint judges and lawyers to head such inquiries, as they are assumed to bring impartiality and independence, plus appropriate skill sets to manage large amounts of information and direct the cross-examination of witnesses.

It is difficult to evaluate just how effective Royal Commissions are. They do have a somewhat dark side historically, in that some Royal Commissions have been used as political mechanisms by various monarchs and governments. However, many Royal Commissions have brought positive social, political, and economic benefits as they gathered information on issues, established fact, helped resolve disputes, and stimulated worthwhile reform. History demonstrates that Royal Commissions have been too diverse and adaptive to be tied down to a single explanatory model, and their intrinsic adaptability and flexibility are likely to ensure their survival into the foreseeable future.

SEE ALSO *Commonwealth, The*

BIBLIOGRAPHY

Gilligan, George. 2002. Royal Commissions of Inquiry. *The Australian and New Zealand Journal of Criminology* 35 (3): 289–307.

George Peter Gilligan

RUBENSTEIN BARGAINING

SEE *Screening and Signaling Games.*

RUGGED INDIVIDUALISM

SEE *Individualism.*

RULE OF LAW

The rule of law characterizes polities where coercive state action is efficiently exercised in accordance with generally applicable authoritative rules, adopted according to an agreed-upon and public procedure, and not contrary to certain fundamental natural rights. The concept is intrinsic to the Western idea of a legitimate legal system.

The most famous exposition of the rule of law was made by British constitutionalist Albert Venn Dicey (1835–1922) in his *Introduction to the Study of the Law of the Constitution* in 1895. Dicey saw the rule of law as embodying three "kindred conceptions": (1) that no one is punishable or can be made to suffer in body or goods except for a distinct breach of law established in the ordinary legal manner before the ordinary courts of the land; (2) that the same general law applies to the rulers as to the ruled; and (3) that individual rights are enforced, not simply proclaimed (Dicey [1895] 1982, pp. 107–122). John Adams (1735–1826), in Article XXX of the 1780 Massachusetts Constitution, added a fourth, quintessentially American contribution to the rule of law: *separation of powers*. "The legislative department shall never exercise the executive and judicial powers, or either of them: the executive shall never exercise the legislative and judicial powers, or either of them: the judicial shall never exercise the legislative and executive powers, or either of them: to the end it may be a government of laws and not of men."

Good organization has been an implicit part of the rule of law since King John (c. 1167–1216) of England was forced to approve the Magna Carta in 1215: "To no one will We sell, to no one will We deny or delay, right or justice" (Magna Carta, c1. 40).

Legalism (respect by the state for, and enforcement of, its laws) is also an important part of the rule of law. This legalism arguably characterized Soviet and, to a large extent, even Nazi rule, however. Legalism is necessary but not sufficient: fundamental individual rights, arguably inherent in Dicey's third kindred conception, are necessary too.

In sum, the rule of law seems to comprise four requirements (five if separation of powers is added):

1. Government is bound by the law.

2. The law is discernible by citizens.

3. Application of the law is well-organized.

4. Ordered liberty is largely maintained; that is, citizens are reasonably secure in their persons and property.

This rule of law can, within these constraints, exist in different legal systems. Republics and parliamentary democracies, civil and common law systems, are compatible with it. Differing tax rates and differing notions of fundamental rights are also compatible with the rule of law. On the other hand, rule-of-law procedural rights, such as the *presumption of innocence* (citizens are to be treated as innocent until they have been proven guilty), *nonretroactivity* (no one can be held accountable for violating a law before it was in effect), and *habeas corpus* (detained persons have the right to have their custody justified both to them and to an independent judicial authority), are intrinsic to the rule of law. Procedure is related to substance here: only if a legal system were substantially and severely unjust might, for example, retroactivity be authorized to eliminate the injustice.

The concept is elusive and fluid, but utterly meaningful. British philosopher Michael Oakeshott (1901–1990) put it best in his essay "The Rule of Law": "The rule of law bakes no bread, it is unable to distribute loaves or fishes (it has none), and it cannot protect itself against external assault, but it remains the most civilized and least burdensome conception of a state yet to be devised" (1983, p. 164).

SEE ALSO *Due Process; Law*

BIBLIOGRAPHY

Belton, Rachel K. 2005. Competing Definitions of the Rule of Law: Implications for Practitioners. Carnegie Endowment for International Peace. Democracy and Rule of Law Project. Carnegie Papers, Rule of Law series, no. 55. http://www.carnegieendowment.org/files/CP55.Belton.FINAL.pdf.

Cass, Ronald. 2001. *The Rule of Law in America*. Baltimore, MD: Johns Hopkins University Press.

Constitution of the Commonwealth of Massachusetts. 1780. http://www.mass.gov/legis/const.htm.

Dicey, Albert Venn. [1895] 1982. *Introduction to the Study of the Law of the Constitution*. Indianapolis, IN: Liberty Fund.

Oakeshott, Michael. 1983. *On History and Other Essays*. New York: Barnes and Noble.

Scalia, Antonin. 1989. The Rule of Law as a Law of Rules. *University of Chicago Law Review* 56: 1175–1188.

Shklar, Judith N. 1998. *Political Thought and Political Thinkers*. Chicago: Chicago University Press.

Tamanaha, Brian Z. The Rule of Law for Everyone? St. John's Legal Studies Research Paper. http://papers.ssrn.com/sol3/papers.cfm?abstract_id=312622.

Michael I. Krauss

RULES VERSUS DISCRETION

The debate of rules versus discretion in economic policy has its origin in the writings of Henry Simons at the University of Chicago. A policy rule can be specific as fixing the quantity of currency and demand deposits, or general as when the Federal Reserve announces to the public the course of action it will take for various states of the economy, putting its reputation behind it. Although rules can be set up in an equation form, such as the Taylor Rule, they require variables such as the natural level of output and expected prices that are only approximate. A rule can be active, as when it requires increasing the money supply when the economy is on a downswing, or passive when the money supply is increased by a fixed percent annually. By definition rules are normative, but some rules are descriptive, meaning that they predict values close to what the authorities actually allow. The danger with rules is the tendency to substitute administrative authority for rules, which tends to impair competition and expand government activities. In 1990, President George H. W. Bush replaced the term "policy rule" with "systematic policy" or "policy system" in his message to Congress.

Discretion requires delegating responsibilities to economic institutions such as the Federal Reserve to decide macroeconomic goals and policies as they see appropriate. According to Kenneth Arrow, the world of uncertainty necessitates discretionary policies. A decision improves with time and experience, which requires information that is available only sequentially. A decision maker such as the Federal Reserve analyzes the problem at hand, and decides on the best policy action to take. Discretionary policy may be inconsistent when it does not change the initial conditions that create a disturbance, or shortsighted when a policy requires lags to materialize.

Economists are divided over whether rules or discretion is the best policy for managing the economy. In the short run, monetary and fiscal policies can affect income, but in the long run, they do not have permanent effects on real income. The monetarist's preferred habitat is the long run, managing the economy through simple rules of the money supply. Milton Friedman believed that the Federal Reserve did not use its discretion to act when the money supply declined by a third during the 1929–1933 period, turning a garden-variety recession into the Great Depression. However, Keynesians find that output, unemployment, and prices can be stabilized in the short run by autonomous expenditures, including those by the government. Franco Modigliani believed that the deep business cycle in 1974 was a consequence of following monetary rules that did not allow the money supply to adapt adequately in both the up and down swings of the cycle.

The debate over rules versus discretion is not settled empirically. If a rule is placed on the money supply, the monetarists look for a causal link between money and prices. The definition of money and a stable velocity-of-circulation function are necessary for empirical investigation. A currency plus demand-deposit definition is not sufficient for rules to work because people hoard and dishoard money, many "near money" substitutes may exist, or wages and prices may be rigid. If wage and price rigidities are only slight, then a rule might work, but it would require the absence of substitutes such as equity or bonds; it would also require that loans be held for long periods so that repayment on principal is not required.

For Simon, such a systemic policy appears paradoxical, as it would require an intelligent monetary system on the one hand, and credibility of rules on the other. Friedman, a student of Simon, moved the research forward by articulating two rules on the money supply, the k-percent rule, and a Friedman rule, which he later referred to as the "5 percent and the 2 percent rules," respectively (Friedman 1969, p. 48). In the 5 percent rule, "the aggregate quantity of money is automatically determined by the requirements of domestic stability" (Friedman 1948, p. 252). To cover the international scene as well, Friedman complemented the 5 percent rule with a flexible exchange rate. The 5 percent rule, however, runs up against rigidities and lag effects in the economy, which are short run in nature. The long-run 2 percent rule requires nominal interest rates to equal the opportunity cost of producing money for the interest rate to be approximately zero.

The test for a stable velocity-of-money function was indirect. Because the velocity function was variable in the short run, Friedman turned to more general evidences, including the use of his permanent-income concept for further empirical analysis. Regression analysis on demand for the money function between money and prices was significant but did not assign causal agency to money alone. The issue became more complicated in the short run when interest rates, a mostly Keynesian variable, turned up significant. Abraham Hirsch and Neil De Marchi examined ruling out common elements in a variety of results tested in order to help identify money as the cause of price changes. Such method of difference testing, coined by John Stuart Mill, cannot be exhaustive.

As more sophisticated models evolved, policy rules became hard to eliminate, and according to Finn Kydland and Edward Prescott, they could improve social optimum. A change in administration leads people to change their expectations and their current decisions. People have expectations about the tax policies of different administrations. Once people have some knowledge of such changes, they adjust their expectations and set into motion a series of iterative changes that may or may not converge to an equilibrium given the current state of the economy. Some policy rules are suboptimal in the sense that their feedback mechanisms depend on initial conditions, and to continue initial policy in subsequent periods is not optimal.

The discretion to print more money can create unexpected inflation. Robert J. Barro and David Gordon argued that people would adjust their expectation of inflation to eliminate surprise inflation, creating a potential for higher money supply and inflations in equilibrium. If policy rules are implemented, such expectations-driven inflation would not occur, but policy makers would have an incentive to break the rule—cheating—because higher inflation means less unemployment and more growth,

according to the Phillips curve. These gaming situations between policy makers and the public can be avoided if policy makers are concerned about their "reputation" or "credibility." The incentive to be credible is based on a substitution of short-term benefits for higher level benefits from lower inflation in the long run.

Other research focuses on ways to pinpoint a rule and extend it into more research areas. William Poole lauds a Taylor Rule that can be refined, much like a scientist would refine a constant. He likens a rule to the choice of using rules to fly a plane rather than letting the pilot have his or her way of navigating. Taylor extended his policy rule to price and nominal income rules for the open economy under fixed versus flexible exchange rates. He found that the nominal income rule outperformed the price rule. Considering the effect of exchange rates on aggregate supply, Richard Froyen and Alfred Guender show that the nominal income rule is weak. V. V. Chari and Patrick Kehoe found that as of 2002, approximately twenty-two countries use some form of rule-based policy.

SEE ALSO *Arrow, Kenneth J.; Central Banks; Economics, Keynesian; Exchange Rates; Friedman, Milton; Great Depression; Macroeconomics; Modigliani, Franco; Monetarism; Policy, Monetary; Taylor Rule*

BIBLIOGRAPHY

Arrow, Kenneth. 1957. Statistics and Economic Policy. *Econometrica* 25 (4): 523–531.

Barro, Robert J., and David B. Gordon. 1983a. A Positive Theory of Monetary Policy in a Natural-Rate Model. *Journal of Political Economy* 91 (4): 589–610.

Barro, Robert J., and David B. Gordon. 1983b. Rules, Discretion, and Reputation in a Model of Monetary Policy. *Journal of Monetary Economics* 12: 101–121.

Chari, V. V., and Patrick J. Kehoe. 2006. Modern Macroeconomics in Practice: How Theory Is Shaping Policy. *Journal of Economic Perspectives* 20 (4): 3–28.

Friedman, Milton. 1948. A Monetary and Fiscal Framework for Economic Stabilization. *American Economic Review* 38 (3): 245–264.

Friedman, Milton. 1969. The Optimum Quantity of Money. In *The Optimum Quantity of Money and Other Essays.* Chicago: Aldine.

Froyen, Richard T., and Alfred Guender. 2000. Alternative Monetary Policy Rules for Small Open Economies. *Review of International Economics* 8 (4): 721–740.

Hirsch, Abraham, and Neil B. De Marchi. 1990. *Milton Friedman: Economics in Theory and Practice.* Ann Arbor: University of Michigan Press.

Kydland, Finn E., and Edward C. Prescott. 1977. Rules Rather Than Discretion: The Inconsistency of Optimal Plans. *Journal of Political Economy* 85 (3): 473–492.

Modigliani, Franco. 1986. *The Debate Over Stabilization Policy.* New York: Cambridge University Press.

Poole, William. 1970. Optimal Choice of Monetary Policy Instruments in a Simple Stochastic Macro Model. *Quarterly Journal of Economics* 84 (2): 197–216.

Poole, William. 1999. Comment. In *Inflation, Unemployment, and Monetary Policy*, eds. Robert M. Solow and John B. Taylor, 78–88. Cambridge, MA: MIT Press.

Simons, Henry C. 1936. Rules versus Authorities in Monetary Policy. *Journal of Political Economy* 44 (1): 1–30.

Taylor, John B. 1993. *Macroeconomic Policy in a World Economy: From Econometric Design to Practical Operation.* New York: Norton.

Lall Ramrattan
Michael Szenberg

RUMBAUT, RUBEN

SEE *Assimilation.*

RUMORS

Rumor is unconfirmed information circulating among persons endeavoring to make sense of a situation that is ambiguous or one that is potentially threatening. Like news, rumor is of current or topical interest and is generally considered important or significant; unlike news, it is never verified. Participants may or may not be aware of the rumor's unstable foundation—they may regard it as fact. Nevertheless, doubtful or deficient supporting evidence is rumor's central defining feature.

FUNCTIONS AND CONTEXTS

Rumors are typically discussed by people trying to make sense of an ambiguous situation or to manage a physical or psychological threat. An example of a sense-making rumor in a school district setting is: "I heard that the real reason the school superintendent was forced to step down was because of certain off-color remarks she made to employees." Faced with a murky state of affairs in which the meaning of current events is not clear or the likelihood of future events is uncertain, people fill the information void with speculation, discussion, and evaluation. Such collective sense-making attempts employ rumors as working hypotheses. Rumors also help people to manage physical threat, sometimes by warning them of how to avoid a potential future negative event, for example: "Get out of town now! A tsunami is headed this way!" More often, rumors simply afford a psychological sense of control over the threat by helping people understand and interpret negative events, for example: "I heard that the department is being downsized despite strong profits this quarter because the new CEO wants short term stock gains (so he can sell his own shares for a windfall before moving on) and doesn't care about long term effects on the company." Rumors may also help manage threats to one's psychological sense of self, often by derogating groups with whom one is not associated; one way of building oneself up is to put others down. An example of one such (false) rumor is: "The Israeli government is behind the events of September 11, 2001: 4,000 Jews were told by the Israeli Secret Service not to show up for work at the World Trade Center that day." Rumors may of course perform more than one of these functions, as when people discuss rumors to make sense of a threatening situation in a way that derogates another social group. Thus rumor is what people collectively do when they find themselves in an unclear or potentially threatening set of circumstances.

COMPARISON WITH GOSSIP

Rumor is often confused with gossip, but there are important differences. Whereas rumor is unverified information circulated to make sense and manage threat, gossip is evaluative social chat about individuals that may or may not be verified. Gossip is idle chit-chat about an individual—typically not present—whose content is often slanderous and personal. Though an important social phenomenon, gossip talk is perceived as less serious, significant, and purposeful than rumor talk. Gossip is part of a relaxed session of shooting the breeze. A classic example is: "Did you hear? Bill and Jennifer are an item!" It matters not whether the statement is firsthand observation or remote speculation; it qualifies as gossip in either case. Thus gossip may or may not be verified, but rumor is never verified. Gossiping to another person tends to strengthen the social bonds between the gossiper and the listener—the listener feels like a privileged insider—and gossip at the same time weakens the social standing of the gossip target. Gossip can be therefore a type of aggression that often attacks another person's relationships and excludes the target from the group. Gossip also serves to convey and reinforce social norms of the group by way of comparison. The statement "Did you hear what Sally did at the Christmas party?" may laud or shame Sally's behavior—depending on the speaker's tone of voice. Though gossip is often negative, it performs a positive function in that it allows people to gain information about a larger group—albeit in a secondhand fashion—that would not be possible if they were limited to firsthand interactions. "Johnny steals from people" is useful social information if a person is deciding who to invite to a party. Finally, gossip is often entertaining—a mutual mood enhancer that again strengthens bonds between participants.

COMPARISON WITH URBAN LEGEND

Urban (also called modern or contemporary) legends also differ from rumors in their characteristic content, function, and context. Whereas rumors are unverified claims circulated in a collective sense-making effort, urban legends are entertaining stories containing themes related to the modern world that are often funny or horrible and usually teach a moral lesson. The urban legend first of all tells a story—it is a narrative with a background, plot, climax, and conclusion; a rumor is typically not that complex and is often a one-liner. Urban legends are often entertaining and tell a morality tale; rumors are not set forth primarily to entertain or propagate norms. For example, when a teenage couple was unable to start their car after necking on a secluded country road, the boyfriend went for help, only to be found dead the next morning hanging upside down above the car, his fingernails scraping against the hood in a macabre fashion. Moral of the story: Don't park! Urban legends are stories about modern themes, such as automobiles, Coca-Cola®, and computers. In addition an urban legend is characteristically migratory, that is, its details vary from time to time and from place to place. However, urban legends may instantiate as specific rumors. For example, stories about the thief who hid underneath a parked car at a shopping mall and—upon the return of the shopper—slashed her exposed ankles with a razor and stole her bags and her car constitute a well-known urban legend. However, "I heard that a woman was slashed on the ankles by a robber at Jonestown Mall last Saturday night" would constitute a rumor.

Of course these forms of informal human discourse sometimes do not fall neatly into one or the other category. Rumors sometimes possess a narrative structure and entertain. Passing a rumor may also endear the speaker to the listener, convey moral norms, and contain slander about an absent third party. Nebulous and intermediate forms do exist. On the whole, however, rumors, gossip, and urban legends tend to possess the divergent qualities discussed above: Rumors are unverified claims circulating during group sense making and threat management, gossip is evaluative social chat, and urban legends are entertaining narratives.

TYPES OF RUMORS

Rumors have been categorized according to a number of different typologies. They have been grouped by subject matter, for example, racial, disaster, organizational, political, and product rumors. They have been classified according to the rumor public—the group through which the rumor circulates. For example, internal organizational rumors circulate among employees, vendors, and stockholders associated with an organization; external rumors circulate among the general public outside of an organization. They have been classified by object of collective concern of the rumor public. For example, pecking order rumors are about changes in management structure and how this might affect job duties and compensation. Stock market rumors circulate among shareholders who want to profit from changing stock values. Organizational change rumors often concern whether or not the change will be effective and how it will affect working conditions. Perhaps the most common rumor typology is by motivational tension. Dread or fear rumors are about potential negative events (e.g., "I heard that twenty-five staff members will be laid off"), whereas wish rumors are about desired positive events (e.g., "We are getting a Christmas bonus this year!"). Wedge-driving rumors derogate other groups (e.g., during World War II "the Catholics are evading the draft" enjoyed audience among non-Catholics).

EFFECTS OF RUMOR

Rumors cause or materially contribute to a variety of outcomes. Rumors can have attitudinal effects, such as sullying a company's reputation (e.g., "Corporation x contributes to the Church of Satan") or fostering hatred toward another group (e.g., "Ethnic Group y greeted the World Trade Center bombing with celebration"). Rumors also result in behavioral outcomes, such as reducing sales (e.g., "Soft Drink Company z is owned by the Ku Klux Klan and puts a substance in their soda that makes black men sterile"), fomenting a riot (e.g., rumors that police caused the death by impalement of a Native Australian by chasing him on his bicycle led to extensive rioting in Sydney), or fostering noninvolvement in disaster relief (e.g., rumors that water flooding New Orleans—after Hurricane Katrina—was toxic kept many workers from participating in rescue operations). Negative rumors in particular affect a variety of organizational attitudes and behaviors, including job satisfaction, organizational commitment, morale, trust in management, productivity, and intention to leave. For example, in a division of one large company, hearing negative rumors about management month after month led to significant increase in negative work attitudes and intentions. Rumors during organizational change are also associated with greater employee stress. Rumors also affect stock market trading behaviors. Experimental investigations have suggested that rumors draw investors away from profitable buy low, sell high trading strategies. And field studies confirm that the stock market is strongly responsive to rumors. Surprisingly, rumors can have these effects even though they are not believed. For example, disaster rumors circulating in 1934 after a catastrophic earthquake in India were not believed but were still acted upon.

FACTORS IN RUMOR TRANSMISSION

Several variables have been associated with rumor transmission. Uncertainty about a situation—being filled with questions about what current events mean or what future events will occur—leads to speculation and rumor as people try to understand their environment and predict what will happen in the future. Anxiety—an emotional state of dread concerning a potential negative event—promotes rumor discussion as people talk with one another in an attempt to thwart the dreaded negative event or to feel better about it by regaining a psychological sense of control. In addition people tend to discuss important rumors—rumors that pertain to an outcome that is personally relevant to them. People also pass along rumors they believe more than those they disbelieve. Poorly managed manufacturing plant layoff situations where employees are given minimal information provide an example of all these factors in action. Employees in such situations are naturally filled with uncertainty; the prospect of losing one's job is anxiety provoking; the topic is an important one; employees often have no control over such decisions; and if trust is low, negative rumors about management are quite believable. Rumors in such situations are rife. Rumor transmission may also be viewed through a motivational lens. People often spread and discuss rumors in order to find facts, that is, to ascertain a true state of affairs in order to deal effectively with real or perceived threats and to make sense of ambiguity. Telling rumors is fundamentally a social act, however, and people may also spread them to enhance their relationships. "I heard that your university is excellent," for example, will tend to improve the teller-listener relationship. Finally, rumors may be told to boost one's self esteem. Self-enhancing rumors typically do this by putting other groups down in order to build up one's own group in contrast—and by association, oneself.

FACTORS AFFECTING RUMOR BELIEF

At least four factors have been associated with belief in rumor. Not surprisingly, rumors in agreement with one's currently held attitudes are more likely to be believed than those that disagree. For example, rumors of government waste and special privilege during the rationing programs necessitated by World War II were more apt to be believed by those opposed to the Roosevelt administration than those in favor of it. Rumors that proceed from a credible source are more likely to be believed than those spread by a non-credible one. In a series of laboratory experiments, rumors about a murder were more likely to be believed when they were heard from someone close to the detective investigating the case than from an elderly busybody with no apparent connection to the case. Repeated hearing of a rumor is also associated with belief. After initial skepticism, a Wall Street stockbroker began to place greater credence in a false rumor that the Clinton White House was covering up the true nature of top aide Vince Foster's death; this occurred solely because he had heard it several times. Finally, hearing a rumor denial reduces belief in the rumor. In one experiment, denying rumors that admittance to a sought-after academic psychology program would be tightened reduced belief in that rumor.

RUMOR ACCURACY

Sometimes collectives are good at ferreting out the facts—and sometimes they are bad at it. For example, rumors circulating in established organizational grapevines tend to be accurate, but rumors following natural disasters tend to be fallacious. Several types of mechanisms have been identified in rumor accuracy. Cognitive mechanisms, such as the narrowing of attention, memory limits, and perceptual biases, tend to reduce accuracy during transmission. Student who serially transmitted rumors—passed them along a chain—tended to pass along parts of a rumor that were more consistent than inconsistent with stereotypes because stereotype consistent information is easier to process. Motivational mechanisms, including fact-finding, relationship-enhancement, and self-enhancement motives, also play a part. Rumors spread by people intent on fact finding tend to become more accurate than those motivated by either relationship- or self-enhancement. Situational features, such as the ability to check on the veracity of the rumor, tend to increase rumor accuracy. Soldiers in one World War II field study could ask superior officers if rumors they heard were false; rumors circulating among this group were highly accurate. Group mechanisms, such as conformity, culture, and epistemic norms, also affect accuracy. In one observational study of rumors among prison inmates, rumors about who was snitching circulated until a consensus was reached, then conformity to that rumor was demanded. Rumors also tend to agree with the cultural axioms and ideas of the rumor public. Finally, social network mechanisms affect transmission and include interaction among participants and transmission patterns. Rumors transmitted serially with interaction between each teller-listener pair in one laboratory study were more accurate than those where discussion was not permitted.

MANAGING RUMOR

Not all rumors are harmful, but those that are remain an object of interest to those interested in preventing or ameliorating such harm. Rumors can be successfully prevented and managed by reducing uncertainty and anxiety, reducing belief in rumor, or reducing dissemination. A sample of experienced public relations officers recommended rumor prevention strategies that reduce uncertainty and enhance formal communications. Strategies rated most highly in effectiveness include stating the values and procedures that will guide organizational change, explaining how decisions will be made, and—if true—confirming the rumor. Increasing trust was also rated highly; in independent research, *dis*trust of management was strongly related to negative rumor transmission in a department facing radical downsizing. Rumor rebuttal—denying the truth of the rumor—is overall an effective rumor management strategy (given that the rumor is indeed false). It is also a more effective strategy than one commonly advocated by some business commentators: no comment. Presenting a no-comment statement to experimental participants who had heard negative rumors about a food manufacturer raised their level of uncertainty and suspicion as much as simply hearing the rumor alone. Some variables moderate the effectiveness of rebuttals; rebuttals proceeding from a source perceived to be appropriate (i.e., knowledgeable regarding the rumor) and honest were most effective in reducing belief in a rumor. Indeed trusted third-party sources of rebuttal are effective. In addition effective rebuttals assist the recipient in attaining a sense of control; for example, rebuttals can include specific actions the hearer can take in order to minimize potential harm from a dreaded negative event. Finally, effective rebuttals can include a rebuttal context that addresses why the rebuttal is being issued; for example, "A competitor is spreading false and malicious rumors, and that is why we are rebutting them today."

SEE ALSO *Collective Wisdom; Equity Markets; Financial Markets; Hearsay; Ignorance, Pluralistic; Lay Theories; Lying; Psychology; Self-Esteem; Social Psychology; Storytelling; Trust*

BIBLIOGRAPHY

Allport, Gordon W., and Leo J. Postman. 1947. *The Psychology of Rumor.* New York: Holt, Rinehart.

Bordia, Prashant, and Nicholas DiFonzo. 2002. When Social Psychology Became Less Social: Prasad and the History of Rumor Research. *Asian Journal of Social Psychology* 5: 49–61.

Bordia, Prashant, and Nicholas DiFonzo. 2004. Problem Solving in Social Interactions on the Internet: Rumor as Social Cognition. *Social Psychology Quarterly* 67 (1): 33–49.

Bordia, Prashant, and Nicholas DiFonzo. 2005. Psychological Motivations in Rumor Spread. In *Rumor Mills: The Social Impact of Rumor and Legend,* eds. Gary Alan Fine, Véronique Campion-Vincent, and Chip Heath, 87–101. New Brunswick, NJ: Aldine Transactions.

Bordia, Prashant, Nicholas DiFonzo, Robin Haines, and L. Chaseling. 2005. Rumor Denials as Persuasive Messages: Effects of Personal Relevance, Source, and Message Characteristics. *Journal of Applied Social Psychology* 35 (6): 1301–1331.

Buckner, H. Taylor. 1965. A Theory of Rumor Transmission. *Public Opinion Quarterly* 29: 54–70.

DiFonzo, Nicholas, and Prashant Bordia. 1997. Rumor and Prediction: Making Sense (but Losing Dollars) in the Stock Market. *Organizational Behavior and Human Decision Processes* 71 (3): 329–353.

DiFonzo, Nicholas, and Prashant Bordia. 1998. A Tale of Two Corporations: Managing Uncertainty during Organizational Change. *Human Resource Management* 37 (3–4): 295–303.

DiFonzo, Nicholas, and Prashant Bordia. 2000. How Top PR Professionals Handle Hearsay: Corporate Rumors, Their Effects, and Strategies to Manage Them. *Public Relations Review* 26 (2): 173–190.

DiFonzo, Nicholas, and Prashant Bordia. 2007. *Rumor Psychology: Social and Organizational Approaches.* Washington, DC: American Psychological Association.

DiFonzo, Nicholas, and Prashant Bordia. 2007. Rumor's Influence: Toward a Dynamic Social Impact Theory of Rumor. In *The Science of Social Influence: Advances and Future Progress,* ed. Anthony R. Pratkanis, 271–296. Philadelphia: Psychology.

Kamins, Michael A., Valerie S. Folkes, and Lars Perner. 1997. Consumer Responses to Rumors: Good News, Bad News. *Journal of Consumer Psychology* 6 (2): 165–187.

Kimmel, Allan J. 2004. *Rumors and Rumor Control: A Manager's Guide to Understanding and Combating Rumors.* Mahwah, NJ: Lawrence Erlbaum Publishers.

Koller, Michael. 1992. Rumor Rebuttal in the Marketplace. *Journal of Economic Psychology* 13 (1): 167–186.

Prasad, J. 1935. The Psychology of Rumour: A Study Relating to the Great Indian Earthquake of 1934. *British Journal of Psychology* 26: 1–15.

Rosnow, Ralph L. 1991. Inside Rumor: A Personal Journey. *American Psychologist* 46 (5): 484–496.

Rosnow, Ralph L., and Gary Alan Fine. 1976. *Rumor and Gossip: The Social Psychology of Hearsay.* New York: Elsevier.

Shibutani, Tamotsu. 1966. *Improvised News: A Sociological Study of Rumor.* Indianapolis, IN: Bobbs-Merrill.

Turner, R. H. 1994. Rumor as Intensified Information Seeking: Earthquake Rumors in China and the United States. In *Disasters, Collective Behavior, and Social Organization,* eds. Russell R. Dynes and Kathleen J. Tierney, 244–256. Newark: University of Delaware Press.

Walker, C. J., and C. A. Beckerle. 1987. The Effect of Anxiety on Rumor Transmission. *Journal of Social Behavior and Personality* 2: 353–360.

Nicholas DiFonzo

RURAL ELECTRIFICATION

SEE *Development, Rural.*

RUSSELL, BERTRAND

SEE *Logic, Symbolic.*

RUSSIAN ECONOMICS

The development of economic theory in Russia is most conveniently divided into a number of separate periods that are bounded by various dramatic changes in the social and political life of the country. Before the emancipation of the serfs in 1861, Russian economics was in many ways imitative of currents of economic theory that were prevalent in the West. Peter the Great (1672–1725) has been interpreted as drawing inspiration from mercantilism for his program of industrial development focused on Saint Petersburg, while physiocracy found expression in the Russian context through the works of Dmitri A. Golitsyn (1734–1803). Classical economics was a major presence across the nineteenth century through the influence of Adam Smith (1723–1790) and his pupils, the first Russian translation of *The Wealth of Nations* (1776) being published in four parts between 1802 and 1806. Heinrich F. Storch (1766–1835) was a noteworthy commentator on Smith's work within Russian borders. Other important Russian economists from the first half of the nineteenth century were Nikolai S. Mordvinov (1754–1845), a supporter of protectionism, and Nikolai I. Turgenev (1789–1871), an advocate of free trade.

After 1861 the originality of Russian economics began to increase dramatically, although Western currents like historical political economy still had a significant influence through Russian representatives such as Ivan K. Babst (1823–1881). Marxists such as Georgii V. Plekhanov (1856–1918) articulated the position that, already in the 1880s, capitalism was successfully developing in Russia, against the populist view that there could never be enough domestic demand for a "mature" form of capitalism to become firmly established. A key issue for Russian economists of this period was the resilience of the peasant commune (or village community), an indigenous institution that practiced the periodic redistribution of arable land. Some argued that such primitive forms of communism were already obsolete, while others maintained that they could be the springboard for future socialist success. Vladimir I. Lenin (1870–1924) argued in favor of the former position, and documented in detail how capitalist industry was rapidly developing within Russian borders. Ironically, given Lenin's assumption of state power in 1917, Karl Marx (1818–1883) came to believe late in his life that the Russian peasant commune could provide a basis for bypassing much of the capitalist phase of historical development, if certain conditions were met. Marx's economic ideas were disseminated in Russia by sympathetic advocates such as Nikolai I. Sieber (1844–1888).

THE GOLDEN ERA

The most inventive and influential "golden era" of Russian economics can be given as occurring between 1890 and 1929, this period being subdivided into prerevolutionary and postrevolutionary segments. In the prerevolutionary golden era, the most significant names in Russian economics were Mikhail I. Tugan-Baranovsky (1865–1919), Vladimir K. Dmitriev (1868–1913), Petr B. Struve (1870–1944), Aleksandr I. Chuprov (1842–1908), Sergei N. Bulgakov (1871–1944), and Dmitri I. Mendeleev (1834–1907). In the postrevolutionary golden era, the most significant names in Soviet economics were Nikolai D. Kondratiev (1892–1938), Eugen E. Slutsky (1880–1948), Alexander V. Chayanov (1888–1939), Evgeny A. Preobrazhensky (1886–1937), Leonid N. Yurovsky (1884–1938), Vladimir G. Groman (1874–1937), Vladimir A. Bazarov (1874–1939), and Grigorii A. Feldman (1884–1958). For reasons of space, the work of only the main aspects of some of the most significant of these economists can be discussed here.

Tugan-Baranovsky's most important contribution to economic theory was *Industrial Crises in Contemporary England* (1894). This book pioneered the empirical description of business cycles by documenting the interrelated movements in gold bullion reserves, interest rates, and exchange rates, plotted alongside shifts in governmental policy regimes. It also presented a theoretical explanation of cycles based upon the accumulation and exhaustion of free loanable capital that fed into debates between economists like John Maynard Keynes (1883–1946) and Dennis H. Robertson (1890–1963) in the United Kingdom in the interwar period. Tugan-Baranovsky's other influential work in economic history was *The Russian Factory in the Nineteenth Century* (1898), which documented various changes in industrial structure, such as the development of possessional factories and the rise and fall of cottage industry. Originally a legal Marxist, Tugan-Baranovsky's economic methodology changed significantly after 1900, favoring an ethical basis to his socialism rather than a class-based approach, to the extent that by 1917 he was employing marginalist ideas in hypothetical planning models. During World War I (1914–1918), Tugan-Baranovsky analyzed the effects of various forms of war finance on future development prospects, and after Russia's exit from the war he assisted in forming the Academy of Sciences in Kiev.

Dmitriev's major work was his *Economic Essays on Value, Competition, and Utility*, first published separately in 1898 and 1902. One of the most well-known elements in these essays was the argument that unrestricted free competition tended to raise production costs above their essential level, that is, above the lowest possible level for any given state of technique. According to Dmitriev, in the competitive battle for sales, accumulating stocks of commodities played the same role as a military arms race did between opposing powers during peacetime. Under free competition, the nonproductive expenditure on commodity storage was higher than under monopoly, due to the need for competing producers to maintain significant levels of dead stock, in fear of others stepping in and gaining market share. Hence free competition had additional economic costs in terms of wasted output, excess inventories, and redundant advertising. Dmitriev was Russia's first mathematical economist, and he was also one of the most significant interpreters of the ideas of David Ricardo (1772–1823) within Russian borders.

Other significant Russian economists from the pre-revolutionary era included Struve, a leading member of the legal Marxists who (after emigration to the United States) became a trenchant critic of Stalinist economic policies; Mendeleev, the inventor of the periodic table of elements, a passionate advocate of industrial protectionism within Russian borders, and creator of the 1891 tariff; Chuprov, the leading representative of historical political economy in Moscow who emphasized the importance of knowledge and scientific invention to understanding economic progress; Bulgakov, a legal Marxist who stressed the international nature of capitalist development; Ivan K. Ozerov, a specialist in public finance and an expert on the structure of taxation in the United Kingdom and Germany; and Petr P. Migulin, a financial theorist who documented the history of currency policy within Russian borders, and also advocated monetary reforms designed to increase the stability of the ruble.

Perhaps the most famous and influential Russian/Ukrainian economist of all was Slutsky, who was also a noted mathematical statistician. He published two articles that had a great and lasting effect on the development of mainstream economics in the West. The first of these articles was "On the Theory of the Budget of the Consumer" (1915) and the second was "The Summation of Random Causes as the Source of Cyclical Processes" (1927). In the former, Slutsky divided the result of a change in demand induced by price changes into income and substitution effects, creating what is called the *Slutsky equation* as a basic tool of microeconomic analysis. In the latter article, Slutsky hypothesized that the summation of mutually independent chance events could generate sinusoidal periodicity, which might imitate the approximate regularity of business cycles, a process that became known in its statistical formulation as the *Slutsky-Yule effect*. Both of these significant contributions are still in use in economics textbooks today. Slutsky also wrote on the praxeological foundations of economics, analyzed the income received by the

Soviet state from currency emission, and invented the concept of the stochastic limit. In the mid-1920s Slutsky transferred from Kiev to become a consultant in the Moscow Conjuncture Institute, which was a pioneering center for the study of business cycles and forecasting headed by Kondratiev.

Kondratiev himself is famous today as the originator of the idea of long cycles of economic development, that is, approximately fifty-year business cycles that are generated by both capital accumulation and technological change. In Kondratiev's account, long cycles coexisted with medium-length economic cycles and also short cycles, within a three-cycle scheme of long-run capitalist development later adopted by Joseph Schumpeter (1883–1950). Kondratiev was initially an agricultural economist who worked on topics such as the effects of war and revolution on the functioning of Russian grain markets. During the New Economic Policy (NEP, 1921–1929) he developed a market-led industrialization strategy for the USSR based on the notion of encouraging the export of primary produce in order to fund capital imports, in direct opposition to Joseph Stalin's (1879–1953) centrally planned strategy of import substitution. Kondratiev also developed a detailed planning methodology based on an indicative rather than an imperative approach that was fully realized in his plan for agriculture and forestry (1924–1928). Some of Kondratiev's colleagues in the Conjuncture Institute, such as Albert L. Vainshtein (1882–1970) and Alexander A. Konyus (1895–1982), survived the political purges of the mid-1930s and became well-known economists in their own right, Vainshtein for work on national wealth estimation and Konyus for work on index number theory.

Other significant Russian economists from the NEP period included Chayanov, an agricultural economist who worked on the structure and motivating drive of peasant farms; Preobrazhensky, a Marxist who developed the notion of primitive socialist accumulation and analyzed the tributary relation between the peasant and the state sectors of the Soviet economy; Yurovsky, a neoclassical economist who masterminded the 1922–1924 currency reform that successfully replaced the depreciating *sovznak* with the stable gold-backed *chervonets*; Groman and Bazarov, two leading members of the State Planning Agency (Gosplan) who documented the restoration processes occurring in the Soviet economy after the end of the Civil War and theorized various planning regularities that were significant to Soviet development policies; and Feldman, who developed an innovative two-sector model of economic growth that was disseminated in the West.

There is some noticeable continuity in the main themes and preoccupations of Russian/Soviet economics between the two golden periods identified above. Before

1917 both business cycles and national development were major topics that were addressed by many Russian economists, in particular in terms of documenting the links between the domestic economy and international capitalism. For example, a significant dispute arose over whether and to what extent Russian business cycles synchronized with those of western Europe, which was related to the degree of penetration of French, German, and British capital within Russian enterprises. After 1917 these general topics were still very significant, although the manner in which they were pursued within the framework of the development of the Soviet centrally planned economy was modified dramatically. National development was fostered not through international cooperation, but through centralized state planning. Another significant issue in discussing the development of Russian economics is its relation to economics being pursued in closely proximate countries such as Ukraine. Some of the most famous names in Russian economics, such as Tugan-Baranovsky and Slutsky, were born in Ukraine, only moving to Russia later in their lives. This dual identity makes the entity identified as "Russian economics" an amorphous grouping, especially when the influence of Western currents is added to the mix.

A significant by-product of the early Soviet period was the emigration of a number of important economists to Europe and the United States. Examples of such émigré economists were Sergei N. Prokopovich (1871–1955), Wasily W. Leontief (1906–1999), and also Struve. Leontief in particular had a significant impact on Western economics through his input-output approach to constructing a balance of the entire national economy. In another category of émigré was Roman Rosdolsky (1898–1967), a leading Marxian scholar and Ukrainian socialist. For a while, Rosdolsky was associated with the Marx-Engels Institute in Moscow. In his writings he was one of the first to highlight the relation between Marx's published work in economics and G. W. F. Hegel's *Science of Logic* (1812–1816) by comparing Marx's *Capital* (1867–1894) with the *Grundrisse* (1857–1858). Rosdolsky also provided a reinterpretation of the Marxian reproduction schemes in which they were seen as only an abstraction of capitalist logic, not a concrete model of actual historical development.

THE STALIN ERA AND AFTER

After 1929 Stalin's ascent to power led to the destruction of the cadre of brilliant Russian economists that had prospered so notably in the golden era. Some, like Kondratiev and Yurovsky, were jailed on fictitious charges and eventually executed, while others, like Slutsky, were forced to leave the subject of economics completely for more neutral areas of research such as statistics. Even so, by the end of the 1930s a new school of mathematical economists led by Leonid V. Kantorovich (1912–1986), Vasilii S. Nemchinov (1894–1964), and Viktor V. Novozhilov (1892–1970) had reintroduced neoclassical ideas in a camouflaged form through the notion of an optimal plan and the idea of a system of optimally functioning economy (SOFE). This mathematical school provided the basis for many of the reform efforts directed at improving the performance of the Soviet economy that occurred sporadically throughout the 1950s and 1960s, but entrenched bureaucratic impediments often hindered the implementation of these attempted reforms. Although Kantorovich was awarded the Nobel Prize for economics in 1975, the 1970s are often described as a period of stagnation in the Soviet economy and also in Soviet economics.

In the Mikhail Gorbachev era (1985–1991), economic reformers like Abel Aganbegyan began to win ascendancy, but were quickly outflanked by a more radical group of pro-market thinkers who desired the dismantling of the Soviet economy and the creation of an entirely new market-based system. This group was triumphant after 1989, leading to full-scale privatization and price liberalization in the early 1990s. The pro-market reform program that was adopted was heavily influenced by Western economists such as Jeffrey Sachs and Richard Layard, and also by Eastern European converts to market economics such as Janos Kornai. Transforming property ownership and achieving free prices were given immediate priority, leaving the legal and institutional environment to fend for itself. Macroeconomic stabilization took some time to achieve, with a significant banking crisis occurring in Russia in 1998. In addition, organized crime grew to occupy a more central position in many post-Soviet economies than it did in the "mature" capitalist economies of the West.

Consequently, whether the transition to a market economy undertaken in Russia after 1989 is regarded as a complete success depends at least in part upon the perspective adopted. Dramatic changes and many improvements have undoubtedly taken place, with some definite winners and also some noticeable losers, but whether the post-Soviet form of mafia capitalism is (all things considered) superior in every respect to the previously existing version of bureaucratic socialism is a debatable point. In terms of the influence of market reform on Russian economics as a discipline, mainstream Western economic theory came to occupy a similar position in Russian universities as it does in the West. The Soviet variety of Marxist economics was totally discredited in the process, but this only had a tenuous relation to the actual ideas of Karl Marx in the first place.

SEE ALSO *Gorbachev, Mikhail; Leontief, Wassily*

BIBLIOGRAPHY

Aganbegyan, Abel. 1988. *The Challenge: Economics of Perestroika.* Trans. Pauline Tiffin. London: Hutchinson.

Barnett, Vincent. 1998. *Kondratiev and the Dynamics of Economic Development: Long Cycles and Industrial Growth in Historical Context.* London: Macmillan.

Barnett, Vincent. 2005. *A History of Russian Economic Thought.* London: Routledge.

Brus, Włodzimierz, and Kazimierz Laski. 1989. *From Marx to the Market: Socialism in Search of an Economic System.* Oxford: Clarendon.

Ellman, Michael. 1973. *Planning Problems in the USSR: The Contribution of Mathematical Economics to their Solution, 1960–1971.* Cambridge, U.K.: Cambridge University Press.

Nove, Alec, and D. M. Nuti, eds. 1972. *Socialist Economics: Selected Readings.* Harmondsworth, U.K.: Penguin.

Sutela, Pekka. 1991. *Economic Thought and Economic Reform in the Soviet Union.* Cambridge, U.K.: Cambridge University Press.

Walicki, Andrzej. 1980. *A History of Russian Thought from the Enlightenment to Marxism.* Trans. Hilda Andrews-Rusiecka. Oxford: Oxford University Press.

White, James. 1996. *Karl Marx and the Intellectual Origins of Dialectical Materialism.* London: Macmillan.

Vincent Barnett

RUSSIAN FEDERATION

According to international law, the Russian Federation from 1992 is the successor state of the Union of Soviet Socialist Republics (USSR), which was created after the First Russian Revolution in October 1917. The USSR was established formally in 1922 and was the successor state of the Russian Empire under the tsarist rule of the Romanov family from 1721.

The founder of the Soviet Union was Vladimir Ilyich Lenin (1870–1924). On the ideological basis of Marxism-Leninism, the Soviet Union existed for seventy-four years as an alternative Eastern political and economic regime, competing with Western democracy and the market economies of the "First World" and thus constituting the so-called Second World. In 1928 the successor of Lenin as leader of the Communist Party was Joseph Stalin (meaning "man of steel"; 1879–1953) from Georgia. The Soviet Union moved from Leninist principles (1922–1927) to a totalitarian Stalinist regime, which lasted from 1928 until Stalin's death in 1953. Stalin was followed by Nikita Khrushchev, the Communist leader until 1964, and Leonid Brezhnev from 1964 to 1982. The Brezhnev era was much less radical than the Stalinist era—with its millions of regime victims—and produced a certain degree of social, economic, and political stability as well as stagna-tion. After the end of the long Brezhnev era, two party leaders, Yuri Andropov and Konstantin Chernenko, had short terms in office until March 1985.

The last important political leader of the USSR after Lenin, Stalin, Khrushchev, and Brezhnev was Mikhail Sergeevich Gorbachev, who came into power in 1985. His policy was to overcome the general stagnation by intro-ducing decisive structural reforms into the Communist economic and political regime. Gorbachev attempted to modernize the USSR so that it could compete successfully with the Western world of democracy and free markets, but it failed in the end. His wide-ranging reforms of the Soviet Union had three main elements. The most impor-tant reform was *perestroika*, a structural reform of the planned economy, and *uskorenie*, the acceleration of these economic changes. The second strand of political reforms focused on *glasnost*, or public openness and transparency about the Stalinist past—with political terror, genocide, and mass murder—and the political history of the USSR. Within these broad areas of economic and political change, Gorbachev started public campaigns against alco-holism and corruption, which proved to be rather unpop-ular in Soviet society. The third dimension of these deep reforms was *demokratisatsiya*, which tried to democratize Soviet society without the introduction of democracy and retaining the Communist one-party state.

In August 1991 conservative Communist forces attempted a coup d'état to stop the structural reforms of the Soviet system that Gorbachev initiated and directed. The Communist coup was stopped within three days by Boris Yeltsin (1931–2007). This attempt to stop the dis-integration of the USSR accelerated it. The Soviet Union ceased to exist on December 31, 1991.

The population of the USSR before the final break-down encompassed 286 million Soviet citizens. The Russian Federation as successor state lost 139 million for-mer Soviet citizens to other Newly Independent States (NIS) and had an initial population of 147 million inhab-itants. During the 1990s, the Russian Federation experi-enced a dramatic decrease in life expectancy, especially among Russian men, and had a population of 143 million citizens in 2005. The Russian demographic crisis has almost been offset by immigration from other former Soviet Republics into the Russian Federation. In the early twenty-first century the Russian Federation is structured into seven federal districts: the Central District around the capital city Moscow, the Northwestern District with Saint Petersburg, the South District that includes the northern Caucasus, the Volga District, the Ural District, the Siberia District, and the Far Eastern District. Russia consists of eighty-six regions and republics, which are integrated into these seven large federal districts.

In June 1991 Yeltsin became president of Russia as part of the Soviet Union after the first Russian presidential elections with 57.3 percent of the vote. In 1996 he was elected as the first president of an independent Russia with 53.8 percent of the valid vote. During his eight years in power, Yeltsin had the difficult task of ending the old political and economic Soviet regime and commencing the transformation toward a democratic system and a market economy in a vast country that covers 11 time zones and about 6.6 million square miles. Weakened by health and alcohol problems, Yeltsin resigned from office on December 31, 1999.

Vladimir Putin (b. 1952) became acting president of Russia on January 1, 2000. He won 52.94 percent of the valid votes in the Russian presidential elections on March 26, 2000. Between 2000 and 2007 he created a hybrid political system, which combines elements of a democratic regime with those of an autocratic regime. The Putin regime is characterized by centralization of power (e.g., appointment of regional governors instead of regional elections), absence of a full rule of law, lack of separation of powers, restricted human and political rights, and suppression of electronic media. President Putin weakened the political powers of the Russian national parliament, the Duma, as well as the Russian party system by favoring a new presidential party with the name United Russia. The Putin era has transformed the Russian Federation into a political system with a historically unique mixture of democratic and autocratic elements. Hence the historical path of Russia toward democracy or autocracy will be decided after the Russian presidential elections in 2008. The Second Russian Revolution, which began in August 1991 with an attempted coup to return to a Communist regime as well as the dissolution of the Soviet Union, has not yet reached a historical conclusion.

SEE ALSO *Brezhnev, Leonid; Communism; Economies, Transitional; Federalism; Gorbachev, Mikhail; Khrushchev, Nikita; Lenin, Vladimir Ilitch; Putin, Vladimir; Russian Revolution; Stalin, Joseph; Union of Soviet Socialist Republics; Yeltsin, Boris*

BIBLIOGRAPHY

Brown, Archie, ed. 2001. *Contemporary Russian Politics: A Reader*. Oxford and New York: Oxford University Press.

Fish, Steven M. 2005. *Democracy Derailed in Russia: The Failure of Open Politics*. New York: Cambridge University Press.

Herspring, Dale R., ed. 2007. *Putin's Russia: Past Imperfect, Future Uncertain*. New York: Rowan and Littlefield.

McFaul, Michael. 2001. *Russia's Unfinished Revolution*. Ithaca, NY: Cornell University Press.

Rose, Richard, William Mishler, and Neil Munro. 2006. *Russia Transformed: Developing Popular Support for a New Regime*. Cambridge, U.K., and New York: Cambridge University Press.

Sakwa, Richard. 2002. *Russian Politics and Society*. 3rd ed. New York: Routledge.

White, Stephen. 2000. *Russia's New Politics: The Management of a Postcommunist Society*. Cambridge, U.K., and New York: Cambridge University Press.

Christian W. Haerpfer

RUSSIAN REVOLUTION

The revolutionary crises of 1917 had their origins in the deep social and political polarization in Russian society that intensified in the first decades of the twentieth century. Peasants suffered from land shortages, periodic hunger, high incidence of disease and early mortality, the burdens of taxation and rents, and military recruitment. Factory workers and artisans lived in squalid tenements or hovels and worked long hours in dangerous conditions. The better-off middle and upper classes were not only more literate, educated, and socially mobile than the peasants, but lived under a different code of law and enjoyed privileges that the ordinary villagers did not. Through the nineteenth century politically-engaged Russian intellectuals gravitated from liberalism and moderation toward revolutionary socialism, at first oriented toward the peasants (populism or *narodnichestvo*) and later, by the 1890s, increasingly focused on the urban workers (Marxism, Social Democracy).

Marxism provided a sociological and economic framework for Russian activists, a view of the way the world worked under capitalism and the European future toward which Russia was headed. Unlike the pro-peasant socialists or populists, who eventually formed the Socialist Revolutionary Party, Marxists believed that Russia could not avoid industrialization and capitalism and had to pass through two successive revolutions, a bourgeois-democratic revolution followed by a proletarian-socialist revolution in which the working people would come to power to build socialism. In 1903 the principal Marxist organization, the Russian Social Democratic Workers' Party, split into two rival factions, the moderate Mensheviks, who were usually more willing to work with other democratic parties, like the populists and liberals, and the more radical Bolsheviks, led by Vladimir Lenin (1870–1924), who generally favored a more rapid transition to the socialist revolution.

However wide the social divide between the state and society in the decades before World War I (1914–1918), the war expanded the gulf and radicalized the workers and peasants. Millions of peasants were turned into soldiers, given guns, and shown that a wider world existed beyond the edges of the village. The February Revolution began on February 23 [Julian calendar] (March 8 on the Gregorian calendar, International Women's Day) with working-class women demanding bread in the cold, dark streets of Petrograd. Within days, hundreds of thousands of Petrograd workers were in the streets, and when Cossacks and ordinary soldiers refused to fire on the crowds, the strike turned into a revolution. The tsar, Nicholas II (1894–1917), abdicated, as did his brother, Grand Duke Mikhail, and the monarchy came to an end.

On March 1 (14), middle-class members of the *duma* formed a provisional government, headed by Prince Georgii Lvov and including leaders of the major liberal and conservative parties. At the same time, workers and soldiers formed their own representative bodies, the soviets (councils) of workers' and soldiers' deputies, for though their leaders were unwilling to take power on their own, they were suspicious of the intentions of the "bourgeois" members of the provisional government. Russia now had not one unchallenged government but "dual power," two competing authorities. In April, the leaders of the Soviet confronted Foreign Minister Paul Miliukov, who insisted on Russia's imperial claims to Constantinople and the Dardanelles. Workers and soldiers poured into the streets, and forced Miliukov to resign. Moderate socialist leaders of the Soviet reluctantly joined the "bourgeois" government, but in the next six months the various coalition governments were unable either to end the world war or to alleviate the social divisions in Russian society. While the government wavered, the Bolsheviks won majorities in the factory committees and successfully agitated against the war at the fronts. Lenin, who had returned to Russia from exile in Switzerland in April, staked out a radical program for transferring all power to the soviets, ending the war, and moving the revolution rapidly into a socialist phase. The Bolsheviks were the only major party that provided a clear alternative to the government and their moderate socialist allies.

To please the Western Allies and contribute to the war effort against the Central Powers, Minister of War Alexander Kerensky launched a disastrous offensive against the enemy in June, but as news of Russian defeats reached the capital, workers, sailors, and soldiers demonstrated against the war and the government, even calling on the Soviet to take power in its own name. The moderate socialists refused, while militant elements supporting the Bolsheviks pushed to seize power. When order was restored by troops loyal to the government and soviets, Lenin was forced to go into hiding in Finland. Lvov resigned, and Kerensky formed a new coalition government. Liberal and conservative forces became more wary of the lower classes and called for an authoritarian government to restore order. The clumsy attempt by General Lavr Kornilov to establish a new authority, however, ended with the lower classes moving swiftly toward the Bolsheviks and electing them the majority party in both the Petrograd and Moscow soviets by early September.

In the second half of October, the Military-Revolutionary Committee of the Petrograd Soviet, led by Leon Trotsky (1879–1940), began establishing its authority over the garrisons of the city. On the morning of October 24 (November 6), Kerensky moved to suppress the Bolsheviks and prevent the insurrection that everyone knew was coming. In the crucial hours, however, the prime minister found his support weak or non-existent. Though workers did not actively participate in the insurrection, the Bolsheviks found the military muscle to take power. By dawn on October 25 (November 7) the city was in the hands of the Military-Revolutionary Committee, and Lenin went before the Second Congress of Soviets and declared that power had passed to the soviets. When the moderate socialists, the Mensheviks and Right Socialist Revolutionaries, protested the Bolshevik seizure of power and walked out of the Congress, they essentially left the Bolsheviks and Left Socialist Revolutionaries to form a new government. Though Lenin preferred a one-party government, within a month he conceded seats to the Left Socialist Revolutionaries, and until March 1918 Soviet Russia had a Left Socialist coalition government.

In November 1917 elections were held to a Constituent Assembly, a kind of founding congress for the new republic. The Bolsheviks failed to win a majority, while the Right Socialist Revolutionaries emerged with the largest plurality. After allowing a single day's meeting (January 5 [18], 1918), however, the Soviet government dispersed the Constituent Assembly, Russia's most freely elected parliamentary body until the early 1990s. In the ensuing civil war the communists did not hesitate to use violence and terror, and as atrocities occurred on both sides, much of the democratic promise of the revolution of 1917 was lost.

SEE ALSO *Bolshevism; Communism; Coup d'Etat; Democracy; Left and Right; Lenin, Vladimir Ilitch; Leninism; Marxism; Monarchy; Revolution; Socialism; Totalitarianism; Trotsky, Leon; Union of Soviet Socialist Republics; Violence*

BIBLIOGRAPHY

Acton, Edward, Vladimir Iu Cherniaev, and William G. Rosenberg, eds. 1997. *Critical Companion to the Russian Revolution, 1914–1921.* Bloomington: Indiana University Press.

Figes, Orlando. 1998. *A People's Tragedy: A History of the Russian Revolution, 1891–1924.* New York: Penguin Books.

Galili, Ziva. 1989. *The Menshevik Leaders in the Russian Revolution: Social Realities and Political Strategies.* Princeton, NJ: Princeton University Press.

Hasegawa, Tsuyoshi. 1981. *The February Revolution: Petrograd 1917.* Seattle: University of Washington Press.

Rabinowitch, Alexander. 1976. *The Bolsheviks Come to Power: The Revolution of 1917 in Petrograd.* New York: W. W. Norton.

Rosenberg, William G. 1974. *The Liberals in the Russian Revolution; the Constitutional Democratic Party, 1917–1921.* Princeton, NJ: Princeton University Press.

Smith, S. A. 1983. *Red Petrograd: Revolution in the Factories 1917–18.* Cambridge, U.K.: Cambridge University Press.

Steinberg, Mark D., and Vladimir M. Khrustalëv. 1995. *The Fall of the Romanovs: Political Dreams and Personal Struggles in a Time of Revolution.* New Haven, CT: Yale University Press.

Suny, Ronald, and Arthur Adams, eds. 1990. *The Russian Revolution and Bolshevik Victory: Visions and Revisions.* 3rd ed. Lexington, MA: D. C. Heath.

Wildman, Allan K. 1980–1987. *The End of the Russian Imperial Army.* 2 vols. Princeton, NJ: Princeton University Press.

Ronald Grigor Suny

RYBCZYNSKI THEOREM

The Rybczynski theorem, along with the Stolper-Samuelson, factor-price equalization, and Heckscher-Ohlin theorems, is one of four key propositions describing the properties of the standard Heckscher-Ohlin model with two goods and two factors. The Polish-born economist Tadeusz M. Rybczynski's (1923–1998) paper, "Factor Endowment and Relative Commodity Prices" (1955), relates changes in an economy's factor supplies to resulting changes in equilibrium outputs and prices.

The simplest version of the Heckscher-Ohlin model assumes that two goods, say autos and textiles, are produced using the same two factor inputs, say labor and capital, but in proportions that differ across the two industries. If the auto industry uses a higher ratio of capital to labor, it is termed the *capital-intensive* industry, while the textile industry is termed *labor-intensive*. Under the usual assumptions of the model, an increase in the supply of either factor, holding constant the supply of the other, results in an outward shift of the production possibility frontier. Thus, the economy can now produce more of both goods, so that most economists prior to Rybczynski's contribution assumed that this kind of biased growth would result in higher equilibrium outputs of each good, though with relatively greater growth of the industry that uses more of the growing factor.

Rybczynski's surprising result is that a given percentage increase in the supply of one factor, say capital, holding constant the supply of the second factor (labor) as well as the relative price of the two goods, must result in a still larger percentage increase in the equilibrium output of the good that is capital-intensive in production (autos), and an absolute *decrease* in the equilibrium output of the good that is labor-intensive (textiles). The result also requires that the economy produce some of each good in both the equilibrium prior to the change in factor supply and the final equilibrium following the change. Rybczynski's proof makes use of the box diagram as applied for the first time to production by Wolfgang Stolper and Paul A. Samuelson in their landmark paper, "Protection and Real Wages" (1941), which presented what is now known as the Stolper-Samuelson theorem. Moreover, Rybczynski builds on Stolper and Samuelson's key insight concerning the basic two-good, two-factor version of the Heckscher-Ohlin model—that the relative price of the two goods uniquely determines factor prices and thus factor proportions.

In general, an economy can adjust to an increase in the supply of capital, holding constant the supply of labor, through some combination of capital-deepening and a changed mix of outputs. This alternative formulation of the Rybczynski theorem was provided by Ronald Jones in his 1965 paper, "The Structure of Simple General Equilibrium Models," which offers the first integrated treatment, as well as a number of generalizations, of the four key theorems of the Heckscher-Ohlin model. To the extent that more capital results in a reduction in its relative cost to producers, firms in both sectors will now opt for a higher ratio of capital to labor. But the Stolper-Samuelson theorem implies that with output prices fixed and both goods produced, factor prices and thus cost-minimizing capital-labor ratios must remain unchanged in the new equilibrium. Thus, the adjustment is achieved entirely through a change in the mix of outputs. Expansion of the capital-intensive industry allows additional capital to be employed, but more labor is also required to maintain that industry's unchanged ratio of capital to labor. This labor (plus additional capital) must be obtained through a contraction in the equilibrium output of the labor-intensive industry, which releases a relatively higher ratio of labor to capital than is required for expansion of the capital-intensive industry. This allows the additional capital to be absorbed at constant factor prices.

The Rybczynski theorem, by indicating what would be produced at unchanged output prices, has clear implications for effects of biased factor growth on actual prices in the resulting equilibrium. Assuming that both goods are normal in consumption—that is, that as incomes rise more of each will be demanded—growth in the supply of capital necessarily means a drop in the relative prices of autos for a closed economy and, not surprisingly, an associated decline in the return to capital, the auto industry's intensively used factor. Moreover, as Stolper and Samuelson demonstrated earlier, the decline is not merely relative; capital's return must fall in real terms. Likewise, the return to labor, the factor now relatively scarcer, must rise in real terms. For an open economy, the Rybczynski theorem allows predictions about the resulting changes in a country's equilibrium trade volume and terms of trade. As the stock of capital grows, desired trade at given terms of trade will increase (decrease) if the country is capital-abundant (labor-abundant) relative to its trading partners. An expansion of the capital stock will thus lead to deterioration (improvement) in the country's terms of trade. Corresponding results hold for an expansion of labor with capital held constant.

Despite its stark assumptions, the Rybczynski theorem, especially as later generalized by Jones, provides powerful insights into the likely consequences of biased factor growth. Like the supply and demand curves of partial-equilibrium analysis, the simple Heckscher-Ohlin model provides the first back-of-the-envelope attack on a wide range of questions. Together with the other theorems of the Heckscher-Ohlin model, the stripped-down basic version of the Rybczynski theorem has become an essential part of the intellectual toolkit of every international economist.

SEE ALSO *Heckscher-Ohlin-Samuelson Model; Stolper-Samuelson Theorem*

BIBLIOGRAPHY

Jones, Ronald W. 1965. The Structure of Simple General Equilibrium Models. *Journal of Political Economy* 73 (6): 557–572.

Rybczynski, T. M. 1955. Factor Endowment and Relative Commodity Prices. *Economica* 23 (88): 352–359.

Stolper, Wolfgang, and Paul A. Samuelson. 1941. Protection and Real Wages. *Review of Economic Studies* 9 (1): 58–73.

Rachel McCulloch

S

SACRED, THE
SEE *Symbols.*

SADAT, ANWAR
1918–1981

Born in Mit Abul Kom, a town north of Cairo, Egypt, Sadat was one of the first students to graduate from a British military school. On graduating, he was posted to a remote government base where he met Gamal Abdel Nasser (1918–1970), a charismatic army major who was to become the nationalist leader of Egypt. They maintained a lifelong friendship. From 1942 on, Nasser secretly organized young cadets and officers to promote a republican, anti-British patriotic movement. The movement's radical ideas were also directed against the corrupt monarchy of King Farouk (1920–1965), whose profligacy and incompetence were partly held responsible for the failures of the Egyptian army against Israel in 1948. In response to these military and political failures, Nasser's group evolved into the Free Officers Movement, which staged a coup on July 23, 1952, against Farouk. Sadat, who became Nasser's public relations minister, remained under the shadow of Nasser during the dramatic events in modern Egyptian history—the Suez crisis (1956) and the Six-Day War (1967)—until Nasser's death in September 1970.

RISE TO INTERNATIONAL PROMINENCE

Sadat was relatively unknown in international politics, despite the many positions he had held during Nasser's period—minister of state (1954), secretary to the National Union (1959), president of the parliament (1960–1968), and vice president and member of the Presidential Council (1964). In his attempt to emulate Nasser, he initially adopted a stridently aggressive stance against Israel, including the surprise attack in the Yom Kippur War of October 1973. The war ended in stalemate; with the Egyptian economy in crisis, Sadat adopted a diplomatic approach to Israel, launching the Sadat Initiative in 1977. This started a peace process that led to the Camp David talks in September 1978 with U.S. President Jimmy Carter and Israeli prime minister Menachem Begin. The peace treaty that was signed in March 1979 involved the return of the Sinai to Egypt, the creation of demilitarized zones, and some autonomy for a Palestinian administration. Both Begin and Sadat received the Nobel Peace Prize, but the peace agreement was opposed by the Palestine Liberation Organization, several Arab states, and right-wing elements in Israel.

DOMESTIC PROBLEMS

Opposition from within Egypt came from Muslim fundamentalists. Sadat attempted to co-opt radical Muslim groups, including the Muslim Brothers, whom Nasser had exiled. He realized that the extreme poverty of the peasantry and urban working class created a breeding ground for religious and political radicalism. To stimulate the Egyptian economy, Sadat in 1975 sought to expand the private sector and to reduce the old Soviet-style economy and state bureaucracy. This economic opening (*infitah*) was combined with a policy of supporting moderate Muslim intellectuals such as Omar Telmesani, who began to publish *Al Dawa* (Call to Islam) in 1976. In return for their political support, Sadat allowed these religious intellectuals considerable cultural freedom.

This political pact began to disintegrate in 1977 when riots broke out in response to the negative consequences of the "open-door" economic policy and a radical group called the Society of Muslims (*Al Takfir wa-l Hijra*) defied the government by kidnapping and murdering a cleric. Sadat's peace process, which involved some recognition of Israeli sovereignty, was rejected by both moderate and radical elements of the Muslim community. The radicals, who became known generally as *takfir*—a devout Muslim who excommunicates other Muslims who are seen to be lapsed—spread their message through much of the Arab world. These movements accepted the teaching of Sayyid Qutb (1906–1966), who, as the founder of the Muslim Brothers, had preached the necessity of violent *jihad* against unbelievers and who was hanged for an alleged plot against Nasser.

In response to this radicalization, Sadat dissolved the Egyptian Students Union and brought a number of key activists to trial. Some 1,600 people were arrested, resulting in significant international and domestic criticism. He also attacked the Coptic community, forcing the Coptic Pope Shenouda III into exile (he was eventually restored by President Hosni Mubarak in 1985). As a result of this political crackdown, the radicals became a clandestine movement among the underclass of the slums of Cairo, declaring a war against Sadat and the moderate clerics who were accused of apostasy. Sadat was assassinated on October 6, 1981, during the yearly 6 October 1973 victory parade by Muslim fundamentalists inside the army. He was buried in the unknown soldier memorial in Cairo and was succeeded by Mubarak as president.

The problems facing Egypt in Sadat's time continue to dominate Egyptian politics. The state bureaucracies remain firmly in control of the economy and, despite President Mubarak's moderate reforms and the recent success of the Egyptian stock market, a democratic culture has been slow to develop. The Muslim Brothers are excluded from parliamentary politics because they are still regarded as an illegal organization. A fragile peace with Israel has, however, been sustained because both governments regard Hamas (*Harakat al-Muqawama al-Islamiyya*) in the West Bank and Hizbullah (the Iranian-backed Party of God) as a threat. Periodic attacks on tourists, Copts, and members of the government have also curtailed the growth of the tourist industry. Between 1993 and 1997, Mubarak responded with ruthless oppression against members of the radical Gamaat Islamiya. In retrospect, Sadat's era was progressive in attempting to secure peace and reform the economy, but he left behind a legacy of authoritarianism.

SEE ALSO *Authoritarianism; Fundamentalism, Islamic; Nasser, Gamal Abdel; Peace Process*

BIBLIOGRAPHY

Kepel, Gilles. 2003. *Muslim Extremism in Egypt: The Prophet and the Pharaoh*. Trans. Jon Rothschild. Berkeley: University of California Press.

Sadat, Anwar el-. 1978 *In Search of Identity: An Autobiography*. New York: Harper and Row.

Bryan S. Turner

SADDLE POINT
SEE *Phase Diagrams; Zero-sum Game.*

SAFETY, OCCUPATIONAL
SEE *Occupational Safety.*

SAHLINS, MARSHALL
1930–

One of the most influential cultural anthropologists of the latter part of the twentieth century, Marshall Sahlins has written seminal works on economic anthropology, social and cultural theory, and the relation of culture and history. In his earliest writings he sought to clarify the social-evolutionist theory of Leslie White, his University of Michigan teacher, but he soon came to reject White's evolutionism and technological determinism. In his mature works, he has elaborated a sophisticated reworking of Claude Lévi-Strauss's structuralism, one that is antithetical to reductionism of all kinds in the study of culture.

In his book *Stone Age Economics* (1972), Sahlins criticized the evolutionist ranking of societies on universalistic criteria such as the intensity of economic production. Influenced by Karl Polanyi, Sahlins argued that economic systems are culturally ordered, serving different ends in different societies. For example, hunter-gatherer societies may seem poor because the people have few possessions, but in fact they enjoy a kind of material plenty precisely by virtue of being unencumbered by things that impede their mobility. Traditionally, such people subsisted on wild foods, and when these grew scarce in one region, they could easily pack up and move to a richer one. Indeed, to the extent that poverty is a social status and a matter of wanting more than one has, hunter-gatherers have far *less* poverty than do the grossly unequal societies of advanced civilization, since their culture leads them to share scarce resources (like meat from the hunt) rather than possessing or consuming them individually. Thus, they exemplify a "Zen road to affluence," or a "want not, lack not" philosophy that shows that the naturalized Western conception of mankind as fundamentally acquisitive and driven by fear of scarcity is ethnocentric (Sahlins 1972, pp. 2, 11).

In *Culture and Practical Reason* (1976), Sahlins took these arguments farther, offering a philosophically compelling, general critique of anthropological theories that explain social and cultural phenomena by appealing to material or functional causes outside the culture itself. Because practical utility and functionality are themselves always relative to particular cultural modes of existence, Sahlins wrote that it is wrong to conceive of them as external to the symbolically organized order of culture.

Structuralism's great shortcoming has been its artificial separation of culture's abstract symbolic structure from the real historical events that perpetuate and transform it. But these are reintegrated in Sahlins's theory of structural history. Since people necessarily act according to their culturally presupposed categories and values, "history is culturally ordered, differently so in different societies" (Sahlins 1985, p. vii). Sometimes actions have unexpected outcomes, however, that can lead people to reconsider their conventionally held cultural meanings. Thus, cultural orders themselves are historical, partly formed and transformed by events. In his writings since 1980, Sahlins developed this theory through extended historical studies of intercultural contact in early colonial Hawaii and Fiji, as well as in the transpacific trade connecting Britain, China, Hawaii, and the Northwest Coast of America in the eighteenth and nineteenth centuries.

A brilliant polemicist, Sahlins has participated throughout his career in important debates on such matters as color perception, sociobiology, world-systems theory, and postmodernism in anthropology. Perhaps the most famous of these was his debate with Gananath Obeyesekere on native rationality and the power of myths. This exchange centered on Sahlins's historical account of the European explorer Captain Cook's visit to Hawaii in 1779, and particularly on the question of whether he was viewed at the time by native priests as a manifestation of a Hawaiian god, Lono. The larger intellectual issue this raised was the politics of depicting cultural difference. Obeyesekere accused Sahlins of exoticizing the Hawaiians and perpetuating a European colonial myth in which irrational natives are naïvely given to mistaking Europeans for gods. In responding, Sahlins marshaled impressive evidence that Cook was treated as Lono in historical fact, and he argued that it is a greater denigration of other peoples

to submerge their cultures' distinctive rationalities under a well-intentioned but ethnocentric portrayal as being essentially just like one's own. Some European colonial writers undoubtedly disparaged cultural Others for confusing certain men with their gods, but these Others may not have shared the European presumption that gods and men are (with one singular exception) nonoverlapping categories, highly distant from one another.

BIBLIOGRAPHY

PRIMARY WORKS

Sahlins, Marshall. 1972. *Stone Age Economics.* Chicago: Aldine-Atherton.

Sahlins, Marshall. 1976. *Culture and Practical Reason.* Chicago: University of Chicago Press.

Sahlins, Marshall. 1981. *Historical Metaphors and Mythical Realities: Structure in the Early History of the Sandwich Islands Kingdom.* Ann Arbor: University of Michigan Press.

Sahlins, Marshall. 1985. *Islands of History.* Chicago: University of Chicago Press.

Sahlins, Marshall. 1995. *How "Natives" Think: About Captain Cook, For Example.* Chicago: University of Chicago Press.

Sahlins, Marshall. 2000. *Culture in Practice: Selected Essays.* New York: Zone Books.

Sahlins, Marshall. 2004. *Apologies to Thucydides: Understanding History as Culture and Vice Versa.* Chicago: University of Chicago Press.

SECONDARY WORK

Obeyesekere, Gananath. 1992. *The Apotheosis of Captain Cook: European Mythmaking in the Pacific.* Princeton, NJ: Princeton University Press.

Ira Bashkow

SAID, EDWARD
1935–2003

Edward Said is recognized as one of the most influential literary critics of the last quarter of the twentieth century. Said's contributions to postcolonial and critical theory, the humanities, cultural studies, social geography, and the social sciences evade easy categorization given the startling breadth and range of his thought. Influenced by Michel Foucault, Giambattista Vico, Georg Lukacs, Antonio Gramsci, Frantz Fanon, and Theodor Adorno and a self-proclaimed admirer of Sigmund Freud, Said was among the first to introduce American academic audiences to structuralism, poststructuralism, and to a lesser extent deconstruction.

A critical scholar nevertheless deeply committed to humanism, Said was also a public intellectual known for his eloquent commitment to Palestinian self-determination. Born in Jerusalem, Said fled with his family to Cairo in 1948 and a few years later relocated to the United States. He studied at Princeton and then at Harvard, where he wrote a PhD dissertation on Joseph Conrad, then joined Columbia in 1963. Unexpectedly moved by the profound injustice of the dispossession of the Palestinians, with whom he increasingly identified as an exiled intellectual, he found the Six Days War of 1967 a politicizing moment and significant turning point in his life. Over the next several decades Said became a frequent commentator on U.S. foreign policy and Middle Eastern politics. He was a regular contributor to *Al-Hayat* (a London-based Arab daily) and *Al-Ahram Weekly* (an Egyptian daily) as well as serving as the music critic for the *Nation*.

Said is best known for his groundbreaking work *Orientalism* (1978). Widely acknowledged as a cornerstone text for postcolonial studies, this acclaimed work has also had profound influences on social geography, cultural studies, and radical history. Drawing on Foucault's notion of discourse, Said exposes Orientalism as a Western system of thought that is linked to imperialism and the establishment of cultural hegemony and is an essentializing discourse that effectively produces the "Orient" as the West's "other." *Orientalism* observes the West observing the Middle East, Arabs, and Islam, and two further volumes in the triology, *The Question of Palestine* (1979) and *Covering Islam* (1981), sustain this focus. In the trilogy's 1993 sequel, *Culture and Imperialism*, Said expands these insights to explore a more generalized relationship between cultural production and empire. In the latter text he draws on European writing (and one musical piece, Verdi's *Aida*) on Africa, India, the Far East, Australia, and the Caribbean to show how an imperialist imagination is embedded in cultural production and how cultures of resistance to imperialism emerge in a context of decolonization.

The Question of Palestine (1979) was Said's first major text on Palestine, and in it he endeavors to establish a broadly representative Palestinian perspective for a Western, and primarily an American, audience. This particular text documents the historical and political dispossession and erasure of the Palestinians by Zionist colonization and thus differs distinctly from *Orientalism*, which drew mainly on literary texts. However, in method Said effectively demonstrates that a hegemonic cultural attitude toward Islam, the Arabs, and the Orient is what makes the ongoing colonial violence against the Palestinians a possibility. Thus the "Palestinian problem" is a materialized effect of Orientalism. *Covering Islam* proceeds similarly but with a focus on the Western media's role in representing, and imagining, Islam. Other books on Palestine include *The Politics of Dispossession* (1994),

After the Last Sky (1986), *Blaming the Victims* (1988), and *The End of the Peace Process* (2000).

Said's wide-ranging and often controversial thought is rooted in literary theory. His dissertation on Joseph Conrad's letters was influenced by the Geneva school, a vein of literary criticism rooted in the phenomenological thought of Husserl and Merleau-Ponty, and became his first book, *Joseph Conrad and the Fiction of Autobiography* (1966). For Said, Conrad's letters revealed the uncertainty, difficulty, and reflexive struggle of a self-exiled Pole, an articulate writer who was nevertheless disoriented and not quite sure of his place in the world. An interest in the condition of the exiled writer, a theme that continues through his life's work, is palpably present in this first book.

Said's second book, *Beginnings: Intention and Method* (1975), began to establish his reputation as one of America's foremost literary critics, as the text drew on contemporary French theory in its concerns to shift from theological "origins" to the problem of a secular "beginning" point for critical theory, where human action makes history, and a history of change. The text explores the relation of literature to philosophy, psychology, and critical theory through an engagement with the writings of Freud, Foucault, Freidrich Nietzsche, and Vico as well as Jacques Lacan, Jacques Derrida, Giles Deleuze, and Claude Lévi-Strauss.

The World, the Text, and the Critic (1983) is an early "bridging" text of Said's thought. This integrative and synthetic work is interested in the material contexts—the "worldliness"—of writing. Increasingly impatient with an academic domestication of poststructuralist and deconstructive theories of textuality, Said argues that critical scholarship must be situated in material struggles so that the critic does not lose sight of the political context in which intellectual pursuits become possible. The text is an early critique of the narrow confines of academic disciplinarity, which Said argues is implicated in a tamed specialization of intellectual inquiry. His deep commitments to humanism are evident in this text, and he returns again to these themes in a series of lectures given at Columbia University, posthumously published under the title *Humanism and Democratic Criticism* (2004). In this text Said reflects on the tensions between humanist, structuralist, and poststructuralist modes, and he suggests that although humanism is critiqued as essentializing and totalizing, a commitment to the humanistic ideals of justice and equality are nevertheless crucial for a critical scholar. Throughout his vast and disparate body of work, Said maintains a critical posture within humanism, a "contrapuntal" awareness perhaps made possible by the condition of being an exilic, border intellectual.

A talented pianist, Said also wrote extensively on music's relation to society, and his critical writings often draw on musical metaphors. *Musical Elaborations* (1991), *Parallels and Paradoxes: Explorations in Music and Society* (2002), and the posthumously published *On Late Style: Music and Literature against the Grain* (2006) exemplify his significant contributions to this interdisciplinary area of humanistic study. In 2003 Said died in New York after a decade-long battle with leukemia.

SEE ALSO *Fanon, Frantz; Foucault, Michel; Freud, Sigmund; Gramsci, Antonio; Humanism; Justice; Lucas Critique; Music; Orientalism; Palestinians; Postcolonialism; Self-Determination*

BIBLIOGRAPHY

Ali, Tariq. 2006. *Conversations with Edward Said.* Oxford: Seagull Books.

Ashcroft, Bill, and Pal Ahluwalia. 1999. *Edward Said: The Paradox of Identity.* London and New York: Routledge.

Bayoumi, Moustafa, and Andrew Rubin, eds. 2000. *The Edward Said Reader.* New York: Vintage.

Bhabha, Homi, and W. J. T. Mitchell. 2005. *Edward Said: Continuing the Conversation.* Chicago: University of Chicago Press.

Hussein, Abdirahman A. 2002. *Edward Said: Criticism and Society.* London and New York: Verso.

Sprinkler, Michael, ed. 1992. *Edward Said: A Critical Reader.* Oxford and Cambridge, MA: Blackwell.

Melissa Autumn White

SALIENCE, MORTALITY

Mortality salience is a psychological state in which thoughts of one's death are prominent, or *salient*, in the individual's conscious mind. The concept was developed by Jeff Greenberg, Tom Pyszczynski, and Sheldon Solomon in 1986 to test hypotheses derived from terror management theory. The theory proposes that the fear of death motivates people to maintain faith in cultural worldviews that makes life seem meaningful and to be enduringly significant contributors to that meaningful reality. In this way, people can believe they will endure beyond their own deaths; this belief in turn helps people control their terror of death.

Greenberg and his colleagues proposed that if the theory is correct, then increasing mortality salience should intensify people's support of their own cultural worldview and striving for self-worth within the context of that worldview. Mortality may become salient in many natural contexts, including following acts of terrorism or war, natural disasters, reading or watching news or crime stories, witnessing automobile accidents, the death of a close friend or family member, or being in close proximity to a cemetery. The most common method to increase mortality salience in experiments is to ask participants to respond to the following: "Please describe the emotions the thought of your own death arouses in you"; and "Jot down, as specifically as you can, what you think will happen to you physically as you die and once you are physically dead."

The first study utilizing this mortality salience induction found that mortality salience led municipal court judges to recommend a much higher bond in a hypothetical prostitution case. This finding supports terror management theory because it shows that mortality salience encouraged the judges to uphold their worldview by punishing someone who violated the morals of that worldview. Subsequent studies found that mortality salience leads people to react positively to anyone who supports one's worldview and negatively to anyone who violates it. Further research has found that mortality salience affects a wide range of judgments and behaviors that preserve faith in either one's worldview or one's self-esteem.

More than 200 studies have made mortality salient, using various methods and comparing mortality salience to many control conditions. Mortality salience has been increased by exposure to death anxiety questionnaires, gory accident videos, and proximity to funeral parlors and cemeteries. Control conditions have reminded participants of neutral topics and aversive topics such as failure, uncertainty, pain, and social exclusion. These findings have supported the specific role of thoughts about death in mortality salience effects.

Research exploring the cognitive processes activated by mortality salience has shown that mortality salience first leads people to distract themselves from thoughts of death. However, after a delay, thoughts of death return to the fringes of consciousness; this is when worldview and self-esteem–bolstering effects of mortality salience occur. Similar effects occur after exposure to very quick subliminal flashes of death-related words on a computer screen. These words appear for 28 milliseconds in between two easily visible neutral words. Because research participants are not aware of them, these briefly flashed words bring death thoughts close to consciousness without making mortality salient. This work suggests that the problem of death exerts its influence outside of conscious awareness.

Mortality salience research supports terror management theory and by so doing suggests that because of the need to control mortality concerns, naturally occurring reminders of death may contribute to nationalism, prejudice, and intergroup aggression, as well as pro-social behavior and valued cultural achievements.

SEE ALSO *Self-Esteem; Terror Management Theory*

BIBLIOGRAPHY

Greenberg, Jeff, Sheldon Solomon, and Tom Pyszczynski. 1986. The Causes and Consequences of a Need for Self-Esteem: A Terror Management Theory. In *Public Self and Private Self*, ed. Roy F. Baumeister, 189–212. New York: Springer-Verlag.

Pyszczynski, Tom, Sheldon Solomon, and Jeff Greenberg. 2003. *In the Wake of September 11: The Psychology of Terror*. Washington, DC: American Psychological Association.

Jeff Greenberg

SALPINGECTOMY

SEE *Sterilization, Human.*

SALT RETENTION HYPOTHESIS

SEE *Slavery Hypertension Hypothesis.*

SAMARITAN'S DILEMMA

SEE *Bequests.*

SAMBA

SEE *Dance.*

SAMBO

The derisive term *Sambo* refers to African American males in a manner that is commonly viewed as racist and unacceptable. The long career of the Sambo stereotype is an important window into the history of black-white U.S. race relations. The term itself is a form of denigration and represents a stereotype that has been used variously to justify the inhumane treatment of slaves, provide a rationale for Jim Crow segregation, and, most often, to pander to the basest racist impulses in the United States to entertain white popular audiences. The Sambo stereotype has had several iterations in U.S. popular culture, ranging from children's literature to minstrel shows of the slavery and post–Civil War eras, radio, motion pictures, television, and dining establishments. In addition, the Sambo stereotype also has a controversial career in the work of academics who studied slavery, particularly Stanley Elkins's 1959 publication *Slavery*. This characterization of black men as

passive buffoons was creatively challenged in Spike Lee's 2000 movie *Bamboozled*.

THE ORIGINS OF SAMBO

One of the first representations of Sambo appeared in an 1808 short story by Edmund Botsford titled "Sambo and Toney: A Dialogue in Three Parts." Much of the Sambo stereotype—subservient, ignorant, and linguistically challenged—was presented in its full form in this early iteration. The story was intended to convey a supposedly accurate conversation between two slaves:

> Sambo: Yes, thank God brother Toney, my mafter good, and I like up the country and cotton planting very well—you got a good mafter, Toney?
>
> Toney: So fo, he do, he give us victual enough and good clothes but he make us work devilifh hard....
>
> Sambo: Well then, why you complain and fay devilifh hard, you know what devilifh mean, Toney? devilifh is fomething wicked, I fear you ufe fuch words, you wicked too, Toney.
>
> Toney: What you call wicked, Sambo?

This dialogue is set in the slave South—though according to Botsford, "Fambo" might be a more appropriate spelling—but the last line is not far from a 1980s equivalent uttered in the television program *Diff'rent Strokes*: "Whatchoo talkin' 'bout, Willis?" A continuous thread of racism pervades U.S. popular culture, and to this day African American actors are often relegated to playing the fool.

SAMBO AND THE MINSTREL SHOW

The Sambo stereotype found its largest audience with the rise of minstrel shows in the 1830s. It was the minstrel show that popularized these caricatures of black slaves with white, working-class audiences. Sambo the stage performer was popularized when a white entertainer named Thomas "Daddy" Rice created the character known as Jim Crow. The accompanying song, entitled "Jump Jim Crow," was penned by Rice and utilized the same exaggerated mispronunciations:

> Weel about and turn about and do jis so,
> Eb'ry time I weel about and jump Jim Crow.

Rice claimed he modeled the character after an old black man he observed in Washington, D.C., and he created this notion of "jumping Jim Crow" as a way to entertain predominately white working-class audiences.

Popular entertainers would perform as black caricatures, with makeup that included the application of burnt cork to the face. They would "act black" by reproducing every stereotype known to the white audiences of the time. "Zip Coon," "Tambo," "Sambo," "Jim Crow," and "Jim Dandy" all corresponded with white stereotypes of black men. In addition, black women were often subjected to the same level of ridicule in the caricatures of "Mammy," "Jezebel," and "Sapphire." Before the Civil War, these stereotypes were often used to justify slavery, for they were meant to show the supposedly inferior essential characteristics of slave men and women. This Sambo stereotype was clearly at work in *Bishop Whipple's Southern Diary, 1834–1844*. The author, an Episcopal clergyman named Henry Benjamin Whipple, wrote of the slaves he encountered on a trip through the South: "They seem a happy race of beings and if you did not know it you would never imagine they were slaves. The loud laugh, the clear dancing eye, the cheerful face show that in this sad world of sin and sorrow they know but very few."

In the separate but unequal period of black-white relations (1865–1964), segregated institutions often found their legitimation in the stereotypical representations of blacks "knowing their place." The minstrel characters included the uppity Zip Coon, who becomes the buffoon because he wrongly thinks he's successful, and the happy, ignorant, subservient Jim Crow and Tambo, who sing and dance their troubles away. At the tail end of the Jim Crow era, Edward R. Murrow aired his famous "Harvest of Shame" broadcast on Thanksgiving evening 1960. Murrow detailed the horrific working and living conditions of white and black migrant farmworkers. A Florida grower in the exposé had this to say about African American workers on his farm: "They love to go from place to place. They don't have a worry in the world. They're happier than we are. Today they eat, tomorrow, they don't worry about [*sic*]. They are the happiest race of people on earth."

POPULAR CULTURE AND BLACKFACE PERFORMANCES

What cannot be overstated is that minstrel shows embodied the first form of popular culture in the United States. There is a direct line from minstrels to vaudeville, Broadway shows, motion pictures, radio, and television. Ziegfeld Follies, Christy's Minstrels, the lyrics and performances of Stephen Foster, and Al Jolson's *The Jazz Singer* mark the most popular performances of antiblack racism in the Jim Crow era. Rather than being an aberration, performing in blackface and invoking racist stereotypes was a mainstay of Hollywood motion pictures. White actors who performed in blackface included Shirley Temple, Al Jolson, Bing Crosby, Eddie Cantor, Bob Hope, Fred Astaire, Judy Garland, Mickey Rooney, and even Mickey Mouse.

Radio and Television One of the most popular radio programs of the pre-television era was *Amos and Andy*, which was performed by two white actors. The show simply took the 1808 Sambo and Toney dialogue and updated it to the times. Many of the first television programs were based on the most popular radio programs of the day. Given the longstanding radio success of *Amos and Andy*, it was no surprise that a television program would be in the works. But two white men performing in blackface did not seem as apropos for the new medium, particularly given the vocal opposition of the NAACP to stereotypical blackface representations. Therefore, the CBS network hired the first all-African American acting crew to re-create the program. But the content of the television show did not veer from the original radio program and the black actors were expected to perform the stereotypes of Sambo, Jezebel, Sapphire, and Zip Coon.

Another early popular television program, *Stepin Fetchit*, took the Sambo stereotype to a similar level. The black actors Bert Williams and Lincoln Perry were both of Afro-Caribbean parentage and did not grow up in the United States. Thus, they were not similarly situated in their upbringing to see how the African American stereotypes of the stupid and docile buffoons they were playing reinforced inferior social conditions for black Americans.

Buffoonery was the main representation of blacks on television. With the advent of children's cartoons, the common tropes deployed in blackface comedies were in evidence. While *Our Gang* and the *Little Rascals* were best known for redeploying the racist caricature of black children as pickaninnies in the characters of Stymie and Buckwheat, the inevitable cartoon explosions, with the resultant blackface or pickaninny image, was frequently used in Warner Brothers, Disney, MGM, Hanna-Barbera, and most other children's cartoons.

Children's Books Children were long subjected to the Sambo stereotype in early picture books and later comic books. *The Story of Little Black Sambo* is the most famous of these products. Written by Helen Bannerman in 1899, the story is a combination of the Sambo and uppity Zip Coon stereotypes though it is set in India, with tigers and allusions to Hindu culture. The story tells of a happy-go-lucky black child who loses his fancy clothes to tigers. It is built on a well-entrenched and blatantly racist structure of storytelling. Over time, the illustrations in various editions of the book increasingly took on the blackface motif for the story's protagonist and his parents (Black Mumbo and Black Jumbo). Updated versions placed the story on a plantation in the U.S. South.

Sambo's Restaurant *The Story of Little Black Sambo* found yet another life when a restaurant chain began to use the images of the book, and the story itself, to encourage children to eat there. The restaurant, named Sambo's, was officially not named to invoke particular stereotypes. The owners, Sam Battistone and Newell "Bo" Bohnett, expressly identified their own names as the basis for the restaurant name, but they quickly incorporated the Little Black Sambo motif into the menu, placemats, advertisements, and promotions.

The Sambo's chain was purchased by the Denny's chain of restaurants in 1984, and for a time the two restaurants coincided with the same signage but distinct names. After social protest and continued pressure from African American organizations, the Sambo's chain ceased to exist. But the more insidious nature of racism would rear its ugly head in the Denny's corporation when, in the 1990s, it faced class action lawsuits by African American customers, who successfully argued that Denny's was guilty of discriminatory practices and routinely not serving blacks.

Denny's and Sambo's were ubiquitously identified by the black community as particularly hostile to black customers, and a series of well-publicized events, occurring across the country, cemented a sense that an informal policy was in place to require its black patrons, and only its black patrons, to prepay for meals. As a result of the branding of Denny's as a racist company, the corporation underwent a major makeover that involved legally required actions and a massive public relations campaign designed to increase the number of minority-owned franchises. Mandatory racial sensitivity training was undertaken, and an explicit nondiscrimination policy, based on a U.S. Department of Justice–enforced consent decree, was established. The claim that stereotypical images are harmless was severely undercut when it became clear that a chain restaurant long steeped in those stereotypes also perpetrated the most grievous practices of discriminatory treatment against the victims of the stereotypes.

SAMBO IN ACADEME

The Sambo stereotype was a staple of popular culture, but academic research was not immune from stereotypical reasoning. Stanley Elkins's 1959 analysis of slavery as a total institution can be credited for sparking the new social history of slavery research. Historians such as Eric Foner, Herbert Gutman, and Eugene Genovese wrote some of the most widely acknowledged analyses of slavery in part to discredit the claims of Elkins. The dubious hypothesis that Elkins sought to verify was that the peculiar system of U.S. chattel slavery caused the Sambo social psychology of slaves: "Sambo, the typical plantation slave, was docile but irresponsible, loyal but lazy, humble but chronically given to lying and stealing; his behavior was full of infantile silliness and his talk inflated with childish exaggeration" (Elkins 1959, p. 87).

Elkins never empirically verifies that Sambos existed, but he assumes their presence. The following generation of historians effectively challenged this assumption with a body of research that found U.S. slaves to be much more contentious, to be purposive as actors fighting against slavery, and to have great strength in maintaining family and cultural ties in spite of oppressive social conditions.

In popular culture, a series of challenges to the Sambo stereotype have also surfaced. In particular, the Spike Lee movie *Bamboozled* (2000) tells the story of an African American television executive, Pierre Delacroix, who creates the impromptu idea for a new millennium minstrel show in order to save his job. To his chagrin, the white executives love the idea, and Lee effectively demonstrates the damage inflicted on the black actors selected to perform in blackface, as well as the larger societal damage inflicted on everybody involved in the production and consumption of racist stereotypes. In the closing scene, when Delacroix finally comes to terms with the monster he has created, he is seen in his office, which is filled with racist memorabilia. A Sambo coin bank takes on a life of its own until Delacroix eventually destroys it, along with all the lawn jockeys, blackface knick-knacks, and Mammy cookie jars.

As much as this movie was intended to put executives and white audiences on the spot for the perpetuation of stereotypes, it is clear that the message has not been fully received. In *Star Wars Episode I: The Phantom Menace* (1999), a character named Jar Jar Binks was introduced, and though his form is frog-inspired, his mode of speech and general demeanor is Sambo-inspired. The continuing struggle for African American actors is to find roles that allow them to play more than the fool. Most of the television shows featuring African American casts are comedic in genre, and they invariably have one or more characters playing the hapless fool. A strong case could be made that the history of being white in America corresponds with a strong fascination with all things black, except for black people. It is within this context that blackface minstrels, television comedies, Eminem, Elvis Presley, and contemporary jazz and blues bars make sense.

SEE ALSO *Blackness; Comic Books; Film Industry; Jim Crow; Memín Pinguín; Racism; Television; Uncle Tom*

BIBLIOGRAPHY

Bean, Annemarie, James V. Hatch, and Brooks McNamara, eds. 1996. *Inside the Minstrel Mask: Readings in Nineteenth-Century Blackface Minstrelsy.* Hanover, NH: Wesleyan University Press.

Boskin, Joseph. 1986. *Sambo: The Rise and Demise of an American Jester.* New York: Oxford University Press.

Elkins, Stanley M. 1959. *Slavery: A Problem in American Institutional and Intellectual Life.* Chicago: University of Chicago Press.

Lott, Eric. 1995. *Love and Theft: Blackface Minstrelsy and the American Working Class.* New York: Oxford University Press.

Roediger, David. 1999. *The Wages of Whiteness.* New York: Verso Books.

Strausbaugh, John. 2006. *Black Like You: Blackface, Whiteface, Insult and Imitation in American Culture.* New York: Penguin Books.

Ronald L. Mize Jr.

SAMPLE

SEE *Censoring, Sample; Sampling; Selection Bias.*

SAMPLE ATTRITION

Sample attrition is a feature of longitudinal or panel data in which individual observations drop out from the study over time. Attrition may occur for a number of reasons, including insufficient compensation for survey response, induction into military services, transfer of residence with no follow-up information, or death of the respondent.

A dataset suffering from attrition is referred to as an attrited sample, whereas individual observations that drop out over the course of the panel are referred to as attriters. Assuming a longitudinal dataset is randomized at the inception of the data collection process, sample attrition would not pose any challenges in estimation of the attrited panel data if sample attrition occurs randomly. This would be the case if the attriters compose a random selection of individuals in the survey, and the underlying causes of attrition are independent of the survey response being studied. However, attrition in actual panel data is rarely random, since the probability of attrition is most often dependent on the observable and unobservable attributes of the individual observations that simultaneously affect the response variable being studied. For example, in firm-level data used to study business firm profits over time, firms could make a decision about whether to shut down (and thus, be removed from the sample) based on observable characteristics, as well as unobservable firm characteristics such as expected operating revenues and productivity, which are either directly or indirectly a determinant of firm profits as well. Thus less productive firms attrite from the sample, leaving a nonrandom sample for analysis. Any quantitative inference about the entire population of firms based on analysis of just the attrited sample would thus be misleading, since the at-trited sample is nonrepresentative of the underlying population. In these cases, estimation of the panel dataset while ignoring sample attrition would lead to biased and inconsistent estimation, and thus incorrect inference.

Sample attrition was first formally described and analyzed in J. Hausman and D. Wise's work *Econometrica* (1979). Using the well-known random-effects specification, Hausman and Wise considered models in which the unobservable errors that determine the attrition decision are naturally correlated with the unobservable errors that determine the response variable. Due to this choice of specification, this model is sometimes referred to as the Selection on Unobservables model. The specification is easily manipulated to illustrate that least squares regression using only the retained data would be biased and inconsistent for the parameters of interest. The model also shows that using only the first period randomized sample leads to biased and inconsistent estimators, if future periods are affected by attrition. The latter is a consequence of the unavoidable correlation of error terms due to latent individual specific effects that do not change over time. Then, under the joint normality assumption on the errors, it is shown, however, that consistent estimators of the parameters of interest can be obtained by the maximum likelihood (ML) procedure. Generalizations, including models with relaxed distributional assumptions, have been since suggested by various researchers, including M. Verbeek and T. Nijman in the *International Economic Review* (1992) and Jeffrey Wooldridge in the *Journal of Econometrics* (1995). Cheng Hsiao provides a review in his *Analysis of Panel Data* (1986).

Several late-twentieth-century theoretical advances have been suggested in the analysis of sample attrition models. These have included models wherein an observable determinant of sample attrition is uncorrelated with the response variable, but possibly correlated with the unobservable determinant of the response variable. This difference from the original attrition model has led to this model being known as Selection on Observables, as studied in John Fitzgerald, Peter Gottschalk, and Robert Moffitt's 1996 research. This model is complementary to the classical attrition model studied by Hausman and Wise; each is formulated on a different assumption and each is of independent interest in empirical research.

A separate consideration in the theoretical work on sample attrition has been the possibility of obtaining a refreshment sample, which refers to supplemental data randomly sampled from the population to augment the attrited sample. This type of approach has been considered by, among others, K. Hirano and colleagues in 2000, who proposed consistent estimators of the parameters of interest when such refreshment samples are available.

In 2004, Mitali Das considered a generalized model of attrition. This model permits the estimand of interest to be either a parameter (as in previous work) or a flexible and unknown function, permits the errors to have unspecified joint distribution, and usefully permits attriters to reappear in future periods.

SEE ALSO *Pooled Time Series and Cross-sectional Data; Research, Longitudinal; Selection Bias*

BIBLIOGRAPHY

Fitzgerald, John, Peter Gottschalk, and Robert Moffitt. 1998. An Analysis of Sample Attrition in Panel Data. *Journal of Human Resources* 33 (2): 251–299.

Cheng Hsiao. 1986. *Analysis of Panel Data.* Cambridge, U.K.: Cambridge University Press.

Robins, James M., Andrea Rotnitzky, and Lue Ping Zhao. 1995. Analysis of Semiparametric Regression Models for Repeated Outcomes in the Presence of Missing Data. *Journal of the American Statistical Association* 90: 106–121.

Wooldridge, Jeffrey M. 2002. Inverse Probability Weighted M-Estimation for Sample Selection, Attrition and Stratification. *Portuguese Economics Journal* 1: 117–139.

Mitali Das

SAMPLING

A *sample* is a subset of items, objects, or elements from a larger group of interest, called the *population*. When an observed sample is used to make inferences about the unobserved population, chance factors must be considered and the risk of being wrong must be assessed. Statistical sampling uses probability to measure this uncertainty. Statistical, or probability, sampling implies that every item or subset of items in the population has a mathematically determined likelihood of being selected; which item or items in the population will be selected is left to chance and not to judgment. A sample consisting of numerical values that have meaning on a number line (for example, numbers on a ruler) is assumed to have been generated by a random variable that has a specific probability distribution.

SIMPLE RANDOM SAMPLING

In *simple random sampling*, each item in the population is equally likely to be selected. For instance, if the population of interest consists of N elements, then each and every possible sample of n elements (where n may equal 1, 2, 3, ...$N-1$) should have a probability of $1/N^n$ of being realized. (Typically, in textbooks, upper case N is used to denote the number of elements in the population, and lower case n gives the number of elements in the sample.) An example would be to blindly draw well-shaken numbered slips of paper from a hat or drum one at a time, with each slip placed back in the hat. Replacement ensures that each number is equally likely on each draw, although computerized random number generators are typically used to simulate it.

In drawing numbers from a hat or in a laboratory experiment, replacement might seem possible; in actual business and economics practices, however, replacement is seldom possible. If the population of interest is extremely large relative to the sample size, then even though the probability of each sample being selected in repeated sampling does not remain fixed, the changes in probability could be trivial. For instance, if $n = 30$ and $N = 30,000$, then for the first sample the probability of drawing 30 items is

$$n!(N-n)!/N! = 2.8(10)^{-88}.$$

On the second sampling, it is

$$n!(N-2n)!/(N-n)! = 3.0(10)^{-88}.$$

As long as N is large relative to n, whether there is or is not replacement will not be critical. In practice, randomization based on the notion of fixed sampling probabilities is more a matter of degree than an absolute.

Putting numbered items in a hat to be shaken or into a revolving drum, may give the appearance of good mixing, but the resulting selections will not necessarily produce a sample that represents the population. For instance, in 1970, during the Vietnam War, military draft status for induction into the U.S. Armed Forces was determined by the order in which birthdays were drawn from a drum. The Selective Service placed 366 capsules in a drum, each representing a birthday. The drum was turned several times and capsules were selected "at random." As Norton Starr discusses in detail, this method looked impressive on television, but the results were not a good representation of birthdays. Randomization suggests that among the first 183 birthdays selected, about one-sixth should be from November and December. Of the first 183 days selected, however, 46 were from November and December, well above the expected 30 or 31. This led to speculation that more than simple random sampling error was involved.

SYSTEMATIC SAMPLING

Systematic random sampling involves the selection of every k-th element (or block of elements) from a list of elements, starting with any randomly selected element. Systematic sampling is a popular way of generating samples in accounting and quality-control work. It is typically less expensive to select every k-th element than to search for the n randomly determined items. In systematic sampling, however, only the first of *n* items can be considered as randomly determined.

Systematic sampling is convenient for populations formed by lists, stacks, or series. For instance, if students with e-mail addresses at a university is the population of interest, systematic sampling could be used to minimize the likelihood that those with the same last name (who may be relatives) would be included in a sample. However, if the data have cyclical components, then systematic sampling may be inappropriate.

STRATIFIED SAMPLING

When the population is known to consist of a number of distinct categories, characteristics, or demographics, the sampling process can be made more efficient (requiring a lower sample size for the same precision) if the population is divided into subgroups that have the common attribute. For example, in a study of starting salaries, recent university graduates might be grouped, or "stratified," by their majors. In a study of higher-education costs, universities might be placed in one of two subgroups: public or private. Heterogeneous populations can always be divided into subgroups that are more homogeneous if those in the population can be identified by the characteristic. These more homogeneous subgroups are called "strata." Either simple random sampling within strata or one of a number of sampling methods is then applied to each stratum separately, where sample size for a strata is made proportional to the stratum's share of the population.

Cluster Sampling If sampling requires face-to-face communication and the members of a population are physically separated from one another (as in different cities), then it would be very costly to visit randomly selected homes. Instead, sampling might be restricted to a few cities. Within these cities, a surveyor visits specific neighborhoods, interviewing an adult from every *i*-th house on *j*-th street. Such sampling is called cluster or area sampling because groups or clusters of elements are first selected and then elements within a cluster are chosen. At each stage, selection can be random or based on nonrandom judgment.

Classical Statistics and Sample Statistics Classical statistics assumes simple random sampling. Random "draws" imply that each sample of size *n* will yield somewhat different values. Thus, the value of any statistic calculated with sample data (for example, the sample mean) varies from sample to sample. A histogram (graph) of these values provides the sampling distribution of the statistic. Many Web sites show how the distribution of the sample means changes with *n*. Robert Wolf, for example, has designed "Statutor," a computer-based tutorial on sam-

pling distributions, estimators, and related topics that can be freely downloaded.

The law of large numbers holds that as *n* increases, a statistic such as the sample mean ($\bar{X}$) converges to its true mean (μ). That is, the sampling distribution of the mean collapses on or degenerates to a spike at the population mean. The central limit theorem, on the other hand, states that for many samples of like and sufficiently large size *n*, the histogram of their sample means will appear to be a normal bell-shaped distribution. As the sample size *n* is increased, the distribution of the sample mean at first becomes normal (central limit theorem) but then degenerates to the population mean (law of large numbers). Only the standardized mean, $(\bar{X} - \mu)\sqrt{n}/\sigma$, maintains its shape as *n* goes to infinity, where σ is the population standard deviation.

Sampling and Inferential Statistics in the Social Sciences Unlike laboratory random experiments, sample data in the social sciences are often "opportunistic," meaning they have been observed with no explicit and certain knowledge as to how they were generated. In such cases, the researcher must have a theory about the data-generating process. For example, one might assume that observation *i* at time *t* on dependent variable Y_{it} was generated by *k* independent variables, $X_{1t}, X_{2t}, X_{3t}, \ldots, X_{kt}$, plus an error term ε_{it} reflecting random chance factors, where the betas are parameters to be estimated:

$$Y_{it} = \beta_0 + \beta_1 X_{1t} + \beta_2 X_{2t} + \ldots + \beta_k X_{kt} + \varepsilon_{it}$$

A maximum likelihood estimator of the betas requires the researcher to make an assumption about the error term (for example, ε_{it} is normal with mean zero and unit standard deviation) and then have a computer program search for values of the betas that maximize the probability of getting the observed sample values of the *X*s and *Y*. Here the sample *Y* values are assumed to come from this model, conditional on the values of the *X*s, with the randomness in *Y* generated by the assumed distribution of the epsilon error term. If the assumed population model of the data-generating process is wrong, then the estimated parameters are meaningless. Unlike data obtained from simple random sampling in a laboratory experiment, opportunistic sample data cannot be used to make inferences without a theory about the nature of the data-generating process.

SEE ALSO *Censoring, Sample; Ex Ante and Ex Post; Exchangeability; Heteroskedasticity; Monte Carlo Experiments; Multicollinearity; Natural Experiments; Policy Experiment; Probability, Limits in; Sample Attrition; Selection Bias; Serial Correlation*

BIBLIOGRAPHY

Starr, Norton. 1997. Nonrandom Risk: The 1970 Draft Lottery. *Journal of Statistics Education* 5 (2). http://www.amstat.org/publications/jse/v5n2/datasets.starr.html.

Wolf, Robert A. Statutor: A Computer Based Teaching Tool for Statistical Concepts. Ann Arbor: University of Michigan, Department of Biostatistics. http://archives.math.utk.edu/software/msdos/statistics/statutor/.html.

William E. Becker

SAMUELSON, PAUL A.
1915–

If one could do a mental time-and-motion study of a modern economic theorist at work, a large fraction of what he or she actually does from day to day would turn out to have its origins in Paul Samuelson's work. In that precise sense, Samuelson has been the economist's economist.

Paul Anthony Samuelson was born in Gary, Indiana, on May 15, 1915. He graduated from Hyde Park High School in Chicago in 1932 and went on to the University of Chicago and an already precocious B.A. in 1935. The next step proved to be important: he moved to Harvard for his Ph.D., studying with Joseph Schumpeter (1883–1950), Gottfried Haberler (1900–1995), Wassily Leontief (1906–1999), and, more to the point, the polymath Edwin Bidwell Wilson (1879–1964), from whom he may have learned some tricks of the trade in dealing with equilibrium systems of equations. From 1937 to 1940 Samuelson was a junior fellow of the Harvard Society of Fellows; that was—and is—a plum appointment, providing a stipend, stimulating company, and three undisturbed years in which to pursue one's own research. In 1940 he was appointed assistant professor of economics at Massachusetts Institute of Technology (MIT), retiring as institute professor emeritus in 1986. If Harvard had retained Samuelson as an assistant professor, the history of economic thought might not have been affected, but the center of gravity of economic teaching would not have shifted so strongly toward MIT. Anti-Semitism certainly played a significant role in Harvard's failure to keep him, but there were other factors as well: Lloyd Metzler and James Tobin also slipped away.

Samuelson has probably been the last great generalist in economics. His five volumes of published papers (with more in the works) range from the pure theory of consumer demand to macroeconomics and the history of economic thought. The place to start, however, is with *The Foundations of Economic Analysis*, published in 1947 (and reprinted with additions in 1983) but already containing the results of earlier articles. It is fair to say that this book was the major influence in the transformation of economics into the mathematical-model-building discipline it is today.

Of course there had been many important prior uses of mathematics in economic theory. What the *Foundations* did was to turn scattered stand-alone efforts into a paradigm, in Thomas Kuhn's (1922–1996) original sense of a standard way to answer standard questions. In particular, Samuelson explained, exemplified, and inculcated the notion of comparative statics, aimed at answering a fundamental class of questions: how do the coordinates of an equilibrium point defined by a system of equations shift when one or more of the given determining parameters changes? Bread-and-butter examples range from determining the effects of a changing excise tax on the price and quantity of a single good to determining the effect of a changing quantity of base money on the basic variables of a macroeconomic model. A second focus of the book was on the logic of constrained maximization, and a third on the importance of explicit dynamic modeling both for its own results and for understanding the stability, and therefore the significance, of a longer-run equilibrium. The wealth of examples was an eye-opener to younger economists.

Despite the broad landscape over which his work has ranged, there are especially important concentrations. His first three articles, dating from 1937 to 1938, are on utility theory and consumer behavior, the pure theory of capital, and welfare economics and international trade. The theory of consumer behavior has been on Samuelson's mind for seventy years.

There is a story that, asked by a science department colleague at MIT to name a theory in economics that was neither false nor trivial, Samuelson named the theory of comparative advantage. True to his word, he has made outstanding contributions to the theory of international trade. They include a complete statement and clarification of the gains from trade, the factor-price equalization theorem (when does free trade in produced goods induce uniform prices of immobile factors, wherever they are, and when does it not), the transfer problem, and more.

Yet another such monument is the theory of public goods (initiated by Erik Lindahl [1891–1960] but worked out in its modern form by Samuelson). These are goods the use of which by one "consumer" does not foreclose use by others. Examples include weather forecasts, national defense, and clean air. Instances with a "public-good element" outnumber the pure public goods, and this adds importance to the problem.

There is room merely to mention only one more of these clusters in Samuelson's work, the theory of finance. Here he has not only made contributions himself—for example, the martingale property of asset prices, and even the beginning of a theory of option pricing—but he has directly inspired the work of others. For further references, comments by specialists, and discussion of Samuelson's contributions to still other branches of economics, see E. Cary Brown and Robert M. Solow (1983) and Michael Szenberg et al. (2006).

What has been described so far was aimed at other economists. Another side of Samuelson's activity has been directed at a broader public. Apart from columns in newspapers and magazines in the United States and elsewhere and many public lectures, there is the famous elementary textbook *Economics.* The first edition was published in 1948, with up-to-date revisions published at approximately three-year intervals until 1985, when it acquired the joint authorship of William D. Nordhaus of Yale. Successive editions have followed, the 2005 edition being the eighteenth. For many years *Economics* was the runaway leader in sales, but it was eventually overtaken by other textbooks, most of which had imitated the form and tone that Samuelson had pioneered.

Economics was an innovator in several respects. The textbook taught economics to beginning students as the model-building enterprise it had become, taught to them in simplified form, of course. Students were expected to use the supply-and-demand apparatus or a simple macroeconomic model as devices for understanding made-up events, and also real-world data. It was a style of teaching that lent itself to problem sets, certainly appropriate at MIT but equally appropriate to the view of economics as a pragmatic discipline, a "How Things Work" discipline. The three-year revisions were intended to keep the noses of students, classroom teachers, and the author to the grindstone of what was actually happening in the economy at large. The unity of theory and practice has been a hallmark of Samuelson's work.

BIBLIOGRAPHY

Brown, E. Cary, and Robert M. Solow, eds. 1983. *Paul Samuelson and Modern Economic Theory.* New York: McGraw-Hill.

Samuelson, Paul A. [1947] 1983. *Foundations of Economic Analysis.* Enlarged ed. Cambridge, MA: Harvard University Press.

Samuelson, Paul A. 1966–1986. *The Collected Scientific Papers of Paul A. Samuelson.* Vols. 1–5. Cambridge, MA: MIT Press.

Samuelson, Paul A., and William D. Nordhaus. 2005. *Economics.* 18th ed. Boston: McGraw-Hill.

Szenberg, Michael, Lall Ramrattan, and Aron Gottesman, eds. 2006. *Samuelsonian Economics and the Twenty-First Century.* New York: Oxford University Press.

Robert M. Solow

SANDINISTAS

The Sandinista Front for National Liberation (FSLN) is a Nicaraguan political party. It was formed to oppose the Somoza family dynastic dictatorship, which ruled from 1936 to 1979. It is named after Augusto Cesar Sandino (1893–1934), a Nicaraguan nationalist and anti-imperialist patriot who fought a seven-year war from 1926 to 1933 against a U.S. occupation force. On February 21, 1934, after putting down his weapons, Sandino was killed at the order of Anastacio Somoza Garcia, the head of the U.S.-formed Nicaraguan National Guard. In 1936 Somoza Garcia consolidated his political power, overthrowing the civilian government and staging a rigged election to install himself as president. He was inaugurated on January 1, 1937. From then until 1979 either he, one of his two sons (Luis and Anastacio Jr.), or—for brief periods—one of their cronies ruled Nicaragua.

The FSLN was originally formed clandestinely in 1961. The organization's founding members included Carlos Fonseca, Silvio Mayorga, and Tomas Borge. Particularly important to the organization's formation and early development, Fonseca is widely credited as the organization's intellectual father. His revolutionary ideology came to be known as *Sandinismo*—which combines elements of Marxist class analysis and Sandino's own nationalist and anti-imperialist ideology as applied to the Nicaraguan social, political, and economic reality. This led the Sandinistas to organize for the military overthrow of the Somozas because they were convinced that the Somozas were completely unresponsive to peaceful demands for democratization and economic reform.

Throughout the 1960s and early 1970s the Sandinistas suffered serious setbacks, including the death in combat of all of its original founders, except Borge. These losses led to a regrouping period in which they sought to accumulate strength in secret while organizing politically. However, it also led to a split into several competing Sandinista factions. The first, called the Prolonged Popular War (Spanish acronym GPP) Tendency, advocated building grassroots peasant support in the countryside. In contrast, the Proletarian Tendency grew out of the urban underground and advocated the organization of union workers into self-defense units. The final faction, called the Terceristas (Third Way), favored a more pragmatic approach combining different forms of struggle and advocated the creation of a broad alliance of all Nicaraguans opposed to Somoza to generate a national insurrection.

THE REVOLUTION

By late 1978 the long awaited national insurrection began and many of Somoza's supporters abandoned him. To take advantage of this opportunity the Sandinistas reunited early in 1979 and created a single nine member National Directorate with three representatives from each faction. The members were Daniel Ortega, Humberto Ortega, and Víctor Tirado (Terceristas); Tomás Borge, Bayardo Arce, and Henry Ruiz (GPP); and Jaime Wheelock, Luis Carrión, and Carlos Núñez (Proletarian faction). On July 19, 1979, the Sandinista Revolution triumphed, ousting Anastacio Somoza Jr.'s regime in a mass popular insurrection.

Once in power the Sandinistas embarked upon ambitious political and economic programs designed to democratize Nicaragua and lift the country out of underdevelopment. Their political agenda called for reforming the country's institutions, including disbanding Somoza's National Guard, and enfranchising the country's vast rural and urban poor through mass organizations affiliated with the FSLN. In 1984 they carried out the first democratic national elections in the country's history, which the Sandinistas won with 66 percent of the vote. Though derided by U.S. president Ronald Reagan's administration as a "Soviet style farce," the elections were designed with the technical assistance of the Swedish Electoral Commission and observed by credible international organizations and European governments. The newly elected Constituent Assembly, with the help of open "town meetings" around the country, promulgated a new constitution in 1987. Simultaneously, the Sandinistas launched aggressive economic reforms to combat the twin evils that had historically plagued Nicaragua: poverty and inequality. To this end they implemented an agrarian reform to distribute land confiscated from Somoza and his cronies (one-fifth of the country's arable land) to individual peasants, cooperatives, and collective farms. In the cities they passed popular economic reforms, such as raising the minimum wage and introducing price controls and subsidies on basic goods and services, and embarked on public works programs to increase employment. These coincided with the Sandinistas' desire to implement a mixed-economy in which private property, state property, and cooperative property would co-exist. Sandinista social policy was equally ambitious, especially in the areas of education, health care, and housing.

From 1979 until Ronald Reagan's inauguration in 1981, U.S.-Nicaraguan relations were cool but nonconfrontational. However, shortly after entering office President Reagan signed a secret executive authorization to begin trying to overthrow the Sandinista government, which the United States accused of supporting the guerrillas in El Salvador, being too closely allied to Cuba, and being Communists. U.S. coercion ranged from diplomatic pressures and economic sanctions to supporting the rebel force known as the Contras and threatening direct U.S. military action. These policies put a huge economic strain on the Nicaraguan economy, and the Sandinistas were forced to respond by shifting much of their trade to Europe and the Soviet Union. Similarly since the early 1980s, sales of weapons from Western countries were also embargoed pushing the Nicaraguans to import most of their weapons from the Socialist Bloc. While the Sandinistas claimed that these weapons were for defensive purposes to fight the U.S.-supported Contra rebels, the Reagan Administration pointed to them as proof that the FSLN were Communists and presented an eminent threat to other countries in the region and ultimately the United States. However U.S. public support for military intervention, whether indirectly by supporting the Contras or directly by U.S. troops, was the most unpopular U.S. foreign military policy of the 1980s. Indeed widespread domestic opposition led to strong public pressure on Congress to limit aid to the Contras. It also eventually led to the outlawing of lethal aid for the Contras from 1984 to 1985.

In turn this led members of the Reagan Administration, notably Oliver North of the National Security Council, to engage in the illegal and covert funding of the Contras by giving them money received from selling arms to a hostile country, Iran, in exchange for the release of U.S. hostages held by Lebanese Hezbollah. When this back-channel funding was uncovered it became known as the "Iran-Contra scandal." An independent counsel, Lawrence E. Walsh, was appointed to investigate the affair. Eventually several members of the Reagan Administration were prosecuted and convicted. However, these convictions were later overturned on appeal or through presidential pardons.

From 1984 through early 2007 the electoral system that the Sandinistas put in place peacefully transferred power four times. The first was in 1990 when the Sandinistas were voted out of office. For the next sixteen years, three conservative administrations held power. However, on November 5, 2006, Sandinista candidate Daniel Ortega was reelected president of Nicaragua on a social democratic platform. The 2006 elections were widely scrutinized by international observers including delegations from Europe, the Organization of American States, and the Carter Center in Atlanta, Georgia. By all accounts they were, with the exception of a few minor irregularities, fair and transparent. In January 2007 Ortega began his new term in office.

SEE ALSO *Anticolonial Movements; Development, Rural; Iran-Contra Affair; Land Reform; Marxism; Peasantry; Reagan, Ronald; Revolution; Socialism*

BIBLIOGRAPHY

Booth, John A., Christine J. Wade, and Thomas W. Walker. 2006. *Understanding Central America: Global Forces, Rebellion, and Change.* 4th ed. Boulder, CO: Westview Press.

Kornbluh, Peter, and Malcolm Byrne, eds. 1993. *The Iran-Contra Scandal: The Declassified History.* New York: New Press.

Sandinista Front for National Liberation. Official Homepage of the Sandinista Front for National Liberation (Spanish). http://www.fsln-nicaragua.com/.

Walker, Thomas W. 2003. *Nicaragua: Living in the Shadow of the Eagle.* 4th ed. Boulder, CO: Westview Press.

Zimmerman, Matilde. 2000. *Sandinista: Carlos Fonseca and the Nicaraguan Revolution.* Durham, NC: Duke University Press.

Héctor Perla Jr.

SANDINO, AUGUSTUS CESAR

SEE *Sandinistas.*

SANITATION

Sanitation (from the Latin *sanitas,* meaning health) refers to the maintenance and delivery of clean, hygienic conditions that help prevent disease through services such as drinking water supply, garbage collection, and safe disposal of human waste. Sanitation is the focal point of public health policy, but in the experience of local communities much more than health is at stake in "sanitation."

GLOBAL STATISTICS

World Health Organization (WHO) reports show that in 2004, 5.3 billion people (83% of the world population) had access to clean water sources (in 1990 that percentage was 78). Of the 1.1 billion people without access to clean drinking water, 84 percent live in rural areas. The situation is particularly critical in sub-Saharan Africa, where 44 percent of the population remains without clean drinking water, and in Eastern and Southern Asia.

Similar statistics apply to the coverage of "basic sanitation" (improved toilet facilities). According to the same 2004 WHO report, only 59 percent of the world population had access to a hygienic toilet in 2004. It is again sub-Saharan Africa (38 percent) and Eastern Asia (45 percent) that have the highest populations without basic sanitation.

Unsanitary conditions are the main cause of ill health and premature death in poor societies. WHO statistics of 2004 report that 1.8 million people die every year from diarrheal diseases (including cholera), 90 percent of whom are children under five. Eighty-eight percent of diarrheal disease is attributed to poor sanitation. Malaria, another sanitation related disease, kills 1.3 million people each year; again, 90 percent of these deaths are children under five. Other diseases that originate in poor sanitary conditions include schistosomiasis (a parasitic infection), intestinal helminthes (ascariasis, trichuriasis, hookworm), and hepatitis-A. Although the health consequences of sanitation are overwhelming, people often have reasons to pursue—or refuse—better sanitation.

EVOLUTIONIST VIEWS: SURVIVAL INSTINCT

Social scientists have developed various theories to interpret or explain human concern about avoiding dirt and promoting hygiene. Evolutionist thinkers believe that there is medical wisdom in the human fear of dirty things. Dirty objects and activities pose a danger, so it is wise to avoid them. Disgust of dirt is a survival strategy (usually a non-conscious one). A 2001 study by Valerie Curtis and Adam Biran list five disgust elicitors derived from research in India, Burkina Faso, The Netherlands, Britain, and an international airport. The five elicitors are: (1) body excretions and body parts; (2) certain animals; (3) decay and spoiled food; (4) certain categories of "other people;" and (5) violations of morality. Bodily excretions were mentioned most frequently as causing disgust and among them, feces topped the list, but vomit, sweat, spittle, blood, pus, and sexual fluids were also regarded with aversion. Animals that were mentioned most often included pigs, dogs, rats, snakes, worms, cockroaches, maggots, lice, and flies. People that were found disgusting were those with signs of sickness, dirt, or deformity, and strangers with whom one was forced to come into close contact, for example in crowded places. People who behaved immorally also evoked aversion.

Curtis and Biran's hypothesis is that humans have evolved behavioral defenses against disease and that "disgust is one of the mechanisms crafted by natural selection to keep our distance from contagion" (Curtis and Biran 2001, p. 22). The researchers found support for their hypothesis by checking the routes of transmission for a selection of common infectious diseases. In all of them, one or more elicitors of disgust were mentioned as playing an important role in transmission. Feces were named as the source of more than twenty infectious diseases. Breath, saliva, lice, rats, and sexual organs were also important sources or transmitters of infection. All of these score high for human disgust.

William Ian Miller's 1997 study of disgust is difficult to place in any disciplinary tradition. His own expertise mainly lies in literature and history but his study also draws on psychologists, moral philosophers, and political and social theorists. Trying to decipher the origin and working of emotion, Miller derives most inspiration from psychology.

The disgust Miller discusses applies to many phenomena and activities, such as defecation, sex, food, and drink. He distinguishes two types of disgust. The first, which is clearly Freudian, prevents the activation of unconscious desire. It defends against pollution, denies access to objects and acts that would block the psychic development of the human person. The evolutionist perspective of disgust as a survival instinct returns here at the level of the human psyche. The second type of disgust is "disgust of surfeit," it punishes after having indulged in a "disgusting" activity. The two types complement each other. In the aversion of things perceived as dangerous because of their power "to contaminate, infect, or pollute by proximity, contact, or ingestion" it is first of all the unconscious reaction to psychic dangers that is at work (Miller 1997, p. 2).

CIVILIZATION PROCESS

Most authors writing on hygiene and sanitation from a sociological point of view refer to Norbert Elias's study on the civilization process. Elias studied etiquette books, letters, and other documents in France and England from the eleventh century onward and describes how the authors of those guides for proper conduct gradually became more particular about body functions, body parts, and body products.

He talks about a general process of civilization, which implies a "privatization" or "intimization" of human behavior. More and more, public activities became shameful and were confined to the private world. The human body was a focal point. The body itself had to be well covered and activities such as sex, sleep, urination, and defecation became embarrassing when carried out in front of other people. Modern hygiene facilities are regarded as expressions of the civilizing process.

CULTURAL SYMBOLICS AND RELATIONAL CONCERNS

The symbolic anthropologist Mary Douglas, in her classic *Purity and Danger*, turns away from evolutionist and "medical materialist" (a term used by American psychologist and philosopher William James, meaning reducing ritual to its supposed positive medical effect) explanations of hygiene and presents dirt as "matter out of place," a definition that became famous for its beautiful simplicity and provocation. Shoes on the table (Douglas's example) are dirty; under the table they are clean. Saliva safely caught in a handkerchief is hygienic, but when it falls in a plate it turns disgusting. Her claim that absolute dirt does not exist opened new windows in the study of hygiene as a cultural phenomenon. Dirt is defined by its context. It is disorder and carries an invitation or rather an obligation to restore order: "Ideas about separating, purifying, demarcating and punishing transgressions have as their main function to impose system on an inherently untidy experience" (Douglas 1970, p. 15). Hygiene, in short, is a basic cultural act: it distinguishes dirt from what is clean and thus, creates cultural order. Enculturation of small children starts with teaching them what is clean and what is not clean. Hygiene is the essence of culture. *What* is dirty is of less importance. Crucial is *that* dirt exists. Without the concept of dirt people could not formulate the norms and values of culture.

RELATIONAL CONCERNS

What makes an object abject and threatening? Douglas suggested: its out-of-place condition. Others claimed it depends on the matter itself. Too little attention has, however, been given to the identity of the person who is directly associated with something dirty, to the social life of the dirty matter. The answer to the question "whose?" determines the experience of disgust much more than has been suggested by Douglas and other authors who wrote about the cultural meaning of dirt. By adding a sociological dimension to dirt, Douglas's theory of matter out of place becomes more true to life and effective as an interpretative tool.

The humanist Erasmus's dictum that one's own shit has a pleasant smell (*Suus cinque crepitus bene olet*) is a humorous exaggeration, but it is not exaggerating to say that people usually are not disturbed by the smell (and sight) of their own feces. Objects, substances, and acts become dirtier as the person behind them is less close or less liked. Animals that produce dirt are also placed in categories of less and more disturbing. Animals that are "part of the family" are experienced as cleaner than those who belong to another family. And so on. Acts and gestures from a loved person that are cherished as dear and intimate (bodily contact, sex) turn into horrifying violence when another person performs them. Good or bad, clean or dirty, in this case, depends entirely on the actor. The "matter" remains the same. The urge for "hygienic action" also depends a great deal on such relational concerns. Washing hands after toilet use or before eating, for example, is as much a social as a healthful act.

SANITATION POLICY

Hygiene, in the medical sense, is a core value in modern societies. Objects, activities, and people are judged by their medical qualities. Food, houses, streets, markets, working places, holiday camps, public transport, and visitors should be clean and not pose a danger to health. Dirty things and people are rejected and rejected things and people are called dirty.

Anthropologists and historians argue, however, that people do not always make that explicit link between health and dirt. After studying the hygienic ideas and practices by mothers in Burkina Faso, Curtis concluded that their cleanliness and dirt avoidance were primarily a matter of "etiquette and social acceptability rather than to avoid illness" (Curtis 1998, p. 110). In a 2005 study, conducted in Bénin, Jenkins and Curtis observed that modern toilets were popular because they were seen as a sign of social prestige and success.

Michel Foucault argues that in the modern state, medicine is a major instrument of control by societal and political institutions. His concept of "Bio-power" suggests that the state can reward or punish its citizens by providing or withholding health. Sanitation, preventive heath care, implies the imposition of a regime. Sanitary policy legitimizes the state's interference in households and private lives of people and thus helps to establish more effective disciplinary power. Bio-power—and sanitation in particular—constitutes the link between macro and micro (Foucault 1990; Gastaldo 1997).

Sanitation policies have been most successful when they also appealed to other values in people's lives, such as social decency, respect, comfort, and religion. Cultural ignorance and lack of respect for local knowledge and practices of hygiene are major problems in sanitation projects by both foreign organizations and local governments in low-income societies. Tiokou Ndonko's 1993 anthropological study in Cameroon for example, analyzed cultural and religious resistance against the government's sanitation policy. Hygiene, seemingly a purely medical concern, lies at the heart of culture and is both a means of political control and resistance.

SEE ALSO *Civilization; Cultural Relativism; Disease; Freud, Sigmund; Health in Developing Countries; James, William; Public Health; Taboos; Toilets*

BIBLIOGRAPHY

Curtis, Valerie. 1998. *The Dangers of Dirt: Household, Hygiene and Health.* PhD diss., Agricultural University Wageningen.

Curtis, Valerie, and Adam Biran. 2001. Dirt, Disgust and Disease: Is Hygiene in Our Genes? *Perspectives in Biology and Medicine* 44 (1): 17–31.

Douglas, Mary. [1966] 1970. *Purity and Danger. An Analysis of Concepts of Pollution and Taboo.* Harmondsworth, U.K.: Penguin.

Elias, Norbert. [1939] 1982. *The Civilizing Process.* New York: Pantheon.

Foucault, Michel. 1990. *The History of Sexuality*, vol. 1: *An Introduction.* London: Penguin.

Gastaldo, Denise. 1997. Is Health Education Good for You? Rethinking Health Education through the Doncept of Bio-power. In *Foucault: Health and Medicine,* ed. Alan Petersen and Robin Bunton, 113–133. London: Routledge.

Goudsblom, Johan. 1986. Public Health and the Civilizing Process. *Milbank Quarterly* 64 (2): 161–188.

Jenkins, Marion W., and Val Curtis. 2005. Achieving the "Good Life": Why Some People Want Latrines in Rural Benin. *Social Science and Medicine* 61 (1): 2446–2459.

Miller, Ian. 1997. *The Anatomy of Disgust.* Cambridge, MA: Harvard University Press.

Ndonko, Flavier Tiokou. 1993. *Répresentations Culturelles des Excrements.* Münster, Germany: Lit Verlag.

World Health Organization. 2004. Water, Sanitation and Health. http://www.who.int/water_sanitation_health/publications/facts2004/en/.

World Health Organization. 2005. *Meeting the MDG Drinking Water and Sanitation Target. The Urban and Rural Challenge of the Decade.* Geneva: World Health Organization.

Sjaak van der Geest

SANSKRITIZATION

The term *Sanskritization* was first coined by the Indian sociologist Mysore Narasimhachar Srinivas (1916–1999) in his Oxford University PhD thesis, which was eventually published as *Religion and Society among the Coorgs of South India* (1952). His research demonstrated that, contrary to the British colonial view, the caste system was not static and pan-Indian, but local, dynamic, and fluid. He captured the dynamics of this stratification system in his theory of Sanskritization. Sanskrit is the canonical language of the Hindu scriptures, including principally the *Upanishads*, and thus Sanskritization is the process by which lower castes attempt to emulate the culture of higher castes. More precisely, this social process involves the adoption by a "low" caste or other group of the customs, rituals, and beliefs of a "high" or "twice-born" caste. One specific example is the adoption of a vegetarian diet, which is not typical of low-caste practice. These social changes are normally followed by a claim to a more elevated position within the hierarchy of castes.

The theory is in fact more complex, because of the difficulties of translation of the notion of "caste," which corresponds to what is locally known as *jati* or *kulam*. Whereas *varna* refers to the four main castes (Brahmin, Kshatriya, Vaisya, and Sudra), *jati* refers to the many smaller groups or subcastes by which the Indian system is internally and locally divided. A caste is characterized by endogamy, hereditary membership, and a specific lifestyle. Although social classes are open, caste in principle is not. Whereas social mobility in class society involves the movement of individuals, in a caste system it is an entire community (typically a *jati*) that moves up or down the system.

This social dynamic is also associated with a contrast between what anthropologists have called the "great" and "little traditions" of peasant society. In his *Peasant Society and Culture* (1956) Robert Redfield argued that a "great tradition" is a culture closely associated with religion that is spread over a large territory and embedded in a literary tradition defended by a stratum of intellectuals such as priests. A "little tradition," by contrast, is localized, limited, and oral. Little traditions can be absorbed into great traditions and become universalized, or there may be a reverse process whereby great traditions may become parochial. Sanskritization can be seen therefore as the process by which a local community immersed in the "little tradition" makes a claim for membership in the "great tradition" by acquiring elements of Sanskrit learning and ritual practice. The whole history of Hinduism can be interpreted as the constant interaction between the Brahmins (as priests and teachers) and the religious customs of other social groups.

The principal ambiguity of Srinivas's theory is whether Sanskritization is a radical or conservative process. One can interpret the social mobility of *jati* as a social "safety valve" in which able and educated but low-status groups move up the hierarchy of caste to claim their place in society, thereby leaving the existing structure in place. Srinivas, however, saw the process as a progressive feature of a society that was becoming more open and democratic. Although Srinivas did not believe that the caste system would simply collapse under the pressure of modernization, he did argue that it would continue to adapt, especially under the impact of electoral politics at the village level. The increased provision of education, urbanization, and industrialization have had an impact on traditional relations between castes, but approximately one-seventh of the Indian population still bear the stigma of untouchability, despite affirmative action programs introduced by the Indian Constitution of November 26, 1949, rejecting untouchability as an infringement of fundamental rights. The Constitution's principal legal architect was Bhimrao Ramji Ambedkar (1891–1956), who, although himself an untouchable, had been invited by the Congress-led government of newly independent India to serve as the nation's first law minister. Ambedkar advocated the expansion of educational provision for the untouchables as an affirmative action program. These legal measures in the Constitution have been continuously reaffirmed in subsequent legislation such as the Untouchability (Offences) Act of 1955. However, given the resilience of untouchability in Indian society, it is evident that sanskritization is not a radical solution for social inequality.

BIBLIOGRAPHY

Betaille, Andre. 1969. *Caste, Class, and Power: Changing Patterns of Stratification in a Tanjore Village.* Berkeley and Los Angeles: University of California Press.

Dumont, Louis. 1998. *Homo Hierarchicus: The Caste System and Its Implications.* Rev. ed. New Delhi: Vedams Books.

Redfield, Robert. 1956. *Peasant Society and Culture: An Anthropological Approach to Civilization.* Chicago: University of Chicago Press.

Searle-Chatterjee, Mary, and Ursula Sharma. 1994. *Contextualising Caste: Post-Dumontian Approaches.* Oxford: Blackwell.

Srinivas, Mysore Narasimhachar. 1952. *Religion and Society among the Coorgs of South India.* Oxford: Clarendon Press.

Bryan S. Turner

SANTA ANNA, ANTONIO LOPEZ DE

SEE *Mexican-American War.*

SANTERÍA

Santería has long been called an Afro-Cuban religion: This designation highlights the origins of many of its elements and early founders but also obscures the fact that Santería has long been a major religion in Cuba practiced by diverse people and has become a global religious movement. Between 1780 and 1850 the Atlantic slave trade transported approximately 1 million enslaved people to Cuba. Nearly 500,000 came from West Africa, where they were in the process of forging the culture now called Yoruba. In Cuba they intermingled with others and forged a popular religion, related to but distinct from the traditional religion of the Yoruba.

WORLDVIEW

The world in which Santería's followers live overflows with diverse kinds of spirits and divinities, and this "theo-diversity" reflects and embodies the natural biodiversity of both tropical West Africa and Cuba. The supreme god, Olodumare, created the natural world in which humans now live as well as a host of *orishas* (divinities, called *orichas* in Cuban Spanish) responsible for its various aspects. Most orishas lived in heaven with Olodumare before descending to the earth. Here they revealed outrageous personalities, led phenomenal lives, and did memorable deeds, and then they ascended into heaven, turned into natural features (e.g., rivers), or disappeared into the earth itself. The stories and rituals for the orishas reveal their specific personalities, complete with foibles, virtues, and preferences for specific foods, objects, metals, and colors. Each orisha rules a specific part of nature and some aspect of human life or society. Most people consider the orishas to be divine representatives or facets of Olodumare.

Elegguá, the mischievous messenger of the other orishas, wears red and black, carries a hooked stick for grabbing things, drinks rum, and smokes cigars. He lives in the forest, the savannah, bars, and crossroads. Always generous, Yemayá is the maternal ocean. A Great Mother figure, she dresses in blue and white, rules motherhood, and eats rams, ducks, pineapples, and watermelons. Obatalá, the father of the orishas, has clean white clothes and a cool, even character. He resides in high places, patiently forms human bodies and other creations, and eats white animals and fruits with white flesh. The sensual Oshún lives in the river and rules childbirth, dance, and erotic love. She loves brass, gold, pumpkins, oranges, and mangoes. Shangó is a fiery king invoked as the fourth ruler of the Yoruba city of Oyo. He wears red and white and makes his presence known through thunder and lightning. In Cuba approximately thirty orishas make up the pantheon, but people acknowledge the existence of an even greater number.

Each human being has a patron orisha and an innate spiritual component thought to reside within the physical head. Chosen by the individual before birth and authorized by Olodumare, this inner head (*orinú*) contains the individual's destiny, character, and special talents, and it reflects the person's essence (*aché*). The individual's aché continues after death and becomes an ancestral spirit (*egun*), whom the living acknowledge and venerate through ritual.

Aché, the inherent essence and power to make things happen, exists in all natural objects and life forms. Certain herbs heal specific illnesses, and healing is their aché. A mixture of herbs sacred to the orishas helps consecrate priests and priestesses, and this is also called *aché*. Particular individuals have special talents that transform circumstances—their aché. Words, spoken or sung, carry aché, and thus the Lucumí language (derived from Yoruba) remains an important part of the religion. Similarly animal blood and certain key parts of sacrificed animals have aché to engage the orishas and the ancestors in human affairs. Santería conceives of the natural world and its aché through polarities: Heaven and earth, white and red, and male and female are just a few of the oppositions that organize the religion's rituals.

RITUALS AND CEREMONIES

Santería's followers mount complex ritual performances to interact with the orishas and other spirits. Through offerings of objects, foods, and animals, people "make *ebó*" to placate and petition the spirits. In divination they use traditional mechanisms (coconut pieces, cowrie shells, or palm nuts) to learn the disposition of the spirits and what sacrifices will create the appropriate balance between humans and the spirits. Most divination results in an *odu*, one of 256 possible divination signs thought to be spirits in their own right; odus contain proverbs, allegories, advice, and myths about the orishas, used to orient people to their circumstances. Specific songs, drum rhythms, and dance steps call the orishas to possess their followers, and the orishas use the human body to dance, sing, salute community members, and give advice. Through rituals and ceremonies, Santería initiates channel the aché of the orishas.

Through various initiations, people intensify their relationships with the orishas. The ceremonial receiving of consecrated necklaces (*elekes*) for the principal orishas creates a link between the individual spiritual head and those orishas; similarly it forges a bond between the individual and the initiators (godparents) and their ritual lineage. The warrior's ceremony gives the new initiate sacred objects (*fundamentos*) through which to engage four important orishas who guide, protect, and invigorate the individual. The initiation of a new priest or priestess unites a large number of participants in a complex seven-day ceremony (*kariocha*) that begins a year-long process of transformation. These rituals forge intense, intimate connections between people and the orishas, and Santería often becomes an encompassing way of life.

Santería's followers have often embraced other religious traditions and sources of divine power. Santería emerged in proximity to the Catholic Church, and the similar spiritual hierarchies made for easy comparisons: Orishas have long been compared with saints. While many scholars imagine Santería simply as a syncretism, a mixture between Yoruba religion and Catholicism, the religion focuses on worshipping the orishas and allows its followers to include or exclude links to Catholicism and other traditions, like the Afro-Cuban religions Palo Monte and Abakuá, which have their primary sources in other African cultures. People often extend the veneration of the ancestors to include spiritism (from France), and its rituals have evolved to include some specifically Cuban forms. Some people borrow ideas and symbols from Freemasonry and astrology.

CONTEMPORARY ISSUES

Cuban immigrants carried Santería beyond the island, and it now enjoys great popularity in the Caribbean, Mexico, Venezuela, Colombia, and the United States, while smaller active communities exist all over Canada and Europe. As in Cuba, the religion unites diverse people, transcending racial and economic differences. Discrimination against the religion has led to strong movements for legal recognition, and in 1993 the U.S.

Supreme Court recognized Santería as a religion and its followers' right to sacrifice animals. Followers of the religion have begun exchanging ideas, images, and ritual practices with both Haitian Vodou and Brazilian Candomblé, each sharing strong historical ties to Yoruba religion. As Santería becomes a global religion spread by traveling elders, published texts, and the Internet, face-to-face relationships remain central to learning the worldview and rituals. Both the orishas and the odus provide flexible conceptual systems with which people can understand and respond to their diverse circumstances.

SEE ALSO *African Diaspora; Animism; Religion; Rituals; Vodou*

BIBLIOGRAPHY

Brown, David H. 2003. *Santería Enthroned: Art, Ritual, and Innovation in an Afro-Cuban Religion.* Chicago: University of Chicago Press.

Clark, Kamari Maxine. 2004. *Mapping Yoruba Networks: Power and Agency in the Making of Transnational Communities.* Durham, NC: Duke University Press.

Mason, Michael Atwood. 2002. *Living Santería: Rituals and Experiences in an Afro-Cuban Religion.* Washington, DC: Smithsonian Institution Press.

Matory, J. Lorand. 2005. *Black Atlantic Religion: Tradition, Transnationalism, and Matriarchy in the Afro-Brazilian Candomblé.* Princeton, NJ: Princeton University Press.

Palmié, Stephan. 2002. *Wizards and Scientists: Explorations in Afro-Cuban Modernity and Tradition.* Durham, NC: Duke University Press.

Michael Atwood Mason

SAPIR-WHORF HYPOTHESIS

SEE *Anthropology; Anthropology, Linguistic.*

SARGENT, THOMAS
1943–

During the 1970s the pioneering work of the American economist Thomas Sargent focused on the implications of rational expectations for econometric research and policymaking. Expectations about the future are a key ingredient of economic decision making, and over the years economic theory has employed different models of expectations formation. The rational expectations hypothesis, initially formulated by John F. Muth Jr. in 1961, swept through macroeconomics during the 1970s. Robert Lucas Jr. and Thomas Sargent, in their 1972 and 1973 articles, led this revolution. The 1981 book by Lucas and Sargent reprints much of the key early literature, while a complete bibliography of Sargent's works can be found in his 2005 interview with George W. Evans and Seppo Honkapohja.

Sargent exposed difficulties in standard procedures and showed how to formulate and conduct valid tests of central macroeconomic relationships under the rational expectations hypothesis. His contributions in this area include studies of the natural rate of unemployment, monetary neutrality of real interest rates, dynamic labor demand, hyperinflation, and tests for the neutrality of money in "classical" models. In the 1980s Sargent developed new econometric methods for estimating rational expectations models, which were presented in his 1980 and 1982 articles with Lars Hansen.

As put forward in articles with Neil Wallace in 1973 and 1975, Sargent also made several key contributions to theoretical macroeconomics, including the saddle-path stability characterization of the rational expectations equilibrium and the policy ineffectiveness proposition for monetary policy. His 1979 graduate textbook integrated these insights into an approach that viewed macroeconomic equilibrium as a dynamic, stochastic process. In later work Sargent continued to extend the rational expectations approach into new areas. Two prominent examples are his 1981 study, with Wallace, of the implications of the government budget constraint for inflation and his 1998 study, with Lars Ljungqvist, of the sources of the European unemployment problem.

Sargent's contributions have not been confined to the development and application of the rational expectations paradigm. The standard formulation of rational expectations makes the strong assumption that economic agents have so much information that their forecast errors are just random noise. Sargent's interest in the theoretical foundations of rationality led him in the 1980s to join a line of research called *learning theory*. In this approach, agents have an imperfect understanding of the economy and try to improve their knowledge over time. Albert Marcet and Sargent's 1989 article showed, in a general setting, that econometric learning could converge to rational expectations equilibrium when certain conditions are satisfied. Sargent's 1999 book called attention to the possibility of "escape routes," that is, occasional large deviations from an equilibrium, and led to a surge of interest in persistent learning dynamics. The 1993 book by Sargent and 2001 book by George Evans and Seppo Honkapohja provide, respectively, an overview and a full treatise on learning and expectations formation in macroeconomics. Closely related to the research on learning are issues of robustness and model uncertainty, to which Sargent has made key contributions, including his book with Hansen in 2003 and with Hansen and Thomas Tallarini in 1999.

In addition to the great intellectual depth and wide range of the contributions outlined above, Sargent has also done important research in economic history. Examples are his 1985 study on episodes of moderate and rapid inflations and his 2002 study, with François Velde, on monetary standards. Sargent discusses the different facets of his research in a 2005 interview with Evans and Honkapohja.

BIBLIOGRAPHY

Evans, George W., and Seppo Honkapohja. 2005. An Interview with Thomas J. Sargent. *Macroeconomic Dynamics* 9 (4): 561–583.

Lucas, Robert E., Jr., and Thomas J. Sargent, eds. 1981. *Rational Expectations and Econometric Practice.* Minneapolis: University of Minnesota Press.

George W. Evans
Seppo Honkapohja

SARTORI, GIOVANNI

SEE *Sociology, Political.*

SARTRE, JEAN-PAUL
1905–1980

Jean-Paul Sartre was born in Paris on June 13, 1905, and died there on April 15, 1980. He studied philosophy at the École Normale Supérieure, achieving his doctorate in 1929, and then taught high school until the publication of his first novel, *Nausea*, in 1938. Sartre was a prisoner of war in World War II from 1940 to 1941, after which he founded a group of resistance intellectuals, *socialism et liberté*, which he disbanded by the time of the 1943 publication of his most famous philosophical work, *Being and Nothingness*. Sartre became a celebrity at the end of the war, which enabled him to be a public intellectual on the world stage for a variety of causes that included fighting against anti-Semitism, supporting Third World liberation and workers' struggles, protesting against the Vietnam War, and joining strikers in the student movement of the late 1960s. Some of Sartre's causes, such as his support of the Algerian struggle for independence, led to assassination attempts on his life. Other causes, such as his support of communism without ever joining the Communist Party, led to attacks on him from extreme liberal and conservative critics. Sartre received many awards, two of

which he refused—the French Legion of Honor in 1945 and the Nobel Prize in 1964. He was co-founder of the influential magazine *Les temps moderne* in 1945.

Although he wished to achieve greatness as a novelist and playwright, Sartre's legacy is primarily as a philosopher, where he contributed to the study of freedom and the challenges it poses for understanding human existence. His writings from the 1930s until the late 1940s gave him a leading and permanent place in existentialism and phenomenology. Phenomenology is the study of things as understood as objects of consciousness. Sartre's motto "Existence precedes essence," argued for in *Being and Nothingness*, became a major theme of existential thought and a rallying cry against essentialism in the study of human beings. Human beings create themselves through living a biography, which is the only real self that will emerge at each person's death. For a living human, choice is not only a constant possibility but is a precondition for itself. Even so-called choosing not to choose is a choice, and the act of choosing must in principle have preceded it. Sartre's most famous play from this period, *No Exit* (1944), explored these themes in a situation, people encountering other people, with literally no material alternative to the "hell" of being forced together.

Many of Sartre's writings in the late 1940s into the mid-1950s addressed existential themes in concrete situations. In *Anti-Semite and Jew*, he examined how the hating of Jews played a role in the construction of Jewish identity and the anti-Semite's. This question of how humans create values that in turn create "us" was taken up in a unique genre (philosophical biography), in his demand for the writer to be politically "engaged," and in his explorations of Marxism, reflected in works such as *Baudelaire* (1947), *What Is Literature?* (1947), and *Critique of Dialectical Reason* (1960). The *Critique of Dialectical Reason* explored the problem of agency in history and in developing existential Marxism, which is dialectical thought without determinism or the crushing of freedom.

Sartre, in effect, said good-bye to literature in *The Words* (1964), in which his hatred for his own class, the bourgeoisie (capitalist class), culminated in his rejection of literature as a bourgeois ideal in favor of devoting the rest of his life to political engagement. Although he continued to protest and sign declarations condemning human rights violations as long as his health permitted, this last period of Sartre's life was marked by his conducting a sustained, multi-volume study of the life of the nineteenth century French novelist Gustave Flaubert, *The Family Idiot* (1971–1972), which he did not write for an audience but for himself. As with his works of philosophical biography, the role of bad faith in the formation of the self is illustrated in minute detail throughout. The text, like many of Sartre's projects, was not completed, which is appropriate for a philosopher whose life was a struggle against ever being pinned down and standing still.

SEE ALSO *Anti-Semitism; Bourgeoisie; Culture, Low and High; Epistemology; Existentialism; Human Rights; Jews; Literature; Marxism; Philosophy; Resistance; World War II*

BIBLIOGRAPHY

Contat, Michel, and Michel Rybalka, eds. 1973. *The Writings of Jean-Paul Sartre.* Evanston, IL: Northwestern University Press.

Contat, Michel, Yvan Cloutier, Michel Rybalka, and Laura Piccioni, eds. 1993. *Sartre: Bibliography, 1980–1992.* Bowling Green, OH: Philosophy Documentation Center.

Sartre, Jean-Paul. [1938] 1965. *La nausée.* Trans. Robert Baldick. Harmondsworth, U.K.: Penguin.

Sartre, Jean-Paul. [1943] 1948. *L'être et le néant; essai d'ontologie phénomologique.* Trans. Hazel E. Barnes. New York: Philosophical Library.

Sartre, Jean-Paul. [1960] 1976. *Critique de la raison dialectique, précédé de Question de méthode,* tome 1, *Théorie des ensembles pratique.* Trans. Alan Sheridan-Smith. London: New Left Books.

Sartre, Jean-Paul. 1972. *L'idiot de la famille: Gustave Flaubert de 1821–1857,* tome 1-3 [The Family Idiot]. Trans. Carol Cosman. 5 vols. Chicago: University of Chicago Press.

Sartre, Jean-Paul. [1985] 1991. *Critique de la raison dialectique,* tome 2, *L'intelligibilité de l'histoire.* Trans. Quintin Hoare. London: Verso.

Lewis R. Gordon

SAT TEST, THE

SEE *Standardized Tests.*

SATANISM

SEE *Magic; Taboos.*

SATIATION

The *Oxford English Dictionary* offers one definition of *satiation* to be the "point at which satisfaction of a need or familiarity with a stimulus reduces or ends an organism's responsiveness or motivation" and thereby encompasses, in principle, the satiety of both needs and desires.

Neoclassical economics, however fuzzily its boundaries are conceived, sits ill at ease with the distinction between needs and desires. By conceiving of a generality in which the particularity of commodities is submerged in an abstract finite or infinite list, or simply postulated as a coordinate-free, infinite-dimensional space endowed with precisely specified mathematical structure, it obliterates the nineteenth-century distinction between use and exchange values. (The loci classici in the case of a finite list of commodities are Samuelson 1947; Debreu 1959; and McKenzie 2002. For an infinite-dimensional space of commodities, see the reference to Gérard Debreu's 1952 paper on *Valuation equilibrium and Pareto optimum* in Debreu 1959 and relevant references in Khan 2008. The source for the use- and exchange-value is Marx 1967, who in turn takes it from chapter 4, book 1 of Smith 1776.) Once food, labor, money, and more popularly current reifications such as fidelity, trust, racial or ethnic characteristics, reputation, and the like are all seen under the same analytical rubric (in addition to Marx 1867, chap. 1, see Hill 1967 for the commodification of labor and Khan 1993 and 2002 for commodification more generally), "wants that spring from the stomach as opposed to those from fancy, appetites of the mind as opposed to hungers of the body" (Marx [1867] 1967, p. 43) are subjected to the same theoretical machinery and tamed by the same indiscriminate calculus, one blind to individual particularities of any commodity. It thus stands to reason that the subject sits ill at ease with the concept of satiation.

Thus *perfect competition*, as formalized in what is referred to as "general equilibrium theory," the existence theorem, the two fundamental theorems of welfare economics, and through its adoption of the monotonicity assumption on preferences, the Debreu-Scarf theorem, all assume individual preferences to be non-satiated and the consumption set on which these preferences are defined to be unbounded from above (see Debreu 1959 and McKenzie 2002 for an explication of these results). To be sure, there is a literature in general equilibrium theory that addresses the assumption of satiation and thereby problems arising from compact consumption sets, but it surely constitutes a peripheral rather than a central stream (see McFadden 1969 and the literature that follows him in Winter 1969; Rader 1980; John and Ryder 1985; Weymark 1985; Mas-Colell 1992. I am supposing Debreu's [1986] verbal proof of the first fundamental theorem to be also relevant here as well as the resurgence of the subject as exemplified in Martins-da-Rocha and Monteiro 2007 and their references.)

At the founding moment of the theory of optimal growth, Frank Ramsey did assume a "bliss point" (a point of *satiation* in the terms of this entry) for his representative agent (see Ramsey 1928 and its finite commodity generalization in Samuelson and Solow 1965). However, by viewing this assumption as a response to an analytical difficulty rather than as a descriptive point of substance to be incorporated into the theory, subsequent work took two alternative routes. In a literature exemplified by Tjalling Charles Koopmans (1965), David Gale (1967), and William A. Brock (1970), the objective function was rendered well-defined by considering deviations from a golden-rule stock, a stock that ensures the highest constant sustainable rate of consumption and thereby ensuring the convergence of the relevant integral of the utility stream. Alternatively, as in Koopmans (1967) and Nancy L. Stokey and Robert E. Lucas Jr. (1989), the undiscounted framework is done away with altogether as something irrelevant to a regimen in which methodological individualism is rather aggressively prescribed to counter the possibility of any sort of governmental paternalism.

There is an irony in that Robinson Crusoe remains a hallowed figure for neoclassical economics even though his needs are limited (obviously so) and his desires have no ready outlet. (In addition to playing a role in Edgeworth 1881, Koopmans's 1957 exposition of general equilibrium theory and the John von Neumann and Oskar Morgenstern 1953 criticism of this theory are based on Robinson Crusoe.) However, moving away from the creations of Daniel Defoe, Paul A. Samuelson, and Frank P. Ramsey, one ought perhaps not forget that the skeptical David Hume was crystal clear about the dampening effect of satiation on commerce and on the progress commerce was to bring in its wake. In his influential essay "Of Refinements in the Arts," he writes:

> Riches are valuable at all times, and to all men; because they always purchase pleasures, such as men are accustomed to, and desire.… In a nation where there is no demand for such superfluities, men sink into indolence, lose all enjoyment of life, and are useless to the public, which cannot maintain or support its fleets and armies, from the industry of such slothful members.… Luxury, when excessive, is the source of many ills; but is in general preferable to sloth and idleness, which would commonly succeed in its place, and are more hurtful both to private persons and the public. (Hume [1742/1752] 1985, pp. 276, 272, 280)

The problem of scarcity of labor as a damper to the growth of colonial (plantation) economies brought about by satiation and self-sufficiency of native labor, and its possible cure in terms of a head tax levied in money, was well understood by colonial governments of all stripes in both the nineteenth and the twentieth centuries (see, for example, Mamdani 1976, chaps. 2 and 3), but even a half-adequate exploration of these theoretical and practical issues goes well beyond the ambit of this brief entry.

SEE ALSO *Arrow-Debreu Model; Competition, Perfect; Economics, Neoclassical; Optimal Growth; Samuelson, Paul A.; Wants; Welfare Economics*

BIBLIOGRAPHY

Brock, William A. 1970. On Existence of Weakly Maximal Programmes in a Multi-Sector Economy. *Review of Economic Studies* 37 (2): 275–280.

Debreu, Gérard. 1959. *The Theory of Value.* New York: Wiley.

Debreu, Gérard. 1986. Theoretic Models: Mathematical Form and Economic Content. *Econometrica* 54 (6): 1259–1270.

Debreu, Gérard, and Herbert E. Scarf. 1963. A Limit Theorem on the Core of an Economy. *International Economic Review* 4 (3): 235–246.

Edgeworth, F. Y. 1881. *Mathematical Psychics.* London: Kegan-Paul.

Gale, David. 1967. On Optimal Development in a Multi-Sector Economy. *Review of Economic Studies* 34 (1): 1–18.

Hill, Christopher. 1967. Pottage for Freeborn Englishmen: Attitudes to Wage Labour in the Sixteenth and Seventeenth Centuries. In *Socialism, Capitalism, and Economic Growth: Essays Presented to Maurice Dobb*, ed. C. H. Feinstein, 338–350. Cambridge, U.K.: Cambridge University Press.

Hume, David. [1742/1752] 1985. *Essays: Moral, Political, and Literary*, ed. Eugene F. Miller. Indianapolis, IN: Liberty Fund.

John, Reinhard, and Harl E. Ryder. 1985. On the Second Optimality Theorem of Welfare Economics. *Journal of Economic Theory* 36 (1): 176–185.

Khan, M. Ali. 1993. On Education as a Commodity. *Pakistan Development Review* 32: 541–579.

Khan, M. Ali. 2002. On Trust as a Commodity and the Grammar of Trust. *Journal of Banking and Finance* 26 (9): 1719–1766.

Khan, M. Ali. 2008. Perfect Competition. In *The New Palgrave Dictionary of Economics*, 2nd ed., ed. Steven N. Durlauf, Lawrence E. Blume, and E. Durlauf. London: Macmillan.

Koopmans, Tjalling Charles 1957. *Three Essays on the State of Economic Science.* New York: McGraw-Hill.

Koopmans, Tjalling Charles. 1965. On the Concept of Optimal Economic Growth. *Pontificiae Academiae Scientiarum Scripta Varia* 28 (1): 225–300.

Koopmans, Tjalling Charles. 1967. Objectives, Constraints, and Outcomes in Optimal Growth Models. *Econometrica* 35 (1): 1–15.

Mamdani, Mahmood. 1976. *Politics and Class Formation in Uganda.* New York: Monthly Review.

Martins-da-Rocha, Felipe V., and Paulo K. Monteiro. 2007. Unbounded Exchange Economies with Satiation: How Far Can We Go? Mimeo. Rio de Janeiro: FGV.

Marx, Karl. [1867] 1967. *The Process of Capitalist Production.* Vol. 1 of *Capital: A Critique of Political Economy*, ed. Frederick Engels, trans. S. Moore and E. Aveling. New York: International Publishers.

Mas-Colell, Andreu. 1992. Equilibrium Theory with Possibly Satiated Preferences. In *Equilibrium and Dynamics: Essays in*

Honour of David Gale, ed. Mukul Majumdar, 201–213. New York: St. Martin's.

McFadden, Daniel. 1969. A Simple Remark on the Second Best Pareto Optimality of Market Equilibria. *Journal of Economic Theory* 1 (1): 26–38.

McKenzie, Lionel W. 2002. *Classical General Equilibrium Theory.* Cambridge, MA: MIT Press.

Rader, Trout. 1980. The Second Theorem of Welfare Economics When Utilities Are Interdependent. *Journal of Economic Theory* 23 (3): 420–424.

Ramsey, Frank P. 1928. A Mathematical Theory of Savings. *Economic Journal* 38 (152): 543–559.

Samuelson, Paul A. 1947. *Foundations of Economic Analysis.* Cambridge, MA: Harvard University Press.

Samuelson, Paul A., and Robert M. Solow. 1956. A Complete Capital Model Involving Heterogeneous Capital Goods. *Quarterly Journal of Economics* 70 (4): 537–562.

Smith, Adam. [1776] 1981. *An Enquiry into the Nature and Causes of the Wealth of Nations*, ed. R. H. Campbell and A. S. Skinner. Indianapolis, IN: Liberty Fund.

Stokey, Nancy L., and Robert E. Lucas Jr. 1989. *Recursive Methods in Economic Dynamics.* Cambridge, MA: Harvard University Press.

Von Neumann, John, and Oskar Morgenstern. 1953. *Theory of Games and Economic Behavior.* 3rd ed. Princeton, NJ: Princeton University Press.

Winter, Sidney G., Jr. 1969. A Simple Remark on the Second Optimality Theorem of Welfare Economics. *Journal of Economic Theory* 1 (1): 99–103.

Weymark, John A. 1985. Remarks on the First Welfare Theorem with Nonordered Preferences. *Journal of Economic Theory* 36 (1): 156–159.

M. Ali Khan

SATIRE

The word *satire* is often thought to be derived from the Latin word *satura*, originally meaning the vessel used for carrying harvest produce. It came to mean a mixture, and then a mixed form of entertainment that people might have at harvest time, consisting of songs, jokes, and other kinds of humor. In its broadest sense, then, satire is a mixed kind of humorous entertainment related to comedy that focuses on people and their behavior.

In a more particular sense, satire is a literary form, traced back to the Romans and in particular to the works of Juvenal (c. 50/60–127 CE) and Horace (65–8 BCE), who both wrote about their own times, though in different tones. Horace is characterized as more urbane and witty, Juvenal as more savage and critical. For these writers, a satire was a particular sort of poem with a strict form and specific content. It was this definition that pervaded

English literature in the work of John Donne (1572–1631), John Dryden (1631–1700), Alexander Pope (1688–1744), and Samuel Johnson (1709–1784) in the seventeenth and eighteenth centuries.

From the Renaissance onward, the works of Horace and Juvenal, together with works by other great Greek and Roman writers, including Homer (ninth to eighth century BCE), Virgil (70–19 BCE), and Ovid (43 BCE–c. 17 CE), were the basis of an educated person's reading. The one hundred years from the Restoration in 1660 constituted the great age of satire in English literature, known as the Augustan Age, referring to the period in ancient Rome when Augustus Caesar (63 BCE–14 CE) was the first emperor. English writers produced their own translations or versions of such classical works. For example, the "Epistle to Arbuthnot" (1735) is Alexander Pope's prologue to his own imitation of Horace's satires, and Dr. Johnson based his *London* (1738) and *The Vanity of Human Wishes* (1749) on Juvenal's *Satires* 3 and 10.

The eighteenth century, however, also saw the rise of prose satire, especially in the works of Jonathan Swift (1667–1745), whose *Gulliver's Travels* (1726) and *A Modest Proposal for Preventing the Children of Ireland from Being a Burden to Their Parents or Country* (1729) have influenced most satirical writers since.

One significant reason for the pervasiveness and popularity of satire in England during the eighteenth century may have been people's reactions to the disorder and division that they experienced during the civil war of the 1640s. Satire became an effective method of drawing attention to the ways in which human behavior falls short of its ideal and of trying to correct that within an accepted political and social framework. The job of the satirist, therefore, became, as Jonathan Swift put it, "to cure the vices of mankind." It is this moral purpose that underlies great satirical achievements.

Along with this moral purpose, features that distinguish satire from other kinds of writing are its flexibility of tone and its consistent use of wit and irony. The most consistent target for satire in any period is hypocrisy, and the predominant method is irony, where the reader always has to be alert to the conflict between the literal and actual meanings of what is being said. Hence, although the golden age is perhaps the greatest age of satire in English and although writing is the dominant form of satire, nevertheless satire appears in many different periods and in many different forms: writing, painting, and more recently television and film.

It is often the case that effective satire can be ephemeral. Particular examples of hypocrisy come and go quickly, and so references can soon become dated as their occasion slips from memory. Obvious examples may be found in the contemporary television series *South Park* or *The Simpsons* or in political caricatures or cartoons.

There is also a sense in which satire is culture bound. Because it depends on wit and irony, it is neither accessible nor thriving in societies and groups where fundamentalism or literalism is the prevailing ethos. Throughout history there have been those who can only read literally and who have therefore missed the whole thrust of a satirical work. This was true of some readers of Swift's *A Modest Proposal*, just as it has been true of some viewers of the satirical film *Borat: Cultural Learnings of America for Make Benefit Glorious Nation of Kazakhstan* (2006).

Peter Buckroyd

SATISFACTION, RELATIONSHIP

SEE *Relationship Satisfaction.*

SATISFICING BEHAVIOR

Herbert Simon coined the term *satisficing behavior* to describe human choice among alternative behaviors recognizing bounded rationality. The information-processing capacity of the human brain cannot examine all possible alternatives and their consequences for human satisfaction. Thus, Simon argued that satisficing was the dominant process, with maximizing playing a lesser role. Consumers, for example, might set an aspiration level and then begin to examine alternative purchases. When the aspiration level is reached, the person is satisfied, the search stops, and the purchase is made. Simon also applied his notion to games: "The players, instead of seeking for a 'best' move, need only to look for a 'good' move" (Simon 1955, p. 108). The aspiration level is conceived of as being learned in a series of choices. If the aspiration level is set too low, too many alternatives qualify, and perhaps the person is bored. If set too high, no alternatives may qualify, and the level is lowered. This makes preferences endogenous to ongoing experience and feedback rather than fixed as is often assumed in neoclassical economics. The new conception has not become standard among economists, but its use is growing.

Search among alternatives is necessarily selective and simplified by applying rules of thumb (heuristics) whether by a consumer or a business considering the mix of products to produce and methods of production. The interruption of routine is the occasion for examining behavior and goals. The learning involved in the examination of

available means may cause goals (ends in view) to be modified. The problem agenda and problem representation are not given in advance but are worked out in the decision process affected by context and events affecting saliency of particular alternatives. This is consistent with a pragmatic view seeing means and ends as interdependent. "If there are goals, they do not so much guide the search as emerge from it" (Simon 1991, p. 367). Simon referred to this process as procedural rationality.

Humans are quite able to rationalize their current behavior. They can find a reason for what they are doing even if it was not in their consciousness before the behavior. The adjustment of aspiration level to the outcome of present behavior is both psychologically healthy and a possible source of disaster as habits can persist long after they are dysfunctional.

Some economists object to the concept of endogenous and evolving preferences because a moving target provides no deterministic standard for defining rationality. It is not easy to distinguish irrationality from learning. A business manager (or voter) may focus on one sub-problem rather than another over time. Saliency is affected by events, framing, context, and emotion. For example, environmental consciousness may result in management finding that former wastes can actually be recycled into profitable products. This would not happen if rationality were unbounded and all profitable alternatives were always being considered. Likewise, a consumer would not be influenced by product placement in the store or by advertising.

Consumers and producers do not have time to examine all possibilities. They collapse their experience into rules of thumb, and new observations cue behavior when the new data is put into a category to which a particular behavior is attached. The human brain can take in data and jump unconsciously to a conclusion and behavior. The fact that the reinforcement of behavior happens unconsciously does not mean that experience is irrelevant. The mind does not waste experience. The ability of the mind to fill in missing data is a strength and weakness. The brain takes in necessarily limited and uncertain data and fills in the rest by itself. This saves us from helpless indecision and at the same time exposes us to disaster when more observation would have led to a different behavior, perhaps affecting our very survival. In the face of very complex computational problems that challenge the capacity of the brain, this jumping to action may be better for profitability and survival than making a mistaken calculation. More data and more calculation are not necessarily better. When the payoff to one firm depends on the choices of other firms and the future is uncertain, the world may be much more predictable if most firms are using the same rules of thumb than if all are calculating their best guesses.

Satisficing is consistent with many observed behaviors, such as simple markup pricing by business (requires less data than profit maximization), lexicographic preferences and choice (requires less data and calculation than utility maximization), and modular budgets. There is experimental evidence that many choices are intransitive. A modular budget allocating one's income initially to categories of expenditures produces what appears to an outsider as intransitive choices. Choices of goods then are made within these accounts without further reexamination of all feasible alternatives.

Consumers and businesses have multiple objectives, and making them commensurable would take considerable mental energy and calculation. The same could be said for attaching subjective probabilities to all outcomes. It is simpler to regard outcomes simply as likely or unlikely (outcomes the consumer or manager would be surprised by).

Bounded rationality implies decision costs. There are necessary tradeoffs between decision costs and better decisions. It is tempting then to suggest a calculated optimal search rule and conclusion of what is good enough. But such a rule has the same problem as that of the brain's limitations.

Satisficing, which focuses attention on how managers and consumers actually make decisions, has implications for research. Scholars must get out of their armchairs to conduct field surveys; such research will always be incomplete and messy, but Simon argued that it would still be better than making assumptions. After surveying the literature, John Conlisk concludes in his 1996 article "Why Bounded Rationality?" that "psychology and economics provide wide-ranging evidence that bounded rationality is important" (p. 692). He argues that "models of bounded rationality adhere to a fundamental tenet of economics, respect for scarcity. Human cognition, as a scarce resource, should be treated as such" (p. 692). Satisficing is consistent with both observations. The point is not that optimization be wholly replaced with satisficing, but that human behavior will, as Conlisk notes, "vary by context, depending on such conditions as deliberation cost, complexity, incentives, experience, and market discipline" (p. 692).

SEE ALSO *Maximization; Minimization; Optimizing Behavior; Simon, Herbert A.*

BIBLIOGRAPHY

Baumol, William J. 2004. On Rational Satisficing. In *Models of a Man: Essays in Memory of Herbert A. Simon*, eds. Mie Augier and James G. March, 57–66. Cambridge, MA: MIT Press.

Conlisk, John. 1996. Why Bounded Rationality? *Journal of Economic Literature* 34 (2): 669–700.

Gigerenzer, Gerd, and Reinhard Selten, eds. 2001. Bounded Rationality: The Adaptive Toolbox. Cambridge, MA: MIT Press.

Simon, Herbert A. 1955. A Behavioral Model of Rational Choice. *Quarterly Journal of Economics* 69: 99–118.

Simon, Herbert A. 1991. *Models of My Life*. New York: Basic Books.

A. Allan Schmid

SAUVY, ALFRED

SEE *Third World.*

SAVING RATE

The ability of a society to defer consumption from the present to the future provides resources for capital accumulation, which in turn creates a basis for increasing labor productivity and improving living standards. As such, positive national saving may beneficially contribute to a country's economic development, although many other factors—such as the state of domestic demand and the effectiveness of financial intermediation—are also involved in influencing the extent to which this potential may be realized. (See the collection of papers in Setterfield 2002 on demand-led growth.)

The total saving undertaken by a country has three components:

a	Domestic private saving	$Y - T - C$	Income earned by households (Y), net of taxes they pay to the government (T), minus what they spend on goods and services (C)
b	Public saving	$T - G$	Any excess in the government's tax revenues (T) over its expenditures (G)
c	International saving	$X - M$	Any excess in the value of the country's exports (X) over the value of its imports (M), which implies an accumulation of wealth abroad

Items (a) and (b) added together are known as "national saving." To facilitate comparisons across countries and over time, saving levels are usually divided by disposable income (for domestic private saving) or national income (for public and national saving), to compute saving rates:

Domestic private saving rate: $(Y - T - C)/(Y - T) \times 100$;

Public saving rate: $(T - G)/Y \times 100$;

National saving rate: $[(Y - T - C) + (T - G)]/Y \times 100$.

Changes in public saving can be expected to change private saving also because they affect expected after-tax income streams—the basis on which households make saving decisions. As a notable example, public pension programs such as U.S. Social Security generally reduce private saving, because people have less burden to accumulate their own savings to cover consumption in retirement. However, the extent to which private and public saving substitute for each other is open to debate. A contested conjecture is the idea of "Ricardian equivalence," which holds that reductions in public saving are offset in full by increased private saving, because households will set aside resources to pay for the greater tax burden they know they will eventually face (Barro 1974). However, the empirical evidence on Ricardian equivalence is fairly mixed.

To see how a country's saving relates to its investment, it is helpful to look at the following re-expression of the national-income accounting identity:

$$I = (Y - T - C) + (T - G) - (X - M)$$

This expression shows that funds for investment (I) can come from domestic private saving, public saving, and/or international *dis*saving. The last term corresponds to the country's trade balance. Because a country that has a trade deficit (X < M) must realize a capital inflow to cover it, the inflow supplements national saving as a source of finance for domestic investment. But if its exports exceed its imports, the surplus entails a capital outflow, reducing financing available for domestic investment in favor of wealth accumulation abroad. This "open-economy" aspect of the saving/investment link has been important for the United States in recent years: The level

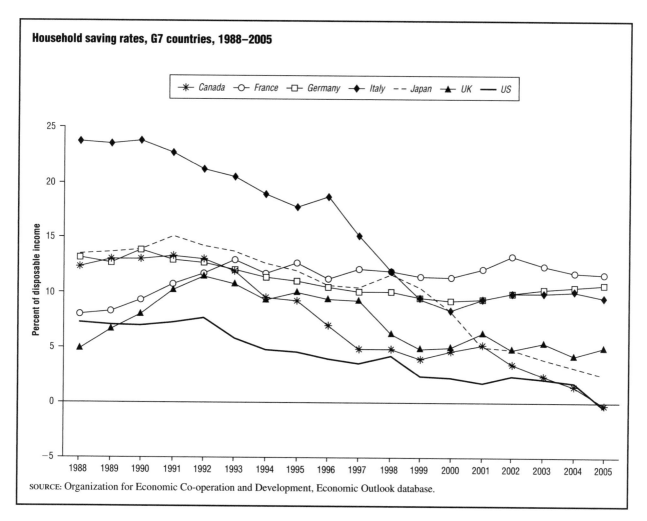

Household saving rates, G7 countries, 1988–2005

SOURCE: Organization for Economic Co-operation and Development, Economic Outlook database.

Figure 1

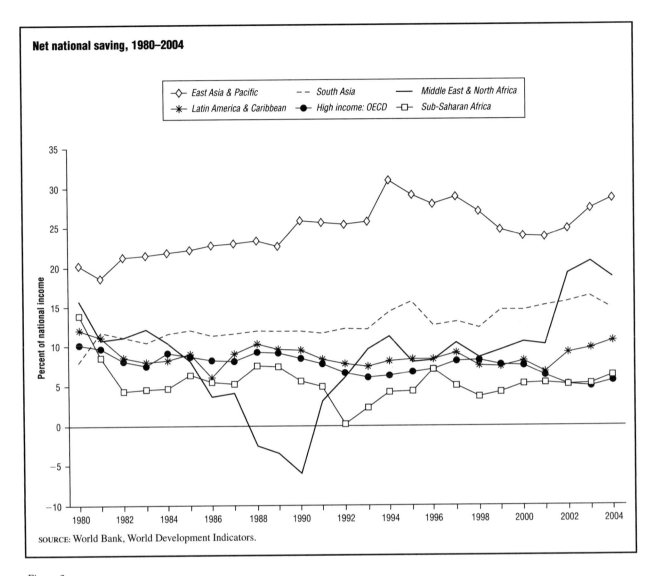

Net national saving, 1980–2004

Legend: East Asia & Pacific; South Asia; Middle East & North Africa; Latin America & Caribbean; High income: OECD; Sub-Saharan Africa

SOURCE: World Bank, World Development Indicators.

Figure 2

of domestic investment has remained healthy despite low national saving due to the willingness of other countries to supply capital to the United States.

It is important to note that saving is a *flow* concept; that is, it measures the excess of income over spending in a given year, which adds to the country's *stock* of wealth. Thus, a decline in household saving does not necessarily imply lower ability to finance consumption in the future—just a slower pace of accumulation of resources toward that end. A related implication is that household wealth can rise, even if saving falls, as long as asset prices are rising. This has probably contributed to the decline in household saving in advanced-industrial countries in recent years (figure 1): Because housing and stock markets have been strong, increases in asset prices have enabled households to scale their saving back while still accumulating wealth.

There are substantial, persistent differences across countries in their saving rates. As shown in figure 2, national saving rates in East Asia and the Pacific tend to be very high by international standards, ranging between 20 and 30 percent in the past twenty-five years. In contrast, saving rates in high-income countries of the Organization for Economic Cooperation and Development (OECD) have drifted down from about 10 percent in 1980 to 5 to 7 percent in the mid-2000s. In Latin America and the Caribbean, saving rates tend to track those of the high-income OECD countries, whereas in South Asia they are higher (10–15%). In sub-Saharan Africa and especially the Middle East and North Africa, national saving rates fluctuate appreciably from year to year, in good part because fluctuating prices of commodity exports impart volatility to public saving.

While the causes of these cross-country differences are not well-understood, several factors are probably involved. First, the "life-cycle" theory of saving (Ando and Modigliani 1957) suggests an important role of demographic variables. The basic proposition of the life-cycle view is that people borrow against future income when young, save in their high-earning middle-age years, and spend down their assets in retirement. Thus, for example, population aging in the advanced-industrial countries might be expected to drive down private saving rates (OECD 1998). Second, periods of rapid economic growth tend to be strongly associated with increased saving, perhaps because consumption takes a while to catch up to permanently higher incomes (Carroll and Weil 1994). Third, the introduction of government social-insurance programs (e.g., unemployment, welfare, disability) alleviates people's need to "save for a rainy day," which may edge national saving down. Fourth, the development of credit markets also reduces precautionary motives to save, as borrowing can be used instead of dissaving to cover consumption needs (Japelli and Pagano 1989). Finally, there are also differences across cultures in the priority placed on saving for the future versus living for today, although it is difficult to disentangle effects of culture on saving from those of other variables.

A growing body of research examines how saving rates vary with household characteristics, using survey data (see Browning and Lusardi 1996 for a valuable review). Many studies find that saving tends to be higher among middle-aged households, *ceteris paribus*, consistent with the life-cycle view. Yet there are also lots of findings that are hard to reconcile with life-cycle theory—for example, that good-sized fractions of households hardly save at all, that older households tend to dissave "too slowly" relative to their life expectancies, and that very rich households save entirely too much for life-cycle motives to be the whole story. Thus, researchers have explored numerous extensions to the life-cycle model to see whether its fit to the data can be improved. These extensions include the possibility that liquidity constraints or asset-limits for social-insurance programs explain low saving among low-income households (Zeldes 1989; Hubbard, Skinner and Zeldes 1995); that uncertainty about time of death and/or bequest motives lie behind slow dissaving in old age (Davies 1981; Abel 1985); and that the very wealthy accumulate wealth for wealth's sake, rather than for the future consumption it assures (Carroll 2000). Nonetheless, given uncertainties about whether intertemporal optimization is a good description of consumption and saving behavior, economic research is also branching out to explore "behavioral" views of household saving, in which households use heuristics to make informationally complex decisions and/or struggle with problems of self-control, in which they know they should be saving for the future but are unable to start doing so today (Sheffrin and Thaler 1988 and Laibson 1997). Behavioral approaches may be especially valuable for investigating whether households save adequately for retirement (Aaron 1999)—which in turn is important for evaluating proposals to shift responsibility for retirement saving back to the private domain.

BIBLIOGRAPHY

Aaron, Henry, ed. 1999. *Behavioral Dimensions of Retirement Economics.* Washington, DC: Brookings Institution Press and Russell Sage Foundation.

Abel, Andrew. 1985. Precautionary Saving and Accidental Bequests. *American Economic Review* 75 (4): 777–791.

Ando, Albert, and Franco Modigliani. 1957. Tests of the Life Cycle Hypothesis of Saving: Comments and Suggestions. *Oxford Institute of Statistics Bulletin* 19: 99–124.

Barro, Robert. 1974. Are Government Bonds Net Wealth? *Journal of Political Economy* 82 (6): 1095–1117.

Browning, Martin, and Annamaria Lusardi. 1996. Household Saving: Micro Theories and Micro Facts. *Journal of Economic Literature* 34 (4): 1797–1855.

Carroll, Christopher. 2000. Why Do the Rich Save So Much? In *Does Atlas Shrug?: The Economic Consequences of Taxing the Rich*, ed. Joel Slemrod, 157–184. New York: Russell Sage Foundation and Harvard University Press.

Carroll, Christopher, and David Weil. 1994. Saving and Growth: A Reinterpretation. *Carnegie-Rochester Conference Series on Public Policy* 40: 133–192.

Case, Karl, John Quigley, and Robert Shiller. 2001. Comparing Wealth Effects: The Stock Market Versus the Housing Market. National Bureau of Economic Research, Working Paper No. 1335.

Davies, James. 1981. Uncertain Lifetime, Consumption, and Dissaving in Retirement. *Journal of Political Economy* 89 (3): 561–577.

Hubbard, R. Glenn, Jonathan Skinner, and Stephen Zeldes. 1995. Precautionary Saving and Social Insurance. *Journal of Political Economy* 103 (2): 360–399.

Jappelli, Tullio, and Marco Pagano. 1989. Consumption and Capital Market Imperfections: An International Comparison. *American Economic Review* 79 (5): 1088–1105.

Kuehlwein, Michael. 1993. Life-Cycle and Altruistic Theories of Saving with Lifetime Uncertainty. *Review of Economics and Statistics* 75 (1): 38–47.

Laibson, David. 1997. Golden Eggs and Hyperbolic Discounting. *Quarterly Journal of Economics* 112 (2): 443–477.

Organization for Economic Cooperation and Development. 1998. *Maintaining Prosperity in an Ageing Society.* Paris: Author.

Setterfield, Mark, ed. 2002. *The Economics of Demand-Led Growth: Challenging the Supply-Side Vision of the Long Run.* Northampton, MA: Edward Elgar.

Sheffrin, Hershel, and Richard Thaler. 1988. The Behavioral Life-Cycle Hypothesis. *Economic Inquiry* 26: 609–643.

Zeldes, Stephen. 1989. Consumption and Liquidity Constraints: An Empirical Investigation. *Journal of Political Economy* 97 (2): 305–346.

Martha A. Starr

SAY, JEAN-BAPTISTE

SEE *Say's Law.*

SAY'S LAW

The French economist Jean-Baptiste Say, in his *A Treatise on Political Economy* (1803), developed a theory of market activity that sited the source of the demand for products not on the quantity of money possessed by individuals but rather on the value of the quantity of products that those individuals supplied. People receive money for producing goods with the purpose of immediately purchasing goods of an equivalent value: "A product is no sooner created, than it, from that instant, affords a market for other products to the full extent of its own value" (Say 1971, p. 134). Money itself has no bearing on the relationship between the production of goods and the quantity of goods that they could fetch. It was in this sense that one might infer from Say's analysis that "supply creates its own demand." Changes in production by one individual thereby affect production in many markets: "The success of one branch of commerce supplies more ample means of purchase, and consequently opens a market for the products of all the other branches; on the other hand, the stagnation of one channel of manufacture, or of commerce, is felt in all the rest" (Say 1971, p. 137).

SAY'S ECONOMICS

Say's views on public policies emanated directly from his understanding of the mechanism by which an economy thrived and grew. The state should not put into effect any policy that would prevent producers from keeping their profits or for income to be diverted to unproductive consumption rather than savings. Anything that promoted the ability to produce more implied the enhanced ability of everyone else to produce *and* consume more goods.

The broader definition of Say's Law as it is customarily accepted relates to the idea that a general glut in commodities for the economy as a whole is impossible. Say, however, at least in the *Treatise*, never imagined the possibility of there being a general glut of all commodities, except as an aside (Baumol 1977, p. 156; Kates 1998, p. 24). He did recognize, though, that in real time one's abil-ity to make a purchase was not automatically equal to what he had intended when measured by the value of the product at the time of production. Gluts in "superabun-dant commodities," as Say called them, might occur if "it has been produced in excess abundance, or because the production of other commodities has fallen short" (1971, p. 135). Neither of these causes could be attributed to anything economy-wide. Rather, gluts in any one com-modity, even the superabundant kind, occurred, at the end of the day, not because of a dearth of money but because of a dearth of supply.

It was left to James Mill (1808) and Robert Torrens (1821) to elaborate on Say's framework, allowing them to conclude that a general glut in the economy as a whole was a logical impossibility. Mill in turn influenced Say's understanding of this issue, which he laid out in later edi-tions of his *Treatise* (see also Say 1967 [1821]). Torrens's explanation was more consistent with Say's perspective in that an economy-wide downturn could be explained by "miscalculations" and particular gluts in the market (Kates 1998, p. 36).

What emerged from these elaborations of Say's origi-nal analysis was a generally held conceptualization that one could think about a *price system* that regulated the flow of resources and goods supplied within a theory of markets. Moreover this price system was understood to be independent from the identification of the absolute nature of those prices, which were determined solely by the stock of money at any moment of time—the so-called classical dichotomy.

KEYNES'S ECONOMICS

In 1936 John Maynard Keynes, in his *The General Theory of Employment, Interest, and Money*, criticized this tradi-tion of economic theory and policy that began with the writings of Say, what he referred to as "classical econom-ics." The intention of Say and others to show that output (and employment) in the economy emanated from activ-ity at the level of the individual firm suffered from a logi-cal flaw, in Keynes's opinion, because the specification of the functional relationships at the level of the individual could be posited only if it was assumed that output as a whole was given and unchanging. Thus the method of describing an economy in terms of the behavior of indi-vidual supply had no theoretical validity except when out-put as a whole was fixed at the point where all resources were employed. Classical economics could explain *relative* movements in output and employment, but they had no method for considering changes in the level of output and employment as a whole. This conclusion followed from the view held by Say and his followers that no one would hold money as a store of value; money therefore had no essential properties in and of itself. Keynes therefore wished to consider, instead, a monetary economy "in which changing views about the future are capable of influencing the quantity of employment and not merely its direction" (1971, p. xxii).

From that criticism of what he considered to be an illogical theoretical system, Keynes sought to develop an alternative framework of analysis with his *theory of effective demand*. Here, he believed, one could think logically about the relationship between activity at the level of each individual or firm and industry as a whole (his *alternative* dichotomy) but without the necessary presumption that output was given at full employment. Keynes's reframing specified those relationships in a form such that each realm (the individual firm or industry and industry as a whole) existed in the context of the other. Either could remain stable or fluctuate without any stipulation that whatever was produced in the economy had to use all of the resources that were available. Keynes therefore felt that he had formulated a *general* theory of employment and output that was not predicated on a price system within a theory of markets in the tradition of Say, independent of the determination of absolute prices in general. Instead, he set the goal of bringing questions of money and prices back into the theory of employment and output as a whole.

This Keynesian revolution, which was intended to overturn the economic theory and policy built on Say's Law, never happened, at least according to one of Keynes's closest students and colleagues, Joan Robinson. Keynes's alternative vision of a monetary theory of production, as well as his mode of reasoning upon which that vision was built, was never embraced by the discipline. Economic theory and policy in the early twenty-first century therefore remained entrenched firmly in the dichotomous framework by which resource allocation is determined in a system of relative prices emanating from the rational behavior of individuals, while absolute prices are determined by the quantity of money.

Modern theoretical debate has been reduced to analyzing the speeds at which prices and quantities adjust. New classical economists, on the one hand, assume that prices adjust instantaneously, meaning that questions of quantity adjustments are never at issue—the classical dichotomy is therefore in place at all times, leading to a clear and limited set of policy prescriptions that eschew any form of discretionary public intervention. The only tool of macroeconomics is the control of inflation through the proper control of the money stock. New Keynesian economists, on the other hand, admit that markets may fail to resolve themselves in the short period, which could lead to greater movements in output than in prices. It should be emphasized that questions of employment and output by new Keynesians are still conceptualized and therefore framed as a mere generalization of individual market activity, the approach Keynes found to be illogical. In these intervals the classical dichotomy might very well be violated, perhaps necessitating policy intervention beyond just monetary policy. But even for most new Keynesian economists, it is just a matter of time before markets make their necessary adjustments, reestablishing the separation of real and monetary sectors.

Both schools of thought do recognize that institutional barriers to full resolution persist even over the longer period. This recognition has led them to construct theoretical edifices such as the "natural rate of unemployment" and the non-accelerating inflation rate of unemployment, allowing them to fit reality back into their theoretical vision. Once resolved, there has emerged a confluence of views on long-term public policies for both new classical and new Keynesian economists limited to the control of inflation by the monetary authorities and the shedding of external barriers to the free market mechanism, allowing it to resolve itself fully.

One should not be surprised that policy to promote *real* economic growth has led to legislation that intends to break down all barriers that might have prevented those who prospered (who made profits either by productive activity or in the form of dividends from equity holding) from keeping the greatest portion of those profits. For they who are the most successful in the market can be expected to increase supply by the greatest amount, "open[ing] a market for the products of all the other branches" (Say 1971, p. 137). These supply-side policies have been disavowed by some new Keynesian economists, although the motivation for their objections has come from political rather than economic foundations. The vision of economics and economic policy has progressed little indeed since Say's *Treatise*, when he suggested that policies should not exist that take away profits from producers unnecessarily and that savings (immediately translating into investment because people do not want to hold onto their money/profits longer than they must) should be encouraged over unproductive consumption.

SEE ALSO *Business Cycles, Empirical Literature; Business Cycles, Real; Economics, Classical; Economics, New Classical; Economics, New Keynesian; Investment; Involuntary Unemployment; Keynes, John Maynard; Mill, James; Natural Rate of Unemployment; Phillips Curve; Robinson, Joan; Savings Rate; Shocks; Voluntary Unemployment; Walras' Law*

BIBLIOGRAPHY

Baumol, William J. 1977. Say's (at Least) Eight Laws, or What Say and James Mill May Really Have Meant. *Economica* 44: 145–161.

Kates, Steven. 1998. *Say's Law and the Keynesian Revolution: How Macroeconomic Theory Lost Its Way*. Cheltenham, U.K.: Elgar.

Keynes, John Maynard. 1971. *The General Theory of Employment, Interest, and Money*. In *The Collected Writings of John Maynard Keynes*. Vol. 7. London: Macmillan and New York: St. Martin's. (Orig. pub. 1936.)

Mill, James. 1966. *Commerce Defended*. In *Selected Economic Writings*, ed. Donald Winch. Chicago: University of Chicago Press. (Orig. pub. 1808.)

Say, Jean-Baptiste. 1967. *Letters to Mr. Malthus on Several Subjects of Political Economy*. New York: A. M. Kelley. (Orig. pub. 1821.)

Say, Jean-Baptiste. 1971. *A Treatise on Political Economy; or, The Production, Distribution, and Consumption of Wealth*. New York: A. M. Kelley. (Orig. pub. 1803.)

Roy J. Rotheim

SCALES

In the social sciences, it is often important to measure attributes of individuals that are not readily observable, such as beliefs, attitudes, emotional experiences, and personality traits. Because such attributes are not readily observable, social scientists rely on scales that allow individuals to report the extent to which they possess or experience them.

SCALES OF MEASUREMENT

A scale provides both *qualitative* information and *quantitative* information about an attribute. The most basic type of scale has an individual simply indicate whether he or she possesses a certain attribute. This type of scale provides only a qualitative indication of the presence or absence of the attribute and is considered to have a *nominal* scale of measurement. A second type of scale has the individual indicate the presence or absence of the attribute in question *and* the quantitative amount of the attribute he or she possesses. For example, a scale of this sort could ask individuals to indicate how much they like ice cream by selecting a number from one to three, where one represents *not at all*, two represents *moderately*, and three represents *extremely*. This type of a scale has an *ordinal* scale of measurement, which provides a rank-order quantitative value of the degree to which the attribute is present. Note that even if these values are related to one another in a rank ordering, the psychological distance between neighboring values may not be equivalent (e.g., in the example above, the psychological difference between *not at all* and *moderately* may not be the same as

the psychological difference between *moderately* and *extremely*). When a scale provides rank-order values of an attribute and equal psychological distances between neighboring values, the scale has an *interval* scale of measurement. Finally if a scale has equal psychological distances between neighboring values and a value that reflects the complete absence of the attribute in question, then the scale has a *ratio* scale of measurement. Most scales used by social scientists are nominal or ordinal in nature because it is very difficult to objectively determine if the psychological distance between neighboring scale values is truly equivalent.

TYPES OF SIMPLE SCALES

Two general types of non-nominal scales are used in the social sciences. The first type is the *Likert scale*, which consists of labeled discrete values located between two labeled endpoint values. The ice cream scale described above is an example of a Likert scale. The second type is the *visual analog scale*, which consists of either discrete unlabeled values or a continuous unlabeled line between labeled endpoints. Likert scales are ordinal and provide only a limited number of values from which to choose, but they yield information about the qualitative degree to which an individual possesses the attribute in question. In contrast, continuous visual analog scales provide a large number of potential values from which to choose, but they yield little information about the qualitative degree to which an individual possesses the attribute in question. Some believe that visual analog scales have an interval scale of measurement, whereas others argue that they possess only an ordinal scale of measurement.

COMBINING SCALES INTO INVENTORIES

Ratings on individual scales are often combined to form an inventory. Inventories are essential when assessing complex attributes. Creating an inventory ensures that an attribute is measured in its entirety, which may be difficult to accomplish with a single scale. In an inventory, individuals respond to a number of statements using the same scale of measurement. For example, an anger inventory may be created by asking respondents to rate how angry, irritated, and mad they feel, each on a discrete visual analog scale. Each statement in the inventory must refer to a single object in order to minimize confusion. It is also useful to include statements that require responses that are the opposite of other statements in the inventory (e.g., How much do you like ice cream? vs. How much do you hate ice cream?) in order to reduce the likelihood that individuals are reporting responses without paying close attention to the scale items.

338

RELIABILITY AND VALIDITY

A scale or inventory must be both reliable and valid. *Reliability* is the extent to which an individual makes similar ratings across time using the same scale or, in the case of an inventory, the similarity of an individual's responses to related items within the inventory. Assuming that a scale or inventory is reliable, it must also have high *construct validity*. Construct validity is the extent to which the scale or inventory accurately measures the attribute in question. High construct validity can be demonstrated in a number of ways. First, one can establish *convergent validity* by showing that responses on the scale or inventory are positively associated with patterns of behavior or responses on another scale or inventory believed to measure the attribute or a similar attribute. Second, one can establish *discriminant validity* by showing that responses on the scale or inventory are not positively associated with patterns of behavior or responses on another scale or inventory believed to reflect an unrelated attribute.

SEE ALSO *Guttman Scale; Likert Scale; Locus of Control; Ordinality; Rotter's Internal-External Locus of Control Scale; Self-Esteem*

BIBLIOGRAPHY

Messick, Samuel. 1995. Validity of Psychological Assessment: Validation of Inferences from Person's Responses and Performances as Scientific Inquiry into Score Meaning. *American Psychologist* 50 (9): 741–749.

Robinson, John P., Phillip R. Shaver, and Lawrence S. Wrightsman. 1991. *Measures of Personality and Social Psychological Attitudes*. San Diego, CA: Academic Press.

David A. Lishner
E. L. Stocks

SCARCITY

The term *scarcity* implies a lack of a given thing, of it not being plentiful or easy to find. It is a term that does not impress one as having anything to do with science. For economics, however, scarcity is the starting point, a state of affairs that gives rise to a series of deductions that build the whole formal structure of economic science.

In the somewhat technical jargon of economics, scarcity represents a situation in which the existing *means* (resources, goods, etc.) are not sufficient for the achievement of all existing *ends* (goals, wishes, desires, etc.). Under such circumstances, it is indispensable to make decisions about which ends one will strive to achieve and which ones will be left unattended to. All such decisions imply the existence of some *benefits* (or *utility*), associated

with the achievement of certain ends, and of some *costs*, corresponding to the benefits associated with the achievement of ends that were forgone. It is in terms of benefits and costs that economists conceive of every decision, and it is through benefits and costs that changes in external conditions have an impact on human behavior.

It is easy to see that in a world where everything was abundant—where scarcity would not apply—all the above categories would be meaningless and economics would not exist. However, scarcity does exist, and it is not a mere empirical coincidence. It is a condition of life as human beings perceive it, and as such it cannot be undone. One can certainly imagine having many times more resources at one's disposal and having more of every good than could possibly be enjoyed (although humans are very far from experiencing this scenario). And yet this would not free one from having to make any decision whatsoever: One would still be forced to choose between different ways of enjoying all those superabundant supplies of goods, for human beings cannot engage in mutually exclusive activities. Thus, due to the inescapable scarcity of time, it is not possible to conceive of a world in which scarcity would not be known. This is why most scholars (or economists, at any rate) consider scarcity to be a universal and necessary human condition.

The presence of the scarcity problem people face, and in particular the need for trade-offs in dealing with scarcity, is reflected in popular common-sense adages such as "there ain't no such thing as a free lunch" (coined by Robert A. Heinlein in *The Moon Is a Harsh Mistress* [1966] and popularized in economics by Milton Friedman). In economic science, it is typically illustrated by the "production possibility frontier," a two-dimensional graph showing maximum amounts of two goods (e.g., "guns and butter") that can be produced with given resources. The frontier, which graphically represents the finiteness of options, also illustrates the concept of cost, for it shows that as long as all resources are being used, the output of one good can be increased only at the expense of a lower output of the other good.

While scarcity may be considered an omnipresent condition of human life, it is possible to view human behavior as a struggle to reduce its acuteness. The extent to which people are successful at narrowing the gap between means and ends can, in turn, be seen as a subjective degree of wealth as perceived by the person in question.

In economics, this process of reducing the problem of scarcity can also be shown with the help of the production possibility frontier. A more efficient use of resources allows for greater production of both goods, which in turn allows for more ends to be achieved and (with given wants) gives rise to a feeling of being wealthier than before. This more efficient use of resources, graphically pictured as an outward shift of the frontier, is usually attributed to three different sources of improvement: (1) improvement in human capital, (2) accumulation in physical capital, and (3) human cooperation (a division of labor and exchange).

The omnipresence of scarcity and its central position in orthodox economics has been challenged both from within economics and from without it. The attack from within has come from progressively minded economists. Believers in the enormous capacities of technological progress and the human mind have claimed there is a possibility of doing away with scarcity at some point in the future by devising ever more efficient ways of using resources, and thus making goods so plentiful as to accommodate all practical needs.

While this theory is usually propounded by some lesser lights among economists, there have been notable exceptions. John Maynard Keynes, for example, insisted that scarcity is kept unnecessarily high by an artificially high interest rate. In a similar vein, John Kenneth Galbraith, not incidentally an admirer of Keynes and a well-known economist as well, undermined the importance of scarcity with his concept of the "affluent society." Our society is supposed to have reached a sufficient degree of affluence to enable it to provide all the genuine needs people may have. The remaining feelings of scarcity are a product of artificial wants, as Galbraith would have it, created by advertising. None of these authors, however, have attacked scarcity directly, nor have they claimed that scarcity would cease to exist altogether. Instead, they have alluded to its man-made, and thus unnecessary, nature, and to a possibility of its substantial elimination through proper government policy.

From outside of economics, the assault on scarcity has come from anthropologists such as Marshall Sahlins. Their point is that a large degree of affluence did exist before the advent of civilization, among the Paleolithic hunter-gatherers. They show that, contrary to conventional wisdom, such societies did not struggle, but rather enjoyed a life of relative plenty, with more leisure time and (some claim) greater happiness than an average modern person would have today. All this, of course, is due to their having had drastically more modest needs.

While these ideas, just like those of Galbraith, can be justly considered as criticism of the modern consumer civilization, they do not show the logical possibility of a world without scarcity. Even the most austere monks living on water would surely have to make some decisions, if only what to meditate about. Thus, these criticisms may well play down the necessity of the scarcity in human affairs (i.e., its severity and centrality in the human mind),

but they will hardly cause the orthodox economics to crumble under its weight.

SEE ALSO *Anthropology; Choice in Economics; Economics; Friedman, Milton; Galbraith, John Kenneth; Keynes, John Maynard; Microeconomics; Opportunity Cost; Poverty; Production Frontier; Sahlins, Marshall; Trade-offs*

BIBLIOGRAPHY

Galbraith, John Kenneth. 1958. *The Affluent Society.* Boston: Houghton Mifflin.

Heinlein, Robert A. 1966. *The Moon Is a Harsh Mistress.* New York: Putnam.

Sahlins, Marshal. 1972. *Stone Age Economics.* Chicago: Aldine-Atherton.

Sievert, Dale M. 1989. *Economics: Dealing with Scarcity.* Waukesha, WI: Glengarry.

Dan Stastny

SCARR, SANDRA WOOD
1936–

Sandra Wood Scarr's career as a psychological scientist spanned more than four decades. During that time, she engaged in scholarly pursuits dedicated to examining genetic influences on development and the importance of quality child care.

Scarr was born in 1936. She received her PhD from Harvard University in 1965 with a dissertation that examined genetic contributions to personality development in identical and fraternal female twins. Scarr's findings, that sociability and activity level were genetically linked, challenged the mainstream belief at the time that environmental influences predominantly affected development. Following graduate school, Scarr held academic positions at the University of Maryland (1965), the University of Pennsylvania (1966–1971), the University of Minnesota (1972–1975), Yale University (1977–1983), and the University of Virginia (1983–1995). She retired in 1995.

While at the University of Pennsylvania, Scarr examined the genetic and environmental predictors of identical and fraternal twins' intellectual development. Although genetic influence accounted for variations in intellectual development overall, environmental influences were more pronounced for black children than white children. Scarr attributed these differences to disparities in the relative opportunities afforded to the white versus the black children.

While at the Institute of Child Development at the University Minnesota, Scarr initiated the Minnesota Adoption Projects with the psychologist Richard A. Weinberg. One of their most controversial and misinterpreted collaborative studies was the Minnesota Transracial Adoption Project, which examined the IQ of 101 black children adopted into white families. Their findings revealed that rearing environments do affect children's performance on intelligence tests; specifically IQ scores of the black children reared in white families relative to those reared in black families were significantly higher. Longitudinal examinations of these same children suggested that the effects of rearing environments are strongest in early childhood and dramatically decrease in adolescence. Although alternative explanations for the decrease in IQ scores may be attributable to environmental factors, such as conflicts surrounding dating and social identity during adolescence or the conflicts that might arise for nonwhite children living in a white environment with their white parents, the reduction of environmental influences in adolescence is well supported in the behavioral genetics literature. Scarr's book *Race, Social Class, and Individual Differences in I.Q.* was published in 1981.

Scarr extended her work on gene-environment interactions through a series of theoretical and empirical papers. She and her colleagues proposed that the environments actively selected by individuals affect the genetic expression of characteristics such as personality. Further individuals' characteristics evoke particular reactions from others in one's environment. Thus the expression of a person's genes has not only passive and active effects but also evocative effects.

Another branch of Scarr's research program was geared toward improving the quality of child care environments. Scarr's research with Margaret Williams, which demonstrated that stimulation practices (e.g., music exposure and rocking) had beneficial effects on premature infants' subsequent growth and development, revolutionized the standards of neonatal care practices in hospital settings.

In 1984 Scarr published *Mother Care/Other Care*, for which she received the American Psychological Association's (APA) National Book Award in 1985. In this book Scarr identified deciding factors that influenced mothers' reasons for entering the workforce as opposed to remaining at home. She also challenged the belief that maternal employment had negative effects on young children's development and maintained that children can be well cared for by someone other than their parents. Her work also addressed the benefits of high-quality child care, particularly the importance of low child to caregiver ratios and stimulating day care environments.

In 1990 Scarr began serving on the board of directors of KinderCare Learning Centers, where she eventually served as chief executive officer from 1995 to 1997. Scarr moved to Hawaii after an investment firm purchased KinderCare.

Throughout her career, Scarr earned numerous awards and honors for her contributions to the science of psychology. In 1988 she received the first APA Award for the Distinguished Contribution to Research in Public Policy, and in 1989 she was elected to the American Academy of Arts and Sciences. Scarr's professional service included serving as the associate editor of *American Psychologist*, as editor of *Developmental Psychology*, and as cofounding editor of *Current Directions in Psychological Science*. Scarr also held several key leadership positions, including serving on the APA's board of directors, as president of the Society for Research in Child Development, and as president of the American Psychological Society.

Ultimately, although controversial, Scarr's contributions to the study of gene-environment interactions and the importance of quality child care defined and paved the intellectual path for contemporary and future generations of psychological scientists.

SEE ALSO *Child Development; Children; Determinism, Environmental; Determinism, Genetic; Developmental Psychology; Intelligence; IQ Controversy; Nature vs. Nurture; Personality; Psychology; Psychometrics; Twin Studies*

BIBLIOGRAPHY

Scarr, Sandra. 1981. *Race, Social Class, and Individual Differences in I.Q.: New Studies of Old Issues.* Mahwah, NJ: Erlbaum.

Scarr, Sandra. 1984. *Mother Care/Other Care.* New York: Basic Books.

Scarr, Sandra W. 2001. Sandra Wood Scarr. In *Models of Achievement: Reflections of Eminent Women in Psychology*, ed. Agnes N. O'Connell and Nancy Felipe Russo, vol. 2, 99–112. Mahwah, NJ: Erlbaum.

Scarr-Salapatek, Sandra, and Margaret L. Williams. 1973. The Effects of Early Stimulation on Low-Birth-Weight Infants. *Child Development* 44: 94–101.

Joann Benigno
Clare Faulhaber

SCHACHTER, STANLEY
1922–1997

Stanley Schachter was trained as a social psychologist at Yale University, Massachusetts Institute of Technology, and the University of Michigan, where he received his

Ph.D. in 1949. After his early collaborative work on social influence with psychologist Leon Festinger (1919–1989), including the classic field study of cognitive dissonance, *When Prophecy Fails* (1956), Schachter produced, on the basis of his own intuitions and distinctive research and analytic style, the prize-winning *Psychology of Affiliation* (1959).

A native New Yorker, Schachter moved in 1961 from the University of Minnesota to Columbia University in New York City, where he spent the remainder of his career, aside from summers (analyzing data) in his beloved Amagansett in New York's Hamptons. He won the American Psychological Association's Distinguished Scientific Contribution Award in 1969 and was elected to the National Academy of Sciences in 1983.

Schachter is primarily associated with the idea that internal and external cues combine to determine human experience. This notion was offered initially in his formula for what constitutes a true emotional experience—namely, the joint presence of physiological arousal and a suitable emotional label or explanation (usually provided by the environment) for that arousal. The absence of either arousal or an appropriate emotional construal leads to an incomplete emotional experience. Empirical support for this notion was not as robust as one might prefer, but the Schachter perspective (Schachter and Singer, 1962) had a powerful impact, largely because of Schachter's creative experimental scenarios and his eloquent and amusing writing style, and also because he and his students extended the formula to the realm of misattribution of emotion, which led to many fascinating and even practical implications.

It is often noted that Schachter's work on obesity and eating grew directly out of his work on emotion. While it is true that both formulations involve internal and external cues, what is often overlooked is that the formula is quite different in the two realms. Whereas a true emotional experience requires both an internal cue (arousal) and an external cue (label), Schachter switched gears when talking about obesity. For one thing, he no longer targeted subjective experience; instead, his work focused on the act of eating rather than the experience of hunger. Moreover, instead of invoking an interaction of internal and external cues to explain eating, Schachter argued that eating could be produced by either sort of cue, acting in isolation. The obese, it appears, are not responsive to internal cues and eat entirely on the basis of external cues (i.e., environmental food cues), whereas normal-weight individuals are responsive to internal cues (and probably to external cues as well). Schachter's internal/external distinction as applied to obesity and eating has been challenged, but once again, his research was so clever and his argumentation so persuasive that he won over a generation of readers.

Schachter went on to study cigarette smoking, where he eventually adopted a radically "internal" perspective, arguing that psychological factors affect smoking only insofar as they affect urinary pH, which in turn influences nicotine reuptake into the bloodstream. He also studied the psychology of money and verbal dysfluencies before retiring in 1992. His legacy is his blend of creativity and the dogged pursuit of data to support his intuitions, which pleased him most when they challenged conventional wisdom.

SEE ALSO *Addiction; Cognitive Dissonance; Festinger, Leon; Obese Externality; Obesity; Overeating; Psychology; Smoking*

BIBLIOGRAPHY

Festinger, Leon, Henry W. Riecken, and Stanley Schacter. 1956. *When Prophecy Fails*. Minneapolis: University of Minnesota Press.

Grunberg, Neil E., Richard E. Nisbett, Judith Rodin, and Jerome E. Singer, eds. 1987. *A Distinctive Approach to Psychological Research: The Influence of Stanley Schachter.* Hillsdale, NJ: Erlbaum.

Schachter, Stanley. 1959. *The Psychology of Affiliation: Experimental Studies of the Sources of Gregariousness*. Stanford, CA: Stanford University Press.

Schachter, Stanley, and Jerome E. Singer. 1962. Cognitive, Social, and Physiological Determinants of Emotional State. *Psychological Review* 69: 379–399.

C. Peter Herman

SCHADENFREUDE

SEE *Sympathy.*

SCHATTSCHNEIDER, E. E.
1892–1971

Elmer Eric Schattschneider received his PhD from Columbia University in 1935. For the remainder of his academic career he taught primarily at Wesleyan University in Middletown, Connecticut, where he was John E. Andrus Professor of Government. He was president of the American Political Science Association from 1956 to 1957. He is best known for his work on political parties, which he used as a prism through which he built a powerful and, despite numerous criticisms, enduring argument on the nature of modern democracy.

Schattschneider first presented his argument regarding parties in *Party Government* (1942). It is probably the most often cited, the most controversial, and the single most influential work on American political parties penned to date. His thesis was that modern democracy is unthinkable except in terms of political parties because they are the umbilical cord that links citizens to their government. If that cord is cut, he thought, both government and citizens would shrivel and die as components of a democratic polity. The weakness of the founding arguments, in *The Federalist* for example, is that the founders' conception of government was not only undemocratic but, because it was essentially nonpartisan, was also built on unrealistic assumptions about democracy. American government became progressively democratic as parties developed. Schattschneider became the best-known advocate for the "responsible party" school in American government, the idea that parties should formulate policy proposals and present them to the voters, thus making elections occasions for major policy decisions. The measure of democracy would largely consist of the ability of parties to translate these policy choices made by the electorate into policy government. The cycle of democracy was one of responsible parties, electoral choice between parties, and party organization of government after the election. Schattschneider further refined and developed his party arguments when he was elected to chair the American Political Science Association Committee on Political Parties. The committee report, *Toward a More Responsible "Two Party" System*, was published in 1950.

The argument for responsible parties was challenged on several grounds. First, responsible parties would necessarily require that ideology, liberal or conservative, would be the organizing principle of policy proposals rather than the more pragmatic consideration of simply winning elections. Responsible parties would intensify political conflict over competing policies. Consensus political scientists argued that the natural tendency of political parties in a winner-take-all system would be toward the center of political gravity because voters would be distributed with varying intensity along a continuum that ranged from liberal to conservative and not merely cluster at the extremes. Second, Schattschneider was challenged on the very purpose of parties in the first place. Do parties exist merely to promote policy government, or do they also serve as intermediary institutions between citizens and their government that should moderate conflict rather than exacerbate it? American political parties, it was pointed out, developed after the ratification of the Constitution and did not so much create a democratic government as they helped provide a means whereby citizens could find a measure of civic peace within a framework that was largely popular from the outset. The founders evidently thought democracy could be conceived of outside the framework of parties.

A measure of Schattschneider's influence is in the literature of political parties since his most important work. It is almost impossible to discuss American political parties in terms of their purpose and role in a democratic system without reference to his arguments. The resulting quarrels over the nature of parties led Schattschneider to publish *The Semisovereign People: A Realist's View of Democracy in America* (1960). It is a deceptively short book—an essay really—that tries to get at, as he puts it, "what makes things happen" in American government (Schattschneider 1960, p.v.). This is his most philosophical work. His conclusion was that "the role of the people in the political system is determined largely by the conflict system, for it is conflict that involves people in politics and the nature of conflict determines the nature of public involvement" (Schattschneider 1960, p. 126). The people, he thought, are powerless unless the system is competitive, and parties are the institutional agents of that competition. *The Semisovereign People* is a fitting epitaph for the work of one of the most influential scholars in American political science.

Schattschneider was right to see parties as the engine of policy changes and innovation. He was also right to see in the development of modern party government a significant departure from the founders' conception of popular government. The extent to which parties are or should be responsible in the sense he advocated is a more debatable proposition.

SEE ALSO *American Political Science Association; Competition; Conflict; Elites; Federalism; Party Systems, Competitive; Political Parties; Political Science; Sovereignty; Voting*

BIBLIOGRAPHY

PRIMARY WORKS

Schattschneider, E. E. 1935. *Politics, Pressures, and the Tariff.* New York: Prentice-Hall.

Schattschneider, E. E. 1948. *The Struggle for Party Government.* College Park: Program in American Civilization, University of Maryland.

Schattschneider, E. E. 1960. *The Semisovereign People: A Realist's View of Democracy in America.* New York: Holt, Rinehart, and Winston.

Schattschneider, E. E. 2004. *Party Government.* New Brunswick, NJ: Transaction Publishers. (Orig. pub. 1942.)

SECONDARY WORKS

Green, John C., and Paul S. Herrnson, eds. 2002. *Responsible Partisanship? The Evolution of American Political Parties since 1950.* Lawrence: University Press of Kansas.

White, John Kenneth. 1992. E. E. Schattschneider and the Responsible Party Model. PS: Political Science and Politics 25 (2): 167–171.

Sidney A. Pearson Jr.

SCHEMAS

A schema is a knowledge structure containing the generic representation of a concept. For example, a schema for chairs includes a flat platform to sit upon, four legs, and a back. While not all chairs fit this description, schemas can be modified to include other versions of the concept (e.g., a three-legged stool or a chair with no legs). Schemas can be held about any concept, are often arranged hierarchically, and affect perception, cognition, and memory.

The concept of a schema can be traced to Immanuel Kant (1724–1804), who in 1781 discussed the concept in *Critique of Pure Reason*. More recently, Frederick Bartlett, in 1932, had participants read foreign folktales and later asked them to recall the details. When reading a Native American folktale, non–Native American participants often changed "canoe" to "boat," left out prominent themes, and made the story more European. Bartlett suggested that memory was not fixed, but changed as people actively reconstructed episodes to fit their preexisting schemas.

Jean Piaget used schemas to explain how children acquire new skills and learn to interact with the world. After being scared by a large, aggressive dog, a child may develop the schema that four-legged creatures are dangerous. When confronted by similar dogs, the child may react with fear. Piaget referred to the application of an existing schema to a different stimulus as "assimilation." However, when exposed to a small, well-behaved dog, the child might react positively. Piaget referred to the modification of an existing schema (or the creation of an entirely new schema) to fit a new stimulus as "accommodation." Piaget suggested that assimilation and accommodation are the bases of adaptation (i.e., learning) and define the stages of cognitive development.

There are many different kinds of schemas (what follows is by no means an exhaustive list): role schemas (e.g., the role of a student vs. that of a teacher), event schemas (e.g., what happens at a cocktail party vs. a football game), self schemas (i.e., what we think of ourselves either globally or in specific domains), relationship schemas (e.g., the relationship with one's mother vs. one's best friend), trait schemas (e.g., what shy people are like vs. outgoing people), procedural schemas (e.g., how to make coffee vs. how to put gas in a car), stereotypes (i.e., schemas concerning members of social groups; e.g., the cognitive ability of the young vs. the elderly), and scripts (i.e., how to act in certain situations; e.g., ordering food at a fast food restaurant vs. a fine dining establishment).

Schemas are thought to be functional. They help to organize and understand the world and to fill in informational gaps. They also reduce ambiguity and serve as memory guides, directing our attention to relevant aspects in the environment. However, the overuse of schemas can result in stereotypes. For example, a 2001 study by Brian K. Payne found that when participants were shown a picture of a person's face followed by a picture of either a tool or a gun, the race of the face influenced whether people misidentified pictures of tools as weapons. Even though participants were told to ignore the first picture showing a person, they were more likely to report tools as weapons when the pictures were paired with black faces. This tendency for previously viewed stimuli to activate schemas and influence perceptions—even in very different situations—is known as priming.

SEE ALSO *Piaget, Jean; Priming; Racism; Script Models; Stereotypes*

BIBLIOGRAPHY

Bartlett, Frederick C. 1932. *Remembering: A Study in Experimental and Social Psychology.* Cambridge, U.K.: Cambridge University Press.

Kant, Immanuel. 1781. *Critique of Pure Reason.* Trans. Norman Kemp Smith. New York: Modern Library, 1958.

Payne, Brian K. 2001. Prejudice and Perception: The Role of Automatic and Controlled Processes in Misperceiving a Weapon. *Journal of Personality and Social Psychology* 81 (2): 181–192.

Piaget, Jean. 1969. *The Psychology of the Child.* Trans. Helen Weaver. New York: Basic Books.

Taylor, Shelly E., and Jennifer Crocker. 1981. Schematic Bases of Social Information Processing. In *Social Cognition*. Vol. 1 of *The Ontario Symposium*, eds. E. Tory Higgins, C. Peter Herman, and Mark P. Zanna, 89–134. Hillsdale, NJ: Erlbaum.

Scott T. Wolf

SCHIZOPHRENIA

Approximately one percent of the population suffers from schizophrenia, a severe and persistent mental disorder that is characterized by a wide range of cognitive, social, behavioral, and emotional symptoms and that has been identified by the World Health Organization as one of the ten most debilitating diseases. As specified in the *Diagnostic and Statistical Manual of Mental Disorders* (*DSM* -IV-TR) (APA 2000), positive symptoms of schizophrenia include hallucinations, delusions, disorganized speech, and grossly disorganized or catatonic behavior. Negative symptoms include affective flattening (a lack of emotional response), alogia (poverty of speech), and avolition (an absence of motivation). In addition, impairment is present in one or more major areas of functioning, such as work, interpersonal relations, or self-care. Subtypes of schizophrenia include paranoid, catatonic, disorganized, undifferentiated, and residual schizophrenia.

The vulnerability-stress model offers a useful way of integrating current thinking about schizophrenia. The model assumes that schizophrenia involves a biogenetic vulnerability or predisposition to develop the disorder. A range of biological and psychosocial factors can interact with this vulnerability to affect the manifestation and course of the illness. Certain risk factors, such as substance abuse, are associated with symptom exacerbation and an increased likelihood of relapse. Protective factors, such as social support and coping strategies, can ameliorate the symptoms of the disorder and make relapse less likely.

Both diagnostic and functional assessment are important in designing individualized treatment and rehabilitation plans. The use of standardized instruments, such as the Structured Clinical Interview for *DSM*-IV-TR (SCID), can increase the likelihood of an accurate diagnosis. Functional assessment focuses on potential deficits in skills and resources that can result in impairment in the ability to function at home, work, and school.

Effective and efficacious psychopharmacological and psychosocial treatments have become available during the past three decades. Since the late 1970s there has been increasing development of new antipsychotic medications. Evidence-based psychosocial interventions have replaced older psychodynamic approaches and accelerated community reintegration of patients who were formerly institutionalized. The benefits of antipsychotic medications include decreased symptoms, reduced risk of relapse, and increased response to psychosocial interventions. Generally combined with medications, psychosocial interventions have demonstrated benefits in the areas of relapse and rehospitalization, housing stability, competitive employment, social functioning, psychotic symptoms, and substance use disorders (Mueser et al. 2003).

Evidence-based psychosocial interventions include assertive community treatment (ACT), family psychoeducation, supported employment, training in illness-management and recovery skills, and integrated dual disorders treatment. The *ACT model* was developed to meet the needs of individuals with a history of high service utilization or severe functional impairment. Services are provided on a twenty-four-hour basis in natural living environments by multidisciplinary treatment and rehabilitation teams. *Family psychoeducation* generally includes services both for people with schizophrenia and for their family members. Components include education about mental illness and its management, skills training, and social support. *Supported employment* services include rapid job search rather than extensive prevocational assessment; competitive wages for jobs in integrated settings; ongoing support once a job has been obtained; and com-

bined vocational and mental health services. Interventions that target *illness management* and recovery are designed to help people with schizophrenia acquire the information and skills needed to collaborate in their treatment, to minimize the effects of the disorder on their lives, and to be able to pursue personally meaningful goals. *Integrated dual disorders treatment* focuses on substance use disorder, which is the most common and clinically significant comorbidity associated with schizophrenia. Integrated mental health and substance abuse programs provide simultaneous treatment of both disorders in a single setting. Social and cultural variables are relevant to the etiology, epidemiology, phenomenology, course, and prognosis of schizophrenia.

Because schizophrenia seemed more prevalent in lower socioeconomic groups, earlier sociologists postulated social stress as a casual factor; others attributed clustering in poor areas to downward social drift. Although psychogenic or sociogenic theories have largely been nullified by biogenetic findings, other correlates of the social environment have apparent etiological significance. For example, maternal exposure to wartime famine or the type A influenza virus during fetal development predicts significantly higher risk for later development of schizophrenia.

World Health Organization studies have consistently shown that despite standardized diagnostic criteria, the prognosis for schizophrenia is significantly better in developing countries than in the industrialized West. Some analysts attribute this to the presence of less virulent variants of the syndrome. Others point to cultural variables that mitigate the impact of schizophrenia in traditional societies, including magical causal theories that view mental disorders as temporary. In developed countries, in contrast, the person and illness are often fused, generating damaged identity. In addition, traditional agrarian societies offer more normalization through flexible work roles and arranged marriages. In these societies, people with schizophrenia are five times more likely to marry than in the industrialized West (Hopper 2004). In developing countries, extended kinship networks relieve the burden often experienced by smaller households in developed countries. The nuclear family structure, with its limited capacity for caregiving, is related to high expressed emotion, which entails hostile criticism or emotional overinvolvement in some family members. High expressed emotion is correlated with patient relapse, but is less frequent in non-Western cultures and is largely remediable with family psychoeducation (Leff and Vaughn 1985).

In contrast to now discredited theories that implicated families in causation, a literature has emerged on the impact of schizophrenia on families. Research indicates that the families of people with schizophrenia face both objective burden, which include the time, energy, and finances devoted to illness management, and subjective burden, which refers to the emotional costs of coping with difficult behaviors and the pain and losses of a loved one. Families have dealt with their distress by organizing into movements throughout the world to improve research and services and to combat stigma. People with schizophrenia suffer the terrors of psychosis, diminished life aspirations, and social devaluation. Social and cultural conceptions range from retribution for personal or ancestral misconduct to the split personality definition that has made the word *schizophrenic* an erroneous synonym for self-contradiction. Media accounts of violence reinforce societal stigma, although people with schizophrenia are more often victims than perpetrators.

In spite of these challenges, many deinstitutionalized patients are functioning well in their communities. Longitudinal studies in Europe and the United States show that more than half of formerly hospitalized, presumably chronic patients with schizophrenia can, with proper treatment, lead satisfying, relatively symptom-free lives. Studies of mostly first-episode patients show from 48 percent to 91 percent experiencing symptomatic remission posthospitalization (Liberman and Kopelowicz 2005). A burgeoning consumer movement of former patients, many with schizophrenia, offers peer services, recovered role models, and hope. With continuing research on improved medications, psychosocial interventions, peer services, and genetic predictors of more exact individualized treatments, the prognosis looks more favorable than ever before.

SEE ALSO *Kinship; Manias; Mental Health; Mental Illness; Psychotherapy; Psychotropic Drugs; Stress; World Health Organization*

BIBLIOGRAPHY

American Psychiatric Association (APA). 2000. *Diagnostic and Statistical Manual of Mental Disorders* (*DSM* -IV-TR). 4th ed., text rev. Washington, DC: Author.

Hopper, Kim. 2004. Interrogating the Meaning of "Culture" in the WHO International Studies of Schizophrenia. In *Schizophrenia, Culture, and Subjectivity: The Edge of Experience*, eds. Janis H. Jenkins and Robert J. Barrett, 62–86. Cambridge, U.K.: Cambridge University Press.

Leff, Julian, and Christine Vaughn, eds. 1985. *Expressed Emotion in Families: Its Significance for Mental Illness*. New York: Guilford.

Liberman, Robert P., and Alex Kopelowicz. 2005. Recovery from Schizophrenia: A Concept in Search of Research. *Psychiatric Services* 56 (6): 735–742.

Mueser, Kim T., et al. 2003. Implementing Evidence-based Practices for People with Severe Mental Illness. *Behavior Modification* 27 (3): 387–411.

Diane T. Marsh
Harriet P. Lefley

SCHLIEMANN, HEINRICH
1822–1890

Born in Neubukow in Mecklenburg-Schwerin, Germany, on January 6, 1822, the son of a Lutheran minister, Heinrich Schliemann received his secondary education in Neustrelitz and became a grocer's apprentice (1836–1841). He took an intensive course in bookkeeping, but finding no suitable employment in Germany, he decided to sail to Colombia to make his fortune there. When the ship ran aground off the coast of Holland, he became a clerk with Schroeder's, a large trading company in Amsterdam, and eventually their agent in St. Petersburg, where he also set up his own business and married Yekaterina Lyshin in 1852. The marriage produced three children but was not a happy one. Schliemann made a great deal of money buying and selling commodities on the St. Petersburg exchange. In 1868 he went on a grand tour through Italy and Greece to the Troad in Turkey, hiring workmen to make tentative excavations on Ithaca and at Pinarbashi (Troad). The British expatriate Frank Calvert, who had made small excavations at Hisarlik, convinced Schliemann that that was the site of Troy. Schliemann resolved to return and dig there. In 1869 he received a doctorate from the University of Rostock for his book *Ithaque, le Péloponnèse et Troie* (Ithaca, the Peloponnesus, and Troy), divorced his Russian wife in Indianapolis, and married Sophia Engastromenos in Athens. This marriage, which was almost as stormy as the first, produced two children.

After an exploratory (and illegal) dig in 1870, he began a campaign of excavations at Hisarlik (1871–1873) with a large number (70–100) of workmen. These revealed a series of nine superimposed settlements. Schliemann reckoned the second oldest of these (Troy II) to be Homeric Troy. This seemed to be confirmed in May 1873 when he found at that level a large hoard of metal objects including gold and silver vessels and jewelry, which he called "Priam's Treasure." Even more important were his excavations at Mycenae (1876). These brought to light an advanced civilization on mainland Greece that predated Periclean Athens by a thousand years. Before Schliemann, no one had dreamed of its existence. The finds in the shaft graves there were richer and far more sophisticated than those at Troy. Attempting to establish clear connections between Troy and Mycenae, Schliemann returned to excavate at Troy in 1878, 1879, 1882, and 1890. Finally, in 1890 conclusive proof emerged that Troy II was far earlier than the shaft grave burials at Mycenae, though Schliemann did not acknowledge this in his 1890 report. Subsequent excavation has shown that Homeric Troy should be dated to the last levels of Troy VI (according to Wilhelm Dörpfeld and recently the German-

American excavation team led by Manfred Kormann) or to Troy VII (according to Carl Blegen, who excavated Troy 1932–1938). Among the many other sites Schliemann excavated, Tiryns and Orchomenos are the most important. He died in Naples on December 26, 1890.

The accuracy of some of Schliemann's archaeological reports has been questioned in recent years. It is now clear, for instance, that "Priam's Treasure" is not a single find, as Schliemann claimed, but a composite of many pieces found over months of excavation. However, much of his work has been confirmed by his successors. He remains a crucial figure in Aegean archaeology.

SEE ALSO *Archaeology*

BIBLIOGRAPHY

PRIMARY WORKS

Schliemann, Heinrich. [1878] 1976. *Mycenae.* New York: Arno Press.

Schliemann, Heinrich. [1881] 1976. *Ilios.* New York: Arno Press.

SECONDARY WORKS

Easton, Donald. 1998. Heinrich Schliemann: Hero or Fraud? *Classical World* 91: 335–343.

Fitton, J. Lesley. 1995. *The Discovery of the Greek Bronze Age.* London: British Museum.

Traill, David A. 1995. *Schliemann of Troy: Treasure and Deceit.* London and New York: John Murray.

Traill, David A. 2000. "Priam's Treasure": Clearly a Composite. *Anatolian Studies* 50: 17–35.

David A. Traill

SCHNEIDER, HERMAN

SEE *Assimilation.*

SCHOMBURG, ARTURO

SEE *Boricua.*

SCHOOL VOUCHERS

The immediate purpose of school voucher programs is straightforward enough: they are designed to provide families with cash subsidies that help defray the costs of a private education. The larger social objectives that school voucher programs purport to serve, however, vary considerably. Some people promote vouchers on the grounds that they inject competitive forces into a monopolistic public education system. Others exalt the perceived benefits of a religious education; namely the teaching of moral values, discipline, and prayer. To some they rescue students trapped in failing public schools, while still others suggest that vouchers are a civil rights issue, extending educational opportunities to predominantly poor, minority, and urban residents that heretofore have been the province of wealthier, whiter populations.

It is little surprise, then, that the specific features of actual voucher programs vary widely. A handful of programs are funded with taxpayer dollars, while numerous others are financed with private donations. Programs intermittently target students with disabilities, students attending chronically underperforming public schools, low-income families, or rural residents who lack ready access to a public school. The particular mix of participating secular and religious schools also varies from program to program, as do the specific requirements and accountability systems with which private schools must comply.

The first voucher experiment in the United States began in 1990 in the city of Milwaukee, where tuition subsidies of up to $2,500 were offered to low-income families. For the first eight years, the program could legally serve no more than 1.5 percent of the city's public school population (approximately 1,700 students), and only secular schools were allowed to participate. In 1996 the state of Wisconsin permitted up to 15 percent of the Milwaukee public school population to participate in the program. The state also expanded the menu of private schooling options to include religious institutions, and it increased the monetary value of the vouchers. A lawsuit objecting to the expanded program's constitutionality delayed its implementation until 1998, when the Wisconsin Supreme Court upheld the program. Since then, the numbers of private schools and students participating in the voucher program have expanded rapidly.

Other publicly funded voucher programs have been implemented in Cleveland, Ohio; Florida; and Washington, D.C. Ohio enacted a pilot voucher program starting in the 2006-2007 school year, and Vermont and Maine have voucher-like tuition programs that assist children residing in rural districts to attend either a secular private school or a public school in another district. In the 2005-2006 school year, roughly 14,200 non-special-education students participated in the voucher program in Milwaukee, while 5,700 did so in Cleveland, 733 in Florida, 1,090 in Washington, D.C., 5,450 in Vermont, and 6,250 in Maine. And thousands more beside have enrolled in privately funded voucher programs in such cities as Dayton, Ohio; Indianapolis, Indiana; San Antonio, Texas; and New York City, as well as a national program operated by the Children's Scholarship Fund.

THE EFFECTS OF SCHOOL VOUCHERS

The origin of the modern voucher movement can be traced to the Nobel laureate Milton Friedman's defense of parental school choice in *The Role of Government in Education* (1955). Friedman promoted vouchers as a way to spark competition, improve the efficiency of public school systems, and improve the actual performance of schools. John Chubb and Terry Moe revived the idea in *Politics, Markets, and America's Schools* (1990), in which they explicated why private institutions have stronger incentives than public ones to mimic "best practices" in education.

In the early twenty-first century, a lively debate persists about whether the threat of losing students (and the dollars attached to them) to other districts or to private schools induces public schools to operate more efficiently. In one especially influential paper published in 2000, Caroline Hoxby found that competition among public school districts improves school productivity by simultaneously raising student achievement and lowering spending. Reanalyzing the same data, Jesse Rothstein came to very different conclusions, which Hoxby then refuted. In a separate exploration of the voucher programs in Milwaukee, Cleveland, and San Antonio, Frederick Hess carved out a middle ground, arguing in 2000 that competition induces only moderate productivity increases, unless the internal structure of the public school system sets performance-based incentives throughout the system.

Whether vouchers raise the performance of those students who use them has been equally controversial. In 1995, John Witte, Troy Sterr, and Christopher Thorn claimed that students who participated in the original, limited voucher program in Milwaukee scored no higher than a random sample of public school students and low-income students. Using the unsuccessful applicants as an alternative control group, Jay Greene and colleagues found in 1996 that the voucher program had a significant positive effect on the students' achievement in math and reading. Using yet another methodology, Cecilia Rouse concluded in 1998 that students participating in the program learned at a faster pace in math and at a similar pace in reading, compared to their peers in public schools.

Because families self-select into public and private school populations, it can be extraordinarily difficult to determine whether observed differences between them are due to the quality of the schools in the two sectors or the kinds of students who choose to attend them. The best evidence regarding vouchers, therefore, comes from randomized field trials, in which vouchers are assigned to an eligible population by means of a lottery. In several privately funded voucher programs in the United States, it was possible to conduct such analyses. After examining such programs in New York City, Washington, D.C., and Dayton, Ohio, William Howell and Paul Peterson found that vouchers had positive effects on African-Americans' test scores but no effect on those of white or Hispanic students. Additionally, as a result of using vouchers, parents did not appear any more or less involved in their children's educational lives; parental satisfaction with their children's schools improved substantially; and the probability that children attended religious services increased, though the frequency of church attendance among parents actually decreased.

Evaluations of voucher programs elsewhere in the world have been similarly mixed. In 2002, Angrist and colleagues found that Colombian students who were awarded vouchers repeated grades less often and achieved higher test scores. In a 2000 study, Edward Fiske and Helen Ladd offered no conclusions about the overall effect of New Zealand's parental choice system, but they argued that the system exacerbated the social stratification of the nation's school system. Both positive and negative effects on Chile's unrestricted voucher program have been reported. Chang-Tai Hsieh and Miguel Urquiola found no evidence that vouchers improved average educational outcomes, though they observed that the best public school students left for private schools as a result of the program. Francisco Gallego, meanwhile, found that the competition increased students' test scores in public and voucher schools alike.

THE POLITICS OF SCHOOL VOUCHERS

In 2002 the U.S. Supreme Court affirmed the constitutionality of the Cleveland voucher program in *Zelman v. Simmons-Harris*, rejecting the claim that the use of public funds to send children to religious schools violated the First Amendment's establishment clause. The Court found the program to be neutral with respect to religion because parents were allowed "to exercise genuine choice among options" that included religious and secular private school, magnet schools, charter schools, and traditional public schools.

Despite *Zelman*, controversy continues to plague voucher initiatives. Voucher programs have faced strong opposition from teachers unions, the existing public school establishment, and such advocacy groups as People for the American Way and the National Association for the Advancement of Colored People. Through legislative battles and lawsuits, these groups have effectively slowed the expansion of school voucher programs. Outside of Milwaukee, where tremendous growth has occurred, only about 7,500 more students around the nation used publicly funded vouchers in 2005 than in 1991. Though considerably more students have participated in privately financed school voucher programs, topping out at over 100,000 in 2000 (Ladner 2001), enrollments over the last several years appear to have either leveled off or declined.

State judges are partially responsible for arresting the expansion of voucher programs. A pilot voucher program enacted in Colorado in 2003 never saw the light of the day because the state's supreme court ruled that it violated the state constitution's requirement that local districts maintain control of locally raised funds and of "any discretion over the character of instruction participating students will receive at district expense" (*Owens v. Colorado Congress of Parents*, 2004). In early 2006, school vouchers suffered another setback when the Florida Supreme Court struck down the state's program in the name of educational "uniformity" in *Holmes v. Bush*. Other voucher programs have been defeated by voters. In November 2000, both California and Michigan voters rejected school-voucher ballot initiatives.

Public support for vouchers has proven difficult to gauge, not least because of survey respondents' sensitivity to the wording of questions. In 2002, for instance, the annual Phi Delta Kappa/Gallup Poll asked for people's opinion about vouchers in two different ways. A majority of respondents supported vouchers if asked one way but opposed them if asked another way. Since 2002 the Phi Delta Kappa/Gallup Poll has left out the more neutral of the two questions, which, incidentally, also yielded higher support for vouchers. Regardless of question wording, however, in 2001 Terry Moe found that low-income, black, and Hispanic residents in disadvantaged school districts constituted the strongest proponents of vouchers, while wealthy white suburban residents constituted the strongest opponents.

Among political elites, support for vouchers varies markedly across party lines. Republicans tend to favor them, championing the supposed power of unfettered markets and small government. Most Democrats, who have close ties to unions and a history of supporting public education, are skeptical of many forms of choice, especially vouchers. Indeed, congressional votes for the 2004 District of Columbia pilot voucher plan split along party lines. In the House, Republicans were 52 percentage points more likely than Democrats to support the plan, while in the Senate they were 42 percentage points more likely to do so.

Looking forward at the national level, school vouchers face an obvious political challenge. Those political elites who are predisposed to support vouchers (Republicans) disproportionately represent constituents who oppose them (suburban whites), while those elites (Democrats) who represent strong proponents of vouchers (urban minorities) also have strong ties to teachers unions, which vigorously oppose them. Despite calls for a national voucher program, the expansion of voucher programs is likely to be the continued result of a combination of privately funded initiatives and an unusual alliance of younger African-American city leaders and Republican mayors and governors.

SEE ALSO *Education; Education, Unequal; Educational Quality; Schooling; Schooling in the USA*

BIBLIOGRAPHY

Angrist, Joshua, Eric Bettinger, Erik Bloom, Elizabeth King, and Michael Kremer. 2002. Vouchers for Private Schooling in Colombia: Evidence from a Randomized Natural Experiment. *American Economic Review* 92 (5): 1535–1558.

Chubb, John E., and Terry Moe. 1990. *Politics, Markets, and America's Schools.* Washington, DC: Brookings Institution Press.

Fiske, Edward B., and Helen F. Ladd. 2000. *When Schools Compete: A Cautionary Tale.* Washington, DC: Brookings Institution Press.

Friedman, Milton. 1955. The Role of Government in Education. In *Economics and the Public Interest*, ed. Robert Solo. New Brunswick, NJ: Rutgers University Press.

Gallego, Francisco A. 2006. *Voucher-School Competition, Incentives, and Outcomes: Evidence from Chile.* Working Paper. Department of Economics, MIT. http://econ-www.mit.edu.

Greene, Jay P., Paul E. Peterson, Jaingtao Du, Leesa Boeger, and Curtis L. Frazier. 1996. *The Effectiveness of School Choice in Milwaukee: A Secondary Analysis of Data from the Program's Evaluation.* Cambridge, MA: Harvard University Program on Education Policy and Governance.

Hess, Frederick. 2002. *Revolution at the Margins: The Impact of Competition on Urban School Systems.* Washington, DC: Brookings Institution Press.

Howell, William G., and Paul E. Peterson. 2006. *The Education Gap: Vouchers and Urban Schools.* Rev. ed. Washington, DC: Brookings Institution Press.

Hoxby, Caroline M. 2000. Does Competition among Public Schools Benefit Students and Taxpayers? *American Economic Review* 90 (5): 1209–1238.

Hoxby, Caroline M. 2005. *Competition among Public Schools: A Reply to Rothstein (2004).* Working Paper 11216. Cambridge, MA: National Bureau of Economic Research.

Hsieh, Chang-Tai, and Miguel Urquiola. 2006. The Effects of Generalized School Choice on Achievement and Stratification: Evidence from Chile's Voucher Program. *Journal of Public Economics* 90: 1477–1503.

Ladner, Matthew. 2001. *Just Doing It 5: Surveying America's Privately Funded School Choice Grants Programs for Growth, Impact, and Progress.* Austin, TX: Children First America.

Moe, Terry. 2001. *Schools, Vouchers, and the American Public.* Washington, DC: Brookings Institution Press.

Rothstein, Jesse. 2005. *Does Competition among Public Schools Benefit Students and Taxpayers? A Comment on Hoxby (2000).* Working Paper 11215. Cambridge, MA: National Bureau of Economic Research.

Rouse, Cecilia Elena. 1998. Private School Vouchers and Student Achievement: An Evaluation of the Milwaukee Parental Choice Program. *Quarterly Journal of Economics* 113 (2): 553–602.

Witte, John F., Troy D. Sterr, and Christopher A. Thorn. 2005. *Fifth-Year Report: Milwaukee Parental Choice Program.* Madison: University of Wisconsin, Department of Political Science. http://www.lafollette.wisc.edu/publications.

William G. Howell
Elena Llaudet

SCHOOL OF LAUSANNE

SEE *Lausanne, School of.*

SCHOOLING

Around the world, organized education, or schooling as it is better known, has long been responsible for socializing members of society to adopt and practice its values and culture. For example, early schooling focused more on indoctrinating children into a collective religious, dynastic, or national identity rather than individual self-expression. From this standpoint, schooling sought to produce self-knowledge within educators so that they might help produce that knowledge in others. For nearly its entire existence, however, formal schooling has been highly selective in determining whom it educates and for what purpose. Until the advent of the Industrial Revolution, schooling was an activity relegated only to the elite members of a society, as its purpose was to perpetuate elitism and maintain class stratification.

Individuals were educated for careers in the clergy, military, government, and academia. In any given country, however, educated citizens made up only a small proportion of the population. The masses, if educated at all, simply learned through the transmission of information from family and other members of the community, as the elite classes did not believe educating the masses to be socially desirable or responsible (Gutek 1993). In the United Kingdom, for example, a majority of the population could neither read nor write until the early nineteenth century. This pattern of schooling remained consistent throughout much of the world until the Industrial Revolution.

With the Industrial Revolution, some societies found themselves in need of a new, educated middle class. Faced with the need to educate large populations, societies began to develop compulsory, state-supported schools. Because the population of citizens to be educated was growing, societies could no longer be as selective in determining who would be educated. As the number of students increased, they exhibited varying degrees of ability. As a result, schooling became a vehicle to sort students into various levels based on their abilities. Students believed to be able to profit most from schooling were tracked into more traditional paths, while those believed to be able to profit least were sorted into paths that led them out of the educational system. This practice of sorting students into different academic tracks, although now more sophisticated, has prevailed in education systems around the world.

As argued by scholars such as Michael Apple, Henri Giroux, Paulo Freire, and Joel Spring among others, there is an undeniable relationship between education, power, and the state. In light of the current globalization of schooling, academic success is almost exclusively defined in terms of "capital accumulation and the logic of the marketplace" (McLaren 2002, p. 34). Not only are working-class students affected by this principle, but middle-class students are as well. American culture, for example, continuously encourages the consumption of commodities as a mechanism to continue the cycle of accumulation, blinding even middle-class students to the self-repressive, oppressive nature of capitalism. The schools mimic this cycle by intellectual dependence in students (Gatto 1992). The focus of educational reform in the United States has been to create a force of "compliant, productive and patriotic workers for a resurgent America" (McLaren 2002, p. 187). Schools, with their factory-like structure, control the process of learning by keeping students on tight schedules regulated by bells and time blocks. Learning, therefore, is at the mercy of the school's schedule, and students learn only what can be taught in the allotted time span. Learning is prescribed by the society, and students are told what to learn, when to learn it, and how (Gatto 1992). Looking at this phenomenon from a Marxist perspective, capitalism diminishes the individual to a commodity with a certain value—labor value—that can be bought and sold all in the name of profit. In essence the ruling class (the capitalists) exploit the working class (the workers) by extracting "a surplus value beyond what is necessary for the working class to survive" (McLaren 2002, p. 198).

Teachers are also prescribed what and how to teach. Many teachers fear losing their jobs if they deviate from the curriculum that society has deemed appropriate for them to follow. From a critical educational standpoint, schooling is a "form of power which reveals its connections to the entrenched interests of capital and the state, exercised 'over the heads of teachers' and through teachers over their students" (Banya 2002). This is evident in the push toward incorporating corporate management pedagogies within the classroom. Teachers are provided "teacher-proof" state-mandated curricula that adopt management-type pedagogies that reduce their role to that of nothing more than a "semi-skilled, low-paid clerk" (McLaren 2002). Furthermore, they are "unwitting pawns in class and cultural domination and exploitation" (McLaren 2002, p. 221).

Society, through schools, teaches us that success can be achieved by intelligence, hard work, and creativity. The school system is built on the spirit of meritocracy—those students who try harder and have more innate intelligence reap their rightful rewards. Students who possess the dominant cultural capital—ways of talking, acting, and socializing—are rewarded, while those possessing the cultural capital of the oppressed are devalued. As a result, schools perpetuate the unjust system of trading in cultural capital for economic capital.

Educational inequality is a persistent problem, particularly in terms of race, gender, and social class. In the United States, for example, women and minorities have historically been limited by and excluded from attaining higher levels of education by discriminatory policies. There are those, however, who argue that "things should be different now" because of the opportunities in the public and private sectors available to those who have a good education.

In terms of race, a growing black middle class has raised new concerns regarding the lagging school performance of many African Americans. The new argument is that "class" and not "race" are the root causes of inequality in America. As middle-class African Americans leave urban, inner-city areas, the largely manufacturing employment sector also leaves, thus creating an "underclass" of citizens who are left behind to endure the brunt of poverty and inequality. Poverty is a major barrier to quality education, as many schools in lower income communities have curricula designed to keep poor people in their place (Spring 1989).

In terms of gender, teachers are more likely to value the opinions of middle-class white male students over those of females (McLaren 2002). Girls, for example, are expected to be composed and passive, while boys are encouraged to be more academically aggressive. As a result, girls are less likely to take math and science courses, more likely to attribute failure to internal factors, and although they start school ahead of boys in reading and math, they graduate from high school with lower scores in both areas.

These practices are not perpetuated by force, however. The dominant culture, rather, is able to exercise power over subordinate classes through hegemony—the maintenance of domination through consensual social practices, social forms, and social structures (McLaren 2002). Students are not taught to question the prevailing capitalist values of the nation, and as a result, the culture has helped produce a "veritable passion for ignorance" (McLaren 2002, p. 217). And the social structures—the church, the schools, the mass media and the family—have all been shaped by the dialectical contradiction between labor and capital.

This marketization of schooling is not solely a Western phenomenon. Educational systems in many West African countries were initially developed in the image of Western-type educational systems during the late 1800s and early 1900s in response to perceived needs of the colonizers (Banya 2006). Schools were established for a variety of reasons—commercial, religious, and political—but rarely were they established for indigenous needs. Initially, Christian churches played a major role in the development of educational facilities, and later trading companies and local colonial governments eventually provided their own (Banya 2006).

The major aims of the school systems were to provide personnel for the activities of government administration, the church, and commerce. In attempting to achieve these aims, the frame of reference was entirely Western. In most countries the systems were elitist, focusing their resources and attention on the students who could successfully negotiate the system and take their place in the colonial structure that was being established. As in Western education, West African schools have the responsibility of socializing students to the values and customs of the society. Primary education, for example, introduces those fundamentals necessary to produce an individual who, at a basic level, is able to contribute meaningfully to life in his or her community. Furthermore, the goals of junior and senior secondary level education are the continued acquisition of basic skills and knowledge and the introduction of subjects encouraging the development of nationally desired and saleable skills. Schooling in this sense is designed to utilize each individual's ability, aptitude and interest to equip individuals with skills to satisfy society's manpower needs. They are also expected to develop a character that would help cultivate desirable attitudes and regard for the nation's well-being (Banya 2006).

While the argument can be made that the function of schooling is to prepare citizens to effectively participate in a global economy, it is also important to understand its role in creating autonomous, independent thinkers. To date, however, educational systems continue to perpetuate inequity and injustice.

SEE ALSO *Black Middle Class; Capitalism; Colonialism; Curriculum; Education, USA; Freire, Paulo; Marxism; Middle Class; Missionaries; Pedagogy; Schooling in the USA; Socialism; Socialization; Stratification; Tracking in Schools; Working Class*

BIBLIOGRAPHY

Banya, Kingsley. 2002. Personal correspondence.

Banya, Kingsley. 2006. Can Continuous Assessment Replace External Examinations? *World Studies in Education* 6 (2): 5–27.

Gatto, John. 1992. *Dumbing Us Down: The Hidden Curriculum in Compulsory Schooling.* Philadelphia: New Society Publishers.

Gutek, Gerald. 1993. *American Education in a Global Society: Internationalizing Teacher Education.* White Plains, NY: Longman.

McLaren, Peter. 2002. *Life in Schools: An Introduction to Critical Pedagogy in the Foundations of Education.* 4th ed. Boston: Allyn and Bacon.

Spring, Joel. 1989. *The Sorting Machine Revisited: National Educational Policy Since 1945.* New York: Longman.

Shelby Gilbert

SCHOOLING IN THE USA

The ancient Greeks believed that education was the optimal means for transmitting and reinforcing societal values through the generations. They believed that religious life should coexist with public life (e.g., society and the state) so that society might flourish by sustaining the prevailing culture's norms and values. For this process to occur, the young must be trained and educated and their character shaped.

COLONIAL EDUCATION

Many U.S. founders adopted a similar theory of education, believing that the republic would not survive without sufficiently educated citizens. For the founders' ideas to thrive, appropriate policies were needed to drive the process of educating young citizens in God and country. The importance of public education and the policies that drive its function have transformed and continuously shaped the identity of the United States since its inception, creating an often turbulent history. Many of the founders of American education focused on education as vital to the continual progression of the republic and, in particular, white Protestant morals. The U.S. educational system and the policies enacted were for white males, by white males, for the purpose of advocating their economic, social, and political interests. After much resistance, women were later granted admission to education, and blacks were the last minority group to gain access.

The linkage between public life and education in the United States was not immediate (Salomone 2000). Seventeenth-century colonists did not believe that religion and public life should coexist. In fact, the founders instituted a separation of church and state. As a result, schools were used primarily to reinforce the religious beliefs of the prevailing white citizenry. Since the colonists' main financial resource was agriculture, education was less critical to the economy. Schooling took place primarily within the home, as the burden of teaching children was laid upon the family unit and the white Protestant church. The few schools that existed at the time were seen as short-term places of learning. Many were held for just ten to twelve weeks out of the year, favored boys, and were substantially influenced by wealthy landowners and the Protestant perspective. Early schools also charged fees, which helped to stretch the minuscule monies spent by towns. Before the American Revolution, "education was neither free nor public" (Kaestle 2001, p. 20). Indeed, a family's race, wealth, and social status heavily impacted the amount of education their children received and their potential outcomes.

THE COMMON SCHOOL

Following the American Revolution, influential men such as Thomas Jefferson, Noah Webster, and Benjamin Rush became concerned at the lack of school expansion and the uneven distribution of education. They advocated statewide education that would be systematically supervised. During the 1790s, Jefferson and Rush made failed attempts to legislate state systems of education in Virginia and Pennsylvania. But with the help of Horace Mann, the first secretary of education for Massachusetts, the idea of a statewide school system finally took hold. Mann devised the "Common School," which replaced the colonial mode of education. These schools would impart a higher quality of education for both boys and girls, giving them a chance for a good life while ensuring the survival of the republic. He proposed that schooling should be free and thus be equally accessible to all, thereby increasing the social capital of all, regardless of social position in life, and enhancing democracy. Mann understood that children of higher social status who could attend school had an advantage because of the cultural capital of belonging to a high-status family with high academic expectations. Following Mann's common schooling initiative, education was to put all children, regardless of cultural capital, on an equal footing. Schools would be headed by women, who many felt were dispositionally designed by God to be the principal educators for the white race. Many young women headed west not only to teach the three R's but also to instill discipline and promote national ideals. The common school became the new direction and principal version of public education throughout the United States.

This approach did not proceed without major conflicts between political parties, such as the Jacksonian

Democrats and the Whigs, who debated the role of the government in school expansion and policies. Resistance to centralized state mandates and government intervention also took place in local communities around the country. But Mann persisted in his fight to end the inequalities of the colonial educational system, and in 1860 state laws were established instituting government control. Finally, schools would be funded by taxes and follow state standards.

THE INDUSTRIAL REVOLUTION AND BEYOND

The purpose of common schools shifted again as a result of the Industrial Revolution and the concomitant increase in immigration. Most white Americans were concerned about the new immigrants, regarding them as poor, socially and morally deviant, and threatening to the predominant white Protestant way of life. Schooling became a critical device for assimilating new immigrants to the ideas of Protestant morals, respect for private property and authority, hard work, patriotism, and accepting one's given second-class citizenship in the social hierarchy, while at the same time training them to understand the political and public affairs that were important to expanding America through the world economy.

The nineteenth century ended with many changes in education and a vast expansion of American schools. Many scholars have noted that the changes in education and educational policy were closely connected to U.S. economic needs (e.g., Vinovskis 1999). The practice of holding school for children until the eighth grade changed because of the new skills demanded of workers. Children were being asked to stay in school longer than they had in previous decades. Later, secondary education was added. In addition, rising curriculum standards, an increased teachers' knowledge base, and additional state and federal control forced the creation of stricter education policies that standardized the practice of education.

Because of government and business influences, education policy transitioned from the philosophy that the role of schools was to provide moral teaching to the philosophy that their role was to provide vocational and industrial education. After World War I, group intelligence tests were used to place children on curricular tracks that purported to demonstrate differences among immigrants, racial minorities, and whites. In the end, the purpose was to show the country that immigration should be restricted. Some proponents of IQ tests felt that they could also be used to assign groups of children to tracks that allegedly offered education that benefited their individual needs. But many saw the educational policies that drove these tests as not simply assigning children to appropriate vocational or academic tracks but as a form of social engineering that restricted the opportunities of immigrants and other minorities.

By the 1950s, many government officials were coming to believe that schools suffered from lower standards that enabled such countries as the Soviet Union to beat the United States in the space race. In response, policy initiatives such as the National Education Defense Act of 1958 provided funding for graduate students to study foreign languages, mathematics, and other sciences. Later, "education, as a form of investment in human capital, was recognized as an important component of economic development in the 1960s" (Vinovskis 1999, p. 153). In decades to come, education policy would be used to provide for the growth of schooling to stimulate economic expansion. This idea of viewing children as human capital was renewed in the 1980s and 1990s and continues in the twenty-first century.

THE CONTEMPORARY SCENE

Although in contemporary America schooling is believed to be universal and connected to the founders' purpose, discussion surrounding public education is more complicated today than ever. Many groups are attempting to reform public education through a variety of initiatives, and many of the same past issues have reemerged. The actors in these conflicts include politicians, administrators, boards of education, special-interest groups, teachers unions, corporations, and foundations. Many functionalists argue that public education and policy have triumphed because education has stayed true to the founders' ideals in continuing the success of the republic. Functionalists accept social inequality as necessary, arguing that social inequality encourages competition, which pushes people to perform to the best of their abilities to attain a desired social level. Therefore, individuals and minority groups without power are in constant conflict, always striving for a better place on the social hierarchy. These theorists believe that an individual or a group's social mobility is determined by their own efforts because everyone, regardless of race or gender, has equal access to education and resources.

Both the Reagan and Bush administrations of the 1980s and 1990s closely adhered to this functionalist doctrine, favoring political approaches to social issues that affected the poor and minority groups. Under the functionalist paradigm, individuals are to blame for their own lack of resources, power, and education. Both administrations blamed the educational system for the failure of public education. The 1980s reports *A Nation at Risk* and *Action for Excellence* blamed public education for the nation's decreased status in the global markets. With Richard Herrnstein and Charles Murray's 1994 book *The Bell Curve*, attention was redirected to children, especially the supposed deficiency of minority and lower-class children, who were blamed for the nation's drop in competitiveness in global markets.

This approach again became prevalent in the George W. Bush administration through policies and legislation such as No Child Left Behind. Supporters of the policy argue that the education reform act "is aimed at addressing the needs of disadvantaged children, closing the gap between the rich and poor kids, improving accountability, and offering schools more financial resources to improve their performance" (Giroux 2003, p. 72). Parents can obtain vouchers to choose and pay for education that fits their child's needs if their current school is not achieving to government standards within three years. Many voters agreed with Bush, voting largely for a presidential candidate who ran on a strong market-based approach to education policy. This market approach is also seen in the concept of charter schools, which first emerged in 1992 in Minnesota as advocates demanded change in urban schools. Proponents of charter schools see them as a way of enhancing competition in public education by focusing on student achievement while at the same time empowering parents with choice. Opponents such as Jonathan Kozol (1992) note that "choice will fragmentize ambition, so that the individual parent will be forced to claw and scramble for the good of her kid and her kid only, at whatever cost to everybody else" (p. 92). But in reality, the market approach and legislation such as No Child Left Behind focus on the academic and social deficits of poor and minority children and not on the structural deficits of the economic and educational institutions. The blaming tactic that focuses on the low achievement of poor and minority children as well as the operation of public schools takes attention away from economic issues that are closely connected to student achievement. It has also galvanized the connection of the corporate world with public education by treating schools as if they were businesses within the marketplace.

RACE, CLASS, AND EDUCATION

Conflict theorists have attempted to deconstruct the functionalist doctrine. They charge that every society operates socially and economically on the grounds of inequality that privileges the wealthy and powerful while attempting to convince lower groups that the gap in power, resources, or education are necessary to the survival of the society. Conflict theorists argue that schools are set up as mechanisms to sort and control minorities in an unequal manner, inhibiting their social mobility. In essence, regardless of effort, some children in U.S. public schools are set up to "lose."

Conflict theorists consider the current schooling issues as a prime example of the inequalities that exist in public education. Miron (1996) states that in a study of an urban school setting in Louisiana, black students articulated a general dislike for the way school officials treated them. Miron asserts that the curriculum was used as a tool to discriminate against black students. In terms of observed behavior and academic practices, whites were found to be subjected to less rigorous observation than black students.

Secondly, despite significant progress during the civil rights era, some scholars today feel that the spirit of "true" integration never occurred in U.S. public schools. In fact, many feel that public schools today have shown signs of de facto segregation where by choice whites are increasingly leaving ethnically diverse inner-city schools for more homogeneous white surroundings in suburbs (Bell 2004; Kozol 2005). This becomes all the more believable when one recalls that the foundation of U.S. public education meant that whites would benefit from a white system of control.

African Americans have a particularly long history of denied and suppressed educational opportunities. For example, in the South, the expansion of the rights, privileges, and access to formally all-white institutions for blacks took place during Reconstruction (1866–1877). Blacks participated and successfully held governmental positions of power, voted in elections, owned land, partook in the economy, and sought education that was once denied to them during the era of slavery. Moreover, the Reconstruction legislation that affected public schooling in the South was the result of the important and influential efforts of ex-slaves not only to shape but also to create a catalyst for an established public school system for all children, which continues to exist in the South today. Ex-slaves' desire for schooling was felt by old and young alike. Blacks at the time believed that obtaining an education enabled them to open the doors to democratic politics in the United States. In order to obtain an education, they appealed to federal and state governments.

Ex-slaves' desire for education was founded on "self-help." Even though blacks held together in securing a decent amount of resources on their own, blacks also knew they needed the assistance of outside white investors, as well as state and federal government funding, physical protection, and legislation that granted equality. Because of this need for assistance, blacks met many obstacles: lack of money, conflicts with northern white missionaries who tried to control the education process, community conflicts, and acts of terrorism. In terms of education, because of the protection of the Thirteenth, Fourteenth, and Fifteenth Amendments and the Civil Rights Acts of 1868 and 1875, blacks for a while enjoyed equal access to education. But this period of radical progressiveness and alliances between whites and blacks did not last long because of such factors as the withdrawal of Northern troops from the South, the ousting of blacks from the Republican Party, physical and emotional terrorism by the Ku Klux Klan, and the Democratic Party's return to political power. The U.S. Supreme Court ruling in *Plessy v. Ferguson* (1896) marked the collapse of Reconstruction by making it constitutionally legal to segregate blacks from whites as long as "equality" existed in their separation.

Two race "worlds" took root within the first decade of the twentieth century (Bell 2004). This was no more evident than in public education, with white and black schools. By separating whites from blacks, the process of schooling was another institutional example of the continuation of racial oppression of blacks. This unequal treatment was observed in the lack of adequate pay for school staff, inferior facilities, and lack of suitable academic resources in black schools compared to white schools. Even in the face of school segregation and considerably unequal financial resources—despite *Plessy's* "separate-but-equal" clause—many black schools thrived because of the adoption of a "counterhegemonic" theme, meaning that they were "organized in opposition to the dominant ideology of white supremacy and Black intellectual inferiority" in order to create literate, academically achieving citizens and leaders who would continue the racial uplift of African Americans (Perry, Steele, and Hilliard 2003, p. 91). W. E. B. Du Bois in *Black Reconstruction* discussed how these schools did not exist in the South without the initiatives of blacks. Shortly after the Civil War, newly elected black officials and their collaborative efforts with the Freedman's Bureau, aid societies, and missionary groups all helped to establish the first state-financed public education system for young and old blacks alike. During Reconstruction, many free blacks began to educate themselves and others. Black women soon filled an important role in establishing and maintaining the schools. These new facilities helped blacks become literate and empowered in the business, economic, and judicial worlds that were foreign to them. Schools provided a place for blacks to be educated on the agenda of the Republican Party, their rights as free blacks, and the importance of voting.

The legal segregation of public schools continued until *Brown v. Board of Education* (1954). In terms of Native Americans, they too were required to attend segregated government schools where they were forced to abandon their tribal traditions, dress, appearance, and customs, in an effort to assimilate them into white customs.

Educational policies and schooling have adapted to the dramatic changes in population, the economy, the push for racial equality, technological advances, war, and cultural transformation. What has remained constant is that elite whites who control power and resources continue to vie for power through policies, including educational policies that have been historically devised to maintain the status quo by denying equal access to education for all citizens. The foundation of inequality set in place by the founders is alive and present in today's education system.

SEE ALSO Brown v. Board of Education, *1954;* Brown v. Board of Education, *1955; Education, Unequal; Norms*

BIBLIOGRAPHY

Bell, Derrick. 2004. *Silent Covenants: Brown v. Board of Education and the Unfilled Hopes for Racial Reform.* New York: Oxford University Press.

Crowson, L. Robert. 2003. The Turbulent Policy Environment in Education: Implications for School Administration and Accountability. *Peabody Journal of Education* 78 (4): 29–43.

Daniels, Ron. 2002. Racism: Looking Forward, Looking Back. In *Race and Resistance: African Americans in the 21st Century,* ed. Herb Boyd, 1–20. Cambridge, MA: South End Press.

Du Bois, W. E. B. 1935. *Black Reconstruction in America: 1860–1880.* New York: Atheneum.

Giroux, A. Henry. 2003. *The Abandoned Generation: Democracy beyond the Culture of Fear.* New York: Palgrave Macmillan.

Gutmann, Amy. 1987. *Democratic Education.* Princeton, NJ: Princeton University Press.

Hahn, Steven. 2003. *A Nation under Our Feet: Black Political Struggles in the Rural South from Slavery to the Great Migration.* Cambridge, MA: Belknap Press of Harvard University Press.

Kaestle, Carl. 2001. *Part One-1770-1900: The Common School.* In *School: The Story of American Public Education,* eds. Sarah Mondale and Sarah B. Patton, 11–60. Boston: Beacon.

Kozol, Jonathan. 1992. I Dislike the Idea of Choice, and I Want to Tell You Why. *Educational Leadership* 50 (3): 90–92.

Kozol, Jonathan. 2005. *The Shame of the Nation: The Restoration of Apartheid Schooling in America.* New York: Crown.

Lubienski, Chris. 2001. Redefining "Public" Education: Charter Schools, Common Schools, and the Rhetoric of Reform. *Teachers College Record* 103 (4): 634–666.

Miron, Louis. 1996. *The Social Construction of Urban Schooling: Situating the Crisis.* Cresskill, NJ: Hampton.

Mondale, Sarah, ed. 2002. *School: The Story of American Public Education.* Boston: Beacon.

Perry, Theresa, Claude Steele, and Asa Hilliard III. 2003. *Young Gifted and Black: Promoting High Achievement among African-American Students.* Boston: Beacon.

Ridenour, Carolyn S., Thomas J. Lasley, II, and William L. Bainbridge. 2001. The Impact of Emerging Market-Based Public Policy on Urban School and a Democratic Society. *Education and Urban Society* 34 (1): 66–83.

Rushing, Wanda. 2000. Inequality and Education Reform: Formulating a Macro-Historical Sociology Perspective. *Race Ethnicity and Education* 4 (1): 29–44.

Salomone, C. Rosemary. 2000. *Visions of Schooling: Conscience, Community, and Common Education.* New Haven, CT: Yale University Press.

Spring, Joel. 1998. *Conflict of Interests: The Politics of American Education.* 3rd ed. Boston: McGraw-Hill.

Vinovskis, A. 1999. *History and Educational Policymaking.* New Haven, CT: Yale University Press.

Williams, Heather. 2005. *Self-Taught: African American Education in Slavery and Freedom.* Chapel Hill: University of North Carolina Press.

Woodson, Carter. 1933. *The Mis-Education of the Negro.* Chicago: African American Images, 2000.

Terence D. Fitzgerald

SCHULTZ, THEODORE

SEE *Labor, Surplus: Conventional Economics; Lewis, W. Arthur; Subsistence Agriculture.*

SCHUMPETER, JOSEPH ALOIS
1883–1950

Joseph Alois Schumpeter was born in Triesch, Moravia (now the Czech Republic), on February 8, 1883, an only child of a textile manufacturer. After his father's premature death his mother married a high-ranking officer in the Austro-Hungarian army. Young Schumpeter enjoyed a typically aristocratic education—strong on the humanities, weak on mathematics and science—at the Theresianum in Vienna.

As a law student at the University of Vienna Schumpeter took courses in economics from Friedrich von Wieser (1851–1926) and participated in Eugen Böhm von Bawerk's (1851–1914) seminars, joining other budding economists such as Ludwig von Mises (1881–1973) and Austro-Marxists Otto Bauer (1881–1938) and Rudolf Hilferding (1877–1941). He received his doctorate in 1906 and published his first book, *Das Wesen und der Hauptinhalt der theoretischen Nationalökonomie* (1908; still untranslated), a methodological treatise on economic theory. In 1909 he was offered a position as an associate professor in Czernowitz, capital of the southeastern crownland of the Austro-Hungarian Empire (now in Ukraine). In 1911 he was appointed to the chair of political economy at the University of Graz. By the outbreak of World War I he had already established an international reputation as an economist of the first rank: at the age of thirty he was awarded an honorary degree by Columbia University.

After unsuccessful excursions into politics and banking following World War I—he had served as secretary of state for finance for seven months in 1919 in the new republican Austrian government, and in 1921 he assumed directorship of the Biedermann Bank in Vienna—he returned to academia for good in 1925 as professor of public finance at the University of Bonn in Germany.

His sojourn in Bonn was overshadowed by the deaths of his beloved second wife and shortly afterward of his mother, blows from which he never recovered. Schumpeter's permanent tenure at Harvard University began on September 1, 1932, and he was connected with the university continuously, except for two sabbatical leaves, until his death on January 8, 1950. Schumpeter was a founding member of the Econometric Society, and served as its president from 1937 to 1941. In 1948 he was elected, as the first European, president of the American Economic Association.

Schumpeter was an encyclopedic scholar, equally versed in history, sociology, and economics, with a stupendous knowledge in the history of economic thought. More than any other economist before him, with the possible exception of German social philosopher Karl Marx (1818–1883), Schumpeter highlighted the role of innovation for the performance of market capitalism. By *innovation* he meant the introduction of new production technologies and new goods, the conquest of a new supply of raw materials, the setting up of new organizations of industries, and the opening up of new markets. For Schumpeter entrepreneurial action conceived as innovation is the central feature of capitalism, and it forms the backdrop to his theories of credit, interest, capital, profit, and the business cycle. In Schumpeter's scheme the entrepreneur as an agent of innovative change is a revolutionary, overturning tried and tested ways, departing from routine, resisting inertia, and producing novelty by putting extant resources to new uses. The carrying out of new combinations in production is the essence of "creative destruction," a task accomplished by entrepreneurs.

Such bold and confident ways represent a distinct economic function. It is distinct from that of the inventor, the imitator, the capitalist, the banker, the manager, the landowner, and the worker. The entrepreneur may be any or all of these things, but if so it would be by coincidence rather than by nature of function. Neither is the entrepreneurial function necessarily tied to possession of wealth although it may be helpful, nor do entrepreneurs form a class in a sociological sense. It is not money per se that motivates entrepreneurs but rather the dream to found a private empire and the joy of getting things done against the odds.

The results of the entrepreneurially fueled innovation process being inherently uncertain, it is refractory to reduce them to mere calculation. The knowledge buttressing innovation need not be new, it is usually available knowledge that has not been deployed before at all, or else it is utilized in new ways. According to Schumpeter innovation is above all an act of will, depending on leadership, and should not be confused with scientific (or otherwise) invention. Schumpeter broke with tradition by denying that profit is a return to risk. Schumpeter argued that risk falls on the capitalist, not on the entrepreneur *as* entrepreneur, the latter as such being bereft of capital.

Schumpeter's final great work published during his lifetime, *Capitalism, Socialism, and Democracy* (1942), focused on sociological aspects of capitalism, in particular the institutional structure of capitalist society. The paradoxical message emanating from his most popular book is that capitalism is doomed, not by its economic failure (as Marx averred) but by its success. Writing in the early 1940s, Schumpeter pointed to concrete tendencies within advanced capitalist society that he perceived as depleting its moral capital. He singled out the resentment capitalism breeds among intellectuals. According to Schumpeter capitalism had been disfigured by various historical tendencies to such an extent that it should really be called "socialism." The transformations included the growth of interventionist governments, the advent of a managerial bureaucracy within both the public and private sectors, and the rise of a professional middle class with a mind-set completely at odds with that of the classic capitalist. These developments had been accelerated by economic depression and war. According to Schumpeter, socialism is merely the acknowledgment that they have taken place.

Among economists Schumpeter has been interpreted (rightly or wrongly) as saying that with the advent of large corporations and their generously funded research and development departments entrepreneurship and innovation would become increasingly routinized. The withering away of entrepreneurship would amount to innovation being reduced to a decision-making process amenable to rational calculation. This is precisely how the Soviet economy and its Eastern European satellites had set up their innovation systems (with disastrous consequences), on the assumption that innovation, being mere routine business, is plannable. Such a rationalistic approach to the innovation process would be incompatible with capitalist institutions.

In recent decades Schumpeter's ideas on capitalism as "a method of evolutionary change" have instigated a renaissance in research on technological change led by economists, such as Richard N. Nelson and Sidney G. Winter (1982), favoring an evolutionary approach to economics.

Indeed Schumpeterian economics is one of the main sources of evolutionary economics.

SEE ALSO *Austro-Marxism; Capitalism; Entrepreneurship; Great Depression; Hilferding, Rudolf; Marx, Karl; Mises, Ludwig Edler von; Socialism; Technological Progress, Economic Growth*

BIBLIOGRAPHY

Allen, Robert Loring. 1991. *Opening Doors: The Life and Work of Joseph Schumpeter.* 2 vols. New Brunswick, NJ: Transaction.

Dopfer, Kurt, ed. 2005. *The Evolutionary Foundations of Economics.* Cambridge, U.K.: Cambridge University Press.

Nelson, Richard R., and Sidney G. Winter. 1982. *An Evolutionary Theory of Change.* Cambridge, MA: Belknap Press of Harvard University Press.

Schumpeter, Joseph A. 1934. *The Theory of Economic Development: An Inquiry into Profits, Credit, Interest, and the Business Cycle.* Trans. Redvers Opie. Cambridge, MA: Harvard University. Translation of the second German edition published in 1926.

Schumpeter, Joseph A. 1939. *Business Cycles: A Theoretical, Historical, and Statistical Analysis of the Capitalist Process.* 2 vols. New York: McGraw-Hill.

Schumpeter, Joseph A. 1942. *Capitalism, Socialism, and Democracy.* New York: Harper and Brothers.

Schumpeter, Joseph A. 1954. *History of Economic Analysis.* Ed. Elizabeth Boody Schumpeter. New York: Oxford University Press.

Stolper, Wolfgang F. 1994. *Joseph Alois Schumpeter: The Public Life of a Private Man.* Princeton, NJ: Princeton University Press.

Swedberg, Richard. 1991. *Joseph A. Schumpeter: His Life and Work.* Cambridge, U.K.: Polity Press.

Stephan Boehm

SCIENCE

The term *science* (in Latin *scientia,* in Greek *epistēmē*) means "knowledge." In philosophy it refers strictly to proven ideas, to the exclusion of hypotheses or speculations. Until the twentieth century, proof remained mysterious, but what it achieves has been clear since antiquity: certainty, truth unshakable by criticism or doubt. In the nineteenth century Newtonian mechanics was admitted as scientific in this strict sense, and its overthrow was an earthquake. Scholars now agree that certitude is limited to logic and mathematics. Thus scientists have shifted their efforts toward securing for science a surrogate certainty—usually probability.

This shift raises many new questions, thus far unstudied. For example, is Isaac Newton's theory still scientific? In 1962 the historian of science Thomas S. Kuhn spoke of "pre-science" and of "petrified science." Which defunct theory should remain in the up-to-date science textbook? Kuhn suggested that it should present only the latest ideas. Which ones? If not proof, what makes an idea scientific? This is one version of the problem of the demarcation of science (as sets of statements) in disregard for other aspects of the scientific enterprise and its context—intellectual, educational, sociopolitical, and so on. Another possible point of departure is the social dimension of science. In the early seventeenth century the English philosopher Francis Bacon said that the advancement of science would improve the human condition, so investing efforts in scientific research would be the most efficient way to spend one's spare time. Georg Wilhelm Friedrich Hegel, the early-nineteenth-century German philosopher, noted that the invention of gunpowder made city walls useless and so altered the political landscape. The German political philosopher Karl Marx in the nineteenth century equated science with technology (*grosso modo*) and declared all social and political changes as due to technological progress. Following on Marx, in 1939 the English physicist J. D. Bernal made the dubious claim that medieval science was superior to ancient science. In 1964 the Marxist philosopher Louis Althusser rejected many of Marx's sweeping generalizations but still declared the humanities mostly errors that express bourgeois ideology; he contrasted this ideology with science proper, which includes both the exact sciences and revolutionary dialectical materialism as he understood it. He did not trouble himself to demarcate these fields sufficiently to invite detailed discussions as to whether a certain theory, say, in physics or in economics, is or is not scientific. In 1919—decades before Althusser—the American economist Thorstein Veblen studied the nature of science in an effort to examine the validity of claims for the scientific status of diverse economic theories, including that of Marx. He demarcated science historically, by reference to the scientific ethos that, he said, these theories represent; this ethos is often called *humanism*, the same ethos that Althusser later dismissed as bourgeois. Veblen also drew attention to the wealth of empirical finds and role of theories as explanatory (as opposed to classificatory).

Twentieth-century social science developed ideas about specific aspects of society, including prestige—social prestige, the prestige of ideas, and the prestige of scientific ideas. (Prestige is enhanced by power over life; thus nuclear physics is most prestigious.) The concept of science must include the gathering of some sort of empirical information and the search for some interconnections between that information and certain ideas. Science then appears to involve intellectual activities of some sort.

Already four centuries ago Bacon deemed science the outcome of the indiscriminate collection of factual information and its use as a solid foundation on which to construct truly scientific ideas. His view, perhaps modified, prevails as the myth of science. (Being a myth proper, it is used at times in its original variant and at other times in modification.) The problem of demarcation then becomes: What do I know, and how can I show that I truly know it? This approach puts science in a psychological context, raising the question, as suggested by the twentieth-century philosopher of science Karl Popper: Is the psychology used to characterize science scientific? Science is also a publicly available fund of knowledge; the traditional view of it as psychological leads to the view (characteristic of the approaches known as reductionism and psychologism) of everything social as inherently psychological.

If science can be viewed as psychological, so too can mathematics, as suggested by Bacon and the nineteenth-century English philosopher and economist John Stuart Mill. The refutation of this notion led to the revolutionary shift of the view of knowledge from psychology to sociology—from my knowledge to ours—opening the way for the study of the enterprise of science, its prestige, and the social class of its practitioners. This in turn opens interesting secondary questions: Are the teaching of science and the administration of science scientific? (Is the dean of the faculty of science a scientist?) Is all science-based technology scientific? The sociology of science, a young discipline hatched in the early twentieth century, has not yet reached these questions. Such questions pose a difficulty: Science is international, but science-based professions are not. (Compare Japanese science with Japanese technology.) Come to think of it, how international is science? (Is establishing some lingua franca for science advisable?)

Here is a general dispute about all human studies: Existentialists and postmodernists want them to be utterly context dependent, case by case; positivists and analysts want them utterly context free. Seeking a middle ground in sociological laws to set limits on fragmentation, one may view social institutions as generalizations that determine the extent of context dependence. Money is one such institution. Rather than speak separately of the interests of every economic agent, we speak of their profit motive, which, as Georg Simmel argued in 1900, is an intermediary. This role of money makes it important and explains the success of the economic theory that eliminates it from its equations (by replacing prices with relative prices). The trouble is, while waiting for sociology to develop, how should social scientists proceed? They can make use of trivial sociology that at times is powerful. The suitable general concept here is that of games or science regulated by recognized rules (usually institutionalized).

Games need not be problematic unless placed under the artificial limitations imposed in game theory, and as in the case of war games, they need not always be frivolous. As to the triviality of the sociology of games, it is advantageous: It stops the question-begging nature of the theory of science from becoming a nuisance. Thus the rules of the game are negotiable. The game of science then might, but need not, exclude science administration, science education, (science-based) technology, and more. Also the rules may be flexible. All this is a secondary issue, as it obviously should be, as long as science remains chiefly the search for ideas and information of a certain kind. The problem of demarcation now reappears: Which kind? Any kind we want.

As this view of science allows excessive freedom, it also invites instituting limitations—to some function, to some tradition, or to some existing paradigms. Paradigms can be ideas (Newton on gravity), preferred ideas (Einstein), institutions (the Royal Society of London, the local medical school, the patent office), traditions, perhaps ways of life. Approaches to problems via paradigms are limited: Taken too seriously, they prove troublesome as too much may depend on an innocent arbitrary choice. The paradigm of this trouble concerns choices of words resting on the view that the commonness of usage is its only justification. We do not want all usage justified, because we want language to function as a useful means for communication.

What then is the function of science? Among several functions, its most conspicuous is explanation, discovery, invention, better living. Jumping a few steps ahead, one can say that its chief function is the search for true explanations (as suggested by Newton, Einstein, and Popper). Its other functions are peripheral. Assuming this to be the case, one can view science as primarily but not solely the enterprise of approaching true explanations of increasing funds of publicly available information.

This is lovely but full of holes. How do we learn from experience? In what way are scientific theories empirical? Popper broke new ground when he said that theories are empirical when they exclude certain observations and to the extent that they do so. Testing them is, then, the search for these observations; the function of testing theories is to refute them so as to usher in their successors. Applying such a test to the theories of Marx and Sigmund Freud, Popper proved them nonempirical. This approach depends on the exact wording of theories, which may become testable by the enrichment of their contents. Popper later tried to square the two ideas: that the empirical is the refutable and that the aim of theorizing is the approximation of the truth (Einstein). The success of his attempt is under debate.

Robert K. Merton approached matters more historically. In 1938, in the wake of Max Weber, the German sociologist of the late nineteenth century and early twentieth century, Merton identified the scientific revolution with the establishment of the Royal Society of London and the motive for it as Protestantism. He then developed a quasi-Weberian model of science, resting on the theory of science of William Whewell (1840, 1858). Merton's views earned much fame and much criticism. The criticism is at times valid, as Whewell's view is outdated, and at times based on trivial evidence that he idealized science (which he frankly admitted), both in the sense of presenting it at its best and in the sense that Weber recommended the developing of an ideal type. Reports on poor examples of laboratory life as if they were representative appeared as alleged refutations of his views, although fraud is hard to eradicate anywhere.

The presentation of science by Michael Polanyi (1958, 1966) is the most intriguing, even though he played down the rationality of science. He compared the sociology of science to that of the arts and deemed both artistic and scientific training as the tacit transmission of ways of life in workshops by way of personal example. Polanyi's view is insightful and beneficial, although it overstresses tradition as endorsement while slighting the traditional encouragement of criticism and of independence (as suggested by Popper). Polanyi was in error when he ignored efforts to render the tacit explicit and open the results to criticism.

Polanyi's views were further developed by Kuhn, who wished to extend the instruction of leaders beyond their immediate personal example limited to their workshops. Their products can travel and serve as substitutes for personal examples. These become chief examples or, in Greek, paradigms. A science is mature, he said, as it gains a ruling paradigm. This notion appealed to those who wanted their products to serve as paradigms, especially in social studies, where the craving for status is strong. Kuhn later admitted that a territory can be divided between paradigms. He also admitted that identifying a paradigm is difficult. This difficulty should not trouble followers of Polanyi, but it does bother followers of Kuhn, as he declared paradigms obligatory. Kuhn's approach runs contrary to the view of Merton about the liberalism of science. Kuhn also declared his theory applicable only to the study of nature, not of society.

How do the studies of nature and society differ? Any discussion of this question has to be in accord with one view of science or another. One may of course go to and fro, using the best view of science to differentiate natural and social science and then taking the best differentiation one has to try to learn what it says about science. One thing is certain: Social sciences have a more important role to play in the discussion of science than was heretofore believed.

SEE ALSO *Althusser, Louis; Existentialism; Freud, Sigmund; Ideology; Knowledge; Marx, Karl; Merton, Robert K; Mill, John Stuart; Paradigm; Philosophy of Science; Popper, Karl; Postmodernism; Revolutions, Scientific; Scientific Method; Scientism; Social Science; Sociology, Knowledge in; Veblen, Thorstein*

BIBLIOGRAPHY

Agassi, Joseph. 1981. Sociologism in Philosophy of Science. In *Science and Society: Studies in the Sociology of Science*, 85–103. Hingham, MA: Kluwer Boston.

Althusser, Louis. 1964. Marxisme et humanisme. *Cahiers de l'Institut de Science Économique Appliquée* 20: 109–133.

Althusser, Louis. 1996. Marxism and Humanism. In *For Marx*. Trans. Ben Brewster, 219–241. London: Verso, 1996.

Bacon, Francis. [1620] 2000. *Novum Organum* [The new organon], eds. Lisa Jardine and Michael Silverthorne. Cambridge, U.K., and New York: Cambridge University Press.

Bernal, J. D. 1939. *The Social Function of Science*. London: Routledge.

Carnap, Rudolf, and Richard C. Jeffrey, eds. 1971–1980. *Studies in Inductive Logic and Probability*. 2 vols. Berkeley: University of California Press.

Einstein, Albert. 1994. *Ideas and Opinions*. New York: Modern Library.

Hegel, Georg Wilhelm Friedrich. [1837] 2004. *The Philosophy of History*. Trans. J. Sibree. University of Idaho, Department of Philosophy. http://www.class.uidaho.edu/mickelsen/texts/Hegel%20-%20Philosophy%20of%20History.htm

Kuhn, Thomas S. 1962. *The Structure of Scientific Revolutions*. Chicago: University of Chicago Press.

Latour, Bruno, and Steve Woolgar. 1986. *Laboratory Life: The Construction of Scientific Facts*. Foreword by Jonas Salk. Princeton, NJ: Princeton University Press.

Levi, Isaac. 1986. *Hard Choices: Decision Making under Unresolved Conflict*. Cambridge, U.K., and New York: Cambridge University Press.

Merton, Robert K. [1938] 2001. *Science, Technology, and Society in Seventeenth-Century England*. New York: Howard Fertig.

Merton, Robert K. 1965. *On the Shoulders of Giants*. New York: Free Press.

Notturno, Mark A. 1985. *Objectivity, Rationality and the Third Realm: Justification and the Grounds of Psychologism: A Study of Frege and Popper*. Dordrecht, Netherlands: Kluwer Academic Publishers.

Polanyi, Michael. 1958. *Personal Knowledge: Towards a Post-Critical Philosophy*. Chicago: University of Chicago Press.

Polanyi, Michael. 1966. *The Tacit Dimension*. Garden City, NY: Doubleday.

Popper, Karl R. 1945. *The Open Society and Its Enemies*. London: Routledge.

Popper, Karl R. 1959. *The Logic of Scientific Discovery*. New York: Basic Books.

Popper, Karl R. 1972. Knowledge without the Knowing Subject. In *Objective Knowledge: An Evolutionary Approach*, 106–152. Oxford: Clarendon.

Russell, Bertrand. 1931. *The Scientific Outlook*. New York: Norton.

Russell, Bertrand. 1948. *Human Knowledge, Its Scope and Limits*. New York: Simon and Schuster.

Simmel, Georg. [1900] 2004. *The Philosophy of Money*, ed. David Frisby. Trans. Tom Bottomore and David Frisby. 3rd ed. London and New York: Routledge.

Veblen, Thorstein. [1919] 1990. *The Place of Science in Modern Civilization and Other Essays*. New Brunswick, NJ: Transaction.

Wettersten, John R. 1995. Preliminary Report on Efforts of Psychologism to Gain Influence in Proper Epistemological, Methodological, and Psychological Societies. In *Critical Rationalism: Essays for Joseph Agassi*, eds. I. C. Jarvie and Nathaniel Laor. Vol. 2. Dordrecht, Netherlands, and Boston: Kluwer Academic Publishers.

Whewell, William. 1858. *Novum Organum Renovatum*. London: John W. Parker.

Whewell, William. 1967. *The Philosophy of the Inductive Sciences, Founded upon Their History*. 2 vols. New York and London: Johnson Reprint Corporation.

Joseph Agassi

SCIENCE FICTION

Science fiction consists of stories, often set in the future and off the planet Earth, that emphasize scientific, sociological, and especially technological innovation. While a writer might imagine what could happen to, say, an Irish Catholic politician who felt attracted to his brother's American Episcopalian wife in the 1960s, a science fiction writer might imagine what could happen to an implant formed from the mental software of a human male and the hardware body and brain of a human female. Similarly, while Henry James (1843–1916), in *Daisy Miller* (1878), imagines a nineteenth-century American heiress involved with a European suitor, the science fiction writer Ursula K. Le Guin, in *The Left Hand of Darkness* (1969), speculates about a human male who comes to know a hermaphrodite humanoid, a Gethenian, who sometimes turns male or sometimes female, depending on its emotional circumstances (the Gethenian often remains neuter if no suitable partner is around). James concentrated his attention on Daisy Miller, her commanding father, her suitor, and so forth, while taking the social, cultural, and biological background for granted. Le Guin, in contrast, imagined a world without gender and in consequence (or she so thought) without war, examining it through the eyes of her human visitor.

Science fiction has been said to begin with Mary Shelley's *Frankenstein* (1818) or with Jules Verne's *From the Earth to the Moon* (1865) and *Twenty Thousand Leagues under the Sea* (1870) or even as far back as Plato's *Timaeus* (c. 300 BCE), his imagined version of Atlantis. However, science fiction as a distinct literary genre, with specialty magazines such as *Amazing Science Fiction* and *Astounding Science Fiction*, dates from the late 1920s and early 1930s. Its "golden age" of the 1950s and 1960s was driven primarily by technological speculations about the future, whether set primarily on Earth or spreading throughout the galaxy (with science fiction heroes typically confronted by rapacious aliens). Early readers of science fiction were often budding engineers and natural scientists. Writers and characters were mostly male. Isaac Asimov (1920–1992), although he began publishing science fiction stories in his teens, became a professor of biochemistry at Boston University, eventually publishing over five hundred books. (He was fired from his tenured professorship, not for writing science fiction but for publishing factual science texts for the general reader—"popularizations"). Many of Asimov's stories concerned robot-human interactions. His Foundation series sketched the psychohistory of a vast galactic civilization, loosely paralleling the decline of the Roman Empire and the rise of the modern era.

Robert Heinlein (1907–1988) and Fritz Leiber (1910–1992) created theories of time travel that have fascinated philosophers and physicists (e.g., if you kill a butterfly in the age of dinosaurs, will this event cascade into a future in which intelligent dolphins dominate the world, or will the future conserve reality by resisting change?). In *Gather, Darkness!* (1943), Leiber anticipated a post–World War III dark age of theocracy in which a religious government maintains control using technology concealed as supposed miracles, only to be challenged by revolutionary forces that clothe their technology as witchcraft, thus making it *real* to the thoroughly medieval mind-set of the populace. Heinlein produced a version of Plato's *Republic*, titled *Space Cadet* (1948), in which he imagined a future where an intelligent elite has engineered a world government that the populace believes to be a democracy. Later, during a period of opposition to the U.S. war against Vietnam (1957–1975), the patriotic Heinlein lost trust in intellectuals and wrote *Starship Troopers* (1959), in which warriors ruled politically. Paradoxically, Heinlein also then wrote *Stranger in a Strange Land* (1961), from which American hippie readers enthusiastically co-opted the term *grok* for intimate understanding (as in free lovemaking), although they misconstrued Heinlein's underlying libertarian attitude. In retrospect, some see Heinlein as typifying male chauvinist science fiction. Paradoxically as

well, his first novel in manuscript, *For Us, The Living*, written in 1939, describes a man who clashes with, and eventually accepts as wholly justified, a 2086 future in which women have social and career equality with men (this rejected manuscript was not published until 2004, after Heinlein's death).

In the late 1960s, science fiction began to draw more female authors and readers. A readership consisting of budding engineers and scientists gave place to social science and humanities students, while technological innovation, space war, and abstract ideas gave way to psychological and stylistic experimentation. The quietly egalitarian 1950s work of such science fiction writers as Judith Merril (1923–1997) and Katherine Maclean gave way to Joanna Russ's brilliantly feminist *Female Man* (1975), Ursula LeGuin's novels, and Alice B. Sheldon's (1915–1987) many short stories (published under the pen name James Tiptree Jr.). There were also "crossover" figures such as Kurt Vonnegut (1922–2007), who began his career in science fiction and then smoothly switched to a broader "mainstream" readership. Doris Lessing established her reputation as a mainstream writer but has also written much that is science fiction in content terms. In 1976 Octavia Butler (1947–2006) published *Kindred*, whose contemporary African American protagonist time travels to the antebellum South. Butler's Exogenesis series explores issues of sexual identity, sexuality, and power, blurring lines between science fiction and other literatures. Butler's work won her a coveted MacArthur Fellowship in 1995. In the 1980s and 1990s, Orson Scott Card dazzled the science fiction community with *Ender's Game* (1985), *Speaker for the Dead* (1986), and *Xenocide* (1991), infusing traditional science fiction with computer gaming and winning a large youth audience. A practicing Mormon who has complained that science fiction did not take religion seriously, Card has also written explicitly scriptural stories.

The term *mainstream* was adapted by the middle of the twentieth century to distinguish "literature" from specialized, not-quite-literary genres such as science fiction, horror stories, romance fiction, spy stories, and crime fiction (bookstores often arrange their shelves in accord with this distinction). At the same time, however, this breakdown can seem increasingly dubious. For one thing, older books tend to migrate to the literature shelves. Mary Shelley's *Frankenstein*, H. G. Wells's *The Time Machine* (1895), and Verne's *From the Earth to the Moon* will be found there, along with Fyodor Dostoyevsky's *Crime and Punishment* (1855) and Edgar Allan Poe's (1809–1849) horror stories. Graham Greene (1904–1991), who made his mark as a crime and espionage writer, is now wholly included in the literature sections of libraries and bookstores. "Classics" sections may include not only Poe, Wells, Greene, and Dostoyevsky, but also Arthur Conan

Doyle's (1859–1930) Sherlock Holmes detective stories and Leguin's and Lessing's writings, alongside such long-celebrated "literary giants" as Ernest Hemingway (1899–1961) and William Faulkner (1897–1962). Moreover, the centrality and celebrity once granted literary figures now generally envelops only writers, stars, and producers of movies and television. Quite simply, story writers such as Mark Twain (1835–1910) and O. Henry (1862–1910) were the most famous, most widely enjoyed, and best-paid professional entertainers of their day. Even as late as 1952, the issue of *Life* magazine that carried Hemingway's *The Old Man and the Sea* sold over five million copies in two days. Arguably, Hollywood and television comprise the only "mainstream" today.

SEE ALSO *Fiction; Le Guin, Ursula K.; Literature*

BIBLIOGRAPHY

Heinlein, Robert. 2004. *For Us, The Living: A Comedy of Customs.* New York: Scribner.

Le Guin, Ursula K. 1969. *The Left Hand of Darkness.* New York: Walker.

Leiber, Fritz. 1950. *Gather, Darkness!* New York: Pellegrini and Cudahy. Originally serialized in *Astounding Science Fiction* in May, June, and July 1943.

Russ, Joanna. 1975. *The Female Man.* New York: Bantam.

Justin Leiber

SCIENTIFIC MANAGEMENT

SEE *Management.*

SCIENTIFIC METHOD

Research is scientific if and only if it follows a procedure known as *scientific method*. A received view of this method has evolved in the seventeenth century as a synthesis of ideas of Bacon, Boyle, and Newton. Roughly, scientific method consists of indiscriminate observations of regularities, gathering information on repeatable phenomena, and using it as a sound basis for theorizing. Scientific method is, then, a talisman for success. Accordingly, researchers strive to show that their work conforms to scientific method—to the point of distortion. Yet, famously, all guarantees of success in research are worthless. Plato declared that the validity of ideas depends on their pedigree. Tradition offers only two views on the source of ideas: It is intuition—intellectualism, apriorism (Plato)—

or it is observation—empiricism, inductivism (Aristotle). Question: Where should thinking or observing begin? No answer. Reliance on both thought and experience as sources of knowledge is impossible, as they may mismatch; yet their judicious use as procedures is possible: Apriorism admits experience as hints; inductivism admits hypotheses as temporary scaffolding.

The promise of success that scientific method grants depends on the unlearning of prejudices. Sir Francis Bacon, the father of the modern scientific method and a precursor of the Enlightenment, was the first to realize that preconceived opinions distort observation, as they invariably confirm themselves; reliable observations come from unbiased minds. So he recommended relinquishing all preconceptions. This is radicalism; it bespeaks utter rationality. The classical rationalists of the Age of Reason viewed humans as utterly rational, with reason as free of local (individual) differences. Their theories ignored these differences; their economic theory concerned only free trade; their political theory deemed the state as taking care of the contracts, including those between ruler and subject; religion they viewed as private, independent of any established church. Social researchers thus viewed individual conduct as purely rational and as yielding to individually endorsed motives exclusively. Thus, their views on scientific method embody a view of humanity as rational and the individual as preceding society.

The received view of scientific method remained excessively rationalist, radical, ahistorical, individualist, and liberal. To date it dominates the natural sciences, economics, and behaviorist and Freudian psychology. After the failure of the French Revolution, the dominant view within social studies had history as its paradigm, and its agenda largely aimed at shunning radicalism by presenting political theory historically, deprecating democracy and science. As views on scientific method differed, so views differed as to whether social studies start with individuals and reach the study of the social whole or vice versa. This was then a backlash against radicalism. Its prime initiator was Georg Friedrich Wilhelm Hegel, who traced the roots of French revolutionary terror to the Enlightenment's dismissal of social authority as resting on prejudice. Scientific method is inapplicable to society, he declared, since societies have historical roots; there is no social prediction even though nations are subject to historical laws. Schelling, Hegel, and others, developed new methods, variants of which some twentieth-century thinkers embraced, especially Henri Bergson and Edmund Husserl. Following Hegel's claim that the methods of the natural and social sciences diverge, Wilhelm Dilthey suggested that whereas the natural sciences employ deductive explanations, the social sciences employ empathy. (Karl Popper endorsed this distinction, incidentally: His theory of explanation—situational logic—encompasses both models, and allows for reference to both individuals and institutions.) Hegel's methodology is still popular among those who ignore scientific method. Conspicuous among his twentieth-century followers are Gabriel Marcel, Paul Ricouer, Martin Heidegger, Hans-Georg Gadamer, Jean-Paul Sartre, and Jacque Derrida. They all adopted variants of Husserl's method. Heidegger preferred poetic truth to scientific truth. Gadamer endorsed Hegel's objection to the Enlightenment movement's sweeping dismissal of prejudice. He recommended the study of texts, not of facts, hoping that certitude is achievable there, with wider conclusions. Derrida objected: There is no one certain way to read a text. Gadamer was adamant, expressing preference for Aristotle's text on physics over modern ones. Sartre first accepted scientific method and endorsed behaviorism. As he was later impressed with psychoanalysis, he gave up both. (Incidentally, Popper considered both violations of the rules of scientific method, as he rejected the received view.)

Hegel also influenced adherents to science, including Henri de St. Simon, Auguste Comte, John Stuart Mill, and Karl Marx. They sought the scientific historical laws that permit predictions. Marx stressed that scientific method sanctify his predictions, rendering them incontestable. (Not all his followers share his respect for science.) Does the use of scientific method validate Comte's theory of the three stages of history or Marx's view of history as propelled by the class struggle? Is dissent a challenge to their scientific credentials? Or did prejudice distort their use of scientific method? These are difficult questions.

William Whewell, a significant nineteenth-century transitional figure, dismissed the fear of prejudice. He contested Bacon's proposal to empty our minds of preconceived opinions, declaring all ideas preconceived. He trusted rigorous tests to eliminate error. Bacon promised that empty minds will follow scientific method and produce true theories; Whewell denied that: We need hypotheses; occasionally, researchers hit upon true ones and verify them empirically, he said. His view won popularity among physicists while social thinkers followed Mill.

Marx challenged the individualist, ahistorical economics with his historical prediction: As markets must be increasingly unstable, capitalism will give way to socialism—probably through civil war. At the end of the nineteenth century, Émile Durkheim and Max Weber, known as the fathers of modern sociology, circumvented him and shifted the debate away from history back to the other question that Hegel had raised: Which is primary, the individual or the social whole? Their writings on society and on scientific method ignore historical laws.

Durkheim's starting point was the claim that some "social facts" are observable (such as conformity to laws).

This is hard to comprehend, but clearly, he wanted to broaden classical individualist methodology to make it recognize collective entities. He steered between Hegel's view of social forces and Marx's view of economic forces. He considered national cultures to be the glue that maintains collectives; in particular, religion is society's representation or celebration of itself.

Durkheim valued individual contributions to culture, as he admired science. Does his view of culture allow for this? He left this question open. Hence, as a response to Hegel, his theory is incomplete. His attention lay elsewhere: He insisted that a culture coheres with its society. He invented functionalism, the view that social wholes are coherent. A clear counterexample to this is crime: It is dysfunctional. He suggested that crime has a function: to remind society of the law. This does not block the counterexample: The need for violent reminders bespeaks incoherence. Once functionalism incorporates dysfunctional aspects, it becomes trivial and abandons coherence. Durkheim was inspired by Claude Bernard's observation that cold-blooded animals are more adapted to the environment but less energetic than warm-blooded ones. He applied this to the division of labor: High specialization enables a striking worker to bring society to a halt and forces it to cohere (organic solidarity). This is too vague to be open to criticism.

Weber rejected "one-sided materialism"—in allusion to Marx—and ascribed social values to ideas. His studies identify typical value-systems of typical members of various classes and societies. Unlike classical individuals who represent humanity in general, Weber's typical individuals represent subcollectives. His theory of scientific method thus steers between classical individualism and collectivism. To emphasize his reluctance to say whether societies are real, he called it "individualism of method."

Georg Simmel (a contemporary of Durkheim and Weber, but influential only after World War II) suggested that individual and society are equally primary, so that conflict is never totally avoidable. Karl Popper suggested considered action as strictly individual but within social contexts—situational logic—thus achieving a view that is in the traditional individualist mode, without being radical. This opens the road for new kinds of explanation—especially for actions aiming at institutional reform.

Popper's suggestion rests on his groundbreaking description of scientific theory as (not proven but) testable, namely, refutable. For success, this is necessary but insufficient: There is no guarantee. Scientific truth is then not *the* truth, but the best available approximation to it. This closes the debate comparing the rules for natural and social studies. For explanations in the social sciences to be refutable, they should center on individual actions.

Science is now increasingly seen as the search for answers to interesting questions that are open to criticism.

Another development is of the systemist outlook: Both individual and society are systems of sorts (Mario Bunge). How is action at all possible? This question is outside the domain of social studies; these take actions as given and center on their unintended consequences (Hayek)—especially actions intended to improve society. Systemism is incomplete without a theory of scientific method. Some variant of Popper's theory is an obvious candidate. This, however, is a matter for future discussions of scientific method adequate for social studies. The starting point of any such study has to be an examination of the history and sociology of the social sciences, especially of the question, what do we owe to the diverse school of thought of the past and to their august members?

SEE ALSO *Positivism*

BIBLIOGRAPHY

Agassi, Joseph. 1977. *Towards a Rational Philosophical Anthropology.* Dordrecht, Netherlands: Kluwer.

Agassi, Joseph, and Ian C. Jarvie, eds. 1987. *Rationality: The Critical View.* Dordrecht, Netherlands: Kluwer.

Aron, Raymond. 1967. *Durkheim, Pareto, Weber.* Vol. 2 of *Main Currents in Sociological Thought.* Trans. Richard Howard and Helen Weaver. Garden City, NY: Doubleday.

Bacon, Sir Francis. 1620. *The Collected Works of Francis Bacon, Volume I Part I, Philosophical Works.* London: Routledge, [1879] 1996.

Bendix, Reinhardt. 1970. *Embattled Reason: Essays on Social Knowledge.* New Brunswick, NJ: Transaction Books.

Bochenski, Joseph M. 1957. *Contemporary European Philosophy.* Trans. Donald Nicholl and Karl Aschenbrenner. Berkeley: University of California Press.

Boyle, Robert. 1661. "Proëmial Essay" to *Certain Physiological Essays.* In *The Works of Robert Boyle.* Vol. 2, eds. Michael Hunter and Edward B. Davis. London: Pickering & Chatto, 1999–2000.

Bunge, Mario. 1996. *Finding Philosophy in Social Science.* New Haven, CT: Yale University Press.

Durkheim, Émile. 1893. *Émile Durkheim on the Division of Labor in Society.* Trans. Louis Coser. New York: Macmillan, 1933.

Durkheim, Émile. 1895. *The Rules of Sociological Method.* Trans. Sarah A. Solovay and John H. Mueller. Chicago: University of Chicago Press, 1938.

Durkheim, Émile. 1912. *The Elementary Forms of the Religious Life.* Trans. Joseph Ward Swain. London: George Allen & Unwin, 1915.

Durkheim, Émile. 1928. *Socialism and Saint-Simon,* ed. Alvin W. Gouldner; trans. Charlotte Sattler. Yellow Springs, OH: Antioch Press, 1958.

Durkheim, Émile, and Marcel Mauss. 1903. *Primitive Classification.* Trans. Rodney Needham. Chicago: University of Chicago Press, 1963.

Hayek, Friedrich von. 1952. *The Counter-Revolution of Science: Studies on the Abuse of Reason.* New York: Free Press.

Hegel, Georg Friedrich Wilhelm. 1837. *Philosophy of History,* ed. Eduard Gans; trans. John Sibree. New York: Dover, 1956.

Marx, Karl. 1849. *Wage-Labor and Capital,* ed. Friedrich Engels; trans. J. L. Joynes. Chicago: C. H. Kerr, 1891.

Marx, Karl. 1859. *A Contribution to the Critique of Political Economy.* Trans. N. I. Stone. Chicago: C. H. Kerr, 1904.

Marx, Karl. 1865. *Wages, Price, and Profit.* Moscow: Foreign Languages Publishing House, 1951.

Marx, Karl, and Friedrich Engels. 1848. *The Communist Manifesto.* Trans. Samuel Moore. New York and London: Verso, 1998.

Mill, John Stuart. 1843. *A System of Logic,* ed. J. M. Robson. London: Routledge & Kegan Paul, 1974.

Newton, Isaac. 1730. "Query 31." In his *Opticks,* 4th ed. (London 1730) New York: Dover, 1952.

Pickering, William S. F., ed. 1975. *Durkheim on Religion: A Selection of Readings with Bibliographies.* London: Routledge.

Popper, Karl. 1935. *The Logic of Scientific Discovery.* London: Hutchinson, 1959.

Popper, Karl. 1942–1943. *The Poverty of Historicism.* London: Routledge, 1957.

Popper, Karl. 1945. *The High Tide of Prophesy: Hegel, Marx, and the Aftermath.* Vol. 2 of *The Open Society and Its Enemies.* London: Routledge.

Simmel, Georg. 1950. *The Sociology of Georg Simmel,* ed. and trans. Kurt H. Wolff. Columbus: Ohio State University Press.

Weber, Max. 1903–1917. *The Methodology of the Social Sciences,* eds. and trans. Edward A. Shils and Henry A. Finch. New York: Free Press, 1949.

Weber, Max. 1904–1905. *The Protestant Ethic and the Spirit of Capitalism.* Trans. Talcott Parsons. New York: Scribner, 1930.

Whewell, William. 1847. *Philosophy of the Inductive Sciences.* 2nd ed. 2 vols. New York: Johnson Reprint, 1967.

Joseph Agassi

SCIENTISM

Scientism, in a broad sense, is a belief in the superiority of science as a way of understanding. There are many different forms or aspects of this belief, but from the perspective of the social sciences, two aspects of scientism have assumed major significance. These are *methodological scientism,* the view that the methods of the natural sciences are the most (or only) appropriate way of understanding social phenomena, and *reductionist scientism* or physicalism, the view that mental and social phenomena can be reduced to or explained in terms of the concepts of the physical sciences. While *scientism* is sometimes used as a positive term by advocates of such positions, it is typically a pejorative label employed by critics.

While scientism has its roots in the work of Francis Bacon, Auguste Comte, Herbert Spencer, and other pretwentieth-century writers, the term itself was first used by French writers in the 1930s. It was introduced into English by the economist Friedrich A. von Hayek (1899–1992) in several publications in the 1940s that were later collected in his book *The Counter-Revolution of Science* (1952). Hayek presented several arguments that later became central to critiques of scientism:

1. that meaning and intention are essential to understanding human action and social phenomena generally and that these are not reducible to physical terms;

2. that the social sciences seek to understand unique, particular phenomena as well as those that can be subsumed under general laws and that context is essential to explaining such phenomena; and

3. that much of the quantification prevalent in the social sciences is inappropriate, copying the form rather than the substance of physical science.

These arguments are prominent in what later became known as the "interpretive" approach to social science. The German theorist Jürgen Habermas (b. 1929) raised additional arguments against scientism, challenging the traditional separation of science and politics as well as asserting the social sciences' need for interpretive and situation-specific understanding.

While the reductionist version of scientism has sometimes been promoted by physical scientists and philosophers, twentieth-century debate in the social sciences largely focused on methodological issues and the ontological assumptions that inform them. The main arguments against scientism have been grounded in social constructivism, the view that we construct, rather than simply discover, the nature of the world. This view entails that scientific knowledge is simply one construction among others and has no exclusive claim to preeminence or truth. These arguments have informed both the methodological debates in the social sciences, often called the "paradigm wars," between quantitative and qualitative approaches and the broader critique of science itself (the "science wars"), most prominently in what has been called the "critical sociology of science." The latter combines social constructivism with Habermas's political analysis of science to argue that the authority of scientific "knowledge" derives not from any legitimate claim to "truth" about the world but from the rhetorical and political strategies used by scientists to promote their claims.

The "paradigm wars" were widely seen as waning during the last decade of the twentieth century, accompanied by increased acceptance of qualitative and interpretive research and the rise of what has been called "mixed methods" research, combining qualitative and quantitative approaches. In the early twenty-first century, however, scientistic views have gained renewed prominence and political support, particularly in British and American educational policies, where experimental methods have been promoted as "science-based" research, in opposition to the diversity of methods traditionally used in educational research. Attempts have been made to develop a middle-ground position, although some of these have been criticized as still incorporating scientistic assumptions.

Philosophers have also attempted to develop a middle ground between scientism and radical constructivism. One such attempt is the development of critical realism as an alternative to both empiricism and constructivism. Critical realism combines a constructivist epistemology (our *understanding* of the world is to a significant extent socially constructed) with a realist ontology (the world exists independently of our constructions and influences the success of those constructions). Similar views are widespread in the philosophy of science. A parallel critique has challenged the narrowly logical definition of science and scientific method promoted by positivist philosophers and emphasizes the grounding of scientific methods and understanding in our commonsense activities as inquirers. In combination these arguments support both the methodological and the antireductionist critiques of scientism and promote a broader understanding of science that is compatible with methodological and conceptual diversity. They do so while avoiding the relativism of radical constructivism and affirming the value for the social sciences of scientific concepts, such as causal explanation.

SEE ALSO *Epistemology; Science*

BIBLIOGRAPHY

Haack, Susan. 2003. *Defending Science—within Reason: Between Scientism and Cynicism.* Amherst, NY: Prometheus Books.

Habermas, Jürgen. 1971. *Knowledge and Human Interests.* Trans. Jeremy J. Shapiro. Boston: Beacon.

Hayek, Friedrich A. von. 1952. *The Counter-Revolution of Science: Studies on the Abuse of Reason.* Glencoe, IL: Free Press.

Sorell, Tom. 1991. *Scientism: Philosophy and the Infatuation with Science.* London: Routledge.

Joseph A. Maxwell

SCOPES, JOHN
SEE *Scopes Trial.*

SCOPES TRIAL

The dramatic Scopes "Monkey Trial" in 1925 involved the prosecution of high school science teacher John T. Scopes (1900–1970) for violating Tennessee's Butler Law, outlawing the teaching of evolution in the state's public schools. The trial was one of American history's landmark courtroom battles and a watershed in what came to be widely understood as a cresting conflict between science and religion.

The publication of Charles Darwin's *Origin of Species* in 1859 was taken by many as a radical challenge to the Biblical accounts of humankind's origin. In the ensuing years, revolutionary advances in science and technology, increasing urbanization, and the growth of religious pluralism fed by mass immigration, buoyed both the self-confidence of science and the appeal of a secular public sphere. Evolutionary theory was applied to social relations to justify the laissez-faire (or hands-off) policies and economic inequalities of the Gilded Age (which many Christians condemned) as naturally occurring instances of the survival of the fittest. Prominent public thinkers increasingly argued that religion was dogmatic, superstitious, and impeded the scientific spirit essential to a more enlightened modernity. The 1920s, however, witnessed a revival of Fundamentalist Protestantism, aimed at fighting these trends, and many of the ideas—like evolution—that undergirded them by undermining the authority of Scripture. Part of the Fundamentalist counterattack involved state-level efforts to outlaw the teaching of Darwinian theory to public school children.

The Scopes trial was self-consciously conceived as a theatrical staging of these broad-ranging social debates. Tennessee's Butler Law was passed largely as a statement of principle. Few of its proponents either intended or expected that it would be aggressively enforced. The proponents of evolutionary theory, scientific investigation, academic freedom, and secular education (including the American Civil Liberties Union) actively recruited John Scopes, a general science teacher substituting as a biology teacher, to admit to having violated the law by teaching a lesson in evolution. They did so in full collusion with local town officials in Dayton, Tennessee (including the prosecutor), who hoped a dramatic public spectacle pitting the claims of science against religion would revive the economic fortunes of the ailing southern town. The town officials bore no ill will toward Scopes, who swam with the opposing side's lawyers during trial recesses. It was understood that, if convicted, Scopes would serve no jail time, but instead pay a fine generously provided by others. The prosecution and defense teams recruited two of the country's most famous lawyers to square off on behalf of science on one hand and the Bible on the other—the radical Chicago attorney (and proud atheist) Clarence Darrow (1857–1938) and the Populist evangelical former presidential candidate and secretary of state William Jennings Bryan (1860–1925), respectively. The trial was conducted in a carnival-like swirl of hot-dog and lemonade hawkers, souvenir vendors, and street-corner orators. The proceedings were broadcast live from Chicago on WGN radio and charted by swarms of reporters, including the celebrated American journalist H. L. Mencken (1880–1956). The sparring between the two lawyers, including Darrow's withering cross-examination of Bryan (who mounted the stand himself as an expert on biblical teaching) became the stuff of legend. Although the jury convicted Scopes, the consensus was that Darrow had effectively humiliated the creationists, striking a powerful blow for science and academic freedom. Many have held the trial's grueling ordeal responsible for Bryan's death only days after the verdict, as well as for the ensuing retreat of many fundamentalist Protestants from the nation's public life.

In subsequent years the Scopes trial retained a rich resonance as a symbol of the dangers of not only religious zealotry, but of religion in general, to the advancement of knowledge and intellectual freedom. These symbolic uses were evident in accounts of it in the most prominent cold war era American history textbooks and, most famously, in the Jerome Lawrence and Robert E. Lee play, *Inherit the Wind* (and its 1960 film adaptation by Stanley Kramer), which took dramatic liberties with real events by building up the depth of John Scopes's commitment to evolutionary theory and academic freedom and the ruthlessness and intolerance of the Dayton townspeople and prosecutors. These reconstructed memories were prominent in the culture at precisely the moment in the early 1960s that the U.S. Supreme Court held—in a run of Establishment Clause cases invalidating Bible reading and prayer in the schools—that the Constitution imposed a "high and impregnable" "wall of separation" between church and state. As evangelical and fundamentalist Christians became newly active in politics in the 1980s (in part in reaction to these judicial rulings) and as a new generation of critics of evolutionary theory and proponents of creationism and "intelligent design" gained influence, the meaning and legacy of the Scopes Trial are being reconsidered once again.

SEE ALSO *Christianity; Church and State; Civil Liberties; Creationism; Cross of Gold; Darwin, Charles; Fundamentalism, Christian; Populism; Science*

BIBLIOGRAPHY

Larson, Edward J. 1997. *Summer for the Gods: The Scopes Trial and America's Continuing Debate Over Science and Religion.* New York: BasicBooks.

Lawrence, Jerome, and Robert E. Lee. 1955. *Inherit the Wind.* New York: Random House.

Scopes, John T., and James Presley. 1967. *Center of the Storm: Memoirs of John T. Scopes.* New York: Holt, Rinehart, and Winston.

Ken I. Kersch

SCOTTISH MORALISTS

The term *moralist* as used here is historically and technically specific. It describes loosely related but mutually supporting intellectual positions in modern metaphysics and epistemology; in morality, civil society, and the law; in economic and political theories; and in cultural history. Therefore the group of Scottish thinkers who are individually and collectively called *moralists*, though without unanimity in the details of their beliefs, share, in a general and in identifiable ways, compatible views on the nature of philosophy, social science, and politics.

These thinkers are easily identifiable in part because their mature professional lives were spent largely in Scotland, particularly—though not exclusively—at the universities of Glasgow and Edinburgh. Furthermore, their ideas blossomed and their influence radiated from Scotland out to the major centers of learning in modern Europe and beyond roughly between 1740 and 1800. It was in these sixty years that the most influential works were published by the Common Sense philosopher Thomas Reid (1710–1796), the Skeptical philosopher and historian David Hume (1711–1776), the economist Adam Smith (1723–1790), the jurist and cultural historian John Millar (1735–1801), and the sociologist and political scientist Adam Ferguson (1723–1816). Others whose works were part of the moralist trend before, during, and after the sixty-year period and who are privileged for the sake of analysis include: Francis Hutcheson (1694–1746), the jurist Henry Home, Lord Kames (1697–1782), the philosopher and biographer of Adam Smith, Dugald Stewart (1753–1828), and the economist James Mill (1773–1836). Also worthy of mention are James Ramsey McCulloch, Thomas Chalmers, Thomas Carlyle, William Robertson, James Boswell, James Hutton, Robert Wallace, and James Watts. Though born in Ireland to Scottish parents, the Utilitarian philosopher Francis Hutcheson is usually associated with the Scottish moralists because of his influence on Hume and Reid. Hutcheson's impact at the University of Glasgow, where he taught for many years, was so profound that some regard him as a founding father of the Scottish Enlightenment.

WHY SCOTLAND, WHY THEN? SOME HISTORICAL BACKGROUND

When the kingdoms of England and Scotland were united under King James VI in 1707, Scotland was in the midst of a series of so-called Jacobinite revolutions: The first occurred in 1690, the second in 1715, and the last in 1745. These social and political upheavals left Scots not just with a sense of cultural and national instability but also faced with economic challenges that would prove transformative. In order to keep up with its English and French neighbors, Scotland was forced to modernize its economy.

But competition with England and France transcended the domains of the purely political or economic. Cultural issues were never far behind. For example, in England and France it had become a matter of national pride among philosophers, scientists, and playwrights to publish or produce in the national vernacular. It was therefore notable when, in 1729 at the University of Glasgow, Hutcheson became the first to give a lecture in English rather than Latin.

A transformed political culture, the search for economic prosperity through modernization in the context of international competition, and the emergence of a dynamic civil society—these are some of the key factors that account for the national, cultural, and class coherence that characterizes a significant number of the group of thinkers and theorists we call the *Scottish moralists*.

SCIENTIFIC AND CULTURAL CONTRIBUTIONS

In its technical details, it is obvious that Scottish moral philosophy could not have been possible without Copernicus, Bacon, Galileo, Kepler, Boyle, and Newton. The works of these men transformed not just what scientists studied but also, more importantly, the method of inquiry itself. The development of fact-based methods of scientific research—as opposed to idealistic speculative rationalism—directly paved the way for a new kind of philosophy: empiricism. As scholastic speculation and discourse became supplanted by physical observation, measurement, and mechanical experimentation, philosophers like Hume responded by developing a skeptical approach toward traditional metaphysical problems. Hume's self-described "new" philosophy aimed to be grounded in, and reconciled with, the Newtonian and other mechanical and materialistic disciplines. For Hume, skepticism about the existence of the soul, causality, and the possibility of miracles were some of the natural results of his effort—to quote the subtitle of his *Treatise of Human Nature*—to "introduce the experimental method of reasoning into moral subjects."

One of the consequences of empiricist epistemology was antifoundationalism, not just in regard to interpretations of religious beliefs (like the belief in miracles), but also in the conceptions of popular morality and social ethics. *Utilitarianism*, inspired both by the empirical sciences and the new political sciences of writers like Hobbes, became a widely accepted perspective. Hutcheson was the first to use this term to mean "the greatest happiness for the greatest number," though he did so in response to Hobbes and Hume. Hobbes claimed that individuals acted, however indirectly, only out of self-interest and never altruistically. Hume's own methodological and substantive skepticism led him to draw the conclusion that the foundations of both individual and social morality were merely customary and conventional: Neither religion nor metaphysics can guarantee that our ideas of the proper and improper, right and wrong, good and bad, or beautiful and ugly are transcendentally grounded.

Empiricism and utilitarianism combined to produce the doctrine that individuals merely act out of self-interest and to seek pleasure and avoid pain. The doctrine in turn made it possible to say that neither religion nor morality nor aesthetics required, for their explanations, theological or metaphysical foundations. Hutcheson, for example, argued that individuals naturally value society and therefore naturally work cooperatively to achieve it, simply because of their naturally based capacity for feeling or sympathy. It is sympathy that leads otherwise unrelated and self-interested individuals to think and act benevolently toward one another. The task of culture and civilization was merely to promote this fellow-feeling, so that in society persons not only compete but also cooperate for the common good. It is ultimately fellow-feeling and a sense of mutual belonging that leads to well-ordered civil society, national peace, and commercial prosperity. One of the obvious consequences of Hutcheson's social and political philosophy is that being virtuous (e.g., doing what is proper, right, or good), because untethered from earlier theological and metaphysical moorings, amounts to a commitment in personal thought and action to increasing the "degrees of happiness" both for oneself and for all.

Empiricist and utilitarian theories also took hold in the sphere of economic thought. Adam Smith not only accepted the idea that individuals acted out of self-interest but also promoted this self-interest both as a particular kind of natural psychology and as a form of social rationality. In *The Wealth of Nations* (1776), a book considered the founding text of modern economics, Smith translated the original insights of utilitarian ethics into the argument that what is economically selfishly good for the individual is also generally good for the welfare of society. Smith notes: "As every individual … endeavours as much as he can both to employ his capital in the support of domestic industry, and so to direct that industry that its produce may be of the greatest value; every individual necessarily labours to render the annual value of society as great as he can" (IV, 2.9).

In his famous phrase, the "invisible hand," Smith captured what he thought was going on in any prosperous economy. Dynamic and free commercial relations occur, in nearly mysterious ways, as a result of equilibrium between supply and demand. This equilibrium occurs not because individuals are acting selflessly, nor is it a result of heavy-handed government regulation or of business cartels and monopoly. Rather, market equilibrium is simply an empirical fact based on the psychology of the individual. The self-interested actor "neither intends to promote the public interest, nor knows how much he is promoting it" (IV.2.9). Thus it is the mere effort to look out for one's own economic interests ("he intends only his own security … he intends only his own gain") that makes the actor automatically "led by an invisible hand to promote an end which was no part of his intention" (IV.2.9). In even more colorful language, Smith anticipates objections to his observations by pointing out that it is "not from the benevolence of the butcher, the brewer, or the baker that we expect our dinner, but from their regard to their own interest" (IV.7.26).

Moreover, Smith believed that a society is worse off in a government-regulated economy. Market forces alone appear to successfully ensure that an individual, "by pursuing his own interest … frequently promotes that of society more effectually than when he really intends to promote it" (IV.2.9). Smith was, accordingly, entirely skeptical about any hope that "much good [can be] done by those who affected to trade for the public good" (IV.2.9). This position provides the reasoning behind the laissez-faire doctrine in classical economics, a doctrine whose origin is rightly attributed to Smith.

What stands out the most in the above-mentioned moral, social, and economic theories is confidence in the autonomy both of the individual and of society. This confidence translates into the belief that a society and its culture—its history—can be consciously made and remade. It inspired the moralist intellectuals to propose progressive theories of history. In their writings, the word *development* acquired an explicitly historical character. Against the feudal worldviews shaped predominantly by traditional attachments to class and land, in which social hierarchies were justified by religion and theology, the moralists proposed a conception of history as a domain controlled by autonomous individuals and their collective quest for rational self-determination. In addition to Smith's *Wealth of Nations*, Lord Kames's *Essays on Principles of Morality and Natural Religion* (1751), John Millar's *Observations Concerning the Distinction of Ranks in Society* (1771),

Ferguson's *An Essay on the History of Civil Society* (1767), and William Robertson's *The History of Scotland* (1794) were each in the forefront of developing the argument that rather than being fated by God or Nature to follow an inexorable path, any society, if based on the psychology of the individual, could be socially progressive and economically prosperous. The scientific study of society and history—in short, the rise as independent and empirical fields of research of such social sciences as psychology, economics, anthropology, sociology, legal history, and cultural theory—had its modern beginnings in many of the insights generated or expanded upon in the works of the Scottish moralists.

The moralists' theory of history helps explain why it is not surprising to discover in some of their writings prejudice against cultures and societies perceived as "backward," static, and nonprogressive. Their evolutionary view of society led them to try to determine the direction of universal progress and to position existing societies and cultures in hierarchical classificatory schemes, using what they supposed were empirical scales of measurement. Smith, for example, believed that societies and ultimately global history progressed through several stages, defined by economic and political activities: The series of stages begins with hunter-gatherers, then progresses through stages characterized by nomadic tribes, sedimentary farmers, feudal states, and mercantile societies, before culminating in industrial urbanization. The secret to industrialization, according to Smith, was division of labor, a method capable of producing the largest quantity of goods for the largest number of people by the most market-efficient methods.

Because of their evolutionary conception of societies, Scottish moralists were not disturbed by imperial expansion and colonial conquest. Imperialism and colonial conquest, in Ferguson's view, for example, promoted commercial activities and transformed culturally and economically "primitive" nations into industrial or industrializing countries or trading partners. Indeed, because of its wide influence the work of the Scottish moralists cannot be decoupled from the contradictions that attended the development of modernity throughout Europe, Africa, and the Americas: Even as the capitals and provinces of Europe and the Americas were championing the idea of historical progress and the "rights of man," a great deal of the growth in the world's local and international economies was based on slave trade and slave labor, imperialism, and colonialism.

INFLUENCE AND LEGACY

The influence of the moralists on the transformation of Scottish society can easily be measured. On January 8, 1696, for example, a young man by the name of Thomas

Aikenhead was executed for blasphemy. A university student, Aikenhead was successfully charged with "denigrating" the Bible. But public records of the proceeding suggest that Aikenhead was viewed to have committed something more offensive. Though he said he believed in the Holy Trinity, he also, by his own confession, believed that moral laws were "the work of governments and men" and had said to fellow students that theological arguments produced to show otherwise were "a rapsodie of feigned and ill-invented nonsense" (Hill N.D.). By 1755, however, Scotland itself had changed. This was the year David Hume was formally charged with an offense anyone might have considered far more grievous, namely, atheism. Moreover, like Aikenhead, Hume had published books arguing that morality was justified entirely by tradition and custom. Yet, the charges brought against him were dropped—for lack of cause.

Beyond Scotland, the moralists were at the cutting edge of the wider social and political movement known as the Enlightenment. In the decades 1740 to 1800 the Enlightenment movement both became a more universal phenomenon and took on local coloration not just in the cities of Glasgow, Edinburgh, Paris, London, Berlin, and Philadelphia, but also in lesser-known centers of commerce and learning such as Bristol, Cartagena, La Fleche, Konigsberg, and Axum. In the same sixty-year period, three of the modern world's most significant political transformations occurred: the American, the French, and the Haitian revolutions. The most direct connections between these revolutionary developments included the international evangelical and moral revivals represented by activist groups like the Society of Friends, popularly known as the Quakers. In London, influential Quakers formed The Meeting on Slave Trade and worked with Thomas Clarkson and William Wilberforce in the cause of abolition of the slave trade. In the Americas, particularly Philadelphia, Quaker leaders of opinion like John Woolman and Anthony Benezet worked with atheists and believers alike—Thomas Paine, Benjamin Franklin, Joseph Priestley, among others—to found in 1775 and promote what became the first abolition society anywhere in the western world: the Pennsylvania Abolition Society. In Paris, revolutionary clerics like Abbé Grégoire formed complementary international abolitionist associations, including *La Societé des amies des noirs*, an organization which became influential as a source of moral and material support for the revolutionary black slave and ex-slave populations of the French colony of San Domingue, today's Haiti. These international networks grew out of strong and deep grassroots moral awakening. For example, at its 1754 governing meeting in Germantown, Pennsylvania, Quaker representatives drafted and adopted a formal declaration that, in the language of the Enlightenment social movement, its members "shall never think of bereaving our fellow creatures of that valuable blessing, liberty, nor endure to grow rich by their bondage." The document goes on to admonish the rest of the world that "to live in ease and plenty by the toil of those whom violence and cruelty have put in our power is neither consistent with Christianity nor common justice" (The Philadelphia Yearly Meeting of the Society of Friends 1754). The influential roles of the Quakers in the abolitionist movement and in the birth of modern world wide human rights campaigns have been chronicled by Adam Hochschild in *Bury the Chains: Prophets and Rebels in the Fight to Free an Empire's Slaves* (2006) and *King Leopold's Ghost: A Story of Greed, Terror, and Heroism in Colonial Africa* (2006).

In technical philosophic and scientific matters, the legacy of the Scottish moralists can be seen throughout the world in the subsequent development of philosophy and in the growth of the social sciences. The antifoundationalist tenor of their works provoked other thinkers to raise questions that had remained hidden. Immanuel Kant, for example, credits Hume's skepticism for helping to awaken in him the questions he formulated and tried to answer in the *Critique of Pure Reason* (1781). The field of modern economics can hardly be said to exist prior to Adam Smith, and Thomas Reid's Common Sense conception of truth and objectivity is echoed in the works of the twentieth-century American psychologist William James and the sociologist George Mead. In fact, in contemporary psychology and medicine, there is a distinct subfield called *symbolic interactionism*, in which it is argued that it is only in society that the most valued human qualities—e.g., our conceptions of the self and of the individual—are generated. In twenty-first-century philosophy, under the name *extended mind* or *external mind*, one finds equivalent social-environmentalism in the conceptions of consciousness and moral agency. Some of these newer research projects in this area draw on the strengths of moralist psychology and social theory while at the same time challenging their ethnocentric aspects.

Some aspects of twentieth-century existentialism also reflect prior developments in "moralist" conceptions of freedom and of history. For example, environmentalism notwithstanding, moralist ego psychology makes it possible to believe that though nature and society may predispose an individual to certain actions, it is only weakness of will or, in the case of illness, natural impairment that robs the individual of control over their decisions, or over the actions based on those decisions.

Finally, social theory from Nietzsche to Marx—specifically, moral psychology and political economy—benefited from the insights of the Scottish moralists. For both Nietzsche and Marx, hypocrisy and lack of transparency in moral and economic relations are "mystifica-tions" that mask the realities of class values and class relations, which are erroneously conceived as products of nature rather than what they truly are: consequences of histories of taste and of social dynamics between individuals and groups within or across national boundaries.

SEE ALSO *Atheism; Civil Society; Economics; Enlightenment; Hume, David; James, William; Liberalism; Marx, Karl; Mead, George Herbert; Mill, James; Morality; Nietzsche, Friedrich; Philosophy; Philosophy, Moral; Religion; Smith, Adam; Social Science*

BIBLIOGRAPHY

PRIMARY WORKS

Ferguson, Adam. 1767. *An Essay on the History of Civil Society.* Edinburgh: A. Kincaid & J. Bell.

Ferguson, Adam. 1792. *Principles of Moral and Political Science.* 2 vols. Edinburgh: W. Creech.

Hill, Andrew. N.D. Thomas Aikenhead. The Aikenhead Society, http://www.uua.org/uuhs/duub/articles/thomasaikenhead.html.

Hume, David. [1739–1740] 2000. *A Treatise of Human Nature.*, eds. David Fate Norton and Mary J. Norton. New York: Oxford University Press.

Hutcheson, Francis. 1747. *A Short Introduction to Moral Philosophy.* 3 vols. Glasgow: Robert Foulis. Originally published as *Philosophiae moralis institutio compendiaria, ethices et jurisprudentiae naturalis elementa continens.* Glasgow: Robert Foulis, 1742.

Hutcheson, Francis. 1755. *A System of Moral Philosophy.* 3 vols. London: A. Millar.

Kames, Henry Homes, Lord. 1732. *Essays upon Several Subjects in Law.* Edinburgh: R. Fleming.

Kames, Henry Homes, Lord. 1751. *Essays on the Principles of Morality and Natural Religion.* 2 vols. Edinburgh: R. Fleming, for A. Kincaid & A. Donaldson.

Millar, John. 1771. *Observations Concerning the Distinction of Ranks in Society.* London: W. & J. Richardson for John Murray.

The Philadelphia Yearly Meeting of the Society of Friends. 1754, The Henry J. Cadbury Library of Philadelphia Yearly Meeting. http://www.pym.org/pm/lib.php.

Reid, Thomas. [1764] 1997. *An Inquiry into the Human Mind on the Principles of Common Sense*, ed. Derek R. Brookes. Edinburgh: Edinburgh University Press.

Robertson, William. [1794] 1828. *The History of Scotland, and an Historical Disquisition Concerning Ancient India.* Paris: Baudry.

Smith, Adam. [1759] 2002. *The Theory of Moral Sentiments*, ed. Knud Haakonssen. Cambridge, U.K., and New York: Cambridge University Press.

Smith, Adam. [1776] 1904. *An Inquiry into the Nature and Causes of the Wealth of Nations*, 5th ed., ed. Edwin Cannan. London: Methuen. http://www.econlib.org/library/Smith/smWNtoc.html.

SECONDARY WORKS

Buchan, James. 2003. *Crowded with Genius: The Scottish Enlightenment: Edinburgh's Moment of the Mind.* New York: HarperCollins.

Eze, Emmanuel Chukwudi. 1997. *Race and the Enlightenment: A Reader.* Oxford: Blackwell.

Herman, Arthur. 2001. *How the Scots Invented the Modern World: The True Story of How Western Europe's Poorest Nation Created Our World and Everything in It.* New York: Crown.

Phillipson, N. T., and Rosalind Mitchison, eds. 1997. *Scotland in the Age of Improvement: Essays in Scottish History in the Eighteenth Century.* Edinburgh: Edinburgh University Press.

Pitts, Jennifer. 2006. *A Turn to Empire: The Rise of Imperial Liberalism in Britain and France.* Princeton, NJ: Princeton University Press.

Sher, Richard B. 1990. *Church and University in the Scottish Enlightenment: The Moderate Literati of Edinburgh.* Edinburgh: Edinburgh University Press.

Shott, Susan. 1976. Society, Self, and Mind in Moral Philosophy: The Scottish Moralists as Precursors of Symbolic Interactionism. *Journal of the History of Behavioural Sciences* 12 (1): 39–46.

Williams, Eric. [1944] 1994. *Capitalism and Slavery.* Chapel Hill: University of North Carolina Press.

Wilson, Robert A. 2004. *Boundaries of the Mind: The Individual in the Fragile Sciences.* 2 vols. New York: Cambridge University Press.

Emmanuel Chukwudi Eze

SCRAMBLE FOR AFRICA

SEE *Imperialism.*

SCREENING AND SIGNALING GAMES

An agent with private information who takes a costly action in order to favorably affect the responses of others is "signaling." A responding agent who precommits to a response that is contingent on the informed agent's action is "screening."

In Michael Spence's seminal paper (1973), a worker signals her value by her choice of education. Firms base their beliefs about a workers' productivity based on her educational choice and compete for her services. In the simplest case there are two types of worker, with values v_1 and $v_2 > v_1$. The cost of achieving an educational credential z for a type t worker is $c_t(z)$. Spence asked under what conditions it would pay the high value worker to signal by choosing to add to her educational credentials, even in the extreme case in which the education had no direct effect on productivity. Suppose that there is such an education level z_2 selected only by a high-value worker. That is, the equilibrium outcome separates the different types. Given that there is separating, competition by firms results in a wage offer of v_1 for those without the educational credential and a wage offer of v_2 to those with the credential. For this to be an equilibrium, each type of worker must have an incentive to take the anticipated action. Hence the following incentive constraints must be satisfied:

$$IC_1: v_1 \geq v_2 - c_1(z)$$
$$IC_2: v_2 - c_2(z) \geq v_1.$$

Let $\underline{z}$ be the education level where the first constraint is satisfied with equality and let $\bar{z}$ be the education level where the second constraint is satisfied with equality. As long as the high-value worker has a lower cost of education, $\underline{z} < \bar{z}$ and any education level $z_2 \in [\underline{z}, \bar{z}]$ satisfies the two incentive constraints. Note that a smaller z_2 is less costly for the high type. Thus, for Pareto efficient separating, the incentive constraint for the low type is binding.

APPLICATIONS

From this basic idea a vast applied literature has emerged. In the insurance industry it has been argued that deductibles are used to separate risk classes, because a good risk has a smaller probability of incurring the deductible and hence a smaller cost of signaling. For new products, advertising has been explained as a signal, because if the quality is low, the firm will incur a loss of revenue due to reduced future sales, as consumers experience the good. Similarly, a high introductory price can signal high quality, as long as there are a sufficient number of fully informed consumers.

In the theory of bargaining between a firm and union, the delay between an offer and a counter-offer is a potential signal. Suppose that bargaining with full information leads to agreement over how the pie should be shared. The firm only knows whether revenue will be high or low. The opportunity cost of delay is lower for a low profit firm, so the union is willing to accept that the pie must be smaller and thus accept a lower wage.

Signaling theory has also been used extensively in finance to show how the underpricing of an initial public offering (IPO), the capital structure, and the issue of double-taxed dividends can all be used to signal a firm's profitability.

In macroeconomic policy analysis it has been argued that a government can credibly signal its commitment to "tough" future economic policy by taking a tough action in the current period. The net cost to taking this action is lower for a government that really does value the future benefits of (for example) a sustained anti-inflationary policy. Similarly, a government can signal its long-term commitment to trade liberalization by taking a tough action in the current period.

DEVELOPMENT OF THE THEORY

Spence's original work followed largely in the Walrasian tradition. Michael Rothschild and Joseph Stiglitz (1976) argued for a formal game-theoretic foundation. In their analysis, the uninformed agents move first, making commitments as to how they will respond. That is, the firms make screening offers. They showed that in such a model there may be no Nash equilibrium, and concluded that competitive markets can perform poorly.

More recent theory has focused on signaling games in which the informed agent moves first. Suppose, in the Spence model, that the informed agent believes he will be paid a high wage if and only if he chooses an education of at least $z_2 \in [\underline{z}, \bar{z}]$. Given such beliefs, the two types separate. Because any education level on this interval will suffice, there is now a continuum of Nash separating equilibria. But what beliefs are plausible if the informed agent chooses a smaller education $\hat{z}$? This question is at the heart of a large theoretical literature on refinements of Nash equilibria (Intuitive Criterion, Divinity, Stability). The most popular of these refinements is the Intuitive Criterion of In-Koo Cho and David Kreps (1987). Their basic idea is that an informed agent will take an out-of-equilibrium action when (1) she will be better off if the responders correctly infer her type, and (2) given this belief, all other types prefer their Nash equilibrium action. The efficient separating equilibrium is the unique Nash equilibrium that satisfies this restriction on beliefs. This is readily illustrated. Consider the education levels z_2 and $\hat{z}$ < z_2 on the interval $[\underline{z}, \bar{z}]$. By construction, a low-value worker is better off earning his true value v_1 than paying for an education at these levels. Thus, by the Intuitive Criterion, a worker choosing $\hat{z}$ will be perceived to be high value. Given such beliefs, high value workers have an incentive to choose the less costly education $\hat{z}$. Arguing in this way, only the Pareto efficient separating Nash equilibrium can satisfy the restrictions on beliefs imposed by the Intuitive Criterion.

SEE ALSO *Evolutionary Games; Game Theory; Noncooperative Games*

BIBLIOGRAPHY

Cho, In-Koo, and David M. Kreps. 1987. Signaling Games and Stable Equilibria. *Quarterly Journal of Economics* 102 (2): 179–222.

Riley, John G. 1979. Informational Equilibrium. *Econometrica* 47 (2): 331–359.

Riley, John G. 2001. Silver Signals: Twenty-Five Years of Screening and Signaling. *Journal of Economic Literature* 39 (2): 432–478.

Rothschild, Michael, and Joseph E. Stiglitz. 1976. Equilibrium in Competitive Insurance Markets: An Essay on the Economics of Imperfect Information. *Quarterly Journal of Economics* 90 (4): 630–649.

Spence, A. Michael. 1973. Job Market Signaling. *Quarterly Journal of Economics* 87 (3): 355–374.

John G. Riley

SCRIPT MODELS

A script is a type of schema, or implicit mental representation, that describes an expected sequence of events. Scripts are developed from experiences with particular situations, from which information is abstracted and organized so as to guide thinking, feeling, and behavior when encountering similar experiences in the future. In a collaboration between the fields of artificial intelligence and social psychology, Roger Schank and Robert Abelson (1977) introduced a script model to explain people's understanding of socially stereotypic events such as eating at a restaurant. From the fields of social, personality, and clinical psychology, a script model has been employed to understand people's experience of emotionally significant and personally idiosyncratic events such as negotiating relationship conflict (Baldwin 1992). For example, a script might specify that in the context of conflict with an intimate other, if the other expresses anger, the self will feel regret and act submissively to achieve resolution of the conflict.

Models of scripts for socially stereotypic events emphasize that scripts enable people to automatically comprehend a variety of experiences through a cognitive structure that provides both power and economy. Models of scripts for personally significant events emphasize that scripts serve an individual's motivation to anticipate and deal with emotional experiences to maximize positive emotion and minimize negative emotion. In either case, script models depict people as creating scripts by extracting the important elements of scenes they have experienced and connecting similar scenes together. Evidence suggests that children less than one year old begin to make such connections between scenes; for example, they cry in anticipation of pain upon seeing a doctor and needle a few months after getting an inoculation. Culture plays a role in the formation of scripts; for example, Utku Eskimos construe being alone as social isolation and feel loneliness, whereas Tahitians see being alone as an opportunity for spirits to cause uncanny feelings and fear. The intrafamilial environment is also important; for example, childhood patterns of relations with parents are significantly related to adult scripts about love relationships.

Research has shown that scripts facilitate processing of and memory for script-relevant information; provide inferences in the face of missing information; guide interpretation of ambiguous situations; promote script-confirming patterns of thought, emotion, and behavior; and are associated with individual differences in personality. Scripts can also have maladaptive consequences if applied when not relevant, leading to inappropriate inferences or recall. Scripts with problematic content can lead to maladaptive thinking, emotion, and behavior patterns associated with psychopathology. In general, scripts are more easily modified by experience when they are first being developed, but at a certain point they become resistant to change in the face of incongruent experience. Mildly inconsistent and peripheral information will be ignored or discounted; however, information that is highly inconsistent and highly central may undermine the script itself. For example, individuals who suffer a traumatic loss are often unable to sustain their construal of the world as meaningful. Methods for changing maladaptive scripts require more research, but one model of therapy proposes that the relationship between therapist and client undermines a maladaptive interpersonal script by presenting recurrent experiences that are emotionally significant and substantially incongruent.

SEE ALSO *Culture; Memory; Personality; Schemas; Social Information Processing; Stereotypes*

BIBLIOGRAPHY

Baldwin, Mark W. 1992. Relational Schemas and the Processing of Social Information. *Psychological Bulletin* 112 (3): 461–484.

Schank, Roger, and Robert Abelson. 1977. *Scripts, Plans, Goals, and Understanding.* Hillsdale, NJ: Erlbaum.

Amy P. Demorest

S-CURVE HYPOTHESIS

SEE *Kuznets Hypothesis.*

SEARCH ENGINES

SEE *Computers: Science and Society.*

SECESSION

Secession is the act of withdrawing territory from a state and converting it into an independent state or joining it to another state. In the latter case, secession is combined with irredentism. Secession is a negative term, one that is more likely to be used by its opponents than its advocates. Supporters of secession prefer to describe themselves as struggling for something positive. For example, those who support Quebec's secession from Canada describe themselves as "sovereigntists" or "independentists," not as "secessionists."

Secession can usefully be distinguished from three other terms with which it is often confused. First, it is not a synonym for "self-determination" but one form that a struggle for self-determination might take. Second, it is different, particularly in the minds of international lawyers, from "decolonization," which involves the separation of a colony from its metropole, with a colony typically defined as a racially distinct territory separated from the metropole by saltwater and whose people do not enjoy metropolitan citizenship rights. Secession, by contrast, is seen as withdrawal from a state, with the territory involved usually a contiguous piece of the state's territory or a nearby island. Third, secession is an act that is initiated and carried out by those who want a new state of their own. It should be distinguished, therefore, from "partition," which implies the fresh division of a territory by an external (third-party) actor (O'Leary 2005). Irish nationalists sought the secession of Ireland from the United Kingdom, but the latter partitioned Ireland, as they later partitioned India and contributed to the partition of Palestine.

Secessions are generally attempted by minority nations that want their own state (or to be joined with another state), though Russia, with a significant majority of the state's population, seceded from the Soviet Union. There is no prospect of immigrant ethnic groups, such as the Chinese community in British Columbia or the Koreans in California, seceding from their respective states, as these are not mobilized as nations. Nor is it foreordained that a minority nation will become secessionist. There is evidence that the timely accommodation of minority nations, involving territorial autonomy and, in the case of sizable minorities, inclusive power sharing (consociational) politics at the center, can reduce support for secession.

States almost invariably oppose secession. Many states explicitly rule it out in their constitutions. Some, such as Ukraine or Turkey, even make it impossible to change their constitutions to allow secession. In these cases, the unity of the state is a higher value than popular sovereignty. Americans need no reminders that states are often prepared to resist secession with considerable force, even if it costs many lives.

As international law is written by states, it is hardly surprising that its provisions on secession are very restrictive. International law recognizes a legal right of "peoples" to "self-determination," but this right was intended to apply only to historic European colonies, that is, to acts of decolonization. It was developed, moreover, at a time when significant numbers of acts of decolonization had already occurred. The right is a "once-only" right, to be exercised at the point of decolonization, and does not extend to minority regions within colonies or to minority or majority regions that intersect colonial frontiers. Oddly, then, the international legal right to "self-determination" is built on the constructs of imperialists. Since World War II (1939–1945), there has been only one clear example of a successful, internationally recognized secession that was opposed by the state's authorities, the case of Bangladesh, which seceded from Pakistan with India's help in 1971. With one questionable exception, all other secessions have either been agreed to by central authorities (East Timor, Eritrea, the Czech Republic and Slovakia) or have been recognized after central authority had collapsed (the fifteen republics that seceded from the Soviet Union). The Soviet Union's republics had the additional advantage of a constitutional right to secession. The questionable exception is Yugoslavia. The secessions of Slovenia, Croatia, and Bosnia-Herzegovina were opposed by Belgrade (Serbia and Montenegro), but the Badinter Commission nonetheless ruled that Yugoslavia was in "a state of dissolution." To bolster its case, the commission also cited a clause in the Yugoslav constitution that gave its republics the right of secession.

The unwillingness of the states system to sanction secession is underlined by a number of "de facto secessions" (Bahcheli, Bartmann, and Srebrnik 2004). Here, secessionist authorities have failed to win recognition from other states even though they have succeeded in monopolizing the sovereign functions of government on their territory, often for years or even decades. These regions include Transnistria (Moldova), Nagorno-Karabakh (Azerbaijan), Somaliland (Somalia), the Turkish Republic of North Cyprus (Cyprus), and Abkhazia and South Ossetia (Georgia). The strangest case of a de facto secession is Kosovo, which was liberated from Serbia's control by an international military alliance in 1999. In spite of this, the international community has so far refused to recognize Kosovo's independence. If it does, it is likely to do so in a way that does not set a precedent for others. It may help Kosovo's case that, while it was not a full republic of the former Yugoslavia, it enjoyed equality with these republics within federal institutions and a similar level of autonomy. This may allow other states to argue that Kosovo is a special case, sufficiently like the full republics of the former Yugoslavia to enjoy similar rights.

While lawyers have debated the legal right to secession, philosophers have argued about the moral right. As liberals are committed to the idea of a legitimate state, it is difficult for them to rule out secession under any circumstances, although some suggest the priority should be to make the state legitimate, not to break it up. The two main liberal schools of thought on secession are based on "just-cause" and "choice" theories (Moore 1998). Just-cause theorists have traditionally taken a restrictive view of secession, arguing that a right to secede exists only when the state has been egregiously abusive. One of their most prominent representatives has recently offered a softer version of this: Minorities can secede if they are denied autonomy (Buchanan 2003). Choice theorists, using democratic arguments based on consent, analogize from marital to political divorce: Minorities should be able to leave if they want to and not just if they have been abused or not accommodated (e.g., Beran 1984).

Some scholars believe that states, particularly Western democracies like Canada and the United Kingdom, are becoming less resistant to secession and less likely to oppose it by force (Kymlicka 2001, pp. 387–393). In 1998, the Canadian Supreme Court established a process whereby a province can secede, providing there is clear support for breakup, and after negotiations with the federal authorities. The prime minister of the United Kingdom, John Major, opined in the early 1990s that Scotland could secede if it wanted to, and in the Belfast Agreement of 1998, London confirmed that Northern Ireland could join the Republic of Ireland, provided that this was approved by referendums in both jurisdictions. Ethiopia's republics have also been given the right to secession, and recent peace settlements in Sudan and Papua New Guinea have extended this right to South Sudan and Bougainville, respectively. From the other side, one academic has argued that minorities, particularly in western Europe, are no longer as insistent on secession, provided they are given autonomy and are included in international (European Union) institutions (Keating 2001). Neither of these trends is universal. In most parts of the world, states are at least as insistent on maintaining unity as they ever were, and there are still many secessionist movements.

The record of secession as a method of conflict resolution has been mixed. In some cases, the transition from one state to two, or several, has been relatively smooth (Czechoslovakia, the Soviet Union, Norway/Sweden). In other cases, breakup had disastrous consequences (Yugoslavia, with respect to Croatia and Bosnia-Herzegovina, but so far not Slovenia or Macedonia). These contrasting cases suggest a straightforward point: Secessions that are opposed by the center and/or a significant community within the secessionist region are more likely to be violent (McGarry 1998).

SEE ALSO *Borders; Confederate States of America; Conflict; Decolonization; Ethnicity; European Union;*

INTERNATIONAL ENCYCLOPEDIA OF THE SOCIAL SCIENCES, 2ND EDITION

Partition; Quebecois Movement; Self-Determination; Sovereignty; U.S. Civil War

BIBLIOGRAPHY

Bahcheli, T., B. Bartmann, and H. Srebrnik, eds. 2004. *De Facto States: The Quest for Sovereignty.* London: Frank Cass.

Beran. H. 1984. A Liberal Theory of Secession. *Political Studies* 32: 21–31.

Buchanan, A. 2003. *Justice, Legitimacy, and Self-Determination: Moral Foundations of International Law.* Oxford: Oxford University Press.

Keating, M. 2001. Nations Without States: The Accommodation of Nationalism in the New State Order. In *Minority Nationalism and the Changing International Order,* eds. Michael Keating and John McGarry, 19–43. Oxford: Oxford University Press.

Kymlicka, W. 2001. Reply and Conclusion. In *Can Liberal Pluralism Be Exported? Western Political Theory and Ethnic Relations in Eastern Europe,* eds. W. Kymlicka and M. Opalski, 347–413. Oxford: Oxford University Press.

McGarry, J. 1998. "Orphans of Secession": National Pluralism in Secessionist Regions and Post-Secession States. In *National Self-Determination and Secession,* ed. Margaret Moore, 215–232. Oxford: Oxford University Press.

Moore, M. 1998. Introduction: The Self-Determination Principle and the Ethics of Secession. In *National Self-Determination and Secession,* ed. Margaret Moore, 1–13. Oxford: Oxford University Press.

O'Leary, B. 2004. Partition. In *The Social Science Encyclopedia,* 3rd ed., vol. 2, eds. A. Kuper and J. Kuper, 708–710. London: Routledge.

John McGarry

SECOND BEST

SEE *Theory of Second Best.*

SECOND RUSSIAN REVOLUTION

SEE *Russian Federation.*

SECOND SIGHT

SEE *Veil, in African-American Culture.*

SECOND-PRICE AUCTION

SEE *Auctions; Value, Subjective.*

SECRECY

Secrecy, according to sociologist Edward Shils, (1911–1995) is a form of concealment reinforced by sanctions against disclosure and differs from privacy in its non-voluntary character. In some societies, secrecy is concealment enforced by tacit and often religious proscriptions or taboos. In other societies, laws and statutes secure secrets and privileges for those who possess them. Regardless of how it is regulated, secrecy is implicated in the maintenance of religious or political hierarchies. Secrecy also plays an essential role in the internal division of groups by limiting access to knowledge.

In many instances, access to knowledge is regulated by membership associations or "secret societies." Secret societies have been significant institutions in virtually all political cultures. For example, among the indigenous people of the Northwest Coast of North America, secret societies provided certain members of hereditary clans exclusive access to mythic, ritual, and political knowledge, which secured them against opposition from other clan members. Among many societies in Australia and Oceania, secret societies are associated with age grades and adult masculinity. Even when secret societies are open to all males, the societies must be entered through elaborate rites of initiation. Membership in such groups may then confer political and economic rights, as well as access to sacred or private historical knowledge.

In China, secret societies often emerged from mutual aid organizations, which represented and protected the interests of particular classes (peasant or aristocrat). Among the Straits Chinese in Southeast Asia, secret societies often worked to preserve language-based cultural traditions and mediated between diasporic and mainland groups, channeling resources and information between the groups. At various times, including revolutionary nationalist and communist wars, secret societies have provided crucial structures for organizing political activity.

Secret societies are associated both with the maintenance of legitimate power and the organization of oppositional movements. Insofar as secrecy is a principle that protects power, secrecy must both display itself and conceal the true nature of power's exclusivity. In other words, political secrecy is public secrecy; people must be led to believe that there is something that they do not know, and that this something underwrites others' power. Hence, secrecy is often associated with elaborate rituals and formalized communicational codes. This is true not only for the infamous sects of esoteric knowledge—such as the cults of Mithra in ancient Greece and the Rosicrucians and Masons or Opus Dei in the Christian tradition—but it also characterizes membership in contemporary political parties and groups such as the Ku Klux Klan in the United States.

The development of secrecy is intensified and accelerated in the context of the state, both in its pre-modern and its modern, bureaucratic forms. The idea that states should withhold knowledge from subjects on the grounds that it would harm them has a long history. This idea can be found in Plato's *Republic*, book 2, where it is suggested that tales of gods warring with gods or performing immoral acts ought to be banned as the subject of poetry, lest these acts encourage similar behavior in humans. In *City of God* book 2, Augustine appraised the Christian church over the Pagan religions precisely because it claimed to oppose a politics of secrecy with a doctrine of universal truth. Nonetheless, state officials within the nations influenced by Christianity never relinquished the practice of secrecy as the basis of power—any more than did those inspired by other theologies.

Both the nature and theory of secrecy received impetus from the institutional and technological developments of modernity. In the nineteenth century, secrecy came to be thought of not only as a phenomenon within society but as an essential principle of social groups in general. German social theorist Georg Simmel (1858–1916) referred to secrecy as one of humanity's "greatest achievements." Simmel's concept, on which Shils built his more elaborate definition, emphasized purposive aggression against a third person. According to Simmel, the concept and phenomenon of secrecy revealed society to be a formation based not on dyadic relations but on the spectral presence of the "third person." By third person, he meant to encompass the total social formation, beyond those with whom one might have dialogic relations—including all those who precede one in history, and all who may come after, but especially those against whom one might forge an oppositional solidarity.

From Simmel's perspective, the value of the secret is intensified by the possibility of its betrayal or revelation. Simmel also remarked that as societies become more complex, what is "public becomes ever more public, and what is private becomes ever more private." A crucial development in this perspective is the emergence of writing and, more specifically, the epistolary form of letter writing, in which writing is linked to the idea of privacy. In the letter, the exclusion of others is simultaneously bureaucratized and made to appear as a necessary condition of interpersonal intimacy.

In German political economist and sociologist, Max Weber's (1864–1920) writings, the link between bureaucracy and secrecy is both explicit and mutually sustaining. According to Weber, bureaucracies produce their relative superiority and claims on professional exclusivity by developing secret knowledge. Hence, while democratic capitalist societies generally presume and espouse the value of openness and transparency, they are increasingly subject to the force of secrecy. In his magisterial work, *Economy and Society*, Weber went so far as to claim that "'the official secret' is the specific invention of bureaucracy." Weber also claimed that secrecy was doomed to fail, as the expert knowledge of private economic interest groups would ultimately come to supplant that of governmental elites.

Weber's sense that government secrecy would ultimately give way to the regime of expert knowledge and, hence, corporate trade secrets has in some senses been realized to the extent that copyright and patent laws dominate the landscape of secrecy legislation. However, in recent years practices of state secrecy have expanded rather than diminished in the United States—despite the anticipation of state secrecy declining following the end of the cold war. (Similar developments have also been seen elsewhere.) According to the U.S. Information Security Oversight Office, acts of original classification (the secreting of primary documents, including "top secret," "secret," and "confidential" materials) decreased in 1995 by more than 36,000 to 167,840. However, that number increased to 258,633 by 2005. Moreover, derivative classifications, materials classified because they include citations of, or reference to, classified documents, increased at an even greater rate. In 1995, reported derivative classifications had decreased by almost 1.2 million to 3,411,665. In 2005, derivative classifications had grown to 13,948,140.

These figures reveal a general trend in the early twenty-first century of an increase in the production of state secrets and an expansion of their sphere of circulation. The latter fact, which derives largely from new digital technologies, enhances the aura of secrecy while the former consolidates the power derived from it.

The result is a doubled development. On the one hand, there are more secrets and more people who are aware that there are more secrets. On the other, fewer and fewer people are authorized to know the content of those secrets. Thus, in the United States, for example, the number of people who are authorized to know and determine the status of government knowledge decreased in the decade between 1995 and 2005 by about 26 percent.

Mitigating the U.S. trends of expanding state secrets are constitutionally authorized mechanisms for accessing information. These mechanisms include acts and procedures gathered together under the title of "Freedom of Information," by which the press and members of the public are entitled to petition for the declassification of documents. The United States also legislates the mandatory termination of classificatory protections, through statutes of limitations on copyrights and patents, as well as limits on government classifications. The 1997 U.S. Senate's *Report of the Commission on Protecting and*

Reducing Government Secrecy termed this built-in obsolescence of government secrecy the "life-cycle" of classification.

However, the legislated dissipation of secrecy protections is different from the mutual entailment of secrecy and revelation that Simmel had observed. Simmel was referring to the intensification of secrecy that comes about through the risk of its revelation. Such a logic can be seen in the transformation of military policies since 1993, when President William Jefferson Clinton signed Public Law 103-160, commonly known as "Don't ask, don't tell." This law promised to limit surveillance activities directed against gays and lesbians in the U.S. armed forces, but it also prohibited people who have same-sex relations from serving in the military. The law also proscribes homosexual and bisexual people who are in the military from revealing their sexual orientation. In 1994 the policies emanating from the law resulted in 617 discharges. That number increased steadily, and in 2001, 1,273 people were dismissed from the armed services. Although dismissals on the basis of sexuality dropped as the U.S. government commenced war after 9/11, dismissals rose again in 2005.

Shils's notion of the enforced secret reaches its apogee in the "Don't ask, don't tell" law. Moreover, the demand for the secreting of homosexuality in the military runs directly counter to the achievements of social movements over the course of the late twentieth century, at least in the Western nations. These movements had made sexual self-disclosure a foundational moment of self-liberation. Such achievements may have limited relevance in societies beyond the West. In the United States however, the logic of "Don't ask, don't tell," appears to confirm Eve Kosofsky Sedgwick's thesis, as articulated in *The Epistemology of the Closet.* Sedgwick states that in modern Western societies the epistemological basis of power operates, as it does elsewhere, in the vacillation between secrecy and revelation but in modernity becomes increasingly focused on questions of sexuality and, more specifically, on the differentiation of populations into hetero and homosexual types.

Inverting the historical relationship between secrecy and power, the "epistemology of the closet" and the policy of "Don't ask, don't tell" makes the possession of a secret (homosexuality) a risk and a source of disenfranchisement. That this inversion takes place while older systems linking secrecy and power are extended and intensified by new technologies of encryption, duplication, and dissimulation, reveals that the classical theories of secrecy are themselves in need of transformation.

SEE ALSO *Bureaucracy; Central Intelligence Agency, U.S.; Cold War; Corruption; Freedom of Information Act; Hot Money; Illuminati, The; Ku Klux Klan; National Security; Plato; Politics: Gay, Lesbian, Transgender,* *and Bisexual; Power; Sexual Orientation, Social and Economic Consequences; Sexuality; Weber, Max; Whistle-blowers*

BIBLIOGRAPHY

Augustine. [c. 419] 1972. *City of God.* Trans. Henry Bettenson. London: Penguin.

The Commission on Protecting and Reducing Government Secrecy. 1997. *Report of the Commission on Protecting and Reducing Government Secrecy,* Senate Document 105-2. Washington, DC: U.S. Government Printing Office.

National Security Oversight Office. 1996. *1995 Report to the President.* Washington, D.C.: National Archives and Records Administration

Plato. [c. 360 BCE] 1930. *The Republic.* Trans. Paul Shorey, ed. G.P. Goold, Cambridge, MA: Harvard University Press.

Sedgwick, Eve Kosofsky. 1990. *Epistemology of the Closet.* Berkeley: University of California Press.

Shils, Edward A. 1956, reissued 1996. *The Torment of Secrecy: The Background and Consequences of American Security Policies.* Chicago: Ivan R. Dee.

Simmel, Georg, 1950. Secrecy and the Secret Society. In *The Sociology of Georg Simmel.* Trans. Kurt H. Wolff, 330–344, and 345–376. New York: Free Press.

Weber, Max. Bureaucracy, from *Economy and Society* [*Wirtschaft und Gesellschaft*], part III, pp. 650–678. Excerpted in Gerth and Mills, *From Max Weber: Essays in Sociology,* 1964, pp.196–244.

Rosalind C. Morris

SECULAR, SECULARISM, SECULARIZATION

The term *secular* arises from the history of Christianity and describes that which is not sacred or not of the church. The term *secularization* thus refers to the process by which human activity and knowledge progressively come under the control of scientific rather than religious understanding. Max Weber (1864–1920) termed this rationalization and intellectualization characteristic of modern times, "the disenchantment of the world" ([1918] 1946, p. 155).

This differentiating of the sacred from the secular is associated with Europe in the seventeenth century. Prior to this time in Europe, and in non-Western cultures generally, the sacred and the secular were not necessarily separate spheres in the context of political rule. Secularism is thus associated with modernity and in the twentieth century has come to refer to two interrelated practices: (1) a mode of political organization in which the state is neutral with reference to all established religions; and (2) later in the century, a political practice of the state that protects the rights of minorities in a multicultural society.

The need to separate church from state arose in seventeenth-century Europe for three broad reasons: (1) the rise of the industrial bourgeoisie that questioned the divine right of kings, against the older landed feudal elites that drew on the political and economic power of the church; (2) the fatigue produced by a century of war in Europe, in which Christian denominations clashed with each other for political power; and (3) the challenge posed to religious knowledge by the great breakthroughs in science.

It is only in the late twentieth century that it became widely recognized that *secular, secularism,* and *secularization* are not neutral descriptive terms of universal applicability, but arise from a specific spatial-temporal context. Charles Taylor (1998), however, argues that despite its specific origins, secularism continues to be relevant for modern democracies everywhere. Even the most diversified societies can be secular, despite differences about religion at the deeper level, by building consensus on a "common political ethic," such as a doctrine of human rights, freedom, and equality. Such a consensus can be brought about even if there is no agreement about the values in which this ethic is embedded.

From the latter half of the twentieth century, however, it is precisely the concepts of human rights, liberty, and equality that have been challenged as being (Western/Christian) culture-specific. The rise of modern political movements based on Islam offers a powerful challenge to the idea that modern societies must be built on the basis of separation between religious and political power. Even within the West, secularism as state neutrality is increasingly challenged by the growing diversity within these societies. It has become evident that, historically, "secularism" was achieved in Western societies only after defeating rival Christian denominations and diverse cultural practices. The religio-cultural formation that was victorious then attained the status of the "universal." What we see today in the West then, is a resurgence of diversity rather than a new phenomenon.

In newer postcolonial democracies such as India, Hindu right-wing politics opposes the protection of minority rights that is an aspect of Indian secularism. A self-critical response from those opposed to such politics has been the acknowledgement that secularism in India has been state-centric and has not engaged sufficiently with beliefs and practices on the ground.

In this context arises the question of the relationship of secularism to democracy. Many contemporary states assume that secularism as a value trumps democracy. To take one instance, Turkey and France legally prohibit symbols of religion in public, over the protests of Muslim believers who want Muslim women to wear head scarves.

Feminist scholars point out that the controversy centers on women's bodies precisely because the patriarchal, patrilineal family is at the heart of modern statecraft. Veena Das suggests that once the idea of God was displaced, secular means had to be crafted to ensure that "the sovereign receives life beyond the lifetime of individual members" (2006, p. 94). In other words, Das suggests that the state has to reimagine its relation to the family in more complex ways than merely assigning the family to the realm of the private.

Samuel Huntington's "clash of civilizations" thesis (1993) argues that current debates over secularism arise from the division of the world into opposing civilizational frameworks, broadly, that of the West and Islam. He traces the conflict between "Western" civilization and "Islamic" civilization to the founding of Islam itself. Thus what we see today is merely an "ancient rival" reacting irrationally to "our Judeo-Christian heritage" and "our secular present."

From this point of view it appears that the contemporary "West" is rational and secular, with its religious heritage lying in the past, while contemporary "Islam" is irrational and trapped in religion. However, scholars have pointed out that the apparent secularism of Western states is built on Christian assumptions; for example, the practice of observing the weekly holiday on Sunday rather than any other day, is biblical in origin. Further, Western secularism involves the continuous regulation of what constitutes religious as opposed to nonreligious practices and institutions. In the United States, the legal apparatus of the state periodically defines what religion is by deciding whether particular forms of public behavior come under the principle of freedom of religion. In France, the antireligious state owns and administers all property belonging to institutions of religions that existed in France in 1905, when the law was passed.

The paradoxes of Western secularism are explained, in Talal Asad's (2003) view, by the fact that the emergence of secularism in modern Europe merely shifted the proper domain of violence from religious communities to nation-states. Henceforth, the nation-state would determine the place of religion, and the only legitimate perpetrator of violence was to be the nation-state, whether the violence was inflicted upon its own citizens, upon other nations, or upon colonized parts of the world.

Ashis Nandy (1990) also makes the link between the violence of the modern nation-state and secularism. Despite its contradictions, the modern state has succeeded in marginalizing all religions, while its own ideologies of secularism, development, and nationalism act as intolerant faiths backed by the coercive state apparatus. Nandy recognizes "religious fundamentalism" (or in India, communalism), as a rational and modern project that seeks to control state power. Religious fundamentalism is thus a product of "secularization" and is as intolerant of the eclecticism of lived religion as is the modern nation-state. A more tolerant society would require the recovery of those resources within religious practices that make it possible to live with "fluid definitions of the self," an idea inimical to both modern state practices and to religious fundamentalism.

SEE ALSO *Christianity; Democracy; Modernity; Religion*

BIBLIOGRAPHY

Asad, Talal. 2003. *Formations of the Secular: Christianity, Islam, Modernity.* Stanford, CA: Stanford University Press.

Das, Veena. 2006. Secularism and the Argument from Nature. In *Powers of the Secular Modern: Talal Asad and his Interlocutors*, eds. David Scott and Charles Hirschkind, 93–112. Stanford, CA: Stanford University Press.

Huntington, Samuel P. 1993. The Clash of Civilizations. *Foreign Affairs* 72 (3): 22–50.

Nandy, Ashis. 1990. The Politics of Secularism and the Recovery of Religious Tolerance. In *Mirrors of Violence: Communities, Riots, and Survivors in South Asia*, ed. Veena Das, 69–93. New York and Delhi: Oxford University Press.

Taylor, Charles. 1998. Modes of Secularism. In *Secularism and Its Critics*, ed. Rajeev Bhargava, 31–53. New York and Delhi: Oxford University Press.

Weber, Max. [1918] 1946. Science as Vocation. In *From Max Weber: Essays in Sociology*, trans. and eds. H. H. Gerth and C. Wright Mills, 129–156. New York: Oxford University Press.

Nivedita Menon

SECULAR EFFECTS
SEE *Period Effects.*

SECULAR HUMANISM
SEE *Humanism.*

SECURE BASE
SEE *Attachment Theory.*

SEEMINGLY UNRELATED REGRESSIONS

The seemingly unrelated regressions (SUR) model explains the variation of not just one dependent variable, as in the univariate multiple regression model, but the variation of a set of m dependent variables; that is, the monthly consumption expenditures of m consumers or the annual voting behavior of m voters, in terms of the variation of general and specific input or independent variables and error terms specific to each individual, problems that are frequently encountered in many sciences. Indeed, John Geweke has written, "The seemingly unrelated regressions (SUR) model developed in Zellner (1962) is perhaps the most widely used econometric model after linear regressions. The reason is that it provides a simple and useful representation of systems of demand equations that arise in neoclassical static theories of producer and consumer behavior" (2003, p. 162).

It is the case that a SUR model is a collection of two or more regression relations that can be analyzed with data on the dependent and independent variables. For many years, the individual regression relations were fitted one by one, usually using least squares techniques and justified by an appeal to single equation estimation optimality properties; That is, the least squares estimators are best linear unbiased estimators according to the well-known Gauss Markov theorem and maximum likelihood estimators when single equation normal likelihood functions are employed. Also in traditional multivariate regression models with the same independent variables in each equation and normal error terms in different equations with zero means, different variances and non-zero covariances, it had been shown that applying the least squares method equation by equation leads to fully efficient maximum likelihood estimators for regression coefficients in different equations. What was overlooked in this pre-1962 literature is the fact that when the error terms in the different regression equations are correlated and different independent variables appear in the equations, the regression equations are related, not unrelated as many assumed incorrectly and hence the term "seemingly unrelated," and that the sample information in other regressions can be employed to improve the precision of estimation of parameters in any given regression equation under a wide range of conditions. That is, new, operational SUR best linear unbiased estimators for the parameters of a set of say m regression equations were put forward that uniformly dominate the single equation least squares estimators under a broad range of conditions.

It was shown that these SUR or generalized least squares (GLS) estimators are best linear unbiased and maximum likelihood and Bayesian estimators under frequently encountered conditions. In addition, by joint analysis of the set of regression equations rather than equation by equation analysis, more precise estimates and predictions are obtained that lead to better solutions to many applied problems; that is, portfolio formation procedures in 2003 work by Jose M. Quintana and colleagues, in which dynamic regression equations with time varying parameters and various input variables were employed to explain the variation of monthly stock prices. By taking account of the fact that the regression equations were related and not unrelated, SUR estimation, prediction, and portfolio formation procedures were utilized to yield improved analyses of the variation of stock prices and to form optimal portfolios with very good rates of return. In Arnold Zellner and Henri Theil's 1962 work, similar techniques were applied to simultaneous equations models to yield a new joint estimator, the three-stage least squares estimator that dominates single equation estimators by taking account of the correlation of error terms in equations of the system by use of joint estimation of coefficients in equations of structural models.

The simplest version of a linear, constant parameter SUR system is one that contains $m \geq 2$ linear regression equations, $y_i = X_i\beta_i + u_i$, $i = 1, 2, \ldots, m$, where y_i is an $n \times 1$ vector of observations on the ith dependent variable, X_i is an $n \times k_i$ matrix with full column rank of observations on the k_i independent variables in the ith regression equation, β_i is a $k_i \times 1$ vector of regression parameters and u_i is an $n \times 1$ vector of zero mean error terms. The usual method of estimating the regression coefficients was to estimate the equations individually by least squares to obtain $\hat{\beta}_i = (X_i'X_i)^{-1}X_i'y_i$, $i = 1, 2, \ldots, m$. However, in Zellner's 1962 work it was shown that when the error terms are correlated across the equations, the equations are related and joint estimation, rather than equation-by-equation estimation, leads to more precise estimates of the regression coefficients and predictions of future values of the dependent variables. Indeed, as explained in the articles and texts cited in this entry's bibliography, these joint SUR estimators are generalized best linear unbiased estimators and, with a normality assumption for the error terms, maximum likelihood and "diffuse prior" Bayesian estimators. Further they reduce to single equation least squares estimators when error terms in the different equations are mutually uncorrelated; that is, the equations are unrelated. In addition, use of SUR techniques leads to improved tests of hypotheses regarding regression coefficients' and other parameters' values.

Similarly, taking account of the error terms' correlations across equations leads to better predictions of future values of the dependent variables, as shown in the 2005 work of Arnold Zellner and Guillermo Israilevich who use SUR techniques in forecasting U.S. economic sectors' output growth rates and aggregate output growth rates. And in works of Sid Chib and Edward Greenberg (1995), John Geweke (2003), and Peter E. Rossi and colleagues (2005) modern Bayesian methods are described that yield optimal finite sample estimation, testing, and prediction techniques for many variants of the SUR model; that is, SUR models with time varying parameters and auto correlated error terms. Similarly, when the dependent vari-

ables are discrete random variables as in multivariate logit or probit models with correlated error terms, the SUR joint estimation, testing and prediction techniques have been found to be useful, as shown in the 1977 work of T. C. Lee and colleagues.

SEE ALSO *General Linear Model; Simultaneous Equation Bias*

BIBLIOGRAPHY

Chib, Sid, and Edward Greenberg. 1995. Hierarchical Analysis of SUR Models with Extensions to Correlated Serial Errors and Time-Varying Parameter Models. *Journal of Econometrics* 68: 339–360.

Geweke, John. 2003. *Contemporary Bayesian Econometrics and Statistics*. Hoboken, NJ: Wiley.

Greene, William H. 2003. *Econometric Analysis*. 5th ed. Upper Saddle River, NJ: Prentice-Hall.

Judge, George G., William E. Griffiths, Robin C. Hill, et al. 1985. *The Theory and Practice of Econometrics*. New York: Wiley.

Lee, T. C., George G. Judge, and Arnold Zellner. 1977. *Estimating the Parameters of the Markov Probability Model from Aggregate Time Series Data*. 2nd ed. Amsterdam: North-Holland.

Meng Xiao-Li and Donald B. Rubin. 1996. Efficient Methods for Estimation and Testing with Seemingly Unrelated Regressions in the Presence of Latent Variables and Missing Observations. In *Bayesian Analysis in Statistics and Econometrics: Essays in Honor of Arnold Zellner*, ed. Donald A Berry, Katheryn M. Chaloner, and John Geweke, 215–227. New York: Wiley.

Percy, David F. 1996. Zellner's Influence on Multivariate Linear Models. In *Bayesian Analysis in Statistics and Econometrics: Essays in Honor of Arnold Zellner*, ed. Donald A Berry, Katheryn M. Chaloner, and John Geweke, 203–213. New York: Wiley.

Quintana, Jose M., Bluford H. Putnam, and David S. Wilford. 1996. *Mutual and Pension Funds Management: Beating the Markets Using a Global Bayesian Investment Strategy*. In 1996 Joint Section on Bayesian Statistical Science, American Statistical Association and International Society for Bayesian Analysis (ISBA). Proceedings volume for papers presented at ISBA Meeting in Istanbul, Turkey, 1995.

Rossi, Peter E., Greg M. Allenby, and Robert McCulloch. 2005. *Bayesian Statistics and Marketing*. Hoboken, NJ: Wiley.

Srivastava, V. K., and David E. A. Giles. 1987. *Seemingly Unrelated Regression Equations Models*. New York: Dekker.

Theil, Henri. 1971. *Principles of Econometrics*. New York: Wiley.

Zellner, Arnold. 1962. An Efficient Method of Estimating Seemingly Unrelated Regressions and Tests for Aggregation Bias. *Journal of the American Statistical Association* 57: 348–368.

Zellner, Arnold. 1963. Estimators for Seemingly Unrelated Regressions: Some Exact Finite Sample Results. *Journal of the American Statistical Association* 58: 977–992; corrigendum, 1972, 67: 255.

Zellner, Arnold, and David S. Huang, 1962. Further Properties of Efficient Estimators for Seemingly Unrelated Regression Equations. *International Economic Review* 3: 300–313.

Zellner, Arnold, and Guillermo Israilevich. 2005. The Marshallian Macroeconomic Model: A Progress Report. *Macroeconomic Dynamics* 9: 220–243 and *International Journal of Forecasting* 21: 627–645.

Zellner, Arnold, and Henri Theil. 1962. Three-Stage Least Squares: Simultaneous Estimation of Simultaneous Equations. *Econometrica* 30: 54–78.

Arnold Zellner

SEGA

SEE *Video games.*

SEGREGATION

Segregation is the practice of keeping racial and ethnic groups separated. This includes, but is not limited to, the separation of racial groups in schools, housing, public facilities, and public transportation. This separation usually involves a dominant racial-ethnic group discriminating against a subordinate racial-ethnic group, as in the U.S. South during legal segregation.

The system of legal segregation in the U.S. South was a totalitarian social system that Southern whites developed and maintained after the abolishment of slavery in 1865. The primary function was to continue the social system of servitude, the racial caste hierarchy, and the economic control of African Americans under the legal fiction of *separate but equal.* Legal and informal segregation practices (Jim Crow) meant comprehensive racial subordination and imposed a badge of degradation on all African Americans in many areas of the United States. The daily practice of legal segregation is "a compulsory ritual denoting first and second-class citizenship." It has more than psychological and social significance, serving also the basic economic and political purpose of facilitating the exploitation of nonwhites by whites, collectively and individually (Kennedy 1959, p. 206).

CHALLENGERS OF SEGREGATION

The social system of legal segregation began in the late 1870s and 1880s, and there were several attempts by African Americans to challenge the laws, the violence, and the inequality that resulted from their implementation. The first challenge began with the U.S. Supreme Court case of Homer Plessy, an African American man, who refused to sit in the colored section on a train. His case went to the Supreme Court in 1896. As a result of that case, the laws of racial segregation were buttressed. The decision stipulated that laws mandating segregated areas and sections for blacks and whites, in theory, could be separate but equal.

In 1954, Thurgood Marshall, at the time a successful black attorney for the National Association for the Advancement of Colored People (NAACP) and later U.S. Supreme Court justice, won the *Brown vs. Board of Education* case before the U.S. Supreme Court; the case ostensibly ended segregation in public schools. However, the laws of segregation did not come to an official end until the enactment of the Civil Rights Act in 1964. This act resulted in large part from the nonviolent civil disobedience of the black-led civil rights movement from the 1950s to the 1970s, which included minister-leaders such as Dr. Martin Luther King Jr.

Dr. King, famous for his "I Have A Dream" speech against segregation given at the Lincoln Memorial in Washington, D.C., in 1963, led the Montgomery bus boycott. Rosa Parks (1913–2005), a member of the NAACP, was arrested for refusing to give up her seat to a white man on a segregated bus. Over decades a great many African Americans, including leaders and intellectuals such as Parks, King, Marshall, Malcolm X, W. E. B. Du Bois, and Ida B. Wells-Barnett, stood up against the injustices of segregation, lynching, and civil rights violations.

CONTEMPORARY ISSUES OF SEGREGATION

Even though the official segregation system was finally outlawed by the 1968 Civil Rights Act, its reality and impact continue into the twenty-first century. The racial attitudes of whites on surveys since found that ever fewer whites publicly subscribe to the earlier views of the Jim Crow era. Nevertheless, segregated schools, neighborhoods, and churches are still prevalent. In the early twenty-first century, the United States remains racially segregated and racial equality remains more of an ideal than a reality.

The continued spatial isolation and segregation of black Americans have been achieved by a conjunction of racist attitudes, covert and overt discriminatory behaviors, and rooted institutional practices that continue to subordinate black Americans in most institutions. Social scientists have shown the serious repercussions of this for blacks and other Americans.

Social science research has also shown that racial segregation in housing and education still adversely affects the health of African Americans and other Americans of color because that segregation helps to reinforce institutional segregation in yet other institutional areas. Economic inequality is closely linked to racial inequality, and both operate as strong determinants of major variations in health status.

Although other subordinated racial groups such as Latinos and Asian Americans, as well as some white ethnic groups, have experienced imposed residential segregation in U.S. history, no group has experienced the high degree of segregation and isolation faced by African Americans, "who are twice as isolated as Hispanics and Asians and about 60% more segregated" (Massey and Denton 1993, p. 67). The social, health, and economic repercussions of this residential segregation are similar to the detrimental results experienced by black South Africans in South Africa's dismantled oppressive system of apartheid.

SOUTH AFRICAN APARTHEID

The oppressive system of apartheid swept through South Africa as a consequence of the electoral victory of the white-racist National Party in 1948. Apartheid embraced a totalitarian racial policy essential to replace the old policy of informal segregation. Legal apartheid controlled and manipulated the space in which black people developed their lives and livelihoods. The main aim of apartheid was total separation of blacks and whites in schools, hospitals, beaches, stores, buses, and housing. Black South Africans were forced to live in subordinate conditions, were separated from their families, were subjected to physical and psychological trauma, and were forced to carry identification cards to move about their country. The white South African government forced black South Africans to live in particular areas called Bantustans and townships. The townships consisted of deplorable one-room shanty houses made of cardboard and scrap metal. Entire families lived in these shanty houses without running water and electricity. These deplorable conditions still exist into the twenty-first century in South Africa. The system of racial apartheid, for many decades during the twentieth century, disproportionately placed all economic, social, and political power in the hands of whites, at the expense of every other racial-ethnic group.

The experiences of apartheid in South Africa for blacks were not unique. The institutionalization of racism there, a process that permeated and perverted every aspect of the individual and collective lives of South Africans, was similar in many aspects to that of the era of legal segregation in the United States. In the early twenty-first century both still have a striking persistence of residential segregation and other racial inequalities in regard to socioeconomic, health, political, and educational resources. South Africa's history of racial, cultural, and economic tensions still affects black South Africans who were used as a cheap source of labor and who were prevented from purchasing land, voting, and interracial marriage.

Black South Africans resisted the system of apartheid just as African Americans resisted legal segregation. Nelson Mandela, an internationally recognized leader in the struggle for black civil rights, was the head of the African National Congress, whose struggle played a major role in finally dismantling racial apartheid. Mandela was imprisoned in 1963 for his participation in the fight for civil rights, and he spent nearly thirty years of his life in prison. He was released in 1990 and served as president of South Africa from 1994 to 1999. His contributions, accomplishments, sacrifices, and commitment to and for civil rights are recognized and celebrated internationally.

Unlike the United States, South Africa was forced to create the Truth and Reconciliation Commission, with the power to interview white oppressors and their victims, to establish historical documents of the events, to unearth the missing dead, and to grant amnesty, in order to secure a democratic society in South Africa. Mandela's message of truth, justice, equality, and reconciliation dominated the early days of transition and aided in the success of ending the oppressive system of apartheid. In contrast, neither the U.S. government nor state governments have ever apologized for the enslavement and segregation of African Americans. A truth and reconciliation commission whose work would recognize that history of racial oppression might do for the United States what it did for South Africa.

SEE ALSO *African National Congress; Apartheid;* Brown v. Board of Education, *1954;* Brown v. Board of Education, *1955; Citizenship; Civil Liberties; Civil Rights; Civil Rights Movement, U.S.; Du Bois, W. E. B.; Integration; Jim Crow; King, Martin Luther, Jr.; Malcolm X; Mandela, Nelson; Marshall, Thurgood; National Association for the Advancement of Colored People (NAACP); Racism; Segregation, Residential; Segregation, School; Separate-but-Equal; Supreme Court, U.S.; Truth and Reconciliation Commissions; Warren, Earl; Wells-Barnett, Ida B.*

BIBLIOGRAPHY

Baldwin-Ragaven, Laurel, Leslie London, and Jeanelle De Gruchy. 2000. *Learning From Our Apartheid Past: Human Rights Challenges for Health Professionals in Contemporary South Africa. Ethnicity and Health* 5 (3/4): 227–241.

Bonilla-Silva, Eduardo. 2003. *Racism without Racists: Color-Blind Racism and the Persistence of Racial Inequality in the United States.* Lanham, MD: Rowman and Littlefield.

Christie, Kenneth. 2000. *The South African Truth Commission.* New York: St. Martin's Press.

Collins, Chiquita A., and David R. Williams. 1999. Segregation and Mortality: The Deadly Effects of Racism? *Sociological Forum* 14 (3): 495–523.

Cornwall, Jo Anne. 1986. The United States and South Africa: History, Civil Rights and the Legal and Cultural Vulnerability of Blacks. *Phylon* 47 (4): 285–293.

Feagin, Joe R. 2006. *Systemic Racism: A Theory of Oppression.* New York: Routledge.

Feagin, Joe R., and Karyn D. McKinney. 2003. *The Many Costs of Racism.* Lanham, MD: Rowman and Littlefield.

Fourie, Ginn J. A. 2000. The Psychology of Perpetrators of 'Political' Violence in South Africa—A Personal Experience. *Ethnicity & Health* 5 (3/4): 283–289.

Gibson, James L. 2004. *Overcoming Apartheid: Can Truth Reconcile a Divided Nation?* New York: Russell Sage Foundation.

Kennedy, Stetson. 1959. *Jim Crow Guide to the U.S.A: The Laws, Customs, and Etiquette Governing the Conduct of Nonwhites and Other Minorities as Second-Class Citizens.* London: Lawrence and Wishart.

Massey, Douglas S., and Nancy A. Denton. 1993. *American Apartheid: Segregation and the Making of the Underclass.* Cambridge, MA: Harvard University Press.

Packard, Jerrold. 2002. *American Nightmare: The History of Jim Crow.* New York: St. Martin's Press.

Patterson, James T. 2002. *Brown v. Board of Education: A Civil Rights Milestone and Its Troubled Legacy.* New York: Oxford University Press.

Smythe, Hugh H. 1948. The Concept of Jim Crow. *Social Forces* 27 (1): 45–48.

Verdun, Vincene. 2005. The Big Disconnect Between Segregation and Integration. *The Negro Educational Review* 56 (1): 67–82.

Williams, David R., Allen Herman, Ronald C. Kessler, et al. 2004. The South Africa Stress and Health Study: Rationale and Design. *Metabolic Brain Disease* 19 (1/2): 135–147.

Joe R. Feagin
Ruth Thompson-Miller

SEGREGATION, OCCUPATIONAL

SEE *Crowding Hypothesis.*

SEGREGATION, RESIDENTIAL

Residential segregation refers to differences among social groups in their spatial distribution. Conceived broadly, the topic subsumes regional and other macro-level patterns of spatial distribution; but the research literature has focused primarily on group differences in distribution across neighborhoods in urban areas. Research on residential segregation constitutes one of the oldest traditions in sociology and has a rich history of cumulative development extending back to the founding of the discipline. Patterns of neighborhood distribution received close attention in W. E. B. Du Bois's *The Philadelphia Negro* (1899), a landmark work often viewed as the first major empirical study in urban sociology. Studies of segregation processes of neighborhood change were integral to the Chicago School tradition spawned by Robert Park and Ernest Burgess's *The City* (1925) and were a mainstay of empirical urban sociology in the 1920s, 1930s, and 1940s.

Quantitative research on racial segregation advanced significantly in the 1950s and 1960s. A key methodological statement by Otis Dudley Duncan and Beverly Duncan (1955) forged a working consensus on measurement approaches, and studies by Duncan and Duncan (1957), Stanley Lieberson (1963), and Karl Taeuber and Alma Taeuber (1965) established exemplars for research on segregation and neighborhood change that remain influential. Five decades of vigorous, cumulative research ensued, marked by steady methodological refinement—in studies such as those by Lieberson (1981), Linda Stearns and John Logan (1986), Douglas Massey and Nancy Denton (1988), and David James and Karl Taeuber (1985)—and a stream of empirical studies assessing trends and patterns in residential segregation—in studies such as those by Lieberson (1980), Reynolds Farley and William Frey (1994), Massey and Denton (1987, 1989, 1993), Paul Jargowsky (1997), Edward Glaeser and Jacob Vigdor (2003), and Logan (2003).

Residential segregation occurs along many lines of demarcation in social life. Segregation is most pronounced on the dimensions of race and ethnicity and socioeconomic status but is also observed in lesser degrees along cultural and religious lines, stage of family-life cycle, and differences in lifestyle. As a result, cities can be described as urban mosaics of heterogeneous neighborhoods marked by relative internal homogeneity in social characteristics. Urban ethnographies identify a multitude of neighborhood types—"old money" elite enclaves, "nouveau riche" gated communities, suburban developments, working-class areas, ethnic villages, areas of immigrant settlement, poverty areas, gay and lesbian districts, artist colonies, and so on—and they document the variation in social life across these areas. Urban theory outlines the micro- and macro-level dynamics involved. Quantitative studies describe the extent to which social differentiation is expressed spatially and assess the impact of the various factors shaping segregation trends and underlying neighborhood change. The literature on racial and ethnic segregation and segregation among socioeconomic groups is especially well developed and establishes that these forms of segregation are maintained both by informal and decentralized social dynamics and by structured institutional forces, including legal and regulatory guidelines.

In the United States the most closely studied aspect of segregation is the white–black residential color line. Historically, white–black segregation has been, and remains, more pronounced than any other form. For most of the twentieth century it was maintained by a welter of interlocking laws, regulations, and institutional practices supplemented by intimidation and violence on the part of whites, which in combination functioned to exclude blacks from white residential areas. The separate-but-equal doctrine established by the *Plessy v. Ferguson* Supreme Court decision of 1896 provided the legal bulwark for the oppressive Jim Crow system in the South that formally separated blacks and whites in schools and public facilities. In the North and Midwest, restrictive covenants, realtor discrimination, so-called mortgage redlining, and related institutional practices combined with informal intimidation and violence by whites to foster levels of white–black segregation and black ghettoization that surpassed even the levels seen in the South. This unparalleled pattern of segregation had severe consequences for African Americans: inferior housing and schooling, sharply restricted life chances, and disproportional exposure to concentrated poverty and attendant social problems such as drug abuse, crime, and gang violence. In short, the residential color line has been at the heart of the extreme social isolation and disadvantage experienced by the African American population in the United States.

The Civil Rights era of the 1960s, following on crucial legal decisions from the 1950s and earlier (e.g., the Supreme Court *Brown v. Board of Education of Topeka* in 1954), brought the dismantling of overt, formal mechanisms of white–black segregation. Initially, change was often more symbolic than consequential. For example, the Fair Housing Act (Title VIII of the Civil Rights Act of 1968) swept aside many practices of overt housing discrimination in principle but in practice was not backed with effective enforcement policies. Effective enforcement of antidiscrimination policy came only with later legislation (e.g., the Fair Housing Amendments Act of 1988) and associated court rulings. Decades later, reductions in housing discrimination, especially the more blatant formally sanctioned practices, became clear. But discriminatory practices have endured in both the informal realm and less obvious institutional practices (e.g., siting of low-income housing). Consequently, changes in residential segregation have been slow in coming despite seemingly sweeping legal reforms. This is evident in patterns of resurging racial segregation in public schools, as documented by Gary Orfield (2001), which is rooted in enduring patterns of racial residential segregation.

The white–black color line presents a special case for segregation theory. Segregation patterns for other ethnic and racial groups in the United States have not involved comparable levels of social isolation and residential disadvantage. Similarly, patterns of residential assimilation observed over time for many other ethnic and racial groups have not been seen for African Americans. To be sure, white–black segregation has not been a constant. It increased, rising from moderate to unprecedented high levels during the era of the Great Migration of African Americans to northern urban areas during the early part of the twentieth century. In 1970, after a half-century of stasis, white–black segregation began slowly declining and by 2000 had returned to levels not previously seen since 1920–1930; this trend has been accompanied by a rapid disappearance of exclusively white residential areas, as shown by Glaeser and Vigdor (2003). Variation in white–black segregation across metropolitan areas also should be noted; generally, segregation is higher in metropolitan areas that were major destination sites of the Great Migration (e.g., Chicago, Cleveland, Detroit, Philadelphia) and lower in metropolitan areas of the South and West that rose to national prominence after World War II (e.g., Houston, Los Angeles, and San Diego). The trends over time and the variation across metropolitan areas are both important. But the key social fact is that white–black segregation remains more pronounced than any other form of segregation. It is quantitatively more severe and, in a pattern not typically seen for other groups, is routinely manifest on multiple dimensions (e.g., uneven distribution, isolation, clustering, concentration, and centralization) simultaneously, a phenomenon observers such as Massey and Denton (1989) characterize as hypersegregation.

White–black residential segregation is also exceptional for the near absence of dynamics of spatial assimilation. Residential segregation of earlier European immigrant groups dissipated slowly over generations as reductions in cultural and socioeconomic differences between groups were accompanied by steady reductions in spatial separation from "old stock" European groups. At the start of the twenty-first century, a similar dynamic appears to be operating for Latino and especially Asian immigrant groups. As Massey (1985) notes, a comparable process has yet to be observed for African Americans. Thus, for example, the rapid suburbanization of the African American population since the 1980s has largely extended white–black segregation to suburban areas rather than fundamentally reducing overall segregation as historically occurred for other groups.

The reasons for enduring high levels of white–black segregation in the post-Civil Rights era are the subject of much consideration. Scholars generally concur that contemporary white–black segregation cannot be explained as a byproduct of economic segregation and group differences in income. In contrast to patterns observed for other groups, segregation among whites and blacks of similar socioeconomic status is scarcely lower than overall white–black segregation. In view of this fact, future research will need to monitor the residential experiences of potential bellwether groups such as middle- and high-status African American households. There also is widespread consensus that racial discrimination continues to be a major factor in contemporary white–black segregation. Most observers, as reported by Massey and Denton (1993) and Margery Turner and colleagues (2002), conclude that blatant forms of exclusionary discrimination have declined; but many, as also reported by Massey and Denton (1993) as well as John Yinger (1995), conclude that less obvious but highly consequential forms of discrimination continue.

Opinion is mixed regarding the relevance of informal residential dynamics outside the purview of existing antidiscrimination law. As Camille Charles (2001) has shown, blacks encounter higher levels of negative stereotyping and prejudice and rank at the bottom in survey responses regarding preferences for potential neighbors. Scholars such as John Yinger (1995) and Douglas Massey and Nancy Denton (1993) discount the role of prejudice in the absence of discrimination, but studies by Thomas Schelling (1978), William Clark (1991, 1992, 2002), Mark Fossett (2006), and Fossett and Warren Waren (2005) suggest that household location decisions governed by such preferences can sustain high levels of segregation even in the absence of discrimination. Consistent with this view, studies of residential movement, such as Ingrid Ellen's (2000), indicate that avoidance of blacks on the part of whites and other groups—a social dynamic outside the scope of existing antidiscrimination law—is an important contributing factor in maintaining segregation. This suggests that significant movement toward residential integration for African Americans will not be observed until greater declines occur in negative stereotyping and prejudice against blacks as well as in exclusionary housing discrimination against blacks.

SEE ALSO *Apartheid;* Brown v. Board of Education, *1954;* Brown v. Board of Education, *1955; Chicago School; Cities; Civil Rights Movement, U.S.; Communalism; Contact Hypothesis; Discrimination; Du Bois, W. E. B.; Ethnicity; Ghetto; Jim Crow; Migration; Nouveaux Riches; Park School, The; Park, Robert E.; Prejudice; Race; Racism; Resegregation of Schools; Segregation; Segregation, School; Separate-but-Equal*

BIBLIOGRAPHY

Charles, Camille. 2001. Processes of Racial Residential Segregation. In *Urban Inequality: Evidence from Four Cities,* eds. A. O'Conner, C. Tilly, and L. D. Bobo. New York: Russell Sage.

Clark, William A. V. 1991. Residential Preferences and Neighborhood Racial Segregation: A Test of the Schelling Segregation Model. *Demography* 28 (1):1–19.

Clark, William A. V. 1992. Residential Preferences and Residential Choices in a Multiethnic Context. *Demography* 29 (3): 451–466.

Clark, William A. V. 2002. Ethnic Preferences and Ethnic Perceptions in Multi-Ethnic Settings. *Urban Geography* 23 (3): 237–256.

Du Bois, W. E. B. [1899] 1996. *The Philadelphia Negro: A Social Study.* Philadelphia: University of Pennsylvania Press.

Duncan, Otis Dudley, and Beverly Duncan. 1955. A Methodological Analysis of Segregation Indices. *American Sociological Review* 20 (2): 210–217.

Duncan, Otis Dudley, and Beverly Duncan. 1957. *The Negro Population of Chicago: A Study of Residential Succession.* Chicago: University of Chicago Press.

Ellen, Ingrid Gould. 2000. *Sharing America's Neighborhoods: The Prospects for Stable Racial Integration.* Cambridge, MA: Harvard University Press.

Farley, Reynolds, and William Frey. 1994. Changes in the Segregation of Whites from Blacks in the 1980s: Small Steps Toward a More Integrated Society. *American Sociological Review* 59 (1): 23–45.

Fossett, Mark. 2006. Ethnic Preferences, Social Distance Dynamics, and Residential Segregation: Theoretical Explorations Using Simulation Analysis. *Journal of Mathematical Sociology* 30 (3–4):185–274.

Fossett, Mark, and Warren Waren. 2005. Overlooked Implications of Ethnic Preferences for Residential Segregation in Agent-Based Models. *Urban Studies* 42 (11):1893–1917.

Glaeser, Edward L., and Jacob L. Vigdor. 2003. Racial Segregation: Promising News. In *Redefining Urban and Suburban America: Evidence from Census 2000,* eds. Bruce Katz and Robert E. Lang, 211–234. Washington, DC: Brookings Institution Press.

James, David, and Karl Taeuber. 1985. Measures of Segregation. *Sociological Methodology* 13: 1–32.

Jargowsky, Paul A. 1997. *Poverty and Place: Ghettos, Barrios, and the American City.* New York: Russell Sage Foundation.

Lieberson, Stanley. 1963. *Ethnic Patterns in American Cities.* Free Press of Glencoe.

Lieberson, Stanley. 1980. *A Piece of the Pie: Blacks and White Immigrants Since 1880.* Berkeley: University of California Press.

Lieberson, Stanley. 1981. An Asymmetric Approach to Segregation. In *Ethnic Segregation in Cities,* eds. Ceri Peach, Vaughan Robinson, and Susan Smith, 61–82. London: Croom Helm; Athens: University of Georgia Press.

Logan, John R. 2003. Ethnic Diversity Grows, Neighborhood Integration Lags. In *Redefining Urban and Suburban America: Evidence from Census 2000,* eds. Bruce Katz and Robert E. Lang, 235–256. Washington, DC: Brookings Institution Press.

Massey, Douglas S. 1985. Ethnic Residential Segregation: A Theoretical Synthesis and Empirical Review. *Sociology and Social Research* 69: 315–350.

Massey, Douglas S., and Nancy A. Denton. 1987. Trends in the Residential Segregation of Blacks, Hispanics, and Asians, 1970–1980. *American Sociological Review* 52 (6): 802–825.

Massey, Douglas S., and Nancy A. Denton. 1988. The Dimensions of Residential Segregation. *Social Forces* 67 (2): 281–315.

Massey, Douglas S., and Nancy A. Denton. 1989. Hypersegregation in U.S. Metropolitan Areas: Black and Hispanic Segregation along Five Dimensions. *Demography* 26 (3): 373–391.

Massey, Douglas S., and Nancy A. Denton. 1993. *American Apartheid: Segregation and the Making of the Underclass.* Cambridge, MA: Harvard University Press.

Orfield, Gary. 2001. *Schools More Separate: Consequences of a Decade of Resegregation.* Cambridge, MA: Civil Rights Project at Harvard University.

Rawlings, Lynette, Laura Harris, and Margery Austin Turner. 2004. Race and Residence: Prospects for Stable Neighborhood Integration. Urban Institute. Neighborhood Change in Urban America Series, no. 3. http://www.urban.org/url.cfm?ID=310985.

Schelling, Thomas C. 1978. *Micromotives and Macrobehavior.* New York: Norton.

Stearns, Linda B., and John Logan. 1986. Measuring Segregation: Three Dimensions, Three Measures. *Urban Affairs Quarterly* 22 (1): 124–150.

Taeuber, Karl E., and Alma F. Taeuber. 1965. *Negroes in Cities: Racial Segregation and Neighborhood Change.* Chicago: Aldine Publishing.

Turner, Margery Austin, Steven L. Ross, George C. Galster, and John Yinger. 2002. *Discrimination in Metropolitan Housing Markets: National Results from Phase I of HDS2000.* Urban Institute. http://www.urban.org/url.cfm?ID=410821.

Yinger, John. 1995. *Closed Doors, Opportunities Lost: The Continuing Cost of Housing Discrimination.* New York: Russell Sage Foundation.

Mark Fossett

SEGREGATION, SCHOOL

Education has been long considered integral to the social health of most nation-states. Despite this regard for its importance, particularly with respect to the frequent promise of education as a "great equalizer," schooling has often been used by dominant groups to engage larger systems of oppression. Indeed, the long and pervasive histories of school segregation that characterize many nations remain glaring proof of such inequities in educational justice.

APARTHEID SOUTH AFRICA

In apartheid South Africa, school segregation was used as one government-directed means to perpetuate racial inequality. The Bantu Education Act of 1953, which gave the state control of all schools, was one of many legislative acts that sought to remove and restrict the lives of non-whites in every possible sphere of life. While schooling for black Africans dramatically expanded under apartheid, this seemingly paradoxical effect was driven by the survival need of the white Afrikaner regime to acculturate the majority black population to the ideological beliefs undergirding apartheid segregation, as well as to limited job horizons, in an effort to both protect white skilled labor from African competition and provide masses of unskilled labor for growing white industry. As Nelson Mandela recounted in his autobiography *Long Walk to Freedom* (1994), this form of education amounted to "intellectual '*basskap*' (domination), a way of institutionalizing inferiority" (p. 145).

Aside from its ideological destructiveness, the segregated schooling imposed through Bantu Education was characterized by a highly inequitable distribution of resources leading to overcrowding, poor facilities, and low-grade teachers. The inequitable conditions institutionalized through Bantu Education would eventually backfire on the Afrikaner regime, as black youth entering their late teens and early twenties "rose up with a vehemence," most notably during the Soweto student uprising of 1976 (Mandela 1994, p. 148).

RACIAL SEGREGATION IN THE UNITED STATES

Tracing the historical progression of school segregation in the United States provides another striking example of the way education becomes incorporated into a system of oppression. In 2002 Peter Irons verified that never has there been a year in U.S. history when even half the country's black children attended schools where a majority of children was white. However, school segregation in the United States exists as but one part of a centuries-old, interconnected system of racial oppression. As Joe Feagin has documented, the white male founders who drafted the U.S. Constitution built into the country's foundation mechanisms designed to maintain African American enslavement. Eight decades would pass before these enslavement mechanisms were removed. Following a short Reconstruction era in the South, during which time public educational opportunities were finally extended to newly freed black Americans (as well as poor whites), the southern white elite, predominantly former slaveholders returning to power, quickly imposed extreme racial segregation as a new form of domination.

In the post-Reconstruction era, African Americans in the North were not exempt from the effects of a broadening racial segregation. There the daily life of black Americans was impacted by an informal de facto segregation, which affected black children's education as well.

Throughout the South, however, where the majority of African Americans lived, segregation became a deeply entrenched way of life, endorsed by law and culture. Legal segregation, called Jim Crow, was a totalitarian system of government-buttressed control that extended to virtually every facet of life. Under the system of legal segregation African Americans faced not only large-scale discrimination by whites in the economy but also met severe restrictions in access to education, housing, political participation, churches, health care, and public accommodations. Indeed, the hand of overt segregation was undergirded by the constant threat of white violence and extended to every corner of lived existence for African Americans, limiting even the cemeteries where one could be interred.

Nowhere was the existence of legal segregation more rampant than in U.S. school systems. With few exceptions, public and private educational institutions—from nursery schools to universities—were segregated in the South. Segregation in schools, as in other institutions, was legally protected, indeed required, by court decisions, climaxing most significantly in *Plessy v. Ferguson.* This 1896 Supreme Court decision upheld the legal mandate for segregated public accommodations and set the infamous "separate but equal" legal precedent. This separate-but-equal standard was a backhanded way to seemingly satisfy the Fourteenth Amendment equal protection clause while paving the way for segregated schooling that ended up being far from "equal" for African Americans.

In practice, southern state and local governments disregarded the education of black youth. As Paul Finkelman stressed, "the disparity in public expenditures guaranteed that blacks would have inferior educational facilities" (2004, p. 45). In 2004 Richard Kluger documented how such disparities operated during legal segregation, with the case of Clarendon County, South Carolina. In 1949 that county government paid $179 per white pupil, while spending only $43 per black pupil there. In this same year the county's 2,375 white children went to twelve different schools, valued at $673,850 (an average value of $56,154 per building); the county's 6,351 black students were dispersed over 61 schools, collectively valued at $194,575 (an average value of $3,190 per building). Many schools were dilapidated, lacking modern heating or indoor plumbing. The racial disparity in spending meant significantly larger class sizes for black students and poorer pay for black principals, supervisors, and teachers. These material inequities served to support the supremacist doctrine that whites intended to communicate through segregation's practice: Whites and blacks are not simply different; whites are superior.

Significantly, black parents and activists have engaged in long struggles for adequate and desegregated schooling since the mid-nineteenth century. They frequently met extreme resistance and were largely legally stifled in their efforts until the period from 1930 to 1950, when successful court cases (most brought by the National Association for the Advancement of Colored People [NAACP], founded in 1909) laid the legal foundation for what Finkelman referred to as "*the* watershed decision of the twentieth century" (2004, p. 35), *Brown v. Board of Education* (1954). As Feagin and Bernice McNair Barnett noted in 2004, the Supreme Court decision in *Brown* effectively dethroned the *Plessy v. Ferguson* doctrine of separate-but-equal that had defined the law, striking down segregation in schooling with the following declaration by the justices: "We conclude that in the field of public education the doctrine of 'separate but equal' has no place. Separate educational facilities are inherently unequal."

Brown was a landmark decision because it was interpreted by numerous judges as a mandate to dismantle state-created segregation in all major institutions, and recognized African Americans as first-class citizens. As T. Alexander Aleinikoff maintained, in *Brown* "Segregation in the public schools is condemned for producing second-class citizenship for African-Americans both because it imposed a stigma on them (as persons not fit to go to school with whites) and because it did not adequately prepare them to be effective citizens" (2002, p. 40).

The reaction to *Brown* by the southern white elite and public ran from general hostility to massive resistance, and few schools were actually desegregated for more than a decade. One of the primary reasons for the failure was the weakness of the 1955 companion case, *Brown v. Board of Education (Brown II)*, which vaguely stipulated that desegregation should proceed "with all deliberate speed." White leaders, including President Dwight Eisenhower, failed to back the Court's decrees with federal authority. Additionally, some state governments passed laws in an attempt to "bypass" the decrees, for example, by issuing grants or tax credits to white families to send their children to segregated private schools, where *Brown*'s reach did not extend. Not until the late 1960s did the Supreme Court and other federal courts finally force meaningful school desegregation in the South.

RESEGREGATION IN THE POST-*BROWN* ERA

Studies examining African American academic achievement document the substantial benefits of desegregated schooling for children of color. Reviewing desegregation's impact, in 2004 Janet Ward Schofield and Leslie R. M. Hausmann found desegregation positively impacted high school graduation rates and black academic achievement. The impact extends beyond primary and secondary schooling, such that African Americans attending integrated schools are more likely to attend college, entertain higher occupational aspirations, gain access to beneficial networks, and acquire better jobs. It is important to note, however, that such positive outcomes are less influenced by the actual racial heterogeneity of desegregated schools than they are by the typically better educational infrastructure that exists in such schools, for example, in terms of resources. In other words, the great crisis of segregated education has not been that children of color cannot be well educated aside other children of color, but rather that segregated educational institutions have been and most often continue to be, as *Brown* reminds, "inherently unequal."

A number of scholars and civil rights advocates have argued for the importance of integrated education, particularly as a way to reduce racial isolation. Participating in diverse educational communities, all students become better prepared to live, learn, work, and participate democratically in an increasingly multiracial world. Additionally, school desegregation creates opportunities to break down stereotypes as students associate with those unlike themselves. Individuals who attended desegregated schools are more likely to live and work in integrated settings, weakening overall racial isolation.

Despite significant progress, by the late 1970s many white liberals began backtracking in their commitment to desegregate U.S. schools. By the 1980s, such backtracking was widespread, primarily as a result of new conservative presidential administrations and courts. Through the 1990s courts allowed many school systems to abandon desegregation plans. Notably, Supreme Court decisions in *Board of Education v. Dowell* (1991), *Freeman v. Pitts* (1992), and *Missouri v. Jenkins* (1995) proved damaging to long-term desegregation, ending federal segregation orders before lasting success could be demonstrated in the interest of returning schools to local white control. In 2004, Lia B. Epperson identified the fault of this local-rights approach, arguing that "It is a standard that treats whites and blacks as if they were similarly situated and ignores the history of segregation and its vestiges.... This very form of local control allowed segregation to flourish in the era before *Brown*, and has done so again in the decade since these decisions" (2004, p. 140).

As Jonathan Kozol attested in 2005, retreat in desegregation has allowed for the persistence of already segregated schools, as well as the rapidly growing resegregation of schools that had been integrated. The Harvard Civil Rights Project reported in 2003 that three-fourths of black and Latino students attended predominantly minority schools, and more than 2 million attended "apartheid schools" where 99 to 100 percent of students were not white. As during legal segregation, racial disparities in per-pupil spending remain extreme.

Even within schools integrated at the facility level, a type of "second-generation segregation" is often imposed through the racially correlated allocation of educational opportunities. For instance, many scholars argue that ability tracking (a practice instituted soon after the *Brown* decision) has led to the emergence of what economist William Darity Jr. refers to as "segregated curriculums." Beginning as early as elementary school, tracking frequently creates an internal racial segregation, as students of color are disproportionately assigned to lower academic tracks and are relatively absent from accelerated tracks (e.g., "gifted" or honors programs). In 2002 Terence Fitzgerald additionally uncovered categorical labeling practices whereby African American students were disproportionately assigned to special education and/or behavioral disordered categories, as well as more frequently expelled or placed in alternative school settings. The effects of such racially stratified practices have far reaching consequences, initiating a discriminatory cycle of restricted educational opportunities for students of color that leads to inferior learning opportunities, diminished school achievement, oppositional responses, and exacerbated racial disparities in school.

As the increasing prevalence of resegregation and second-generation segregation displays, and as Feagin and Barnett urge, efforts to end racial segregation require "constant renewal, for established arrangements of centuries have a strong social inertia" (2004, p. 1104). Beyond the U.S. and South African legacies, school segregation targeting ethnic or cultural minorities has been documented in many other nations, including England, the Czech Republic, Hungary, Bosnia, and Croatia. Only with continued resistance to the de facto segregation of schools around the globe, acknowledgement of the benefits of integrated education for all, and renewed commitment to actions that will ensure more equitable, integrated societies, can the promise of education be fulfilled.

SEE ALSO *Education; Resegregation of Schools; Tracking in Schools*

BIBLIOGRAPHY

Aleinikoff, T. Alexander. 2002. *Semblances of Sovereignty: The Constitution, the State, and American Citizenship.* Cambridge, MA: Harvard University Press.

Auerbach, Franz, and David Welsh. 1981. Education. In *Race Discrimination in South Africa*, ed. Sheila Van der Horst, 66–89. Cape Town: David Philip.

Beinart, William, and Saul Dubow, eds. 1995. *Segregation and Apartheid in Twentieth-Century South Africa.* New York: Routledge.

Bell, Derrick. 2004. *Silent Covenants:* Brown v. Board of Education *and the Unfulfilled Hopes for Racial Reform.* New York: Oxford University Press.

Darity, William, Jr. 2006. Correspondence: Acting White. *Education Next* (Spring): 6.

Darity, William, Jr., Domini Castellino, Karolyn Tyson, et al. 2001. *Increasing Opportunity to Learn via Access to Rigorous Courses and Programs: One Strategy for Closing the Achievement Gap for At-Risk and Ethnic Minority Students.* Report prepared for the North Carolina Department of Public Instruction.

Diseko, Nosipho J. 1990. Prelude to 1976: The Implementation and Response to Bantu Education, 1954–76. In *Repression and Resistance: Insider Accounts of Apartheid*, eds. Robin Cohen, Yvonne Muthien, and Abebe Zegeye, 117–141. London: Hans Zell Publishers.

Epperson, Lia B. 2004. Resisting Retreat: The Struggle for Equity in Education Opportunity in the Post-*Brown* Era. *University of Pittsburgh Law Review* 66 (1): 131–154.

Feagin, Joe. 2000. *Racist America: Roots, Current Realities and Future Reparations.* New York: Routledge.

Feagin, Joe R. 2004. Heeding Black Voices: The Court, *Brown*, and Challenges in Building a Multiracial Democracy. *University of Pittsburgh Law Review* 66 (1): 57–81.

Feagin, Joe R. 2006. *Systemic Racism: A Theory of Oppression.* New York: Routledge.

Feagin, Joe R., and Bernice McNair Barnett. 2004. Success *and* Failure: How Systemic Racism Trumped the *Brown v. Board of Education* Decision. *University of Illinois Law Review* 2004 (5): 1099–1130.

Finkelman, Paul. 2004. The Radicalism of Brown. *University of Pittsburgh Law Review* 66 (1): 35–56.

Fitzgerald, Terence D. 2002. *The Circumvention of Public Law 94-142 and Section 504: The Sorting and Controlling of Black Males.* Ph.D. diss., University of Illinois, Urbana-Champaign.

Frankenberg, Erica, and Chungmei Lee. 2003. *Charter Schools and Race: A Lost Opportunity for Integrated Education.* Harvard Civil Rights Project. http://www.civilrightsproject. harvard.edu/research/deseg/Charter_Schools03.pdf.

Frankenberg, Erica, Chungmei Lee, and Gary Orfield. 2003. *A Multiracial Society with Segregated Schools: Are We Losing the Dream?* Harvard Civil Rights Project. http://www. civilrightsproject.harvard.edu/research/reseg03/reseg03_full. php.

Irons, Peter. 2002. *Jim Crow's Children.* New York: Penguin Books.

Johnston, Ron, Deborah Wilson, and Simon Burgess. 2004. School Segregation in Multiethnic England. *Ethnicities* 4 (2): 237–265.

Kluger, Richard. 2004. *Simple Justice: The History of* Brown v. Board of Education *and Black America's Struggle for Equality.* New York: Vintage.

Kozol, Jonathan. 2005. *The Shame of the Nation.* New York: Crown Publishers.

Louw, P. Eric. 2004. *The Rise, Fall, and Legacy of Apartheid.* Westport, CT: Praeger.

Mandela, Nelson. 1994. *Long Walk to Freedom.* Boston: Little, Brown and Company.

Mickelson, Roslyn Arlin. 2001. Subverting *Swann:* First- and Second-Generation Segregation in the Charlotte-Mecklenburg Schools. *American Educational Research Journal* 38: 215–252.

Oakes, Jeannie. 2005. *Keeping Track: How Schools Structure Inequality.* 2nd ed. New Haven, CT: Yale University Press.

Orfield, Gary. 1997. Unexpected Costs and Uncertain Gains of Dismantling Desegregation. In *Dismantling Desegregation: The Quiet Reversal of* Brown v. Board of Education, eds. Gary Orfield and Susan E. Eaton, 73–114. New York: New Press.

Schofield, Janet Ward, and Leslie R. M. Hausmann. 2004. The Conundrum of School Desegregation: Positive Student Outcomes and Waning Support. *University of Pittsburgh Law Review* 66 (1): 83–112.

Tushnet, Mark V. 1995. Brown v. Board of Education: *The Battle for Integration.* New York: Franklin Watts.

Tyson, Karolyn, William Darity Jr., and Comini Castellino. 2005. It's Not "a Black Thing": Understanding the Burden of Acting White and Other Dilemmas of High Achievement. *American Sociological Review* 70: 582–605.

U.S. Department of State. 2006. *2005 Country Reports on Human Rights Practices.* Washington, DC: U.S. Department of State. http://www.state.gov/g/drl/hr/c1470.htm.

Wood, Peter B., and Nancy Sonleitner. 1996. The Effect of Childhood Interracial Contact on Adult Anti-Black Prejudice. *International Journal of Intercultural Relations* 20: 1–17.

Jennifer C. Mueller
Joe R. Feagin

SELECTION BIAS

An important aspect of empirical investigations in the social sciences is to draw inferences for the whole population of interest when one has data only on a subsample from that population. A first step in conducting such inference is to assume that the subsample under examination is drawn randomly from the population. However, in many instances in economics, or in the social sciences in general, it is not possible to make such an assumption. For example, suppose one is interested in drawing inferences regarding the determinants of wages for women when one has information on wages only for women working in market employment. If the sample of market-employed women "differs" from the population in some systematic way, then using the sample of employed women may lead to incorrect inferences regarding the determinants for all women. This issue, where the inference based on subsample is not appropriate for the entire population, is known as *selection bias*.

The example of employed women is useful for further illustrating the concept of selection bias. In fact, the original papers on selection bias were motivated by empirical work on precisely this topic. Suppose one has a sample of women of which, without loss of generality, half are employed in market employment and half are not. Furthermore, suppose each woman is characterized by observable characteristics, such as race, age, and education, and unobservable characteristics, such as motivation and ability. Also assume that these unobservable characteristics are uncorrelated with the observable characteristics so as to demonstrate that selection bias arises even with exogenous conditioning variables. Suppose the objective of the researcher is to explore the relationship between the observable characteristics and wages for all women by using only the data on the subsample of workers.

First assume that the decision to work in market employment is random. That is, each individual tosses a coin and on the basis of the coin toss decides whether or not to work. In this case examining the subsample leads to correct inferences because the process of selection for the sample, which is used to draw inferences, is random; thus there are no differences between the employed sample and the nonemployed sample. As a result there is no selection bias.

Second, now suppose that only the highly educated individuals in the population are observed to be working in market employment. In this case the working sample would be overrepresented by individuals with higher levels of education. Thus, the sample of employed workers will have different average characteristics from those observed to be not working in market employment.

However, since the topic of interest is how the individual's characteristics affect wages, one can control for the role of any observable characteristics when performing estimation over the employed sample. Thus differences in observable characteristics alone will not lead to selection bias.

Finally, consider the case in which all the highly motivated individuals in the sample of women are those that are observed to work in market employment. If motivation affected only the decision to be employed but not the wage, then this would not induce selection bias; even though the sample of working women would have a higher level of motivation on average than the whole population, one could still directly control for all the determinants of wages when examining the relationship between these determinants and wages. However, consider a case in which motivation does affect wages as well as the market work decision. In this case, the sample of employed women would have wages that were determined by the observable characteristics, which one could control for, and their level of motivation, which one could not control for. Moreover, as one has only a sample of motivated individuals working, one must conclude that for this employed sample the role of motivation, on average, is to increase wages. Failure to account for the role of motivation leads to a selection bias and incorrect inferences regarding the determinants of wages. Thus, in general, selection bias occurs when the unobservable features determining the probability of being observed in the subsample used for inference (in this example the sample of employed women) are correlated with the unobservables determining the outcome of primary interest (i.e., wages).

The issue of selection bias arises in a large number of empirical investigations in economics. Accounting for selection bias has therefore become a critical feature of empirical work in economics. One can see from the example above that adjusting for selection bias essentially requires controlling for the role of the unobservables. The first efforts to account for selection bias were conducted in a fully parametric setting. That is, the distribution of all the unobservables in the model were fully stated up to unknown parameters. This approach was suggested by James J. Heckman (1974, 1979) and ever since has had a substantial impact on both theoretical and empirical microeconometrics. Subsequent theoretical and empirical work in this area focused on relaxing the distributional assumptions in the model and thus attempted to make inference more robust to the assumptions employed in the earliest investigations. The 1998 article by Francis Vella surveys these departures from the original Heckman formulation and treatment. Another important innovation, as discussed by Charles Manski's 1989 article, has been the use of bounds in this literature. According to this approach, one attempts to infer the upper and lower bounds on the object of interest (for example, the impact determinants of wages) when one relaxes various assumptions underlying the process determining selection bias.

SEE ALSO *Classical Statistical Analysis; Descriptive Statistics; Heckman Selection Correction Procedure; Sampling*

BIBLIOGRAPHY

Heckman, James J. 1974. Shadow Prices, Market Wages, and Labor Supply. *Econometrica* 42 (4): 679–694.

Heckman, James J. 1979. Sample Selection Bias as a Specification Error. *Econometrica* 47 (1): 153–161.

Manski, Charles F. 1989. Anatomy of the Selection Problem. *Journal of Human Resources* 24 (3): 341–360.

Vella, Francis. 1998. Estimating Models with Sample Selection Bias: A Survey. *Journal of Human Resources* 33 (1): 127–169.

Francis Vella

SELECTION BIAS REGRESSION

SEE *Heckman Selection Correction Procedure.*

SELECTIVE ATTENTION

Selective attention involves the ability to attend to relevant information while ignoring irrelevant information. In early research on this topic, a critical question was whether attention occurs before (early selection) or after (late selection) the information is processed for meaning. One of the tasks used to answer this question is the dichotic listening task. In this task, participants listen to different passages of text presented in each ear through headphones. Researchers found that when questioned about the message in the unattended or ignored ear, participants detected changes in perceptual characteristics (e.g., pitch, volume) but did not notice other meaning-based changes. This result suggests the existence of a perceptual filter that selects information based on features such as volume or pitch. This filter serves to limit the amount of information entering short-term memory (i.e., the "bottleneck" in processing). However, other evidence suggests that unattended information also passes through the filter, though at an attenuated level, whereas still other results suggest that attention occurs much later, after all information has been processed for meaning. One current model of selective attention proposes that attention can occur early or late, depending on the perceptual and memory demands imposed by the task.

Selective attention is also investigated employing tasks using reaction time, measured in milliseconds, as the variable of interest. In the Stroop task, participants name the color of the ink in which a word is printed. Individuals are slower to respond in an incongruent condition (e.g., the word *red* printed in green ink) compared to a congruent condition (e.g., the word *red* printed in red ink), because the relatively automatic word-naming response must be inhibited in the incongruent condition. This interference is more pronounced with increased age, even in relatively healthy older adults. In visual search tasks, participants identify a target item among irrelevant distractor items. Under difficult conditions, when distractors are physically similar to the target, search becomes less efficient, particularly for older adults. However, under conditions in which the target is a unique item and tends to "pop out" from the distractors, search performance is comparable for younger and older adults. Using these tasks with brain-imaging techniques has allowed researchers to identify a frontoparietal network of brain regions involved in selective attention. Healthy older adults show increased activations, compared to younger adults, in this frontoparietal network, combined with decreased activations in visual cortical regions. The increased activation may serve as a compensatory mechanism for age-related declines in visual processing.

Other causes of individual differences in selective attention include attention deficit hyperactivity disorder (ADHD), which has typically been associated with global deficits in attention. However, recent research using visual search tasks suggests no differential impairment in selective attention between ADHD children and matched control children, although ADHD-related deficits have been observed in other components of attention, such as the ability to switch between two different tasks. Although there is little evidence of sex differences in selective attention, a few studies using the dichotic listening and visual search tasks have found moderate differences in selective attention favoring women.

SEE ALSO *Attention-Deficit/Hyperactivity Disorder; Neuroscience*

BIBLIOGRAPHY

Lavie, Nilli, Aleksandra Hirst, Jan W. de Fockert, and Essi Viding. 2004. Load Theory of Selective Attention and Cognitive Control. *Journal of Experimental Psychology: General* 133 (3): 339–354.

Wolfe, Jeremy M. 2003. Moving Towards Solutions to Some Enduring Controversies in Visual Search. *Trends in Cognitive Science* 7 (2): 70–76.

Barbara Bucur
David J. Madden

SELECTIVE SERVICE

During major military conflicts in which the United States has been involved throughout its history, the government has utilized various programs and forms of military conscription in order to draft male citizens to the armed forces. While no draft has been in place since 1973, the Selective Service exists as an independent agency within the federal government to administer the registration of eighteen-year-old males, which is required by law, and conduct a draft should a need for military manpower over and above a volunteer force arise. An individual who is appointed by the president of the United States and confirmed by the U.S. Senate directs the Selective Service System.

HISTORICAL PERSPECTIVE

Congress passed the first military conscription act on March 3, 1863, during the Civil War. The act authorized President Abraham Lincoln (1809–1865) to draft men between the ages of twenty and forty-five into military service for the Union forces. The law, which included the option of draftees to pay a *commutation fee* of $300 to escape enlistment, provoked protests in New York City by those who saw it as unfairly protecting the wealthy.

Lincoln was forced to send federal troops to quell violent mobs. The Confederate States also instituted conscription in 1862, and it proved just as unpopular in the South as in the North. The next military draft law in the United States was passed in 1917; the Selective Service Act gave the president the power to conscript men for service during World War I.

As American involvement in World War II approached, President Franklin D. Roosevelt (1882–1945) signed the Selective Training and Service Act of 1940. This act created the first peacetime draft and established the Selective Service as an independent federal agency. The original legislation called for a service commitment of twelve months but was expanded to eighteen months following direct U.S. engagement in hostilities. Men between the ages of eighteen and forty-five who registered with the Selective Service were eligible to be inducted into the army and Marine Corps, and more than 10,000,000 men were inducted between 1940 and 1947. New legislation in 1948 reduced the mandatory registration age range to between eighteen and twenty-six. Military conscription continued during the Korean War in the 1950s and, most notably and controversially, during the Vietnam War.

Beginning in 1964, President Lyndon B. Johnson (1908–1973) was authorized by Congress to increase the number of troops in Vietnam, and by early 1968 the United States had more than 500,000 troops there. Tens of thousands of young men were drafted through the Selective Service lottery, while thousands of others avoided service through exemptions—also called deferments—granted by the several regional Selective Service draft boards around the nation based on educational commitments, membership in the clergy, medical restrictions, membership in the National Guard, and other obligations. Critics of the draft process noted an inordinate number of minorities had been selected, and questioned the randomness of the lottery. As in the past, the draft was seen as unfairly singling out those without the economic means to avoid service. As the number of U.S. soldiers killed in action rose and the war became increasingly unpopular, the draft became a focal point for antiwar protestors. In 1973 President Richard M. Nixon (1913–1994) signed legislation that ended the draft, and those joining the military thereafter did so as volunteers.

THE SELECTIVE SERVICE IN THE EARLY-TWENTY-FIRST CENTURY

Despite the end of the draft, in the early-twenty-first century the Selective Service exists as a contingency in the event of a draft. All males in the United States must register within thirty days of their eighteenth birthdays;

that requirement applies to citizens and aliens alike. Registrants may sign up via mail, at a U.S. post office, or on a student federal financial aid form. Because the Selective Service does not apply draft status classification to registrants when there is no draft, disabled men must also register. Similarly men who are conscientious objectors to war must register with the Selective Service, since there is no place on the registration form to indicate objection to induction into the armed services. The mere act of registering, however, does not guarantee a man will be inducted in the event of a draft. As it did during previous wars where a draft was in place, the Selective Service would classify registrants to determine eligibility for induction and deferments when and if a draft is reinstated. Additionally, according to its mission statement, the Selective Service would devise an alternative service program for those classified as conscientious objectors.

Females are not required to register with the Selective Service. Congress has explicitly stated in all Selective Service legislation that only males are required to register. In a 1981 case challenging the constitutionality of that particular clause (*Rostker v. Goldberg*), the Supreme Court ruled that Congress was well within its authority to exclude women from registration with the Selective Service because the purpose of the legislation is to raise and regulate armies and navies for combat action, and women are excluded from nearly every type of military combat. President William J. Clinton (b. 1946) ordered a review of the policy regarding females and Selective Service registration in 1994, and the Department of Defense reported that the process of exclusion remained justifiable because of combat regulations and restrictions but noted the need to revisit the issue as the roles of female soldiers expand in the future.

In the event Congress passes legislation reinstating the draft, a National Draft Lottery would be conducted to determine the order in which men would be drafted for induction. The lottery would be based upon the birth dates of registrants, beginning with those men twenty years of age during that calendar year. A major difference from the Vietnam draft-era is that registrants who are eighteen and nineteen years old during the year of the draft would most likely not be called, as opposed to the great number of men under the age of twenty called to Vietnam. The lottery would be conducted in public and under the auspices of the National Institute of Standards and Technology in order to insure as random a lottery as possible.

SEE ALSO *Civil-Military Relation; Military; National Service Programs; Pacifism; Peace Movements; U.S. Civil War; Vietnam War; World War I; World War II*

BIBLIOGRAPHY

Flynn, George Q. 2002. *Conscription and Democracy: The Draft in France, Great Britain, and the United States.* Westport, CT: Greenwood.

Graham, John R. 1980. *Constitutional History of the Military Draft.* Hudson, WI: Ross & Haines.

Holmes, Richard. 1985. *Acts of War.* New York: Free Press.

Huntington, Samuel P. 2005. *The Soldier and the State: The Theory and Politics of Civil-Military Relations.* Cambridge, MA: Belknap Press.

Kusch, Frank. 2001. *All American Boys: Draft Dodgers in Canada from the Vietnam War.* Westport, CT: Praeger Publications.

McNamara, Robert S. 1995. *In Retrospect: The Tragedy and Lessons of Vietnam.* New York: Random House.

Rostker v. Goldberg, 453 U.S. 57 (1981).

Selective Service System. http://www.sss.gov.

Matthew May

SELECTORATE THEORY

SEE *Stability, Political.*

SELF DISCREPANCY THEORY

Self discrepancy theory was introduced by psychologist E. Tory Higgins (1987) with the purpose of explaining the relationship between aspects of the self and affect. In this theory, Higgins posits that individuals possess different types of *self-guides*, or standards, against which they compare their current self. These comparisons yield information that individuals are either near their self-guides or are distant from them. In the case of proximity to self-guides, individuals experience positive affect. In the case of discrepancy from self-guides, individuals experience negative affect. This affect is differentiated by the type of self-guide being used in comparison. Individuals may compare themselves to an *ideal self-guide*, which represents their hopes or wishes. Or they may compare themselves to an *ought self-guide*, which represents their obligations or responsibilities. Comparisons made to ideal self-guides result in affect along an elation-dejection spectrum: Proximity to ideal standards yields affect such as happiness and joy, while discrepancy from ideal standards yields affect such as depression and sadness. Comparisons made to ought self-guides result in affect along a relief-agitation spectrum: Proximity to ought self-guides yields affect such as calmness and contentment, while discrepancy from ought self-guides yields affect such as nervousness and guilt. The magnitude of discrepancy is related to the experience of negative affect such that the greater the discrepancy, the greater the negative affect.

Timothy Strauman (1992) applied self discrepancy theory to psychological disorders of emotion. He found that individuals reporting symptoms of depression had larger discrepancies from their ideal selves, while individuals reporting symptoms of anxiety had larger discrepancies from their ought selves.

Self discrepancy assumes that self-regulation occurs in response to the negative affect experienced as the result of a discrepancy. This self-regulation occurs through a discrepancy-reducing feedback process in which individuals exert changes on their behavior in response to a noticed discrepancy. Feedback about individuals' progress toward self-guides is transmitted back to the individual, and behavioral change is either continued or terminated.

An expansion of this theory by Higgins (1997) suggests that individual differences in self-guides are chronic and related to personality. He labeled individuals who tend to have accessible ideal self-guides as *promotion-oriented* and individuals who tend to have accessible ought self-guides as *prevention-oriented*. These different types of goal orientations are expected to influence the types of goals individuals pursue, as well as the contexts under which they will experience the most successful goal pursuit.

Measurement of discrepancies often occurs through the Selves Questionnaire. On this questionnaire, individuals list attributes associated with each of the different *self-states* (own-actual, own-ideal, own-ought, other-actual, other-ideal, other-ought). Correlations and partial correlations among the self-states are computed to determine magnitude of discrepancy. Some researchers may opt to use only the self-states from the individuals' own perspective.

SEE ALSO *Self-Guides*

BIBLIOGRAPHY

Higgins, E. Tory. 1987. Self-discrepancy: A Theory Relating Self and Affect. *Psychological Review* 94 (3): 319–340.

Higgins, E. Tory. 1997. Beyond Pleasure and Pain. *American Psychologist* 52 (12): 1280–1300.

Strauman, Timothy J. 1992. Self-guides, Autobiographical Memory, and Anxiety and Dysphoria: Toward a Cognitive Model of Vulnerability to Emotional Distress. *Journal of Abnormal Psychology* 101: 87–95.

Michelle Sherrill

SELF-ACTUALIZATION

Self-actualization is the process by which an organism or person realizes its full potential. The concept was first introduced by the Gestalt psychologist Kurt Goldstein in his 1939 book *The Organism*. It was soon adopted and developed by several early proponents of the humanistic psychology movement, such as Carl Rogers (1902–1987), the founder of client-centered therapy. Nonetheless, self-actualization is most strongly associated with the work of Abraham Maslow (1908–1970), another early humanistic psychologist. It is for that reason that this article will focus on Maslow's original formulation of self-actualization and subsequent research on that formulation.

HIERARCHY OF MOTIVES

Maslow's first discussed self-actualization in the context of his argument for a motive hierarchy. This hierarchy was put forward in his article on "A Theory of Human Motivation" published in a 1943 issue of *Psychological Review*. According to this early formulation, human needs could be ordered according to their relative *pre-potency*. That is, a particular need will not manifest itself until a more basic, pre-potent need is first satisfied. The most pre-potent motives are physiological and pertain to self-preservation. These include the needs to breathe, to drink water, to eat food, to dispose of bodily wastes, to sleep, and to regulate body temperature. If these needs are reasonably well satisfied, another set of motives are evoked, namely, those that concern safety. This includes the desire for physical security, such as the need to live in a secure, predictable environment free of violence and threat. Once this set of needs is also gratified the individual advances to love needs, which include the desire for affection, intimacy, and belongingness.

After physiological, safety, and love needs are satisfied, the person can move to esteem needs. These involve the enhancement of one's self-confidence and self-respect. Only upon the gratification of esteem needs can an individual progress to the need for self-actualization. According to Maslow, this "refers to the desire for self-fulfillment" or "the desire to become more and more what one is, to become everything that one is capable of becoming" (1943, p. 383). Because each individual human being has a distinct intrinsic potential, self-actualization is the most divergent of the needs in the hierarchy. Everyone can appreciate the desire for a breath of fresh air, the need to feel safe from danger, and the push to feel good about one's self. But where one person might self-actualize by becoming a scientist, another might do so by becoming an athlete or chef. There are as many ways to self-actualize as there are distinguishable individuals. However, because a large number of persons never are able to satisfy more pre-potent needs, self-actualizing individuals tend to be relatively rare.

From 1943 until Maslow's death in 1970, this formulation underwent several modifications and elaborations. One important change was the later distinction between *deficiency* and *being* needs. The former "D-needs" encompass the physiological, safety, love, and esteem needs. To experience these needs is to succumb to "D-cognition," or the awareness of a deficiency—of a negative condition that must be removed. The latter "B-needs," in contrast, concern "B-cognition," or the awareness of pure being—a positive state that is actively enjoyed. In this second group Maslow placed not just self-actualization but also various higher motives, such as the needs for knowledge, for aesthetics and beauty, and for self-transcendence, a spiritual need. Unlike the deficiency needs, Maslow's conception of the being needs changed over the course of his career. These changes involved both their number and their placement within the hierarchy.

CHARACTERISTICS OF SELF-ACTUALIZERS

Having placed self-actualization at or near the apex of the motive hierarchy, Maslow felt it necessary to investigate the attributes of those personalities whose lives are dominated by B- rather than D-cognition. This presented a methodological problem because, according to his theory, self-actualizing individuals should be relatively rare. In fact, he reported that in student populations—the most common source of research participants in psychological research—only 1 out of 3,000 students managed to get beyond deficiency needs. As a consequence, Maslow adopted an unconventional investigative strategy. Rather than study self-actualizing students he would examine eminent personalities whose acts of self-actualization had driven them to major achievements. His sample included, among others, first lady and humanitarian Eleanor Roosevelt, the African American abolitionist Frederick Douglass, the physicist Albert Einstein, the psychologist and philosopher William James, the German poet Johann Wolfgang von Goethe, the Spanish violoncellist and conductor Pablo Casals, and the French painter Pierre-Auguste Renoir.

For each of the sampled self-actualizers Maslow collected biographical information about their personal characteristics. From that information he abstracted a sketch of the typical self-actualizing personality. In particular, self-actualizers were found to have more accurate perceptions of reality, to be more accepting of themselves and others, to display a freshness of appreciation for the world around them, to be more spontaneous, to be more problem centered rather than self centered, to exhibit a strong need for privacy, to maintain deep personal relationships with just a few select individuals, to harbor a powerful sense of kinship to fellow human beings as well as a great deal of humility and respect for others, to have strong but somewhat unconventional ethical standards, to concentrate on ends rather than means, to be autonomous and to resist enculturation, to project a more intellectual than aggressive sense of humor, to be more creative, and to undergo special cognitive-emotional moments that Maslow called *peak experiences*. The latter experiences were especially important as motivators in the self-actualization process.

EMPIRICAL RESEARCH

Because Maslow was reacting against the predominant behaviorism of his day, his research on self-actualization did not meet contemporary standards for scientific rigor. For instance, his motivational hierarchy was not based on a series of laboratory experiments regarding the relative strengths of various human needs. Although he could be said to have collected data for his global profile of the self-actualizing personality, his analyses were qualitative and subjective rather than quantitative and objective. Moreover, his criteria for identifying certain individuals as being self-actualizers appear in retrospect to be somewhat haphazard or idiosyncratic.

Nevertheless, subsequent researchers have tried to scrutinize Maslow's theory using more conventional methods. Some of this research has focused specifically on the hierarchy of motives. On this point it soon became clear that the empirical data did not lend much if any support to the hypothesized ordering of needs. Not only is the drive priority unstable or variable within the set of D-needs, but also it is the case that B-needs can sometimes take precedence over D-needs. This possibility is suggested by the proverbial image of the "poor starving artist in the attic" who places self-actualization before the supposedly pre-potent needs for food, companionship, and a warm bed. Although Maslow himself acknowledged that the motivational priorities can sometimes be upset in particular cases, he often viewed these departures as pathological rather than healthy. Furthermore, once one allows for individual differences in the hierarchical placement of the motives the whole concept becomes seriously weakened as a scientific explanation. A hierarchy that can assume almost any form across separate personalities can hardly be viewed as a legitimate hierarchy.

A far larger body of empirical research has concentrated on Maslow's profile of the self-actualizing person. Unlike Maslow's own work, this research has relied on the development and application of psychometric instruments that directly assess a person's self-actualization. The first such measure was the Personal Orientation Inventory created by researcher Everett L. Shostrom in 1963.

Although this instrument was used extensively throughout the 1970s and 1980s, it was also subjected to numerous criticisms with respect to validity and reliability. In the late 1980s and 1990s alternative measures appeared, including the Jones and Crandall (1986) Short Index of Self-Actualization and the Sumerlin and Bundrick (1996) Brief Index of Self-Actualization. Taken together, research using these instruments has helped validate much of what Maslow had concluded from his eminent creators and leaders. For instance, self-actualizers tend to display superior mental health, to have higher self-esteem, to have lower anxiety, to have more purpose in life, and to be more creative, hopeful, optimistic, and independent. Furthermore, investigations have indicated some of the factors that help increase the level of self-actualization, such as specific meditation practices and therapeutic interventions. Hence, there is little doubt that self-actualization is an observable and significant psychological phenomenon.

CRITICAL EVALUATION

By the twenty-first century self-actualization had acquired a somewhat ambivalent position in the psychological sciences. On the one hand, the concept of self-actualization—including Maslow's formulation of its placement in a hierarchy of motives—remains extremely well known. The word continues to be used by many applied psychologists, especially those active in clinical, counseling, educational, and industrial psychology. Moreover, numerous introductory textbooks in psychology still include an almost obligatory section on Maslow's motive hierarchy. On the other hand, empirical research on self-actualization waned considerably after the 1990s. Indeed, an article on the subject has not been published in a top-tier psychology journal since the 1980s. All of these trends may suggest that its utility as a psychological concept has diminished to the point that its status has become more historical than scientific. Even so, it is hard to imagine that the idea will disappear from popular psychological thought. The concept of self-actualization has entered mainstream culture in a manner almost comparable to the ideas of the Austrian neurologist Sigmund Freud, the father of psychoanalysis. Therefore, it is unlikely that the concept will ever completely retreat into the history books. Furthermore, interest in the construct has undergone something of a revival in the mid-2000s with the advent of the positive psychology movement, which concerns itself with the empirical study of human virtues.

BIBLIOGRAPHY

Jones, Avin, and Rick Crandall, eds. 1991. *Handbook of Self-Actualization*. Corte Madera, CA: Select Press.

Maslow, Abraham H. 1943. Theory of Human Motivation. *Psychological Review* 50: 370–396.

Maslow, Abraham H. 1970. *Motivation and Personality*. 2nd ed. New York: Harper and Row.

Rogers, Carl R. 1961. *On Becoming a Person*. Boston: Houghton Mifflin.

Runco, M. A. 1999. Self-Actualization. In *Encyclopedia of Creativity*, Vol. 2, eds. Mark A. Runco and Steven R. Pritzker, 533–536. San Diego, CA: Academic Press.

Snyder, C. R., and Shane Lopez, eds. 2002. *Handbook of Positive Psychology*. New York: Oxford University Press.

Dean Keith Simonton

SELF-AFFIRMATION THEORY

Sometimes people have thoughts and experiences that threaten their self-image. According to Claude Steele's (1988) self-affirmation theory, when people's self-image has been threatened they are motivated to affirm the integrity of the self. Moreover, people have a desire to restore their general self-image, not simply to resolve the specific threat. The unique prediction that self-affirmation theory makes is that people have a strong desire to maintain a positive self-image; therefore, when people experience a specific self-threat, they can overcome the unpleasant arousal associated with the threat by affirming an equally important, yet unrelated, aspect of the self. This can work to restore self-esteem even without resolving the specific threat.

Self-image threats can arise from several sources. One important source is when people hold inconsistent cognitions or engage in behaviors that are inconsistent with their beliefs. For example, some people fail to practice safe sex on a regular basis, although they are aware of the health risks associated with such actions. Likewise, some people do not drive energy efficient cars, although they profess to have positive attitudes toward environmental issues. When people hold two conflicting cognitions or when they behave in a way that is contrary to how they think they should act, they often experience an unpleasant psychological state that is referred to as *cognitive dissonance*. The inconsistency between one's cognitions and behavior can be arousing and threatening to the self because it suggests that people are irrational, immoral, and even unintelligent.

According to cognitive dissonance theorists, people often try to reduce this unpleasant psychological state by engaging in one of three actions. First, people may attempt to change their behavior to make it more consistent with their cognition. For example, smokers can stop smoking. Second, people can attempt to reduce cognitive dissonance by changing their cognitions. Smokers, for example, can lower their perception of the health risks associated with smoking. Finally, people can attempt to reduce cognitive dissonance by adding new cognitions to their belief system. For example, smokers can focus on counterexamples to the health risk by focusing on people who smoke but have lived a very long life. Additionally, smokers may justify their behavior by emphasizing how much smoking reduces their stress level. These three basic ways of reducing cognitive dissonance involve changing beliefs and actions within the domain in which the self has been threatened. For example, in order to restore their self-regard, smokers must engage in some affirmation strategy that is directly relevant to smoking behavior. Self-affirmation theory, however, predicts something different. It states that when people experience a self-image threat after engaging in an undesirable behavior in one domain, they can restore their self-image by affirming another aspect of the self. As with the smoking example, smokers can restore their self-image by reminding themselves that they contribute to charities for impoverished children or that they have a lot of friends. In this example, contributing to charities or focusing on being well liked are unrelated to the domain of smoking and yet serve the function of making people feel good about themselves after a threat.

Threatening thoughts and experiences can also arise from the way people are treated or are perceived to be treated by other individuals. The perceptions and behaviors of other individuals can pose a threat to a person's personal self-worth. For example, being accused of being uncooperative may threaten a person's self-esteem because most people desire to appear cooperative. Additionally, other individuals' perceptions and behaviors can pose a threat to a person's collective self-worth. For example, being considered unintelligent because one is black may threaten a person's collective self-esteem or sense of self as a member of a particular group. When people feel threatened because they sense that they are judged or treated in terms of social stereotypes or that they might do something that could inadvertently confirm the stereotype, they experience what Steele (1997) refers to as a *stereotype threat*. According to self-affirmation theory, when people experience a stereotype threat they can reaffirm the self even in a domain unrelated to the stereotyped domain. For example, an African American student who is stereotyped by his teacher as unintelligent can reaffirm the self by thinking about how great he is at negotiating interpersonal conflict.

Self affirmation theory suggests that there are many possible ways that people can protect their self esteem when it is under threat. Specific threats may come from inconsistencies in thoughts and behaviors that may lead to a state of cognitive dissonance or the presence or perceived presence of societal stereotypes of a particular group. Whatever the source, research has found that affirming an aspect of the self that may even be unrelated to the self threat is effective in making people feel good about themselves, at least in the short term.

SEE ALSO *Cognitive Dissonance; Self-Esteem; Stereotype Threat*

BIBLIOGRAPHY

Steele, Claude M. 1988. The Psychology of Self-Affirmation: Sustaining the Integrity of the Self. In *Advances in Experimental Social Psychology*, Vol. 21, ed. Leonard Berkowitz, 261–302. San Diego, CA: Academic Press.

Steele, Claude M. 1997. A Threat in the Air: How Stereotypes Shape Intellectual Identity and Performance. *American Psychologist* 52: 613–629.

J. Nicole Shelton
Laura Smart Richman

SELF-AWARENESS THEORY

Self-awareness is the capacity to take oneself as the object of thought—people can think, act, and experience, and they can also think about what they are thinking, doing, and experiencing. In social psychology, the study of self-awareness is traced to Shelley Duval and Robert Wicklund's (1972) landmark theory of self-awareness. Duval and Wicklund proposed that, at a given moment, people can focus attention on the self or on the external environment. Focusing on the self enables *self-evaluation.* When self-focused, people compare the self with *standards of correctness* that specify how the self ought to think, feel, and behave. The process of comparing the self with standards allows people to change their behavior and to experience pride and dissatisfaction with the self. Self-awareness is thus a major mechanism of self-control.

Research since the 1970s has strongly supported self-awareness theory (Duval and Silvia 2001). When people focus attention on the self, they compare the self with standards, try harder to meet standards, and show stronger emotional responses to meeting or failing to meet a standard. The tendency to change the self to match a standard depends on other variables, particularly perceptions of how hard it will be to attain the standard. Remarkably, many experiments have shown that when people are not self-focused, their actions are often unrelated to their personal standards—self-awareness is needed for people to reduce disparities between their actions and their ideals.

Self-awareness theory was enriched by new research methods. According to the theory, anything that makes people focus attention on the self will increase self-awareness. Researchers accomplish this by placing people in front of large mirrors, videotaping them, having people listen to recordings of their voices, or making people feel like they stick out. Momentary levels of self-awareness are measured by people's use of self-referential words and pronouns and by how quickly people recognize self-relevant information.

Self-awareness theory remains a fruitful and controversial theory. One new direction is the application of self-awareness theory to clinical disorders involving negative self-evaluation (e.g., depression) and excessive self-consciousness (e.g., social anxiety). One controversy, reviewed by Paul Silvia and Guido Gendolla (2001), is whether self-awareness enables accurate judgments of the self. Many researchers have proposed that self-awareness creates clearer perceptions of internal states, emotions, and traits. Other researchers, however, have noted that the self-concept is fluid, complex, and contextual—it is not a static object that can simply be apprehended and examined. Ironically, by making some aspects of the self especially salient, self-awareness may exaggerate and bias judgments of what the self is like.

SEE ALSO *Anxiety; Self-Consciousness, Private vs. Public; Self-Esteem; Self-Monitoring; Self-Perception Theory*

BIBLIOGRAPHY

Duval, Shelley, and Robert A. Wicklund. 1972. *A Theory of Objective Self Awareness.* New York: Academic Press.

Duval, Thomas Shelley, and Paul J. Silvia. 2001. *Self-Awareness and Causal Attribution: A Dual Systems Theory.* New York: Kluwer Academic Press.

Silvia, Paul J., and Guido H. E. Gendolla. 2001. On Introspection and Self-Perception: Does Self-Focused Attention Enable Accurate Self-Knowledge? *Review of General Psychology* 5: 241–269.

Paul J. Silvia

SELF-CLASSIFICATION

Self-classification occurs anytime an individual reports an identity, characteristic, or membership within a social group. Though the use of self-classification as a discrete form of measurement coincides with the twentieth-century popularization of social surveys in Britain and the United States (Gordon 1973), the origins of classification have roots in antiquity. Efforts to systematically distinguish plants from animals began with Aristotle, and following the influential work of the Swedish botanist Carolus Linnaeus (1707–1778), classification became the scientific standard for expressing organizational hierarchies in the natural world (Frängsmyr, Lindroth, Eriksson, and Broberg 1983). Taxonomic classification groups individual units by the number of properties they share, with broad, loosely related parent categories subdivided into more detailed, closely related subcategories. Societies are also organized hierarchically, and to the extent that population groups differ on outcomes of interest to social scientists, classification can be viewed as a prerequisite of all comparative research and studies of inequality in particular.

In the natural sciences units are classified by the investigator, and taxonomies are assumed to represent objective groupings based on universal laws. Social taxonomies are embedded within social relations, however, and cannot be viewed as objective or universal (Durkheim [1912] 1965). Subjects often classify themselves in social research, and many surveys, polls, and population censuses are composed entirely of self-reported data.

In many ways self-classification has revolutionized social research, particularly in areas of attitude and opinion polling. Self-reports of personal well-being, self-esteem, and presidential approval are common examples of types of subjective measures widely used in cross-sectional comparisons and trend analyses. Even objective information such as height and weight can be self-classified without incurring the costs of direct measurement.

Because self-reports are inherently subjective, however, they sometimes provide inaccurate or unreliable measures of objective characteristics. People may lack relevant knowledge about their personal histories; even seemingly straightforward measures, such as the place and timing of birth, are unknown in certain instances. In other cases, individuals may misrepresent themselves, particularly on measures that are perceived to be intrusive or potentially stigmatizing, as with measures of income, substance abuse, and even height or weight (Strauss 1999). Although advances in questionnaire design and interview techniques have improved the quality of self-reported data, there are limits to what these advances may achieve. For example, many individuals are unwilling to self-classify as perpetrators of discrimination on survey questionnaires, which has spurred the development of "deception designs," such as housing and job search audits, that can be used to circumvent respondents' reluctance to admit socially undesirable behavior (Yinger 1986).

Discrepancies between self-classification and direct measures are also a risk when the constructs underlying those measures reflect a combination of objective and subjective realities. Many axes of inequality fit this criterion. Though concepts such as race, class, and gender can be reduced to ostensibly objective terms (ancestry, income, and sex, respectively), these simplifications ignore the social embeddedness of identity, which is shaped by the dynamic interplay between social actors, institutional forces, and historical contingencies. Systems of racial hierarchy evolved quite differently in North and South America (Graham 1990), for example, so it is plausible for similar-looking individuals from each region to self-classify in different ways. Because identities reflect the social construction of race in each region, however, it is inappropriate to view one identity as more accurate than the other, much less to justify the use of "objective" criteria, such as ancestral descent, which may have little bearing on the social consequences of race in these regions.

SEE ALSO *Audits for Discrimination; Ethnicity; Gender; Identification, Racial; Identity; Identity, Social; Race; Racial Classification; Self-Identity; Social Categorization; Social Constructs; Subjectivity: Analysis*

BIBLIOGRAPHY

Durkheim, Émile. [1912] 1965. *The Elementary Forms of the Religious Life.* New York: Free Press.

Frängsmyr, Tore, Sten Lindroth, Gunnar Eriksson, and Gunnar Broberg. 1983. *Linnaeus: The Man and His Work.* Berkeley: University of California Press.

Gordon, Michael. 1973. The Social Survey Movement and Sociology in the United States. *Social Problems* 21 (Fall): 284–298.

Graham, Richard. 1990. *The Idea of Race in Latin America, 1870–1940.* Austin: University of Texas Press.

Mason, Patrick L. 2004. Annual Income, Hourly Wages, and Identity among Mexican-Americans and Other Latinos. *Industrial Relations* 43 (4): 817–834.

Strauss, Richard. 1999. Comparison of Measured and Self-Reported Weight and Height in a Cross-Sectional Sample of Young Adolescents. *International Journal of Obesity* 23: 904–908.

Yinger, John. 1986. Measuring Racial Discrimination with Fair Housing Audits: Caught in the Act. *American Economic Review* 76: 881–893.

Anthony Daniel Perez

SELF-CONCEPT

The self has a long history of study within the psychological tradition, dating back to early work by William James in his seminal book *The Principles of Psychology* (1890). Throughout the next century of study, self-concept was examined by numerous researchers who emphasized both internal characteristics and external influences on the self-concept. Though some researchers have looked at self-concept as a global construct, many agree that the self-concept is composed of multiple components. Much of the research has focused on the cognitive structure of the self-concept as well as the related evaluative component of self-esteem. In general, the self-concept is an individual's perceptions of the self arising from multiple components, including how one sees oneself in interaction with others as well as how one views oneself in isolation.

DEVELOPMENT

Susan Harter wrote extensively about self-concept development in her book *The Construction of Self: A Developmental Perspective* (1999). Her detailed account of the emergence of self-concept begins as the self-concept appears around the age of two, first manifesting as a recognition of the self as a distinct physical entity. The development of autobiographical memory is important in the emergence of self-concept in that before the age of two, children may have generic memories but do not yet have a memory of the self. Through discourse with parents in which past events involving the child are recounted, children begin to form autobiographical memories and an evolving autobiographical portrait of the self. Another important influence on the emerging self-concept of children is the attachment relationship with the caregiver. From the attachment relationship, children form internalized representations of others and how the self fits into the social world. This is important to the child's asserting his or her unique influences on the world and to viewing the self as a unique entity interacting with the external world.

Increasing cognitive and social demands cause the development of the child's self-concept to change from being based upon only a few components or poorly clarified to a more organized and clear formulation based on several clearly distinct domains. Different roles that are required of children as development progresses require the child to develop different sets of behaviors and personality characteristics according to the current role. Some of these roles and traits may clash, such as when a child sees him- or herself as warm and friendly with peers and moody and unresponsive with parents. As the child moves into adolescence, cognitive capabilities enable the child to integrate all of these roles and clashing components into a coherent sense of self.

SELF-WORTH AND SELF-ESTEEM

Another important component of Harter's account of the development of self-concept is the idea of self-worth. Self-worth is determined from the evaluation of the components of the self; Harter stresses that self-worth is formed primarily from areas that are important to the self. This echoes the ideas of William James and asserts that not only is the self formed of multiple components, but also that these components differ in their importance to the individual. Each component is evaluated separately, such that individuals may feel they are skilled in some domains and not as skilled in other areas. Harter contends that these areas of importance are developed through feelings of competence in different areas. In an individual with a positive sense of self, the areas in which he or she feels competent are more highly weighted than those areas in which he or she does not feel competent.

This close connection between self-concept and self-worth suggests that self-concept is closely related to its evaluative side, frequently termed *self-esteem*. Though often talked about as separate constructs, these two areas may be difficult to separate, as Harter points out that many of the components of the self are evaluative in nature. For example, when asked to define the self-concept, an individual might list adjectives such as "smart," "funny," or "good-looking." However, these words are in themselves evaluative. Thus the self-concept and self-esteem are two constructs that are discussed as though they are separate, but in fact they are closely related.

STRUCTURE

Another area subject of study closely related to the self-concept is the cognitive structure of the self. Social cognition researchers view the self-concept as an organized set of knowledge about the self, and as such, how the different components are organized becomes important. Herbert Marsh and Richard Shavelson developed an influential theory of the self as organized in a hierarchical structure (1985): A stable sense of self is at the apex of the hierarchy, which then branches into academic and nonacademic components, and each of these further differentiates into more specific self areas.

Patricia Linville made important contributions to the literature on the self-concept structure with her self-complexity theory (1985), which asserts that the knowledge about the self is organized into multiple cognitive structures known as "self-aspects." These self-aspects are organized in relation to each other, with related aspects being linked in a network structure. Different social contexts and cognitions activate different self-aspects, which in turn activate other linked aspects. The complexity of the self-concept is a result of both the *number* of self-aspects and the *interrelatedness* of those aspects. A complex self-concept is composed of a large number of independent aspects.

Linville further asserted that having a complex self-representation is positive for mental health. This is due to the network structure of the self. When a negative event occurs in an area related to one self-aspect, the individual is likely to experience negative affect in that area. A simple self structure may have two important consequences. First, if there are few self-aspects, the negatively affected area represents a large part of the self, and so a negative event leads to negative feelings about the self. Second, if the self-concept is composed of highly interrelated aspects, then this negative event is likely to trigger negative feelings in all other associated areas; Linville referred to this as *affective spillover*. In these two ways a simple self-concept is more affected by any one event, whereas a more complex self-concept has more stability. According to Linville, a complex self-concept leads to more stability in affect, which is associated with better mental health. Later studies have questioned these ideas and aimed to clarify the effects on self-complexity on mental health.

One example of this is Carolyn Showers's 1992 investigation of how positive and negative self-aspects may be separated or related. Showers found that how they are related matters to levels of self-esteem and depression. When positive self-aspects are important to overall self-worth, compartmentalization of positive and negative aspects results in higher self-esteem and reduced levels of depression. In contrast, when negative self-aspects are important, compartmentalization is associated with negative effects, and furthermore, when negative self-aspects are important, a more complex self is better for positive psychological well-being. Therefore, one modification to Linville's 1985 theory has been that the content of the structure matters to the buffering impact as well as to the structure. Other clarifications have also been made to more fully understand the impact of self structure.

Some theorists have argued that the content and structure of the self-concept are unrelated, whereas others, such as Showers, argue that they work in concert. Although there is a distinction between what can be defined as content and structure in the self-concept, several studies suggest that both of these areas are important.

FLEXIBILITY

Another topic in the self-concept literature is the debate about whether the self-concept is dynamic or stable. Some scholars argue that the self-concept is stable once formed; others maintain that it is a more malleable construct. Some social cognition researchers view the self-concept as both stable and changing: There are components to the self that are stable across situations, but there are also components that may change in their expression depending on the context. For example, when asked about his self-concept, a young man in school might mention intelligence as an important part of himself, but in a social setting he might stress social skill as more important. Context as well as self-presentation issues may come into play as important in terms of viewing the self as stable or malleable.

MEASUREMENT ISSUES

With such a broad field of study, there are many ways to measure self-concept. Explicit measures of self-concept are often used to assess different areas that an individual might find important to the self. Examples of commonly used explicit measures include the Piers-Harris "Children's Self-Concept Scale" (1969), Susan Harter's "Self-Perception Profile" (1985), and Marsh and colleagues' "Self-Description Questionnaire" (1984). Implicit measures of self-concept and self-esteem are also used; one example is the "Implicit Association Test." This measure examines response times between sets of stimuli and is based on the idea that items that are cognitively related should have a faster association than items that are unrelated (Greenwald, McGhee, and Schwartz 1998).

SEE ALSO *Child Development; Identity; James, William; Self-Esteem; Self-Schemata; Social Cognition; Social Cognitive Map*

BIBLIOGRAPHY

Greenwald, Anthony G., Debbie E. McGhee, and Jordan L. K. Schwartz. 1998. Measuring Individual Differences in Implicit Cognition: The Implicit Association Test. *Journal of Personality and Social Psychology* 74: 1464–1480.

Harter, Susan. 1985. *Self-Perception Profile for Children: Manual.* Denver, CO: University of Denver Press.

Harter, Susan. 1999. *The Construction of the Self: A Developmental Perspective.* New York: Guilford Press.

Linville, Patricia W. 1985. Self-Complexity and Affective Extremity: Don't Put All of Your Eggs in One Cognitive Basket. *Social Cognition* 3: 94–120.

Marsh, Herbert W., and Richard Shavelson. 1985. Self-Concept: Its Multifaceted, Hierarchical Structure. *Educational Psychologist* 20: 107–123.

Marsh, Herbert W., Jennifer Barnes, Len Cairns, and Marjorie Tidman. 1984. Self-Description Questionnaire: Age and Sex Effects in the Structure and Level of Self-Concept for Preadolescent Children. *Journal of Educational Psychology* 76: 940–956.

Piers, E. V. 1969. *Manual for the Piers-Harris Children's Self Concept Scale.* Nashville, TN: Counselor Recordings and Tests.

Wylie, Ruth C. 1974. *The Self-Concept.* Rev. ed., vol. 1. Lincoln: University of Nebraska Press.

Melanie B. Hoy

SELF-CONSCIOUSNESS, PRIVATE VS. PUBLIC

Many organisms exhibit at least a rudimentary form of self-awareness by which they experience themselves as distinct from their environment. However, humans are capable of more profound and consequential forms of self-awareness that make possible uniquely human capacities such as introspection and self-reflection. Although all normal-functioning people are sometimes self-aware, some people are consistently aware of themselves. The tendency to consistently direct attention toward the self is referred to as self-consciousness.

According to Arnold Buss, to whom the seminal research on self-consciousness is attributed, the tendency to consistently direct attention toward the self is evidenced in the highly self-conscious person in the following ways:

- An intense focus on behavior—past, present, and future
- A heightened sensitivity to privately experienced feelings
- Recognition of positive and negative characteristics in oneself
- A tendency to introspect
- Imagining oneself
- An awareness of how one appears to others
- Concerns about others' appraisals

A distinction typically is drawn between forms of self-consciousness corresponding to the two distinct vantage points from which people can direct attention toward themselves and the different aspects of the self experienced from those vantage points. Private self-consciousness is the tendency to focus on oneself from a personal vantage point and attend to aspects of the self that are not readily apparent to others, such as one's thoughts and feelings. Public self-consciousness is the tendency to focus on oneself from the perceived vantage point of real or imagined others and to attend to aspects of the self that are observable by others, such as facets of one's appearance and behavior.

The origins of the contemporary empirical literature on self-consciousness can be traced to the 1975 publication of the Self-Consciousness Scale by Allan Fenigstein, Michael F. Scheier, and Arnold H. Buss. Although the measure includes a set of items that reflect social anxiety, the primary use of the measure is for the item sets corresponding to the two major forms of self-consciousness. These items are used in virtually all empirical research on individual differences in the tendency to direct attention toward the self. Respondents indicate the extent of their agreement or disagreement with statements such as "I'm generally attentive to my inner feelings" (private) and "I'm usually aware of my appearance" (public). Composite scores on these item sets serve to index private and public

self-consciousness. These scores are modestly correlated, suggesting that the tendency to focus on oneself from one vantage point is not necessarily accompanied by a tendency to focus on oneself from the other vantage point.

Psychometric analyses of the Self-Consciousness Scale have routinely identified a schism in the set of private self-consciousness items. Not only do the items reliably cluster in two sets, but scores on these item sets are not strongly related to each other and are differentially related to other variables. Internal state awareness is a rudimentary, nonevaluative form of private self-consciousness, typified by the statement, "I reflect about myself a lot." Scores on internal state awareness are positively correlated with variables that indicate psychological health. Self-reflectiveness is an evaluative form of private self-consciousness, typified by the statement, "I'm constantly examining my motives." Scores on self-reflectiveness are positively correlated with a set of variables that, on the whole, indicate poor psychological health. In comprehensive models of self-awareness, internal state awareness is an instance of objective self-awareness, not unlike the rudimentary forms of self-awareness experienced by nonhuman species. Self-reflectiveness is an instance of symbolic self-awareness, the uniquely human form of self-awareness that makes self-evaluation possible and inevitable.

Research in which these forms of self-consciousness as measured by the Self-Consciousness Scale are studied in relation to other variables does not allow for an evaluation of the extent to which self-consciousness is a causal factor. That evaluation requires experimental research, which involves randomly assigning people to manipulated levels of self-consciousness. Indeed, it is now evident that laboratory manipulations of self-consciousness produce relations with other variables that mirror the relations evidenced when self-consciousness is measured using the Self-Consciousness Scale. Private self-consciousness has been manipulated in several ways. The most frequently used method involves exposing people to an image of their face in a small mirror. Other manipulations include having people listen to their own voice or their own heartbeat; instructing people to focus on themselves; and having people write a story in which they are the main character. Public self-consciousness has received less attention in experimental research but has been successfully manipulated by exposing people to an image of their body in a full-length mirror or having people watch themselves on video. Using these manipulations, people who have been induced to focus attention on themselves can be compared to people who have not been so induced on outcome variables of interest to evaluate the potential causal influence of self-consciousness on those variables.

Findings from research using the Self-Consciousness Scale and laboratory experiments in which self-consciousness is manipulated indicate that self-consciousness is implicated in a host of social attitudes, emotions, and behaviors. Private self-consciousness is associated with better access to self-knowledge, and a greater interest in new self-knowledge regardless of whether that knowledge is positive. As a result, the self-knowledge of people high in private self-consciousness plays a more prominent role in their behavior. For instance, compared to people low in private self-consciousness, their attitudes are more predictive of their behavior; they are less likely to conform when their opinions are challenged; and they are more resistant to inaccurate suggestions about their own sensations. Private self-consciousness also is associated with emotional experience. Because introspection often leads to self-criticism, private self-consciousness can give rise to negative emotion. In addition, attention directed toward private self-aspects appears to intensify current emotional experience—positive or negative.

Public self-consciousness is associated with phenomena that involve perceptions of how other people view the self. For instance, public self-consciousness is associated with a greater concern for appearance as evidenced by wearing more makeup and showing greater concern about balding. Compared to people low in public self-consciousness, people high in public self-consciousness are more likely to conform to group pressure; they are more accurate in their perceptions of how others perceive them; and they are more likely to experience aversive social emotions such as shyness and social anxiety.

Self-consciousness in its two forms—private and public—is a fundamental human trait relevant to a broad range of attitudes, emotions, and behaviors of interest to social scientists. Because humans experience forms of self-consciousness that no other organism experiences, the study of self-consciousness addresses the fundamental question of what it means to be human.

SEE ALSO *Attitudes; Conformity; Emotion; Psychometrics; Scales; Self-Awareness Theory; Self-Perception Theory; Self-Representation; Social Psychology; Trait Theory*

BIBLIOGRAPHY

Buss, Arnold. 2001. *Psychological Dimensions of the Self.* Thousand Oaks, CA: Sage Publications.

Fenigstein, Allan, Michael F. Scheier, and Arnold H. Buss. 1975. Public and Private Self-Consciousness: Assessment and Theory. *Journal of Consulting and Clinical Psychology* 43 (4): 522–527.

Sedikides, Constantine, and John J. Skowronski. 1997. The Symbolic Self in Evolutionary Context. *Personality and Social Psychology Review* 1 (1): 80–102.

Rick H. Hoyle

SELF-CONSCIOUSNESS SCALE

SEE *Self-Consciousness, Private vs. Public.*

SELF-CONTROL

Self-control has been defined as the capacity that individuals have to exert control over their own thoughts, emotions, impulses, and performance. A central component of this definition is that self-control involves overriding or inhibiting something that would otherwise occur. A wide variety of concepts related to self-control have been studied in the field of psychology. These include self-regulation, willpower, and delay of gratification.

Many scholars have used the terms *self-control* and *self-regulation* interchangeably. *Self-regulation* can be defined as the self-governing process by which individuals monitor, evaluate, and modify their behavior in regard to standards. In this process behavior is evaluated in terms of standards or reference values. After the evaluation phase, an operation phase ensues. During this phase, individuals' current behavior is compared to a desired or undesired end state. If a discrepancy is noticed between one's self and standard, the results are negative and imply that individuals should change their behavior in a way that brings them more in line with their standards. If no discrepancy is noticed, the results are positive and imply that individuals should maintain their present course of behavior. The process of exerting self-control is often thought to parallel that of self-regulation. Exerting self-control is probably best viewed as a particular case of self-regulation in which overriding or suppression of an undesired response occurs. Hence any event that requires self-control occurs in the larger framework of self-regulation. However, it is not the case that any event that involves self-regulation could be described as requiring self-control.

The predominant view of self-control has been as a personality characteristic. This trait is influenced by temperament, parental factors such as socialization, attachment, and warmth, and demographic factors such as neighborhood safety and family socioeconomic status. In adults personality characteristics related to self-control include impulsivity, sensation seeking, conscientiousness, and emotional stability. Impulsivity and sensation seeking are negatively correlated with self-control, whereas conscientiousness and emotional stability are positively correlated with self-control.

SELF-CONTROL AND BEHAVIOR

As a trait, self-control is connected with a wide variety of behaviors and problems. In their 2004 work the researchers June Tangney, Roy Baumeister, and Angie Boone showed convincingly that high levels of self-control are associated with better adjustment whereas low levels of self-control are associated with poorer adjustment and interpersonal problems. In their research high self-control was associated with lower levels of alcoholism, higher grade point averages, less eating disorder symptomatology, and less aggression. Other research has shown that poor self-control skills are related to problems with weight control and overeating, alcohol misuse and drug addiction, impulsive consumer purchasing and behavior, and crime and delinquency. In fact self-control is a central component of the general theory of crime proposed in 1990 by Michael Gottfredson and Travis Hirschi. In this theory self-control is related to crime because individuals with varying levels of self-control consider the consequences of their behavior to different extents. Individuals with high self-control consider the long-term consequences of their behavior, while individuals with low self-control do not.

A different line of research on self-control has focused on the differences between attending to short-term and long-term benefits of behavior. Delay of gratification is a particular type of impulse control in which individuals opt to wait for more preferred rewards in lieu of taking a less preferred reward immediately. In 1988 Walter Mischel showed that the ability to delay gratification is one that increases with age. Additionally his research on delay of gratification supports viewing self-control as a personality variable. In one 1990 study Mischel and his colleagues Yuichi Shoda and Phillip Peake showed that children who waited for longer periods of time to earn rewards became adolescents with better overall adjustment and had higher SAT scores. David Funder, Jeanne Block, and Jack Block provided evidence in the 1980s that the ability to delay gratification is related to a variety of positive outcomes. Children who were better at delaying gratification tended to be calmer, less irritable, less easily frustrated, and less aggressive. They were also better at concentrating and received higher grades then children who were lower in self-control.

Models of self-control vary in the extent to which they view self-control as a skill, as knowledge, or as strength. The largest body of support exists for viewing self-control through a strength model, where self-control is compared to a muscle. In this model individuals have limited regulatory resources or resources available to exert self-control. Individuals who exert self-control suffer a cost in that they may be less able to exert self-control on a subsequent task. In their 1998 work Mark Muraven, Diane Tice, and Roy Baumeister showed that when individuals exert self-control, their regulatory resources become depleted and individuals' performance on simultaneous activities requiring self-control is impaired. Furthermore exerting self-control on an activity impairs performance on consecutive tasks. This resource for self-control is used for tasks related to regulating affect, behavior, and cognition. Activities that require an individual to exert self-control in one domain can lead to deficits in performance in another domain. For example, individuals who are asked to regulate their emotions by refraining from feeling or expressing them while they watch a sad film clip persist for a shorter period of time at a physical task than individuals who watch the same sad film clip without regulating their emotions. Other tasks that deplete individuals' resources to exert self-control include making personally relevant and important choices, ostracizing liked others, refraining from temptations, and overriding habits. Individuals can practice exerting self-control and strengthen this "muscle" so that at later times engaging in the practiced activity does not lead to as much resource depletion.

Although the traditional view of self-control is a response to an unwanted event, individuals may exert self-control by avoiding situations that may contain temptations or distractions. This type of self-control is referred to as counteractive self-control. In 1997 Peter Gollwitzer and Veronika Brandstatter provided evidence that implementation intentions can increase the success of goal pursuit, even in the face of obstacles or temptations. An implementation can best be construed in terms of a "when, then" statement. An example might be "when my alarm clock goes off in the morning, then I will get out of bed to exercise." These intentions connect the desired behavior with the context in which that behavior is expected to occur.

The economist Thomas Schelling defined a similar construct of precommitment. Individuals may exert self-control in this way by planning activities that will preclude, or limit, their potential behaviors. A classic example of this would be a general who commands the army to burn the bridges after it crosses them, thereby limiting the army's likelihood of retreat. The relationship between intentions, planning, and behavior has sparked other research in self-control. Specifically Judy Fitch and Elizabeth Ravlin studied willpower as it relates to the role of the self in motivation and goal pursuit. Their 2005 work approaches willpower as a subfactor of the personality trait of conscientiousness. Willpower is defined as persistency and determination, or the ability to exert extra effort to attain a desired goal. In their research Fitch and Ravlin found that willpower moderated the relationship between intention and behavior. In other words, individuals who have stronger willpower are more likely to engage in behaviors that reflect their intentions.

Temptations may not always act as obstacles to successful self-control. In 2003 Ayelet Fishbach, Ronald Friedman, and Arie Kruglanski found that the presence of temptations is automatically associated with relevant goal pursuit. Individuals who were primed with temptations that might distract them from their goal were more likely to engage in choices and activities related to that goal. When individuals perceived the goal they were pursuing to be important, they were even more likely to associate temptations with goal pursuit. It should be noted that the priming manipulation in this study occurred at a nonconscious level. That is, temptations were not actually present when the goal pursuit of individuals was being assessed. In regard to self-control, this research implies that thinking about temptations ahead of time may increase an individual's ability to resist them when they are physically present.

In summary, understanding self-control requires viewing it as a function of both the person and the environment. Like many psychological phenomena, both individual and situational factors influence the ways that self-control occurs. Researchers know that individuals vary across personality factors and in their ability to exert self-control and that these differences are attached to meaningful outcomes. They also know that contextual factors such as the presence of temptations lead to fluctuations in how individuals control their thoughts, emotions, and behaviors. Indeed individuals can even influence their own later ability to exert self-control through detailed planning.

BIBLIOGRAPHY

Fishbach, Ayelet, Ronald S. Friedman, and Arie W. Kruglanski. 2003. Leading Us Not into Temptation: Momentary Allurements Elicit Overriding Goal Activation. *Journal of Personality and Social Psychology* 84: 296–309.

Fitch, J. L., and E. C. Ravlin. 2005. Willpower and Perceived Behavioral Control: Influences on the Intention-Behavior Relationship and Postbehavior Attributions. *Social Behavior and Personality* 33: 105–124.

Funder, David C., Jeanne H. Block, and Jack Block. 1983. Delay of Gratification: Some Longitudinal Personality Correlates. *Journal of Personality and Social Psychology* 44: 1198-1213.

Gollwitzer, Peter M., and Veronika Brandstatter. 1997. Implementation Intentions and Effective Goal Pursuit. *Journal of Personality and Social Psychology* 84: 296–309.

Gottfredson, Michael R., and Travis Hirschi. 1990. *A General Theory of Crime.* Stanford, CA: Stanford University Press.

Mischel, Walter, Yuichi Shoda, and Phillip K. Peake. 1988. The Nature of Adolescent Competencies Predicted by Preschool Delay of Gratification. *Journal of Personality and Social Psychology* 54: 687–696.

Muraven, Mark, Roy F. Baumeister, and Diane M. Tice. 1998. Ego-Depletion: Is the Active Self a Limited Resource? *Journal of Personality and Social Psychology* 74: 1252–1265.

Schelling, T. C. 1985. *Choice and Consequence: Perspectives of an Errant Economist.* Cambridge, MA: Harvard University Press.

Tangney, June P., Roy F. Baumeister, and Angie K. Boone. 2004. High Self-Control Predicts Good Adjustment, Less Pathology, Better Grades, and Interpersonal Success. *Journal of Personality* 72: 271–322.

Michelle Sherrill

SELF-DEFEATING BEHAVIOR

A self-defeating behavior is any behavior leading to a lower reward/cost ratio than is available through an alternative behavior or behaviors. Self-defeating behaviors include choosing to suffer, self-handicapping, failure to achieve potential, fear of success, learned helplessness, and procrastination. Such behaviors are learned in a variety of ways but usually are initially adaptive in preventing greater suffering or in obtaining rewards in the situations in which they are originally learned. For example, parents may be less punitive if children are self-critical after doing something the parents do not like than if children do not derogate and punish themselves. Self-defeating behaviors often occur as a consequence of situations that are uncontrollable. For example, if children are punished even when they believe they have behaved well, or if they are rewarded even when they have behaved poorly, they may gain the sense that their behavior does not matter. Then "learned helplessness" is said to occur because the child does not feel as if he or she is in control of what is happening.

Self-handicapping can occur when people receive positive information that they feel may be unwarranted. In order to protect a possible positive view of themselves, people may engage in some sort of excuse making in advance in order to protect a positive, but precarious, self-view or self-esteem. Self-handicapping involves engaging in a behavior known to hurt performance, such as getting too little sleep, using a harmful substance, not studying, or not working hard. A person may choose a task so easy that success is meaningless or so difficult that success is unlikely. Success and failure in such situations do not provide information about one's comparative ability. Persistence can become counterproductive when it prevents people from engaging in more valuable experiences or when it leads people to exhaust their resources in futile endeavors.

Roy Baumeister and Steven Scher (1988) identified three potential types of self-defeating behaviors: (1) primary self-destructiveness; (2) tradeoffs; and (3) counterproductive strategies. They found no evidence for primary or deliberate self-destructiveness among normal individuals. Tradeoffs occur when people act to gain short-term benefits despite long-term costs—behaviors especially likely to occur when people are emotionally aroused or highly self-aware. For example, shy people may avoid social situations out of a fear of making a bad impression. Their avoidance of people may lead to greater social exclusion in the future, leading them to be even less confident. They trade the possibility of intimacy to avoid short-term rejection. Or, the cost of medical treatment may lead people to fail to continue it when they do not or no longer perceive symptom relief. Failure to comply may exacerbate their condition in the long run. Counterproductive strategies involve misjudging one's capabilities or the realities of the situation. An example is "choking under pressure." In this scenario, one may carefully monitor performance in order to do one's best, but the monitoring itself may lead to more anxiety and a poorer performance.

Self-defeating behaviors often simply reflect expectancy-confirmation processes. If we think that we are not good at a particular task, we do not try our best and then perform more poorly than if we had expected that we could excel. People often internalize the expectations held for their gender, race, or social class or by significant others and then engage in self-fulfilling prophecies. If such expectations are negative, then they are self-defeating. A frequent cause of self-defeating behaviors is a desire to maximize self-esteem. There are no consistent effects for high self-reported self-esteem, however. Overconfidence and lack of confidence can both lead to problems.

Sometimes people appear to "choose to suffer" in an effort to (magically) improve their outcomes in other situations. Such behavior may stem from an unrealistic extension of the work ethic. Research has shown that people expecting an unpleasant event are more likely to choose to engage in another unpleasant activity during the waiting period if they change their beliefs about themselves, such as thinking that they are brave or that they deserve to suffer. If they change their beliefs about the situation, such as thinking it will not be so bad after all, they are less likely to engage in an unpleasant activity during the waiting period.

CLINICAL DISORDERS AND TREATMENT

All clinical disorders could be considered as forms of self-defeating behaviors. A "self-defeating personality disorder" was considered briefly by the American Psychiatric Association, drawn largely from characteristics that had been noted by clinicians since Sigmund Freud (1856–1939) as masochistic. The criteria for the proposed self-defeating personality disorder, however, overlapped too much with those for dysthymic disorder (depression) and other personality disorders, such as dependent personality. Furthermore, feminists were concerned that women who

were abused might get labeled as having a personality disorder that brought on abuse, thus leading victims of abuse to be blamed.

All forms of psychotherapy are designed to treat some form of what might be called self-defeating behavior. When people are frightened of situations, behavioral treatments are often the most effective. When people are not clear as to what the problem entails, a treatment involving talking and ascertaining feelings that are necessarily conscious may be appropriate. For example, psychoanalysis has been oriented especially toward understanding if fears of hurting parents or other loved ones interfere with achieving personal goals, such as leaving loved ones all alone, being more successful than they are, or not fulfilling loved ones' desires to impress other people. Lack of motivation, anxiety, mood disorders, and unrealistic thinking are also treated with medication in combination with psychotherapy.

SEE ALSO *Learned Helplessness; Psychotherapy; Psychotropic Drugs; Punishment; Shyness*

BIBLIOGRAPHY

Baumeister, Roy, and Steven. J. Scher. 1988. Self-Defeating Behavior Patterns Among Normal Individuals: Review and Analysis of Common Self-Destructive Tendencies. *Psychological Bulletin* 104 (1): 3–22.

Curtis, Rebecca Coleman. 1989. *Self-Defeating Behaviors: Experimental Research, Clinical Impressions, and Practical Implications.* New York: Plenum.

Rebecca C. Curtis

SELF-DETERMINATION

Self-determination, in the most general sense, refers to the capacity to control one's own destiny, free of interference by others. Historically, the right to self-determination has meant the right of a subjugated nation or colonized population to establish a sovereign, independent state—to secede from a multinational state or to dissolve colonial ties of dependency to an imperial "mother country." It has also been invoked in support of demands for local autonomy or self-government at the sub-state level as a means to preserve the culture or safeguard the security of national or aboriginal minorities. Since the 1960s, however, many social movement activists (particularly proponents of a postmodernist "politics of identity") have sought to invest the principle with a much looser meaning.

NATIONAL SELF-DETERMINATION

The concept of national self-determination is a modern one, despite the fact that struggles by subjugated peoples against occupation, colonialism, and enslavement have occurred for many thousands of years. Its advent was predicated on the prior emergence of such defining features of capitalist modernity as the discourse on rights, the ideology of nationalism, and the European nation-state system.

A nation-state is a form of state power in which territorial sovereignty is ostensibly exercised on behalf of a specific nation—a relatively homogeneous aggregation of people who typically share a common language, economic life, and cultural tradition as an "imagined community" (to use Benedict Anderson's expression). The nation-building projects of modern European states were undertaken to strengthen their positions relative to major rivals and often involved attempts to unify and homogenize the population within the borders of the nation-state, usually through coerced assimilation or "ethnic cleansing" (including forced population transfers and genocide in some circumstances). For several of the major European powers, it also involved the conquest and colonial subjugation of other, far-flung territories and peoples with the aim of consolidating empires whose purpose was to enrich and empower the imperial nation-state or "mother country." Political domination, military subjugation, and economic exploitation of colonies stimulated the emergence of anti-imperialist movements and nationalist projects within colonized populations otherwise divided along tribal, religious, and linguistic lines.

Independence struggles by the colonial possessions of the major imperial powers began long before the term *self-determination* came into use. The first such struggle was waged against Britain by several of its "settler colonies" in North America, and its success resulted in the founding of the United States of America in 1776. Encouraged by revolutionary events in France, the black population of Haiti rose up against French rule in the 1790s, eventually establishing an independent republic in 1804. By the late nineteenth century, Spain had lost most of its colonial possessions in the Americas. The success of these New World independence struggles heightened the nationalist aspirations of subjugated nationalities in the multinational states—the Austro-Hungarian, Ottoman, and Russian empires—that dominated much of Eurasia and the Middle East prior to World War I.

Within the imperial nations themselves, few supported the right to self-determination of national minorities at home or colonized peoples abroad. The major exception before 1914 was the international socialist movement. Thus, Karl Marx argued that English wage workers could never achieve their emancipation as a class so long as they remained complicit in the national oppression of the Irish. At its 1896 congress, the Marxist Second International adopted a resolution affirming the right of all nations to self-determination.

In Russia, Vladimir Lenin saw the aspirations of the oppressed nationalities of what he called the czarist "prison house of peoples" as integral to the broader struggle for democracy, insisting that the only way to forge working-class unity across national lines was to combat "great Russian chauvinism" and recognize the right of Ukrainians, Georgians, and other nationalities to establish their own independent states. However, Lenin distinguished between recognizing the *right* to self-determination and actually advocating independence. The right to self-determination, he wrote, is similar to the right to divorce; one can affirm the right without advising the action. After the victory of the Bolshevik Revolution in 1917, Lenin established the right of nations to self-determination as a fundamental programmatic plank of the Third (Communist) International, advocating national liberation struggles in the colonial world and waging an unsuccessful, deathbed struggle against the Russian chauvinist policies of Joseph Stalin and his acolytes in 1923. The subsequent consolidation of bureaucratic rule under Stalin transformed the Soviet Union into a Russian-dominated multinational state in which the right of the constituent, nationally based republics to secede was extinguished.

At the end of World War I, the principle of national self-determination found a new ostensible champion in the American president Woodrow Wilson, acquiring currency, for the first time, in liberal political discourse. " 'Self determination' is not a mere phrase," Wilson declared in 1918, "it is an imperative principle of action which statesmen will henceforth ignore at their peril" (Moynihan 1994, pp.78-79). But Wilson soon qualified his support for the idea, recognizing the dangers that the principle could pose to European stability. Subsequently, U.S. advocacy of the right of national self-determination proved inconsistent. After World War II, the United Nations, under American leadership, upheld a principle of international law that affirmed the right of colonies to independence from overseas empires but that recognized no right of secession for national minorities within established states.

In the post–World War II era, formal political independence was achieved by the great majority of former colonies in Africa, Asia, and the Western Hemisphere, opening the way, in most cases, to their neocolonial economic and political subjugation by the great powers. However, the demand for self-determination continued to be vigorously asserted by Northern Irish Republicans and Scots in the United Kingdom, Québécois in Canada, Basques in Spain, Tamils in Sri Lanka, and by many would-be nationalist movements operating within the hundreds and perhaps thousands of "imagined communities" that had defined themselves as nations. Under the watchword of self-determination, the 1990s saw the rapid breakup of the Soviet Union and the Yugoslav federation and the emergence of a plethora of new nation-states in Europe and Asia.

The dispossessed status of the Palestinian people, resulting from the creation of the state of Israel in 1948 and the consolidation of a Hebrew-speaking nation on territory claimed by both Jews and Palestinians as a home-land, remains an intractable national problem at the beginning of the twenty-first century. Here the question arises: Under what conditions can two "interpenetrated peoples" reconcile their mutually conflicting claims to self-determination?

SELF-DETERMINATION AND THE POLITICS OF IDENTITY

The radical ferment of the 1960s inspired a much looser definition of the concept of self-determination, such that it was often used to describe the aspirations of any group confronting putatively oppressive treatment. The original impetus to this redefinition was provided by the 1960s Black Power movement in the United States. Reacting against the liberal, integrationist perspective of the main-stream Civil Rights movement, many African American activists (notably Malcolm X, Stokely Carmichael, and the Black Panthers) embraced black nationalism. Having defined African Americans as an "oppressed nation" or as an "internal colony" (however problematically), these activists proclaimed the right of the black population to various forms of "self-determination"—sometimes through proposals for "separation" from "White America" but more commonly through demands for "black control of the black community." It is notable that few of these schemes were implemented—their most enduring legacy probably being black studies programs in higher education.

The stage was thus set for the emergence of a decid-edly amorphous notion of self-determination, one with which other marginalized or oppressed sectors could easily identify. The concept was also extended to notions of "empowering" individual victims of abuse or poverty through community organizing. Self-determination merged with the broader notion of "liberation" and was invoked by activists who championed not only the rights but also the unique identities of racial and ethnic minori-ties, women, gays, and the disabled. Indeed, for many advocates of a postmodern "politics of identity," self-deter-mination became virtually synonymous with unfettered expression of sectoral identity based not only on national-ity but on gender, race, or sexual orientation as well.

SEE ALSO *Anticolonial Movements; Autonomy; Black Power; Colonialism; Colony, Internal; Communalism; Dependency Theory; Indigenous Rights; Lenin, Vladimir Ilitch; Liberation; Marx, Karl; Minorities;* *Nationalism and Nationality; Palestinians; Politics, Identity; Secession; Separatism; United Nations*

BIBLIOGRAPHY

Anderson, Benedict. 2006. *Imagined Communities: Reflections on the Origin and Spread of Nationalism.* Rev. ed. London and New York: Verso.

Hobsbawm, Eric J. 1992. *Nations and Nationalism since 1780.* 2nd ed. Cambridge, U.K. and New York: Cambridge University Press.

Lenin, V. I. [1914] 1977. *The Right of Nations to Self-Determination: Selected Writings.* Westport, CT: Greenwood Press.

Löwy, Michael. 1998. *Fatherland or Mother Earth?: Essays on the National Question.* London and Sterling, VA: Pluto Press.

Moynihan, D. P. 1994. *Pandaemonium: Ethnicity in International Politics.* Oxford: Oxford University Press.

Murray Smith

SELF-DETERMINATION THEORY

Self-determination theory (SDT) is a macro-theory of human motivation, personality development, and well-being. The theory focuses especially on volitional or self-determined behavior and the conditions that promote it, as well as a set of basic and universal psychological needs, namely those for autonomy, competence, and relatedness, the fulfillment of which is considered essential to vital, healthy human functioning.

SDT begins with the assumption that people are active organisms, with inherent tendencies toward psycho-logical growth and development. This active nature is manifest in the phenomenon of *intrinsic motivation*, the innate tendency to seek out novelty, challenges, and oppor-tunities to learn. It is also evident in the phenomenon of *internalization*, or the tendency of persons to adopt, and attempt to integrate, ambient social mores and values.

Although the growth tendencies underlying intrinsic motivation and internalization are "natural," this does not mean that they operate automatically. Instead, these propensities require nutriments from the social environ-ment. These are specified using the concept of *basic psy-chological needs*, defined as those supports that are essential and necessary for psychological health. Within SDT there are but three basic psychological needs: autonomy, relat-edness, and competence. When these needs are supported and satisfied within a social context, people experience more vitality and self-motivation, as well as enhanced well-being. Conversely, the neglect or thwarting of basic needs is implicated in most forms of psychopathology and maladjustment (Ryan, Deci, Grolnick, and LaGuardia 2006).

SDT has evolved as a set of four mini-theories. Each mini-theory was developed to explain a set of motivationally based phenomena that emerged from laboratory and field research.

Cognitive evaluation theory (CET) addresses the effects of social contexts on intrinsic motivation. It stresses the importance of autonomy and competence, and it specifically addresses how factors such as rewards, deadlines, feedback, and pressure affect feelings of autonomy and competence and thus enhance or undermine intrinsic motivation.

Organismic integration theory (OIT) addresses the process of internalization of extrinsic motivation. Here the focus is on the continuum of internalization, extending from external regulation to introjection, identification, and integration. These forms of regulation, which can be simultaneously operative, differ in their relative autonomy, and the more autonomous the overall motivation, the greater the person's persistence, performance, and well-being. OIT further suggests that internalization and integration is facilitated by contextual supports for autonomy, competence, and relatedness.

Causality orientations theory (COT) describes individual differences in how people orient to different aspects of the environment in regulating behavior. When *autonomy-oriented*, people orient to what interests them and act with congruence; when *control-oriented*, people primarily regulate behavior by orienting to social controls and reward contingencies; and when *impersonally oriented*, people focus on their lack of personal control or competence.

Finally, *basic psychological needs theory* (BPNT) elaborates the concept of basic needs. BPNT posits that each need exerts independent effects on wellness and, moreover, that the impact of any behavior or event on well-being is largely a function of its relations with need satisfaction. Based on BPNT, for example, research has shown that materialism and other extrinsic goals such as fame or image do not enhance well-being, even when one is successful at attaining them. By contrast, goals such as personal growth or giving to one's community are conducive to need satisfaction, and thus facilitate health and wellness.

Together these four mini-theories constitute SDT. Given its scope, SDT has also spawned active research in numerous areas. One controversial issue has been the impact of rewards, which CET argues can powerfully control behavior, but often at the cost of intrinsic motivation. Another controversy is the cross-cultural generalizability of SDT. SDT suggests that whether collectivist or individualist, Eastern or Western, people function most effec-

tively and experience greater mental health when their behavior is autonomously regulated. Still another issue has been the characterization of well-being. Richard Ryan and Edward Deci (2001) maintained that wellness is not well captured by hedonic measures of "happiness." Instead, SDT employs the concept of *eudaimonia*, or wellness defined as the vital, full functioning, as a complementary approach. Finally, because autonomy is facilitated by reflective awareness, SDT stresses the role of *mindfulness* (Brown and Ryan 2003) in self-regulation and wellness.

The practical implications of SDT in healthcare, education, work, parenting, psychotherapy, religion, and sport contexts are manifold, and the theory has catalyzed considerable applied research and numerous interventions (see Ryan, Deci, Grolnick, and LaGuardia 2006; Deci and Ryan 2000).

SEE ALSO *Psychology, Agency in*

BIBLIOGRAPHY

Brown, Kirk W., and Richard M. Ryan. 2003. The Benefits of Being Present: Mindfulness and Its Role in Psychological Well-Being. *Journal of Personality and Social Psychology* 84: 822–848.

Deci, Edward L., and Richard M. Ryan. 2000. The "What" and "Why" of Goal Pursuits: Human Needs and the Self-Determination of Behavior. *Psychological Inquiry* 11: 227–268.

Ryan, Richard M., and Edward L. Deci. 2001. To Be Happy or To Be Self-Fulfilled: A Review of Research on Hedonic and Eudaimonic Well-Being. In *Annual Review of Psychology*, vol. 52, ed. Susan T. Fiske, 141–166. Palo Alto, CA: Annual Reviews.

Ryan, Richard M., Edward L. Deci, Wendy S. Grolnick, and Jennifer G. LaGuardia. 2006. The Significance of Autonomy and Autonomy Support in Psychological Development and Psychopathology. In *Theory and Methods*. Vol. 1 of *Developmental Psychopathology*, 2nd ed., eds. Dante Cicchetti and Donald J. Cohen, 795–849. New York: John Wiley and Sons.

Richard M. Ryan
Edward L. Deci

SELF-DISCLOSURE

Revealing private personal information to other people is a fundamental characteristic of interpersonal communication. A great deal of research in the social sciences has examined the factors that affect such self-disclosure. Sidney Jourard's 1964 book *The Transparent Self* energized self-disclosure research, particularly in the fields of social psychology, clinical and counseling psychology, and communications. Jourard defined self-disclosure as the extent to which people made themselves "transparent" (or clear) about their inner thoughts and feelings in their self-related communications with others. Jourard's popular Self-Disclosure Questionnaire contains a broad range of topics including a person's attitudes and values, tastes and interests, personality, body, and sexuality. On this and similar measures, respondents typically indicate how much they would tell a target person about each topic.

Research suggests that self-disclosure is a fundamental way that relationship bonds are established, developed, and maintained. For example, self-disclosure helps relationship partners to clarify their own actions and intentions and to understand those of their partners. Self-disclosure also helps to increase feelings of intimacy, acceptance, trust, and self-worth within a relationship. For instance, research shows that more intimate self-disclosures are associated with greater liking, and that having disclosed to others increases people's liking of those persons.

Much research has examined the "disclosure reciprocity" effect, or the tendency for interaction partners to disclose intimate information in a reciprocal fashion. Social scientists have suggested that interaction partners may feel normative pressure or an obligation to reciprocate the intimacy level of information that is shared in the relationship. Failing to attend to the normative aspects of disclosure reciprocity can lead to relationship problems. For example, telling another person too much about oneself too early in a relationship or failing to reciprocate another person's self-disclosures may inhibit the development of that relationship.

Researchers have consistently found that females tend to show more self-disclosure than males. Although a relatively small effect, this gender difference can be moderated by target, measure, or topic. For example, women disclose much more to those with whom they have a relationship (e.g., a friend or parent) than do men. Developmental researchers have found that as adolescents enter puberty, they disclose increasingly more to peers than to parents. Research also suggests that cultures with a greater emphasis on nuclear and extended families (e.g., Hispanic populations) are more self-disclosing than cultures with less closely knit social or family structures (e.g., non-Hispanic white Americans). Members of Eastern cultures (such as China and Japan) tend to report less frequent self-disclosures than members of Western cultures (such as the United States).

In addition to positive consequences for relationships, disclosing emotional self-related experiences has positive effects on physical health. However, sometimes disclosing a personal secret can lead to negative relationship consequences. For example, self-disclosures can make a person vulnerable to the rejection, indifference, alienation, or exploitation of others. In more applied settings, there is much discussion and debate about whether and to what extent therapists should self-disclose to their clients. The nature of self-disclosure in online relationships has also seen increased attention from researchers.

BIBLIOGRAPHY

Derlega, Valerian J., Sandra Metts, Sandra Petronio, and Stephen T. Margulis. 1993. *Self-Disclosure*. Newbury Park, CA: Sage Publications.

Jourard, Sidney M. 1971. *The Transparent Self*. Rev. ed. New York: Van Nostrand Reinhold.

Thomas M. Brinthaupt

SELF-EFFICACY

Among all the thoughts that affect human functioning, and standing at the core of psychologist Albert Bandura's social cognitive theory, are *self-efficacy* beliefs, the judgments that individuals make about their capability to accomplish tasks and succeed in activities. Self-efficacy beliefs touch virtually every aspect of people's lives—whether they think productively or self-debilitatingly; how well they motivate themselves and persevere in the face of adversities; their vulnerability to stress and depression; and the life choices they make. People with a strong sense of efficacy approach difficult tasks as challenges to be mastered rather than as threats to be avoided. They have greater intrinsic interest and deep engrossment in activities, and they set themselves challenging goals and maintain strong commitment to them. High self-efficacy also helps create feelings of serenity in approaching difficult tasks and activities. As a consequence, self-efficacy beliefs powerfully influence the level of accomplishment that one ultimately achieves.

Self-efficacy should not be confused with self-esteem, which is a broad evaluation of one's self, complete with the judgments of self-worth that accompany such evaluations. When individuals tap into these two self-beliefs, they ask themselves quite different types of questions. Self-efficacy beliefs revolve around questions of *can* (Can I drive a car? Can I solve this problem?), whereas self-esteem beliefs reflect questions of *feel* (Do I like myself? How do I feel about myself as a father?). Moreover, one's beliefs about what one can do may bear little relation to how one feels about oneself. Many bright students are able to engage their academic tasks with strong self-efficacy even while their academic skills are a source of low self-esteem, having been labeled by their classmates as nerds or eggheads.

Individuals form their self-efficacy beliefs by interpreting information primarily from four sources, the most influential of which is their past mastery experience. Successes typically raise self-efficacy; failures lower it. People also form their self-efficacy beliefs through the vicarious experience of observing the actions of models. Observing models contributes to the belief in one's own capabilities: "If they can do it, so can I." Individuals also create and develop their efficacy beliefs as a result of the social persuasions they receive from significant others. Finally, somatic and emotional states such as anxiety, stress, arousal, and mood provide information about efficacy beliefs. When people experience negative thoughts and fears about their capabilities, those affective reactions can lower self-efficacy perceptions and trigger additional stress and agitation that help ensure the inadequate performance they fear.

Because individuals operate collectively as well as individually, self-efficacy is both a personal and a social construct. Collective systems develop a sense of collective efficacy—a group's shared belief in its capability to attain goals and accomplish desired tasks. For example, schools develop collective beliefs about the capability of their students to learn, of their teachers to teach and otherwise enhance the lives of their students, and of their administrators and policymakers to create environments conducive to these tasks. Organizations with a strong sense of collective efficacy exercise empowering and vitalizing influences on their constituents.

SEE ALSO *Self-Discrepancy Theory; Self-Esteem; Self-Monitoring*

BIBLIOGRAPHY

Bandura, Albert. 1977. Self-efficacy: Toward a Unifying Theory of Behavioral Change. *Psychological Review* 84 (2): 191–215.

Bandura, Albert. 1982. Self-efficacy Mechanism in Human Agency. *American Psychologist* 37 (2): 122–147.

Bandura, Albert. 1997. *Self-efficacy: The Exercise of Control.* New York: Freeman.

Pajares, Frank, and Tim Urdan, eds. 2006. *Self-efficacy Beliefs and Adolescence.* Greenwich, CT: Information Age.

Frank Pajares

SELF-EMPLOYMENT

An individual who is self-employed works for himself or herself rather than as an employee of another individual or organization, obtaining an income through ownership of a business or professional practice in which he or she contributes much of the labor needed to produce or distribute a good or service. According to the Organization for Economic Cooperation and Development, the self-employed include employers, own-account workers, members of producers' cooperatives, and unpaid family members. However, the designation "self-employed person" does not usually apply to those who are in a position to hire a large workforce (that is, to upper-management personnel who have a significant stake in the assets of the firm in which they are nominally self-employed). Such individuals are more appropriately referred to as "capitalists," who derive their income primarily from ownership and investment rather than from the performance of labor. Since 1967 the Current Population Survey conducted by the U.S. federal government has asked self-described self-employed individuals whether the businesses they operate are incorporated. Those who answer affirmatively are deemed to be salaried employees; those who answer in the negative are defined as self-employed.

A self-employed person operating a small-scale, unincorporated business such as a family farm, a retail outlet, a service-contracting firm, or a professional practice may rely on the labor of assistants, whether waged or unwaged, in producing or providing a good or service, but most of the value added is contributed by the self-employed person. The self-employed include many farmers and professionals (e.g., medical doctors, dentists, lawyers, architects) as well as "freelance" workers such as writers, consultants, musicians, and artists who sell the products of their labor (rather than their ability to work) on the market, or who work on an "individual assignment" basis.

The developed capitalist world has seen a secular decline in the number of self-employed since the end of World War II (1939–1945). In 2005 the self-employed constituted 7.5, 12.4, and 14.7 percent of the labor force in the United States, Germany, and Japan, respectively. In the United States, as in most other industrialized countries, the downward trend in the self-employment rate is overwhelmingly attributable to the decline of small-scale agriculture and the movement of much of the self-employed farm population to waged and salaried employment, usually in nonagricultural sectors. However, the trend also reflects a more general decline of small and medium-sized businesses and the concomitant concentration of capital in large corporations. Changing tax laws have encouraged many small business proprietors to incorporate, with the consequence that they have been redefined as salaried employees. New corporate practices, such as franchising, have also had an impact on the measurement of self-employment.

Corporate downsizing, cutbacks in social assistance to the economically indigent, and efforts to reduce the size of the public sector since the profitability crises of the 1970s have contributed to a slowing or even a partial reversal of the long-term trend toward a decline in self-employment. Although sometimes presented as a revival of "entrepreneurial spirit," an increase in small-business activity may actually reflect the disappearance of "good" corporate or public-sector jobs for highly skilled, formerly salaried employees or for semiskilled or unskilled wage earners. During periods of high unemployment and underemployment, a spike in self-employment is likely to occur. In the 1990s, for example, Canada led the industrial nations in a "shift to self-employment" (with self-employment accounting for 18% of all employment by 1998) over a period in which unemployment and under-employment reached near-record levels (Lowe 2000).

Three additional empirical facts about self-employment deserve to be highlighted. First, self-employment is highest among those who are the most and the least educated, with the well educated typically receiving above-average earnings and the poorly educated below-average earnings, relative to employed workers. Second, the gender gap in earnings is greater between self-employed men and women than it is between their employed counterparts. And finally, the self-employed tend to put in longer hours for their earnings than do the employed, raising quality of life concerns that are magnified by their need to independently finance—or go without—the "benefits" (e.g., pensions, health care insurance, etc.) that are received by many employed workers.

At the ideological level, the persistence of self-employment (and small business in general) in the developed capitalist countries contributes significantly to obscuring the central dynamic of modern capitalism: the division, interdependence, and conflict between capital and wage labor. The self-employed, in Marxist terms, constitute a "petty bourgeoisie" within a global economy whose productive assets are decisively concentrated in the hands of several hundred huge transnational corporations that employ a tiny fraction of the world's workforce. As such, self-employed persons are compelled to "exploit themselves" or face economic ruin. At the same time, their atomized existence, precarious competitive position, and sometime dependence on wage labor predispose them to embrace the ideological nostrums of "free enterprise" and "self-responsibility" to an extreme degree, to view the labor movement with suspicion or outright hostility, and to oppose more generous welfare-state policies.

In 2005 the self-employed constituted 34.9, 35.7, and 45.8 percent of the labor force in Brazil, Mexico, and Turkey, respectively. In the countries of the global South, the destruction of traditional subsistence agriculture and "independent commodity production" by export-led, neoliberal development has produced a new class of impoverished urban "entrepreneurs" struggling to survive with the most meager of economic assets. This phenomenon, which has taken on massive proportions in the bar-rios and shantytowns surrounding major Latin American cities, is a striking reminder that "self-employment" is very often a manifestation of chronic unemployment and underemployment, of which about one-third of the global labor force (1 billion people) were the victims in the year 2000.

SEE ALSO *Bourgeoisie, Petty; Education, USA; Employment; Globalization, Social and Economic Aspects of; Middle Class*

BIBLIOGRAPHY

David, Mike. 2004. Planet of Slums. *New Left Review* 26 (March–April): 5–34.

Lowe, Graham S. 2000. *The Quality of Work: A People-Centred Agenda.* Toronto: Oxford University Press.

Organization for Economic Cooperation and Development. 2006. *Labor Force Statistics.* Paris: Author.

Yates, Michael D. 2003. *Naming the System: Inequality and Work in the Global Economy.* New York: Monthly Review Press.

Murray Smith

SELF-ENHANCEMENT

Self-enhancement refers to an unduly inflated self-image and to the processes that make it so. As a process, self-enhancement is a motivated attempt to seek and emphasize positive feedback and to shield the self from negative feedback (where the shielding is more properly termed *self-protection*). Successful performance, social victories, or acceptance by others can be selectively recalled or embellished in memory, whereas failures, social defeats, or rejections can be reinterpreted, forgotten, or outright rejected. This operation of motivated self-enhancement is constrained by the motive of self-verification, which calls for the construction and maintenance of a stable self-image. The conflict between these two motives is apparent only when self-esteem is low. High self-esteem enables thoughts that are simultaneously self-enhancing and self-verifying. Hence, the process of self-enhancement can provide a buffer against depression (Bernichon, Cook, and Brown 2003).

Some processes of self-enhancement are conscious and strategic. Optimistic predictions regarding future events, such as a high perceived probability of succeeding at a job or a low perceived probability of contracting a dreaded disease, can be self-enhancing. When people care more about the hit rate of their predictions than about the false positive rate, self-enhancement may be the expression of rational decision utilities. These utilities are malleable: Predictions become more modest when people are accountable to others or when their actual outcomes are soon to be revealed. Mood states and the task difficulty also moderate predictions, such that a positive mood heightens self-enhancement and a difficult task lowers it.

Other processes are implicit or even unconscious. People with positive self-images automatically associate their own attributes with positive feelings and approach behavior. For example, the initials of one's own name and the date of one's birth come to be seen as highly desirable through repeated exposure. As a consequence, people like others who share these attributes, however irrelevant they might be for social behavior. When relocating, for example, people prefer to move to states whose names begin with the same letter as their own.

The prevalence of self-enhancement has spawned studies on stable individual differences. As a trait construct, self-enhancement is derivative because it is assessed as a discrepancy between the positivity of a person's self-image and some index of what the person is "really like." The idiographic approach is to ask people how they see themselves relative to the average person. This approach is problematic because many people who claim to be better than average may actually be better. The alternative approach is nomothetic in that it uses the discrepancy between a self-judgment and the aggregate judgment made by observers as a measure of self-enhancement. This method seeks to solve the criterion problem by statistical aggregation over observer judgments, assuming that observers are on average unbiased (Krueger 1998).

The methodological debate over how best to capture individual differences is bound up with the substantive question of whether self-enhancement is beneficial or detrimental to a person's well-being. This question remains open because the answer strongly depends on the method used. Idiographic studies suggest adaptive advantages, whereas nomothetic studies suggest that self-enhancers are narcissistic and disliked.

SEE ALSO *Self-Affirmation Theory; Self-Serving Bias; Self-Verification*

BIBLIOGRAPHY

Bernichon, Tiffiny, Kathleen E. Cook, and Jonathon D. Brown. 2003. Seeking Self-Evaluative Feedback: The Interactive Role of Global Self-Esteem and Specific Self-Views. *Journal of Personality and Social Psychology* 84: 194–204.

Krueger, Joachim. 1998. Enhancement Bias in the Description of Self and Others. *Personality and Social Psychology Bulletin* 24: 505–516.

Joachim I. Krueger

SELF-ESTEEM

Self-esteem is one of the most frequently studied constructs in the social sciences. Popular culture and public policy discussions also make frequent reference to self-esteem. Yet, despite its familiarity and wide usage, there is no generally accepted definition of self-esteem among social scientists. The earliest use of the term was by philosopher/psychologist William James in what became an influential chapter, "The Consciousness of Self," in *The Principles of Psychology* (1890). James included self-esteem in a group of "self-feelings" that emerge from the conscious awareness of self in relation to others. He offered two definitions of self-esteem that, in their inconsistency, typify the confusion and disagreement associated with the term. In the best-known of James's definitions, self-esteem is "determined by the ratio of our actualities to our supposed potentialities; a fraction of which our pretensions are the denominator and the numerator our success: thus, Self-esteem = Success / Pretensions" (p. 310). Alternatively, according to James, self-esteem is "a certain average tone of self-feeling which each one of us carries about with him, and which is independent of the objective reasons we may have for satisfaction or discontent" (p. 306). These seemingly incompatible definitions highlight a valid and important distinction between self-esteem that is contingent on circumstances and self-esteem that transcends them.

Most of the empirical research on self-esteem in the social sciences works from definitions similar to James's "average tone of self-feeling." The best-known of these is offered by the sociologist Morris Rosenberg in his *Society and the Adolescent Self-Image*, where self-esteem is defined as "a favorable or unfavorable attitude toward the self" (1965, p. 15). The brief self-report measure that Rosenberg developed for his research on adolescents, the Self-Esteem Scale, is the most widely used measure of self-esteem in social science research. In another influential book, *The Antecedents of Self-Esteem*, Stanley Coopersmith offered a similar conceptualization of self-esteem as "the evaluation the individual makes and customarily maintains with regard to himself" (1967, p. 4). Both Rosenberg and Coopersmith operate from the assumption that people's attitude toward or customary evaluation of self underlies their overall sense of self-worth. The definitions offered in these two classic works and assumed by much of the empirical work on self-esteem describe a particular form of self-esteem that is traitlike, consistent across time and situations, and global, concerned with all aspects of the self. This definition also corresponds well to usage of the term in popular culture and public policy settings.

Two alternative conceptualizations of self-esteem depart from these classic definitions by dropping the assumption that self-esteem is global or that it is a trait. Domain-specific conceptualizations accept the premise that self-esteem is an attitude toward or customary evaluation of the self but contend that it is not necessarily global. Thus, for instance, it is possible to have a high opinion of oneself in the social domain but a relatively modest, or even negative, opinion of oneself in the academic domain. Whether self-esteem is viewed as global or domain-specific, it may be conceptualized as a state rather than a trait. This form of self-esteem is like James's ratio of successes to pretensions definition in that it is contingent on circumstances. State self-esteem typically rises when circumstances are positive and drops when they are negative. Neither the domain-specific nor the state conceptualizations are necessarily inconsistent with the global trait conceptualization because it can be shown that weighted combinations of domain-specific self-evaluations are highly predictive of global self-esteem and that state self-esteem varies in a relatively narrow range around the level of trait self-esteem to which it typically returns.

Classic conceptualizations of self-esteem and the questionnaire measures they have spawned assume that people are willing and able to accurately report their self-esteem, an assumption that now seems at least partially unfounded. Drawing on basic research on attitude formation and change, social scientists now make a distinction between self-esteem as traditionally measured—explicit self-esteem—and self-esteem measured using procedures that do not require or allow people to consciously indicate their attitude toward themselves—implicit self-esteem. As with attitudes toward any object, research indicates that explicit and implicit attitudes toward self are not strongly associated. Indeed, different patterns of correspondence between explicit and implicit self-esteem are now viewed as evidence of qualitatively different forms of self-esteem. For instance, a person who is high on explicit but low on implicit self-esteem is described as having defensive self-esteem. A person who is high on both explicit and implicit self-esteem is described as having genuine self-esteem. This work raises questions about the likely success of policies and practices designed to bolster self-esteem that focus only on explicit attitudes toward self (e.g., positive "self-talk").

Furthermore, other important qualitative distinctions in self-esteem indicate that there is more to self-esteem than whether it is high or low. One such distinction is stability of self-esteem, defined as the degree of variability in a person's self-esteem across time. Stability of self-esteem is only modestly associated with level of self-esteem, meaning that people at any given level of self-esteem will vary in the stability of their self-esteem. The combination of level and stability of self-esteem allows for more precise predictions about the role of self-esteem in behavior. For instance, people with high but unstable self-esteem are more likely to react with hostility to provocation than people with stable high self-esteem. Another qualitative distinction is contingency of self-esteem, defined as the degree to which self-esteem is responsive to changes in circumstances. Contingency is moderately correlated with level of self-esteem, indicating that lower self-esteem is accompanied by greater contingency. Contingency of self-esteem typically is indexed at the domain-specific level, allowing for distinctions between people not only in terms of how contingent their self-esteem is, but also in terms of the specific domains in which it is contingent.

In popular usage, self-esteem often is used as a generic label for a variety of similar constructs from which it should be distinguished. Principal among these is self-concept, a much broader term that, according to Rosenberg, is "*the totality of the individual's thoughts and feelings having reference to himself as object*" (1965, p. 7, emphasis in original). Another construct often erroneously referred to as self-esteem is self-efficacy, a narrower construct than self-esteem—even in its domain-specific form—that reflects people's perceptions of their ability to enact a specific behavior. It is directly influenced by prior experience with the behavior and is only indirectly influenced by or reflective of self-esteem.

In popular culture and public policy settings, self-esteem is perceived as critically important to healthy functioning. The strength of this perception is evident in the efforts of groups such as the National Association for Self-Esteem and the California Task Force to Promote Self-Esteem and Personal and Social Responsibility, the latter concluding that "self-esteem is the likeliest candidate for a social vaccine" (1990, p. 232). This conclusion stands in stark contrast to the empirical research literature, which indicates that self-esteem is not strongly associated with behavior—desirable or undesirable—and that, when there is an association, self-esteem is not a causal factor. In an influential *Scientific American* article, "Exploding the Self-Esteem Myth," Roy Baumeister and colleagues summarized this literature by stating, "we have found little to indicate that indiscriminately promoting self-esteem in today's children or adults … offers society any compensatory benefits" (2005, p. 91). This conclusion has led social scientists to examine more closely their assumptions about the origins and functions of self-esteem. Emerging accounts suggest that self-esteem is best viewed as a reflection of other characteristics such as healthy family relationships and social acceptance; it is these constructs that warrant the attention given to self-esteem.

Self-esteem is at once simple and complex. The widely accepted definition of the construct as simply people's attitude toward themselves is at odds with the social and psychological structures and processes that underlie it, as well as the wide range of opinions as to its importance for individuals and society. Concerns about whether it is important at all have inspired social scientists to probe more deeply the origins and underpinnings of self-esteem to determine how, if at all, it matters. The result is one of the most richly described, frequently studied, and intriguing constructs in the social sciences.

SEE ALSO *Guttman Scale; James, William; Mental Health; Psychology; Rosenberg's Self-Esteem Scale; Scales; Self-Awareness Theory; Social Science; Trait Theory*

BIBLIOGRAPHY

Baumeister, Roy F., Jennifer D. Campbell, Joachim I. Krueger, and Kathleen D. Vohs. 2005. Exploding the Self-Esteem Myth. *Scientific American* 292 (1): 84–91.

California Task Force to Promote Self-Esteem and Personal and Social Responsibility. 1990. *Toward a State of Esteem.* Sacramento: California Department of Education.

Coopersmith, Stanley. 1967. *The Antecedents of Self-Esteem.* San Francisco: W. H. Freeman.

James, William. 1890. *The Principles of Psychology.* Vol. 1. New York: Henry Holt. (Cambridge, MA: Harvard University Press, 1981.)

Rosenberg, Morris. 1965. *Society and the Adolescent Self-Image.* Princeton, NJ: Princeton University Press. (Revised edition, Middletown, CT: Wesleyan University Press, 1989.)

Rick H. Hoyle

SELF-FULFILLING PROPHECIES

Psychological theory proposes that people's beliefs construct reality. The emphasis on the construction of reality dates back to the 1940s and 1950s. During this time, "New Look in Perception" research challenged the idea that people perceive reality accurately by proposing that what people perceive is heavily influenced by their motives, emotions, and expectations. The *self-fulfilling prophecy* is a quintessential process of this perspective because it involves people's beliefs changing social reality. A self-fulfilling prophecy occurs when one person causes her or his own false belief about another person to become true.

A self-fulfilling prophecy includes three steps. First, one person must hold a false belief about another person. For example, a teacher may overestimate a student's ability, believing that the student is more capable than the student really is. Second, the person holding the false belief must treat the other person in a manner that is consistent with it. A teacher who overestimates a student's ability would have to treat the student as if she or he is highly

capable. The teacher may often call on that student, spend extra time with that student, teach that student especially difficult material, and provide that student with feedback contingent on performance (Rosenthal 1973). Third, the person about whom the false belief is held must, in response to the treatment she or he receives, confirm the originally false belief. The student who is treated as if she or he is highly capable may enjoy and value school and, consequently, invest more time and effort on school work than other students do. In turn, this student may ultimately learn more than other students in the class, thereby confirming the teacher's originally false belief that she or he was highly capable.

The term *self-fulfilling prophecy* was introduced to the social sciences by Robert Merton (1948). A sociologist by training, Merton proposed that the self-fulfilling prophecy was capable of creating large-scale social problems such as social inequalities. For example, he described how in the early part of the twentieth century African Americans were barred from joining labor unions on the grounds that they were strikebreakers. This left African American laborers with few job opportunities, forcing them to take any work that presented itself, including work that became available as a result of white laborers going on strike. Thus, according to Merton, the belief that African Americans were strikebreakers caused them out of necessity to become strikebreakers, thereby creating a self-fulfilling prophecy.

SELF-FULFILLING PROPHECY RESEARCH

Merton's contribution to the field's understanding of the self-fulfilling prophecy was purely theoretical, meaning that he explained how self-fulfilling prophecies may operate, but never actually tested whether they occur. Nonetheless, his analysis resulted in hundreds of experimental tests of the process that have provided clear evidence that the self-fulfilling prophecy is a real phenomenon that occurs in a variety of settings.

For example, Robert Rosenthal (a professor at Harvard University) and Lenora Jacobson (an elementary school principal in San Francisco) tested whether teachers' false beliefs about their students' intelligence create self-fulfilling prophecies. Rosenthal and Jacobson (1968) were concerned that one reason disadvantaged students may perform poorly in school is because that is what their teachers expect of them, and they wondered if disadvantaged students might perform better if their teachers expected them to improve academically. To test this, they told elementary school teachers that Harvard researchers had created a new IQ test that could identify "intellectual blooming." They then told the teachers which of their students had been identified by this test as one of these "late bloomers"—students who would have substantial gains in their IQs over the course of the school year. In reality, there was no special test to measure intellectual blooming; students had simply been administered a typical IQ test, and random assignment determined which students would be labeled as the late bloomers. Because the late bloomers were chosen at random, they were really no different from any other students intellectually. The only difference between the students labeled late bloomers and those not so labeled was their teachers' expectations for them. Therefore, any difference between their IQs at the end of the school year could be attributed only to a self-fulfilling prophecy, which is exactly what Rosenthal and Jacobson found. By the end of the school year, the late bloomers had significantly greater gains in their IQs than did the other students.

THE MAGNITUDE AND IMPLICATIONS OF SELF-FULFILLING PROPHECIES

The large body of research on self-fulfilling prophecies shows that people's false beliefs can influence the behavior of others. However, the magnitude by which they do so is usually modest, meaning that, on average, people's false beliefs only influence other people's behavior through self-fulfilling prophecies a little bit. Even so, there are conditions under which self-fulfilling prophecy effects are larger than average. For example, self-fulfilling prophecy effects are strongest among individuals who are stigmatized, including African American students, girls in math classes, students who are tracked into low-ability groups within their classrooms, and students who have histories of poor academic achievement (Jussim, Eccles, and Madon 1996).

Self-fulfilling prophecy effects can also become larger than average through a process of accumulation. In a typical day an individual interacts with many people, each of whom may hold a false belief about that individual and have a self-fulfilling effect on that individual's behavior. When the false beliefs that different people hold about the same individual are similar, their independent self-fulfilling effects may combine, thereby causing small self-fulfilling prophecy effects to become large. Consistent with this process, research has shown that parents have the strongest self-fulfilling effects on their children's alcohol use when both hold false and unfavorable beliefs about their child's likelihood of drinking alcohol (Madon, Guyll, Spoth, and Willard 2004). The accumulation of self-fulfilling prophecy effects across people has particularly important implications for stereotyped individuals because such individuals are disproportionately exposed to false and unfavorable beliefs from many different people.

Although any single person's stereotypic beliefs may have only a small self-fulfilling effect on another's behav-

ior, that effect may combine with the self-fulfilling effects of other people's stereotypic beliefs to ultimately have a large and harmful impact on the outcomes of stereotyped individuals such as women and minorities.

SEE ALSO *Merton, Robert K.; Pygmalion Effects; Stereotype Threat; Stereotypes*

BIBLIOGRAPHY

Jussim, Lee, Jacquelynn Eccles, and Stephanie Madon. 1996. Social Perception, Social Stereotypes, and Teacher Expectations: Accuracy and the Quest for the Powerful Self-Fulfilling Prophecy. In *Advances in Experimental Social Psychology*, vol. 28, ed. Mark P. Zanna, 281–388. San Diego, CA: Academic Press.

Madon, Stephanie, Max Guyll, Richard L. Spoth, and Jennifer Willard. 2004. Self-Fulfilling Prophecies: The Synergistic Accumulation of Parents' Beliefs on Children's Drinking Behavior. *Psychological Science* 15: 837–845.

Merton, Robert K. 1948. The Self-Fulfilling Prophecy. *Antioch Review* 8: 193–210.

Rosenthal, Robert. 1973. *On the Social Psychology of the Self-Fulfilling Prophecy: Further Evidence for Pygmalion Effects and Their Mediating Mechanisms.* New York: MSS Modular Publications.

Rosenthal, Robert, and Lenore Jacobson. 1968. *Pygmalion in the Classroom: Teacher Expectation and Pupils' Intellectual Development.* New York: Holt, Rinehart, and Winston.

Stephanie Madon
Jennifer Willard
Ashley A. Buller
Kyle Scherr

SELF-GUIDES

Self-guides are constructs in social psychology that refer to representations of the self. Self-guides are desired self states that have motivational implications and are involved in the process of self-regulation.

The various types of self-guides, proposed by psychologist E. Tory Higgins (1987), are the *actual self, the ideal self,* and the *ought self.* The actual self refers to the way individuals view themselves currently. The ideal self refers to the person that individuals would like to be, and the ought self refers to the person that individuals feel they should be. Individuals' ideal self-guides tend to be associated with hopes and wishes, while their ought self-guides tend to be concerned with safety and responsibility. These ought self-guides represent the internalization of expectations of others and society.

The source of self-guides can also be distinguished as being from the self or from an other. For instance, an individual might have a self-guide that represents who he would ideally like to be, as well as a self-guide that represents who his father thinks he ought to be.

Comparisons can occur between any of these self-guides. Individuals may compare their own ideal selves with others' ideal selves for them. Or they may compare their own actual self with their own ought self-guide. It is through these comparisons that self-guides are associated with self-regulation. Individuals may experience a discrepancy between their actual self and either their ought or ideal self. Such discrepancies lead to the experience of *negative affect*. It is assumed that this experience of negative affect motivates individuals to change their behavior in the hopes of reducing the discrepancy between their actual self and a self-guide. A reduction in this discrepancy then leads to a reduction in the experience of negative affect. Successful self-regulation is equated with lacking a discrepancy and is associated with experiencing positive affect. Failure to self-regulate is equated with experiencing a discrepancy and is associated with negative affect.

Research has found that the positive and negative affect experienced can be differentiated by the type of self-guide used in comparison. Discrepancies between actual selves and ideal selves are associated with dejection-related affect, such as depression and sadness. Discrepancies between actual selves and ought selves are associated with agitation-related affect, such as anxiety and guilt.

Individuals may differ in regard to the type of self-guide that is chronically accessible for them. These differences carry implications for goal pursuit and information processing. Higgins (1997) expanded his theory to suggest that individuals with chronic ideal self-guides tend to pursue goals that are related to promotion or growth, whereas individuals with chronic ought self-guides tend to pursue goals that are related to prevention or safety. Lisa Evans and Richard Petty (2003) show that individuals pay more attention to and more thoroughly process information that is presented in a way consistent with their more prevalent self-guide.

SEE ALSO *Self-Discrepancy Theory*

BIBLIOGRAPHY

Evans, Lisa M., and Richard E. Petty. 2003. Self-Guide Framing and Persuasion: Responsibly Increasing Message Processing to Ideal Levels. *Personality and Social Psychology Bulletin* 29 (3): 313–324.

Higgins, E. Tory. 1987. Self-discrepancy: A Theory Relating Self and Affect. *Psychological Review* 94 (3): 319–340.

Higgins, E. Tory. 1997. Beyond Pleasure and Pain. *American Psychologist* 52 (12): 1280–1300.

Michelle Sherrill

SELF-HATRED

Much of the psychological research in the area of self-hatred owes its origin to the work of the American philosopher and social psychologist George Herbert Mead (1863–1931) and his idea of the "looking-glass self." Mead claimed that people pay attention to the view that others have of them, and when that view is largely negative, a person can internalize it and develop self-hatred. Mead's other major contribution to this area of social research was the importance he placed on the role that language and symbols play in society. A number of later researchers pointed out that American symbols were major conveyers of negative views of blacks and other ethnic groups. At least one prolific author, Sander L. Gilman, has gone so far as to suggest that persecution is inherent in a society's language. Erving Goffman (1922–1982), another influential sociologist, claimed that ethnic (and other minority) groups were often "stigmatized" by society's negative symbolic interaction and the internalization of such stigmatization (often termed "racism") is a major cause of self-hatred.

There is, however, some controversy among scholars concerning the degree to which ethnic group identity affects the development of self-hatred. Some researchers take the position that mere membership in an ethnic group, whether freely chosen or not, is sufficient to cause the individual member to develop feelings of self-hatred if the group is negatively viewed by the majority group. Other researchers take the position that it is not group membership per se that results in self-hatred but the degree to which the individual identifies with the group in question. High or strong identification with one's own ethnic group can sometimes block or ameliorate the kind of psychological damage that results in self-hatred. Ethnic group membership can thus be viewed as a protection against self-hatred as opposed to a cause.

Because of their unique experiences with racism and oppression, blacks and Jews have been the populations most heavily studied in the area of self-hatred. Many of the early researchers were themselves Jews who sought to understand the people in their communities who exhibited visible signs of self-hatred. The founder of psychoanalysis, Sigmund Freud (1856–1939), wrote *Moses and Monotheism* in part to explain Jewish self-hatred produced by external oppression in Europe during the 1930s. The "self-hating" or "self-loathing" Jew has become an archetype in modern American social science, as the term is often used to disparage those Jews who are viewed as anti-Zionist or anti-Israel or for any Jew who is "not Jewish enough." A similar term, "Uncle Tom," has been used to describe the African American who is deemed to possess a high degree of self-hatred. (The term *Uncle Tom* comes from the title character of Harriet Beecher Stowe's antislavery novel *Uncle Tom's Cabin.*) *Apples, bananas,* and *coconuts* are terms that have been used to describe people whose external features are nonwhite (red, yellow, and brown respectively) but whose internal thought patterns are said to be white and reflective of a high degree of self-hatred. The individuals who are the recipients of such negative appellations defend themselves by claiming that it is possible to assimilate some values of the dominant society while at the same time rejecting those (such as white superiority) that they find offensive. Research in support of the possibility of such selective socialization is sparse.

The feminist-oriented research in this area is a reminder that self-hatred is not restricted to members of marginalized groups or subcultures. It is found in the wider society and has been linked to symptoms of depression, substance abuse, and general anxiety. What is perhaps unique about this type of self-hatred is that it does not seem to be related to anything other than a sense of personal failure. It has proven difficult, if not impossible, for researchers to specify a causal link among the possible variables. Self-hatred is as much a cause of as well as a result of depression, anxiety, substance abuse, and gender ambiguity. It can therefore be viewed as both the hub and a spoke of the wheel of social misfortune. As a hub it represents the central role that the self, however damaged or elevated, plays in the dynamics of social life. As a spoke self-hatred represents one of the negative consequences of the socialization process itself.

SEE ALSO *Anxiety; Assimilation; Depression, Psychological; Ethnicity; Feminism; Freud, Sigmund; Gender; Goffman, Erving; Identity; Jews; Looking-Glass Effect; Mead, George Herbert; Multidimensional Inventory of Black Identity; Nationalism and Nationality; Race; Racism; Sexual Orientation, Social and Economic Consequences; Socialization; Stigma; Uncle Tom*

BIBLIOGRAPHY

Freud, Sigmund. 1967(1955). *Moses and Monotheism*. New York: Vintage.

Gilman, Sander L. 1990. *Jewish Self-Hatred: Anti-Semitism and the Hidden Language of the Jews*. Reprint ed. Baltimore, MD: John Hopkins University Press.

Goffman, Erving. 1986. *Stigma: The Management of a Spoiled Identity*. New York: Simon and Schuster.

Mead, George Herbert. 1955. *Mind, Self, and Society from the Standpoint of a Social Behaviorist*. New York: Vintage.

Carolyn B. Murray

SELF-HELP ORGANIZATIONS

SEE *Volunteerism.*

SELF-IDENTITY

The notion of the social self has been of particular interest in the social sciences because it reflects a concern with how people's social behavior varies not only as a function of different social roles but also as a function of the kind of social others with whom a person interacts. Within the social sciences, a distinction is made between personal identities, self-identities, and social identities (Hogg, Terry, and White 1995; Thoits and Virshup 1997). Personal identities consist of self-definitions in terms of unique and idiosyncratic characteristics. Social identities, on the other hand, reflect identification of the self with a social group or category. *Self-identities*, the focus of this article, are conceptualized as a definition of self as a person who performs a particular role or behavior.

Self-identity refers to a person's self-conception, self-referent cognitions, or self-definition that people apply to themselves as a consequence of the structural role positions he or she occupies or a particular behavior he or she engages in regularly. Self-identities reflect the "labels people use to describe themselves" (Biddle, Bank, and Slavings 1987, p. 326). For example, a person's self-identities may include the fact that she is a mother, a wife, a daughter, a social worker, and a blood donor. Self-identities provide meaning for the self, not only because they refer to concrete role specifications or behaviors but also because they distinguish roles or actions from counterroles or opposing behaviors (Lindesmith and Strauss 1956). For example, "the role of mother takes on meaning in connection with the role of father, doctor in connection with nurse, and so on" (White and Burke 1987, p. 312).

Theoretically, the importance of the concept of self-identity is derived from identity theory (Stryker 1968, 1980; Burke 1980; Stryker and Serpe 1982; Wiley 1991), which views the self not as an autonomous psychological entity but as a multifaceted social construct that emerges from people's roles in society and the behaviors they perform. Symbolic interactionists such as Mead (1934) and Cooley (1902) considered the self to be a product of social interaction: It is through social interaction that identities actually acquire self-meaning and people come to know who they are. It is important to note that identity theory focuses on the self-defining roles that people occupy in society rather than on the wider range of different social attributes, such as gender, race, or ethnicity, that can be ascribed to the self. Thus, the general perspective of identity theory forms the basis for a relatively large body of microsociological literature concerned with predicting role-related behavior (Simon 1992; Thoits 1991). Within social psychology, however, researchers have been more interested in using self-identity to improve our understanding and prediction of the relationship between attitudes and action.

The concept of self-identity is pivotal in the link between social structure and individual action. Self-identities, by definition, imply action (Callero 1985) and are a set of expectations prescribing behavior derived from a person's social position and considered appropriate by others. Satisfactory enactment of roles or behaviors not only confirms and validates a person's self-identity (Callero 1985), it also reflects positively on self-evaluation. The perception that one is enacting a role satisfactorily should enhance feelings of self-esteem, whereas perceptions of poor role performance may engender doubts about one's self-worth and may even produce symptoms of psychological distress (Thoits 1991; Hoelter 1983; Stryker and Serpe 1982).

THE APPLICATION OF SELF-IDENTITY IN THE ATTITUDE-BEHAVIOR RELATIONSHIP

Within the field of social psychology, the greatest interest in self-identity has been shown by researchers in the attitude-behavior field. Within this field, it has been argued that self-identities can determine intentions and behaviors. For example, political activists may participate in protest actions because activism has become a central part of their self-concepts, and blood donors may give blood because being a donor has become an important part of their self-definition. Self-identity may have a predictive effect on intentions, independent of attitudes and other constructs, because self-identity encapsulates people's goals or interests that are distinct from those expressed by their attitudes. Indeed, as noted by Sparks (2000), the integration of self-identity into the theory of planned behavior "offers the opportunity to examine the social, moral, and emotional dimensions of people's attitudes and behaviour in greater detail" (p. 45).

Several authors have addressed the extent to which self-identity might be a useful addition to the dominant models of the attitude-behavior relationship, namely the theories of reasoned action (Fishbein and Ajzen 1974) and planned behavior (Ajzen 1991). Self-identity has been found to contribute significantly to the prediction of behavior across a number of domains, including altruistic behavior such as blood donation (Charng, Piliavin, and Callero 1988), political behavior such as voting (Granberg and Holmberg 1990), environmental behavior such as recycling (Terry, Hogg, and White 1999), health behaviors such as exercise behavior (Theodorakis 1994) or licit and illicit drug use (Conner and McMillan 1999), and consumer behavior such as food choice (Sparks and Shepherd 1992). On the basis of past research, Conner and Armitage (1998) argued that it is reasonable to assume that there are certain behaviors for which self-identity is an important determinant of intentions (Armitage and Conner, 2001).

THE INTERPLAY BETWEEN SELF-IDENTITY AND PAST BEHAVIOR

One important question for self-identity researchers is the nature of the interplay between self-identity and past behavior. Identity theory assumes that self-identity and past behavior interact to influence intentions. That is, with repeated performance of a behavior, that behavior is more likely to be seen as an important part of the self-concept, increasing the predictive power of self-identity. However, support for this hypothesis has been equivocal: Some studies have found that self-identity is more predictive of intentions at higher levels of past behavior (Charng et al. 1988), some tests have found no evidence that the effects of self-identity vary as a function of past performance of the behavior (Astrom and Rise 2001; Terry et al. 1999), and other tests have found that self-identity is more predictive of intentions at lower levels of past behavior (Conner and McMillan 1999; Fekadu and Kraft 2001). Conner and McMillan argued that the stronger impact of self-identity on intention at lower levels of past behavior may reflect the role that initial experiences play in strengthening the relevance of identity to intentions. However, as behavior is repeated, intentions become less under the control of cognitive factors such as self-identity and more under the control of habitual forces such as past behavior. Given these inconsistencies, more research on the interplay of self-identity and past behavior, using a wide range of populations and behaviors, is needed in order to understand more fully the role of self-identity in the attitude-behavior context.

ASSESSING SELF-IDENTITY

Within the literature, self-identity is assessed in a number of ways. Initially, researchers used direct and explicit statements to measure the extent to which a particular role or behavior was integrated as part of the self. For example, researchers working within the theory of planned behavior have asked people to indicate their level of agreement with statements such as, "I think of myself as the sort of person who is concerned about the long-term health effects of my food choices" (Sparks and Guthrie 1998), "Blood donation is an important part of who I am" (Charng et al. 1988), or "I am not a type of person oriented to engaging in contraception" (Fekadu and Kraft 2001).

Such measures have been found to be reliable and to predict behavioral intention; however, several criticisms have been noted. First, explicit statements require people to declare in public his or her identification with a particular role and behavior, therefore increasing the salience of that behavior (Sparks, Shepherd, Wieringa, and

Zimmermanns 1995). Second, it has been argued that measures of self-identity serve as measures of past behavior, with people possibly inferring their self-identities from an examination of their past behavior (Sparks 2000). Finally, Fishbein (1997) has argued that self-identity measures may essentially constitute measures of behavioral intention.

In the past decade, however, researchers have developed alternate measures of self-identity. Drawing on marketing research, Mannetti and colleagues (2002, 2004) have used an identity-similarity measure that reflects the degree of similarity between the person's self-image and that of the stereotypical or idealized person who engages in the target behavior. After obtaining independent descriptions of the two images, the distance or nearness between them is computed as a difference score, which is then used as an identity-similarity measure. This type of measure, which is less direct and explicit as well as more specific than other measures, does not increase the salience of behavior, and is independent of behavioral intention, has been found to be a large and significant predictor of behavioral intention (Mannetti, Pierro, and Livi 2002, 2004).

FUTURE DIRECTIONS

Theory and research within the social sciences has highlighted the important role that self-identities play in shaping and guiding action, but future research is needed to tease apart its specific roles. One important direction for future research is to examine the interplay among self-identity and other constructs identified as important in attitude-behavior research and to track the development of self-identities over time. Another important research direction, given the criticisms leveled at self-identity measures, is to develop measures that avoid both the conceptual issues highlighted above and the statistical issues involved in using difference scores. Interest in self-identity and its implications for behavior is widespread, and it is likely that interest in this area will persist for a long time.

SEE ALSO *Choice in Psychology; Decision-making; Identity; Self-Concept; Self-Esteem; Social Identification; Social Psychology; Sociology, Micro-*

BIBLIOGRAPHY

Ajzen, I. 1991. The Theory of Planned Behaviour. *Organizational Behavior and Human Decision Processes* 50 (2): 179–211.

Armitage, C. J., and M. Conner. 2001. Efficacy of the Theory of Planned Behaviour: A Meta-Analytic Review. *British Journal of Social Psychology* 40: 471–499.

Astrøm, A. N., and J. Rise. 2001. Young Adults' Intentions to Eat Healthy Food: Extending the Theory of Planned Behaviour. *Psychology and Health* 16: 223–237.

Biddle, B. J., B. J. Bank, and R. L. Slavings. 1987. Norms, Preferences, Identities, and Retention Decisions. *Social Psychology Quarterly* 50 (4): 322–337.

Burke, P. J. 1980. The Self: Measurement Requirements from an Interactionist Perspective. *Social Psychology Quarterly* 43 (1): 18–29.

Callero, P. 1985. Role-Identity Salience. *Social Psychology Quarterly* 48 (3): 203–215.

Charng, H. W., J. A. Piliavin, and P. L. Callero. 1988. Role Identity and Reasoned Action in the Prediction of Repeated Behaviour. *Social Psychology Quarterly* 51: 303–317.

Cooley, C. 1902. *Human Nature and Social Order*. New York: Scribner's.

Conner, M., and C. J. Armitage. 1998. Extending the Theory of Planned Behaviour: A Review and Avenues for Future Research. *Journal of Applied Social Psychology* 28: 1429–1464.

Conner, M., and B. McMillan. 1999. Interaction Effects in the Theory of Planned Behaviour: Studying Cannabis Use. *British Journal of Social Psychology* 38: 195–222.

Fekadu, Z., and P. Kraft. 2001. Self-Identity in Planned Behaviour Perspective: Past Behaviour and Its Moderating Effects on Self-Identity-Intention Relations. *Social Behavior and Personality* 29: 671–686.

Fishbein, M. 1997. Predicting, Understanding and Changing Socially Relevant Behaviours: Lessons Learned. In *The Message of Social Psychology*, eds. C. McGarty and S. A. Haslam, 77–91. Oxford: Blackwell.

Fishbein, M., and I. Ajzen. 1974. Factors Influencing Intentions and the Intention-Behaviour Relation. *Human Relations* 27 (1): 1–15.

Granberg, D., and S. Holmberg. 1990. The Intention-Behavior Relationship Among U.S. and Swedish Voters. *Social Psychology Quarterly* 53 (1): 44–54.

Hoelter, Jon W. 1983. The Effects of Role Evaluation and Commitment on Identity Salience. *Social Psychology Quarterly* 46 (2): 140–147.

Hogg, M. A., D. J. Terry, and K. M. White. 1995. A Tale of Two Theories: A Critical Comparison of Identity Theory with Social Identity Theory. *Social Psychology Quarterly* 48: 203–215.

Lindesmith, A. R., and A. L. Strauss. 1956. *Social Psychology*, rev. ed. New York: Dryden Press.

Mannetti, L., A. Pierro, and S. Livi, 2002. Explaining Consumer Conduct: From Planned to Self-Expressive Behaviour. *Journal of Applied Social Psychology* 32 (7): 1431–1451.

Mannetti, L., A. Pierro, and S. Livi. 2004. Recycling: Planned and Self-Expressive Behaviour. *Journal of Environmental Psychology* 24: 227–236.

Mead, G. 1934. *Mind, Self, and Society*. Chicago: Chicago University Press.

Simon, R. W. 1992. Parental Role Strains, Salience of Parental Identity, and Gender Differences in Psychological Distress. *Journal of Health and Social Behavior* 33: 25–35.

Sparks, P. 2000. Subjective Expected Utility-Based Attitude-Behavior Models: The Utility of Self-Identity. In *Attitudes, Behaviour, and Social Context: The Role of Norms and Group*

Membership, eds. D. J. Terry and M. A. Hogg, 31–46. Mahwah, NJ: Laurence Erlbaum.

Sparks, P., and C. A. Guthrie. 1998. Self-Identity and the Theory of Planned Behaviour: A Useful Addition or an Unhelpful Artifice. *Journal of Applied Social Psychology* 28 (15): 1393–1410.

Sparks, P., and R. Shepherd. 1992. Self-Identity and the Theory of Planned Behaviour: Assessing the Role of Identification with Green Consumerism. *Social Psychology Quarterly* 55 (4): 388–399.

Sparks, P., R. Shepherd, N. Wieringa, and N. Zimmermanns. 1995. Perceived Behavioural Control, Unrealistic Optimism and Dietary Change: An Exploratory Study. *Appetite* 24: 243–255.

Stryker, S. 1968. Identity Salience and Role Performance: The Relevance of Symbolic Interaction Theory for Family Research. *Journal of Marriage and the Family* 30: 558–564.

Stryker, S. 1980. *Symbolic Interactionism: A Social Structural Version*. Menlo Park, CA: Benjamin/Cummings.

Stryker, S., and R. T. Serpe. 1982. Commitment, Identity Salience, and Role Behaviour: Theory and Research Example. In *Personality, Roles, and Social Behaviour*, eds. W. Ickes and E. S. Knowles, 199–218. New York: Springer-Verlag.

Terry, D. J., M. A. Hogg, and K. M. White. 1999. The Theory of Planned Behaviour: Self-Identity, Social Identity, and Group Norms. *British Journal of Social Psychology* 38: 225–244.

Theodorakis, Y. 1994. Planned Behaviour, Attitude Strength, Role Identity, and the Prediction of Exercise Behaviour. *Sports Psychologist* 8: 149–165.

Thoits, P. A. 1991. On Merging Identity Theory and Stress Research. *Social Psychology Quarterly* 54 (2): 101–112.

Thoits, P. A., and L. K. Virshup. 1997. Me's and We's: Forms and Functions of Social Identities. In *Self and Identity: Fundamental Issues*, eds. R. D. Ashmore and L. Jussim, 1: 106–133. Oxford: Oxford University Press.

White, C. L., and P. J. Burke. 1987. Ethnic Role Identity among Black and White College Students: An Interactionist Perspective. *Sociological Perspectives* 30: 310–331.

Wiley, M. G. 1991. Gender, Work, and Stress: The Potential Impact of Role-Identity Salience and Commitment. *Social Psychology Quarterly* 32: 495–510.

Deborah J. Terry
Joanne R. Smith

SELF-IMAGE

SEE *Body Image; Self-Concept.*

SELFISHNESS

SEE *Generosity/Selfishness.*

SELF-JUSTIFICATION

People are rational beings, highly capable of exercising careful judgment and judicious evaluation before taking action. Research shows that people are often rationalizing creatures as well, quite facile in their ability to justify their own actions, beliefs, and feelings after the fact. This phenomenon, known as *self-justification*, involves convincing oneself (and others) that what one did, felt, or thought was logically appropriate, even going so far as to invent plausible explanations when it is not immediately apparent why one acted, felt, or thought as one did.

The research that first brought attention to people's tendency to self-justify was a study of the rumors that arose after an earthquake in India in the 1930s. The report noted a perplexing pattern of rumor transmission: Individuals who lived in an area minimally affected by the devastating event were the ones spreading various stories of future calamities. Why would people who suffered little or no negative effects of the earthquake engage in concocting and communicating ideas that would seemingly only provoke fear and dread? Upon reflecting on these findings, social psychologist Leon Festinger (1919–1989) had the insight that this behavior was not fear-provoking in nature, rather it was fear-justifying. Festinger reasoned that although these individuals were spared the worst of the earthquake, they nonetheless were afraid. Yet the circumstances in their case, having escaped disaster, could not adequately or fully account for the anxiety they were experiencing, which Festinger argued motivated them to create future bleak scenarios that were more commensurate with the dread they already felt, and thus served to justify it.

Festinger went on to develop his *cognitive dissonance* theory, which provided a conceptual basis for this and other instances of self-justification phenomena. He argued that people have a need for their cognitions (i.e., thoughts, beliefs, and attitudes) to be consistent with one another. When people become aware that an inconsistency exists among two or more cognitions, an unpleasant tension state known as cognitive dissonance arises. People are motivated to reduce the dissonance and do so by changing old, or adding new, cognitions to eliminate the inconsistency.

One of the earliest tests of cognitive dissonance theory and possibly the first systematic demonstration of self-justification consisted of research participants working on an extremely boring task—turning wooden knobs again and again—and then being asked to convince another person that the task was actually quite enjoyable. Participants were offered either $1 or $20 as compensation for agreeing to this latter request, which they all did. Later, participants provided their own evaluation of the knob-turning task. Participants who were promised $20 to convince another person that the knob-turning task was a pleasant experience rated the task very negatively, no different in fact than another group of participants who performed the task but were not asked to misrepresent it to someone else. Those promised $1, however, rated the knob-turning task more positively than did the other two groups of participants. In explaining this result, Festinger and his colleagues argued that unlike $20, $1 in compensation was not psychologically sufficient to justify the discrepancy between what participants really felt about the dull task and their contrary public expression that the task was enjoyable. To diminish this contradiction, and the corresponding dissonance associated with it, participants altered their attitude toward the knob-turning task in a positive direction. Participants' public expression that the task was interesting was now better justified by their "corrected" attitude.

Later research demonstrated that self-justification helps explain the ubiquity of initiation rituals across human cultures. Elliot Aronson and Judson Mills had participants undergo either a severe, mild, or no screening session (effectively serving as an initiation) before being allowed to take part in what was anticipated to be an interesting discussion on the psychology of sex. All participants then listened to a portion of an ostensibly ongoing group discussion of secondary mating habits in lower animals, which was designed to be dull and banal. Finally, participants were asked to provide their reactions to the discussion and group. Participants who underwent the severe initiation, which required them to exert the most effort and endure the most suffering to gain admittance to the group, expressed more positive reactions than did those who experienced only a mild initiation or no initiation at all. Aronson and Mills argued that the severe initiation was too painful for participants to deny; hence they justified their exertions (simultaneously reducing dissonance) by inflating their estimate of the attractiveness of the group. This particular type of self-justification is often referred to as *effort justification*.

A particularly troubling manifestation of self-justification occurs when people engage in what has become known as *victim derogation* or *defensive attribution*. When we observe bad things happening to good people for no apparent reason, we tend to rationalize that they must have had it coming. Blaming the victim enables us to maintain the perception that the world is a just place in which random victimization does not occur. Similarly, perpetrators of harm often belittle their victims in order to convince themselves that the victims deserved exactly what they got.

SEE ALSO *Attribution; Cognitive Dissonance; Festinger, Leon; Natural Disasters; Rituals; Rumors*

BIBLIOGRAPHY

Aronson, Elliot. 2004. *The Social Animal.* 9th ed. New York: Worth.

Carli, Linda L. 1999. Cognitive Reconstruction, Hindsight, and Reactions to Victims and Perpetrators. *Personality and Social Psychology Bulletin* 25 (8): 966–979.

G. Daniel Lassiter

SELF-KNOWLEDGE

SEE *Self-Perception Theory.*

SELF-LOVE

SEE *Narcissism.*

SELF-MONITORING

Self-monitoring is a construct referring to individual differences in the way people monitor and manage their presentations of self, behaviors, and emotions. It was first proposed by psychologist Mark Snyder in 1974 in his article "Self-Monitoring of Expressive Behavior." According to Snyder's formulation, people vary in the degree to which they attend and respond to social and situational cues regarding what behaviors are most appropriate. Essentially, variations in self-monitoring refer to variations in how willing or able people are to regulate their behavior and self-presentations in specific situations.

The Self-Monitoring (SM) Scale, developed by Snyder, captures differences in the kinds of cues to which individuals respond. It consists of items assessing how respondents observe, control, or regulate their expressive behavior in different settings. While there were twenty-five true-false items in the original scale, a revised eighteen-item scale is now more frequently used by researchers.

Individuals who score high on the SM Scale (high self-monitors) are concerned with the situational appropriateness of their behavior and are sensitive to social cues about what is correct behavior. They would agree with a scale item like "I would probably make a good actor." Regardless of how he or she really feels, a high self-monitor might be one of the most mournful of the mourners at a funeral held in the morning and then one of the happiest people at a party or wedding held later that same day. In contrast, those scoring low on the SM Scale (low self-monitors) are controlled more by their perceived internal feelings and attitudes and make little effort to fit the social situation. They would agree with a scale item like "I have trouble changing my behavior to suit different people and different situations." Low self-monitors might find it hard to hide their good mood even at a funeral. Alternatively, low self-monitors are more likely to show unhappiness at a party if they happen to be in a bad mood that day.

A great deal of research has examined behavioral differences between the two self-presentational orientations. For example, high self-monitors show greater cross-situational variability in their behavior than low self-monitors. Alternatively, low self-monitors are more likely to show high correspondence between inner attitudes and overt behaviors than are high self-monitors. These differences reflect the fact that high self-monitors are more likely to monitor their social environments, whereas low self-monitors are more likely to monitor themselves. Thus, it follows that among high self-monitors, aspects of the social self are more important, whereas the existential, experiential self (i.e., how one experiences oneself) is more important to the low self-monitor.

With regard to how these two self-types are related to psychological health, Snyder considers high self-monitors to be more pragmatic (or sensitive and strategic) across a number of social situations. Low self-monitors, on the other hand, tend to be more consistent with their principles and less responsive to situational or social pressures. Research suggests that personal problems are no more common among high or low self-monitors and that neither type is more susceptible to mental illness. Self-monitoring also seems to be unrelated to measures of neuroticism, anxiety, and depression.

SEE ALSO *Anxiety; Depression, Psychological; Neuroticism; Self-Control; Self-Presentation; Stereotype Threat*

BIBLIOGRAPHY

Gangestad, S. W., and M. Snyder 2000. Self-Monitoring: Appraisal and Reappraisal. *Psychological Bulletin* 126 (4): 530–555.

Snyder, M. 1974. Self-Monitoring of Expressive Behavior. *Journal of Personality and Social Psychology* 30 (4): 526–537.

Thomas M. Brinthaupt

SELF-PERCEPTION THEORY

Psychology has long recognized that people must know themselves in order to survive and adapt in life. The value of self-knowledge stems from the fact that the self represents the only constant throughout life. Because of this if the self is well defined, it can provide a solid basis of val-

ues, preferences, and attitudes to manage the many decisions of daily life. Clear self-knowledge helps people to quickly decide and express their views on issues such as capital punishment, the ideal profession, or their tastes in music, whereas the absence of clear self-knowledge can leave an individual paralyzed by these decisions. Given the importance of self-knowledge, psychologists have spent a great deal of time attempting to understand how people come to know themselves.

Self-perception theory represents one of the most influential theories of how self-knowledge unfolds. Developed by social psychologist Daryl Bem self-perception theory consists of two basic claims. First the theory claims that people come to know their own attitudes, beliefs, and other internal states by inferring them from their own behavior and the circumstances under which they occur. So a student who observes that he or she constantly reads psychology books may infer an interest in psychology. Second the theory claims that when internal cues are weak, the individual is in the same position as an outside observer who must rely upon the external cues of their behavior to infer their own inner characteristics. In this case people's conclusion that they genuinely like psychology will be reinforced if there are no external incentives to explain their behavior (e.g., grades), and they have no clear prior opinions regarding psychology. Thus people simply use their behavior and the circumstances in which it occurs to infer their own beliefs and attitudes.

One reason why self-perception theory has been so influential stems from its simplicity as an explanation for how self-knowledge develops. That is people come to know themselves merely by observing their own behavior. Beyond its simplicity, however, self-perception theory has been so influential because it provides an important contrast to the most famous psychological theory of how behavior shapes self-knowledge: cognitive dissonance theory. Cognitive dissonance theory assumes that people are motivated to maintain consistency between self beliefs and experience an unpleasant state of dissonance when they hold two inconsistent beliefs about the self. Thus the inconsistency between the thoughts "I do not like psychology" and "I constantly read about psychology" arouses dissonance, and people are motivated to reduce dissonance by changing one of those thoughts. The most direct way to resolve dissonance is to change the prior belief ("I do not like psychology") to align with the behavior ("I spend a great deal of time learning about psychology"). That is the person can resolve dissonance by making their initial attitude more favorable (I really do like psychology) and, hence, consistent with their behavior.

There are two differences between cognitive dissonance theory and self-perception theory. First unlike cognitive dissonance theory, self-perception theory does not assume that any motivational state (e.g., dissonance reduction) is necessary for change in self-knowledge. In fact self-perception theory only requires people's willingness to infer their own attitudes and beliefs by considering the environmental and dispositional causes for their own actions for changes in self-knowledge to occur. Second self-perception theory claims that people can use their own behavior to infer self-knowledge when the internal cues of prior beliefs are ambiguous or weak, whereas cognitive dissonance theory assumes that people adjust self-knowledge only when the internal cues of prior beliefs are clear and conflict with their freely chosen behavior. Taken together these two differences have led psychologists to suggest that both self-perception theory and cognitive dissonance theory can explain the adjustment of self-knowledge under different conditions. Self-perception theory explains *the creation of new self-knowledge* following behavior *that does not conflict with clear initial self-views* whereas cognitive dissonance explains *change in existing self-knowledge* following freely chosen behavior *that does conflict with clear initial self-views.*

The resolution of the self-perception theory versus cognitive dissonance theory debate represents one of the greatest contributions of self-perception theory. Indeed psychology only becomes better when old theories are challenged and complemented by new theories. However the contribution of self-perception theory extends beyond cognitive dissonance theory through its ability to account for a wider variety of self-attribution phenomenon. Most notably self-perception theory can explain how people develop self-knowledge from behavior even when there is no inconsistency between prior beliefs and behavior. So self-perception theory can explain how people infer that they intrinsically enjoy engaging in an activity (psychology) that they once found intrinsically unenjoyable (behavior-belief inconsistency) *when there are not* obvious situational incentives to explain their behavior (e.g., money for grades). In addition, however, self-perception theory can explain how people infer that they do not intrinsically enjoy engaging in an activity (psychology) that they once found intrinsically enjoyable (behavior-belief consistency) *when there are* obvious situational incentives that can explain their behavior (e.g., money for grades). Cognitive dissonance theory cannot explain this type of change in self-views because the behavior of task engagement (reading psychology) is not inconsistent with the initial belief that they enjoy the task. Self-perception theory can explain this type of change in self-beliefs because it does not assume that an inconsistency must exist between initial beliefs and behavior for people to adjust self-knowledge. That is people infer that they must be engaging in the task to earn the external rewards rather than to satisfy their intrinsic interest in the activity. Self-

perception theory not only explains the change in self-views produced by external rewards that cannot be explained with cognitive dissonance but also emphasizes the dangers of offering people incentives to engage in tasks that they are already interested in. The ability to explain changes in self-knowledge under a wide range of conditions makes self-perception theory one of the most influential theories of how people get to know themselves.

SEE ALSO *Behavior, Self-Constrained; Cognitive Dissonance; Knowledge; Psychology; Self-Control; Self-Justification; Self-Monitoring*

BIBLIOGRAPHY

Bem, Daryl J. 1972. Self-Perception Theory. In *Advances in Experimental Social Psychology*, vol. 6, ed. Leonard Berkowitz, 1–63. New York: Academic Press.

Festinger, Leon. 1957. *A Theory of Cognitive Dissonance.* Evanston, IL: Peterson.

Kunda, Ziva. 1990. The Case for Motivated Reasoning. *Psychological Bulletin* 108 (3): 480–498.

Patrick J. Carroll

SELF-PRESENTATION

Self-presentation is the process by which individuals represent themselves to the social world. This process occurs at both conscious and nonconscious (automatic) levels and is usually motivated by a desire to please others and/or meet the needs of the self. Self-presentation can be used as a means to manage the impressions others form of oneself. Strategic or tactical self-presentation (impression management) occurs when individuals seek to create a desired image or invoke a desired response from others.

The concept of self-presentation emerged from the symbolic interactionist (SI) tradition. The SI tradition is a uniquely sociological contribution to the field of social psychology that attends to the processes by which individuals create and negotiate the social world. SI proposes that it is through interaction and the development of shared meanings (symbolism) that individuals navigate the social world. The works of Erving Goffman, especially *The Presentation of Self in Everyday Life* (1959), exemplify the SI tradition and are seminal contributions to the study of impression management and self-presentation.

Goffman employs a dramaturgical metaphor in which he maps elements of social interaction to the stage. Working at the microsociological level, Goffman focused on the process by which actors construct roles and portray them to an audience. The social actor works to create a front that is both believable and elicits the approval of others. Goffman's work on impression management and self-presentation provides a roadmap for understanding human behavior and the tension between the individual and society.

Subsequent to Goffman's early articulations of ideas of self-presentation, experimental social psychologists such as Edward E. Jones and Barry R. Schlenker devised experimental methods for the study of self-presentation. This fruitful work provided empirical data about self-presentation that fueled the development of theoretical accounts of self-presentation (e.g., Schlenker 1975). Jones's important text *Ingratiation* presented ingratiation as a form of impression management by which actors can elicit positive responses from others (Jones 1964). One taxonomy of self-presentation strategies includes ingratiation, intimidation, self-promotion, exemplification, and supplication (Jones and Pittman 1982).

Self-presentation is an important part of social life and is largely a prosocial way that individuals negotiate social interactions. Yet, for the individual, the process of self-presentation may be fraught with tension. These tensions were presented in Goffman's pioneering work, which provided a sensitive account of internal tensions that can arise in the trade-offs between the need for social approval and the desire for authenticity. Arlie Russell Hochschild's *The Managed Heart* (1983) focuses on the emotional work involved in self-presentation. Other scholars (e.g., Erickson and Wharton 1997) have also addressed the conflicts that can arise in self-presentation. Not all individuals attempt or are willing to portray an inaccurate image to their audiences. For some people, psychological needs other than the need for social approval drive behavior.

Self-presentation is complex: It is both an individual difference variable and a function of social situations. Self-presentation strategies differ across individuals but also are influenced by environmental factors. In addition to self-presentation differences observed according to age, gender, and culture, researchers have observed differences in self-presentation based on environmental factors. That is, individuals may elect to alter their self-presentations in response to cues from the social environment. As used here, cues refer to both environmental cues such as the social context (i.e., how public the setting is) and interpersonal cues such as the perceived responses of others. Individuals may also differ in the extent to which they engage in self-monitoring. Self-monitoring is the extent to which individuals monitor their behavior and self-presentation in response to real or perceived interactional cues.

Self-presentation is both an individual experience and a social phenomenon and highlights the tensions inherent in human interaction.

SEE ALSO *Goffman, Erving; Ingratiation; Self-Concept; Self-Esteem; Self-Monitoring; Self-Representation; Social Psychology*

BIBLIOGRAPHY

Erickson, Rebecca, and Amy S. Wharton. 1997. Inauthenticity and Depression: Assessing the Consequences of Interactive Service Work. *Work and Occupations* 24: 188–213.

Goffman, Erving. 1959. *The Presentation of Self in Everyday Life*. New York: Anchor.

Hochschild, Arlie Russell. 1983. *The Managed Heart: Commercialization of Human Feeling*. Berkeley: University of California Press.

Jones, Edward E. 1964. *Ingratiation: A Social Psychological Analysis*. New York: Meredith.

Jones, Edward E., and Thane S. Pittman. 1982. Toward a General Theory of Strategic Self-Presentation. In *Psychological Perspectives on the Self*. Vol. 1, ed. Jerry Suls, 231–262. Hillsdale, NJ: Erlbaum.

Schlenker, Barry. R. 1975. Self-Presentation: Managing the Impression of Consistency when Reality Interferes with Self-Enhancement. *Journal of Personality and Social Psychology* 32: 1030–1037.

Alexis T. Franzese

SELF-REFLECTION

SEE *Ethnography; Observation, Participant.*

SELF-REGULATION

SEE *Self-Monitoring.*

SELF-REPORT METHOD

Social scientists use many methods to collect data. The most common method is self-report, in which people respond to questions about themselves regarding a wide variety of issues such as personality traits, moods, thoughts, attitudes, preferences, and behaviors. In fact, much of social science knowledge and theory are based largely on self-report data.

ADVANTAGES OF SELF-REPORT

The main advantage of self-report is that it is a relatively simple way to collect data from many people quickly and at low cost. A second advantage is that self-report data can be collected in various ways to suit the researcher's needs. Questionnaires can be completed in groups or individually and can be mailed to respondents or made available on the Internet. Self-report data can also be collected in an interview format, either in person or over the telephone. Researchers can thus obtain data from respondents across a large geographic area or to whom they do not have direct access.

Furthermore, researchers can collect data regarding behaviors that cannot be observed directly or are unethical to simulate in the laboratory (i.e., activities typically done in private and behaviors that would cause embarrassment if done in public). The only person with direct access to mental events and some behaviors is the self; therefore, the self is the best person to report on these variables. Also, respondents completing pencil-and-paper questionnaires with the assurance of confidentiality and anonymity might be more willing to accurately report on a variety of behaviors and characteristics.

DISADVANTAGES OF SELF-REPORT AND POSSIBLE SOLUTIONS

There are several disadvantages of self-report that threaten the reliability and validity of measurement. Researchers must ensure that measures are reliable—meaning the outcomes of measurements are repeatable—and valid—meaning the intended variable is measured.

Some threats to validity derive from the way the measure is designed, such as using ambiguous words or words that are not appropriate for the reading level of the respondents. This is especially problematic when different groups (e.g., men and women, adolescents and adults) are likely to interpret words differently or have different reading levels. Researchers must choose words carefully to convey their desired meaning precisely and at an appropriate reading level. Another way to ensure consistent interpretation of items is to provide respondents with a reference group. For example, respondents may be instructed to indicate their level of shyness in relation to people of their same age and gender. It may also be important to provide additional information to ensure that respondents interpret and use response scales correctly, such as providing examples of portion sizes when asking questions about eating habits.

The order of items may also influence how a person responds. For example, people may report different levels of happiness depending on whether they answer this question before or after reporting how many dates they had last month. Researchers should consider how questions might influence answers to subsequent questions. Furthermore, when asking about controversial or potentially embarrassing information, researchers might plan to ask less controversial questions first so that respondents feel comfortable at the outset and thus will be more likely to provide honest responses to more difficult questions.

Other threats to the validity of self-report are due to respondent characteristics. One such well-known threat is socially desirable responding, or the attempt by respondents to make themselves look good. Researchers avoid this problem by using neutral items; by using the Q-sort method of response, in which the respondents are allowed to rate only a certain number of items as highly descriptive of themselves; and by informing respondents that answers are anonymous and/or confidential, thereby encouraging honest responding. Finally, researchers may choose not to use data from respondents who score high on measures of social desirability.

Respondents may have other biases unrelated to item content. They might tend to embrace or avoid extreme responses, or they might exhibit acquiescence, a tendency to agree with statements. These threats can be reduced by requiring respondents to choose one answer from a list. To reduce acquiescence bias, researchers can use measures with items keyed in different directions so that agreeing with some items lowers the total score.

An especially harmful threat to self-report occurs when respondents are intentionally dishonest. Dishonest responding can be decreased by ensuring confidentiality (and anonymity, if possible). Data from people who score high on measures of lying or faking (in both negative and positive directions) can also be excluded from further analyses.

Experimenters may pose threats to the validity of self-report by unintentionally influencing how people respond to questions, which is especially likely with an interview format. Typically, this threat results from experimenters expecting people to respond in line with hypotheses. To lessen this threat, experimenters and interviewers should be unaware of the research hypotheses, and several interviewers should be used to reduce systematic influences of any one interviewer.

The situation and location of interviews may also influence self-report measures. For example, people interviewed on college campuses may agree with the statement "The government should give more money to education" in greater numbers than people interviewed in a park. The situation may serve as a cue to the respondents about the desirable answer, and they may respond accordingly. Even when the respondent is not consciously aware of contextual cues, he or she may still be influenced by them on a subconscious level.

A final threat to validity can occur if all data have been collected with self-report because this is likely to artificially inflate correlations; this problem is known as method variance. In fact, collecting data with any single method has its pitfalls. Researchers who use a single method for collecting data need to be aware of method variance so they can correctly interpret the magnitudes of the correlations found between various measures.

METHODS OTHER THAN SELF-REPORT

Multiple methods can be used to gain a multifaceted understanding of variables of interest and to determine consistency between self-reports and other measurements. Other-report (asking another person about the person of interest) is increasingly being used to examine variables that were previously primarily measured with self-report. Behavioral observation is another method for gathering information about variables commonly assessed with self-report, although this method is more time-consuming and expensive than self-report. To check for accuracy, self-reports can be compared with archival data (e.g., criminal records).

Researchers must keep in mind the purpose of their research to determine which method(s) of data collection to use. If researchers are interested in people's subjective experience of their own thoughts and behaviors, then self-report is appropriate. However, if researchers are interested in more than people's subjective experience of themselves, then a multimethod approach should be used to ensure reliable and valid measurement. Social science researchers are often concerned with more than subjective experience and are beginning to embrace multimethod approaches to data collection. This shift in data collection methods is likely to increase the quality of data available to test and revise social science theories.

SEE ALSO *Ethics in Experimentation; Informed Consent; Mood; Personality; Privacy; Reliability, Statistical; Self-Disclosure; Self-Presentation; Self-Serving Bias; Survey; Validity, Statistical*

BIBLIOGRAPHY

Block, Jack. 1977. Advancing the Psychology of Personality: Paradigmatic Shift or Improving the Quality of Research. In *Personality at the Crossroads: Current Issues in Interactional Psychology*, eds. David Magnusson and Norman S. Endler, 37–63. Hillsdale, NJ: Erlbaum.

Moskowitz, D. S. 1986. Comparison of Self-Reports, Reports by Knowledgeable Informants, and Behavioral Observation Data. *Journal of Personality* 54 (1): 294–331.

Paulhus, Delroy L. 1991. Measurement and Control of Response Bias. In *Measures of Personality and Social Psychological Attitudes*, eds. John P. Robinson, Philip R. Shaver, and Lawrence S. Wrightsman, pp. 17–59. San Diego, CA: Academic Press.

Tera D. Letzring

SELF-REPRESENTATION

How people define themselves in relation to others greatly influences how they think, feel, and behave, and is ultimately related to the construct of identity. Self-development is a continuous process throughout the lifespan; one's sense of self may change, at least somewhat, throughout one's life. Self-representation has important implications for socio-emotional functioning throughout the lifespan.

Philosopher and psychologist William James (1842–1910) was one of the first to postulate a theory of the self in *The Principles of Psychology*. James described two aspects of the self that he termed the "I Self" and "Me Self." The I Self reflects what people see or perceive themselves doing in the physical world (e.g., recognizing that one is walking, eating, writing), whereas the Me Self is a more subjective and psychological phenomenon, referring to individuals' reflections about themselves (e.g. characterizing oneself as athletic, smart, cooperative). Other terms such as *self-view, self-image, self-schema,* and *self-concept* are also used to describe the self-referent thoughts characteristic of the Me Self. James further distinguished three components of the Me Self. These include: (1) the material self (e.g., tangible objects or possessions we collect for ourselves); (2) the social self (e.g., how we interact and portray ourselves within different groups, situations, or persons); and (3) the spiritual self (e.g., internal dispositions).

In the late twentieth century, researchers began to argue that the self is a cognitive and social construction. Cognitive perspectives suggest that one's self-representation affects how one thinks about and gives meaning to experiences. Like James, psychologist Ulric Neisser distinguished between one's self-representation connected to directly perceived experiences and that resulting from reflection on one's experiences. The "ecological self," connections of oneself to experiences in the physical environment, and the "interpersonal self," connections of oneself to others through verbal or nonverbal communication, comprise direct perception of experience. Neisser proposed that these two types of self-representation develop early in infancy. Regarding reflections on one's experiences, Neisser identified three types of self-representation that emerge in later infancy and childhood with cognitive and social maturation. The temporally "extended self" is based on memories of one's past experiences and expectations for the future. The "private self" emerges with the understanding that one's experiences are not directly perceived by others, but rather must be communicated to be shared. The "conceptual self," one's overarching theory or schema about oneself based on one's reflection on experiences within social and cultural context, parallels terms such as *self-concept* and *self-schema*. In a 1977 article, psychologist Hazel Markus showed that one's self-representation or self-schema guides information processing and influences one's behavior.

As psychologist Roy Baumeister pointed out in *Identity: Cultural Change and the Struggle for Self,* because self-representation develops through one's experience of the world, cultural and social factors are important in who we are and what we think about ourselves. Philosopher George Herbert Mead (in *Mind, Self, and Society*) postulated that acquisition of self-representation emerges from socialization practices. Mead argued that individuals are socialized to adopt the values, standards, and norms of society through their ability to perceive what others and society would like them to be. Psychologists Tory Higgins, Ruth Klein, and Timothy Strauman further suggested that self-representation includes ideas about who we are (actual self), who we potentially could be (ideal self), and who we should be (ought self), both from one's own perspective and from one's perception of valued others' perspectives. Discrepancies between the actual self and the ideal self or ought self may result in depression or anxiety, respectively.

Attachment theory likewise demonstrates how the self is socially constructed and, in turn, affects how people evaluate themselves (i.e., their self-esteem). Thus, relationships with others play an important role in people's self-representation and self-esteem. Psychologist John Bowlby focused on caregiver-child relationships. Securely attached children feel safe in the environment and are able to actively explore their surroundings. Through experiencing secure attachment to a consistent caregiver, children develop a belief that they are good and worthy of love. This forms the basis of self-esteem. In contrast, an insecure attachment, in which the child does not feel confi-

dent in the caregiver's protection, may result in feeling unworthy of love, anxious and distressed, and relatively low self-esteem.

The beginnings of self-representation emerge early in infancy, with the recognition that one is a separate physical being from others. Self-representation development continues throughout adulthood. Because self-representation involves social and cognitive constructions, changes in self-representation occur with individuals' cognitive and social development. Psychologist Susan Harter has conducted highly influential research on the developmental course of self-representation. Excerpts from Harter's summary of self-representation development from early childhood through adolescence (Harter, 1988) are presented in the Table 1.

In addition to cognitive and social maturation, changes in one's social context may be equally important influences on self-representation. For example, Susan Cross (in "Self-construals, Coping, and Stress in Cross-cultural Adaptation") notes that cultural values influence self-development. As an individual moves from one cultural context (e.g., Eastern culture) to another (e.g., Western culture), changes in self-representation may emerge. Individuals can learn to adopt a self-representation that embraces multiple cultures.

SEE ALSO *Attachment Theory; Bowlby, John; Child Development; Developmental Psychology; James, William; Mead, George Herbert; Mental Health;*

	Early childhood	Middle childhood	Adolescence
Content	specific examples of observable physical characteristics, behaviors, preferences, etc.	trait labels, focusing on abilities, interpersonal characteristics, and emotional attributes	abstractions about the self involving psychological constructs, focusing on different relationships and roles
Organization	little coherence, due to inability to logically organize single self-descriptors	logically organized, integrated within domains that are differentiated from one another	ability to construct a formal theory of the self in which all attributes across and within role domains are integrated and should be internally consistent
Stability over time	not stable over time	recognition of and interest in continuity of self-attributes over time	Intrapsychic conflict and confusion over contradictions and instability within the self, concern with creation of an integrated identity
Basis	fantasies and wishes dominate descriptions of behaviors and abilities	use of social comparison due to ability to simultaneously observe and evaluate the self in relation to others	intense focus on the opinions that significant others hold about the self, especially peers and close friends

Table 1

Psychology; Self-Awareness Theory; Self-Consciousness, Private vs. Public; Self-Guides; Self-Perception Theory; Self-Schemata; Social Psychology; Stages of Development

BIBLIOGRAPHY

Baumeister, Roy F. 1986. *Identity: Cultural Change and the Struggle for Self.* New York: Oxford University Press.

Bowlby, John. 1969. *Attachment and Loss.* New York: Basic Books.

Cross, Susan. 1995. Self-construals, Coping, and Stress in Cross-cultural Adaptation. *Journal of Cross-Cultural Psychology* 26 (6): 673–697.

Harter, Susan. 1988. Developmental Processes in the Construction of the Self. In *Integrative Processes and Socialization: Early to Middle Childhood*, eds. Thomas D. Yawkey and James E. Johnson, 45–78. Hillsdale, NJ: Erlbaum.

Harter, Susan. 1999. *The Construction of the Self: A Developmental Perspective.* New York: Guilford.

Higgins, Tory, Ruth Klein, and Timothy Strauman. 1985. Self-concept Discrepancy Theory: A Psychological Model for Distinguishing Among Different Aspects of Depression and Anxiety. *Social Cognition* 3: 51–76.

James, William. 1890. *The Principles of Psychology.* New York: Henry Holt.

Kanagawa, Chie, Susan Cross, and Hazel Rose Markus. 2001. Who Am I?: The Cultural Psychology of the Conceptual Self. *Personality and Social Psychology Bulletin* 27 (1): 90–103.

Markus, Hazel. 1977. Self-schemata and Processing Information about the Self. *Journal of Personality and Social Psychology* 35 (2): 63–78.

Mead, George Herbert. 1934. *Mind, Self, and Society.* Chicago: University of Chicago Press.

Neisser, Ulric. 1988. Five Kinds of Self Knowledge. *Philosophical Psychology* 1 (1): 35–59.

Pa Her
Julie C. Dunsmore

SELF-SCHEMATA

Psychologists have spent a great amount of time and energy studying the self-concept, or how individuals construe themselves. In research on the self-concept, the construct of self-schemata was introduced by psychologist Hazel Markus (1977). Self-schemata are cognitive representations of the self that have implications for information processing and self-regulation.

Schema are blocks of knowledge that help individuals categorize, organize, and process information. Markus built on this idea by suggesting that individuals possess schemas about themselves. These blocks of self-knowledge were coined *self-schemata*, or *self-schema*. Self-schemata correspond to characteristics or traits that individuals might use to describe themselves. They may also correspond to the social roles individuals would describe themselves as possessing. Taken together, self-schemata describe an individual's self-concept.

Markus and Paula Nurius (1986) expanded on the idea of self-schemata from the present to the future. These possible selves, or representations of who individuals might become in the future, are considered to be an extension of the self-concept. Future self-schemata may be positive (hoped-for selves) or negative (feared selves). Possible selves provide an evaluative context for current behavior. Additionally, they provide motivational directions for behaviors in the future by clarifying specific desired or undesired end states.

A frequent method of measuring self-schemata is to record the response speed of individuals as they respond to characteristics presented on a computer screen. Individuals are asked to hit buttons that correspond to the phrases "me" or "not me." The more quickly an individual is able to respond to an idea, whether the response is positive or negative, the more schematic that individual is in that domain. An alternative way of measuring schematicity is to have individuals list characteristics they view as relevant to their self-concept. The former methodology has the advantage of reducing the influence of social desirability.

John Kihlstrom and colleagues (1988) show that individuals who are schematic are more likely to notice information relevant to that schema and more likely to perceive their own and others' behavior as relating to that schema. Further research by Ann Ruvolo and Markus (1992) shows that both self-schemata and possible selves are associated with increased memory. This research is consistent with the self-referent effect, the tendency of individuals to more easily remember information that is relevant to themselves. The explanation for these effects is that schema relating to the self are highly accessible.

Research on possible selves suggests that future-oriented self-schemata are related to self-regulation. When possible-self standards are salient for individuals, they are more likely to behave in ways that help them approach hoped-for selves and avoid feared selves. Markus and Daphna Oyserman (1990) extended possible-selves theory by showing that self-regulation is most successful for individuals who possess both a salient hoped-for and salient feared self in the same domain.

SEE ALSO *Schemas; Self-Concept; Self-Discrepancy Theory; Self-Monitoring*

BIBLIOGRAPHY

Kihlstrom, John. F., et al. 1988. Information Processing and the Study of the Self. In *Social Psychological Studies of the Self: Perspectives and Programs.* Vol. 21 of *Advances in Experimental Social Psychology*, ed. Leonard A. Berkowitz, 145–178. San Diego, CA: Academic Press, 1988.

Markus, Hazel. 1977. Self-schemata and Processing Information about the Self. *Journal of Personality and Social Psychology* 35: 63–78.

Markus, Hazel, and Paula Nurius. 1986. Possible Selves. *American Psychologist* 41: 954–969.

Oyserman, Daphna, and Hazel Markus. 1990. Possible Selves in Balance: Implications for Delinquency. *Journal of Social Issues* 46: 141–157.

Ruvolo, Ann P., and Hazel Markus. 1992. Possible Selves and Performance: The Power of Self-relevant Imagery. *Social Cognition* 10: 95–124.

Michelle Sherrill

SELF-SERVING BIAS

A self-serving bias is any cognitive or perceptual process that is distorted by the need to maintain and enhance self-esteem. When individuals reject the validity of negative feedback, focus on their strengths and achievements but overlook their faults and failures, or take more responsibility for their group's work than they give to other members, they are protecting the ego from threat and injury. These cognitive and perceptual tendencies perpetuate illusions and error, but they also serve the self's need for esteem.

Self-serving biases are particularly evident when individuals formulate attributions about the causes of personal actions, events, and outcomes. When explaining positive actions and experiences, their attributions emphasize the causal impact of internal, dispositional causes, but when identifying the causes of negative events, they stress external, situational factors. The boy who believes his skillful play earned him his victory, the employee who blames her troubles at work on the boss rather than herself, the student who attributes a poor grade to bad luck or the difficulty of the test, and the A student who traces the grade back to hard work and innate ability are all displaying this self-serving attributional bias. Because failure undermines self-confidence and self-worth, individuals seek an external factor that can be blamed for the failure. When they succeed, however, they can bolster their self-esteem by attributing this positive outcome to personal factors (Weiner 1985).

Some people are less susceptible to this bias than are others. Individuals who are depressed or who suffer from chronically low self-esteem tend to take the blame for their failures but deny responsibility for their successes. People

in many non-Western cultures also frequently attribute outcomes that lead to negative consequences to themselves rather than external factors. Individuals with an external locus of control consider both positive and negative outcomes to be caused by factors beyond their control, and those with an internal locus of control assume that they, personally, are responsible for their outcomes (Rotter 1966). Overall, however, the tendency to externalize failure and internalize success occurs in a wide range of educational, athletic, and interpersonal situations. Researchers have also isolated the effects of performance feedback on attributions experimentally by giving research participants false positive or negative feedback about their work on a laboratory task. Invariably, those told they failed attribute performance to such external factors as bad luck, task difficulty, or the interference of others, and those told they succeeded point to the causal significance of such internal factors as ability and effort.

Researchers now recognize that a number of cognitive, motivational, and psychological factors combine to create the tendency to internalize success and externalize failure. As Dale T. Miller and Michael Ross (1975) suggest, individuals internalize success and externalize failure because they are usually optimistic when predicting their outcomes and experiences. They expect to pass tests, get good jobs, and have long-lasting relationships rather than fail, get fired, or divorce. Because negative experiences are unexpected, people tend to attribute them to external factors rather than stable, personal ones. Miller and Ross thus conclude that these biases do not always "serve the self," but are in some cases produced by "cold," cognitive processes as well as "hot" motivations and needs.

SEE ALSO *Attribution; Self-Enhancement; Self-Esteem*

BIBLIOGRAPHY

Miller, Dale T., and Michael Ross. 1975. Self-Serving Biases in the Attribution of Causality: Fact or Fiction? *Psychological Bulletin* 82 (2): 213–225.

Rotter, Julian B. 1966. Generalized Expectancies for Internal Versus External Control of Reinforcement. *Psychological Monographs* 80: 1-28.

Weiner, Bernard. 1985. An Attributional Theory of Achievement Motivation and Emotion. *Psychological Review* 92 (4): 548–573.

Donelson R. Forsyth

SELF-SYSTEM

Social scientists have long been concerned with describing the structure and functions of the human self—the constellation of self-referent thoughts, feelings, and motives that constitute the individual's experience of himself or herself in relation to the world. These descriptions range from intrapsychic to cultural in focus, and the accounts of structure and functions range from those that portray the self as a stable, monolithic entity, to those that outline a complex, dynamic system of interrelated elements and processes. These latter accounts typically refer to the self as the *self-system*.

System-oriented accounts of the self comprise two features: (1) They specify a set of self-aspects—constituents of a differentiated but unified whole; and (2) they posit mechanisms that give rise to the different self-aspects, the interplay between them, and the interplay between the self-system and the experienced world. System accounts often trace their origin to the work of philosopher/psychologist William James (1842–1910), who, in his oft-quoted *Principles of Psychology* (1890), first described the self as a differentiated entity. James specified two dimensions of differentiation. One is distinctly social, describing self-aspects as internalized representations of the self in relation to significant others. The other dimension positions these representations in the social self, which, along with the material self and the spiritual self, constitute the full self-system.

Although many models of the self-system draw on James's description, it does not fully describe the self in system terms because it does not posit mechanisms by which the social, material, and spiritual selves arise, and it does not offer a systematic account of the interplay between these self-aspects or between the self-system and the experienced world. In perhaps the earliest fully drawn model of the self-system, Harry Stack Sullivan (1892–1949), in *The Interpersonal Theory of Psychiatry* (1953), outlined the interpersonal processes that give rise to the self-system. The *good-me* arises from positive interactions between the infant and caregiver. The *bad-me* arises from interactions with the caregiver that engender anxiety. Finally, the *not-me* encompasses interpersonal aspects of the self-system that are nonconscious—the "private mode of living." These self-aspects are a joint product of interpersonal reward and anxiety that, in the mentally healthy individual, function cooperatively to promote security and guard against anxiety in interpersonal relations.

The cognitive revolution of the 1960s provided social scientists with the conceptual and methodological tools for developing and studying models that proffer more detailed accounts of the structure of the self-system and richer accounts of processes that operate within the self-system and between the self-system and the environment. In terms of structure, these models generally view the self-system as a highly organized network of knowledge structures that are either activated directly through self-directed attention or by stimuli in the environment or indirectly as a result of their association with other knowledge structures that have been activated. Once activated, these constituents of self-knowledge influence attention, perception, emotion, and behavior, typically, in a manner that ensures the stability and continuity of the self-system across situations and over time.

SEE ALSO *Cognition; Emotion; James, William; Psychoanalytic Theory; Psychology*

BIBLIOGRAPHY

Hoyle, Rick H., Michael H. Kernis, Mark R. Leary, and Mark W. Baldwin. 1999. *Selfhood: Identity, Esteem, Regulation.* Boulder, CO: Westview.

Sullivan, Harry S. 1953. *The Interpersonal Theory of Psychiatry,* eds. Helen Swick Perry and Mary Ladd Gawel. New York: Norton.

Rick H. Hoyle

SELF-VERIFICATION

Self-verification theory proposes that people want others to see them as they see themselves. For example, those who see themselves as relatively dominant want others to see them as dominant, and those who see themselves as relatively submissive want others to recognize them as submissive. The theory was developed by William B. Swann Jr. (1983). Drawing on earlier theorizing, he assumed that people form self-views so that they can predict the responses of others and know how to act toward them. Thus, for example, those who see themselves as intelligent expect that others will notice their insightfulness and so are inclined to pursue activities that require intelligence. Because self-views play a critical role in making sense of their experiences and guiding their actions, people become invested in maintaining them by obtaining self-confirming information.

Among persons with positive self-views, the desire for self-verification complements another important motive, the desire for self-enhancing or positive evaluations. For example, those who view themselves as "organized" find that their desires for both self-verification and self-enhancement compel them to seek feedback that confirms their positive, "organized" self-view. People with negative self-views, however, find that the two motives conflict: Although the desire for self-verification compels such persons to seek negative evaluations, the desire for self-enhancement compels them to seek positive evaluations. Self-verification theory points to the conditions under which people with negative self-views resolve this conflict by seeking self-verification rather than self-enhancement.

Considerable evidence supports self-verification theory (Swann 1996). In one study, researchers asked participants with positive and negative self-views whether they would prefer to interact with evaluators who had favorable or unfavorable impressions of them. Those with positive self-views preferred favorable partners, but contrary to self-enhancement theory, those with negative self-views preferred unfavorable partners.

Many replications of this effect using diverse methodologies have confirmed that people prefer self-verifying evaluations and interaction partners. For example, not only do self-verification strivings influence the relationships people enter initially, they also influence whether or not people remain in certain relationships. Research on married couples, college roommates, and dating partners show that people gravitate toward partners who provide verification and drift away from those who do not—even if this means withdrawing from positive partners. And even if people wind up with partners who do not see them in a self-verifying manner, they may correct the situation by changing their partners' minds. College students who were mildly depressed, for instance, were especially likely to solicit negative evaluations from their roommates, and such activities made their roommates more inclined to derogate and reject them at the semester's end. And even if people should somehow fail to elicit self-confirming evaluations, information-processing biases in attention, memory, and interpretation may make their social works appear to be more confirming than they actually are, thus stabilizing their self-views.

Self-verification strivings are adaptive for most people because most people have positive self-views, and self-verification processes enable them to preserve these positive self-views. Also, within small groups, verification of negative as well as positive self-views may also facilitate commitment and performance. Yet for people with negative self-views, self-verification strivings may have undesirable consequences, causing them to gravitate toward partners who undermine their feelings of self-worth.

The major criticism of self-verification theory has been that, relative to self-enhancement, it is a rare phenomenon that is restricted to people with terribly negative self-views. As evidence, critics cite hundreds of studies indicating that people prefer, seek, and value positive evaluations more than negative ones. Such critiques overlook two important things. First, because most people have relatively positive self-views, the fact that they display a preference for positive evaluations may reflect a preference for evaluations that are self-verifying (as well as self-enhancing). Second, self-verification strivings are not limited to people with globally negative self-views; even people with

high self-esteem seek negative evaluations about their flaws, and even people with moderately positive self-views withdraw from spouses who evaluate them in an exceptionally positive manner.

BIBLIOGRAPHY

Swann, William B., Jr. 1983. Self-Verification: Bringing Social Reality into Harmony with the Self. In *Social Psychological Perspectives on the Self*. Vol. 2, eds. Jerry Suls and Anthony G. Greenwald, 33–66. Hillsdale, NJ: Erlbaum.

Swann, William B., Jr. 1987. Identity Negotiation: Where Two Roads Meet. *Journal of Personality and Social Psychology* 53: 1038–1051.

Swann, William B., Jr. 1996. *Self-Traps: The Elusive Quest for Higher Self-Esteem*. New York: Freeman.

Swann, William B., Jr., Chris De La Ronde, and J. Gregory Hixon. 1994. Authenticity and Positivity Strivings in Marriage and Courtship. *Journal of Personality and Social Psychology* 66: 857–869.

William B. Swann Jr.

SELIGMAN, MARTIN
1942–

Born in 1942 Martin E. P. Seligman is a noted psychologist whose contributions to psychological science include a better understanding of depression and the stimulation of interest in the positive aspects of personal growth and development. He earned his bachelor's degree summa cum laude in philosophy at Princeton University in 1964 and his doctor of philosophy in experimental psychology at the University of Pennsylvania in 1967.

In his early work Seligman focused on animal models of learned helplessness. Among his discoveries he found that when dogs were subjected to inescapable shocks, they later failed to attempt escape or to avoid such shocks, at least temporarily. His research also demonstrated that the learned helplessness could be reduced with appropriate training. According to Seligman and his fellow researchers, the animals had learned that their attempts at escape behaviors were not rewarded, so those attempts were extinguished.

Subsequently psychologists extended his work with the animal model to include discussion of such behavior in people. Psychologists addressed the question of why people sometimes fail to escape from untenable situations when escape is possible. As psychology, as a discipline, moved from behavioral to cognitive explanations of behavior, researchers focused less on reinforcement contingencies and more on thought processes, such as the expectation with learned helplessness that one could not control one's environment, so action would be futile.

Subsequent to his investigation of learned helplessness and its connections to depression, Seligman began focusing on coping and adaptation, developing the emerging field called positive psychology. This approach has at its heart the idea that people are motivated to thrive; it concerns itself with healthful approaches to life by individuals and by institutions. Positive psychology focuses on understanding (1) positive emotions like contentment with the past and hope for the future; (2) positive individual traits like the capacity for work and love, curiosity, integrity, and self-control; and (3) positive institutions that foster the creation of justice, civility, and tolerance (Positive Psychology Center 2007).

To promote positive psychology Seligman created the Positive Psychology Center at the University of Pennsylvania. The center is designed to promote research and dissemination of positive psychology. The domain has generated research programs and innovative ideas; at the same time, another of Seligman's goals is to foster societal action that promotes psychological growth within communities. The combination of theoretical, empirical, and applied ideas led in 2006 to the creation of the *Journal of Positive Psychology*.

Seligman has written many books including *Biological Boundaries of Learning* (1972), *Learned Optimism* (1991), *The Optimistic Child* (1996), *Authentic Happiness: Using the New Positive Psychology to Realize Your Potential for Lasting Fulfillment* (2002), and *Character Strengths and Virtues: A Handbook and Classification* (2004). Many of his books have been translated into multiple languages.

Seligman has been recognized for his contributions in numerous ways. In 1998 he was elected the president of the American Psychological Association (APA), the largest organization of psychologists in the world. Prior to that he served as president of Division 12 (Clinical Psychology) of the APA. In addition he has been elected fellow of seven APA divisions: General Psychology, Experimental Psychology, Behavioral Neuroscience and Comparative Psychology, Society of Clinical Psychology, Adult Development and Aging, Health Psychology, and International Psychology. Seligman is also a fellow of the Association for Psychological Science, the Behaviour Research and Therapy Society, and the Pennsylvania Psychological Association.

He has received fellow status in nonpsychological organizations as well, including the American Association for the Advancement of Science and the Society of Behavioral Medicine. He has garnered honorary doctorates from Uppsala University in Sweden, Massachusetts College of Professional Psychology, and Complutense University in Madrid.

SEE ALSO *American Psychological Association; Behaviorism; Learned Helplessness; Positive Psychology; Psychology; Reinforcement Theories*

BIBLIOGRAPHY

Positive Psychology Center. 2007. http://www.ppc.sas.upenn.edu/.

Seligman, Martin E. P. 1975. *Helplessness: On Depression, Development, and Death*. San Francisco: W. H. Freeman.

Seligman, Martin E. P. 1991. *Learned Optimism*. New York: Knopf.

Seligman, Martin E. P. 1994. *What You Can Change and What You Can't: The Complete Guide to Successful Self-Improvement: Learning to Accept Who You Are*. New York: Knopf.

Seligman, Martin E. P. 2002. *Authentic Happiness: Using the New Positive Psychology to Realize Your Potential for Lasting Fulfillment*. New York: Free Press.

Bernard C. Beins

SELLING LONG AND SELLING SHORT

In the field of finance selling long (or going long) on a security or an investment means that an investor buys that security or investment with the prospect of keeping it for some time because he or she believes that its price (or value) is going to increase in the long run. This investment action is called a long position in that particular security or investment.

The opposite practice is known as selling short or short selling a security or an investment. An investor who gets involved in short selling believes that the price of the underlying security is going to decrease in the near future. Hence, that investor borrows shares of the security he or she anticipates will have a price decrease and then sells those shares at the current market price, expecting to pay back the loan in stocks when the price of the security drops. This way the investor makes a profit by selling high and buying low, but he or she sells first and buys later. Thus, because the investor does not own the underlying security but only borrows and sells it, it is considered that that investor is in a short position regarding that particular security. Of course, a high risk is involved in such investment actions because the price of the security or investment in which someone has a short position could rise instead of fall, and then the investor has to pay more and loses money instead of gaining as he or she anticipated.

In general, an investor will go long or have a long position in a security or an investment when that investor expects the price to rise and will have a short position when he or she expects the price to drop. However, short selling is not allowed in all countries. The term *short* is used because it indicates an inadequacy, and in finance it is applied to situations in which investors sell securities that they do not own. Therefore, such a sale is called short sale because it creates an inadequacy, a negative position, in the sold security. In a portfolio the percentage that shows the portion of the security that is in a short position is negative. The securities in which a long position is held have positive percentages in portfolio weights. The sum of the portion of each security that makes up a portfolio is always equal to one despite any long or short positions in the participating securities.

SHORT SELLING IN THE UNITED STATES

In the United States the process of short selling proceeds as follows:

1. An investor interested in short selling borrows shares of a security from a brokerage firm. However, in the United States there is a rule that the investor has to deposit cash in his or her brokerage firm amounting to 50 percent of the value of the borrowed shares (this is called a margin).

2. The investor then sells the borrowed shares and credits the proceeds from the sale at his or her cash account in the brokerage firm.

3. At a specified time agreed on with the brokerage firm the investor must close the position by buying back the shares from the market.

4. The investor must return the shares to the broker (lender) as was agreed. If the price of the underlying shares increases, the investor suffers a loss. If that price decreases as expected, the investor makes a profit.

Furthermore, by law since 2005 regulated broker-dealers in the United States do not allow their customers to short sell securities if the customers have not arranged for a broker-dealer to confirm that the brokerage firm is able to deliver the underlying securities. This process is called locating. The brokerage firms can borrow shares in many ways, facilitating locates and delivering the short-selling securities. U.S. brokers can borrow stocks from leading custody banks such as JP Morgan Chase (New York), Citibank (New York), Mellon Bank Corp. (Pittsburgh), the Bank of New York (New York), the Northern Trust Company (Chicago), State Street Corporation (Boston), Robeco (Netherlands), UBS

(Zurich), fund management companies, and even their customers who have long positions in those stocks.

In the United States, to avoid a high amount of loss, short sellers can place a stop loss order with the brokerage firm after selling a stock short. Then the broker has to cover the position if the price of the underlying stock increases to a certain level, limiting the loss to the customer.

A short-selling investor has to pay a fee at the brokerage company that facilitates that investor's short-selling activities. Usually this is a standard commission fee, as with buying a security.

If the price of the shares in a short position rises instead of falling, the broker will deduct money from the investor's cash account and transfer it to the investor's margin account. If the price continues to increase and there are not enough funds in the investor's cash account to cover the investor's position, the investor will have to borrow on margin and will begin to accrue margin interest charges. Furthermore, if the stock on a short position pays dividends and the dividend date passes while the investor is short on the stock, the dividend will be deducted from the investor's account.

THE BENEFITS AND HISTORY OF SHORT SELLING

According to Jones and Lamont (2001), short selling makes an important contribution to the efficiency of the stock market. There are limits to arbitrage. Specifically, some stocks can become overpriced. A group of investors may realize this and adopt a short position in those overpriced stocks. When the stocks are sold in the market, their prices are driven downward (high supply, low prices), and eventually they reach an equilibrium price level.

Historically, short-selling practices were reported in the seventeenth century during the scandal that arose after the violent fall of the Dutch tulip market. In the eighteenth century England banned short selling. In the nineteenth century the term *short* was used in the United States. In the early twentieth century the short-selling activities of traders were blamed for the Wall Street crash of 1929. After that time severe regulations on short selling were implemented in 1929, 1938, and 1940. Legislated rules that banned mutual funds from engaging in such activities were lifted in 1997. In 2005 the Securities and Exchange Commission established locate and close-out requirements for brokerage firms.

SEE ALSO *Arbitrage and Arbitrageurs; Banking; Efficient Market Hypothesis; Financial Instability Hypothesis; Financial Markets; Great Depression; Great Tulip Mania, The; Interest Rates; Interest, Own Rate of; Returns; Speculation; Spot Market; Stock Exchanges*

BIBLIOGRAPHY

Aitken, Michael J., Alex Frino, Michael S. McCorry, and Peter L. Swan. 1998. Short Sales Are Almost Instantaneously Bad News: Evidence from the Australian Stock Exchange. *Journal of Finance* 53: 2205–2223.

D'Avolio, Gene. 2001. *The Market for Borrowing Stock.* Harvard University Working Paper. Boston, MA: Harvard University, Graduate School of Business Administration.

Dechow, Patricia M., Amy P. Hutton, Lisa Meulbroek, and Richard G. Sloan. 2001. Short-Sellers, Fundamental Analysis and Stock Returns. *Journal of Financial Economics* 32: 125–158.

Diamond, Douglas W., and Robert E. Verrecchia. 1987. Constraints on Short-Selling and Asset Price Adjustment to Private Information. *Journal of Financial Economics* 18: 227–311.

Fabozzi, Frank J. 2004. *Short Selling: Strategies, Risks, and Rewards.* Hoboken, NJ: Wiley.

Jones, C. M., and O. A. Lamont. 2001. Short Sale Constraints and Stock Returns. *Journal of Financial Economics* 67: 207–239.

Whitney, Richard, and William R. Perkins. 1932. *Short Selling.* New York and London: D. Appleton.

Katerina Lyroudi

SELLOUTS

The label *sellout* has referents in cultural, social, political, and economic communities. In idiomatic use, sellouts are people affiliated with a person or group (who typically have subordinate social status) who are perceived to have betrayed that person or group, their interests, and/or an ideology or cause. To sell out is to betray a group and/or cause.

Sellouts are often accused of betraying groups to which they had belonged previously, and which have a subordinate status to the group in power. These groups might be family, kin, or friendship-based groups, or larger, socially constructed or imagined communities based on nationality, race, gender, sexual orientation, or class. Or the groups might be collectives, such as musicians of a marginalized style of music, environmentalists, members of business conglomerates, or international business partnerships seeking to maximize national profits in a competitive global economy.

These groups often have a specific ideological orientation that requires solidarity or a cause, and sellouts are said to be traitors to the cause. The sellout's attempt to benefit himself socially, culturally, politically, or economically has negative implications for the subordinate group and a positive effect for the group in power—often referred to as the mainstream.

In their work on the economics of identity, William Darity, Patrick Mason, and James Stewart (2006) imply that there is an underlying relationship of domination and subordination between groups (in their work, racial groups) that leads to conflicts and the creation of alternative social norms. Darity et al. contend that the incentives for conflict relate to inequalities in material resources persistent in a society such as the United States with a racialized economic equilibrium that favors whites over other racial groups. This results in racialized individuals and racialized groups pursuing either a racialist or an individualist identity strategy.

A racialist identity strategy permits access to intragroup altruism while identifying individuals for othergroup antagonism—that is, minorities versus whites and vice versa. People working under this system have strong loyalties to their racial group and the causes of the collective membership, especially members of the oppressed racial group. Thus, sellouts are individuals from the subordinate group who reject the racialist identity strategy in favor of an individualist strategy, opting for alternative social norms for personal gain rather than for the norms and practices of racialist altruism. The sellout's actions often hinder the collective racial advancement toward the group cause.

In Latina/o communities in the United States, *Vendido/a* ("sellout"), *Tío Taco* ("Uncle Taco"), and "coconut" ("brown on the outside and white on the inside") are often used as derogatory labels for sellouts who betray their loyalties to the Latina/o group or their cause against white domination. Similarly, in Asian American communities a "banana" is a person who is said to be "yellow on the outside and white on the inside," and in American Indian communities, an "apple" is "red on the outside and white on the inside." The most articulate definition of the concept and label in the African American community is documented by Geneva Smitherman, who defines a sellout as "an African American who isn't DOWN WITH the Black cause, one who betrays the race and compromises the COMMUNITY'S principles, usually for personal gain.... By extension, anyone who GOES FOR SELF and abandons his or her group's collective mission" (Smitherman 2000, p. 200). Other referents to sellouts in the African American community include "passing" (for white) and the labels "Oreo" (the cookie, "black on the outside and white on the inside") and "Uncle Tom" (from the 1851–1852 Harriet Beecher Stowe novel *Uncle Tom's Cabin*). Studies on this topic in the field of education were originally framed under the concept of "acting white" (Fordham and Ogbu, 1986).

Assimilation and acculturation are forms of selling out on a large scale through dissociating from the cultural, gender, class, racial, or sexual orientation norms and practices of subordinate group membership.

Besides gaining access to resources denied the subordinate group, sellouts may have a more altruistic motivation, such as a desire to work within the system for change; nevertheless, they may be accused of selling out. Others may be motivated to sell out for personal security—that is, to avoid physical and or ideological persecution by the oppressing group. Sometimes sellouts are co-opted by the dominant group to promote their agenda, then "disposed of" without receiving the expected benefits. Or they may feel guilty for abandoning their original (subordinate) group and never achieve full acceptance by the dominant group.

Luis Urrieta Jr.'s work with Chicana/o activist educators (2005) highlights the complexity of the issue of selling out, illustrating that there is more of a gray area than the "either/or" dichotomy allows. The tipping point of when people are in danger of becoming sellouts is rather arbitrary, and selling out is idiomatically understood differently in various communities, thus eluding a standardized definition.

SEE ALSO *Acting White*

BIBLIOGRAPHY

Darity, William A., Jr., Patrick L. Mason, and James B. Stewart. 2006. The Economics of Identity: The Origin and Persistence of Racial Identity Norms. *Journal of Economic Behavior and Organization* 60 (3): 283–305.

Fordham, Signithia, and John Ogbu. 1986. Black Students' School Success: Coping with the Burden of "Acting White." *Urban Review* 18 (3): 176–206.

Smitherman, Geneva. 2000. *Black Talk: Words and Phrases from the Hood to the Amen Corner*. New York: Houghton Mifflin.

Urrieta, Luis, Jr. 2005. "Playing the Game" versus "Selling Out": Chicanas' and Chicanos' Relationship to Whitestream Schools. In *Performance Theories in Education: Power, Pedagogy, and the Politics of Identity*, ed. Bryant K. Alexander, Gary Anderson, and Bernardo B. Gallegos, 173–196. Mahwah, NJ: Lawrence Erlbaum.

Luis Urrieta Jr.

SEMANTIC MEMORY

In 1972 the cognitive scientist Endel Tulving (b. 1927) argued that conscious recollection (i.e., declarative memory) is composed of two separate memory domains, each having distinct functionality, knowledge access, and neurological localization. Whereas *episodic memory* involves our conscious recall of past events within some specific context, *semantic memory* involves our recall of factual knowledge that is not context-dependent.

Psychologists have assessed semantic memory through a large array of tests. For example, in recalling a previously studied list of words, participants often recall groups of words in sequence (i.e., cluster) on the basis of thematic or taxonomic relations, even though the words were ordered randomly at presentation. Measures of the time required to make various forms of judgments also reflect semantic memory structure. Variation in the time required to name visually presented words, or to discriminate words from nonwords (lexical decision), reflects access to semantic information about words. Similarly, the time required to make category judgments, such as whether a robin is a bird, can be used to infer some properties of semantic memory structure.

Analyses of lexical access and category judgment tasks have led to the development of network models, which describe how the components of semantic information (e.g., concepts) are organized within semantic memory. In a hierarchical network model, for example, access to each lower-level item depends on the higher-order category (e.g., robin–bird). In contrast, other models propose that semantic memory is not organized hierarchically, though information is related to varying degrees. In these latter models, memory retrieval occurs in parallel, as a result of the activation of related information within the network. Recently, connectionist models have furthered this notion and have depicted semantic memory networks as highly distributed yet unitary systems whose multiple elements work largely in parallel.

The network and connectionist models are based on accounts of behavioral data and mathematical simulation. The question of how semantic and episodic memory abilities are represented in the brain is currently controversial. Studies of neurological patients suggest that damage to medial temporal regions of the brain can impair episodic memory while leaving semantic memory largely intact. Neuroimaging studies of healthy individuals also indicate some degree of differentiation in the pattern of brain activation occurring during episodic and semantic memory tasks, but there is also a substantial degree of overlap. Though details vary according to task demands, neuroimaging research suggests that left prefrontal regions, medial temporal regions, ventral visual processing areas, the hippocampal formation, and parts of parietal cortex can all play a role in semantic memory processing. Accessing semantic information, however, can also be a form of episodic encoding. That is, the best way to prepare for a later episodic test is to encode the meaning of the information to be remembered (as opposed to its physical structure). Typically, the left prefrontal region of the brain is implicated in both semantic retrieval and episodic encoding, and the right prefrontal region is implicated in episodic memory retrieval. This complex network of cortical involvement reflects the growing recognition among researchers that semantic memory comprises several component processes.

SEE ALSO *Neuroeconomics*

BIBLIOGRAPHY

Chang, Tien Ming. 1986. Semantic Memory: Facts and Models. *Psychological Bulletin* 99 (2): 199–220.

Martin, Alex, and Linda L. Chao. 2001. Semantic Memory and the Brain: Structure and Processes. *Current Opinion in Neurobiology* 11 (2): 194–201.

Matthew C. Costello
David J. Madden

SEMINOLES

SEE *Osceola.*

SEMIOTICS

Toward the end of the seventeenth century John Locke (1632–1704) partly hoped for, partly prophesied, and partly proposed a new field of inquiry called "semeiotike." That "doctrine of signs," which he characterized as "aptly enough also, logic," invites the reader to "consider the nature of signs, the mind makes use of for the understanding of things, or conveying knowledge to others" (Locke [1690] 1996, p. 337). Locke's proposal was neglected until the American logician-philosopher-mathematician Charles Sanders Peirce (1839–1914) picked up its charge in his writings from1866 until his death in 1914. In keeping with what he considered the "ethics of terminology," Peirce named this effort, which he describes as "the doctrine of the essential nature and fundamental varieties of" possible sign-activity, *semeiotic* (emphasizing the diphthong *ei* in *semeion* [sign] in its spelling to indicate the word's Greek origin), though he sometimes used the term *semiotic.*

Independently of Peirce and Locke, the Swiss linguist Ferdinand de Saussure (1857–1913) determined to study the "life of signs in social life" and named his "new" science *semiology.* In contrast to Peirce's writings, his lecture notes, which were compiled and published posthumously in 1966 by his students as *Cours de Linguistic Générale,* caught the attention of several leading linguists and "signophiles" soon after his death.

NOMENCLATURE

In addition to *semiology, semeiotic,* and *semiotic,* there were also available the labels, *semiotics, significs,* and *signology.* However, the struggle for recognition was between *semiology* and *semiotics,* and *semiotics* won the day. Apart from the deliberated extension of their inquiries into extralinguistic sign systems and their choice of a label to describe their work, most self-styled semioticians were semiologists by another name and the *Cours* remained their foundational text. Among the rest, *semeiotic* and *semiotic* were to become associated with those whose research followed more or less Peircean lines. Nevertheless, there have been considerable crossovers in the use of labels and some mixing up of theoretical orientations as well. Many Peirceans use *semiotics* and non-Peirceans use *semiotic,* though the latter employ it mostly as an adjective rather than as a noun in their writings. *Semeiotic* is never used by Saussurians, and Peirceans who use that term do so to mark the difference of their approach to the sign from that of the Saussurians.

SAUSSURE AND SEMIOLOGY

A linguistic sign as defined by Saussure is a two-sided phenomenon, a relationship that links an acoustic image and a concept, or a signifier and a signified. The link is not between a thing and its name but between a sound pattern and a concept. That relationship is internal to language, internal to the mind, and independent of external reality. Therefore, a linguistic sign does not "stand for" an external world but construes it. Thus, a tree that is signified by the word *tree* is not an actual tree but the concept "tree." Similarly, a signifier does not stand for the signified but instead construes it. The signifier and the signified are "functives" that are copresent or co-occurrent, although on different strata, with the first being more abstract than the second. In their respective strata they "exist" in a context of other signifiers and signifieds, respectively. Each is held together with and held apart from the other signifieds and signifiers in their respective strata by similarities and differences; that is what makes them part of a system or structure.

Which signifier pairs with which signified is determined by convention; it is arbitrary from an empirical point of view. The external world is brought into a relationship with the internal structure by the projection of the internal structure on the external world. That logocentric view overly simplifies a being's living-in-the-world and its engagement with that world to the point of solipsism. The semiologically structured internal relationship of the signifier to the signified analogically structures, organizes, and orients sign users to the flux of percepts they receive from the external world. This is a nominalistic view of both language and the world.

There are many reasons why the semiological model of the sign—dyadic, nonmaterial and confined to a hermetically sealed system called language—came to assume paradigmatic power over semiotics generally. The foremost reason is structural: Only human beings have culture. Not all the features that constitute culture are uniquely human, but language is. What makes human language unique is *la langue*. The linguistic sign is the defining element of *la langue*. The defining feature of the linguistic sign is its binary structure, in which the elements of the dyad are held together by a relationship that is arbitrary or conventional (as opposed to natural). From this it is hypothesized that even though the uniquely human institution called culture is not identical to language, because its only assuredly human feature is language, the elementary form of culture must be structured along the lines of the elementary form of language: the linguistic or semiological sign.

PEIRCE AND SEMEIOTIC

One can find as many as eighty-eight definitions of the sign in Peirce's published and unpublished writings. Peirce defined and adjusted the definition of the sign to a range of contexts, a short list of which includes mathematics, logic, philosophy, pendulum experiments, chemistry, psychology, language, history, realism-nominalism debates, scholasticism, metaphysics, theories of mind, and discussions of truth. He often bent his definitions for the benefit of his interlocutors and correspondents' comprehension.

Peirce had a pansemeiosic view of the world. The sign easily transgressed such dichotomies as mind-body, nature-culture, human-animal, internal-external, and matter-spirit. For Peirce the universe is "perfused with signs." He considered thought as semeiosic sign activity but "not necessarily connected with a brain. It appears in the work of bees, of crystals, and throughout the purely physical world." He claimed that "not only is thought in the organic world, but it develops there," granting that "signs must have a Quasi-mind." His belief that "there can be no isolated sign" was frustrated by demands for a definition of the sign, for he considered a sign only as part of a semeiotic process (Peirce 1934, vol. 4, para. 551; vol. 5, para. 448).

Peirce held that even "a person is not absolutely an individual" but a state of consciousness. Every state of consciousness was an inference for Peirce, and therefore life itself was a sequence of inferences or a train of thought. "At any instant then man is a thought." Moreover, if consciousness is taken to mean thought, he reminds the reader that thought "is more without us than within. It is we that are in it, rather than it in any of us." Here Peirce anticipates Michel Foucault's idea of episteme and discourse as well as his critique of the overrating of

"agency" by modern individualism. Man's "thoughts are what he is 'saying to himself,' that is, saying to the other self that is just coming into life in the flow of time. When one reasons, it is that critical self that one is trying to persuade." Human "thought," he opined, was a sign, "mostly of the nature of language." Given that language is by and large constituted of symbols, and that "at any instant ... man is a thought, and ... thought is a species of symbol, the general answer to the question what is man? is that he is a symbol" (Peirce 1934, vol. 5, para. 421; 1958, vol. 7, para 583; 1958, vol. 8, para. 256).

DIFFERENCES BETWEEN SAUSSURE AND PEIRCE

There are many differences between Saussure's and Peirce's concepts of the sign. The Saussurian sign is dyadic, originating in linguistics, whereas the semeiosic sign is irreducibly triadic and based on logic. Also, logic as semeiotic is a normative or formal science, in contrast to the empirical sciences such as linguistics and psychology, which Peirce classified as special sciences. As a formal science, semeiotic is concerned with the necessary conditions for what makes something a sign as such, the bases on which to determine its truth, and the conditions that are required for the communication and growth of signs.

Peirce derived the proof for the sign's triadicity from logic, mathematics, and phenomenology. With a certain amount of familiarity with a number of his scattered definitions of the semeiosic sign, one can begin to appreciate the complexity of the sign and the work it does. In the triadic sign, the first thing to know is that the first correlate of the triad is the sign (at times called the representamen), the second correlate is the object, and the third is the interpretant. Thus, the semeiosic *Sign* (uppercase) is constituted by an irreducible triadic correlation in which a *sign* (lowercase) stands for an *object* to an *interpretant*. The sign as the conveyer of meaning mediates between the object and the interpretant; the interpretant mediates between the sign and the object to interpret the meaning; the object mediates between the interpretant and the sign to ground the meaning. If any one of the three correlates is removed, the Sign as such will not be an actual Sign but merely a potential Sign.

Despite his numerous attempts to fix the sign in a definition, Peirce's fundamental conception of semeiotic was the process of "sign-ing" or semiosy rather than the sign per se. This is evident in the following definition: "The *sign* is anything which determines something else (its *interpretant*) to refer to an object to which itself refers (its *object*) in the same way, the *interpretant* becoming a *sign* in turn, and so on *ad infinitum*" (Peirce 1934, vol. 2, para. 303). When defined in this way, the sign brings out the open and dynamic nature of sign activity or semiosy.

Semiosy is the very life of the sign. When semiosy ceases, the sign either dies or goes into hibernation until an interpretant-sign predisposed to receiving its representation of the object arrives. Thus, a potsherd from an antique goblet would "hibernate" until a knowledgeable archaeologist found it, realized it, and represented it as a sign of an antique goblet to a student. The student would, as the next interpretant-sign along the chain of revivified semeiosis who was fit to receive (by training) the representation, then translate and communicate the meaning of the represented object to yet another interpretant-sign (that student's own students, say) even as the professor's representation of the potsherd as representing the original goblet was communicated to the original student. And then the represented object will be represented to someone else, that is, yet another interpretant, ad infinitum. The very structure of the semeiotic sign establishes it as fundamentally and minimally dialogic.

At the most abstract level there are three types of interpretants: the immediate, the dynamic, and the final. Peirce describes the immediate interpretant as the immediate pertinent possible effect in its unanalyzed primitive entirety (Robin 1967). A dynamic interpretant is the actual manifestation of a significant effect. A final interpretant is the teleological growth of a sign that makes its home an interrelated system of signs. The three interpretants that correspond in human experience to these abstract interpretants are the emotional, the energetic, and the logical interpretants. The feeling of déjà vu would be an example of an emotional interpretant; the bodily reaction of a person at whom the command "halt!" is barked out by a soldier after the declaration of a curfew would be an example of an energetic interpretant; the habitualized mode of conditional reasoning such as "if the light turns red, I will not cross the road" would be a logical interpretant. The dynamic interpretant does not possess meaning but is a brute reaction; neither does an emotional interpretant that remains at the level of a mere feeling before being put into words have meaning. A logical interpretant is meaningful. The path a river takes is a final interpretant: a habit carved into the earth. There are many other triadic sets of sign types and other triadic phenomena in Peirce's writings. They are generated by the logic of Peirce's phenomenological categories of Firstness, Secondness, and Thirdness; the possible, the actual, and the general, or "mood, the moment, and mind," respectively (Daniel 1996, pp. 104–134).

SEE ALSO *Anthropology, Linguistic; Culture; Foucault, Michel; Linguistic Turn; Logic; Symbols*

BIBLIOGRAPHY

Daniel, E. Valentine. 1996. *Charred Lullabies: Chapters in an Anthropography of Violence*. Princeton, NJ: Princeton University Press.

Deeley, John. 1982. *Introducing Semiotic: Its History and Doctrine*. Bloomington: Indiana University Press.

Hodge, Robert, and Gunther Kress. 1988. *Social Semiotics*. Ithaca, NY: Cornell University Press

Liszka, James Jakob. 1996. *A General Introduction to the Semeiotic of Charles Sanders Peirce*. Bloomington: Indiana University Press.

Locke, John. [1690] 1996. *An Essay Concerning Human Understanding*, ed. Kenneth P. Winkler. Indianapolis, IN: Hacket.

Peirce, Charles S. 1849–1914. *Papers*. Manuscript Collection in the Houghton Library, Harvard University.

Peirce, Charles S. 1934. *Collected Papers*, vols. 1–6, eds. Charles Hartshorne and Paul Weiss. Cambridge, MA: Harvard University Press.

Peirce, Charles S. 1958–1966. *Collected Papers*, vols. 7–8, ed. Arthur Burks. Cambridge, MA: Harvard University Press.

Peirce, Charles S. 1980–1996. *The Writings of Charles S. Peirce: A Chronological Edition*, vols.1–5, ed. Max H. Fisch. Bloomington: Indiana University Press.

Robin, Richard S. 1967. *Annotated Catalogue of the Papers of Charles S. Peirce*. Amherst: University of Massachusetts Press.

Saussure, Ferdinand de. 1974. *Course in General Linguistics*, eds. Charles Bally and Albert Sechehaye; trans. Wade Baskin. London: Fontana.

Thibault, Paul J. 1997. *Re-reading Saussure: The Dynamics of Signs in Social Life*. London and New York: Routledge.

E. Valentine Daniel

SEMIPARAMETRIC ESTIMATION

Econometrics and other statistical sciences deal with the estimation of various functions (models) such as conditional density function, regression function (conditional mean), heteroskedasticity function (conditional variance), and auto-covariance function (conditional covariance). For empirical research, economic theory suggests the types of variables that can be used in these models under consideration, but often it does not provide the functional form of these models. In view of this, empirical and theoretical work in econometrics is usually done by assuming linear or nonlinear parametric functional forms of these models (see Hartley 1961 and Gallant 1987). However, these parametric models may be false and may therefore provide biased and misleading estimates and inferences. In view of this, econometrics moved in the direction of data-based local modeling for studying these econometric models of unknown functional forms. This approach is also called the "nonparametric (NP) method" or "NP smoothing." There are various NP methods, including spline methods, series methods, differencing methods, and neural-network methods, but the NP kernel smoothing method has become particularly popular because of its vast applicability, its simplicity, and its well-developed theoretical results. NP kernel methods involve local averaging; for example, a consistent estimate of the regression model is obtained by locally averaging those values of the dependent variable that are "close" in terms of the values taken on by the regressors, and these are determined by a "window width." The NP kernel estimation procedure was developed in the seminal works of Murray Rosenblatt (1956), Elisbar Nadaraya (1964), and Geoffrey Watson (1964). (See also Fan and Gijbels 1996 and Pagan and Ullah 1999 for a detailed development on this subject.)

A major complication in a purely NP method is the "curse of dimensionality." The cost associated with using the NP method is the need for very large data, especially when the number of variables in the model is large, if an efficient measurement of the model is to be made. This problem leads to the idea that one might try to restrict some variables, say in a regression model, to have a linear parametric impact while allowing others to have an unknown functional form. As an example, in the female wage model the wage is considered as being linearly affected by the females' personal characteristics, but the variable, the number of years of job experience, can be of an unknown functional form. Effectively, estimation involves a combination of parametric and NP methods, leading to the estimators being described as semiparametric (SP). In general, SP models contain both parametric and NP models, and over the years, a large class of SP models have appeared in the econometrics literature (see Robinson 1988; Linton 1995; and Pagan and Ullah 1999).

Suppose one wanted to estimate the function g in the regression function

$$y_i = g(x_i) + u_i, \ i = 1, \ldots, n \qquad (1)$$

where y_i is the dependent variable, x_i is a vector of q regressors, and u_i is an additive error. A parametric approach fits the data to a parametric model $g(x_i) = g(x_i, \theta)$, often a linear model with $g(x_i, \theta) = \alpha + x_i\beta$, where θ is a parameter set of the model. The least squares estimator $\hat\theta$ is obtained by minimizing

$$\sum_{i=1}^{n} [y_i - g(x_i - \theta)]^2 \qquad (2)$$

over θ, and this estimator is consistent and asymptotically normally distributed (see Gallant 1987). In the NP estimation method, first the regression function $g(x_i)$ is considered as a local polynomial regression, say linear, as $y_i = \alpha(x) + (x_i - x)\beta(x) + u_i$ for x_i in $x \pm h/2$. Then the NP local

linear regression estimation method leads to the following weighted squared loss minimization

$$min \sum_{i=1}^{n} (y_i - \alpha(x) - (x_i - x)\beta(x))^2 K(\frac{x_i - x}{h}) \qquad (3)$$

where $K(\cdot)$, a nonnegative weight (kernel) function, is a decreasing function of distances of x_i from the point x, and h is a window width that determines how rapidly the weights decrease as the distance of x_i from x increases (see Pagan and Ullah 1999).

The SP estimation method deals with the SP models where one component is parametric and the other is NP. A popular SP model is $g(x_i, \theta) = x_{i1}\beta + g(x_{i2})$, where x_{i1} and x_{i2} are q_1 and $q_2 (q = q_1 + q_2)$ sets of variables and the model is linear in x_{i1} but the functional form in x_{i2} is unknown. The SP estimation of β involves the parametric least squares estimation of β in the regression of y_i^* on x_i^*, where $y_i^* = y_i - E(y_i|x_{i2})$ and $x_i^* = x_{i1} - E(x_{i1}|x_{i2})$ are generated by first estimating the conditional means appearing in them by the NP method. Another SP model arises where $g(x_i, \theta)$ is taken to be a known parametric model and where the distribution function of the error u is unknown and not assumed to be normal. In this case, the SP estimation of θ is done by writing the likelihood function of the model under the density specified by its NP kernel estimator. The efficiency properties of these estimators have been extensively studied (see Robinson 1988; Bickel, Klaassen, Ritov, and Wellner 1992; and Pagan and Ullah 1999). Other SP models' estimation includes the situations where $g(x_i, \theta) = x_i\beta$, but $V(u_i|x_i) = \sigma^2(x_i)$ or the serial correlation in u_i is of unknown form. In addition, there is an extensive class of applied SP models with limited dependent variables (see Linton 1995; Horowitz and Lee 2002; and Pagan and Ullah 1999).

Extensive work on the empirical applications of SP models has begun to appear in both cross-section and time-series econometrics, especially in labor econometrics and financial econometrics. Although some related work is being done, several challenging research issues remain. The first is the development of a unified approach toward a data-driven window width and the development of user-friendly software. Others include the systematic development of work on SP estimation of panel-data models, especially when the time-series component is nonstationary, and the development of the theory of SP estimation of models with both continuous and discrete variables (see Racine and Li 2004).

The SP estimation method is a fast-growing area of research in econometrics and statistics. With advances in computer technology the applications of the SP approach are rapidly increasing. In a wide sense, the frontier of this research area has moved on, and it is expected to continue growing in both theory and applications.

SEE ALSO *Nonparametric Estimation; Parameters*

BIBLIOGRAPHY

Bickel, Peter J., Chris A. J. Klaassen, Ya'acov Ritov, and Jon A. Wellner. 1992. *Efficient and Adaptive Estimation for Semiparametric Models.* Baltimore, MD: Johns Hopkins Press.

Fan, Jianqing, and Irene Gijbels. 1996. *Local Polynomial Modeling and Its Applications.* London: Chapman Hall.

Gallant, A. Ronald. 1987. *Nonlinear Statistical Models.* New York: Wiley.

Hartley, Herman O. 1961. The Modified Gaus-Newton Method for the Fitting of Nonlinear Regression Functions by Least Squares. *Technometrics* 3: 269–280.

Horowitz, Joel L., and Sokbae Lee. 2002. Semiparametric Methods in Applied Econometrics: Do the Models Fit the Data? *Statistical Modeling* 2: 3–22.

Linton, Oliver B. 1995. Estimation in Semiparametric Models: A Review. In *Advances in Econometrics and Quantitative Economics: Essays in Honor of C. R. Rao,* ed. Gangadharrao. S. Maddala, Peter C. B. Phillips, and Thirukodikaval N. Srinivasan. Oxford: Blackwell.

Nadaraya, Elisbar. 1964. On Estimating Regression. *Theory of Probability and Its Applications* 9: 141–142.

Pagan, Adrian, and Aman Ullah. 1999. *Nonparametric Econometrics.* New York: Cambridge University Press.

Racine, Jeffrey S., and Qi Li. 2004. Nonparametric Estimation of Regression Functions with Both Categorical and Continuous Data. *Journal of Econometrics* 119: 99–130.

Robinson, Peter M. 1988. Semiparametric Econometrics: A Survey. *Journal of Applied Econometrics* 3: 35–51.

Rosenblatt, Murray. 1956. Remarks on Some Nonparametric Estimates of a Density Function. *Annals of Mathematical Statistics* 27: 642–669.

Watson, Geoffrey S. 1964. Smooth Regression Analysis. *Sankhya* 26 Series A: 359–372.

Aman Ullah

SEN, AMARTYA KUMAR
1933–

Amartya Kumar Sen was born November 3, 1933, in Santiniketan, India. He is a central figure in modern welfare economics, social choice, and development economics. Equal parts philosopher and economist, Sen is unique among modern economists in insisting on the centrality of values and ethics. His most influential works include theoretical contributions to social choice theory, theories of inequality, and the mechanisms underlying poverty.

Sen's early arguments questioned the foundational assumptions of the mainstream approach to social welfare analysis. In 1970, two seminal works greatly expanded social choice theory (the study of the aggregation of individual preferences to form a collective choice). In *Collective Choice and Social Welfare,* Sen showed that Arrow's impossibility theorem (the idea that no voting system meets a desired set of criteria when there are three or more choices) collapses once interpersonal comparisons are allowed. He also established the feasibility of several approaches to constructive social decisions. In "The Impossibility of a Paretian Liberal," he showed that the critical assumption of pareto optimality (an allocation of resources in which no one can be made better off without making someone else worse off) is not value-neutral, as previously supposed. Instead, it conflicts with other fundamental liberal norms, particularly the importance of liberty in the personal domain. Later, in "Rational Fools" (1977), he contested the narrow behavioral assumption that rationality is interchangeable with self-interest, showing it to be an inadequate characterization of human motivation.

These advances in social choice theory allowed for the construction of several non-paretian criteria for social welfare functions. Sen's own explorations (with various authors) were in the areas of inequality, poverty, and distribution-adjusted national income measures. In his explorations of distributive justice and poverty, Sen developed the use of entitlement analysis and the capability approach to development. In *Poverty and Famines* (1981), he presented a theory of famine causation that concentrated on a collapse of people's entitlements (the commodities that different persons can acquire), and he investigated different economic processes that can lead to famines, arguing that they need not necessarily connect with a low or decreasing food supply. He illustrated this theory with detailed case studies of many actual famines, including the Bengal famine of 1943 and the Ethiopian famine of 1973 and 1974.

For Sen, development is seen as the expansion of capabilities and associated human functionings. *Capabilities* are the constituent elements of development, comprising wide-ranging substantive freedoms such as the ability to feed oneself or to participate in economic and political activities. *Functionings* are the actual things humans may wish to do or be. Poverty, therefore, is not simply the deprivation of income, but a deprivation in capabilities.

The growth of additional practical indicators of social welfare and advances in understanding capabilities contributed to alternative methodologies to evaluate development. A direct result of this was the genesis of the United Nations' *Human Development Report.* Sen has also been at the forefront of incorporating discussion of gender inequalities and the role of women in development. In "Missing Women" (1992), he addressed the role of gender inequalities in mortality in parts of the developing world. This was supplemented by a 2003 study of the new phenomenon of selective abortion of female fetuses.

Sen has taught in India, the United Kingdom, and the United States, and he is the recipient of numerous awards, including the 1998 Nobel Prize in Economics.

BIBLIOGRAPHY

Sen, Amartya Kumar. 1970. *Collective Choice and Social Welfare.* San Francisco: Holden Day.

Sen, Amartya Kumar. 1970. The Impossibility of a Paretian Liberal. *Journal of Political Economy* 78 (1): 152–177.

Sen, Amartya Kumar. 1973. *On Economic Inequality.* Oxford: Oxford University Press.

Sen, Amartya Kumar. 1973. On the Development of Basic Income Indicators to Supplement the GNP Measure. *United Nations Bulletin for Asia and the Far East* 24 (2-3): 1–11.

Sen, Amartya Kumar. 1976. Poverty, an Ordinal Approach to Measurement. *Econometrica* 44 (2): 219–223.

Sen, Amartya Kumar. 1976. Real National Income. *Review of Economic Studies* 43: 19–39.

Sen, Amartya Kumar. 1977. Rational Fools: A Critique of the Behavioral Foundations of Economic Theory. *Philosophy and Public Affairs* 6 (4): 317–344.

Sen, Amartya Kumar. 1979. The Welfare Basis of Real Income Comparisons: A Survey. *Journal of Economic Literature* 17 (1): 1–40.

Sen, Amartya Kumar. 1981. *Poverty and Famines: An Essay on Entitlement and Deprivation.* Oxford: Oxford University Press.

Sen, Amartya Kumar. 1983. Poor, Relatively Speaking. *Oxford Economic Papers* 35 (2): 153–169.

Sen, Amartya Kumar. 1985. *Commodities and Capabilities.* Amsterdam: North Holland.

Sen, Amartya Kumar. 1992. *Inequality Reexamined.* Cambridge, MA: Harvard University Press.

Sen, Amartya Kumar. 1992. Missing Women. *British Medical Journal* 304 (6827): 587–588.

Sen, Amartya Kumar. 1999. *Development as Freedom.* Oxford: Oxford University Press.

Sen, Amartya Kumar. 2003. "Missing Women" Revisited. *British Medical Journal* 327.

Arjun Jayadev

SENECA

The Senecas are an American Indian group from northeastern North America. One of the six nations of the Iroquois Confederacy, or Haudenosaunee, Senecas call themselves Onodowaga, meaning "People of the Great Hill." Traditional Senecas determine group membership matrilineally (through the mother's line) and speak a language in the Northern Iroquoian language family. It is likely that several previously autonomous groups coalesced to form the Seneca nation in the fifteenth or sixteenth century, prior to Seneca entry into the Iroquois Confederacy. Seneca material culture begins to correspond closely to that found on eastern Iroquois sites slightly after 1600, perhaps reflecting Seneca participation in the Iroquois Confederacy. When first documented by Europeans, Seneca territory stretched across what is now western New York State from the Genesee River to Seneca Lake; the approximately four thousand Senecas subsisted through agriculture (primarily of maize, beans, and squash), hunting, fishing, and gathering.

Seneca life was altered tremendously by the European fur trade, interaction with European colonial powers, and American territorial encroachment. Senecas began trading beaver pelts for European manufactured goods during the sixteenth century, initially using Native intermediaries. Starting in the 1630s, recurrent European-borne epidemics had major impacts on Seneca communities. Jesuit missionaries resided with the Senecas intermittently from 1668 to 1709. Seneca warriors featured prominently in Iroquois conflicts with the Hurons, Eries, Neutrals, and Susquehannocks from the 1630s through the 1670s. During the seventeenth and eighteenth centuries, Senecas also established satellite communities north of Lake Ontario, at the Niagara portage, and in Pennsylvania and Ohio.

After 1680 the Confederacy and the Senecas increasingly became enmeshed in imperial politics. French forces destroyed all four homeland Seneca villages in 1687. After 1701 Senecas and other Iroquois established a policy of neutrality between European powers, receiving diplomatic benefits by playing European groups off one another. Senecas built smaller, dispersed villages across the region and began producing deerskins for trade with Europeans after 1715. Following the 1760 surrender of New France to Great Britain, Seneca opportunities for diplomatic maneuvering diminished. Western Senecas were key players in the multinational Indian revolt against the British from 1763 to 1766. During the American Revolution (1775–1783), the Senecas sided with Great Britain. American expeditions led by John Sullivan (1740–1795) and Daniel Brodhead (1736-1809) razed approximately thirty Seneca villages in 1779; Seneca survivors spent a difficult winter at Fort Niagara under British protection. Many Senecas subsequently reoccupied their homelands, while others founded new settlements, most notably Buffalo Creek.

From the Revolution to the present day, Senecas have faced major pressures on their lands, resources, and culture from the United States. A series of controversial treaties and agreements, starting with the Treaty of Fort Stanwix in 1784, divided Senecas and confined them to smaller and smaller reservations. A fraudulent 1838 treaty almost transferred the four remaining Seneca reservations to the Ogden Land Company; a renegotiated 1842 treaty still resulted in the loss of the Buffalo Creek reservation. Following passage of the U.S. Indian Removal Act of 1830, Senecas living in Ohio negotiated exchange of their lands for territory in what is now Oklahoma; their descendants officially formed the Seneca-Cayuga Tribe of Oklahoma in 1937.

Christian missionaries became fixtures on Seneca reservations in the 1790s. In 1799 an Allegany Seneca named Handsome Lake (c. 1735–1815) received visions for a new religious code that reconciled Iroquois traditions with the limitations of reservation life. His teachings (the Gaiwiio) eventually spread to other Iroquois communities. In 1848 Senecas at Cattaraugus and Allegany replaced their traditional government with an American-style elective council; Tonawanda Senecas maintained traditional governance, ending political ties between the groups. The Thomas Indian School, a state-run boarding school promoting Indian assimilation, operated at Cattaraugus from 1855 to 1957. From 1959 to 1964 federal officials took one-third of the Allegany reservation for the construction of the Kinzua Reservoir, forcing relocation of 550 people.

Senecas long have fought American encroachments on their territory and rights. Some efforts have succeeded, including the 1990 renegotiation of non-Indian leases of Seneca property in Salamanca, New York, and the 2002 compact between New York State and the Seneca Nation of Indians that allowed casino development in Salamanca, Niagara Falls, and Buffalo. Other efforts, such as the Seneca claim for Grand Island, have been rejected by American courts. Today, approximately 10,000 Senecas reside in several jurisdictions across the United States and Canada. In New York State, the Seneca Nation of Indians controls territories at Allegany, Cattaraugus, and Oil Spring; the Tonawanda Band of Seneca Indians have a separate reservation. Senecas also reside in Oklahoma and on the Six Nations Reserve in Ontario, Canada. Many other Senecas live off reservations, particularly in Buffalo, Rochester, and Erie.

SEE ALSO *American Revolution; Iroquois; Native Americans; Tribe*

BIBLIOGRAPHY

Abler, Thomas S., and Elisabeth Tooker. 1978. Seneca. In *Handbook of North American Indians*, Vol. 15: *Northeast*, ed. Bruce G. Trigger, 505–517. Washington, DC: Smithsonian Institution.

Bilharz, Joy A. 1998. *The Allegany Senecas and Kinzua Dam: Forced Relocation through Two Generations*. Lincoln: University of Nebraska Press.

Morgan, Lewis Henry. [1851] 1962. *League of the Iroquois*. New York: Citadel.

Wallace, Anthony F. C. 1969. *The Death and Rebirth of the Seneca*. New York: Vintage.

Kurt A. Jordan

SENECA FALLS
SEE *Suffrage, Women's.*

SENILITY
SEE *Dementia.*

SENSATIONALISM

Certain events, even when reported accurately and without exaggeration, elicit intense reactions. Some such sensational stories—illustrated by O. J. Simpson standing trial in 1995 for a double homicide and R. Gordon Wasson's description in 1957 of an ancient religious ritual in which psychedelic mushrooms were eaten—are justifiable given the novelty of the phenomena described. Reports tainted by fraud or disregard for truth deserve censure.

Fraudulent reports are often sensational. For example, a *Washington Post* reporter, Janet Cooke, won a Pulitzer Prize in April 1981 for her tall tale about "Jimmy," an eight-year-old boy allegedly addicted to heroin since age five. Cooke's story aroused considerable pity among readers. Washington, D.C., Mayor Marion Barry and other city officials promptly started searching for Jimmy, the innocent victim of a heroin dealer. Before Cooke's fabricated story was published in the *Post* on September 28, 1980, Cooke lied to enlist her editors' sympathy, claiming she could not reveal her "sources" because she "promised them anonymity and her life was threatened by the drug pushers involved" (Stein 1993, p. 130). Cooke's credibility was shattered after autobiographical information she supplied to the Pulitzer Prize committee was released—and was proven to be false. *Washington Post* editors subsequently scrutinized some 145 pages of notes and tape-recorded interviews but discovered no evidence that "she actually interviewed a heroin-addicted child" (Stein 1993, p. 131). Cooke confessed and resigned, at the

Post's request. The Pulitzer Prize was returned, for the first time in its sixty-four-year history.

Mayor Barry, the Pulitzer Prize committee, and Cooke's colleagues were blinded by their pity for an innocent child, combined perhaps with anger at his mother and the drug dealers blamed for having addicted them. Cooke feigned fear to circumvent her editors' request that she identify Jimmy and other "sources" for her then unpublished story.

Pity, fear, and anger—powerful emotions Cooke exploited to sell her story—are integral to pathos, an emotionally oriented persuasive device discussed in Aristotle's *Rhetoric*. The Greek word *pathos* is the root of the English word "pathetic," a term whose negative connotations imply unjustifiable sensationalism.

Sensational stories often are written by reporters afflicted with excessive pathos, usually arousing the same emotions in their audience that interfered with their own capacity for critical thinking. The "yellow journalism" of William Randolph Hearst and Joseph Pulitzer is a famous example. Their newspapers' coverage of Cuban-Spanish conflicts between 1895 and 1898 routinely exaggerated the suffering of Cuban rebels in order to arouse pity for them and anger at allegedly tyrannical Spaniards. Anti-Spanish media propaganda involved some deceit, as well as outrageous yet unverified reports, as when the American battleship *Maine* exploded and sank in Havana harbor in 1898. Many reporters, especially Hearst employees, rushed to judgment, proclaiming that Spain had mined the *Maine*, killing 260 Americans. Most historians agree that America's decision to wage war against Spain was partly the result of such careless reporting. Research conducted in the 1970s concluded that an accident caused the *Maine*'s destruction.

Pathos-driven accounts of breast implants in the 1990s illustrate irresponsible sensationalism without intentional deceit. The journalist John Stossel has explained how and why victims' anecdotes alleging that silicone breast implants caused cancer and autoimmune disease became fashionable during the 1990s. Scientific facts and evidence were ignored because "the women's fear and anger were palpable" (Stossel 2004, p. 105). According to doctors, about 1 percent of all women who had breast implants had connective tissue disease. Most reporters saw that as proof of causality, ignoring the fact that 1 percent of all women who had not had transplants also got that disease (Stossel 2004, p. 106). If silicone implants truly cause connective tissue disease, then the percentage of women afflicted by that disease would be significantly higher than the percentage of women who never had breast implants. Media hysteria prompted a federal prohibition on silicone breast implants from 1992 to 2006, unless prescribed for reconstructive surgery following mastectomy.

Anthropologists have been implicated in scandals after publishing controversial claims before diligently attempting to verify their facts. Ashley Montagu, commenting on the anthropologist Robert Zingg's acceptance of unverified claims about two feral "wolf-children" allegedly found inside a den near a village in India, warned that "no scientist can accept as true any statement … until it has been independently confirmed by others" (quoted in Zingg 2004, p. 233). Zingg's startling book, *Wolf-Children and Feral Man* (1942), was abhorrent to most social scientists, for whom verification is indispensable to achieving the primary purpose of scientific research: accumulating accurate information.

Margaret Mead's sensational declaration that Samoan teenagers enjoyed premarital sexual freedom was welcomed by most social scientists eager for evidence that nurture rather than nature produced adolescent stress. Mead's book *Coming of Age in Samoa* (1928) was, by the 1960s, the most widely read of all anthropology books (Freeman 1996, p. 105). Mead's seductive story about Samoan sexuality became indefensible after one of her adolescent female informants confessed in 1987 to Derek Freeman (1996, p. viii) that she and a friend had gleefully concocted anecdotes implying that premarital sex was standard Samoan practice. Mead erred by rushing to endorse—and publish—those hoaxers' accounts, even though, as Freeman notes, her own research data indicated that at least 60 percent of the adolescent females in her sample were virgins.

More infamous anthropological examples of sensationalism involve outright deception For forty years Piltdown Man, excavated near Sussex, England, was celebrated as the "missing link"; proof that humans evolved from apes. In 1953, scientific tests showed that this six-hundred-year-old skull was spurious; a new orangutan jaw and teeth had been cleverly filed and attached to the human skull. For financial gain, in 1971 Manuel Elizalde fabricated the Tasaday tribe, an allegedly "Stone-Age" people surviving in the Philippines. Carlos Castaneda's claim, that he was the apprentice of a Yaqui Indian sorcerer, made him a best-selling author and a doctor in anthropology before he was denounced as a hoaxer. Whatever these tricksters' motives, they intended to benefit by using deception to persuade people that their astonishing allegations were true.

Preventing or reducing the number of reports that are concocted (e.g., Elizalde, Castaneda) or careless (e.g., Zingg, Mead) probably requires both the enforcement of harsher professional penalties for such malpractice and increasing the rewards for researchers (debunkers) whose critical thinking and adherence to high scholarly standards advance social scientific knowledge. Deterring journalists from publishing stories infected with unjustified sensationalism, however, will be difficult given America's deep commitment to freedom of the press and the media's imperative to sell news. Readers need skepticism and intellectual ability to identify unjustified sensationalism and unverified stories, distinguishing those from honest, verified, and important news or scholarly reports.

SEE ALSO *Castaneda, Carlos; Drug Traffic; Journalism; Mead, Margaret; Propaganda*

BIBLIOGRAPHY

Fikes, Jay C. 1993. *Carlos Castaneda, Academic Opportunism, and the Psychedelic Sixties.* Victoria, B.C.: Millenia.

Fikes, Jay C., and Phil C. Weigand. 2004. "Sensacionalismo y etnografía: El caso de los Huicholes de Jalisco." *Relaciones* 25 (98): 50–68.

Freeman, Derek. 1996. *Margaret Mead and the Heretic: The Making and Unmaking of an Anthropological Myth.* Victoria, Australia: Penguin Books Australia.

Mead, Margaret. 1928. *Coming of Age in Samoa: A Psychological Study of Primitive Youth for Western Civilisation.* New York: Morrow.

Singh, J. A. L., and Robert M. Zingg. 1942. *Wolf-Children and Feral Man.* New York: Harper.

Stein, Gordon. 1993. *Encyclopedia of Hoaxes.* Detroit, MI: Gale Research.

Stossel, John. 2004. *Give Me a Break: How I Exposed Hucksters, Cheats, and Scam Artists and Became the Scourge of the Liberal Media.* New York: HarperCollins.

Zingg, Robert M. 2004. *Huichol Mythology.* Tucson: University of Arizona Press.

Jay Courtney Fikes

SENTIENCE

SEE *Consciousness.*

SEPARABILITY

Separability is a pivotal economic concept introduced independently by Masazo Sono (1945) and Wassily Leontief (1947) in order to deal with aggregation problems in both utility and production theory. Specifically, this concept was employed by Robert Strotz (1957) to analyze two-stage optimization in utility theory: Given separability, the first stage involves partitioning commodities into subsets and optimizing intensities within each subset. While holding the within-subset intensities fixed, the between-subset intensities are optimized in the second stage.

In formal terms, Leontief and Sono defined two factors i and j to be *separable* from factor k if and only if

$$\frac{\partial}{\partial p_k} \left(\frac{\frac{\partial C(Y, p_1, ..., p_n)}{\partial p_i}}{\frac{\partial C(Y, p_1, ..., p_n)}{\partial p_j}} \right) = 0 \iff$$

$$\frac{\partial^2 C}{\partial p_i \partial p_k} \frac{\partial C}{\partial p_j} - \frac{\partial^2 C}{\partial p_j \partial p_k} \frac{\partial C}{\partial p_i} = 0, \quad (1)$$

where $C(Y, p_1, p_2, ..., p_n)$ is a twice differentiable cost function with nonvanishing first and second partial derivatives with respect to input prices $p_1, ..., p_n$ (Blackorby and Russell 1976, p. 286). A similar definition also applies to any twice differentiable production function $F(x_1, x_2, ..., x_n)$ (see, e.g., Berndt and Christensen 1973, p. 404).

For aggregation purposes, the economic literature commonly distinguishes *strong* from *weak* separability, a terminology coined by Strotz (1957). A cost function $C(Y, p_1, p_2, ..., p_n)$ or a production function $F(x_1, x_2, ..., x_n)$ is said to be *weakly separable* if condition (1) holds for all $i \in N_s, j \in N_s$, and $k \notin N_s$, where N_s is a subset of the set of input factors $N = \{1, 2, ..., n\}$. Accordingly, cost function is said to be strongly separable if condition (1) holds for all $i \in N_s, j \in N_t$, and $k \notin N_s \cup N_t$, where N_t is another subset of N.

Steven Goldman and Hirofumi Uzawa (1964) prove that weak and strong separability impose specific restrictions on the underlying cost and production functions. Weak separability with respect to any partition R of r mutually exclusive and exhaustive subsets $N_1, N_2, ..., N_r$ is necessary and sufficient for a production function to be of the form $F(X_1, X_2, ..., X_r)$, where the aggregate X_s is a function of only the elements of N_s. Similarly, strong separability implies that the production function is of the form $F(X_1 + X_2 + ... + X_r)$.

In empirical applications it is often indispensable to invoke separability assumptions if data on some production factors are lacking. For instance, numerous empirical studies investigating the substitutability of capital (K) and labor (L) have assumed that both inputs are weakly separable from energy (E) and materials (M), implying the so-called "value-added" specification of production technologies, $F(V = G(K, L), E, M)$. This assumption, it is commonly asserted, allows for focusing on the capital-labor aggregate $V = G(K, L)$ when estimating the degree of substitution between capital and labor, whereas energy and materials inputs can be safely ignored (Berndt and Wood 1975, p. 265).

This example illustrates that the concept of separability is intimately associated with the notion of substitutability of production factors and consumer goods (see, e.g., Berndt and Christensen 1973 and Blackorby and

Russell 1976). The natural intuition about the separability of a nonnegligible production factor, such as energy after the oil crises, from all other factors is that the substitution elasticity estimates of nonenergy inputs remain the same, irrespective of whether energy is included in any substitution analysis (Hamermesh 1993, p. 34).

This intuition, however, does not apply to the typically employed substitution measures, such as the Allen and Morishima elasticities of substitution, or cross-price elasticities, because the classical Leontief-Sono condition (1) only implies that the *input proportion* x_i/x_j remains unaffected by changes in the price p_k of factor k:

$$\frac{\partial}{\partial p_k}\left(\frac{x_i(p_1, p_2, \ldots, p_n)}{x_j(p_1, p_2, \ldots, p_n)}\right) = 0, \qquad (2)$$

where Shephard's Lemma $\frac{\partial C}{\partial p_i} = x_i$, has been inserted into condition (1). When replacing the cost function by its dual production function $F(x_1, x_2, \ldots, x_n)$, the primal analogon of condition (1) suggests that the *marginal rate of substitution* between any two 2 inputs i and j,

$\frac{\partial F(x_1, x_2, \ldots, x_n)}{\partial x_i} \Big/ \frac{\partial F(x_1, x_2, \ldots, x_n)}{\partial x_j}$, is independent from

the input x_k of factor k (Berndt and Christensen 1973, p. 404).

Yet, virtually no empirical study measures the ease of substitution between i and j in terms of either their input proportion or their marginal rate of substitution. Manuel Frondel and Christoph Schmidt (2004) therefore suggest an empirically oriented definition of separability that guarantees the invariance of cross-price elasticities

$\eta_{x_i p_j} := \frac{\partial \ln x_i}{\partial \ln p_j}$ and $\eta_{x_j p_i} := \frac{\partial \ln x_j}{\partial \ln p_i}$ due to changes in the

price p_k:

$$\frac{\partial}{\partial p_k}\eta_{x_i p_j} = 0 \qquad \text{and} \qquad \frac{\partial}{\partial p_k}\eta_{x_j p_i} = 0. \qquad (3)$$

It can be shown that this definition represents a stronger requirement than the classical Leontief-Sono separability condition (1). In other words, the Leontief-Sono condition (1) is necessary, but not sufficient, for the separability definition (3) to hold (Frondel and Schmidt 2004, p. 221). Frondel and Schmidt (2004, p. 220) argue, however, that only these stronger conditions capture a separability notion coming close to Hamermesh's (1993) intuition.

SEE ALSO *Elasticity; Leontief, Wassily; Optimizing Behavior; Production Function; Utility Function; Uzawa, Hirofumi*

BIBLIOGRAPHY

Allen, R. G. D. 1938. *Mathematical Analysis for Economists.* London: Macmillan.

Berndt, Ernst R., and Laurits R. Christensen. 1973. The Internal Structure of Functional Relationships: Separability, Substitution and Aggregation. *Review of Economic Studies* 40: 403–410.

Berndt, Ernst R., and David O. Wood. 1975. Technology, Prices, and the Derived Demand for Energy. *Review of Economics and Statistics* 57: 259–268.

Blackorby, Charles, and R. Robert Russell. 1976. Functional Structure and the Allen Partial Elasticities of Substitution: An Application of Duality Theory. *Review of Economic Studies* 43: 285–292.

Frondel, Manuel, and Christoph M. Schmidt. 2004. Facing the Truth about Separability: Nothing Works without Energy. *Ecological Economics* 51 (3–4): 217–223.

Goldman, Steven M., and Hirofumi Uzawa. 1964. A Note on Separability in Demand Analysis. *Econometrica* 32: 387–398.

Hamermesh, Daniel S. 1993. *Labor Demand.* Princeton, NJ: Princeton University Press.

Leontief, Wassily W. 1947. Introduction to a Theory of the Internal Structure of Functional Relationships. *Econometrica* 15: 361–373.

Morishima, M. 1967. A Few Suggestions on the Theory of Elasticity. *Keizai Hyoron* (Economic Review) 16:145–150.

Sono, Masazo. 1945. The Effect of Price Changes on the Demand and Supply of Separable Goods. *International Economic Review* 2: 1–51.

Strotz, Robert H. 1957. The Empirical Implications of a Utility Tree. *Econometrica* 25: 269–280.

Manuel Frondel
Christoph M. Schmidt

SEPARATE-BUT-EQUAL

During the post–Reconstruction era, southern states passed laws reestablishing white advantages and privilege by reviving pre–Civil War practices requiring blacks and whites to attend separate schools, ride in separate train cars, and sit in separate sections of theaters. Soon after the Interstate Commerce Commission (ICC) was created in 1887, it received complaints from blacks who had purchased first-class train tickets but were forced to ride in less comfortable dirty train cars reserved for blacks only. In response, the ICC ruled that in trains under its jurisdiction, if racial segregation was practiced, then equal-quality cars must be provided for "white" and "colored" races. Louisiana (and other southern states) then passed laws stipulating that "all railway companies carrying passengers in their coaches in this State shall provide equal but separate accommodations for the white and colored races, by providing two or more passenger coaches for each passenger train, or by dividing the passenger coaches by a partition so as to secure separate accommodations.... No person or persons shall be admitted to occupy seats in coaches other than the ones assigned to them on account of the race they belong to."

In a U.S. Supreme Court case of tremendous importance, *Plessy v. Ferguson* (1896), Homer Plessy, a black man, challenged that Louisiana law. He argued that determining where people should sit based solely on their race was an unconstitutional violation of citizens' rights; for example, the Fourteenth Amendment prohibits laws that abridge the privileges or immunities of U.S. citizens or deny people equal protection of the laws. The Supreme Court's decision, however, rejected Plessy's claim, and, for the next sixty years, its ruling that "separate-but-equal" segregation is permissible and not harmful was the foundation on which racial segregation was legitimated.

Plessy v. Ferguson's doctrine of "separate-but-equal" racial segregation rested on three closely related arguments, each of which was later challenged by civil rights proponents. First, the Court argued that the Fourteenth Amendment only guarantees that blacks and whites have equality with regard to political rights (e.g., to vote or hold office) and legal rights (e.g., to serve on juries, to own property), not with regard to social rights or social equality. Second, *Plessy v. Ferguson* asserted that state governments had the right to permit or require racial separation provided that the segregation laws are "reasonable" and "enacted in good faith for promotion for the public good, and not for the annoyance or oppression of a particular class." Third, this "separate-but-equal" doctrine contended that enforced separation of the races did *not* stamp the colored race "with a badge of inferiority." Instead *Plessy v. Ferguson* claimed that if the two races are socially unequal, this inequality is the result of "racial instincts" that either put one group lower than the other or cause people to believe they are superior or inferior, and the Court held that altering either of these is beyond the power of legislation or judicial decision-making—that is, that "natural" inequalities and prejudices linked to race can not be overcome by government-required commingling of the two races.

What is evident in *Plessy v. Ferguson*'s "separate-but-equal" doctrine is the absence of a serious concern about whether the separate facilities assigned to "white" and "colored" races really were of equal quality. Nowhere in the Court's decision is there mention of any test to be used to judge whether the separate facilities are in fact equal, nor is there a clear statement directing those in authority to provide equal facilities to both races. In fact, shortly after *Plessy v. Ferguson*, the Supreme Court ruled on whether a board of education in Georgia was required to provide a high school for blacks since they did so for

whites. The Court ruled that the school board did not have to do so, and this decision (*Cumming v. Richmond County Board of Education*, 1899) became a precedent for providing "separate and unequal" facilities to blacks.

CONSEQUENCES

The legacy of "separate but (un)equal" was that white-dominated state and local governments created and institutionalized a gulf or color line in public life separating blacks and whites. W. E. B. Du Bois, in the early 1900s, called this color line "the problem of the 20th century" (Du Bois 1901). Gross inequities were permitted under the guise of "separate but equal." In health care, hospitals and doctors in the North and South routinely refused to treat blacks in need of medical attention, and black medical students were denied training and internship experience in "white" hospitals. In education, southern states in the 1930s spent for blacks' education less than one-third what they spent for whites. Residential neighborhoods and housing policies were organized to exclude blacks from the better areas and prevent them from living among whites, for example, by racial zoning ordinances, racially restrictive covenants, discriminatory mortgage lending, and outright refusal to rent apartments or sell homes to blacks. Atlanta blacks comprised one-third of the city's population but resided on less than 20 percent of its land—the most overcrowded and run-down areas. Residential segregation was not just a southern phenomenon; in the 1940s and 1950s many northern cities, including Chicago, Cleveland, and Detroit, were among the most highly segregated cities (and remained so in the mid-2000s).

Perhaps the most visible consequence of the "separate but (un)equal" color line was the demarcation of "white" and "colored" public spaces in parks, beaches, movie theaters, sports stadiums, restaurants, buses and transit waiting rooms, restrooms, and water fountains. People of color who transgressed the color line by using a facility reserved for whites were frequently arrested, jailed, physically beaten, or killed by the police or by secretive groups of whites who took it upon themselves to guard racial boundaries.

Another consequence of racial segregation imposed by the "separate but (un)equal" doctrine was the development of notable African American communities in most large U.S. cities. As migrating blacks were forced into a few neighborhoods, their growing numbers and initiatives for survival and success expanded many black institutions that would greatly influence local (sometimes national) cultural, social, economic, and political life. Amid squalor and poverty in these African American districts arose successful banks and businesses, vibrant churches, innovative music and arts scenes, active social and labor groups, and organizations devoted to racial solidarity, uplift, and the struggle against racism. In well-known black communities, such as New York's Harlem, and in less well-known ones, the broadened social-class structure, the accumulation of resources, and development of leadership gradually stimulated a movement that would challenge and defeat state-sponsored racial segregation.

Although the "separate but (un)equal" doctrine originated from whites' racial prejudices, once institutionalized it nurtured and amplified racial prejudices, mainly in two ways. First, by denying blacks opportunities for good education, jobs, homes, medical care, and social dignity, it forced many into impoverishment and desperation, and many whites interpreted behavioral symptoms associated with this as a sign of black inferiority. Second, isolating blacks from whites prevented the kind of social interaction that can dispel prejudice, that is, equal-status intergroup cooperation toward common goals, which reveals personal information that disconfirms common negative stereotypes.

OVERTURNING "SEPARATE BUT (UN)EQUAL"

In a limited sense the *Brown v. Topeka Board of Education* (1954) decision overturned the "separate but (un)equal" doctrine. It dealt with de jure segregation in public schools, in which governmental agents (school boards) required blacks and whites to attend different schools. The Court ruled this an unconstitutional violation of blacks' Fourteenth Amendment rights because it "has a detrimental effect upon the colored children" in that it suggests an inferiority among blacks that weakens their motivation to learn and negatively affects their hearts and minds, thereby depriving them of equal educational opportunity. Because of delaying tactics by many state and local officials, little racial integration occurred in schools for ten years. In truth, the *Brown* decision was the tip of the iceberg that punctured the "separate but (un)equal" doctrine. It was based on prior precedent-setting lawsuits by the National Association for the Advancement of Colored People (NAACP) that challenged racial segregation and on the dissemination of psychological and sociological research on the negative effects of racial segregation. Finally, and perhaps most importantly, victory against segregation beyond the schools was the product of social activism and pressure created by public protests, boycotts, and disruptions of the status quo (including the Montgomery bus boycott, sit-ins, and riots after the assassination of Dr. Martin Luther King Jr.) that forced many authorities to see that they had more to lose than to gain in preserving state-sanctioned racial segregation.

SEE ALSO Brown v. Board of Education, *1954; Discrimination; Discrimination, Racial; Jim Crow; Public Rights; Segregation; Segregation, School; Supreme Court, U.S.; White Supremacy*

BIBLIOGRAPHY

Bell, Derrick. 1992. *Race, Racism, and American Law.* 3rd ed. Boston: Little, Brown.

Du Bois, W. E. B. 1901. The Freedmen's Bureau. *The Atlantic Monthly* 87 (March): 354.

Meier, August, and Elliott Rudwick. 1976. *From Plantation to Ghetto.* 3rd ed. New York: Hill and Wang.

Charles Jaret

SEPARATION AND POOLING GAMES

SEE *Screening and Signaling Games.*

SEPARATION ANXIETY

Separation anxiety is characterized by infants' and toddlers' intense emotional reactions to the departure of a person with whom they have established an emotional attachment. Having its roots in psychodynamic theory, according to which infants' attachment to their mothers is a learned response to being fed, the ethological theory of attachment (Bowlby 1980) frames the development of emotional attachment as an innate behavioral need that not only satisfies infants' hunger, but also keeps them safe from danger and allows for a secure base from which they can explore their surroundings. According to attachment theory, separation anxiety is a normal developmental stage in which infants have formed a representation of their caretakers as reliable providers of comfort and security.

The strange situation procedure (Ainsworth et al. 1978), in which infants and toddlers are observed during brief separations from and reunions with the parent, is often used by researchers to determine if infants have reached the stage of separation anxiety and if their attachments with caregivers are healthy and secure. Using such procedures, researchers have found that separation anxiety is a fairly universal phenomenon that emerges around six to eight months, with signs of distress peaking around fourteen to twenty months, at which age toddlers may follow or cling to caregivers to prevent their departure.

Typically, separation anxiety lasts only a few minutes; however, many factors, such as tiredness, illness, changes in the household routine, family changes such as birth of a sibling, divorce, death, or a change in caregiver or routine at a day-care center, can contribute to more intense episodes. The intensity of distress also varies depending on: (1) the availability of another person with whom the child has a close bond; (2) the familiarity of the situation; (3) previous experience with the caretaker leaving; and (4) the child's sense of control over the situation. Separation anxiety diminishes as children develop a sense of safety and trust in people other than parents, become familiar with the environment, and trust in the parent's return.

Although separation anxiety is part of normal development for infants and toddlers, for older children, adolescents, or adults such anxieties and behaviors may represent symptoms of a serious disorder known as separation anxiety disorder, or what are also referred to as disorders of attachment. In addition to excessive distress when separated from the primary caregiver, symptoms of disorders of attachment include sleep disturbances such as difficulty falling asleep, nightmares, or fears at bedtime; depressed or withdrawn behavior; apathy; difficulty concentrating; and somatic complaints (e.g., dizziness, nausea, or palpitations). Children may also fear losing the parent or worry about the parent being harmed. Their need to stay close to the parent or home makes it difficult to form healthy relationships with others, such as peers or teachers. Older individuals with separation anxiety disorder may have difficulty moving or getting married and may, in turn, worry about separation from their own children and partner. To reach the diagnostic threshold for this disorder, the anxiety or fear must cause distress or affect social, academic, or job functioning.

SEE ALSO *Anxiety; Attachment Theory; Child Development; Children; Neuroticism; Psychology*

BIBLIOGRAPHY

Ainsworth, Mary D. S., M. C. Blehar, E. Waters, and S. Wall. 1978. *Patterns of Attachment: A Psychological Study of the Strange Situation.* Hillsdale, NJ: Lawrence Erlbaum.

American Psychiatric Association. 1994. *Diagnostic and Statistical Manual of Mental Disorders.* 4th ed. Washington, DC: Author.

Bowlby, John. 1980. *Loss: Sadness and Depression.* Vol. 3 of *Attachment and Loss.* New York: Basic Books.

Becky Kochenderfer-Ladd

SEPARATION OF POWERS

The separation of powers is normally understood as a constitutional doctrine according to which political freedom is best guaranteed by separating the powers of government into legislative, executive, and judicial branches, each with its own jurisdiction. The purpose of this arrangement is to ensure that no single group or individual can control all the levers of power and, thereby, rule despotically. The legislature has primary responsibility for lawmaking, while the impartial interpretation of the law and the application of it to particular cases falls under the purview of the judiciary. The executive must obey the rules established by the legislature and enforced by the judiciary.

Charles-Louis de Secondat, baron de Montesquieu (1689–1755), provided the separation of powers with its canonical statement in *The Spirit of the Laws* (1752), but early intimations of the idea can be found in ancient Greece and Rome, where the systematic study of constitutions first began. Aristotle was the first comparative political thinker to notice that all constitutions have deliberative, judicial, and executive elements. Although he did not argue that government should be organized into separate branches, he believed that different types of constitutions (democratic, aristocratic, or monarchic) should be "mixed," so as to counteract the tendencies to corruption inherent in all pure constitutions. Greek historian Polybius (c. 200–c. 118 BCE) used this theory to explain Roman history, as did Renaissance Florentine thinker Niccolò Machiavelli. The immediate precursor to the development of the separation of powers, however, was seventeenth-century English political thought, particularly the work of John Locke.

The separation of powers is an inherently conservative doctrine, in that it was intended to prevent the use of state power to promote radical social change, and yet it contributed to the rise of constitutional democracy. It offered a constitutional design that promised simultaneously to check monarchical abuses of power and limit the growing ambitions of legislators. It appealed to the nobility, who felt squeezed between overweening absolutist monarchs and pressures to expand popular participation. Although the separation of powers is not a theory of democratic government—it can be, and was, adopted by constitutional monarchies—it gave impetus to the spread of democracy by offering a way of reconciling the will of the people with the rule of law. As such, the doctrine was celebrated in the *Declaration of the Rights of Man and the Citizen* (1789) during the French Revolution, and it was the subject of intense debate by the framers of the Constitution of the United States.

Over the course of the nineteenth century the doctrine lost relevance, and its meaning was gradually restricted to a more specific distinction among types of democratic constitutions—specifically, presidential versus parliamentary government. Critics of Montesquieu charged that he had misread the English constitution, by failing to appreciate how in Westminster parliamentary systems the legislature and executive were fused in the cabinet and in the office of the prime minister. Such a fusion of powers made parliamentary systems elective dictatorships, or so claimed the critics. The Constitution of the United States, with its separate election of president and congress, came to be seen as the closest approximation of the separation of powers.

Montesquieu's critics misunderstood the separation of powers, however. They imagined a watertight separation of branches of government in which no person or group could be a member of more than one branch at a time and no branch could encroach upon the powers of another. This view, which is more of a caricature than a description of any observed political system, had no expositors: No major constitutional theorist ever called for such an absolute separation. James Madison (1751–1836) was the first to reject this caricature, not only because it misrepresented Montesquieu, but, more importantly, because the partial encroachment of branches of government was necessary as a check against the abuse of power: Ambition should counteract ambition; checks and balances, rather than watertight separation of branches of government, would limit tendencies toward abuse of power. Madison was firmly of the same mind as Montesquieu in his conviction that only power can check power.

In the twentieth century the idea of the separation of powers continued to occupy a respected place in legal scholarship and jurisprudence, but lost appeal among social and political theorists. The development of the administrative functions of the state, especially with the expansion of the welfare state, placed more public-sector activity outside the sphere of legislation and into the hands of specialized agencies and experts. The rise of totalitarianism by electoral means in Italy and Germany suggested that the separation of powers was a feeble bulwark against modern antidemocratic and illiberal movements. Political freedom depended more on the degree of social and economic equality, the competitiveness of political-party systems, and a culture of constitutionalism, than on the constitutional separation of powers. Above all, as political science became a more scientific discipline, the language of the separation of powers seemed outdated and formalistic. A new view of institutions arose, building on economic and organizational theory, in which the separation of powers was understood to mean the separate election of executive and legislature in a presidential system of government.

The Anglo-American tendency to treat the separation of powers as a virtual synonym of presidentialism has been resisted by continental political theorists, especially in recent work on deliberative democracy. German philosopher Jürgen Habermas argued that the various branches of government in constitutional democracies correspond to different logics of argumentation, and their separation is necessitated by these discourses. The legislature is the chief deliberative body, yet it has little administrative power. The weakness of the legislature as an administrative body ensures that its deliberations are insulated from the temptations inherent in the exercise of such power and hence oriented toward the production of general laws for the public good.

The purpose of the separation of powers, according to Habermas, is to bind the exercise of administrative power to the deliberative power of citizens acting in concert. The executive administers policies consistent with parliamentary law; it represents the need for action within the rule of law. Equally important is the separation of power between legislature and judiciary. The role of the judiciary is to impartially enforce the law, and court procedures reflect this imperative. The fact that judges can deny citizens their most basic liberties requires that the rules and procedures for doing so be established not by the judges themselves but by the legislature as a body that represents the collective, deliberative power of the whole community. Critics of deliberative democracy object to its highly abstract and normative tone, while exponents see it as a promising beginning for a renewed discussion of the separation of powers.

SEE ALSO *Constitutions; Checks and Balances; Democracy; Government; Habermas, Jürgen; Judicial Review; Judiciary; Locke, John; Parliaments and Parliamentary Systems; Totalitarianism*

BIBLIOGRAPHY

Habermas, Jürgen. 1996. *Faktizität und Geltung: Beiträge zur Diskurstheorie des Rechts und des demokratischen Rechsstaats* [Between Facts and Norms: Contributions to a Discourse Theory of Law and Democracy]. Trans. William Rehg. Cambridge, MA: MIT Press.

Hamilton, Alexander, James Madison, and John Jay. [1787–1788] 1982. *The Federalist Papers.* New York: Bantam Books.

Montesquieu, Charles-Louis de Secondat, baron de. [1752] 1949. *De l'esprit des lois* [The Spirit of the Laws]. Trans. Thomas Nugent, with introduction by Franz Neumann. New York: Hafner Publishing.

Vile, M. J. C. 1998. *Constitutionalism and the Separation of Powers.* 2nd ed. Indianapolis, IN: Liberty Fund.

Maxwell A. Cameron

SEPARATISM

Separatism is the ideas or activities advocating separation of a group or a territorial unit from a state (country), state institutions, or a larger group, usually in the form of autonomy or independence. Examination of complex relationships between the intensity of separatism and its goals and motivations cross-nationally or within individual states is one of the central lines of inquiry in social sciences. Systematic analyses of this phenomenon are available in political science, sociology, anthropology, social psychology, and geography.

With regard to intensity, scholars distinguish between latent separatism in the form of beliefs, attitudes, narratives, ideologies, as well as collective memories of past autonomous or independent status, and active separatism that can be peaceful (petitions, noncompliance with national laws, formation of separatist movements, and rallies or demonstrations) or violent (destruction of property, beatings, riots, guerrilla attacks, terrorist acts, and civil wars). The intensity of separatism also relates to the scale and nature of separatist demands. At the lowest end of the scale are group- or community-level demands for a larger share of economic revenues or for enhancing the status of their culture and lifestyle that do not involve changing the constitutions or other legal foundations of a nation-state. Examples are most manifestations of municipal or tribal separatism in the United States; provincial separatism in Europe, China, and the Russian Federation; and sectarian dissidence (e.g., Nation of Islam in the United States, Old Believers in the Russian Orthodox Church). In the latter case, sectarian refers to breaking away from the main arm of the group's base religion and dissidence refers to these groups seeking to stand apart from society and government in important ways.

At a higher level are demands to change constitutions or other fundamental state laws to decentralize government authority within a state in favor of constituent administrative units (provinces), usually with respect to electoral processes, government appointments, taxation, control over natural resources and principal economic activities, language use, education, regulation of churches, and other cultural and symbolic issues. In the late twentieth and early twenty-first centuries this type of separatist demand was systematically illustrated by the movement known as the "parade of sovereignties" in post-Soviet Russia (1991–1999). This movement resulted in a negotiated federal treaty, a redefinition of the political status of Russia's eighty-nine constituent units (provinces, republics, and districts) in the Russian constitution, and the signing of power-sharing treaties between the federal government and more than fifty constituent unit governments.

The strongest form of separatism is demand for independent statehood (full secession), complete with granting the separatist units the monopoly on legitimate use of violence within its borders and international recognition of the new state's sovereignty. Reflecting the drive for self-determination, these demands take the form of civic or ethnic nationalism or, typically, a combination of both. Prominent examples at the global level both past and present are separatist movements in Spain (Basques), Canada (Quebec), Turkey (Kurds), Great Britain (Northern Ireland), the Soviet Union (Estonia, Lithuania, Latvia), the Russian Federation (Chechnya), former Yugoslavia (Croatia, Kosovo, Bosnia, Slovenia), Georgia (Abkhazia, South Ossetia), Indonesia (Aceh, East Timor), China (Tibet, Xingjiang), India (Kashmir), Mexico (Chiapas), Nigeria (Biafra), Ethiopia (Eritrea), the United States (the Confederacy), and elsewhere. In the majority of cases where these types of secessionist claims have had strong social support, they have also been accompanied by mass political action, from demonstrations and referenda to the formation of rebel armies and protracted wars.

SEPARATISM: A COMPLEX AMALGAM

Most separatist ideologies or movements are complex amalgams of political, ethnic/racial, religious, and socioeconomic separatisms. Only rarely does one find any of these distinct forms of separatism in their pure form. Political separatism represents contestation over the design and control of political systems and their constituent institutions. Mobilized political ideologies are paramount. This was the case of monarchist, socialist, and liberal-democratic separatist movements that seized power in provincial governments and mobilized military forces to unsuccessfully contest the Bolshevik takeover of Russia's central government in November 1917. The central element of the separatist movements that later galvanized the disintegration of the Soviet Union was anti-communism. The latter enabled the coming together of pro-democracy and nationalist movements that had few reasons to join forces otherwise. Russia's first elected president, Boris Yeltsin, mobilized a distinctly anti-Soviet separatist movement advocating secession from Soviet institutions, such as the Communist Party, the KGB (the security and intelligence organization of the Soviet Union), and the state planning agency.

Ethnic, racial, and religious separatism presupposes claims for enhanced status, autonomy, or independence of individual ethnic, racial, or religious groups from the state or a larger group. At the center of ethnic/racial movements are claims to cultural and/or linguistic distinctiveness and privilege (as in Quebec, Basque Country, and Corsica). Religious separatist movements arise within major religions (Catholic-Protestant conflict in Northern Island, Shiite-Sunni conflict in Iraq) or across major religions (Hindu-Muslim conflict over Kashmir, Islam-Christianity distinctions in Bosnia). In their most extreme form these movements claim the need to ensure physical survival of an entire ethnic/racial and/or religious group (Abkhazia, Chechnya, Xingjiang). Separatism of ethnic, racial, and religious minorities may also take a form of resistance to discrimination, oppression, forced resettlement, ethnic cleansing, or mass extermination initiated against them by the politically dominant ethnic or racial groups within a state (i.e., those who control the army, police, security forces, mercenaries, and paramilitaries). In the latter instances, separatist conflicts become particularly intense, brutal, and protracted as action-retaliation patterns escalate, become intractable, and constrain conflict resolution efforts by third parties within or outside the state. One of the prominent empirical questions in social sciences is to what extent the intensity of separatist movements depends on whether ethnic, linguistic, religious, and other identity cleavages in a society are cross-cutting (India) or overlapping (Russia). Economic separatism, on the other hand, is typified by the slogan of the American colonists seeking independence from the British Empire—"no taxation without representation"—but when economic interests are predominant, separatist movements are more likely to end in bargains with central authorities rather than in state disintegration.

MOTIVATION BEHIND SEPARATIST MOVEMENTS

Social scientific research identifies three sources of motivation behind separatist movements: (1) structural conditions (macroeconomic performance and intergroup differentials, demographic trends and distribution of ethnic populations, polity type, ethnofederalism, geography and terrain); (2) behavioral microfoundations (intergroup bias, frustration-aggression psychology, cognitive processes, emotions); and (3) interactivity (bargaining or "games" within and outside the state, conflict precedent, demonstration effects). Debates within and across disciplines are predominantly about the relative importance of these factors. Research methodology includes ethnographic accounts; historical case studies; small-group experiments; and statistical analysis of surveys, aggregate statistics, and event data. Examples of the latter are the Minorities at Risk, State Failure Task Force, and Global Events Data Systems projects based in the United States, which draw on large datasets documenting cases of separatism from nation-states or empires throughout the world from 1800 to the early 2000s.

SEE ALSO *Autonomy; Decentralization; Ethnic Conflict; Ethnic Fractionalization; Ethnicity; Nationalism and Nationality; Partition; Secession; Segregation; Segregation, Residential; Segregation, School; Self-Determination; Self-Determination Theory; Sovereignty*

BIBLIOGRAPHY

Alexseev, Mikhail A., ed. 1999. *Center-Periphery Conflict in Post-Soviet Russia: A Federation Imperiled.* New York: St. Martin's.

Fearon, James D., and David D. Laitin. 2003. Ethnicity, Insurgency, and Civil War. *American Political Science Review* 97 (1): 75–90.

Gurr, Ted Robert. 2000. *Peoples Versus States: Minorities at Risk in the New Century.* Washington, DC: United States Institute of Peace Press.

Horowitz, Donald L. 1985. *Ethnic Groups in Conflict.* Berkeley: University of California Press.

Roehner, Bertrand M. 2002. *Separatism and Integration: A Study in Analytical History.* Lanham, MD: Rowman and Littlefield.

Zartman, I. William, ed. 1995. *Collapsed States: The Disintegration and Restoration of Legitimate Authority.* Boulder, CO: Lynne Rienner.

Mikhail A. Alexseev

SEPHARDIM

SEE *Jews.*

SEPTEMBER 11, 2001

On September 11, 2001, or "9/11," a series of terrorist attacks on the United States killed approximately 3,000 people. On a sunny Tuesday morning four commercial airplanes were hijacked and used as flying bombs to destroy prominent symbols of American economic and political power. The plan, a coordinated attack conducted by four separate teams of hijackers with at least one in each team trained in the basics of airplane flight, commandeered American Airlines flight 11, United Airlines flight 175, American Airlines flight 77, and United Airlines flight 93. They flew two of the aircraft into the Twin Towers of the World Trade Center in Manhattan, New York, and one into the Pentagon in Washington, D.C. The fourth plane, United flight 93, after a violent struggle between the passengers, crew, and hijackers, did not reach its intended target and crashed into a field in rural Pennsylvania.

THE ATTACKS

Two of the early-morning flights, flights 11 and 175 from Logan Airport in Boston and bound for Los Angeles, were hijacked soon after takeoff at 8:00 and 8:15. Flight 77 from Dulles Airport in Washington, DC, also bound for Los Angeles, was hijacked soon after takeoff at 8:10. The fourth plane, flight 93 from Newark Airport in New Jersey, bound for San Francisco, was hijacked after takeoff at 8:40. The planes, loaded with fuel for lengthy cross-country flights, were selected to create maximum destruction on their targets. The hijackers, carrying mace or tear gas and box-cutter knives and claiming to have bombs, took control of the aircraft after killing or assaulting the pilots, flight attendants, and at least one passenger.

Flight 11, reported by morning commuters to be flying at a dangerously low altitude south along the Hudson River in New York, veered east over lower Manhattan before crashing into the North Tower of the World Trade Financial Center (WTC) at 8:46. At approximately 9:02 flight 175 crashed into the South Tower of the WTC. The crash of the second plane was seen live on television by many who were watching the news of the first crash, including the parents of one of the passengers on United 175, who were on the phone with their son, who was calling from aboard the doomed plane. Throughout the day television stations broadcast live images of the morning attacks and the human tragedy that ensued.

Many inside the WTC, believing they would quickly be rescued, were instructed not to evacuate the building. Soon hundreds of New York City firefighters and police and Port Authority Police officers descended on the scene to provide assistance, attempting to fight the fires that quickly engulfed the buildings and evacuate the surrounding area. While some in the office complex fled safely, thousands remained in the building, trapped by fire and smoke. Hundreds watched in shocked disbelief from the streets below as people jumped to their deaths from the burning buildings. Those trapped on the floors above the flames tried to make their way to the roofs of the towers in the vain hope they would be rescued, only to perish as the smoke and heat overcame them in locked stairwells.

At 10:05, the South Tower of the WTC, crippled by the intense jet-fuel-fed fire that destabilized the structure, collapsed. A massive cloud of debris and smoke surrounded the area. Less than thirty minutes later the North Tower collapsed, sending more debris and smoke into the air. Within minutes Lower Manhattan was enveloped in a dark plume of debris and smoke. Most of the rescuers who entered the building lost their lives, including 343 members of the New York City Fire Department, twenty-three New York City police officers, and thirty-seven Port Authority police. Additionally, over 2,000 people in the towers or on the ground were killed. Among those who evacuated the buildings immediately following the attacks, many expressed both sadness and admiration for the rescue personnel who had entered the burning buildings to battle the fires and assist the injured, many of

whom had called emergency service operators to plead for assistance until the moment the buildings collapsed.

While these events unfolded in New York City, another hijacked plane, flight 77, crashed into the Pentagon at 9:37, killing all aboard and 125 civilian and military personnel on the ground. At 10:03, about the same time the South Tower of the WTC collapsed, the last of the four hijacked aircraft crashed into a field in rural Pennsylvania, killing all forty-four people aboard. Flight 93 crashed after numerous passengers learned from family and coworkers on the ground through cell phone calls that other planes had been hijacked earlier and flown into buildings. The passengers tried to overpower the hijackers and regain control of the plane to avoid further attacks. The crash was believed to have occurred as a result of the hijackers either deliberately crashing the plane or losing control of it. The National Commission on Terrorist Attacks Upon the United States, referred to as the 9/11 Commission, later issued a report determining that flight 93 was targeted to hit the U.S. Capitol.

The events of September 11 were marked by confusion and error at the highest levels of government and in the media. Conflicting and erroneous reports about additional hijackings or explosions were rife on the morning of September 11. The 9/11 Commission later outlined the national government's breakdown in general command, communication, and control. At the time of the attacks in New York City, Mayor Rudy Giuliani emerged as a symbol of grace under pressure as he appeared throughout the day and into the night on television and radio from the devastated site to reassure New Yorkers that the city would endure. In the days and months to follow New York City was overwhelmed with support and assistance from construction, health care, police, fire, and rescue personnel from governments and individuals around the world, many of whom came to Manhattan with no intention but to selflessly assist in the recovery effort. For months after the attacks, many people sought out assistance from mental health professionals to cope with the events and the impact it had on their lives. New York City residents often refer to their life experiences as either pre- or post-9/11.

MOTIVES

The September 11 attack was not the first terrorist attack against the WTC. In 1993 an explosives-laden truck detonated in the center's underground parking garage, killing six and injuring hundreds. In the aftermath ten men were arrested, tried, and sentenced to life in prison. Investigation revealed that the terrorists intended to damage the WTC enough so that it would collapse. The terrorist organization that funded the attack, Al-Qaeda, initially a collection of loosely aligned Islamic paramilitary organizations, had formed in the 1980s in response to the

Soviet Union's occupation of Afghanistan, later broadening its activities to include the United States for its support of Israel and for having troops stationed in Saudi Arabia. Osama Bin Laden emerged as the leader of this group in 1988.

Al-Qaeda had carried out numerous attacks against the United States dating back to 1992. It bombed hotels in Yemen where U.S. troops routinely stopped; it supported groups battling U.S. forces in Somalia in 1993; it carried out car bombings in Saudi Arabia outside a joint Saudi-U.S. facility in 1995; it detonated a truck bomb outside a residential complex that housed U.S. soldiers in Saudi Arabia, killing nineteen, in 1996; it bombed U.S. embassies in Tanzania and Kenya in 1998; it conducted the attack on the *USS Cole*, a destroyer docked in Yemen, killing seventeen and wounding forty, in 2000. In a 2004 statement, Bin Laden acknowledged Al-Qaeda's involvement in many of these earlier attacks, including the attacks of September 11.

RESPONSE

In the aftermath of the September 11 attacks, President George W. Bush's approval ratings soared. Some criticized the president for not being decisive on the morning of the attacks after he was seen on television visiting with grade school children in Florida and later in the day flew from Florida to Louisiana and then Nebraska before returning to Washington, D.C., in the evening. On October 7, 2001, after the United States declared a war on terrorism, a U.S.-led coalition launched an invasion of Afghanistan called Operation Enduring Freedom in an effort to capture Bin Laden and eliminate his base of support. The invasion failed to capture Bin Laden but did topple Afghanistan's Taliban government, which was believed to have supported Bin Laden and Al-Qaeda. Later, in March 2003, another U.S.-led coalition initiated Operation Iraqi Freedom, an attack on Iraq in an effort to eliminate alleged weapons of mass destruction and Iraq's alleged support for international terrorism. No weapons of mass destruction or evidence of Iraq's cooperation with international terrorist organizations were proven, but Iraq's government under Saddam Hussein collapsed. A French citizen, Zacarias Moussaoui, arrested in August 2001 on an immigration violation after trying to enroll in flight training courses, was convicted of conspiring to kill Americans as part of the September 11 terror attacks. He is now serving a life sentence in a federal prison in Colorado as the only person convicted of the crimes that occurred on September 11.

In the aftermath of the attacks the U.S. Congress passed the USA Patriot Act, increasing the power of the federal government, particularly the executive branch. Congress also created the Department of Homeland Security and facilitated a greater role for the National Security Agency, the nation's leading eavesdropping organization, in the pursuit of terrorism both within the United States and abroad. Some of the president's aggressive assertions in the war on terror, including the establishment of military commissions to try suspected terrorists, were later determined by the U.S. Supreme Court to be unconstitutional violations of executive authority.

SEE ALSO *Al-Qaeda; bin Laden, Osama; Guantánamo Bay; Hussein, Saddam; Iraq-U.S. War; Jingoism; Nationalism and Nationality; Patriotism; Supreme Court, U.S.; Terrorism; Terrorists*

BIBLIOGRAPHY

Clarke, R. 2004. *Against All Enemies: Inside America's War on Terror.* New York: Simon and Schuster.

CNN.com. 2001. *September 11: Chronology of Terror.* http://archives.cnn.com/2001/US/09/11/chronology.attack/index.html.

National Commission on Terrorist Attacks Upon the United States. 2004. The 9-11 Commission Report. Washington, DC: U.S. Government Printing Office.

Senate Select Committee on Intelligence and House Permanent Select Committee on Intelligence. 2002. Intelligence Activities Before and After the Terrorist Attacks of September 11. Washington, DC: U.S. Government Printing Office.

James Freeman

SEQUOYAH
c. 1770–1843

Sequoyah, a Cherokee also known as George Guess, Guest, or Gist, developed a Cherokee syllabary that brought literacy to his people. Sequoyah's mother was Cherokee and a member of the Paint clan, one of the seven Cherokee clans; she was descended from Oconostota, an eighteenth-century warrior and ruler. His father's lineage is uncertain. Some scholars claim he was George Guess, a German trader, or Nathaniel Gist, friend of George Washington. Sequoyah was born near the ancient capital Echota and Fort Loudon (in the vicinity of Tellico Blockhouse in Monroe County, Tennessee) on the Little Tennessee River among the Overhill or Upper Cherokees. In the early 1800s, seeking to avoid attacks from marauding settlers, he migrated with fellow Cherokees to the southernmost edge of the Cherokee Nation and made his home at Willstown, in present-day Dekalb County (Alabama). Though lame, during the War of 1812 he was a horse-mounted combatant serving in the

Cherokee regiment under Colonel Gideon Morgan. As part of a campaign directed by General Andrew Jackson, he fought against the Alabama Red Stick Creeks in the Battle of Horseshoe on March 27, 1814.

In his private life Sequoyah sought solitude, partly because of his lameness, but also because he wished to develop his talents as a silversmith engraver. Sequoyah's involvement with engraving spurred his intense interest in "talking leaves," the term he used for written material, and in classical and European writing conventions. Though opposed in his efforts by his first wife and neighbors, he began to create his writing method in 1809 and finished his arduous task ten years later, with assistance from his young daughter. He started with a pictograph system and ended up with a system using true phonetic symbols.

Though not an English speaker, Sequoyah recognized the power that written speech, or "talk on paper," could bring to those who had previously only transmitted ideas orally. In 1821 he introduced his syllabary, representing consonant-vowel combinations, six vowels, and the consonant *s*. Sequoyah and his young daughter first showed the system to Sequoyah's cousin, George Lowery. Mike Waters, the brother of Sally Waters, Sequoyah's second wife, was the first person to learn the syllabary. The initial Sequoyahan composition dealt with the boundary lines between the Cherokee Nation, Georgia, and Tennessee. A short time later Sequoyah brought a suit in Indian Court, held at Chatooga (northeastern Georgia), and presented his case by reading aloud from a document written in his syllabary. The audience was amazed and news of his invention spread quickly. Within months, the Cherokees had attained literacy. This was impressive not only for Sequoyah's ability to instill Cherokee literacy, but also for the efficiency with which the Cherokees learned the syllabary.

In 1823 Sequoyah left the Cherokee Nation in the Southeast to live with his kinsmen who migrated westward and settled along the Arkansas River, near present-day Indian Territory. He continued to teach his syllabary to the western Cherokee. In recognition of his contributions, Sequoyah was invited to Washington, D.C., in 1825 to receive $500 from Congress; once there, he had his portrait painted by the famed Charles Bird King. Sequoyah became an Indian activist. In 1828 he traveled to Washington, D.C., as a delegate representing some eight thousand Cherokees in land negotiations with the U.S. government in the Treaty of 1828. He was successful in adjudicating contested Arkansas lands claimed by the Osages for exchange of lands beyond the Arkansas River (present-day Oklahoma).

That same year the Cherokee National Council at New Echota (Georgia) acquired a printing press and had type cases set in both Sequoyahan and English characters,

creating the only bilingual Indian newspaper, the *Cherokee Phoenix*. The newspaper, printed partially in the syllabary, contained Cherokee shamans' sacred formulae used for ceremonial purposes, as well as accounts of the manners and customs of the Cherokee. It also featured news of the day and political announcements about district candidates for National Council seats, and printed the 1827 Cherokee Constitution establishing a republican government. The press brought literacy to the illiterate and turned out more than 225,000 pages before Georgia citizens seized it in 1834 because of the *Cherokee Phoenix*'s anti-Indian removal editorials. Because he had already left the Southeast, Sequoyah escaped the bitter factionalism that marked the declining days of the Cherokee Nation (East) after U.S. policymakers forced Cherokees out of their ancestral lands in 1838 in a relocation known as the Trail of Tears.

After Cherokees reunified their nation in Indian Territory, Sequoyah's syllabary was the nucleus of unification for both traditional and acculturated Cherokees. On December 29, 1843, survivors of the removal and Old Settlers, Cherokees who had moved to Indian Territory before mandatory displacement, bestowed upon their beloved scholar a lifetime annual income of $300, probably the first literary pension in American history. Ever mindful of his fellow Cherokees' welfare, Sequoyah constantly taught the syllabary, both to Cherokees in Indian Territory and to those living beyond its borders. Sequoyah left the Cherokee capital, Tahlequah (in Oklahoma), with his son Teesy in an oxcart for Mexico, where he hoped to teach the syllabary to Mexican Cherokees. On his way to Mexico, he visited with Texas Cherokees, who were plotting revenge against Texan residents who had killed many of their relatives, and convinced them to join the members of the recently restored Cherokee Nation (Tahlequah). After reaching northern Mexico, Sequoyah became deathly ill; he died in 1843 and was buried in a cave near San Fernando de las Rosas.

Today, Sequoyah's syllabary is central to the educational programs of both the Cherokee Nation Tahlequah (in Oklahoma) and the Eastern Band of Cherokees (in Cherokee, North Carolina), the latter being remnant Cherokees not included in the compulsory removal of 1838. Cherokee education includes total immersion in the syllabary beginning at a very young age. Literacy in the syllabary is also enhanced by two Cherokee publications, the *Cherokee Phoenix* (Tahlequah) and the *Cherokee One Feather* (Cherokee, North Carolina); both papers print in the historical bilingual tradition. Correspondence between East and West Cherokees is greatly facilitated by the syllabary, both because it is so widely studied and because its efficiency permits Cherokees to become proficient writers after a few days' study. Indeed, Sequoyah's syllabary has contributed in no small way to the cultural revitalization that reverberates throughout both Cherokee domains.

SEE ALSO *Cherokees; Trail of Tears*

BIBLIOGRAPHY

Bender, Margaret Clelland. 2002. *Signs of Cherokee Culture: Sequoyah's Syllabary in Eastern Cherokee Life*. Chapel Hill and London: University of North Carolina Press.

Fogelson, Raymond D. 1996. Sequoyah. In *Encyclopedia of North American Indians*, ed. Frederick E. Hoxie, 580–582. Boston: Houghton Mifflin.

Kilpatrick, Jack Frederick. 1965. *Sequoyah of Earth and Intellect*. Austin, TX: Encino Press.

King, Duane H. 1988. Sequoyah or George Guess (Gist). *Journal of Cherokee Studies* 13: 36–38.

Rowena McClinton

SERBS

Serbs are South Slavic people who predominantly live in Serbia, Montenegro, Bosnia-Herzegovina, and Croatia. They are also a significant minority in the Republic of Macedonia and Slovenia.

Serbs constitute about 66 percent of the population of Serbia. The largest urban populations of Serbs in the former Yugoslavian region are in Belgrade and Novi Sad (in Serbia) and in Banja Luka (in Bosnia-Herzegovina). Serbs are also present as a sizable minority in all capitals of the former Yugoslavian republics. They make up 2 to 3 percent of the population of Zagreb, Skopje, Ljubljana, and Sarajevo. Another 1.6 million used to live in Bosnia and Herzegovina and 600,000 lived in Croatia prior to the Yugoslav wars, but they have now been largely expelled from the latter.

Serbian culture was largely influenced by the Byzantine Empire starting in the ninth century and throughout much of the Middle Ages. Another source of persistent influence is the Serbian Orthodox Church. However, prior to the Ottoman invasion in the fourteenth century Serbs were strongly influenced by the Catholic Church, especially in the coastal areas such as Montenegro and Croatia. Austrians and Hungarians have also been highly influential among Croatian Serbs, Serbs of Vojvodina, and Bosnian Serbs to a smaller extent. Serbian culture declined during the five-hundred-year rule of the Ottoman Empire. After Serbia became autonomous in 1817, there was a resurgence of Serbian culture that remains strong today in Central Serbia. The Socialist Federal Republic of Yugoslavia, which was formed following World War II and was in existence until the wars of the 1990s, was part of the Soviet Bloc of Communist countries, but in recent decades there has been a growing influence from the West as well as a resurgence in traditional culture.

Serbs have played a major role in world history. In 1914 Gavrilo Princip (1894–1918), a Bosnian Serb, assassinated Archduke Franz Ferdinand (1863–1914), heir to the imperial throne of the Austro-Hungarian Empire. This act precipitated the crisis that would lead to World War I. In more distant history Djordje Petrovic Karadjordje (died 1817) led the 1804 rebellion against the Turks, who were then in power. Serbs have played a significant role in the development of the arts and sciences as well. Prominent Serbs include the scientists Nikola Tesla (a Croatian Serb; 1856–1943), Michael Pupin (1858–1935), Jovan Cvijić, and Milutin Milankovic; the famous composers Stevan Mokranjac and Stevan Hristic; literary authors Ivo Andrić (1892–1975) and Milos Crnjanski; and Vuk Stefanović Karadžić (1787–1864), credited with reforming the Serbian language. Other famous members of the Serbian community are sports stars Vlade Divac, Peda Stojakovic, and Nemanja Vidic; and actor Karl Malden (Mladen Sekulovich). From the entertainment arena there are movie directors such as Dusan Makavejev, Peter Bogdanovich, and Emir Kusturica, and TV producer Paul Stojanovich.

SEE ALSO *Croats; Ethnic Conflict; Ethnicity; Identity; Milosevic, Slobodan; Nationalism and Nationality; Ottoman Empire; World War I*

BIBLIOGRAPHY

Cirkovic, Sima M. 2004. *The Serbs*. Malden, MA: Blackwell.

Radan, Peter, and Aleksandar Pavkovic. 1997. *The Serbs and Their Leaders in the Twentieth Century*. Brookfield, MA: Ashgate.

Dagmar Radin

SERFDOM

SEE *Servitude*.

SERIAL CORRELATION

Serial correlation is a statistical term that refers to the linear dynamics of a random variable. Economic variables tend to evolve parsimoniously over time and that creates temporal dependence. For instance, as the economy grows, the level of gross national product (GNP) today depends on the level of GNP yesterday; or the present inflation rate is a function of the level of inflation in previous periods since it may take some time for the economy to adjust to a new monetary policy.

Consider a time series data set $\{Y_t, X_{1t}, \ldots, X_{kt}\}$ for $t = 1, 2, \ldots, T$. Our interest is to estimate a regression model like $Y_t = \beta_0 + \beta_1 X_{1t} + \ldots, \beta_k X_{kt} + \varepsilon_t$. For instance, Y_t is the inflation rate, and $X_{1t}, \ldots, X_{kt}$ is a set of regressors such as unemployment and other macroeconomic variables. Under the classical set of assumptions, the *Gauss-Markov theorem* holds, and the *ordinary least squares* (OLS) estimator of the β_i's is the *best, linear, and unbiased estimator* (BLUE). Serial correlation is a violation of one of the classical assumptions. Technically, we say that there is serial correlation when the error term is linearly dependent across time, that is, the $\text{cov}(\varepsilon_t, \varepsilon_s) \neq 0$ for $t \neq s$. We also say that the error term is *autocorrelated*. The covariance is positive when on average positive (negative) errors tend to be followed by positive (negative) errors; and the covariance is negative when positive (negative) errors are followed by negative (positive) errors. In either case, a covariance that is different from zero will happen when the dependent variable Y_t is correlated over time and the regression model does not include enough lagged dependent variables to account for the serial correlation in Y_t. The presence of serial correlation invalidates the Gauss-Markov theorem. The OLS estimator can still be *unbiased* and *consistent* (large sample property), but it is no longer the best estimator, the *minimum variance estimator*. More importantly, the OLS standard errors are not correct, and consequently the t-tests and F-tests are invalid.

There are several models that can take into account the serial correlation of ε_t: the autoregressive model AR(p), that is, $\varepsilon_t = \rho_1 \varepsilon_{t-1} + \rho_2 \varepsilon_{t-2} + \ldots \rho_p \varepsilon_{t-p} + v_t$, where v_t is now uncorrelated with zero mean and constant variance; the *moving average* MA(q) $\varepsilon_t = \theta_q v_{t-q} + \ldots + \theta_1 v_{t-1} + v_t$; or a mixture model ARMA(p,q). Testing for serial correlation in the error term of a regression model amounts to assessing whether the parameters ρ_i's and θ_i's are statistically different from zero. A popular model within economics is the AR(1) model: $\varepsilon_t = \rho_1 \varepsilon_{t-1} + v_t$. Within this model, the null hypothesis to test is H_0: $\rho_1 = 0$. If we reject the null hypothesis, we conclude that there is serial correlation in the error term. To implement the test, we proceed by running OLS in the regression model. We retrieve the OLS residuals $\hat{\varepsilon}_t$ and, assuming that the regressors $X_{1t}, X_{2t}, \ldots, X_{kt}$ are strictly exogenous, we regress $\hat{\varepsilon}_t$ on $\hat{\varepsilon}_{t-1}$. A t-statistic for H_0: $\rho_1 = 0$ will be asymptotically valid. If the autoregressive model is of a large order, an F-test for a joint hypothesis as H_0: $\rho_1 = \rho_2 = \ldots = \rho_p = 0$ will also be valid. If the regressors are not strictly exogenous, the auxiliary regression of $\hat{\varepsilon}_t$ on $\hat{\varepsilon}_{t-1}$ should be augmented with the set of regressors $X_{1t}, X_{2t}, \ldots, X_{kt}$ for the t-test and F-test to be valid. There is also a very popular statistic, the *Durbin-Watson*, which also

requires strict exogeneity that tests for AR(1) serial correlation. The main shortcoming of this test is the difficulty in obtaining its null distribution. Though there are tabulated critical values, the test leads to inconclusive results in many instances.

Once we conclude that there is serial correlation in the error term, we have two ways to proceed depending upon the exogeneity of the regressors. If the regressors are strictly exogenous, we proceed to model the serial correlation and to transform the data accordingly. A regression model based on the transformed data is estimated with generalized least squares (GLS). If the regressors are not exogenous, we proceed to make the OLS standard errors robust against serial correlation. In the first case, let us assume that there is serial correlation of the AR(1) type, that is, $\varepsilon_t = \rho_1 \varepsilon_{t-1} + v_t$. In order to eliminate the serial correlation, we proceed to transform the data by quasi-differencing. For simplicity, suppose that the regression model is $Y_t = \beta_0 + \beta_1 X_{1t} + \varepsilon_t$. The following transformation will produce a regression model with an uncorrelated error term:

$$Y_t - \rho_1 Y_{t-1} = \beta_0(1 - \rho_1) + \beta_1(X_{1t} - \rho_1 X_{1t-1}) + \varepsilon_t - \rho_1 \varepsilon_{t-1} = \beta_0(1 - \rho_1) + \beta_1(X_{1t} - \rho_1 X_{1t-1}) + v_t$$

If ρ_1 is known, it is easy to obtain the quasi-differenced data, that is, $Y_t - \rho_1 Y_{t-1}$ and $X_t - \rho_1 X_{t-1}$, and proceed to run OLS in the model with the transformed data. This will produce a GLS estimator of the β_i's that now will be BLUE as the new error term v_t is free of serial correlation. In practice, ρ_1 is not known and needs to be consistently estimated. The estimate $\hat{\rho}_1$ is obtained from the auxiliary regression of $\hat{\varepsilon}_t$ on $\hat{\varepsilon}_{t-1}$. We proceed by quasi-differencing the data, $Y_t - \hat{\rho}_1 Y_{t-1}$ and $X_t - \hat{\rho}_1 X_{t-1}$, and as before, running OLS with the transformed data. The estimator of the β_i's now is called the *feasible GLS estimator* (FGLS), which is a biased estimator, though asymptotically is still consistent. In practice, the FGLS estimator is obtained by iterative procedures known as the *Cochrane-Orcutt procedure*, which does not consider the first observation, or the *Prais-Winsten procedure*, which includes the first observation. When the sample size is large, the difference between the two procedures is negligible.

In the second case, when the regressors are not strictly exogenous, we should not apply FGLS estimation because the estimator will not be even consistent. In this instance, we modify the OLS standard errors to make them robust against any form of serial correlation. There is no need to transform the data as we just run OLS with the original data. The formulas for the robust standard errors, which are known as the HAC (heteroscedasticity and autocorrelation consistent) standard errors, are provided by Whitney Newey and Kenneth West (1987). Nowadays, most of the econometric software calculates the HAC standard errors, though the researcher must input the value of a parameter that controls how much serial correlation should be accounted for. Theoretically, the value of this parameter should grow with the sample size. Newey and West advised researchers to choose the integer part of $4(T/100)^{2/9}$ where T is the sample size. Although by computing the HAC standard errors we avoid the explicit modeling of serial correlation in the error term, it should be said that they could be inefficient, in particular when the serial correlation is strong and the sample size is small.

SEE ALSO *Least Squares, Ordinary; Pooled Time Series and Cross-sectional Data; Properties of Estimators (Asymptotic and Exact); Time Series Regression; Unit Root and Cointegration Regression*

BIBLIOGRAPHY

Newey, Whitney K., and Kenneth D. West. 1987. A Simple, Positive, Semi-Definite Heteroskedasticity and Autocorrelation Consistent Covariance Matrix. *Econometrica* 55: 703–708.

Gloria González-Rivera

SEROTONIN

Serotonin, like dopamine and norepinephrine, is a brain neurotransmitter. When the brain produces serotonin, tension is eased and the subject feels less stressed and more focused and relaxed. In contrast, when it produces dopamine or norepinephrine there is alertness in thinking and acting. Serotonin is called the "calming chemical." It can be obtained naturally by eating sugar or other carbohydrates, which raise the insulin level in the blood, triggering a greater ratio of a chemical (actually, an enzyme) called *tryptophan*. This in turn rushes to the brain, where it produces serotonin. Vitamin C is required for the conversion of tryptophan into serotonin. Tryptophan is found in foods such as bananas, plums, turkey, and milk. A diet poor in omega-3 fatty acids may lower brain level serotonin and cause depression.

CHEMICAL COMPOSITION AND ACTION

Serotonin was isolated and named by Maurice M. Rapport, Arda Green, and Irvine Page in 1948. First, Rapport identified it as a vasoconstrictor substance in the blood serum, and because it is a serum agent that affected vascular tone he called it *serotonin*. Later, in 1950, Rapport identified serotonin chemically and gave it the chemical name 5-hydroxytryptamine. The chemical name of serotonin is 3-(2-aminoethyl)-1H-indol-5-ol, and in pharmacological terminology 5-HT.

The chemical formula of serotonin is $N_2OC_{10}H_{12}$. Its molecular mass is 176.2182 g/mol, its monoisotopic mass is 176.0950 g/mol, and its composition is as follows: N (15.8970 percent), O (9.0793 percent), C (68.1598 percent), and H (6.8638 percent).

Specifically, serotonin is a monoamine neurotransmitter that is synthesized in the central nervous system by the serotonergic neurons and in the gastrointestinal tract by the enterochromaffin cells. Serotonin is formed by the hydroxylation and decarboxylation of tryptophan. The greatest concentration of serotonin is found in the enterochromaffin cells of the gastrointestinal tract (90 percent), and the rest is found in platelets and in the central nervous system. The effects of serotonin are mostly felt in the cardiovascular system, with additional effects in the respiratory system and the intestines.

The function of serotonin is exerted upon its interaction with specific receptors. Several serotonin receptors have been cloned, such as 5HT1, 5HT2, 5HT3, 5HT4, 5HT5, 5HT6 and 5HT7. Within each group there are subtypes that affect various aspects of bodily functions.

More specifically, serotonin can be found in the human gastrointestinal tract and in the bloodstream. In the human body, serotonin can be synthesized from the amino acid tryptophan by a short metabolic pathway that consists of two enzymes: tryptophan hydroxylase and amino acid decarboxylase. The first enzyme, tryptophan hydroxylase, has two forms, one that is present in several tissues and the other one in a brain-specific isoform. In contrast, in the central nervous system serotonin can also be synthesized by the neurons of the Raphe nuclei that are distributed along the length of the brainstem in nine pairs. Specifically, there are swellings, called *varicosities*, along the axon that release serotonin into the extraneuronal space. From there, serotonin can be diffused to activate special receptors that exist on the dendrites, the cell bodies, and the presynaptic terminals of the adjacent neurons.

Serotonin plays an important role in the regulation of mood, sleep, appetite, vomiting, sexuality, memory and learning, temperature regulation, cardiovascular function, and endocrine regulation. Low levels of serotonin have been associated with migraines, bipolar disorders, apathy, fear, feelings of worthlessness, insomnia, fatigue, anxiety, and depression (www.chm.bris.ac.uk/motm/serotonin/depression.htm). Autopsies on suicide cases have revealed very low levels of serotonin in the brain. In turn, low levels of serotonin can be caused by an anxiety disorder because serotonin is required for the metabolism of stress hormones. The most concrete evidence for the connection between serotonin and depression is the decreased concentrations of serotonin in the cerebrospinal fluid and brain tissues of people suffering from depression.

Extremely high levels of serotonin in the body cause toxic effects, and are even fatal in some cases; this is termed "serotonin syndrome."

In 2005 scientific evidence emerged that genetic polymorphisms in the enzyme tryptophan hydroxylase in both its forms can affect susceptibility to depression and anxiety (Nash et al. 2005; Zhang et al. 2005). Furthermore, a study in 2006 showed that ovarian hormones can affect the expression of tryptophan hydroxylase, triggering postnatal depression and premenstrual stress syndrome (Hiroi et al. 2006). Also, where infants have abnormal serotonergic neurons—those neurons on the brain stem that synthesize serotonin—there is a high possibility of sudden infant death syndrome (SIDS) (Weese-Mayer, et al. 2003). Based on recent research, by Lesurtel et al. (2006), serotonin mediates liver regeneration and induces cell division throughout the body.

The pharmacology of serotonin is very complex because there is a large and diverse range of serotonin receptors in the human body. At least seven types of such receptors have been identified in different places of the body, and they all have different effects. Serotonin receptors can be stimulated by psychoactive drugs such as ecstasy (MDMA), LSD, DMT, and psilocybin (a substance found in psychedelic mushrooms). A small dose of ecstasy, for example, stimulates a big release of serotonin in the body, causing feelings of well-being, comfort, and tactile sensitivity. High doses of such substances can produce feelings of emotional empathy, or entactogenesis.

The 5-HT3 receptor is an antiemetic agent used mainly in cases of postoperative nausea and nausea caused by anticancer chemotherapy using cytotoxic drugs. It is also used to treat depression and other mental and psychological conditions. The 5-HT 1B/D receptor is an agent to treat migraines. The role of 5-HT receptors is a topic of intense research, so more therapeutic applications may be discovered in the future.

If depression is severe as a result of serotonin deficiency, antidepressants—that is, pharmaceutical agents that increase the level of serotonin in the brain—may be used. If depression is mild, it can be cured without medications because levels of serotonin can be increased with rigorous exercise. Studies have shown that the amount of serotonin in the brain is increased with increased activity, and the production of serotonin is raised for some days after exercise.

TYPES OF SEROTONIN MEDICATIONS

There are certain psychiatric medications that modulate the levels of serotonin in the human body. These have been classified into four general categories: (1) monoamine oxidase inhibitors, (2) tricyclic antidepressants, (3) atypical antipsychotics, and (4) selective serotonin reuptake inhibitors.

Monoamine oxidase inhibitors (MAIOs) are used to prevent the breakdown of monoamine neurotransmitters (one of which is serotonin). Hence, they increase the concentrations of serotonin in the brain. They are used for patients suffering from depression, but they may have serious side effects, including adverse drug interactions such as hypertensive crisis. Trycyclic antidepressants (TCAs) inhibit the reuptake of both serotonin and norepinephrine. Selective serotonin reuptake inhibitors (SSRIs) are also used in the treatment of depression. They are newer drugs and inhibit only serotonin's reuptake, hence they are safer, having fewer side effects and fewer adverse drug interactions. One of their side effects is anorgasmia, or a delay of sexual climax.

SSRIs available in the United States (with trade names given in parentheses) include:

Citalopram (Celexa, Cipramil, Emocal, Sepram, Seropram);

Escitalopram oxalate (Lexapro, Cipralex, Esertia);

Fluoxetine (Prozac, Fontex, Seromex, Seronil, Sarafem);

Fluvoxamine maleate (Luvox, Faverin);

Paroxetine (Paxil, Seroxat, Aropax, Deroxat, Paroxat);

Sertraline (Zoloft, Lustral, Serlain);

Dapoxetine (no known trade name).

SSRIs are prescribed for treatment of major depression, anxiety disorders, panic disorders, obsessive-compulsive disorders (OCD), social phobia, eating disorders, irritable bowel syndrome (IBS), and premature ejaculation (which affects up to 60 percent of men).

Briefly, the mechanism of brain cells is as follows: The messages in the brain are passed between two nerve cells through a synapse, which is a small gap between the cells. The sender (presynaptic) cell releases neurotransmitters such as serotonin, dopamine, and norepinephrine into that gap. These neurotransmitters are recognized by special receptors on the surface of the receiver cell (postsynaptic), which, upon this stimulation, relays the signal. During this process, approximately 10 percent of the neurotransmitters are lost; the remaining 90 percent are released from the receptors to be taken back by monoamine transporters into the sender cell (presynaptic). This process is called "reuptake." When there is a problem in this operation, some type of disorder appears in the person's behavior.

According to some theories, a lack of stimulation of the receiver cell (a postsynaptic neuron) at a synapse can cause depression. In order to stimulate this receiver cell, SSRIs, as their name implies, inhibit the reuptake of serotonin only from the three neurotransmitters. In contrast, TCAs inhibit the reuptake of both serotonin and norepinephrine. When medication is used, serotonin stays in the synaptic gap longer than it normally would so that it can be recognized again by the receptors of the postsynaptic cell and the process can be repeated, thus the postsynaptic cell can finally be stimulated fully, as it should have been originally.

MEDICATION SIDE EFFECTS

Adverse effects of SSRIs include general side effects, suicidality, sexual side effects, and "discontinuation syndrome." Specifically, during the first four weeks of treatment with SSRIs symptoms may include nausea, drowsiness, headache, changes in weight and appetite, changes in sexual behavior, increased feelings of depression and anxiety, tremors, and increased sweating. These symptoms usually disappear after the adaptation period, but they are highly individual and drug-specific.

Regarding suicidality, there have been many accusations by patients and their families that SSRIs cause suicidal ideation and behavior. However, there is little scientific support for these claims, and manufacturers of SSRIs usually have vehemently denied them. But in early 2006 GlaxoSmithKline announced to the media that new meta-analysis of their clinical trial data revealed a statistically significant higher frequency of suicidality in patients treated with their SSRI, paroxetine (Paxil) (GlaxoSmithKline, May 2006, "Clinical Worsening and Suicide Risk," Press release; www.healthfoundation. healthspace.eu/health/antidepressants-paxil.php).

Regarding the sexual side effects, SSRIs can cause various types of sexual dysfunctions such as anorgasmia, erectile dysfunction, and diminished libido (Landen et al. 2005; Hu Xh et al. 2004). It is believed that sexual dysfunction is caused by an SSRI-induced reduction in dopamine. If the postsynaptic receptors 5-HT2 and 5-HT3 are stimulated, they decrease dopamine release from the Substantia Nigra. Because of these problems, the SSRI fluoxetine (Prozac) was recently classified as a reproductive and developmental toxin by the Center for the Evolution of Risks to Human Reproduction (CERHR), which is an expert panel at the National Institute of Environmental Health Sciences and people were advised to avoid it.

Finally, regarding the discontinuation syndrome, SSRIs have not been found to be addictive. However, a sudden discontinuation of their use may cause both somatic and psychological withdrawal symptoms that collectively are called the "SSRI discontinuation syndrome." These reactions are different from and usually less significant than the withdrawal symptoms of drugs such as opium, alcohol, or cocaine, but occasionally they have been extreme, and some patients can never withdraw completely from the SSRI drugs. In some cases, stopping the use of SSRIs can cause unpredictable and irregular acts and behaviors (e.g., violent rages, suicidal ideation), as well as an intensification of previous symptoms. In Europe, SSRI products cannot be advertised as "non-habit-forming," as they are in the United States. According to the World Health Organization, SSRIs meet the definition of "addictive" (Tamam and Ozpoyraz 2002).

Serotonin toxicity, commonly referred to as "serotonin sydrome," is a toxidrome (a form of poisoning) caused by medical treatment. Increased serotonin levels in the central nervous system can result from the use of archetypal serotonergic drugs, examples being the specific or selective serotonin reuptake inhibitors (SSRIs). The toxicity of SSRIs increases with greater dosages, but overdose of an SSRI alone is not fatal in healthy adults. The toxicity can be fatal, however, when drugs with different mechanisms are mixed together. The most common combination of therapeutic drugs likely to raise serotonin to a fatal level is the combination of MAOIs with SRIs or TCAs (Gillman 2004; Isbister et al. 2004). The duration of an episode of serotonin toxicity depends on the type of drugs that precipitated it. Many of them have durations of less than twenty-four hours, and side effects or toxicity will subside over this time, without specific treatment, if one or all of the offending drugs are reduced or ceased completely. As of the mid-2000s there was no evidence of permanent or long-term neurological effects or damage from serotonin toxicity (Whyte 2004).

In approximate order of seriousness (from least to most serious), the symptoms of serotonin toxicity, according to Dunkley (2003), include:

1. neuromuscular hyperactivity: tremor, clonus, myoclonus, hyperreflexia, and (only in late or severe stage) rigidity, which may effect truncal muscles;

2. altered mental status: excitement, agitation, and (only in late or severe stage) confusion;

3. autonomic hyperactivity: diaphoresis (excessive sweating), fever, mydriasis (eye dilation), tachycardia (elevated heart rate), moderately elevated blood pressure, and tachypnoea (rapid breathing).

The usual clinical picture is of a hypervigilant or agitated patient with tremor and hyperreflexia. Clonus and myoclonus (involuntary muscle contractions) usually begin in lower limbs and may spread and become generalized. Pyramidal rigidity (a rigidity of certain muscles) is a late development (usually it happens when MAOIs have beed mixed with SRIs) and may impair respiration if it affects truncal muscles. Serious toxicity is indicated by high rigidity, a fever higher than 38.5 degrees Celsius, and an increasing PaCO2 (arterial carbon dioxide pressures).

SEE ALSO *Anxiety; Depression, Psychological; Dopamine; Drugs of Abuse; Emotion; Neuroscience; Psychoneuroendocrinology; Psychopathology; Suicide*

BIBLIOGRAPHY

Aghajanian, George K., and G. J. Marek. 1999. Serotonin and Psychedelics. *Neuropsychopharmacology* 21 (2 suppl): 16S–23S.

De Kloet, E. Ronald. 2003. Hormones, Brain, and Stress. *Endocrine Regulations* 37 (2): 51–68.

Depression. University of Bristol. www.chm.bris.ac.uk/motm/serotonin/depression.htm.

Dunkely, E. J. C., et al. 2003. Hunter Serotonin Toxicity Criteria: A Simple and Accurate Diagnostic Decision Rule for Serotonin Toxicity. *Quarterly Journal of Medicine* 96: 635–642.

Gillman, P. K. 2004. Moclobemide and the Risk of Serotonin Toxicity (or Serotonin Syndrome). *Central Nervous System Drug Reviews* 10: 83–85.

Hiroi, Ryoko, Ross A. McDevitt, and John F. Neumaier. 2006. Estrogen Selectively Increases Tryptophan Hydroxylase-2 mRNA Expression in Distinct Subregions of Rat Midbrain Raphe Nucleus: Association between Gene Expression and Anxiety Behavior in the Open Field. *Biological Psychiatry* 60: 288–295.

Hoyer, Daniel H., Jason P. Hannon, and Graeme R. Martin. 2002. Molecular, Pharmacological, and Functional Diversity of 5-HT Receptors. *Pharmacology, Biochemistry, and Behavior* 71 (4): 533–554.

Hu Xh, et al. 2004. Incidence and Duration of Side Effects and Those Rates as Bothersome with Selective Serotonin Reuptake Inhibitor Treatment for Depression: Patient Report versus Physician Estimate. *Journal of Clinical Psychiatry* 65: 959–965.

Isbister, G. K., S. Bowe, A. Dawson, and I. Whyte. 2004. Relative Toxicity of Selective Serotonin Reuptake Inhibitors (SSRIs) in Overdose. *Journal of Toxicology, Clinical Toxicology* 32, no. 3: 277–285.

Jones, Brian J., and Thomas P. Blackburn. 2002. The Medical Benefit of 5-HT Research. *Pharmacology, Biochemistry, and Behavior* 71 (4): 555–681.

Landen, M., P. Hogberg, and M. Thase. 2005. Incidence of Sexual Side Effects in Refractory Depression during Treatment with Citalpram or Paroxetine. *Journal of Clinical Psychiatry* 66: 100–106.

Leonard, Brian E. 2001. The Immune System, Depression, and the Action of Antidepressants. *Progress in Neuropsychopharmacology and Biological Psychiatry* 25 (4): 767–804.

Lesurtel, Mickael, Rolf Graf, Boris Aleil, et al. 2006. Platelet-Derived Serotonin Mediates Liver Regeneration. *Science* 312 (April 7): 104–107.

Nash, Matthew W., K. Sugden, P. Huezo-Diaz, R. Williamson, A. Sterne, S. Purcell, S. Sham, P. C. Sham, and I. W. Craig. 2005. Association Analysis of Monomine Genes with Measures of Depression and Anxiety in a Selected Community of Sample Siblings. *American Journal Medical Genetics Part B: Neuropsychiatric Genetics* 135: 33–37.

Rapport, Maurice, Arda A. Green, and Irvine H. Page. 1948. Serum Vasoconstrictor (Serotonin). IV. Isolation and Characterization. *Journal of Biological Chemistry* 176, no. 3: 1243–1251.

Tamam, L., and N. Ozpoyraz. 2002. Selective Serotonin Reuptake Inhibitor Discontinuation Syndrome: A Review. *Advances in Therapy* 19: 17–26.

Weese-Mayer, D. E., E. M. Berry-Kravis, B. S. Maher, J. M. Silvestri, M. E. Curran, and M. L. Marazita. 2003. Sudden Infant Death Syndrome: Association with a Promoter Polymorphism of the Serotonin Transporter Gene. *American Journal of Medical Genetics* 117, no. 3 (March 15): 268–274.

Whyte, I. M. 2004. Serotonin Uptake Inhibitors. In *Medical Toxicology*, ed. R. C. Dart, 843–851. Baltimore: Lippincott, Williams and Wilkins.

Zhang, Xiaodong, Raul R. Gainetdinov, Jean-Martin Beaulieu, et al. 2005. Loss-of-Function Mutation in Tryptophan Hydroxylase-2 Identified in Unipolar Major Depression. *Neuron* 45: 11–16.

Katerina Lyroudi

SERVICE, SELECTIVE

SEE *Selective Service.*

SERVITUDE

Servitude is a relationship between two people in which one person, the servant, has to work for the benefit of another person, the master, without the right to quit and seek other employment freely. Typically, the master may sell or give the servant away under some conditions and may be thought of as having a property right in that person. In some cases, the master may be a corporate entity such as a government or business. Normally, the servant receives only basic food, shelter, and clothing from the master, although the servant's rights to own or receive property vary widely.

Servitude has existed throughout human history, and ancient civilizations organized almost all labor under some type of master-servant relationship. The peak periods for servitude in Western civilization were during the late Roman Republic (late second to mid-first centuries BCE), when almost all productive labor was performed by slaves, and during the seventeenth, eighteenth, and early nineteenth centuries in the European colonies of the Americas, where the majority of workers producing for the market worked under some form of servitude.

The relationship between master and servant is both economic and personal. Masters and servants have an unequal relationship, of course. But this does not prevent masters from seeing servants as social as well as economic assets and taking care of them beyond the minimum required to keep a valuable worker productive. And it does not prevent servants from seeing their masters as patrons as well as employers. These sorts of feudal relationships may be more or less present, depending on a number of variables, including the connection of the plantation or workshop to a wider marketplace; the potential profits to be gained from servants' labor; whether master and servant live together; whether they share a common language, ethnicity, culture, or religion; and the values taught by their culture and religion.

In addition, there are generally capitalist elements to the master-servant relationship: The servant is also a worker who produces the goods that the master needs. Often the master is a participant in a competitive marketplace where productivity is all-important and the servant has little stake in the master's success in the market. The balance between feudal and capitalist elements in the master-servant relationship is responsible for many of the differences in servants' treatment under different forms of servitude.

Servitude and free labor are normally incompatible. Free laborers resent servants and masters because servitude depresses wage rates and because they may feel discriminated against by the feudal relationship to the extent that any exists. For example, working people in the Northern United States in the early nineteenth century opposed slavery in the Southern states not so much because of their belief in universal principles of human rights, but because they feared that the "slave power" of the Southern planters might impair their own freedom. By their response that Southern slaves were treated better than Northern workingmen, Southern apologists for slavery actually fed these fears. Rural landholders who are heavily invested in being masters, both in economic terms and as a part of their identity, tend to resist the end of servitude, but the bourgeois often see servitude as inefficient and ideologically unsound. Thus servitude tends to change forms or decline as capitalist free labor rises.

Servitude has existed in many forms around the world and in virtually all times and places. Among the forms of servitude are slavery, indenture, debt servitude, serfdom, prison labor, conscription or corvée, and ethnic or lineage servitude.

SLAVERY

Slavery is distinguished from other forms of servitude by being lifelong and heritable. In Western traditions, the children of an enslaved woman are usually slaves regard-less of the status of the father, although this may not be true in some non-Western slave systems. The slave is the personal property of the master, and that property right can be transferred for cash. Slave systems, like other forms of servitude, have always had legal and customary restrictions on the masters' right to exploit slaves' labor, abuse or neglect slaves, or transfer them to another owner. Free people can be enslaved, most commonly as a result of capture in wartime, but also as a legal punishment. Slaves can be freed, or manumitted, by their masters as a reward for service or in return for payment, although there are often legal and customary restrictions to the practice.

One tends to think of slavery as being tied to race, and in the Americas in the early modern period this was certainly the case. Prior to the fifteenth century, however, most slaves in Europe, Asia, and the Middle East were of similar ethnicity to their masters, and this was commonly true of slaves in antiquity. Certainly the equation of slavery and African origins did not exist before the fifteenth century. Having the same or a similar ethnicity and religion as one's master, however, conferred few or no legal rights enforceable against the master.

Millions of people came from Africa to the Americas, the Middle East, and the Mediterranean as slaves between the fifteenth and nineteenth centuries. The modern African diaspora is mostly the product of the slave trade. In the Islamic world, slaves were commonly employed as personal retainers—household employees, administrators, and soldiers—rather than agricultural laborers. As in the Western world, most Islamic slaves were brutally exploited, but some were able to rise to positions of great power, delegated by their master but no less real. Egypt was ruled by a *junta* of slave soldiers, the Mamluks, for several centuries. The Ottoman Empire was ruled by a sultan but administered by a grand vizier and his assistants, who were the sultan's slaves.

Most countries abolished slavery in the nineteenth century, and as a legally sanctioned system it is very rare today. Most of what is called slavery in modern times, such as the imprisonment of young women in the sex trade or of workers in sweatshops, is more properly classified as indenture or debt servitude. Slavery in the individual, permanent, heritable sense still exists in a few African and Middle Eastern countries. Slavery is formally outlawed everywhere but is accepted by custom and social practice in Mauretania, Sudan, Yemen, Somalia, and many other areas in the region not under the effective jurisdiction of national governments.

INDENTURE

Under indenture, the property right of a master in a servant is transferable but limited in time, and the children of the servant are usually free. The conditions under which indentured servants work are governed by contract, custom, and sometimes by law. Indenture typically occurs when free people more or less voluntarily agree to indenture themselves for a period of time in exchange for some benefit, usually financial, although they might be tricked or coerced into signing a contract.

Many European immigrants to the Americas in the seventeenth and eighteenth centuries came as indentured servants, having agreed to work for a period of five or seven years in exchange for transportation to America and a small grant of land, livestock, and farm equipment at the end of the contract. Some were prisoners or were forced to accept indenture in order to avoid imprisonment, while others were actually kidnapped off the street; but most signed up willingly enough in order to escape horrible poverty in Europe.

In general, indenture is no longer legal, but it is still quite common. Many people sign employment contracts, and those contracts can legally contain penalties for nonfulfillment, but individuals are not forced to work against their will. Outside the law, however, many illegal migrants from East Asia sign indenture contracts with the smugglers who bring them to the United States, the Middle East, or elsewhere. These contracts are not legal in any country, but they can be enforced by extralegal means by the criminal masters. In some cases, masters have considerable power in local political systems and are able to enforce theoretically illegal contracts using governmental power, so it is harder to claim that indenture has been completely outlawed.

DEBT SERVITUDE

In debt servitude, the master gains a property right over the servant similar to indenture, and that property right can be bought and sold. However, instead of the servitude being limited in time, it lasts until the servant pays off a debt. The master is typically in charge of the accounting so this may take quite a while. In some systems, the debt is heritable, as is the servant status. This is called peonage.

In Spanish America after the collapse of the *encomienda* system (a sort of ethnic servitude) in the sixteenth century, wealthy landowners ensured a steady supply of farm labor by subjecting the local peasants to peonage. The peons were required to buy their goods at the landowner's store and were paid in scrip that could only be exchanged there. They were encouraged to borrow against the value of the coming year's crop, and inevitably found their debt, and thus their labor obligation, increasing year by year.

A modern form of debt servitude is common in the sex industry. Young rural women are sold by their parents in order to satisfy a debt and find themselves working in brothels until the creditor is satisfied. This frequently lasts until age or disease makes the woman unfit for profitable work in prostitution.

As in indenture, the limited nature of debt servitude tends to weaken the feudal ties between master and servant. Masters generally have little compunction about "releasing" servants who become unprofitable, often leaving them destitute. No country's laws permit debt peonage today, but influential masters often get the support of local officials and criminals are able to enforce debt servitude without benefit of police power.

SERFDOM

Serfs were servants tied to the land under a feudal system. Serfs worked for the owner of the land under conditions typically fairly tightly regulated by law and tradition. A wide variety of rules applied, but typically the master could call upon a serf to perform a specific set of tasks (tend a certain field, for example) or provide a certain amount of labor (so many days or so many hours a day, for example) during the agricultural cycle. The serf could not be bought or sold without the land to which he or she was attached. Medieval peasant villages often provided much of their own government, but the master-serf relationship generally gave the master some sort of legal jurisdiction as well as a right to labor service, and the serf gained some right to protection, support in illness and old age, and other social services from his or her master. The serfs' traditional rights to use the soil as they saw fit often kept landowners from developing their land, and the abolition of serfdom proved advantageous to progressive landlords in the early modern period, if not to the serfs themselves.

In seventeenth-century Russia, on the other hand, masters gained the right to transfer serfs fairly easily from one piece of land to another in response to the rapid expansion of agriculture into eastern lands captured from nomadic peoples. Subsequently, by a legal fiction, serfs could be transferred from one master to another without a transfer of land, and the condition of the Russian serf became similar to that of a slave, subject to being bought and sold as an individual. In medieval Western Europe, on the other hand, serfs had stability in their villages and could be locally influential farmers with considerable wealth and security.

No country permits serfdom today, and relationships of this type are rare.

PRISON LABOR

In a prison labor system, property rights to servants are owned not by an individual but by the government. Governments might exercise this right directly or transfer it to a private party in return for rent. The servitude is a punishment for a real or pretended crime, is limited in time by the prisoner's sentence, and is not heritable.

In nineteenth-century Australia, much of the productive labor was performed by prisoners, whose labor was leased by free settlers. Free laborers resented prison labor, though, as it drove down wages and discouraged free migration, so as each state's economy matured, it stopped accepting transported prisoners. In the American South in the aftermath of the Civil War, imprisonment was a tool of social control over the newly freed black population. Landowners rented prisoners' labor, which helped defray the cost of the huge prison systems. Other prisoners worked on chain gangs to build new infrastructure or produce products the state needed. In Stalinist Russia, prisoners performed much of the labor used to develop the Siberian industrial plants, which produced the weapons that helped win World War II.

Prison labor is very common today. The United States has laws against the importation or transport across state lines of products made by prisoners, but states still use prison labor for many items used by their governments, the most famous being license plates. Chinese factories sometimes contract with the prison system for labor, although this must be concealed if the products are to be exported.

CONSCRIPTION OR CORVÉE

In conscription or corvée systems, free individuals are required to work for their government for a certain period of time as a condition of citizenship or residence. Conscription generally refers to military service, while corvée implies forced civilian service, often as labor on infrastructure projects. The service is generally limited in time, either for the duration of a conflict or for a certain fixed period.

Conscription reached its height in the age of mass armies in the first half of the twentieth century. Millions of conscripts, often serving very much against their will, fought on all sides of the world wars of that period. Conscription into the British navy during the seventeenth and eighteenth century was less organized, accomplished by press-gangs of sailors who would literally kidnap men and force them onto ships, where they would serve for years.

Corvée labor was a feature of colonial practice during the second great wave of European colonialism in the nineteenth century. The most notorious example is the forced recruitment of rubber collectors in the Belgian Congo. Workers' families would be kidnapped and raped or beaten if the worker ran away, and if workers didn't bring in enough product, their hands might be cut off by colonial soldiers. Nazi Germany also used corvée labor in which civilians taken from occupied territories were used to supplement prison labor in the arms industry.

Conscription is still very common today. Many countries consider military service obligations to be a part of civic education for their citizens. Corvée labor is still found in many developing countries on a limited scale, often used for road repair or urban beautification campaigns.

ETHNIC OR LINEAGE SERVITUDE

As with prison labor and conscription, in ethnic or lineage servitude the owner is a group: an ethnic group, a powerful family, or a government. The servants generally owe their labor collectively as well. A particular ethnic group, defeated nation, family, village, or other collective entity will be required to furnish a certain amount of labor to their masters under conditions set by custom or law.

The best-known example of this in European-controlled territories is the *encomienda* system in Spanish America during the colonial era. After the Spanish conquest, the defeated native peoples were required to pay tribute in the form of products and labor: so many bushels of corn and so many men for such an amount of time from each village. The government used some of the labor on its own infrastructure projects, to build cathedrals, fortifications, viceroys' palaces, and the like. Most labor service, though, was assigned to Spanish *conquistadors* on a temporary basis, not as a property right but as a payment for the masters' service to the state. Spanish masters might employ the laborers on their own land as agricultural workers, and the situation of the indigenous people in some cases approached that of serfs under Western European feudalism. Many *encomienda* Indians were sent to work in mines, where they were brutally exploited. The *encomienda* system deteriorated as the native population declined through the fifteenth century. Indians could also escape the *encomienda* system by leaving their villages and moving to the cities or living on lands owned by Europeans, who would employ them as wage laborers or peons.

Lineage slavery was prevalent in west Africa, as, for example, among the Fulani of Guinea. After the conquest of the Fouta Djallon highlands in the seventeenth century, the defeated peoples were adopted into Fulani clans but given distinctive surnames. The members of the "slave" lineage groups were given land to plant crops on, while the descendents of the conquerors continued their pastoral lifestyle. The obligation of farmers to pay in-kind tribute and labor service to herders continued under French colonial rule, but was abolished after independence. The sense of status remains, however, governing marriage choice, leadership within communities, and patron-client relationships, even though as servitude the system has ended.

THE AFTERMATH OF SERVITUDE

It is common for all forms of servitude to have lingering repercussions. Individuals can escape servitude, either at the end of their term of service, by flight, or by manumission. Whole populations can escape through changes in laws and customs. But even a profound social revolution cannot erase the cultural memories of servitude, which continue to affect relationships between the descendants of masters and the descendants of servants for many generations. When mixed with racial differences, as can be seen in the United States in the twenty-first century, this can produce poisonous social dysfunction.

Sometimes, however, the aftermath is more positive. In the Roman Empire after the first century CE, for example, as the tide of conquest stopped and, with it, the flow of new slaves dried up, the gradual manumission of most slaves led to the establishment of a fairly benign system of patron-client relationships between patricians and the descendents of their freedmen. This patronage system formed the basis for the remarkable strength of Roman culture even after the barbarian invasions starting in the fourth century CE.

SEE ALSO *Capitalism; Exploitation; Feudal Mode of Production; Feudalism; Latifundia; Mode of Production; Prison Industry; Prison Psychology; Prisons; Selective Service; Slave Trade; Slave-Gun Cycle; Slavery; Slavery Industry; Working Class*

BIBLIOGRAPHY

Curtin, Philip D. 1998. *The Rise and Fall of the Plantation Complex: Essays in Atlantic History.* 2nd ed. Cambridge, U.K.: Cambridge University Press.

Du Bois, W. E. B. 1999. *Souls of Black Folk.* New York: Norton & Co. (Orig. pub. 1903.)

Gaspar, David, and Darlene Hine. 1996. *More Than Chattel: Black Women and Slavery in the Americas.* Bloomington: Indiana University Press.

Hochschild, Adam. 1998. *King Leopold's Ghost: A Story of Greed, Terror, and Heroism in Colonial Africa.* Boston: Houghton Mifflin.

Klein, Herbert S. 1999. *The Atlantic Slave Trade.* Cambridge, U.K.: Cambridge University Press.

Kolchin, Peter. 1987. *Unfree Labor: American Slavery and Russian Serfdom.* Cambridge, MA: Belknap Press.

Patterson, Orlando. 1982. *Slavery and Social Death: A Comparative Study.* Cambridge, MA: Harvard University Press.

Solzhenitsyn, Aleksandr. 2002. *The Gulag Archipelago, 1918–1956.* Trans. Thomas P. Whitney and Harry Willetts, ed. Edward Ericson. New York: Harper Perennial.

Stewart R. King

SETTING, PRICE

SEE *Price Setting and Price Taking.*

SETTLEMENT

The term *settlement* has a number of meanings attributed respectively to the areas of law, finance, archaeology, and history. The legal definition generally refers to the act of settling a dispute or disagreement and reaching an agreement on the case, which then settles the claim. Often both sides of a lawsuit have a strong incentive to settle, chiefly to avoid costs. Courts can enforce settlements, and the party in default can be sued for breach of contract. In modern litigation, most suits are either withdrawn or settled, and settlements have become an important feature of the legal process. In rarer instances, the process of giving real estate, land, or some other heritage to someone is called a settlement, as is the respective document.

In finance the term generally describes the settling or payment of an account. More specifically, a settlement delivers securities or interests in securities to fulfill contractual obligations. This is usually preceded by trading and involves a purchase price. Before the introduction of the electronic settlement system in the 1990s, securities settlement was associated with a certain financial risk because it involved the physical movement of paper instruments, which were relatively easy to steal or forge. The transition from paper-based to electronic settlement is accomplished by immobilization, which means that securities are held by depositaries that are electronically linked to a settlement system. The ultimate goal is to dispense with paper instruments entirely (dematerialization).

The term *settlement* is also used to describe a specific human habitat that may include all sizes of human settlements, from hamlets to cities. More specifically, a settlement is the most rudimentary form of human habitation in a formerly uninhabited area. The term also refers to archaeological sites of human habitation. Settlement patterns and landscape approaches, which record material traces of human habitation, have become central for contemporary archaeology because they help explain long-term cultural and behavioral change. Thus archaeologists believe that the first European settlement in North America occurred around 1000 CE, when Viking explorers made their way to Vinland, which is probably modern Newfoundland.

For reasons unknown, European contact with the North American continent was interrupted until the sixteenth century, when the Spaniards reached Florida. In 1565 the Spaniards established the first permanent European settlement at Saint Augustine, a base for missionaries and (slave) traders. A few decades later rival European powers founded settlements along the east coast of the continent. Around 1600 the French assumed control over the Saint Lawrence Valley, founded the settlements of Quebec (1608) and Montreal (1642), and during the century succeeded in bringing a few hundred settlers to Louisiana. While the Dutch controlled the Hudson River valley for much of the seventeenth century, the major settlements of the English Crown were established in Jamestown (1607) and Plymouth (1620). At the same time the Spanish also started to settle in the Southwest of the continent; however, it took them over 150 years to establish outposts on the coast of the Pacific.

In the Southwest and West the Spanish eventually yielded to American settlers who claimed the territory during the nineteenth century, a claim that not only involved land but also expressed a belief in individual liberty and economic opportunity. The settlement of the West was hastened by the Homestead Act of 1862, which granted 160 acres to any family that lived on the land for five years. In the American West a small village or collection of houses was called a settlement.

In the antebellum South, the term *settlement* sometimes referred to the living quarters of the slaves on a plantation. In urban areas of the United States, the word *settlement* acquired a different meaning. The term *social settlement* originated in London's East End, where Samuel Barnett and a group of Oxford students founded Toynbee Hall in 1884 by "settling" in a working-class area, not only to help their neighbors but to learn firsthand about the mounting problems of urbanization. Only two years later the first settlement house was founded in the United States, and the settlement movement grew rapidly, with Hull-House in Chicago, College Settlement in New York, and South End House in Boston becoming the most famous social settlements. Because settlements mainly worked for and among ethnically diverse urban populations, they became central to the reform efforts of the Progressive Era. The settlement idea also spread to western Europe, South Asia, and Japan; and the International Federation of Settlements and Neighbourhood Centres was founded in 1926 as a worldwide association of national, regional, and local organizations working to strengthen communities in society.

SEE ALSO *Agricultural Industry; Cities; Colonialism; Finance; Law; Peasantry; Plantation; Settlement, Negotiated; Settlement, Tobacco; Settlements; Slavery*

BIBLIOGRAPHY

Billman, Brian R., and Gary M. Feinman, eds. 1999. *Settlement Pattern Studies in the Americas: Fifty Years since Virú.* Washington, DC: Smithsonian Institution Press.

Carson, Mina. 1990. *Settlement Folk: Social Thought and the American Settlement Movement, 1885–1930.* Chicago: University of Chicago Press.

Middleton, Richard. 2002. *Colonial America: A History 1565–1776.* Oxford: Blackwell.

Milner, Clyde A., Carol A. O'Connor, and Martha A. Sandweiss, eds. 1994. *The Oxford History of the American West.* New York: Oxford University Press.

Wahlgren, Erik. 1986. *The Vikings and America.* New York: Thames and Hudson.

Weber, David J. 1992. *The Spanish Frontier in North America.* New Haven, CT: Yale University Press.

Anja Schüler

SETTLEMENT, NEGOTIATED

A settlement is a contract between two or more parties to resolve a legal dispute without a trial. Most civil cases are decided by settlement, and the contract usually incorporates the desire of the parties to give up their legal claims against one another in return for certain conditions written into the settlement agreement. When a settlement agreement is reached, it is usually submitted to the court with jurisdiction over the dispute in the form of a joint stipulation by the parties to be incorporated into an order. In suits where the plaintiff's claims have been satisfied by the payment of money, the plaintiff can simply file a notice with the court that the case has been dismissed.

Because litigation is expensive and parties may not have the financial resources to afford protracted legal proceedings, settlement is encouraged. A court may request, or order, the parties to a dispute to participate in a settlement conference or mediation to attempt to resolve their dispute before a trial is held. A mediation or settlement conference provides the parties with an opportunity to resolve their differences without a costly and time-consuming trial. Settlement talks also reduce the risks associated with a trial. In many cases, settlement negotiations lead to a more favorable outcome for the parties than a trial because the parties retain more control over the process. Courts tend to favor settlement negotiations as a way to promote judicial efficiency and reduce the backlog of cases on the docket.

In the interest of facilitating settlement, the law treats settlement discussions as confidential and the substance of such discussions as inadmissible at trial and other proceedings. In highly sensitive cases, if a settlement agreement is achieved, the agreement may require the parties to keep its contents confidential. It is important to note, however, that confidentiality is not possible in class action cases in the United States. Pursuant to Rule 23 of the Federal Rules of Civil Procedure and complementary state court rules, all settlements are subject to approval by the courts, and notice to be bound by a settlement must be directed to all class members. Class action lawsuits are more likely to be resolved by a negotiated settlement given the number of parties and the scale of the potential damages involved. Other types of lawsuits that tend to result in settlement include personal injury lawsuits and product liability actions.

Courts will enforce a settlement in the same way they enforce other valid contracts. If a party breaches a settlement agreement, that party can be sued for breach of contract. In some jurisdictions, the original civil action can be revived if a party breaches the settlement agreement.

Settlements are exclusive to civil cases. In criminal proceedings, a prosecutor and defendant may enter into a plea bargain prior to trial. Similar to the class action context in civil proceedings, the judge in a criminal proceeding must approve the plea bargain reached by the parties.

SEE ALSO *Law; Settlement, Tobacco*

BIBLIOGRAPHY

Coben, James R., and Peter R. Thompson. 2006. Disputing Irony: A Systematic Look at Litigation about Mediation. *Harvard Negotiation Law Review* 11: 69–70.

Corpus Juris Secundum. 2002. Vol. 15An, 61–172. Saint Paul, MN: Thompson West.

George, James P. 2006. Access to Justice, Costs, and Legal Aid. *American Journal of Comparative Law* 54 (suppl.): 293–316.

Shaw, Margaret L., and Linda L. Singer. 2005. Settlement, Post-Settlement, and More: Issues in Mediating Class Action. *Alternatives to the High Cost of Litigation* 23: 61–73.

Klinton W. Alexander

SETTLEMENT, TOBACCO

From 1954 to 2006 three separate waves of civil litigation in the United States occurred against the tobacco industry based on claims of severe health problems associated with tobacco use. Tobacco industry corporations sued during this period included Philip Morris, R. J. Reynolds, Brown and Williamson, American Tobacco, United States Tobacco, British American Tobacco, Lorillard, and the Liggett Group. Also sued during this period were tobacco industry–affiliated organizations including the Tobacco Institute, Center for Indoor Air Research, and Council for Tobacco Research. All three of these affiliated organizations became defunct in 1999 due to the 1998 Master Settlement Agreement signed by the tobacco industry and attorneys general from forty-six states.

THREE WAVES OF TOBACCO LITIGATION

From 1954 to 1978 the first wave of 125 individual personal injury lawsuits mostly related to lung cancer were filed against the tobacco industry based on the legal theories of negligence, misrepresentation, and breach of warranty. The tobacco industry argued in its defense that there was no proven connection between smoking and disease. Few of these cases went to trial and none were decided against the tobacco industry.

From 1979 to 1993 a second wave of about two hundred individual personal injury lawsuits were filed against the tobacco industry using the legal theories of negligence, misrepresentation, breach of warranty, breach of product liability, and negligent failure to inform. In 1964 after the United States surgeon general's landmark report linked smoking to lung cancer, the tobacco industry continued to maintain in litigation that while there was no proven link between smoking and disease, smokers also assumed the risk when using tobacco due to health warning labels on cigarette packs. Cigarette warning labels were mandated by the federal Cigarette Labeling and Advertising Act of 1965.

Only eighteen of these cases were litigated with only one case filed in 1983 in New Jersey, *Cipollone v. Liggett Group, Inc.*, decided against Liggett Tobacco Company. In 1985 a jury awarded $400,000 to Tony Cipollone, the husband of the original plaintiff Rose Cipollone who had previously died of cancer. This decision was partially overturned when in 1992 the United States Supreme Court ruled there was no liability due to failure to warn of health dangers because of federal cigarette pack warning labels. The United States Supreme Court sent the case back to the New Jersey federal court to rule on the remaining legal claims. However, due to the expense of further litigation the plaintiff dismissed the lawsuit.

In the third wave of cases from 1994 to 2006, several individual and private class action lawsuits primarily in California, Florida, Oregon, Kansas, and Puerto Rico were decided against the tobacco industry using legal theories of torts, fraud, conspiracy, misrepresentation, breach of warranty, breach of product liability, and negligent failure to inform. Legal theories used in state class action cases included using statistics to ascertain if a percentage of Medicaid smokers suffered from disease due to smoking and violation of state tort, consumer protection, antitrust, and racketeering laws. This theory was used to make it easier to sue and win. It was much more difficult to win arguing direct causation between tobacco use and a disease and death. Statistical trends represent an easier form of proof.

The first important private class action lawsuit was *Castano v. American Tobacco* filed in federal court by sixty plaintiffs' law firms on May 9, 1994, on behalf of all nicotine addicted individuals. While the class was certified by federal district Judge Okla Jones on February 17, 1995, this class was later decertified on May 23, 1996, by the U.S. Fifth Circuit Court of Appeals. The court ruled this class certification was inappropriate because there were too many differences in the plaintiffs' claims and wide differences in state laws making the case unmanageable. This decision initiated several new private and state class action lawsuits. The first state lawsuit was filed by Mississippi in 1994 followed by Florida, Texas, and Minnesota. Florida and Mississippi settled in 1997 and Texas and Minnesota settled in 1998 for a combined total of $40 billion allocated over twenty-five years adjusted for inflation and no spending restrictions.

In 1998 the Master Settlement Agreement with the other forty-six states was signed. Payments of $206 billion over twenty-five years adjusted for inflation were awarded to the states. Due to the lack of spending restrictions in the settlement, most states by 2006 had not provided minimal funding for state anti-tobacco programs as defined by best practices by the Centers for Disease Control and Prevention. These state anti-tobacco programs were to include community programs, school programs, youth enforcement, counter-marketing, cessation, and state anti-tobacco education programs.

2006 FEDERAL COURT DECISION

In the federal district court case of *United States of America v. Philip Morris USA Inc., et al.* filed by the United States Justice Department in 1999 and decided in 2006, Judge Gladys Kessler ruled that the tobacco industry's fundamental defense in litigation from 1954 to 2006 was a purported claim of insufficient evidence linking smoking to disease. Internally, however, the tobacco industry long acknowledged that cigarettes were harmful and also addictive.

Judge Kessler also ruled that those in the tobacco industry were racketeers as defined under the federal Racketeering Influenced and Corrupt Organizations Act. The court decision also ordered the tobacco industry to permanently refrain from making misleading statements regarding the health and safety of cigarettes and to make public corrective statements on the dangers of cigarette addictiveness and the serious health effects of smoking and secondhand tobacco smoke. This ruling was appealed by the tobacco industry and will be reviewed by a higher court.

EVOLUTION OF LEGAL FINDINGS

While the tobacco industry was highly successful in the first two waves of litigation that were filed from 1954 to 1994 on behalf of individual plaintiffs, the third wave of litigation from 1994 to 2006 represented a dramatic reversal of legal fortune for the industry. This reversal of legal fortune has been due to the advent of new legal theories including state Medicaid reimbursement and revelations of significant industry misconduct revealed in previously secret industry tobacco documents.

SEE ALSO *Disease; Foundations, Charitable; Settlement; Settlement, Negotiated; Smoking; Tobacco Industry*

BIBLIOGRAPHY

Blanke, Douglas. 2002. *Towards Health with Justice: Litigation and Public Inquiries as Tools for Tobacco Control.* Geneva, Switzerland: Tobacco Free Initiative, World Health Organization.

Givel, Michael. 2006. Failure to Change Through Multiple Policy Instruments and Venues the Tobacco Industry Policy Subsystem in the States from 1990 to 2003. *Policy Studies Journal* 34 (3): 453–457.

Givel, Michael, and Stanton A. Glantz. 2004. The "Global Settlement" with the Tobacco Industry: 6 Years Later. *American Journal of Public Health* 94 (2): 218–224.

U. S. District Court for the District of Columbia. 2006. *U.S. of America, Plaintiff, Civil Action No. 99-2496 (GK) and Tobacco-Free Kids Action Fund, American Cancer Society, American Heart Association, American Lung Association, Americans For Nonsmokers' Rights, and National African American Tobacco Prevention Network, Intervenors, v. Philip Morris USA, Inc., (f/k/a Philip Morris, Inc.), et al., Defendants.*

U.S. Supreme Court. 1992. *Cipollone v. Liggett Group* (90-1038), 505 U.S. 504. http://caselaw.lp.findlaw.com/scripts/getcase.pl?court=US&vol=505&invol=504.

Michael Givel

SEVEN YEARS WAR

SEE *Quebecois Movement.*

SEX, INTERRACIAL

Public disapproval of and legal restrictions on interracial sex, or racial exogamy, have varied widely in civilization, but sex between members of different racial groups has remained common whenever people of different races have lived together. Attitudes toward interracial relationships have evolved since the Age of Discovery and are connected with trends in society, culture, politics, and economics.

THE SIXTEENTH AND SEVENTEENTH CENTURIES

The few people of color in England and in the English colonies in the late sixteenth century and early seventeenth century seemed to have been able to have white sexual and marital partners without great difficulty. Famously, John Rolfe (not Captain John Smith) married Pocahontas and brought her back to England to live with him in the 1630s. In other European countries at the time, interracial sexual relationships, both informal and sanctified by marriage, were not uncommon. In Spain and Portugal there was a long tradition of *mestizaje*, or race mixing, between whites, Moors (including people from black Africa), and Jews. These relationships were completely unremarkable until after 1492, when increasing restrictions on "New Christians" meant that those in mixed relationships and their mestizo children had a social handicap to overcome. Also after 1492 Spaniards and Portuguese began to have relations with Indians and Africans in the New World, and the mestizos who resulted from these unions often rose to high ranks in their colonial societies. *Limpieza de sangre*, or purity of blood, was an officially defined characteristic that could be purchased by someone whose ancestry was actually partly Indian or African. Nonetheless, mixed ancestry was a handicap for the children of the conquistadores and their Indian partners.

THE EIGHTEENTH AND NINETEENTH CENTURIES

From being somewhat unusual, culturally exotic, and a slight handicap for the resulting children in the sixteenth century, interracial sex and marriage became taboo (although still enthusiastically practiced) by the nineteenth century. White indentured servant women in Virginia in the eighteenth century who had children of color found their own indentures extended and sometimes their children sold into slavery despite the general legal provision that children follow the free or slave status of the mother. Thomas Jefferson's long-lasting relationship with his slave Sally Hemings was potent political ammunition for his opponents. Federalist newspapers at the time brought up the rumored relationship, and even centuries afterward defenders of his reputation try to explain away the evidence and deny that any relationship took place. Jefferson overcame these attacks—he was reelected despite the fact that the rumors were widely heard and apparently also believed. Many white men in the U.S. South before 1865 had unacknowledged informal sexual relationships with their slaves, and these relationships sometimes had negative consequences for the white partners if they became known. The increasing strength of racial separatist ideologies meant that these white men had to engage in a sort of hypocritical double-

think, supporting the idea of racial separation in their public lives while practicing interracial sex in private. By the mid-nineteenth century the southern diarist Mary Chesnut reflected the views of women of her class in her acid criticism of wealthy white men who fathered children with their slaves. In other slave societies in the Americas, the situation was somewhat less difficult for those white men who were involved in long-term sexual relationships with women of color. Men who wished to marry women of color generally had to give up some of their civil rights, and those in acknowledged long-term relationships could suffer in social regard and economic relationships with other whites. Men of color who had sexual relations with white women anywhere in the Americas were in great peril—the penalty could be death or, at a minimum, brutal physical punishment and sale to a faraway master. Outside the United States, white men who had informal sexual relations with women of color (as opposed to seeking marriage with them) faced few penalties in social regard and none at all under law. This led to a situation of considerable license, of which some men took enthusiastic advantage.

The traditional interpretation of interracial sex between whites and African American slaves (and between Spanish conquistadores and Indian women) is that these were rapes. Much recent research suggests that most children of mixed race in the slave societies of the Americas were the product of lasting relationships that produced a number of children. Often these relationships were between poor white men and slave or Indian women they worked or lived alongside, as, for example, that between Toussaint Charbonneau and Sacagawea from around 1800 until her death after 1810. It is unclear what inducements led the women to join and remain with their partners. However, in slave societies, although the children of a slave woman and a free man were born slaves, they had a much greater chance of gaining their freedom than did the children of two slaves. And the social price paid by a poor white man for being in an interracial relationship would be less than that paid by a wealthy planter such as Jefferson. Moreover, the price a slave owner or hacendado paid for regularly raping his slaves or peons was unrest in his workforce, and by the beginning of the nineteenth century there was a price paid in social regard in white society, especially in North America. Indeed the most notorious rake, Thomas Thistlewood of Jamaica, had numerous run-ins with his neighbors because of his general brutality toward slaves.

THE TWENTIETH CENTURY

After the abolition of slavery, restrictions on interracial sex became even more pronounced in most former slave societies in the Americas. These prejudices began to strengthen even in places where there had been few or no slaves, such as in the northern states of the United States and in Britain and France. In former slave societies an ideology of white solidarity, reinforced by legal segregation, meant that even relationships between poor white men and women of color became less common. In contrast, in areas where there were many native people, such as Mexico and the Andean region of South America, informal relations between the races had always been common, but mixed marriages became more common and tolerated after independence from Spain. In Latin America there was a racial hierarchy, but sexual relationships and marriages between people from different levels of the hierarchy were not harshly punished. In the United States, though, by the early twentieth century antimiscegenation laws were common, affecting all interracial relations, not just those between blacks and whites. These laws remained in force until 1967, when they were ruled unconstitutional by the U.S. Supreme Court in *Loving v. Virginia*. Germany adopted harsh miscegenation laws under National Socialism (Nazism). South Africa had miscegenation laws under apartheid, and Israel in the early twenty-first century does not recognize marriage between Jews and non-Jews, although there is no attempt to hinder informal interracial sex. In other areas there have been no laws against mixed marriages or informal relationships, but in many places people in such relationships and their children have faced significant social handicaps, including active interference by the state in child rearing, as in Australia, where children of mixed native and white ancestry were routinely taken away from their parents by the state and raised in orphanages until the 1970s.

Informal restrictions and bureaucratic impediments to interracial sex have been much more pervasive and long-lasting than formal laws. In many places in the U.S. South and in the former slave societies of the Americas until the middle of the twentieth century, a man of color could be beaten or killed with impunity for having or even suggesting sex with a white woman. "Quadroon balls" in southern cities functioned to pair white men with women of color, but men sought to conceal their participation, and overt relationships with women of color had grave social consequences.

In the early twenty-first century throughout Europe and North America, men of color who are in sexual relationships with white women continue to suffer social penalties from both whites and fellow members of their minority group. Although white men in these societies often seek out women of color for casual sex—taking advantage of still-extant racial power differentials—more formal relationships invite some social consequences. Mixed-race couples in the United States still report cases of housing discrimination at higher rates than same-race minority families. The most serious prejudice in this regard is against relationships between blacks and whites—exogamy between whites and other racial groups is somewhat better tolerated by both those groups and white society. However, even exogamy between groups that are traditionally the targets of racial discrimination—as between blacks and Latinos or Asians in the United States—has attracted opponents within those groups.

However, restrictions on interracial sex and marriage are much weaker in the early twenty-first century than they were even in the mid-twentieth century. Popular culture bears witness, with interracial couples in movies and television not raising any eyebrows, and powerful people have successful political careers while married to members of other races (for instance, Clarence Thomas, associate justice of the U.S. Supreme Court).

EXPLANATIONS

The traditional explanation for prohibitions on exogamy is that people naturally fear the unfamiliar and find it distasteful. This begs the question of why many men from dominant groups in racially mixed societies often seek out women of other races for informal sex. Of course in some cases, as in sixteenth-century Mexico, there were few white women available, but even when there are many white women, white men often seek out women of color for at least informal relationships. Sociobiologists such as Jared Diamond (*The Third Chimpanzee*) argue that men seek to control sexual access to women they control—members of their own group—while undermining such attempts by males of other groups, thus providing a neat explanation for both restrictions on interracial sex and informal white male exogamy. The problem with sociobiological explanations is that human genetics changes slowly, whereas popular resistance to racial exogamy in Europe and North America has waxed and waned during the last five hundred years, a blink of the eye in evolutionary terms.

Much of the explanation for popular opposition to racial exogamy must lie in the realms of socioeconomic, cultural, and ideological changes. In the area of ideology, Christian religious teaching in the 1400s held that human beings had a single origin—as children of Adam and Eve. All people were human and fully eligible for all the sacraments, including marriage. Reformation thinkers did not deny this scriptural analysis, but the period saw the establishment of national churches in Protestant Europe, and membership in the national church meant citizenship. Inasmuch as slave owners and colonial masters were reluctant to grant the rights of citizenship to their racial subordinates, they also were reluctant to think of them as fellow Christians and marriageable. In any case, the Enlightenment reduced the influence of Christian teaching over Europeans and also raised the possibility that the various races had separate origins. Eighteenth- and nineteenth-century racial ideologies tended to dehumanize the racial other and encouraged whites to preserve racial distinctions in all things, including sex and marriage. The high point of this ideological current was in the early twentieth century, when a harsh racial climate, given scientific sanction by the eugenics movement, spurred the adoption of antimiscegenation laws in most states in the United States that did not already have them. The Virginia law overturned by *Loving*, for example, was enacted in 1924 and specifically cited eugenics as one of its motivations. There had been miscegenation laws on the books in a number of states in the South before the Civil War, but all such laws in former Confederate states were wiped off the books during Reconstruction. (Maryland was an exception since it remained loyal during the Civil War and was not "reconstructed.") When the laws returned in the period of Jim Crow, they generally used eugenic arguments. The eventual failure of these laws is a signpost of the generalized decline in the power of racist ideologies in the late twentieth century.

Larger historical forces also had an impact on public attitudes toward interracial sex. At the end of the fifteenth century Europeans had little contact with the racial other outside of Iberia, and it was precisely in Spain and Portugal where there were some restrictions on interracial sex. Those few non-Europeans who lived outside of Spain and Portugal had no difficulty selecting partners of other races. As Europe spread its economic and political control over the entire globe, Europeans felt a need for racial solidarity in the face of much more numerous subject peoples. Support for racial endogamy can be seen as part of a package of ideological responses to the problems presented by colonialism. One strong argument for this point of view is that restrictions on interracial sex and marriage were strongest in those places where Europeans (or their descendants born in the Americas) ruled over large numbers of non-European peoples: in Spanish and Portuguese America in the sixteenth and seventeenth centuries and in the United States and South Africa in the late eighteenth century, the nineteenth century, and the early twentieth century. As non-Europeans gained political power in the late twentieth century, these restrictions began to diminish. However, this explanation does not account for the persistence of popular resistance to racial exogamy or for the opposition among groups traditionally the subject of racial discrimination.

BIBLIOGRAPHY

Burnard, Trevor. 2003. *Mastery, Tyranny, and Desire: Thomas Thistlewood and His Slaves in the Anglo-Jamaican World.* Chapel Hill: University of North Carolina Press.

Diamond, Jared. 2006. *The Third Chimpanzee: The Biological Roots of Human Behavior.* New York: Harper Perennial.

Gordon-Reed, Annette. 1997. *Thomas Jefferson and Sally Hemings: An American Controversy.* Charlottesville: University of Virginia Press.

Pilkington, Doris. 2002. *Rabbit Proof Fence: The True Story of One of the Greatest Escapes of All Time.* New York: Miramax Books.

Romano, Renee. 2003. *Race Mixing: Black-White Marriage in Postwar America.* Cambridge, MA: Harvard University Press.

Vasconcelos, José. 1977. *The Cosmic Race.* Baltimore, MD: Johns Hopkins University Press.

Stewart R. King

SEX AND MATING

Humans in all cultures engage in various forms of mating, including marriage or committed pair-bonding as well as short-term, casual sexual relationships. Given that reproduction is at the heart of natural selection, decisions about mating are of central adaptive significance. Accordingly, mating is one of the most heavily studied areas in the biological and social sciences. Recent theoretical and empirical findings in human mating research have identified key sex differences in mate preferences, as well as neural and hormonal correlates of mating.

ENTERING RELATIONSHIPS AND THE TRAITS THAT ARE VALUED

Mate preferences may be separated into broad questions of "whether and what" (Li and Kenrick 2006). For long-term relationships, the sexes tend to be equally careful about *whether* to enter. When considering minimum requirements for a marriage partner, both sexes have equally high standards. However, men tend to be more eager than women to enter short-term sexual relationships, and report significantly lower standards for them, especially for one-night stands. When approached by an opposite-sex stranger who immediately makes an invitation for casual sex, 75 percent of men said yes whereas 100 percent of women said no.

To explain men's lower short-term mating thresholds and mate preferences in general, at least two major theories have been proposed. Though often presented as competing explanations and hotly debated, sociocultural and evolutionary theories may be compatible in that the former focuses on more immediate, proximate causations, whereas the latter looks to more distal, ultimate explanations. Sociocultural theories explain sex differences by looking to social norms and the influence of larger groups. According to this view (Eagly and Wood 1999), societal norms tend to influence men to be more agentic and women to be more passive across many endeavors, including sexual behaviors. Thus, the difference in willingness to enter short-term relationships may be due to gender role differences, whereby men are socialized to be sexually autonomous and women are socialized to be sexually restrained.

According to evolutionary theorists (Buss and Schmitt 1993; Gangestad and Simpson 2000), mating psychologies may have developed in response to specific adaptive issues that long- and short-term mating pose to women and men. Men's eagerness for sex can be traced back to differences in minimum obligatory parental investment. Whereas men are physiologically required to contribute only a few sex cells to offspring, women must provide substantial pre- and postnatal resources if offspring are to survive. Because offspring present much higher potential costs to women if they are the results of uncommitted sex, short-term relationships are reproductively less favorable for women than for men. For long-term relationships such as marriage, both sexes invest substantially in the relationship and in raising children, so both sexes may have evolved to be selective about taking on a long-term partner.

Given that a relationship will occur, an equally important consideration concerns *what* characteristics are valued. When considering long-term mates, men not only value physical attractiveness more than women do, but they also prioritize finding a minimum level of physical attractiveness in their partners. Women value social status more than men do, and women prioritize obtaining a minimum level of social status in long-term mates. Beyond satisfying these priorities, both sexes favor other characteristics such as kindness and intelligence, and ideally prefer a well-rounded mate. For short-term mates, both sexes tend to prioritize having a certain level of physical attractiveness before being concerned about other characteristics.

From a sociocultural perspective, women have less access to status, power, and economic resources than men do. To achieve upward mobility, women place relatively greater emphasis on status-related traits in their marriage partners. However, if the intended mating duration is short-term, then economic constraints should be less relevant and both sexes should be free to prioritize the physical attributes of their potential short-term mates, as men do for long-term mates.

Why is physical appearance prioritized over other desirable traits? Because of time constraints and variation in women's reproductive capacity, ancestral men may have had a need to first and foremost identify long- and short-term partners who were healthy and fertile. Accordingly, men are inclined to place initial value on physical features

that signal youth, sexual maturity, and fecundity. However, other characteristics are also important for long-term relationships, and once a moderate amount of physical attractiveness has been verified, more attention is paid to other desirable characteristics.

In contrast to female fertility, male fertility remains relatively constant over the life span. However, men vary in their ability to provide resources for offspring. Because ancestral men who were higher in status had better access to resources, women may have evolved to prioritize social status in long-term mates to ensure essential resources for offspring. For short-term mates, resources are less relevant, and women may value physical attractiveness in response to the adaptive issue of identifying partners with desirable heritable characteristics.

According to this "good genes" theory (Gangestad and Simpson 2000), pathogens encountered during development can lead to visible deviations from bilateral symmetry. A healthy set of genes and immune system allow a person to resist such pathogens. Because testosterone suppresses the immune system, those who simultaneously exhibit testosterone-rich features and bilateral symmetry effectively advertise having genes that are resistant to local pathogens. That is, only those with desirable good genes can afford to be loaded with potentially damaging testosterone *and* remain symmetrical in appearance. Indeed, male symmetry is correlated with testosterone-mediated secondary sexual characteristics such as muscularity and masculinity, and men whom women consider physically attractive exhibit more facial masculinity and bilateral symmetry. Symmetrical men are more desirable as short-term affair partners and have more sexual partners than asymmetrical men. In ancestral environments, women who mated with physically attractive men may have accrued reproductive benefits by passing on good genes to offspring.

PHYSIOLOGICAL MECHANISMS INVOLVED IN MATE CHOICE

For humans and other biparental species, trade-offs exist between parenting and mating, and individual hormonal profiles likely mediate both male and female reproductive strategies along these lines (Clutton-Brock 1991). In order for conception to occur during a woman's menstrual cycle, a set of hormonal conditions must be present. First, a mid-cycle rise in luteinizing hormone must occur, signaling impending egg maturation. Second, the ovarian hormones estradiol and progesterone must be at optimal levels, with estradiol rising prior to ovulation and progesterone hitting peak levels after ovulation has occurred. Natural selection may have shaped women's mating psychologies to parallel such changes in physiology.

For females, it would be reproductively ideal to find mates who can provide both material and genetic benefits to offspring; however, obtaining both sets of features in one male is difficult. Therefore, most women may need to make strategic trade-offs by selecting long-term partners who are higher in investment potential than sexual attractiveness. Moreover, these trade-offs may have selected for a dual-mating psychology in which women seek primary partners who provide investment while obtaining better genes through extra-pair mating (i.e., mating with individuals other than one's primary partner).

Indeed, around ovulation, female sexual desire becomes stronger and the number of sexual fantasies increases. However, these are directed not toward primary partners, but toward potential affair partners. This is particularly true if the primary partner is less physically attractive and lacks indicators of genetic fitness, including strength, social dominance, and symmetry. When near ovulation, women prefer masculine and symmetrical faces in men, and the scent of symmetrical men. For women who are in a steady relationship, in-pair sex tends to occur consistently across the cycle, whereas extra-pair sex occurs significantly more often on high-fertility days.

Males also face strategic trade-offs involving differential allocation of effort to mating or parenting. The resolution of these trade-offs depends on cues from the environment. Men tend to allocate more effort to mating to the extent to which they possess indicators of good genotypic quality. When men do not have the attributes that make them attractive to females, or otherwise face limited sexual opportunities, they tend to invest more heavily in a single mate's offspring. For example, African tribal evidence shows that men of high status have more wives and spend less time on parenting than men of low status.

Testosterone is a steroid hormone that plays a key role in mediating trade-offs in male mating strategies. Higher testosterone levels are associated with greater promiscuity and less parenting. Men with higher testosterone are less likely to have ever married and, if they do marry, are more likely to engage in extramarital sex. The testosterone of men who marry falls as they transition from bachelor to husband, and testosterone remains low among stably married men.

At the neural level, the hormones oxytocin and vasopressin appear to be involved in the formation of pair bonds between males and females. Recent insight into the neuroendocrine basis of monogamous pair bond formation comes from the comparative study of two rodent species. The prairie vole and the meadow vole are two very closely related species that differ markedly in mating strategies. Male and female prairie voles form lifetime pair-bonds, whereas meadow voles are highly promiscu-

ous. During copulation, oxytocin and vasopressin are released in the brain. Oxytocin facilitates affiliation and partner preference behavior in female prairie voles, and vasopressin facilitates affiliative and parenting behavior in male prairie voles. Exogenous injections of vasopressin to the male prairie vole and oxytocin to the female facilitate mate preference behavior without the occurrence of mating. Likewise, blocking the receptors for these hormones will prevent pair-bonding from occurring after copulation. In contrast, similar injections do not influence social behavior in the meadow vole.

Though human brains release oxytocin and vasopressin during sex, relatively little is known about their precise functions in humans. Nevertheless, findings from other species provide a starting point, and ongoing efforts to understand the changes in gene expression for oxytocin and vasopressin receptor density may help to clarify individual differences in human mating strategies.

SEE ALSO *Evolutionary Psychology; Romance*

BIBLIOGRAPHY

Baker, R. Robin, and Mark A. Bellis. 1995. *Human Sperm Competition: Copulation, Masturbation, and Infidelity.* London: Chapman and Hall.

Booth, Alan, and James M. Dabbs, Jr. 1993. Testosterone and Men's Marriages. *Social Forces* 72: 463–477.

Bullivant, Susan B., Sarah A. Sellergren, Kathleen Stern, et al. 2004. Women's Sexual Experience During the Menstrual Cycle: Identification of the Sexual Phase by Noninvasive Measurement of Luteinizing Hormone. *The Journal of Sex Research* 41: 82–93.

Buss, David M., and David Schmitt. 1993. Sexual Strategies Theory: An Evolutionary Perspective on Human Mating. *Psychological Review* 100: 204–232.

Clark, Russell D., and Elaine Hatfield. 1989. Gender Differences in Receptivity to Sexual Offers. *Journal of Psychology and Human Sexuality* 2: 39–55.

Clutton-Brock, Tim H. 1991. *The Evolution of Parental Care.* Princeton, NJ: Princeton University Press.

Eagly, Alice H., and Wendy Wood. 1999. The Origins of Sex Differences in Human Behavior: Evolved Dispositions Versus Social Roles. *American Psychologist* 54: 408–433.

Gangestad, Steven W., and Jeffry A. Simpson. 2000. The Evolution of Human Mating: Trade-Offs and Strategic Pluralism. *Behavioral and Brain Sciences* 23: 573–587.

Gangestad, Steven W., Randy Thornhill, and Christine E. Garver-Apgar. 2005. Women's Sexual Interests Across the Ovulatory Cycle Depend on Primary Partner Development Instability. *Proceedings of the Royal Society of London* B 272: 2023–2027.

Hewlett, Barry S. 1991. *Intimate Fathers: The Nature and Context of Aka Pygmy Paternal Infant Care.* Ann Arbor: University of Michigan Press.

Johnston, Victor S., Rebecca Hagel, Melissa Franklin, et al. 2001. Male Facial Attractiveness: Evidence for Hormone

Mediated Adaptive Design. *Evolution and Human Behavior* 21: 251–267.

Kenrick, Douglas T., Edward K. Sadalla, Gary Groth, and Melanie R. Trost. 1990. Evolution, Traits, and the Stages of Human Courtship: Qualifying the Parental Investment Model. *Journal of Personality* 58: 97–116.

Li, Norman P., and Douglas T. Kenrick. 2006. Sex Similarities and Differences in Preferences for Short-Term Mates: What, Whether, and Why. *Journal of Personality and Social Psychology* 90: 468–489.

Møller, Anders P., and Randy Thornhill. 1998. Developmental Stability and Sexual Selection: A Meta-Analysis. *American Naturalist* 151:174–192.

Penton-Voak, I. S., D. I. Perrett, D. Castles, et al. 1999. Female Preference for Male Faces Changes Cyclically. *Nature* 399: 741–742.

Symons, Donald. 1979. *The Evolution of Human Sexuality.* New York: Oxford University Press.

Thornhill, Randy, and Steven W. Gangestad. 1994. Fluctuating Asymmetry and Human Sexual Behavior. *Psychological Science* 5: 297–302.

Thornhill, Randy, and Steven W. Gangestad. 1999. The Scent of Symmetry: A Human Pheromone That Signals Fitness? *Evolution and Human Behavior* 20: 175–201.

Trivers, Robert L. 1972. Parental Investment and Sexual Selection. In *Sexual Selection and the Descent of Man, 1871–1971*, ed. Bernard Campbell, 136–179. Chicago: Aldine.

Young, Larry J. 1999. Oxytocin and Vasopressin Receptors and Species-Typical Social Behaviors. *Hormones and Behavior* 36: 212–221.

Norman P. Li
Kristina M. Durante

SEXISM

Sexism commonly describes attitudes, statements, acts, strategies, or methods that lead to the discrimination, marginalization, or oppression of individuals or groups based on their sex. Coined by the New Women's Movement during the 1970s, the term was rapidly employed by the newly developing fields of women's and gender studies as a tool to analyze processes that discriminated against and marginalized women. Sexism against women pervades all areas of their lives, public and private, legal and economic, educational and social, religious and psychological, and gender relations in particular. It chiefly manifests itself in disparaging attitudes and behavior toward women and can legitimize their harassment, rape, and trafficking. Like racism, sexism has affected the lives of women worldwide and throughout history.

In philosophical thought, sexism is considered a subcategory of *essentialism*, a term British philosopher Karl Popper (1902–1994) introduced in 1935. In present-day women's and gender studies, the term essentialism usually has a pejorative, or derogatory, meaning, due to the models of biological determinism associated with it. For example, essentialist positions claim that all members of a group share a permanent and inalterable list of characteristics, such as the idea that women across all historical and cultural boundaries exhibit certain "womanly" attributes like motherliness. Essentialist thought has contributed to establishing gender as a distinct category of analysis, a distinction that a number of feminist authors, most notably Judith Butler (b. 1956), started to dismiss in the 1990s. Essentialist arguments, especially in gender discourses, tend to side with conservative political thought and the upholding of the status quo, thus often contributing to sexism. They are, however, sometimes used by progressive political groups such as the gay rights movement, which claims that homosexuality is rooted in biology.

Extreme forms of sexism against females are called *misogyny*, or hatred of women. Misogyny, or its weaker form, *gynophobia* (fear of women or femininity), is usually ideologically or psychologically founded. It is expressed in sexist attitudes and practices and can be institutionalized in political or social structures. Unlike antifeminism, a term that is often used synonymously but refers to attitudes against women's emancipation, misogyny implies an inherent inferiority of women and thus represents essentialist ideas of femininity. A second form of sexism commonly identified is sexism against men, also known as *reverse sexism*. Like sexism against women, it can develop extreme forms, called *misandry*, or hatred of men. A milder form is called *androphobia* (fear of men or masculinity). While the sexist view that women are superior to men is not as prevalent, it has become part of the public discourse.

The publication of Kate Millet's *Sexual Politics* (1970), which challenged the myth of a "natural" difference between the sexes and the resulting hierarchical social structures that considered men superior, laid the groundwork for a comprehensive critique of sexism by feminists, mainly in the United States and Europe. Millet's book focused on dominant theories in literary analysis and revealed the sexist nature of the literary canon, but she also analyzed psychological, sociological, and anthropological theories that cause and reinforce existing hierarchies between the sexes and define a woman as something that deviates from the (male) norm.

In the 1970s other feminist scholars and activists in the United States and Europe began to analyze and challenge sexist practices in schools and other educational institutions and identified various ways schools discriminated against girls. Among their most important grievances were sex-biased curricula and textbooks, practices of classroom interaction favoring boys, sex-typed course and career counseling, and male domination in math and science classes as well as in educational administration. Obviously, some of these problems are easier to rectify than others—policy decrees, for example, can successfully be employed to change the contents of textbooks but may be less effective in altering sexist classroom interaction.

The study of sexist language, gestures, and behavior became another focus of feminist academics and activists who identified various strategies employed to ignore women in academic and everyday discourse to make them "invisible" or silence them by sexist jokes or male "codes." Other studies found that sexist attitudes and practices were widespread in the workplace to marginalize women and keep them away from higher paying jobs, both white and blue collar, which are considered fields reserved for men.

SEXUAL HARASSMENT

Feminist legal scholars and lawyers started to battle sexism, specifically sexual harassment, in the economic world. Originally defined as treatment that persistently provokes, pressures, frightens, and otherwise discomforts coworkers, harassment has increasingly acquired a sexual component not restricted to demanding sexual favors but rather identifying discriminatory demands such as wearing gendered forms of dress or performing stereotypical feminine duties not included in the job description. In 1991 the media coverage of Supreme Court Justice Clarence Thomas's confirmation to the U.S. Supreme Court, which spotlighted the claims of sexual harassment alleged by his former employee Anita Hill, was central to installing both forms, *quid pro quo* and hostile work environment harassment, into the public mind. Largely an American invention, sexual harassment continues to generate much controversy. While a narrow sexual definition of harassment has undergone some criticism in the United States, chiefly due to supposed vague standards and an infringement of the right to free speech, this definition has begun to spread to other nations around the globe.

In the United States in particular, the antidiscrimination measures of the 1970s and 1980s have largely succeeded in making sexist attitudes and practice socially unacceptable. Many experts think, however, that the rapid changes in gender roles that occurred in the family and the workplace during those decades were the main cause for the transformation of gender relations in other areas of social life. Some scholars find that at the beginning of the twenty-first century, sexism ceased to be an exclusively female problem and sexist attitudes against men are on the rise. Masculinist movements and fathers' rights organizations, for example, have started to promote men's rights and have addressed a number of legal issues in particular, such as paternity leave and equal access to children. Other

experts contend that sexism is becoming less relevant altogether, at least in industrial societies. Undoubtedly, gender biases and sexist practices remain more intact in societies where women are limited to the private sphere.

SEE ALSO *Affirmative Action; Discrimination; Discrimination, Wage, by Gender; Essentialism; Family; Family Functioning; Family Structure; Femininity; Feminism; Gender; Gender Studies; Masculinity; Misogyny; Motherhood; Political Correctness; Women's Studies*

BIBLIOGRAPHY

American Association of University Women. 1999. *Gender Gaps: Where Schools Still Fail Our Children*. New York: Marlowe.

Butler, Judith. 1993. *Bodies That Matter: On the Discursive Limits of "Sex."* New York: Routledge.

MacKinnon, Catharine A., and Reva B. Siegel, eds. 2004. *Directions in Sexual Harassment Law*. New Haven, CT: Yale University Press.

Millett, Kate. 1970. *Sexual Politics*. Garden City, NY: Doubleday.

Schor, Naomi, and Elizabeth Weed, eds. 1994. *The Essential Difference*. Bloomington: Indiana University Press.

Anja Schüler

SEXUAL ABUSE

SEE *Torture.*

SEXUAL HARASSMENT

Sexual harassment is the creation of an overtly sexualized work or school dynamic that adversely affects the experience of one or more workers or students. The "sexual" in *sexual harassment* relates to motive rather than content; while sexual harassment may involve sexually explicit language, images, or actions, the key is that the person being harassed is targeted because of his or her gender. Sexual harassment may be perpetrated by an individual or a group; perpetrators and victims may be of opposite genders or the same gender, men or women. In many jurisdictions, sexual harassment is illegal; workers or students who are adversely affected by harassing behavior may seek compensation through the courts.

In the United States, Title VII of the Civil Rights Act of 1964 prohibits gender-based discrimination in the context of employment and imposes civil liability on employers who engage in or tolerate such behavior. The text of Title VII makes it "an unlawful employment practice for an employer … to discriminate against any individual with respect to his compensation, terms, conditions, or privileges of employment, because of such individual's … sex." Originally, lawmakers and judges understood the statute to prohibit disparate treatment of men and women with respect to the tangible and economic aspects of employment: hiring, promotion, retention, pay, and economic benefits.

Even under this limited understanding of Title VII, courts recognized that one form of sexual harassment—called "quid pro quo sexual harassment"—was prohibited. This most explicit form of sexual harassment involves a person in a position of authority making express sexual demands on a subordinate with an implied or overt threat of retaliation if the sexual demands are not met. For example, if a supervisor tells a subordinate that he can keep his job only if he is willing to engage in sexual acts with the supervisor, that is quid pro quo sexual harassment.

In 1986, the U.S. Supreme Court recognized a more subtle—and more controversial—form of actionable sexual harassment: "hostile work environment" sexual harassment. A hostile work environment may be created through unwanted sexually suggestive remarks, sexually charged jokes, or sexual touching. The key difference between a claim of quid pro quo sexual harassment and hostile work environment sexual harassment is the injury or harm experienced by the victim; in a hostile work environment claim, the alleged harm is psychological stress rather than an explicit deprivation of job benefits. Sometimes hostile work environment claims involve an allegation of "constructive discharge": The work environment was so hostile, so unbearable, that the victim felt compelled to quit and was thus constructively discharged from employment.

Champions of equal rights hail laws prohibiting both quid pro quo and hostile work environment sexual harassment as important tools for equalizing the economic opportunities of men and women. One of the more controversial sexual harassment cases in U.S. history, *Jensen et al. v. Eveleth Taconite Company*, involved women hired to work in a taconite processing facility in Eveleth, Minnesota; the case was significant because it was the first sexual harassment case successfully brought as a class action. In journalistic accounts of the litigation, many of the women noted that the mines offered wages dramatically higher than those offered by any other employers in the area. For many of the women involved in the litigation, they had to work at the mine or collect welfare benefits to feed their children.

Critics of hostile work environment claims charge that the line between a relaxed and collegial work environment and a hostile environment is not clear enough for employers to develop workable human resources policies.

The U.S. Supreme Court has attempted to address this issue by insisting that Title VII is not a "general civility code" (*Oncale v. Sundowner Offshore Services, Inc.*, 523 U.S. 75 [1998]); "[w]hen the workplace is permeated with discriminatory intimidation, ridicule, and insult that is sufficiently severe or pervasive to alter the conditions of the victim's employment and create an abusive working environment, Title VII is violated" (*Harris v. Forklift Systems, Inc.*, 510 U.S. 17, 21 [1993]).

Although most sexual harassment law focuses on the work environment, sexual harassment can occur and even be legally actionable in other contexts. Most notably, as mentioned above, sexual harassment may occur in a school environment. In the United States, Title IX of the Education Amendments of 1972 prohibits gender discrimination in education. Courts have construed Title IX to prohibit sexual harassment; students who are sexually harassed by teachers, administrators, or even other students may have a cause of action against the school that tolerated the harassment.

SEE ALSO *Discrimination; Inequality, Gender; Law; Patriarchy; Political Correctness; Sexism; Workplace Relations*

BIBLIOGRAPHY

Beiner, Teresa M. 2005. *Gender Myths v. Working Realities: Using Social Science to Reformulate Sexual Harassment Law.* New York: New York University Press.

Bingham, Clara, and Laura Leedy Gansler. 2002. *Class Action.* New York: Doubleday.

Wendy L. Watson

SEXUAL ORIENTATION, DETERMINANTS OF

A person's sexual orientation concerns whether he or she is sexually attracted to people of the same sex, the opposite sex, or both. Starting in the nineteenth century, scientists, physicians, and mental health specialists have offered numerous theories of how people develop sexual orientations. What determines a person's sexual orientation remains a question of much scientific, psychological, and social scientific controversy. Current biological theories focus on genes, brains, and hormones.

For much of the twentieth century, scientists believed that gay men and lesbians had gender-atypical hormone levels in their bodies; for example, they thought that lesbians had more testosterone and less estrogen in their systems than did heterosexual women. Recent studies have shown that almost all lesbians and gay men have the same circulating hormone levels as their heterosexual counter-parts. In response, current hormonal theories propose a link between sexual orientation and prenatal hormone levels. As prenatal hormone levels play a role in the organization of the developing brain, the idea is that different prenatal hormones levels could explain sexual orientation differences among adults. This prenatal hormonal hypothesis is premised largely on observations that early hormone exposure determines both the repertoire of mating behaviors exhibited by laboratory animals and the morphology of particular brain regions believed to modulate those behaviors.

BRAINS

Over the past few decades, confirmed sex differences in the size of several brain structures in various laboratory animals have lead to speculation regarding parallel differences in the human brain associated with sex and sexual orientation. Several of the structural sex differences identified in animals involve specific cell groups in a region of the rodent hypothalamus involved in regulating particular mating behaviors. One such anatomical sex difference in rodents develops in response to sex differences in early exposure to sex hormones and involves a part of a rodent's hypothalamus called the sexually dimorphic nucleus of the preoptic area (SDN-POA). In the laboratory, damage in the vicinity of the SDN-POA decreases mounting behavior, and electrical stimulation of the region elicits mounting behavior. These observations established the belief that the SDN-POA participates in regulating male sexual behavior. That belief lacks critical support because the destruction of the SDN-POA of male rats does not, however, disrupt mounting behavior. The function of the SDN-POA remains to be elucidated.

The belief that the SDN-POA participates in regulating sex behavior in rats led to the search for a comparable nucleus in humans. The human third interstitial nucleus of the anterior hypothalamus (INAH3) has been identified as the most promising candidate. This nucleus is much larger and contains substantially more neurons in presumed heterosexual men than in women. By extrapolation from animal work, this human sex difference is widely believed to reflect sex differences in early hormone exposure, but this hypothesis is exceedingly difficult to test in humans. The AIDS epidemic has, however, made it possible to study this nucleus in men whose medical records indicate homosexual behavior. These studies suggest that the volume of INAH3 may be smaller in homosexual men than in heterosexual men; however, that finding must be viewed tentatively for various reasons, including that all the homosexual men in these studies died from complications of AIDS.

Researchers have also sought to identify variation with sex and sexual orientation in the bundles of fibers that connect the left and right hemispheres of the brain. These studies have produced conflicting results regarding variation with both sex and sexual orientation.

GENES

Inside each person's cells are chains of DNA that act as a recipe for making that person. Determining the role a portion of genetic material plays in the development of a particular human trait is complicated, although there has been some success for specific anatomical and physiological traits. It is much more difficult to identify genetic material that influences complex psychological traits such as sexual orientations. One way to infer the extent to which a trait is genetic is to study twins. Identical twins share 100 percent of their genetic material. Fraternal twins are genetically only as closely related as non-twin biological siblings, sharing only 50 percent of their DNA. Because identical twins are genetically identical, differences between them are due to their pre- or post-natal environment, not genes. This inference does not work in the other direction. If identical twins have the same trait, it might be because they were raised in the same environment.

Sophisticated studies have assessed sexual orientation in identical twins, same-sex fraternal twins, non-twin biological siblings, and similarly-aged unrelated adopted siblings. The idea is that if sexual orientation is genetic, identical twins should have the same sexual orientation, and the rate of homosexuality among the adopted siblings should be equal to the rate in the general population. If, on the other hand, identical twins and adopted siblings are as likely to have the same sexual orientation, then genetic factors make very little contribution to sexual orientation. Subjects recruited through ads in gay publications looking for volunteers with twins of the same sex were asked to rate their own sexual orientation, the sexual orientation of their relatives, and for permission to contact their siblings. In these studies, identical twins of gay men and lesbians were substantially more likely to share their sibling's sexual orientation than were fraternal twins.

The result of such twin studies are difficult to interpret because gays and lesbians seem more likely to volunteer themselves and their twin siblings for such studies when they have gay or lesbian siblings. When the proportions of identical and fraternal twins who are concordant for homosexuality are examined in databases of twins who were not selected on the basis of sexual orientation, the estimates for heritability of homosexuality are much lower than when subjects are selected from newspaper ads recruiting on the basis of sexual orientation.

Building on the twin studies, scientists have tried to isolate the portion of the human genome that hypothetically influences sexual orientation. One such study began with the observation that some studies had found that homosexuality in men seems to follow the maternal line of the family. Some have interpreted this pattern among gay men's families, which has only sometimes been observed, as suggesting that male homosexuality, similar to color blindness, is inherited from one's mother on the X chromosome. To test the hypothesis that the X chromosomes contains genes that influence sexual orientation, families with at least two gay brothers were recruited from a sample of families in which homosexuality appeared to follow the maternal line. DNA samples were obtained from two gay brothers in each subject families. Samples were then analyzed using linkage analysis to determine how frequently the gay brothers had inherited markers from the same X chromosome of their mother. Because mothers have two X chromosomes but only pass one to their sons, one would expect two sons to have a 50 percent chance of sharing markers from the same maternal X chromosome. One research team, however, reported that when both sons were gay, 64 percent appeared to have inherited a particular portion of the same maternal chromosome (known as the Xq28 region). This finding was interpreted as suggesting that genes influencing sexual orientation in men may reside on the Xq28 region. That suggestion must be viewed cautiously because it has been criticized on the basis of multiple technical and statistical concerns, and two independent research teams have failed to replicate it.

More generally, linkage analysis is best suited for discovering the genetic basis of traits determined in a genetically simple manner rather than traits that are influenced by several genes working in concert. This technique has mistakenly indicated that a specific genetic sequence plays a role in the development of a particular trait. Such mistakes are especially likely in the case of genetically complex traits, cognitively mediated psychological/behavioral traits, or those traits strongly affected by environmental factors.

In addition to linkage analysis, some studies have looked for differences related to sexual orientation in candidate genes chosen on the basis of their involvement in the hormonal mechanisms of sexual differentiation and development. To date, these studies have not produced positive findings.

In any event, genes in themselves cannot directly cause a behavior or a psychological phenomenon. Genes direct RNA synthesis that in turn leads to the production of a protein that may influence the development of psychological dispositions and particular behaviors. There are many intervening pathways between a gene and a behavior or a behavioral disposition and even more intervening variables between a gene and a cognitively mediated behavior.

None of the most popular scientific theories of the determinants of sexual orientations are well supported. This does not mean, however, that sexual orientations are not biological in the sense that all psychological phenomena require the activity of a living brain. Rather than asking whether or not sexual orientations are biological, the more salient question is what role biology plays in the development of sexual orientations. Biology would still be a factor in sexual orientation if there are multiple pathways to the development of a particular sexual orientation. Biological factors may also play a role if they influence temperamental or personality factors that shape how a person interacts with the environment and experiences of it, which in turn affects the development of one's sexual orientation.

SEE ALSO *AIDS; Gender; Gender, Alternatives to Binary; Sexual Orientation, Social and Economic Consequences; Sexuality; Twin Studies*

BIBLIOGRAPHY

Byne, William, et al. 2001. The Interstitial Nuclei of the Human Anterior Hypothalamus: An Investigation of Variation with Sex, Sexual Orientation and HIV Status. *Hormones and Behavior* 40: 86–92.

Hamer, Dean, and Peter Copeland. 1994. *The Science of Desire: The Search for the Gay Gene and the Biology of Behavior.* New York: Simon and Schuster.

LeVay, Simon. 1996. *Queer Science: The Use and Abuse of Research into Homosexuality.* Cambridge, MA: MIT Press.

Mustanski, B. S., M. L. Chivers, and Bailey J. Michael. 2002. A Critical Review of Recent Biological Research on Human Sexual Orientation. *Annual Review of Sex Research* 13: 89–140.

Stein, Edward. 1999. *The Mismeasure of Desire: The Science, Theory and Ethics of Sexual Orientation.* New York: Oxford University Press.

Edward Stein
William Byne

SEXUAL ORIENTATION, SOCIAL AND ECONOMIC CONSEQUENCES

Sexual orientation is generally considered a personal characteristic that reflects an individual's sexual behavior, attraction, or self-identity. Individuals can have a primary orientation toward others of the same sex (gay, lesbian, or homosexual people), toward people of both sexes (bisexual people), or toward people of a different sex (heterosexual people). Social scientists have studied the influence of sexual orientation on social and economic outcomes by comparing the experiences of lesbian, gay, and bisexual (LGB) people with those of heterosexual people. Overall, research shows that sexual orientation is an important influence on health and on economic and social well-being.

In discussions of the social and economic effects of sexual orientation, most interest is focused on LGB people. While controversy exists over exactly how many LGB people live in the United States or other countries, most studies find that 2 to 6 percent of people report sexual behavior, attractions, or a self-identity toward people of the same sex, making people who are LGB a clear sexual minority in numerical terms. Furthermore, heterosexuality is generally the socially accepted sexual orientation, while being LGB is often considered an inferior and stigmatized status. Stigma puts LGB people at a social and economic disadvantage and implies that their lives may be affected by prejudice and discrimination.

One important characteristic of sexual orientation influences the kind of disadvantages experienced by LGB people. Sexual orientation is not a visible characteristic, unlike age, race, or sex, and therefore LGB people can sometimes keep their sexual orientation invisible or allow others to assume that they are heterosexual. Invisibility sometimes allows LGB people to escape ill-treatment, but the activities and effort required to hide sexual orientation—commonly known as being "in the closet"—may be considerable and can cause psychological and physical stress, not to mention social discomfort.

When LGB people "come out" of the closet and become more visible in their families, workplaces, and communities, they may be subjected to behavior that reflects prejudice, such as vocal disapproval, social rejection, discriminatory treatment, or even physical violence. Both actual rejection and disapproval and the fear of rejection and discrimination reduce the participation of LGB people in their families, in religious organizations, and in some community activities. The personal effects of prejudice also sometimes include increased depression and anxiety, as well as other physical and mental health conditions. Numerous studies also show that LGB young people are more likely to consider suicide. In contrast, studies show that supportive workplace policies, laws, and coworkers create environments that encourage LGB people to come out, which often improves their workplace lives and mental health.

When some businesses tried to tap into an affluent untapped market by wooing LGB consumers beginning in the 1990s, some people and policymakers wondered whether LGB people actually face economic discrimination. However, many studies by economists show that the reality of economic disadvantage trumps the myth of gay affluence. Gay men earn less than heterosexual men with the same job-related characteristics, with a pay gap of 10 to 32 percent in the United States. Lesbians earn no more than comparable heterosexual women, and in some studies they earn more than heterosexual women. However, the gender pay gap means that a lesbian couple always earns less than a heterosexual married couple and less than a gay male couple, so lesbians are also not the "dream market" that businesses are said to seek. Also, many employer benefits policies extend health care or survivor benefits to the spouses of employees, but only a minority of employers grant those same rights to LGB employees' same-sex partners, resulting in lower total compensation for LGB employees.

Scholars do not agree on the causes of the wage patterns. Some argue that gay men's earnings disadvantage reflects discrimination in the labor market, an argument bolstered by the fact that few states (or countries) forbid employment discrimination based on sexual orientation. Others argue that the wage variances stem from variations in family formation for LGB and heterosexual people. A gay man who partners with another man may not need to support a partner and children, reducing gay men's incentives to gain added job skills and experience and eventually reducing gay men's earnings relative to heterosexual men who might plan to be a sole provider for a family. However, the fact that gay men have more education than heterosexual men suggests that gay men's commitment to investing in job-related skills is at least as strong as for heterosexual men. Likewise, lesbians know that they will not have a male partner, so they might have more skills and experience than heterosexual women, who might also be more likely to leave the labor market for short periods to raise children or do other family-related work. This compensation for differences in family structures could disguise or compensate for any less visible discrimination that lesbians might face that would otherwise reduce their earnings.

The issue of partnership highlights another realm of social and economic disadvantage for LGB people in creating families. Census 2000 counted roughly 600,000 same-sex couples in the United States, with one in three female couples and one in five male couples raising children under eighteen years old. However, in most places LGB people form these families in the absence of access to marriage or full parental rights. Several countries (beginning with the Netherlands, Belgium, Spain, and Canada) and the state of Massachusetts allow same-sex couples to marry, while some other states and European countries provide a different and usually lesser form of legal recognition for same-sex couples. Without the right to marry, couples have no access to important legal rights and benefits that enhance family security and economic well-being.

The social and economic differences in treatment across sexual orientation outlined here have prompted a growing social and political movement around the world to reduce stigma and prejudice and to improve the well-being of LGB people. As a result of these efforts, more LGB people are living open lives, more jurisdictions forbid discrimination based on sexual orientation, more employers treat LGB and heterosexual employees equally, and more states and countries are granting rights to same-sex couples.

BIBLIOGRAPHY

Badgett, M. V. Lee. 2001. *Money, Myths, and Change: The Economic Lives of Lesbians and Gay Men.* Chicago: University of Chicago Press.

Cochran, Susan. 2001. Emerging Issues in Research on Lesbians' and Gay Men's Mental Health: Does Sexual Orientation Really Matter? *American Psychologist* 56: 932–947.

Gates, Gary J., and Jason Ost. 2005. *The Gay and Lesbian Atlas.* Washington, DC: Urban Institute Press.

U.S. Bureau of the Census. 2003. Married-Couple and Unmarried-Partner Households: 2000. Census 2000 Special Reports (CENSR-5). http://www.census.gov/prod/2003pubs/censr-5.pdf.

Woods, James D. 1994. *The Corporate Closet: The Professional Lives of Gay Men in America.* New York: Free Press.

M. V. Lee Badgett

SEXUAL SELECTION THEORY

Although Charles Darwin is best known for his theory of evolution by natural selection, he was also fascinated by the differences between males and females in all species. His 1871 book, *The Descent of Man and Selection in Relation to Sex*, documented these differences and suggested an explanation for them. Darwin pointed out that traits such as peacock tails that occur in only one sex could be of two types: The primary sexual characters enable males to produce sperm and females to produce and nurture eggs; the evolution of these traits is easy to explain via natural selection. The secondary sexual characters, such as the long tails and bright colors of many male birds or antlers on male deer, are often detrimental to survival, either because they make males more conspicuous to predators, or because they are physiologically costly to produce.

Darwin said that secondary sexual characters could evolve in one of two ways. First, they could be useful to one sex, usually males, in fighting for access to members of the other sex. Weapons like the antlers on male ungulates or horns on male beetles are advantageous because better fighters get more mates and have more offspring. The second way was more problematic. Noting that females often pay attention to traits like long tails and elaborate plumage during courtship, Darwin concluded that the traits evolved because the females preferred them. The sexual selection process, then, consisted of two components: male-male competition, which results in weapons, and female choice, which results in ornaments.

Although competition among males for females seemed reasonable to Darwin's Victorian contemporaries, the idea that females could do anything as complex as discriminate between males with different degrees of development of a character like colorful plumage was one they could not swallow. Alfred Russel Wallace, who independently arrived at some of the same conclusions about evolution and natural selection as Darwin, was particularly vehement in his objections.

Largely because of this opposition to the idea of female choice, sexual selection as a theory lay dormant for several decades. It was not until the 1960s that evolutionary biologists began to reconsider the portrait they had painted of animal social life. Probably the most important new insight came from work by Robert Trivers, who pointed out that females and males differ in how they put resources and effort into the next generation, which he termed parental investment. Females are limited by the number of offspring they can successfully produce and rear. Because they are the sex that supplies the nutrient-rich egg and often the sex that cares for the young, they leave the most genes in the next generation by having the highest quality young they can. Which male they mate with is important because a mistake in the form of poor genes or no help with the young could mean that they lose their whole breeding effort for an entire year.

Males, on the other hand, can leave the most genes in the next generation by fertilizing as many females as possible. Because each mating requires relatively little investment, a male mating with many females sires many more young than a male mating with only one female. Hence males are expected to compete among themselves for access to females, and females are expected to be choosy and to mate with the best possible male they can.

A classic example is the elephant seal. These animals spend most of the year at sea. In late fall males arrive at isolated beaches and establish a dominance hierarchy, often by vicious fighting and throwing around of their weight, which can exceed three tons. Female elephant seals, about a third the size of males, arrive later, already pregnant. Males herd them when they get to shore; after having her pup, a female is sexually receptive and mates with (usually) the male who has herded her and controls her movements. Males that can sequester more females have a chance for enormous payoffs: A study of an elephant seal colony showed that, in one year, a single male fathered about 90 percent of the pups in the colony. It thus pays to compete with other males because males that do so leave more genes in succeeding generations. Females, on the other hand, have one pup regardless of how many males they mate with. This species is oriented more toward male-male competition than female choice, and the best fighter wins.

In other species female choice predominates. For example, satin bowerbirds are members of a family in which males build elaborate structures during the breeding season. The male collects objects and carefully places them around the bower, after which he waits by it for a female to appear. If she does, he begins a species-specific display that may involve song, complicated courtship dances, or other enticements. Sometimes the female is won over, stays with the male, and mates. Sometimes she watches for a while and leaves. Either way, her choice determines the outcome.

In a handful of species the usual pattern is reversed: Males provide a large contribution to females and offspring, while females benefit by mating with many different males. Katydid males, for instance, sing to attract females for mating. But once a female arrives, she stands to gain much more than a fertilization of her eggs. The males of many katydids produce a gelatinous, nutrient-rich structure called a spermatophylax, which is given to females along with a packet of sperm and which the female eats while the sperm is fertilizing her eggs. It supplies her with protein she often does not get in her usual diet, which enables her to lay more eggs. Females with larger nuptial gifts, as they are called, have more offspring.

But the gifts have an even bigger return if the female recipient is herself relatively large, because larger females lay more eggs. A male cannot give many spermatophylaxes to females in a season, as they can average up to 30 percent of his weight. Therefore, in many species of katydids, male choice rather than female choice occurs, with males seeming to gauge the size of prospective mates and rejecting them if they are too light. Male competition in katydids is much less important than male mate choice; instead, female competition may be a major force, and males choose from among available females. This further supports the notion that the crucial factor is which sex limits the reproductive capacity of the opposite sex.

SEE ALSO *Alpha-male; Darwin, Charles; Fertility, Human; Hierarchy; Natural Selection*

BIBLIOGRAPHY

Andersson, Malte. 1994. *Sexual Selection*. Princeton, NJ: Princeton University Press.

Andersson, M., and Simmons, L. W. 2006. Sexual Selection and Mate Choice. *Trends in Ecology and Evolution* 21 (6): 296–302.

Darwin, Charles. [1871.] 1989. *The Descent of Man and Selection in Relation to Sex*. New York: New York University Press.

Trivers, R. L. 1972. Parental Investment and Sexual Selection. In *Sexual Selection and the Descent of Man 1871–1971*, ed. Bernard Campbell, 136–179. Chicago: Aldine.

Marlene Zuk

SEXUAL TRAFFICKING

SEE *Pimps; Prostitution.*

SEXUALITY

Surveys of human sexuality serve several purposes. They provide reports of sexual norms to supplement information from sources such as media, church, and medicine. They expand the vocabulary for discussing sexual desire and behavior. They offer a unique and fascinating lens through which to examine social trends. Finally, findings from scientific sex surveys provide evidence for public policy initiatives, education, treatment, and funding regarding sexual health and the prevention of sexually transmitted infections.

Nearly 750 sex surveys were conducted in twentieth-century America. These range from massive nationwide investigations to small scholarly studies to questionnaires in consumer magazines such as *Redbook, Cosmopolitan*, and *Playboy*. The focus of these surveys ranges widely as well, covering subjects as diverse as marriage, divorce, fertility, contraception, masturbation, intercourse, orgasm, abstinence, gender equality, homosexuality, rape, adolescence, aging, sex education, pornography, and sexually transmitted infections. This entry highlights a few of the large American sex surveys and indicates their contributions and the story they tell about our culture.

OUR VICTORIAN FOREMOTHERS

The earliest American sex survey was a study of forty-five wives by Stanford physician Clelia Mosher (1863–1940), conducted between 1892 and 1912. Mosher's findings

Notable twentieth-century sex surveys

How the questionnaires were focused

Survey author	Date	Survey sample	Number of respondents	Men's attitudes	Women's attitudes	Physical aspects of sex	Social aspects of sex	Spiritual aspects of sex
Clelia Mosher	1892–1912	Married women	45		X	X	X	X
Katharine B. Davis	1929	Women	2,200		X	X	X	X
Gilbert Hamilton	1929	Married couples	200	X	X	X		
Alfred Kinsey et al.	1948	Men	5,300	X		X	X	
Alfred Kinsey et al.	1953	Women	5,940		X	X	X	
Morton Hunt	1974	Women and men	2,026	X	X	X	X	
Shere Hite	1976	Women	3,019		X	X	X	
Alan Bell and Martin Weinberg	1977	Gays and lesbians	4,639	X	X	X	X	
Carol Tavris and Susan Sadd	1977	Women	100,000		X	X	X	
Karla Jay and Allen Young	1979	Gays and lesbians	5,000	X	X	X	X	
Philip Blumstein and Pepper Schwartz	1983	Heterosexual and gay couples	6,066	X	X	X	X	
Edward Brecher	1984	Women and men over age fifty	4,246	X	X	X	X	
Edward Laumann et al.	1994	Women and men	3,432	X	X	X	X	
Carol R. Ellison and Bernie Zilbergeld	2000	Women	2,632		X	X	X	
Gina Ogden	1999–2002	Women and men	3,810	X	X	X	X	X

Table 1

suggest that women at the turn of the twentieth century may have been much more erotically responsive than the stereotypical corseted, repressed Victorian housewife. In fact, for Mosher's respondents, marital unhappiness was caused less by wifely frigidity than by sexual desires their husbands were unable to gratify.

In 1929 another female physician, Katharine Bement Davis (1860–1935), surveyed 2,200 women, including unmarried women and lesbian women. Her findings reveal how little sex education was available to women at that time. Although 56 percent of her sample reported that they had had "adequate instruction" before marriage, their responses show that information was limited to anatomical facts and that these women longed for more knowledge about the relational aspects of sex and the "sex emotions." (Davis 1929, p. 64). Again, these women were more sexually responsive than one might predict of early twentieth-century women. Nine percent of Davis's respondents reported intercourse daily or more often, some over a span of many years. Many reported sexual fantasies, frequent masturbation, and also mutual masturbation with male and with female partners. One woman reported experiencing sleep orgasms (Davis 1929, p. 359), another said she became "drunk on erotic passages in books" (p. 291), and another reported the ability for spontaneous orgasm, that is, orgasm without physical touch: "I

can induce 'that queer feeling' almost any time by thinking about it" (p. 191). The sexological literature did not investigate the phenomenology of spontaneous orgasm until more than sixty years later, when researchers Gina Ogden and Beverly Whipple did so (Whipple, Ogden, and Komisaruk 1992).

INVESTIGATING MARRIAGE: NARROWING THE DEFINITION OF SEX

During the 1920s, 1930s, and 1940s, sex surveys were generally conducted by male researchers and funded by universities or government agencies, practices that have continued into the first decade of the twenty-first century. The best-known surveys of this period focused on preserving the institution of marriage—at a time when social values had been disrupted by economic depression, two world wars, and increased independence for middle-class women, who were moving into workplaces traditionally occupied by men. While Davis was conducting her survey, psychiatrist Gilbert Hamilton (1877–1943) surveyed one hundred white, married, "highly cultured" New York couples. His questions were based on assumptions that narrowed the definition of sex and laid down the pattern for subsequent surveys. Some of these assumptions were:

- *Sex* meant penis-vagina intercourse, whereas romance, kissing, and petting meant preparation for intercourse (hence the notion of *foreplay*).

- *Sexual satisfaction* meant physiological orgasm with vaginal spasms that could be measured.

- *Sexual interest* was proportional to the number of partners a respondent reported.

Hamilton's survey did not inquire about physical aspects of sexual response beyond intercourse, or about the emotions or meanings of sex. This and subsequent surveys found men to have more interest in sex than women—more partners, more frequent intercourse, and earlier first intercourse. Women were found to be less interested and satisfied—with some 80 percent anorgasmic on intercourse.

KINSEY AND FOLLOWERS: THE QUANTIFICATION OF SEX

Alfred Kinsey (1894–1956) and his colleagues introduced quantitative methods and random sampling that set the gold standard for all future sex survey methodology. The Kinsey Reports were the first massive investigations of American sexual behavior. *Sexual Behavior in the Human Male* (5,300 men) was published in 1948. *Sexual Behavior in the Human Female* (5,940 women) was published in 1953. These Kinsey surveys addressed six "outlets" of sexual response: masturbation, petting, homosexuality, premarital intercourse, extramarital intercourse, and intercourse with animals. Perhaps Kinsey's best-known contribution was his notion that sexual orientation is not necessarily fixed, but often fluctuates over a range of behaviors and fantasies during the lifespan. He placed heterosexuality and homosexuality on a continuum—using a zero-to-six scale. On this scale, "zero" indicates that sexual desires and behaviors involve only partners of the opposite sex, and "six" indicates that sexual desires and behaviors involve only same-sex partners. Most of us fall somewhere between, said Kinsey—hence a "Kinsey-three" indicates bisexuality.

The Kinsey questionnaires were exhaustive, with hundreds of questions, many doubling back to validate earlier ones. In addition, Kinsey trained interviewers to ask questions that were designed to be nonjudgmental and to minimize yes-or-no evasions. He assumed that all of his respondents had rich sexual experiences. For instance, to explore the still taboo subject of masturbation, Kinsey instructed his interviewers to ask: "How do you masturbate?" rather than "Do you masturbate?" This technique placed the burden of negative proof on the respondents—and as illustrated in the 2004 movie *Kinsey*, gave permission for even shy respondents to tell eloquent stories.

Far-reaching as these Kinsey questions were, they nonetheless focused on the performance aspects of sex and omitted emotions and meanings, which Kinsey stated had no place in scientific inquiry. For Kinsey, orgasm was the index of sexual health, and number of partners was the index of sexual interest.

Two large random surveys acted as follow-ups for American sexual attitudes in the generations after Kinsey. Morton Hunt's 1974 survey of 2,026 women and men, *Sexual Behavior in the 1970s*, was sponsored by *Playboy* magazine and showed an increase in oral sex and intercourse outside of marriage. Edward Brecher's (1911–1989) survey of 4,246 women and men, *Love, Sex, and Aging* (1984), sponsored by the Consumer's Union, showed that the Kinsey generation, now age fifty and older, was still sexually active.

THE SEXUAL REVOLUTION: GAYS, LESBIANS, AND WOMEN

In 1969 the Stonewall riots in New York City ignited national consciousness about gay rights (Carter 2004). During the 1960s and into the pre-AIDS 1980s, a number of sex surveys focused on gay and lesbian behaviors. Allen Bell and Martin Weinberg (1977) surveyed 4,639 gay men and lesbian women. Their questionnaire, too, was based on performance; the findings suggested that gay men were more interested in sex—as defined by genital stimulation, physical orgasm, and number of partners—and that lesbian women were more interested in romantic emotional commitment. *The Gay Report* (1979) by Karla Jay and Allen Young surveyed another 5,000 gays and lesbians and came to a more complex conclusion: that lesbians engaged in plenty of sex, but defined it more broadly than gay men did—including love, relationship, and their partners' pleasure, as well as genital stimulation and multiple partners. In 1983 sociologists Philip Blumstein and Pepper Schwartz corroborated this view in their survey of heterosexual and gay couples—a total of 6,066 individuals. In their report, *American Couples*, they wrote that lesbians' reports of sex were usually not genitally focused and that heterosexual men and women diverged on what they considered sexual experience to include.

The changing roles of women were a major focus of this period. Sociologist Shere Hite's 1976 survey of 3,019 women popularized the notion of clitoral orgasm to challenge the male-centered focus on penis-vagina intercourse. Her findings were criticized by the scientific establishment because her respondents, drawn largely from the National Organization for Women (NOW), were self-selected rather than randomly selected. Nonetheless, *The Hite Report* became an international best seller as it reflected women's political and medical advances toward sexual freedom. In 1960 the birth control pill had provided a means of avoiding unwanted pregnancy, in 1973 the U.S. Supreme Court's *Roe v. Wade* decision legalized abortion throughout the country, and various sex-positive books for women had paved the way for Hite's material, especially *Our Bodies, Ourselves* (1970), Betty Dodson's *Liberating Masturbation* (1974), and Lonnie Barbach's *For Yourself* (1975).

Hite's popularity ushered in a boom of further sex surveys by women in the 1980s and 1990s, especially questionnaires in large-circulation women's magazines. *The Redbook Report on Female Sexuality* (1977) by social psychologists Carol Tavris and Susan Sadd had over 100,000 respondents—married women, who disclosed "the good news about sex." Yet these women's surveys reverted to the usual indicators for sexual satisfaction: interest in intercourse, number of partners (usually heterosexual), and orgasm as goal.

THE GENDER GAP IN SATISFACTION

The last large institutional sex survey of the twentieth century (3,432 men and women) was conducted by Edward Laumann and three colleagues: John Gagnon, Robert Michael, and Stuart Michaels. Published in 1994 as *The Social Organization of Sexuality*, the survey's purpose was to research risk factors for HIV/AIDS and other sexually transmitted infections. But the findings harked back to pre-Kinsey surveys that focused on commitment and marriage while downplaying affairs, casual sex, and gay and lesbian relationships. Also like the pre-Kinsey surveys, the Laumann findings underscored the sexual shortcomings of women. The highly publicized statistic that emerged from the Laumann findings is that 43 percent of the women respondents reported sexual dissatisfaction or dysfunction, as distinct from 31 percent of the men. This gender discrepancy in satisfaction was reaffirmed in Laumann's 2006 survey of 27,500 people in twenty-nine countries and reflected what has become a thematic limitation of sex survey research: focus on intercourse and omission of meaningful issues such as attraction, love, intimacy, and commitment.

In the late 1990s, two large independent surveys were conducted by sex therapists. Their survey questions, largely drawn from their clinical practices, focused on feelings and meanings. Carol Rinkleib Ellison's 2000 study of 2,632 women, *Women's Sexualities*, conducted with Bernie Zilbergeld, underscored the developmental and intergenerational aspects of sex and love. Gina Ogden's study, "Integrating Sexuality and Spirituality" (ISIS) (2002), showed that for 3,810 American women and men, sexual experience involved emotional, intellectual, and spiritual dimensions as well as physical. Her multidimensional ISIS

model is in *The Heart and Soul of Sex: Making the ISIS Connection* (2006).

Into the first decade of the twenty-first century, however, institutional sex surveys continued to explore intercourse as the primary index of sexual behavior—as evidenced by the fourth cycle of the Guttmacher Institute's National Survey of Family Growth from 1982 to 2002 (38,000 men and women), which reported that nine in ten Americans engaged in premarital intercourse. But this study did not explore the emotional or cultural dynamics that might help us understand the motivations for premarital sex, or why it is important for us to know about this behavior.

CONCLUSIONS

Sex surveys influence the national conversation about sex, but their definitive value is limited. First, these surveys skew the overall understanding of human sexual experience by omitting significant portions of the population, such as the immigrant, uneducated, and poor, who are also most at risk of sexual violence and disease, and also top echelons of the upper class, who control many of our ideas and institutions. Another limitation of sex surveys is their attempt to reduce sexual experience to numbers, which tends to reinforce stereotypes and assumptions rather than provide the nuanced information needed for assessing norms, medical interventions, and public policy initiatives. Another limitation is researcher bias. Institutional sex surveys, such as the Kinsey and Laumann studies, profess scientific objectivity. But true objectivity is impossible; all sex surveys are effectively prejudged by the questions they ask and by how the results are interpreted.

For sex surveys to expand their usefulness and influence, researchers at the institutional level need to acknowledge the intrinsic complexity of sexual experience and broaden their focus to include feelings and meanings as well as intercourse-related frequencies. In addition, they need to reach populations previously undersurveyed. Perhaps some may be reached via the Internet if the constraints of electronic reporting do not further oversimplify questions, answers, and analysis of results.

SEE ALSO *Gender; Gender Gap; Hite, Shere; Kinsey, Alfred; Marriage; Romance; Sexual Orientation, Determinants of; Sexual Orientation, Social and Economic Consequences*

BIBLIOGRAPHY

Bell, Allen P., and Martin S. Weinberg. 1977. *Homosexualities: A Study of Diversity among Men and Women*. New York: Simon and Schuster.

Blumstein, Philip, and Pepper Schwartz. 1983. *American Couples: Money, Work, Sex*. New York: William Morrow.

Brecher, Edward M. 1984. *Love, Sex, and Aging: A Consumers Union Report*. Boston: Little, Brown.

Carter, David. 2004. *Stonewall: The Riots that Sparked the Gay Revolution*. New York: St. Martin's.

Davis, Katharine Bement. 1929. *Factors in the Sex Life of Twenty-Two Hundred Women*. New York: Harper.

Ellison, Carol Rinkleib. 2000. *Women's Sexualities: Generations of Women Share Intimate Secrets of Sexual Self-Acceptance*. Oakland, CA: New Harbinger.

Eriksen, Julia A., with Sally A. Steffen. 1999. *Kiss and Tell: Surveying Sex in the Twentieth Century*. Cambridge, MA: Harvard University Press.

Hamilton, Gilbert V. 1929. *A Research in Marriage*. New York: Lear.

Hite, Shere. 1976. *The Hite Report: A Nationwide Study of Female Sexuality*. New York: Macmillan.

Hunt, Morton. 1974. *Sexual Behavior in the 1970s*. Chicago: Playboy.

Jay, Karla, and Allen Young. 1979. *The Gay Report: Lesbians and Gay Men Speak Out about Sexual Experiences and Lifestyles*. New York: Summit.

Kinsey, Alfred C., Wardell B. Pomeroy, and Clyde E. Martin. 1948. *Sexual Behavior in the Human Male*. Philadelphia: Saunders.

Kinsey, Alfred C., Wardell B. Pomeroy, Clyde E. Martin, and Paul H. Gebhard. 1953. *Sexual Behavior in the Human Female*. Philadelphia: Saunders.

Laumann, Edward O., John H. Gagnon, Robert T. Michael, and Stuart Michaels. 1994. *The Social Organization of Sexuality: Sexual Practices in the United States*. Chicago: University of Chicago Press.

Mosher, Clelia Duel. 1892–1912. *Statistical Study of the Marriages of Forty-Seven Women*. Microfilm: 1 reel. 1975. Redwood City, CA: Mark Larwood. Originals at Stanford University Archives.

Ogden, Gina. 2002. *Sexuality and Spirituality in Women's Relationships: Preliminary Results of an Exploratory Survey*. Working Paper 405. Wellesley, MA: Wellesley College Center for Research on Women.

Ogden, Gina. 2006. *The Heart and Soul of Sex: Making the ISIS Connection*. Boston: Shambhala.

Whipple, Beverly, Gina Ogden, and Barry Komisaruk. 1992. Physiological Correlates of Imagery-Induced Orgasm in Women. *Archives of Sexual Behavior* 21 (2): 121–133.

Gina Ogden

SHADOW PRICES

A shadow price of a resource is its value to the decision maker. Shadow prices frequently equal market prices, but there are many instances in which they differ from each other. Methods for measuring shadow prices are closely related in the constrained optimization literature of math-

ematical programming, and in the econometrics literature. Within the constrained theoretical optimization framework, the shadow price (often called a "dual value") is the change in the objective function of the optimal solution, which is the result of a small change in the value of a constraint. Each constraint has an associated shadow price, which is represented by a Lagrange multiplier. This can be illustrated by considering the Lagrange multiplier associated with revenue maximization based on the sale of a commodity x at price p, where the firm faces the constraint that the amount available to sell cannot exceed X. The optimal solution is for the firm to sell X units of x, and the shadow price of x is p. If one considers this same problem, but subject to a production function constraint, namely $x = f(L)$, where L is the quantity of labor employed, the intuitive result is that the shadow price of a unit of output equals its marginal cost.

If the individual is assumed to maximize utility, then the interpretation of a shadow price becomes less intuitively obvious. Let us assume that the individual wishes to maximize the utility derived from leisure and consumption of good x, subject to two constraints: (1) money stock plus earned income must equal or exceed his expenses, and (2) leisure plus work hours cannot exceed total available hours. In this case, each constraint will be binding (since neither money nor time will be wasted), and each shadow price has an interesting interpretation. The shadow price of time equals the marginal utility of leisure. The shadow price of money (expressed in "utils" per dollar) equals the marginal utility of consumption divided by the price of the good x. This outcome shows that all scarce resources have a positive price, even if it is only expressed in terms of utility. That is, even if a scarce good or input is not sold directly in a market, it still has a shadow, or implicit, price. In a decentralized market, the ratio of market prices equals the ratio of shadow prices, and shadow prices are expressed in terms of utility, while actual prices are expressed in terms of dollars. When the Lagrangian takes the value of zero, its associated constraint is nonbinding. With more than one constraint, additional Lagrangian multipliers are used, each with a shadow price interpretation for that resource. In economics, it is assumed that both goods and time are scarce, so that zero shadow prices do not occur.

In many cases, the shadow price differs from the actual price for a good or an input. In the industrial organization literature, this could be due to rate-of-return regulation as illustrated by Scott Atkinson and Robert Halvorsen (1984). Further, monopoly power, monopsony power, labor union regulations, distortionary taxes, sticky prices, and export/import regulations are just some of the many constraints that can cause divergences between actual and shadow prices. In the case of rate-of-return regulation for electric utilities, the shadow price of capital exceeds the actual price of capital, causing the utility to over-invest in capital. (Färe and Primont [1995] and Mas-Colell et al. [1995] provide many more examples of constrained cost minimization, utility maximization, profit maximization, and revenue maximization in a mathematical programming framework. In particular, Färe and Primont stress the dual relationship between various constrained optimization models.)

Econometricians have focused on estimating shadow prices (sometimes called virtual prices) for inputs and outputs that are not marketed, so that actual prices are not observed, and for inputs and outputs where shadow prices differ from actual observed prices. Robert Halvorsen and Tim Smith (1991) employ a restricted cost function to estimate the time path of the shadow price of an unextracted resource, whose actual price is not observable because of the prevalence of vertical integration in the industry. The basic technique involves taking partial derivatives of the restricted cost function with respect to the quasi-fixed input, and then employing Hotelling's lemma.

Hedonic prices have also been estimated as shadow prices of attributes whose market prices are not available due to bundling. Hedonic regressions have a reduced form: The equilibrium price of a commodity is regressed on its attributes, which are typically not available in an unbundled form, and therefore are not separately priced. Examples are automobile price as a function of automobile attributes and housing price as a function of housing attributes. (For examples of these regressions see Atkinson and Halvorsen [1990] and Atkinson and Crocker [1987].) Hedonic prices have also been calculated to determine the value of human life, as shown by W. KipViscusi (2004).

Atkinson and Jeffrey Dorfman estimate the shadow price for tradable sulfur dioxide emission permits by calculating partial derivatives of the distance function with respect to sulfur dioxide emissions. Following Rolf Färe and Daniel Primont (1995), one divides the partial derivative of the distance function with respect to a good by its derivative with respect to sulfur dioxide, and then equates this to the ratio of the market price of this good to the unknown shadow price of sulfur dioxide. One then solves for the latter. The estimated shadow price can then be usefully compared to the market price for traded permits, as this market is quite thin.

A large additional literature has developed that maintains the hypothesis that shadow prices to the firm may differ from actual or market prices in instances where actual prices are observed. Shadow cost, shadow distance, and shadow profit systems have been developed and estimated. With shadow-cost systems, if ratios of estimated shadow prices differ from ratios of actual prices, then the firm is allocatively inefficient. Atkinson and Halvorsen (1984) and Atkinson and Christopher Cornwell (1994) assume shadow-cost minimization and estimate shadow-cost functions to compute the allocative efficiency of electric utilities and airlines, respectively. Panel data facilitates the estimation process, as shown by Atkinson and Cornwell. Atkinson and Primont (2002) extend this analysis to an estimation of a shadow-distance system, which employs the first-order conditions for cost minimization. A shadow-distance system estimates the dual to a shadow cost system by computing shadow quantities rather than shadow prices. After assuming shadow-profit maximization by firms, a shadow-profit system was devised by Atkinson and Halvorsen (1980) and Atkinson and Cornwell (1998). This system is used to estimate the shadow prices of inputs and outputs, where the latter are measures of monopoly power. Shadow prices for inputs and outputs have also been estimated to compute the extent of monopoly and monoposony power by Atkinson and Joe Kerkvliet (1989).

Attempts have been made to translate shadow-price estimates into the potential savings from eliminating allocative inefficiency. (See, in particular, Kumbhakar [1997].) However, Atkinson and Dorfman (2006) show that any such decomposition is not unique, unless at least one input's shadow price can be related to its actual price via a factor of proportionality.

BIBLIOGRAPHY

Atkinson, Scott E., and Christopher Cornwell. 1994. Parametric Measurement of Technical and Allocative Inefficiency with Panel Data. *International Economic Review* 35: 231–245.

Atkinson, Scott E., and Christopher Cornwell. 1998. Profit versus Cost Frontier Estimation of Price and Technical Inefficiency: A Parametric Approach with Panel Data. *Southern Economic Journal* 64 (3): 753–764.

Atkinson, Scott E., and Thomas Crocker. 1987. A Bayesian Approach to Assessing the Robustness of Hedonic Property Value Studies. *Journal of Applied Econometrics* 2 (1): 27–45.

Atkinson, Scott E., and Jeffrey Dorfman. 2006. Chasing Absolute Cost Savings in a World of Relative Inefficiency. Working paper. Department of Economics, University of Georgia.

Atkinson, Scott E., and Robert Halvorsen. 1984. Parametric Efficiency Tests, Economies of Scale, and Input Demand in U.S. Electric Power Generation. *International Economic Review* 25 (3): 647–662.

Atkinson, Scott E., and Robert Halvorsen. 1990. The Valuation of Risks to Life: Evidence from the Market for Automobiles. *Review of Economics and Statistics* 72: 133–136.

Atkinson, Scott E., and Joe Kerkvliet. 1989. Dual Measures of Monopoly and Monopsony Power: An Application to Regulated Electric Utilities. *Review of Economics and Statistics* 71 (2): 250–257.

Atkinson, Scott E., and Daniel Primont. 2002. Measuring Productivity Growth, Technical Efficiency, Allocative

Efficiency, and Returns to Scale Using Distance Functions. *Journal of Econometrics* 108: 203–225.

Färe, Rolf, and Daniel Primont. 1995. *Multi-Output Production and Duality: Theory and Applications.* Boston: Kluwer Academic Publishers.

Halvorsen, Robert, and Tim R. Smith. 1991. A Test of the Theory of Exhaustible Resources. *Quarterly Journal of Economics* 106 (1): 123–140.

Kumbhakar, Subal C. 1997. Modelling Allocative Inefficiency in a Translog Cost Function and Cost Share Equations: An Exact Relationship. *Journal of Econometrics* 76: 351–356.

Mas-Collel, Andreu, Michael D. Whinston, and Jerry R. Green. 1995. *Microeconomic Theory.* Oxford: Oxford University Press.

Viscusi, W. Kip. 2004. The Value of Life: Estimates with Risks by Occupation and Industry. *Economic Inquiry* 42 (1): 29–48.

Scott E. Atkinson

SHAMANS

Shamans represent humanity's most ancient forms of healing, spirituality, and community ritual. In *Shamanism: Archaic Techniques of Ecstasy* (1964), Mircea Eliade characterized the shaman as someone who enters ecstasy to interact with spirits on behalf of the community. Although some have challenged his suggestion of the universality of shamanism, the cross-cultural research of Michael Winkelman has established the universal validity of the concept of the shaman, as well as the characteristics of Shamans, particularly their differences with respect to other types of magico-religious practitioners. In *Shamanism: The Neural Ecology of Consciousness and Healing* (2000), Winkelman illustrates how the cross-cultural similarities in shamans relate to humans' evolved psychology. Shamanism was an important evolution of human culture and consciousness and created practices to expand ancient primate activities for ritual healing and group integration.

THE NATURE AND UNIVERSALITY OF THE SHAMAN

While shamans and priests are both religious practitioners, they differ in many basic ways. Shamans enter into a direct relationship with the spiritual world, for example, while priests mediate with respect to deities. Winkelman's research, particularly in *Shamans, Priests, and Witches: A Cross-Cultural Study of Magico-Religious Practitioners* (1992), provides empirical evidence for these differences: Shamans of hunter-gatherer societies reflect biological adaptations to an evolved psychology involving altered states of consciousness (ASC), while priests reflect adaptations to the social leadership needs of agricultural groups.

Unlike priests who generally acquire their positions by virtue of social position in class or kinship ranks, the shaman is thought to be chosen by the spirits. Shamans acquire their special status through experiences of the spirit world. While most people in shamanic cultures may deliberately seek contact with the spirit world in a vision quest, only a few will have the benefit of being chosen by the spirits for special experiences and powers. Spirit-world experiences occur spontaneously in illness, hallucinations, dreams, and visions, and they are further induced through vision quests involving prolonged fasts; the ingestion of emetics, tobacco, and hallucinogen drugs; and other arduous techniques that provoke profound alterations of consciousness, which are interpreted as entry into the spirit world. Ritual inductions of spirit-world experiences generally employ drums, rattles, and other percussion, as well as singing and chanting.

The universals of human culture associated with shamanism involve the use of techniques for altering consciousness to produce an experience of interacting with the spirit world. These experiences are key to providing healing and information for the community. The altered states of consciousness associated with shamanism are a human universal derived from human biology, reflecting extraordinary aspects of normal systemic reactions of the brain and nervous system in maintaining homeostasis, or internal balance (Laughlin, McManus, and d'Aquili 1992; Winkelman 2000). The psychiatrist Arnold Mandell has characterized this neurobiological transcendence in terms of activation of the serotonergic linkages between the limbic (emotional) brain and the R-Complex (behavioral) brain (1980). This activation produces strong slow-wave (theta, 3-6 cycles per second) brain discharges that induce synchronized brain waves across the levels of the brain and between the frontal hemispheres.

The particular form of altered consciousness associated with shamanism is called a *soul journey, soul flight*, or some other similar term referring to the departure of some aspect of the self, particularly one's soul or spirit, from the body in order to journey to the spirit world. This shamanic soul journey is distinct from the possession experiences associated with the altered states of consciousness of more complex societies. Possession involves experiences in which a person's sense of personal consciousness and volition is replaced by the controlling influences of a spirit entity who possesses the person's body and controls it (Bourguignon 1976). This divine control of one's person is not typically associated with shamanic practice. The shaman remains aware of self during the soul journey, while possessed people typically report a lack of awareness of the experience following possession. Winkelman has integrated cross-cultural and interdisciplinary explanations that suggest important influences on the nature and form of altered states of consciousness from a variety of dietary, social, political, and ritual practices. The shaman's awareness during the soul journey reflects the active engagement in altered states through early ritual practices, while the possessed person's sense of external dominance by the possessing entity reflects influences external to the self, such as endocrine imbalances from nutritional deficiencies and dissociate experiences induced by oppressive social conditions.

ASPECTS OF SHAMANIC PRACTICE

Shamans have additional universal characteristics that differentiate them from the priests and possessed mediums of more complex societies. Cross-culturally, shamans are characterized as charismatic leaders whose community rituals generally involve healing and divination. Other characteristics of shamans are:

- They undergo an altered state of consciousness (ASC), characterized as a "soul journey."

- They perform rituals involving chanting, music, drumming, and dancing.

- They have had initiatory death-and-rebirth experiences and guardian spirit encounters.

- They have close relationships with animals in control of spirits and development of personal powers.

- They use therapeutic processes to recover lost souls, defined as the separation of some vital aspect of personal essence due to attacks by spirits and sorcerers.

Shamans typically engage the entire local community in all-night ceremonies. During hours of dancing, drumming, and chanting, the shaman may dramatically recount mythological histories and enact struggles in the spirit world. Shamans also have the capacity to engage in sorcery and malevolent magic to harm others.

VISIONARY TECHNIQUES EMPLOYED FOR SUPERNATURAL ENGAGEMENT

Shamans use rituals to induce the altered state of consciousness (ASC) typified in a soul journey, where a spiritual aspect departs the body and travels to the spirit world. The ASC is typically produced through drumming and dancing to the point of collapse (or deliberate repose), and it may be potentiated by dietary and sexual restrictions and medicinal plants. The overall physiological dynamics of ASC induction involve excitation until exhaustion, which induces the relaxation response, a natural recuperation process. The shaman's ASC includes: a death-and-rebirth experience, producing a self-transformation; a flight to the lower, middle, and upper levels of the spirit world, reflecting transformations of consciousness; and personal transformation into an animal, enabling the shaman to travel and use special powers.

The shamanic ASC stimulates the reptilian and paleomammalian levels of the brain, and the associated preverbal processes. The ASC synchronizes diverse brain regions with theta brain wave discharges, which are produced by serotonergic linkages that propel these discharges from the brain stem and limbic areas into the frontal cortex. This produces an integration of lower brain processes into consciousness; an interhemispheric synchronization of the frontal cortex; and a synthesis of emotion, thought, and behavior. ASCs induce information integration, social bonding, stress reduction, and healing through enhancement of visual representation faculties. Humans have a visual symbolic system utilized in the dream mode of consciousness and illustrated in the typically visual (as opposed to verbal) material manifested in dreaming. This visual presentational symbolism (as opposed to the verbal representational system) provides a medium for manifestation of information from the preverbal levels of the unconscious. Winkelman (2000, 2002) discusses how shamanic rituals elicited and integrated this symbolic capacity to produce a new level of mental evolution underlying the development of the modern cultural capacity during the Middle/Upper Paleolithic transition approximately 40,000 years ago.

Shamanism focuses on internal mental images, evoking them through ASC and ritual practices for integrating dream processes, particularly overnight ritual activities. Shamanic visions engage psychobiological communication processes that integrate unconscious psychophysiological information with affective and cognitive levels. Shamanic images provide analysis, synthesis, and planning through integrating the informational and personal processes associated with dreaming, a visual symbolic system of self-representations involving the paleomammalian brain. Shamanic traditions recognize this use of the dream capacity in terms such as *dream time*. This process engages ASC induction activities that produce theta waves and induce awareness of this emotionally salient material. This integration of normally unconscious content into conscious processes produces a sense of interconnectedness and transpersonal healing experiences.

SHAMANISM AND HEALING: PSYCHOINTEGRATION

Shamans are the preeminent healers of premodern societies. Their roles as healers include medical and psychiatric functions, addressing physical disease as well as a variety of psychological conditions. Shamanism provides mechanisms for inducing healing through systemic psychological integration using ritual, symbols, and ASC. Shamans' practices represent the evolution of a "holistic imperative," a drive toward more integrated levels of consciousness (Laughlin, McManus, and d'Aquili 1992). Shamanic traditions produce integrative responses that synchronize divergent aspects of human cognition and identity through several mechanisms, including: (1) using ASC, ritual, and symbols to activate synchronizing brain processes; (2) the stimulation of processes of lower-brain structures and subconscious aspects of personality and self; and (3) incorporating people into community rituals that strengthen social support and identity. These therapeutic processes still have relevance in the modern world, as evidenced by the modern resuscitation of the ancient shamanic practices.

SEE ALSO *Animism; Magic; Mental Health; Mental Illness; Miracles; Purification; Religion; Rituals*

BIBLIOGRAPHY

Bourguignon, Erika. 1976. *Possession*. San Francisco: Chandler and Sharpe.

Eliade, Mircea. 1964. *Shamanism: Archaic Techniques of Ecstasy*. New York: Bollingen Foundation.

Laughlin, Charles, Jr., John McManus, and Eugene d'Aquili. 1992. *Brain, Symbol, and Experience: Toward a Neurophenomenology of Consciousness*. New York: Columbia University Press.

Mandell, Arnold. 1980. Toward a Psychobiology of Transcendence: God in the Brain. In *The Psychobiology of Consciousness*, eds. Julian Davidson and Richard Davidson. New York: Plenum.

Winkelman, Michael. 1986. Magico-Religious Practitioner Types and Socioeconomic Conditions. *Behavior Science Research* 20 (1–4): 17–46.

Winkelman, Michael. 1990. Shaman and Other "Magico-Religious" Healers: A Cross-Cultural Study of Their Origins, Nature, and Social Transformations. *Ethos* 18 (3): 308–352.

Winkelman, Michael. 1992. *Shamans, Priests, and Witches: A Cross-Cultural Study of Magico-Religious Practitioners*. Anthropological Research Paper No. 44. Tempe: Arizona State University.

Winkelman, Michael. 2000. *Shamanism: The Neural Ecology of Consciousness and Healing*. Westport, CT: Bergin and Garvey.

Winkelman, Michael. 2002. Shamanism and Cognitive Evolution. *Cambridge Archaeological Journal* 12 (1): 71–101.

Winkelman, Michael. 2004. Shamanism As the Original Neurotheology. *Zygon Journal of Religion and Science* 39 (1): 193–217.

Michael Winkelman

SHAME

Shame occupies an important place both among the emotions and as a key component in social relationships. It might well be called "the master emotion" for reasons to be discussed below. But why so much attention to one emotion? This emphasis has been difficult for many people to follow. What about other primary emotions, such as love, fear, anger, grief, and so on? To the average reader in modern societies, the focus on shame seems arbitrary.

Not so, however, in traditional societies. These societies, because of their exclusive concern with social relationships rather than individuals, overemphasize shame. An excellent introduction to the consciousness of shame in a traditional society can be found in Joan Metge's 1986 study of the emotion lexicon in the Maori language.

Modern societies, since they emphasize the isolated, self-reliant individual, hide shame. Consciousness of this emotion would betray the extent of each individual's dependence on the views of others, and therefore the social nature of the self.

C. H. Cooley's (1864–1929) idea of the "looking-glass self" suggested an elementary link between shame and selfhood: "A self-idea of this sort seems to have three principal elements: the imagination of our appearance to the other person; the imagination of his judgment of that appearance; and some sort of self-feeling, such as pride or mortification (shame)" (Cooley 1922, p. l84).

Erving Goffman (1922–1982), whose work often centered on embarrassment, provided another justification. He argued that embarrassment, and by implication shame, had universal importance in social interaction: "Face-to-face interaction in any culture seems to require just those capacities that flustering seems to destroy. Therefore, events which lead to embarrassment and the methods for avoiding and dispelling it may provide a cross-cultural framework of sociological analysis" (Goffman 1956, p. 266).

Christian Heath further justifies this focus:

> Embarrassment lies at the heart of the social organization of day-to-day conduct. It provides a personal constraint on the behavior of the individual in society and a public response to actions and activities considered problematic or untoward. Embarrassment and its potential play an important part in sustaining the individual's commitment to social organization, values and convention. It permeates everyday life and our dealings with others. It informs ordinary conduct and bounds the individual's behavior in areas of social life that formal and institutionalized constraints do not reach. (Heath 1988, p. 137)

Beyond these considerations, there is another, broader one that is implied in Goffman's ideas, particularly the idea of impression management. Most of his work implies that every actor is extraordinarily sensitive to the exact amount of deference being received by others. Even a slight difference between what is expected and what is received, whether too little or too much, can cause embarrassment.

Thomas J. Scheff (2006) followed Goffman's lead by proposing that embarrassment and shame are primarily social emotions, because they usually arise from a threat to the bond, no matter how slight. The degree of social connectedness, of accurately taking the viewpoint of the other, is the key component of social bonds. A discrepancy in the amount of deference conveys judgment, and so is experienced as a threat to the bond. Since even a slight discrepancy in deference is sensed, embarrassment or the anticipation of embarrassment would be a virtually continuous presence in interaction.

In most of his writing, Goffman's every-person was constantly aware of her own standing in the eyes of others, implying almost continuous states of self-conscious emotion—embarrassment, shame, humiliation, and in rare instances pride—or anticipation of these states. Their sensitivity to the eyes of others makes Goffman's actors seem three-dimensional, since they embody not only thought and behavior, but also feeling.

Helen Lynd (1896–1982) was one of the first to focus on shame as a key to personal identity (1958). Silvan Tomkins (1911–1991) devoted an entire book (1963) to describing the concept of shame and its psychological and social functions. Helen Lewis (1913–1987) has shown the key role of unacknowledged shame in failed psychotherapy sessions (1971), and John Braithwaite's work (1989) on the role of reintegrative shame in restorative justice has attracted a considerable following.

Shame and embarrassment are crucial because they have both psychological and social functions. For brevity, this entry will discuss only the three most important functions. First, for individuals, shame appears to be an automatic signal of moral trespass; the conscience has an instinctive shame component (Scheff and Retzinger 1991). This type of shame can be suppressed, but only at great cost. For most people, shame provides unmistakable signals of where they stand in their moral universe at any particular moment.

Second, normal shame signals the state of the social bond. Embarrassment and other shame signals warn us when the self or other is feeling too close (exposed, violated) or too far (invisible, rejected). If these signals are suppressed or ignored, it may be almost impossible to know where one stands with another person. Interaction takes on a stiff and formal character, with individuals flustered or distracted, which interferes with understanding and trust. Engulfment and isolation produce, and are produced by, the denial of shame. Recognition of shame and embarrassment signals in others is a way of becoming aware of their humanity. Seeing that the other is embarrassed or ashamed is an elemental path toward understanding that they are persons much like ourselves.

It now seems likely that shame is a genetically inherited emotion that is a human universal. Since shame identifies threats to the social bond and to the integrity of the self, it makes sense that sensitivity to shame signals would be adaptive, and that this kind of sensitivity would have survival value for the individual and the group.

Third, shame seems to be the primary regulator of all emotions, including shame itself (shame about shame). This kind of regulation poses no problem with normal shame, because it is easily acknowledged and resolved. As indicated above, it is merely a signal of the state of the bond. But unacknowledged shame can interfere with the resolution of all the emotions, including anger, fear, grief, and shame itself. The basic reason that people hide their emotions is that they have learned to be ashamed of them. The exception is angry displays: Most people, especially men, have learned to flaunt anger and aggression as a way of masking vulnerable emotions (such as fear, shame, and grief) because they have been taught that these emotions are signs of weakness.

Since shame is a self-conscious emotion, persons and groups may fall into traps of self-consciousness that interfere with normal biological, psychological, and social paths that allow the resolution of painful emotions. For example, in the absence of unacknowledged shame, persons and groups with conflicting interests are able to find the most-beneficial or least-destructive compromise. Unacknowledged shame paralyzes both the ability and desire to reach a compromise. For this reason, unacknowledged shame and alienation may be keys to understanding interminable impasses and quarrels (Scheff and Retzinger 1991; Retzinger 1991; Scheff 1994).

For these reasons, pride and shame play an equal part with solidarity and alienation in determining the degree of social integration in a society, its capacity for cooperation and survival under stress, and its potential for fragmentation or violent disruption. Because we live in a highly individualized society, these matters have only recently come to our collective attention. Denial of shame goes hand in hand with denial of interdependence. An accurate and effective social science requires that shame and interdependence be brought to the light of day.

SEE ALSO *Alienation; Emotion; Goffman, Erving; Humiliation; Looking-Glass Effect; Self-Consciousness, Private vs. Public; Self-Hatred; Sin; Social Psychology; Stigma*

BIBLIOGRAPHY

Braithwaite, John. l989. *Crime, Shame, and Reintegration.* Cambridge, U.K.: Cambridge University Press.

Cooley, Charles H. 1922. *Human Nature and the Social Order.* New York: Scribner's.

Goffman, Erving. 1956. Embarrassment and Social Organization. *American Journal of Sociology* 62: 264–271.

Heath, Christian. 1988. Embarrassment and Interactional Organization. In *Erving Goffman: Exploring the Interaction Order*, ed. Paul Drew and Anthony Wooton. Cambridge, U.K.: Polity.

Lewis, Helen. B. 1971. *Shame and Guilt in Neurosis.* New York: International Universities Press.

Lynd, Helen M. 1958. *On Shame and the Search for Identity.* New York: Harcourt.

Metge, Joan. 1986. *In and Out of Touch: Whakamaa in Cross Cultural Perspective.* Wellington, New Zealand: Victoria University Press.

Retzinger, Suzanne M. 1991. *Violent Emotions: Shame and Rage in Marital Quarrels.* Newbury Park, CA: Sage.

Scheff, Thomas J. 1994. *Bloody Revenge: Emotions, Nationalism, and War.* Chicago: University of Chicago Press.

Scheff, Thomas J. 2006. *Goffman Unbound! A New Paradigm for Social Science.* Boulder, CO: Paradigm.

Scheff, Thomas J., and Suzanne M. Retzinger. 1991. *Emotions and Violence: Shame and Rage in Destructive Conflicts.* Lexington, MA: Lexington Books.

Tomkins, Silvan. 1963. *Affect, Imagery, Consciousness.* Vol. 2: *The Negative Affects.* New York: Springer.

Thomas J. Scheff

SHARECROPPING

A sharecropping arrangement is an agrarian contract between a landlord and a tenant in which the tenant pays a fraction of the crop to the landlord in exchange for the right to exploit the landlord's plot of land. In addition to the crop rent, there may or may not be a fixed component to the contract in the form of a side payment either from the landlord to the tenant (a wage) or from the tenant to the landlord (a fixed rent). As a result, sharecropping (or share tenancy) is an alternative to (1) a wage contract, in which the landlord pays the tenant a wage but gets to keep all of the crop; and (2) a fixed rent contract, in which the tenant pays the landlord a fixed rent (either in cash or in kind) but gets to keep all of the crop. Sharecropping should therefore not be confused with a crop fixed rent contract, in which the tenant exploits the land in exchange for a fixed amount of crop per unit of land paid as rent (e.g., 1 ton of grain per hectare).

Terence J. Byres in his introduction to a collection of essays and case studies on sharecropping (1983) provides a historical perspective on share tenancy and recounts how the institution is mentioned in historical documents from ancient Greece (594–593 BCE); ancient China (722–481 BCE); ancient India (fourth century BCE); the Roman Empire (61–112 CE); western Europe, especially France, where the institution is referred to as *métayage* (ninth century CE); southern Europe, especially Italy, where the institution is referred to as *mezzadria* (ninth century CE); Russia, where the institution is referred to as *polovnik*, under the Mongol Empire (thirteenth and fourteenth centuries); and China and India during the twentieth century.

Sharecropping has long been reviled by social scientists—most notably by Marx-inspired economists such as Amit Bhaduri (1973) and Robert Pearce (1983), who perceived it as a mechanism by which capital (i.e., landed individuals or households) exploits labor (i.e., landless individuals or households)—but also by most economists up to Joseph E. Stiglitz (1974), as related by Alexander F. Robertson (1980). Although the Marxist critique of share tenancy may have been true during some historical periods and in some regions of the world (e.g., in the postbellum southern United States; see Reid 1973), it does not explain the persistence of sharecropping contracts that both parties enter into voluntarily, in places as diverse as the United States (Young and Burke 2001), Brazil (Stolcke and Hall 1983), Ethiopia (Pender and Fafchamps 2006), Madagascar (Bellemare 2006), India (Pandey 2004), Pakistan (Jacoby and Mansuri 2006), and so on.

THEORIES OF SHARECROPPING: THE QUASI MONOPOLY OF ECONOMICS

The study of sharecropping by social scientists has been almost the exclusive preserve of economists, and it dates back to Adam Smith's *An Inquiry into the Nature and Causes of the Wealth of Nations* (1776, 1976), which viewed *métayage* (Smith used the French term for sharecropping, since share tenancy was still unheard of in England) as an inefficient contract between slavery and the English (i.e., fixed rent) system. Alfred Marshall, in the eighth and last edition of his *Principles of Economics* (1920), was the first social scientist to apply a rigorous analytical framework to the study of sharecropping, allowing him to identify the moral hazard problem associated with share tenancy. Assuming that supervision of the tenant by the landlord is prohibitively costly, the tenant will provide labor only up to the point where the value of his marginal product of labor equals the opportunity cost from entering the contract (i.e., the wage the tenant would derive from alternative employment). But then, because the tenant receives only a fraction of the value of the marginal product of labor, and given that the marginal product of labor is assumed to be decreasing, the tenant will underprovide labor with respect to a fixed rent contract. In the years following the publication of the last edition of *Principles of Economics*, the moral hazard problem associated with sharecropping—that is, the underprovision of labor by the tenant due to the fact that the landlord cannot supervise labor—has thus come to be known as "Marshallian inefficiency."

It was not until much later, in the 1960s, that Steven N. S. Cheung, then a graduate student at the University of Chicago, sought to reestablish the efficiency of share tenancy, although an effort had been made in that direction by D. Gale Johnson, who argued that tenants have every incentive to produce efficiently given the threat of eviction by the landlord in a repeated interaction setting (Johnson 1950). By assuming that the landlord can costlessly enforce the tenant's level of effort, Cheung showed that sharecropping can be as efficient as a fixed rent contract in a static framework (1968).

Two schools of thought were thus born. On the one hand, the Marshallian view argued that sharecropping was inefficient because it assumed that enforcing the landlord's preferred level of effort was prohibitively costly. On the other hand, the Cheungian (or "transactions costs") view argued that sharecropping was efficient because it assumed that the landlord could costlessly enforce her preferred level of effort.

Taking a deliberately Marshallian view, Stiglitz was the first to fully formalize the institution of sharecropping using the tools of microeconomic theory (1974). In a paper that presents and solves one of the first complete principal-agent models in economics, Stiglitz asked why sharecropping in developing countries was perceived as an inefficient (and often irrational) arrangement when the same type of contract did not raise any questions when observed under the form of commission sales in industrialized countries. Stiglitz showed that when the absentee landlord is risk-neutral and the tenant is risk-averse, sharecropping provides a useful trade-off between incentives and risk-sharing. In this case, a wage contract provides the weakest incentives to the tenant, who is also fully insured against production risk, whereas a fixed rent contract provides the strongest incentives to the tenant, who is also exposed to all the production risk. By trading off the tenant's comparative advantage in labor supervision with the landlord's comparative advantage in risk-bearing, a sharecropping contract remains the optimal choice among the set of inefficient contracts, i.e., it is second-best, following the terminology of contract theory. Stiglitz's work, which contributed to the birth of the so-called information revolution in economics along with that of George Akerlof (1970) and A. Michael Spence (1973), also reestablished the rationality of sharecropping.

The theory of share tenancy put forth by Stiglitz provided the canonical model of sharecropping, but it has been refined in many ways. David M. G. Newbery incorporated a second type of uncertainty, namely uncertainty over the tenant's wage from alternative employment, in the framework (1977). Mukesh Eswaran and Ashok Kotwal in 1985 considered the contracting problem under two-sided moral hazard—that is, moral hazard in the provision of managerial ability by the landlord and moral hazard in the provision of labor by the tenant—and showed that when each party is highly inefficient in providing the other party's inputs (i.e., when the tenant is highly inefficient at providing managerial ability and when the landlord is highly inefficient at providing labor supervision), sharecropping emerges as the optimal contract. Clive Bell and Pinhas Zusman, instead of adopting the principal-agent framework, used the tools of cooperative game theory to study sharecropping (1976). William Hallagan abstracted from moral hazard considerations and instead chose to introduce adverse selection into the model to explain selection by the tenants into different contracts (1978). Douglas Allen and Dean Lueck took into account the fact that, in certain parts of the world, the landlord and the tenant share the cost of inputs, and that when the crop share is set equal to the cost share, sharecropping is again an efficient arrangement (1992, 1993). Maitreesh Ghatak and Priyanka Pandey showed that in the presence of limited liability, if the tenant can choose between agricultural techniques that differ in their levels of expected yield and variance, the landlord may choose a sharecropping contract in order to curb the tenant's risk-taking behavior (2000). Marc F. Bellemare developed theoretical explanations to account for the emergence of reverse share tenancy (i.e., sharecropping between a poor, risk-averse landlord and a richer, risk-neutral tenant), a contract that remains a theoretical impossibility under the canonical Stiglitzian theory of share tenancy (2006). This list of works is nonexhaustive, given that sharecropping is one of the most studied problems in economics and in the social sciences.

EMPIRICAL EVIDENCE ON SHARECROPPING

Empirically, social scientists have sought to answer two major questions regarding sharecropping: (1) Do incentives matter in land tenancy agreements—that is, are tenants less productive under share tenancy than under fixed rent, or is there Marshallian inefficiency?; and (2) Do the contract shapes observed in the data correspond to theoretical predictions? As in much of the applied literature on contracts (Prendergast 1999), the second question has received much less attention, mostly because of lack of data. Most empirical researchers asking the first question have found at least partial support for the hypothesis of Marshallian inefficiency (Bell 1977 and Shaban 1987 in India; Laffont and Matoussi 1995 and Ai, Arcand, and Éthier 1996 in Tunisia; Jacoby and Mansuri 2006 in Pakistan). As regards the second question, Daniel Ackerberg and Maristella Botticini found that risk-sharing concerns indeed do drive contract choice once the possibility that landlords and tenants match endogenously is taken into account in a data set of land tenancy contracts in early Renaissance Tuscany (2002); Pierre Dubois found that fertility considerations make landlords more likely to choose a sharecropping contract in an effort to curb tenants' incentives to overuse the land and deplete soil fertility in a dataset of land tenancy contracts in a rural area of the Philippines (2002); and Bellemare found that asset risk (i.e., the possibility of losing their claim to the land) makes landlords more likely to choose sharecropping over fixed rent in a dataset of land tenancy contracts in Madagascar (2006).

BIBLIOGRAPHY

Ackerberg, Daniel A., and Maristella Botticini. 2002. Endogenous Matching and the Empirical Determinants of Contract Form. *Journal of Political Economy* 110: 564–591.

Ai, Chunrong, Jean-Louis Arcand, and François Éthier. 1996. Moral Hazard and Marshallian Inefficiency: Evidence from Tunisia. Working Paper, Université de Montréal.

Akerlof, George. 1970. The Market for Lemons. *Quarterly Journal of Economics* 89: 488–500.

Allen, Douglas, and Dean Lueck. 1992. Contract Choice in Modern Agriculture: Cash Rent Versus Cropshare. *Journal of Law and Economics* 35: 397–426.

Allen, Douglas, and Dean Lueck. 1993. Transaction Costs and the Design of Cropshare Contracts. *RAND Journal of Economics* 24: 78–100.

Bell, Clive. 1977. Alternative Theories of Sharecropping: Some Tests Using Evidence from Northeast India. *Journal of Development Studies* 13: 317–346.

Bell, Clive, and Pinhas Zusman. 1976. A Bargaining-Theoretic Approach to Cropsharing Contracts. *American Economic Review* 66: 578–588.

Bellemare, Marc F. 2006. Three Essays on Agrarian Contracts. PhD diss., Cornell University.

Bhaduri, Amit. 1973. A Study in Agricultural Backwardness Under Semi-Feudalism. *Economic Journal* 83: 120–137.

Breman, Jan. 1974. *Patronage and Exploitation*. Berkeley: University of California Press.

Byres, Terence J. 1983. *Sharecropping and Sharecroppers*. London: Frank Cass.

Cheung, Steven N. S. 1968. Private Property Rights and Sharecropping. *Journal of Political Economy* 76: 1107–1122.

Dubois, Pierre. 2002. Moral Hazard, Land Fertility, and Sharecropping in a Rural Area of the Philippines. *Journal of Development Economics* 68: 35–64.

Eswaran, Mukesh, and Ashok Kotwal. 1985. A Theory of Contractual Structure in Agriculture. *American Economic Review* 75: 352–367.

Ghatak, Maitreesh, and Priyanka Pandey. 2000. Contract Choice in Agriculture with Joint Moral Hazard in Effort and Risk. *Journal of Development Economics* 63: 303–326.

Hallagan, William. 1978. Self-Selection by Contractual Choice and the Theory of Sharecropping. *Bell Journal of Economics* 9: 344–354.

Jacoby, Hanan G., and Ghazala Mansuri. 2006. Incentives, Supervision, and Sharecropper Productivity. Development Economics Research Group Working Paper. Washington, DC: World Bank.

Johnson, D. Gale. 1950. Resource Allocation under Share Contracts. *Journal of Political Economy* 58: 111–123.

Laffont, Jean-Jacques, and Mohammed S. Matoussi. 1995. Moral Hazard, Financial Constraints, and Sharecropping in El Oulja. *Review of Economic Studies* 62: 381–399.

Marshall, Alfred. 1920. *Principles of Economics*. 8th ed. London: Macmillan.

Newbery, David M. G. 1977. Risk-Sharing, Sharecropping, and Uncertain Labor Markets. *Review of Economic Studies* 44: 585–594.

Pandey, Priyanka. 2004. Effects of Technology on Incentive Design of Share Contracts. *American Economic Review* 94: 1152–1168.

Pearce, Robert. 1983. Sharecropping: Towards a Marxist View. In *Sharecropping and Sharecroppers*, ed. Terence J. Byres, 48–52. London: Frank Cass.

Pender, John, and Marcel Fafchamps. 2006. Land Lease Markets and Agricultural Efficiency in Ethiopia. *Journal of African Economics* 15: 251–284.

Prendergast, Canice. 1999. The Provision of Incentives in Firms. *Journal of Economic Literature* 37: 7–63.

Reid, Joseph D. 1973. Sharecropping as an Understandable Market Response: The Post-Bellum South. *Journal of Economic History* 33: 106–130.

Robertson, Alexander F. 1980. On Sharecropping. *Man* 15: 411–429.

Shaban, Radwan A. 1987. Testing between Competing Models of Sharecropping. *Journal of Political Economy* 95: 893–920.

Smith, Adam. [1776] 1976. *An Inquiry into the Nature and Causes of the Wealth of Nations*. Chicago: University of Chicago Press.

Spence, A. Michael. 1973. Job Market Signaling. *Quarterly Journal of Economics* 87: 355–374.

Stiglitz, Joseph E. 1974. Incentives and Risk-Sharing in Sharecropping. *Review of Economic Studies* 41: 219–255.

Stolcke, Verena, and Michael M. Hall. 1983. The Introduction of Free Labor on São Paulo Coffee Plantations. In *Sharecropping and Sharecroppers*, ed. Terence J. Byres, 170–200. London: Frank Cass.

Young, H. Peyton, and Mary A. Burke. 2001. Competition and Custom in Economic Contracts: A Case Study of Illinois Agriculture. *American Economic Review* 91: 559–573.

Marc F. Bellemare

SHARON, ARIEL
1928–

Born on February 27, 1928, in the British Mandate of Palestine, Israeli leader Ariel Sharon's long and controversial military and political career embodies the tension between pragmatism and idealism inherent in modern nationalist movements. Oscillating between extremist Jewish ethno-nationalism and pragmatic secular Zionism, Sharon's leadership has triggered strong and contradictory responses. It provokes hate and revulsion among the many who see him as a dogmatic and reckless bully and a war criminal. Others view Sharon with great appreciation as a brilliant strategist and pragmatic statesman who took courageous steps toward making peace with Egypt and ending the Israeli occupation in Gaza.

Sharon joined the Israeli Haganah, an underground paramilitary organization, at age fourteen. In the 1948 Arab-Israeli War he served as a platoon commander and was severely wounded in the Battle of Latrun against the Jordanian Legion. In 1953 Sharon commanded a special commando unit ("101"), which carried out retaliatory military raids against Palestinian infiltrators from refugee camps who harassed the new border settlements, trying to reappropriate property or kill Israelis. Because of the political impact of Unit 101's controversial operations, which targeted both civilians and Arab soldiers, Sharon obtained direct access to Prime Minister David Ben-Gurion (1886–1973) and to Army Chief of Staff Moshe Dayan (1915–1981).

Throughout his career, Sharon exploited his privileged position to undertake military operations, often despite the objections of his direct superiors. In the 1956 Suez War, Sharon led a controversial operation to conquer the Mitla Pass against orders. In the 1967 Six-Day War, Sharon distinguished himself as a strategist commanding the most powerful armored division on the Sinai front.

Sharon resigned from the army in June 1972 and was instrumental in creating the right-wing Likud Party. In October 1973 he was recalled to service following the Yom Kippur War. Commanding a reserve armored division, Sharon located a breach between the Egyptian forces, which he then used to capture a bridgehead and lead a crossing of the Suez Canal. Sharon again violated his orders by exploiting this success to cut off and encircle the Egyptian Third Army. Because of this move, which was regarded as the turning point of the war, Sharon is considered by many in Israel as a war hero who saved Israel from defeat.

After Likud won the 1977 elections, Sharon became the minister of agriculture. In all his subsequent ministerial posts—defense (1981–1983), industry and commerce (1984–1990), construction and housing (1990–1992), infrastructure (1996–1998), and foreign affairs (1998–1999)—Sharon found ways to support and encourage the settlement activities in the occupied territories to prevent the possibility of returning them. Yet, during the peace negotiations with Egypt, he persuaded the Likud government to remove the settlements in Sinai.

As minister of defense, Sharon was the architect of the 1982 Lebanon War, bringing about the destruction of the Palestine Liberation Organization (PLO) infrastructure in Lebanon. What started as a limited operation developed under Sharon's command into a full-scale war with controversial military operations and far-reaching political goals, many of which were never approved by the Israeli cabinet. Sharon was forced to resign as defense minister after a government commission found him indirectly responsible for the Sabra and Shatila massacres, in which hundreds of Palestinian civilians in refugee camps were killed by Lebanese Christian-Maronite militias.

In 2000, shortly after the breakdown of the Camp David peace negotiations, Sharon visited the Al-Aqsa Mosque (Temple Mount) in Jerusalem. His visit was followed by a bloody Palestinian uprising (the Al-Aqsa Intifada), marking the end to the Oslo peace process and the fall of Ehud Barak's left-wing government.

In February 2001 Sharon was elected prime minister of Israel. With Palestinian violence escalating, Sharon ordered in 2002 the reoccupation of West Bank towns and the building of a controversial security fence between Israel and the occupied territories. Sharon later accepted, however, the internationally supported "road map" to peace in 2003, and in 2005 he withdrew the Israeli Army and settlers from the Gaza Strip, citing security issues. This move was opposed by many in Likud and forced Sharon into a coalition with the Labor Party. He eventually formed a new centrist party, Kadima, and declared a new election. In January 2006, just two months before the election, Sharon suffered a stroke that left him hospitalized in a coma. Kadima was temporarily leaderless until Ehud Olmert took over the party and won narrowly in the ensuing elections.

BIBLIOGRAPHY

Kimmerling, Baruch. 2003. *Politicide: Ariel Sharon's Wars Against the Palestinians.* London and New York: Verso.

Miller, Anita, Jordan Miller, and Sigalit Zetouni. 2002. *Sharon: Israel's Warrior-Politician.* Chicago: Academy Chicago Publishers and Olive Publishing.

Nadav Gabay

SHARP, GRANVILLE
1735–1813

Born in Durham, England, on November 21 (November 10, old style), 1735, Granville Sharp is best known as being the prime mover in the abolition of slavery in England; one might even say that he was the force behind the British abolitionist William Wilberforce. He also launched a Bible society, saved a Christian denomination from annihilation, and even founded a nation. Such activities were matched only by his literary efforts. Although he had little formal education, his writings covered seemingly disparate topics—from Greek and Hebrew to theology, music, agriculture, and social causes, especially the cause of freedom for the black slave. An Englishman who never set foot outside his homeland, Sharp influenced the causes of liberty in three American wars (the Revolutionary War, the War of 1812, and the Civil War) by his theological-political writings.

As an indefatigable abolitionist, Sharp initiated a legal case in 1772. A slave from Virginia, James Somerset, had come to England with his master. Sharp successfully argued that either none of the laws of Virginia applied in England or all of them did. The verdict was pronounced on June 22, 1772: "As soon as any slave sets his foot on English ground, he becomes free."

On May 22, 1787, he was elected the chairman of the newly formed Society for the Abolition of the Slave Trade because he was, in the words of his biographer, the "father of the cause in England." Although Wilberforce was the spokesman for the society before Parliament, Sharp was especially active in getting public opinion on its side. After a twenty-year battle, in March 1807 Parliament banned the slave trade. However, the abolition of slavery from the British Empire—Sharp's ultimate goal—would not occur until 1833, twenty years after his death, on July 6, 1813, in London.

After the American Revolution, many former slaves who had fought on the side of the British in exchange for their freedom were now homeless in the streets of London. Several of them wanted to return to their native continent, and they sought Sharp for advice. He was able to procure ships and funds from the British government, as well as a large piece of land in West Africa. The new colony, Sierra Leone, was founded in April 1787. Granville Town was the name they gave their first settlement in honor of Sharp, though the name was later changed to Freetown. In 1961 Sierra Leone became an independent state.

Sharp made three major contributions to the Christian faith, to which he was deeply committed. First, he rescued the Episcopalian denomination in America. The clergy were required to swear allegiance to the crown, an ethical impossibility after the Revolutionary War. Even as early as 1777, Sharp worked toward an independent Episcopacy in America. Ten years later, principally because of Sharp's influence, American clergy could be ordained without taking such an oath of allegiance. Second, in 1804 he became the first chairman of the British and Foreign Bible Society, the first Bible society in the world. Third, Sharp's many writings (nearly seventy books and pamphlets) focused especially on integrating social causes with Christian beliefs, as well as on the original languages of the Bible (Greek and Hebrew). He is especially known for the "Granville Sharp rule," a principle of Greek syntax that he discovered as affirming the New Testament teaching of the deity of Christ.

SEE ALSO *Slavery*

BIBLIOGRAPHY

Hoare, Prince. 1828. *Memoirs of Granville Sharp, Esq. Composed from His Own Manuscripts and Other Authentic Documents in the Possession of His Family and of the African Institution.* 2nd ed. 2 vols. London: Henry Colburn.

Wallace, Daniel B. 1998. Granville Sharp: A Model of Evangelical Scholarship and Social Activism. *Journal of the Evangelical Theological Society* 41 (4): 591–613.

Daniel B. Wallace

SHARPEVILLE MASSACRE OF 1960
SEE *Apartheid.*

SHEPPARD'S LEMMA
SEE *Separability.*

SHERIF, MUZAFER
1906–1988

Born in Turkey, Muzafer Sherif built a productive career as an experimental social psychologist. Upon receiving his master's degree at Istanbul University, he continued his studies in the United States, earning a master's degree at Harvard in 1932 and a PhD at Columbia in 1935. After spending the World War II years (1939–1945) in Turkey, Sherif returned to the United States as a postdoctoral fellow at Princeton and Yale. He then became a research professor of psychology at the University of Oklahoma and later a distinguished professor of sociology at Pennsylvania State University. His tenure in these two rather different departments illustrates his unwavering commitment to social psychology as an interdisciplinary enterprise.

SHERIF AND NORM FORMATION

Sherif produced many creative studies, and his publications spanned five decades. He was most noted for three lines of research. The first was the focus of his doctoral dissertation, "A Study of Some Social Factors in Perception." Inspired by the work of the French sociologist Émile Durkheim (1858–1917) and the British anthropologist Bronislaw Kasper Malinowski (1884–1942), Sherif recognized the importance of the process of norm formation in a group situation. The dynamics of this process occurred when individuals faced a recurrent situation in which they were interdependent. In one of his studies Sherif looked at people's judgments of the extent of movement of a pinpoint of light. He noted that when a person sees a small light in an otherwise completely dark room, it appears to move even though it is stationary. This *autokinetic effect* provided a suitable setting since it was an ambiguous situation when estimations were made of how far the light moved, thus lending itself to a variety of judgments.

Sherif had subjects give their perceptions individually over 100 trials and then in subsequent sessions in group situations. When estimating individually, subjects tended to form their own personal reference scales, but when brought together in a group, they tended to converge in their estimations. This *convergence* was regarded by Sherif as the essence of *norm formation*, one of the basic forms of social influence. In a variation in design Sherif sought to demonstrate that norms formed in a group situation would carry over into a situation in which other group members were not present.

INTERGROUP STUDIES

The second line of research for which Sherif is responsible involved a series of intergroup summer camp studies. This series culminated in a 1954 study at Robbers Cave State Park, Oklahoma. There, twenty-two eleven-year-old boys faced tasks that divided them into groups. Those groups then competed vigorously for mutually exclusive goals and finally cooperated to achieve *superordinate goals*. The latter refers to goals that are highly desired by two groups but that can only be achieved through cooperation.

Groups grew into units with their own distinctive norms and status structure as a result of repeated interaction in situations of interdependence. When the groups interacted with antithetical goals, they formed negative stereotypes of each other and gave vent to hostility and aggression in many forms. Most importantly, when hostile groups interacted in a series of superordinate goals, hostility was diminished, and the stereotypes became more positive. Sherif's interest in intergroup relations was undoubtedly influenced by the turbulent events he witnessed as a Turkish youth as well as the American psychologist and philosopher William James's (1842–1910) 1906 essay "The Moral Equivalent of War" (1910).

SHERIF AND ATTITUDE CHANGE

The third line of research Sherif was responsible for initiating was his unique take on the subject of attitude change. His social judgment theory held that one's reaction to a communication, in terms of positive or negative attitude change, would depend on where one placed the communication. Misplacing a communication in the direction of one's own attitude, called *assimilation*, facilitated positive attitude change. Distortion of a communication away from one's own attitude position was called *contrast*, and when that occurred, attitude change in the direction opposite to that advocated by the communicator was predicted. *Ego-involvement* and *discrepancy* were also important concepts in social judgment theory. As involvement increased, positive attitude change decreased. As discrepancy increased, positive attitude change increased up to the point of inflection and decreased beyond that. Sherif's view was that it is more useful to think of an attitude as a series of zones (*latitudes of acceptance*, *noncommitment*, and *rejection*) than as a single point on a numerical scale. In connection with this theory, two innovative measuring instruments were devised, the *own categories procedure* and the *method of ordered alternatives*.

SHERIF'S OTHER CONTRIBUTIONS

Although Sherif is best known for his empirical contributions, he did have an overarching theory. That theory was centered on the concept of a *frame of reference*, conceived as the totality of external and internal factors operating at a given time. This concept was accompanied by a set of twelve propositions, as he outlined in his 1969 book published with Carolyn Wood Sherif. In that book he noted, "The more unstructured the external stimulus situation, the greater the contribution of internal factors" (Sherif and Sherif 1969, p. 62).

Another of Sherif's contributions to social psychology had to do with the role of experimentation in the research process. For Sherif, experimentation came late in the research process, only after one had gained an intimate knowledge of the phenomenon under consideration. In this way Sherif believed one could be confident that his or her research would have a bearing on real world events. Sherif saw himself as committed to doing basic research, but the implications were there for anyone interested in applied research.

SEE ALSO *Attitudes; Durkheim, Émile; James, William; Malinowski, Bronislaw; Norms; Superordinate Goals*

BIBLIOGRAPHY

Granberg, Donald, and Gian Sarup.1992. Muzafer Sherif: Portrait of a Passionate Intellectual. In *Social Judgment and Intergroup Relations: Essays in Honor of Muzafer Sherif*, ed. Donald Granberg and Gian Sarup, 3–54. New York: Springer-Verlag.

Sherif, Muzafer. 1936. *The Psychology of Social Norms*. New York: Harper.

Sherif, Muzafer. 1966. *In Common Predicament: Social Psychology of Intergroup Conflict and Cooperation*. Boston: Houghton Mifflin.

Sherif, Muzafer, and Carolyn Wood Sherif. 1969. *Social Psychology*. New York: Harper and Row.

Donald Granberg

SHINING PATH

SEE *De Soto, Hernando.*

SHINTO

Shinto is the indigenous religion of Japan. Although its origins extend back into Japan's prehistory, Shinto has undergone significant periods of development throughout the country's history, and it continues to be an important part of Japanese culture.

ORIGINS AND HISTORICAL DEVELOPMENT

Although Shinto can be traced back to Japan's Jomon period (c. 11,000–400 BCE), it was during the Yayoi period (c. 400 BCE–250 CE) that the key elements associated with its development—wet rice agriculture, fertility rituals, and stable, long-term communities—appeared. During this time, local shrines were established and many of the beliefs and practices seen in Shinto today came into existence. During the Kofun period (c. 250–592 CE), Shinto became associated with a large-scale process of political consolidation. Although there remained small shrines in local communities, large Shinto shrines were built at Ise and Izumo on the eastern and western sides of the central Japanese island of Honshu, reflecting the more centralized political structure that was emerging. By the early Nara period (early eighth century), the first written histories of Japan—the *Kojiki* (712) and the *Nihon shoki* (720)—included myths associated with Shinto that served to legitimize the imperial line and the leadership of the Japanese state. Primary among these was the mythic descent of the first Japanese emperor, Jimmu, from the sun goddess, Amaterasu.

The introduction of Buddhism into Japan from China around the middle of the sixth century also brought a new dimension to the development of Shinto. Buddhism, which had a much more extensive theology and culture (art, architecture, and literature) associated with it, came over time to coexist peacefully with Shinto, rather than to compete with it. The two religions—Shinto, with its connections to fertility and life, and Buddhism, with its theology reaching beyond the present world—grew to support one another. Beginning in the eighth century, Buddhist temples and Shinto shrines were often located together on the same site. In 743 the Shinto deity Amaterasu and the cosmic buddha Vairocana were officially declared to be two dimensions of the same reality. In the centuries that followed, the syncretistic relationship between Shinto and Buddhism continued to develop.

During the Tokugawa period (1600–1868), a shift away from Buddhism occurred, and a stronger connection to Confucian thought (introduced into Japan during earlier contact with China) developed. During this time, Shinto came to be used as a mechanism of support for political and social unity. This role of Shinto reached its peak during the Meiji period (1868–1912) and the pre–World War II and wartime portions of the Showa period (1926–1989), when Shinto branched off into Sect Shinto (retaining its local characteristics and Buddhist connections) and State Shinto (which became an official state religion and was used to instill a sense of loyalty to the country). Under State Shinto an Office of Shinto Worship (Jingikan) was established, and a system of national shrines was given official support and patronage. Reverence for the emperor, who was now considered to be a Shinto deity—"sacred and inviolable" in the words of the Meiji Constitution (1889)—and support for the Shinto concept of *kokutai* (body politic or national essence) was required in Japanese schools. Following Japan's defeat in World War II (1939–1945), State Shinto was banned, the emperor was forced to renounce his divine status, and Shinto in large degree returned to its earlier pattern of local shrines and its connections with Buddhism. With key modifications, the religion continues in modern times to play a significant role in Japanese culture.

CORE BELIEFS AND PRACTICES

A central feature of Shinto lies in a belief in the existence of spirits or deities in nature known as *kami*. These spirits are usually associated with natural phenomena, such as a mountain, a waterfall, a large tree, or an unusual rock.

The surrounding area then comes to be considered sacred, and a shrine (*jinja*) is erected there. Various rituals are performed at the shrine, among the most important being food offerings and rites of purification. In the beginning, the shrines were strictly local in character, and agricultural fertility was a central purpose of the rituals performed there. Annual shrine festivals (*matsuri*) were events of great importance in the local community. Over time, certain shrines came to be thought of as connected with particular needs and serve as places to pray for human fertility, success in business, or even (in modern times) success in passing college entrance exams. Some shrines assumed regional significance. Other shrines—as mentioned in the preceding section—reflected a larger, national purpose.

Over time also, shrine architecture came to follow certain basic styles or types. The earliest shrines (exemplified today by the great Ise Shrine dedicated to Amaterasu) were constructed of unpainted wood, but after the introduction of Buddhism, many shrines were painted a brilliant vermillion red, displaying the Chinese Buddhist influence. Large gateways (*torii*)—also of varying styles—mark the entrance or approach to a shrine. Other important shrine features include stone dogs (*komainu*) guarding the shrine entrance, a place of purification (*chozuyu*) where worshippers stop to wash their hands and rinse their mouths prior to approaching the main shrine building, the main sanctuary (*honden*) where the *kami* is believed to reside, the collection box (*saisen-bako*) where money is thrown to express gratitude to the *kami*, and a special bell (*suzu*) connected to a rope, which worshippers ring to announce their arrival.

In addition to participation in the annual shrine festival, people also visit shrines on national holidays such as New Year's (*shogatsu*) or the summer Bon festival (*obon*). Most Japanese are married in a Shinto wedding ceremony, and there are other shrine ceremonies celebrating various life passages, such as the first shrine visit for a newborn child (*hatsu-miyamairi*) or national Coming-of-Age Day (*seijin-no-hi*) for twenty-year-olds, which takes place on January 15. Finally, many traditional Japanese sports (*sumo*, for example), as well as other forms of traditional culture, have their roots in Shinto.

IMPORTANCE TODAY

Since the end of World War II and the banning of Shinto as an official state religion, Shinto practice has focused primarily on its role as an aspect of traditional culture. More than 100,000 shrines existed in the country in 2003, ranging from small neighborhood shrines to large shrines of national significance. Japanese tourists flock to the famous shrines in historic cities like Kyoto and Nara. National holidays and family rites of passage, as well as

matsuri, are celebrated at local or neighborhood shrines. It remains common for people to have a small Shinto family altar (*kamidana*, "god shelf") located above the entrance to their homes. Although occasional controversies surface regarding holdovers from Shinto's earlier role as a state religion—the periodic controversy, for example, surrounding the Yasukuni Shrine commemorating the war dead in Tokyo—Shinto, for the most part, is a colorful and happy form of religious expression, the darker side of human existence being left to Buddhism with its funeral rituals and ideas concerning the next life. Most Japanese consider themselves, at some level at least, adherents of both religious traditions.

SEE ALSO *Buddhism; Imperialism; Meiji Restoration; Nationalism and Nationality; Religion; Rituals; Symbols; World War II*

BIBLIOGRAPHY

Inoue, Nobutaka, ed. 2003. *Shinto: A Short History.* Trans. Mark Teeuwen and John Breen. London: RoutledgeCurzon.

Kodansha. 1983. *Kodansha Encyclopedia of Japan.* 9 vols. Tokyo: Author.

Littleton, C. Scott. 2002. *Shinto: Origins, Rituals, Festivals, Spirits, Sacred Places.* Oxford: Oxford University Press.

Nelson, John K. 2000. *Enduring Identities: The Guise of Shinto in Contemporary Japan.* Honolulu: University of Hawai'i Press.

Scott Wright

SHIPPING INDUSTRY

Shipping has been a major means of transporting bulky commodities since prehistoric times; the stones used to construct Stonehenge were moved by sea and those used in the Egyptian pyramids came by barge down the Nile. The shipping sector was central to the economies of many early Mediterranean civilizations and, for example, provided the bulwark for Minoan power. Shipping became entwined with early financial institutions as individuals in Athens financed the long lead times between investments and returns, although it was not until the ninth century that the first mercantile bank was established. The Roman Empire and those in China depended extensively on their commercial shipping for trade and to bring the fruits of distant domains back to the core regions.

The role of shipping was subsequently a facilitator in the growth of the more explicit maritime powers after the fall of Rome. The Vikings exerted their influence from Greenland to Russia and down into modern Turkey almost exclusively through their control over trade and the quality of their military vessels. Commercial shipping has always been entwined, because of the lags and uncertainties involved in voyages, with insurance and banking; and the emergence of sophisticated finance markets in Italy in the fourteen and fifteenth centuries led expansions in Mediterranean maritime activities. The Spanish financed their sixteenth-century European wars more directly with gold brought back by galleons from their colonies in the New World.

Subsequently the Dutch and British empires were founded upon powerful navies that complemented and protected extensive civilian trading fleets. In particular, in the early phases of the Industrial Revolution when land transportation remained difficult, maritime trade allowed new export markets to be served and new sources of raw material to be exploited. Many of the major seaports in Britain, such as Liverpool and Bristol, and in the southern states of the United States, such as Charleston, South Carolina, grew on the back of the triangular trade routes carrying manufactures, raw materials, and slaves that linked Europe, Africa, and the Americas. In Asia, the growth of maritime trade in spices and commodities using oceangoing junks underlaid the prosperity of Indian and Chinese coastal areas. In addition to the transportation role, the shipping industry made direct contributions to production in the fishing and whaling industries that grew to feed and supply industrializing nations with food and oil.

The advent of the steam engine made for more reliable and safer shipping services but also, in the context of its linking with the railways that provided feed and distribution service to ports, increased the potential markets that could be served. Technological developments (such as refrigerated ships and steel hauls), the demands for new products (such as oil) in the late nineteenth century, and the emergence of new technologies (such as the container and the mega-ships) in the late twentieth century have helped to maintain the momentum of the industry.

Much of the emergence of the scale of the modern shipping industry can also be traced by the impetus given it by World War I and World War II that not only required a large mercantile marine for military logistics reasons, but also subsequently dumped a stock of vessels on the market that allowed entrepreneurs to build up commercial fleets at relatively low capital costs and with suitable discharged sailors available to man them.

In the early twenty-first century the international shipping industry carries about 90 percent of global trade by weight. While much of this involves transoceanic movements, short-sea shipping plays an important role in many large freight markets. Shipping also provides important ferry and passenger services. In 2005 globally there were approximately 42,200 registered ships with a combined tonnage of nearly 600 million gross tons. Of these more than 20,000 were general cargo vessels, 6,100 bulk

carriers, 3,200 container vessels, 11,300 tankers, and nearly 5,700 passenger ships. This pattern reflects the changing technologies and production priorities of the larger supply chain (e.g., the advent of containers from the 1960s and just-in-time production) and the types of commodities carried (e.g., the increased demands for oil.) The global fleet is registered (flagged) in a variety of countries with registration often depending on local tax structures rather than the locations of shipping activities. The widespread registration under "flags-of-convenience" reflect these financial considerations.

Cargo activities can be divided between unscheduled, tramp shipping, which involves the leasing of a ship for a particular trade, and liner activities. The latter provide regular sailings and carry partial loads. Liner activities have existed from the 1870s when steamship technology allowed for reliable scheduling of sailings and often involved some form of cartel arrangements between shipping companies. These have evolved through "conferences" that coordinate services and rates, allocate capacity between members, and offer loyalty discounts for specific, often unidirectional, routes; through "consortia" from the 1970s whereby some conference members offered joint services; and through alliances that engage in cross-route rationalization and do not issue a common tariff. These tendencies toward a degree of collusion are often seen as important to ensure that regular services can be provided and that shipping companies can make a reasonable return on their large capital investments in what would otherwise be an excessively competitive market. Economic regulatory bodies, especially in the United States, however, have regularly been concerned about the potential monopoly power they might create.

Policy challenges remain, and many extend beyond conventional market regulation. Shipping has always been closely associated with the environment. Classical times saw Greece being denuded of trees to build fleets and a similar fate nearly befell the British oak tree in the eighteenth century. From a different perspective, it was shipping that brought the Black Death pandemic to Europe in the fourteenth century that killed one-third of the population. In the early twenty-first century, the high visibility of major maritime disasters, especially when there are major adverse environmental implications, poses challenges, as does the concern that ships or their cargos may form the basis for terrorist actions. The problems are seen to be growing as scale economies stimulate the use of larger vessels (e.g., post Panamax ships), which have the potential for inflicting massive environmental damage in the event of an accident, and as the general growth in world trade, both in aggregate and in the diversity of nations involved, makes policing the shipping industry more complex. The growth in the number of vessels operating under flags of convenience adds to these difficulties.

In order to confront the more traditional challenges posed by the shipping industry, as well as the newer ones, industry is heavily regulated at several levels—most notably at the global level by the United Nation's International Maritime Organization (IMO) that oversees safety and environmental matters and the International Labor Organization (ILO) that focuses on labor standards in the shipping industry. National governments control movements within territorial waters, register vessels, and regulate within their antitrust policies the nature of the services that can be used for their trading activities, for example, the particular features of any cartel arrangements. But shipping is also regulated in a de facto way by local governments that often own and, inevitably, control ports that form the terminals for shipping operations. Integrating the roles and activities of this hierarchy of institutions so that effective maritime policies can be achieved has often proved elusive.

SEE ALSO *Automobile Industry; Aviation Industry; Railway Industry; Transportation Industry*

BIBLIOGRAPHY

Kendall, Lane C., and James J. Buckley. 2001. *The Business of Shipping*. 7th ed. Centreville, MD: Cornell Maritime Press.

Sjostom, W. 2004. Ocean Shipping Cartels: A Survey. *Review of Network Economics* 3 (2): 107–134.

Kenneth Button

SHKLAR, JUDITH
1928–1992

Judith Nisse Shklar was Cowles Professor of Government at Harvard University and one of the most influential political theorists of the late twentieth century. Though her studies were wide-ranging in focus, her work centered on the problems of cruelty, exclusion, oppression, and fear in liberalism.

Born in Riga, Latvia, to Jewish parents, Shklar was still fairly young when her family fled Europe to avoid Nazi persecution. Perhaps accordingly, her first major work, *After Utopia: The Decline of Political Faith* (1957), wrestles with the intellectual legacy of twentieth-century totalitarianism. In a time when the political application of comprehensive ideologies has led to so much horror, is there any future for the discipline of political theory? Shklar found it unlikely that its future would look like its past; political theory had little chance of returning to the high levels of hope and optimism that had once marked it, particularly during the Enlightenment. In this postfa-

natical age, she argued, political philosophers would do best to take up the gauntlet of intellectual history and avoid future entanglements with "-isms." Shklar thus articulated an argument that would mark her career: Philosophy needs to separate and extricate itself from ideology.

Shklar herself found much to defend in classical liberalism, which she described in her seminal essay "The Liberalism of Fear" as resting on the proposition that "every adult should be able to make as many effective decisions without fear or favor about as many aspects of her or his life as is compatible with the freedom of every other adult." For Shklar, unlike others who find more aspiration in the liberal framework, liberalism has no positive, moral aim outside this basic commitment to political and social freedom.

In that sense, Shklar's liberalism rests upon a pessimistic or skeptical sensibility. Her version of liberalism does not aim for the best; rather, it is concerned with averting the worst. And the worst, for Shklar, is the kind of partisan injustice and cruelty that might also be called political evil.

Shklar's dedication to this kind of "barebones liberalism," as she called it in her second and favorite book, *Legalism: Law, Morals, and Political Trials* (1964), is evident throughout her corpus. Even in her treatments of individual thinkers—she composed full-length books on the political theories of Georg Hegel, Montesquieu, and Jean-Jacques Rousseau—Shklar remained invested in supporting liberalism but divesting it of any perfectionist associations.

Any account of Shklar's life and works would be remiss not to mention that she was one of the first women to achieve success in the field of political philosophy—and, in fact, the first woman to serve as president of the American Political Science Association. Though Shklar acknowledged that her career, especially in its earliest days, had been made more difficult by the pervasive sexism of the age, she resisted being classified as what she called a "real feminist." To identify herself with a collective ideology, she argued, would be to undermine her own intellectual project.

SEE ALSO *American Political Science Association; Enlightenment; Freedom; Holocaust, The; Law; Liberalism; Nazism; Political Theory; Sexism; Social Exclusion; Totalitarianism*

BIBLIOGRAPHY

Shklar, Judith N. 1957. *After Utopia: The Decline of Political Faith*. Princeton, NJ: Princeton University Press.

Shklar, Judith N. 1964. *Legalism: Law, Morals, and Political Trials*. Cambridge, MA: Harvard University Press, 2006.

Shklar, Judith N. 1989. The Liberalism of Fear. In *Liberalism and the Moral Life*, ed. Nancy L. Rosenblum, 21–38. Cambridge, MA: Harvard University Press.

Shklar, Judith N. 1998. *Political Thought and Political Thinkers*, ed. Stanley Hoffman. Chicago: University of Chicago Press.

Susan J. McWilliams

SHOCKS

In economics a shock is an unexpected change in the economy or a component of the economy. The hypothesis of rational expectations holds that individuals will incorporate all available and relevant information into their decision-making processes. From a behavioral standpoint, shocks are important in that they alter individuals' behaviors by altering the information that goes into their decision-making processes. This alteration in behaviors in turn has economic consequences.

Because of people's ability to anticipate changes in the economy, shocks are difficult to measure. In the past, changes in economic measures have been taken as proxies for shocks. For example, if inflation increased from 3 percent to 4 percent, economists would say that a 1 percent positive shock to inflation had occurred. This approach is not entirely satisfactory as the greater the ability of individuals to anticipate the change, the less the change represents a shock. For example, a rise in the price of gasoline from $2.50 to $2.75 would have represented a shock of $0.25 only if people expected that the price of gas would remain at $2.50. If people had expected the price of gas to rise from $2.50 to $2.75 and the price of gas actually did rise from $2.50 to $2.75, then the change in the price would have represented no shock at all. If, however, people had expected that the price of gas would rise from $2.50 to $2.75 but in fact the price only rose from $2.50 to $2.60, then the change in the price of gas would have been $0.10 and the shock would have been *negative* $0.15. That is, people would have anticipated an additional $0.15 price increase that never materialized. The difficulty in measuring shocks lies in the difficulty of knowing how much of a change in an economic measure was anticipated and how much was unanticipated.

While an unanticipated change in any economic measure can be described as a shock, economists give most attention to inflationary shocks (unanticipated changes in inflation), production shocks (unanticipated changes in the growth rate of real gross domestic product [RGDP]), and leading shocks (unanticipated changes in leading economic indicators). Positive inflation shocks represent unanticipated price growths and lead to reduced real wages and a slowdown in consumption. Positive production shocks represent unanticipated increases in real economic activity and can lead to an unanticipated reduction in inflation and growth in real wages. Leading economic indicators typically change direction prior to a turning point in business cycles. Unanticipated changes in leading economic indicators can indicate the approach of a turning point in the business cycle.

Methods for measuring economic shocks require *multidimensional panel forecasts*. A multidimensional panel forecast data set is a set of forecasts generated by multiple forecasters over multiple time periods and forecasting at multiple time horizons. For example, forecasters A, B, and C (multiple forecasters) will forecast inflation for the year in January, again in February, again in March, and so on (multiple horizons), and they will repeat this every year over a number of years (multiple time periods). Assuming that economic forecasters are rational, the forecasts can be taken to be reasonable measures of people's expectations about the future, and even if the forecasters are biased, the biases can be filtered out such that estimates of economic shocks can be extracted from what is left. Measures of shocks and volatilities of shocks can be extracted from multidimensional panel forecasts via econometric methods.

The volatility of shocks is the variance of the shocks hitting the economy over time. For example, the economy may experience a sequence of large positive and negative shocks that mutually cancel each other out such that the net shock over the period is zero. However, the volatility of the shocks over the period will be nonzero as the shocks rose to positive levels then fell to negative levels. Consumer and investor uncertainty is a function of both shocks and the volatility of shocks. Uncertainty in turn impacts economic growth. The more uncertain consumers are about the future, the less likely they are to engage in transactions and so the slower is economic growth. Similarly the more uncertain investors are about the future, the less likely they are to invest and so the slower is economic growth. Studies indicate that the relationship between shocks and volatility is asymmetric. Negative shocks tend to be associated with greater volatility than positive shocks. This is typically interpreted as individuals regarding bad news of a given magnitude as being more influential on their decisions than is positive news of the same magnitude.

SEE ALSO *Business Cycles, Empirical Literature; Business Cycles, Real; Expectations; Expectations, Implicit; Expectations, Rational; Involuntary Unemployment; Natural Rate of Unemployment; Phillips Curve; Risk; Say's Law; Uncertainty; Voluntary Unemployment; Walras' Law*

BIBLIOGRAPHY

Davies, Antony. 2006. A Framework for Decomposing Shocks and Measuring Volatilities Derived from Multi-Dimensional Panel Data of Survey Forecasts. *International Journal of Forecasting* 22: 373–393.

Engle, Robert F., and Victor K. Ng. 1991. Measuring and Testing the Impact of News on Volatility. National Bureau of Economic Research Working Paper No. W3681.

Parkin, Michael. 2005. *Macroeconomics.* Boston: Addison Wesley.

Antony Davies

SHORT PERIOD

Economists measure periods in units of economic time. In the market period, time is compressed so that supply cannot vary. In the short period (SP), time occupies an interval in which fixed investments cannot change; in the long period, time is sufficient to allow all inputs to vary. Fixed investments include specialized skill and ability, machinery, and organizational structure. In the SP, one can only mix and match fixed investment to meet changing demand and supply conditions. Alfred Marshall (1842–1924), the reigning British economist of his day who is credited with these views, was aware that no sharp line of demarcation could be drawn between the short and the long periods ([1929] 1982). A day gives an intuitive feel for the market period. For the SP, one considers not only the given supply of, say, bread for that day, but goes back to the planting of wheat, which started approximately a year before, and the expected prices set at that time. The expected price may reach its normal values from two months to a year, bracketing the SP.

One problem with the SP is whether fixed investments should extend beyond the production period. Plough or die-casting equipments may last for only one production period, and the stock of capital should reflect the life of such short-lived equipment. If the adjustment spreads over time based on available price signals, then the SP definition is in jeopardy. Alternatively, one can deduct values from equipment in the previous period. Another problem in the SP is that various industries take different time intervals to produce a product with the same plant units, making it impossible to have an aggregate SP for the whole economy. The preeminent economist John Maynard Keynes (1883–1946) answered these problems by using the concept of prime cost, which is the sum of factor and user costs in defining income and its components of savings and investments; by using the concepts of *exante* vs. *expost* for equating saving and investment; and finally by settling on the more logical concept of national income identity.

Post-Keynesians have many interpretations of the Keynesian short period. A counter long-period view is that long-period expectations are not realized yet. One argument is that Keynes's view is a special case of the classical system. Richard Kahn's (1989) view that short run average cost was constant with a reversed L-shape up to a maximum level of output seems to counter Keynes's view of a Z curve in chapter 3 of the *General Theory*. On the special case characteristics, Lawrence Klein (1966) stated that the SP Walrasian (named for the French economist Léon Walras [1834–1910]) equilibrium might not exist in the Keynesian model because of interest inelastic investment or very high interest elastic demand for money due to market imperfections. Marshall's protégé Arthur Pigou (1877–1959), in correspondence with Keynes, was the first to draw a reversed L-shape labor supply curve for the SP. From the dominant textbook perspective, Keynes's SP solution made output and employment depend on investment through a multiplier and made the equality between saving and investment follow from two logical premises—income is the sum of consumption and investment, and saving is income less consumption. Keynes appears to fix all capital stock for the whole economy in the SP, analogous to Marshall's fixing production units for a single industry. Although Keynes dealt with liquidity preference and marginal efficiency of capital schedules that vary with long-term expectation, he defined SP expectation as a day and restricted long-period expectation to the view of mass psychology, which plays out in three months to a year, corresponding to Marshall's market period and SP, respectively.

Following Keynes, John Hicks (1904–1989) created a temporary (sequential) equilibrium model that reflected Keynes's SP. Prices are determined in the market period, Monday, and production varies during the rest of the week to meet varying market conditions. The past week, $t - dt$ to t, or the future week, t to $t + dt$, is an infinitesimal period during which production can change. The long period is a link of various Mondays and weeks together.

For modern policy analysis, the SP equilibrium is reflected in a downward sloping Phillips curve at a position of nonaccelerating inflation rate of unemployment (NAIRU). For the monetarists and the new classical school, adjustments for SP differences between actual and expected prices enables convergence of the aggregate SP supply schedule to the long-period natural level where desired expectations are fulfilled. Robert Lucas and Thomas Sargent (1981), who extended the Walrasian and Marshallian concepts of price taking to the case where price provides information, were not concerned with long- and short-run characterizations, but with drifts in structural parameters of their models. The modern literature also developed an SP non-Walrasian equilibrium concept that depends on current prices and the expectation of future prices based on past and current prices. Thus the economic agents are able to carry out all their preferred actions in current markets.

SEE ALSO *Capital; Demand; Expectations; Long Period; Long Run; Long Run Prices; Market Clearing; Short Run; Supply*

BIBLIOGRAPHY

Hicks, John. 1946. *Value and Capital.* 2nd ed. London: Clarendon Press.

Hicks, John. 1965. *Capital and Growth.* London and New York: Oxford University Press.

Hicks, John. 1981. *Wealth and Welfare: Collected Essays on Economic Theory.* Cambridge, MA: Harvard University Press.

Kahn, Richard. 1989. *The Economics of the Short Period.* New York: St. Martin's.

Keynes, John Maynard. 1936. *The General Theory of Employment, Interest, and Money.* London: Macmillan and New York: Harcourt Brace.

Keynes, John Maynard. 1973. *The General Theory and After,* Part II: *Defense and Development.* Vol. 14 of *The Collected Writings of John Maynard Keynes.* London: Macmillan and New York: St. Martin's.

Klein, Lawrence R. 1966. *The Keynesian Revolution.* 2nd ed. New York: Macmillan.

Lucas, Robert E., Jr., and Thomas J. Sargent. 1981. After Keynesian Macroeconomics. In *Rational Expectations and Econometric Practice,* vol. 1, eds. Robert E. Lucas Jr. and Thomas J. Sargent, 295–319. Minneapolis: University of Minnesota Press.

Marshall, Alfred. [1929] 1982. *Principles of Economics.* 8th ed. London: Macmillan.

Michael Szenberg
Lall Ramrattan

SHORT RUN

The term *short run* refers to a period of time in which at least one factor (input) of production cannot be immediately modified. This concept determines exactly how a firm's decision-making is constrained. Factors of input may be constrained by past decisions or a decision that cannot immediately be implemented. The short run contrasts with the long run, in which all input factors that can be variable are variable. The short run does not specify any exact length of time, such as three months or one year. The short run can be five minutes or five years, depending on the exact characteristics of the fixed factors. Examples of circumstances that would place a firm in a short-run situation include but are not limited to: contracts that cannot be broken on rented machinery, the

time required to build a bigger factory, rental agreements on factory space, the time required to purchase and assemble additional machinery, and the time required to find a renter for owned capital.

In the perfectly competitive model, the short run constrains firms to change only the amount of variable costs, typically the amount of labor employed. In the classic example, a firm can increase (decrease) production only by increasing (decreasing) its labor force. The amount of capital is fixed in the short run because the rental or purchase of large machinery and factory space requires long-term contracts that are not immediately revised. Contrasting this to the long run, labor is still variable, but now each individual firm has the option to purchase more capital or to not renew contracts and employ less capital.

In the short run, a firm will choose the level of variable inputs that maximizes its profit taking given its level of fixed inputs. The profit-maximizing output level may be chosen at zero, implying the short-run shutdown decision. In this case when the price at which a firm can sell its goods lies below the average variable costs of the firm, the firm would lose money on each additional unit of good that it produces, leaving it better off not to produce at all. A firm may not exit the industry in the short run, however, because of existing fixed costs. Once all fixed costs become variable, the firm has entered the long run, and is no longer in the short run. This gives the firm more opportunities to lower costs and increase profits by altering its inputs to achieve the most efficient production techniques. If the firm is unable to become profitable in the long run, it has the long-run option to exit the industry.

There are short-run and long-run versions of supply, demand, and the entire family of cost curves (marginal cost, average cost, total cost). It is important to recognize that in the short run, a firm has variable costs and fixed costs, represented by two separate curves. In the long run, all fixed costs become variable, eliminating the fixed cost curve and causing the variable cost and the total cost curves (and thus the corresponding average variable and average total cost curves) to collapse into one total cost and average cost curve. Typically, the short-run version of each curve is *less* elastic than its corresponding long-run version.

Jacob Viner presented these concepts in his 1931 work, "Cost Curves and Supply Curves," which formalized the graphical and analytical analysis of short-run and long-run cost curves. This work is visible in the economics textbooks of the early twenty-first century as the graphical representations of markets and firms that are used to determine market equilibrium and firm behaviors.

In the field of macroeconomics, Milton Friedman (1912–2006) developed short-run and long-run concepts differentiated from one another with respect to expectations. In the short run, expectations about the future are not fully realized, and conversely in the long run, expectations are fully realized. For example, Edmund S. Phelps (b. 1933) and Friedman provide a distinction between the "short-run" and "long-run" Phillips curves. The Phillips curve, originally formulated by the New Zealand economist A. W. H. Phillips (1914–1975), displays the inverse relationship between unemployment and inflation. In the short run, expansionary monetary or fiscal policies will raise nominal wages as the demand for labor increases. These same policies will also have the effect of raising the overall price level, resulting in smaller real wage changes relative to the nominal wage change. Workers will eventually realize the inflationary effect on their real wages and insist on wage changes that keep pace with inflation. Those who entered the labor force because of higher nominal wages will exit once they realize that real wages are no higher than before the policy modification. The result is that in the short run, workers may supply more labor in response to expansionary policies in the absence of fully realized expectations, but in the long run, once expectations of price inflation have adjusted, unemployment will increase back to the previous natural level, while nominal prices and wages remain at their higher levels because of the original expansionary stimulus. This results in a deviation from the traditional Phillips curve, which Friedman refers to as the expectations-augmented Phillips curve. The faster the worker's expectations are realized, the sooner the short run transitions into the long run, and the less effective expansionary policies will be.

In conclusion, the short run and the long run may be summarized as follows:

- Short run: Some inputs variable, at least one fixed. Firms can choose a level of production only by changing the amount of a variable input. Choosing an output of zero implies the shutdown decision. New firms do not enter the industry, and existing firms do not exit. Supply, demand, and cost curves are less elastic (more inelastic).

- Long run: All inputs variable, firms can enter and exit the marketplace. Supply, demand, and cost curves are more elastic.

SEE ALSO *Long Period; Long Run; Phillips Curve; Short Period*

BIBLIOGRAPHY

Baumol, William J., and Alan S. Blinder. 2006. *Economics: Principles and Policy.* 10th ed. Mason, OH: Thomson South-Western.

Black, John. 2002. *A Dictionary of Economics.* 2nd ed. Oxford: Oxford University Press.

Viner, Jacob. [1931] 1952. Cost Curves and Supply Curves. In *Reading in Price Theory*, eds. George J. Stigler and Kenneth E. Boulding, 198–226. Chicago: Richard D. Irwin.

Raymond A. Farkouh

SHTETL

The *shtetl*, Yiddish for "small town" (plural *shtetlekh*), was the archetypal eastern European Jewish community for over half a millennium. Moreover, it emerged during the twentieth century as a social paradigm of Jewish communal life and became the subject of extensive Jewish memory practices in the wake of the Holocaust. As early as the thirteenth century, Jews settled in small towns in Poland, where they played a central role in the local economy as merchants, artisans, and managers of property owned by the aristocracy. Eventually these towns, in which Jews sometimes comprised the majority population, stretched the length and breadth of eastern Europe. Here the Jewish population surged during the eighteenth century, making shtetlekh home to the majority of world Jewry for over a century.

Jewish shtetl life received little analysis until Jews began leaving these towns in large numbers during the latter half of the nineteenth century as a result of urbanization and immigration. The shtetl figured centrally in early works of modern Yiddish literature—most famously by Sholem Aleichem (Sholem Rabinovitsh, 1859–1916)—many of which offered astute critiques of traditional Jewish mores and provincial society through satire. The early twentieth century witnessed a new interest in traditional eastern European Jewish life among modernizing Jews, prompting early ethnographic efforts to collect folklore in both the shtetl and the rural village (Yiddish: *dorf*). The most famous early example was the 1912–1914 expedition in Ukraine led by S. Ansky (Solomon Rappoport, 1863–1920), who subsequently drew on the materials collected to write *The Dybbuk* from 1912 to 1917, the best known work of modern Yiddish drama.

During the interwar years, scholarly efforts to study shtetl life were organized by the YIVO Institute for Jewish Research in Vilna, Poland (now Vilnius, Lithuania), and researchers in state-supported institutes in the Soviet Union. These undertakings included grassroots projects, such as a pamphlet published in Minsk in 1928, which exhorted amateur folklorists, *"Forsht ayer shtetl"* (Research your town). Individual ethnographies, memoirs, literary works, and journalistic accounts of shtetl life also appeared during this period in Yiddish, Hebrew, Polish, Russian, German, and other languages.

Following the genocide of European Jewry during World War II (1939–1945), many former residents of shtetlekh initiated efforts to memorialize their own local histories, customs, and murdered townsfolk, most notably by compiling *yisker-bikher* (communal memorial books). At the same time, American anthropologists undertook a major project to write a composite study of prewar eastern European Jewish life based on research from a pioneering wartime "anthropology-at-a-distance" project overseen by Margaret Mead (1901–1978) and Ruth Benedict (1887–1948). The resulting book, *Life Is With People* (1952), quickly became the standard work in English on shtetl life. As folklorist Barbara Kirshenblatt-Gimblett has observed, this book's approach offers an idealized, paradigmatic vision of the shtetl—timeless, uniform, insular—that is as problematic as it was appealing in the aftermath of the Holocaust. The impact of *Life Is With People* has been extensive, influencing, among other works, *Number Our Days* (1978), anthropologist Barbara Myerhoff's (1935–1985) study of elderly American Jewish immigrants from eastern Europe. More recently, return travel to shtetlekh has been the subject of ethnographic films (e.g., Marian Marzynski's *Shtetl* [1996]) and studies of Jewish memory practices.

BIBLIOGRAPHY

Kugelmass, Jack, and Jonathan Boyarin, eds. and trans. 1998. *From a Ruined Garden: The Memorial Books of Polish Jewry.* 2nd ed. Bloomington: Indiana University Press.

Myerhoff, Barbara. 1978. *Number Our Days.* New York: Dutton.

Zborowski, Mark, and Elizabeth Herzog. [1952] 1995. *Life Is With People: The Culture of the Shtetl.* New York: Schocken.

Jeffrey Shandler

SHYNESS

Shyness can be defined by the presence of anxious reactions, excessive self-consciousness, and negative self-evaluation in response to real or imagined social interactions to the degree that it produces enough discomfort to interfere with and inhibit one's ability to perform successfully in social situations and also to the extent that it disrupts one's personal and professional goals. The symptoms of shyness can be affective (e.g., heightened feelings of tension and anxiety), physiological (e.g., racing heart, dryness of the mouth), cognitive (e.g., heightened self-consciousness and excessive thoughts of critical self-evaluation), and behavioral (e.g., increased interpersonal distance, inhibited verbal participation, and lack of eye contact). The number of adults who consider themselves to be chronically shy (e.g., shy their entire lives) is approximately 40 percent (Carducci 1999).

Subtypes of shyness include situational shyness (temporary shyness triggered by specific situations such as meeting a famous person), shy extroversion (outgoing appearance coexisting with a high degree of anxiety and negative self-evaluation, often experienced by entertainers), and transitional shyness (an extended period of shyness brought on by life changes such as moving to a new town). Introversion is not considered a subtype of shyness. Although shyness and introversion are similar in their overt expressions of behavior, they differ in their underlying motives. Introverts do not necessarily fear social situations, but simply prefer more solitary activities. Shy individuals, like extroverts, prefer social activities but are restrained in their participation by the experience of shyness. This approach-avoidance conflict is a source of distress for shy individuals.

The characteristic features of shyness include an excessive degree of self-consciousness, negative self-evaluation, and negative self-preoccupation. Shy individuals also demonstrate a slow-to-warm tendency characterized by an extended period of adjustment to social situations, especially those that are novel. Situational shyness is the transitory experience of shyness that can be triggered by a variety of situations, the most frequent being interactions with authorities, one-to-one interactions with members of the opposite sex, and unstructured social settings.

The most frequently used measure of shyness is the Revised Shyness Scale (RSS). The RSS contains fourteen items assessing the three principal dimensions of shyness: affective/physiological (e.g., "I feel tense with people I don't know"), cognitive (e.g., "I feel painfully self-conscious when I am around strangers"), and behavioral (e.g., "it is hard for me to act natural when I am meeting new people"). The RSS uses a five-point Likert scale, with responses ranging from 1 ("very uncharacteristic or untrue, strongly disagree") to 5 ("very characteristic or true, strongly agree"). Scores on the RSS demonstrate acceptable test-retest reliability and validity by correlating highly with other measures of shyness, social avoidance, and interpersonal difficulty.

Distinctions have been made between shyness and other socially related constructs. Like shyness, embarrassment is characterized by heightened self-consciousness, but unlike shyness, embarrassment includes feelings of guilt and is a response that occurs after an inappropriate social response in the presence of others. Individuals do not experience embarrassment prior to the performance of an inappropriate response or when others are not present. In contrast, the affective (e.g., anticipatory feelings of anxiety), cognitive (e.g., assuming one's comments will be judged unfavorably by others), and behavioral (e.g., not approaching others) responses characteristic of shyness can occur prior to the actual performance and in the absence of others (e.g., before entering a social situation). Social anxiety, like shyness, involves anxiety and self-critical evaluation in novel social settings, but to a greater degree: Individuals affected by social anxiety have greater difficulties in social situations (e.g., parties) and therefore may avoid them, but there is little disruption in other social aspects of their public lives (e.g., riding on public transportation, eating in a restaurant, or going shopping). Social phobia, which is experienced by approximately 8 percent of the population, is a clinically diagnosed psychiatric condition that, like shyness and social anxiety, involves feelings of anxiety and excessive critical self-evaluation, but to such a greater degree that it has a much more pervasive and disruptive influence on one's ability to participate in everyday situations.

Causes of shyness can be psychological (e.g., the result of family dynamics), biological (e.g., determined by hormonal and neurotransmitter levels), genetic (e.g., inherited temperament), neurological (e.g., bed nucleus of the striate terminals), or cultural (e.g., prioritizing the individual over the collective). The evolutionary benefits of shyness include cautionary behavior in novel and potentially threatening situations and the facilitation of social exchange and cooperation through the reduced tendency for self-serving expression. The personal costs of shyness include increased personal blame for interpersonal failures, loneliness, and substance abuse; the social costs, particularly for males, include less stable marriages, career delay, and lower levels of career advancement.

Interventions available for dealing with shyness include informational Web sites, self-help books, self-directed programs, online and offline social support groups, and structured clinical programs. Different treatment approaches are utilized depending on which component of shyness is targeted. Approaches for dealing with the affective component of shyness tend to focus on the reduction of bodily arousal, such as progressive relaxation techniques and biofeedback. Approaches for dealing with the cognitive component of shyness typically emphasize cognitive modification, such as revising self-perceptions, altering attributions, and adjusting expectations for defining success in social situations. Approaches for dealing with the behavior component of shyness emphasize the acquisition and development of social skills, such as strategies for approaching others, techniques for initiating and maintaining conversation, and procedures for entering ongoing conversations. Structured clinical programs typically involve combining elements from all the approaches, such as cognitive modification to identify which situations produce the most critical self-evaluations and structured role-playing exercises within the context of systematic desensitization to reduce anxiety, teach appropriate behavioral responses, and build self-confidence. An emerging, controversial view of shyness links it to more serious psy-

chiatric conditions such as social phobia and emphasizes its treatment with prescription drugs, such as those based on selective serotonin reuptake inhibitors (SSRIs).

SEE ALSO *Anxiety; Neuroscience; Personality; Psychotherapy; Temperament; Trait Theory*

BIBLIOGRAPHY

Carducci, Bernardo J. 1999. *Shyness: A Bold New Approach*. New York: HarperCollins.

Crozier, W. Ray. 2001. *Understanding Shyness*. Basingstoke, U.K.: Palgrave.

Hernderson, Lynne, and Philip G. Zimbardo. 2001. Shyness as a Clinical Condition: The Stanford Model. In *International Handbook of Social Anxiety: Concepts, Research, and Interventions Relating to the Self and Shyness*, eds. W. Ray Crozier and Lynn E. Alden, 431–447. New York: John Wiley and Sons.

Schmidt, Louis A., and Jay Schulkin, eds. 1999. *Extreme Fear, Shyness, and Social Phobia: Origins, Biological Mechanisms, and Clinical Outcomes*. New York: Oxford University Press.

Bernardo J. Carducci

SIBLING RELATIONSHIPS

Sibling relationships are the longest lasting relationships of most people's lives, and about 85 percent of all people have at least one sibling. Studies by researchers such as Judy Dunn, Victor Cicirelli, Wyndol Furman, and Susan McHale have contributed to our understanding of how sibling relationships develop from early childhood to adulthood, and how siblings influence each other. Research has focused on four broad areas: development of the relationship across the life course, the links between sibling and other family relationships, the impact of siblings on individual health and well-being, and the ongoing discussion of why siblings are so different.

Sibling relationships begin the day the second child arrives, and sometimes even earlier as parents talk about the arrival of a new baby. Judy Dunn and Carol Kendrick (1982) used interviews and in-home observations of mothers, firstborns, and infant siblings to understand why some sibling pairs develop relationships that are warm and supportive while others develop relationships that are hostile and conflictual. Their research, along with other studies, finds that a positive sibling relationship is more likely to develop when parents include the firstborn child in care of the baby and when they talk about the new baby as a person with needs and feelings just like their "big sister or brother." At the other end of the life span, researchers such as Victoria Bedford, Victor Cicirelli, and Ingrid Connidis have demonstrated that social support is an important function of sibling relationships in adulthood and that childhood rivalries can reemerge when siblings spend more time together as adults. More recently, research is growing on siblings during adolescence and early adulthood. For example, Katherine Jewsbury Conger, Chalandra M. Bryant, and Jennifer Meehan Brennom (2004) used observations of sibling interactions and information reported by siblings to explain the changing nature of the sibling relationship in adolescence and the implications for social support in adulthood.

Parents are clearly recognized as important figures in the lives of young children, but for many, siblings are also important. Older siblings play many roles as playmates, teachers, role models, advisors, therapists, friends, and even bossy babysitters. Younger siblings play complementary roles as playmates, students, advice seekers, competitors, friends, and unwilling participants in activities devised by helpful older siblings. In fact, studies of cultures around the world find that four- and five-year-old siblings in some societies begin teaching their younger siblings as early as two and three years of age about language and proper behavior (Zukow 1989). Thomas S. Weisner (1989) presents a theoretical framework that takes family relationships and culture into account in explaining the unique contribution of siblings to social, emotional, and cognitive development. Cicirelli (1995) provides a comprehensive review of the varied theoretical and methodological approaches that researchers have used to study the association between parent-child and sibling relationships and the link between sibling relationships and those with friends and classmates. Laurie F. Kramer and Amanda K. Kowal (2005) report that positive behaviors between first-borns and their friends in early childhood are related to positive relationships with their younger siblings in childhood and early adolescence. Kramer's research on resolving conflict between siblings will be of particular interest to parents.

The parents' marital relationship is another important factor in the lives of siblings. Research by Clare Stocker and others reports that spousal conflict is related to conflict between siblings and can interfere with siblings' ability to develop a positive relationship. Other research finds that some siblings bond more closely during difficult times such as a divorce or death of a parent. And research on stepfamilies finds that sibling relationships often suffer when parents divorce and remarry. Remarriage also adds the complexity of half-siblings and step-siblings.

Evidence is accumulating that siblings can promote competent behaviors as well as encourage problem behaviors. A special issue of the *Journal of Family Psychology* (December 2005) was devoted to research on siblings, and the studies demonstrate the exciting new advances made in this area. The editors, Laurie Kramer and Lew Bank, selected eighteen articles designed to "illustrate the ways in which sibling relationships serve as important contexts for both individual development and family functioning" (p. 483). Many of the studies use sophisticated statistical analyses that allow social scientists to examine sibling relationships within families across multiple points in time. These studies, conducted with a broad range of ethnically diverse families, demonstrate the increased appreciation for the importance of siblings' roles in family life and individual development. Interested readers will also want to refer to Frits Boer and Judy Dunn's 1992 book, *Children's Sibling Relationships: Developmental and Clinical Issues*, which provides a summary of clinical and developmental issues, including the impact of a sibling's illness or disability on individual development and sibling relationships.

One frequently asked question is why siblings are so different if they grew up in the same family. The ongoing debate centers on nature (a person's genetic makeup) and nurture (shared and nonshared experiences in the family such as parenting and other social settings). The field of behavior genetics uses comparisons between twins, full siblings, and adoptive siblings to explain individual similarities and differences in personality and behavior (Dunn and Plomin 1990; Lytton and Gallagher 2002). One example illustrates why there are no easy answers to this ongoing debate. Everyone can understand why identical twins (monozygotic, or conceived with one egg) are similar because they share 100 percent of their genetic material, so if differences are observed they are the result of the environment such as experiences with parents and friends. However, their environment also is likely to be more similar because these twins are the same sex and arrive at the same time in the family. Fraternal twins (dyzygotic, or conceived with two eggs) also arrive in the family at the same time but share only about 50 percent of their genes and they may be the same or opposite sex. For these siblings, some factors are pushing them toward similarity and others toward difference. Full siblings (the most common variety) also share about 50 percent of their genetic material, but each sibling arrives at a different point in the family's life. Even though they all live in the same family, the experiences of one sister may be quite different from those of her sister or brother.

Differential parental treatment has been identified as one factor that explains why siblings in the same family might be so different (McGuire 2001). Parents, and most children, agree that parents should treat siblings differently because of age, sex, temperament, and other individual characteristics. However, if parents play favorites and the siblings feel the treatment is unfair, then there can be negative consequences. Several researchers (e.g., Gene

Brody, Katherine Conger, Shirley McGuire, Susan McHale, and Robert Plomin) have found that differential parental treatment may be related to negative relations between siblings, child behavior problems, and conflictual family relations. Moreover, siblings can also influence the parenting behaviors. The exploration of shared and non-shared environments as explanations for sibling similarities and differences continues to be a promising area for research.

SEE ALSO *Child Development; Children; Determinism, Biological; Determinism, Environmental; Family; Family Structure; Heredity; IQ Controversy; Marriage; Nature vs. Nurture; Parenting Styles; Twin Studies*

BIBLIOGRAPHY

Boer, Frits, and Judy Dunn, eds. 1992. *Children's Sibling Relationships: Developmental and Clinical Issues.* Hillsdale, NJ: Erlbaum.

Brody, Gene H., ed. 1996. *Sibling Relationships: Their Causes and Consequences.* Norwood, NJ: Ablex Publishing.

Cicirelli, Victor G., ed. 1995. *Sibling Relationships across the Lifespan.* New York: Plenum Press.

Conger, Katherine Jewsbury, and Rand D. Conger. 1994. Differential Parental Treatment and Change in Sibling Differences in Delinquency. *Journal of Family Psychology* 8 (3): 287–302.

Conger, Katherine Jewsbury, Chalandra M. Bryant, and Jennifer Meehan Brennom. 2004. The Changing Nature of Adolescent Sibling Relationships: A Theoretical Framework for Evaluating the Role of Relationship Quality. In *Continuity and Change in Family Relations: Theory, Methods, and Empirical Findings*, eds. Rand D. Conger, Frederick O. Lorenz, and K. A. S. Wickrama, 319–344. Mahwah, NJ: Erlbaum.

Dunn, Judy, and Carol Kendrick. 1982. *Siblings: Love, Envy, and Understanding.* Cambridge, MA: Harvard University Press.

Dunn, Judy, and Robert Plomin. 1990. *Separate Lives: Why Siblings Are So Different.* New York: Basic Books.

Furman, Wyndol, and Richard Lanthier. 2002. Parenting Siblings. In *Handbook of Parenting*, 2nd ed. Vol. 1: *Children and Parenting*, ed. Marc H. Bornstein, 165–188. Mahwah, NJ: Erlbaum.

Kramer, Laurie F., and Lew Bank, eds. 2005. Sibling Relationship Contributions to Individual and Family Well-Being: Introduction to the Special Issue. *Journal of Family Psychology* 19 (4): 483–485.

Kramer, Laurie F., and Amanda K. Kowal. 2005. Sibling Relationship Quality from Birth to Adolescence: The Enduring Contributions of Friends. *Journal of Family Psychology* 19 (4): 503–511.

Lytton, Hugh, and Lin Gallagher. 2002. Parenting Twins and the Genetics of Parenting. In *Handbook of Parenting*, vol. 1: *Children and Parenting*, ed. Marc H. Bornstein, 227–253. Mahwah, NJ: Erlbaum.

McGuire, Shirley. 2001. Nonshared Environment Research: What Is It and Where Is It Going? *Marriage and Family Review* 33 (1): 31–56.

Weisner, Thomas S. 1989. Comparing Sibling Relationships across Cultures. In *Sibling Interaction across Cultures: Theoretical and Methodological Issues*, ed. Patricia Goldring Zukow. New York: Springer-Verlag.

Zukow, Patricia Goldring, ed. 1989. *Sibling Interaction across Cultures: Theoretical and Methodological Issues.* New York: Springer-Verlag.

Katherine Jewsbury Conger

SIBLING RIVALRY
SEE *Sibling Relationships.*

SICKNESS
SEE *Disease.*

SIGNALING MODELS
SEE *Screening and Signaling Games.*

SIGNALS

The word *signal* comes from the Latin word *signum*, meaning "sign," and from the Late Latin word *signalis*, meaning "of a sign." A *signal* is an event, message, activity, or, generally, any means of communication that encodes or transmits a message or some information between at least two parties, the sender and the receiver of the message.

In economics, a signal is a means by which one party (the agent) conveys some meaningful information about itself to another party (the principal). The action of sending a signal is called *signaling*. In business, a signal is a means by which a firm conveys to the market (investors, financial analysts, banks, bondholders, stockholders, and all stakeholders) information about its current position and future prospects.

In a perfect market, all information is accessible to all at zero cost and simultaneously. However, markets in reality are not perfect and manifest a deviation from perfect information called *asymmetric information*. In some economic transactions, the participants have different access to information pertinent to their decision-making: One party has more or better information than the other, and this inequality of information access disrupts normal market behavior. Michael Spence (1973, 2002) suggests that two parties with different exposure to needed information could overcome this problem of asymmetry by having one party send a signal to the other, revealing some pertinent information. The receiving party could interpret this signal and adjust their behavior accordingly. Interpretation, of course, is subjective and can lead to erroneous inferences. Thus, there is need for a lot of caution in signal interpretation.

There are types of sellers who usually have better information than buyers, such as used-car dealers, salespeople, mortgage brokers, loan originators, stockbrokers, real estate agents, and company insiders (managers). There are also circumstances in which the buyer usually has better information than the seller, such as estate sales as specified in a last will and testament, sales of old art pieces without prior professional valuation, and purchases of health insurance by consumers (or clients) with various risk levels. Asymmetric information can result in one party being defrauded by the other. Because information is easy to create and spread, but difficult to control and trust, it complicates many standard economic theories.

In finance, signaling theory has been applied to the problem of asymmetry of information between a firm's insiders (managers) and outsiders (stockholders, stakeholders, bondholders, and investors). This theory mainly concerns two aspects of a firm's strategic decisions: capital structure and dividend policy decisions. Stephen Ross (1977), the first to apply signaling theory to finance, argues that the market values a firm's perceived returns, not its actual returns. Managers, as insiders, have monopolistic access to pertinent information about a firm's prospects and expected cash flows. Therefore, when it is in their strategic interest, they can use project financing or dividend policy to send signals to investors about their firm's future. For instance, increased financial leveraging can be used by managers to signal optimistic future prospects. Hayne Leland and David Pyle (1977) assume that owners (entrepreneurs) have better information about the expected value of their firms' future investment projects than outsiders have. If a firm increases its dividend payout, this is perceived as a positive signal about expected future cash inflows. The market interprets this increase as a sign that the firm will be able to generate enough cash inflows to cover all its debt payments and its dividend payments without increasing the probability of bankruptcy (see Fama, Fisher, Jensen, and Roll 1969; Asquith and Mullins 1983; Richardson, Sefcik, and Thompson 1986).

SEE ALSO *Finance; Information, Asymmetric; Information, Economics of; Screening and Signaling Games*

BIBLIOGRAPHY

Asquith, Paul, and David W. Mullins Jr. 1983. The Impact of Initiating Dividend Payments on Shareholders' Wealth. *Journal of Business* 56 (1): 77–96.

Fama, Eugene F., Lawrence Fisher, Michael C. Jensen, and Richard Roll. 1969. The Adjustment of Stock Prices to New Information. *International Economic Review* 10 (1): 1–21.

Leland, Hayne E., and David H. Pyle. 1977. Informational Asymmetries, Financial Structure and Financial Intermediation. *Journal of Finance* 32 (2): 371–387.

Richardson, Gordon, Stephan E. Sefcik, and Rex Thompson. 1986. A Test of Dividend Irrelevance Using Volume Reactions to a Change in Dividend Policy. *Journal of Financial Economics* 17 (2): 313–333.

Ross, Stephen A. 1977. The Determination of Financial Structure: The Incentive-Signaling Approach. *Bell Journal of Economics* 8 (1): 23–40.

Spence, Michael. 1973. Job Market Signaling. *Quarterly Journal of Economics* 83 (1): 355–374.

Spence, Michael. 2002. Signaling in Retrospect and the Informational Structure of Markets. *American Economic Review* 92 (3): 434–459.

Katerina Lyroudi

SIKHISM

Sikhism, a religion that emerged in the Punjab region of India in the fifteenth century, can be said to be the cultural product of the collision between Hinduism and Islam. As such, it combines elements of Islam, such as monotheism and iconoclasm, with certain features of Hinduism, such as the doctrines of reincarnation, karma, and nirvāna. While Sikhism is often regarded as a syncretic religion, this interpretation is offensive to Sikhs, who regard their religion as a direct and separate revelation. Crucial to the distinctive character of Sikhism, however, was the rejection of the caste system and its associated rituals and legal apparatus by the Sikh Gurus, or teachers.

Sikhism was founded by Guru Sri Guru Nanak Dev Ji (1469–1539), who was born at Talwandi, a village that is now known as Nankana Sahib, near Lahore in Pakistan. Leaving home to gain religious knowledge, Nanak is said to have encountered Kabir (1440–1518), a saintly figure who was revered by the followers of many religious traditions. Nanak promoted religious tolerance and the equality of women. His most famous saying was: "There is no Hindu, there is no Muslim." Nanak undertook four extensive journeys around and beyond India, spreading his teaching in Bengal and Assam, in Shri Lanka via Tamil Nadu, in the north toward Kashmir, Ladakh, and Tibet, and finally toward Baghdad and Mecca.

As a system of religious philosophy, Sikhism was traditionally known as the Gurmat (the teachings of the gurus) or Sikh dharma. There were ten Gurus who led the community from the time of Nanaka until 1708. These Gurus came from the Khatri *jati*, a mercantile caste. The term *Sikhism* comes from the Sanskrit root *sisya*, signifying a "disciple" or "student." Sikhs, who now number over twenty-three million adherents around the world, are predominantly inhabitants of the Punjab, where they represent 65 percent of the population. In practical terms, Sikhs are distinguished by the custom in which baptized Sikhs wear the *panj kakke* (the Five Ks): uncut hair, a small comb, a metal bracelet, a short sword, and a special undergarment. Sikhs served in the British army between 1870 and 1947, and many of them settled outside the Punjab after they were discharged. Thus, there is now a large Sikh diaspora.

Nanak emphasized personal devotion to and intimate faith in God. The principal belief is faith in *Vahiguru*, or God, who is conceived without gender as a single, personal, and transcendental creator God. *Vahiguru* is omnipresent and can be comprehended by the "heart" of the true disciple, who achieves religious enlightenment through meditation. The chief obstacles to knowledge and salvation are human attachment to worldly pursuits and interests that determine human involvement in the endless cycle of birth and death, or *samsara*. This collection of beliefs about sin, responsibility, rebirth and release can be referred to as the *dharma-karma-samsara* system that Sikhism shares with other religions of the Indian subcontinent. The pursuit of material interests is an illusion, or *maya*, which is evident in the Five Evils of egoism, anger, greed, attachment, and lust. These evils can only be avoided by intense meditation and verbal repetition of the name of God. In terms of its social teaching, in addition to rejecting caste, Nanak taught that Sikhs should respect the rights of all creatures, especially of human beings. Sikh teaching also underlines egalitarianism, charity, and the sharing of resources.

There are two sources of scriptural authority in Sikhism: the Guru Granth Sahib and the Dasam Granth. The Guru Granth Singh may be referred to as the Adi Granth, or the First Volume. The Adi Granth is the scriptural version created by Arjun Dev in 1604, while the Guru Granth Sahib is the final version produced by Gobind Singh. These teachings take the form of hymns arranged into thirty-one *ragas* (musical forms) in which they were originally composed. These hymns were originally written in many different languages, and there are both Sanskrit and Arabic portions. The Granth is regarded as the living embodiment of the eleven teachers, and great respect is required in reading them, such as covering the head with a turban or piece of cloth.

Under the guruship of Nanaka, Sikhism was an informal collection of followers, but it eventually came to have a political identity. Guru Ram Das (1534–1581) created the city of Ramdaspur, subsequently known as Amritsar. Guru Arjun Dev (1563–1606) built the Golden Temple (Harimandir Sahib), which was completed in 1601, and prepared the sacred text of the Adi Granth. As a result of conflicts with the Mughal authorities, the Sikhs founded the Khalsa (brotherhood and sisterhood of followers who join the community at puberty by undertaking certain rituals) in 1699 to provide for the defense of the community or *Panth*. As the Sikh community developed a military and political organization, Sikhism became a considerable force in medieval India.

With the death of Banda (Guru Tegh) Bahadur (1621–1675), the ninth Guru of the Sikh faith, the *misls*, a confederation of Sikh warrior bands, was formed. Toward the end of the Mughal Empire (1526–1858), a Sikh kingdom arose under Maharaja Ranjit Singh, with a capital in Lahore and outer boundaries from the Khyber Pass to China. Eventually, this kingdom (1799–1849) came under British control after the Anglo-Sikh Wars (1845–1846 and 1848–1849).

The partition of India occurred in 1947, and the Sikhs suffered greatly from the resulting violence. Millions were forced to leave their ancestral homeland in the West Punjab. Although the Sikhs eventually prospered, there has been a movement (*Damdami Taksal*), led by Jarnail Singh Bhindranwale (1947–1984), to create an independent state of Khalistan. This movement led to clashes with the government and communal violence. Bhindranwale was killed in June 1984 in the Golden Temple during a clash with the Indian army. In retaliation, Prime Minister Indira Gandhi was assassinated by her Sikh bodyguard in October 1984.

The attempt to remove Bhindranwale was known as Operation Blue Star in the Indian army, but for Sikhs it represented a desecration of the sacred Golden Temple and the Sikh community. As a result of the military attack, Bhindranwale acquired the status of a martyr, and following Indira Gandhi's assassination there was further communal killing of Sikhs. The consequence of these conflicts was to reinforce the sense of Sikh identity, but also to stimulate the exodus of Sikhs to Europe, North America and East Africa, thereby augmenting the already large Sikh diaspora.

SEE ALSO *Gandhi, Indira; Hinduism; Islam, Shia and Sunni; Monotheism; Reincarnation; Religion; Secession; Supreme Being*

BIBLIOGRAPHY

Cole, W. Owen. 1984. Sikhism. In *A Handbook of Living Religions*, ed. John R. Hinnells, 237–255. Harmondsworth, Middlesex, U.K.: Penguin.

Mann, Gurinder Singh. 2001. *The Making of Sikh Scripture.* New York: Oxford University Press.

Singh, Khushwant 2006. *The Illustrated History of the Sikhs.* Delhi: Oxford University Press.

Smart, Ninian 1989. *The World's Religions.* Englewood Cliffs, NJ: Prentice Hall.

Bryan S. Turner

SILICON VALLEY

Silicon Valley, California, USA, is widely hailed as the driving force behind the new high-tech economy. This region has a long history of economic and social struggle that predates and sets the stage for the contemporary terrain of sleek high-technology firms with billionaire chief executive officers (CEOs). Santa Clara Valley (as the region is also known) has been the site of continuous struggles between Native Americans and newcomers, wealthy business owners and low-income workers, and Anglos and people of color and immigrants. This includes the time of the Spanish conquest (beginning in 1769), the gold-rush period (during the mid-1800s), the agricultural period (during the late 1800s through the mid-1900s [Zavella 1987]), and the present-day electronics or high-technology era. During each of these periods, the Santa Clara Valley has been the site of battles over economic and political power that resulted in the relegation of indigenous peoples, immigrants, and people of color to the lowest positions in the social hierarchy. Each period of struggle also saw enormous harm visited upon the natural environment as corporations extracted raw materials for production and sale in global consumer markets (Park and Pellow 2002).

International Business Machines (IBM) built its first West-Coast plant, its Pacific headquarters, in San Jose, California, in 1943. Soon companies such as FMC, Lockheed, General Electric, Sylvania, Fairchild, Memorex, National Semiconductor, and dozens of others located to the area and built what eventually became known as Silicon Valley, producing industrial and consumer electronics that constituted the high-tech revolution.

While a number of industrialists became extraordinarily wealthy as a result of the electronics boom, social inequality was a continuous hallmark of economic development in the region. By 1995, although there was great racial diversity in Santa Clara County (as the total Latino population constituted 23 percent of the county's residents, Asian Pacific Islanders were 20 percent, and the white population less than 53 percent), Silicon Valley was experiencing ever-increasing wage inequality by race, class, and gender at rates much greater than in the United States as a whole. In 1970 women and people of color constituted an exceedingly small fraction of professional and managerial positions in the valley while these same groups were concentrated in the lower-paid, higher-risk occupations of craft worker, operative, and laborer. As of the early twenty-first century, these patterns remained virtually unchanged, except for class bifurcation among Asian populations as many skilled Chinese and South Asian immigrants moved into higher-paid positions while the Vietnamese population remained concentrated in the lowest-paid positions. Thus, race, class, and gender each operated in ways that generally disadvantaged people of color and women in Silicon Valley.

Despite these social inequalities, Silicon Valley promoters were always able to boast about the environmentally safe image of the high-technology industry and how this sector was distinct from other manufacturing industries because it was "pollution free." The pollution-free image was shattered in December 1981 when it was discovered that the well that supplied drinking water to homes in south San Jose was contaminated with thousands of gallons of the deadly chemical trichloroethane (TCA), a solvent used to remove grease from microchips and printed circuit boards after they are manufactured. The toxic waste materials had been leaking from an underground storage tank for at least a year and a half. The responsible party was the Fairchild Semiconductor Corporation, a major firm in the valley.

Most persons working to produce computers and semiconductor chips inside Silicon Valley's electronics firms are women, immigrants, and people of color. Much of the ethnic and gender segregation in the industry is the result of conscious and selective recruiting on the part of managers (Hossfeld 1990). Compounding the exposure of these workers to the pollution in their neighborhoods is the fact that they hold jobs that are more toxic than those found in any other basic industry. Up to 1,000 different chemicals and metals are used in the various processes required to produce semiconductor chips around the world. Toxic spills that have enraged communities located near chip plants have also impacted the health of workers inside the plants.

Outsourcing of jobs overseas has been a major concern among Silicon Valley workers since the 1980s. Despite earlier *no lay-off pledge* declarations by high-technology industry leaders, this sector is not fundamentally different from any other with regard to the impact of globalization. The electronics industry is a global industry with investors, owners, factories, workers, and consumer markets the world over. Firms have worked to continuously minimize costs and maximize profits, and this often means importing workers through the H1B visa program (the program that allows foreign workers to come to the

United States to work for one company for a set period of time before they return home, which some critics have labeled a modern form of indentured servitude) or moving factories overseas to find cheap labor in other countries. Electronics firms have moved from the United States to Mexico and then to China, for example, in an effort to hold down costs and boost earnings. Predictably, these practices are accompanied by low-wage, hazardous working conditions and often result in serious occupational health hazards and environmental harm. If Silicon Valley (and those communities around the globe that host a high density of electronics firms) is to have a hopeful future, it will have to be transformed and characterized by social equity and ecologically sustainable economic practices.

SEE ALSO *Technological Progress, Economic Growth; Technology*

BIBLIOGRAPHY

Hossfeld, Karen. 1990. Their Logic Against Them: Contradictions in Sex, Race, and Class in Silicon Valley. In *Women Workers and Global Restructuring*, ed. Kathryn Ward. Ithaca, NY: ILR Press.

Pellow, David N., and Lisa Sun-Hee Park. 2002. *The Silicon Valley of Dreams: Environmental Injustice, Immigrant Workers, and the High-Tech Global Economy.* New York: New York University Press.

Zavella, Patricia. 1987. *Women's Work and Chicano Families: Cannery Workers of the Santa Clara Valley.* Ithaca: Cornell University Press.

David N. Pellow
Lisa Sun-Hee Park

SILK ROAD

The term *Silk Road* (*die Seidenstrasse*) was first coined by the nineteenth-century German explorer Baron Ferdinand von Richthofen (1833–1905). It broadly describes the ancient trading routes stretching across the Eurasian continent from China to Europe. While silk was clearly one of the earliest and most important commodities traded along the route, precious metals and stones, spices, porcelain, and textiles also traveled the road. More significantly, the Silk Road was an avenue for the exchange of ideas. The technologies of silk production, paper making, gunpowder manufacture, and block printing made their way west across Asia via this highway. Buddhism, Islam, and Christianity entered China via the Silk Road. Migrants, merchants, explorers, pilgrims, refugees, and soldiers brought along with them religious and cultural ideas, products, flora and fauna, and plagues and disease in this gigantic cross-continental exchange.

Thus, the Silk Road is a symbol of the globalization of trade, technology, and ideology for the premodern world.

Although Chinese silk was found in Europe as early as 500 BCE, well recorded trading started only when China gained control of its western frontier during the Western Han dynasty (202 BCE –9 CE). The first route started from China's capital at the time, Chang-An (now Xian), and continued through the northwest frontier of China and the elaborate trading networks of major Eurasian civilization zones in Central Asia, Persia, and Roman Europe. Traffic along the Silk Road was disrupted at times of political disintegration, such as the collapse of the Han dynasty around 220 CE. A second, "southern" Silk Road started in southwest China, passing through China's Sichuan and Yunan provinces and Burma to reach India. Trade in silk between China and India increased substantially between the fourth and sixth centuries when the northern route became unstable.

During the first two hundred years of the Tang dynasty (618–907 CE) silk trade via the northern route thrived again, only to decline toward the end of dynasty when Tang lost control of the northwestern territories to the Arabs. The route was significantly revived under the Mongol Empire established by Genghis Khan (1167–1227). Safe trade routes, effective post stations, the use of paper money, and the elimination of trade barriers marked the high stage of East-West exchange, which saw the famous travels of Marco Polo.

As shipbuilding technology progressed, maritime routes became easier and safer; this was the most important contributing factor to the relative decline of the overland Silk Road from around the fourteenth century. A significant breakthrough came in 1488 when Portuguese ships found their way to East Asia by bypassing the mighty Ottoman barrier and rounding the Cape of Good Hope. Meanwhile, in China the centers of economic and cultural activities began to shift decisively southward, with the lower Yangzi delta area (roughly in the Jiangsu and Zhejiang provinces) emerging as the most important center of production of luxury goods, including silk. This development helped accelerate the geographic shift in Eurasian trade from the overland to the sea route, which is sometimes called the maritime Silk Road.

Accompanying the trade in silk was the slow but cumulative diffusion of the craft of silk-making, which traveled from China through Central Asia, Persia, Anatolia, North Africa, and Eastern and Southern Europe, and finally, in the seventeenth and eighteenth centuries, took hold in the newly discovered American continent.

SEE ALSO *Trade*

BIBLIOGRAPHY

Boulnois, L. 1966. *The Silk Road.* Trans. Dennis Chamberlin. London: Allen & Unwin.

Franck, Irene M., and David M. Brownstone. 1986. *The Silk Road: A History.* New York: Facts on File.

Liu, Xinru. 1988. *Ancient India and Ancient China: Trade and Religious Exchanges, AD 1–600.* Delhi: Oxford University Press.

Ma, Debin. 2005. The Great Silk Exchange: How the World Was Connected and Developed. In *Textiles in the Pacific, 1500–1900,* ed. Debin Ma, pp. 1–32. Aldershot, U.K.: Ashgate.

Debin Ma

SILVER INDUSTRY

The world silver industry consists of miners, refiners, traders, and fabricators. Generally speaking, the silver industry overall grew in the decade from 1996 to 2005, with mine supply increasing to meet rising fabrication demand and refiners and traders handling greater volumes to facilitate this growth.

While silver prices were generally flat through most of this decade, prices began rising out of the US$4 to US$5 per ounce range where they had been trapped in 2003. During 2005 and the first half of 2006, silver prices rose sharply, reaching a decade-long high of more than US$9 per ounce in late 2005 and soaring further to nearly US$15 per ounce by April 2006. While low prices hurt the mining sector through much of the 1990s and early 2000s, they had a long-run effect of spurring fabrication demand, particularly nontraditional uses of silver in diverse areas from electronics to medicine.

According to a 2006 report by Peter Klapwijk, world mine production of silver was generally on the increase between 1996 and 2005, during which time production rose from just under 500 million ounces to approximately 642 million ounces. William E. Brooks reported in 2006 that approximately two-thirds of mined silver worldwide is produced as a by-product of copper, lead, zinc, and gold production. As a consequence, silver is mined and enters the market regardless of the price.

Silver resources are spread over all continents (excluding Antarctica and Greenland, where resource estimates are unavailable). The largest producing country in 2005 was Peru, which accounted for slightly more that 15 percent of world output. Peru was followed by Mexico, Australia, China, Chile, Russia, Poland, and the United States. Estimated minable world silver reserves—that is, silver contained in ore that can be mined at a profit—amount to approximately 8.7 billion ounces (Brooks

2006). It is not known, however, how many of these ounces could be recoverable through primary rather than by-product production.

LABOR CONDITIONS AND ENVIRONMENTAL ISSUES

Labor conditions and the degree of unionization in the silver mining industry vary widely around the world. In the United States, for example, every mine worker undergoes safety training before being employed and takes a periodic refresher course. Silver mining, and hard-rock mining in general, however, is significantly safer than coal mining. Coal mining involves digging into a combustible material, which is the cause of many coal mine accidents. This is not the case with hard-rock mining.

Because silver mines tend to be fairly large-scale operations employing several hundred workers at a moderate size mine, the workforce is amenable to unionization. The degree of unionization, however, varies widely depending on national and state or provincial laws. In the western United States, where most of U.S. output comes from, mine workers tend not to be unionized, but many of the specialized tradespeople, such as electrical workers, pipe fitters, and some construction workers, do tend to be unionized. In general, whether union members or not, mine workers are typically among the highest paid industrial workers.

Environmental reclamation laws also vary widely around the world. In the United States environmental laws concerning discharge of pollutants and reclamation are generally administered by state agencies in compliance with U.S. Environmental Protection Agency regulations. In other countries similar regulations may or may not be in force. Nevertheless, international banking concerns typically make compliance with U.S. environmental standards a general condition of financing mine development in other countries. These conditions are generally imposed by lenders to prevent environmental degradation being used as a rationale for nationalization and confiscation of a mining property. Not all mines, however, are financed through international lenders, and in these cases compliance is less certain although there is still an incentive for operators to avoid confiscation and nationalization.

REPROCESSING, REFINING, AND COMMODITY EXCHANGES

In addition to mining, silver also makes its way into the world supply chain from the reprocessing of scrap metal that comes from various fabrication processes and via sales from government stockpiles. In 2005 mined silver accounted for approximately 70 percent of the total supply, while scrap accounted for 21 percent. Historically, reprocessing photographic wastes has been the major source of scrap, but this is changing because of a variety of factors. Other major sources of scrap include jewelry and silverware manufacturing. In addition to reprocessing scrap, government sales account for 7 percent of the silver supply and producer hedging for 2 percent (Klapwijk 2006). All of these sources combined for a total supply of 911.9 million ounces in 2005 (Klapwijk 2006).

In the case of mined silver, producers ship unrefined product to a refinery for reduction to a commercial grade product. There are many refineries around the world that can process unrefined product, with more than twenty of them located in the United States. These refineries also melt down and refine other types of scrap material to produce a commercial grade product. These commercial grade products can range from products that are alloyed with other metals for special purposes and sold under contract to jewelers and other fabricators to silver bullion that is 99.99 percent pure silver.

Many major commodity exchanges around the world make a market in bullion silver. These include markets in London, New York, and Tokyo, but perhaps the largest is the London Bullion Market Association. Traders in these markets sell silver in "spot" markets, that is, for immediate delivery, and deal in futures and options contracts for delivery in the future.

PRODUCTS

As noted, fabrication demand has increased since the mid-1990s. The more interesting story behind this increase, however, has been the change in the mix of products fabricated. Historically, the major uses of silver were the minting of coins and the fabrication of jewelry, silverware, and objects of art such as candlesticks and bowls. During the twentieth century photographic processing emerged as a major use of silver, and from the middle of the twentieth century the use of silver for coinage diminished, though substantially only in the United States. Fabrication demand for photography has started to decline as consumers shift from film-based photography to digital cameras. At the same time, however, in spite of the decline in the traditional uses of silver in coinage and photography, demand for silver has been growing as new uses have been found for this metal based on its particular qualities, such as its being an excellent electronic conductor and having high degrees of malleability and reflectivity.

Silver is commonly used in a variety of batteries, from most quartz watch batteries to batteries used in the aerospace industry. Silver batteries are lighter weight and can deliver more power per weight than traditional lead-acid batteries.

Because silver alloys or combines with other metals well, it is commonly used as a coating for bearings in jet engines and for brazing and soldering in electronics and other manufacturing. Perhaps one of the most common uses of silver as a coating is in the manufacture of mirrors. Silver is also used in windows that reflect solar radiation and heat and in eyeglasses. In addition the metal is also an important catalyst used in manufacturing a variety of plastics and chemicals.

The use of silver in the electronics industry is also growing. Because of its conductivity and resiliency, silver contacts are widely used in many industries. High-voltage contacts at power plants and in manufacturing plants frequently are made of silver or are silver coated. Automobiles have silver contacts in ignition systems, other electronic systems, and safety systems, such as air bags. Silver is also widely used for contacts and circuitry in computers, including the contacts under computer keyboard keys.

In medicine silver has long been used as a biocide. Since before 500 BCE it has been known that water, milk, vinegar, and other foods resist spoilage better when stored in silver vessels than in other containers. This characteristic of silver has led to its use in water purification systems, bandages, and other antibacterial, antifungal, and antiviral applications.

BIBLIOGRAPHY

Brooks, William E. 2006. Silver. In *Mineral Commodity Summaries*, January 2006. Washington, DC: U.S. Geological Survey.

Klapwijk, Peter. 2006. *World Silver Survey*. London: Gold Fields Mineral Services.

John L. Dobra

SIMILARITY/ ATTRACTION THEORY

Similarity/attraction theory posits that people like and are attracted to others who are similar, rather than dissimilar, to themselves; "birds of a feather," the adage goes, "flock together." Social scientific research has provided considerable support for tenets of the theory since the mid-1900s. Researchers from a variety of fields such as marketing, political science, social psychology, and sociology have contributed to and gleaned information from empirical tests of similarity/attraction theory. The theory provides a parsimonious explanatory and predictive framework for examining how and why people are attracted to and influenced by others in their social worlds.

A large body of research investigates the role that similarity of attitudes plays in attraction. According to studies by Ellen Berscheid and Elaine H. Walster (1969) and Donn Byrne (1971) in general people are most attracted to others who share similar attitudes. Additionally people who share similar important attitudes (e.g., attitudes concerning home and family) are more likely to be attracted to each other than those who share less important attitudes (e.g., attitudes toward certain fabric softeners).

There are several reasons why people prefer the company of others who espouse attitudes, especially important attitudes, which are similar to their own (Berscheid and Walster 1969; Byrne 1971). Most importantly perhaps, sharing similar attitudes provides corroboration that a person is not alone in his or her belief; they might even be correct to hold the attitude in question. Other possible reasons suggested for why people prefer others who are similar to themselves are that (1) knowledge of similar attitudes may help people to predict others' future behaviors, providing a predictive "window" into the other's behavioral predilections, and (2) people may be more likely to assume that others who hold similar attitudes to themselves have a greater chance of being attracted to them, a "likeness begets liking" explanation.

In addition to people's inclinations to be attracted to those who share similar attitudes, people are also attracted to others who manifest personality characteristics (e.g., optimism, self-esteem, shyness, conscientiousness) that are similar to their own. In fact people may choose to associate with certain others because they have similar personalities. For example friends are more likely to share personality traits than nonfriends. Moreover, marital partners share more similar personalities than people in randomly assigned pairs. Indeed personality similarity may play a key role in marital happiness and longevity (Berscheid and Walster 1969; Byrne 1971).

Furthermore people are attracted to romantic partners who share similar physical characteristics and levels of physical attractiveness. Tall people are more likely to marry tall partners than short ones, and attractive people are more likely to marry attractive partners than unattractive ones.

People's preference for similarity in social partners is not limited to the aforementioned domains, though. Research has demonstrated that people report greater liking for and attraction to people who are like them in the following areas as well: socioeconomic status, religious beliefs, social habits (e.g., frequency of attending parties), bad habits (e.g., drinking and smoking), ethnicity, and intelligence.

Similarity/attraction theory may not hold in all social instances, however. For example some scholars have suggested that people may be more likely to be attracted to partners who complement rather than replicate certain attributes. This *complementarity* view of attraction

explains, for example, why attractive younger women may form successful marital unions with much older, wealthier men. Along similar lines people may not like others who share negative personality traits with them. Rather than be constantly reminded of their faults in a given dimension through the presence of someone similar, people may prefer to interact with others who they believe will "bring out the best" in them.

Additionally some researchers, such as Milton Rosenbaum in a 1986 study, have suggested that attitudinal dissimilarity, rather than attitudinal similarity, drives the similarity-liking link. According to the *dissimilarity-repulsion* view people's motivation to avoid social interactions with dissimilar others is stronger than, or at least as strong as, people's desire to affiliate with like-minded others. Indeed a 2000 study by Ramadhar Singh and Soo Yan Ho revealed that, under certain circumstances, the influence of attitudinal similarity and dissimilarity may exert equivalent and opposite effects on liking. Further in some cases, dissimilar attitudes may have a stronger influence on interpersonal attraction than similar attitudes (Singh and Ho 2000).

In summary similarity-attraction theory attempts to explain and predict interpersonal liking by asserting that people are attracted to others who are similar to themselves. Consistent with this view, research has revealed that people prefer to affiliate with those who share similar attitudes, personalities, physical attributes, and a host of other characteristics compared to others who do not. Though similarity/attraction theory explains many cases of interpersonal attraction, it may not accurately predict all attraction outcomes. In some cases complementarity or avoidance of dissimilar others may better explain certain patterns of human liking.

SEE ALSO *Attitudes; Friendship; Personality; Personality, Cult of; Psychology; Romance; Social Relations; Trait Theory*

BIBLIOGRAPHY

Berscheid, Ellen, and Elaine H. Walster. 1969. Rewards Others Provide: Similarity. In *Interpersonal Attraction*, 69–91. Reading, MA: Addison-Wesley.

Byrne, Donn. 1971. *The Attraction Paradigm*. New York: Academic Press.

Rosenbaum, Milton E. 1986. The Repulsion Hypothesis: On the Nondevelopment of Relationships. *Journal of Personality and Social Psychology* 51 (6): 1156–1166.

Singh, Ramadhar, and Soo Yan Ho. 2000. Attitudes and Attraction: A New Test of the Attraction, Repulsion and Similarity-Dissimilarity Asymmetry Hypotheses. *British Journal of Social Psychology* 39 (2): 197–211.

Jorgianne Civey Robinson

SIMON, HERBERT A.
1916–2001

Born on June 15, 1916, in Milwaukee, Wisconsin, Simon was the second son of Arthur Simon, an immigrant German who was an electrical engineer and inventor, and Edna Merkel Simon, a third-generation American who was an accomplished pianist. Determined to become a mathematical social scientist, he bid farewell to Milwaukee at age seventeen to enter the hall of academe in Chicago, where he obtained his BA in 1936 and his graduate degree in 1943, both in political science. During his professional career, he was affiliated with the University of California at Berkeley, the Illinois Institute of Technology, the Cowles Commission, the Rand Corporation, and Carnegie-Mellon University, which was still known as the Carnegie Institute of Technology when Simon moved there in 1949. At the time of his death, he was the Richard King Mellon Professor of Computer Science and Psychology at Carnegie.

Starting off in political science and then moving through several disciplinary domains such as management theory, economics, cognitive psychology, and artificial intelligence, Simon's entire academic career was focused on understanding human decision-making and problem-solving processes and their implications for social institutions. In economics, Simon has become mostly known for his psychology-inspired criticism of the rationality postulate. In particular, he criticized the four basic assumptions of neoclassical economics: (1) the presupposition that each economic agent had a well-defined utility or profit function; (2) the idea that all alternative strategies were presumed to be known; (3) the assumption that all the consequences that follow upon each of these strategies could be determined with certainty; and (4) the presumption that the comparative evaluation of these sets of consequences was driven by a universal desire to maximize expected utility or expected profit. For Simon, these four assumptions clashed with insights from psychology that there were external, social constraints and internal, cognitive limitations to decision-making, upon which he based the opposing assumptions of his bounded rationality program.

Simon argued that, first, the bounded rationality program assumed that decision-makers were confronted by the need to optimize several, sometimes competing, goals. Second, Simon's bounded rationality program postulated a process for generating alternatives. Third, Simon argued that individuals mostly applied approximate solutions to problems. Finally, Simon's bounded rationality theory proposed a satisficing strategy. It sought to identify, in theory and in actual behavior, procedures for choosing that were computationally simpler and argued that individuals picked the first choice that met a preset acceptance crite-

rion. Simon also became known for contributions such as the so-called Hawkins-Simon conditions for stability, his findings on certainty equivalence, his research on size distributions of firms and organizations, and his insights on causality, identifiability, and aggregation.

In 1978, Simon received the Nobel Prize in economics for what the Nobel committee called "his pioneering research into the decision-making process within economic organizations." Bounded rationality has received renewed attention in recent years from, among others, behavioral economists, game theorists, and rational expectations economists. Yet, whereas Simon saw bounded rationality as an alternative to mainstream economics, many contemporary theorists attempt to use his ideas to solve some of the problems in their neoclassical program.

BIBLIOGRAPHY

Ando, Albert. 1979. On the Contributions of Herbert A. Simon to Economics. *Scandinavian Journal of Economics* 81 (1): 83–93.

Baumol, William J. 1979. On the Contributions of Herbert A. Simon to Economics. *Scandinavian Journal of Economics* 81 (1): 74–82.

Cicarelli, James, and Julianne Cicarelli. 1989. Herbert Alexander Simon. In *Nobel Laureates in Economic Sciences: A Biographical Dictionary*, ed. Bernard S. Katz, 264–276. New York: Garland.

Sent, Esther-Mirjam. 2001a. Sent Simulating Simon Simulating Scientists. *Studies in History and Philosophy of Science* 32 (3): 479–500.

Sent, Esther-Mirjam. 2001b. Herbert A. Simon as a Cyborg Scientist. *Perspectives on Science* 8 (4): 380-406.

Sent, Esther-Mirjam. 2004. The Legacy of Herbert Simon in Game Theory. *Journal of Economic Behavior and Organization* 53 (3): 301–317.

Simon, Herbert A. 1955. A Behavioral Model of Rational Choice. *Quarterly Journal of Economics* 69 (1): 99–118.

Simon, Herbert A. 1956. Rational Choice and the Structure of the Environment. *Psychological Review* 63 (2): 129–138.

Simon, Herbert A. 1972. Theories of Bounded Rationality. In *Decision and Organization*, eds. C. B. McGuire and Roy Radner, 161–176. Amsterdam: North-Holland.

Simon, Herbert A. 1991. *Models of My Life*. New York: Basic Books.

Esther-Mirjam Sent

SIMULTANEOUS EQUATION BIAS

Simultaneous equation bias is a fundamental problem in many applications of regression analysis in the social sciences that arises when a right-hand side, X, variable is not truly exogenous (i.e., it is a function of other variables). In general, ordinary least squares (OLS) regression applied to a single equation from a system of simultaneous equations will produce biased, that is, systematically wrong, parameter estimates. Furthermore, the bias from OLS does not decrease as the sample size increases. Estimating parameters from a simultaneous equation model requires advanced methods, of which the most popular today is two-stage least squares (2SLS).

UNDERSTANDING OLS AND BIAS

Consider the following single-equation regression model:

$$y_i = \beta_0 + \beta_1 x_i + \varepsilon_i.$$

This data generation process (DGP) says that each value (denoted by the i subscript) of the dependent variable, y, is produced by taking β_0 and adding β_1 times the value of the independent variable, x, and adding a draw from the random error distribution, ε_i.

To estimate the value of the slope parameter, β_1, from a sample of x, y observations, we fit a line using ordinary least squares, so named because coefficients are chosen to minimize the sum of squared residuals. A residual is the vertical distance between the actual and predicted value. The equation of the fitted line is

$$\text{Predicted } y = b_0 + b_1 x.$$

The slope coefficient from the OLS fitted line, b_1, is our estimate of the unknown parameter β_1. Because we are dealing with a finite sample, we know that our estimate, b_1, is probably not exactly equal to the parameter value, β_1. If we generated another sample, we would get another value of b_1 for that sample. This shows that the slope coefficient from the OLS fitted line is actually a random variable.

Figure 1 provides a concrete example of the abstract ideas underlying OLS. The points in the graph correspond to those in the table. The estimated slope, 4.2, does not equal the true slope, 5, because of the random error term, which in this case is normally distributed with mean zero and standard deviation of 50. A new sample of ten observations would have the same X values, but the Ys would be different and, thus, the estimated slope from the fitted line would change.

There are other estimators (recipes for fitting the line) besides OLS. The circle in Figure 2 represents all of the possible estimators. The vertical oval contains all of the linear estimators. This does not refer to the fitted line itself, which can have a curved or other nonlinear shape, but to the algorithm for computing the estimator. All of the unbiased estimators are included in the horizontal oval. *Unbiasedness* is a desirable property referring to the accuracy of an estimator. Unbiased estimators produce estimates that are, on average, equal to the parameter value. *Bias* means that the estimator is systematically wrong, that is, its expected value does not equal the parameter value. The area where the ovals overlap in Figure 2 is that subset of estimators, including OLS, which are both linear and unbiased.

According to the Gauss-Markov Theorem, when the DGP obeys certain conditions, OLS is the best, linear, unbiased estimator (BLUE). Of all of the linear and unbiased estimators, OLS is the best because it has the small-

An example OLS regression

X_i	Y_i
10	87.35
20	75.31
30	144.09
40	260.45
50	243.45
60	211.76
70	306.17
80	333.08
90	371.28
100	508.81

DGP: $y_i = 10 + 5x_i + \varepsilon_i.$

$\varepsilon \sim N(0, 50)$

Predicted $y = 23.7 + 4.2x$

Figure 1

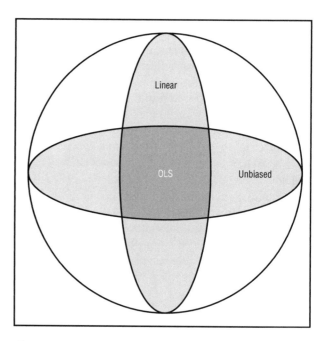

Figure 2

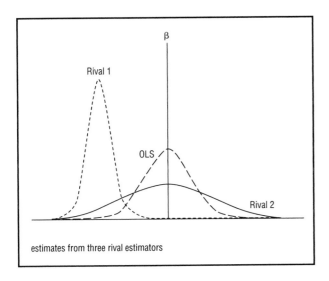

estimates from three rival estimators

Figure 3

est variance. In other words, there are other estimators that are linear and unbiased (centered on β_1), but they have greater variability than OLS. The goal is unbiased estimators with the highest precision, and the Gauss-Markov Theorem guarantees that OLS fits the bill.

Figure 3 shows histograms for three rival linear estimators for a DGP that conforms to the Gauss-Markov conditions. The histograms reflect the estimates produced by each estimator. Rival 1 is biased. It produces estimates that are systematically too low. Rival 2 and OLS are unbiased because each one is centered on the true parameter value. Although both are accurate, OLS is more precise. In other words, using OLS rather than Rival 2 is more likely to give estimates near the true parameter value. The Gauss-Markov Theorem says that OLS is the most precise estimator in the class of linear, unbiased estimators.

SIMULTANEOUS EQUATION BIAS

Suppose one faces a simultaneous equation DGP like this:

$$y_{1i} = \beta_0 + \beta_1 x_i + \beta_2 y_{2i} + \varepsilon_{1i}$$
$$y_{2i} = \alpha_0 + \alpha_1 y_{1i} + \varepsilon_{2i}.$$

There are two dependent (or endogenous) variables, y_1 and y_2. Each equation has a regressor (a right-hand side variable) that is a dependent variable.

If one is interested in the effect of y_1 on y_2, can one toss out the first equation and treat the second equation as a single-equation model? In other words, what happens if one ignores the simultaneity and simply runs an OLS regression on an individual equation? One gets simultaneous equation bias. The OLS estimator of α_1, the slope parameter in the second equation, will be biased, that is, it will not be centered on α_1. With every sample to which

one applies the OLS recipe, the resulting estimates will be systematically wrong. OLS is now behaving like the Rival 1 estimator in Figure 3 (although one does not know if the bias centers OLS above or below the true parameter value).

Consider the following concrete example. A researcher is interested in estimating the effect of the crime rate (number of crimes per 100,000 people per year) on enforcement spending (dollars per person per year). As the crime rate rises, more police officers and prison guards are needed, so enforcement spending will rise. The researcher is interested in estimating the slope coefficient, β_1, in the following model:

$$Enforcement\ Spending_i = \beta_0 + \beta_1\ CrimeRate_i + \varepsilon_i.$$

Unfortunately, in this situation, as in most social science applications, the real world does not follow a single-equation DGP. Although it is true that government policy makers allocate resources to enforcement spending depending on the crime rate, criminals make decisions based on enforcement spending (and other variables). Increased crime causes more enforcement spending, but more enforcement spending causes less crime. This kind of feedback loop is common in the social sciences. The appropriate model is not a single-equation DGP because the crime rate is not a truly exogenous variable. Instead, the researcher must cope with a simultaneous system of equations where both enforcement spending and crime rate are dependent variables.

If the researcher naively applies OLS to the single equation, her estimate of the effect of crime on enforcement spending, β_1, will be biased. Because ignoring the fact that the crime rate is actually a dependent variable with its own DGP equation causes this bias, it is called *simultaneous* equation (or simultaneity) bias.

The source of the poor performance of the OLS estimator lies in the fact that we have a violation of the conditions required for the Gauss-Markov Theorem: The crime rate is a right-hand side variable that is not independent of the error term. In a given year a high crime rate will result in high enforcement spending, but that will trigger a low crime rate. Conversely, a low enforcement spending year will lead to more crime. When the error term is correlated with a regressor, OLS breaks down and is no longer an unbiased estimator.

AVOIDING SIMULTANEOUS EQUATION BIAS

Estimating an equation with dependent variables on the right-hand side requires advanced methods. It is important to recognize that increasing the sample size or adding explanatory variables to the single-equation regression will not solve the problem.

The approach typically taken is called two-stage least squares (2SLS). In the first stage, an OLS regression utilizes truly exogenous variables (called instrumental variables) to create artificial variables. In the second stage, these artificial variables are then used in place of the endogenous, right-hand side variables in each equation in the system.

In the enforcement spending and crime rate example, the researcher would first regress the crime rate on a set of truly exogenous variables to create a Predicted Crime Rate variable. Determining the instruments to be used in the first stage regression is a crucial step in the 2SLS procedure. In the second stage, she would substitute the Predicted Crime Rate for the Crime Rate variable and run OLS. It can be shown that as the sample size increases, the expected value of the 2SLS estimator gets closer to the true parameter value. Thus, unlike OLS, 2SLS is a consistent estimator of a parameter in a simultaneous equation model.

In practice, two separate regressions are not actually run. Modern statistical software packages have an option for 2SLS that performs the calculations, computing appropriate standard errors and other regression statistics, in one step. As a practical matter, even if there are strong theoretical reasons to suspect the presence of simultaneous equation bias, it need not be a particularly large bias.

A BRIEF HISTORY OF SIMULTANEOUS EQUATION BIAS

Attempts to estimate demand curves in the first quarter of the twentieth century led economists to model supply and demand equations as a simultaneous system. This work culminated in the probabilistic revolution in the 1940s. In "The Probability Approach in Econometrics," Trygve Haavelmo called for explicit description of the data generation process, including the source of variation in the error term and the use of a simultaneous system of equations to model complicated interrelationships among variables.

Haavelmo's program was supported by Tjalling Koopmans and others at the Cowles Commission, a research think tank housed at the University of Chicago from 1939 to 1955. These econometricians made progress in several key areas, including the identification problem, understanding the nature of simultaneous equation bias, and methods for properly estimating an equation embedded in a simultaneous system. They concentrated their simultaneous equation estimation efforts on full- and limited-information maximum likelihood. Two-stage least squares, a much more efficient computational approach, was not discovered—independently by Henri Theil and Robert Basmann—until the 1950s.

SUMMARY

Simultaneous equation bias occurs when an ordinary least squares regression is used to estimate an individual equation that is actually part of a simultaneous system of equations. It is extremely common in social science applications because almost all variables are determined by complex interactions with each other. The bias lies in the estimated coefficients, which are not centered on their true parameter values. Advanced methods, designed to eliminate simultaneous equation bias, use instrumental variables in the first stage of a two-stage least squares procedure.

SEE ALSO *General Linear Model; Instrumental Variables Regression; Least Squares, Three-Stage; Least Squares, Two-Stage; Ordinary Least Squares Regression; Regression; Regression Analysis*

BIBLIOGRAPHY

Christ, Carl F. 1994. The Cowles Commission's Contributions to Econometrics at Chicago, 1939–1995. *Journal of Economic Literature* 32 (1): 30–59.

Haavelmo, Trygve. 1944. The Probability Approach in Econometrics. In *The Foundations of Econometric Analysis*, eds. David F. Hendry and Mary S. Morgan, 1995. Cambridge, U.K. and New York: Cambridge University Press.

Hendry, David F., and Mary S. Morgan, eds. 1995. *The Foundations of Econometric Analysis*. Cambridge, U.K. and New York: Cambridge University Press.

Morgan, Mary. 1990. *The History of Econometric Ideas*. Cambridge, U.K. and New York: Cambridge University Press.

Wooldridge, Jeffrey M. 2006. *Introductory Econometrics: A Modern Approach*. 3rd ed. Mason, OH: Thomson/South-Western.

Humberto Barreto

SIMULTANEOUS EQUATIONS, SYSTEM OF

SEE *Linear Systems; Nonlinear Systems.*

SIN

Sin, in most religions, may be rooted in human "being" but shows itself in human action. This action is of a negative character and represents what the Catholic theologian Karl Rahner (1904–1984) described as an awareness that "things are not the way they ought to be" (Rahner 1961–1979, p. 164). In some faiths the stress is on the corporate character of sin: what causes it, how it is manifested, and what a community does with it. Thus when ancient Israel offended against the way "things ought to be" as prescribed by Yahweh, the people together experienced punishment by this God and recognized a need to atone for sin, to bring the lives of the community and individuals in it in line with the way "things ought to be."

The source of that sense of "ought" may relate to the ways humans in the earliest and simplest of circumstances sensed that there must be a right way, but they were not able to attain it or resisted attainment. Or the source may be in conscience. How the separate faiths account for conscience or any other inner apparatus that inspires and informs conduct tells much about what each considers to be sin and what each prescribes to be a remedy, often called *atonement*. Alongside a primitive sense of "oughtness" and "conscience," a third way of discerning the source of sin is in divine revelation. Ordinarily this means that gifted and charismatic individuals, prophets within the tradition, judge people against the standard of what some holy book has described as conformity to the proper way or prescribed as atoning action.

In cultures informed by the Bible of the Jews and Christians, the definitions and experiences of sin come to focus in a witness to a living creator God who interacts with people, stipulating how they should live, and who in a sacred scripture sets forth a covenant, a divine-human pact that must be followed if God is to be pleased or given an opportunity to show mercy. Whether on a communal or an individual level and whether on gross or trivial scales, sin is seen as a free violation of what God commands and expects. In Christianity there is a similar stress on locating the errant individual in light of how he or she affirms or departs from a divine-human covenant. Christianity preaches that God is both just and merciful. Being merciful, God can recognize value in the efforts of those who try to live in accord with divine commands and can extend mercy even where there is failure.

Sin in most Christian traditions is seen against the background of what Christians call *original sin*, which they perceive as a reality even if they have difficulty accounting for it along with other negative features and experiences in a universe created and governed by a good God. Traditionally original sin, the factor in human experience that makes it impossible for anyone to live a perfect life, is traced to Adam and Eve, the first humans, according to the account in Genesis. Tempted by an external agent, "the serpent," they willingly responded and went against the express decree of God. When, acting upon this evil agency in and around them, their heirs, all humans, engage in *actual sin*—also a technical term—they are breaking the

covenant. In some biblical language, *sin* means "missing the mark" or "transgressing God's boundaries."

In Judaism and Christianity various paths of return to the covenant and God's good graces are prescribed and are called *atonement* or *reconciliation* to God. The same God who set forth the mark that was missed or the boundary transgressed and who can be wrathful and will exact punishment is also witnessed to as merciful. Through atoning activities, for Christians in the agency of Jesus Christ as God's Son who is offered up in a loving sacrifice for others, believers are set on a path that allows them to approach hitting the mark, staying in the boundaries, pleasing God, and receiving a reward, thanks to the grace of this covenanting God. One of the main differences between Roman Catholic and Protestant varieties of Christianity is the stress in the former on human participation in redeeming activities through "good works," while for Protestantism, which also expects good works, the accent is more on God's grace.

In virtually every faith, though terms like *original sin* and *transgressing* may be absent, there is some pattern or ideal to be followed to place human individuals or the community in a positive relation to the highest power or source. This is usually "God," under a variety of names, such as for Muslims Allah. Allah has created an ordered universe, but humans who violate the laws of Allah cause disorder and are evil or act evilly. While Islam does not employ concepts such as original sin, Muslims know that they are in a universe where something is expected of them that they do not and cannot achieve on their own. Practicing rites of prayer, almsgiving, and submission to Allah represents a turning from sin and the threat of punishment and makes room for Allah the All-Merciful to show mercy.

Religious communities that either do not witness to God or gods, such as Buddhism, or where deity is represented by various supernatural beings, as in Hinduism, will not speak in terms of a covenant with a merciful God that humans choose to follow or break. Thus in Buddhism, which cannot connect human evil with a covenanting God because there is no witness to God, the concern is to deal with negative forces and actions, summarized in the term *karma*. Individual actions are measured in the light of whether the intention of an act was positive or negative, with the goal of dealing with suffering, which is a universal human experience, by disciplines and practices that in their intention make room for good and positive karma and actions.

In Hinduism there is also no covenant with the one God (monotheism) or original sin, yet there are also prescribed paths for conduct pleasing to the deities adored in Hinduism. In Hinduism, as well as most other faiths, there are actions equivalent to atoning ones in monotheistic faiths, actions that through conduct and proper ritual or meditation lead one to positive conduct and reward. In almost all faiths atoning activities that counter sin or bad karma have positive rewards in this life and, in many faiths, in life after death. This is so in Christian resurrection or Hindu reincarnation. In none of the faiths is the realistic note wholly lost. That is, they do not envision a complete overcoming of evil as expressed in human sin but teach ways to live and think in the face of such evil that resides in the external world and in the self.

SEE ALSO *Christianity; Hell; Hinduism; Judaism; Punishment; Purification; Reincarnation; Religion; Supreme Being*

BIBLIOGRAPHY

Häring, Bernard. 1974. *Sin in the Secular Age.* Garden City, NY: Doubleday.

Park, Andrew Sung. 1993. *The Wounded Heart of God: The Asian Concept of Han and the Christian Doctrine of Sin.* Nashville, TN: Abingdon.

Rahner, Karl. 1961–1979. Anonymous Christianity. In *Theological Investigations*, vol. 12. Baltimore: Helicon.

Smith, C. Ryder. 1953. *The Bible Doctrine of Sin and of the Ways of God with Sinners.* London: Epworth.

Martin E. Marty

SINGER, HANS
1910–2006

Hans Wolfgang Singer was born on November 29, 1910, in Elberfeld, Germany, into a Jewish family. When the Nazis rose to power, he fled Germany to study at Cambridge University, where he completed a PhD in economics on a refugee scholarship. After a brief academic career, he joined the United Nations (UN). After his extensive work (1947–1969) with the UN, he joined the newly established Institute for Development Studies (IDS) at the University of Sussex. Until his death on February 26, 2006, he maintained his academic contact with IDS.

Singer was widely acclaimed because of his association with the Prebisch-Singer hypothesis. He got the idea while preparing a UN report in 1949. The report was a follow-up of the League of Nations 1945 report noting that during the sixty years preceding 1938, primary product prices had fallen relative to prices of manufactures. On the basis of the UN report, the Argentine economist in charge of the UN Economic Commission for Latin America (ECLA), Raul Prebisch, and Singer raised the issue of declining terms-of-trade of primary products and

the primary-producing less developed countries (LDCs) vis-à-vis manufactures and the manufacture-exporting developed countries (DCs). They questioned the dominant classical policy prescription of free trade and international division of labor according to the Ricardian dictum of comparative advantages.

The Prebisch-Singer hypothesis was virtually discarded in mainstream economics in the face of strong statistical objections against it. Nevertheless, Singer continued to believe it to be a fact, although he did not necessarily know how to go about proving it. In 1986 the economist Prabirjit Sarkar provided a strong statistical support in favor of it. This encouraged Singer to collaborate with Sarkar to work further in this field, which led in 1991 to the Sarkar-Singer extension of the hypothesis in the field of manufacture exports of the LDCs to pay for their manufacture imports from the DCs. This extension provided a further support to the Prebisch-Singer hypothesis, particularly its core that is primarily concerned with the relationships between types of *countries* (unequal relationships between the LDCs and the DCs)—not just with the relationships between types of *commodities* (primary products and manufactures). In the process it has become more relevant to the early twenty-first century world with increasing trade of manufactures between the LDCs and the DCs.

Throughout his life Singer maintained a voluminous flow of professional publications on all aspects of development—from long-term trends in prices to short-term commodity price instability, food security, and welfare of children. He advocated food aid, concessional loans for the development and management of the affairs of debt-ridden LDCs.

Singer was a follower of the original scheme of the English economist John Maynard Keynes regarding the then future world economic system tabled at the Bretton Woods Conference (1944) for its consideration. He shared Keynes's concern for commodity price stability for the sake of stability of the world economy. Like Keynes, he believed that surplus and deficit in balance of payments were two sides of the same coin, and so both sides should bear the burden of adjustment in balance of payments disequilibrium. But the system that came up with the International Monetary Fund (IMF) and the World Bank penalizes the deficit countries in spite of their role in increasing effective demand and thereby promoting world output and employment. He identified this as one major cause of the agony of the LDCs. He was critical of the neoliberal one-size-fit-for-all policy prescriptions of the IMF and World Bank for the debt-ridden LDCs. He anticipated much of the writings of the dissident World Bank economist Joseph Stiglitz on the discontents of globalization.

SEE ALSO *Prebisch, Raúl; Prebisch-Singer Hypothesis; Terms of Trade*

BIBLIOGRAPHY

League of Nations. 1945. *Industrialization and Foreign Trade.* Geneva: Author.

Sarkar, Prabirjit. 1986. The Singer-Prebisch Hypothesis: A Statistical Evaluation. *Cambridge Journal of Economics* 10: 355–371.

Sarkar, Prabirjit, and Hans Singer. 1991. Manufactured Exports of Developing Countries and Their Terms of Trade since 1965. *World Development* 19: 333–340.

Sarkar, Prabirjit, and Hans Singer. 1992. *Debt Crisis, Commodity Prices, Transfer Burden, and Debt Relief.* Discussion Paper no. 2 97. Sussex, U.K.: IDS, University of Sussex.

United Nations. 1949. *Relative Prices of Exports and Imports of Under-developed Countries.* New York: Author.

Prabirjit Sarkar

SINGH, V. P.
1931–

V. P. Singh is a senior leader of the Janata Dal political party. He was a cabinet minister in the Janata Party–led central government of India from 1977 to 1980, and later he was prime minister of India briefly in 1989–1990.

Born in 1931, V. P. Singh came from a north Indian aristocratic Hindu princely family. His political rise began when Prime Minister Indira Gandhi picked him to be the chief minister of the Hindi-speaking state of Uttar Pradesh, India's most populous state. When Rajiv Gandhi won an overwhelming victory in the 1984 national elections, Singh was appointed finance minister by the new prime minister. Known for his honesty and courage, Singh began to crack down on corruption, alienating a number of wealthy supporters of Rajiv Gandhi and the Congress Party. As finance minister, he began investigations into various defense procurements, including allegations of bribes and payoffs in the Swedish Bofors gun purchase contract that threatened to expose even Prime Minister Rajiv Gandhi. Because he was a Congress Party member of the Lok Sabha (the lower house of parliament) since 1971, and then prime minister of India from 1989 to 1990, he was instrumental in implementing the recommendations of the Mandal Commission.

Singh was dismissed from his post and subsequently left the Congress Party. He started a new party called the Jan Morcha, which later merged with the Janata Party, the Lok Dal, and the Congress Party's socialist faction to form a new party called the Janata Dal. The Janata Dal forged a coalition with the Bharatiya Janata Party (BJP) on the right and the Communist Party on the left and defeated the Congress Party in the 1989 general elections. After various political struggles among the coalition groups, Singh was asked to take the mantle of prime minister of India. His minority Janata Party government was dependent on support in parliament from the Congress Party and the Communist Party. When the Congress Party withdrew its support, the Singh government fell.

Singh was known for his promotion of just causes, calling for justice for Muslims in Kashmir and Sikhs in Punjab while maintaining the territorial integrity of India. After serving as prime minister for less than a year, he faded from state and national politics, especially when he was diagnosed with cancer, which remained in remission in early 2007.

SEE ALSO *Caste; Congress Party, India; Ethnic Conflict; Ethnic Fractionalization; Gandhi, Indira; Janata Party; Quota Systems*

BIBLIOGRAPHY

Chand, Attar. 1990. *V. P. Singh and His Politics: New Challenges.* Delhi, India: Batra Book Service.

Mustafa, Seema. 1995. *The Lonely Prophet: V. P. Singh, A Political Biography.* Delhi, India: New Age International.

Shourie, Arun. 1991. *The State as Charade: V. P. Singh, Chandra Shekhar, and the Rest.* New Delhi, India: Roli Books.

Suri, Surindar. 1990. *The Rise of V. P. Singh and the 1989 and 1990 Elections.* New Delhi: Konark Publishers.

Raju G. C. Thomas

SINGLE MOTHERS
SEE *Female-Headed Families.*

SINN FEIN
SEE *Irish Republican Army.*

SISTERHOOD
SEE *Feminism, Second Wave; Women's Liberation.*

SIT-INS
SEE *Civil Rights Movement, U.S..*

SITTING BULL
1831–1890

Sitting Bull was most likely born in the winter of 1831 at Many Caches, along the Grand River near present-day Bullhead, South Dakota. Originally named Jumping Badger, he was the son of a Hunkpapa Lakota chief, Tatanka Iyotanka (Sitting Bull), and Her Holy Door. The son would become one of the most famous American Indian leaders in history, a great war chief and spiritual leader who earned lasting fame as the man most responsible for the defeat of Colonel George Armstrong Custer at the Battle of Little Big Horn in 1876.

After counting his first coup at the age of fourteen, Jumping Badger received his father's name, Sitting Bull. He early established himself as a courageous warrior and a highly skilled hunter. He also earned the status of a *wichasha wakan*, or holy man, who could interpret visions and dreams from the spirits. He was also known for his generosity and for his devotion to family members. All of these qualities collectively earned him widespread esteem and helped him to rise to the position of perhaps the most revered Indian leader of the Plains.

As the United States government sought to force tribes onto reservations, Sitting Bull increasingly came to represent, for both Indian and Euro-American, resistance to United States expansion into the Plains. However, he adopted a defensive strategy, fighting only when he perceived a clear threat to his people.

That strategy worked reasonably well until 1876 when General Alfred H. Terry led an expedition against Sitting Bull's camp. Terry's plan was for Colonel John Gibbon (accompanied by Terry) and the Seventh Cavalry under Custer to converge simultaneously on the camp from different directions.

By late June, seven thousand or more Lakotas and Cheyennes had joined his village, and Sitting Bull's vision in which he saw soldiers falling upside down into the camp had helped convince his people of their coming victory. In addition, a successful battle against General George Crook's troops along the Rosebud River in southeastern Montana had further bolstered their confidence.

When Custer arrived at Sitting Bull's encampment along the Little Big Horn, he chose not to wait for Terry and Gibbon. Instead, he attacked on June 25 after further eroding his chance for victory by dividing his forces. Custer and everyone with him died in what would become perhaps the most famous defeat in U.S. military history and be immortalized as Custer's Last Stand.

A lingering controversy regarding Sitting Bull's role in the battle originated with accusations by Gall, a rival of Sitting Bull's, that the Hunkpapa chief was not present during the battle and played no role in it. Historians now agree that Gall was wrong.

The victory for Sitting Bull was short-lived. Faced with a relentless pursuit by Colonel Nelson Miles, Sitting Bull made his way to Canada, arriving in May 1877. Finally, he surrendered to U.S. officials at Fort Buford in northwestern Dakota Territory on July 20, 1881. He spent most of his remaining years on Standing Rock Reservation, located in central North and South Dakota.

For about four months in 1885, Sitting Bull toured with Buffalo Bill Cody's Wild West Show. During this time, he befriended the young shooting specialist Annie Oakley.

By 1890, a mystical ceremony known as the Ghost Dance was spreading across reservations. Proponents believed that the dance would reverse time, removing soldiers from the land, bringing the buffalo back, and restoring the Indian way of life.

Questions have lingered regarding Sitting Bull's attitude toward the Ghost Dance. He seemed to believe that the new religion might possess some truth and had encouraged the dance at Standing Rock while not participating himself. Perhaps to test the validity of the dance, he was planning a trip to Pine Ridge Reservation in southwestern South Dakota, a hotbed of Ghost Dance activism. Officials grew concerned that Sitting Bull might use the movement as a means to stir up resistance, even war, against the government.

To prevent Sitting Bull from leaving, James McLaughlin, the Standing Rock agent, ordered his arrest. Early in the morning of December 15, 1890, a contingent of Lakota police arrived at his cabin. As they attempted to arrest Sitting Bull, supporters came to his defense. Violence soon erupted, and Sitting Bull was shot twice, the second time in the head, and killed. As historians learned more about his life, Sitting Bull gradually emerged during the twentieth century as a great American leader—a complex man who did much more than defeat the Seventh Cavalry at Little Big Horn.

SEE ALSO *Battle of the Little Big Horn; Mysticism; Native Americans; Resistance*

BIBLIOGRAPHY

Gray, John S. 1976. *Centennial Campaign: The Sioux War of 1876.* Ft. Collins, CO: Old Army Press.

Utley, Robert M. 1994. *The Lance and the Shield: The Life and Times of Sitting Bull.* New York: Ballantine Books.

Vestal, Stanley. 1989. *Sitting Bull: Champion of the Sioux.* 2nd ed. Norman: University of Oklahoma Press. (Orig. pub. 1957.)

Edward J. Rielly

SIX-DAY WAR

SEE *Arab-Israeli War of 1967.*

SKEWNESS

SEE *Descriptive Statistics.*

SKILL

Skill is usually understood as an ability to do something well, either manually, mentally, or both. In contrast to terms that denote only potential for acquiring some ability (such as natural ability, talent, aptitude, or capacity), the term *skill* usually means actual competence that has been acquired by training, schooling, or practice. The concept is used in several disciplines (most importantly economics, sociology, psychology, education, and ergonomics), has many meanings, and is applied for different purposes and in a variety of contexts.

The term *skill* is used mainly to refer to (1) a level of individual performance, in the sense of accuracy and speed in performing particular tasks, or (2) qualities required for successful performance in particular jobs and tasks. Economists and educational psychologists tend to use the concept of skill in the first sense: to describe the abilities acquired by an individual such as a worker, which may include cognitive skills, manual dexterity, knowledge, and social skills. These researchers often take skill as an independent variable and use it, for example, in predicting wage levels. In sociology, on the contrary, skills are often taken as qualities required of a particular job, in terms of the range and complexity of the tasks involved, level of discretion over work and time, and the knowledge and training needed to learn the job. Many sociologists thus view skill as a dependent variable and try to explain variations in the level of skill within occupations, economies, and/or over time. For analysis of changing skills levels over time, the historical example of craft workers often stands as a benchmark.

Although *skill* has always been a somewhat ambiguous and rarely precisely defined term, in the past it had a much narrower meaning than today. It tended to be equated with craft, technical know-how, and manual dexterity. Gradually, however, the importance of mental qualities was acknowledged and motor skills and cognitive skills were distinguished. While motor skills require voluntary body movement to achieve a goal, cognitive skills do not involve muscular movement and involve activities such as problem solving, memory, or reading (Tomporowski 2003). More recently, the concept of skill was further broadened. In addition to "hard skills" (both

motor and cognitive), the importance of "soft skills" was underlined. They include effective communication, creativity, flexibility, change readiness, leadership, team building, and so on. Much discussion has also been given to the distinction between "generic" (also "transferable" or "key") skills on the one hand and occupational or job-specific skills on the other. While occupation-specific skills have value only in one particular sector or industry, generic skills have value in a number of sectors. The tendency to re-label as skills personal traits and attitudes and to term many concrete and abstract human dispositions as "skills" further broadened and blurred the concept.

THEORIES

In social theories, the concept of skill is usually linked to the labor market, education, and technology. Authors, however, differ fundamentally on the role skills are supposed to play. The origins of the skill concept are often connected with Karl Marx. The dominant interpretation of Marx's work suggests that capitalists, through mechanization of labor and the manufacturing system, reduced skills requirement to increase productivity and profits and to increase control over workers and work organization. This line of reasoning was followed in so-called de-skilling theory, assuming a process of job degradation (Braverman 1974). In sharp contrast, the thesis of postindustrial and/or knowledge societies posits a general upgrading of skills and stresses the growing importance of cognitive skills. Human capital theory also stresses the importance of knowledge and skills to economic performance and assumes that employers adjust earnings to reflect both skills and educational attainment. Workers with scarce skills are supposed to obtain better-paid and more secure jobs than those without them, and skills and education are assumed to be highly correlated. In contrast, credential theory (Collins 1979) views education as a biased indicator of skill and asserts that colleges function more as a rationing device in job allocation than as skills provider. Educational credentials are supposed to be a much more important determiner of labor force reward than skill.

Theoretical positions also differ in the extent to which skill level is supposed to be objective or socially constructed (Spenner 1990). Neoclassical demand-side perspectives (for example, the theory of the firm) as well as supply-side perspectives (such as human capital theory) tend to take the nature of skills as objective, determined by market mechanisms and the logics of efficiency and return on capital. An opposing view is that skill level is not an objective phenomenon but a social construct. Occupations and jobs are labeled as skilled, semiskilled, or unskilled on the basis of custom and practice, such as union negotiation or job regulation. The most direct method of enhancing an occupation's power is to remove itself from market competition (so-called social closure), establishing a monopoly over some tasks and thus gaining the ability to increase the price of services and therefore prestige (Attewell 1990). Occupations that can restrict entry, require a lengthy period of training, and remove themselves linguistically from lay language (consider Latin in medicine or slang in many professions) can create a public perception of work that requires exceptional knowledge and skill. In contrast, certain types of work may thus objectively require a high level of technical skill but go unrewarded in the labor market.

APPROACHES TO MEASUREMENT

From the epistemological point of view, positivists and ethnomethodologists can be determined (Attewell 1990). Positivists treat skill as an attribute that has an objective character independent of the observer and is amenable to more or less objective measurement. They also reflect the Cartesian division of intellect and body and regard the former as superior. Skill is acquired when one achieves knowledge about general and abstract principles and rules that are context free. Not surprisingly, they take cognitive skills, especially the most complex and abstract ones, as higher-level skills. In sharp contrast, ethnomethodologists suggest that all human activities, even the most mundane such as walking or carrying on a conversation, are quite complex and require a complex coordination of perception, movement, and decision. Because these mundane activities are extraordinarily complicated, they cannot be attended consciously. Conscious reflection of activity is thus an indication of incomplete learning rather than mastery. Skill means the ability to do things without thinking about them. A master's skills are not based on conscious, abstract, and context-free knowledge but rather on tacit and context-bound knowledge. In consequence, ethnomethodologists consider abstract rules as being at a much lower level of skill and challenge positivist and quantitative approach to measuring skills.

Empirical research on skills usually follows the positivist approach. Based on the distinction between skill as an individual competence and as a job requirement, skill supply and skill demand measures are usually distinguished. Both skill supply and skill demand can be measured both directly and indirectly. As for skill demand (that is, skill requirements of jobs), direct measures involve (1) job classification based on some kind of external judgment, and (2) self-reported (by the jobholder) requirements. Indirect measures include the average or typical education among job incumbents. Because of lack of data, many researchers use indirect measurement or infer skill demand from data on skill supply (usually education) and wages. This approach, however, has an important limitation—it conflates the supply and demand sides of skill

(workers and jobs). Many studies have found that education, skill, and labor reward are not equivalent concepts and that their interchangeability precludes testing of the various theories stated earlier. Thus, direct measures of skills requirements, though not without problems, are preferred. The most widely used direct measures of skill demands are occupational schemas, such as the American Dictionary of Occupational Titles (DOT). As for skill supply (workers' skills), only indirect measures are usually available. These include the sum of years of vocational or formal education, years of on-the-job experience, or wage rates. In the 1990s large-scale international surveys such as International Adult Literacy Survey (IALS) were introduced, allowing direct and international measurement of cognitive skills (OECD 2000).

IMPLICATIONS

The concept of skill must be always used with care, and one must bear in mind that different theoretical approaches define and measure skills in quite different ways, especially since skill theory and measurement have several fundamental and direct policy implications. From the policy point of view it is important to know (1) whether capitalism and/or new technologies are de-skilling or up-skilling work, how skills needs change over time, and what skills will be needed in the future; (2) how much (and what type) of education is needed in the labor market and what causes skills mismatches; (3) to what extent unequal labor force rewards are determined by education, skills, or discrimination; (4) how skills are distributed within and between countries, and whether the distribution is increasingly polarized; (5) how skills are created in different education and training systems; (6) how to measure and classify skills in a standard way to ensure labor mobility and qualification recognition; (7) what type of skills are needed in nonmarket relationships, such as family or community; and (8) to what extent education should provide students with generic or specific skills. Because the concept of skill is difficult to define and started to be measured directly only very recently, it is not possible to give a definite answer to any of these eight questions. Analyses done so far (e.g., Kerckhoff, Raudenbush, and Glennie 2001), however, confirmed that skill is not a redundant term but an empirically independent factor, one that needs to be taken as a separate theoretical construct.

SEE ALSO *Credentialism; Knowledge Society; Labor Market; Soft Skills*

BIBLIOGRAPHY

Attewell, Paul. 1990. What Is Skill. *Work and Occupations* 17 (4): 422–448.

Braverman, Harry. 1974. *Labor and Monopoly Capital: The Degradation of Work in the Twentieth Century.* New York and London: Monthly Review Press.

Collins, Randall. 1979. *The Credential Society: An Historical Sociology of Education and Stratification.* New York: Academic Press.

Kerckhoff, Alan C., Stephen W. Raudenbush, and Elizabeth Glennie. 2001. Education, Cognitive Skill, and Labor Force Outcomes. *Sociology of Education* 74 (1): 1–24.

OECD and Statistics Canada. 2000. *Literacy in the Information Age: Final Report of the International Adult Literacy Survey.* Paris: Organisation for Economic Co-operation and Development/Statistics Canada.

Spenner, Kenneth I. 1990. "Skill: Meanings, Methods, and Measures." *Work and Occupations* 17 (4): 399–421.

Tomporowski, Phillip D. 2003. *The Psychology of Skill: A Life-Span Approach.* Westport, CT: Praeger.

Arnost Vesely

SKINNER, B. F.
1904–1990

B. F. Skinner, an American psychologist, provided the experimental foundations of contemporary behavior analysis and its applications. He introduced the terminology of operant behavior and elaborated on the concept of reinforcement. He interpreted verbal behavior in terms of those foundations and was outspoken about the differences between the methods of behavior analysis and those of cognitive psychology. His contributions provided the foundations for extensions to a variety of applications both within and outside of psychology (e.g., education, psychopharmacology, behavioral economics).

Born on March 20, 1904, in Susquehanna, Pennsylvania, Burrhus Frederic Skinner (later known mostly as B. F.) grew up while the inventions of Thomas Edison and others were changing life in small-town America. From an early age, Skinner was a tinkerer, building gadgets and devices. At Hamilton College, he majored in English, also taking courses in science and philosophy. He sent some short stories to Robert Frost after graduation. Frost's reply encouraged him to take a year off from academic pursuits to try a career in writing. But Skinner concluded that he had nothing to say and called the time his "dark year."

Having read Pavlov and others, Skinner turned from English to psychology and entered the doctoral program at Harvard University, where he began experiments on the behavior of rats that led to more than two dozen journal articles and culminated in his 1938 book, *The Behavior of Organisms.* In 1936 he moved to the University of Minnesota, where he continued basic research. World War II occasioned a project on training pigeons to guide missiles that got only to the point of a demonstration of feasibility, but a fringe benefit was the discovery of shaping, a technique for teaching new behavior. One other consequence was that pigeons began to replace rats as the dominant organism of the operant laboratory.

Another product of those days was the Aircrib, which Skinner built for his wife and second daughter. The windowed space with temperature and humidity control improved on the safety and comfort of ordinary cribs while making child care less burdensome. Rumors to the contrary, it was not used for experiments with the infant. Skinner noted that there was nothing natural about standard cribs; he had simply invented a better one.

In 1945 Skinner became Chair of the Department of Psychology at Indiana University. After his 1947 William James Lectures at Harvard University, on verbal behavior, he returned permanently to Harvard. His 1948 novel, *Walden Two,* which at first received little notice but later became widely read, described a utopia the most important feature of which was its experimental character: Any practice that did not work was to be modified until a more effective substitute was found.

Meanwhile, at Columbia College, Fred S. Keller and W. N. Schoenfeld created an undergraduate psychology curriculum based on Skinner's work, including a one-year introductory course with a laboratory. With research now located at several universities, meetings of those interested in behavior analysis became a series of annual conferences. Eventually a formal division for the Experimental Analysis of Behavior (Division 25) was established within the American Psychological Association. During those years, while the Harvard Pigeon Laboratory provided students of operant behavior opportunities to develop their own independent lines of research, Skinner created the subject matter of reinforcement schedules in collaboration with Charles B. Ferster and built the first of his teaching machines. Soon after, Keller began his innovations in college teaching that introduced self-paced courses and behavioral definitions of teaching objectives. The *Journal of the Experimental Analysis of Behavior* began publication in 1958; within a decade, the increased activity in applications of operant theory led to a companion journal, the *Journal of Applied Behavior Analysis.*

In 1953, in his book *Science and Human Behavior,* Skinner dropped the formal structures of his early theorizing, modeled after theory in the physical sciences, and made the ties to biology explicit in his many references to evolutionary contingencies. He also began explicitly to extend the principles of his early research to human behavior. Here were treatments of self-control as competition between short-term and long-term contingencies involving consequences of different magnitude, of thinking as covert behavior, of reports of private events as verbal behavior shaped by verbal communities that had access only to public correlates, of social behavior, and of selves as functionally organized systems of responses. There was hardly a significant aspect of human endeavor that was not captured in one way or another by the net that Skinner had so widely cast.

Skinner retired from the laboratory in 1962, returning to it only briefly nearly 20 years later, but continued his writing throughout his life. His books include the controversial *Beyond Freedom and Dignity* in 1971, *About Behaviorism* in 1974, and a three-volume autobiography. In *Beyond Freedom and Dignity*, Skinner pointed out that some controversies about freedom result from confusions between two sources of the language of freedom. The issue of freedom versus determinism is a philosophical question with a long history, but the issue of freedom from coercion is an empirical problem that involves the consequences of various social and political practices. In our daily lives, we are typically concerned not so much with whether our choices are determined as with how our choices are determined and by whom. Doing something at the point of a gun is different from doing it under other circumstances.

Skinner learned of his leukemia in 1989. On August 10, 1990, at his final public appearance, he accepted a Lifetime Achievement Award from the American Psychological Association. His remarks criticized cognitive science as the creationism of the twentieth century, in that it sought causes of behavior inside the organism instead of in the organism's environment. A week later, in hospital, Skinner put finishing touches on his last journal article, "Can psychology be a science of mind?," for the *American Psychologist*. He died the next day, August 18, 1990. His last word, upon receiving a drink of water, was "Marvelous."

THE ANALYSIS OF BEHAVIOR

Skinner followed Pavlov in insisting on the primacy of data and the study of individuals rather than groups but diverged from Pavlov in many ways. For Skinner, behavior was not to be taken as a symptom of something else. As interaction between organism and environment, it should be studied in its own right, not to resolve problems of physiology or to open the way to cognitive or other levels of analysis. Skinner did not disapprove of physiology but argued that without a science of behavior neuroscientists would not know what to look for in the nervous system.

In Pavlovian conditioning, a conditional stimulus comes to produce responses related to those elicited by an unconditional stimulus. The prototypical example is the elicitation of salivation by some stimulus that consistently

precedes food. In Skinner's operant behavior, the contingencies are different: A stimulus sets the occasion on which responses have some consequence; absent that stimulus, responses do not do so. The prototypical example is the rat whose lever presses produce food only in the presence of a light. The rat comes to press the lever only when the light is on. Such stimuli, colloquially called signals or cues, do not elicit responses; instead, they set the occasions on which responses have consequences. Such behavior, called operant because it operates on the environment, does not entail associations or stimulus-response connections. The three-term contingency, in which stimuli set the occasion upon which responding has consequences, is not reducible to pair-wise stimulus and response relations.

Here was a profoundly simple concept: The consequences of current behavior reinforce or select the behavior that will occur later. Associationism had been replaced by selectionism. Reinforcement operates on populations of responses within individual lifetimes much as evolutionary selection operates on populations over successive generations in Darwinian natural selection. The populations, operants, are classes of responses defined by their effects rather than by what they look like (Skinner also considered implications of a third variety of selection, sometimes called cultural or memetic selection, that occurs when behavior is passed on from one organism to another, as in imitation).

Shaping, which creates novel behavior through reinforcement of responses that successively approximate it, illustrates reinforcement as selection. For example, if the strongest of a rat's initially weak lever presses are reinforced, the force of pressing increases and the reinforcement criterion can be moved up to the strongest of the new population. With continuing force increases and criterion changes, the rat soon presses with forces that would never have been observed without shaping. Shaping opened up education, developmental disabilities, behavioral medicine and even the training of pets to applications of behavior analysis. When research produced variable results, solutions were sought not by averaging over more subjects but by refining procedural details to identify sources of variability. The applied analysis of behavior is recognized for both effectiveness and accountability; treatment of early autism is among its several notable successes.

The discovery that behavior could be maintained easily even when responses were reinforced only occasionally led to schedules of reinforcement, which arrange reinforcers based on number of responses, the times when they occur, or various combinations of these and other variables. Different schedules produce different temporal patterns of responding. A device that Skinner called the cumulative recorder allowed these temporal patterns to be visualized in considerable detail. Schedules are now used widely in studies ranging from psychopharmacology to behavioral economics.

VERBAL BEHAVIOR

In his 1957 book, *Verbal Behavior*, Skinner extended his analyses to the functions of words. His approach differs from linguistics, the study of language, in that linguists describe practices of verbal communities in terms of the grammars, vocabularies, and phonetic units characterizing different languages; these descriptions of language structure tell little about their functions. This behavioral distinction is analogous to that between physiology (function) and anatomy (structure) in biology. Behavior analysis, following from Skinner's work, deals mainly with function (i.e., how does behavior work, what does it do), whereas cognitive science deals more often with structure (e.g., organization in what is perceived or learned).

Skinner's book was mainly about language function. A critical 1959 review by the linguist Noam Chomsky was more concerned with language structure than with the functional content of Skinner's account. *Verbal Behavior* provided a taxonomy of function rather than structure (for example, identifying verbal classes by their effects rather than by their topographies), applying it to a broad range of verbal phenomena. Later expansions extended the taxonomy to the origins of novelty in verbal behavior. Skinner did not reply to Chomsky's review because it had missed the point, but unfortunately some interpreted his failure to reply as a sign that he could not do so. Skinner and others addressed Chomsky's review only long after.

One function of verbal behavior is instruction; people often do things because they are instructed to do them. Following instructions has social consequences and is crucial to many social institutions—families, schools, industry, the military—so it is important to understand not only how instructions work but also how they can go wrong (e.g., as in following unethical orders without question). Skinner called behavior that depended on words rule-governed behavior, though it is now more often called verbally governed behavior. In verbal governance, what we say about what we do often determines what we do. Contemporary analyses of verbal behavior include experimental studies of how verbal governance comes about and the conditions under which it occurs.

BEHAVING AND KNOWING (BEHAVIOR AND COGNITION)

Skinner's analyses were also about how we come to know ourselves. We think we have privileged access to private events such as feelings and thoughts, but how do we learn to talk about them? Parents who see the colors that a child sees can respond appropriately to the child's color naming and so can teach the names, but how can a verbal community without access to relevant stimuli create and maintain verbal responses? In referred pain, a bad tooth in the lower jaw may be reported as a toothache in the upper jaw; here the dentist is a better judge than the patient of where the bad tooth really is. If we can be mistaken even about the location of a toothache, how can other reports of private events be reliable?

Skinner did not deny the private, but noted that common vocabularies can be based only on what is mutually accessible to both speakers and listeners. If private feelings do not have public correlates, how can one tell when anyone else has them? If one cannot tell, how can one ever teach appropriate words? This is a problem because much of the language of cognitive thought originates in the vocabulary of private events.

According to Skinner, processes called cognitive (e.g., thinking, visualizing) are kinds of behavior. Skinner did not deny events taking place inside the skin, but maintained that they should be called private rather than mental. When Skinner criticized representations in cognitive psychology, the issue was not whether lasting effects are produced by stimuli (an organism that has responded to a stimulus is a changed organism). Rather, it was about the form the change takes. Skinner opposed copy theories of behavior or perception. A representation is not necessarily a copy (a spoken letter may represent a seen one but has no visual properties in common with it), so it is of interest that the most successful cognitive accounts do not involve representations that function as copies. In this regard, behavior analysis shares its views with cognitive scientists who are advocates of neural nets and connectionist systems.

SEE ALSO *Behaviorism; Cognition; Determinism; Linguistic Turn; Operant Conditioning; Pavlov, Ivan; Reinforcement Theories; Skinner Box*

BIBLIOGRAPHY

Lattal, Kennon A., ed. 1992. Reflections on B. F. Skinner and Psychology. *American Psychologist* 47: 1269–1533.

Skinner, B. F. 1938. *The Behavior of Organisms.* New York: Appleton-Century-Crofts.

Skinner, B. F. 1957. *Verbal Behavior.* New York: Appleton-Century-Crofts.

Skinner, B. F. 1990. Can Psychology Be a Science of Mind? *American Psychologist* 45: 1206–1210.

Skinner, B. F. 1999. *Cumulative Record.* 4th ed. Acton, MA: B. F. Skinner Foundation.

A. Charles Catania

SKINNER BOX

In behavioral studies, researchers study the relationship between environmental events and measures of a target behavior, termed a *respondent* (in classical conditioning) or *free operant* (in operant conditioning). In the 1930s, as B. F. Skinner was developing the laws of operant conditioning, he constructed an apparatus, technically called an *operant chamber* but popularly known as a "Skinner box," that deprives an animal of all external stimuli other than those under the control of the experimenter (Skinner 1935). Generally, a Skinner box is soundproof and light-resistant, and usually contains a bar or lever to be pressed by the animal to either gain a reward or avoid a painful stimulus. An operant chamber allows the researcher to experimentally manipulate environmental stimuli and measure their impact on operant behavior. Additionally, the use of the chamber allows data on the animal's responses to be monitored and collected electromechanically twenty-four hours a day, seven days a week, thus eliminating the need for an external observer to record behavior.

Employed for more than seventy years in basic operant research, the operant chamber recently has been used to study topics such as how previous conditioning influences the acquisition of new responses under delayed and immediate reinforcement (Snycerski, Laraway, Huitema, and Poling 2004); discrimination training (Nevin, Davison, and Shahan 2005); how drugs affect responding (Pinkston and Branch 2004); concurrent schedules (Sealey, Sumpter, Temple, and Foster 2005); and sophisticated data analysis techniques (e.g., Li and Huston 2002).

Although there have been organized contests to train a rat to complete a series of complex activities using live animals and an operant chamber (Banister-Marx 1996), maintaining an animal laboratory with operant chambers is expensive, and often beyond the resources of those not engaged in ongoing research programs. As a result, researchers have developed software such as "Sniffy the Virtual Rat" (Alloway, Willson, and Graham 2005) to simulate how schedules of reinforcement and extinction effect responding. Another software simulation program allows students to learn to modify a bird's behavior (Hay 2004). Nick Yee suggests that role-playing games such as "EverQuest" have all the elements of a virtual Skinner box (2001a, 2001b).

The Skinner box is sometimes confused with the baby tender, a device Skinner developed to provide one of his infant daughters with a comfortable, protective environment in which to sleep (Skinner 1945). The rumor that Skinner left his infant daughter in the device for such long periods of time that she was traumatized and later committed suicide in her twenties is completely untrue—in fact, Deborah Skinner Buzan wrote an article in 2004 about the myth (Buzan 2004). Nevertheless, the story has continued to circulate and is included in an historical account of major events in psychology (Slater 2004).

SEE ALSO *Behaviorism; Classical Conditioning; Operant Conditioning; Pavlov, Ivan; Reinforcement Theories; Skinner, B. F.*

BIBLIOGRAPHY

Alloway, Tom, Greg Wilson, Jeff Graham, Lester Krames. 2000. *Sniffy the Virtual Rat: Pro Version 2.0.* Belmont, CA: Thomson Wadsworth.

Banister-Marx, John. 1996. The Annual Skinner Box Rat Training Competition. The National Health Museum. http://www.accessexcellence.org/AE/AEC/AEF/1996/banister-marx_rat.html.

Buzan, Deborah Skinner. 2004. I Was Not a Lab Rat. *Guardian,* March 12.

Hay, John. 2004. Operant Conditioning: Programmable. University of Maryland University College, PsycLab Online. http://pantherfile.uwm.edu/johnchay/PL06/OC/OC.html.

Li, Jay-Shake, and Joseph Huston. 2002. Nonlinear Dynamics of Operant Behavior: A New Approach Via the Extended Return Map. *Reviews of the Neurosciences* 13 (1): 31–57.

Nevin, John A., Michael Davison, and Timothy A. Shahan. 2005. A Theory of Attending and Reinforcement in Conditional Discriminations. *Journal of the Experimental Analysis of Behavior* 84: 281–303.

Pinkston, Jonathan W., and Marc N. Branch. 2004. Repeated Post- or Presession Cocaine Administration: Roles of Dose and Fixed-Ratio Schedule. *Journal of Experimental Analysis of Behavior* 81: 169–188.

Sealey, Diane M., Catherine E. Sumpter, W. Temple, and T. Mary Foster. 2005. Concurrent Second-Order Schedules: Some Effects of Variations in Response Number and Duration. *Journal of the Experimental Analysis of Behavior* 84: 19–35.

Skinner, B. F. 1935. Two Types of Conditioned Reflex and a Pseudo Type. *Journal of General Psychology* 12: 66–77.

Skinner, B. F. 1945. Baby in a Box. *Ladies' Home Journal* (October): 30–31, 135–136, 138.

Slater, Lauren. 2004. *Opening Skinner's Box: Great Psychological Experiments of the Twentieth Century.* New York: Norton.

Snycerski, Susan, Sean Laraway, Bradley E. Huitema, and Alan Poling. 2004. The Effects of Behavioral History on Response Acquisition with Immediate and Delayed Reinforcement. *Journal of Experimental Analysis of Behavior* 81 (1): 51–64.

Yee, Nick. 2001a. The Norrathian Scrolls. http://www.nickyee.com/eqt/home.html.

Yee, Nick. 2001b. The Virtual Skinner Box. http://www.nickyee.com/eqt/skinner.html.

William G. Huitt
John H. Hummel

SKOCPOL, THEDA
1947–

Victor S. Thomas Professor of Government and Sociology and director of the Center for American Political Studies at Harvard University, Theda Skocpol was president of the American Political Science Association (2001–2003) and of the Social Science History Association (1996). She has made major contributions to historical and comparative sociology and to political science in her work on revolutions. Her theory of revolutions and the state has been influenced by the approach of sociologist and political scientist Barrington Moore (1913–2005) in his *Social Origins of Dictatorship and Democracy* (1966).

In *Vision and Method in Historical Sociology* (1984), Skocpol advocated the use of secondary data and sources to undertake macrohistorical and comparative work—an approach that she pioneered in her major work, *States and Social Revolutions: A Comparative Analysis of France, Russia, and China* (1979), which received the C. Wright Mills Award of the Society for the Study of Social Problems, as well as the American Sociological Association Award for a Distinguished Contribution to Scholarship. With this work, Skocpol produced a distinctive theory of revolution through the study of three *anciens régimes*. Skocpol argued that revolutions occur because states are exposed to endogenous socioeconomic processes, particularly class conflict. Her theory rejects any significant role for human agency in such revolutions. They are not produced by the revolutionary will of revolutionaries themselves, but they are the unintended consequence of the decomposition of the state system and its agrarian bureaucracy. Skocpol examined the causal constraints—class relations, the repressive character of the state, and the external military—on state activities resulting from objective historical circumstances. The distinctive aspect of her initial theory was to reject any attempt to absorb the state into society, since the repressive actions of the state have independent causal consequences for revolutions.

Skocpol conducted research on the historical origins of American social policy in *Social Policy in the United States: Future Possibilities in Historical Perspective* (1995), *Protecting Soldiers and Mothers: The Political Origins of Social Policy in the United States* (1992), and *The Missing Middle: Working Families and the Future of American Social Policy* (2000). In *Diminished Democracy: From Membership to Management in American Civic Life* (2003), Skocpol criticized liberal theories that claim that the vigor of civic life depends on the absence of the state. By contrast, her study of voluntary associations demonstrates that vigorous democratic politics nourish a participatory civil society. She contributed to the study of contemporary political life in *Boomerang: Clinton's Health Security Effort and the Turn Against Government in U.S. Politics*

(1996) and (with Morris P. Fiorina) *Civic Engagement in American Democracy* (1999).

Skocpol's "state autonomy theory" was severely criticized by G. William Domhoff (1996), who claims that she abandoned her original position, increasingly putting emphasis on social movements, women's lobby groups, and voluntary associations in civil society. By contrast, Domhoff argues that support for disability pensions for Civil War veterans is explained by the interests of the corporate community (or capitalists). The differences between welfare provision in the United States and Europe is explained by the strength of the American capitalist class and the racial and ethnic divisions in the American working class.

SEE ALSO *Capitalism; Civil Society; Democracy; Mills, C. Wright; Power Elite; Volunteer Programs; Volunteerism*

BIBLIOGRAPHY

Domhoff, G. William. 1996. *State Autonomy or Class Dominance? Case Studies on Policy Making in America.* Hawthorne, NY: de Gruyter.

Moore, Barrington, Jr. 1966. *Social Origins of Dictatorship and Democracy: Lord and Peasant in the Making of the Modern World.* Boston: Beacon.

Bryan S. Turner

SLAVE LIVES, ARCHAEOLOGY OF

The archaeology of slavery is a branch of historical archaeology focused on the analysis and interpretation of slavery through the use of material remains. The archaeology of slavery was originally referred to as *plantation archaeology* because the excavations were concentrated on former plantations throughout the southern United States. In the early days of plantation archaeology, the primary focus was on the maintenance and promotion of nationally significant historic sites; however, as a result of a movement to develop a deeper understanding of ethnicity and diversity within American society, in the late 1960s there was a shift in the field to include a broader understanding of the lives of enslaved Africans. Archaeological studies of slavery provide information on the living conditions of enslaved people by looking at housing and household composition, diet, personal possessions, household goods, health care, and other aspects of their material world. This subset of historical archaeology is used to understand the human experience of African American life and positively contribute to the ever-expanding notion of black cultural identity. Although the first archaeological sites that focused on slavery were in the southern United States, there has been a great deal of work conducted in other parts of the African diaspora, including such regions as Central and South America and the Caribbean.

THE ARCHAEOLOGY OF RACE AND GENDER

Early archaeological interpretation took its lead from traditional history. Much of the analysis was based on the search for general patterns that reinforced accepted notions of the experience of slavery. These early sites highlighted archaeology as a method to fill in the gaps of historical analysis with the use of artifacts. The archaeology of slavery, however, shifted from a general perspective of plantation life to the examination of specific enslaved communities.

The archaeological study of plantations has begun to employ an anthropological methodology known as *critical theory*. As an ideology, critical theory encourages movement beyond the boundaries of academia into the community. Critical theory is an approach that engages contemporary social issues in various ways. The form of critical analysis used in the archaeology of slavery is a form of activist archaeology that recognizes and supports the role of descendant communities in order for them to retrieve histories from their own perspectives. The archaeology of slavery has become much more visible to the public, and the interpretations and contributions the field makes take into consideration groups of people traditionally marginalized.

The shift toward a more collaborative research methodology that allows archaeology to become a respected voice in public discourses about contemporary notions of race and racism was a direct response to the events surrounding the African Burial Ground project in New York City in the early 1990s. The political struggles between the local African American community and archaeologists marked a turning point in the relationship between the archaeological community and the public. The practice of engaged or activist archaeology became synonymous with the field as a result of this site.

In an effort to understand the lives of enslaved communities, archaeologists investigate the multiple meanings of environment and space. Plantation landscapes often include areas of domestic production, also known as slave quarters, and other sites where the everyday activities of enslaved communities took place. These household-related activities included basic food preparation, childcare and health care, laundry, clothing repair, recreational storytelling, music making, and game playing. These quartering areas ultimately became sites to strengthen social relationships and ensure the survival of the enslaved community.

In 2001 Maria Franklin first proposed a black feminist archaeology that would contribute to a deeper analysis of multiple forms of oppression and pay closer attention to the role of gender by highlighting the unique experience of enslaved women. A black feminist approach emphasizes how gender and race affect a specific community. This approach also demystifies contemporary misconceptions of the role of enslaved women within the household, taking into account the fluid nature of the enslaved family and alternative ways to understand how enslaved women were integral yet not solely responsible to black cultural production. When archaeological investigations of plantation societies during the colonial and antebellum period have focused on households, there is an emphasis on spaces dominated by women. However, enslaved communities performed domestic tasks communally. A gendered approach identifies how enslaved women played an essential role in social and cultural reproduction and acknowledges the role of gender and race in analyzing the multiple forms of oppression experienced by all members of the enslaved community. The result of this methodology inherently serves as a means to produce holistic and politically aware accounts of the African-American past.

ATLANTIC AFRICA AND THE AMERICAS: AFRICAN DIASPORA ARCHAEOLOGY

The archaeology of the African diaspora has expanded the scope of research and established a dialogue between Africa and the Americas during the slave trade era. This dialogue has allowed for a comparative and transnational methodology that produces a new direction in the archaeological interpretation of slavery. Current trends in African diaspora archaeology acknowledge the complexity of how Africans in the Americas negotiated their identities and incorporated aspects of African culture in the African experience throughout the diaspora. Archaeologists also recognize ways in which the diaspora influenced the continent of Africa. Archaeologists therefore, are considering the global dimensions of African cultural transformations throughout the modern era.

The social memory of people of African descent is linked to the experience of slavery, from the way a community shaped its built environment, the material remains of social and cultural activity, and how the distant past acts as the foundation of contemporary notions of black identity. The artifacts, architecture, and archaeological deposits at different sites allow for a close and unique way of looking at the institution of slavery. The archaeology of slavery has moved beyond the boundaries of plantations in the southern United States. After more than twenty years of excavations, the conversation between archaeologists working in the Caribbean, United States, and Western Africa has resulted in an enhanced study of the system of slavery. These links are essential to the future of the field; the things that have been shared between sites across the diaspora and continental Africa have led to a more holistic approach to the study of African people.

SEE ALSO *African American Studies; African Diaspora; African Studies; Archaeology; Burial Grounds; Burial Grounds, African; Collective Memory; Critical Theory; Feminism; Plantation; Slavery*

BIBLIOGRAPHY

Barile, Kerri, and Jamie Brandon, eds. 2004. *Household Chores and Household Choices: Theorizing the Domestic Sphere in Historical Archaeology.* Tuscaloosa: University of Alabama Press.

Conkey, Margaret W., and Sarah H. Williams. 1991. Original Narratives: The Political Economy of Gender in Archaeology. In *Gender at the Crossroads of Knowledge: Feminist Anthropology in the Postmodern Era*, ed. Micaela di Leonardo, 102–139. Berkeley: University of California Press.

Franklin, Maria. 2001. A Black Feminist Inspired Archaeology? *Journal of Social Archaeology* 1 (1): 108–125.

Franklin, Maria, and Larry McKee, eds. 2004. African Diaspora Archaeologies: Present Insights and Expanding Discourses. *Historical Archaeology* 38 (1): 1–9.

Gero, Joan M., and Margaret W. Conkey, eds. 1991. *Engendering Archaeology: Women and Prehistory.* Oxford: Blackwell.

LaRoche, Cheryl, and Michael Blakey. 1997. Seizing Intellectual Power: The Dialogue at the New York African Burial Ground. *Historical Archaeology* 31 (3): 84–104.

McDavid, Carole. 1997. Descendants, Decisions, and Power: The Public Interpretation of the Public Archaeology of the Levi Jordan Plantation. *Historical Archaeology* 31 (3): 114–131.

Orser, Charles E. 1999. The Challenge of Race to American Historical Archaeology. *American Anthropologist* 100 (3): 661–668.

Singleton, Theresa, ed. 1999. *I, Too, Am America: Archaeological Studies of African-American Life.* Charlottesville: University of Virginia Press.

Singleton, Theresa, and Mark Bograd. 1995. *The Archaeology of the African Diaspora in the Americas.* Glassboro, NJ: Society for Historical Archaeology.

Whitney Battle-Baptiste

SLAVE MODE OF PRODUCTION

Although one of the least developed Marxist concepts, slave mode or organization of productive relations has spawned rich intellectual debate. There are four major lines of inquiry. Must the number of productive workers be the dominant form of labor? What is the significance of surplus extraction (profit through exploitation) in the organization of production, and how does it define a social formation? Is there one mode of production or several competing social formations at any one time? What was the historical evolution of the slave mode of production?

Although Karl Marx's primary concern was with the historical evolution of capitalism, not pre-capitalist social formations, he occasionally referred to the slave mode of production. The *German Ideology* identified the first historical form of property as communal, containing within it familial and slave relations (1978, p. 151). The *Communist Manifesto* recognized three forms of class society: capitalist and proletarian during the bourgeois epoch, lord and serf during feudalism, and master and slave during antiquity (1978, p. 474). The *Grundrisse* described the second system of historical development as antiquity characterized by dynamic, urban, warlike conditions, with chattel-slave relations (1965, pp. 36, 71–75). Despite these references, Marx provided little conceptual explanation for the origins and nature of slavery. In contrast to his analysis of the conditions of modern capitalism, he gave little attention to the internal dynamic of the slave mode of production and how this mode rises out of past social formations and dissolves under new historical conditions.

SLAVES IN ANTIQUITY

Unlike Marx, scholars of antiquity have long debated the nature of classical slavery. According to Moses Finley, slavery was insignificant both temporally and geographically in the Greco-Roman world. The dominant labor force produced under various degrees of "unfreedom" in a society with different relations of production. The key question, concludes Finley, is "whether the relations of production were sufficiently different to preclude the inclusion of such societies within a single social formation in which the slave mode of production was dominant" (1991, p. 496). On the one hand, Ellen Meiksins Wood argues that peasant-citizens rather than slaves constituted the productive basis of Athenian democracy and that forms of tenancy, leasing, and management, not slavery, formed the basis for surplus extraction (1988, pp. 64–82). Geoffrey E. M. de Ste. Croix agrees that non-slave producers accounted for the demographic majority during antiquity, but argues that the dominant form of exploitation was slavery because slaves provided the surplus extraction for a wealthy elite. According to Ste. Croix, Marx's concentration on the distinctive feature of society "is not the way in which the bulk of the labour of production is done, but how the extraction of surplus from the immediate producer is secured" (1981, p. 52). It was slavery's increase in surplus extraction that accounts for "the magnificent achievements of Classical civilization" (1981, p. 40). Perry Anderson agrees on the importance of slave surplus extraction during antiquity, although he argues that the imperial state played a more important role in organizing the actual process of extraction (1992, pp. 19–22).

Another key question concerns the historical evolution of ancient slavery into new social formations. Marx simply described the movement of "progressive epochs in the economic formation of society" (1978a, p. 5). In contrast, Ste. Croix explains that slavery as the most efficient form of surplus extraction was transformed once Roman frontiers stabilized and the number of war-supplied slaves trailed off. The consequence was increased slave-breeding as landowners sought to maintain their labor force. The crucial factor was female slave reproduction over slave production. To make up for the lost surplus, landowners extended exploitation to hitherto free laborers, with the result of the emergence of a uniform class of coloni whose rate of exploitation was down, but volume had expanded. Thus, the ancient world was destroyed by a social crisis from within and finished off by the so-called barbarians from without (1991, p. 503). Anderson agrees on the internal social crisis but pays equal attention to external factors. "The dual predecessors of the feudal mode of production," he argues, "were the decomposing slave mode of production on whose foundations the whole enormous edifice of the Roman Empire had once been constructed, and the distended and deformed primitive modes of production of the Germanic invaders" (1974, pp. 18–19).

NEW WORLD SLAVES

Although Marx's own historical moment was dominated by the capitalist mode of production, slavery was not a peculiar institution in the mid-nineteenth century. When Marx was forty-two years old in 1860, there were about six million enslaved Africans in the New World, two-thirds of whom were imprisoned in the American South. Numerous scholars have debated this duality. Eugene Genovese argues that southern slavery was in conflict with capitalism and created a "powerful and remarkable social class" (1967, pp. 3–4). In contrast, John Blassingame has focused upon slave non-productive relations, especially communal and cultural formations. Other scholars insist on the centrality of productive relations. Ira Berlin and Philip Morgan insist that work "engaged most slaves, most of the time" (1993, p. 1). Still others insist on the exploitative nature of slavery and the role of surplus extraction. Eric Williams argued that slavery built up capitalism, while capitalism destroyed slavery. Robin Blackburn has recently argued that the profits from colonial slavery's surplus extraction—what he dubs "extended

primitive accumulation"—fueled Britain's remarkable industrial takeoff. The passage from pre-modern to modern society was not that of the classic Marxist transformation of agrarian property relations, but rather "exchanges with the slave plantations helped British capitalism to make a breakthrough to industrialism and global hegemony ahead of its rivals" (1997, p. 572). Unlike economic arguments for the shift from antiquity to feudalism, political explanations for passages from slavery to modernity, especially slave revolts in the New World, have been persuasively made by W. E. B. Du Bois, C. L. R. James, Robin Blackburn, and others.

SLAVES IN AFRICA

The debates on slave surplus extraction, competing social formations, and historical evolution have been extended to Asia and Africa. Walter Rodney argues that there was no "epoch of slavery" in pre-fifteenth-century Africa because of the absence of "perpetual exploitation." He prefers the notion of competing social formations to one mode of production with pre-colonial Africa in transition from communal agriculture to feudalism (1982, p. 38). Claude Meillassoux agrees that the absence of perpetual "relations of exploitation and the exploiting class" ensured there was no system of slavery in Africa and that there were several social formations (1991, pp. 36, 235). But he goes further. Slavery was not only a relationship of production, but also a "mode of reproduction" (1991, p. 324). In contrast to Ste. Croix's argument for antiquity, this reproductive slavery had little to do with procreation and much more to do with the economy of theft through war, abduction, and brigandage (1991, pp. 76, 92). "Wars of capture and markets," Meillassoux argues, "had their counterpart in the sterility of the women slaves who, despite their sex and their numbers, were deprived of reproductive functions" (1991, pp. 85, 278). Although John Thornton does not subscribe to Marxist concepts such as mode of production and surplus extraction, he does insist on the centrality of slavery to the continent's historical development, and his argument has been quite influential. Specifically, ownership or control of labor (in contrast to land ownership in feudal Europe) was the dominant principle of property relations in African societies, and "slavery was rooted in deep-seated legal and institutional structures of African societies" (1998, p. 74). This view has been correctly criticized for downplaying the qualitative change wrought by the advent of the Atlantic slave trade.

Returning to the lines of inquiry above, there are some key points. The number of productive workers does not have to be dominant. This was as true of slaves in antiquity as of slaves in the New World. Surplus extraction is critical to particular social formations.

Slaves in antiquity and the New World helped build magnificent civilizations. Slavery is a modern as well as an ancient social formation. Kevin Bales counts twenty-seven million slaves today operating as part of the global economy (1999, p. 9). Slavery plays a role in the historical evolution of social formations in terms of both reproduction and production. There is no one passage from slavery into other social formations.

SEE ALSO *Anderson, Perry; Capitalist Mode of Production; Conjunctures, Transitional; Du Bois, W. E. B.; Feudal Mode of Production; James, C. L. R.; Labor, Surplus: Marxist and Radical Economics; Marx, Karl; Marxism; Mode of Production; Surplus*

BIBLIOGRAPHY

Anderson, Perry. 1974. *Passages from Antiquity to Feudalism.* London: NLB.

Anderson, Perry. 1992. Geoffrey de Ste Croix and the Ancient World. In *A Zone of Engagement*, 1–24. London and New York: Verso.

Bales, Kevin. 1999. *Disposable People: New Slavery in the Global Economy.* Berkeley: University of California Press.

Berlin, Ira, and Philip D. Morgan, eds. 1993. *Cultivation and Culture: Labor and the Shaping of Slave Life in the America.* Charlottesville: University of Virginia Press.

Blackburn, Robin. 1988. *The Overthrow of Colonial Slavery, 1776–1848.* London and New York: Verso.

Blackburn, Robin. 1997. *The Making of New World Slavery: From the Baroque to the Modern, 1492–1800.* London and New York: Verso.

Blassingame, John W. 1972. *The Slave Community: Plantation Life in the Antebellum South.* New York: Oxford University Press.

Du Bois, W. E. B. 1992. *Black Reconstruction in America, 1860–1880.* New York: Atheneum. (Orig. pub. 1935.)

Finley, Moses I. 1991. "Ancient Society" and "Slavery." *A Dictionary of Marxist Thought*, ed. Tom Bottomore. Oxford, U.K., and Cambridge, MA: Blackwell.

Genovese, Eugene. 1967. *The Political Economy of Slavery: Studies in the Economy and Society of the Slave South.* New York: Vintage. (Orig. pub. 1961.)

James, C. L. R. 1963. *The Black Jacobins: Toussaint Louverture and the San Domingo Revolution.* New York: Random House.

Marx, Karl. 1965. Grundrisse. In *Pre-Capitalist Economic Formations.* Trans. Jack Cohen. Ed. Eric J. Hobsbawm. New York: International Publishers. (Orig. pub. 1941.)

Marx, Karl. 1978a. Communist Manifesto. In *The Marx-Engels Reader*, ed. Robert D. Tucker. New York: Norton. (Orig. pub. 1848.)

Marx, Karl. 1978b. German Ideology. In *The Marx-Engels Reader*, ed. Robert C. Tucker. New York: Norton. (Orig. pub. 1932.)

Meillassoux, Claude. 1991. *The Anthropology of Slavery: The Womb of Iron and Gold.* Chicago: University of Chicago Press.

Rodney, Walter. 1982. *How Europe Underdeveloped Africa.* Washington, DC: Howard University Press. (Orig. pub. 1972.)

Ste. Croix, G. E. M. de. 1981. *The Class Struggle in the Ancient Greek World: From the Archaic Age to the Arab Conquests.* Ithaca, NY: Cornell University Press.

Thornton, John. 1998. *Africa and Africans in the Making of the Atlantic World, 1400–1800.* Cambridge, U.K., and New York: Cambridge University Press.

Williams, Eric. 1944. *Capitalism and Slavery.* Chapel Hill: University of North Carolina Press.

Wood, Ellen Meiksins. 1988. *Peasant-Citizen and Slave: The Foundations of Athenian Democracy.* London and New York: Verso.

J. R. Kerr-Ritchie

SLAVE RESISTANCE

Demographic realities and power relationships in the British mainland colonies and later, following independence, in the United States, militated against the type of large-scale slave conspiracies that took place in South America and the Caribbean. The presence of a heavily armed white majority in every state except South Carolina (and, toward the very end of the antebellum period, Mississippi), the lack of an impregnable hinterland in which to create maroon colonies from which runaways could besiege plantations, the relatively dispersed nature and small size of slaveholding, and the fact that the landlord class was in residence (not absentee) combined to make massive slave rebellions far less common than day-to-day resistance or individual acts of self-threat. In the years after the Revolution, as harsher forms of colonial patriarchalism began to metamorphose into paternalism—a complex and ongoing process of negotiation and brutality that many scholars regrettably reduce to a simplistic model of accommodation—slaves achieved enough living space to build stable families and rich spiritual communities. Given the odds against success, it is hardly surprising that the handful of slaves bold enough to rise for their freedom found their rebellions reduced to unsuccessful conspiracies and their fellows doomed to die in combat or on the gallows.

Despite persistent attempts by historians to force a uniformity of vision and goals on rebel leaders, insurgent slaves in the eighteenth and nineteenth centuries differed from one another fully as much as white revolutionaries in the same era. Jemmy, an Angolan who led an agrarian uprising in 1739 near Stono River, South Carolina, tried to hasten his African followers across the border into Spanish Florida. Caesar Varick, who only two years later in 1741 conspired to burn New York City, lived in one of

North America's largest urban centers with an Irish wife. Gabriel, a young, secular rebel who had turned away from African traditions, hoped to stay and work in a more egalitarian Virginia. Denmark Vesey, an aged free black who bought his freedom the year before Gabriel died in 1800, expected to achieve a limited exodus for his family and followers out of Charleston to Haiti. Vesey and his chief lieutenant, "Gullah" Jack Pritchard, an East African priest, fused African theology with the Old Testament God of wrath and justice, whereas Nat Turner relied on Christian millennial themes and hoped to bring on the day of jubilee for black Virginians. Beyond their obvious abilities as leaders and their equally obvious desire to breathe free, bond rebels in the United States fit no simple pattern.

If slave rebellions in North America correspond to any one model, it is that they proliferated during times when the white majority was divided against itself in significant ways. Colonial insurgents in South Carolina and New York City turned to violence at a time when their masters were at war with France and Spain. Gabriel, the most politicized of all the slave rebels, formulated his plans during the divisive election of 1800, when Federalists and Republicans threatened to take up arms against one another. The rebels in the Tidewater area of Virginia, despite the memory of the repression that followed Gabriel's death, began to organize again during the chaos of the War of 1812. Having read of the Missouri debates in Charleston newspapers, Vesey prayed that northern whites would prove tardy in riding to the rescue of the estranged Southerners. Slaves near Natchez, Mississippi, began to plan for their freedom in 1861, following the outbreak of the Civil War.

Most of all, slaves, who well knew what they were up against and rarely contemplated suicidal ventures, plotted for their freedom only when safer avenues had been closed to them. For most of the seventeenth century, for example, when the high death rate in the Southern colonies made inexpensive white indentured servants far more numerous than costly African slaves, enterprising bondpersons relied more on self-purchase than the sword. The economic possibilities in early Virginia produced more runaways than rebels; the practice of buying one's own body even produced several black entrepreneurs—such as Anthony Johnson, a former slave who became a wealthy planter and who named his estate Angola after the land of his birth. It was only after landless whites and hard-used white indentured workers under the command of Nathaniel Bacon burned Jamestown in 1676 that Southern planters made a concerted effort to replace white servants with African slaves. The comprehensive Virginia Slave Code of 1705, the first of its kind in colonial North America, crushed the hope of industrious slaves that they might be upwardly mobile. Only then, as North American racial walls rapidly hardened, did desperate slaves turn to physically hazardous

paths toward freedom. During the last days of Queen Anne's War in April 1712, a determined band of twenty-five Coromantee Africans burned several buildings in New York City and killed nine whites. (Unfree labor had been legalized in New York by the Duke's Law of 1665.) Having made a commitment to unfree labor, equally determined whites revenged themselves on the rebels. Several rebels committed suicide before they could be captured, but those taken alive were broken on the wheel and hanged in chains as a warning to future rebels.

In the early eighteenth century, even though the constant threat of war between Britain and its continental neighbors provided endless opportunities for daring slaves, mainland revolts rarely posed much real danger to the slaveholding regime. Because the Atlantic slave trade was at its peak, every colony included large numbers of native Africans who sought to escape from bondage by building isolated maroon communities. Most runaways fled into the hinterland, where they established maroon colonies and tried to re-create the African communities they had lost. Even the two most significant rebellions of the period—that of Stono, South Carolina, and the subsequent attempt to burn New York City—were led by Africans who dreamed only of ending their own bondage, not of ending unfree labor in general. Aware of Spanish promises of freedom in colonial Florida, Angolan soldiers under Jemmy tried to escape across the border. To the north, New York City bondmen planned to torch the wooden city and flee to French Canada, which was then at war with the rebels' masters. The price of failure was high. New York authorities ordered Caesar Varick and twelve of his followers burned alive; eighteen others were hanged—two of them in chains—and seventy more bondmen were banished from the colony.

Given the odds against them, most enslaved men and women resisted their condition through other methods. Young men, especially those who had not yet married, ran away, often in homogenous groups. Before the early nineteenth century, slaves in the Southern colonies fled toward Spanish Florida, while those in the North sought freedom in French Canada; with the gradual emancipation of slavery in the Northern states and the American acquisition of Florida, bondmen journeyed toward the free states or remained truants within the South. Some women, particularly domestic servants, occasionally fought back through poison. Although it is hard to know whether the illness of white masters was due to toxins or natural causes, colonies like South Carolina passed legislation in 1751 against "the detestable crime of poisoning [that] hath of late been frequently committed by many slaves" (Rucker 2005, 112).

The onset of the American Revolution alternately discouraged and stimulated slave rebellions. Although the

British invasion and the animosity between patriots and Tories presented slaves with a unique opportunity to organize, most slaves chose instead to take advantage of the dislocation of war to escape with their families into the growing cities or behind British lines. (The Revolution was the one time in North American history when as many female slaves as males ran away.) Because the aggressive bondmen who cast their lots with the military forces of King George were precisely the sort of bold, determined slaves who normally tended to organize slave conspiracies, the bloody fighting in the Southern states after 1778 actually diminished the prospect that a mainland counterpart of Toussaint Louverture would rise out of the tobacco plantations.

Nonetheless, as Eugene D. Genovese suggested in his influential study *From Rebellion to Revolution* (1979), the age of revolution, and especially the slave revolt in Saint Domingue in 1791, marked a change in patterns in black resistance. The Caribbean rebels under the leadership of Boukman and Toussaint Louverture sought not only to destroy the power of their Parisian absentee masters but to join the societies in which they lived on equal terms. For black Americans determined to realize the egalitarian promise of the American Revolution, the news from the Caribbean reminded them that if they dared, the end of slavery might be within their reach. Whereas Jemmy and his African recruits hoped only to escape the chains of colonial South Carolina, the slave Gabriel of Virginia, born in the year 1776, wanted to join political society on equal terms. Gabriel and his lieutenants, who instigated the most extensive plot in Virginia history, hoped to force the white patriot elite to live up to its stated ideal: that all men were created free and equal. Leading a small army of slaves in Henrico County, the young blacksmith planned to march into Richmond under a banner emblazoned with the words "Death or Liberty." He assured one supporter that "poor white people," who had no more political power than the slaves, "would also join" them in the struggle for equality. Although trial testimony makes little mention of events in Saint Domingue, white authorities like Governor James Monroe harbored no doubts that Toussaint Louverture's victories had an enormous "effect on all the peoples of colour" in the early national South (Egerton 1993, 169).

In several cases, bondmen who had been carried from revolutionary Saint Domingue by their masters participated in North American slave revolts. In 1792 slaves on Virginia's eastern shore proposed to "blow up the magazine in Norfolk, and massacre its inhabitants" (Aptheker 1943, 228).

Norfolk County had a white majority, but Northampton and Elizabeth City counties, just across the Chesapeake Bay, had an enslaved majority. Although the

rebel leader Caleb, a favored servant and driver, was evidently American-born, several of his recruits were Haitian refugees, and all—according to the trial testimony—had been inspired by the example of Saint Domingue. Two decades later, in 1811, one of the most extensive conspiracies in the history of the United States erupted in southern Louisiana, only a few miles upriver from New Orleans. Slaves led by a mixed-race driver named Charles Deslondes announced their intention of marching on the city "to kill whites" (Aptheker, 249). Although Deslondes, contrary to myth, was not Haitian, many of the roughly two hundred slaves who rose with him had resided in the French Caribbean.

After Gabriel's execution and the death of twenty-five of his followers in the fall of 1800, slave rebellions on the eastern seaboard became both less common and less politically conscious. Slaves who worked along the rivers in southern Virginia and Halifax County, North Carolina, under the leadership of Sancho, a ferryman, formed a highly decentralized scheme to rise on Easter Monday of 1802. But Sancho, despite having been involved in Gabriel's plot, shared little of Gabriel's dream of a multiracial republic. The lack of an ideological dimension appeared even when the dislocation brought on by the War of 1812 and a second British invasion of the Chesapeake once more gave bondmen in Virginia an opportunity to rise for their liberty. Gloucester County authorities jailed ten slaves in March 1813, and the following month found rebels in Lancester County and Williamsburg "condemned on a charge of conspiracy & insurrection" (Aptheker, 255). By the late summer and early fall, rumors of revolt unnerved inhabitants of Norfolk and Richmond as well.

If the relative ease with which white authorities crushed these isolated rebellions did not extinguish the desire for freedom, it nonetheless reminded leaders in the slave community that the determined white majority in the American South presented insurgents with a formidable obstacle. Denmark Vesey of Charleston, perhaps the most pragmatic of all the rebel leaders, realized that Gabriel's dream of forcing mainland elites to accommodate blacks' aspirations to freedom and economic justice was impossible.

Vesey plotted, therefore, not to end slavery in South Carolina, but instead to lead a mass escape from Charleston to the Caribbean, where he had lived and worked as a boy. Hoping to take control of the city on the night of July 14, 1822, Vesey's recruits—many of them Africans—intended to slaughter the inhabitants of the city and seize bank reserves before fleeing to Haiti, an embattled black republic sorely in need of capital and skilled labor. If Vesey, a prosperous freeman, doomed those who remained behind to renewed repression by whites, he can scarcely be faulted: He understood that his followers had virtually no hope of bringing down the peculiar institution in South Carolina.

Even Vesey's unsuccessful exodus, which may be regarded more as mass flight than a revolution, indicated the difficulties of planning an effective strategy amidst large numbers of ever-vigilant whites. Like virtually all rebel leaders in the United States, Vesey recognized the danger of openly recruiting in the countryside. Word of the Charleston plot probably reached several thousand slaves—which is not to say that even half that number committed themselves to the struggle—and there was always a danger that a black Judas would hear the whispers and inform the master class. White authorities had long ago perfected the art of dividing the slave community by offering a tempting reward—freedom—to those who would turn their coats. Like Jemmy and Gabriel before him, Vesey, whose army had more officers than soldiers, planned to rise quickly and present the low country's black majority with a fait accompli. The victorious armies would not be recruited or armed in advance but raised by the captains as they marched.

Ironically, the bloodiest slave revolt in the United States took place in the decade after Vesey's failure, at a time when rebellion—as opposed to other forms of resistance—had become virtually suicidal. The slaves in Southampton County, Virginia, who rose with Nat Turner in 1831 shared neither Gabriel's trust in a second American Revolution nor Vesey's hope of fleeing to the Caribbean. Although Turner may have expected to establish a maroon colony in the vast Dismal Swamp, his plot gave little evidence of planning or rational preparation. Most likely, the messianic Turner hoped that God would protect and guide his army as the Lord had guided the Israelites. At least fifty-seven whites perished in the revolt, but local militiamen easily routed the ill-equipped rebels; three companies of federal artillery, together with seamen from two warships in the Chesapeake, reached Southampton only three days after the insurrection began.

Although the secession of the Southern states in the winter of 1860–1861 presented militant blacks with precisely the sort of division that rebel leaders typically tried to take advantage of, the Civil War channeled black resistance into patterns acceptable to the politicians of the free states. During the first year of the conflict, as Confederate soldiers repulsed northern invasions, militant slaves across the cotton-growing South saw few options but to pull down the rebel government from within. The plot in Natchez, Mississippi, still shrouded in mystery, stands as but one example of collective resistance during the months before the Confederate debacle at Antietam Creek. Rumors of black resistance spread in New Orleans and Columbia, South Carolina. Seven slaves swung from the gibbet in Charleston in April 1861. The Confederate brigadier general R. F. Floyd urged the governor of Florida to declare martial law in the hope of eradicating a "nest of traitors and lawless negroes" (Aptheker, 301).

Most slaves, however, understood, as Herbert Aptheker suggested in his definitive work on *American Negro Slave Revolts* (1943), that "the Army of Lincoln was to be the Army of Liberation" (p. 84). Aged slaves with long memories counseled patience and waited for the arrival of Northern forces. Following the Emancipation Proclamation, Northern freemen and Southern runaways, eager and willing to fight, donned blue uniforms in the name of liberty for blacks. Despite the Confederates' threat to execute black soldiers as slave insurgents, thousands of bondmen fled the countryside, planning to return and liberate their families. By the end of the war, 180,000 African Americans (one out of every five males in the republic) had served in Union forces. Those former slaves who marched back toward the plantations of their birth singing "General Gabriel's Jig" rightly understood themselves to be a part of the largest slave rebellion in the history of the United States.

SEE ALSO *American Revolution; Gabriel (Prosser); Haitian Revolution; Toussaint Louverture; Turner, Nat; U.S. Civil War; Vesey, Denmark*

BIBLIOGRAPHY

Aptheker, Herbert. 1943. *American Negro Slave Revolts.* New York: Columbia University Press.

Dubois, Laurent. 2004. *Avengers of the New World: The Story of the Haitian Revolution.* Cambridge, MA: Harvard University Press.

Egerton, Douglas R. 1993. *Gabriel's Rebellion: The Virginia Slave Conspiracies of 1800 and 1802.* Chapel Hill: University of North Carolina Press.

Egerton, Douglas R. 1999. *He Shall Go Out Free: The Lives of Denmark Vesey.* Lanham, MD: Rowman and Littlefield.

Frey, Sylvia R. 1991. *Water From the Rock: Black Resistance in a Revolutionary Age.* Princeton, NJ: Princeton University Press.

Genovese, Eugene D. 1979. *From Rebellion to Revolution: Afro-American Slave Revolts in the Making of the Modern World.* Baton Rouge: Louisiana State University Press.

Hoffer, Peter Charles. 2003. *The Great New York Conspiracy of 1741: Slavery, Crime, and Colonial Law.* Lawrence: University of Kansas Press.

Rucker, Walter C. 2005. *The River Flows On: Black Resistance, Culture, and Identity Formation in Early America.* Baton Rouge: Louisiana State University Press.

Douglas R. Egerton

SLAVE TRADE

The history of most modern societies has involved, in some form or fashion, the use of coerced labor, including the institution of slavery and the exploitation of slave labor. And where slavery existed—defined as a system in which the production process is carried out by human beings owned by other human beings—a mechanism for supplying slaves was necessary. This mechanism is called the slave trade. While slavery and the slave trade as concepts and as practices have an ancient pedigree and global itineraries, their relationship to the history, practices, and realities of modern societies continues to stir considerable concern and controversy. The tools of historians must be combined with tools and insights from economics, political science, and other social sciences to explore how empirical data and theoretical debates have animated our understanding of the slave trade's global history, especially the transatlantic slave trade.

Slavery was commonplace in many ancient societies, including Greece, Rome, and Egypt. Slaves were forced to work in almost all sectors—agriculture, mining, domestic service, and even as gladiators and soldiers. Many of these slaves were captured in war, but formal mechanisms to supply slaves were also well established. Rome drew its slaves from all over its expanding empire, for example, and at one point there were as many slaves as there were Roman citizens. The slave trade was also a prominent feature of medieval societies, with Africans being enslaved and shipped to the Muslim world across the Sahara, the Red Sea, and the Indian Ocean. Scholars have estimated that as many as 19 million people from sub-Saharan Africa were shipped to the Muslim world between 650 and 1890.

Until the fifteenth century, the major destination for the slave trade was the Muslim world, with slaves coming from Africa and from Europe. In fact, the word *slave* is derived from the word *slav*, the name for a large ethnic and linguistic group residing in eastern and southeastern Europe, including Russians, Ukrainians, Poles, Czechs, Slovaks, Bulgarians, and others. In the fifteenth and sixteenth centuries, Africa became the major source of slaves, and the international slave trade was dominated by Portugal, reflecting the development of European colonies in the Americas that needed labor. In the seventeenth century, Britain emerged as the largest carrier of slaves.

THE NUMBERS

There have been three waves of estimates regarding the numbers of Africans who were traded as commodities in the slave trade across the Atlantic Ocean. The first wave included estimates ventured by scholars who repeated earlier numbers gleaned mainly from popular writing and not based on systematic analysis—W. E. B. Du Bois's

approximation of 100,000,000 Africans lost to the slave trade was a prime example. Such estimates were the main target of Phillip Curtin's *The Atlantic Slave Trade: A Census* (1969), one of the pioneering studies seeking to provide more accurate numbers. The second wave of estimates, to which Curtin contributed, was based on more extensive compilation and synthesis of available data and estimates using statistical inferences based on population changes in importing countries, but not on research into original sources. Curtin provided an estimate of 9,566,100 Africans between 1451 and 1870, concluding provocatively that it was unlikely that new scholarship would alter his estimate by a number greater than 10 percent. Noel Deerr's *The History of Sugar* (1949–1950) was an earlier representative of this tradition extended but not initiated by Curtin's census. The major impact of Curtin's work was not its originality but its method, comprehensiveness, and timing, appearing at a time when concerns over race and race relations were mounting, and drastically lower estimates of the number of Africans traded were bound to provoke controversy.

Joseph Inikori (1976, 1982) provided one of the earliest critiques of these census efforts. He pointed to his own research and synthesized the work of other scholars as the basis for concluding that Curtin's estimate required a 40 percent upward adjustment. Most important was his discovery of new shipping data that provided more accurate numbers of slaves carried. Beyond confirming that all such estimates are far from complete or final, the continuing debate underscores the centrality of intellectual history in exploring heated disagreements in historical interpretation where perspectives are shaped by the dynamics of color, class, nationality, morality, disciplinary paradigms, ideological orientations, and claims about objectivity.

A third wave is represented by scholars who have compiled the Trans-Atlantic Slave Trade Database (TSTD), sponsored by Harvard University's Du Bois Institute and published in 1999. With data on more than 27,000 slave voyages, TSTD concluded that 11,062,000 Africans were transported from Africa between 1519 and 1867, with 9.6 million landing in the Americas, figures not substantially different from Curtin's. More than half were carried between 1700 and 1799, and about 30 percent after the abolition of the slave trade by Great Britain and the United States in 1807. Beginning with Prince Henry's traders in 1441, Portugal was the major carrier in the trade involving Africans, and 75 percent of all slaves were carried by the Portuguese in the first 150 years of the trade. Overall, however, British citizens transported 46 percent of all Africans, followed by the Portuguese (29.1%), France (13.2%), Spain (4.8%), the Netherlands (4.7%), and Denmark (1%). Only 2.5 percent of all slaves were transported by slave merchants based in the United States and British

Caribbean. Up until 1820, more Africans were transported across the Atlantic than Europeans—8.4 million Africans to 2.4 million Europeans.

TSTD enables more detailed attention to the geographical distribution of the origins and destinations of enslaved Africans and the resulting demographic and cultural shape of the "diaspora" in which Africans were dispersed or scattered. Almost 45 percent of all slaves came from the West African coast that is today Ghana, Togo, Ivory Coast, Burkina Faso, Benin, and parts of Nigeria, for example. As destinations, 41 percent of enslaved Africans were shipped to present-day Brazil, 27 percent to British America, 11 percent to French territories, and 13 percent to Spanish territories. And there was method in the madness, with European slave traders and slave-purchasing areas in the Americas showing preference for Africans from particular regions (e.g., rice-growing South Carolina preferred slaves from Gambia and rice-growing regions of West Africa).

There have also been substantial updates to TSTD, bearing out earlier and unwelcome insistence that all such estimates were only provisional. A new revised TSTD now includes over 34,000 slaving voyages. It recognizes "major gaps" in the 1999 database, especially with regard to the early history of the slave trade and that of Brazil, the largest importing nation. It adds 7,000 new voyages and provides additional information on more than 10,000 voyages in the 1999 database.

POLITICAL ECONOMY

Political economy generally denotes an approach that focuses on the relationship of economic activity—trade and commerce as well as production—and their interrelationships with the activities of government, politics, and the broader society. To paraphrase Adam Smith's 1776 title for his pioneering volume in this tradition, the slave trade and slavery's contribution to "the wealth [and poverty] of nations" was critical. This line of thinking was continued in the next century by Karl Marx, who pondered in Vol. 1 of *Capital,* "the turning of Africa into a warren for the commercial hunting of Black skins" as an initial source for early investment in capitalist production. The approach is also closely related to Walter Rodney's *How Europe Underdeveloped Africa* (1974) and similar discussions by such scholars as J. M. Blaut (1992, p. 206) of "the role played by colonialism in industrial production."

Meeting the need for labor in the Americas was essential if European nations were to realize the goals of mercantilism—favorable trade balance, increased amounts of precious metals, and the like. Therefore, beyond the issue of how many Africans were taken from the continent into slavery in the Americas—especially the horrendous treatment during the middle passage between Africa and the Americas—and who played what role in enslaving them, is the need to understand the contribution of African labor to wealth production in the various nations that were carriers of slaves and beneficiaries from the economic productivity of slave labor.

Expectedly, sharp differences have emerged as well over this area, generally termed "profitability" of the slave trade, an assessment dependent in part on calculations of the number of slaves traded. For example, Roger Anstey (1975) suggested 9.6 percent as the rate of profit in the British slave trade between 1761 and 1897, calculating profits by using data on the number of slaves landed, slave prices, and other data on cost and revenue. Inikori (1976) provided evidence pointing to underestimations in the number of slaves landed in the West Indies and the average price for which slaves were sold. William Darity (1985) used these corrected figures to demonstrate a plausible increase in the rate of profits from 9.6 percent to 30.8 percent, a figure consistent with the conclusion of Eric Williams in *Capitalism and Slavery* (1944).

Efforts to calculate the contribution of the slave trade to economic development became more controversial when prominent scholars concluded that profits from the slave trade were not large enough to make a significant contribution to British industrialization, a view that diverged from the long-held conventional wisdom about the impact of what had been called "the triangular trade" (Anstey 1975; Engerman 1972; Davis 1984, p. 73). Darity (1990), Barbara Solow (1991), and others highlighted the impact that different definitions, theoretical assumptions and economic models can have in calculating rates of profits, concluding that the slave trade was a relatively important source of industrial capital. Moreover, Ronald Bailey (1986, 1990) has given the term "slave(ry) trade"—activities related both to the slave trade and slavery and closer to the "multiplier effect" concept used by some economists—as the source of profits that should be utilized in calculating contributions to industrialization and not just profits from buying and selling slaves. Substituting profits from the Caribbean trade in place of profits solely from the sale of slaves, he concluded that enough profits could have been generated to finance the British industrial revolution several times over. (As an additional example, the 7,000 new voyages added to the 1999 TSTD database discussed above requires a recalculation of the slave trade's impact on the expansion of the ship-building and shipping industry.)

In this approach, this contribution from the "slave(ry) trade" would include the important role and economic significance of agricultural crops produced by slave labor in the colonies, including sugar, tobacco, rice, coffee, and cotton, as well as profits generated in related shipping, banking and insurance, and manufacturing, a central thesis in Williams's *Capitalism and Slavery* and argued by Inikori (2002). Importantly, this approach facilitates a sharper focus on the role of slavery and the slave trade in U.S. history, an emphasis admirably treated, for example, by Du Bois (1896) and in the chapter on "Black Merchandise" in Lorenzo Greene's *The Negro in Colonial New England* (1942).

MORALITY OF THE SLAVE TRADE

Ships in the transatlantic slave trade rarely carried Europeans and were rarely owned and operated by Africans. This color/race and class dynamic helps to explain why the controversy over the slave trade provokes sharp debates over morality and ethics. It is so potent because modern capitalist nations, which early prohibited the enslavement of Europeans, were the world's leaders in the enslavement and trade of Africans, a legacy related to both poverty and racism that hovers over world history and the history of many nations and peoples. Even more perplexing, the slave trade and slavery were consolidated and expanded at the same time as the rise of the progressive transatlantic philosophical movement called the Enlightenment in the late eighteenth century, and such practices were enshrined and extended, not abolished, by the American Revolution and the U.S. Constitution. Edmund S. Morgan, a scholar of early America, was provoked to probe the paradoxical marriage of convenience he called "American slavery/American freedom."

Ideas about abolition surfaced as early as the late 1600s with the work of the Quakers and other religious groups, but it was not until 1807 that legislation to end the slave trade was enacted in Great Britain and in the United States. It was another eighty years before such practices were finally outlawed by all of the nations whose citizens had been involved as slavers and beneficiaries of slavery. Scholarly debates regarding the root causes of abolition and the slow unfolding of its success have been as intense as those regarding the causes and consequences of slavery and the slave trade, with some scholars emphasizing humanitarian motives and others stressing economic and political dynamics. That the system of U.S. slavery that fueled the transatlantic slave trade necessitated for its abolition a civil war resulting in the deaths of more than 620,000 people will guarantee that discussion and debate will continue in the decades to come.

Two hundred years after the 1807 abolition of the slave trade in Great Britain and the implementation of a similar measure in the U.S. Constitution, the slave trade continues to rest uncomfortably in scholarship and in social memory. In recent times, the controversy has taken the form of calls for and debates over apologies for participation in the slave trade and slavery, and over the payment of some form of "reparations" similar to what was provided to Jews and other victims of the Holocaust and to U.S. citizens of Japanese ancestry incarcerated in World War II camps. And there are growing contemporary movements to grapple with new forms of slavery, poverty, and economic coercion in a deepening globalized economy. Research, thinking, and writing about the history of the slave trade should provide a solid foundation for understanding and acting in the present and future.

SEE ALSO *Caribbean, The; Cotton Industry; Du Bois, W. E. B.; Engerman, Stanley; Holocaust, The; Immigrants to North America; Incarceration, Japanese American; Inikori, Joseph; James, C. L. R.; Jews; Marx, Karl; Mercantilism; Plantation; Race; Racism; Rodney, Walter; Roma, The; Slave-Gun Cycle; Slavery; Slavery Industry; Smith, Adam; Sugar Industry; White Supremacy; Williams, Eric; World War II*

BIBLIOGRAPHY

Anstey, Roger. 1975. *The Atlantic Slave Trade and British Abolition, 1760–1810.* Atlantic Highlands, NJ: Humanities Press.

Bailey, Ronald W. 1986. Africa, the Slave Trade, and the Rise of Industrial Capitalism in Europe and the United States: A Historiographic Review. *American History: A Bibliographic Review* 2: 1–91.

Bailey, Ronald W. 1990. The Slave(ry) Trade and the Development of Capitalism in the United States: The Textile Industry in New England. *Social Science History* 14 (3): 373–414; reprinted in Stanley Engerman and Joseph Inikori. *The Atlantic Slave Trade: Effects on Economics, Societies, and Peoples in Africa, the Americas, and Europe.* Durham, NC, and London: Duke University Press, 1992.

Blaut, J. M. 1992. *The Colonizer's Model of the World: Geographical Diffusionism and Eurocentric History.* New York: Guilford.

Curtin, Phillip. 1969. *The Atlantic Slave Trade: A Census.* Madison: University of Wisconsin Press.

Darity, William, Jr. 1985. The Numbers Game and the Profitability of the British Trade in Slaves. *Journal of Economic History* 45 (3): 693–703.

Darity, William, Jr. 1990. British Industry and the West Indies Plantations. *Social Science History* 14 (1): 117–149.

Davis, David Brion. 1984. *Slavery and Human Progress.* New York: Oxford University Press.

Deerr, Noel. 1949–1950. *The History of Sugar.* 2 vols. London: Chapman and Hall.

Drake, St. Clair. 1987–1990. *Black Folk Here and There: An Essay in History and Anthropology.* 2 vols. Los Angeles: University of California Center for Afro-American Studies.

Du Bois, W. E. B. 1896 [1999]. *Suppression of the African Slave-Trade to the United States of America.* Mineola, NY: Dover.

Eltis, David. 2001. The Volume and Structure of the Transatlantic Slave Trade: A Reassessment. *William and Mary Quarterly*, 3rd Ser., 58: 17–46.

Eltis, David, Stephen D. Behrendt, David Richardson, and
Herbert S. Klein. 1999. *The Trans-Atlantic Slave Trade: A
Database on CD-ROM*. Cambridge, U.K., and New York:
Cambridge University Press. The revised database, released
February 2007, was sponsored by the Arts and Humanities
Research Council and is accessible at http://www.data-
archive.ac.uk.

Engerman, Stanley. 1972. The Slave Trade and British Capital
Formation in the Eighteenth Century: A Comment on the
Williams Thesis. *Business History Review* 46: 430–443.

Greene, Lorenzo. 1942. *The Negro in Colonial New England,
1620–1776*. New York: Columbia University Press.

Inikori, Joseph. 1976. Measuring the Atlantic Slave Trade: An
Assessment of Curtin and Anstey. *Journal of African History*
17: 197–223.

Inikori, Joseph, ed. 1982. *Forced Migration: The Impact of the
Export Slave Trade on African Societies*. New York: Africana
Publishing.

Inikori, Joseph. 2002. *Africans and the Industrial Revolution in
England: A Study in International Trade and Economic
Development*. New York: Cambridge University Press.

Rodney, Walter. 1974. *How Europe Underdeveloped Africa*.
Washington, DC: Howard University Press.

Solow, Barbara, ed. 1991. *Slavery and the Rise of the Atlantic
System*. Cambridge, U.K., and New York: Cambridge
University Press.

Thomas, Hugh. 1997. *The Slave Trade: The Story of the Atlantic
Slave Trade, 1440–1870*. New York: Simon and Schuster.

Williams, Eric. 1944. *Capitalism and Slavery*. Chapel Hill:
University of North Carolina Press.

Ronald W. Bailey

SLAVE-GUN CYCLE

For the first two centuries of European trade in western
Africa (roughly 1441 to 1650), gold was the main product of trade. But as demand for slave labor in the Americas
expanded following the phenomenal growth of plantation
agriculture and mining from the seventeenth century,
European demand in western Africa shifted decisively
from gold and other products to captives, leading to the
transportation of millions of Africans for enslavement in
the Americas between the 1650s and the 1860s. The
impact of this trade in captives on African societies has
been debated since the late eighteenth century—first,
between the abolitionists and the slave traders and, later,
among modern historians. One contested issue is the role
of the trade in the scale and frequency of wars in western
Africa between the 1650s and the 1860s. This is the context for the notion of the *slave-gun cycle*—that guns were
employed in wars that generated captives for export, the
proceeds from which were employed to buy more guns to

fight more wars that generated more captives. Historians
disagree on the quantity of firearms imported during the
period and their contribution to the scale and frequency
of wars. This entry examines the issue of quantity and the
linkages to war. It argues that the linkages presented by
both sides of the debate appear to be simplistic. A combination of new evidence and a more complex analysis sheds
more light on the subject.

Because of inadequate evidence and the difficulty of
interpreting what is available, quantifying various aspects
of the transatlantic slave trade is fraught with controversy.
An estimate based on a variety of British records—merchants' private papers, customs records, and parliamentary
papers—puts the mean total annual import into western
Africa from all regions of the Atlantic basin at between
300,000 and 400,000 guns in the second half of the eighteenth century (Inikori 1977). Other estimates based on
more limited archival sources are smaller—190,000 for
the 1780s; 140,000 for the 1820s; about 200,000 for the
1860s (Eltis and Jennings 1988).

The debate on the contribution of imported guns to
the scale and frequency of wars in western Africa during
the era of the transatlantic slave trade has been conducted
largely within short time periods with all of western Africa
taken as a unit of study. This methodology conceals information that region-specific study covering long time
periods reveals. This entry, therefore, takes the major subregions of western Africa involved in the transatlantic
slave trade, comprised of the Gold Coast (modern southern Ghana), the Bight of Benin (modern Togo, Republic
of Benin, and southwest Nigeria), the Bight of Biafra
(southeastern Nigeria and southern Cameroon), and
West-Central Africa (the area from modern Gabon to
modern Angola); discusses changes in the commodity
composition of their imports from the early years of their
trade with the Europeans; and combines the information
with other relevant evidence. The Gold Coast and West-
Central Africa began significant trading with the
Europeans early in the fifteenth and sixteenth centuries;
the Bights of Benin and Biafra came in relatively late during the middle decades of the seventeenth century. For
this reason, British records employed in the analysis provide better coverage for the commodities imported into
the Bights of Benin and Biafra in the early years.

For the Bight of Benin, cowries (sea shells employed
in local trade as all-purpose currency) overwhelmingly
dominated the imports in the seventeenth century, being
consistently more than one-half of the total value of
imports before the last decade of the century. The invoices
show no firearms, again, until the last decade of the century. From the latter period, the volume and ratio of
imported cowries declined continuously, while that of
firearms rose—from approximately 3 percent in 1690/

1692 to 9 percent in 1724. In the Bight of Biafra, copper rods, weighing about one pound each (employed in local trade as all-purpose currency), constituted about two-thirds of the total value of imports in most years between the 1660s and 1680s. In most years from the 1660s to 1690s, there were no firearms at all in the invoices; the ratio of firearms in the invoices for 1661 and 1662 is approximately 7 percent each. Like the Bight of Benin, currency imports declined over the eighteenth century, while firearms increased—from approximately 3 percent in 1701 to 40 percent in 1790. From 1827 to 1839, firearms imported into both regions ranged between 21 percent and 35 percent of total imports, and 14 to 18 percent from 1840 to 1850. During these twenty-four years (with data unavailable for 1844), a total of 1.2 million guns were imported into the two regions from Britain alone, the bulk of which went to Yorubaland, where European traders' choice of Lagos as their headquarters in the late eighteenth century and the collapse of the Oyo Empire in the early nineteenth century led to almost a hundred years of wars (Inikori 1992).

Detailed study of imports into the Gold Coast and West-Central Africa in the fifteenth and early sixteenth centuries is yet to be conducted. However, a Portuguese gold trade ledger for Elmina (Gold Coast), covering 1529 to 1531, shows that metals (without guns) made up 50 percent of imports and cloth 25 percent; no firearms were imported. From the seventeenth century, firearms flooded into the Gold Coast and West-Central Africa, at a time when the Bights of Benin and Biafra hardly imported any firearms.

When the import data is combined with other evidence, we get a much clearer linkage between imported firearms and wars in western Africa during the transatlantic slave trade era. There is clear evidence showing that local and interregional long-distance trade was expanding in western Africa (the geographical region from Mauritania to Namibia), especially West Africa (the political region from Mauritania to Nigeria), at the time Europeans arrived in the mid-fifteenth century. The early European trade in African products, particularly gold, further stimulated the ongoing trade expansion. Cowries and copper rods were already all-purpose currencies in the pre-European trade. The proportionately large import of these currencies in the early decades of European trade is a reflection of the growing local demand for currency to meet the needs of the expanding local and interregional trade. The low demand for firearms in the early years of European trade shown by the commodity composition is, again, a reflection of the general prevalence of peaceful conditions in the kin-based small-scale polities on the coast and in the hinterland. The minor skirmishes that broke out occasionally between neighbors were brief in duration, and prisoners (if any) were ransomed at the end (Meillassoux 1991, p. 33). For as long as European

demand was overwhelmingly dominated by African products, the situation remained largely unchanged.

The massive shift of European demand from products to captives changed everything. As individuals and groups of bandits engaged in kidnapping and raids within polities and across political boundaries in response to growing export demand for captives, the small polities were unable to maintain law and order within, while raids across political boundaries provoked wars between neighbors, wars whose scale and consequences increased considerably. These wars disrupted the preceding interregional trade and shifted demand from currency to firearms. Initially, therefore, the wars were not caused by the import of firearms. The shift of European demand from products to captives was the main cause. However, in due course, the massive import of firearms and their distribution among bandits created conditions that fueled the wars and made them endemic. Because exporting captives provided virtually the only access to firearms, given the nature of European demand, polities in conflict were compelled to sell captives for export, which by itself provoked retaliation and continuation of hostility. On the other hand, the sale of war captives in exchange for firearms made war self-financing, which helped to prolong wars. All these developments were experienced by virtually all the polities in western Africa from Senegambia to Angola at different points in time between 1450 and 1850.

A combination of import data and other evidence thus makes it clear that the slave-gun cycle notion, as often employed in the literature, is simplistic. So, too, is the attempt to distinguish between economic and political causes of war during the Atlantic slave trade period. In the main, the wars were political in nature, but were caused largely by the political complications arising from the actions of individuals and groups of bandits responding to the growing export demand for captives, in the first instance (Inikori 1992, pp. 25–39). Given the small size and the politico-military weakness of the polities on the coast and in the hinterland when the Europeans arrived in the mid-fifteenth century, comparative arguments based on the ratio of imported firearms to population (Eltis and Jennings 1988) are not well-founded. Also erroneous is the argument that Europeans and their firearms made no difference to the wars of the slave trade era because before the arrival of Europeans political leaders in western Africa were regularly engaged in wars for the accumulation of slaves as a form of wealth owing to land laws that prevented private accumulation of land and capital as wealth (Thornton 1992). Linguistic and other evidence from West-Central Africa (Hilton 1985; Vansina 1989) and archival and oral evidence from other regions show that the largely kin-based polities on the coast and in the hinterland, and even the Kongo kingdom in West-Central Africa, were not engaged in slave gathering wars in the fifteenth century,

541

and they had no accumulated slaves for domestic use or for sale when the Europeans arrived. A few captives were being exported across the Sahara at the time, but that trade was centered in the interior savanna; most coastal polities and their hinterlands were not involved. What is more, the evidence shows unambiguously that there were no legal barriers to the private investment of capital in land and agriculture when market conditions were appropriate. Finally, wars continued in western Africa for some decades after the abolition of the transatlantic slave trade in the mid-nineteenth century because the conditions for sociopolitical conflict created by the export demand for captives continued to exist even after abolition.

BIBLIOGRAPHY

Eltis, David, and Lawrence C. Jennings. 1988. Trade Between Western Africa and the Atlantic World in the Pre-Colonial Era. *American Historical Review* 93 (4): 936–959.

Hilton, Anne. *The Kingdom of Kongo.* 1985. Oxford: Clarendon.

Inikori, Joseph E. 1977. The Import of Firearms into West Africa, 1750 to 1807: A Quantitative Analysis. *Journal of African History* 18 (3): 339–368.

Inikori, Joseph E. 1992. *The Chaining of a Continent: Export Demand for Captives and the History of Africa South of the Sahara, 1450–1870.* Kingston, Jamaica: Institute of Social and Economic Research.

Inikori, Joseph E. 1996. Slavery in Africa and the Transatlantic Slave Trade. In *The African Diaspora*, eds. Alusine Jalloh and Stephen Maizlish, 39–72. College Station: Texas A&M University Press.

Inikori, Joseph E. 2002. The Development of Entrepreneurship in Africa: Southeastern Nigeria During the Era of the Transatlantic Slave Trade. In *Black Business and Economic Power*, eds. Alusine Jalloh and Toyin Falola, 41–79. Rochester, NY: University of Rochester Press.

Inikori, Joseph E. 2003. The Struggle against the Transatlantic Slave Trade: The Role of the State. In *Fighting the Slave Trade: West African Strategies*, ed. Sylviane A. Diouf, 170–198. Athens: Ohio University Press.

Meillassoux, Claude. 1991. *The Anthropology of Slavery: The Womb of Iron and Gold.* Trans. Alide Dasnois. Chicago: University of Chicago Press.

Thornton, John. 1992. *Africa and Africans in the Making of the Atlantic World, 1400–1680.* Cambridge, U.K.: Cambridge University Press.

Vansina, Jan. 1989. Deep-Down Time: Political Tradition in Central Africa. *History in Africa* 16: 341–362.

Wilks, Ivor. 1977. Land, Labour, Capital, and the Forest Kingdom of Asante: A Model of Early Change. In *The Evolution of Social Systems*, eds. John Friedman and M. J. Rowlands, 487–534. London: Duckworth.

Joseph E. Inikori

SLAVEOWNERS

SEE *Slavery.*

SLAVERY

It has been common for many generations to begin essays on American slavery by noting how commonplace slavery is: It is sanctioned in the Old Testament and has appeared in some form throughout recorded human history, from ancient Egypt to the capture and enslavement of European Christians by Muslims in the Middle Ages to the present. Writers also commonly note that slavery existed in Africa, that Africans sold other Africans into slavery, and—though this is a relatively recent addition to the "stock" essay—that western Europeans ended slavery in a relatively short compass, from about the time of the American Revolution, when northern states began to adopt abolition statutes, through the 1860s.

All of this is true. However, the emphasis has important political implications. For that picture of slavery makes it look natural. It employs the "everybody does it" argument to demystify a practice of immense horror. In fact, those arguments were employed with great facility by proslavery thinkers to justify the continuation of the institution. During debates over the Fugitive Slave Act, Senator John Bell of Kentucky said that slavery has been "contributing in a hundred various forms and modes, through a period of thousands of years, to the amelioration of the condition of mankind generally, though sometimes abused and perverted, as all human institutions, even those of religion, are" (U.S. Congress 1850, 1105).

Senator Bell (who ran unsuccessfully for president of the United States in 1860) found that slavery was "still contributing to advance the cause of civilization through, if you please, having its origins in individual cupidity, still mysteriously working out a general good" (U.S. Congress 1850, 1105). He went so far as to reason from there that slavery was not inconsistent with God's law.

Moreover, saying that every society engaged in slavery is misleading. The nature of African American slavery was different in kind from slavery in many other societies. This is frequently lost on those who seek to make African American slavery look commonplace and thus minimize the nature of the harm. Grecian and Roman slavery was nonracial and temporary, for example. The children of people enslaved in one generation might rise to the ranks of free people, and slaves were incorporated into the society more generally.

It is now becoming more common to emphasize other parts of the institution of slavery that resulted in the forced migration of 11 million people to America, nearly one-half million of whom came to English-speaking

North America from the seventeenth through the mid-nineteenth centuries. (The importation of slaves into the United States was outlawed in 1808, although some people were imported illegally after that.) The institution built on centuries of European experience with slavery. Slavery survived in parts of Spain through the 1500s; soon slavery spread to Spain's colonies in America. In fact, in 1495 Columbus brought 500 Native American slaves back to Spain. But there were important differences. The slavery that developed in the Americas was brutally violent and perpetual. Slaves were often isolated from free people and left with no hope of having even their children escape from slavery.

The institution was revived and expanded in light of extraordinary needs for labor. Violence permeated it, including the forced separation of families, wars of conquest in Africa encouraged by the European market for humans, the middle passage to America, and brutalization on plantations in America.

ORIGINS

Many historians debate the origins of slavery: in European practices such as slavery in Spain in the 1400s, in a legal tradition that stretched back to Roman law, in cultural patterns that encompassed slavery in the Old Testament, in economic needs, and in race prejudices. The legal traditions came largely from Spain—and through Spanish law, from Roman law. European-imposed slavery came ashore in the West Indies in the late 1400s and early 1500s, then spread from the Caribbean to the mainland. Historians have spent much time trying to discern how and when slavery came to British North America. The first black people brought to Virginia in the 1620s seem to have had a status similar to that of indentured servitude, where they worked for a limited period of time and then became free. But by the 1660s, it appears that a system of inherited slavery had emerged in Virginia and elsewhere in mainland British North America. Children's status followed that of their mothers, so the offspring of slave mothers were also slaves. The best answer as to why appears to be that a combination of economic interests, racism, and cultural practices created the American slave system. And while race lies at the center of the institution of slavery, not all blacks were slaves. No whites were slaves, either.

And yet the human spirit longed to be free, even as the system of slavery grew in British North America and statutory laws grew up around it. In 1739 the Stono Rebellion took place along the coast of South Carolina. Something like sixty slaves began the rebellion by stealing weapons along the Stono River. In the wake of the rebellion, the statutory law of South Carolina became harsher and working conditions deteriorated. Shortly afterward,

in 1741, there was an alleged plot by slaves in New York City, where 10 percent of the population was enslaved. The extent of the plot remains in dispute, but more than two dozen slaves were executed in the aftermath.

SLAVERY AND AMERICAN REVOLUTION

Even as the slave population and the importance of slavery as a labor system were increasing, many in British North America began thinking in the Enlightenment's terms of a universal right to freedom. American revolutionists gave consideration to the terms of slavery. In a draft of the Declaration of Independence, Thomas Jefferson included the slave trade as one of the offenses of the English Crown, but that indictment was subsequently removed. Like the delegates to the Continental Congress, Americans at the time of the Revolution were more generally unwilling to act on antislavery values. One of the great paradoxes of American history is the question of how Americans could fight a war based on the idea of freedom while still maintaining slavery. Or, in the words of Dr. Samuel Johnson, "How is it that we hear the loudest yelps for liberty among the drivers of negroes?"

There was, then, in the ideology of republicanism popular in early America—that conjunction of faith in widely spread property holdings, independence from economic dependency, and political independence as well—a strange relationship with slavery. Harriet Beecher Stowe drew out the contradiction in her 1852 novel *Uncle Tom's Cabin* when a boy beat his slave. The boy's uncle asked whether that was consistent with the republican principle that "men are born free and equal." The boy's father said that the phrase was

> [o]ne of Tom Jefferson's pieces of French sentiment and humbug. It's perfectly ridiculous to have that going the rounds among us, to this day.... we can see plainly enough that all men are not born free, nor born equal; they are born anything else. For my part, I think half this republican talk sheer humbug. It is the educated, the intelligent, the wealthy, the refined, who ought to have equal rights and not the canaille. (Stowe 1852, p. 74)

Such an exchange pointed out one of the abolitionists' arguments: that slaveholders cared little for the equality of anyone, white or black. Some abolitionists argued, instead, that the slavery of Africans was but a step on the way to further inequality.

Historian Edmund Morgan's 1975 book, *American Slavery, American Freedom*, takes up the paradox of Americans' claims for freedom in the Revolution and their concomitant respect for slavery. His answer is that slavery provided the social and intellectual setting for whites' freedom. In essence, slaves made it economically possible for white men to have democracy. Moreover, the presence of slavery alerted white men to how awful servitude might be—and thus led them to be vigilant in the protection of their rights. This draws in some ways from the insight of South Carolina senator James Henry Hammond, who spoke in 1858 about slaves as the "mudsill class" who made white freedom and equality possible. Though Hammond turned to this argument as a basis for continuing slavery, later historians have used his theory for insight into the nature of political ideology and slavery. In essence, they looked to Hammond to decode why slavery, so inconsistent with the American language of freedom, had such a powerful hold on the minds of white men.

POSTREVOLUTIONARY CHANGES

In the aftermath of the American Revolution, the institution of slavery grew in popularity in the United States, even as the movement opposing slavery also grew. In the northern states, gradual abolition plans began the process of ending slavery. For example, Massachusetts and Pennsylvania passed statutes that would emancipate slaves born afterward, following a period of apprenticeship. The statutes also freed slaves brought into the states. Thus, by about the middle of the nineteenth century, no more slaves would live in those states; those who were enslaved prior to the enactments would have died, and the others would have been freed. One effect of this was to encourage owners to sell their slaves to southern states, where they and their children would continue to be slaves.

The Enlightenment continued to have some adherents. Thomas Jefferson noted in 1784 in his *Notes on the State of Virginia* that "The whole commerce between master and slave is a perpetual exercise of … the most unremitting despotism on the one part, and degrading submission on the other. … I tremble for my country when I reflect that God is just; that His justice cannot sleep forever" (Jefferson 1984, pp. 288–289). Events elsewhere also contributed to the debate over slavery. In Haiti, Enlightenment ideas and the human impulses to resist slavery led to a revolution among the half-million slaves in 1791, which resulted by 1803 in the end of slavery in Haiti. The free black state was close to alone in the world; the United States would not receive an ambassador from Haiti or even recognize Haiti. The revolution included extraordinary violence. Hundreds of whites died; some white refugees fled from Haiti to South Carolina, where they provided living reminders of what might happen in a slave society. The United Kingdom ended slavery in its colonies in 1833, at a great financial cost, following decades of abolitionist agitation.

CAPITALISM AND ANTISLAVERY SENTIMENTS

There remains substantial question about the origins of antislavery sentiments. They grew in conjunction with the development of the market economy, which has led some historians to ask, "What is the relationship between capitalism and abolitionism?" One might think at first that there is some tension, in that the institution of slavery seems to have been a fairly effective way of obtaining (relatively) inexpensive labor. Anyone wondering about how important slavery was in the development of the southern agricultural economy might perform a simple experiment: Spend an afternoon—just an afternoon—working in a field in Alabama in July. Then ask, would anyone perform this kind of labor unless forced to do so?

However, the market economy seems to have had a positive effect on antislavery sentiments; in part it made people aware of their fellow humans, in part it led to competition with free labor. Thus, free laborers had both sentimental and economic reasons for opposing slavery. That did not necessarily mean that white voters always welcomed the idea of recently freed slaves living in their community; but for reasons of self-interest, they often had a desire to end slavery. In these cases, the economic interests of many voters merged with the humanitarian sentiments of others to give strength to the antislavery cause, even as proponents of property rights in the South clung tightly to the institution.

One might also consider that Adam Smith was the author of an important treatise, *Theory of Moral Sentiments*, as well as *The Wealth of Nations*. As the market economy led the way for the development of middle-class sentiments that recognized the need for promotion of humanity (Harriet Beecher Stowe's *Uncle Tom's Cabin* is a prominent example here), it also led the way for economic competition by free workers with slavery. The Republican Party's slogan in the 1850s, for example, was "Free Soil, Free Labor, Free Men."

W. E. B. Du Bois discussed this in his 1935 book *Black Reconstruction*, one of the most important works ever written on slavery and its aftermath. The book was an important corrective to the then-dominant school of historical scholarship that relegated slavery to the sidelines in the discussion of the Civil War and that decried the domination of the South by corrupt and lawless Yankees and blacks during Reconstruction. Du Bois dealt with the differing meanings of slavery for white workers—the impact of slave labor on driving down wages, as well as the presence of free black workers in driving down wages. Du Bois wrote, for example, that white immigrants "blamed blacks for the cheap price of labor. The result was race war; riots took place which were at first simply the flaming hostility of groups of laborers fighting for bread and butter" (Du

Bois 1935, p. 18). Du Bois pointed out the complex relationship between white workers and slaves and free blacks, which made it sometimes difficult to tell how voters would define and express their preferences.

GROWING TENSIONS OVER SLAVERY AND ANTISLAVERY

In the United States there was other action. Congress outlawed the importation of slaves from outside the United States in 1808 (the earliest date permitted under the Constitution). That had the effect of increasing the prices of enslaved people and also encouraging better treatment because of their increased value. The controversy over the extension of slavery to newly acquired territories continued as well. The Northwest Ordinance of 1789 had prohibited slavery in the Northwest Territory (including Ohio and Michigan), which Virginia had ceded to the United States. Southern states worried that if free states were admitted, the South would gradually lose political power. In 1820, Congress passed the Missouri Compromise, which prohibited slavery in territories north of Missouri's southern border. For a while that contained discord over slavery. Thomas Jefferson wrote—with great foresight—about the compromise that "this momentous question, like a fire bell in the night, awakened and filled me with terror. I considered it at once as the knell of the Union." He predicted that although sectional divisions over slavery were quelled for the time being, "a geographical line, coinciding with a marked principle, moral and political, once conceived and held up to the angry passions of men, will never be obliterated; and every new irritation will mark it deeper and deeper" (Ford 1904–1905, vol. 12, pp. 158–160).

Subsequent events proved Jefferson correct. By the early 1830s, the politics of slavery grew more divisive. Nat Turner's August 1831 rebellion in southern Virginia led to the deaths of at least fifty-five white people—and to a serious debate in the Virginia legislature about a gradual abolition plan. The plan failed, narrowly; in other southern states, there was growing reluctance even to discuss the possibility of termination of slavery. In 1835, when abolitionists attempted to use the U.S. mail to deliver abolitionist literature, southern states further closed ranks. After 1835, there was little serious antislavery talk in the South; the nation was on a course toward Civil War and then, emancipation.

After 1835, southern congressmen imposed the "gag rule," which prohibited discussion of the abolition of slavery (or even the receipt of abolitionist petitions) in Congress. Southerners seem to have made an already degrading slavery harsher as well, for instance, by taking seriously statutes prohibiting the teaching of slaves how to read and by generally policing slaves more closely than they had before. Moreover, in the nineteenth century southern states moved to make emancipation of slaves harder and in some cases to require them to leave the states shortly after receiving freedom. College professors in southern institutions wrote important proslavery tracts, including Thomas R. Dew of William and Mary, Albert Taylor Bledsoe of the University of Virginia, R. H. Rivers of Alabama Wesleyan College (now the University of North Alabama), and William Smith of Randolph Macon College. Staples of the proslavery argument were that slavery was ubiquitous in history and that slave societies profited greatly from the institution. They concluded that slavery was not a drag on society but a principle cause of civilization. Moreover, they argued that economic and social stability required slavery. They pointed to Haiti and suggested the dangers to white society from the abolition of slavery.

In 1850, Congress again passed a comprehensive compromise (known as the "Compromise of 1850") that, among other things, required northern states to assist in the return of fugitive slaves. But that could not settle the issue for long. The Supreme Court invalidated the Missouri Compromise in 1857 in the *Dred Scott* case, as it attempted to install southern constitutional thinking on slavery as the law of the land. In 1860, Abraham Lincoln won election, and shortly thereafter South Carolina, fearing for the future viability of slavery, seceded. Other southern states followed and the Civil War began in 1861. During the secession discussions, southern politicians frequently spoke about the importance of preservation of slavery, and some advocated the reopening of the slave trade.

DIFFERENCES OF SPANISH AND FRENCH AMERICAS

Slavery was present in Spanish and French America, as well as in English-speaking America. In Spanish and French America, unlike English-speaking America, there seems to have been intermarriage between owners and slaves, and slaves seem to have had more formal legal protection. That has led to much discussion of whether the slave systems of Spanish and French America were more benign than in English-speaking America. There was, as many have pointed out, extraordinary violence in the slave systems throughout the Americas. After the Civil War finally ended slavery throughout the nation in 1865, slavery continued for a few more years in other parts of the Americas. Brazil finally ended slavery in 1888, which marked its termination in the Americas.

SEE ALSO *American Revolution; Cox, Oliver C.; Declaration of Independence, U.S.; Engerman, Stanley; Fogel, Robert; Freedom; Haitian Revolution; Human Rights; Jefferson, Thomas; Liberation*

BIBLIOGRAPHY

Davis, David Brion. 2006. *Inhuman Bondage: The Rise and Fall of Slavery in the New World.* New York: Oxford University Press.

Du Bois, W. E. B. 1935. *Black Reconstruction in America, 1860–1880.* New York: Russell and Russell.

Ford, Paul Leicester, coll. and ed. 1904–1905. *The Works of Thomas Jefferson.* Vol. 12. New York and London: G. P. Putnam's Sons.

Gross, Ariela. 2000. *Double Character: Slavery and Mastery in the Antebellum Southern Courtroom.* Princeton, NJ: Princeton University Press.

Harris, Leslie. 2003. *In the Shadow of Slavery: African Americans in New York City, 1626–1863.* Chicago: University of Chicago Press.

Jefferson, Thomas. 1984. *Notes on the State of Virginia*, ed. Merrill D. Peterson. New York: Library of America, Literary Classics of the United States.

Jordan, Winthrop. 1968. *White over Black: American Attitudes Towards the Negro, 1550–1812.* Chapel Hill: University of North Carolina Press.

Morgan, Edmund S. 1975. *American Slavery–American Freedom: The Ordeal of Colonial Virginia.* New York: Norton.

Roediger, David. 1991. *The Wages of Whiteness: Race and the Making of the American Working Class.* London and New York: Verso.

Stowe, Harriet Beecher. 1852. *Uncle Tom's Cabin; or, Life among the Lowly.* Boston: John P. Jewett.

Tannenbaum, Frank. 1947. *Slave and Citizen: The Negro in the Americas.* New York: Knopf.

U.S. Congress. 1850. *Congressional Globe*, 31st Cong., 1st sess., July 6.

Watson, Alan. 1989. *Slave Law in the Americas.* Athens: University of Georgia Press.

Williams, Eric. 1994. *Capitalism and Slavery.* Chapel Hill: University of North Carolina Press.

Alfred L. Brophy

SLAVERY HYPERTENSION HYPOTHESIS

Early in the twentieth century, before chronic high blood pressure (hypertension) was even recognized as a serious medical condition, colonial physicians in Africa had already developed an interest in the apparent absence of hypertension among indigenous black populations. Rather than interpreting these observations as some sort of natural advantage possessed by Africans, they attributed the difference to a carefree traditional life, uncomplicated by the stresses of industrialized society. In the United States, on the other hand, evidence emerged by the 1930s that black Americans had a higher prevalence of hypertension than whites, and this observation spawned many theories about anatomic and physiologic differences that might explain the disparity.

Despite extensive research since the mid-twentieth century on social and behavioral factors that contribute to hypertension, there has been a persistent impulse in American biomedicine to view racial groups as representing human subspecies. Explanations for racial health disparities therefore tend to be couched reflexively in terms of hypothesized genetic factors. This tradition of racial essentialism led to a surfeit of ad hoc hypotheses about hypertension, such as relating blood pressure levels directly to skin pigmentation or to excess testosterone levels in black men. Some authors suggested that because blacks originated from hot and humid environments, they possessed innate capacities for sodium retention that proved maladaptive in other settings. Others proposed that salt supplies for the sub-Saharan progenitors of African Americans were historically limited.

A POPULAR HYPOTHESIS

One of the most widely disseminated of these "just so" stories is the "slavery hypertension hypothesis," an evolutionary theory that relates excess hypertension risk in New World blacks to natural selection during the "Middle Passage" for the trait of retaining sodium. The theory was posited at least as early as 1983, and it was adopted in the late 1980s by the hypertension researcher Clarence Grim, who has championed the idea energetically in the subsequent decades. Grim speculated that sodium loss from sweating, diarrheal stools, and vomit during the transatlantic voyage led to high levels of mortality from dehydration, and therefore to selection pressure against genes coding for greater sodium excretion in the kidneys.

As this hypothesis grew in popularity, some researchers began to voice skepticism, arguing against the theory on the basis of population genetics, details of the physiology of hypertension, and basic evolutionary biology. For example, Philip Curtin, a historian of the slave trade on whose work Grim had drawn heavily, denied any historical validity to the proposition that Africa had traditionally been "salt-scarce." Curtin asserted that his own work had been misquoted on this point. He also disputed the mortality estimates cited by Grim, noting that these figures were not only incorrect or outdated, but that they were referenced so poorly that their original source could not be identified. Curtin argued that Grim's proposition that a majority of deaths were due to diarrheal disease was equally baseless, and he concluded that Grim's hypothesis not only lacked supporting evidence, but that what little evidence did exist directly contradicted the theory.

Grim has largely avoided responding to specific criticisms, and in response to these arguments he countered vaguely that Curtin had "failed to grasp several key physiological and epidemiological principles underlying the hypothesis." Other defenders of the hypothesis have been similarly oblique in print. The editor of the journal *Psychosomatic Medicine*, for example, dismissed critics of the Slavery Hypothesis as "left-thinking" people, admonishing them that race and ethnicity are "too important to be ignored or politicized" (Dimsdale 2001, p. 325).

THE SLAVERY HYPOTHESIS TODAY

The slavery hypertension hypothesis remains widely accepted, as evidenced by the numerous hypertension textbooks that describe the theory in detail, often without mention of any criticism. The hypothesis is frequently invoked in the medical literature to justify the more general proposition of innate biologic difference in cardiovascular disease risk and treatment efficacy. For example, the editor of the *American Journal of Cardiology* wrote in 2001 that "[i]t is this selective survival among the descendants of surviving slaves of genes responsible for an increased ability to hold on to salt that is now responsible for the exceptionally high prevalence of hypertension in African-Americans" (Roberts 2001, p. 1344).

The theory also reappears periodically in the popular press. In a 2005 feature about the Harvard economist Roland Fryer Jr. for example, the *New York Times Magazine* depicted the slavery hypothesis as a new and exciting idea from the young academic superstar. "Fryer's notion that there might be a genetic predisposition at work was heightened when he came across a period illustration that seemed to show a slave trader in Africa licking the face of a prospective slave," wrote the profile's author, Stephen Dubner. He continued, "a person with a higher capacity for salt retention might also retain more water and thus increase his chance of surviving. So it may have been that a slave trader would try to select, with a lick to the cheek, the 'saltier' Africans. Whether selected by the slavers or by nature, the Africans who did manage to survive the voyage—and who then formed the gene pool of modern African-Americans—may have been disproportionately marked by hypertension" (Dubner 2005, p. 56).

In this instance, the reasoning happens to be exactly backwards, as the "saltier" Africans would be exactly the ones who were not retaining sodium. Disregarding this logical error, what is remarkable is the perpetual recurrence of

the theory as so new and exciting that no actual data (e.g., a measurement of a genetic marker for sodium metabolism) is required. The single piece of "evidence" cited in this account is a 1764 antislavery engraving, the interpretation of which as a depiction of tasting for salt is dubious at best.

BEYOND THE SLAVERY HYPERTENSION HYPOTHESIS

In the case of the slavery hypothesis, a vague suggestion has achieved considerable scientific and popular dissemination, despite a dearth of evidence and denunciations by many critics that have generally gone unanswered. Respected researchers cite the theory readily, in many cases even expressing their aesthetic attraction to the idea. This is echoed in the popular press, where writers have further exaggerated the simplistic genetic determinism and essential black abnormality that are implicit in the hypothesis. Racial groups have been portrayed as fundamentally distinct in physiology, conforming to the stark distinctions that are common in the social sphere. Moreover, the casual acceptance of this outright speculation has become an edifice upon which to construct further elaborations, such as race-specific therapies, and the many facets of this mythology have come to reinforce each other and create the impression of evidence, when in fact there is little or no evidence at all.

SEE ALSO *Disease; Hypertension; Race; Slavery*

BIBLIOGRAPHY

Curtin, P. D. 1992. The Slavery Hypothesis for Hypertension among African Americans: The Historical Evidence. *American Journal of Public Health* 82 (12): 1681–1686.

Dubner, S. J. 2005. Toward a Unified Theory of Black America. *New York Times Sunday Magazine*, March 20: 54–59.

Grim, C. E., J. P. Henry, and H. Myers. 1995. High Blood Pressure in Blacks: Salt, Slavery, Survival, Stress, and Racism. In *Hypertension: Pathophysiology, Diagnosis, and Management*, eds. John H. Laragh and Barry M. Brenner, 2nd ed., 171–207. New York: Raven Press.

Kaufman, J. S., and S. A. Hall. 2003. The Slavery Hypertension Hypothesis: Dissemination and Appeal of a Modern Race Theory. *Epidemiology* 14 (1): 111–118.

Roberts, W. C. 2001. High Salt Intake, Its Origins, Its Economic Impact, and Its Effect on Blood Pressure. *American Journal of Cardiology* 88: 1338–1346.

Jay S. Kaufman

SLAVERY INDUSTRY

The word *industry* (from the Latin *industria*, meaning "diligent activity directed to some purpose") generally refers to a combination of business operations related to a primary economic product or process. Hence, *slavery industry* refers to business activity related to the institution of slavery, including not just the process of supplying slaves but also the relationship of slavery-related activity to linked activity in manufacturing, agricultural production, commerce, shipping, and financial institutions. The main issue involves exploring whether Africa, the slave trade, and slavery-related economic activity—conventionally characterized as the *triangular trade* or what Ronald Bailey (1992) calls the *slave(ry) trade*—was important to the development of commerce and industry in Europe, especially Great Britain, and the United States.

An estimate of the numbers of Africans taken as slaves was produced by Harvard University's Transatlantic Slave Trade Database in 1999. It provided up to 226 pieces of information for more than 27,233 slaving voyages. Some 11,062,000 Africans were transported between 1519 and 1867, though these numbers are constantly revised upward. About 55 percent were transported between 1700 and 1799, and 29.5 percent between 1800 and 1849. Surprisingly, about 30 percent were transported after Britain's slave trade abolition acts of 1807.

British slave traders (including those living in British colonies) carried almost 46 percent of all slaves, and the Portuguese were responsible for about 29.1 percent. The remaining Africans were carried by France (13.2%), Spain (4.8%), the Netherlands (4.7%), and the United States (2.5%). British slave traders dominated in the all-important period in the eighteenth century when European industrialization surged. Some 280,000—about 2.5 percent of all slaves—were imported into the United States, and 48 percent of these were imported after the beginning of the American Revolution (1775–1783).

Some scholars have called the forced importation of Africans into the New World cauldron before the nineteenth century "the Africanization of the Americas," one of the most significant demographic transformations in world history. Up to 1820, Africans outnumbered Europeans by a ratio of over 3 to 1 among those people who were transported across the Atlantic: almost 8.4 million Africans and 2.4 million Europeans. This had an obvious impact on population trends in Africa (depopulation) and in the Americas. The black population of the West Indies, for example, grew from 15,000 to 434,000 between 1650 and 1770—an increase of almost 2,793 percent—while the white population remained almost static, increasing from 44,000 to 45,000. The need to "repeople" the Americas resulted in part from the demand for labor and the almost genocidal impact that European settlement had on the Native American population. Thus, African peoples composed an even larger proportion of the labor force in all of the American regions associated with expanded Atlantic commerce than is generally known.

Beyond the number of Africans who were enslaved, the most hotly debated issue has been the impact that enslaved African labor had on the economic development of slave-trading nations. This was the central thesis in a book by Eric Williams (1911–1981), historian and former prime minister of Trinidad and Tobago, titled *Capitalism and Slavery* (1944). Williams's book is, in his words, "strictly an economic study of the role of Negro slavery and the slave trade in providing the capital which financed the Industrial Revolution in England and of mature industrial capitalism in destroying the slave system" (1944, p. v). Both aspects of his argument continue to provoke considerable debate, especially whether or not British abolition resulted more from economic forces than from humanitarian impulses. This issue has particular relevance to the late eighteenth and early nineteenth centuries, when large-scale manufacturing using machines became the dominant activity in industrial capitalist economies, especially in Great Britain and the United States, with cotton textiles as the leading sector.

For example, British colonies in the Caribbean and in the South, where slavery thrived, produced an average of more than 80 percent of the total value of British America's exports in the seventeenth, eighteenth, and nineteenth centuries. Enslaved African labor played a central role in the production of rice, sugar, tobacco, and cotton and in other key sectors, including the mining of gold, silver, and precious metals. Sugar and cotton, however, are the two most important sectors, and data in Joseph Inikori (2002, p. 489) bear this out: from 1752 to 1754, sugar's share of British American imports into Britain was 49 percent as compared to cotton's 2 percent. By 1814 to 1816, sugar's share was 52 percent and cotton's only 22 percent. By the 1854–1856 period, however, cotton dominated with 48 percent as compared to sugar's 15 percent.

Sugar and its cultivation provide the first context and a key link in the story of the evolution of racial slavery in the Americas, a point early recognized by Noël Deerr, who concluded that trying "to write a history of sugar without at the same time treating of slavery was like trying to produce Hamlet with the part of Laertes omitted" (1949–1950). Sugar was the crop for which large-scale plantation slavery was constructed, first on European islands in the Atlantic and then in the Caribbean. It was brought over to Hispaniola (now Haiti) in 1493 by Christopher Columbus (1451–1506), who had learned about its cultivation from his Italian father-in-law on Madeira Island, a Portuguese territory. Once transferred to the so-called New World, sugar production became a crucible with an incessant demand for labor of any type—first Native American and then European indentured servants, before the industry fastened onto African labor that was more accessible, available, abundant, and cheap. Scholars have estimated that between 60 and 70 percent of all the Africans who survived the transatlantic slave trade ended up as slaves on the sugar plantations of the Americas.

Cotton was the most decisive raw material for the British and U.S. industrial revolution in textiles, the leading industrializing sector in both nations. The industry was spurred by the invention and improvement of such technologies as the flying shuttle (1733), the spinning jenny (1764), the mule (1779), and the power loom (1785). But the labor of enslaved Africans was also crucial. In 1860 enslaved Africans working on only 3 percent of the earth's land mass in the South produced 2.3 billion pounds of cotton, or 66 percent of the world's total crop, up from 160 million pounds in 1820. This was the sole source for 88.5 percent of British cotton imports in 1860, and even supplied the growing needs of a rapidly expanding cotton textile industry centered in New England after 1790. African and slave-based economies in the Caribbean also provided important markets for British and later American manufactured cloth. Moreover, economist Robert North and others concluded that incomes from marketing slave-produced cotton, tobacco, rice, and sugar—products "sold in the markets of the world"—shaped the pattern of regional specialization and the division of labor that helped to consolidate the U.S. national economy before the Civil War (1861–1865).

Beyond its pivotal contribution to consolidating the first global commercial and industrial economies centered around the Atlantic Ocean, the "slave(ry) trade" was also a focal point of intense national rivalries among European powers. Such rivalries were part and parcel of the rise of new nation-states, initial "testbeds" in which the policies and techniques associated with mercantilism, international diplomacy, colonial administration, and war were refined.

Many historical aspects of the slavery industry involving people of African descent from the fifteenth century to the nineteenth century continue to have contemporary consequences. Slavery and the slave trade helped shape the persisting inequities that have historically existed in the economic and social conditions of peoples of African descent all over the world, a theme provocatively captured in the title of Walter Rodney's *How Europe Underdeveloped Africa* (1972). Second, the slavery industry played a key role in fostering and sustaining racism, an ideology that groups human beings into socially constructed biological categories labeled *races*, and then treats these groups as if they are inherently "inferior" or "superior" in the allocation of economic, political, and social resources and opportunities.

Inequality based on class and race has historically been the target of social protests from the earliest days of the slavery industry and continuing through the civil rights and Black Power movements up to the present. Recent calls for reparations—which demand apologies and various forms of compensation to "repay" people of African descent for their contribution to the profits and developmental success of nations, companies, and citizens with historical ties to the slave trade and slavery—have sparked considerable controversy. Some governmental units have demanded full disclosure of corporate ties to the slave trade and slavery as a precondition for granting contracts. Other recent movements, however, do not distinguish between historical forms and consequences of slavery and the slave trade that linked African peoples to the rise of capitalism from more recent systems of exploitation and oppression, such as the growing international traffic in human beings associated with contemporary globalization. Such continuing debate and ongoing struggles will undoubtedly shape these movements for social change for many decades to come.

SEE ALSO *African Americans; Cotton Industry; Industrialization; Liverpool Slave Trade; Reparations; Servitude; Slave Trade; Slavery; Sugar Industry*

BIBLIOGRAPHY

Bailey, Ronald W. 1992. The Slave(ry) Trade and the Development of Capitalism in the United States: The Textile Industry in New England. In *The Atlantic Slave Trade: Effects on Economics, Societies, and Peoples in Africa, the Americas, and Europe,* ed. Stanley Engerman and Joseph Inikori, 205–246. Durham, NC: Duke University Press.

Blackburn, Robin. 1997. *The Making of New World Slavery: From the Baroque to the Modern, 1942–1800.* London: Verso.

Darity, William, Jr. 1990. British Industry and the West Indies Plantations. *Social Science History* 14 (1): 117–149.

Deerr, Noël. 1949–1950. *The History of Sugar.* 2 vols. London: Chapman and Hall.

Eltis, David, Stephen D. Behrendt, David Richardson, and Herbert S. Klein. 1999. *The Trans-Atlantic Slave Trade: A Database on CD-ROM.* Cambridge, U.K., and New York: Cambridge University Press.

Inikori, Joseph. 2002. *Africans and the Industrial Revolution in England: A Study in International Trade and Economic Development.* Cambridge, U.K.: Cambridge University Press.

Rodney, Walter. [1972] 1981. *How Europe Underdeveloped Africa.* Rev. ed. Washington, DC: Howard University Press.

Solow, Barbara, ed. 1991. *Slavery and the Rise of the Atlantic System.* Cambridge, U.K.: Cambridge University Press.

Thomas, Hugh. 1997. *The Slave Trade: The Story of the Atlantic Slave Trade, 1440–1870.* New York: Simon and Schuster.

Williams, Eric. 1944. *Capitalism and Slavery.* Chapel Hill: University of North Carolina Press.

Ronald W. Bailey

SLAVS

SEE *Croats; Serbs.*

SLEEPER EFFECTS

People receive hundreds of persuasive messages on a given day. Naturally, they discount a great majority of these messages by relying on cues such as the credibility of the message source. In general, it is expected that noncredible sources present invalid arguments. Therefore, communications associated with noncredible sources generally do not bring about substantial attitude change in response, and may be regarded as ineffective influence attempts. Decades of research on the *sleeper effect*, however, suggests that it would be misleading to reach that conclusion without measuring attitudes down the line again. People are not very good at remembering the original context of everything that they learn, and as a result, it is possible that they may continue to remember the message well but have a hard time remembering its source. Thus, forgetting the noncredible source of the message or simply dissociating it from the message may bring about a delayed increase in persuasion. This possibility, known as the *sleeper effect*, is counterintuitive because the impact of a persuasive message is usually greater at the time of exposure than some time after exposure.

As a data pattern, the sleeper effect was identified in the early 1930s. However, systematic study of the effect and its mechanisms started much later, in the 1950s (e.g., Hovland and Weiss 1951). During World War II Carl Hovland and colleagues were interested in evaluating the impact of propaganda films commissioned by the army on the morale and opinions of enlisted U.S. soldiers. In one of their studies (Hovland, Lumsdaine, and Sheffield 1949), soldiers watched a film from the *Why We Fight* series and reported their opinions either five days or nine weeks after exposure to the film. Measures of opinions taken five days after the presentation of the film suggested that the film did not have an impact on the opinions of the soldiers. When measured again nine weeks after exposure, however, the researchers found that the opinions of those who had watched the film shifted in the direction of advocacy, whereas the opinions of those who had not watched the film remained unchanged. Thus, the film had an effect, but it required some time to surface. The term *sleeper effect* was coined after this observation.

Several mechanisms have been considered to account for the effect. However, variants of the *discounting cue explanation* have been especially popular (for a review of primary explanations, see Kumkale and Albarracín 2004; see also Pratkanis, Greenwald, Leippe, and Baumgardner 1988). According to this theory, a noncredible message

source induces suspicions of invalidity and temporarily decreases the impact of an otherwise persuasive message; consequently, little or no persuasion takes place at the time of exposure. Over time, though, the attitudes of the recipients shift in the direction of advocacy, either because the recipients forget the discounting information (*forgetting hypothesis*) or because they do not spontaneously associate the discounting cue with the message any longer (*dissociation hypothesis*). When they identified the sleeper effect for the first time, Hovland and colleagues (1949) suggested that the recipients might have forgotten the noncredible source of the message but remembered the message itself. In a follow-up study Hovland and Weiss (1951) found evidence for the sleeper effect again, but measures of recall for the message source suggested that the recipients could still remember the source of the message. Based on this finding, Hovland and colleagues proposed that forgetting the discounting cue was not necessary for the sleeper effect to take place; a weakened association between the message and the discounting cue could generate the effect as well. To the extent that the discounting cue becomes less accessible than the message over time, the likelihood of observing the sleeper effect should increase significantly. For several decades researchers concurred that the sleeper effect could be guided by either of these processes. Despite widespread acceptance of these earlier findings, subsequent research revealed that the effect might not be as strong or reliable as once thought. A recent synthesis of the relevant literature, however, revealed that the sleeper effect takes place reliably under certain circumstances, such as when the recipients deeply think about the communications at the time of receiving the communications (Kumkale and Albarracín 2004). At the very least, this synthesis verified that there is evidence for the sleeper effect in persuasion.

BIBLIOGRAPHY

Hovland, Carl I., and Walter Weiss. 1951. The Influence of Source Credibility on Communication Effectiveness. *Public Opinion Quarterly* 15: 635–650.

Hovland, Carl I., Arthur A. Lumsdaine, and Fred D. Sheffield. 1949. *Experiments on Mass Communication*. Princeton, NJ: Princeton University Press.

Kumkale, G. Tarcan, and Dolores Albarracín. 2004. The Sleeper Effect in Persuasion: A Meta-Analytic Review. *Psychological Bulletin* 130 (1): 143–172.

Pratkanis, Anthony R., Anthony G. Greenwald, Michael R. Leippe, and Michael H. Baumgardner. 1988. In Search of Reliable Persuasion Effects III: The Sleeper Effect Is Dead. Long Live the Sleeper Effect. *Journal of Personality and Social Psychology* 54 (2): 203–218.

G. Tarcan Kumkale

SLUMS

Slums are squalid sections of a city or town, areas in which most inhabitants are in or near poverty, stores and residences are cheap and dilapidated, and streets are narrow and blighted. Slums have been created in various locations; where they arise depends upon political and economic conditions in a community. In early industrial cities of England and the United States, slums housed the lowest paid workers not far from the center of the city, close to factories gates. To this day, slums in English and U.S. cities are typically located in these areas, though often the factories have closed down. In other cities, where central areas retained high land and rent value, large public housing projects were built on the outskirts and slums developed and still exist on peripheral areas (e.g., Paris). Perhaps the world's largest slum (Dharavi) is on the northern edge of the city of Mumbai (formerly Bombay). In Mexico City and other cities of Latin America, Africa, and Asia, slums exist both near the heart of the city and on the outskirts. The latter are impoverished shanty settlements created and inhabited by squatters, many of whom are relatively recent migrants.

SLUM CONDITIONS AND CAUSES

Slums are usually the most stigmatized parts of a city or town (other areas carrying high social stigma, such as skid rows, red-light districts, and docks, often are located near slum neighborhoods). In the mind of the general public, the disrepute and stigma of the slum area washes onto the people who frequent or inhabit it. When most people think of a slum they think of residents who deviate from the morals, norms, and standards of public decency held up by the wider conventional community (i.e., people involved in serious crime, drug and alcohol abuse, juvenile delinquency, gang violence). People also frequently invoke the concept of "social disorganization" to describe the slum; in other words, they see it as an area lacking the sociocultural institutions, order, coherence, and predictability found in more economically stable environments.

Sociologists and anthropologists, however, paint a more nuanced picture of slum life. Research shows that a broad range of individuals and households live in slums, from the "routine-seekers" and "decent" residents, who abide by the norms and values of the larger society, to the "action-seekers" and "street" folk, who are more likely to flout or reject those standards (Gans 1962; Anderson 1999). Additionally, research on slums often highlights the ways in which ongoing life is organized rather than disorganized. Communication channels, interpersonal obligations, status symbols, local institutions, and public etiquette usually do exist in a slum, although these may be quite different from those of middle-class neighborhoods

in a city or suburb. As the literature on local community organizing in slum areas shows, outsiders often are surprised at how much potential or actual organization exists (e.g., in the form of leadership and engagement in local social networks) even in allegedly disorganized poor neighborhoods. Having said this, one must not romanticize slums as bastions of salt-of-the-earth authenticity; all too often life in them is short and brutal, with miserable living conditions and wasted human potential.

It is tempting to think that slums are an urban anomaly produced only when something goes terribly wrong in a city. However, the high prevalence of slums and the ease with which they grow suggests that their causes lie in conventional and institutionalized routines of business as usual. Urban space is stratified as the most powerful people or those with the greatest wealth occupy the most desirable parcels of land. In cities where land and housing are commodities, the most desirable land is expensive, and the worst locations (e.g., noisy, wet, polluted) are cheap. Early slums developed when people built crowded substandard housing on the cheapest land and rented it to poor households with earnings too low to allow them to live in better but more costly areas. Beyond that simple process, the creation of slums involves more subtle causes of concentrated poverty and property decline.

By definition, cities and towns that have in their neighborhoods a mixture of housing types and the full price range in housing, from cheapest to most expensive, are places that do not have highly concentrated poverty, since the poor can live dispersed in fairly close proximity to the nonpoor. Also by definition, places where only the affluent reside are places that have no concentrated poverty in them; although, by excluding the poor, such places may contribute to the concentration of poverty in other locales. For concentrated poverty to occur, the nonpoor must have the desire and ability to distance themselves from the poor. This desire arises from several sources. One is the search for status (prestige and respectability); the poor are often perceived as uncouth, ignorant, or disreputable, and the nonpoor gain status by disassociating themselves from the poor. This is especially true if, as is often the case, the poor belong to a stigmatized racial or ethnic group. One's address becomes a prestigious status symbol if one lives in an area reserved for the "right" kinds of people. Such class consciousness coupled with aversive racism creates a related motive for concentrated poverty: fear of declining property value and/or the desire for property value appreciation. When the poor and/or racial-ethnic minorities are seen as harmful threats to community health and stability (e.g., lowering the quality of schools, raising the crime rate, spreading disease, not keeping up their yards or homes), then attempts to exclude them are made, which if successful leaves them in areas of highly concentrated poverty. On the other hand, if efforts to exclude the poor are unsuccessful and some do enter a neighborhood, then under certain conditions, a self-fulfilling vicious circle of out-movement and avoidance of the area by the affluent coupled with declining property values occurs, as affluent people refuse to pay "top dollar" for housing in or close to areas in which "the undesirables" live and instead move to other more secure, better locations.

METHODS OF EXCLUSION

Historically, the institutionalized mechanisms the affluent have utilized to distance themselves from the poor, thereby relegating those with low incomes to impoverished areas, are restrictive covenants, zoning ordinances, building codes, and political control over the location of public housing projects. With these devices (which control the types and size of housing units that are built, the size of the lots homes are built on, and whether or not apartments are allowed to be built) those in control create sections of cities or whole towns that are simply too expensive for poor people to live in. Beyond these forms of class exclusion, African Americans have faced racial exclusion (e.g., denial of mortgage loans for homes in suburban areas). This combination of restrictions forced most middle- and working-class black households to live near or in predominantly poor black areas, thereby minimizing their ability to accumulate wealth through appreciating values of their homes. Since 1980, as successful blacks became able to obtain better housing outside old black city neighborhoods, the out-movement of the middle- and working-class—in combination with loss of jobs due to deindustrialization, plus minimal investment in poor urban areas by government and the private sector—left many areas devastated with extraordinarily high rates of poverty. In rare instances, such as in Mt. Laurel, New Jersey, some state courts have ruled that suburban towns' reliance on exclusionary land use control to keep the poor out of their towns and penned up in high poverty sections of cities, like Camden or Newark, is illegal. In the 1990s, programs aimed at increasing home ownership among blacks and replacing public housing projects with mixed income developments have reduced the extent of concentrated urban poverty.

CAUSES OF DETERIORATION

A slum is more than an area of concentrated poverty; it is an area of physical and social deterioration. Several mechanisms cause this deterioration. One is "red-lining" by financial and insurance institutions. Older areas with less affluent residents are perceived as not profitable enough for home or business loans and insurance coverage, which prevents the repair and improvement of dwellings and buildings. Inability to obtain insurance coverage makes it difficult or unwise for businesses or home owners to remain in red-lined neighborhoods. Absentee landlords and speculators also play a role if they are unwilling or unable to properly maintain properties and instead extract from their buildings maximum rent while investing the minimum in upkeep, until they become dilapidated or uninhabitable. Boarded up or semi-abandoned buildings get used by transients or for drug use and become the objects of arson (for insurance money or "kicks"), and a "broken windows" phenomena may emerge as residents or outsiders commit further damage and criminal acts because they see nothing to restrain destructive impulses (Wilson and Kelling 1982). Outsiders dump garbage in the neighborhood, crime increases, and most people who seek to better themselves leave the area if they are able.

SEE ALSO *Ghetto; Segregation, Residential*

BIBLIOGRAPHY

Anderson, Elijah. 1999. *Code of the Streets.* New York: W. W. Norton.

Eckstein, Susan. 1990. Urbanization Revisited: Inner-City Slum of Hope and Squatter Settlement of Despair. *World Development* 18: 165–181.

Gans, Herbert J. 1962. *The Urban Villagers.* New York: The Free Press.

Medoff, Peter, and Holly Sklar. 1994. *Streets of Hope: The Fall and Rise of an Urban Neighborhood.* Boston: South End Press.

Philpott, Thomas Lee. 1978. *The Slum and the Ghetto.* New York: Oxford University Press.

Suttles, Gerald D. 1968. *The Social Order of the Slum.* Chicago: University of Chicago Press.

Wilson, James Q., and George L. Kelling. 1982. The Police and Neighborhood Safety: Broken Windows. *Atlantic Monthly* 127 (March): 29–38.

Wilson, William J. 1996. *When Work Disappears.* Chicago: University of Chicago Press.

Charles Jaret

SMITH, ADAM
1723–1790

The eighteenth-century Scottish economist Adam Smith is widely acknowledged as both the father of modern economics and the apostle of free trade. His cornerstone work, *The Wealth of Nations* (1776), was popular in Smith's era (six editions were published before Smith's death in 1790) and figures prominently in modern discussions of economic theory.

LIFE AND CHARACTER

Adam Smith was born on June 5, 1723, in Kirkcaldy, Scotland, a posthumous child. His mother was in her early twenties, and she was widowed after less than three years of marriage. The bond between mother and son was very close, and as Smith never married, those who believe in psychoanalytic explanations have seen significance in this. Whenever it was feasible he lived with his mother, and a spinster cousin joined them in the 1760s.

Smith went to Glasgow University in 1737 at age fourteen. In 1740 he was sent to Balliol College, Oxford, where he stayed until 1746. Smith declined entering the church, a profession many thought advisable, and spent two unemployed years back at home in Scotland. Lord Kames and other friends then invited Smith to lecture on Rhetoric and Belles-Lettres in 1748, as a reigning Scottish fashion was to learn how to speak and write English like the English. Smith was considered a capital instructor for this purpose, and his lectures were well attended.

In 1751 Smith succeeded in being appointed to the professorship of moral philosophy at Glasgow. For the next twelve years his fame grew steadily, especially after the publication of his first book in 1759, *The Theory of Moral Sentiments* (*TMS*). *TMS* not only gave Smith a European reputation, it also appears to have gained him the position of tutor to the Duke of Bucceluch. This was a lucrative appointment, and it guaranteed Smith financial independence. Scottish University students paid their individual professors, and Smith behaved admirably in repaying his students their fees.

Smith had provided distinguished and valuable services to the university, not only as a teacher but also as an administrator. Since Smith's absentmindedness and lack of address are undoubted, having been noted in a variety of historical sources, Smith's success as an administrator shows that he had the ability to concentrate fully on a given task and to persuade his colleagues to do the same. He was college quaestor (treasurer) for six years, an unusually long term, and at the end of his time at Glasgow he was dean of faculty, vice-rector, and chairman of a special committee on internal university affairs. On accepting Smith's resignation, the university minutes record sincere regret "at the Removal of Dr. Smith, whose distinguished Probity and amiable qualities procured him the esteem and affection of his Colleagues" (Campbell and Skinner 1982, p. 125).

The European tour with the Duke of Bucceluch took nearly three years, and from 1764 to 1767 Smith had the opportunity to meet most of the eminent European literati, including the school of French economists known as the physiocrats. The lectures Smith delivered at Glasgow had dealt, in part, with economic topics, but it was during his stay in France that Smith appears to have begun writing *An Inquiry into the Nature and Causes of the Wealth of Nations* in earnest. Perhaps from 1764 onward, and certainly from 1767 to 1776, with very few interruptions, Smith's constant concern was the writing of his most prominent work.

Smith's appointment as commissioner of customs in 1777 was due to the influence of the Duke of Bucceluch with the prime minister, Lord North. A humorous consequence of his new position was Smith's realization that he had "scarce a stock, a cravat, a pair of ruffles, or a pocket handkerchief which was not prohibited to be worn or used in Great Britain." In order to set an example he "burnt them all" (Smith 1987, p. 245). As Smith's duties involved the control of smuggling, scholars have wondered how Smith could wish to punish the smuggler, who was not really blamable according to the dictates of natural liberty set out in *The Wealth of Nations*? The issues raised by Smith's acceptance of such a position have been most forcefully posed by the scholars Gary Anderson, William Shugart, and Robert Tollison: "The author of the *Wealth* and Commissioner Adam Smith were one and the same person ... there is strong evidence that Smith sought the position and that it represented a reward not so much for intellectual accomplishment as for services he had rendered to the government" (1985, p. 742).

Consciously assertive of his originality, as early as 1755 Smith read a lecture strongly defending his priority for the idea of a system of natural liberty. Smith believed that several of his contemporaries, all major figures of the Scottish enlightenment, had plagiarized some of his thoughts. Adam Ferguson's (1723–1816) work on the division of labor and William Robertson's (1721–1793) economic interpretation of history provide two well-known examples of potentially plagiarized work while Hugh Blair (1718–1800) may have cooled relationships by his (acknowledged) use of Smith's lecture notes on the subject of rhetoric in Blair's *Lectures on Rhetoric* (1783). Smith had several eccentricities; among his personal habits, it was the absentminded consuming of sugar lumps, even in company; in conversation, he is said to have often taken opposite views of the same subject, according to his humor. Smith ended his days among admiring friends in Scotland, busy in his official duties and revising his publications, the last substantial revision being that of *TMS*. After ailing visibly for a while, Smith died on July 17, 1790.

EARLY WRITINGS

Smith's first love was rhetoric and literature. Dugald Stewart, Smith's successor to the Edinburgh chair, records that "the variety of poetical passages which he was not only accustomed to refer to occasionally, but which he was able to repeat with correctness, appeared surprising even to those whose attention had never been attracted to more important acquisitions" (Rae 1965, p. 34). One of Smith's most pleasant and instructive writings is the *Essay on the History of Astronomy*, which was published by Smith's executors some five years after Smith's death. The most interesting feature of the essay is Smith's discussion of the principles that guide good philosophy and that hence serve to persuade readers. Smith asserts that "philosophy is the science of the connecting principles of nature" (Smith 1982, p. 45) and so good philosophy provides individuals connections from the familiar to the unfamiliar in such a natural manner that they are convinced of its truth. The essay considers the subject of astronomy from this perspective and concludes by praising the English physicist and mathematician Sir Isaac Newton (1642–1727) for providing "the greatest and most admirable improvement that was ever made in philosophy" (Smith 1982, p. 98). Smith was coy about the reality of the Newtonian system; his own principles suggest that all such systems are imaginary but he also wrote that the weight of evidence is such that one is forced to admit that the principles seem so natural, the arguments so well connected, and the evidence so overwhelming that one is insensibly led to speak of Newtonianism as real.

The most careful and sustained expositions of *TMS*, by twenty-first-century analysis the standard view, have been articulated by Alec Macfie, Roy H. Campbell, and David D. Raphael; the most interesting contrasts in the last two decades are those of Laurence Dickey and John Dwyer. Dickey argued forcefully that Smith changed his mind on the virtue of selfishness in the last edition of *TMS* (1986), while Dwyer showed how the circles Smith moved in were emphatic in asserting that the sympathetic passions were the most beneficial for society (1998).

Smith viewed moral philosophy as facing two main questions: What is the content of ethics and how does one come to accept one's ethical precepts? He was very perceptive on the second question but only marginally illuminated the first. In modern language, *TMS* is probably best appreciated as a book on the socialization of morality rather than on the nature of right and wrong, which also explains why sociologists have been more struck with *TMS* than philosophers of ethics. Even though Smith did not illuminate practical ethics, it is notable that he insisted upon virtue being instinctive and not based upon calculation, as well as upon the reality of benevolence.

In *TMS*, humankind's acceptance of moral rules is grounded upon the need for social approval. Individuals internalize morality by looking for the admiration of those who see them. This explanation serves well for children, or when adults are in company. Smith extended the application to adults who debate moral problems when alone by introducing the concept of an "impartial spectator"—

someone who examines one's moral quandaries with detachment and whose approval serves to sustain us when we suffer reverses of fortune.

The standard view argues that the sympathetic imagination of *TMS* leads to humankind's codes of ethics and of law, while self-interest is the basis of economic behavior; the conflict between *TMS* and *The Wealth of Nations* is only apparent because the two books deal with different levels of social reality. Posterity has accorded fame to *The Wealth of Nations* and only appreciation to *TMS* because the link between self-interest and economic phenomena can be satisfactorily indicated, while a link of similar clarity between sympathy and ethics still awaits us. A late twentieth-century trend to interpret Smith's economics through the lens of *TMS* faces the difficulty that only in the preface to the last edition of *TMS*, shortly before his death, did Smith make any public attempt to mention the two books together. Five editions of *The Wealth of Nations* (and of *TMS*) came and went without Smith ever trying to soften *The Wealth of Nations* with *TMS*. Scholars argue that if Smith had wanted modern-day readers to qualify the selfishness of *The Wealth of Nations* with the stoicism of *The Theory of Moral Sentiments* he would have done so himself.

THE WEALTH OF NATIONS

The manner of writing of *The Wealth of Nations* is modern in its frequent separation of theory from policy. In Books I through IV, Smith explained that free trade is the ideal policy for all nations. In Book V he explained the obvious practical requirement that governments must raise taxes to meet essential expenses. So the combined effect of all five books is to advocate a policy that imposes taxes for revenue but not for protection. This is the same policy that was supported in the popular literature of the 1740s in the pamphlets of William Richardson and Sir Matthew Decker. However, the separation of pure theory, which supports free trade, from practical policy, which recognizes the need for taxes, makes the ideas of *The Wealth of Nations* more attractive.

Much of the charm of Smith's work arises from the casual fluidity of his language. He expressed commonplace ideas forcefully and provided homely illustrations; Smith's arguments are axiomatic, but he interrupted his exposition with much ordinary illustration. These nuances in his writing have led modern-day scholars to frequent, and perhaps endless, discussion about whether he was really inductive or deductive. Perhaps the most effective use of everyday thought was the phrase "invisible hand" to describe the harmony of the market. Moral philosophers had consistently rejected the use of the market as socially beneficial because they could not fathom how the universal prevalence of selfishness—the motivation of the market—could lead to a harmonious society. It was one of several euphemisms used by contemporaries to refer to God as the beneficent controller of the universe. When Smith came to proving this difficult point, he found it convenient to finesse the argument by referring instead to the invisible hand as one that provides coherence through the market. Smith knew he could count on the subliminal persuasiveness of the "invisible hand" to quash any doubts readers might have about the goodness of the market. Ferguson and Robertson, while serving as army chaplains, had each used the phrase to exhort their soldiers in 1747. Whether Smith himself believed in a Christian God is beside the point; it is his rhetorical skill that needs to be appreciated.

The fairest treatment of Smith's contributions to economic theory would portray Smith's ideas along with those of his contemporaries. Space does not permit and readability perhaps does not require such discussion. With a brief glance at contemporary thought, the focus herein is on the internal logic of Smith's arguments, with the topics being chosen by their importance for modern economics. In considering Smith's contributions to economic theory it is useful to begin with microeconomics, then to macroeconomics, and finally to international trade.

Jacob Viner provided a penetrating assessment of Smith's contributions to micreconomics when he wrote, "On every detail, taken by itself, Smith appears to have had predecessors in plenty. On a few details was Smith as penetrating as the best of his predecessors" (1928, p. 118). The theoretical constructs of demand and supply, used by modern economists, had been widely and effectively used by economists for more than a century when Adam Smith wrote. A brief overview of Smith's microeconomic theory shows that Smith's attempted innovations were severely limited.

Smith distinguished between "natural" and "market" price, regarding the former as clearly the more fundamental of the two. What then determines natural price? Smith began by explaining to readers that in every society, at any given time, there exists an ordinary or average rate of wages, profits, and rent; these average rates for each factor of production Smith called the natural rate. He then defined the natural price as the sum of the natural rates of wages, profits, and rents. This price is distinguished from the market price, which is merely another name for whatever price reigns in the market at any given time. The demand of those individuals who are willing to pay the natural price of a commodity constitutes what is called the "effectual demand," and market price is said to arise out of the interplay of the *actual* supply and the desires of the *effectual* demanders. The explicit theoretical construct thus consists of an awkward juxtaposition of a point supply and a point demand. If, however, one glosses over the

location of equilibrium, that is, the natural price, and asks instead how Smith described what happens when the world is not in equilibrium, the treatment is excellent.

Since natural price is defined as the sum of natural wages, profits, and rents, this requires an explanation of the natural rates of wages, profits, and rents. The natural rates are naturally regulated by the structure of the economy and its growth, "partly by the general circumstances of the society, their riches or poverty, their advancing, stationary, or declining condition; and partly by the particular nature of each employment" (1976, I, 72, 159). The subsequent chapters, however, fail to show readers how to use structure and growth to find natural wages or profits in any particular situation.

Smith had claimed that product prices are to be explained by factor prices; this dichotomy between the forces determining product and factor prices was an innovation. He subsequently claimed that factor prices, and hence product prices, are to be explained by structural and growth factors. Somehow, microeconomics has disappeared. The procedure has led some rigorous critics such as Mark Blaug, to exclaim, "To say that the normal price of an article is the price that just covers money costs is to explain prices by prices. In this sense, Adam Smith had no theory of value whatever" (1985, p. 39).

How did Smith convince so many ordinary readers of the merits of the market? He does provide readers many convincing illustrations of opportunity cost and of the equalization of returns in different uses. Chapter X of Book I deals with the inequalities of wages and profits across different occupations. It is a beautiful exercise in tracing how differences in prestige or risk can account for such inequalities in money wages. While such explanations can be couched in the modern language of demand and supply, since Smith did not apply the modern apparatus, one has to ask if there are other, perhaps simpler, ways of getting to such results.

Suppose Smith began by *assuming* that any violation of natural liberty was both morally wrong and economically harmful; such a position could itself provide the grounds to condemn several institutions of Smith's day. Such "politically based" arguments are convenient in that they need to consider the absence of competition on only one side of the market. For example, in the case of the Law of Settlements, which hindered the mobility of workers, it was enough to condemn the Laws that the rights of workers were being violated. Second, if one assumes that a market reaches a stable equilibrium, then the belief in one-sided competition alone suffices to provide several analytical results. For example, in the usual version of Ricardian rent theory, the same final outcome is reached whether only farmers compete (for land) or only landlords compete (for farmers). This one-sided analytical procedure works best when there are constant returns to scale and the assumption of fixed proportions, used on several occasions by Smith, is perhaps a consequence of his analytical method.

Smith's contribution to microeconomics requires some care to elucidate: He did not advance scholars' understanding of the equilibrium theory, involving demand and supply; he even confused matters by dichotomizing product and factor prices. But, from his very earliest lectures, Smith thoroughly appreciated the fundamental fact that liberty and competition lead to zero-profits. This observation was repeatedly and successfully applied to such fields as the choice of occupations, the preference for pasturage over tillage, and the determination of joint prices. It even sufficed to move analysts toward the "natural price," wherever that might be. It is a form of argument that is attractive, easy to learn, and independent of the more intricate demand-supply apparatus, and accounts for Smith's hold on the general public.

There is no direct concern for macroeconomic problems in *The Wealth of Nations*. By omitting any systematic discussion of unemployment in *The Wealth of Nations*, Smith made macroeconomic concerns seem chimerical and succeeded in focusing attention on capital accumulation and upon long-run issues. So perhaps the most notable victory of *The Wealth of Nations* was a silent one. When Smith did touch upon unemployment, the primary concern for his contemporaries, he used three separate arguments to de-emphasize that concern. Smith provided readers with a model of the economy as a giant corn farm, which employs workers by keeping aside a portion of last year's harvest in order to feed the workers until the next harvest. Smith called this the "wages fund," and since it is predetermined by last year's decision, one cannot increase the numbers to be employed since the model provides the food for only so many. A second argument claimed that the soldiers disbanded after the Seven Years' War found new jobs within a short space of time, and Smith used this as proof that persistent unemployment is not a real possibility. Finally, Smith made the "global" assertion that "what is annually saved is as regularly consumed as what is annually spent, and nearly in the same time too; but it is consumed by a different set of people" (1976, I, 337-338). The implication that aggregate demand always equals aggregate supply, regardless of how much or little is saved, probably had great impact upon Smith's contemporaries. The cumulative impact of the several arguments was to suggest to readers that the market economy is globally stable, and if only it were left free, it would also be efficient.

An important idea, never quite explicitly stated yet pervading the entire book, is the superiority of commercial society over feudalism. This led Smith to the concepts of productive labor, which roughly correspond to economic activity that produces a measurable output, and to contrast it with unproductive labor or services. Without such a framework, one would be hard pressed to explain why a fully employed commercial society, making cloth and machines, is superior to a fully employed feudal one, making swords and monasteries. Much of the framework of modern national income accounting is set up at different points of *The Wealth of Nations*. To grasp the concept of national income one has to have all of a nation's economic activity in one's mind. A very important by-product, appropriate to someone who believed in unintended consequences, was the image of the economy as a whole. This constantly recurring background to all parts of *The Wealth of Nations*, the image of the economy as a complex machine always working away, has led scholars, such as Samuel Hollander, to argue that Smith was an early general equilibrium theorist (1976).

The effort to conceive of the economy as a whole and represent it by some number had a second potent conclusion. Since bundles of apples and oranges cannot be compared physically but only as economic values, the numerical concept led to a focus upon monetary values. In turn, this enabled Smith to conclude that growth is not based upon acquiring a surplus of some physical balance, as with mercantilism and bullion or with physiocracy and agriculture, but rather a value surplus—that of income over expenditure. In this sense, it has been well said that Smith's novelty lay in the cumulative "shifts of focus" in *The Wealth of Nations* (Winch 1996, p. 22).

The issue that bridges macroeconomics and trade is monetary policy. Smith broke cleanly with the past and argued that the market was sufficient to provide whatever amount of circulating medium was necessary. Mercantilist arguments in favor of an influx of metals as a wartime buffer or for providing ample liquidity to the markets were all specious. Just as one does not try to regulate trade in pots and pans but trusts the market to provide them as needed, so too could the market suffice for money.

> To attempt to increase the wealth of any country [by interfering with the trade in gold and silver] … is as absurd as it would be to increase the good cheer of private families, by obliging them to keep an unnecessary number of kitchen utensils (Smith 1976, IV, pp. 439–440).

From the time of publication of *The Wealth of Nations* until the middle of the twentieth century, Smith was viewed primarily as the source of laissez-faire ideas. According to Wesley Mitchell in his *Types of Economic Theory* (1967), the benefits of economic freedom can be argued on the basis of three axioms:

1. Individuals desire to maximize their wealth.

2. Individuals know better than governments how to maximize their own wealth.

3. National wealth is the sum of individual wealth (1967, pp. 61–64).

Axioms 1 and 2, in conjunction, prove that individual wealth is maximized when government leaves individuals alone. Axiom 3 then says that maximizing individual wealth suffices to maximize national wealth. If one describes the axioms loosely as greed, knowledge, and additivity, then greedy and knowledgeable individuals surely do not need government in order to maximize their wealth, and additivity suffices to assure one that, since the aggregate is the simple sum of the individuals, the aggregate also does not need government to maximize economic growth. Modern readers, familiar with externalities in the form of, say, pollution, will probably be most curious about the validity of axiom 3, but in most developing economies axioms 1 and 2 are also worth questioning.

The two most important policy measures of Smith's time were bounties for infant industries in foreign trade and preventing speculation in food markets in domestic trade. Smith firmly rejected both bounties for infant industries and interference in food markets. He argued the case against bounties as follows: He noted that no one argues against natural advantages, and he went on to illustrate this with his famous example of growing grapes in hothouses in Scotland. Then he transferred the argument without any further reasoning to cases where there is no suggestion of natural advantage. "Whether the advantages which one country has over another, be natural or acquired, is in this respect of no consequence" (1976, IV, p. 458). One could ask how others acquired such an advantage and why anyone might not acquire it as well? This is just what all economists who urged "catch-up" to their countries did argue. Smith could have said that choosing which infant industries have promise requires too much knowledge and discrimination or that such infants have a persistent tendency not to want to grow up. He did neither. So strong was his feeling on the matter that he simply bypassed the argument.

If one wonders about the incongruity of the putative father of economics providing so many examples of indifferent economic analysis, one should remember that a critic found many proofs in Euclid's *Elements* to be "more complicated than older versions … essential axioms of order and separation are entirely overlooked, the postulates inadequate to prove even the first theorem" (Goodstein 1951, p. 3). Modern-day scholars seem to remember historical figures as much for their intentions as for their achievements. Smith wrote at a time when his liberal cosmopolitanism won him many converts, especially outside Britain; the support of elite politicians probably mattered, especially when Smith could be used in support of conservative economic policies during scarcities; and the benefits to Britain of appealing to free trade when Britain was the leader in manufacturing meant that economic truth was supported by self-interest. How far Smith's superior fame was due to these noneconomic factors is a question that only bias can solve.

It is appropriate to close by continuing with the words of Jacob Viner who wrote of Smith that he was only applying to society forms of reasoning that had long been utilized by theologians and philosophers to general phenomena and that only on a few details was Smith's analysis superior: "But Smith made an original forward step when he seriously applied himself to the task of analyzing the whole range of economic process with the purpose of discovering the nature of the order which underlay its surface chaos" (1928, p. 118). It was not so much any refinement in analysis but Smith's ambitious undertaking and his faith in the overall harmony of free trade that constitute his principal legacy.

BIBLIOGRAPHY

PRIMARY WORKS

Smith, Adam. 1976. *An Inquiry into the Nature and Causes of the Wealth of Nations*, eds. Andrew S. Skinner and R. H. Campbell. Oxford: Clarendon Press.

Smith, Adam. 1982. *Essays on Philosophical Subjects*, eds. William P. D. Wightman and J. C. Bryce. Indianapolis, IN: Liberty Classics.

Smith, Adam. 1987. *The Correspondence of Adam Smith*, eds. Ernest C. Mossner and Ian S. Ross. Indianapolis, IN: Liberty Classics.

SECONDARY WORKS

Anderson, Gary, Robert Tollison, and William F. Shugart III. 1985. Adam Smith in the Customshouse. *Journal of Political Economy* 93 (4): 740–759.

Blaug, Mark. 1985. *Economic Theory in Retrospect*. Cambridge, U.K: Cambridge University Press.

Campbell, R. H., and Andrew Skinner. 1982. *Adam Smith*. New York: St. Martin's Press.

Dickey, Laurence. 1986. Historicizing the 'Adam Smith Problem': Conceptual Historiographical, and Textual Issues. *The Journal of Modern History* 58 (3).

Dwyer, John. 1998. *The Age of the Passions: An Interpretation of Adam Smith and Scottish Enlightenment Culture*. East Linton, Scotland: Tuckwell Press.

Eden, F. M. 1928. *The State of the Poor*, ed. A. G. L. Rogers. London: Routledge.

Goodstein, R. L. 1951. *The Foundations of Mathematics*. Leicester, U.K.: University College of Leicester.

Hollander, Samuel. 1976. *The Economics of Adam Smith*. Toronto: University of Toronto Press.

Mitchell, Wesley. 1967. *Types of Economic Theory*. New York: Kelley.

Rae, John.1965. *Life of Adam Smith*. New York: Augustus M. Kelley. (Orig. pub. 1895).

Viner, Jacob. 1928. Adam Smith and Laisse-Faire. In *Adam Smith 1776–1926*. Chicago: University of Chicago Press.

Winch, Donald. 1996. *Riches and Poverty*. Cambridge, U.K.: Cambridge University Press.

Salim Rashid

SMITH, VERNON L.
1927–

American economist Vernon Lomax Smith was born in Wichita, Kansas, on January 1, 1927. In 2002 Smith became the co-laureate of the Nobel Prize in Economics "for having established laboratory experiments as a tool in empirical economic analysis, especially in the study of alternative market mechanisms" (Nobel Foundation 2002). In awarding Smith the prize, the Nobel committee recognized the well-known observation that Smith is the father of the discipline of experimental economics.

Smith's official Nobel autobiography (Nobel Foundation 2002) provides a moving description of life in the Depression-era Kansas of railroads, farming, oil drilling, and relatives who die too young. This was also a world in which a graduate of a one-room schoolhouse who became a distracted "C" student in high school could gain admission to one of the world's finest universities, the California Institute of Technology (Caltech), by passing the rigorous admission exam. By 1955 Smith was a graduate of Caltech (B.S., 1949), the University of Kansas (M.A., 1951), and Harvard University (Ph.D., 1955), with a faculty position at Purdue University in Indiana.

Smith's initial research areas were in capital theory, investment, and financial economics. At about this time, a fortunate synergy among teaching and research emerged. The behavior of the stock market is certainly relevant to capital theory and financial economics, and Smith pondered how to get these ideas across in his classes. He recalled from his days as a graduate student at Harvard that economist Edward Hastings Chamberlin (1899–1967) had created a simulated "random meetings" market in a classroom, in which demand and supply curves were constructed from hypothetical benefits and costs assigned to the students. Chamberlin's markets famously failed to find the competitive equilibrium. Smith's changes were initially to use a different trading institution, the oral double auction (an analog of stock exchange trading rules), and to repeat the markets across time. Later, after conversations with psychologist Sidney Siegel (1916–1961), Smith made a third important inno-

vation: costs and valuations were no longer hypothetical, and participants were actually paid according to their earnings. The Chamberlin findings dissolved; the markets converged to the competitive predictions. Smith's first research results in experimental economics were published in the *Journal of Political Economy* in 1962. Further exploration of the double auction institution followed. Then, Smith applied the methodology to a different institution, the sealed bid auction (as used in U.S. Treasury securities auctions). Along the way, Smith continued to make seminal contributions in financial economics, environmental economics, and economic anthropology.

During a visiting appointment at Caltech in 1974, Smith found that a former Purdue faculty member, Charles Plott, had moved to Caltech and become an enthusiastic proponent of experimental methodology. This began a period of fruitful collaboration between them. Smith left for the University of Arizona in 1976 and then George Mason University in 2001. Smith's reputation as the "father of experimental economics" coalesced, due not only to the original Purdue innovations but also to the breadth of his new applications and the development of key methodology treatises on laboratory experiments. In the former category, Smith's work expanded to include public goods provision mechanisms, oral auctions, industrial organization, asset pricing, and the concept of computer assisted "smart markets." His methodological articles address the concept of "induced valuation" (reflecting his earlier decision to pay subjects based upon earnings). In 1982 his tour de force, "Microeconomic Systems as an Experimental Science," was published. Nationally and internationally, the number of researchers adopting the methodology increased dramatically. Smith was the driving force behind the founding of the Economic Science Association in the mid-1980s.

In his Nobel autobiography, Smith singles out two books in economics that attracted his attention prior to graduate school, one by American economist Paul Samuelson, the other by Austrian economist Ludwig von Mises (1881–1973). This observation is a foreshadowing of Smith's career. His lifetime of contributions to traditional mathematical microeconomic theory (the Samuelson stream) by themselves would be stellar, but his work in experimental economics is equally important. For Smith, experimental economics is immersed in a different way of looking at the world. Smith's mother had strong socialist leanings, and his graduate training at Harvard in the early 1950s was hardly an incubator for a libertarian worldview, certainly not foreshadowing his later active involvement with the Mont Pelerin society. But Smith's economics (not merely his experimental economics) are very different from that which his early background might suggest. This could be due to his early reading of von Mises and German economist Friedrich von Hayek (1899–1992). It could also reflect the striking observation from his first experiments: markets that do not efficiently capture gains from exchange under one institution will do so under another. Whatever the history, there is no better place to find Smith's views than in his 2002 Nobel lecture, "Constructivist and Ecological Rationality in Economics." The lecture has obvious overtones of Austrian economics, but Smith presents a tantalizing paradox. Experimental economics can be viewed as buttressing a Hayekian view of economics, but Hayek himself seemed to anticipate, and then reject, the methodology of experiments.

SEE ALSO *Austrian Economics; Constructivism; Economics, Experimental; Hayek, Friedrich August; Mises, Ludwig Edler von; Mont Pelerin Society; Samuelson, Paul A.*

BIBLIOGRAPHY

Chamberlin, Edward H. 1948. An Experimental Imperfect Market. *Journal of Political Economy* 56: 95–108.

Nobel Foundation. 2002. The Bank of Sweden Prize in Economic Sciences in Memory of Alfred Nobel 2002. Press Release, Autobiography, and Prize Lecture. http://nobelprize.org/nobel_prizes/economics/laureates/2002/.

Smith, Vernon L. 1962. An Experimental Study of Competitive Market Behavior. *Journal of Political Economy* 70: 111–137.

Smith, Vernon L. 1982. Microeconomic Systems as an Experimental Science. *American Economic Review* 72: 923–955.

Smith, Vernon L., Gerry L. Suchanek, and Arlington W. Williams. 1981. Bubbles, Crashes, and Endogenous Expectations in Experimental Spot Asset Markets. *Econometrica* 56: 1119–1151.

Robert Mark Isaac

SMOKING

Cigarette smoking has great societal and clinical significance. It is a major cause of several diseases, including a variety of cancers. The practice of cigarette smoking is pervasive; about a quarter of all adult Americans smoke cigarettes, and smoking rates are even higher in many other countries. Despite the high personal cost associated with cigarette smoking, it is a prototypical addictive disorder manifesting such features as tolerance, withdrawal, and chronic use. The peak age for smoking prevalence is between eighteen and twenty-five years. Retrospective data from the National Household Survey on Drug Abuse suggests that the average age of first use of tobacco products in 1999 among all persons who ever used in their lifetime was 15.4 for cigarettes, 20.5 for cigars, and 16.7 for

smokeless tobacco across all age groups (Kopstein 2001). Data from the National Comorbidity Survey suggests that the onset of nicotine dependence is delayed for at least one year after the onset of daily smoking. Smoking rates decline among people who have reached their mid-twenties, but these declines are modest in comparison to other forms of substance use. This may be due to the fact that cigarette smoking is highly addictive, legal, and not immediately performance-impairing.

BIOLOGICAL ASPECTS OF NICOTINE ADDICTION

Nicotine, independently, yields the trademark effects of an addictive drug. It produces tolerance and physical dependence, and heightened doses produce euphoria and satisfaction (Corrigall 1999; USDHHS 1998). Smokers will not self-administer tobacco on a chronic basis if it does not contain nicotine. Nicotine is essential for the development and maintenance of a smoking habit. However, once nicotine dependence is established, cues related to nicotine release become greatly influential in controlling self-administration behaviors. When a cigarette is smoked, about 80 percent of the inhaled nicotine is absorbed in the lungs (Armitage et al. 1975). Absorption is both efficient and extremely rapid. Despite the overall recognition that the rapid onset of drug action promotes addictive drug use, it remains unclear why this is so. Researchers do not fully understand which characteristics of drug pharmacokinetics are most determinant of addictiveness.

BEHAVIORAL ASPECTS AND ENVIRONMENTAL INFLUENCE

Data published in 2002 suggest that smoking among American adolescents is fairly common, with 27 percent of twelfth graders, 18 percent of tenth graders, and 11 percent of eighth graders reporting that they had smoked in the past month (Johnston et al. 2002). This level of smoking prevalence represents a decline from peaks in the mid-1990s. Much less is known about the epidemiology of tobacco dependence in adolescents. *Dependence* is a term often correlated with addiction, and adolescent smokers are less likely to be diagnosed with tobacco dependence than are adult smokers (Colby et al. 2000), although many adolescent smokers consider themselves addicted. Adolescents who are dependent report the same symptoms as do dependent adults, including cravings, withdrawal, tolerance, and a desire to reduce smoking (Colby et al. 2000). Compared to adults at the same level of self-reported intake, adolescents who smoke are more likely to be diagnosed as dependent, which suggests that adolescents may be especially vulnerable to dependence or sensitive to the effects of nicotine (Kandel and Chen 2000).

Before they experiment with cigarettes, adolescents form beliefs and attitudes about the effects of smoking. These attitudes and beliefs prospectively predict both the onset and escalation of smoking. Many adolescents believe that there are no health risks related to smoking in the first few years, and they believe that they will stop smoking before any damage is done. Existing evidence suggests that adolescents and adults exhibit unrealistic optimism about the personalized risks of smoking (Arnett 2000; Weinstein 1999). Whether adolescents are any more likely than adults to underestimate the personalized risks of smoking is unclear.

Evidence indicates that as smokers become more dependent, there is a shift in the motivational basis for their tobacco use. Social motives and contextual factors are rated as influential to beginner smokers, while heavy smokers emphasize the importance of control over negative moods and urges, and the fact that smoking has become involuntary (Piper et al. 2004). When smoking becomes less linked to external cues and more linked to internal stimuli, smokers are classified as *dependent.* There is also evidence suggesting that smoking cigarettes may lead to the use of illicit drugs. Cigarette smoking is endemic among substance abusers, with rates as high as 74 percent to 88 percent (Kalman 1998), compared to 23 percent of the general population (CDC 2002).

Greater parental education is associated with less likelihood of smoking in offspring. Additionally, girls appear to be more influenced by peer smoking than boys (Mermelstein 1999). In the United States, the highest smoking rates are among American Indian and Alaska Native adolescents, followed by whites and then Hispanics, with lowers rates among Asian Americans and African Americans. While studies that sample multiethnic groups are sparse, research has suggested that African American and Asian American adolescents report stronger antismoking socialization messages from parents and that African American parents report feeling particularly empowered to influence their children's smoking (for reviews, see Mermelstein 1999; USDHHS 1998). Peer smoking is a relatively weak predictor of smoking for African American adolescents compared to white adolescents.

Adolescents sometimes start smoking as a result of self-image. The social image of an adolescent smoker is an ambivalent one, with negative aspects but also images of toughness, sociability, and precocity that may be particularly valued by "deviance-prone" adolescents who are at risk to smoke (Barton et al. 1982). Additionally, adolescents may start smoking and continue smoking because of their perception of the effect that smoking has on weight control and dieting. The belief that smoking can control body weight has been shown to predict smoking initiation among adolescent girls, but not boys (Austin and

Gortmaker 2001). In addition, this belief is held more widely by white girls than by African American girls (Klesges et al. 1997). Despite the above-mentioned indicators, peer smoking is the most consistently identified predictor of adolescent smoking (Derzon and Lipsey 1999). In addition to cigarette smoking by peers, affiliation with peers who engage in high levels of other problem behaviors also prospectively predicts smoking initiation, as does self-identification with a high-risk social group (Sussman et al. 1994).

SMOKING CESSATION AND PREVENTION

The tobacco industry spends millions of dollars per day on advertising and promotional materials to keep their products in the public eye. Beyond such reminders of the availability of tobacco products, smoking is not an easy habit to break. Smokers must not only break the physical addiction to nicotine, but also the habit of lighting up at certain times of the day. Successful quitters confess that quitting is often a lengthy process that involves several unsuccessful attempts. Although one-third of smokers attempt to quit each year, 90 percent or more of those who attempt to quit will fail.

Nicotine replacement therapies (NRTs) have been used to help some people quit smoking. The two most common forms of NRTs are chewing gum and the nicotine patch, both of which are available over the counter. Nicorette, a prescription chewing gum containing nicotine, is often used to help reduce the consumption of nicotine over time. Users have reported experiencing fewer cravings for nicotine as the dosage is reduced, until they are completely weaned. The nicotine patch was first marketed in 1991 for smokers with a desire to quit. Generally, the nicotine patch is used in conjunction with a comprehensive smoking-behavior cessation program. Additionally, a nicotine nasal spray, nicotine inhaler, and nicotine pill have been approved by the FDA to help cigarette smokers quit smoking. In order to prevent the initiation and maintenance of smoking, there has been an increase since the mid-1980s in the development and implementation of smoking cessation and prevention programs, especially for young people and adolescents.

GLOBAL ECONOMICS OF SMOKING

Approximately 80 percent of the world's 1.1 billion smokers live in low- and middle-income countries. In 1998 about four million people died of tobacco-related disease worldwide (WHO 1999). This number is projected to increase to ten million annually by 2030, with 70 percent of these deaths occurring in low-income countries. Death counts of this magnitude could be prevented if current smokers quit, but it is rare for smokers living in low- to middle-income countries to attempt to quit smoking (Jha and Chaloupka 2000). Although few dispute that smoking is damaging to human health on a global scale (Peto and Lopez 2000), governments have avoided taking action to control smoking. This is mainly due to concerns that such interventions might have harmful economic consequences, such as permanent job losses. Despite these concerns, several common measures aimed at the control of smoking, such as higher tobacco taxes, consumer information, bans on advertising and promotion, and regulatory policies, have had a significant impact. Each will be discussed below.

An increase in tobacco taxes is the single most effective intervention to reduce the demand for tobacco. A review by Prabhat Jha and Frank Chaloupka (2000) suggests that a price increase of 10 percent would reduce smoking by 4 percent in high-income countries and by about 8 percent in low- and middle-income countries. This evidence also implies that young people, individuals on low incomes, and those with less education are more responsive to price changes (Chaloupka et al. 2000). Policies to improve the quality and extent of tobacco information can also reduce smoking, particularly in low- and middle-income countries. For example, in the 1960s and 1970s, the promulgation in the United States and Britain of new evidence on the health risks of smoking helped reduce consumption between 4 and 9 percent. In addition, warning labels on cigarette packages were also found to reduce consumption during that era (Kenkel and Chen 2000). In a review of 102 countries and econometric analyses of income, Henry Saffer and Chaloupka (2000) revealed that bans on advertising and promotion led to considerable reductions in tobacco consumption.

Enforcing regulatory policies designed to prevent smoking in public places, worksites, and other facilities can also significantly reduce cigarette consumption worldwide (Yurekli and Zhang 2000). Attempts to impose restrictions on the sale of cigarettes to young people in high-income countries have mostly been unsuccessful (Siegel et al. 1999). Furthermore, it may be difficult to implement and enforce such restrictions in low-income countries. Evidence indicates that freer trade in tobacco products has led to an increase in smoking and other types of tobacco use. One solution is for countries to adopt measures that effectively reduce demand and apply those measures to both imported and domestically produced cigarettes (Taylor et al. 2000).

SEE ALSO *Addiction; Adolescent Psychology; Disease; Peer Effects; Tobacco Industry; Tolerance, Drug*

BIBLIOGRAPHY

Armitage, A. K., C. T. Dollery, C. F. George, et al. 1975. Absorption and Metabolism of Nicotine from Cigarettes. *British Medical Journal* 4: 313–316.

Arnett, Jeffrey Jensen. 2000. Optimistic Bias in Adolescent and Adult Smokers and Nonsmokers. *Addictive Behavior* 25: 625–632.

Austin, S. Bryn, and Steven L. Gortmaker. 2001. Dieting and Smoking Initiation in Early Adolescent Girls and Boys: A Prospective Study. *American Journal of Public Health* 91: 446–450.

Barton, John, Laurie Chassin, Clark Presson, and Steven J. Sherman. 1982. Social Image Factors as Motivators of Smoking Initiation in Early and Middle Adolescence. *Child Development* 53 (6): 1499–1511.

Centers for Disease Control and Prevention (CDC). 2002. Cigarette Smoking among Adults—United States, 2000. *Morbidity and Mortality Weekly Report* 51: 642–645.

Chaloupka, Frank J., Teh-Wei Hu, Kenneth E. Warner, et al. 2000. The Taxation of Tobacco Products. In *Tobacco Control in Developing Countries*, eds. Prabhat Jha and Frank Chaloupka, 237–272. Oxford: Oxford University Press.

Colby, Suzanne, Stephen T. Tiffany, Saul Shiffman, and Raymond S. Niaura. 2000. Are Adolescent Smokers Dependent on Nicotine? A Review of the Evidence. *Drug Alcohol Dependence* 59 (suppl.): 83–95.

Corrigall, William A. 1999. Nicotine Self-Administration in Animals as a Dependence Model. *Nicotine Tobacco Resistance* 1: 11–20.

Derzon, James H., and Mark W. Lipsey. 1999. Predicting Tobacco Use to Age 18: A Synthesis of Longitudinal Research. *Addiction* 94: 995–1006.

Jha, Prabhat, and Frank J. Chaloupka. 2000. The Economics of Global Tobacco Control. *British Medical Journal* 321: 358–361.

Johnston, Lloyd D., Patrick M. O'Malley, Jerold Bachman, and John E. Schulenberg. 2002. *National Survey Results on Drug Use from the Monitoring the Future Study, 1975–2002*. Vol. 1: *Secondary School Students*. Rockville, MD: U.S. Department of Health and Human Services, Public Health Service, and National Institutes of Health.

Kalman, David. 1998. Smoking Cessation Treatment for Substance Misusers in Early Recovery: A Review of the Literature and Recommendations for Practice. *Substance Use and Misuse* 33: 2021–2047.

Kandel, Denise B., and Kevin Chen. 2000. Extent of Smoking and Nicotine Dependence in the United States, 1991–1993. *Nicotine and Tobacco Research* 2: 263–275.

Kenkel, Donald, and Lisa Chen. 2000. Consumer Information and Tobacco Use. In *Tobacco Control in Developing Countries*, eds. Prabhat Jha and Frank Chaloupka, 177–214. Oxford: Oxford University Press.

Klesges, Robert C., Vanessa E. Elliot, and Leslie A. Robinson. 1997. Chronic Dieting and the Belief that Smoking Controls Body Weight in a Biracial Population-based Adolescent Sample. *Tobacco Control* 6: 89–94.

Kopstein, Andrea. 2001. Tobacco Use in America: Findings from the 1999 National Household Survey on Drug Abuse. Rockville, MD: U.S. Department of Health and Human Services, Substance Abuse and Mental Health Services Administration.

Mermelstein, Robin. 1999. Ethnicity, Gender, and Risk Factors for Smoking Initiation: An Overview. *Nicotine and Tobacco Research* 1 (suppl.): 45–51.

Peto, Richard, and Alan D. Lopez. 2000. The Future Worldwide Health Effects of Current Smoking Patterns. In *Critical Issues in Global Health*, eds. C. Everett Koop, Clarence E. Pearson, and M. Roy Schwartz, 154–161. San Francisco: Jossey-Bass.

Piper, Megan E., Thomas M. Piasecki, E. Belle Federman, et al. 2004. A Multiple Motives Approach to Tobacco Dependence: The Wisconsin Inventory of Smoking Dependence Motives (WISDM). *Journal of Consulting in Clinical Psychology* 72 (2): 139–154.

Saffer, Henry, and Frank J. Chaloupka. 2000. Tobacco Advertising: Economic Theory and International Evidence. *Journal of Health Economics* 19: 1117–1137.

Siegel, Michael, Lois Biener, and Nancy A. Rigotti. 1999. The Effect of Local Tobacco Sales Laws on Adolescent Smoking Initiation. *Prevention Medicine* 29: 334–342.

Sussman, Steve, Clyde W. Dent, Lou Anne McAdams, et al. 1994. Group Self-identification and Adolescent Cigarette Smoking: A 1-year Prospective Study. *Journal of Abnormal Psychology* 103: 576–580.

Taylor, Allyn L., Frank J. Chaloupka, Emmanuel Guindon, and Michaelyn Corbett. 2000. The Impact of Trade Liberation on Tobacco Consumption. In *Tobacco Control in Developing Countries*, eds. Prabhat Jha and Frank Chaloupka, 343–364. Oxford: Oxford University Press.

U.S. Department of Health and Human Services (USDHHS). 1998. *Tobacco Use among US Racial/Ethnic Minority Groups: African Americans, American Indians, and Alaska Natives, Asian Americans and Pacific Islanders, Hispanics, Report of the Surgeon General*. Atlanta, GA: USDHHS, Centers for Disease Control and Prevention, National Center for Chronic Disease Prevention and Health Promotion, Office on Smoking and Health.

Weinstein, Neil D. 1999. Accuracy of Smokers' Risk Perceptions. *Nicotine and Tobacco Research* 1 (suppl.): 123–130.

World Health Organization (WHO). 1999. *Making a Difference, World Health Report 1999*. Geneva, Switzerland: Author.

Yurekli, Ayda A., and Ping Zhang. 2000. The Impact of Clean Indoor-Air Laws and Cigarette Smuggling on Demand for Cigarettes: An Empirical Model. *Health Economics* 9: 159–170.

Daphne C. Watkins

SNCC

SEE *Student Nonviolent Coordinating Committee.*

SOCIAL ACCOUNTING MATRIX

A social accounting matrix (SAM) gives a snapshot of all the transactions between different actors or agents in an economy (Pyatt 1988). The economy can be that of a nation, a province, or even a city. The scope of a SAM—that is, how many groups of actors are considered or the level of disaggregation within a group—depends on the availability of data. Transactions are organized in the form of a square matrix. The (i, j) element of the matrix represents the expenditure of actor j on actor i. Equivalently, it is also the income of actor i that originates from the activities of actor j. Expressed in accounting jargon, the concept of SAM is simply that of a double-entry bookkeeping in which the incomings of an actor are also the outgoings of another actor. Thus each row sum must be equal to the corresponding column sum.

It is the choice of actors that distinguishes SAM from both traditional national accounts and an input-output matrix. In terms of broad groups of actors, SAM typically considers production sectors, households, factors of production, and institutions. Each broad group is further disaggregated. For example, a typical SAM involves specific types of households and specific factors of production in order to reflect the economic and social structure of the economy under consideration. Production activities create incomes for various factors of production. These incomes then get distributed to different types of households and corporations. Household and corporate incomes generate private consumption and savings/investments. Government income is generated from direct taxation of household and corporate incomes and from indirect taxation and is translated into public expenditure and investments. The actual task of collecting and collating the information necessary to construct a SAM is quite formidable. Often data from different sources need to be combined. For this and many other reasons, the row and column sums frequently differ. There are, however, numerical methods to reconcile these differences.

The concept of representing transactions between actors in an economy in the form of a matrix was first introduced by Wassily Leontief in his classic work *The Structure of American Economy* (1941, 1951). For Leontief, the actors were mainly producing sectors, and the matrix represented intermediate inputs in production. However, in one of his later reviews of input-output analysis, he writes:

> Households must not necessarily be considered to be part of the exogenous sectors. … In dealing with problems of income generation in its relation to employment, the quantities of consumers' goods and services absorbed by households can be considered (in a Keynesian manner) to be structurally dependent on the total level of employment in the same way as the quantities of coke and ore absorbed by blast furnaces are considered to be structurally related to the amount of pig iron produced by them. (Leontief 1966, pp. 141–142)

From these conceptual foundations, Leontief extends the input-output matrix to include transactions between households, factors of production, and so on.

The applications of SAMs can be wide-ranging. They can, and often do, form the backbone of computable general equilibrium models. SAMs are particularly useful for any exercise in which a researcher or policy maker is interested in analyzing the distributional implications of particular policy measures (Pyatt and Round 1979, 1985, and 2006). In such cases, the overall matrix multiplier (which gives the total "activity" level of all the actors in an economy to produce a given level of final use as the sum of direct activity levels and an infinite series of indirect ones) is typically broken down into a number of multiplicative components (Pyatt and Round 1979). Each of these components represents a particular connection between or within groups' effects. An analysis of these disaggregated multipliers not only tells us the effects of an injection of a particular shock to various socioeconomic groups, it also tells us the mechanisms through which such effects come about. There are now many studies that construct SAMs for developing countries and examine the distributional consequences of policy measures (Pyatt and Round 1985). One hopes that as time goes by, SAMs for more and more countries will be constructed, as they could only help in the formulation and effective implementation of development policies benefiting the poor.

SEE ALSO *Development Economics; General Equilibrium; Income Distribution; Input-Output Matrix; Leontief, Wassily; Macroeconomics; Models and Modeling; Multisector Models*

BIBLIOGRAPHY

Leontief, Wassily. 1951. *The Structure of American Economy, 1919–1939: An Empirical Application of Equilibrium Analysis.* 2nd enlarged ed. New York: Oxford University Press. Originally published as *The Structure of American Economy, 1919–1929* (Cambridge, MA: Harvard University Press, 1941).

Leontief, Wassily. 1966. *Input-Output Economics.* New York: Oxford University Press.

Pyatt, Graham. 1988. A SAM Approach to Modeling. *Journal of Policy Modeling* 10 (3): 327–352.

Pyatt, Graham, and Jeffery I. Round. 1979. Accounting and Fixed Price Multipliers in a Social Accounting Matrix Framework. *Economic Journal* 89 (356): 850–873.

Pyatt, Graham, and Jeffery I. Round, eds. 1985. *Social Accounting Matrices: A Basis for Planning.* Washington, DC: World Bank.

Pyatt, Graham, and Jeffery I. Round. 2006. Multiplier Effects and the Reduction of Poverty. In *Poverty, Inequality, and Development: Essays in Honor of Erik Thorbecke,* eds. Alain de Janvry and Ravi Kanbur, 233–259. New York: Springer.

Sajal Lahiri

SOCIAL ANXIETY

Social anxiety refers to the fear of being humiliated, embarrassed, negatively evaluated, or rejected in social situations. A common human experience, social anxiety exists on a continuum of severity from infrequent and mild feelings of discomfort in social situations to chronic and pervasive distress in many different social settings. An individual's experience of social anxiety may be limited to one specific type of social situation, such as public speaking, or it may be so pervasive that anxiety and fear are experienced in nearly any situation in which other people are present. When an individual's social anxiety is excessive and results in significant distress or impairment, the person may be diagnosed with social anxiety disorder (or social phobia).

Social anxiety disorder is the third most prevalent psychiatric condition in the United States, with a lifetime prevalence rate of approximately 13 percent in the general population. The majority of individuals with excessive social anxiety, or social anxiety disorder, also report co-morbid anxiety, mood, or substance abuse (e.g., alcohol) conditions. Although excessive social anxiety is a relatively common psychological condition, the exact cause of the phenomenon remains unclear. Several researchers have noted the possibility of a genetic predisposition for social anxiety that appears to contribute to familial patterns of the condition. Developmental researchers point to temperamental characteristics in shy, fearful, and behaviorally inhibited children and the increased likelihood that these children will develop excessive social anxiety later in life. Other researchers believe that a predisposition may interact with early learning to reinforce the perception that social interactions are threatening and that estimated costs of social failures outweigh the possible benefits (e.g., intimacy).

As a coping strategy, people with excessive social anxiety often attempt to alter or control negative feelings associated with social evaluative concerns and avoid or escape situations in which these feelings may occur. These efforts may lead to increased apprehension of future social events, increased use of alcohol and other maladaptive coping strategies (e.g., rumination), and social withdrawal and isolation. As a result, excessive social anxiety is related to functional impairment in a variety of domains including school, work, leisure, and physical health. Socially anxious individuals also report a number of interpersonal problems, including fewer friends, less perceived social support, an increased likelihood of being single, and less romantic relationship satisfaction. Thus excessive social anxiety may be what therapists call a "life-limiting" condition in that it interferes with interpersonal functioning and results in fewer positive emotional experiences and events.

Social anxiety may be treated effectively with a variety of psychological and pharmacological interventions. Evidence suggests that both individual and group cognitive-behavioral therapy may be effective in reducing symptoms and distress associated with social anxiety. Cognitive-behavioral therapies tend to target dysfunctional thoughts, beliefs, and behaviors and teach individuals different, more adaptive, ways to manage their behavior and respond effectively in social situations. In addition, several medications, including benzodiazepines and the class of antidepressants called SSRIs (selective serotonin reuptake inhibitors) appear to be effective and well-tolerated.

SEE ALSO *Addiction; Anxiety; Neuroticism; Psychology; Psychotherapy; Stages of Development*

BIBLIOGRAPHY

Heimberg, Richard G., Michael R. Liebowitz, Debra A. Hope, and Franklin R. Schneier, eds. 1995. *Social Phobia: Diagnosis, Assessment, and Treatment.* New York: Guilford.

Hofmann, Stefan G., and Patricia Marten DiBartolo, eds. 2001. *From Social Anxiety to Social Phobia: Multiple Perspectives.* Boston: Allyn and Bacon.

Rapee, R. M., and R. G. Heimberg. 1997. A Cognitive-Behavioral Model of Anxiety in Social Phobia. *Behaviour Research and Therapy* 35 (8): 741–756.

William E. Breen
Todd B. Kashdan

SOCIAL CAPITAL

In a broad and nonessentialist sense, social capital means that the relations humans enter into are a potential source of utility and benefit for them. However, the concept of social capital is perceived in divergent ways with a plurality of approaches and empirical operationalizations. Unfortunately, there is little discussion among dissenting viewpoints.

After an earlier emergence in the work of Lydia Hanifan (1916) or Jane Jacobs (1961), the term *social capital* resurfaced in the 1970s in the work of economist Glenn Loury. For Loury, the social context in which one finds oneself embedded strongly conditions one's achievement. This is profoundly evident whenever social divisions that structure inequalities, such as race or class, are at play. In such a context, Loury describes social capital as the impact of one's own social position, which acts to further or impede the acquisition of human capital (the market-valued assets of education and skills) (Loury 1977, pp. 175–176).

PIERRE BOURDIEU, JAMES S. COLEMAN, AND SOCIAL CAPITAL

Pierre Bourdieu (1930–2002) was the first to conceptualize social capital in an explicitly sociological manner that is at variance with Loury's view. For Bourdieu, capital consists of accumulated human labor that either assumes a distinct material form or an integrated form as part of an objective or subjective structure, the latter being the predispositions of mind and body (Bourdieu 2001, p. 98). Bourdieu also understands capital in the sense of power and resources (Bourdieu and Wacquant 1992).

Bourdieu is concerned with three forms of capital: economic, cultural, and social, each operating in a different field. Among them, social capital, which neither derives from nor is independent of the other forms, comprises social responsibilities, connections, or linkages, and under certain circumstances is convertible into economic capital. Bourdieu also considers the family to be a basic source of social capital, mainly found among the socially powerful in the upper middle class or *haute bourgeoisie*; the ideal-typical institutionalized form of social capital is the nobility title (Bourdieu 2001, p. 98). By contrast, the lower social strata do not possess capital, including social capital (Bourdieu 1986).

Social capital is formed, more or less consciously, via integration into networks. Unlike economic capital, social capital has no specific material form. It is also characterized by a certain indeterminacy, so that there can be, for example, a residual sense of unspecified obligation. Social capital is, in a sense, "suspended" in midair, like social structures. This, according to Bourdieu, is an inevitable dimension of social capital. If it were clear and specific, it would simply be a series of ordinary nonmarket transactions. Social capital, according to Bourdieu, is "the sum of active or potential resources that are connected through the possession of a network of permanent relations of mutual acquaintance and recognition, which are more or less institutionalized, or, in other words, with the inclusion into a group" (Bourdieu 1994, p. 90). Participation in a group provides each member "with the backing of the collectivity-owned capital, a 'credential' that entitles them to credit in the various senses of the word" (Bourdieu 2001, p. 103). Importantly, the agent of action is the separate individual member of the group.

Transactions between group members require a minimum degree of homogeneity, and the profits that accrue from membership form the basis of the solidarity that makes such transactions possible. Bourdieu clearly holds that the reproduction of social capital requires a continuous effort of "sociability" and continual repeated contacts during which mutual recognition by group members is confirmed in order to sustain group cohesion (Bourdieu 2001, p. 104).

For his part, while studying school failure and aiming at the reinforcement of human capital, James Coleman (1926–1995) came to regard social capital as a means of support. In particular, he claims that social capital strengthens students' school and university performance and, therefore, the generation of human capital. This view is much in line with Loury's conceptualization of social capital, yet here social capital is explicitly a positive and enhanceable quality (Coleman and Hoffer 1987; Coleman 1988).

Coleman uses this notion of social capital in connection with other forms of capital, such as economic-financial, natural, and human capital. Specifically, social capital results from changes that take place between individuals, facilitating social action (Coleman 1990, p. 302).

Coleman defines social capital on the basis of its function, as a range of entities with two common attributes: These entities are all aspects of social structures, and they all facilitate certain actions within structures, by individual or collective agents (Coleman 1988, p. S98). Social capital may assume three forms: "obligations and expectations, which depend on trustworthiness of the social environment, information-flow capability of the social structure, and norms accompanied by sanctions" (p. S119). Coleman, like Bourdieu, stresses the nonconcrete, nonmaterial, and indefinite character of social capital as compared to other forms of capital. However, in contradistinction to Bourdieu, he notes that unlike other forms of capital, social capital is a public good, because those who generate social capital enjoy only a limited part of its benefits (pp. S116–S118). Social capital is not solely a property or benefit of the individual agent who generates it, but also of other individuals, as well as of the community. Because social capital is embedded within the social context, certain characteristics of social relations can facilitate its appearance, including trust and reciprocity among the members of the inner-group, effective normative regulations, and open social structures (pp. S102–S105, S106).

It is important to distinguish resources from the ability to acquire them, through participation in networks or social structures. This distinction is clear in Bourdieu, but vague in Coleman. By equating social capital with the resources through which it is acquired, or which it creates, one is led toward tautology and a vicious circle. In this sense, it can be argued that Coleman's conceptualization gets blurred and eventually loses much of its value.

ROBERT D. PUTNAM, SOCIAL CAPITAL, AND CRITIQUE

Parallel to the ongoing sociological interest in social capital, this notion has also been adopted by other disciplines. Political scientist Robert Putnam, for example, has developed his ideas in relation to social capital especially. He points out that social capital is formed by "features of [*social organizations, or*] *social life*—networks, norms, and trust—that enable participants to act together more effectively to pursue shared objectives" (Putnam 1995, pp. 664–665, emphasis added; Putnam 1993, p. 67).

Putman broadens the notion of social capital from the level of individual and collective actors to the level of organizations and communities (Wollebaek and Selle 2002, p. 34; Portes 2000), and from there to social life as a whole. The latter includes cities, regions, and even entire countries. Coleman had already attempted such an expansion of meaning, as we have seen. However, the problem of silence relating to the supposedly neutral character of horizontal ties, raised in sociological discussions of Coleman's definition of social capital, cannot be tolerated in Putnam's conceptual transference. In the neopluralistic participatory context that the latter has adopted, differences in economic, social, or other forms of power do not raise a significant issue; hence what prevails is participation as such and the extent to which it appears.

Participatory attitudes within the context of community networks seem to generate additional forms of social capital. Thus, social capital can do the "bonding," "bridging," or even "linking" of social groups. This means, respectively, forming ties between people in similar situations, bringing together people in different situations who belong to different social groups (Svendsen 2006), and mustering heterogeneous social groups together (Woolcock 2001). All result in synergies that effect positive outcomes in virtually all fronts. Undoubtedly, in this way networks appear to be vehicles of social capital.

In fact, in Putnam's approach, social capital stock is equal to the participatory attitude in a community. Specifically, social capital is not researched directly, but instead proxies are used: Social capital is operationalized through indices such as, primarily, the degree of participation in volunteer organizations (Welzel et al. 2005, p. 121); trust toward authorities or others; the reading of newspapers, which reflects an interest in public affairs; and similar indices that mostly apply to the mezzo- and macro-levels (Putnam 2000). So, the key in researching social capital is the keenness of participation, or more broadly civic values or the ethos of "civicness" from which willingness to participate originates.

Attempts at deconstruction and critical recomposition of social capital have been made by sociologist Alejandro Portes and his associates, among others. Portes and Julia Sensenbrenner (1993) suggest a clear distinction between the sources of social capital and the results of its action. They recognize four sources from which social capital originates: (1) internalization of values; (2) transactions of a reciprocal character; (3) forms of collective solidarity; and (4) the trust imposed by negative or positive sanctions. It is accepted that the sources of social capital are embedded in the motives of network/group members to provide resources. These include consummatory motives, and those cultivated within the community, with solidarity strikes being a typical case. They may also originate from instrumental motives involving the expectation of reciprocity and trust (e.g., the sponsor is secured against fraud) (Portes and Sensenbrenner 1993; Portes 1998, p. 8).

The various sources of social capital lead to its composite formation so that social capital is the ability to secure benefits via "participation in networks and other social structures" (Portes 1998, p. 6). Of course, the idea that interconnections favor individual upward mobility may also be found in writers like Mark Granovetter (1973, 1983) who avoid the term *social capital.*

While Bourdieu does not take an interest in whether the effects of social capital are positive or negative, in Coleman's work, social capital is presented as exerting a fundamentally positive social influence, especially in the case of social problems tackled through the effectiveness of social capital. For Putnam too, social capital is a "blessing" that reduces anomie, promotes democracy, and produces wealth. However, Portes and his associates reject this all-positive account of social capital and its effects as one-dimensional, while stressing a number of negative aspects: Of prime importance is the exclusion of non-members, and the excessive demands made upon rich members of the social capital network (or group) for compliance, uncensored acceptance, and so forth.

Portes's interventions offer a more balanced understanding of social capital and its potential. The notion is not rejected but rationalized, with emphasis on the need to systematically study the effects of social capital and avoid attributing irrelevant, accidental, or spurious effects to it (Portes 1998, 2000; Portes and Landolt 2000; Portes and Mooney 2002). This perception has led to conceptualizations of social capital more akin to the micro-level that focus on the individual's relationships to her or his network of social connections and the benefits and resources she or he may muster. Such approaches tend to restrict the agentic impact, even if they give a place to it, while underlying that of social structure (Lin 2000, 2001). In such explorations, which tend to utilize qualitative methods, one of the main concerns is to decipher causality in generating and activating social capital (Mouw 2005; Smith 2003).

The wider promotion of the contentious notion of social capital, and the strengthening and broadening of its usage, mainly took place through the work of Putnam, who came to influence key politicians, including U.S. president Bill Clinton, plus a series of international organizations like the World Bank, the Organization for Economic Cooperation and Development (OECD), and the European Union. At the same time, social capital has come to be used in ever-increasing ways as a recipe for non-economic solutions to social problems (Halpern 2005). The overextension of its meaning and the consequent slackening of its application have led to contestation about its true content. It now appears that the notion of social capital has, to a significant extent, been taken over by agents of ideological and political intervention (Koniordos 2006). However, the social capital notion is certainly of social-scientific interest if its use is suitably restricted to what it may substantively explain.

SEE ALSO *Authority; Bourdieu, Pierre; Conformity; Ethnic Enclave; Ethnocentrism; Networks; Networks, Communication; Pluralism; Putnam, Robert; Solidarity; Trust*

BIBLIOGRAPHY

Bourdieu, Pierre. 1986. *Distinction: A Social Critique of the Judgement of Taste.* Trans. Richard Nice. London: Routledge and Kegan Paul.

Bourdieu, Pierre. 1994. Social Capital: Preliminary Notes. In *P. Bourdieu: Sociological Texts*, ed. Nikos Panagiotopoulos, 91–95. Athens: Delfini (in Greek).

Bourdieu, Pierre. 2001. Forms of Capital. In *The Sociology of Economic Life*, eds. Mark Granovetter and Richard Swedberg, 96–111. 2nd ed. Boulder, CO: Westview.

Bourdieu, Pierre, and Loïc Wacquant. 1992. *An Invitation to Reflexive Sociology.* Cambridge, U.K.: Polity.

Coleman, James S. 1988. Social Capital in the Creation of Human Capital. *American Journal of Sociology* 94: S95–S120.

Coleman, James S. 1990. *Foundations of Social Theory.* Cambridge, MA: Harvard University Press.

Coleman, James S., and Thomas Hoffer. 1987. *Public and Private Schools: The Impact of Community.* New York: Basic Books.

Granovetter, Mark. 1973. The Strength of Weak Ties. *American Journal of Sociology* 78 (6): 1360–1380.

Granovetter, Mark. 1983. The Strength of Weak Ties: A Network Theory Revisited. *Sociological Theory* 1: 201–233.

Halpern, David. 2005. *Social Capital.* Cambridge, U.K.: Cambridge University Press.

Koniordos, Sokratis M. 2006. Social Capital: Between Theoretical Clarity and Confusion. *Science and Society* 16 (Spring-Summer): 1–38 (in Greek).

Lin, Nan. 2000. Inequality in Social Capital. *Contemporary Sociology* 29 (6): 785–795.

Lin, Nan. 2001. Building a Network Theory of Social Capital. In *Social Capital: Theory and Research*, eds. Nan Lin, Karen Cook, and Ronald Burt, 3–31. New York: de Gruyter.

Loury, Glenn C. 1977. A Dynamic Theory of Racial Income Differences. In *Women, Minorities, and Employment Discrimination*, eds. Phyllis A. Wallace and Annette LaMond, 153–186. Lexington, MA: Heath.

Mouw, Ted. 2005. Social Capital and Finding A Job: Do Contacts Matter? *American Sociological Review* 68: 868–898.

Parkin, Frank. 1978. *Class Inequality and Political Order*. London: MacGibbon & Kee.

Portes, Alejandro. 1998. Social Capital: Its Origins and Applications in Modern Sociology. *Annual Review of Sociology* 24: 1–24.

Portes, Alejandro. 2000. The Two Meanings of Social Capital. *Sociological Forum* 15: 1–12.

Portes, Alejandro, and Patricia Landolt. 2000. Social Capital: Promise and Pitfalls of Its Role in Development. *Journal of Latin American Studies* 32: 529–547.

Portes, Alejandro, and Margarita Mooney. 2002. Social Capital and Community Development. In *The New Economic Sociology: Developments in an Emerging Field*, eds. Mauro F. Guillén et al., 303–329. New York: Russell Sage Foundation.

Portes, Alejandro, and Julia Sensenbrenner. 1993. Embeddedness and Immigration: Notes on the Social Determinants of Economic Action. *American Journal of Sociology* 98 (6): 1320–1350.

Putnam, Robert D., with Robert Leonardi and Raffaella Y. Nanetti. 1993. *Making Democracy Work: Civic Traditions in Modern Italy*. Princeton, NJ: Princeton University Press.

Putnam, Robert D. 1995. Tuning In, Tuning Out: The Strange Disappearance of Social Capital in America. *Political Science and Politics* 28: 664–683.

Putnam, Robert D. 2000. *Bowling Alone: The Collapse and Revival of American Community*. New York: Touchstone.

Smith, Sandra S. 2003. "Don't Put My Name On It": Social Capital Activation and Job-Finding Assistance among Black Urban Poor. *American Journal of Sociology* 111 (1): 1–57.

Svendsen, Gunnar L. H. 2006. Studying Social Capital *in Situ*: A Qualitative Approach. *Theory and Society* 35: 39–70.

Welzel, Christian, Ronald Inglehart, and Franziska Deutsch. 2005. Social Capital, Voluntary Associations, and Collective Action: Which Aspects of Social Capital Have the Greatest "Civic Payoff"? *Journal of Civil Society* 1 (2): 121–146.

Wollebaek, Dag, and Per Selle. 2002. Does Participation in Voluntary Associations Contribute to Social Capital? The Impact of Intensity, Scope, and Type. *Nonprofit and Voluntary Sector Quarterly* 31 (1): 32–61.

Woolcock, Michael. 2001. The Place of Social Capital in Understanding Social and Economic Outcomes. *Canadian Journal of Policy Research* 2 (1): 65–88.

Sokratis M. Koniordos

SOCIAL CATEGORIZATION

Social categorization—the collective definition and naming of categories of perceived phenomena—is fundamental to human cognition and culture. Given that it is so fundamental, it is not surprising to find that it has inspired a range of divergent social science approaches. These can be crudely divided into contrasting emphases on content or process.

To take content first, writing in 1903, Émile Durkheim and Marcel Mauss (1963) argued that social structures generate classificatory systems; culturally specific categorizations of the human body, animals, and the wider world, and the relationships between those categories, symbolize and rework relationships of opposition and alliance within and between groups. Later works in this structuralist vein, such as Claude Lévi-Strauss's *Totemism* (1963), developed the notion that the natural world provides classificatory material that is "good to think with," particularly about social relationships.

The basic axiom, that the social categorization of the world represents or dramatizes social structure, underlies Mary Douglas's anthropological discussions of cosmology, ritual, and symbolism (1966). Pierre Bourdieu took the idea further in analyzing modern French relationships between stratification, consumption, and categories of taste, style, and symbolic value (1984). Other authors, even though abandoning the structuralist underpinnings, have since explored similar territory (Lamont and Fournier 1992). The theme that the categories of culture are systematically related to social structure has inspired the academic fields of cultural studies and social studies of consumption.

Within social psychology, the study of social categorization has emphasized process. The most prominent contemporary theoretical school derives from Henri Tajfel's "minimal group" experiments. These provided evidence that when people are arbitrarily placed in one of two groups in a laboratory setting, with no history of animosity and nothing at stake, intergroup negative discrimination results (1970). Reflecting the human need to create cognitive and social order, social categorization is, it is argued, sufficient in itself to generate identification of and with in- and out-groups. A large literature continues to develop and critique this paradigm (Brewer and Hewstone 2004, pp. 145–318).

Finally, another processual approach hinges upon the distinction, originally methodological, between "groups" and "categories": The first is a human collectivity that is defined by and meaningful to its members, the second a collectivity that is defined from outside (during a census or survey, for example). This leads to a contrast between processes of group identification and of social categorization and the argument that identification is always a matter of internal self- or group identification, external categorization by others, and the relationship between the two (Jenkins 2004). Power—whose definition prevails—thus becomes central to our understanding of social categorization.

SEE ALSO *Racial Classification; Self-Classification*

BIBLIOGRAPHY

Bourdieu, Pierre. 1984. *Distinction: A Social Critique of the Judgement of Taste.* Trans. Richard Nice. London: Routledge and Kegan Paul.

Brewer, Marilynn B., and Miles Hewstone, eds. 2004. *Self and Social Identity.* Oxford: Blackwell.

Douglas, Mary. 1966. *Purity and Danger: An Analysis of Concepts of Pollution and Taboo.* London: Routledge and Kegan Paul.

Durkheim, Émile, and Marcel Mauss. [1903] 1963. *Primitive Classification.* Trans. Rodney Needham. London: Cohen and West.

Jenkins, Richard. 2004. *Social Identity.* 2nd ed. London: Routledge.

Lamont, Michèle, and Marcel Fournier, eds. 1992. *Cultivating Difference: Symbolic Boundaries and the Making of Inequality.* Chicago: University of Chicago Press.

Lévi-Strauss, Claude. 1963. *Totemism.* Trans. Rodney Needham. Boston: Beacon Press.

Tajfel, Henri. 1970. Experiments in Intergroup Discrimination. *Scientific American* 223: 96–103.

Richard Jenkins

SOCIAL CHANGE

The concept of social change is central to the social sciences and, in particular, to sociology. The work of many of the pioneers of sociology, including the central triumvirate (Émile Durkheim [1858–1917], Max Weber [1864–1920], and Karl Marx [1818–1883]), involves a sustained reflection upon the changes they believed that they were witnessing in their societies and the new social forms they saw emerging (e.g., organic solidarity, modernity, bureaucracy, and industrial capitalism).

In certain respects change is an inherent feature of societies rather than a periodic event that they undergo or something extraneous that acts upon or happens to them. At whatever level one pitches the concept, a society is not a thing but a process. It comprises a vast web of interactions that unfold through time and, as such, is in a perpetual state of becoming. Any society is constantly in motion and, like the proverbial river, is therefore never quite the same from one moment to the next. The key question, from this point of view, is not why things change but why many social forms persist for as long as they do: that is, why and how they are reproduced. Nevertheless, forms do change, sometimes on a grand scale, and much social science is focused on the question of why this is so.

A key distinction can be found in classical and early modern social theories between *revolutionary* and *evolu-*

tionary theories of change. This distinction hinges on the question of whether change happens in short dramatic bursts (revolutions) or more gradually, over the long term—the most likely answer being "both ways," as the two modes are not mutually exclusive. Political revolutions, such as the French Revolution of 1789, are obvious exemplars for the revolutionary model, but we also refer to "the industrial revolution," to "scientific revolutions," and to such "cultural revolutions" as the Reformation or Enlightenment. Evolutionary change is more difficult to pinpoint because, by definition, it is gradual and occurs over long stretches of time, but it is easily revealed through comparisons of historically distant snapshots of social life.

Evolutionary theories often refer to interaction between the social form said to be evolving and its wider (social and/or natural) environment. Changing environments are said to "select" the forms that proliferate within them. This position can entail teleology; that is to say, it may rest upon an assumption, generally deemed erroneous by contemporary social theorists, that social forms serve a purpose within the wider systems to which they belong and, more problematically, come into being because they serve that purpose. Functionalist accounts, when not criticized on the grounds that they cannot explain change, are often criticized for making such assumptions. Evolutionary accounts are not necessarily teleological, however, even when they work with the notion of environmental fit. Darwin's theory of evolution by natural selection, for example, is non-teleological. Biological "adaptations" do not emerge because they fit with the environment, in Darwin's view. Their emergence is purely contingent—though they "die out" if they do not fit with their environment or lose out to better-fitting "adaptations" in the struggle for survival. Moreover, insofar as evolutionary accounts do rest upon teleological assumptions, this does not serve to distinguish them from revolutionary accounts, which can be equally prone to teleology. Not only, for example, do some variants of (revolutionary) Marxism adopt functionalist explanations, some also adhere to the teleological notion that history is propelled in the direction of a pre-given endpoint and thus revolution is inevitable. Furthermore, the "laws" of social change, which are said to propel society in a particular direction and which one finds in some Marxist accounts, while not necessarily teleological, are problematic on account of what Karl Popper calls their "historicism." Popper's critique of historicism (1969) defies brief summation. Suffice it to say, however, that he is critical of the claims of some Marxists to have discovered "iron" laws of historical necessity and change because, he argues, our knowledge of these laws inevitably changes our behavior and thereby changes the course of history itself, such that the "laws" could not have been "laws" in the first place. In part this is a claim about the role of knowledge and ideas in steering the course of change and a critique of materialist theories that ignore or deny their role. More profoundly, however, it is a claim about the role of reflexivity in history. We are not condemned to follow a particular historical trajectory, according to Popper, because we have the capacity to reflect upon the flow of history and this affords us the opportunity to act differently than we would otherwise have done.

Both revolutionary and evolutionary accounts of social change have come under attack in recent social science, particularly in the context of "postmodern" and "poststructuralist" theories. In addition to challenging "grand narratives" of history (i.e., accounts that purport to tell the story of human history *in toto* and in the singular), these theories have challenged the notion of progress that, they argue, underpins such narratives. In part this critique has been informed by a dissatisfaction with the ethnocentric assumptions built into many accounts of progress; that is, the tendency for writers to treat their own society and standpoint as the furthest point hitherto achieved by any society along a continuum that all societies can be measured against. At a deeper level it is informed by a suspicion of all forms of evaluative discourse, centered ultimately on claims regarding the impossibility of arriving at an unprejudiced or rational basis by which to establish criteria of evaluation.

The more extreme claims of postmodernists can be challenged by reference to the pragmatic possibility of deriving local and specific criteria by which to evaluate change: For example, if we are prepared to agree that reducing infant mortality is a good thing, then we can argue that Western societies, insofar as their rates have reduced, have progressed in this respect. We do not need to establish a universal standard against which all societies should be measured or, conversely, to eliminate the value judgment that something is a "good thing" in order to make meaningful claims about progress, as long as we can derive mutually agreeable criteria upon which to base our assessment. However, much contemporary debate on change is framed in postmodern terms. Whereas classical social theory was centered on the emergence of modern society, contemporary social theory is centered on the transition to postmodern society. Paradoxically, postmodernism has become something of a "grand narrative" of history, and a dominant one at that.

SEE ALSO *Marx, Karl; Marxism; Postmodernism; Revolution; Social Movements*

BIBLIOGRAPHY

Boudon, Raymond. 1986. *Theories of Social Change: A Critical Appraisal.* Trans. J. C. Whitehouse. Cambridge, U.K.: Polity.

Giddens, Anthony. 1971. *Capitalism and Modern Social Theory: An Analysis of the Writings of Marx, Durkheim, and Max Weber.* Cambridge, U.K.: Cambridge University Press.

Harvey, David. 1989. *The Condition of Postmodernity: An Enquiry into the Origins of Cultural Change.* Oxford: Blackwell.

Lyotard, Jean-François. [1979] 1984. *The Postmodern Condition.* Trans. Geoff Bennington and Brian Massumi. Manchester, U.K.: Manchester University Press.

Popper, Karl. 1969. *The Poverty of Historicism.* 2nd ed. London: Routledge.

Nick Crossley

SOCIAL CLASS

SEE *Class.*

SOCIAL CLASSIFICATION

SEE *Social Categorization.*

SOCIAL COGNITION

Social cognition is the branch of social psychology that studies how people think about themselves and other people. It focuses on the steps people take and the conclusions they reach as they strive to make sense of their social environment. The field tends to view people as information processors, something like a computer, who take in information from the outside world, sort that information out and interpret it, calculate a judgment, and then choose a behavior in response. In doing so, the field examines what information people pay attention to, how they analyze it, how they reach judgments based on that information, how those judgments guide their behaviors, and then which parts of the information they remember.

Work in social cognition is wide-ranging and explores a breathtaking diversity of topics. For example, some social cognitive researchers investigate how people develop opinions and attitudes about social issues. Others examine whether people's judgments of others are distorted by stereotypes. Others look at whether people reach decisions that are wise and rational versus faulty and costly. Others study how people reach impressions of themselves that lead to high versus low self-esteem.

Social cognition principles carry a wide variety of implications for real world pursuits. Social cognition principles, for example, explain why people make right versus wrong decisions about their health. It suggests the best ways to teach students to remember school material. It explains the pitfalls that prevent people in negotiations from reaching harmonious settlements. It explains how people can commit discrimination against people from other ethnic or social groups without even knowing it. It describes why and when people make poor decisions about their money.

One can claim that social cognition has always been a featured part of social psychology, even when the rest of psychology has neglected, or even denied, the importance of people's internal thought processes. In particular, in the early to mid-twentieth century, the bulk of psychology was dominated by the *behaviorist* tradition, led by B. F. Skinner (1904–1990) and others, which emphasized how organisms reacted to rewards and punishments while studiously avoiding any talk of that organism's internal psychological world. During this era, many social psychologists squarely examined that internal life, exploring how people developed their attitudes toward social issues, as well as how they formed stereotypes about social groups, or made attributions about the causes of other people's behavior.

However, in the 1960s, with the advent of the *cognitive revolution*, things changed dramatically. The mainstream of psychology became fascinated with the organism's internal life—how that organism perceived, thought about, and remembered the world around it. Cognitive psychologists, in particular, generated many sophisticated and powerful theories describing thought and memory. Social psychologists quickly adopted these theories and methods to explore in finer detail how people strive to comprehend events in their social world. Today, work on social cognition remains a vigorous and prominent branch of social psychology.

Although work in social cognition is too diverse to be captured in a simple catalogue, one can point to dominant ideas and themes that social cognitive research has repeatedly demonstrated.

SCHEMATA: THE BUILDING BLOCKS OF SOCIAL COGNITION

One prominent theme focuses on the building blocks of people's thoughts. People carry with them information about individuals, social groups, objects, and events arranged in *schemata* (singular: *schema*). A schema is a knowledge structure containing the features and examples associated with a person, group, object, or event. For example, people's schema of *bird* usually contains such characteristics as *wings*, *feathers*, *a beak*, and *flight*, as well as some common examples of birds, such as *robin* and *duck*. Usually schemata are described as *associative networks*, that is, as a web of linked associations. Thus, when the concept of *bird* comes to mind, these associative links activate the relevant features and examples (e.g., wings,

duck) connected to the concept, thus also bringing those notions to mind.

Schemata are tremendously helpful for social life. If a friend tells you, for example, that he or she went to a restaurant last night, you can easily surmise, because you possess a special type of schema for an event called a *script*, that the person looked at a menu, ordered food, ate it, paid the bill, and left a tip. Your friend does not need to specify these details; you already know.

That said, schemata can also be misleading or harmful, especially when people try to recall the past. For example, if someone asks George to remember the words *drowsy*, *bed*, *pillow*, *snoring*, and *nighttime*, he will probably remember most of these words. But he will also probably mistakenly recall the word *sleep* because all those terms listed above are linked to *sleep* through the associative network (the schema) of this concept. Memory errors prompted by schemata can be quite profound. For example, people witnessing a crime may misremember that the culprit had a gun, a disguise, or unkempt hair if it fits their schema of the event they witnessed. Schemata also explain how stereotypes can distort memory. If, for example, a friend describes a professor as distant, smart, and assertive, one might also mistakenly recall that the friend said the professor was arrogant—if that attribute fits one's schema of a professor.

The impact of schemata on social judgment, interpretation, and memory has been shown to be profound in a wide array of studies, and there has been a good deal of discussion about the specific form that schemata take. According to the *prototype* view, schemata consist of the features associated with an object or event (such as wings and feathers to a bird). According to an *exemplar* view, schemata consist of typical examples of a concept (such as a robin being a typical example of a bird). Research ultimately suggests, however, that schemata tend to be a blend of both features and examples.

ERRORS AND BIASES IN SOCIAL JUDGMENT

One additional prominent theme in social cognitive research scrutinizes cognitive habits that lead people to make errors and biases in their judgments. For example, one such consequential habit is *confirmation bias*. Research on this bias shows that when people ask a question (e.g., "Is Jerry outgoing?"), they tend to look for information that would confirm the question in the positive (e.g., "He does go to parties") and not for information that would disconfirm it (e.g., "He said last week he hated talking in front of large groups"). When the opposite question is asked (e.g., "Is Jerry shy?"), people instead search for information that would confirm that reverse hypothesis, leading to very different conclusions.

Confirmation bias can lead to several problems in judgment. For example, it can lead people to be *overconfident* in their predictions about themselves and others. When people consider a question soliciting a prediction (e.g., "Will I get a good grade in this class?"), they tend to consider information that suggests that the answer is "yes." This can lead them to overconfidence about the chance that their prediction will prove to be accurate. That is, they may say that they are 90 percent sure their prediction will be correct even when the real chance is closer to 70 percent. Indeed, when people say they are 100 percent certain of their prediction, they tend to be wrong roughly one time out of five. Some researchers have suggested that a valuable habit for avoiding overconfidence is to also ask how an event might go in the opposite direction from that posed in the question (e.g., ask the reasons why one might get a poor grade). This *consider-the-opposite* strategy has been shown to reduce overconfidence in people's predictions.

People also suffer from *illusory correlations*, seeing relationships between variables even when they do not exist. Some illusory correlations are inspired by schemata and stereotypes. For example, in an experiment described in a 1967 article, Loren J. Chapman and Jean P. Chapman showed participants a series of drawings, some of which were purportedly drawn by people suffering from paranoia. Participants in the study tended to conclude that the drawings of paranoid individuals more often than not included people with larger eyes—even when there was no relationship between eye size and mental illness in the drawings they looked over.

Other illusory correlations are inspired by what people find easier to remember. For example, people tend to remember unusual behaviors (e.g., riding a unicycle) performed by rare groups (e.g., Alaskans), as reported by David L. Hamilton and Robert K. Gifford in a 1976 article. Thus, when asked if there is any relation between a rare behavior and a rare group (e.g., do Alaskans participate in odd sports?), people report that such a relationship exists, even if the evidence they have reviewed fails to support this conclusion. Because rare-rare combinations are memorable, they lead to illusory correlations.

People also fall prey to the *fundamental attribution error* (also known as the *correspondence bias*), which means that they give too much weight to a person's personality in explaining, evaluating, and predicting social behavior and too little weight to situational forces. That is, people look primarily to a person's internal character to explain his or her actions, and not to factors outside the person that could have produced the behavior. This bias most commonly arises when people make *attributions* for another person's behavior; that is, they try to identify the causes for why the behavior occurred. For example, if you say that

"John stumbled while learning the dance," people tend to leap to the conclusion that John is clumsy (i.e., something about his internal personality) rather than that the dance was difficult (e.g., something about the outside situation).

Several studies have provided powerful demonstrations of the fundamental attribution error. Consider the classic Milgram experiment, completed in the 1960s, in which Stanley Milgram (1933–1984) demonstrated that a majority of participants, if asked, would continue to shock another participant if an authority figure asked them to—even if the other participant suffered heart problems and had stopped answering, and for all practical purposes might be dead. Almost everyone who hears about the study denies that they would "go all the way," complying with the experimenter until the session is curtailed. However, up to two-thirds of people in this situation do go all the way. The situation is extremely powerful even though people do not see it, and there are few indicators from a person's personality that reliably predict whether that person will comply or defy the command to shock another person who has stopped answering.

People also make errors because they rely on quick heuristics to reach their judgments, according to the work of Amos Tversky (1937–1996) and Daniel Kahneman. One such example is the *availability heuristic*, in which people judge the odds, frequency, or truthfulness of an event based on how quickly examples of it spring to mind. For example, if one asks how commonly words of the form ———-n- appear in English, people tend to say that there are not many. However, if asked how many words of the form ———-ing appear, people say quite a few, mostly because such words are easily brought to mind. Of course, all ———-ing words are also ———-n- words, so the latter type of word, paradoxically, must be more frequent.

People also rely on the *representativeness heuristic*. This heuristic refers to the fact that people judge the odds, frequency, or truthfulness of an event based on how well it matches a schema in their head. For example, suppose you were told that Linda is politically liberal and a philosophy major. Which of the following descriptions do you think is the most likely to be true and which the least: that Linda is a feminist, that she is a bank teller, or that she is both a feminist and a bank teller. Most people rate "feminist" as most likely and "bank teller" as least, although that is necessarily an error. Mathematically, the least likely event must be that Linda is both a feminist and a bank teller. Why? If Linda is both, then she is already a bank teller—and there is an added chance that she might be a bank teller without being a feminist. Thus, the single description of "bank teller" must be more probable than being both a teller and a feminist.

This *conjunction fallacy* (i.e., rating a combination of two events as more likely than one of its two individual component events) is caused by the representativeness heuristic. People form a schema of Linda and then quickly compare the various events (e.g., is a bank teller) to this stereotype. If the event matches the schema (e.g., is a feminist), it is seen as probable. If it does not (e.g., is a bank teller), it is seen as improbable. However, in using this heuristic, people commonly violate the simple mathematics inherent in the situation, and thus reach conclusions that cannot be right.

In the following heuristics, people also ignore other valuable information that would lead them to more accurate predictions. For example, people tend to neglect the *base rates* of events, even though these rates have a large impact on what will happen. Base rates refer to the commonness of an event. A high base rate means an event is common (e.g., people tend to have ten toes); a low base rate means that an event is rare (e.g., people tend not to have more than ten toes, although some do). The overall base rate of an event is a valuable indicator about whether or not it will occur in the future, but people, relying on availability and representativeness heuristics, tend not to factor base rates into their judgments and predictions. For example, let's say that you know someone who is over seven feet tall and athletic. Is he more likely to be an NBA basketball player or an accountant? Most people quickly predict that this person is an NBA player, because that fits their schema of a professional basketball player (the representativeness heuristic at work), but they should actually predict that he is an accountant, because accountants far outnumber NBA basketball players. That is, the base rate of accountants is several times higher than the base rate of being an NBA basketball player. Because being an accountant is the much more common event, it is the event one should predict.

DUAL SYSTEMS IN SOCIAL THOUGHT

In another predominant theme, social cognitive work has also increasingly recognized that people possess two very different modes of thought. *System 1* is a rapid mode of thought, in which people reach their judgments quickly through simple associations and heuristics, like the availability heuristic. *System 2* is slower, conscious, deliberate, effortful, rule-based, and analytical.

Anyone who has solved a complex math problem is familiar with system 2. This is the system in which people consciously apply rules to compute some sort of judgment. People may not be as familiar with the operation of system 1. Indeed, at its extreme, system 1 may work so rapidly that a person is not even aware of its operation.

System 1 thinking is often associated with being *automatic*. There are many senses in which thought can be automatic. First, automatic thought can be quick. For example, people recognize the faces of their friends and family in an instant, without conscious deliberation. Second, automatic thought can be efficient, in that it does not detract from other tasks that people apply themselves to. For example, people can drive a car along a familiar route while fully engaged in other tasks, such as listening to the car stereo or talking to a passenger. Third, automatic thought can be completed without monitoring. People can form perfectly grammatical sentences, for example, without consciously monitoring the construction of each single phrase. Fourth, automatic can mean that the thought is outside of the control of the individual—that it just happens. Indeed, it often requires no conscious goal to set itself in motion. For example, few Americans can hear the date "September 11" without reflexively thinking of terrorism.

Finally, and perhaps most importantly, automatic thought can occur without one being aware of it. When this occurs, the thought is usually described as *nonconscious* (i.e., below awareness) or *preconscious* (i.e., occurring before any thought reaches consciousness). Ultimately, this means that the conclusions people reach can be shaped by influences they are not aware of.

These influences are most directly shown in studies of *priming*, in which people are exposed to incidental material that later shapes their conclusions about some seemingly irrelevant situation. For example, if people complete a sentence-completion task that contains such words as *hostile*, *mean*, and *unfriendly*, they will judge a person they encounter soon afterward as more unpleasant and aggressive than they would if exposed to the words *kind*, *generous*, and *sociable*. The influence of priming can occur even when people are not aware of the prime. For example, John A. Bargh, Mark Chen, and Lara Burrows (1996) exposed college students to words associated with elderly people (e.g., *wisdom*, *Florida*) so quickly that the students were not aware that they had been shown any words at all. They thought they were merely seeing flashes on a computer screen. Despite this fact, as students left the experiment, exposure to these primes caused them to walk more slowly (a stereotypical attribute of the elderly) to the elevator as they left the experiment.

System 1, and the automatic thoughts that come with it, produces wide-ranging consequences. For example, the accuracy of people's judgments, as described above, is heavily influenced by rapid use of availability and representativeness heuristics. Some forms of system 1 thinking can also be shown to trump system 2 thought. Norbert Schwarz and colleagues in a 1991 article showed how system 1 elements can have more influence than the actual content of conscious thoughts. In one study, they asked college students to write down six examples of their own assertive behavior. Students found this task easy. Another group was asked to write down twelve examples and found this task difficult. Later, when asked to rate their assertiveness, the first group saw themselves as more assertive than the second group—even though the second group had generated a greater number of examples indicating that they were assertive. Schwarz and colleagues argued that the first group had perceived themselves as more assertive because they were relying on the availability heuristic. Generating six examples was so easy and available that it tended to convince students that they were assertive. System 1 (the availability heuristic) in this case was a more powerful influence than system 2 (the actual number of examples in conscious thought).

The impact of system 1 thought is also evident in social attribution. People appear to reach attributions about others quickly and spontaneously, through system 1, even without a conscious goal of trying to understand those people. For example, if you mention that Janice helped the elderly woman carry her groceries to the car, many people will rapidly and unknowingly classify the behavior as *helpful*. (There is an ongoing debate about whether people think of the behavior or the person, Janice, as helpful.) Indeed, if cued with the word *helpful* later, people will be more likely to remember the sentence that inspired the thought.

Such spontaneous system 1 attributions may explain the fundamental attribution error. Daniel T. Gilbert and colleagues (1988) have proposed that people make rapid attributions to another person's personality. Once made, people correct these quick personal attributions by considering the impact of the situation in a more effortful, conscious, system 2 way. In support of this idea, Gilbert and colleagues have shown that people make greater attributions to someone's personality if they are distracted by some other task, because they are deprived of the cognitive capacity necessary to correct for the quick personal attributions produced by system 1.

System 1 also carries consequences for stereotyping. Patricia G. Devine (1989) has suggested that people apply stereotypes in their judgments of others in a quick, system 1 way. Importantly, these stereotype-inspired thoughts even occur to those who wish not to be influenced by them. People who consciously deny stereotypes based on gender, race, or age know that those stereotypes exist and what they are—and these stereotypes will produce automatic, system 1 associations even among these people. In response, those who wish to avoid using stereotypes must apply more effortful system 2 thought to correct for the impact of those stereotypes. However, when people do not have the cognitive capacity to perform this system 2 correction, they will commit stereotypical thinking even though they wish to prevent it. This may happen when they are tired or distracted by some other task.

System 1 also influences attitudes and persuasion. As Shelly Chaiken and Yaacov Trope (1999) have pointed out, people can be persuaded to hold an attitude via two different routes. Through a heuristic route, people can be persuaded in a system 1 way through rapid associations and rules of thumb. For example, people can be persuaded of a viewpoint if the person trying to persuade them is physically attractive, or has an impressive title, or just rattles off a large number of arguments. This type of persuasion occurs when people are not motivated to think deeply about what they are being told. However, when people are motivated, they more effortfully and consciously deliberate over what they are told. This is the *systematic* route to persuasion, and depends on whether people find the arguments they are given to be strong. (John T. Cacioppo and Richard Petty's *elaboration likelihood model* offers a similar treatment of system 1 and 2 routes to persuasion).

IMPLICIT VERSUS EXPLICIT ATTITUDES

The presence of system 1 also means that people may hold multiple, and sometimes contradictory, attitudes about social groups and issues. For example, at a conscious, *explicit* level, people may harbor no negative attitudes toward people from other racial groups, or the elderly, or the political party opposite their own. However, at an *implicit* level, below conscious awareness or control, people may hold such prejudices. That is, they may hold automatic negative associations to those groups that they are not aware they have.

Much research has shown how attitudes at the implicit level may differ from those at an explicit level. For example, people tend to deny explicitly having any negative opinions of racial groups different from their own. However, if placed in a performance task that assesses their automatic, implicit associations, such negative links are often found. For example, in one version of the *implicit association task*, people are asked to complete two tasks simultaneously. In one task, they are asked whether a face is of a European American or an African American, pressing a button with their left hand if the face is European and with their right if the face is African. Intermixed with this task, they are also shown words (e.g., *puppy, disease*) and asked if each is positive or negative in nature, using their left hand to indicate the former and their right the latter. They then perform these two intermixed tasks again, but this time the hands indicating positive and negative words are switched.

Most European Americans find this second version of the task to be more difficult, in that they are using the same hand to indicate *European* and *negative* (an association they may not have at the automatic level) and the other hand to indicate *African* and *positive* (again, an association they may not possess at the automatic level). African American participants find the second version of the task to be easier than the first, presumably because it matches associations (e.g., *African* and *positive*) that they possess at an implicit level.

NEW DIRECTIONS

Work in social cognition has moved vigorously in several directions since 1990. For example, all the work described so far paints social perceivers as cold, machinelike calculators, calmly using systems 1 and 2 to determine some judgment about their social worlds. More recent work since the 1990s has recognized that cognition need not only be "cold," it can also be "hot," involving vivid and full-blooded emotions. Thus, recent work in social cognition increasingly focuses on the role of emotions in social thought. For example, research has shown that emotional arousal prompts people to pay attention more to the evaluative charge of information in their environment—that is, to whether it is positive or negative—over other aspects of that information. Fear and anxiety also narrow attention to central and salient aspects of a situation, at the expense of more peripheral features.

Emotions also lead people to make different assumptions about a situation. When people become fearful, for example, they perceive themselves to lack control over a situation. Thus, they become more pessimistic and reluctant to take on risks. However, when people are angry, they perceive themselves as more in control and more likely to seek risks out. This was directly shown in a survey taken after the terrorist attacks in the United States on September 11, 2001. Those asked first to describe how the attacks made them fearful perceived the United States to be more at risk for future attacks than did those asked to describe how the attacks made them angry.

Work in social cognition since 1990 has also begun to explore the role played by culture, taking pains to study how social cognition operates around the world. In doing so, researchers have found that culture has a profound impact on the ways people think about their social world and the conclusions they then reach. Differences in culture also appear to extend even to perception of the physical world. For example, if people are shown a scene, North Americans are more likely to describe and remember central components of the scene. East Asian respondents, relative to their North American counterparts, are more likely to describe and remember the context surrounding those central components, better recalling peripheral details of a scene.

This different degree of attention paid to the center versus the context is echoed in social judgment. People from East Asia also tend to avoid the fundamental attribution error, more frequently emphasizing situational factors that may have produced a person's behavior, in contrast to what is emphasized by their North American counterparts. In essence, people from East Asia tend to emphasize the surrounding situational context in their explanations for the behavior of other people, whereas North Americans tend to emphasize the central actor.

Finally, social cognition research since 2000 has increasingly delved into the neurophysiology of social thought, examining the brain structures that support judgments and decision making. By using such techniques as fMRI (functional magnetic resonance imaging) or ERP (event-related brain potentials), psychologists can determine which neural structures in the brain are active as people reach decisions. For example, people who possess negative implicit attitudes toward ethnic groups different from their own (as measured by the implicit association test described above) show more activation of the amygdala, a part of the brain associated with emotional learning and evaluation.

Studies of this type have also begun to map different neural routes that people take to reach conclusions about their social world. In a study on moral judgment by Joshua D. Greene and colleagues (2001), participants were asked how they would respond to the following two moral dilemmas. One dilemma concerned whether participants would switch the track that a train was traveling on to keep it from hitting and killing five people, knowing that the train on its new track would unfortunately kill one other individual. The second dilemma concerned whether participants would push a person in front of a train, killing him, in order to stop the train from killing five people further down the tracks. Although the two scenarios share the same overall structure (i.e., sacrificing one person to save five), people tend to reach different decisions about how to act, being more likely to switch the train track in the first scenario than to push the person onto the tracks in the second.

Participants also tend to reach these decisions via different neural routes. Participants in this study appeared to solve the first dilemma in a calculated system 2 way, analyzing the benefit of switching the train track. In support of this observation, fMRI measurements suggest that as people considered the scenario their parietal lobes, as well as the right middle-front gyrus, were active—areas associated with the "working memory" people use as they think through a decision. In contrast, people appeared to solve the second dilemma by going with their initial emotional reaction, with brain areas associated with emotion (e.g., the right and left angular gyrus, the bilateral posterior cingulate gyrus, and the bilateral medical frontal gyrus) being most active.

CONCLUDING REMARKS

Social cognition is a vibrant area of research. Its influence is also increasingly felt in other scientific and professional disciplines, as scholars in medicine, law, business, education, and philosophy comb its insights to provide knowledge to address questions in those areas of endeavor. In a sense, this vibrancy should not come as a surprise. Every day, people expend a great deal of effort in social cognition, trying to make sense of themselves and the people around them. It is a safe bet that they will never find a point in their lifetime when they can stop doing this task. If this is true of people in everyday life, then it must also be true of the social cognition researcher, who, after all, is also just trying to make sense of what other people do.

SEE ALSO *Attitudes; Attribution; Cognition; Decision-making; Perception, Person; Prototypes; Stereotypes*

BIBLIOGRAPHY

Bargh, John A., Mark Chen, and Lara Burrows. 1996. Automaticity of Social Behavior: Direct Effects of Trait Construct and Stereotype Priming on Action. *Journal of Personality and Social Psychology* 71: 230–244.

Chaiken, Shelly, and Yaacov Trope, eds. 1999. *Dual-Process Theories in Social Psychology*. New York: Guilford.

Chapman, Loren J., and Jean P. Chapman. 1967. Illusory Correlation as an Obstacle to the Use of Valid Psychodiagnostic Signs. *Journal of Abnormal Psychology* 72: 193–204.

Devine, Patricia G. 1989. Stereotypes and Prejudice: Their Automatic and Controlled Components. *Journal of Personality and Social Psychology* 56: 5–18.

Gilbert, Daniel T., Brett W. Pelham, and Douglas S. Krull. 1988. On Cognitive Busyness: When Person Perceivers Meet Persons Perceived. *Journal of Personality and Social Psychology* 54: 733–740.

Gilovich, Thomas, Dale Griffin, and Daniel Kahneman, eds. 2002. *Heuristics and Biases: The Psychology of Intuitive Judgment*. New York: Cambridge University Press.

Greene, Joshua D., R. Brian Sommerville, Leigh E. Nystrom, et al. 2001. An fMRI Investigation of Emotional Engagement in Moral Judgment. *Science* 293: 2105–2108.

Greenwald, Anthony G., David E. McGhee, and Jordan L. K. Schwarz. 1998. Measuring Individual Differences in Implicit Cognition: The Implicit Association Test. *Journal of Personality and Social Psychology* 74: 1464–1480.

Hamilton, David L., and Robert K. Gifford. 1976. Illusory Correlation in Interpersonal Perception: A Cognitive Basis of Stereotypic Judgments. *Journal of Experimental Social Psychology* 12: 392–407.

Kunda, Ziva. 1999. *Social Cognition: Making Sense of People*. Cambridge, MA: MIT Press.

Lerner, Jennifer S., Roxanne M. Gonzalez, Deborah A. Small, and Baruch Fischhoff. 2003. Effects of Fear and Anger on Perceived Risks of Terrorism: A National Field Experiment. *Psychological Science* 14: 144–150.

Moskowitz, Gordon B. 2005. *Social Cognition: Understanding Self and Others*. New York: Guilford.

Nisbett, Richard E. 2004. *The Geography of Thought: How Asians and Westerners Think Differently … and Why*. New York: Free Press.

Phelps, Elizabeth A., Kevin J. O'Connor, William A. Cunningham, et al. 2000. Performance on Indirect Measures of Race Evaluation Predicts Amygdala Activation. *Journal of Cognitive Neuroscience* 12: 729–738.

Schwarz, Norbert, Herbert Bless, Fritz Strack, et al. 1991. Ease of Retrieval as Information: Another Look at the Availability Heuristic. *Journal of Personality and Social Psychology* 45: 513–523.

David Dunning

SOCIAL COGNITIVE MAP

In their 1985 study Robert B. Cairns, Jane E. Perrin, and Beverly D. Cairns defined the Social Cognitive Map (SCM) procedure as a peer-report method for identifying social groups of children or adolescents in school settings. The SCM procedure, originated by developmental psychologist Robert Cairns, involves three distinct steps: collecting peer reports of social groups, aggregating those peer reports in a single matrix, and analyzing similarity patterns in the matrix to identify peer groups.

To collect peer reports of groups, each participating youth is asked: "Are there any kids here (at your school/in your classroom) who hang around together a lot?" The question can be posed during an individual interview or with a group administered questionnaire. In either case respondents are encouraged to identify each member of as many groups as they can recall. Sometimes a roster of peers in the setting is provided to facilitate recall, but respondents are never required to classify all peers into groups. Each respondent's report can be considered the individual's "social cognitive map" of the setting. These individual social cognitive maps are aggregated into a symmetric matrix containing one row and one column for each individual in the setting, regardless of whether or not the individual provided a report of groups. Off-diagonal cells summarize conominations: For example, the total number of times that individuals i and j were named to the same group is placed in cell c_{ij}. Each cell along the diagonal (e.g., c_{ii}) contains the total number of times that an individual was named to any group. Algorithms are applied to the conomination matrix to identify dyads that interact more than one would expect by chance or to identify peer groups. Developmental psychologists typically have identified groups based on similarity in conomination patterns (e.g., intercorrelating the columns of the conomination matrix, then using decision-rules or standard data reduction procedures to identify group structures), but software developed for social network analysis provides a wide range of alternative group-detection algorithms.

The SCM procedure is based on two assumptions: first that there is some degree of consensus among youth regarding peer affiliation patterns, and second that youth are expert participant-observers in peer social networks whose reports have some connection to observable interaction patterns. These assumptions have been validated in several empirical studies. For example, conomination matrices routinely reveal greater than chance levels of agreement among peer respondents; and observational studies document that youth interact with members of their SCM-identified peer groups at rates three to four times higher than with other same-sex classmates.

The SCM procedure focuses on identifying relational ties linking individuals in a setting, which distinguishes it from widely used peer-report methods that focus on measuring the status or behavior of individuals (Cairns 1983). For example aggregating respondents' reports of peers whom they "like most" and "like least" yields powerful measures of peer acceptance and rejection, respectively; and aggregating respondents' nominations of peers who match specific behavioral descriptors (e.g., "starts fights") provides robust measures of aggression. It is possible to derive individual-level measures from the SCM conomination matrix, but the SCM procedure's most unique feature is its explicit focus on relational ties and structures.

Among methods for assessing relational ties among peers, the advantages and disadvantages of the SCM procedure are best understood in the context of alternative procedures. Direct observations have face validity and can produce dense interaction matrices for analysis, but they are costly to gather and may be impractical among older youth because researchers typically lose access to important settings for peer interaction. Self-reported friendships or social groups provide unique information on subjectively valued relationships, but they are vulnerable to self-enhancement biases and result in missing data when individuals decline to participate. There is little data documenting the validity of teacher and parent reports of youths' school-based peer relationships.

In this context the SCM approach has several notable strengths: The necessary data is relatively inexpensive to collect; the multi-informant method produces dense conomination matrices that provide a robust basis for applying a wide range of social network analysis tools (Gest, Moody, and Rulison 2007); and the resulting peer group structures capture reliable and valid patterns of relational ties among all members of the network, even those who do not provide individual reports.

SEE ALSO *Adolescent Psychology; Friendship; Identity Matrix; Peer Effects; Peer Influence; Self-Enhancement*

BIBLIOGRAPHY

Cairns, Robert B. 1983. Sociometry, Psychometry, and Social Structure: A Commentary on Six Recent Studies of Popular, Rejected, and Neglected Children. *Merrill-Palmer Quarterly* 29: 429–438.

Cairns, Robert B., Jane E. Perrin, and Beverly D. Cairns. 1985. Social Structure and Social Cognition in Early Adolescence: Affiliative Patterns. *Journal of Early Adolescence* 5 (3): 339–355.

Gest, Scott D., James Moody, and Kelly L. Rulison. 2007. Density or Distinction? The Roles of Data Structure and Group Detection Methods in Describing Adolescent Peer Groups. *Journal of Social Structure* 8. http://www.cmu.edu/joss/content/articles/volume8/GestMoody/.

Scott D. Gest

SOCIAL COMPARISON

A simple but powerful insight about how people evaluate themselves is that these evaluations often result from comparisons with others. How do people know if they can run fast? Do they run around a track and simply examine their times? No, they compare their times with that of others. How do people know if their opinions are correct? Is there an objective standard to which they can turn? No, people are likely to consult the views of those around them and conform to the majority view.

A THEORY OF SOCIAL COMPARISON PROCESSES

Although an age-old idea and variously found as a building block for many theories of social behavior across disciplines, this insight was first systematically thought through by the social psychologist Leon Festinger in his now classic 1954 paper, "A Theory of Social Comparison Processes." Festinger pointed out that most judgments about the self, in the absence of objective criteria, must be based on social comparisons. In fact, he claimed that this lack of objective criteria was the typical state of affairs, leading to the conclusion that much of what people infer about themselves has relativistic roots.

Festinger also posited a human drive to self-evaluate because accurate self-evaluation should be adaptive. It was to the human organism's benefit to know its abilities accurately and to assess the prevailing attitudes of others.

Another claim of the theory was that similar others are sought for self-evaluation because they are most useful for accurate self-evaluation. More precisely, people prefer comparisons with others who are similar on attributes that are relevant for the comparison. A male high school student would not compare his running time with that of an inexperienced, female middle school student. He would use the running times of other male runners of similar age and training. Likewise, with regard to opinions, people seek out and usually conform to the opinion of people with whom they share important group characteristics.

Festinger's claim for the adaptive implications of seeking social comparisons fits well with evolutionary psychology. Ranking on various characteristics often determines survival and access to resources that lead to reproductive success. Human beings, by this logic, should be highly attuned to social comparisons and the variations in rank that they reveal.

ADVANCES IN SOCIAL COMPARISON THEORY

Social comparison theory has evolved in a number of directions. Philip Brickman and Ronnie J. Bulman (1977) pointed out that the potentially weighty implications for the self resulting from social comparisons mean that these comparisons can produce both pain and pleasure. Upward social comparisons, with individuals who are superior to oneself, can often undermine feelings of self-worth. Such social comparisons might often be avoided as much as sought. Downward social comparisons, with individuals who are inferior to oneself, may bolster feelings of self-worth. Social comparisons of this sort may be sought and savored. Thus, because of either their self-threatening or bolstering effects, social comparisons may serve as much to protect or enhance the self as to further accurate self-evaluation.

Brickman and Bulman focused largely on the pain of inferiority and the pleasures of superiority, but more recent thinking emphasizes that people are quite capable of having either positive or negative reactions to both upward and downward social comparisons. One might suppose that upward comparisons would typically lead to contrast effects, that is, the conclusion of relative inferiority. But partly because of robust judgmental biases allowing individuals to construe themselves as better than they are, an upward comparison can actually boost self-evaluation. In this sense, people assimilate toward the social comparison target, enhancing self-views. Also, one might think that downward comparisons would typically lead to contrast effects and the conclusion of relative superiority. But, downward comparisons, despite self-serving biases, can also produce assimilation effects. This might occur when another person's inferior status suggests a similar fate for oneself, producing anxiety rather than a pleasing sense of superiority.

What determines assimilation versus contrast? Perceptions of control seem to be especially important. In the case of upward social comparisons, if people believe that another's superiority suggests something attainable, then pleasing assimilative reactions can occur. If the superiority suggests an unattainable goal, however, then displeasing contrastive reactions should result. Thus, a freshman might look at the success of a senior as hopeful indication of what he or she might end up achieving; but an underachieving fellow senior might experience this comparison in a depressive, contrastive fashion. Indeed, one way of suggesting how much social comparisons influence everyday life is to note the many emotions that people feel as a result of social comparisons, depending on whether the comparisons are upward or downward, contrastive or assimilative. Upward comparisons, when they produce contrastive effects can lead to the painful, often hostile emotions of envy, resentment, or shame. When they are assimilative in nature, they can lead to the pleasing, beneficent emotions of admiration and inspiration. Downward comparisons, when contrastive, can produce such emotions as pride and contempt; when they are assimilative, they can produce worry, fear, or pity.

Social comparison processes continue to find a central place in many efforts to explain social behavior. One example is the vast amount of influential research inspired by social identity theory (Tajfel and Turner 1979), which assumes that a large part of a person's identity follows from social comparisons between in-group and out-group. Another example is the research on social norms and social influence (Blanton and Christie 2003). Yet another example is the extensive, developing literature on the implications of social comparison for subjective well-being and health (Buunk and Gibbons 1997).

Research and theorizing on social comparison processes continue unabated. Festinger's claims about why and how social comparisons influence people's self-evaluations has received considerable support and has moved far beyond its original scope. There is little doubt about the pervasive and foundational role of social comparisons in determining self-evaluations, in influencing people's behavior, and in shaping people's understanding of their experiences.

SEE ALSO *Cognition; Locus of Control; Motivation; Self-Esteem; Self-Perception Theory; Social Identification*

BIBLIOGRAPHY

Blanton, Hart, and Charlene Christie. 2003. Deviance Regulation: A Theory of Identity and Action. *Review of General Psychology* 7 (2): 115–149.

Brickman, Philip, and Ronnie J. Bulman. 1977. Pleasure and Pain in Social Comparison. In *Social Comparison Processes:*

Theoretical and Empirical Perspectives, eds. Jerry M. Suls and Richard L. Miller, 149–186. Washington, DC: Hemisphere.

Buunk, Bram P., and Frederick X. Gibbons, eds. 1997. *Health, Coping, and Well-Being: Perspectives from Social Comparison Theory.* Mahwah, NJ: Erlbaum.

Festinger, Leon. 1954. A Theory of Social Comparison Processes. *Human Relations* 7 (2): 117–140.

Suls, Jerry M., and Ladd Wheeler, eds. 2000. *Handbook of Social Comparison: Theory and Research.* New York: Kluwer Academic/Plenum.

Tajfel, Henri, and John C. Turner. 1979. An Integrative Theory of Intergroup Conflict. In *The Social Psychology of Intergroup Relations*, eds. William G. Austin and Stephen Worchel, 33–47. Monterey, CA: Brooks/Cole.

Richard H. Smith

SOCIAL CONSTRUCTIONISM

The process of creating social reality by individuals, groups, or organizations in interaction with social structure is often termed social construction. Sociologist W. I. Thomas defined the concept of the situation as, "If men define situations as real, they are real in their consequences" (Thomas and Thomas 1928, p. 572). And this theorem demonstrates that human perceptions in large and small ways create the social world.

While individuals actively participate in creating social reality, simultaneously, they are influenced by social reality. Human behaviors, everyday interactions, and social life do not occur in random fashion; rather daily experiences in the social world are patterned based on the organizing of individuals, groups, and organizations. As Peter Berger and Thomas Luckman presented, "Society is a human product. Society is an objective reality. Man is a social product" (Berger and Luckman 1966, p. 61).

Different perspectives and research approaches are used to investigate social construction and its results. Social scientists have used the term *social construction* to emphasize how identity, roles, statuses, knowledge, and institutions are created and maintained relating with other members of society in socio-historical context. Postmodern theorists demonstrate how social reality is constructed by deconstructing in various ways what is taken as reality. For instance, some postmodern researchers deconstruct knowledge to demonstrate a totalizing general theory or an ultimate truth is misguided.

The creation of identity, the sense of self, demonstrates how the social construction works at the individual level, how significant it is to an individual in various contexts, and how individual identity creation is a reflection of social structure. Individual identity is formed by social processes in different socio-historical contexts. So identity can be fluid, situated, multidimensional, and interactive between individual consciousness and social structure. Identity is created, re-created, and maintained by reacting upon the given social structure and personal characteristics.

Social psychological studies have focused on how social structure intersects with individuals' construction of identity. Many studies focus on people experiencing identity struggles, especially managing lower status in the hierarchical order of social life. For example, creation of sexual identity in relation to majority culture is complicated and is a particular struggle for those belonging to marginalized or stigmatized groups, such as homosexuals. It is through interacting with others and by learning cultural norms and values that individuals become aware of which sexual identity is desirable and appropriate in society. Thus, for homosexuals, construction and maintaining of their sexual identity is the socio-political process of obtaining legitimacy.

Social scientists have incorporated various types of research methods to explore the process and consequence of social construction. These include in-depth interviews, participant observation, ethnomethodology, documentary-historical studies, discourse analysis, experiments, and surveys.

SEE ALSO *Interactionism, Symbolic; Sociology, Micro-*

BIBLIOGRAPHY

Berger, Peter L., and Thomas Luckman. 1966. *The Social Construction of Reality: A Treatise in the Sociology of Knowledge.* New York: Doubleday.

Calhoun, Craig, et al. 2002. *Contemporary Sociological Theory.* Maiden, MA: Blackwell.

Howard, Judith. 2000. Social Psychology of Identities. *Annual Review of Sociology* 26: 367–393.

Seidman, Steven. 1994. The End of Sociological Theory. In *The Postmodern Turn: New Perspectives in Social Theory*, ed. Steven Seidman. Cambridge, U.K.: Cambridge University Press.

Thomas, William I., and Dorothy Thomas. 1928. *The Child in America: Behavior Problems and Programs.* New York: Knopf.

Hyejin Iris Chu

SOCIAL CONSTRUCTS

Social constructs or social constructions define meanings, notions, or connotations that are assigned to objects and events in the environment and to people's notions of their relationships to and interactions with these objects. In the domain of social constructionist thought, a social construct is an idea or notion that appears to be natural and obvious to people who accept it but may or may not represent reality, so it remains largely an invention or artifice of a given society.

Games are an example of socially constructed entities and often exist because of certain sets of conventional rules. These sets of social conventions and agreement to abide by them give games their meaning in any given social context. The game of football could be played in any way, but there have developed over the years known conventional rules governing the players, spectators, and the game's organization. The meaning given to games is therefore socially constructed.

Gender, which represents ways of talking, describing, or perceiving men and women, is also a socially constructed entity. Generally distinguished from sex (which is biological), notions of gender represent attempts by society, through the socialization process, to construct masculine or feminine identities and corresponding masculine or feminine gender roles for a child based on physical appearance and genitalia.

Social class is yet another socially constructed entity. While most scholars agree that class appears to represent a universal phenomenon, its meaning is often contextually located because what determines class varies from one society to another, and even within a culture different people may likely have different notions of class determinants.

Depending on the constructionist perspective, social construction may be the outcome of human choices rather than of immutable laws of nature. Here, then, lies the core issue over which social scientists diverge. Are human ideas and conceptions generated more on subjective criteria than on objective realities? Debates have raged in the social sciences along the divide of science versus objective truth. In the social construction of reality, the question has often been asked: To what extent is our claim to knowledge supported by reality? In other words, to what extent is this claim a social construct? Some writers believe that to the extent that knowledge is aligned with reality, it approximates objective truth; anything less represents a social construct. According to this thinking, even morality is a social construct. However, others believe that all knowledge is social construction.

The basis of this debate—in fact the point of departure among scholars—is the claim that social constructions are based on social facts and surrounding social conventions. Thus constructions based on "facts"—facts that are not ontologically dependent on the social structures and conventions of society—are not. However, Ian Hacking (1999) believes that there are few if any "universal constructionists," in which case few people would argue that the sun or DNA are socially constructed, existing entirely independently of that construction. On the contrary, the social arena is quite different, as vital social realities are socially constructed, existing by virtue of that

social construction by people over time and space. This seeming narrow threshold between scientific construction and social constructs presents problems in social analysis—indeed hard nuts that need to be cracked and cracked satisfactorily.

In the resulting ongoing science wars, one side argues that scientific results, including even those of basic physics, are socially constructed. Others protest, arguing that these results are usually discoveries about our world; they are not the production of society but exist independently of consciousness. However, some sociologists, such as Barry Barnes and David Bloor (1982), have taken a relativist view of social construction, claiming that any notion is as good as the other. Thus, for instance, if a new social construction of the Holocaust emerges, arguing that claims about Nazi extermination camps are exaggerated and that the gas chambers are a fiction, that view may well then be at par with other beliefs about the same phenomena, though this may represent historical revisionism. Nevertheless, the fact remains that constructionists attempt to sort out their notions and beliefs using standards of their own convictions and culture.

Peter Cohen (1990), in his discussion of drug use as a social construct, argues that concepts used to describe and explain the phenomenon of drug use are surrounded by bias, a bias produced by a cultural dependency rather than drug use itself. The so-called scientific analysis of drug use, he argues, has often been used as an instrument for survival of the most powerful; power is not only relevant to decision making and resource allocation but also to the social construction of ideology and morality. Scientific constructions and concepts are thus developed according to the interests and tastes of people in power (a trend that is inescapable though may not be justified), and so these constructions often fit into conventional standpoints on topics of research.

The implications of these varying constructionist positions is that, once again, it is not often clear what is, or what should be, socially constructed. Radical constructionism best underscores this basic problem in social construction. Radical constructionists are concerned, for instance, with the domain of technology, with showing how social processes affect the content of technology and what it means for technology to be seen as working. They claim that the meaning of technology, including facts about its workings, are themselves social constructs. Similarly, on the social construction of reality, radical constructionists believe that the process of constructing knowledge regulates itself and that knowledge is a self-organized cognitive process of the human brain, a construct rather than a compilation of empirical data. If this is so, it is impossible to determine the extent to which knowledge reflects an ontological reality.

The problem of social construction has become more pronounced in different constructions of race based on diverging claims on racial distinctions. For instance, while William A. Darity Jr. (2003) has argued that race does not exist because there is no biogenetic basis for racial classifications, studies from Stanford University tend to contradict this claim by suggesting that the way people classify themselves by race reflects real and clear genetic differences among them. They argue that people of different races, even within the same population, have different ancestries, meaning that different genes are inherited from ancestors. However, Hacking (1999) insists that research studies have tended to challenge the idea of race by presenting evidence that the scientific basis for racial distinctions is based on shaky grounds.

Attempts to confine race to social construction appear to be based on the potential dangers of emotions that may be triggered by suggestions that racial differences reflect meaningful biogenetic differences. This has meant that some experts are inclined to publicize the idea that race does not exist. For instance, the *New England Journal of Medicine*, a prestigious medical journal, editorialized on May 3, 2001, "In medicine there is only one race, the human race."

But as a social construct, connotations of race change as social, political, historical, and economic structures of society change. Rodney D. Coates (2004) argues that notions of race are created for people to fit into, to raise consciousness in line with conceptual boxes so created, and often to generate racial outcomes, for instance, notions of racial inequality to produce racial superiority. He observes that the construct "black" has in fact changed over time and space, and he questions whether our conceptions of "blacks" have correspondingly changed with the lived experiences and reality of blacks. This invariably reveals the dynamic nature of social reality. If constructions of this lived reality fail to reflect that dynamism, it may become an invalid analytic or discursive unit, that is, a unit or object of analysis or discussion and debate.

Stephen Spencer (2000) has further asked: If race is a social construct, of what is it precisely constructed if not the scientifically invalid false consciousness of biological race? He argues that it is as necessary to problematize the social construction of race as it is to question its scientific construction. He concludes that for those who believe in biological construction of race but not in its social construction, the basis of their construction has an underlying biological conception, whether or not they admit that. Such constructions often create false consciousness, producing uncertainty as to what are or are not social differences and ultimately creating a new consciousness, a new social reality.

These questions highlight the problem of what is and what is not a social construct. The answer may well lie in the fact that it all depends on the researcher's politics, theoretical orientation, discipline, position in the class structure, or cultural context. It remains that people may often attempt to justify self-serving definitions, but this raises yet another fundamental question: Can this alter consensus on the validity of concepts? It is apt at this point to note that the use of invalid concepts in social research, public discourse, or policy debates may in fact lead to reification. However, in scientific construction, researchers must move outside the boxes of existing notions of matters of investigation to evaluate and analyze issues on such matters from radically different assumptions, even the assumptions of their disciplines (Coates 2004).

SEE ALSO *Communication; Critical Theory; Femininity; Gender; Linguistic Turn; Masculinity; Meaning; Race; Social Theory*

BIBLIOGRAPHY

Barnes, Barry. 1974. *Scientific Knowledge and Sociological Theory.* London and Boston: Routledge and Kegan Paul.

Barnes, Barry, and David Bloor. 1982. Relativism, Rationalism, and the Sociology of Knowledge. In *Rationality and Relativism*, eds. Martin Hollis and Stephen Lukes, 21–47. Cambridge, MA: MIT Press.

Berger, Peter L., and Thomas Luckmann. 1966. *The Social Construction of Reality: A Treatise in the Sociology of Knowledge.* Garden City, NY: Doubleday.

Coates, Rodney D., ed. 2004. *Race and Ethnicity: Across Time, Space, and Discipline.* Boston: Brill Academic Publishers.

Cohen, Peter. 1990. Drugs as a Social Construct. PhD diss., Universiteit van Amsterdam, Amsterdam, Netherlands.

Darity, William A., Jr. 2003. Racial/Ethnic Employment Discrimination, Segregation, and Health. *American Journal of Public Health* 93 (2): 226–231.

Darity, William A., Jr., and P. L. Mason. 1988. Evidence on Discrimination in Employment: Codes of Color, Codes of Gender. *Journal of Economic Perspectives* 12 (2): 63–90.

Hacking, Ian. 1999. *The Social Construction of What?* Cambridge, MA: Harvard University Press.

Kalekin-Fishman, Devorah, Hanan Bruen, and Miriam Ben-Peretz. 1986. Perception and Interpretation of Vocal Music: Constructs of Social Groups. *International Review of the Aesthetics and Sociology of Music* 17 (1): 53–72.

Pinker, Steven. 2002. *The Blank Slate: The Modern Denial of Human Nature.* New York: Viking.

Spencer, Stephen. 2000. Popular Culture and the Rural Dream: Cultural Contexts and the Literary History of the Good Earth. *Atenea* (June): 125–138.

Spencer, Stephen. 2000. "Racing" Whiteness: American Culture and Construction of Race. Paper presented at the Northeast Modern Language Association Conference, April 8.

Frederick Ugwu Ozor

SOCIAL CONTRACT

A social contract is an agreement that can explain and justify a citizen's rights and responsibilities. It can also give an account of our moral obligations and the legitimacy of the state. Social contract theory explores the scope, content, role, and possible justification of any such social contract.

In his dialogue *Crito*, Plato (c. 427–347 BCE) illustrates the power of the notion of a social contract. He depicts Socrates (c. 469–399 BCE) arguing against escaping his prison cell on the eve of his execution. His voluntary residence in Athens and acceptance of the benefits of Athenian society, Socrates claims, show he has implicitly agreed to do the state's bidding—including accepting its unjust death sentence.

Writers often describe the state of nature as the human condition outside political society. Thomas Hobbes (1588–1679) famously argued that the state of nature is a state of war where life is "solitary, poor, nasty, brutish, and short" (1968, p. 186). Without any settled conceptions of justice, people come to universal and violent conflict. In *Leviathan* (1651) Hobbes describes how individuals secure safety and prosperity only by agreeing with one another to submit themselves completely to an absolute sovereign power. Despite his authoritarian conclusions, Hobbes is one of the founders of the liberal political tradition, which traces political legitimacy and political obligation to the free consent of the governed.

John Locke (1632–1704) denied that the state of nature is necessarily a total war but admitted it has inconveniences (e.g., unfair enforcement of the law of nature). People thus agree to a limited state whose right to rule they may rescind if it is abused. Lockean liberalism thereby justifies a right of revolution. Not all subjects explicitly agree to a state's rule, so Locke argued that residence in a state's territory is implicit consent to the state's authority. Later commentators, such as David Hume (1711–1776) and, more recently, A. John Simmons (b. 1950), criticized the idea that such tacit consent can make a state legitimate or obligate individuals to obey the laws.

Jean-Jacques Rousseau (1712–1778) believed that both Hobbes and Locke built distorting effects of civilization into their accounts of the state of nature. In Rousseau's view, civilization introduces all pernicious inequalities (such as in wealth and status), so society should fashion a social contract in order to secure human freedom. The "general will" is properly sovereign; it wills neither private goods nor aggregates of them but wills the common good. Individuals who then voluntarily will the general will best realize their own freedom by sharing in the public good.

More recently, John Rawls (1921–2002) rooted a theory of justice in a social contract whose participants are in an "original position" marked by a fair bargaining situation. Behind a "veil of ignorance" where they are denied knowledge of morally irrelevant features about themselves such as race, sex, class, or religion, individuals unanimously select two principles to govern the basic structure of society. First, everyone has an equal right to maximal basic liberties consistent with a similar amount for all others. Second, once fair equality of opportunity is secure, any inequalities in social and economic goods must advantage all—especially the least well-off.

Contemporary social contract scholarship explores the scope, number, and power of the agreements. Scholars consider, for instance, whether the social contract is national or international, whether participants are actual or hypothetical persons, and whether and how the contract includes nonhuman animals and the disabled.

SEE ALSO *Liberalism; Locke, John; Rawls, John; Rousseau, Jean-Jacques; Sovereignty*

BIBLIOGRAPHY

Hobbes, Thomas. [1651] 1968. *Leviathan*, ed. C. B. Macpherson. New York: Penguin.

Hume, David. [1748] 1987. Of the Original Contract. In *Essays: Moral, Political, and Literary*, ed. Eugene F. Miller. Indianapolis, IN: Liberty Classics.

Locke, John. [1690] 1960. *Two Treatises of Government*. Cambridge, U.K.: Cambridge University Press.

Plato. 1892. *Crito*. In *The Dialogues of Plato*. 3rd ed. Trans. Benjamin Jowett. London: Oxford University Press.

Rawls, John. 1971. *A Theory of Justice*. Cambridge, MA: Belknap Press.

Rousseau, Jean-Jacques. [1762] 1987. On the Social Contract and Discourse on the Origins of Inequality. In *The Basic Political Writings*. Trans. Donald A. Cress. Indianapolis, IN: Hackett.

Simmons, A. John. 1979. *Moral Principles and Political Obligations*. Princeton, NJ: Princeton University Press.

Andrew I. Cohen

SOCIAL COST

Social cost and social benefit constitute two parts of one phenomenon. They reflect the effect of an economic activity of someone (producer or consumer) on the economic position of someone else who is not directly involved in that activity. Any individual economic decision, and its resulting activity, implies cost in terms of an opportunity foregone, such as opportunity cost. For instance, the labor used for the production of "x" excludes its use for the production of "y." If the activity causes cost to a third party, this cost must be added to the privately borne opportunity cost. An activity that benefits a third party's economic position may be defined as a negative cost. The sum of the private cost and the third-party cost is the social cost. The concept of social cost results from economic interdependence.

THE DEVELOPMENT OF INTERDEPENDENCE

British economist Alfred Marshall (1842–1924), in his *Principles of Economics*, introduced the interdependence phenomenon as "external economies." Marshall restricted himself to production. For example, external economies concern a localized industry that benefits from the neighborhood of a pool of skilled workers (Marshall [1890] 1920, pp. 266–267). The growth of an industry creates a pool of skilled workers that changes the production technology and its costs. Marshall also gave an external-diseconomies example: "English miners have opened out mines of ore which diminished the foreign demand for many of England's products" (Marshall [1890] 1920, p. 274). English miners and mechanics have aided foreign countries to compete successfully with England's products. For England its reduced competitiveness will be seen as negative external economies.

In 1931 economist Jacob Viner (1892–1970) launched a distinction in the term interdependence that is relevant to the concept of social cost; technological versus pecuniary external effects. A technological external effect concerns the indirect effect of an activity on consumption bundle, utility function, or production function of someone else. Marshall's skilled-workers example regards a technological external effect. It implies that privately borne marginal costs differ from social marginal costs. Marginal cost is the extra total cost of an additional unit of production. The disparity between private and social marginal cost results in inefficiency, as the economic decision does not take into account all the relevant costs. Efficiency will be reached if marginal benefits equalize marginal costs, without ignoring the social marginal cost (both positive and negative) on others. The equality concerned is called a Pareto-efficient social-welfare situation. It is a social welfare optimum in which it is impossible to improve someone's welfare without harming the welfare of someone else. Therefore, disparity between private and social cost offers room for Pareto-efficient changes. Social welfare may profit from changing production or consumption until private marginal costs and social marginal costs are equal to each other, without a loss for anyone. This demonstrates the relevance of the concept of social cost.

A pecuniary external effect concerns an activity of some that has a direct impact on the market prices of others. Person A's purchase may increase Person B's input prices. It is similar to a zero-sum game: A's benefit is B's loss. Marshall's miners example is a pecuniary effect. Pecuniary external effects concern redistribution of rent, irrelevant to the concept of social cost. However, in an international context this redistribution may result nationally in welfare effects and social cost.

EXTERNAL EFFECTS THAT RELATE TO SOCIAL COST

In the 1920s British economist Arthur C. Pigou (1877–1959) formulated a remedy to welfare inefficiencies due to inequalities between private and social marginal cost. If private marginal cost exceeds social marginal cost, there is a positive external effect. A subsidy that equalizes private and social cost enables governments to prompt social welfare. For instance, the privately borne cost of education may exceed its social cost due to the social benefits of education, i.e., negative social costs. A subsidy to the education consumer will prompt education, equalizing private to social cost, enhancing Pareto-efficiency. The subsidy will induce additional activity that promotes social good. In the reverse case, there is a negative external effect that ought to induce governments to levy a tax on the activity that causes a negative effect on society.

The Pigovian procedure is beset by a multitude of difficulties. First, the discrepancy between private and social cost depends on the scope of the external effect. Should future generations be taken into account as being part of the harmed or favored third party? Second, cost differs substantially over time. In the short run it is hard to adapt to an effect. Therefore, in the long run the cost issue of an external effect will weaken. Third, costs and benefits pertain to individuals who may value these in a subjective manner. This subjectivity blocks an objective aggregation.

Even a compensation test in which winners compensate losers is not possible without a normative element. After compensation, winners as well as losers might reverse their valuation. While applying the compensation test, a normative assumption about the distribution desired must be made. All these implementation difficulties turn the Pigovian welfare device in what, later on, economist Ronald H. Coase (b. 1910) typifies as "blackboard economics" (Coase 1988, p. 19). Pigou does not take the informational problems into account that surround his proposal. In particular, the tax-subsidy instrument becomes arduous because of diffuse external effects.

Nevertheless, the Pigovian approach is a popular line of thought in designing public policy. In particular cost-benefit analysis endeavors to cope with the measurement and aggregation problems discussed, making explicit the integral (net) sum of private and social cost. Such an analysis may, for instance, imply an appraisal of the negative social cost of safety investments in terms of the cost of a human life.

THE PROBLEMS OF SOCIAL COST

In 1960 Coase wrote *The Problem of Social Cost*, a paper that addressed the basic cause of the discrepancies between private and social cost. Why do markets fail to bring parties together that might be mutually profitable? For instance, Person A's activity inflicts a harm on Person B. It is in line with the Pigovian approach to tax Person A, to prohibit A's activity, or to make A liable for the harm inflicted on Person B. However, according to Coase, this "traditional approach has tended to obscure the nature of the choice that has to be made" (Coase 1960, p. 2).

The choice in the social-cost issue is a reciprocal choice. For example, to prohibit Person A's activity will certainly favor Person B, but, simultaneously, it will harm A. If A's activity brings in a benefit of $50, and if this activity harms B for $20, banning A's activity is socially inefficient. This perspective opens new insights. Person A's activity and Person B's harm should be formulated in terms of property rights. Consequently, A and B will start negotiations about their conflicting rights. A market emerges, and the social-cost concept turns out to be irrelevant. A precondition is that the transaction cost is zero. This is the Coase Theorem in a nutshell.

His theorem aims to underline that in reality, transaction cost is positive. In particular, transaction cost will be substantial if great numbers of parties are involved in an external effect. These abound in modern industrialized economies (e.g., air pollution due to production and consumption). The Coasean program aims to design social arrangements that internalize social cost and minimize transaction cost. Internalized social cost will be borne by optimizing economic agents and, consequently, minimized. The Kyoto Protocol in 1997, which established CO_2-emission rights among nations, is such a social arrangement. Trade on emission rights has emerged, which reduces social cost.

SEE ALSO *Coase, Ronald; Coase Theorem; Cost-Benefit Analysis; Externality; Welfare Analysis; Welfare Economics*

BIBLIOGRAPHY

Coase, Ronald H. 1960. The Problem of Social Cost. *Journal of Law and Economics* 3: 1–44.

Coase, Ronald H. 1988. *The Firm, the Market, and the Law*. Chicago: University of Chicago Press.

Marshall, Alfred. [1890] 1920. *Principles of Economics*, 8th ed. London: Macmillan and Co.

Pigou, Arthur C. [1920] 1978. *The Economics of Welfare*, 4th ed. London: Macmillan. New York: AMS Press.

Stigler, George J., and Kenneth E. Boulding, eds. 1953. *Readings in Price Theory*. London: George Allen & Unwin.

Viner, J. 1931. Cost Curves and Supply Curves. *Zeitschrift für Nationalökonomie*. Reprinted in *Readings in Price Theory*. George J. Stigler and Kenneth E. Boulding, eds. 1953. London: George Allen & Unwin.

Piet de Vries

SOCIAL DEVIANCE

SEE *Deviance.*

SOCIAL DISTANCE

SEE *Social Isolation; Tolerance, Political.*

SOCIAL DOMINANCE ORIENTATION

Social dominance theory proposes that humans have an evolved tendency to form group-based social hierarchies because such social structures were adaptive in evolutionary history. Influenced by Marxism, the theory observes that group-based hierarchies are cross-culturally universal and are stratified according to three criteria: age, gender, and arbitrary-set group memberships, including socially constructed categories such as ethnicity and social class. Social dominance theory describes how sociostructural, psychological, institutional, and ideological factors interact to produce and maintain hierarchically organized social structures that foster discrimination and oppression within society.

Social dominance orientation is the psychological component of social dominance theory. According to Jim Sidanius and Felicia Pratto (1999), social dominance orientation reflects the degree to which people are predisposed to achieve and maintain hierarchically organized social structures in which some groups dominate and have more power than others, versus social structures in which all groups are equal and no one group has more power than any other. This global orientation encompasses the competitive-driven motivation to achieve and maintain group-based dominance and unequal power relations between any given set of social groups, regardless of the particular categories or characteristics used to define those groups (e.g., gender, ethnicity, social class). Social dominance orientation is measured by assessing the extent to which people agree with ideological/attitudinal items such as "Some groups of people are simply inferior to other groups" and disagree with items such as "No one group should dominate in society."

Social dominance theory states that the motivation for group-based dominance and superiority (indexed by social dominance orientation) is a proximal cause underlying the many different manifestations of prejudice and discrimination (e.g., sexism, racism, homosexual prejudice), and also explains why some people are more likely to seek out positions of power and status. Consistent with this perspective, research demonstrates that people who are prejudiced toward one group will also tend to be prejudiced toward other (often unrelated) groups, and that the generality of prejudice toward multiple groups is reliably predicted by individual differences in social dominance orientation. These effects occur because, regardless of qualitative differences in content, prejudice and related ideologies (such as meritocracy and cultural elitism) function as legitimizing myths that produce and maintain hierarchically organized social structures. Accordingly, group-based hierarchies should tend toward stability to the extent that such ideologies are consensually shared across both dominant and subordinate groups within society (a phenomenon referred to as behavioral asymmetry).

Social dominance orientation explains an aspect of prejudice that is not accounted for by other constructs, such as right-wing authoritarianism or political conservatism. Individual differences in social dominance orientation are caused by a combination (and possible interaction) of biological factors (men are typically higher in social dominance orientation than women), sociostructural factors (group membership and exposure to competitive social environments), personality or temperament, and schematic beliefs about the competitive (versus cooperative) nature of the social world. Although there is some debate regarding the extent to which social identity might contextually activate social dominance orientation, most researchers nevertheless agree that the orientation functions as a mechanism through which the aforementioned factors produce individual differences in prejudice and hence institutionalized discrimination and oppression.

SEE ALSO *Authoritarianism; Conservatism; Cults; Discrimination; Elitism; Evolutionary Psychology; Groups; Hierarchy; Identity, Social; Marxism; Measurement; Meritocracy; Prejudice; Racism; Scales; Sexism*

BIBLIOGRAPHY

Pratto, Felicia, Jim Sidanius, Lisa M. Stallworth, and Bertram F. Malle. 1994. Social Dominance Orientation: A Personality Variable Predicting Social and Political Attitudes. *Journal of Personality and Social Psychology* 67 (4): 741–763.

Sidanius, Jim, and Felicia Pratto. 1999. *Social Dominance: An Intergroup Theory of Social Hierarchy and Oppression.* Cambridge, U.K., and New York: Cambridge University Press.

Chris G. Sibley
John Duckitt

SOCIAL ECONOMY

The social economy is generally taken to be a third sector of mixed capitalist economies distinct from the private and public sectors. The social economy is based on cooperative, not-for-profit, and voluntary rather than paid activities carried out within communities, across national economies, and internationally. It is variously referred to as the *nonprofit sector*, the *économie sociale*, and the *Gemeinwirtschaft*, and has a long history coincident with the rise of market economies (Nitsch 1990).

The social economy is defined by the collection of different social objectives of the various organizations that make it up. According to the European Commission, social economy organizations are classified as cooperatives, mutual societies, voluntary organizations, foundations, and social enterprises. All are based on voluntary participation and membership, and are guided by their social objectives rather than a need to make a return on capital. Many social economy organizations simply deliver services to their members or others they aim to serve without making use of the market. Other social economy organizations, known as *social enterprises*, engage in trade activities in order to benefit their members or those they serve. In this latter case, any surpluses or profits earned are reinvested in the enterprise, distributed to stakeholder groups, or used for the benefit of those served by the enterprise. Governance typically operates through the "one member, one vote" principle or through enterprise trustees.

A diverse range of examples of social economy organizations includes building and mortgage societies, credit unions, charities and philanthropic organizations, neighborhood organizations and community groups, trade unions, insurance mutuals, sports associations, hospitals, self-help groups, school organizations, religious groups, environmental groups, arts groups, clubs of many kinds, political organizations, producer cooperatives, trade and professional associations, and job-training organizations.

Recognition of the economic importance of social economy enterprises—treated as nonprofits in the economics literature—is relatively recent (e.g., Rose-Ackerman 1986; Weisbrod 1988; Ben-Ner and Gui 1993). But social economy enterprises, or nonprofits, are now seen to play significant economic roles in addressing needs unmet by the private and public sectors, competing with for-profit enterprises, enhancing economic productivity, improving delivery of public services, promoting economic and social development, and providing employment. In addition, because worldwide trends are toward both increasing services production and privatization of government services, social economy or nonprofit enterprises, many of which address these domains, are likely to play larger economic roles in the future. This is reflected in more explicit recognition of the social economy in the national economic policies of many countries, including the United Kingdom, Spain, France, Canada, and a number of Latin American countries.

SEE ALSO *Associations, Voluntary; Community Economic Development; Development; Foundations, Charitable; International Nongovernmental Organizations (INGOs); Justice, Social; Nongovernmental Organizations (NGOs); Philanthropy; Social Capital; Volunteer Programs; Volunteerism*

BIBLIOGRAPHY

Ben-Ner, Avner, and Benedetto Gui, eds. 1993. *The Nonprofit Sector in the Mixed Economy*. Ann Arbor: University of Michigan.

Nitsch, Thomas. 1990. Social Economics: The First 200 Years. In *Social Economics: Retrospect and Prospect*, ed. Mark Lutz. Boston: Kluwer.

Rose-Ackerman, Susan, ed. 1986. *The Economics of Nonprofit Institutions: Studies in Structure and Policy*. New York: Oxford University Press.

Weisbrod, Burton A. 1988. *The Nonprofit Economy*. Cambridge, MA: Harvard University Press.

John B. Davis

SOCIAL EXCHANGE THEORY

While the general study of market exchange is the domain of the discipline of economics, the social, interactional components of exchange (in a market context or not) interest other social scientists. As German sociologist Georg Simmel noted: "Exchange is not merely the addition of the two processes of giving and receiving. It is, rather, something new. Exchange constitutes a third process, something that emerges when each of those two processes is simultaneously the cause and the effect of the other" ([1907] 1971, p. 57).

Noneconomic investigations of exchange appeared in anthropology in the 1920s. For example, in 1922, Bronislaw Malinowski published a study of islander life that analyzed status components of exchanges that were different from (although related to) simple consumption or material interests. Other anthropological studies followed that emphasized the importance of gift giving and reciprocity for the maintenance of cohesive relationships.

A series of sociological and psychological studies of exchange emerged in the 1950s. George Homans adapted behavioral or operant learning tenets to describe behavior among individuals. Because operant principles emphasize how individuals act on the basis of previous experience,

Homans's formulation also focused on the past as predictive of future behavior. He presented human exchanges as involving rewards and costs and argued that people responded to these exchanges so that benefits outweighed costs. Somewhat different from Homans's approach, Peter Blau developed a more economic framework in his exchange formulations. So, for example, in his analysis of bureaucracies, he pointed out that people compete for scarce resources and trade different social commodities (such as advice).

In psychology, John Thibaut and Harold Kelley developed their theories of social power that involved the idea that the amount of power one individual or group possesses is determined, in part, by the alternatives present. Thus, individuals gauged whether to engage in exchanges dependent upon the value of the exchange itself and if alternatives were available. Alternatives also affected the way comparisons among activities were perceived; that is, what was experienced in the past affected how attractive or unattractive a particular option appeared.

Richard Emerson's formulation of power-dependence theory in social relations took these previous conceptualizations and developed an overarching theory. It specified a relational aspect to power that placed the exchange relation as central. Power was inversely related to dependence: For a given exchange relation, the more powerful an individual or group, the less dependent on the relation. Further, Emerson's theory posited a continual balancing mechanism in exchange relations. If people had power, they used it because it gave them advantage. But, if power was used, it was (incrementally) lost. This shift of power leads to *balancing*.

Further distinctions in different kinds of exchanges emerged in work that followed. Specifically, Linda Molm distinguished two types of exchanges that had different properties. Negotiated exchange involves bargaining and negotiation and then agreement upon the terms of the exchange. In contrast, reciprocal exchange does not involve negotiation but, instead, is comprised of individual acts performed for an other or others without knowledge about future reciprocation. Given equivalent costs and benefits, reciprocal exchanges generate more trust and affect than do negotiated exchanges. Part of the reason for this is that, at least under some conditions, risk generates trust.

Molm investigated coercive power in these nonnegotiated exchanges as well. Coercive power (in the sense of punishing others) is seen by participants as intentional and most likely to be used when an actor has little reward power. This is probably the case because coercion is risky and can decrease the possibilities of future beneficial exchanges. So, even though punishment can be an effective strategy if it is consistently and contingently applied, actors do so relatively infrequently.

While there are differences between negotiated and reciprocal exchanges, there are similarities as well. One important similarity rests with the negative emotion that can be generated with power use. For example, the conflict spiral, a theory about bargaining processes, documents that unequal power, even without punishment, can produce negative emotion.

Much of the research on negotiated exchange has focused upon the idea of alternatives to valued resources and so has considered exchange networks. Relative power of positions in simple networks can be analyzed by calculating the alternatives to a given position. Depending upon the number and extent of alternatives within the network, different kinds of relationships can be defined. Particularly important for the exercise of power is the ability to exclude others. The network then can define strong, equal, or weak power. There have been a number of attempts to find methods of predicting power in networks that vary in structure and size. There is the graph theoretic approach, a game theory approach, and an expected value mode, among others.

Emotion is also implicated in the exchange process. The affect theory of social exchange, for example (see, in particular, Lawler 2001), maintains that while social exchange has an instrumental and individual function, the exchange itself involves a group product that fosters emotional, affective processes. While rational choice formulations had examined how commitment in exchange networks was fostered by uncertainty reduction, it has been demonstrated that affect, in and of itself, can also generate commitment. Productive exchanges provide particularly strong arenas for emotion. These exchanges occur in settings in which group members have equal power, coordination issues exist and must be solved, and interdependence of group members is necessary for production of the outcome.

While the study of exchange has always been important to group dynamics, the addition of emotion and notions of risk, trust, and uncertainty has transformed early investigations of simple cost and benefit. The transformations have expanded both the depth and scope of exchange formulations. For example, depth has been transformed by analysis of actors' strategies in the face of contingencies, and scope has been transformed by analysis of the network configurations under which exchange occurs. In this regard, different disciplines have contributed different insights to the study of social exchange: game theory in economics has focused upon strategies, anthropology has emphasized the cultural components implied in cohesive groups, psychology has investigated issues related to risk and uncertainty, and sociology has focused upon the network structure under which exchange occurs.

SEE ALSO *Blau, Peter M.; Groups; Norms; Reciprocity*

BIBLIOGRAPHY

Blau, Peter M. 1964. *Exchange and Power in Social Life.* New York: Wiley.

Cook, Karen S., and Richard Emerson. 1978. Power, Equity and Commitment in Exchange Networks. *American Sociological Review* 43: 721–739.

Emerson, Richard M. 1972. Exchange Theory, Part I: A Psychological Basis for Social Exchange. In *Sociological Theories in Progress*, Vol. 2, eds. J. Berger, M. Zelditch Jr., and Bo Anderson, 38–57. Boston: Houghton Mifflin.

Homans, George C. 1958. Social Behavior as Exchange. *American Journal of Sociology* 63: 597–606.

Lawler, Edward J. 2001. An Affect Theory of Social Exchange. *American Journal of Sociology* 107: 321–352.

Malinowski, Bronislaw. 1922. *Argonauts of the Western Pacific.* New York: Dutton.

Molm, Linda D. 1997. *Coercive Power in Social Exchange.* Cambridge, U.K.: Cambridge University Press.

Molm, Linda D., Nobuyuki Takahashi, and Gretchen Peterson. 2000. Risk and Trust in Social Exchange: An Experimental Test of a Classical Proposition. *American Journal of Sociology* 105: 1396–1427.

Simmel, Georg. [1907] 1971. *On Individuality and Social Forms*, ed. Donald N. Levine. Chicago: University of Chicago Press.

Thibaut, John W., and Harold H. Kelley. 1959. *The Social Psychology of Groups.* New York: Wiley.

Willer, David, ed. 1999. *Network Exchange Theory.* Westport, CT: Praeger.

Jane Sell

SOCIAL EXCLUSION

Social exclusion is less a single issue capable of empirical exploration than a way of viewing, or an orientation toward, society. The term itself implies on the one hand groups of people who are in some sense marginalized from society and on the other a societal mainstream composed of people who are not excluded. The range of excluded groups is very wide, extending from those subject to racism to older people, from those who are unemployed to those subject to homophobia, from those who are disabled to disillusioned youth, from the mentally ill to teenage mothers (Sheppard 2006).

There are, perhaps inevitably, an equally large number of definitions, although most contain the common "mainstream-marginalization" theme. The definition that perhaps best expresses the meaning of social exclusion was provided by the Child Poverty Action Group: Social exclusion "refers to the dynamic process of being shut out, fully or partially from any of the social, economic, political and cultural systems which determine the social integration of the person in society" (Walker and Walker 1997). This definition gives the sense of being "outsiders," unable to participate fully in society, and that the problem was systemic, in that it involved—whatever the cause—social systems.

THE CONCEPT

Discussions of social exclusion reflect the effects of the great range of groups to which the term is applied. As a response to the conceptual difficulty of embracing such a range, one approach is to focus on a particular group, providing a "practical marker" for social exclusion. Unemployment, in particular, has provided such a focus, as it is regarded by many as the key issue liable to be associated with social exclusion, and also to be part of the situation confronted by many excluded groups such as the racially disadvantaged, disillusioned groups, and poor families.

The primary factor in social exclusion, from this perspective, is unemployment. At an individual level it has a profoundly demoralizing effect when sustained, and at societal level, it provides a threat to social cohesion and stability. The experience in pre–World War II Europe of the political effects of unemployment, and its association with the rise of fascism, provides a background in recent history of the societal threat presented to social order, both within and between [nation-] states. Late-twentieth-century structural changes in the European economies, which saw higher rates of long-term unemployment, fueled a concern for social inclusion policies (Commission for the European Community 1992).

In Britain, France, Germany, and the Netherlands, social exclusion policies have emphasized unemployment and reemployment. By this logic, policies promoting social inclusion should first and foremost be focused on reintegrating the unemployed into the workforce and enabling this to occur through appropriate economic and social measures. In doing so, such policies would be expected to have a secondary effect on other features of social exclusion. Unemployment often has been used as a practical "shorthand" for poverty, underlying a range of issues of social concern relating to poor workforce skills, low income, poor housing, high crime environments, bad health, and family breakdown (Atkinson and da Voudi 2000, p. 435).

A more abstract, and hence more embracing, notion has connected social exclusion and inclusion to the "realization of human potential." Individuals and groups suffer social exclusion to the extent that society does not offer them the opportunity to realize their potential. This notion of rights—that people have a right to achieve their potential, in conjunction with their fellow citizens—is embedded in the very heart of the European Union (EU). It takes precedence over, and makes sense of, some of the union's most fundamental aims: "economic and social progress," states the Comité des Sages, an official group of prominent experts from the EU whose task is to inform policy development, "must be subordinate to this aim" (1996, p. 26). It also links social exclusion with equality of opportunity. In Britain this was formulated by Chancellor Gordon Brown, who argued that everyone deserves to be given an equal chance to fulfill "the potential with which they are born" (1997). Poverty and unemployment could provide obstacles to this, but so could other disadvantages, which are multidimensional, such as health, disability, and age.

A range of responses could be made to these obstacles to inclusion and full social participation in the spheres of education, welfare, and the economic sector. For example, good educational provision, universally provided, provides a strong basis of opportunity for individuals to achieve their potential. All these strategies help promote an idea of "citizenship," which is closely associated with the realization of potential. Citizenship involves participation and involvement in society, and hence the realization of human potential becomes, in part, an active concept focused on social participation.

Education can actively enhance the capacity for citizenship. However, other provisions, for example, the range of welfare support, can counteract or ameliorate the effects of disadvantage that prevent individuals or groups from being citizens. Citizenship stands as a means for curbing the excesses of the market, particularly through the welfare state (Marshall 1963). Material issues of economic inequality are important in this respect, but so too are prejudice and stigma suffered by some groups, affecting their life opportunities, sense of identity, and self-esteem.

Social citizenship involves living "the life of a civilised being according to the standards prevailing in society" (Marshall 1963, p. 74; Kymlicka and Norman 1995). What, it is asked, do people need in order to participate in society fully as citizens? One approach is that of "passive recipient," in which professionals, as experts, identify and design responses to need. The doctor, counselor, or social worker is entrusted with ensuring that an individual's needs are met. An alternative—with more active involvement—emphasizes the capacity of citizens to define, and act upon, their own needs. This rebalances the relationship between service provider and recipient. The service user becomes the "expert" in assessing his or her own needs, and the service provider becomes the facilitator of the response to that need (Smale et al. 1993). This covers the individual level, but it can apply also to groups or communities. In such a scenario, local communities come together in groups actively to improve their own lives, involving, say, community action in relation to run-down neighborhoods or local crime. When a group is active, they are taking up and enacting their rights as citizens. This notion of citizenship involves "realization of potential" in two respects. First, it becomes an aim of their actions, and second, it is embedded in the processes by which they seek to achieve these aims. As active citizens they are enacting their potential.

SOCIAL EXCLUSION AND THE PROBLEM OF ORDER

Human potential may underlie one aspect of social exclusion. Another aspect is the problem of order. One (politically liberal-left) approach relates social exclusion and social order to the notion of the "just society." Walter Runciman suggested that peoples' sense of justice, and hence their sense of grievance, arose in the context of reference groups (1972). They measure their own situation, and rewards, by reference to others whom they consider to be like them. For example, plumbers might compare themselves with electricians, and expect similar rewards, but be unworried by being rewarded less than doctors.

A sense of justice and fairness, and therefore of inclusion and exclusion, involves those to whom people make reference. They do so in two ways. First, there are groups within society with whom people compare themselves, and second, on a wider basis, the general wealth of their own society, and its distribution, provides a reference. No one expects standards appropriate to nineteenth-century European societies to provide a reference for those same societies in the twenty-first century.

Runciman argued that three principles could justify distribution of wealth and status: those of need, merit, and contribution to the common good. However, there should be a limit to the degree of inequality. Following John Rawls (1971), he argued that the test of inequality was whether it could be justified to the losers, and for the winners to do this, they must be prepared, in principle, to change places (Runciman 1972, p. 307). It is also a test for a sense of inclusion, because acceptance would indicate commitment to a set of common fundamental norms and expectations widely accepted in society.

A just distribution of resources, then, is necessary to avoid a sense of social exclusion liable to feed political instability. The danger presented by poverty relative to others is that it could lead to a feeling of exclusion "from normal living patterns" (Townsend 1979, p. 32) and hence of alienation from participation in social life. Poverty, therefore, is not just material but emotional. The promotion of social inclusion should be at societal level,

including incomes policy, full employment, higher social security, and a more redistributivist tax structure.

A (liberal-right) alternative to this societal distribution approach is one that emphasizes personal responsibility. A range of writers (Murray 1994; Field 1996; Etzioni 1995, 1998) have expressed concern about the development of a "moral underclass" not committed to the values of mainstream society, which might have a corrupting impact on mainstream society. According to these writers, welfare dependency, high crime rates, single parenthood, teenage pregnancies, and a decline in traditional family values characterize this underclass.

Amitai Etzioni considered parenting deficits to be the underlying feature in the development of a moral underclass (1998): When parents do not commit themselves enough to their children, a moral deficit amongst the young emerges. Children from single-parent and broken (particularly divorced) families are particularly vulnerable. Etzioni emphasized the need for moral renewal based on socialization, which would create shared norms helping bind society together. The key agencies of this [re]socialization are education and child welfare. Policies supporting parents—including welfare-to-work and penalties for parents whose children are school nonattendees—also would encourage them to engage better with their moral responsibilities.

Charles Murray considered a large proportion of welfare-dependent families were in circumstances of their own making (1994). According to Murray, on the one hand, this group increasingly makes the wrong moral choices, including sustained unemployment, crime, and illegitimate childbirth; on the other, welfare policies, specifically social security benefits, create perverse incentives for them to remain welfare-dependent. For example, teenage pregnancy (and motherhood) is encouraged by the state's giving the impression that once a child is born, housing and other financial benefits will be made available. Social policy needs to be directed not just at resocialization at the personal level, but also in policies (such as low benefits) that are a disincentive to welfare dependency.

Although undoubtedly influential on government policy making (Prideaux 2005), Murray's concept of the underclass has been heavily criticized. The concept, it is argued, diverts attention from wider social, economic, and political causes of poverty (Williams and Pilinger 1996). A commonly accepted assumption about the underclass is that poverty is "intergenerationally transmitted" (i.e., that it passes down from generation to generation), but Murray has emphasized culture, and more recently genetics, as key factors (Fitzpatrick 2001). However, evidence indicates that the benefits bestowed by wealth (or disadvantages associated with its absence) and "networks of association" (who you know) also are important features (Bartholomae et al. 2004). Where these facets are not recognized, the danger arises of "blaming the victim"—that is, erroneously presenting the victim's poverty, disadvantage, and welfare dependence as being his own fault (Ryan 1976).

Teenage pregnancy, an example of an issue of wide concern in developed countries, shows the impact of these two (liberal-left and liberal-right) orientations. It is associated with other social concerns—poverty, unemployment, criminality, and so on—and has a negative impact on life chances. Countries with social policies that reduce inequalities, including Norway, Sweden, and Holland, have the lowest rates of teenage pregnancies, whereas more unequal countries, such as the United Kingdom and United States, have much higher rates. Nevertheless, even countries that have been only moderately successful at reducing teen pregnancies have included education and contraception as policy responses, underlain by normative, personal responsibility features (UNICEF Innocenti Research Center 2001).

THE FUNCTIONALISM OF SOCIAL EXCLUSION

Underlying all these approaches is a consensus functionalism that would be recognizable to Talcott Parsons (1951) and Émile Durkheim (1947). This is reflected in an emphasis on the widespread adoption of common norms that would create order and stability in society, which would also be in the interests of individuals and groups. The means by which this would be achieved vary, depending on the ideological commitment of the protagonists.

Criticisms of social exclusion as an approach arise because of the ideological nature of the very term. Its use, some think, does a disservice to the vast range of phenomena with which it deals, drawing attention away from the specific issues attached to each of them. Furthermore, it assumes that those who are socially excluded should aspire to the values of mainstream society: This may not be what they want, and they may see no reason to do so. Lastly, it has an implicit notion of the "good society" encapsulated in these mainstream values. This notion may itself be contested.

BIBLIOGRAPHY

Atkinson, Rob, and Simin da Voudi. 2000. The Concept of Social Exclusion in the European Union: Context Development and Possibilities. *Journal of Common Market Studies* 38 (3): 427–448.

Bartholomae, Suzanne, Jonathan J. Fox, and Patrick C. McKenry. 2004. The Legacy of Welfare: Economic Endowments or Cultural Characteristics? *Journal of Family Issues* 25: 783–810.

Brown, Gordon. 1997. Why Labour Is Still Loyal to the Poor. *The Guardian*. August 2.

Comité des Sages. 1996. *For a Europe of Civic and Social Rights.* Report of the Comité des Sages, chaired by Maria de Joudes Pintasilgo. Luxemburg: Office for Official Publications of the European Communities.

Commission for the European Community. 1992. *Towards a Europe of Solidarity: Intensifying the Fight against Social Exclusion, Fostering Integration.* COM (92) 542 final, December 23.

Durkheim, Émile. 1947. *The Division of Labour in Society.* Glencoe, IL: Free Press.

Etzioni, Amitai, ed. 1995. *New Communitarian Thinking.* Charlottesville: University of Virginia Press.

Etzioni, Amitai, ed. 1998. *Essential Communitarian Reader.* Lanham, MD: Rowman and Littlefield.

Field, Frank. 1996. Britain's Underclass: Countering the Growth. In *Charles Murray and the Underclass: The Developing Debate,* ed. R. Lister, 58–61. London: Institute of Economic Affairs.

Fitzpatrick, Tony. 2001. Before the Cradle: New Genetics, Biopolicy, and Regulated Eugenics. *Journal of Social Policy* 30: 589–612.

Kymlicka, Will, and Wayne Norman. 1995. Return of the Citizen: A Survey of Recent Work on Citizenship Theory. In *Theorizing Citizenship*, ed. Ronald S. Beiner, 283–322. Albany: State University of New York Press.

Marshall, Thomas H. 1963. Citizenship and Social Class. In *Sociology at the Crossroads and Other Essays*, 67–127. London: Heinemann.

Murray, Charles. 1994. *Underclass: The Crisis Deepens.* London: Institute of Economic Affairs in association with the *Sunday Times.*

Parsons, Talcott. 1951. *The Social System.* London: Routledge and Kegan Paul.

Prideaux, Simon. 2005. *Not So New Labour: A Sociological Critique of New Labour's Policy and Practice.* Bristol, U.K.: Policy Press.

Rawls, John. 1971. *A Theory of Justice.* Cambridge, MA: Harvard University Press.

Runciman, Walter G. 1972. *Relative Deprivation and Social Justice: A Study of Atttitudes to Social Inequality in Twentieth-Century England.* Harmondsworth, U.K.: Penguin.

Ryan, William. 1976. *Blaming the Victim.* New York: Vintage Books.

Sheppard, Michael. 2006. *Social Exclusion and Social Work: The Idea of Practice.* Aldershot, U.K.: Ashgate.

Smale, Gerald, Graham Tuson, Nina Biehal, and Peter Marsh. 1993. *Empowerment, Assessment, Care Management, and the Skilled Worker.* London: National Institute for Social Work.

Townsend, Peter. 1979. *Poverty in the United Kingdom: A Survey of Household Resources and Standards of Living.* Harmondsworth, U.K.: Penguin.

UNICEF Innocenti Research Center. 2001. *A League Table of Teenage Births in Rich Nations.* Florence, Italy: Author.

Walker, Alan, and Carol Walker, eds. 1997. *Britain Divided: The Growth of Social Exclusion in the 1980s and 1990s.* London: Child Poverty Action Group.

Michael Sheppard

SOCIAL EXPERIMENT

A social experiment is the random assignment of human subjects to two groups to examine the effects of social policies. One group, called the "treatment group," is offered or required to participate in a new program, while a second group, the "control group," receives the existing program. The two groups are monitored over time to measure differences in their behavior. For example, a social experiment can compare a program that gives unemployed individuals a financial reward for finding a job with one that does not. Or, a social experiment might compare students in schools that receive a new curriculum with students in schools that do not. Because the randomization procedure guarantees that the two groups are otherwise similar, the measured differences in their behavior can be causally attributed to the new program. The behavioral differences are sometimes called the "impacts" of the program. Commonly measured behavioral outcomes in social experiments include earnings, employment, receipt of transfer payments, health, educational attainment, and child development. Sample sizes in social experiments have ranged from under 100 to well over 10,000.

Some social experiments have more than one treatment group. In such cases, each treatment group is assigned to a different program. The various treatment groups may be compared to each other to determine the *differential* impacts of two of the tested programs, or they may be compared to the control group to determine the impact of the program relative to the status quo. The human subjects may be chosen randomly from the general population or, more commonly, may be chosen randomly from a target population, such as the disadvantaged.

Social experiments have been used extensively since the late 1960s. According to Greenberg and Shroder (2005) almost 300 social experiments have been conducted since then. Social experiments are very much like medical laboratory experiments in which the treatment group is given a new drug or procedure, while the control group is given a placebo or the standard treatment. Laboratory experiments have also been used extensively in the field of economics, since the 1970s (Smith 1994), but they differ from social experiments in that they are used mainly to test various aspects of economic theory, such as the existence of equilibrium or the efficiency of market transactions, rather than the effects of a social program. Also, economics laboratory experiments usually do not have a control group; instead, cash-motivated members of a treatment group are given the opportunity to engage in market transactions in a controlled environmental setting to determine whether they behave in a manner consistent with the predictions of economic theory. Some laboratory experiments in economics have been used to test public policy alternatives.

HISTORY OF SOCIAL EXPERIMENTS

Much of the foundation of the modern approach to social experimentation can be traced back to the work of the famous statistician Ronald Fisher in the 1920s. Fisher refined the notion of random assignment and pointed out that no two groups could ever be identical. He noted that allocation of subjects to treatment and control groups by pure chance (by the flip of a coin or from a table of random numbers, for example) ensures that differences in the average behavior of the two groups can be safely attributed to the treatment. As a result, the direction of causality can be determined using basic statistical calculations. Fisher also recognized that randomization provides a means of determining the statistical properties of differences in outcomes between the groups.

The first major social experiment was the New Jersey Income Maintenance Experiment, which was initiated in the United States in 1968. Although a few smaller social experiments preceded the New Jersey Experiment (such as the Perry Preschool Project in 1962), they were much smaller in scope and much less sophisticated. The New Jersey Experiment tested the idea of a negative income tax (NIT), first proposed by the economists Milton Friedman and James Tobin in the 1960s. The New Jersey Experiment was the first of five NIT experiments conducted in North America (four in the United States and one in Canada) that had very sophisticated designs and many treatment groups. Problems evaluating certain aspects of these complex experiments led to much simpler experimental designs in ensuing years.

From the 1970s to the present, social experiments have been conducted in numerous social policy areas, including child health and nutrition, crime and juvenile delinquency, early child development, education, electricity pricing, health services, housing assistance, job training, and welfare-to-work programs. Notable experiments include the Rand Health Insurance Experiment, which tested different health insurance copayment plans; the Moving to Opportunity Experiments, which tested programs enabling poor families to move out of public housing; four unemployment insurance experiments that tested the effects of various financial incentives to induce unemployed individuals to return to work; and a number of welfare-to-work experiments that tested ways of helping welfare recipients find jobs.

LIMITATIONS OF SOCIAL EXPERIMENTS

Although widely acknowledged as the ideal way to determine the causal effects of proposed social policies, social experiments have several important limitations. First, and perhaps most importantly, social experiments require that a control group be denied the policy change given to the treatment group. Because control groups in social experiments are typically disadvantaged, denial of program services may be viewed as constituting an ethical breach, thus limiting social experiments to places where resources prevent all eligible individuals from being served. Also, treatments that make a participant worse off are also viewed as unethical and politically infeasible.

Second, although well-designed experiments have a high degree of *internal validity* (inferences are valid for the tested sample), they may not have *external validity* (they are not generalizable to other settings). One common criticism of experiments is that because of their limited size, they do not generate the macroeconomic, "community," effects that a fully operational program would generate. For example, a fully operational job training program may affect the wages and employment of nonparticipants and may affect social norms and attitudes, whereas a limited size experiment would not. Additionally, there is no way of knowing for sure whether a successful experiment in one location would be successful in another location, especially because social experiments are typically conducted in places that are chosen not randomly, but for their capability and willingness to participate in an experiment.

Third, social experiments take time to design and evaluate, usually several years. Policymakers may not want to wait the required time to find out if a particular program works.

Finally, in practice, it has often proven difficult to implement random assignment. For one reason or another, individuals may not be willing to participate in a research study, and in cases where collaboration between researchers and government agencies is required, some may be unwilling to participate. As a result, the treatment and control groups that are tested may turn out to be unrepresentative of the target population.

Because of the various limitations of social experiments, other means of evaluating the effects of social policies have been developed. These are generally termed "nonexperimental" or "quasi-experimental" methods. Nonexperimental methods monitor the behavior of persons subjected to a new policy (the treatment group) and select a "comparison group" to serve the role of a control group. But because randomization is not used to select the two groups, it is never known for sure whether the comparison group is identical to the treatment group in ways other than receipt of the treatment. Many researchers match treatment group members to persons in the nonparticipating population to make the groups as similar as possible. The matches are usually done using demographic and economic characteristics such as age, education, race, place of residence, employment and earnings history, and so on. One popular matching technique is *propensity score matching*, which uses a weighted average of the observed

economic and demographic characteristics of the nonparticipating population to create a comparison group.

A particularly attractive nonexperimental method is the "natural experiment." Natural experiments often are used to test the effects of social policies already in place. The natural experiment takes advantage of the way a new policy has been implemented so that the comparison group is almost a true control group. For example, military conscription (being draft eligible) during the Vietnam War was done by a national lottery that selected individuals for military service solely according to their date of birth. Thus, theoretically the group selected for military service should be identical to those not chosen, because the only difference is date of birth. Researchers wanting to test the effects of military conscription on individuals' future behavior could compare outcomes (for example, educational attainment or earnings) of those conscripted with those not conscripted and safely attribute the "impacts" to conscription (Angrist 1990). Because not all conscripted individuals actually serve in the military and because some non-conscripted individuals volunteer for military service, it is also possible to estimate the impact of actual military service on future behavior by adjusting the impacts of conscription for differences in the proportion serving in the military in the treatment and comparison groups. However, the validity of this procedure rests crucially on the comparability of the military service veterans in the two samples.

THE FUTURE OF SOCIAL EXPERIMENTS

Social experiments have changed in character since the late 1960s. Many early social experiments such as the NIT experiments, the Unemployment Insurance Experiments, and the Rand Health Insurance Experiment tested a "response surface" in which subjects were given "quantifiable" treatments of varying tax or subsidy rates. In contrast, most of the more recent social experiments are "black box," meaning that a package of treatments is given to the treatment group, and it is not possible to separately identify the causal effects of each component of the package.

Black-box experiments have been criticized because they tend to have much less generalizability than response-surface experiments. Hence, many researchers have called for a return to nonexperimental evaluation as the preferred method of analyzing the effects of social policies. However, those favoring experimental methods have countered that social experimentation should remain the bedrock of social policy evaluation because the advantages are still great relative to nonexperimental methods (Burtless 1995). In an attempt to "get inside the black box," those sympathetic with the social experiment as an evaluation tool have proposed ways of combining experimental and nonexperimental evaluation methods to identify causal effects of social policies (Bloom 2005). Nonexperimental methods are necessary because of a selection bias that arises when members of the treatment group who receive certain components of the treatment are not a random subset of the entire treatment group. In the future, social policy evaluation may make greater use of both evaluation methodologies—using experiments when feasible and combining them with nonexperimental methods when experiments cannot answer all the relevant policy questions.

SEE ALSO *Negative Income Tax*

BIBLIOGRAPHY

Angrist, Joshua D. 1990. Lifetime Earnings and the Vietnam Era Draft Lottery: Evidence from Social Security Administrative Records. *American Economic Review* 80 (3): 313–336.

Bloom, Howard S., ed. 2005. *Learning More from Social Experiments*. New York: Russell Sage Foundation.

Burtless, Gary. 1995. The Case for Randomized Field Trials in Economic and Policy Research. *Journal of Economic Perspectives* 9 (2): 63–84.

Greenberg, David, and Mark Shroder. 2005. *The Digest of Social Experiments*. 3rd ed. Washington, DC: Urban Institute Press.

Greenberg, David, Donna Linksz, and Marvin Mandell. 2003. *Social Experimentation and Public Policymaking*. Washington, DC: Urban Institute Press.

Smith, Vernon. 1994. Economics in the Laboratory. *Journal of Economic Perspectives* 8 (1): 113–131.

Philip K. Robins

SOCIAL FACILITATION

In 1898 Norman Triplett reported an experiment in which schoolchildren turned a fishing reel under two conditions: first alone and then standing beside a competitor. Triplett claimed that the competitor's presence inspired many of his subjects to perform the reel-turning task more quickly. In his 1924 textbook *Social Psychology*, Floyd Allport offered a behavioral interpretation of Triplett's result. As Allport explained, responses elicited by a nonsocial stimulus can be augmented by a social stimulus. Allport regarded Triplett's finding as evidence of this *social facilitation* and offered some evidence of his own. In Allport's research, college students solved simple multiplication problems and cancelled vowels from English text more quickly when working alongside other students than when alone.

In contemporary usage, the term *social facilitation* has a broader meaning, referring to any influence of the pres-

ence of others on the individual. The others who are present may be doing the same thing as the individual (that is, coacting), or they may simply be observing. Most often, researchers study influences on the individual's performance of a task. Sometimes they find that individuals perform tasks better in the presence of others than when alone, but often they find the opposite: worse task performance when others are present. Both performance improvements and performance degradations are termed *social facilitation*, as the phrase is currently used.

When does the presence of others benefit task performance and when does it impair task performance? Robert Zajonc offered an answer to this question in 1965. According to Zajonc, the presence of others improves the performance of simple tasks and disrupts the performance of complex tasks. Although subsequent research provided some support for Zajonc's assertion, a large-scale review showed in 1983 that the presence of others impairs complex performances more strongly than it facilitates simple performances (Bond and Titus 1983).

What accounts for these effects? Zajonc proposed an answer to this question too. Zajonc wrote that the presence of others functions as a source of generalized drive, enhancing dominant response tendencies. According to this analysis, the dominant tendency is to give the correct response on simple tasks and to make mistakes on complex tasks. By enhancing these tendencies, the presence of others facilitates simple task performance and impairs complex performance, Zajonc's drive theory claims.

Other theories of social facilitation have been proposed. These note that the presence of others can induce many psychological states, including self-awareness, distraction, and evaluation apprehension. Psychophysiological theories have been proposed. Whereas an older theory claimed that the presence of others increases general arousal (Guerin 1993), Jim Blascovich and colleagues offered a different view in 1999: When others are present, people who are performing simple tasks manifest physiology indicative of challenge; those who are attempting complex tasks manifest physiology indicative of threat.

The presence of others influences more than task performance. It can encourage the display of prejudice. It can increase, and sometimes decrease, how much people eat. It has many effects on animal behavior. A rudimentary form of social influence, social facilitation has captured psychologists' attention for more than a century.

BIBLIOGRAPHY

Allport, Floyd. 1924. *Social Psychology*. Boston: Houghton Mifflin.

Blascovich, Jim, Wendy B. Mendes, and Sarah B. Hunter. 1999. Social "Facilitation" as Challenge and Threat. *Journal of Personality and Social Psychology* 77: 68–77.

Bond, Charles F., Jr., and Linda J. Titus. 1983. Social Facilitation: A Meta-Analysis of 241 Studies. *Psychological Bulletin* 94: 265–292.

Guerin, Bernard. 1993. *Social Facilitation*. Cambridge, U.K.: Cambridge University Press.

Zajonc, Robert B. 1965. Social Facilitation. *Science* 149: 269–274.

Charles F. Bond Jr.

SOCIAL HISTORY

SEE *History, Social.*

SOCIAL HUMANISM

SEE *Humanism.*

SOCIAL IDENTIFICATION

How do people perceive the self and what do they perceive as the self? People look outside of the self to the social context because the views of the self are shaped by the world individuals encounter. Social identification theories demonstrate how identity is defined, as a conception of the self, the content of the self, or the knowledge about who I am, constructed in terms of rules and orders applying to social contexts.

Symbolic interactionists have delineated the procedure of constructing the self-concept by evoking the significance of the relationship between the individual and the social structure. George Herbert Mead (1984) differentiates "me" from "I" to explain the concept of social self and how self is constructed through interactions with others. Charles Horton Cooley (1998) presents the concept of the "looking-glass self," noting that the self is constituted through interaction with its surroundings and that the self-concept is achieved by speculating the imaginative evaluation from others. For Mead and Cooley, self is not an a priori or pre-given because it develops only through contact with others.

For Erving Goffman the construction of self is a series of presentations or performances to others: "The very structure of the self can be seen in terms of how we arrange for such performances" in the society (Goffman 1997, p. 23). Social interaction is viewed as a performance influenced by cultural environment, concerning the other people, constructed to provide appropriate impressions.

In this way, the individual develops identity by interacting with others, through presenting desirable impressions according to the social expectations in a particular sociocultural context.

In *The Reproduction of Mothering* (1999) Nancy Chodorow provides a psychological analysis of the construction of gender identity in the intimate social surroundings of family. According to Chodorow, gender identity is the consequence of a specific family form in which women are exclusively responsible for the nurturing of children. Children build their gender identity by differentiating themselves from their primary caregivers, usually their mothers. Because the early social environment differs and is experienced differently by male and female children, Chodorow argues that individuals develop different gender identities based on sex. Her research has been particularly influential in explaining how patriarchal practices of Western cultures affect individual identification processes.

Individuals understand and identify themselves in reference to groups. Social identities—national, ethnic, racial, gender, religious, occupational, and so on—comprise critical aspects of the self-concept and are derived from perceived membership of particular social groups. Originally developed to understand the psychological basis of intergroup discrimination, Henri Tajfel and John C. Turner's social identity theory describes processes significant for an individual's identification with large-scale social groups or categories. The social identification process starts from an "individual's subjective location" in the network of social relationships (Tajfel 1982, p. 503). Identification processes are experienced differently by individuals in terms of their locations in the hierarchically organized social relations of a society—as members of nations; as members of gender groups; as members of racial/ethnic groups; as members of religious groups; and in other social locations. After being categorized based on group membership, individuals seek to achieve positive self-esteem by differentiating their in-group (we/us) from a comparison out-group (them/others). This in-group/out-group comparison process reflects commonly shared ideas or attributions applied to social groups. In other words, the in-group bias leads to discrimination toward out-groups; at the same time, though, some group members identify themselves based in part on socially assigned but negative or undesirable attributions.

In her study of racial-identity development of minority adolescents, Beverly Tatum argues that adolescents of color are more likely to be actively engaged in exploration of their racial or ethnic identity than are white adolescents because they receive more intensive "racial content" messages from their surroundings and they perceive how their racial identity is presented to other racial group members (Tatum 1997, p. 54). In contrast, whites in the United

States often deemphasize explicit racial content, partly because they take it for granted and are privileged through various social domains. Illustrating this, Eduardo Bonilla-Silva (2003) explores different dimensions of white privilege and demonstrates how whiteness is constructed in the U.S. society through narratives.

In a wide range of social settings, individuals struggle to establish social desirability or legitimacy of the identities they possess. Individuals recognize how the groups they belong to are perceived by other group members, and they react to this. Being a member of a particular group sometimes results in exaltation for the individual, but it can also result in unequal treatment, punishment, or marginalization. Distinctiveness often relates to the political boundaries established by the society. For example, identity politics postulates that difference is taken as a political motivation for action. Lesbian and gay activists struggle over their sexual identities to claim the same rights as heterosexuals to marriage, child-rearing, property ownership, and other social practices often forbidden to them.

In recent years social identification theories have expanded the range of research into interdisciplinary areas. Various social-scientific concepts and perspectives are increasingly incorporated as central aspects of social identification processes such as collective protest, political rhetoric, diversity, and system-justification beliefs (Hogg and Ridgeway 2003). However, social identification theories have been criticized for the treatment of identities as individual status categories, such as race/ethnic or gender categories. By focusing on the development of particular social-status categories, identification theorists often ignore structural issues, such as specific historical and cultural backgrounds or the political consequences of identification experiences in a given society. For instance, individual development of racial identity in the United States is deeply associated with the historical and cultural contexts of the United States. Through history, particular racial or ethnic groups have been projected with specific images, cultural notions, and political practices by other racial or ethnic groups. Thus, racial/ethnic identification processes not only mean developing social status categories at an individual level, but also imply structural power relations among racial/ethnic groups directly related to the historical and cultural context.

In the social sciences, studies use various methods—interviews, participant observation, ethnomethodology, discourse analysis, survey, and experiments—to investigate the social identification process at the individual level and how this process is related to the social structure.

SEE ALSO *Blackness; Ethnicity; Goffman, Erving; Groups; Identity; Mead, George Herbert; Nationalism and Nationality; Race; Religion; Social Movements; Sociology; Stigma; Whiteness*

BIBLIOGRAPHY

Abrams, Dominic, and Michael A. Hogg, eds. 1990. *Social Identity Theory: Constructive and Critical Advances.* New York: Springer-Verlag.

Aronson, Elliot, Timothy D. Wilson, and Robin M. Akert. 2002. *Social Psychology.* Englewood Cliffs, NJ: Prentice Hall.

Bonilla-Silva, Eduardo. 2003. *Racism without Racists: Color-Blind Racism and the Persistence of Racial Inequality in the United States.* New York: Rowman and Littlefield Publishers.

Brown, Kathleen M. 1996. *Good Wives, Nasty Wenches, and Anxious Patriarchs: Gender, Race, and Power in Colonial Virginia.* Chapel Hill: University of North Carolina Press.

Chodorow, Nancy. 1999. *The Reproduction of Mothering: Psychoanalysis and the Sociology of Gender.* Berkeley and Los Angeles: University of California Press.

Cooley, Charles Horton. 1998. *Charles Horton Cooley on Self and Social Organization,* ed. and with an introduction by Hans-Joachim Schubert. Chicago: University of Chicago Press.

Goffman, Erving. 1997. *The Goffman Reader,* eds. with introductory essays by Charles Lemert and Ann Branaman. Oxford: Blackwell Publishers.

Hogg, Michael A., and Cecilia L. Ridgeway. 2003. Social Identity: Sociological and Social Psychological Perspectives. *Social Psychology Quarterly* 66: 97–100.

Howard, Judith. 2000. Social Psychology of Identities. *Annual Review of Sociology* 26: 367–393.

Mead, George Herbert. 1984. *George Herbert Mead on Social Psychology,* ed. with an introduction by Anselm Strauss. Chicago: University of Chicago Press.

Tajfel, Henri, ed. 1982. *Social Identity and Intergroup Relations.* Cambridge, U.K.: Cambridge University Press.

Tatum, Beverly Daniel. 1997. *"Why Are All the Black Kids Sitting Together in the Cafeteria?" and Other Conversations about Race.* New York: Basic Books.

Hyejin Iris Chu

SOCIAL INFLUENCE

Of the myriad topics, questions, and issues of greatest moment to social psychologists, social influence has been the cornerstone of the field. From the earliest inception of modern social psychology, it has been the defining issue. For example, the first experiment in social psychology (Triplett 1898) probed a phenomenon referred to as *social facilitation*—or the tendency for individuals engaging in like behavior to spur on the actions of one another. In this study, Norman Triplett determined that the presence of a competing cyclist upped the level of performance of bicycle riders when compared to their performance levels as they pedaled against the clock. Similarly, Triplett observed school-aged children who were instructed to turn fishing reels as fast as they could. He found that when they worked in pairs, their performance was superior to what it was when they worked alone.

As Aristotle (384–322 BCE) noted in detail, we are indeed social beings. The mere presence of others affects us beyond our awareness of those effects. The study of social influence has branched from simple demonstrations of socially facilitated behavior to research on such topics as attitude formation and change, conformity, group consensus, obedience, groupthink, prestige suggestion, political socialization, stereotype formation, and many other socially embedded consequences of social influence. This entry will focus on a description of social influence phenomena in the "classic" studies of and approaches to such influence. These classic studies will be separated into two categories: laboratory-experimental research and field-nonexperimental research.

CLASSIC LABORATORY-
EXPERIMENTAL RESEARCH—
SHERIF'S AUTOKINETIC EFFECT

If a stationary pinpoint of light is viewed in an otherwise completely dark room, the light will appear to move. This illusory effect, known as the *autokinetic effect*, was used by Muzafer Sherif (1935) in early studies of social influence. Participants, who were not told that the light was actually stationary, were asked to indicate any movement they perceived by pressing a key that turned off the light. When a group of participants viewed the light at the same time, the fastest-acting participant turned off the light. After the light was turned off, the participants reported orally on the extent of movement. The results indicated that participants who viewed the light in groups showed a gradual convergence toward an agreed-upon extent of movement. Later, when tested alone, individuals continued giving the group-established judgment.

Sherif interpreted his results as indicating that the groups established a norm that influenced judgments. As will be discussed below, later researchers also emphasized the importance of norms as a determinant of social influence.

Asch's Perceptual-Judgments Research Because Sherif's demonstration of social influence involved public communication, it was more dramatic than the social influence that occurred in the social-facilitation paradigm. Still, the judgments were of an illusion. This was not the case, however, in an influential series of studies by Solomon Asch (1952). In Asch's initial study, eight individuals, all but one of whom were confederates of the experimenter, made eighteen consecutive judgments in which they matched the length of a standard line with one of three comparison lines. On each of the eighteen trials, judgments were publicly announced in the order in which

the group members sat, and the single naïve participant always sat next to last. On twelve of the trials, the confederates responded incorrectly. The results revealed marked individual differences, with three-fourths of the participants being influenced on at least one trial and one-third influenced on half or more of the trials.

Asch later reported a series of interesting follow-up experiments. In one such study, he found that the *conformity effect* was maximized with three confederates, was greatly reduced with two confederates, and all but disappeared with one confederate. In another study, he found that when a single confederate responded incorrectly in a group of participants, the confederate's incorrect judgments created amusement and laughter. In still another study, he found that when the confederate who sat in the fourth position responded correctly, the social influence of the group on the participant sitting next to last was dramatically reduced. This latter finding is an early demonstration of *minority influence*—a topic later pursued by Serge Moscovici (1976, 1980) and others.

Milgram's Obedience-to-Authority Research Asch's research on perceptual judgment did produce dramatic results. However, momentary judgments regarding the perceived length of lines may, in the final analysis, be of no great import. Such is not the case, however, for Stanley Milgram's (1965) research on obedience to authority.

Milgram's initial idea was to provide a test of the extent to which individuals would harm someone when given direct orders to do so. History is replete with instances in which such cruelty has occurred. One of the more notable examples was the mass murdering of Jews at such German concentration camps as Auschwitz, Buchenwald, and Dachau during World War II (1939–1945). During the Vietnam War (1957–1975), there is the example of the 1968 My Lai massacre by American troops. A still more recent example is the murdering in 1978 of children and infants by parents and "nurses" at Jonestown in Guyana.

Milgram's participants had responded to a newspaper advertisement to take part in a study of learning and memory at Yale University. They were all male and ranged in age between twenty and fifty years, and were of both white-collar and blue-collar backgrounds. Participants believed they were being tested in pairs, but one member of the pair was actually a confederate of the experimenter. Following a rigged drawing, the participant was assigned the role of "teacher" and the confederate was assigned the role of "learner" in a supposed test of the effect of punishment on memory. The participant-teacher witnessed the confederate-learner being strapped into an "electric chair" in a room immediately adjacent to the room containing the "shock-generator"—an apparatus containing a series of thirty switches that supposedly delivered increasingly intense shocks to the confederate-learner. The switches were accompanied by labels indicating increasing danger, finally ending with the label "XXX." The participant-teacher's task was to deliver increasingly intense shocks whenever the confederate-learner made an error in memory for the word that had been previously associated with a paired stimulus word. The confederate had been trained to make a standard series of errors. If the participant-teacher hesitated, the experimenter delivered a series of four prods, beginning with "please continue" and ending with "you have no other choice, you must go on." The experiment was terminated if the participant-teacher refused to continue after the fourth prod.

Milgram asked forty psychiatrists from a "leading medical school" to predict the results of the study. These experts on human behavior expected that only 1.25 percent of participants would continue to the top step. In fact, Milgram found that 62.5 percent proceeded to that level. The sizable error in the psychiatrists' predictions provides evidence that even among "experts" there is a tendency to underestimate the extent of social influence.

Zimbardo's Stanford Prison Experiment One might suppose that no one could "top" Milgram's research on obedience to authority. However, that was arguably accomplished in Philip Zimbardo's Stanford Prison Experiment (Zimbardo et al. 1973). The participants in this study were twenty-one males between seventeen and thirty years of age who responded to a newspaper advertisement to take part in a study of prison life. Participants were randomly assigned to be either prison guards or prisoners. Zimbardo and colleagues arranged for the prisoners to be unexpectedly arrested by local police officers, fingerprinted, and jailed. After remaining in a cell for a while, the prisoner's were blindfolded, taken to a mock jail (actually the basement of the Stanford psychology building), "stripped naked, skin-searched, deloused and issued a uniform, bedding, soap and towel" (Zimbardo et al. 1973, p. 38). On the first day, the guards began the routine of having the prisoners line up, cite the prison rules, and repeat their individual ID numbers. On the second day, the prisoners rebelled but the rebellion was put down harshly by the guards, who first called in other guard shifts for reinforcement. On subsequent days, the cruelty and abusiveness of the guards intensified, and the prisoners became increasingly passive and demoralized. Not all guards acted the same way. Some were cruel and some were not, but the "good" guards did nothing to protect the prisoners from the cruel guards. Likewise, not all prisoners acted, or reacted, in the same way. On progressive days, five of the prisoners had emotional breakdowns requiring that they be released. The experiment was terminated after six of the originally planned fourteen days.

In this experiment, the social influence came not from the experimenter, as in the Milgram experiment, but was a dynamic consequence of the interaction between two groups and the learned roles associated with these groups. Following this most dramatic demonstration of social influence, there have been no further attempts at even more dramatic demonstrations of social influence, and, primarily for ethical reasons, there have been no further experimental studies of a prison-like environment.

A CLASSIC FIELD-NONEXPERIMENTAL STUDY—NEWCOMB'S BENNINGTON STUDY

One field-nonexperimental study that has, quite deservedly, received wide attention is Theodore M. Newcomb's (1943, 1958) research on Bennington College students and subsequent follow-ups of those students (Newcomb et al. 1967; Alwin et al. 1991). Newcomb collected the initial data in 1935, the first year in which the then new Bennington College had a senior class, and data collection was continued until 1939. Since the student body was small, approximately 250 women, it was possible to collect data from almost all of the students and to follow the initial freshman in 1935 until they were seniors in 1939. An important circumstance was that the college was physically isolated and relatively self-sufficient. Tuition was high and the majority of the students came from wealthy families with conservative social attitudes. On the other hand, the faculty was relatively liberal and "felt that its educational duties included the familiarizing of an oversheltered student body with the implications of a depression-torn America and a war-threatened world" (Newcomb 1958, p. 421).

Data collected from most of the students, and in-depth interviews with a subsample of them, indicated that there was an increasing trend toward liberalism with each additional year in college. A questionnaire assessing various social and economic issues (e.g., public relief and the right of labor to organize) revealed a consistent trend toward liberalism. A straw vote in the 1936 presidential campaign indicated that 62 percent of Bennington's freshman favored the Republican candidate (Alfred Landon), while only 15 percent of the juniors and seniors did so. Consistent with this difference, 29 percent of freshman favored the Democrat candidate (Franklin D. Roosevelt), while 54 percent of the juniors and seniors did so. An even greater ratio of difference occurred for the Socialist and Communist candidates; this varied from 9 percent for the freshman to 30 percent for the juniors and seniors. In observing changes from the freshman to the senior year, Newcomb documented changes toward liberalism that were particularly marked among the more popular students. Newcomb interpreted his results as indicating that the Bennington College community became a positive reference group for most of the students.

Newcomb's initial data are striking, but the profound effect of social influence was made more obvious by the results of two follow-up studies. Interview data from the first follow-up study (reported in Newcomb et al. 1967) were collected from 1959 to 1960 when the women were in their mid-forties. The results indicated that over the twenty to twenty-five year period, most of the women had retained their liberal political attitudes. Newcomb and colleagues pointed out that the persistence of these liberal attitudes might be partially explained by the fact that they had married men with similar liberal attitudes. Data for the second follow-up study were collected in 1984, the year of Newcomb's death, when the women were sixty-five to seventy years old (Alwin et al. 1991). Interviews were conducted with 335 of the original sample of 527 women. Most of the interviews were conducted by telephone, but twenty-eight of the interviews were conducted in three-hour, face-to-face sessions. The results indicated that 70 percent identified themselves as "liberal" and agreed with the positions of the 1984 Democrat presidential candidate, Walter Mondale, on such issues as the responsibility of government to improve the social positions of African Americans and other minorities. The women furthermore confirmed that their attitudes had grown more liberal while they were at Bennington.

The persistence of acquired liberal attitudes over an approximately fifty-year period provides strong evidence for the potentially profound effect of social influence. The Bennington study and the follow-up interviews make clear that social influence is not restricted to short-term judgments or behaviors (for example, judgments regarding which line is longer), but can be life changing.

DEUTSCH AND GERARD ON NORMATIVE AND INFORMATIONAL SOCIAL INFLUENCE

Morton Deutsch and Harold Gerard are widely referenced for interpreting social influence as due to two factors: *normative* social influence and *informational* social influence. They define normative influence as "influence to conform to the positive expectations of another" (Deutsch and Gerard 1955, p. 629). The idea is that agreement with another person, another group, or even the self (in the case of internalized norms) leads to expectations of positive feelings. For conformity to internalized norms (and resistance to the influence of others), they add another process. This is that such conformity "leads to feelings of self-esteem or self-approval" (p. 630). As speculated below, acceptance of the influence of others may also be related to self-esteem.

Deutsch and Gerard define informational influence as "influence to accept information obtained from another as evidence about reality" (Deutsch and Gerard 1955, p. 629). They rely on Leon Festinger's (1950) argument that "where no physical reality basis exists for the establishment of the validity of one's belief, one is dependent upon social reality (i.e., upon the belief of others)" (Deutsch and Gerard 1955, p. 630). Following his 1950 article, Festinger (1954) elaborated his basic argument into a theory—*social comparison* theory—which became one of the more influential theories in social psychology. The theory assumes that we have a drive to evaluate our beliefs in terms of their correctness or validity. The validity of our beliefs can sometimes be determined through simple observation, but, when this cannot be done—and only when this cannot be done—we evaluate the validity of our beliefs through social comparison with the beliefs of others.

The idea that the beliefs of others are a source of information determining social influence has become very influential. However, one could argue that even social comparison theory underestimates the informational value of social influence. For example, a dramatic study by Bibb Latané and John Darley (1970) demonstrated that the assumed danger indicated by an increasing amount of smoke pouring into a room was influenced by the number of seemingly unconcerned others. The greater the number of unresponsive others—actually confederates of the experimenter—the longer it took for the single participant to leave the room. This experiment provides a clear example of how, contrary to social comparison theory, social influence can alter even the judgments of physical reality.

Despite the fact that Deutsch and Gerard speculated about both informational social influence and normative social influence, their research primarily focused on normative social influence. As in Asch's research, Deutsch and Gerard had participants and confederates make length-of-line judgments. They made a number of comparisons among their various conditions, but two of these bear most directly on the influence of group norms. One comparison was between a condition in which the groups were told that each member of the five (out of twenty) groups that made the fewest errors would receive a pair of tickets to a Broadway play versus a condition in which there was no mention of competition among the groups. There was more conformity in the former, competitive condition—presumably because the competition increased the anticipated positive feelings resulting from conformity to the group norm.

The second comparison was between a condition in which the participant (and the confederates) responded publicly, and a condition in which the participant (but not the confederates) responded privately on sheets of paper that were subsequently discarded. There was more conformity in the former, public condition—presumably because only with public responding could the participant's feelings be influenced by the anticipated reactions of the group members.

What about evidence for informational social influence? Deutsch and Gerard provide no evidence directly bearing on informational social influence, but they do point out that such influence is suggested by a further comparison between the private condition and a control condition in which the participants were alone. Participants made fewer errors in the direction of the group in the alone condition.

THE IMPORTANCE OF BEING RIGHT AND THE IMPORTANCE OF BEING LIKED

Chester Insko and colleagues (Insko et al. 1983; Insko et al. 1985) completed research that they believed could show whether individuals would in fact go along with obviously erroneous opinions of others if they had a chance to learn the true answer subsequently. They set forth a related, but alternative, account of Deutsch and Gerard's (1955) explanations in which they argued that going along with others involves joint concerns of being right (or not being wrong) and being liked (or not being disliked), and that both are consistent with the general tendency of people to think—or want to think—well of themselves. Specifically with regard to informational influence, and following from the social comparison theory assumption that others' beliefs provide a social reality for validating one's own beliefs, they argued that such validation is important because being right, or being correct, is consistent with positive self-esteem, or the general tendency of people to think well of themselves. Similarly, with normative social influence, they argued that agreeing with others creates not only the anticipation of being right but also the anticipation of being liked, and that being liked is consistent with positive self-esteem, or, again, the general tendency of people to think well of themselves.

Insko and colleagues (1983, 1985) conducted two studies, both of which followed the Asch procedure of having a series of confederates and a single participant seated in a row of chairs, with the true participant seated next to last. Unlike in Asch's research, the judgments were not of line lengths but of colors—for example, whether the blue-green in the middle was more like the blue on the left or the green on the right. On twelve of the eighteen trials, the confederates responded incorrectly. Both studies included two cross-cutting independent variables, thereby creating four cells or conditions. One independent vari-

able was whether the participants responded publicly or privately.

The other independent variable related to whether or not the correct answer supposedly could be accurately determined by a spectrometer. In the so-called determined condition, it was explained that a printout of the spectrometer reading would be available for examination at the end of the experiment. In the so-called undetermined condition, no printout was made available and it was explained that spectrometers could not accurately read mixed wavelengths. Assuming that the judgments of the confederates were used as a valid source of information, and assuming that participants were concerned with being right or being correct, it follows that there should have been more conformity to the confederates' judgment in the determined than the undetermined condition.

The results indicated that there was more conformity to the confederates' judgments when the judgments were made publicly rather than privately (regardless of whether the correct answers supposedly could or could not be determined), and there was more conformity when the correct answers supposedly could be determined rather than not determined (regardless of whether the participants responded publicly or privately). These results are consistent with expectations based on the assumed joint concerns of being right (or not being wrong) and being liked (or not being disliked). Thus, both the reduction of epistemic uncertainty and the desire to be liked seem to be factors promoting the power of social influence.

THE SOCIAL CONFORMITY DILEMMA

While social psychologists have typically studied the darker side of our dependence on social norms and collective information such as slavish conformity, destructive obedience, normative error, interpersonal cruelty, and bystander "apathy," there are instances of the collective benefits of social influence that are abundantly evident—for example, in the acquiring of knowledge, the prevention of harmful behavior, and the coordination of activities. The fact that research on social influence has tended to focus on negative consequences should not be taken as an indication that social psychologists necessarily subscribe to the bias implicit in Western, individualistic culture that individual action and choice are always preferable to social conformity. It is obviously the case that many norms are adaptive, and that conformity to such norms, and social learning generally, can be beneficial. One of the profound dilemmas of human existence relates to when we should, or should not, conform to the behavior and judgments of others.

SEE ALSO *Asch, Solomon; Attitudes; Authority; Cognitive Dissonance; Conformity; Experiments; Experiments,*

Human; Experiments, Shock; Groupthink; Milgram, Stanley; Norms; Obedience, Destructive; Persuasion; Prisons; Reality; Sherif, Muzafer; Social Comparison; Social Facilitation; Social Psychology; Socialization; Sociology; Zimbardo, Philip

BIBLIOGRAPHY

Allport, Floyd H. 1920. The Influence of the Group Upon Association and Thought. *Journal of Experimental Psychology* 3: 159–182.

Alwin, Duane F., Ronald L. Cohen, and Theodore M. Newcomb. 1991. *Political Attitudes over the Life Span: The Bennington Women after Fifty Years.* Madison: University of Wisconsin Press.

Asch, Solomon E. 1952. *Social Psychology.* Englewood Cliffs, NJ: Prentice Hall.

Baumrind, Diana. 1972. Some Thoughts on Ethics of Research: After Reading Milgram's "Behavioral Study of Obedience." In *The Social Psychology of Psychological Research,* ed. Arthur G. Miller, 106–111. Toronto, Ont.: Collier-Macmillan.

Deutsch, Morton, and Harold Gerard. 1955. A Study of Normative and Informational Social Influences upon Individual Judgment. *Journal of Abnormal and Social Psychology* 51: 629–636.

Festinger, Leon. 1950. Informal Social Communication. *Psychological Review* 57: 271–282.

Festinger, Leon. 1954. A Theory of Social Comparison Processes. *Human Relations* 7: 117–140.

Insko, Chester A., Sarah Drenan, Michael Solomon, et al. 1983. Conformity as a Function of the Consistency of Positive Self-evaluation with Being Liked and Being Right. *Journal of Experimental Social Psychology* 19: 341–358.

Insko, Chester A., Richard H. Smith, Mark D. Alicke, et al. 1985. Conformity and Group Size: The Concern with Being Right and the Concern with Being Liked. *Personality and Social Psychology Bulletin* 11: 41–50.

Latané, Bibb, and John M. Darley. 1970. *The Unresponsive Bystander: Why Doesn't He Help?* New York: Appleton-Century Crofts.

Milgram, Stanley. 1965. Some Conditions of Obedience and Disobedience to Authority. *Human Relations* 18: 57–76.

Moscovici, Serge. 1976. *Social Influence and Social Change.* Trans. Carol Sherrard and Greta Heinz. London: Academic Press.

Moscovici, Serge. 1980. Toward a Theory of Conversion Behavior. In *Advances in Experimental Social Psychology,* ed. Leonard Berkowitz, Vol. 13, 209–239. New York: Academic Press.

Newcomb, Theodore M. 1943. *Personality and Social Change: Attitude Formation in a Student Community.* New York: Dryden.

Newcomb, Theodore M. 1958. Attitude Development as a Function of Reference Groups: The Bennington Study. In *Readings in Social Psychology,* ed. Eleanor E. Maccoby, Theodore M. Newcomb, and Eugene L. Hartley. 3rd ed. New York: Holt.

Newcomb, Theodore M., Kathryn E. Koenig, Richard Flacks, and Donald P. Warwick. 1967. *Persistence and Change: Bennington College and Its Students after Twenty-five Years.* New York: Wiley.

Orne, Martin T. 1962. On the Social Psychology of the Psychology Experiment: With Particular Reference to Demand Characteristics and their Implications. *American Psychologist* 17 (11): 776–783.

Orne, Martin T., and C. H. Holland. 1972. On the Ecological Validity of Laboratory Deceptions. In *The Social Psychology of Psychological Research,* ed. Arthur G. Miller, 122–137. Toronto, Ont.: Collier-Macmillan.

Sanna, Lawrence J. 1992. Self-efficacy Theory: Implications for Social Facilitation and Social Loafing. *Journal of Personality and Social Psychology* 62 (5): 774–786.

Sanna, Lawrence J., and Paul A. Pusecker. 1994. Self-efficacy, Valence of Self-Evaluation, and Performance. *Personality and Social Psychology Bulletin* 20: 82–92.

Sanna, Lawrence J., and R. Lance Shotland. 1990. Valence of Anticipated Evaluation and Social Facilitation. *Journal of Experimental Social Psychology* 26: 82–92.

Sherif, Muzafer. 1935. A Study of Some Social Factors in Perception. *Archives of Psychology* 27 (187): 1–60.

Triplett, Norman. 1898. The Dynamogenic Factors in Pacemaking and Competition. *American Journal of Psychology* 9 (4): 507–533.

Zimbardo, Philip G., W. Curtis Banks, Craig Haney, and David Jaffe. 1973. The Mind Is a Formidable Jailer: A Pirandellian Prison. *New York Times Magazine,* April 8: 38–60.

Chester A. Insko

SOCIAL INFORMATION PROCESSING

Social information processing theory describes a set of cognitive-emotional mechanisms specifying how the way in which children interpret a particular event influences how they will respond to that situation. This framework takes into account the database of prior experiences with parents and peers that children bring to new situations. As a result of prior social interactions, children develop cognitive schemas that influence their processing of social information in new situations.

Nicki R. Crick and Kenneth A. Dodge (1994) have proposed six steps in a model of social information processing. First, encoding of external and internal cues is the process of taking in information from the environment. Second, making attributions (or interpretations and mental representations of cues) involves deciding what motivates the behavior of other people. On the basis of information children encode from a particular situation, they could decide that others acted with benign, hostile, or ambiguous intent. Third, selecting a goal involves deciding what the desired outcome is in a given situation. Fourth, generating responses is the process of thinking of possible behavioral actions. Fifth, evaluating responses occurs when children assess whether a response is a good one to use in a particular situation and whether that response will bring about desired outcomes. Sixth, enacting responses is the manner in which a child actually behaves.

Deficits at each of these steps have been found to be related to aggressive behavior. At the first step, aggressive children, compared to nonaggressive peers, encode a smaller number of social cues, seek additional information in ambiguous social situations less frequently, and attend selectively to hostile and threatening social cues. At the second step, aggressive children are more likely than nonaggressive children to interpret ambiguous social cues as threatening. At the third step, selecting instrumental (e.g., winning a game) rather than interpersonal (e.g., maintaining a friendship) goals is associated with behaving more aggressively. At the fourth step, generating fewer behavioral responses overall and a higher proportion of aggressive responses to problems is related to behaving more aggressively. At the fifth step, positively evaluating the likely interpersonal and instrumental outcomes of aggression is related to behaving more aggressively. At the sixth step, skill in enacting aggressive responses is related to behaving more aggressively.

Social information processing mechanisms deal with specific links among environments, cognition, and behavioral outcomes. For example, problematic parent–child and peer relationships are associated with a host of social information processing deficits. Children who have been physically maltreated, for instance, become more attentive to hostile cues in the environment and less attentive to other relevant social cues; poor encoding is, in turn, related to higher levels of subsequent aggression. Similarly, children with insecure attachments to their parents are more likely to have social information processing problems than are securely attached children; these problems appear to stem from relationship schemas involving others' lack of emotional and instrumental availability. Children who are rejected by their peers also are more likely to have social information processing deficits that then carry over into future social and behavior problems. Thus, social information processing problems serve as cognitive mediators of the association between environmental risk factors and subsequent behavioral outcomes.

SEE ALSO *Aggression; Attribution; Information, Economics of; Script Models*

BIBLIOGRAPHY

Crick, Nicki R., and Kenneth A. Dodge. 1994. A Review and Reformulation of Social Information-Processing Mechanisms in Children's Social Adjustment. *Psychological Bulletin* 115 (1): 74–101.

Dodge, Kenneth A., and Nicki R. Crick. 1990. Social Information-Processing Bases of Aggressive Behavior in Children. *Personality and Social Psychology Bulletin* 16 (1): 8–22.

Jennifer E. Lansford

SOCIAL ISOLATION

In the social sciences, the term *social isolation* has two distinct usages. When applied to individuals, social isolation refers to a lack of social ties in general. When applied to social groups, social isolation refers to a lack of social and institutional ties to mainstream society. A group can be socially isolated even if the individuals within the group share a dense network of social ties with one another.

Individual social isolation is a relatively straightforward concept. It can be measured by either the percentage of the population in question that lives alone as calculated from census data or an index of social isolation constructed from survey-based social network data (e.g., the Berkman-Syme index). Given such measurements, researchers in social psychology, gerontology, public health, and many other fields have evaluated trends in social isolation and used standard methods of cross-sectional data analysis to measure the apparent effect of social isolation. This research owes much to the analysis of social isolation and schizophrenia by the Chicago school sociologist Robert E. L. Faris in the 1930s. Social isolation has been found to be a significant risk factor for many health problems and is a particular health issue for the elderly. This literature is often subject to the criticism that the simple relationship between isolation and outcomes may actually be an artifact of some unmeasured third factor (for example, alcoholism may produce both social isolation and heart disease). However, ethnographic and clinical research has also tended to support the idea that individual social isolation matters.

Group-level social isolation has been a key theoretical concept in urban sociology since the publication of William Julius Wilson's *The Truly Disadvantaged* (1987), an influential study of troubled inner-city communities. Wilson argues that the limited social contact of residents with the institutions of mainstream society is the primary cause of various community social pathologies such as high rates of out-of-wedlock births, welfare dependency, school dropout, crime, and exit from the labor force. Wilson's later work more explicitly identifies the role of high community rates of joblessness in producing social isolation. In this analysis, macroeconomic changes such as the decline in manufacturing employment combined with the departure of the black middle class from the inner city become the underlying source of inner-city social isolation and social pathology. Wilson's focus on social isolation is distinct from those theories that trace high rates of inner-city social pathology directly to racial discrimination or individual poverty. It is also distinct from "culture of poverty" theories that argue that a substantial proportion of ghetto residents have internalized a pathological set of social values. Wilson's work has inspired a vast empirical literature on "neighborhood effects" in sociology and in other social sciences. This literature only rarely has aimed to measure group-level social isolation directly; typically it focuses on the relationship between neighborhood-level measures of poverty concentration and various individual or family outcomes.

Wilson's work has also influenced economists to incorporate social isolation into economic models of inequality. Work in this literature, surveyed by Yannis Ioannides and Linda Datcher Loury (2004), usually combines formal social network theory with microeconomic models of search and matching. Group social isolation is conceptualized here in terms of the properties of a network of connections between individuals, rather than Wilson's more holistic but difficult to quantify concept of connections between individuals and both institutions and values. One key insight from the economics literature on group social isolation is that group-level isolation, unlike individual-level isolation, is characterized by externalities. That is, a group member who takes costly effort to form social ties with mainstream society will provide benefits to other group members, and these benefits cannot be appropriated by the individual who forms the social tie. As a result, the number of social ties to the mainstream will tend to be inefficiently low.

The closely related concept of social exclusion can be considered a special case of social isolation in which blame is assigned. Brian Barry (2002) notes that "exclusion" implies that the larger society prevents social integration, whereas "isolation" in principle can be voluntary or involuntary and beneficial or malevolent. The concept of social exclusion originated in continental Europe, whereas the notion of social isolation is associated with social scientists based in the United States.

BIBLIOGRAPHY

Barry, Brian. 2002. Social Exclusion, Social Isolation, and the Distribution of Income. In *Understanding Social Exclusion*, ed. John Hills, Julian Le Grand, and David Piachaud. Oxford: Oxford University Press.

Brashears, Matthew E., Miller McPherson, and Lynn Smith-Lovin. 2006. Social Isolation in America: Changes in Core Discussion Networks over Two Decades. *American Sociological Review* 71 (June): 353–375.

Ioannides, Yannis M., and Linda Datcher Loury. 2004. Job Information Networks, Neighborhood Effects, and Inequality. *Journal of Economic Literature* 42 (4): 1056–1093.

Wilson, William Julius. 1987. *The Truly Disadvantaged: The Inner City, the Underclass, and Public Policy*. Chicago: University of Chicago Press.

Brian V. Krauth

SOCIAL JUDGMENT THEORY

Social judgment theory was developed by psychologist Muzafer Sherif, with significant input from Carl I. Hovland and Carolyn W. Sherif. Rooted in judgment theory, which is concerned with the discrimination and categorization of stimuli, it attempts to explain how attitudes are expressed, judged, and modified. The theory details how attitudes are cognitively represented, the psychological processes involved in assessing persuasive communications, and the conditions under which communicated attitudes are either accepted or rejected. It offers a commonsense plan for inducing attitude change in the real world.

There are five basic principles in social judgment theory. The first asserts that people have categories of judgment with which they evaluate incoming information. When an individual encounters a situation in which he or she must make a judgment, a range of possible positions can be taken in response. For example, if an individual is asked to make a monetary contribution to a charity, the possible positions range from "absolutely not" to "most certainly." Along this inclusive continuum there are categories of positions that an individual may find acceptable or unacceptable, and also a range for which no significant opinion is held. These ranges are referred to as the *latitude of acceptance*, the *latitude of rejection*, and the *latitude of noncommittment*, respectively. An individual's most preferred position, located within the latitude of acceptance, is referred to as the *anchor*.

The second principle states that as people evaluate incoming information, they determine the category of judgment, or latitude, to which it belongs. In the above-mentioned example, individuals with a favorable view of the charitable cause would most likely place the request for a donation within the latitude of acceptance. Conversely, those who hold an unfavorable view of the charitable cause will locate their attitude within the latitude of rejection. Those with no significant opinion either way will locate it in the latitude of noncommitment.

The third principle asserts that the size of the latitudes is determined by the level of personal involvement, or *ego-involvement*, one has in the issue at hand. People may or may not have opinions regarding the communicated information, and this will affect whether or not the persuasive message is accepted or rejected. These same opinions (or their lack) also affect the size of latitudes. The higher the level of ego-involvement, the larger the latitude of rejection becomes. For instance, an individual who is solicited for a donation to a cancer society will have a smaller latitude of acceptance if his or her mother suffers from cancer, as compared to someone who has no personal connection to the malady. For that individual, contributing to the charity is imperative, and any other response is unacceptable. Therefore, the latitude of acceptance and noncommitment will be small compared to the latitude of rejection.

Principle four states that people distort incoming information to fit their categories of judgment. When presented with a persuasive message that falls within the latitude of acceptance, and is close to the individual's anchor, people will *assimilate* the new position. That is, they will perceive the new position to be closer to their attitude than it actually is. When the persuasive message is relatively far from the anchor, however, people tend to *contrast* the new position to their own, making it seem even more different than it actually is. In both cases, individuals distort incoming information relative to their anchor.

These distortions influence the persuasiveness of the incoming message. If the message is too close to the anchor, assimilation will occur and it will be construed to be no different than the original position. If contrast occurs, the message will be construed to be unacceptable and subsequently rejected. In both cases, social judgment theory would predict that attitude change is unlikely to occur.

The fifth principle asserts that optimal persuasion occurs when the discrepancies between the anchor and the advocated position are small to moderate. In such cases, assimilation or contrasting will not occur, allowing for consideration of the communicated message. Under these conditions, attitude change is possible.

A major implication of social judgment theory is that persuasion is difficult to accomplish. Successful persuasive messages are those that are targeted to the receiver's latitude of acceptance and discrepant from the anchor position, so that the incoming information cannot be assimilated or contrasted. The receiver's ego-involvement must also be taken into consideration. This suggests that even successful attempts at persuasion will yield small changes in attitude.

SEE ALSO *Attitudes, Behavioral; Cognitive Dissonance; Persuasion; Psychology; Sherif, Muzafer; Social Psychology*

BIBLIOGRAPHY

Sherif, Carolyn W., and Muzafer Sherif, eds. 1967. *Attitude, Ego-Involvement, and Change.* New York: Wiley.

Sherif, Carolyn W., Muzafer Sherif, and Roger E. Nebergall. 1965. *Attitude and Attitude Change: The Social Judgment-Involvement Approach.* Philadelphia: Saunders.

Sherif, Muzafer, and Carl I. Hovland. 1961. *Social Judgment: Assimilation and Contrast Effects in Communication and Attitude Change.* New Haven, CT: Yale University Press.

Paul A. O'Keefe

SOCIAL JUSTICE
SEE *Justice, Social.*

SOCIAL LEARNING PERSPECTIVE

From the 1930s through the 1950s the behavioral theory of operant conditioning, with its emphasis on the application of consequences to influence behavioral change, was the dominant perspective in U.S. psychology. With the reintroduction of a cognitive perspective in the 1950s (e.g., Miller 1956; Miller, Galanter, and Pribram 1960), researchers began to look for ways to integrate the behavioral and cognitive perspectives. Social learning theory, as developed by Neal Miller and John Dollard (1941), Robert Sears (1951), and Albert Bandura (1977), contributed to connecting behavioral and cognitive approaches to learning and is an important step toward modern versions of learning theory.

Bandura (1962), building on the earlier work of Miller and Dollard (1941), proposed that learning first occurs cognitively through imitation and then is modified through the application of consequences. In contrast to a purely behavioral approach, social cognitive theorists propose that individuals are active participants in their own learning. Based on a series of studies during the 1960s and 1970s (e.g., Bandura 1963, 1965a), Bandura in 1977 proposed a four-step process for how individuals learn through observing others' behavior. This process has been referred to as observational learning, or modeling, and involves:

attention—the individual notices something in the environment;

retention—the individual remembers what was noticed;

reproduction—the individual produces an action that is a copy of what was noticed;

motivation—the environment delivers a consequence that changes the probability that the behavior will occur again (reinforcement and punishment).

Through the careful observation of others, individuals learn numerous new behaviors such as emotional reactions and how to use tools in their environments. Bandura (1965b) demonstrated that individuals modify their own behaviors based on the consequences (e.g., reinforcement or punishment) that others receive. He called this phenomenon *vicarious learning*. Individuals tend to model their behavior on persons who are similar to themselves, persons who are of higher status than themselves, and persons who are either reinforced for their behavior or not punished for it. One example of the power of imitation is found in the results of the infamous "Bobo doll study" (Bandura, Ross, and Ross 1961). In this study preschool children who observed adults mistreating a Bobo doll were more likely to engage in similar aggressive behavior than children who had not observed the adults' aggressive behavior.

In more recent years, Bandura turned his attention to the importance of self-efficacy, self-regulation, and the desire of individuals to develop agency over their lives (Bandura 1986, 1989, 2001). To describe the learning process from this perspective, Bandura developed a concept called *reciprocal determinism*, which details a three-way relationship between a person, his or her behavior, and the environment. In the social-cognitive model each of the three elements are equally important and influence the other elements. Thus, an individual's unique characteristics interact with overt behaviors and environmental models and feedback.

SEE ALSO *Bandura, Albert; Behaviorism; Determinism, Reciprocal; Motivation; Psychology, Agency in; Self-Efficacy; Social Cognition; Social Cognitive Map*

BIBLIOGRAPHY

Bandura, Albert. 1962. *Social Learning Through Imitation.* Lincoln: University of Nebraska Press.

Bandura, Albert. 1963. The Role of Imitation in Personality Development. *Journal of Nursery Education* 18 (3): 207–215.

Bandura, Albert. 1965a. Influence of Models' Reinforcement Contingencies on the Acquisition of Imitative Responses. *Journal of Personality and Social Psychology* 28 (2): 117–148.

Bandura, Albert. 1965b. Vicarious Processes: A Case of No-Trial Learning. In *Advances in Experimental Social Psychology*, ed. Leonard Berkowitz, vol. 2, 1–55. San Diego, CA: Academic Press.

Bandura, Albert. 1977. *Social Learning Theory.* New York: General Learning Press.

Bandura, Albert. 1986. *Social Foundations of Thought and Action: A Social-Cognitive Theory.* Englewood Cliffs, NJ: Prentice Hall.

Bandura, Albert. 1989. Social Cognitive Theory. In *Six Theories of Child Development.* Vol. 6 of *Annals of Child Development*, ed. Ross Vasta, 1–60. Greenwich, CT: JAI Press.

Bandura, Albert. 2001. Social Cognitive Theory: An Agentic Perspective. *Annual Review of Psychology* 52: 1–26.

Bandura, Albert, Dorothea Ross, and Sheila A. Ross. 1961. Transmission of Aggression Through Imitation of Aggressive Models. *Journal of Abnormal and Social Psychology* 63: 575–582.

Miller, George. 1956. The Magical Number Seven, Plus or Minus Two: Some Limits on Our Capacity for Processing Information. *Psychological Review* 63: 81–97.

Miller, George, Eugene Galanter, and Karl Pribram. 1960. *Plans and the Structure of Behavior.* New York: Holt.

Miller, Neal, and John Dollard. 1941. *Social Learning and Imitation.* New Haven, CT: Yale University Press.

Sears, Robert R. 1951. A Theoretical Framework for Personality and Social Behavior. *American Psychologist* 6: 476–483.

William G. Huitt
David M. Monetti

SOCIAL MEMORY

SEE *Collective Memory.*

SOCIAL MOVEMENTS

A *social movement* can be defined as a collectivity with mutual awareness in sustained interaction with economic and political elites seeking to forward or halt social change. Social movements are usually comprised of groups outside of institutional power that use nonconventional strategies (e.g., street marches, sit-ins, dramatic media events) along with more conventional ones (e.g., petitions, letter-writing campaigns, etc.) to pursue their aims (Tarrow 1998; Snow et al. 2004). The outsider status and nonconventional tactics of social movements distinguish them from other political entities such as lobbying organizations and political parties (though these more formal organizations may originate from social movements). Most people participate in movements as volunteers and offer their time, skills, and other human resources to maintaining movement survival or achieving goals. Examples of social movements range from community-based environmental movements to transnationally organized economic-justice movements attempting to place pressure on national governments and international financial institutions. The modern social-movement form arose with the spread of parliamentary political systems and nationally integrated capitalist economies in the nineteenth century (Tilly 2004).

EMERGENCE

Social movements are most likely to arise when a particular collectivity comes under threat or receives signals from the political environment that advantages may be forthcoming if groups decide to mobilize. In other words, either "bad news" or "good news" may motivate episodes of collective action (Meyer 2002). Under bad-news conditions, a community or population perceives that its situation will become worse if it fails to act and that it may lose collective goods (e.g., loss of land, rights, employment, etc.). In the good-news political environment, groups sense that they will acquire new collective goods if they act in concert (e.g., new rights, higher wages, greater environmental quality, etc.). Often, bad-news and good-news protest campaigns are triggered by government policies that signal to would-be challengers that the state is becoming less or more receptive to the issues that are most meaningful to the population in question.

Besides these motivations for movement emergence, some type of organizational base needs to be in existence to mobilize large numbers of people (McAdam 1999). These organizational assets may be traditional, such as solidarities based on village, religious, regional, or ethnic identities, or they may be associational, rooted in secondary groups such as labor unions, social clubs, agricultural cooperatives, educational institutions, and more formal social-movement organizations (SMOs) (Oberschall 1973). Without preexisting solidarity ties and organizational links, either formal or informal, it is unlikely that threats or opportunities will convert into social-movement campaigns. Hence, social-movement scholars give special attention to variations in organizational resources across localities and over time in explaining social-movement emergence (Edwards and McCarthy 2004).

OUTCOMES

Perhaps the most important social-movement arena involves movement impacts. That is, what kinds of changes in the political environment can be attributed to the existence and actions of a social movement? What aspects of social change can be explicitly associated with the activities of a movement? Students of social movements examine various aspects of social-movement outcomes. The enduring changes associated with movements include the impacts on movement participants, changes in the political culture, influence on state policies, and "spillover" into other social movements (Meyer and Whittier 1994). In comparison to movement emergence, there is less scholarly consensus on social-movement outcomes (Jenkins and Form 2005). Often, it is difficult to decipher the particular contribution of a social movement to a specific outcome while attempting to control for non-movement influences. Despite these scientific shortcomings, major movements of oppressed social groups in the United States greatly improved their social standing. Participants of such movements obtained major policy changes because they engaged in social-movement-type struggles, especially the women's movement and the African American civil rights movement in the late twentieth century.

A classic study on movement outcomes by William Gamson (1990) found in a representative sample of fifty-three voluntary associations in the United States between 1800 and 1945 that groups that maintained single-issue demands, used more assertive strategies and tactics, and organized themselves along more bureaucratic lines were more successful in achieving their goals than movements that lacked these properties. In terms of state-oriented social movements, or movements with political aims that largely target the government, linking with sympathetic groups inside the state enhances probabilities of movement success (Banaszak 2005). For example, a 2004 study of national environmental politics in Japan by Linda Brewster Stearns and Paul Almeida found that antipollution movements were much more successful in winning new environmental policies when they formed loose alliances with actors inside the government, such as city councils, sympathetic federal agencies, oppositional political parties, and the courts.

THEORIES OF SOCIAL MOVEMENTS

Between the 1960s and the 1980s, a clear succession of social-movement theories took shape—from collective behavior to resource mobilization to political-process perspectives. Since the mid-1990s, social-movement scholarship places much more emphasis on a synthetic approach that combines resource mobilization, political opportunity, and framing perspectives into a larger comprehensive framework of social-movement dynamics. Individual scholars, though, still tend to specialize in one of the three subareas of this larger synthesis.

Resource mobilization scholarship emphasizes the role of formal and informal organizations in collective action. Resource mobilization scholars also attempt to define the population of SMOs within movements and societies using such terms as *social-movement sector, social-movement industry,* and *organizational field* (McCarthy and Zald 1977; McAdam and Scott 2005; Minkoff and McCarthy 2005). More recent work in the resource mobilization subfield has expanded into sophisticated network analysis of the means by which different components of SMOs, participants, and sponsoring organizations are structurally connected to one another and how the variations in those structures affect collective-action dynamics (Diani and McAdam 2003).

The political-process tradition centers on the larger political environment and how differentially configured political contexts shape social-movement emergence, forms of mobilization, and movement outcomes. Important features of the political environment are referred to as *political opportunities*. Five key dimensions of political opportunity shaping collective action within political-process theory include:

1. institution access (i.e., the opening of state agencies)

2. elite conflict (between political or economic elites)

3. electoral realignments (i.e., changing electoral coalitions)

4. influential allies (i.e., experts, mass media, religious institutions, etc.)

5. a relaxation in state repression.

The more these five elements of opportunity are present in a political environment, the greater the probability of the emergence of a large and efficacious social movement. Some versions of political-process theory contend, however, that high levels of political opportunity lead to more institutional forms of politics and less need for social-movement mobilization (Eisinger 1973; McAdam 1996; Meyer 2004; Tarrow 1998).

The *framing perspective* derives from the interpretive tradition in sociology with a special concern for how activists construct social grievances. It is now largely understood that injustice and organizational resources alone do not explain the timing and location of social-movement-type mobilization. Movement leaders and activists must construct norm violations, grievances, and experiences of oppression and injustice in socially meaningful and convincing ways that will motivate the targeted populations to participate in collective action (Snow et al. 1986; Snow and Benford 1988). In other words, social and political activists must "frame" the social world in such a manner that it resonates with rank-and-file movement supporters as well as sympathizers and fence-sitters.

Students of social movements often discuss the ability of political movements to develop *collective-action frames* that will generate large-scale support for the challengers' objectives. The collective-action frame of "civil rights" in the African American freedom struggle in the 1950s and 1960s is considered a particularly potent frame consonant with the political culture and values of the United States, bringing in large numbers of white Americans in solidarity with the grievances of black Americans. In addition, the success of the "civil rights" frame led to several other movements adopting a variant version in subsequent decades. Such movements include the women's, gay/bisexual, Mexican American, Asian American, and disability movements, as well as more conservative movements, such as the pro-life, home schooling, or pro-creationism movements, which invoke civil rights in their claims-making activities.

One avenue for categorically deciphering collective-actions frames is to divide them into their diagnostic, prognostic, and motivational functions. A diagnostic frame defines particular social problems and injustices and assigns blame to the agent(s). Prognostic framing develops an action plan to resolve the social problem or grievance, while motivational framing includes the actual mobilization appeals to persuade people to join the movement or participate in a particular action. David Snow and Robert Benford (1988) view these three core framing tasks as a fundamental part of sustaining social-movement mobilization.

RECRUITMENT

Social-movement recruitment and individual-level participation draw on microlevel models of collective action. Early explanations of social-movement recruitment and participation emphasized the irrationality aspects of mass movements. Political movements of the unruly were viewed as fulfilling psychological deficits for movement participants—a kind of therapy to overcome sentiments of alienation and social strain inherent in fast-paced industrialized urban societies (McAdam 1982). By the late 1970s and early 1980s, scholars began to look at more than just the beliefs and psychological profiles of movement participants. They also examined the microstructural context of mobilization, namely the social ties and networks of potential movement recruits (Snow et al. 1980; McAdam 1986). This newer empirical research found that movement participants were often highly socially integrated in their everyday lives and more likely to belong to civil society associations and clubs than those who did not participate in social movements. In addition, the connections individuals maintained with movement sympathetic organizations and individuals made them much more likely to join a protest campaign, whereas those connected to organizations and individuals opposed to such activities were much more likely not to participate (McAdam 1986). Finally, movement mobilization occurs at a faster rate when entire groups and organizations are recruited en masse as opposed to organizing single individuals one at a time—a process termed *bloc recruitment* (Oberschall 1973).

Movement-recruitment research also distinguishes between low cost/low risk activism versus high cost/high risk activism (McAdam 1986). *Cost* refers to the time and resources put into a particular movement campaign. *Risk* involves the level of personal harm that may result from activism (e.g., reputation, imprisonment, physical safety). For high cost/high risk activism, such as occurs in extremely oppressive regions or societies (e.g., a racially segmented society, a military dictatorship, etc.), a deeper level of integration into a social-movement culture by the individual needs to take place, including previous participation in several rounds of low cost/low risk activism.

NONDEMOCRACIES AND STATE REPRESSION

The majority of social-movement studies focus on movements in industrialized democracies in the global north (McAdam et al. 1996). However, a growing body of literature now exists for political contexts outside of the democratic West. The more stable forms of government in Western democracies allow for a greater upkeep of social-movement-type organizations and more space to launch largely nonviolent campaigns. In nondemocratic and quasi-democratic nations (e.g., monarchies, dictatorships, military juntas), where associational freedoms are proscribed and regular multiparty elections do not occur, scholars face challenges in explaining when social movements will arise and what forms they will take. One fruitful avenue investigates "cracks in the system," small political openings, or larger moves toward political liberalization in nondemocracies. These conditions often provide a conducive environment for a few entrepreneurs in civil society to attempt to form civic associations and possibly even begin to seek small reforms. Other movements may be launched in institutions outside the purview of state control, such as religious institutions (mosques, religious schools, Catholic youth groups, etc.) or remote territories not completely controlled by the administrative state apparatus and army. Foreign governments and movements may also support a fledgling movement in a nondemocratic context.

In the twentieth century, nondemocratic countries were much more likely to experience a radical revolutionary challenge from below than democratic states (Goodwin 2001). Revolutionary movements can be seen as a special type of social movement that seeks the overthrow of the government as its central goal, rather than piecemeal policy change. Often, revolutionary movements begin as reformist movements during a period of regime liberalization and only radicalize once the regime closes down the reform process. The violent repression of reform-minded groups transforms popular conceptions of the entire political system and provides incentives for the formation of more radical and revolutionary political organizations. Such a scenario developed in El Salvador during the 1960s and 1970s, as well as in Guatemala in the 1950s and 1960s, and more recently in Algeria and Nepal.

CONSERVATIVE MOVEMENTS

In the United States, conservative social movements have been on the rise since the 1980s. The emergence of an evangelical protestant Christian Right in alliance with the Republican Party has provided a favorable political context for conservative movements that seek to halt certain social policies perceived as morally reprehensible (e.g., same-sex marriage, legalized abortion, secularism in public schools, etc.). The movement's success resides in its capacity to form coalitions with different levels of government and to employ bloc recruitment strategies (e.g., mobilizing entire church congregations). Since the early 1990s, the Christian Right has won seats in hundreds of school boards, city councils, and state and national legislatures. The movement has also influenced the selection of Supreme Court justices (Micklethwait and Wooldridge 2004). In the 1990s and early 2000s, researchers found that extremist right-wing activity in the form of hate crimes and paramilitary militia groups in the United States was associated with job loss, economic restructuring, and lack of contact between educated and less-educated populations in the regions where these movements arise (Van Dyke and Soule 2002; McVeigh 2004).

TRANSNATIONAL SOCIAL MOVEMENTS

A major area of research involves the expansion of transnational social movements that link members and organizations across more than one country. Two noteworthy transnational movements in the early twenty-first century include international Islamic solidarity and the global justice movement. Internationally connected Islamic movements benefit from the concept of *umma*— the larger community of believers that links the Muslim world beyond national borders (Lubeck 2000). With global migration flows and new communications technology, Islamic-based social movements easily mobilize internationally. Early signs of this emerging process occurred in the 1980s during the Afghan-Soviet war. Thousands of Muslims and Arabs traveled from dozens of countries in the Middle East, North Africa, and beyond to Afghanistan to fight in a jihad (holy war) as the mujahideen (guerrilla fighters) against the secular Soviet Union, which invaded the country in 1979. The foreign Islamic fighters felt an international sense of solidarity with their fellow Muslim Afghans suffering under Soviet occupation. This struggle served as the base of the Al-Qaeda movement, which built a large multinational network out of the social contacts made in Afghanistan. This network of transnational Islamic insurgents has since been used to send foreign contingents to wars in Bosnia, Chechnya, Iraq, Somalia, and other places.

The global justice movement (sometimes referred to by critics as the antiglobalization movement) is another major transnational movement that emerged in the late twentieth century. Supporters of this movement use global communications technologies to mobilize constituents. The global justice movement arose almost simultaneously with the expansion of the global Internet infrastructure between the mid-1990s and the early 2000s. Several organizations in Europe and Canada, including the Council of Canadians, Jubilee 2000, People's Global Action, and ATTAC, began to work with nongovernmental organizations in the developing world to place pressure on newly emerging and older transnational governing bodies and economic institutions such as the United Nations, the World Trade Organization (WTO), the International Monetary Fund, the World Bank, the Group of Eight (G8), and the European Union.

The demands of the global justice movement vary but tend to focus on third world economic justice, environmental protection, and the need for more transparency in decision making among the elite transnational economic and political institutions mentioned above. Though the movement held several major protests in the late 1990s outside of WTO and G8 meetings in Europe, a massive demonstration at the 1999 WTO meetings in Seattle, Washington, served as a breakthrough for the global justice movement. It was the largest sustained protest in an American city in several decades (Almeida and Lichbach 2003). Global justice activists coordinated the arrival of participants around the country and world via the Internet and organized the protests in the streets of Seattle with cell phones. Dozens of countries across the globe also experienced protests in solidarity with the actions in Seattle. The success of the Seattle mobilizations provided a template for organizing dozens of similar global days of action during major international financial conferences or free trade meetings in the first years of the twenty-first century.

SEE ALSO *European Union; G-8 Countries; Globalization, Social and Economic Aspects of; Justice, Social; Mobilization; Revolution; United Nations; World Bank; World Trade Organization*

BIBLIOGRAPHY

Almeida, Paul D., and Mark I. Lichbach. 2003. To the Internet, from the Internet: Comparative Media Coverage of Transnational Protest. *Mobilization* 8 (3): 249–272.

Banaszak, Lee Ann. 2005. Inside and Outside the State: Movement Insider Status, Tactics, and Public Policy

Achievements. In *Routing the Opposition: Social Movements, Public Policy, and Democracy*, eds. David S. Meyer, Valerie Jenness, and Helen Ingram, 149–176. Minneapolis: University of Minnesota Press.

Diani, Mario, and Doug McAdam, eds. 2003. *Social Movements and Networks: Relational Approaches to Collective Action.* Oxford: Oxford University Press.

Edwards, Bob, and John D. McCarthy. 2004. Resources and Social Movement Mobilization. In *The Blackwell Companion to Social Movements*, eds. David Snow, Sarah Soule, and Hanspeter Kriesi, 116–152. Malden, MA: Blackwell.

Eisinger, Peter. 1973. The Conditions of Protest Behavior in American Cities. *American Political Science Review* 67: 11–28.

Gamson, William. 1990. *The Strategy of Social Protest.* 2nd ed. Belmont, CA: Wadsworth.

Goodwin, Jeff. 2001. *No Other Way Out: States and Revolutionary Movements, 1945–1991.* Cambridge, U.K.: Cambridge University Press.

Jenkins, J. Craig, and William Form. 2005. Social Movements and Social Change. In *The Handbook of Political Sociology: States, Civil Societies, and Globalization*, eds. Thomas Janoski, Robert Alford, Alexander Hicks, and Mildred Schwartz, 331–349. Cambridge, U.K.: Cambridge University Press.

Lubeck, Paul M. 2000. The Islamic Revival: Antinomies of Islamic Movements under Globalization. In *Global Social Movements*, eds. Robin Cohen and Shirin Rai, 146–164. London: Althane.

McAdam, Doug. 1986. Recruitment to High-Risk Activism: The Case of Freedom Summer. *American Journal of Sociology* 92 (1): 64–90.

McAdam, Doug. 1996. Conceptual Origins, Current Problems, Future Directions. In *Comparative Perspectives on Social Movements: Political Opportunities, Mobilizing Structures, and Cultural Framings*, eds. Doug McAdam, John D. McCarthy, and Mayer N. Zald, 23–40. Cambridge, U.K.: Cambridge University Press.

McAdam, Doug. 1999. *Political Process and the Development of Black Insurgency, 1930–1970.* 2nd ed. Chicago: University of Chicago Press.

McAdam, Doug, John D. McCarthy, and Mayer N. Zald. 1996. Preface. In *Comparative Perspectives on Social Movements: Political Opportunities, Mobilizing Structures, and Cultural Framings*, eds. Doug McAdam, John D. McCarthy, and Mayer N. Zald, xi–xiv. Cambridge, U.K.: Cambridge University Press.

McAdam, Doug, and W. Richard Scott. 2005. Organizations and Movements. In *Social Movements and Organization Theory*, eds. Gerald Davis, Doug McAdam, W. Richard Scott, and Mayer Zald, 4–40. Cambridge, U.K.: Cambridge University Press.

McCarthy, John D., and Mayer N. Zald. 1977. Resource Mobilization and Social Movements: A Partial Theory. *American Journal of Sociology* 82 (6): 1212–1241.

McVeigh, Rory. 2004. Structured Ignorance and Organized Racism in the United States. *Social Forces* 82 (3): 895–936.

Meyer, David S. 2002. Opportunities and Identities: Bridge-Building in the Study of Social Movements. In *Social Movements: Identity, Culture, and the State*, eds. David S.

Meyer, Nancy Whittier, and Belinda Robnett, 3–21. New York: Oxford University Press.

Meyer, David S. 2004. Protest and Political Opportunity. *Annual Review of Sociology* 30: 125–145.

Meyer, David S., and Nancy Whittier. 1994. Social Movement Spillover. *Social Problems* 41 (2): 277–298.

Micklethwait, John, and Adrian Wooldridge. 2004. *The Right Nation: Conservative Power in America.* New York: Penguin.

Minkoff, Debra C., and John D. McCarthy. 2005. Reinvigorating the Study of Organizational Processes in Social Movements. *Mobilization* 10 (2): 289–308.

Oberschall, Anthony. 1973. *Social Conflict and Social Movements.* Englewood Cliffs, NJ: Prentice-Hall.

Snow, David, and Robert Benford. 1988. Ideology, Frame Resonance, and Participant Mobilization. *International Social Movement Research* 1: 197–217.

Snow, David, E. Burke Rochford, Steven Worden, and Robert Benford. 1986. Frame Alignment Processes, Micromobilization, and Movement Participation. *American Sociological Review* 51: 464–481.

Snow, David, Louis Zurcher, and Sheldon Ekland-Olson. 1980. Social Networks and Social Movements: A Microstructural Approach to Differential Recruitment. *American Sociological Review* 45: 787–801.

Snow, David, Sarah Soule, and Hanspeter Kriesi. 2004. Mapping the Terrain. In *The Blackwell Companion to Social Movements,* eds. David Snow, Sarah Soule, and Hanspeter Kriesi, 3–16. Oxford: Blackwell.

Stearns, Linda Brewster, and Paul D. Almeida. 2004. The Formation of State Actor-Social Movement Coalitions and Favorable Policy Outcomes. *Social Problems* 51 (4): 478–504.

Tarrow, Sidney. 1998. *Power in Movement: Social Movements and Contentious Politics.* 2nd ed. Cambridge, U.K.: Cambridge University Press.

Tilly, Charles. 2004. *Social Movements, 1768–2004.* Boulder, CO: Paradigm.

Van Dyke, Nella, and Sarah A. Soule. 2002. Structural Social Change and the Mobilizing Effect of Threat: Explaining Levels of Patriot and Militia Organizing in the United States. *Social Problems* 49: 497–520.

Paul Almeida

SOCIAL NORMS

SEE *Norms.*

SOCIAL POLICY INTERVENTIONS

SEE *Interventions, Social Policy.*

SOCIAL PSYCHOLOGY

Social psychology is the scientific study of how people think about, influence, and relate to one another. By studying social thinking, social psychologists examine how, and how accurately, we view ourselves and others. By studying social influence, social psychologists examine subtle forces related to conformity, persuasion, and group influence that pull our strings. By studying social relations, social psychologists examine what leads people to hate and hurt one another, or to love and help one another.

Social psychology as a field lies between personality psychology and sociology. Metaphorically speaking, personality psychologists study boats, sociologists study the ocean, and social psychologists study how those boats float. When a person (boat) arrives in an environment (ocean), social psychologists want to understand how they move on the winds and currents.

Social psychology considers many of the same questions as those sociology considers but favors answers that focus on the individual actors (such as the way they perceive their situations) rather than on answers that apply to the group level (such as poverty or family cohesion). It is also distinct from personality psychology, being less interested in individual differences (such as in aggressiveness or unhappiness), though it often considers individual differences that interact with situations (such as when a person with high self-esteem responds to a relationship threat by liking his or her partner more).

Compared to other social sciences, social psychology has few grand theories or revered old masters; it has no Freud or Durkheim. Instead it interweaves smaller, more focused studies that cover topics as diverse as the self, culture, persuasion, group dynamics, prejudice, and eyewitness identification. Despite its enormous scope, social psychology has several themes running through it, including:

- We construct our social reality
- Our social intuitions are often powerful but sometimes perilous
- Social influences shape our behavior
- Personal attitudes and dispositions also shape behavior
- Social behavior is also biological behavior
- Social psychology's principles are applicable in everyday life

As practiced in North America, social psychology is overwhelmingly experimental. It has also exhibited a willingness to engage social issues such as prejudice, violence, and public health.

HISTORY

Norman Triplett's 1898 experiments are generally regarded as the first social psychological studies. He showed that people would wind reels faster when others were present, an effect now referred to as *social facilitation*. Social psychology remained a small field until World War II, at which point the U.S. Army's sudden interest in personnel selection and stress responses led it to sponsor some highly innovative work. In the decade after the war the field exploded: Gordon Allport wrote an enormously influential book called *The Nature of Prejudice* (1954), Solomon Asch (1951) conducted experiments on conformity, Stanley Milgram (1974) conducted his famous experiments inducing people to give supposedly powerful electric shocks to a mild-mannered man, and Leon Festinger (1957) proposed his influential cognitive dissonance theory.

In the last quarter of the twentieth century, social psychology was dominated by a cognitive perspective that asked how we process social information. During the 1990s and beyond, it also has had a growing interest in "warmer" motivational processes and broad cultural influences.

METHODS AND ETHICS

Modern social psychology favors experimental research, with many published articles describing two to seven experiments or quasi-experiments that explore and refine some central idea. Correlational studies are also used, but often given short shrift in favor of experimental evidence. The field also puts great stock in meta-analyses that combine many previous empirical studies. Experiments use diverse manipulations, ranging from the subliminal presentation of words, to interaction with confederates, to false feedback on IQ tests.

Social psychological research is now subject to oversight by institutional review boards that safeguard ethical standards. While these are widely regarded as necessary in light of the ethical controversies that centered on some prominent early studies, social psychological experiments are almost never, in any real sense, hazardous.

PARTS OF THE SOCIAL MIND

Psychologists separate affect (emotions), from behavior, from cognition (thoughts), then study how they interact. Affect has broad consequences. People who are in a good mood tolerate more frustration, choose long-term rewards over immediate small payoffs, and see others in a more optimistic light. A growing movement in psychology known as positive psychology focuses specifically on well-being and how it can be enhanced.

Attitudes, in social psychological parlance, are the affect people bear toward some object or activity. Social psychologists study how attitudes form and change, how strong and durable they are, and how much they predict actual behavior. The answer to the latter question, under many circumstances, is "somewhat, but not as much as you might think."

Since the 1980s cognition has increasingly become a focal point for social psychologists. They study when cognitions are activated (come to mind), how they are organized into schemas, and when people are motivated to think things through systematically as opposed to using heuristic mental shortcuts. Some influential models, such as the theory of reasoned action, describe how a person's beliefs about an object ("it's big, loud, and emits black smoke") are combined to produce an overall attitude ("I hate it").

Affect and cognitions influence behavior, but behavior can also influence affect and cognition. Under the right conditions, both saying and doing can lead to belief (if you say that you like something enough, or just keep buying it, and you might really end up liking it). Even just arranging your face muscles into the shape of a smile can make you feel happier.

Although affect, behavior, and cognition are social psychologists' central organizing principles, other parts of the mind have also been of interest, such as memory and physiological arousal. The self is an enormous area of study, encompassing thoughts about who one is (self-concept or identity) and attitudes toward oneself (self-esteem).

People organize knowledge about themselves into well-integrated pictures, or self schemas, that help them quickly sift and sort the world. People better remember things that are relevant to their self schema, and spontaneously make social comparisons between themselves and others. Self-serving biases describe the ways we distort the world to make ourselves look better (for example, by taking more responsibility for our successes than our failures). Self-monitoring describes people's tendency to engage in impression management—altering their social identity to fit different roles in different places (friend at school, son at home, employee at the office). Manipulations that affect people's self-awareness (the presence of mirrors, seeing one's own name) encourage people to act more in line with their stated attitudes.

DYNAMICS OF THE SOCIAL MIND

Scholars have devoted much attention to social influence—the ways in which individuals and groups come to change others' thinking or behavior. Early dramatic studies showed that people seemed remarkably vulnerable to social influence. In Asch's famous experiment, they doubted their own eyes when others claimed to see things that were patently untrue, and in Milgram's experiment, they gave extremely painful electrical shocks on command. People can, however, resist social influence. Even in these seminal studies compliance was far from universal, and rates of conformity were rapidly deflated by small changes, such as a lack of unanimity among influencers and a greater distance from authority figures. Much work has gone into who conforms to what, when, and why, with several important factors identified in the study of persuasion. These include who (attractive person, authority figure) says what (reasoned vs. emotional message, one- or two-sided appeals) to whom (audience pays close attention or not).

In the 1990s social psychologists started directing their attention more towards "warm" or motivated cognition—people's attempts to arrive at the answers they would like to. People bring this convenient brand of reasoning to many tasks, including forming impressions of themselves and others, attributing motives for actions, and judging the desirability of various outcomes. They do this, though, with some constraints imposed by reality—most consider themselves more moral than average, but few claim saintliness.

Scholars have become increasingly interested in automatic processing, in which judgments, associations, or even actions are made quickly and efficiently with little conscious guidance. For example, work has focused on negative stereotypes that rapidly come to mind when people encounter minority groups. A number of "dual-process models" have been proposed for processes like impression formation, attitudes, persuasion, and stereotyping. In these models people first have a fast, efficient, automatic and uncontrolled reaction that is later adjusted, if the person is so motivated, by conscious thought. Upon seeing a stranger fall over, for example, a fast, effortless inference might be drawn that this person is clumsy. If one liked the person, however, within less than a second one might start searching more deliberately for outside factors and conclude that the person was pushed, or that the floor was slippery, overruling (at least partly) one's initial verdict.

Attraction and intimacy form another major dynamic of interest. Liking is influenced by factors such as proximity, familiarity (the "mere exposure" effect), physical attractiveness, and the sharing of things about one's self. One of the more prominent models of intimate relationships, Robert Sternberg's triangular theory (1988), describes any given relationship in terms of passion (infatuation), intimacy (liking), and commitment (a desire to stick it out). Sternberg argues that a relationship may have only one of these (friends typically have intimacy but no passion), two (good friends would add commitment), or all three (which he calls "consummate love").

When people get together, the resulting groups take on dynamics of their own. People in them work harder when their contributions are visible (social facilitation), but coast when their contributions are unidentifiable (social loafing). Group discussions also sometimes accentuate initial attitudes and actions (group polarization). Sometimes large groups of people will engage in behaviors that none of their members would have contemplated doing on their own (such as chanting for suicidal people to jump), partly because the individual members become "deindividuated"—they lose the self-awareness that anchors them to their personal standards.

APPLICATIONS

Social psychological work has been applied to a great many real-world settings. Researchers have brought it to the study of health behaviors, such as smoking and use of condoms, and in doing so have offered practical advances. They have spearheaded, for example, graphic pictures of decayed teeth and lungs on boxes of cigarettes in Canada. Political psychologists have, likewise, been interested in models of persuasion and attitude formation and change. Organizational psychologists have applied social psychological theories of group processes, satisfaction, and enjoyment to the context of the work place.

Law is another area that has seen widespread application of social psychological research. Psychological work has revealed that eyewitness identification, long a linchpin of legal evidence, is often flawed. It is often very difficult for people to accurately identify even those at whom they have had a good long look. Research has been used to improve identification lineup procedures to produce fairer results with fewer false positives, for example by instructing witnesses that the suspect may or may not be in the lineup. Social psychologists have also been involved in great controversies over the accuracy of "recovered memories"—recollections of past abuse that people believe they have rediscovered later in life. Research shows that, though some such cases may be genuine, some are almost certainly not, as it is not difficult to create false memories in people.

HOT AREAS

As brain imaging technology advances, rapid strides are being made into understanding the brain functioning associated with attitudes, emotions, and behaviors. Early attempts were sometimes dismissed as "color phrenology"—attempts to put people in a scanner and simply catalogue which areas lit up. Newer work compares the known functions of brain regions with their activation during social behaviors. For example, researchers might note that in some types of people subliminal exposure to African American faces simultaneously activates areas associated with alarming stimuli and areas associated with cognitive control. They might infer from this that an emotional reaction is taking place, alongside an effortful attempt to control it.

SEE ALSO *Allport, Gordon; Asch, Solomon; Cognition; Conformity; Emotion; Experiments, Shock; Festinger, Leon; Groupthink; Herd Behavior; Lay Theories; Milgram, Stanley; Neuroscience; Persuasion; Prejudice; Psychology; Role Conflict; Schemas; Self-Consciousness, Private vs. Public; Social Facilitation; Social Science; Socialization; Sociology*

BIBLIOGRAPHY

Allport, Gordon W. 1954. *The Nature of Prejudice.* Cambridge, MA: Addison-Wesley.

Aronson, Elliot. 2004. *The Social Animal.* 9th ed. New York: Worth.

Asch, Solomon. 1951. Effects of Group Pressure upon the Modification and Distortion of Judgment. In *Groups, Leadership and Men*, ed. M. H. Guetzkow, 117–190. Pittsburgh, PA: Carnegie.

Bargh, John A., and Tanya L. Chartrand. 1999. The Unbearable Automaticity of Being. *American Psychologist* 54: 462–479.

Cialdini, Robert B. 2001. *Influence: Science and Practice.* 4th ed. Boston: Allyn and Bacon.

Eagly, Alice H., and Shelly Chaiken. 1993. *The Psychology of Attitudes.* Fort Worth, TX: Harcourt Brace Jovanovich College.

Festinger, Leon. 1957. *A Theory of Cognitive Dissonance.* Stanford, CA: Stanford University Press.

Gilbert, Daniel T., Susan T. Fiske, and Gardner Lindzey, eds. 1998. *The Handbook of Social Psychology.* 4th ed. New York: Oxford University Press.

Milgram, Stanley. 1974. *Obedience to Authority.* New York: Harper and Row.

Sternberg, Robert J. 1988. *The Triangle of Love.* New York: Basic Books.

Zanna, M., ed. 2004. *Advances in Experimental Social Psychology.* Vol. 36. San Diego, CA: Academic Press.

Alexander J. Gunz
David G. Myers

SOCIAL RELATIONS

Social relations are patterned human interactions that encompass relationships among individuals, informally organized groups, and formally organized groups, including the state. Modern-day approaches to social relations are represented by individualist, structuralist, and institutionalist theoretical frameworks. Exemplary thinkers have been selected in the field of labor relations and in the study of political processes to illustrate these different approaches.

Individualist theories explain social relations as the response of the rational individual to the outside environment. Individuals are assumed to be able to determine, and then act, on their personal self-interest. Thomas Malthus (1766–1834) and John Stuart Mill (1806–1873) were key figures in systematizing individualist thought. In the social sciences, particularly in economics, individualist explanations have historically exerted great influence, and since the 1960s they have enjoyed renewed popularity in political science and sociology in the form of rational choice theory.

Structuralist theories emphasize the presence of underlying structures in human relations. These structures have a systematic character, including mechanisms of self-regulation and self-transformation. Karl Marx's theory that capitalist development is driven by a contradiction between the forces of production and the social relations of production is a prime example of a structuralist theory. The *forces of production* refer to labor processes, such as mechanization, the reorganization of the workplace, and the education of the working class. The *social relations of production* refer to the relations between capitalists, who enjoy a monopoly control over the means of production, and workers, who rely exclusively on their own labor power. When the forces of production and the relations of production get seriously out of joint, revolution occurs and leads to the creation of a new system of production with different social relations of production.

Institutionalist theories, in contrast, focus on the role of institutions possessing organization, rules, and shared goals in the shaping of social relations. Institutions are not seen as reflections of underlying structures but as at least partially autonomous units. John R. Commons (1862–1945), Karl Polanyi (1886–1964), and Thorsten Veblen (1857–1929) are among the founders of institutionalism. Long a minority current and largely confined to economics, since the 1990s a "new institutionalism" has won growing support among economists, sociologists, and political scientists.

LABOR RELATIONS

These different approaches can be seen in labor relations, a field to which individualists, structuralists, and institutionalists have contributed significantly. They have all been concerned with labor militancy, but each analyzes militancy in distinctive ways and poses different central questions. Individualists ask why a rational worker would join a trade union or participate in strikes. The economist Mancur Olson, in *The Logic of Collective Action* (1965), questions why workers would join a trade union when the results of collective actions are "collective goods" (defined as goods that benefit all). These results are thus shared by all workers, whether or not they participated in the collective action. A rational worker would let others join and pay the costs of striking, while waiting to achieve any collective good their action might produce. To overcome a rational worker's objections to collective action, Olson suggests that unions often use selective incentives, or benefits confined to group members, such as the exclusion of nonunion workers from employment (closed shops), to make sure that the rewards of collective action are confined to participants in collective action. While Olson's analysis offers insights into some problems of labor relations, it conflicts with observed worker behavior. Strike-prone French and Italian workers have historically lacked benefit packages and closed shops.

In contrast to Olson's individualist focus, John Kelly's Marxist approach asks how militant collective identities are formed at the workplace. To Kelly, social relations play a big role. In *Rethinking Industrial Relations* (1998), he argues that capitalists' monopoly over the means of production enables them to exploit workers, and that workers' experiences at work give them a limited consciousness of their own exploitation. But when do workers come to see their exploitation as class injustices rather than as flaws of particular employers or the products of local circumstances? Emphasizing that consciousness emerges from the interaction of labor processes and social relations, Kelly focuses on the role of ideologically motivated activists on the workshop floor who persuade workers through talk and by collective action that their fate is inextricably bound up with that of the class collectivity. Kelly emphasizes that workers' ideologies and workplace struggles—their social relations—are as important as productive forces in the evolution of worker radicalism.

While social relations play a major role in Kelly's Marxist analysis of labor relations, structural forces also remain crucial. Kelly argues that the decline in labor militancy in the United Kingdom and much of the contemporary Western industrial world is a cyclical phenomenon produced by Kondratieff waves, which are decades-long waves of economic activity. During the upswing of Kondratieff waves, employment increases and the workers' bargaining position strengthens. The opposite occurs during downswings, however, and turning points correspond to historical changes in systems of labor organization. The contemporary decline in unionism in the private sector in the United Kingdom and many industrialized nations does not constitute a dissolution of class as much as it represents the triumph of aggressive capitalism during a favorable historical period.

Kelly's argument puts a good deal of weight on the role of radical political action within trade unions in promoting class identities, but little information is presented about what motivates activists or how militant organizations are sustained. A Kondratieff wave is a good example of a deep structure, one that exerts great influence but that may escape detection entirely by contemporaries. But Kondratieff waves are also problematic because so little is known about their causes. In addition, because the number of cycles is so small, the possibility exists that random forces are at work.

Institutionalist labor relations acknowledge both class and individualist concerns, but they focus major attention on institutional regulation, emphasizing the constructed character of social relations. Institutionalists ask why various industrialized nations possess very different systems of industrial relations. A good example of an institutionalist approach is that of Bo Rothstein, who argues that the character of unemployment insurance programs explains why Scandinavians have significantly higher union membership than other Europeans (1992). According to Rothstein, government-subsidized, union-controlled unemployment insurance programs prevail in Scandinavia, while compulsory national unemployment systems dominate elsewhere. A union-organized unemployment system, the so-called Ghent system, allows Scandinavian unionists to limit benefits to unionized workers, to decide what jobs are suitable for unemployed workers and, as a consequence, to increase labor's control over the labor supply. In Sweden, for example, the union-dominated Ghent system was implemented by Social Democrats with these ends in view. The welfare system actually promotes unionization, accounting for as much as 20 percent of Sweden's lead in unionization over major non-Scandinavian European nations.

Although individualists, structuralists, and institutionalists pose different questions about labor relations and pursue different research agenda, there is some room for common ground. Rothstein underlines the importance of the autonomous creation of Ghent system type welfare programs but also stresses that such institutions may be seen as an example of the selective incentives dear to Mancur Olson. Rothstein also adds that Marxist theories of class formation help explain why trade unionists entered politics to pursue class objectives in the first place.

POLITICAL PROCESSES

Social relations concern not just questions of collective action but also issues of political process of concern to social scientists. Recent debates over the evolution and effects of democratization show how individualist, structuralist, and institutionalist approaches can be applied to political issues.

Many individualists emphasize the importance of reciprocity in understanding political processes, as well as the role of democratic polities in fostering norms of reciprocity. In democracies, such norms are formed in repeated social exchanges that define appropriate behavior and promote collective benefits. Over the course of repeated interactions, individuals learn the value of cooperation and can reasonably expect that their contributions will be rewarded by others' contributions at a later stage of the game. An application of an individualist approach to politics processes can be seen in *Consent, Dissent, and Patriotism* (1997), Margaret Levi's study of conscription and conscientious objection. Levi argues that, however patriotic, rational draftees might be expected to stay home and let others bear the brunt of the battle. Patriotism makes sense when prospective conscripts can be sure that others will also answer the call. Surveying military service in six countries over extended periods of time, Levi found that young men are most likely to respond when they trust that the government is making policy and implementing it fairly, when they see that others are obeying, and when they receive information that confirms government trustworthiness and popular responsiveness. Thus, faith in government's equity and capacity breed civic trust.

A structuralist perspective on democratization and distrust can be seen in Quintan Wiktorowicz's book *The Management of Islamic Activism* (2001). Wiktorowicz studied the response of Islamic movements to Jordan's post-1989 democratic reforms, and he shows how Islamic movements that have adopted formal organizational structures and subjected themselves to state regulation have been systematically manipulated and denied the ability to articulate independent political positions. Charitable societies, religious judges, Mosque preachers, and the Ramadan religious period are carefully policed and regulated by the Jordanian state. One important political-religious group, the Muslim Brotherhood, benefits from state largesse, encouragement, and even facilitation, and it has become a politically moderate ally of the Jordanian state. In contrast, Salafi Muslims have avoided integration and have remained informally organized. Salafi networks possess significant influence in religious education where they advocate social justice and Islamic practices that contrast with the regime's support of the status quo. Rejecting efforts at government control, Salafis have resisted formal organization and, in the underworld of informal organization, reformist Salafis have often established contacts and have been influenced by more radical Islamic Salafis.

Wiktorowicz shows that Jordan's allegedly democratic reforms have not produced democracy. Still, changes in state structure have not been ineffectual. Changes in state structures have profoundly affected the character not only of Jordan's quiescent formal political organizations, but also that of the government's rebellious, informally organized opposition.

From an institutionalist perspective scholars have also been interested in how allegedly democratic reforms can actually restrict democratic politics and undercut the agents of state capacity. Ezra Suleiman's book *Dismantling Democratic States* (1997) is a "new institutionalist" study of governmental deregulation and de-democratization in some important industrial nations. Suleiman suggests that debates over governmental reform changed in the 1980s and 1990s. During these decades, encouraged by advocates of a "New Public Management" policy, attacks on bureaucratization no longer focused on creating a more efficient public civil service but on championing a privatization that, Suleiman believes, weakens democracy. Privatization, he argues, necessarily destroys the public space in which contemporaries can debate political options, while broadsides against bureaucratization undermine faith in the civil servants and governmental institutions that represent the most practical civic alternative to markets. At the higher levels of government, there is increasingly little place for the career civil servant, while business experience is taken as a desirable and sufficient qualification for those charged with serving the public good. But if states no longer foster institutions that possess autonomous power, why debate politics at all? When consumers replace citizens, political authority and democratic politics necessarily contract.

In the case of political processes, as in that of collective action, individualist, structuralist, and institutionalist theories all offer valuable insights. Levi's study of conscription shows how democratic governments can build trust by creating institutions that treat citizens equally and that are sufficiently transparent to let citizens see they are being treated fairly. Wiktorowicz's study of political integration in Jordan shows what happens when state administration is inequitable and when it denies equal treatment to political groups, bringing some into the government and condemning dissenters to the murky world of informal organization and secrecy. Finally, Suleiman demonstrates the growing danger of replacing democratic institutions with markets. Such a situation provides little room for citizens to engage in the kind of debate and civic interaction that Levi argues builds trust, and it provides no vehicles for integrating dissent into the political order.

In conclusion, a look at individualist, structuralist, and institutionalist theories shows a clear difference in their central organizing questions and their root conception of fundamental social relations. Yet each offers valuable insight into important aspects of collective action and political process. The current challenge seems to be not so much to dismiss or discard theories, but to look for new ways to integrate significant contending theories.

SEE ALSO *Democracy; Institutionalism; Interactionism, Symbolic; Labor; Labor Union; Malthus, Thomas*

*Robert; Marxism; Mill, John Stuart; Sociology;
Structuralism; Workplace Relations*

BIBLIOGRAPHY

Elster, Jon, ed. 1986. *Rational Choice.* Oxford: Basil Blackwell.

Granovetter, Mark. 1985. Economic Action and Social Structure: The Problem of Embeddedness. *American Journal of Sociology* 91: 481–510.

Kelly, John. 1998. *Rethinking Industrial Relations: Mobilization, Collectivism, and Long Waves.* London: Routledge.

Lazonick, William. 1991. *Business Organization and the Myth of the Market Economy.* Cambridge, U.K.: Cambridge University Press.

Levi, Margaret. 1997. *Consent, Dissent, and Patriotism.* Cambridge, U.K.: Cambridge University Press.

McAdam, Doug, Sidney Tarrow, and Charles Tilly. 1997. Toward an Integrated Perspective on Social Movements and Revolutions. In *Comparative Politics: Rationality, Culture, and Structure,* eds. Mark Irving Lichbach and Alan S. Zuckerman. Cambridge, U.K.: Cambridge University Press.

Olson, Mancur. 1965. *The Logic of Collective Action: Public Goods and the Theory of Groups.* Cambridge, MA: Harvard University Press.

Rothstein, Bo. 1992. Labor Market Institutions and Working-Class Strength. In *Structuring Politics: Historical Institutionalism in Comparative Analysis,* eds. Sven Steinmo, Kathleen Thelen, and Frank Longstreth, 33–56. Cambridge, U.K.: Cambridge University Press.

Suleiman, Ezra. 1997. *Dismantling Democratic States.* Princeton, NJ: Princeton University Press.

Wiktorowicz, Quintan. 2001. *The Management of Islamic Activism: Salafis, the Muslim Brotherhood and State Power in Jordan.* Albany: State University of New York Press.

Michael Hanagan

SOCIAL SCIENCE

An eclectic and sometimes polarizing term, *social science* is a broad umbrella linking multiple fields, with contention regarding which fields should be included under its purview. Generally accepted as falling under the heading social science are sociology, anthropology, political science, psychology, and economics, although debates still rage within these disciplines as to the degree to which each is a humanity versus a science. Disciplines such as history and linguistics, while still addressing social life, are less often included as social sciences. In general, social science can be regarded as the scientific method's application to all things social. It should be noted, however, that most social sciences manifest, to a greater or lesser degree, a humanities emphasis as well as a scientific one.

There is still some debate regarding the use of the term *social science,* with criticism generally aimed at the word *science.* Traditionally, the natural sciences, or "hard sciences," have been characterized by the use of the scientific method, which involves generating testable hypotheses in order to predict future outcomes and the ability to falsify these hypotheses. When applied to the natural world, the scientific method allows for high degrees of predictability, due to science's ability to recognize and understand universal laws governing empirical reality. When applied to the social world, however, comparable levels of prediction and discoveries of analogous universal laws governing human behavior have proven to be more allusive. Due to the social sciences' limited success in employing the scientific method, they are often referred to as the "soft sciences."

ORIGINS

No definitive date can be given for the birth of social science—its emergence is in fact due to a large number of circumstances spanning centuries and some of its rudimentary ideas can be traced to multiple origins, some dating as far back as Plato. It is generally accepted that an important era in the emergence of contemporary social science began with the Enlightenment and its emphasis on rationality, logic, and methodology as applied to the empirical world. There are scholars, however, such as Lynn McDonald, who contend that the foundation of social science should be traced back to the sixth century (McDonald 1993). Maurice Duverger (1961) has argued that the social sciences, despite early roots in Grecian inquiries into the nature of man, did not emerge as a distinct form of research until the eighteenth century, when social philosophy bearing a "philosophical attitude" gave way to a new scientific emphasis. This shift from social philosophy to social science was given impetus by the emergence of positivism as a widely accepted mode of knowledge. First articulated by August Comte and best described in his 1848 work *A General View of Positivism,* positivism moved almost entirely away from metaphysical speculation and instead focused on the scientific method's ability to produce facts and falsifiable statements about the empirical world.

At first, much of this new scientific inquiry focused nearly exclusively on the natural world. Great gains were made in physics, chemistry, biology, astronomy, and other fields dealing with the natural environment. It was not long, however, before the methods employed to achieve these gains were utilized in attempts to describe, explain, and predict human behavior. Hewing closely to positivism's tenets, the social sciences sought to discover laws governing the social realm—in effect, laws that allow the predictability of human interaction. Subsequent years have shown just how elusive are the levels of predictability and precision found in the natural sciences when sought in the social sphere.

MORAL COMPONENTS

The need for a social science also emerged from widespread and often violent revolutions sweeping European intellectual, political, and economic spheres beginning in the seventeenth century. Economic crisis spurred on by widespread migration to urban centers, widening inequality, and the imperialist ambitions of some European states led many to apply scientific approaches to social behavior, in an attempt to understand and predict social phenomena. Implicit in this project was a distinctly moral component, which scholars such as Alan Wolfe argue is still central to the social sciences, even if it is not always evident in their practice (Wolfe 1989). While social science attempts an objective evaluation of human and social behavior, by its very nature it must grapple with questions of equality, fairness, cohesion, and happiness, and thus with moral issues.

SOCIAL SCIENCE'S METHODOLOGIES

As was the case with the natural sciences, much of the early social science literature relied heavily on human observation in deriving its conclusions. Not until the publication of Émile Durkheim's *Suicide* in 1897 was statistical analysis incorporated into social scientific writings. With the subsequent increase in statistical analysis looking at all forms of social behavior, a divide was created within the social sciences between those using quantitative and those using qualitative methods. The proponents of quantitative methods often cite their predictive powers and the ability to develop generalizable properties via random samples—allowing social scientists the ability to sample the behavior, opinions, or values of a relatively small number of individuals and apply their findings fairly accurately to larger populations. Qualitative methodologists argue that their approach results in a more detailed and specific understanding of a given area of study. While at the start of the twenty-first century this divide still exists within the social sciences, a recognition of the need for a more integrative approach is beginning to emerge.

A third and somewhat distinct methodology emerged during the 1800s from the work of Wilhelm Wundt, generally considered to be the father of psychology. Wundt was one of the first intellectuals to utilize human experiments as a methodological tool for the social sciences—a method still predominant within psychology, but found to a lesser degree in the other social sciences.

ETHICAL CONSIDERATION

Throughout social science's history, ethical as well as moral considerations have played an important and interesting role in shaping types of studies and areas of inquiry. It is this ethical and moral dimension that to a degree sets the social sciences apart from the natural sciences. With its main area of inquiry being the human animal, it has long been recognized that social science, if misused, poses a certain level of danger.

While they are rare, there have been social scientific studies that were physically or emotionally harmful to the individuals under study. Stanley Milgram's electrical shock experiments in the early 1960s and Philip Zimbardo's 1971 Stanford prison experiment are two of the more infamous cases of disregard for the ethical treatment of study subjects. Milgram, conducting authority experiments, led test subjects to believe they were applying dangerously high levels of electric shocks to other experiment volunteers. In reality, volunteers seemingly receiving shocks were accomplices who only acted as if they were being shocked. Despite being told of the deception after their participation in the experiment, some of the volunteers who were instructed to apply electrical shocks continued to suffer emotional stress caused by their initial belief that they had severely harmed or even killed another individual. Likewise, in 1971 Zimbardo, hoping to explore the nature of human evil, created a mock prison at Stanford University, subdividing volunteers into two groups—prisoners and guards. After only six days the experiment was shut down due to sadistic behavior on the part of the guards and the onset of depression in many of the prisoners. Much was learned from both of these classic social scientific investigations—which are still being studied several decades after they ended—but both also dramatically highlight the potential harm experiments can cause tests subjects.

Another ethical issue confronted by social scientists concerns the use of scientific evidence to further dangerous or prejudiced ideologies, and the ways in which such ideologies can shape research results. In *The Mismeasure of Man* (1981), Stephen Jay Gould argues that racial and ethnic prejudices can influence social scientific research in such a way that the scientist's ideological beliefs are reified by flawed research results. Gould shows how early craniometrical research attempting to link skull size to intelligence, and ultimately to a hierarchical ordering of races, produced severely flawed results that mirrored the preconceived prejudices of the scientists conducting the studies. The racist undertones of these and other early attempts at blending biology and the study of human behavior (to produce what was later coined sociobiology) have made many social scientists suspicious of biological explanations for social behavior. Nonetheless, by the second half of the twentieth century achievements in evolutionary biology and genetics had sparked new interest in the link between genetics and social behavior.

Social scientists must also consider who will use their findings and the manner in which the findings will be used—especially when utilized by government and military institutions. While social science can provide much insight useful for the formulation of beneficial public policy, it also has the potential to be utilized in unethical ways. Such was the case in the United States after the September 11th attacks of 2001 which led to the War on Terror. The U.S. military turned to the social sciences, mainly psychology, to aid them in extracting information from combatants in custody. Questions were raised regarding the ethics of social scientists utilizing their expertise on human behavior to aid military and government interrogators extracting information from detainees in coercive ways, possibly amounting to torture. Ultimately, the American Psychological Association ruled its members could participate in the interrogations as consultants so long as noncoercive methods were utilized (American Psychological Association Task Force 2005, Behnke 2006).

SOCIAL SCIENCE'S BRANCHES

Differing perspectives on how social scientific inquiry should be applied and what it should be applied to led to the advent of several branches of social science, which, however, display greatly overlapping interests and methods and share a number of major thinkers in common.

Psychology Psychology, or the science of the mind, which is often traced to the work of Wilhelm Wundt in the mid- to late 1800s, attempts to explain the behavior of individuals through the mechanisms of the psyche. The related field of social psychology explores the mind's operations in the context of interactions within a group. Increasingly, however, subfields within psychology have come to be seen as more akin to the natural than to the social sciences. With its increasing emphasis on biological development and on functions within the brain, psychology, perhaps more than other social sciences, is beginning to blur the line between the natural and social sciences.

Anthropology Anthropology is generally regarded as the scientific study of the origin, the behavior, and the physical, social, and cultural development of humans. According to Wolfe (1989) and others, anthropology's general emphasis on origins has tended to make it only indirectly focus on contemporary society. While it is a broad field, most of its studies can be classified as belonging to one of four subfields: cultural anthropology, physical anthropology, linguistic anthropology, and archaeology.

Economics As with the other social sciences, there are multiple—if similar—definitions of economics. It is perhaps best defined as the study of the creation, consumption, and distribution of scarce resources. The field is broadly categorized into one of two subfields: macroeconomics and microeconomics. Macroeconomics emphasizes national-scale economies and their interactions, whereas microeconomics tends to focus on interactions between agencies, corporations, and individuals. While focusing primarily on markets, economics also explores how markets influence and shape other cultural phenomena.

Political Science Like social science's other branches, political science is a diverse and broad field of inquiry. It is best understood as the study of power and its transfer through political behavior. Political science as a coherent and recognized branch of social science did not develop until the mid-1800s, although it is widely acknowledged that scholars and intellectuals before that time had been pursuing insights into political behavior for many centuries.

Sociology Sociology as a coherent and established field of study is the newest of the social sciences, and perhaps the most difficult to define. With its area of scientific inquiry being all things social, sociology is often seen by its practitioners as analogous to social science itself and as integrating the work done in anthropology, psychology, political science, and economics. Such a view is confirmed by the diversity of the thinkers sociology considers influential—many of whom came from other social-scientific disciplines. Karl Marx and Max Weber, recognized as two of sociology's founders, were trained as an economist and a lawyer, respectively. George Herbert Mead, a philosopher, has had a lasting influence on sociology, as has Talcott Parsons, who had graduate training in economics. Likewise, anthropologist Margaret Mead, psychoanalyst Sigmund Freud, and many other non-sociologists continue to influence sociological research.

While at the start of the twenty-first century sociology, anthropology, political science, psychology, and economics are seen as separate and distinct branches within the social sciences, these disciplines continue to be linked together by a common grounding in the writings of a number of key thinkers. Among those that are still read by more than one social science branch are Adam Smith, John Locke, Sigmund Freud, Karl Marx, Émile Durkheim, and Erick Erickson, to name only a few.

CONTEMPORARY ATTACKS ON SOCIAL SCIENCE

During the 1960s, two then-emerging intellectual movements known as *poststructuralism* and *postmodernism* first articulated an attack on some branches of social science that continues to this day. As Pauline Marie Rosenau argues in *Postmodernism and the Social Sciences* (1992), from their birth both poststructuralism and postmodernism took very similar positions, and by the end of the twentieth century they were generally seen as synonymous with each other. Poststructuralism emerged from continental Europe in the 1960s in reaction to *structuralism*—the belief that basic structures governing human interaction can be found, despite its changing and oftentimes contradictory nature. Postmodernists shared the same reaction against structuralism but applied their critique to larger cultural entities. Because of their many commonalities, by the end of the twentieth century the term *postmodernism* was often used as an all-encompassing word to refer to both movements.

Postmodernism has many historical roots, but its direct origins can be traced to the work of poststructuralists such as Michel Foucault. By the late twentieth century, Jean Baudrillard had emerged as postmodernism's leading theorist. Baudrillard as well as other postmodernists often draw inspiration from Friedrich Nietzsche's nihilistic anti-Enlightenment philosophy, which questioned notions of truth. All claims to objective truth or knowledge, especially those produced through scientific inquiry, are seen by postmodernists as subjective "narratives" that need to be deconstructed and decentered, to reveal them as attempts at exercising and enforcing social power. Furthermore, the existence of ordered reality is denied, and the concept of "evidence" is attacked.

While postmodern thought can largely be attributed to French philosophers such as Baudrillard, Jacques Derrida, and Foucault, there are also American forerunners of postmodern discourse—namely C. Wright Mills, David Riesman, and Berger and Luckmann. Though not generally seen as postmodern thinkers, these Americans hinted at many aspects of postmodern thought prior to the emergence of the postmodern label.

THE SOCIOLOGY OF SCIENCE

Questions about the objectivity of social science have been raised not only by its critics, but from within the social sciences as well. Recognizing the inherently social nature of scientific inquiry, social science has been able to apply its methodology to the practice of science itself—and in so doing has called into question the claims of science, both natural and social, to be objective. Work by academics such as Thomas Kuhn, particularly his landmark publication *The Structures of Scientific Revolutions* (1962), as well as advances in the subfield of the sociology of knowledge, have called into question how objective scientific practices really are, and have begun to show that politics, personalities, and larger cultural trends often inform scientific endeavors. Science (and by default social science) is no

longer seen as a steady accumulation of more and more data leading to incremental advances in knowledge. Instead, science and the knowledge it produces are seen as the product of social forces that often lead to revolutions within scientific fields, and dramatic paradigm shifts in what any particular science claims to be true at a given point in time. This realization during the mid-twentieth century marked a dramatic turning point in social science's development. Social science, which previously had relied on the natural sciences as a model to emulate in its own development, could now apply its own knowledge and methods to the natural sciences—which were seen as areas of social behavior in need of study.

SOCIAL SCIENCE IN THE UNITED STATES

Social science achieved perhaps its purest form in America. For a number of reasons, metaphysical and epistemological concerns have largely been ignored within the United States, leaving such "philosophical speculation" to European counterparts—although British social science is more akin to that found in the United States. Academics such as Dorothy Ross in her 1991 work *The Origins of American Social Science* have argued that America's particular brand of social science is the result of pre–Civil War American exceptionalism—the belief that America held an exceptional place in the world, outside of the historical currents that were leading to class uprisings and mass poverty elsewhere. By the mid-1800s, with the rapid industrialization of the United States, American social scientists were, however, finally forced to recognize the influence of historical forces on American society.

SOCIAL SCIENCE IN THE TWENTY-FIRST CENTURY

Social science's direction at the start of the twenty-first century is difficult to discern. Increasing attacks from postmodernist thinkers provide some reason for concern. Perhaps more alarming, however, are the internal divisions confronting the social sciences. A wide array of sometimes competing methodologies and theories has led to frequent infighting among social science practitioners, and the absence of an accepted grand theory creates some level of worry about future directions. Some of social science's branches, however, namely economics and psychology, seem to be gaining in prestige. In the case of economics, this is mainly due to the increasing weight given to the marketplace as a predictor of many facets of human behavior; in the case of psychology, it is due to the field's growing ties to the biological sciences.

There are other positive developments afoot as well. Social science, especially within sociology and anthropology, has increasingly recognized the need for minority perspectives. As a result, an increasing number of minority scholars have made their way into the social sciences since the 1960s. New areas of study loosely affiliated with the traditional social science disciplines have also emerged: African American studies, Chicano studies, queer theory, and women's studies, all of which have made important contributions to the social sciences. Furthermore, the social sciences have increasingly found a place in governmental and corporate entities, tackling everyday issues confronting society.

SEE ALSO *Anthropology; Economics; Political Science; Social Psychology; Sociology*

BIBLIOGRAPHY

American Psychological Association Task Force. 2005. [O]n Psychological Ethics and National Security. http://www. apa.org.

Baudrillard, Jean. 1981. *Simulacra and Simulation.* Trans. Sheila Faria Glaser. Ann Arbor: University of Michigan Press, 2002.

Behnke, Stephen. 2006. Ethics and Interrogations: Comparing and Contrasting the American Psychological, American Medical, and American Psychiatric Association Positions. *Monitor on Psychology* 37 (7): 66–67. http://www.apa.org/ releases/PENSfinal_061606.pdf.

Comte, Auguste. 1848. *A General View of Positivism.* Trans. J. H. Bridges. London: Routledge and Sons, 1907.

Durkheim, Émile. 1897. *Suicide.* Trans. John A. Spaulding and George Simpson. New York: Free Press, 1966.

Duverger, Maurice. 1964. *An Introduction to the Social Sciences.* Trans. Malcolm Anderson. New York: Praeger.

Gould, Stephen Jay. 1981. *The Mismeasure of Man.* New York: W. W. Norton.

Kuhn, Thomas S. 1962. *The Structure of Scientific Revolution.* Chicago: University of Chicago Press.

Lyotard, Jean François. 1979. *The Postmodern Condition: A Report on Knowledge.* Trans. Geoff Bennington and Brian Massumi. Minneapolis: University of Minnesota Press, 1984.

McDonald, Lynn. 1993. *The Early Origins of the Social Sciences.* Montreal: McGill-Queen's University Press.

Mead, George Herbert. 1934. *Mind, Self, and Society.* Chicago: University of Chicago Press.

Milgram, Stanley. 1963. Behavioral Study of Obedience. *Journal of Abnormal and Social Psychology* 67 (4): 371–378.

Ross, Dorothy. 1991. *The Origins of American Social Science.* Cambridge, U.K., and New York: Cambridge University Press.

Smith, Roger. 1997. *The Norton History of the Human Sciences.* New York: W. W. Norton.

Weber, Max. 1921. *Economy and Society.* eds. Guenther Roth and Claus Wittich; trans. Ephraim Fischoff. Berkeley: University of California Press, 1978.

Wolfe, Alan. 1989. *Whose Keeper? Social Science and Moral Obligation.* Berkeley: University of California Press.

Wundt, Wilhelm. 1897. *Outlines of Psychology.* Trans Charles H. Judd. St. Clair Shores, MI: Scholarly Press, 1969.

Zimbardo, Philip. 1972. Pathology of Imprisonment. *Society* 9 (6): 4–8.

Keith Kerr

SOCIAL SCIENCE, VALUE FREE

The German sociologist Max Weber (1864–1920) is the originator of the demand for freedom from value judgments in the social sciences, an ideal he referred to as *Werturteilsfreiheit* (value-freedom). Weber argued that there is a logical gulf—it is not a matter of degree—separating the causal hypotheses and empirical generalizations of science from value judgments, that is, one's moral, political, and aesthetic preferences. The "truth" of a social scientific hypothesis is in no way a matter of these preferences. No preference is, in turn, "required" by any given set of facts. Since this is so, it behooves social scientists to keep the two realms—fact and value, is and ought, science and values—separate.

In Weber's day, this separation was not observed by everyone. "Professorial prophets," as Weber called them, preached worldviews (*Weltanschauungen*) from university lecterns as if from the pulpit. It was for Weber a matter both of personal integrity and professional duty that this propagation of practical political ideals be brought to a stop (although he found it immensely hard to persuade his colleagues, who represented a range of "human" disciplines, to accept this view). These self-appointed "prophets," Weber argued, indulged in a form of showing off. Worse, their pronouncements impaired the clear perception of reality (Weber's own scientific vocation): Ultimate questions were addressed "in the name of science," which is a logical impossibility. Such professorial "prophets" were paid from state funds (unlike religious preachers), were unsupervised, and did not anticipate any debate; the student audience in the lecture hall could not answer back, so academic power was abused. According to Weber, scholars and teachers should stick to their scientific vocation, for they have a job to do that requires addressing in a businesslike manner. In Weber's philosophy, meaning cannot be given to the whole of existence, as the "prophets" seemed to believe. The teachers' task is instead to present facts, even ones they may find personally unpalatable, and to always see these facts as separate from their own evaluations.

Weber was influential because he called attention to the vocation of the scholar in the human sciences—a job that demands a professional approach—at a time when such a view was rare. What, he asked, is the responsibility of scholars to their discipline and to themselves, both as scholars and as political or moral beings?

VALUE-RELEVANCE

Weber held that values influence the way in which research is conducted in the social sciences (in addition to other non-essential ways common to natural and social science) and that values themselves could be affected by the results of research. The holder of a value position may learn that a course of action is unworkable or that, if pursued, other values might, collaterally, be infringed or impeded. Facts can be brought to bear on values, potentially affecting one's holding of them. However, this does not weaken by one iota a given value's freely-chosen status. On the research side of the human disciplines, evaluations enter into the subject matter. Using *verstehendes Erklären* (understanding explanation), that is, the subject's evaluations seen in relation to the conditions of his or her action, the researcher can hope to sort out the decisive motives of the actor studied. In research, the scrutiny of values permits a discussion between investigators that can clarify the (evaluative) points of view each brings to bear.

Science is served, Weber believed, by an empirical, critical treatment of values. Ultimate values can come into view, and the implications of such values, when particular situations are judged in practical terms in their light, can be traced. In addition, the factual consequences of such judgments can be seen, and new ultimate values can be revealed (with their own implications) of which the maker of the judgment was not at the time aware. The choice of any given value is always, of necessity, "free," that is, incapable of being determined by any fact. It is free because it is a value. It is a choice because there are many values and they are radically at odds, in Weber's view (he called them "warring gods"), in the modern, areligious world.

Both the investigator and the investigated are caught up in culture. "We are," Weber says, "cultural beings" (1968, p. 180). If culture is to be their object, social scientists must recognize that the precondition for a cultural science is that, as cultural beings, humans can take up an attitude to the world and give it meaning and significance—some part of the world becomes culture for them. It is "values" that permit this. And, of course, concrete cultural values and hence "problems" in cultural science change with culture, shifting over time. "Value-relevance" (*Wertbeziehung*) was an idea Weber took from his friend Heinrich Rickert (1863–1936), a philosopher, although he modified it in the process. But his basic attitude to all of science is neo-Kantian in cast. Values are a component of human action and can be empirically investigated. Only their validity is unprovable empirically. It was Weber's intense concern for reality that convinced him of the heterogeneity and historical nature of values, despite

the teachings of the dogmatists who believed the world as a whole had but one meaning and of those philosophers who were striving to provide the means for finding such a meaning on the transcendental level. Weber believed that human beings must choose for themselves. Science must accordingly be kept value free. A concern for values underlaid Weber's commitment to freedom from value judgments in science (and teaching).

THE VALUE-FREEDOM DEBATE

Weber's idea of value-freedom and value-relevance has been an object of continuous discussion since he formulated it. Critics have appeared in several guises. Analytical philosophers, for example, are concerned with the is/ought distinction; descriptivists maintain that all qualities of objects are assimilable to their factual properties; and some empirical sociologists argue that value-freedom is a conservative professional ideology. Given that society is dichotomously divided—between, for example, men and women, white and black, bourgeoisie and proletariat—and the dominant is biased, the sociologist must take sides; if the sociologist falls on the side of the weaker, he or she must be biased too. For critical theorists, Weber advocates "decisionism," that is, he implies that value choice is blind faith and "private"; Weber is thus a (subtle) positivist. A public consensus on value matters (ideals and projects) is, however, possible via human action.

Similarly, but from the perspective of natural law theory, Leo Strauss (1899–1973) argued that Weber was ultimately a nihilist in moral matters, whereas a return to the tradition of classical political philosophy would make it possible to settle whether or not values are heterogeneous and in conflict, as Weber maintains. Weber provided a middle way between positivism and idealism that was itself a finely wrought solution to the key questions involved in the possibility of a "social" science. These questions continue to be asked, and Weber's answers continue to be dissected by fresh generations faced with the conflict between reason and faith, science and values, theory and practice, and detachment and involvement. They share Weber's insight that science "cannot save us" but believe, with him, that commitment alone is not enough.

SEE ALSO *Methodology; Positivism; Weber, Max*

BIBLIOGRAPHY

Bruun, Hans Henrik. 1972. *Science, Values, and Politics in Max Weber's Methodology.* Copenhagen: Munksgaard.

Gouldner, Alvin W. 1973. Anti-Minotaur: The Myth of a Value-Free Sociology. In *For Sociology: Renewal and Critique in Sociology Today*, 3–26. London: Allen Lane.

Strauss, Leo. 1953. *Natural Right and History.* Chicago: University of Chicago Press.

Weber, Max. [1922] 1968. *Gesammelte Aufsätze zur Wissenschaftslehre*, ed. Johannes Winckelmann. Tübingen, Germany: Mohr-Siebeck.

Weber, Max. 1949. *Max Weber on the Methodology of the Social Sciences*. Trans. and eds. Edward A. Shils and Henry A. Finch. Glencoe, IL: Free Press.

Ian Varcoe

SOCIAL STATICS

The concept of social statics relates to the assumption that the order of society is knowable. Without this basic premise, the study of the social sciences lacks rational predictability.

Social statics is the order of society. This order includes structural components (e.g., family, government, and economics) and the interaction between these components. Auguste Comte, the father of sociology, based social statics on the positivistic philosophy. In creating the science of sociology, Comte moved the explanation of the hows and whys of society away from the theological and metaphysical toward the rational and scientific. This is similar to Plato's basic assumption that the order of society is knowable and explainable, as illustrated in *The Republic*.

Comte identified the elements of "spontaneous order" of social statics as the individual, family, and society. Sociology does not focus on the study of the individual in the way that psychology does. For Comte, the simplest form of a social unit is the family. All other social units build upon the family unit. The reason Comte included the individual as one of the elements in social statics was to illustrate a primary function of the family as a social unit: to socialize the individual into a functioning member of society. The result of successful socialization is the expression of appropriate forms of interaction with all elements of society.

The interaction of the family social unit with the rest of society illustrates Comte's concept of the division of labor. The division of labor is an operational definition of social statics. The interdependency of the division of labor holds together social structure and interaction in an orderly fashion. In the family structure there are roles that the husband, wife, and offspring play. For example, the role of the husband is interdependent upon the role of the wife. The family unit cannot fulfill its defined social purpose to reproduce and socialize offspring without the interdependency between husband and wife. Interactions focus on socialization of the members of the family unit for the benefit of the greater society as a form of social control. The division of labor creates not only interde-

pendency but also social control through the socialization process. Social control of sexual relations and reproduction is limited to the family unit, since this is the ideal method for providing for the basic needs of offspring and socializing them.

Social dynamics is the progressive change in social statics. Comte's "law of human progress" is the foundation for social dynamics. The order of society changes over time in a progressive, positive direction. A new social order succeeds an existing social order. In Comte's law of human progress, society had moved from the stage of theological to metaphysical and then to positivistic.

For Herbert Spencer, society is superorganic, which tends toward a state of equilibrium. This biological concept defines social statics as the major institutions of society (e.g., familiar, governmental, religion, and industrial) and interaction represented by the division of labor. Spencer expanded the detailed explanation of social statics to include regulatory, operative, and distributive components. Social dynamics is a progressive evolutionary process. As society progresses, new elements of society are created, and unfit elements decay and drop away. The nature of society moves from homogeneity toward heterogeneity; there is greater differentiation. In primitive times the structure of society was very simple with a minimal division of labor. As society progresses, the division of labor becomes more complex with the addition of new elements of social structure and new customs (interactions). In addition the level of interdependency increases as there is greater differentiation through increased stratification. Stratification is the ranking and ordering of this interdependency and is usually the first social static to change due to increased differentiation. In modern terms stratification is the ranking of abilities and training to fulfill the needs of society. The purpose of stratification is to identify the most important resources needed for societal survival and progress.

Social statics is the foundation for the structural-functionalist tradition in sociology. This tradition studies society at a macro level, identifying the components of social structure and their corresponding functions. Within this tradition, Émile Durkheim's expanded theory of the division of labor incorporates social statics and social dynamics based on social solidarity. Structural components and their functions hold society together and create organic solidarity through increasingly complex interdependency. Talcott Parsons's theory of social system and social action continues in the structural-functionalist tradition by using the concepts of social statics and social dynamics to explain social structure, social order, socialization, and social change.

SEE ALSO *Comte, Auguste; Division of Labor; Durkheim, Émile; Hierarchy; Parsons, Talcott; Prediction; Social*

Science; Society; Spencer, Herbert; Stratification; Structuralism

BIBLIOGRAPHY

Comte, Auguste. 1855. *The Positive Philosophy of Auguste Comte.* Trans. Harriet Martineau. New York: AMS, 1974.

Plato. 1943. *The Republic.* Trans. Benjamin Jowett. New York: Pocket Books. (Orig. written 360 BCE.)

Spencer, Herbert. 1877. *Social Statics: The Conditions Essential to Human Happiness Specified, and the First of Them Developed.* 2nd ed. New York: Robert Schalkenbach Foundation, 1954.

Turner, Jonathan H., Leonard Beeghley, and Charles H. Powers. 2007. *The Emergence of Sociological Theory.* 6th ed. Belmont, CA: Thomson Higher Education.

Ronald Keith Bolender

SOCIAL STATUS

Social status has been used throughout history to differentiate individuals and groups of people in order to maintain hierarchical systems of inequality between and among people and to enforce the idea that certain groups of people are, by nature, born to a certain level of existence.

Social status is often described as one's "standing" in society; the word *status* is derived from the Latin *statum*, meaning "stand." In a narrow sense, the term refers to one's legal or professional standing within a group; in a broader sense, it means one's value and importance in the eyes of the world (de Botton 2004, p. vii). At various points in history, the belief that inequality was a way of life was subscribed to by both the oppressed and their oppressors in terms of religion, law, and cultural norms. History, law, and cultural artifacts show that in nearly every society, certain groups of people were held in high esteem while others were ignored or ridiculed. Historical events such as the French Revolution, the American Revolution, and the civil rights movement largely transformed societies, moving them away from hierarchical ladders that restricted upward mobility because of heredity, lineage, family, gender, race/ethnicity, skills, physical attributes, religion, accent, and temperament.

The desire for social status can spur individuals to act on their dreams, achieve goals, and form a common bridge with others. Often, though, individual achievement has not been considered a factor when comparing one's social standing in a community. According to Alain de Botton in *Status Anxiety* (2004), "what mattered was one's identity at birth, rather than anything one might achieve in one's lifetime through the exercise of one's faculties. What mattered was who one was, seldom what one did" (p. 87).

HISTORICAL PREVALENCE

According to de Botton, the characteristics of groups that historically have been considered high status can be traced from Sparta in 400 BCE to Brazil in 1960. Such characteristics have ranged from military training, wealth, power, sainthood, knighthood, social graces, and hunting ability to those with the ability—physical, intellectual, and artistic—to persuade and/or bully other groups into offering respect or a redistribution of favor. Derrick Bell, in *Silent Covenants: Brown v. Board of Education* (2004), relates social status to race/ethnicity, access to opportunity, and the reflection of persons of color when discussing issues of privilege and status. According to Bell (2004), "Du Bois reminds us that to compensate their low wages, segregation gave whites a 'public and psychological wage'.... David Roediger adds that status and privileges could be used to make up for alienating and exploitative class relationships, North and South" (p. 81).

THEORETICAL DEVELOPMENT AND RESEARCH

Theories have been developed to describe social status, class, and identity. Similarly, social status has been described in terms of international dominance and competitiveness between countries. Thye and Lawler (2005) note that "status characteristics theory investigates the effect that individual properties such as age, gender, and ability have on interaction. The theory asserts that these status characteristics are indicative of task ability. In collective task settings, members act as if status characteristics give clues suggesting how capable each individual is of contributing to the successful completion of the group's task" (p. 126). Status characteristics theory, in essence, attributes rewards, influence, and value to certain groups based on characteristics and expectations of competency. Edward Said (2003) has described the use of social status to plunder other nations in the quest for international superiority. Said frames social status in terms of a country's plunder and conquest under the aegis of "a civilizing mission, the idea that some races and cultures have a higher aim in life than others; this gives the more powerful, more developed, more civilized the right to colonize others in the name of a noble ideal" (p. 333). The historical underpinnings of social status can be traced to the Greeks. Said states that "each culture defines its enemies, what stands beyond it and threatens it. For the Greeks beginning with Herodotus, anyone who did not speak Greek was automatically a barbarian, an Other to be despised and fought against" (p. 335).

Social status is often viewed through the lens of comparing groups along specific criteria and the relationship between groups. According to Suls and Wheeler (2000), Newcomb's 1943 analysis of college student political attitudes revealed that "people use groups or social aggregates as standards or frames of reference when evaluating their abilities, attitudes, or beliefs" (p. 85). Similarly Suls and Wheeler state that "Roper (1940) first introduced the idea of a reference group by suggesting that individuals' perceptions of their own status depends on where they stand in relationship to other people" (p. 85). Abowitz (2005) conducted a recent study of undergraduate college students to ascertain their views of the American class system. Based on a survey of a random sample of 154 undergraduate students, Abowitz reported that college students believe that they can achieve a certain social status through individual factors that are part of, as the author states, an achievement ideology, "the idea that success and social standing are largely a product of individual effort and not a product of family privilege and connections" (p. 716).

SOCIAL STATUS MEASUREMENT

According to classical research conducted to understand the role of student persistence in college, background characteristics of students and their social status were some of the most reliable predictors of success. Similarly, Toutkoushian and Curtis (2005) found that the socioeconomic status of specific school districts can help explain variations in students' average standardized test scores, college attendance, and school rankings. Sociometry, a systematic method for investigating relationships, was used in Kosir and Pecjak's (2005) study to determine whether students were categorized by their peers as having social status and popularity. Based on the results of their research, Kosir and Pecjack found that peer-perceived popularity is a construct that is distinct from sociometric popularity.

Other studies of social status involve the predictive value of subjective assessments of social status with an individual's health status. Research by Operario, Adler, and Williams (2004) based on a national sample of 500 adults, ages eighteen and over, used the Scale of Subjective Status. Participants were instructed to do the following:

> Think of a ladder with 10 steps representing where people stand in the United States. At step 10 are people who are the best off—those who have the most money, the most education, and the most respected jobs. At step 1 are the people who are worst off—those who have the least money, least education, and the least respected jobs or no job. Where would you place yourself on this ladder? (p. 241)

For this portion of the research, "the sample rated themselves on average above the midpoint of the scale at both baseline and follow-up" (Operario et. al. 2004, p. 241). Including measures of global health and health risk factors, the authors found predictive utility in self-report measures of socioeconomic status and individual health status.

Levin (2004) measured social dominance by groups that want to have a higher status than other groups using such distinctions as religion, ethnicity, and gender. Using a social status questionnaire, Levin found that differences in social dominance between arbitrary groups (e.g., ethnicity and religion) was greater when the status gap between the groups was perceived to be larger.

Thus, social status, depending on the historical time frame, country, and culture, can be delineated through one's resources and achievement. However, the hierarchy suggested by comparing one's standing with others still exists and is prevalent in societies where resources and power define the influence that one or a group has. This power and influence permeate aspects of governance and the place each person subscribes to with reference to an individual's or a group's relative value and standing.

SEE ALSO *Lifestyles; Sociometry*

BIBLIOGRAPHY

Abowitz, Deborah A. 2005. Social Mobility and the American Dream: What Do College Students Believe? *College Student Journal* 39 (4): 716–728.

Alcoff, Linda M., and Eduardo Mendieta, eds. 2003. *Identities: Race, Class, Gender, and Nationality*. Malden, MA: Blackwell.

Bell, Derrick. 2004. *Silent Covenants: Brown v. Board of Education and the Unfulfilled Hopes for Racial Reform*. New York: Oxford University Press.

De Botton, Alain. 2004. *Status Anxiety*. New York: Pantheon Books.

Kosir, K., and S. Pecjak. 2005. Sociometry as a Method for Investigating Peer Relationships: What Does It Actually Measure? *Educational Research* 47 (1): 127–144.

Levin, S. 2004. Perceived Group Status Differences and the Effects of Gender, Ethnicity, and Religion on Social Dominance Orientation. *Political Psychology* 25 (1): 31–48.

Operario, D., N. E. Adler, and D. R. Williams. 2004. Subjective Social Status: Reliability and Predictive Utility for Global Health. *Psychology and Health* 19 (2): 237–246.

Said, Edward. 2003. The Clash of Civilizations. In *Identities: Race, Class, Gender, and Nationality*, eds. Linda M. Alcoff and Eduardo Mendieta, 333–335. Malden, MA: Blackwell.

Suls, Jerry, and Ladd Wheeler, eds. 2000. *Handbook of Social Comparison: Theory and Research*. New York: Kluwer Academic/Plenum Publishers.

Thye, Shane R., and Edward J. Lawler, eds. 2005. *Social Identification in Groups*. Vol. 22 of *Advances in Group Processes*. Boston: Elsevier.

Toutkoushian, R. K., and T. Curtis. 2005. Effects of Socioeconomic Factors on Public High School Outcomes and Rankings. *Journal of Educational Research* 98 (5): 259–271.

Marci M. Middleton

SOCIAL STRATIFICATION

SEE *Stratification.*

SOCIAL STRUCTURE

Social structure refers to durable features of sustained, large-scale, social coexistence that shape individual conduct. Attempts to summarize the nature of human society are often said to offer accounts of social structure. Such accounts vary but typically include claims addressing five facets: (1) collective features, process, or patterns that are (2) consistent across large populations and (3) persist for long periods and that are (4) manifest as impersonal and implacable influences that strongly condition (5) the lives that individuals can lead. Claims to priority for particular accounts are sometimes advanced as "structuralism"—assertions of precedence for particular impersonal, extra-individual, or collective features. In polemic usage, the label has accompanied wide and varied claims of displacing superficial or shallow alternatives in favor of deep, overarching generalizations about human conduct, language, or cognitive capacities.

All social sciences incorporate some variants of the concept, but the issues posed by social structure roughly coincide with the disciplinary charter of sociology. Seminal contributions (and their authors) are often lauded for providing distinctive visions of social structure. Since such efforts address the ultimate nature of human society, they are best understood as charter statements that unite followers (and antagonists) into schools whose agreements (and disagreements) extend to the nature, content, and value of the master texts.

Karl Marx (1818–1883) traced the origin of social structure back to the necessity for humans to wrest sustenance from nature through labor. However, the results of labor include matter that has been gathered and reshaped and that if put aside today will add to the fruitfulness of any further labor. Thus fields cleared of forest, iron forged into plows, or grain not eaten but kept for seed become means of production—products of past labor that can be added to future labor to make it more fruitful.

Any society thus must address the problem of who will be assigned control of the means of production. Marx observed that the products of work, built up over generations, became the property of a relative few, who could then assign to themselves the lion's share of the product of future work, without themselves having to do it. He suggested that collective life, including religion and politics, would be constrained to perpetuate such a division of the population into unequal classes. Individual outlooks and actions would tend to conform to interests arising from class positions. And the classes would be linked into antagonism until the growing scale of factories would insure the ascendance of the propertyless in a revolution abolishing property and bringing on a new social structure of a classless society.

Émile Durkheim (1858–1917) underscored that matter was not property unless nonowners respected owners' claims. Markets required moral solidarity to ensure that contracts were honored, for example, constraining buyers and sellers from grabbing away goods or payments without relinquishing what they had offered in return. More broadly, Durkheim argued that absent moral limitation supplied by society, humanity's inherently insatiable desires would lure humans into vice and unreliability as workers, family members, or citizens.

Durkheim argued that moral sentiments shared in common formed social facts—enduring, extensive, external forces that constrained individuals into moral conformity. He offered three complementary accounts of how this might work.

First, Durkheim suggested that the force of society would wax and wane with the overall volume of interaction in a population, suggesting that the impact on individuals rises and falls as moral messages are repeated to them more or less frequently. In turn, the average frequency (and consistency) of moral messages arriving at each individual reflects the totals received and retransmitted by the individual's interaction partners, taken en masse. In this manner, the moral sentiment impinging on individuals arises from collective, accumulated experience that is external and beyond individual control. Second, Durkheim also suggested that participation in collective celebrations, notably religious worship, would amplify and reinforce moral sentiments expressed through such ceremonies. Third, Durkheim feared that inconsistent messages, generated by participation in diverse groups that upheld contrasting normative outlooks or participation in groups unwilling to specify clear moral standards, would result in a state of normative dissonance and weakened moral regulation that he termed *anomie*.

Max Weber (1864–1920) also took issue with Marx's insistence on the primacy of economic factors. He called attention to contrasts rooted in religious outlooks and in other sources of diverging worldviews. Weber thought the common element uniting social structures was learned adherence to schemes of values—abstract ideals spelling out goals and pitfalls. These might include how to serve God (after specifying what God or gods to serve), or the unlimited pursuit of gain, or putting obligations to kin ahead of obligations to the ruler.

Values are highly abstract and often are only expressed indirectly through parables, stories, sermons, and the writings of sages. From these, readers, commentators, and legislators work at deriving further rules that people should follow. For Weber, uniform or structural regularity across a population was the result of enmeshing in a web of norms—morally binding rules that reflected values held in common. While Weber recognized that values and their derivative norms could derive from tradition, or from religious inspiration he termed *charisma*, he also emphasized that rules were subject to extension and elaboration through reasoning by experts who were learned in the code. He feared that such expanding rationality would come to confine humanity in an "iron cage" of intricate but colorless regulation.

Specialists continue to seek to purify and refine seminal visions. Most sociologists accept that many categorical contrasts, such as race, class, and gender, are collective durable features of large populations that shape lives. Many would extend this list to include the principle categories used to sort and count people in censuses and surveys—the demographic variables including age, ethnicity or national origin, religion, education, and so forth. All of these variables strongly condition a wide range of behaviors including friendship, marriage, political preferences, consumer choices, and much more.

Why and how this occurs remains open. Some would insist that such regularities require that individuals act as if extant rules and social definitions are binding. The puzzle is what (if anything) is adequate to account for assent to unequal outcomes on the scale that is required.

An alternative is that durable features reflect how (and in what degree) categories channeled persons into different settings, social pairings, and uses of time. A principal motive is that power-holders can address recurrent organizational dilemmas by drawing on widely understood social classifications to allocate work, authority, or rewards. Any population consists of individual histories that incorporate the (variable) past degree of such sorting, along with assorted consequences and correlates. Classifications are guides (of varying accuracy) to similarities and contrasts in past experience that, in turn, influence individuals and power-holders in subsequent choices over settings, pairings, and time use.

SEE ALSO *Caste; Culture; Hierarchy; Marxism; Stratification; Structuralism*

BIBLIOGRAPHY

Durkheim, Émile. 1951. *Suicide: A Study in Sociology.* Trans. John A. Spaulding and George Simpson. Glencoe, IL: Free Press.

Marx, Karl, and Friedrich Engels. 1970. *The German Ideology*, ed. C. J. Arthur. New York: International Publishers.

Weber, Max. 1978. *Economy and Society: An Outline of Interpretive Sociology*, eds. Guenther Roth and Claus Wittich, trans. Ephraim Fischoff et al. Berkeley: University of California Press.

Steven Rytina

SOCIAL SYSTEM

The concept of social systems became central to sociology with *The Social System* of Talcott Parsons, published in 1951. Parsons's formulations were modeled on concepts of homeostasis developed in physiology rather than simpler notions of equilibrium used by Vilfredo Pareto and other earlier theorists. Parsons portrayed equilibria in social systems not as static balances among forces but as complex interdependencies involving mutual adjustments among many independent components. He emphasized that social systems are moving equilibria that accommodate change while maintaining overall stability. He noted that equilibria can break down, resulting in anomie, strain, and conflict.

SCOPE OF THE CONCEPT

For the system concept to be useful in sociology, Parsons held, it required adaptation to the empirical nature of social reality. Social systems are not concrete, directly observable entities but rather analytically defined domains of objects. They can be identified only by abstracting social interaction, relationships, and institutions from environing phenomena—physical-chemical, biological, psychological, and cultural. Yet, social systems also interpenetrate, or share elements with, their environments. They exist in time, space, and ecological settings. They gain structure by institutionalizing values and norms that have their sources in cultural systems. Their members' affective attachments to normative orders and motivation to pursue socially validated goals derive from personality systems.

Social systems vary in size and duration. Brief interactions between individuals can be treated as social systems. So can large-scale societies that endure for centuries, such as Chinese civilization. Institutions of intermediate scale—the business corporation, medical practice, or electoral politics—are social systems. Complexes of institutions, such as modern metropolises or global trade, may be analyzed as social systems. Individuals participate in many social systems, typically adopting different social roles in each—employees in business firms, members of political parties, fathers or mothers in families.

Parsons viewed social interaction as a dynamic give-and-take of expectations among independent actors. Actors support their expectations with sanctions, invoked contingently on others as rewards when expectations are met or as punishments when expectations are broken. Parsons held that an actor's behavior, even in simple relationships, is doubly contingent, dependent on expectations and sanctions held by both the actor and other parties. Because of different experience and exposure to social strains, actors often hold conflicting expectations for performance of their own or others' roles. Conflicts in expectations emerge in everyday interaction, as between parents and children, and in role relations of macrosocial importance, as between a president and members of Congress over legislative oversight.

Conflicts over role expectations may release powerfully motivated pressures to change roles and the institutions that coordinate them. After adjustment in roles and underlying norms and values, new equilibria may emerge. Motivation that is deviant from previous role expectations may thus be a source of creative social change. Yet, role incumbents mobilize sanctions to counter deviant expectations and are generally able to suppress potential change. Social institutions tend to reimpose established equilibria, whether through informal interaction, the procedures of formal organizations, or legal procedures.

THE FOUR-FUNCTION PARADIGM

Parsons identified four general system problems that all social systems confront. He called them functions and treated them as general dimensions of the organization of social systems. The idea of a closed and ordered set of functions applicable to all social systems was a radical innovation. Previous functional theories had been based on open-ended lists of functions without limitation in theoretical principle. The *four-function paradigm* provided the conceptual frame for Parsons's work after the mid-1950s.

The four functions are:

1. Adaptation, or the gaining of control over conditions in environments of the system. Adaptive processes involve developing new resources or improving allocations of resources to strengthen a system's capabilities and efficiencies.

2. Goal attainment, or the processes of organizing the activities of social units to bring about a valued state in the system's relationships to its environments, typically including other social systems.

3. Integration, or the processes of mutual adjustment among a system's components to promote their long-term dependence on one another and attachment to the system.

4. Pattern maintenance, or the processes of developing long-term commitment to values and other principles that distinguish the system from its environments.

Parsons proposed that the four-function paradigm might outline the primary dimensions of structural differentiation in societies. He thus developed a theory of four functionally specialized subsystems of society, with each subsystem treated as a complex set of interdependent institutions, even subsystems of their own. The four subsystems of society are:

1. The economy serves the adaptive function. In modern societies, it includes the markets for labor and capital, the business corporation, entrepreneurial roles, and the legal institutions of property, contract, credit, and employment.

2. The polity serves the goal-attainment function. In modern societies, it includes government agencies, including administrative, executive, legislative, and judicial authorities.

3. The societal community serves the integrative function. It encompasses ties of social solidarity, including social classes, status groups, voluntary associations, lifestyle groups, ethnic groups, and extended kinship groups. Phenomena of integration, stratification, and conflict are shaped largely by institutions of class structure, status order, and primordial ties, but also by common law, informal normative orders, and public opinion.

4. The fiduciary system serves the pattern-maintenance function, centering on development of the shared values and culture of a society. Its major institutions concern religion, family, socialization, and education. Following Max Weber's emphasis on religious ethics, Parsons argued that change in fiduciary systems has been the greatest source of long-term macrosocial change.

Parsons's theory of societal subsystems was never fully detailed, despite two decades of efforts to analyze the institutional structures of the four systems. He argued that each subsystem has its own forms of inequality, and the chief institutions of the respective subsystems—economic exchange, relationships of political authority, solitary ties in status groups, and socialization in family life—are intertwined with factors such as race and ethnicity, gender, cultural background, and educational differences, although in historically variable ways. He also argued that institutions in each subsystem integrate normative and interest-driven elements and ideal and material factors. Where social control is effective, the pursuit of self-interest reinforces the controlling normative institutions, as when the conduct of business relies on institutions of property, contract, and employment.

THE GENERALIZED MEDIA

Functional theory holds that the differentiated subsystems of society are mutually dependent. Each subsystem can fulfill its specialized function only if the other subsystems fulfill their functions. Applying this proposition to social processes as well as structures, Parsons hypothesized that each subsystem needs resources from the other subsystems to carry out its own processes. He developed a model in which the four subsystems are linked through six *double interchanges*, or exchanges of resources, between pairs of subsystems. A basis of this model was the economists' treatment of *circular flow* between business firms and households (wages for labor, consumer spending for goods and services), which Parsons identified as the interchange between the economy and the fiduciary system. He then outlined five other double interchanges.

Noting that money is an essential mediator of economic processes, including circular flow, Parsons identified additional *symbolic media* that regulate processes for the other three societal subsystems. He proposed that power is the symbolic medium of the polity, influence is that of the societal community, and commitments are that of the fiduciary system. Identifying the set of symbolic media that regulate processes within and across the boundaries of the four subsystems greatly advanced theoretical analysis of equilibrium processes in society.

LUHMANN AND AUTOPOETIC SYSTEMS

In the years after Parsons's theory of social systems reached maturity with the concepts just discussed, the most original thinking about social systems came from German sociologist Niklas Luhmann. Luhmann was influenced by Parsons and retained some of his terminology but developed a distinct theory.

Luhmann's conception of social systems emphasizes not equilibrium but *autopoesis*, a term he adopted from biological theory. Autopoetic (literally, self-producing) systems are capable of self-reproduction of their components. Luhmann emphasized the self-organizing, self-sustaining qualities of social systems and their components, not balances among components, as in equilibrium theories. Luhmann adhered to functional analysis but treated function as a relationship between a system and its multiple environments. Presenting his conception as continuous with Darwinian natural selection, he suggested that autopoetic systems are adaptive within specific ecological settings.

Luhmann emphasized that autopoetic systems of all kinds emerge by reducing the complexities of organization among the various systems in their environments. Every system represents a reduction of antecedent environmental complexities. Biological systems reduce the complexi-

ties of their physical and chemical environments. Psychic and social systems emerged as reductions of biological as well as physical-chemical environments. Once social systems evolved, they maintained intricate dynamic relationships with their environments—psychic, biological, and physical-chemical. The relationships with psychic systems are especially important as they, too, are systems of meaning, and meanings pass back and forth between psychic and social systems. Social systems themselves evolve to complexity as a natural process of adapting to their varied and intricately organized environments. Their complexity then creates opportunities for the emergence of new systems within themselves—subsystems—by the same principle of reduction of complexity.

COMMUNICATION AND SOCIAL SYSTEMS

Luhmann, defining social systems as systems of communication, used information theory and cybernetics to analyze processes of communication. He criticized *transfer* theories of communication, emphasizing that one does not give up anything when communicating ideas to another. Moreover, what the other receives is not necessarily the message originally intended. He accordingly focused the analysis of communication on how it changes the recipient. Communication in this view selects among open possibilities, confirming some possibilities while ruling out others. After receiving a communication, a person knows to orient future conduct to certain possibilities and leave others aside. Communication often occurs simply in physical gestures, but its meaning may be shaped, conveyed, or amplified through three classes of media: language, as used in everyday exchanges between individuals; the media of dissemination in written, print, or electronic forms, which can reach large or specialized audiences over extended times and places; and the symbolically generalized media that act on the relation between motivation and the selective effects of communication. The symbolic media help to connect communication with macrosocial structures, but Luhmann did not match the media to specific subsystems of society, as did Parsons. He gave different lists of symbolic media in his works, but generally included truth, love, money, power or law, and religious or ideological belief.

The symbolic media also serve, Luhmann suggested, as catalysts for the differentiation of society. He rejected Parsons's four-function theory of societal subsystems, maintaining that subsystems emerge only by exploiting particular opportunities to reduce complexity in environing systems. Thus, the emergence of subsystems in particular societies can be identified only through analysis of the historical conditions that created the opportunities for reduction of complexity. Nevertheless, Luhmann identified law, politics, economy, religion and ideology, and science as common subsystems of modern societies. Each of the subsystems contains historically evolved semantic codes for regulating communication, codes that also regulate uses of the symbolic media. Issues of discrimination by race, ethnicity, gender, or cultural background can be understood by analyzing the semantic codes of specific media.

CONCLUSION

Parsons's conceptual scheme was designed to guide empirical research in sociology and related social sciences. Over a period of several decades, a substantial body of empirical studies has been conducted in its terms, with many of the studies standing as major contributions. Luhmann developed his theory of social systems with greater concern for meta-theoretical issues than empirical research. Its long-term influence will likely derive from the critical perspective it provides on other theories. Both bodies of theory demonstrate the importance of theoretical analysis of social systems, yet both also leave significant issues open to further investigation.

SEE ALSO *Communication; Discrimination; Functionalism; Media; Pareto, Vilfredo; Parsons, Talcott; Role Conflict; Role Theory; Sociology, Parsonian; Structuralism; Systems Theory*

BIBLIOGRAPHY

Luhmann, Niklas. 1982. *The Differentiation of Society*. Trans. Stephen Holmes and Charles Larmore. New York: Columbia University Press.

Luhmann, Niklas. 1986. *Love as Passion: The Codification of Intimacy*. Trans. Jeremy Gaines and Doris L. Jones. Cambridge, MA: Harvard University Press.

Luhmann, Niklas. 1989. *Ecological Communication*. Trans. John Bednarz Jr. Chicago: University of Chicago Press.

Luhmann, Niklas. 1990. *Essays on Self-Reference*. New York: Columbia University Press.

Luhmann, Niklas. 1995. *Social Systems*. Trans. John Bednarz Jr. and Dirk Baecker. Stanford, CA: Stanford University Press.

Parsons, Talcott. 1951. *The Social System*. Glencoe, IL: Free Press.

Parsons, Talcott. 1969. *Politics and Social Structure*. New York: Free Press.

Parsons, Talcott. 1971. *The System of Modern Societies*. Englewood Cliffs, NJ: Prentice-Hall.

Parsons, Talcott, and Gerald M. Platt. 1973. *The American University*. Cambridge, MA: Harvard University Press.

Parsons, Talcott, and Neil J. Smelser. 1956. *Economy and Society: A Study in the Integration of Economic and Social Theory*. Glencoe, IL: Free Press.

Victor Lidz

SOCIAL THEORY

Social theory begins with ordinary questions, like why do some passively accept authority while others respond with political violence? Religions provided answers in a distant past. Social theory emerged as a secular alternative, often joining ethical and positive elements. Three traditions of social theory are important for the social sciences.

A first tradition comes from Thomas Hobbes (1588–1679). After years of bloody warfare between Catholics and Protestants, Hobbes's *Leviathan* (1651) offered a worldly theory of social order. What was really at issue was power. As an early example of what would be termed *ideology critique*, Hobbes asks "cui bono?"—whose interest does this idea serve? People obey, he argued, because of fear of violent death. Social order thus turns on who has ultimate power over violence. If there is not one final authority, there would be war of all against all, and life would be "solitary, poor, nasty, brutish, and short." Better, he argued, is a society founded on fear of a great leviathan, whose power guarantees stability.

Leviathan relied on no Absolute Good, whether God or Nature. In tracing all "higher" ideas to "lower" things—power, fear, death, the body, violence—Hobbes set the tone for one main strand of social theorizing. This approach continued in writers from Karl Marx (1818–1883) to Michel Foucault (1926–1984) and Pierre Bourdieu (1930–2002). While each differs, they are Hobbesian in asking "cui bono?"—and answering with a complex power struggle, even if it is denied, for example, in art, religion, and morality. This first type of social theory ferrets out hidden power structures behind everyday interactions and institutions.

Hobbes's stress on fear led others to ask: Does not social order depend on more? What of obligation or love? How could the passions of a millennium and a half of Christianity be redirected onto earth, without producing the disastrous consequences Hobbes feared?

Such questions led to a second strand of social theory, stemming from Jean-Jacques Rousseau (1712–1778). He emphasized not fear but devotion as the foundation of social order. In our long-forgotten natural condition, Rousseau argued, we were independent, loving ourselves for ourselves; but society creates new needs, *amour propre*. We love ourselves based upon how much others love us. Not power, but the struggle for recognition and status regulates social order.

For Rousseau, justice can transcend nature and inequality. Justice depends in turn on the *social contract*, wherein each person must totally submit to the general will. Private freedom, he argued, depended on public equality, which required a "lawgiver." Moreover, the social bond, to last, should be held sacred.

Karl Marx (1818–1883) and V. I. Lenin (1870–1924) transformed the lawgiver into the revolutionary vanguard; the redefined social contract was the abolition of private property, as the condition of freedom and justice. Émile Durkheim (1858–1917) later pursued Rousseau's connections between social solidarity and religious sentiment.

Critical theorists—Theodore Adorno (1903–1969), Max Horkheimer (1895–1973), Herbert Marcuse (1898–1979), Axel Honneth—explored how modern societies create vast inequalities, not only in wealth, but respect and self-worth. They expanded Rousseau's ideas that culture can create unnecessary dependencies, focusing on the "culture industry"—the popular press, music, movies, advertising, and fashions. These sought to promote "needs" like Marx's false consciousness, where people became blinded to their own interests and dependent upon corporate and political masters. Some, like David Riesman (1909–2002), extended Rousseau's *amour propre* to the 1950s conformism of American "other-directedness," while others, like Daniel Bell, analyzed how politicians and corporations could shift the erotic into a political ideology. Thus social theory identified key foundations of power, even if exercised in subtle arenas.

These first two traditions invoke a strong state to right social wrongs, as theoretically defined. The third tradition is more cautious. Alexis de Tocqueville (1805–1859) was equally concerned with the roots of order and governance, but took a different course. Writing after the French Revolution (1789–1799), Tocqueville the aristocrat pondered the implications of equality. Societies emphasizing equality—like postrevolutionary America and France—were hostile toward exceptional talent and excellence; they could level out uniqueness and difference, generating a middling mediocrity. Moreover, equality threatened social identity and meaning: In a hierarchical society, one knew one's place and did not have to anxiously make one's place. In equalized societies, all is in doubt: Foreign observers regularly noted that Americans suffered a permanent "identity crisis," which was spreading globally at the beginning of the twenty-first century.

Traveling across America, Tocqueville commented on the deleterious effects of equality, and potential remedies. Loosed from primordial hierarchies, Americans, he argued, developed a passion for voluntary associations. The town hall and the local church were key examples, sustained by their members' voluntary efforts more than the weight of tradition or the power of elites (or a leviathan or lawgiver). What mattered was commitment by each participant, and Americans were joiners. The strongest social structures, Tocqueville argued, emerged not just through struggles for power or regard of others, but by citizens voluntarily developing shared commitments in local associations, which trained future leaders.

Tocqueville's voluntaristic, bottom-up approach informs a third strand of social theorizing. Max Weber (1864–1920) stressed voluntarism in probing the religious roots of capitalism. Capitalists did not just strive to make money. Rather, Weber argued, Puritan sects encouraged their members to seek salvation in voluntary, committed "good works"—against the old nobility that valued leisure over work. Capitalism was the unintended consequence. Though Weber felt we inherited an "iron cage" of capitalist society that we did not choose, his response was voluntaristic: If you are a scholar, do it as a "vocation," not as a heartless specialist; if you are a politician, lead, do not act as a technocratic bureaucrat. Voluntary commitment was key. In egalitarian America, every social interaction among equal citizens became a source of identity, obligation, and meaning, following G. H. Mead (1863–1931), C. H. Cooley (1864–1929), and Herbert Blumer (1900–1987). Talcott Parsons (1902–1979) extended voluntarism to critique past social theories, but like Weber joined basic values with individual choices. Edward Shils (1911–1995) and Daniel Elazar (1934–1999) continued Tocqueville's concern for hierarchy, honor, and glory, noting that even within an egalitarian society, they remain social powers. Still others, such as Robert Putnam, suggest that the individualistic strain in voluntarism has gone so far in contemporary American life that the commonwealth Tocqueville saw had weakened, as more Americans "bowl alone." Some postmodernists are so individualistic and egalitarian that they deny the possibility of meaning beyond the minds of separate individuals.

These three traditions have been revised and combined in efforts to interpret deep social changes. Consider the rise of industry, the division of labor, and bureaucratic organization in the theories of Marx, Durkheim, and Weber.

Marx, working in London, wrote of the English countryside transformed by industrial manufacturing; he saw people from all races and religions living near factories. These proletarians were a nascent class, opposed to capitalist/owners of the forces of production. In his theory, conflicts between such classes drove history.

Durkheim saw similar changes, but focused on the division of labor. Traditional societies, he argued, held together from pressures toward homogeneity. Modern societies are more like organisms. Social cohesion arises from interdependence; individuals perform specialized functions and develop a heightened sense of uniqueness. But without some firm social regulation, normlessness or "anomie" can undermine differentiated societies. Talcott Parsons and Niklas Luhmann (1927–1998) extended Durkheim's social differentiation into multiple, interconnected subsystems that fill different social functions, while others, such as Robert Merton (1910–2003), developed the idea of anomie and deviance as central to modern life.

Max Weber, writing in Germany, stressed the hierarchical rationality of government bureaucratic officials. Bureaucracies are ancient, but Weber stressed how modern organizations grew ever larger, more rational, and more hierarchical. Not only was the bureaucrat's personality stunted by his duties, everyone risked bureaucratization—since it was balanced increasingly less by the charisma of religion or respect for tradition. Seeking a "value-neutral" perspective, Weber posited that modern society is increasingly subject to "rational authority," as opposed to "traditional" or "charismatic authority." But the theory also had a quasi-moral intent, namely, to provide modern models for styles of action—rooted in the bonds of tradition or the electricity of charisma—which Weber saw threatened by the cold, abstract rationalism of bureaucracy.

Rationality was a political weapon that Enlightenment philosophers used to attack the "irrationality" of the ancient regime before the French Revolution of 1789. The secular theories of Hobbes and Rousseau helped refocus thinking on specific secular arrangements, rather than divinities or kings. But the legacy of this rational approach proved so powerful that Weber feared its excess. Analysis and criticism of rationalism in modern society have been among the most doggedly pursued strands of twentieth-century social thought, especially by Jürgen Habermas and other critical theorists and postmodernists.

Since Marx, Durkheim, and Weber, social theories have continued to stretch the imagination, seeking to capture the times and perhaps guide them. New topics emerge with new social forces: the massive rise of cities and new urban lifestyles; mass media, electronic media, and mass education; increased global interconnection; general increase in leisure time across societies; and a resurgence in the global power of religions are but a few of the subjects whose causes and meanings social theorists continue to pursue.

SEE ALSO *Associations, Voluntary; Blumer, Herbert; Bourdieu, Pierre; Bureaucracy; Class; Critical Theory; Durkheim, Émile; Egalitarianism; False Consciousness; Foucault, Michel; Hobbes, Thomas; Identity Crisis; Individualism; Lenin, Vladimir Ilitch; Lonely Crowd, The; Marcuse, Herbert; Marx, Karl; Mead, George Herbert; Nationalism and Nationality; Parsons, Talcott; Protestant Ethic; Revolution; Rousseau, Jean-Jacques; Social Psychology; Social Science; Sociology; Tocqueville, Alexis de; Weber, Max; World-System*

BIBLIOGRAPHY

Lemert, Charles, ed. and commentator. 2004. *Social Theory: The Multicultural and Classic Readings*. 3rd ed. Boulder, CO: Westview Press.

Parsons, Talcott, Edward Shils, Kaspar D. Naegele, and Jesse R. Pitts. 1965. *Theories of Society*. 2 vols. London: Collier-Macmillan.

Daniel Silver
Terry Nichols Clark

SOCIAL TRANSFORMATION

SEE *Social Change.*

SOCIAL WELFARE FUNCTIONS

Social welfare functions have occupied the center stage of welfare economics since the philosopher Jeremy Bentham (1748–1832) and other utilitarian theorists advocated that humans should seek the greatest total welfare, understood as the sum of individual utilities. The noted economists Abram Bergson (1914–2003) and Paul A. Samuelson (b. 1915) generalized the concept. Following the seminal work of the economic theorists Kenneth J. Arrow (b. 1921) and Amartya K. Sen (b. 1933), the theory of social choice has examined the various possible forms of such functions in detail.

In the most standard form, a social welfare function is a mapping that determines the level of social welfare as a function of individual levels of welfare. In fact, a numerical measure of social welfare is not really needed for the evaluation of social situations; the only relevant part of a social welfare function is how it ranks social situations from the best to the worst.

The theory of social choice analyzes two important features of a social welfare function. The first feature is its degree of aversion to inequalities between individual levels of welfare. For instance, the utilitarian function, computed as the sum of individual indices of welfare, is indifferent to inequalities because only the total matters. In contrast, the maximin function, which identifies social welfare with the welfare of the worst-off individuals in the population, displays an infinite aversion to inequalities since it gives absolute priority to the worst off. There are countless intermediate possibilities between these two extreme functions. The second important feature of a social welfare function is the information about individual indices that is used by the function. For instance, the utilitarian function focuses on individual gains and losses when it compares two situations: A situation is better than another if the sum of welfare gains when one moves to it is greater than the sum of losses. By contrast, the maximin function focuses on individual levels: A situation is better if the level of welfare of the worst-off individuals is greater. The link between the two features—inequality aversion and informational basis—has been thoroughly scrutinized by the theory of social choice. For surveys, see Walter Bossert and John A. Weymark's "Utility in Social Choice" in the *Handbook of Utility Theory* (Barberà, Hammond, and Seidl 2004, pp. 1099–1178) and Claude D'Aspremont and Louis Grevers' "Social Welfare Functionals and Interpersonal Comparability" in the first volume of the *Handbook of Social Choice and Welfare* (Arrow, Sen, and Suzumura 2002, pp. 459–542).

The link between the measurement of social welfare and the measurement of inequalities has also been clarified. The level of social welfare in a given situation can be decomposed into the positive contribution of total welfare and the negative contribution of inequalities. More precisely, it is generally possible to write social welfare as the difference of two terms. One is the sum of individual indices of welfare. The other, which comes as a deduction, is computed as the product of an inequality index and the sum of individual indices. In other words, one can typically say that inequalities reduce social welfare by a certain percentage, and this percentage itself is the value of an inequality index. Classical analyses of this link are provided by Anthony B. Atkinson in his essay "On the Measurement of Inequality" (1970) and Amartya K. Sen and James Foster in their book *On Economic Inequality* (1997).

A controversial issue has been the possibility of constructing social welfare functions on the sole basis of individual ordinal and noncomparable preferences over the social situations. The standard social welfare function relies on individual indices of welfare, but in its most general form it can simply define a ranking of social situations as a function of the preference rankings of these situations for each member of the population. This is important because there is much skepticism in economics about the possibility of making interpersonal comparisons of welfare in a consensual way. Bergson and Samuelson argued that the construction of a purely ordinal social welfare function was possible, but Arrow, in *Social Choice and Individual Values* (1951), provided an impossibility theorem and identified a deep problem in the idea of "aggregating" individual ordinal preferences. This problem has been questioned, however, because Arrow's theorem involved restrictive conditions that do not appear compelling and are not even considered in important branches of welfare economics, such as the theory of fair allocation or cost-benefit analysis. It is now emerging that interesting social welfare functions can be based on individual ordinal and noncomparable preferences, in particular on the basis of the equity concepts developed by the theory of fair allocation. Overviews of the controversies can be found in Marc Fleurbaey and Peter Hammond's contribution, "Interpersonally Comparable Utility," to the *Handbook of Utility Theory* (Barberà, Hammond, and Seidl 2004, pp. 1179–1285) and in an article by Marc Fleurbaey and Philippe Mongin (2005).

RECENT DEVELOPMENTS

Recent developments have dealt with the refinements of social welfare functions to incorporate a variety of fairness concepts or to make it possible not only to compare social situations for a given population, but also to compare social situations across different populations. The latter is important to make judgments about the desirable size of the population, and deep dilemmas plague this issue. A social welfare function such that every addition of an individual with positive welfare is considered to improve the social situation will generate extreme populationist evaluations—for example, the judgment that a larger population always makes a situation better, provided the larger population is large enough, no matter how low individual welfare is in this situation. However, a social welfare function that is based on some notion of average individual welfare is likely to be Malthusian because any addition of an individual with less-than-average welfare is considered undesirable. The compromise proposed in *Population Issues in Social-Choice Theory, Welfare Economics, and Ethics* (Blackorby, Bossert, and Donaldson 2005) is to define a critical level such that the addition of an individual is good only if his welfare is above this threshold.

An important issue in fairness concepts has been the incorporation of considerations of freedom and individual responsibility, motivated by theories of justice such as that of John Rawls (1971). Social welfare functions have been developed that are based on the idea of measuring individual situations in terms of opportunities or resources rather than ultimate welfare. A variety of functions have been proposed, in particular because there are different possible interpretations of the implications of individual responsibility. In one interpretation, individual responsibility removes the need for redistribution, which has motivated the construction of social welfare functions that disregard individual characteristics for which the individuals are responsible and focus on the compensation of inequalities for which individuals are not responsible. In another interpretation, individual responsibility removes the need for inequality aversion in the evaluation. Along this vein, social welfare functions have been proposed that are of the utilitarian sort along the responsibility dimensions of individual characteristics and of the maximin sort along the non-responsibility dimensions. Surveys of this field can be found in John E. Roemer's book *Theories of Distributive Justice* (1996).

SEE ALSO *Arrow Possibility Theorem; Objective Function*

BIBLIOGRAPHY

Arrow, Kenneth J. 1951. *Social Choice and Individual Values.* New York: Wiley.

Arrow, Kenneth J., Amartya K. Sen, and Kotaro Suzumura, eds. 2002. *Handbook of Social Choice and Welfare.* Vol. 1. Boston: Elsevier.

Atkinson, Anthony B. 1970. On the Measurement of Inequality. *Journal of Economic Theory* 2 (3): 244–263.

Barberà, Salvador, Peter J. Hammond, and Christian Seidl, eds. 2004. *Handbook of Utility Theory.* Vol. 2. Boston: Kluwer Academic Publishers.

Bergson, Abram. 1938. A Reformulation of Certain Aspects of Welfare Economics. *Quarterly Journal of Economics* 52 (2): 310–334.

Blackorby, Charles, Walter Bossert, and David Donaldson. 2005. *Population Issues in Social-Choice Theory, Welfare Economics, and Ethics.* Cambridge, U.K.: Cambridge University Press.

Fleurbaey, Marc, and Philippe Mongin. 2005. The News of the Death of Welfare Economics Is Greatly Exaggerated. *Social Choice and Welfare* 25 (2): 381–418.

Rawls, John. 1971. *A Theory of Justice.* Cambridge, MA: Harvard University Press.

Roemer, John E. 1996. *Theories of Distributive Justice.* Cambridge, MA: Harvard University Press.

Samuelson, Paul Anthony. 1947. *Foundations of Economic Analysis.* Cambridge, MA: Harvard University Press.

Sen, Amartya K. 1970. *Collective Choice and Social Welfare.* San Francisco: Holden-Day.

Sen, Amartya K., and James Foster. 1997. *On Economic Inequality,* rev. ed. Oxford: Clarendon Press.

Marc Fleurbaey

SOCIAL WELFARE SYSTEM

The social welfare system refers to "the whole set of modern social programs offering income maintenance in cases of unemployment, industrial accident, illness, forced retirement, loss of a family breadwinner, or extreme deprivation, as well as various sorts of educational, preventive, and regulatory programs" (Orloff 1993, pp. 4–5). President Franklin D. Roosevelt's New Deal policies, especially the Social Security Act of 1935, are regarded as the inauguration of the modern social welfare system in the United States. Social scientists and historians tend to have a much more expansive view of welfare than that put forth in the popular media, which associates welfare with certain types of aid to the poor. From the 1950s to the 2000s, scholars have been concerned with explaining both the origins of social welfare systems and the substantial variation in its form among advanced industrial countries.

THE EMERGENCE OF WELFARE STATES

An early and influential approach to understanding the origins of welfare states argued they emerged as part of the "logic of industrialism." That is, scholars such as Harold Wilensky and Clark Kerr, among others, stressed that complex societies require a modern social welfare system in order to ensure a healthy, well-trained workforce and care for retired workers. Scholars criticized this view on a number of grounds. For example, in *Protecting Soldiers and Mothers* (1992) Theda Skocpol noted that in some places welfare provisions predated industrialization. In addition, Skocpol and other scholars such as Gøsta Esping-Anderson noted that the logic of industrialism approach failed to explain the variation among welfare state systems.

Another group of scholars emphasized the humanitarian or idealistic motives for the expansion of welfare programs in the 1960s. This perspective argued that President Lyndon B. Johnson and other proponents of the Great Society programs implemented these policies and programs in response to the needs of the poor and oppressed. In *Regulating the Poor* (1971) Frances Fox Piven and Richard Cloward criticized this view, emphasizing that political and economic elites were primarily concerned with controlling the poor, not helping them out of poverty. Through an historical discussion of early reform efforts in England and the New Deal era in the United States, Piven and Cloward noted that welfare relief expanded during times of crisis so as to quell social unrest and then was retracted after the crisis was averted.

THREE WORLDS OF WELFARE CAPITALISM

Whether or not and to what extent elites could roll back welfare provisions depended, according to Esping-Anderson, on the strength of political class coalitions. In his *Three Worlds of Welfare Capitalism* (1990), Esping-Anderson argued modern welfare state systems emerged in response to the political class coalitions of workers and farmers in the late nineteenth and early twentieth centuries. Then welfare states expanded or contracted depending on the strength of the coalition of the working and middle classes. These political class coalitions sought state policies that enabled individuals to live outside the demands of the market, what Esping-Anderson termed *decommodification*. For example, workers have historically organized to demand unemployment compensation, pensions, health care, and other programs. These provisions enable individuals to exist without having to work. This improves the quality of life for workers and enables them to demand better work conditions from their employers.

Furthermore, welfare states in advanced capitalist countries display significant variation in the levels of decommodification each system provides for its citizenry. In fact, Esping-Anderson argued they can be grouped together into what he called three worlds of welfare capitalism: the conservative (e.g., Germany), the liberal (e.g., United States), and the social democratic (e.g., Sweden).

For example, in liberal welfare regimes, such as the United States, working class movements and parties have been historically weak. In these countries workers were unable to forge durable coalitions with farmers and later with the new middle classes. As a result, the welfare system in liberal regimes is relatively small and dualistic. That is, instead of a universal system where everyone benefits from welfare policies and programs, it creates two segments in society: one group receives benefits based on their tax contributions while a second group receives benefits regardless of whether or not they pay into the system. In the United States, social security and unemployment insurance are considered contributory entitlements. For most workers, a portion of each paycheck goes toward funding these programs. The second group of welfare recipients is comprised of those who receive aid without making a contribution. This type of aid is means-tested; that is, recipients have to demonstrate they qualify for relief and have to submit to government surveillance, else forfeiting the aid. In addition, in this dualistic system recipients of entitlements (e.g., Social Security) are not stigmatized while those who receive non-contributory aid (e.g., Aid to Families with Dependent Children [AFDC]) are heavily stigmatized. This stigma is supposed to provide a disincentive to receiving aid. For Esping-Anderson decommodification in liberal welfare regimes is low.

In conservative welfare regimes, such as Germany, working class movements are stronger and successfully forge coalitions first with farmers and later with the middle class. However, all social policy is cast in the light of Catholic ideals of tradition and stability. Emphasis is placed on maintaining the traditional family, with a male breadwinner and female homemaker. Thus decommodification is higher than in liberal regimes; yet feminists have pointed out that conservative regimes maintain a subordinate role for women.

In social democratic welfare regimes, such as Sweden, working class movements are strong and successfully forge alliances with farmers and the middle class. Thus for Esping-Anderson decommodification is the highest in social democratic welfare regimes. In these countries, taxes are relatively high, and instead of a dualistic system, benefits are granted on a universal basis, thus preventing the negative consequences of dualism and assuring continued support from the middle classes.

MODERN INTERPRETATIONS

Feminists such as Skocpol have criticized class-based explanations of welfare state systems for failing to take seriously the role of state managers in the production of social policy. Skocpol argued that class-based scholars have emphasized the role of working class (male) movements in provoking the rise of welfare states. As such, they have offered an explanation of the so-called paternal welfare state. Skocpol argued that in the United States a maternalist welfare state predated the paternalist one.

Skocpol found that the earliest efforts at social provision focused on taking care of Northern Civil War veterans in the late 1800s. This was an early and important form of old age pension. In addition, she traced the efforts of early feminists who played key roles in gaining pensions for women and policies that helped children in the early twentieth century. These feminists successfully influenced the creation of a welfare state that sought to protect soldiers and mothers.

Linda Gordon studied many of the same early feminists as Skocpol and offered important insights into maternalist welfare states and the origins of welfare in the United States. In *Pitied but Not Entitled* (1994) Gordon argued that feminists played key roles in agitating for and making governmental policy, noting that early welfare policies sought to reinforce traditional understandings of femininity, especially those that emphasized homemaking and caregiving. Thus the maternalist policies aimed at "protecting soldiers and mothers" were also paternalist, premised on the idea that men should work and women should be subordinate to them, taking care of the housework and the children. Moreover, Gordon demonstrated how welfare policies of the early twentieth century emphasized care for white women who were married with children. Single mothers and women of color were excluded from policies that were designed to complement the "family wage" earned by male husbands/workers. As such, the role of welfare aid was to help maintain the integrity of the traditional white family without usurping the role of male breadwinner. However, a substantial number of male workers had a very hard time earning enough money to support their families, a situation even more pronounced for single mothers.

In addition, Gordon maintained that New Deal welfare policies did more to help the nonpoor than the poor. Policy makers restricted the kinds of jobs that could contribute to Social Security and unemployment insurance. Due to the kinds of jobs they had, such as in agriculture or as domestic help, most women and blacks, for example, were not eligible for these benefits. This gendered and racialized nature of early welfare policies in part reflected the power of southern elites who influenced social policy so as to maintain a loose agricultural labor market in the

South. As a result of concerted political behavior of southern elites, the New Deal welfare policies were enacted unevenly in the South, if they were enacted at all. In the South, welfare provisions were meager, while in the industrialized North they were more generous.

This point is expanded upon by Jill Quadagno, who studied welfare policies from the New Deal through President Johnson's Great Society programs of the 1960s. In *The Color of Welfare* (1994), Quadagno showed how the Great Society programs sought to incorporate blacks and other minorities into the welfare state for the first time. However, such efforts resulted in a conservative backlash that pushed for a retrenchment of welfare to deny blacks an equal footing in society. This retrenchment, inaugurated by President Jimmy Carter, became a key platform of President Ronald Reagan, and was capped off by the signing of President Bill Clinton's "End Welfare as We Know It" bill in 1996, which ended the U.S. government's commitment to providing a safety net for the poor. The 1996 welfare reform bill transformed the pivotal AFDC program into TANF (Temporary Assistance to Needy Families), premised on the belief that instead of aid the government should provide inducements to work. Under these so-called workfare programs, there is a lifetime limit of five years of support, recipients must find work within two years or perform free community service, unmarried mothers must identify fathers to receive aid, and immigrants as well as unmarried teen parents are denied access to welfare programs.

SEE ALSO *Poverty; Welfare; Welfare State*

BIBLIOGRAPHY

Esping-Anderson, Gøsta. 1990. *The Three Worlds of Welfare Capitalism.* Princeton, NJ: Princeton University Press.

Gordon, Linda. 1994. *Pitied but Not Entitled.* New York: Free Press.

Orloff, Ann. 1993. *The Politics of Pensions.* Madison: University of Wisconsin Press.

Piven, Frances Fox, and Richard Cloward. 1971. *Regulating the Poor.* New York: Vintage Books.

Quadagno, Jill. 1994. *The Color of Welfare.* New York: Oxford University Press.

Skocpol, Theda. 1992. *Protecting Soldiers and Mothers.* Cambridge, MA: Harvard University Press.

Robert Sean Mackin

SOCIAL WORK

Social work is a both an academic discipline and a profession. The discipline of social work teaches theory, methods, and practice of the profession. Like many other disciplines within the social sciences, social work studies human behavior in a social environment. Social work is also a practice where individuals can work with individuals, families, groups, organizations, and communities in various settings, such as schools, hospitals, mental health clinics, domestic violence shelters, senior centers, elected offices, private practice, advocacy organizations, and a host of other public and private agencies. The ultimate goal of social work is to enhance the well-being and level of functioning for all people and to create positive social change by improving social conditions and creating more humane practices and policies for vulnerable populations.

Despite the overlap among social work, sociology, and psychology, there remain distinct differences between the disciplines. Social work seeks to intervene between people and their environments. Further, social work addresses social and economic conditions that affect individuals, families, groups, organizations, and communities and highlights the importance of a multicultural understanding of both people and communities. Sociology is an academic discipline—not a professional activity—that studies social groups, organizations, institutions, and societies. Psychology studies and treats individual behavior and mental processes.

Social work is driven by various ideological perspectives. The three most prevalent ideologies are conservative, liberal, and radical. The conservative ideology within social work focuses on a microlevel analysis of the individual, and the primary goal is to assist an individual and perhaps a family with their individual difficulties. This view holds the individual and family responsible and embraces private over public solutions. A liberal orientation in social work holds that social and institutional arrangements affect individual and societal well-being. A liberal view holds that government intervention is crucial and that a private response is insufficient: Government should provide a safety net, according to liberal ideology. This focus is typically considered a mezzo-level analysis. Lastly, the radical tradition of social work adopts a macro focus that confirms the need to restructure social, political, and economic institutions so they may provide a more equitable, universal, and democratic system. This radical view can be critical of the profession, most often targeting the conservative view as reproducing societal inequities and abandoning the historical roots of social work. Further, the radical tradition within the profession has been critical of social work practice as being tied to the state apparatus, which ultimately perpetuates poverty and inequality.

Ideological tension within the profession has historical roots, and there continues to be conflict today about the relevance and effectiveness of micro versus macro practice, although contemporary social workers have begun to recognize that what makes social work unique is the ability to locate social problems within the complex interconnectedness of individuals, families, communities, and societies. This multiple perspective of understanding social problems is one of the profession's assets.

Another view of the social work profession offers poignant criticism. Many authors have addressed the unique quandary that social workers face given the complexities of the U.S. social welfare system and its relationship to capitalist ideology and institutions. In Frances Fox Piven and Richard Cloward's seminal work *Regulating the Poor* (1971), they highlight that social welfare does not curb capitalist institutions; instead, it supports and enhances them. Moreover, the social worker is often the vehicle to ensure capitalism's survival. The profession must deal with this contradiction spelled out by Piven and Cloward, along with others, whereby social workers work in and are committed to the very institutions and agencies that perpetuate inequality, yet social workers rely on these same agencies for their livelihood.

As the various ideological perspectives of the profession reveal, there are numerous and varying accounts of the social work profession. In sum, many believe the profession to be driven by altruistic and humanistic motives, whereas others focus on the history's middle-class do-gooder who seeks professionalization. Still others describe social work as a profession that exerts social control over the poor, further legitimizing capitalism. In fact, social work's historical development embodies each of these realities.

HISTORY OF THE PROFESSION

The profession of social work dates back to the mid-1800s, when state charities began and institutions were established to deal with dependent populations such as the mentally ill, poor children, and people with disabilities. Prior to state intervention, mostly local churches and philanthropic organizations attempted to tackle social problems. But by the end of the nineteenth century these state-run institutions were failing and no longer providing quality care. Simultaneously, two movements emerged offering new ways of dealing with the poor and vulnerable in society: Charity Organization Societies and the Settlement House Movement. Each of these movements, both of which had roots in England, had approaches of dealing with social problems that embraced an ideological stance. The former adopted a conservative view that held that eradicating poverty meant that individual behavior had to be changed. The latter embraced a radical ideology that confirmed the need for fundamental social change.

Abraham Flexner (1866–1959), an educator who was considered an expert in evaluating professional standards and advocated for radical change in the way that medical schools trained doctors in the United States and Canada, said in 1915 that social work had not yet achieved profession status due to its lack of professional standards. Flexner was the author of the famous *Flexner Report* (1910), which had argued for increased standards in medical schools. He concluded that in order to be considered a profession, social work, like medicine, must have its own set of skills and specialized education that is based on scientific knowledge. Social work used this conclusion as an impetus to create and expand the types of setting for social work practice and paid attention to developing a knowledge base that was unique to social work. As a result of new practices, partly driven by the expansion of social welfare provisions in the 1930s, social work became acknowledged as a legitimate profession.

During the Great Depression of the 1930s the field witnessed an expansion in both the number of social workers and the type of work they did. Social work played a crucial role in helping shape and develop the United States's first institutional welfare program. In fact, a notable social worker, Harry Hopkins (1890–1946), headed Franklin Delano Roosevelt's emergency relief program, and another social worker, Jane Hoey (1892–1968), was the head of the Federal Bureau of Public Assistance. Since the 1930s social workers have been central in organizing and running governmental programs that aid the poor and needy.

After the New Deal and Social Security Act were passed, public perception about the profession of social work became more positive, and social work practice expanded greatly. Professional standards increased as well as academic requirements. Given the proliferation of services available to the public, the numbers in the profession increased greatly during these years. Social workers had a renewed sense that social reform was fundamental to their mission. From the 1940s to the 1970s social work was a growing field, expanding into many new arenas and continuing its professionalization project. The 1980s and 1990s were difficult for the social work profession, with massive government cuts to social spending and social welfare services. New social problems emerged that posed new challenges to social workers, such as high rates of incarceration, HIV/AIDS, and the crack epidemic. Some social problems that had been around for centuries—homelessness and domestic violence—increasingly became more politicized and addressed. The 1990s brought decentralization, whereby the federal government assumed less responsibility for the poor and needy, and states were required to do more to respond to vulnerable populations. This historical shift had implications for the social work profession, such as less federal funding and less support, and, as a result, social workers have had to continue developing creative alternatives to remedy social problems.

SOCIAL WORK EDUCATION

Social workers can be trained on a bachelor's (BA or BSW), master's (MSW), or doctoral level (PhD or DSW) of education. Each level produces a specialty of knowledge and depth of skill. Bachelor-level social workers are typically referred to as "frontline workers" who adopt a generalist orientation to social problems and who work in fields ranging from child welfare to domestic violence to services for the aging. Masters-level social workers are also educationally trained as generalist practitioners, but they receive additional training in a particular field such as clinical practice; children, youth, and families; gerontology; substance abuse; public policy; and not-for-profit management. Doctoral-level education in social work provides students with all of these, as well as training to assume leadership positions in agency work or to become faculty members at colleges and universities. In 1952 the Council on Social Work Education (CSWE) was established to oversee curricula within schools of social work. The council is the accrediting body of schools of social work on both the bachelors and masters levels.

SOCIAL WORK'S PUBLIC IMAGE

Today there are approximately 600,000 people who hold social work degrees. According to the Bureau of Labor Statistics, social work is one of the fastest-growing careers in the United States. Given this rise, the profession has received increased public attention, both positive and negative. Public perception of the profession is often misinformed. According to the 2000 census, 845,000 individuals self-identified as social workers. Many individuals who work in the field of human services identify themselves as social workers, yet they do not have any formal social work education. This contributes to the misinformation about the profession, its scope of work, and the educational training required by schools of social work. Many states have passed legislation to protect the title "social worker," restricting it to those who have completed a social work degree from an accredited institution of higher learning.

In 1955 the National Association of Social Workers (NASW) was formed. NASW is the largest membership organization representing professional social workers. It "works to enhance the professional growth and development of its members, to create and maintain professional standards, and to advance sound social policies" (National Association of Social Workers 2006).

Social work is a complicated profession. Like sociology and psychology, there are competing views and traditions, ranging from conservative to liberal to radical, each of which embraces a different ideology and set of practices. Social work has a long and rich history, becoming institutionalized in state programs and during the New Deal in federal programs. Today, there are nearly one million social work professionals in the United States practicing in nearly every setting. Social work's growth is likely to continue, producing positive outcomes in the lives of individuals as well as institutions.

SEE ALSO *Interventions, Social Skills*

BIBLIOGRAPHY

Axinn, June, and Mark J. Stern. 2001. *Social Welfare: A History of the American Response to Need.* Boston: Allyn and Bacon.

Bailey, Roy, and Mike Brake. 1976. *Radical Social Work.* London: Edward Arnold Publishers.

Cloward, Richard A., and Frances Fox Piven. 1977. The Acquiescence of Social Work. *Society* 14 (2): 55–63.

Jansson, Bruce. 2001. *The Reluctant Welfare State.* Belmont, CA: Brooks/Cole.

Katz, Michael. 1986. *In the Shadow of the Poorhouse: A Social History of Welfare America.* New York: Basic Books.

Leiby, James. 1979. *A History of Social Welfare and Social Work in the United States.* New York: Columbia University Press.

Lubove, Roy. 1965. *The Professional Altruist: The Emergence of Social Work as a Career, 1890–1930.* Cambridge, MA: Harvard University Press.

National Association of Social Workers. 2006. http://www.naswdc.org.

Piven, Frances Fox, and Richard A. Cloward. 1971. *Regulating the Poor.* New York: Pantheon Books.

Reisch, Michael, and Janice L. Andrews. 2001. *The Road Not Taken: A History of Radical Social Work in the United States.* Philadelphia: Brunner-Routledge.

Trattner, Walter. 1979. *From Poor Law to Welfare State: A History of Social Welfare in America.* New York: Free Press.

Susanna Jones

SOCIALISM

Socialism can be defined as a political ideology that endorses the equality of power. Socialists believe that the existence of unequal material relationships is evidence of unequal political and social power in any given society. The goals of all socialists are the same: collective living and working arrangements, equal distribution of wealth, and equality of power. The attainment of these goals would guarantee a moral human society with happiness, equality, brotherhood, and community as foundational values.

The methods used to attain these goals have differed according to unique historical circumstances. Some socialists have endorsed industrial efficiency, while others have argued for a return to a "primitive," nonindustrial stage of human history. Additionally, certain socialists have valued organization, control, discipline, hierarchy, leadership by experts, compulsion, violent revolution, and messianic elitism over gradual change, democratism, and pacifism to develop a socialist society. Socialists have sometimes appealed to nationalism and patriotism to recruit supporters. Other times they have proposed a more cosmopolitan philosophy of human organization. The role of the state has often been at the heart of these contradictory approaches. Some socialist states have created dictatorial governments to destroy traditional society and replace it with a pseudosocialist one. Other socialist movements have called for the creation of a just welfare state to take the primary responsibility for providing adequate housing, health care, pensions, and unemployment benefits to all citizens. Alternately, Communists have worked to eradicate the state apparatus entirely, instead offering a purely democratic structure of power relationships.

HISTORICAL EXPLANATION FOR THE RISE OF SOCIALISM

The formulation of socialism as a political ideology occurred between 1815 (the end of the Napoleonic era) and 1848 (the publication year of Karl Marx's *Communist Manifesto* and a year of liberal, nationalist revolutions across Europe) as a particular response to the French Revolution and the Industrial Revolution. The French Revolution of 1789 began the slow destruction of the ancien régime in Western Europe and ushered in the modern period of liberal democracy and industrialization. During this process, the bourgeoisie replaced the aristocracy as the dominant social class, and as the abolition of serfdom swept across Europe during the Napoleonic Wars, European peasants left the villages and migrated to the cities to work in the new industries of the nineteenth century. The population of European cities exploded during this era of urbanization, and the new industrial working classes suffered tremendously from horrid living and working conditions.

The "dual revolution," as the simultaneous liberal and industrial revolutions of the nineteenth century are called, created a social, political, and economic system that destroyed the traditional identities of Europeans, a system that had been founded on values of community, and instead legitimized an individualism that favored white, male property owners. The promotion of a minority of the European population at the expense of the workers, peasants, and women of all social classes angered socialist intellectuals, who criticized the failure of liberal democracy to extend fundamental human rights to all peoples. Though professing that liberalism would bring about progress in Europe through the destruction of legally defined social groups and the introduction of the right to vote, the right to free assembly, an end to censor-

ship, equality before the law, social mobility, and economic freedom, socialists charged that liberal democracy merely created a new bourgeois-dominated social hierarchy that exploited the working classes for personal gain. They saw the liberal promise of economic freedom as a dangerous one because it guaranteed only workers' rights to sell their labor to the highest bidder, and since wages in a capitalist system are tied to market forces, industrial society justified its exploitation of workers as being a kind of natural economic state. Socialists thus viewed liberal capitalism as an immoral system.

Liberal democracy and socialism in the nineteenth century were therefore antithetical: Whose rights should be protected—those of the bourgeoisie to possess private property or those of the working classes against the vagrancies of capitalism? At the heart of this dispute were differing ideas of the intrinsic goodness and value of private property. Liberal capitalists viewed private property as the most sacred of all human rights, while socialists viewed it as the root of all evil in the modern world. Another controversial debate was the natural state of humanity: Is communal organization the foundation of natural law? Can and should we use some definition of natural law to judge existing social institutions? Early nineteenth-century socialists agreed with Enlightenment thinker Jean-Jacques Rousseau (1712–1778), who argued that men are social by nature and naturally want to do and be good. Humanity therefore had the ability to return to this "natural" state through a process of purification. Rousseau also argued that the fall of humanity began with the introduction of private property.

Rousseau inspired the first French socialists, the egalitarians, who reacted violently to the fact that the French Revolution did not bring about social equality or abolish material wealth in the early nineteenth century. Egalitarians urged the people to seize power, do away with social hierarchy, and institute a commonwealth. They also advocated the use of terrorism to dispossess the wealthy and redistribute private property equally among all members of society. In this early stage of socialist development, the abolition of private property was not yet part of the political agenda and the goal was to end the misery of the poor. The egalitarians introduced the idea that the community was more valuable than individuals in isolation. Egalitarianism also endorses a pure democracy without party divisions. Service, devotion, and sacrifice for the sake of community were the hallmarks of egalitarianism.

Socialism took on a more organized form with the rise of utopianism in the 1830s. Charles Fourier (1772–1837), often referred to as the father of utopian socialism, argued that industrialization and liberal democracy did not constitute historical progress. He firmly placed the critique of bourgeois society in the greater context of the rise of the materialization of humankind. Bourgeois society, he argued, reflected a fundamental departure from the foundation of human social life. Fourier rejected the progressive function of industry and technology and instead advocated for the creation of communal organization based upon agricultural units he called *phalanstères*. Along with this rejection of industrial capitalism, Fourier demanded minimum public regulation of individuals and a maximum level of individual freedom. Total gender equality, guaranteed by the destruction of marriage as a social institution, was also a major component of his philosophy.

Fellow utopian socialist Henri de Saint-Simon (1760–1825) rejected Fourier's denunciation of industry and focused his critique of liberal capitalist society on increasing workers' economic and political power, clearly defining socialism as an economic doctrine. Saint-Simon argued that order and efficiency were natural characteristics of humans. Since the interests of entrepreneurs and workers were identical—to increase political status through productivity—human beings would naturally agree to a collective social and economic construction once they realized how profitable such an arrangement could be. Private property, Saint-Simonians charged, was therefore incompatible with the efficiency of the industrial system. By transferring private property to the state, which would be controlled by an association of workers, privileges of birth would disappear. Additionally, the banking system, acting as a social institution, would coordinate the economy for the entire society. Saint-Simon also advocated for female emancipation and special care for paupers and criminals, all of whom he considered to be victims of the immoral bourgeois capitalist state. These radical changes would allow for the moral regeneration of society to occur. Fourier's and Saint-Simon's contradictory critiques of industrial society and visions of the future illuminated the controversial aspects of socialist thought in its early years.

The French utopian socialists greatly influenced German philosopher, historian, sociologist, and economist Karl Marx in the mid-nineteenth century. The *Communist Manifesto*, published by Marx and his partner Friedrich Engels in 1848, presented a theory of history in which an inevitable communist revolution led by industrial workers, the proletariat, would destroy bourgeois capitalist society. While utopian socialism in its various manifestations can loosely be defined as a worldview that promised individuals a full sense of belonging to a progressive communal society, Marx's Communist theory at this early point in his career outlined a specific path toward the attainment of this goal. Marx viewed the history of mankind as being propelled forward by class warfare. He argued that human beings' identities are defined by their economic relationships to one another, not by

religion or other social constructs. The dominant social class, therefore, uses its political and economic position to exploit the subordinate social classes. The struggle between social groups, and the revolutionary attempts of the subordinate classes to destroy the ruling class, is what moves history forward. He called this process dialectical materialism.

In the context of nineteenth-century European industrial society, Marx forecast that the industrial proletariat would overthrow the capitalist bourgeoisie and the revolutionary cycle would end because, for the first time in history, the revolutionary class would represent the majority of the population. The revolution, Marx predicted, would occur on a worldwide scale as members of the proletariat in every industrialized country would spontaneously revolt. Industry would quickly spread to nonindustrialized portions of the world and all societies would become one large "workers' paradise." In the process, nations would cease to exist as primary determiners of an individual's identity. The new communist system would guarantee total equality among all people through collective ownership of the means of production (such as land, machines, factories, tools, and animals), the abolition of private property, and collective living arrangements. The establishment of a complete democracy under such conditions would allow for the "withering away" of the state apparatus and the complete spiritual fulfillment of each individual.

The failure of the Paris Commune (1871) to install a socialist society in France prompted Marx to question this early assertion that a spontaneous and violent revolution was the only path toward socialism. In his later works, Marx tacitly acknowledged the possibility of a peaceful transition to socialism in those societies with mature democratic political systems. This move away from the notion that the excesses of liberal capitalism would naturally produce a proletariat revolution laid the foundation for democratic socialism to emerge as a Marxist political ideology in the late nineteenth century. This inconsistency in Marx's philosophy of revolution allowed future communists and social democrats alike to claim him as the founding father of their radically different processes of revolutionary change. However divergent in their methods, atheistic socialist revolutionary movements around the world shared a common belief in Marx's materialist interpretation of the human experience, one that charged religion with being the "opiate of the people" in the twentieth century.

HISTORICAL EXAMPLES OF SOCIALISM

Vladimir Ilyich Lenin led the world's first socialist revolution in Russia in 1917. Lenin compromised the democratic foundation of Marx's vision by using dictatorial revolutionary tactics to destroy the Russian autocracy and establish socialism. Because Russia lacked the large industrial proletariat needed to complete the Communist revolution, Soviet leaders created a totalitarian version of socialism. Each individual was equally submissive to the dictator—stripped of basic human rights, controlled by secret police forces and spy networks, educated by socialist propaganda, and forced to conform to a new identity as a Soviet socialist citizen. With its focus on industrialization, Marxian socialism in the Soviet Union became an ideology of modernity instead of communism.

The Soviet revolutionary model was widely adopted around the world in the 1940s and 1950s. After World War II, Stalin's takeover of Eastern Europe imposed Soviet communism there. In 1949, Mao Zedong led a nationalist and anti-imperialist Communist revolution in China where the peasantry, rather than the proletariat, was considered to be the revolutionary class. Mao's socialist revolution was also a political and military struggle against imperialist powers (most notably Japan) instead of a Marxist class struggle. Guerrilla warfare, therefore, drove the revolution, rather than the organization of a labor movement or a political party. This pattern of socialist revolution was repeated in North Vietnam in 1954 by Ho Chi Minh. In both the Chinese and Vietnamese cases, the Soviet Union offered heavy support to the revolutionaries in order to extend its sphere of influence across Asia.

In 1959, Cuban leader Fidel Castro established the first socialist government in Latin America. Castro's revolution, however, concerned itself more with the conquest of power than ideology. After a short period of euphoric hope that Latin America might be able to throw off imperialist control through the adoption of Castro's socialism, many Latin American socialists in the 1960s and 1970s rejected his dictatorial model. They also repudiated Marx's atheism and used the power of their Catholic faith to fight against unjust socioeconomic structures. Liberation theology, as the movement was called, argued that the Church's preferential treatment of the poor be involved in political struggles.

Socialism in Africa emerged after the exit of colonial powers in the 1960s. African socialists generally condemned capitalism and worked to protect human dignity, though their goals and methods varied from region to region. Africans' desire to create a postcolonial national identity free from imperialist economic exploitation accounts for this variety.

Alternatively, revisionist socialists in Eastern and Western Europe in the 1950s and 1960s attempted to resurrect the social democratic foundation of Marxism. They rejected the Soviet dictatorial model of communism as well as the Western liberal capitalist model of modernity.

Supporters of the New Left of the 1970s and 1980s dedicated themselves to establishing just social, economic, and political domestic and international structures. The fall of the Soviet Union in the early 1990s effectively destroyed the dictatorial socialist model in Europe, with most European countries working to develop liberal capitalist societies that guarantee freedoms and rights for all individuals.

SEE ALSO *Capitalism; Castro, Fidel; Communism; Cuban Revolution; Egalitarianism; French Revolution; Left and Right; Lenin, Vladimir Ilitch; Liberalism; Marx, Karl; Marxism; Materialism; Minh, Ho Chi; Nationalism and Nationality; Patriotism; Peasantry; Philosophy, Political; Planning; Political Theory; Russian Revolution; Stalin, Joseph; Totalitarianism; Union of Soviet Socialist Republics; Vietnam War; Welfare State*

BIBLIOGRAPHY

Blackburn, Robin, ed. 1991. *After the Fall: The Failure of Communism and the Future of Socialism.* New York: Verso.

Harrington, Michael. 1989. *Socialism: Past and Future.* New York: Arcade.

Howe, Irving, ed. 1986. *Essential Works of Socialism.* New Haven, CT: Yale University Press.

Kilroy-Silk, Robert. 1973. *Socialism Since Marx.* New York: Taplinger.

Lichtheim, George. 1970. *A Short History of Socialism.* New York: Praeger.

Radice, Giles. 1966. *Democratic Socialism: A Short Survey.* New York: Praeger.

Sassoon, Don. 1996. *One Hundred Years of Socialism: The West European Left in the Twentieth Century.* New York: New Press.

Ulam, Adam B. 1979. *The Unfinished Revolution: Marxism and Communism in the Modern World.* Boulder, CO.: Westview Press.

Tracey A. Pepper

SOCIALISM, AFRICAN

There are two basic models of African socialism that represent its variations and development on the continent (Rosberg and Callaghy 1979). The first, more populist type refers to a "first wave" of socialist regimes that emerged during the early years of independence—from the late 1950s throughout the following decade. Flexible, pragmatic, and attuned to local conditions, these first socialist governments in Africa recovered the communalism of traditional culture after breaking free from colonial domination. The second leading model represents a "second wave" of more militant regimes that consolidated power during the 1970s, favoring scientific socialism, an exclusive vanguard party, and a command-style economy while renouncing the false consciousness of traditional culture. These two models are of course abstractions and should not obscure the discrepancies between theory and practice, rhetoric and realpolitik, as well as principles and personalities found within each "ideal type." If a populist-socialist such as Julius Nyerere (Tanzania) could force resettlement in Ujamaa villages (Khapoya 1994, p. 202), a vanguard Leninist such as Marien Ngouabi (Congo-Brazzaville) could protect French interests in phosphates and timber (Decalo 1979, pp. 258–259). Indeed, given that all African economies remain fundamentally mixed and export oriented, African socialism may well be more about the political manipulation of ideological resources than the public ownership of the means of production, particularly in the geopolitical context of the cold war. Nonetheless, the rise and fall of such powerful ideologies illuminates the broader historical forces that shaped African socialism and account for its different forms. One must begin with a discussion of the ideological origins of African socialism before moving on to its first and second "waves" of implementation.

HISTORICAL ANTECEDENTS: THE GENEALOGY OF AN IDEA

The mythic origins of African socialism are found in Victorian evolutionism, with primitive hordes, group marriages, and the glaring absence of private property representing the earliest stages of society. Ethnologists such as E. B. Tylor and Lewis Henry Morgan established unilineal pathways from savagery to civilization that reinforced the racial hierarchies of imperial ideology with blacks at the bottom and whites at the top. The influence of this evolutionary perspective was pervasive, informing Sir Henry Maine's transition from status to contract in comparative law, Ferdinand Tönnies's sociological distinction between *Gemeinschaft* and *Gesellschaft*, and of course the "primitive communism" of Marx's pre-alienated man. When mapped onto the ur-terrain of the Dark Continent, a romanticized image of an original socialist Africa took shape, laying the foundation for the varieties of Pan-Africanism that developed in the first half of the twentieth century.

Edward Blyden (1832–1912) is generally acknowledged as a founding father of Pan-Africanism and its associated socialist traditions. Born in Saint Thomas and raised in Venezuela and the United States, Blyden moved to Liberia, where he advocated the repatriation of blacks to Monrovia. His ethnographic forays into West African hinterlands—commissioned by the British Crown—inspired such important works as *Christianity, Islam, and the Negro Race* (1887) and *African Life and Customs* (1908), in which he moved away from Christianity toward Islamic and indigenous frameworks for African government and self-determination. Of "pagan Africa" he wrote: "Social life … is communistic or co-operative. All work for each, and each work for all," citing such proverbial wisdom as "What is *mine* goes; what is *ours* abides" (Blyden 1979, pp. 81, 89). Challenging Victorian myths of primitive savagery with utopian counter-myths of African socialism, Blyden's stylized portrait of the continent would be refined in the writings of W. E. B. Du Bois (1939), Carter G. Woodson (1936), and in the Négritude of Leopold Sédar Senghor, all of which effected an important ideological transformation. Reworking the imperial opposition between civilization and barbarism, in which racial stereotypes between whites and blacks were largely preserved, Pan-Africanism reversed the hierarchy itself. The individualistic, hyperrational, industrializing societies and economies of the West were no longer signs of superior civilization but symptoms of profound alienation, expressed by the very separation of mind and body diagnostic of Western enlightenment. Africans, by contrast, were more "organic," integrating mind and body, feeling and thought, and most importantly, self and community into collective forms of ownership and everyday life. Africa emerged as a positive foil against which the West was negatively recast, with its crime rates, rapacious greed, and growing inequality. The historical arrows were similarly reversed. Whereas the racist Hamitic Hypothesis of imperial discourse attributed the cultural achievements of Africa—such as political centralization or the invention of iron—to exogenous infusions of "Hamitic" or "caucasoid" blood, the Pan-African vision attributed Africa's decline to the depredations of foreign conquerors and slavers who undermined the traditional fabric of economy and community. Identified and recovered, the socialist underpinnings of Pan-African culture would restore Africa's rightful place in the world.

The Pan-African project took shape against the formal frameworks of European colonization at the turn of the twentieth century. The important Pan-African philosophies of this movement, including Léopold Senghor's "Négritude" and Kwame Nkrumah's "African Personality," cannot be separated from the congresses and colloquia that brought together activists and intellectuals from Africa and the African diaspora. (One of the best comparisons of Négritude and African personality remains Irele [1990]). The four Pan-African congresses organized by Du Bois in 1919, 1921, 1923, and 1937 were framed primarily in terms of race, challenging the "color-bar" through Pan-African alliances that included British socialists such as Sidney and Beatrice Webb, Harold Laski, and H. G. Wells. But the fifth, so-called Manchester Congress held in 1945, reflecting the rising influence of George Padmore, signaled an explicit shift toward decolonization, mobilizing Africans in discourses of trade unionism, socialism, and self-government. It also influenced the careers of Nkrumah, Azikiwe, and Kenyatta, who became icons of independent nationhood. Nkrumah went on to organize the Union of African States (1960) with Guinea and Mali joined by Morocco, Algeria, and Egypt to form the Casablanca group (1961) with a militant commitment to continental unity.

Thus formed a "militant wing" of the Pan-Africanist movement, countered by the more pragmatic Brazzaville and Monrovia groups seeking socialist solutions through economic regionalism. Tensions between militant and moderate socialisms; between national, regional, and continental priorities; between North African and sub-Saharan "cultural" divides; and between inherited colonial philosophical dispositions persisted within the Pan-African community, not only in the Dakar Colloquium (1962), where Senghor reasserted Négritude's universalism, but also within the Organization of African Unity after it was founded in 1963. Nonetheless, a general model of "open" African socialism emerged (Senghor 1964), emphasizing state-directed public-sector development, trade unionism, marketing cooperatives, people's banks, limited land reform, independence from foreign export markets, political mobilization through mass party organization, commitment to egalitarianism, and relative geopolitical autonomy based on the indigenous values of African cultural unity. Principled autonomy from the Soviet Union was also a major theme of the Afro-Asiatic Bandung Conference in 1955, a conference considered by Senghor (1959, p. 3) as the twentieth century's equivalent of the 1847 Congress of the Federation of Communists, which commissioned "The Communist Manifesto." Pan-African in rhetoric, African socialism took root after independence within the political confines of the new nation-states.

THE FIRST WAVE: POPULIST-SOCIALIST REGIMES

It is difficult to separate the first socialist experiments in Africa from the charismatic leaders who brokered independence, such as Kwame Nkrumah in Ghana, Léopold Senghor in Senegal, Sékou Touré in Guinea, Modibo Keita in Mali, Amilcar Cabral in Guinea-Bissau, Kenneth Kaunda in Zambia, and Julius Nyerere in Tanzania. Nkrumah's brand of socialism is hard to pin down as it shifted between nationalism and Marxism, public-sector development and multinational capital, respect for traditional socialist values and disdain for traditional "reactionary" chiefs, and finally, between the mass principles and exclusionary practices of its ruling Convention People's Party (Apter 1972). Squeezing cocoa farmers through its

extractive marketing boards, the state sought to underwrite industrialization and infrastructural development, but as debt increased and productivity dropped, the economy slid into a downward spiral. Fearing political conspiracies within and neocolonial enemies from abroad, Nkrumah became increasingly radicalized and isolated and was ousted by a coup d'état in 1966. In similar trajectories of socialist development and decline, Modibo Keita in resource-poor Mali and Sékou Touré of mineral-rich Guinea collectivized agriculture, nationalized banking, and blended Marxism with African cultural models. In both cases, peasant producers lost out in the reforms, and agriculture stagnated. Whereas Keita was overthrown by a coup in 1968, Touré, who died in 1984, gradually abandoned his socialist policies for Western economic investment.

The most extensive socialist project based on "African" principles was Nyerere's Ujamaa villagization scheme, in what became the hallmark of Tanzania's commitment to self-reliance. In *Ujamaa: Essays on Socialism* (1968), Nyerere offers a doctrine of traditional extended "familyhood" (*ujamaa*) as a blueprint for African unity and development. Enshrined in the Arusha Declaration of 1967, this doctrine rejected heavy industrialization, with its dependency on foreign capital, in favor of collectively organized agricultural production in newly formed Ujamaa villages. What began as "voluntaristic, grass-roots, cooperative socialism," however, became "socialism imposed from above" (Young 1982, pp.114–115) as recalcitrant peasant producers in scattered peasant homesteads were relocated into cooperative communities. Dean McHenry (1979, p. 43) estimates that 91.3 percent of the rural population was living in ujamaa villages by 1976. Although villagization, combined with Scandinavian aid, improved education, medical care, and public utilities in the rural areas, an overall decline in peasant production, including severe food shortages in 1974, eventually brought the experiment to an end. Nyerere resigned in 1985 to make way for neoliberal reforms, but his legacy of national unity and the correlative absence of ethnic politics in Tanzania has endured.

THE SECOND WAVE: SCIENTIFIC-SOCIALIST REGIMES

If the first wave of African socialist states in the 1960s sought the recovery of cultural traditions (Senegal and Tanzania more than Ghana and Guinea), the scientific socialist regimes of the 1970s emphasized more radical ruptures—from the shackles of tradition, from colonial domination, and from preceding military juntas. Elevating a Leninist-styled vanguard party to control the state, these more centralized regimes used the language of class analysis in claiming peasants and workers as their social base, attacking incipient class formation, and thereby justifying coercion in the persecution of political dissidents and internal enemies. In many areas, however, ideological principle was tempered by realism: If foreign owned banks and insurance companies were easily nationalized, more capital-intensive and productive multinationals were given freer rein as revenue-generating engines of growth. In geopolitical terms, greater solidarity with the Soviet bloc in the United Nations did not translate into firm Soviet trade relations and aid. Many of the Afro-Marxist regimes remained interested in Western capital investment, and thus economically nonaligned.

Crawford Young (1982) distinguishes military Marxist regimes from those that grew out of national liberation movements against Portuguese colonialism. Among the former, Congo-Brazzaville was the first to establish a Marxist regime in 1969, when Marien Ngouabi declared a People's Republic and inaugurated the Parti Congolais du Travail (PCT). Somalia followed under Mohammed Siad Barre in 1970, when Soviet military interests enabled Somali national consolidation within an enduring Islamic idiom. In the Republic of Benin, Major Mathieu Kerekou created the Leninist Parti Révolutionaire du Peuple Beninois (PRPB) in 1975, developing new public corporations and peasant cooperatives without sacrificing economic relations with France. A more radical Marxist-Leninist state was implemented in Ethiopia by the revolutionary Derg ("committee"), a secret inner circle of the military who deposed Emperor Haile Selassie in 1975 and instituted major reforms, including the nationalization of land ownership and tenancy to undermine the Amharic feudal aristocracy. Given its notorious "Red Terror" and rule through fear and intimidation, however, the Derg never secured popular legitimacy (Donham 1999).

Notable among national liberation movements were the protracted struggles in Angola and Mozambique against entrenched Portuguese settlers and political overrule that lasted until 1975. In Angola, a bloody civil war became a cold war battleground where a sizable force of Soviet and Cuban soldiers (20,000) and technicians (17,000) backed the Movimento Popular de Libertação de Angola (MPLA) against Jonas Savimbi's reactionary União Nacional para a Independencia Total de Angola (UNITA), supported by South Africa and the United States. (Angola's political identification with the former Soviet Union still resonates from the hammer and sickle on its national flag.)

By the 1990s, the Leninist role of the MPLA degenerated into coveted disbursements of economic and political patronage based on control over oil and diamonds (Hodges 2004). In Mozambique, socialism developed through similar struggles against the Portuguese and, after independence, during a long civil war with South African-

backed Renamo rebels. Samora Machel's revolutionary vanguard party, FRELIMO, emerged as a highly disciplined organization supporting liberation movements in former Rhodesia and South Africa while promoting women's rights, peasant collectives, state farms, and heavy industry at home. The dislocations of the civil war, however, and the atrocities of the Renamo fighters, exacted a heavy toll on the country and economy after a cease-fire was signed in 1992.

If socialism in Africa, like elsewhere, lost ground after the collapse of the Eastern bloc and the rising tide of neoliberal reforms, its central concerns have not withered away (Saul 2001). These remain the role of the state in regulating trade, the growing inequalities associated with economic liberalization, the political economy of "tribalism," and the complex character of class formation in postcolonial Africa. Like the colonial heritage that it fought and opposed, socialism in Africa—even when disavowed—remains deeply embedded in the politics of national development (Pitcher and Askew 2006).

SEE ALSO *Anticolonial Movements; Capitalism; Christianity; Civilization; Collectivism; Colonialism; Decolonization; Dependency Theory; Du Bois, W. E. B.; Ethnology and Folklore; Gemeinschaft and Gesellschaft; Leninism; Liberalization, Trade; Liberation Movements; Neocolonialism; Neoliberalism; Nkrumah, Kwame; Nyerere, Julius; Pan-Africanism; Primitivism; Socialism; Socialism, Christian; Socialism, Islamic; Union of Soviet Socialist Republics*

BIBLIOGRAPHY

Apter, David E. 1972. *Ghana in Transition.* 2nd ed. Princeton, NJ: Princeton University Press.

Blyden, Edward W. 1979. Extracts from *African Life and Customs.* In *Ideologies of Liberation in Black Africa, 1856–1970: Documents on Modern African Political Thought from Colonial Times to the Present,* ed. J. Ayo Langley, 78–87. London: Rex Collings.

Decalo, Samuel. 1979. Ideological Rhetoric and Scientific Socialism in Benin and Congo/Brazzaville. In *Socialism in Sub-Saharan Africa: A New Assessment,* ed. Carl Rosberg and Thomas Callaghy, 231–264. Berkeley, CA: Institute of International Studies.

Donham, Donald. 1999. *Marxist Modern: An Ethnographic History of the Ethiopian Revolution.* Berkeley: University of California Press.

Du Bois, W. E. B. 1939. *Black Folk, Then and Now: An Essay in the History and Sociology of the Negro Race.* New York: Henry Holt.

Engels, Friedrich. 1972. *The Origin of the Family, Private Property, and the State, in the Light of the Researches of Lewis H. Morgan.* New York: International Publishers.

Hodges, Tony. 2004. *Angola: Anatomy of an Oil State.* 2nd ed. Oslo: Fridtjof Nansen Institute (in association with James

Currey, Oxford, U.K., and Indiana University Press, Bloomington).

Irele, Abiola. 1990. *The African Experience in Literature and Ideology.* Bloomington: Indiana University Press.

Khapoya, Vincent B. 1994. *The African Experience: An Introduction.* Englewood Cliffs, NJ: Prentice Hall.

McHenry, Dean E. 1979. The Struggle for Rural Socialism in Tanzania. In *Socialism in Sub-Saharan Africa: A New Assessment*, ed. Carl Rosberg and Thomas Callaghy, 37–60. Berkeley, CA: Institute of International Studies.

Nyerere, Julius. 1968. *Ujamaa: Essays on Socialism.* London: Oxford University Press.

Pitcher, M. Anne, and Kelly M. Askew. 2006. African Socialisms and Postsocialisms. *Africa* 76 (1): 1–14.

Rosberg, Carl, and Thomas Callaghy, eds. 1979. *Socialism in Sub-Saharan Africa: A New Assessment.* Berkeley, CA: Institute of International Studies.

Saul, John. 2001. *Millennial Africa: Capitalism, Socialism, Democracy.* Trenton, NJ: Africa World Press.

Senghor, Léopold S. 1959. *African Socialism: A Report to the Constitutive Congress of the Party of African Federation.* Trans. Mercer Cook. New York: American Society of African Culture.

Senghor, Léopold S. 1964. *On African Socialism.* Trans. Mercer Cook. New York: Praeger.

Young, Crawford. 1982. *Ideology and Development in Africa.* New Haven, CT: Yale University Press.

Woodson, Carter G. 1936. *The African Background Outlined; or, Handbook for the Study of the Negro.* Washington, DC: Association for the Study of Negro Life and History.

Andrew Apter

SOCIALISM, CHRISTIAN

In 1848 Karl Marx dismissed Christian Socialism as "the holy water with which the priest consecrates the heart-burnings of the aristocrat" (Marx [1848] 1967). His immediate, if unstated, target was the group of Anglicans around the theologian F. D. Maurice, who that year in London began a short-lived publication, *The Christian Socialist.* The occasion for their emergence—sympathy with Chartism—was political, and an important part of their activity was practical social witness, such as Maurice's foundation of the Working Men's College in 1854. Their Christian Socialism was thus reformist rather than radical and operated within a theological as well as a political context. As Maurice explained, he chose the term Christian Socialist to differentiate them from both "the unsocial Christians and the unChristian socialists" (quoted in Wilkinson 1998). The former were targets because of the pietistic emphasis on individual salvation of contemporary evangelicalism, and for political reasons. At the time Christian views of political economy were prima-

rily shaped by emphases on responsibility: either in Malthus's warnings about the demoralizing effects of the Poor Law or in the comforting commonplace of the time that he who pursues his own best interests is also supplying the interests of the community as a whole. Maurice attacked such views and the laissez-faire orthodoxy they reflected. Socialism for him, however, seems to have been largely about the church addressing the people inclusively rather than individually, not least through reformist social activity rather than the establishment of an alternative political economy.

Although the term *Christian Socialism* was popularized in this distinctive nineteenth-century context, it drew, as even Marx acknowledged, upon both biblical and ecclesiastical precepts. It may have been at this point that Christian Socialism began to emerge as a distinct witness, but those who followed in Maurice's footsteps could associate their views with a much longer tradition. From the Old Testament the providence of land and the Jewish institution of Jubilee implied divine sanction of equal shares in the means of production and divine prohibition of private accumulation, while the prophets provided examples of denunciations of injustice. The New Testament furnishes strictures against the rich and the money changers, while Christ's message that, instead of the love of self implied by such accumulation, people should love one another became, by the late nineteenth century, the basis for claims that Jesus was the first socialist. And the sharing of all things in common and their distribution according to need in the early church (Acts 2: 44–47; 4: 32–37) suggested protosocialist communities.

There were a number of attempts to re-create such communities in the early nineteenth century. Étienne Cabet in France saw the rise of the medieval church as having corrupted early Christianity, the ideals of which he sought to recapture in utopian communities. The non-Christian Robert Owen simultaneously experimented with such communities in Britain and America. Although his ideas were to influence Maurice, both his and Cabet's communities ended in failure. Meanwhile, the shadowy League of the Just founded in 1836 and largely composed of German exiles in London was transformed from a body calling for the realization of the Kingdom of God on Earth through universal brotherhood in 1847 into the purported commissioners of Marx's *Communist Manifesto*, which sought to achieve the ideal society through class struggle instead.

Some Christians accepted this diagnosis, while rejecting both the materialistic basis of Marxism and its facile assumption that an ideal society requires merely the expunging of class exploitation. They were, however, in a new situation, in which positivistic secular creeds sought to explain the human condition or express social ideals without necessarily having recourse to religious frameworks. Socialism could still benefit from the imprimatur of Christianity, but it could also become a rival creed to churches seen as more focused on salvation in the next world rather than this one. In continental Europe, as well, papal hostility to this challenge in Pius IX's *Syllabus of Errors* (1864), as well as the extent to which Catholicism had become associated with defense of the established order, meant that nineteenth-century socialism there frequently had a distinctly anticlerical flavor. Despite the efforts of, for instance, Bishop Kettler of Mainz in the 1860s, this antipathy was not to be mitigated until after Leo XIII's encyclical *Rerum Novarum* in 1891, which, while still condemning socialism, was much more open to labor organizations.

The more pluralistic political and religious culture of the Anglophone world produced different effects. An emphasis on the Incarnation and the corporate life of the church led Anglo-Catholics such as Stewart Headlam to revive Christian Socialism in the 1870s and 1880s. Walter Rauschenbusch's emphasis in the 1890s on the Kingdom of God as an endeavor for this life, not the next, was also to have wide influence. It led to a positive view of state intervention. Contemporary economic and social developments, especially the emergence of more rigid class differences and secular socialist parties, were also prompting this trend. A "Social Gospel," intended to bridge the gulf to the working classes by a mixture of social work in poorer areas and a generalized language of social welfare, appeared in both Britain and America around the end of the nineteenth century.

In America such figures as Washington Gladden emphasized a new concordat between capital and labor, not least through just wages and profit sharing. Meanwhile, in Edwardian Britain, the more radical idea of Guild Socialism came into vogue. This was an attempt to find ways for workers themselves to directly control their production and entrench the dignity of labor against the materialism of collective socialism. Grounded in part in medieval romanticism, practical expression was most nearly achieved by the guild organization in the building trades established by Quaker businessman Malcolm Sparks after World War I. Such ideas, however, did not long survive in the difficult economic climate of the interwar years.

Anglo-Catholic enthusiasm for a corporate and social expression in faith led instead to experiments such as the Christendom Group around Maurice Reckitt. Meanwhile, within the Roman Catholic Church, while the rise of Catholic Action as a means of engaging with modern conditions prompted a growing accent on social welfare by the 1930s, the theocratic nature of much of Catholic political thought militated against its being expressed in radical political ways. Exceptions included

the Catholic Worker Movement founded by Dorothy Day and Peter Maurin in New York in 1933.

Significant change came with Vatican II in the early 1960s. In particular, its more active approach to pastoral care opened the way for political engagement. This was particularly true in Catholic Latin America, where popular protest against the extreme social inequalities of the Continent were already gathering strength in the wake of the 1958 Cuban revolution. Bishops meeting in Medellín in 1968 concluded that the Church had to be not only for the poor but of the poor. The focus, as developed in Gustavo Gutiérrez's *A Theology of Liberation* (1971), was on God's preferential love for the poor and oppressed, expressed, not least, by Christ himself identifying with their suffering on the cross. This perspective was subsequently to find wide application, particularly in the developing world.

Christian Socialism, then, is to some extent contextual and does not involve a single political or theological viewpoint. It has developed in relation both to secular socialist movements—some of which, like the British Labour Party, now have affiliated Christian organizations—and the wider churches. What is distinctive throughout, however, is the view that a more socially just society requires changes in people's attitudes toward one another rather than simply in the social system.

SEE ALSO *Christianity; Egalitarianism; Jesus Christ; Labour Party (Britain); Liberation Theology; Malthus, Thomas Robert; Marx, Karl; Roman Catholic Church; Socialism; Vatican, The*

BIBLIOGRAPHY

Bryant, Chris. 1996. *Possible Dreams: A Personal History of the British Christian Socialists.* London: Hodder and Stoughton.

Gutiérrez, Gustavo. 1971. *A Theology of Liberation: History, Politics, and Salvation.* Maryknoll, NY: Orbis.

Jones, Peter d'A. 1968. *The Christian Socialist Revival 1877–1914: Religion, Class and Social Conscience in Late-Victorian England.* Princeton, NJ: Princeton University Press.

Marx, Karl. 1848. *The Communist Manifesto.* Harmondsworth, U.K.: Penguin, 1967.

Maurice, Frederick Denison. 1838. *The Kingdom of Christ.* London: Dent, 1906.

Wilkinson, Alan. 1998. *Christian Socialism: Scott Holland to Tony Blair.* London: SCM Press.

Peter Catterall

SOCIALISM, ISLAMIC

Islamic socialism is a discourse that seeks to integrate Islamic spirituality and socialism, promoting religious behavior, state ownership, and greater distribution of resources. Some of the most prominent examples of Muslim nation-states associated with the ideology are discussed below.

One of the first attempts was developed by Pakistani statesman Zulfikar Ali Bhutto (1928–1979) and the Pakistan People's Party (PPP), who adopted the term in response to severe criticism from conservative *ulema* about their un-Islamic socialism. To help alleviate criticism, Bhutto often referred to the "equality of Islam" (Raza 1997). From 1971 he introduced a range of socialist populist policies aimed at greater redistribution of resources. Overall though, particularly after 1973, Bhutto failed to reconcile the differing expectations of his supporters and urban industrialists and rural landlords, and he became ideologically distanced from Islamic socialism (Noman 1988; Raza 1997; Syed 1992) until he was overthrown in a military coup in 1977.

Islamic socialism is most widely associated with Muammar Abu Minyar al-Qadhafi of Libya, who came to power in 1969. He had been heavily influenced by the leadership of, and Arab socialist nationalism expounded by, the Egyptian leader Gamal Abdel Nasser (1918–1970). Qadhafi sought to bring about political, social, economic, and cultural change. The Third Universal (or International) Theory was introduced and expounded in Qadhafi's *Green Book*, which was published in three parts (1975, 1977, 1978). Qadhafi was critical of the excessive materialism and inequalities associated with capitalism, as well as communism's atheism and stifling of individual development. His new doctrine was to be an alternative to the dominant metanarratives, and he incorporated elements of Arab nationalism, Islam, and socialism. The *Green Book* addressed perceived problems within liberal democracy, economics, and social relations. A number of key concepts and practices were promoted, including *Jamahiriya* (state of the masses), "popular democracy" through direct participation in congresses and committees (Qadhafi 1975, p. 25), state welfare, equity, and religious behavior and morals. Large-scale private ownership and opportunities for "exploitation" were restricted (El-Kikhia 1997; Monti-Belkaoui and Riahi-Belkaoui 1996).

Since 1969, modernization processes have been implemented in Libya that have resulted in vastly improved communication and transportation networks and health and education facilities. However, the economy is overreliant on imports and oil revenues that have largely funded the advancements. Qadhafi's regime has been widely associated with repression of political dissidents, armed interference in neighboring states, and international terrorism. Following the drop in oil revenues in the 1980s, the onset of trade sanctions, periodic shortages of basic goods, and political isolation, Libya's economic

and political policies were revised. Measures of economic liberalization have been introduced at the expense of Islamic socialist doctrine; these include privatization, expansion of public sector companies, and foreign investment, particularly after the lifting of United Nations sanctions in 2003.

During the 1970s, Islamic socialism, or *scientific socialism* as it was called by the regime, was also implemented by President Mohammed Siad Barre (1919–1995) in Somalia. Scientific socialism also sought to integrate religion and socialism and placed emphasis upon community development through self-reliance. But shifting alliances in the late 1970s contributed to closer ties with the West and a restructuring of debt that resulted in a loss of state macroeconomic control, greater liberalization, and the effective end of "scientific socialism."

Today, Islamic socialism attracts little support. The inability of "Islamic socialist" regimes to deliver their promises contributed to the doctrine losing credibility and being replaced by political Islam as the "third way."

SEE ALSO *Pan-Arabism; Qadhafi, Muammar al*

BIBLIOGRAPHY

El-Kikhia, Mansour. 1997. *Libya's Qaddafi: The Politics of Contradiction*. Gainesville: University Press of Florida.

Monti-Belkaoui, Janice, and Ahmed Riahi-Belkaoui. 1996. *Qaddafi: The Man and his Policies*. Aldershot, U.K.: Ashgate.

Noman, Omar. 1988. *The Political Economy of Pakistan, 1947–85*. London: KPI.

Qadhafi, Muammar. 1975. *The Green Book*. Pt. 1: *The Solution of the Problem of Democracy*. Tripoli, Libya: Public Establishment for Publishing, Advertising, and Distribution.

Qadhafi, Muammar. 1977. *The Green Book*. Pt. 2: *The Solution of the Economic Problem—Socialism*. Tripoli, Libya: Public Establishment for Publishing, Advertising, and Distribution.

Qadhafi, Muammar. 1978. *The Green Book*. Pt. 3: *The Social Basis of the Third Universal Theory*. Tripoli, Libya: Public Establishment for Publishing, Advertising, and Distribution.

Raza, Rafi. 1997. *Zulfikar Ali Bhutto and Pakistan, 1967–1977*. Oxford: Oxford University Press.

Syed, Anwar. 1992. *The Discourse and Politics of Zulfikar Ali Bhutto*. London: Macmillan.

Stephen Vertigans

SOCIALISM, MARKET

Market socialism became recognized as a concept in the 1960s as a result of the ferment in Soviet bloc countries, whose economies were administered nonmarket entities.

As a concept it generally embraced the idea of a nationalized economy embedded in a market.

The process began in 1952, when Josef Stalin's *Economic Problems of Socialism in the U.S.S.R.* announced that a market existed in consumer goods. In the Soviet Union Professor Evsei Liberman (1897–1983) of Kharkov University put forward market-type proposals in 1962. These were taken up briefly by Alexey Kosygin (1904–1980) when he was the Soviet Union's premier, but were dropped again in 1968. In Czechoslovakia the reform ferment under Alexander Dubček (1921–1992), the Communist Party secretary, led to proposal of a limited market in 1968. This was aborted by the Soviet invasion of that year. Poland and Hungary proceeded more slowly toward the introduction of market-type reforms. The final denouement came when Mikhail Gorbachev (b. 1931), general secretary of the Soviet Communist Party, passed a series of laws in the Soviet Union that were intended to introduce the market, beginning in 1986 with the Law on the State Enterprise.

For most economists market socialism ceased to have any meaning because the issue had been settled in favor of capitalism. The Polish economist Wlodzimierz Brus and the Hungarian economist János Kornai effectively accepted capitalism. The concept, however, has continued to play a role in debates among Marxists and socialist theorists. Historically there were, and remain, two debates. The first concerns the possibility of the market being embedded in socialism. The debates in the U.S.S.R. and in other East European countries were variants of this question. The second concerns whether the market could coexist (or would be in conflict) with planning in a transition period to socialism. Nikolai Bukharin took the first view and Yevgeni Preobrazhensky the second. As an orthodox Marxist, however, Preobrazhensky rejected the view that a market (law of value) could exist in a communist society. At a 1924 debate on the subject in the Communist Academy, Ivan Stepanov-Skvortsov, the main speaker, appeared to argue for market socialism, but Preobrazhensky and Bukharin both opposed the concept very strongly, though they differed as above.

The Austrian Ludwig von Mises (1881–1973) argued in *Socialism: An Economic and Sociological Analysis* (1922) that calculation was impossible under socialism because value would be abolished. Oskar Lange (1904–1965), a Polish economist and later a member of the postwar Polish Communist government, took up the cudgels to argue that it was possible, writing in reply "On the Economic Theory of Socialism" (1936), as well as an essay with Abba Lerner. His argument hinged on a hypothetical pricing scheme worked out by planners, who in turn would base their studies on minimum costing. The idea that the market economy could be written into a series of equations, assuming equilibrium pricing, was already well established in orthodox economics. Lange was arguing that economic calculation was possible under socialism because it would plan as if it were a market economy. Lange was not a Marxist economist and therefore could not see that the essence of socialism, as perceived by Marxists, would be negated by this form of top-down "planning" because it involved control and discipline of workers by the planners. Leon Trotsky (1879–1940) writing at the same time argued that planning had to be democratic or else it would malfunction.

In a sense, Lange's concept of socialism anticipated the later Soviet bloc reformers and their critiques. One of these was taken up by von Mises's fellow countryman the Austrian Friedrich von Hayek (1899–1992), who pointed to the difficulty in calculating the millions of prices involved, a problem which the Soviet Union could not solve: At the time, the Soviet Union had 25 million prices that involved a huge process of calculation, given the interrelationships involved. Today Hayek would receive the reply that modern computing advances could solve the issue. However, few would want a central planner or planning ministry to decide all economic and social issues, even if computing would ensure consistency. In principle, computing could use either the Lange system of administered shadow prices or its own alternative schemes; that debate continues. Logically, in the interests of maximum control from below, there has to be a high level of devolution. The role of the market in a devolved economy is also a matter of continuing debate.

Alec Nove's 1983 book *The Economics of Feasible Socialism* prompted a series of debates, most particularly with Ernest Mandel, in the *New Left Review*, and with others in the pages of the *New Statesman*. Nove argued that the central premise of a communist society—that it would be a society of relative abundance—was utopian, and hence it could not exist. Instead, it was necessary to adapt market forms and criteria to an economy with nationalized property. His book was a recipe for market reforms in the Soviet Union, and he later provided advice to the Soviet Union under Gorbachev.

The Soviet bloc countries of Hungary, Poland, and Czechoslovakia experimented with market forms, as did the Soviet Union. However, the reforms were always suspect among the working class, for whom they meant rising unemployment, greater inequality, and harder work, even if consumer goods were generally more available at lower prices. Reformers argued that the partial reforms were insufficient.

Departing from the classic case of market socialism, which presupposes an economy with most or all enterprises nationalized, but operating within a simulated or real market, the Scandinavian countries, Sweden in particular, generally have been regarded as successful examples of the coexistence of a large state sector and a developed welfare system, with a market economy. But the relatively high level of taxation and large state sector are regarded by some economists as responsible for lessening Swedish competitiveness in a global economy. The election in 2006 of a right-wing government that complained of a very high level of unemployment and promised to privatize and alter the taxation system seems to indicate a limit to the experiment. Debate continues on the reasons for the relative stability of the Swedish case.

The discussion on the role of the market, whether in the transition period to socialism or in socialism/communism, continues among Marxists. Debates around the subject of market socialism were held at the New York–based Socialist Scholars Conferences in the late 1990s and after. Most anti-Stalinist orthodox Marxists continue to maintain that the market will be abolished in socialism/communism. The difference among theorists as to whether the market is inimical to planning or whether it can exist in socialism/communism mirrors degrees of acceptance of orthodox economics.

BIBLIOGRAPHY

Kornai, Janos. 1992. *The Socialist System: The Political Economy of Communism*. Oxford: Clarendon Press.

Lange, Oskar, and Fred M. Taylor. 1938. *On the Economic Theory of Socialism*, intro. and ed. Benjamin E. Lippincott. Minneapolis: University of Minnesota Press.

Mandel, Ernest. 1988. The Myth of Market Socialism. *New Left Review* 1 (May–June): 108–120.

Mises, Ludwig von. [1922] 1981. *Socialism: An Economic and Sociological Analysis*. Indianapolis, IN: Liberty Classics.

Nove, Alec. 1983. *The Economics of Feasible Socialism*. London: Allen and Unwin.

Nove, Alec, and Ian D. Thatcher, eds. 1994. *Markets and Socialism*. Cheltenham, U.K.: Edward Elgar.

Ollman, Bertell, ed. 1998. *Market Socialism: The Debate among Socialists*. New York: Routledge.

Hillel Ticktin

SOCIALISM, NATIONAL

SEE *Nazism.*

SOCIALIZATION

Socialization is a concept that is studied in many different areas of social science and can be adequately explained by any number of disciplines. The general topic of socialization forms the backdrop for numerous lines of research in diverse academic areas such as anthropology, sociology, criminology, and all areas of psychology. The study of socialization differs according to academic domain. For instance, in sociology, socialization is studied in terms of groups of institutions where socialization occurs, whereas anthropology looks at socialization in the larger culture. In this entry, socialization is approached from a psychological perspective, focused on the development of characteristics related to social behavior in individuals.

The term *socialization* refers to the process by which people learn culture, roles, and norms in order to function within a society. The socialization of culture includes learning the language, beliefs, and social structure of the culture in which an individual lives. The socialization of roles includes providing structure and instruction as to how to act in different situations individuals are likely to encounter within their culture. Finally, socializing group norms refers to learning the expected and appropriate behavior in a society in order to productively interact with others. Each of these three elements is integral to successful participation in society.

Though socialization is essential to functioning in society, it sometimes may have negative consequences. Some socialization experiences induce conformity and discourage independent thought: An example of this occurs in certain religious cults where conformity is encouraged and dissent is viewed harshly. Another example of the negative consequences of socialization is the internalizing of various stereotypes. Regardless of whether the socialization experience encourages conformity or independent thought, the end goal is to have individuals who are able to successfully interact within a given society.

Socialization occurs throughout one's lifetime, but it is particularly important during childhood, when the child's personality is taking shape. In early childhood children are socialized to learn the fundamentals of language and culture, which will affect behavior and outcomes throughout their lives. In addition, the way children are socialized and what behaviors are learned as appropriate and acceptable affect personality development with consequences that affect their entire lives. But socialization continues throughout one's entire life as new roles are undertaken and expected behaviors in each role are learned.

In many cultures, women are the first socializing agents in their capacity as the infant's primary caregiver. Primary caregivers of infants and young children have the unique task of socializing the child into the culture and society in which the child lives. These caregivers often are influential in teaching acceptable behaviors and rules as well as fundamental skills such as language development.

Beyond the primary caregiver, the family as a whole has a large role in socialization. This venue is the first social structure for the child, and much social behavior is learned in this arena. As the child develops, teachers, schools, and peer groups become important socializing agents. Mass media also socializes throughout the life span, and religious influences are also important. Each of these domains is somewhat controlled by the family. Family influence on children's neighborhoods and peer groups affects what types of socializing agents the child has access to. On a wider level, each of these domains is influenced by the government. The government exerts influence on socialization through creating experiences common to all children, such as schooling. In this domain, government has a powerful role in determining what can and cannot be learned, thus implicitly socializing the child to what things are and are not acceptable. Through the creation of laws and enforcement of acceptable behaviors, government also affects the family; for example, by enforcing laws that state that parents are not permitted to physically harm their children, the government dictates what types of behaviors children are subject to and, more generally, what types of behaviors are desirable and undesirable in society.

Research has suggested that socialization is not a unidirectional phenomenon. In *reciprocal socialization* parents socialize children and children in turn socialize parents. Children act as socializing agents to parents in a most basic sense as parents must be socialized to the parent role—infants demand certain care and have fundamental needs of their parents. In addition, various outside influences act on children in ways that affect parents and change their behaviors as well. For example, schooling may affect parental behaviors by placing increasing demands on children which parents must accommodate. In addition, increasing peer influences may require parents to modify strategies and behaviors in interacting with their child. Individual characteristics of children, such as their levels of attractiveness and temperaments, may also be factors in the socialization of parents. Newly arrived immigrant families provide a clear example of reciprocal socialization. Parents in these families may learn much of the new country's language and culture from their children as the children have more opportunities to learn (e.g., in school) and are more able to learn new expected roles. In this way, children socialize parents to new roles, and parents socialize children in basic behaviors.

MECHANISMS

Socialization occurs through a variety of mechanisms, both directly and indirectly. Direct socialization occurs through the formal teaching of behaviors and includes reinforcement of accepted behaviors. Schooling, an important source of direct influence, is very controlled: Roles are highly defined and behaviors are explicitly taught and reinforced. Direct socialization occurs throughout one's life. In professional socialization individuals are explicitly taught new behaviors and accepted patterns of social interaction. Although socialization during childhood provides the backdrop for which individuals can successfully maneuver within society, as people age, their socialization becomes more specialized as they learn how to act in specific social situations and be successful in specific arenas.

Indirect socialization, on the other hand, is more informal. This type of socialization may occur anywhere and at any time. Noting what behaviors are successful for others and then imitating these behaviors is an example of indirect socialization. By providing access to situations and restrictions from other situations, socializing agents informally affect what roles and behaviors are learned. Through this method, children are not explicitly taught about acceptable behaviors, but nonetheless are socialized to them.

The psychologist Albert Bandura proposed a theory often used to understand socialization experiences, advocating a social-learning approach in which children learn social behaviors via a variety of ways. Children learn through observational learning of others' behaviors and through modeling these behaviors, as well as through reinforcement. This reinforcement can be directly given to the child, or the child may learn through vicarious reinforcement, in which another individual is observed to be rewarded or punished for behaviors; through this process the child learns which behaviors are acceptable and which are not.

In both direct and indirect methods of socialization it is important to note that socialization is a process both of learning and of being taught. Both experiences are important socializing influences. The process of learning emphasizes the active role of children, who must make sense of their social world in active ways that allow them to explore possible avenues of behavior. In addition, children have individual traits that affect socialization such as temperament, which predisposes each individual to different types of socialization and socializing agents.

Different factors have been found to affect the effectiveness of socialization. Two often studied factors are attachment to parents and parenting style. Attachment theory suggests that infants' relationships with their caregivers form working models of relationships in general that in turn affect children's understanding of the world and their interactions within social arenas. How children form these attachment relationships is an important factor in socialization in that it is through these relationships that they indirectly learn how to behave in the world interpersonally and to form expectations about other people. This process provides an important source of experience upon which children draw to learn to act within their social worlds.

Diana Baumrind (1967) studied parenting style in terms of two dimensions: demandingness and responsiveness. She initially proposed three parenting styles: authoritarian (demanding but unresponsive parenting), authoritative (demanding and responsive parenting), and permissive (not demanding but responsive). Maccoby and Martin (1983) later added a fourth category, neglectful, encompassing parenting styles that are neither demanding nor responsive. In relation to socialization, parenting styles influence the methods by which the parents socialize their child and the effectiveness of the messages parents attempt to transmit. The emotional climate that is created through parenting style affects how children receive messages and how they are interpreted.

EFFECTS

Socialization has many effects on individual behavior and personality. First, it is integral to forming personalities in children. The very nature of socialization dictates that some beliefs and attitudes are reinforced and that there is only selective exposure to other possible attitudes. Children are thus given a set of acceptable behaviors and attitudes from which to form their personalities, creating a firm boundary of possibilities for personality formation.

Children also learn values through the process of socialization. Different sources of socialization including parents, teachers, and the media all have influences on what values the child learns are important. For example, from watching various sources of media in western cultures, most children learn that physical appearance is highly valued, and they mirror this belief in their own value systems. These influences provide the lens through which children view their social world and shape how they will continue to view the world into adulthood.

Socialization processes also affect the developing child through the learning of social and automatic biases about individuals and groups of people. As a part of socialization, children may learn what behaviors are expected and acceptable for different groups of people and may thus form stereotypes about these groups; a common set of stereotypes formed in this way are gender stereotypes. Through these socialization processes the roots of various psychological phenomena studied in social psychology, such as in-group biases, may be found.

TYPES OF SOCIALIZATION

Socialization is often studied in relation to specific roles that individuals take within society. Two primary examples of this line of research are gender socialization and racial socialization. The term *gender socialization* refers to the process by which children learn expectations of behavior for males and females. In children, gender socialization begins through differential treatment based on sex. Boys and girls are treated differently by important adult socializing agents according to what is considered to be acceptable gendered behaviors. Social learning theory is often applied to gender socialization as children are seen to be rewarded and punished for acceptable behaviors, and because they imitate same-sex gender models. This theory posits that children are passive recipients of these messages, but evidence suggests that children selectively and actively process the information they choose to imitate. A more active theory of gender socialization, gender schema theory, posits that children actively form cognitive sets of ideas about gender that help to organize information within their social world.

Racial and ethnic socialization refers to the transmission of messages about how different racial groups fit within society and the relationships between different racial and ethnic groups. Racial socialization is heavily emphasized within some families and in other families it is not considered an important aspect of socialization. As a part of this process, children are taught what behaviors to expect from others based on the race or ethnicity of individuals the child encounters, and they are taught various strategies with which to respond. Racial socialization is directly related to the racial identity that an individual adopts as he or she ages.

BIBLIOGRAPHY

Bandura, Albert. 1969. Social-Learning Theory of Identificatory Processes. In *Handbook of Socialization Theory and Research*, ed. David A. Goslin, 213–262. Chicago: Rand McNally.

Baumrind, Diana. 1967. Child Care Practices Anteceding Three Patterns of Preschool Behavior. *Genetic Psychology Monographs* 475: 43–88.

Darling, Nancy, and Lawrence Steinberg. 1993. Parenting Style as Context: An Integrative Model. *Psychological Bulletin* 113: 487–496.

Goslin, David A. 1969. Introduction. In *Handbook of Socialization Theory and Research*, ed. David A. Goslin, 1–21. Chicago: Rand McNally.

Jacklin, Carol Nagy, and Chandra Reynolds. 1993. Gender and Childhood Socialization. In *The Psychology of Gender*, eds. Anne E. Beall and Robert J. Sternberg, 197–214. New York: Guilford Press.

Maccoby, Eleanor E., and John A. Martin. 1983. Socialization in the Context of the Family: Parent-Child Interaction. In *Socialization, Personality, and Social Development.* Vol. 4 of *Handbook of Child Psychology*, eds. P. H. Mussen and E. M. Hetherington, 1–101. New York: Wiley.

Marshall, Sheree. 1995. Ethnic Socialization of African American Children: Implications for Parenting, Identity Development, and Academic Achievement. *Journal of Youth and Adolescence* 24 (4): 377–397.

Parke, Ross D., and Raymond Buriel. 1998. Socialization in the Family: Ethnic and Ecological Perspectives. In *Social, Emotional, and Personality Development.* Vol. 3 of *Handbook of Child Psychology*, eds. William Damon and Nancy Eisenberg, 463–552. New York: Wiley.

Melanie B. Hoy

SOCIALIZATION OF INVESTMENT

The idea of socializing investment was introduced in 1936 by John Maynard Keynes in his *General Theory of Employment, Interest, and Money.* In the concluding chapter of the book, Keynes identified three major tasks to be undertaken in order to save capitalism from its own demise: "parting with liquidity," "euthanizing the rentiers," and socializing investment. The three are inevitably interrelated in Keynes's theory, as he argued that effective demand is the engine of the capitalist economy and that spending by consumers, firms, and the government is what keeps the economy going.

According to Keynes, economic agents operate in real historical time under conditions of uncertainty in which the future is unknowable and the past is unchangeable. Faced with such an environment, individuals make arbitrage decisions with regard to which asset they wish to hold over time. Each asset gets a return composed of four components: $q - c + l + a$; where q is the expected yield, c is the carrying cost, l is the liquidity premium, and a is the appreciation or depreciation.

At equilibrium, all assets earn the same expected return. If an asset has a demand price higher than its supply price, then firms will produce more of it, but as its production increases, its return will fall and becomes equal to the returns of all other assets. When consumers and firms are optimistic about the future and feel confident about their financial situation, the expected returns on capital equipment rises above the expected return on money (the interest rate), which leads to an increase in investment, thus boosting output and employment. Conversely, when the economy is overtaken by pessimistic expectations, consumers and firms prefer to remain liquid, thus abstaining from spending on consumption and investment goods, which leads to a rise in unemployment. According to Keynes, this is due to money's very specific nature as the most liquid asset in the economy with a near zero elasticity of production, small elasticity of substitution, and no carrying cost. In other words, when people want to hold more money (liquidity), no significant amount of labor is directed to producing it (unlike, for instance, capital equipment).

Therefore, Keynes's conclusion was that an environment must be created that is conducive to more investment and less hoarding of money. Hence his three policy recommendations: (1) "parting with liquidity" (giving up liquid assets in exchange for employment-creating illiquid assets); (2) "euthanizing the rentiers" by lowering the interest rate so much that nobody will find it profitable to save money (because expected returns on money are less attractive than expected returns on capital); and (3) socializing investment through the creation of a new kind of capitalist culture of cooperation between private and public authorities.

Keynes's overall preference for discretionary fiscal spending led many to misunderstand his use of the term *socialization of investment*, despite the fact that Keynes made it very clear that he did not mean "socialism." Keynes explained that socializing investment does not require that the government assume ownership of the means of production and dictate the terms of economic activity to the rest of the economy. According to Keynes, "[i]t is not the ownership of the instruments of production which it is important for the State to assume. If the State is able to determine the aggregate amount of resources devoted to augmenting the instruments and the basic rate of reward to those who own them, it will have accomplished all that is necessary" (Keynes 1936, p. 378).

Furthermore, Keynes emphasized the fact that the socialization of investment does not conflict with the basic features of capitalism. He repeatedly stressed the importance of protecting individualism, private property, freedom of choice, and competition. According to Keynes, the socialization of investment calls for no revolution—it is, rather, a gradual adjustment between the propensity to consume and the inducement to invest for the sole purpose of ensuring an adequate level of effective demand that is consistent with full employment.

The policy framework that is closest to Keynes's idea of socializing investment is to be found in the Swedish (corporatist) model developed after World War II by trade union economists Gösta Rehn and Rudolf Meidner, who envisioned two essential elements that would characterize the Swedish economy for more than four decades: (1) highly centralized wage bargaining; and (2) active labor market policies. The model focused on the socialization of investment and offered a practical alternative to welfarism by putting a strong emphasis on "the right to work" rather than "the right to income." The model strongly encouraged private investment despite high tax rates on profits. Firms were allowed to put their "excess profits" into tax-exempt "investment funds," thus encouraging capital accumulation. Under this model, Sweden was able to keep its unemployment rate below 3 percent for decades without any significant inflationary pressure.

SEE ALSO *Aggregate Demand; Economics, Keynesian; Government; Investment; Keynes, John Maynard*

BIBLIOGRAPHY

Keynes, John Maynard. 1936. *The General Theory of Employment, Interest, and Money.* New York: Harcourt, Brace and World.

Marshall, Mike. 1995. Lessons from the Experience of the Swedish Model. In *The Political Economy of Full Employment: Conservatism, Corporatism, and Institutional Change*, ed. Philip Arestis and Mike Marshall, 202–216. Cheltenham, U.K., and Northampton, MA: Edward Elgar.

Fadhel Kaboub

SOCIETY

A society is a system for facilitating interdependent social relationships according to the values, norms, and ideologies of a shared culture while, at the same time, providing sanctions against individuals who engage in what are seen as antisocial behaviors. Among the primates, humans are unique in their capacity to develop large-scale systems of interdependence by means of culturally transmitted, group-level social systems; in other primate species, cooperation is generally limited to relatives, there is little division of labor, there is little or no social cooperation to care for the sick or wounded, and there are no formal social mechanisms (let alone cultural norms) to stop dominant males and females from taking whatever they wish from weaker members of their group.

As the term is generally understood in sociology as well as in commonsense usage, a *society* is assumed to have three fundamental characteristics: (1) it is bounded by readily discernible territorial borders; (2) it is structurally and culturally distinctive; and (3) it possesses an objective existence that is independent of the wills or actions of individuals.

Generally (if problematically), a society's boundaries are assumed to be those of a nation: Thus we speak of "Canadian society" versus "American society." Moreover, the boundaries of all of a society's institutions, including economics, kinship, and religion, as well as politics, are assumed to be roughly coterminous. A society is not hermetically sealed from others, of course; every day, thousands of Americans and Canadians cross the U.S.-Canada border, and U.S.-Canadian trade is a vital component of the economies of both countries. Still, the fact that a society is essentially a culturally mediated system for facilitat-

ing interdependence means that, in principle, such relationships are more easily undertaken within the society rather than with outsiders. At the same time, it is clear that, with the advent and gathering momentum of globalization, a global society is emerging that is characterized, in part, by the formation of mutually beneficial social structures of unprecedented scope and size, including a new international division of labor in manufacturing.

Each society is unique in the way its various components have been altered and adapted so that they can be integrated with each other. Canada's system of parliamentary democracy is modeled after the British system; however, it has had to adapt to the existence within Canada of a large, French-speaking, and potentially separatist regional minority, centered in Quebec. In part to address the legitimate language discrimination grievances that fuel Quebec separatism, the Canadian system has moved away from the British model toward that of a constitutional democracy with enumerated rights for French speakers. Despite their internal differences, the members of a society are aware of their society's distinctiveness and their vast store of shared experience, and this awareness informs their identity. When asked what is important or very important to their identity, many Canadians mention language, but nearly all of them stress the uniqueness of their society and their country's unique historical experience.

Society has an objective existence that precedes the individuals who live within it, exists independent of their will and subjective perception, and constrains their thought, beliefs, and behavior. This is so because a society consists not only of one-to-one relationships, which to some extent can be negotiated and altered, but also of organizations (such as courts, schools, legislatures, and hospitals) that possess vastly greater power and resources than any individual could muster. In addition, the members of a society are affected by collective outcomes of one-to-one relationships, such as economic recessions and depressions, which again are beyond the capacity of individuals to control.

Taken together, these assumptions argue strongly for a social science that seeks social explanations for social phenomena, and these assumptions collectively define what might be termed the classical sociological perspective (c. 1880s to 1960s). At the same time, each assumption is problematic. Contemporary sociology examines these assumptions critically and asks whether they can be shown to apply empirically.

LINGUISTIC ORIGINS

The English word *society* has its origins in the Indo-European sek^{w-1}, "to follow," from which derives the Latin *societas*, "partnership, fellowship, association, alliance"— that is, followers of a common, mutual interest or common ideal. In line with its Latin origins, the English word can be applied not only to collective historical formations such as "Canadian society," but also to *de novo* associations that are deliberately created to provide mutual benefit, such as professional societies or mutual assistance societies. In popular usage, *society* is sometimes intended to refer to a leisured, cultured, wealthy, and fashionable elite ("high society").

The word *society* can be used scientifically only with caution and critical reflection. It connotes systems of mutually beneficial relationships into which individuals, perceiving the benefits, freely engage. Whether social interdependence is indeed mutually beneficial, let alone entered into freely, is an empirical question.

SOCIETY VERSUS COMMUNITY

All modern societies are capable of creating large-scale structures that facilitate interdependence, such as markets and the division of labor. The resulting structure extends to *communities* within the society, but more importantly, it also draws into its web of interdependence people who have never met each other and never will. As traditionally defined, a community is a group, such as a neighborhood or the congregation of a synagogue, that is characterized by face-to-face interaction in the context of shared local customs and traditions. As understood in classical sociology, communities are necessarily limited both in population and geographic extent because they depend on face-to-face interaction (rather than large-scale interdependence) as a means of achieving group solidarity,

In classical sociology, the modern distinction between society and community owes much to Ferdinand Tönnies (1855–1936), who redefined two German words to capture the distinction. *Gemeinschaft* (community) and *Gesellschaft* (society). In the *Gemeinschaft*, people are held together by organic ties and communal ideology; in the *Gesellschaft*, social relations are impersonal and based on a perception of mutual interest. Tönnies believed, pessimistically, that *Gesellschaft* would obliterate the remnants of *Gemeinschaft*, to the detriment of the human social experience.

Today, most sociologists accept that communities arise, not necessarily from face-to-face interaction, but rather from shared meanings. Because they are capable of promulgating shared meanings on an unprecedented scale, new communication and media technologies (including newspapers, motion pictures, radio, television, and computer-based communications) are capable of creating communities that vastly transcend the limits of face-to-face interaction.

SOCIETY VERSUS THE STATE

In contemporary usage, a society's boundaries are frequently assumed to be the same as that of the nation-state with which it is equated, a fact that testifies to the growing ability of states during the past two centuries to circumscribe the sphere of social relationships in which their subjects engage. It should be noted, however, that the concept of society is by no means synonymous with the concept of a state. A state is a political formation that is fundamentally concerned with the acquisition, use, and protection of power. In contrast, the term *society* refers to all the culturally mediated, patterned forms of social interaction, including political interaction, that create the conditions for interdependence among a society's members.

The term *civil society* is often used to differentiate between the state and society. Classically, the term refers to a zone of public social interaction that is positioned between the state, on the one hand, and the private lives of individuals and families, on the other. It consists of a variety of public but nongovernmental institutions and organizations such as voluntary associations, clubs, youth organizations, mutual benefit societies, community organizations, coffeehouses, charities, trade unions, social movements, and media such as newspapers. In a prosperous society, it is assumed, civil society is vibrant.

One of the most crucial functions of civil society lies in its capacity to foster the *public sphere*, a zone of public social communication in which free, open, rational, and critical conversation can take place concerning the proper ends of society—and, especially, whether the state's policies are serving those ends. For some theorists, especially Jürgen Habermas, a healthy public sphere is a vital component of democratic self-governance.

THEORIES OF SOCIETY

It is possible to find antecedents of the society concept in classical Greek philosophy and, especially, in the work of the Islamic social historian Ibn Khaldun (1332–1406); however, the concept of society as it was understood in classical sociology is generally traced to the mid-nineteenth-century work of Auguste Comte (1798–1857), who is also regarded as the founder of sociology, the English social philosopher Herbert Spencer (1820–1903), and especially Émile Durkheim (1858–1917).

Observing what Durkheim took to be the decline of communities held together by religion and tradition, the anonymity of an increasingly urbanized society, and the prospect of endemic conflict caused by the increasingly violent confrontation between capital and labor, he asked whether modern societies possessed a core of common sympathies that could serve the integrative function formerly provided by rural folk communities and traditional cultures. Of crucial concern to Durkheim was the increasing division of labor generated by urbanization and industrialization. To the cynics of the time, the widening gulf between capital and labor presaged the collapse of social solidarity and, ultimately, the end of European civilization; for example, Karl Marx (1818–1883) believed that the conflict between capital and labor testified to a fundamental contradiction in capitalist society that would inevitably result in revolution, peaceful or otherwise. Yet Durkheim had read Comte and Spencer, and was able to counter this view with the *organic analogy*, which interprets the various components of society as if they were organs in a body: Each of them contributes, in its own differentiated way, to the mutual benefit that stems from their cooperation.

From this analogy, Durkheim went on to argue that the widening division of labor in industrial society did not necessarily raise the specter of social disintegration. On the contrary, Durkheim argued, to the extent that society is understood as an interdependence-fostering structure, the widening scale and scope of industrializing societies would require a corresponding intensification of new modes of social differentiation to serve as the foundation for subsequent, mutually beneficial interdependence. In addition, Durkheim argued that, despite the apparently widening gulf between capital and labor, there still existed enough shared culture and shared identity to overcome the divisiveness seemingly inherent in the new industrial economies. The key, Durkheim argued, lies in recognizing that shared culture and shared identity are not causal factors in themselves, but rather epiphenomena that result from sustained, mutually beneficial, and socially structured interaction. For this reason, Durkheim did not doubt that industrial societies would generate cultural and moral orders capable of social integration on an unprecedented scale, and history has vindicated his prediction.

Durkheim's understanding of society was informed by likening its constituent elements to an advanced, highly differentiated organism. Scientific and technological advances in the twentieth century made new metaphors available to sociological theorists. Drawing on the emerging fields of cybernetics and systems theory, in the 1930s American sociologist Talcott Parsons (1902–1979) depicted the interdependence of social phenomena in terms of a hierarchy of intercoupled systems and subsystems. Niklas Luhmann (1927–1998), a student of Parsons, drawing on chaos theory, depicted society as a complex, self-organizing system.

Beginning in earnest in the 1960s, sociologists revisited and often criticized or rejected the core assumptions of Durkheimian sociology, often adopting new metaphors to capture their perspectives. With the rise of symbolic interactionism, ethnomethodology, and particularly the work of Erving Goffman (1922–1982), society could be understood as a stage on which performers create and shape social reality. Drawing increasingly on resource mobilization theory, work on social movements suggested

that society is like a game in which teams compete with each other, both to acquire necessary economic, social, and political resources and also to frame their activities symbolically in a winning way. As Marxist perspectives found their way into universities in the 1960s, society came to be seen as a battle between social classes with fundamentally opposed interests. Still, rational action theorists, such as James Coleman (1926–1995), depicted society as an economy in which actors develop elaborate networks as they attempt to maximize their self-interest.

Influenced by developments in semiotics and French literary criticism, some postmodern sociologists have likened society to a battle between contending texts or a discourse of signs; others have argued that capitalism has so infected our consciousness that virtually all social activities can be understood by comparing them to producers and consumers in a media-driven marketplace. The production of new analogies shows no sign of abating; for example, society has recently been compared to a restaurant menu, a theme park, a collection of machines, and a set of warring tribes.

CRITICISMS OF THE CONCEPT

Criticisms of the classical concept of society focus on its several problematic aspects, including the assumptions that societies are neatly bounded, that the interdependence fostered by social relationships is mutually beneficial, that society has an objective existence, and that meaning and affect are mere epiphenomena of social relations.

Until recently, sociologists have paid little attention to the problems created by uncritical assumptions regarding a society's boundedness. To the extent that it is meaningful to talk about "Canadian society," for example, it is because Canadian society constitutes a field of social interaction within which Canadians are more likely to interact with each other than with outsiders. Yet, in the context of globalization, Canadians will increasingly interact with foreigners; at the same time, it is clear that Quebec could be seen as a society within a society. For some critics, sociology's willingness to equate societies with nations shows that the discipline has made an uncritical accommodation to nationalist ideology. New directions in sociological theory employ spatial and ecological analogies to tackle the boundedness problem; the boundaries of social interaction are seen as a matter to be determined by empirical investigation rather than facile assumption. In addition, cultural sociologists are developing new approaches for understanding the dynamics of multicultural societies.

At the core of the concept of society is an assumption that amounts to a quid pro quo: By giving up the opportunity to pursue private interest without constraint, people take part in social relations that are, in the end, mutually beneficial. Still, it is obvious that many social relations are founded on asymmetries of power, and result in concomitantly unequal distributions of benefits. Critical sociologists argue that the quid pro quo concept masks asymmetries of power, which are, in their view, a key component of all or nearly all of society's structures and institutions.

Sociologists readily assume that society has an objective existence that can be scientifically studied, even though there is no physical object in the world that one can point to and say, "That is a society." Within sociology, a field called *symbolic interactionism* begins by rejecting the concept that a society has an objective existence that determines the way individuals behave. In contrast, people are seen to act according to the meanings they ascribe to situations. These meanings are learned by engaging in social relations. Action arises as individuals interpret situations in light of the meanings they have learned. Although symbolic interactionism has been influential, most sociologists believe that societies are quite capable of placing people into situations in which an actor's interpretation of the situation is not the sole determinant of social outcomes. People who live in African American slum communities, for example, interpret their situation in differing ways, but this fact has little effect on the overriding social toxicity of these racially isolated neighborhoods. Still, symbolic interactionism served to alert sociology to the need to take meaning and affect seriously and, in so doing, has contributed to the rise of cultural sociology, which is arguably the most important development within sociology to have taken place in a century. In classical sociology, meaning and affect were seen as the outcome of social relationships rather than their cause. Today's cultural sociology (e.g., Alexander 2003) shares with symbolic interactionism a commitment to taking meaning and affect seriously; however, it also recognizes that some social structures are indeed independent of individual will and are unaffected by the meanings people ascribe to them. Cultural sociology views social relations as the outcome of processes in which meaning, affect, and social forces interplay in ways that must be determined empirically rather than by theoretical fiat.

SEE ALSO *Comte, Auguste; Cooperation; Critical Theory; Durkheim, Émile; Ethnicity; Ethnomusicology; Functionalism; Gemeinschaft and Gesellschaft; Gender; Goffman, Erving; Habermas, Jürgen; Interactionism, Symbolic; Marxism; Mexican Americans; Mills, C. Wright; Parsons, Talcott; Postmodernism; Public Sphere; Race; Semiotics; Separatism; Social Statics; Social Structure; Social System; Social Theory; Sociology; Sociology, Latin American; Sociology, Parsonian; Sociology, Post-Parsonian American; Sociology, Urban; Spencer, Herbert; State, The; Structuralism*

BIBLIOGRAPHY

Alexander, Jeffrey C. 2003. *The Meanings of Social Life: A Cultural Sociology.* Oxford and New York: Oxford University Press.

Blumer, Herbert. 1986. *Symbolic Interactionism.* Berkeley: University of California Press.

Durkheim, Émile. 1933. *The Division of Labor in Society.* New York: Free Press.

Tönnies, Ferdinand. 1957. *Community & Society.* Trans. and ed. Charles P. Loomis. East Lansing: Michigan State University Press.

Bryan Pfaffenberger

SOCIETY, MANAGERIAL

SEE *Managerial Class.*

SOCIOBIOLOGY

The scientific study of the social behavior of biological systems from an evolutionary perspective is known as sociobiology, a term coined by the entomologist and biologist Edward O. Wilson in 1975. Researchers from a diverse array of disciplines including biology, psychology, sociology, anthropology, and archaeology study social behavior from a sociobiological perspective. According to this perspective, the social behavior of animals, including humans, has been shaped by the process of natural selection in which any behavior that increases the ability of an individual to live to reproductive age and to successfully reproduce subsequently becomes more prevalent in future generations. Sociobiologists therefore attempt to understand how current social behavior would have provided a reproductive advantage to individuals of previous generations. To facilitate this process researchers identify problems that social beings recurrently faced over evolutionary history and then determine the behaviors that would have been adaptive to successfully deal with these problems. The term sociobiology has now largely been replaced with the term *evolutionary psychology.* Using this approach, researchers have found empirical support for the evolutionary origins of a number of social behaviors including mate attraction and selection, helping behaviors, and aggression.

MATE ATTRACTION AND SELECTION

One of the most influential theories of mating behavior is the parental investment theory proposed by Robert L. Trivers in 1972. Trivers postulated that in sexually reproducing species the sex that invests the most in offspring will be more selective in whom they choose as mates whereas the sex that invests the least in offspring will compete more with each other for sexual access to the more selective sex. In humans, the minimal parental investment that a woman must expend on a child involves the nine months of gestation and parturition, plus a period of lactation that can last from several months to a few years. For men, the minimal parental investment can conceivably involve a single sexual encounter. Given that women are a more limited reproductive resource, competition among men to mate with women should have been stronger during evolutionary history than competition among women to mate with men. Consistent with the predictions derived from this theory, research has shown that men are more willing than women to take advantage of short-term sexual opportunities with different mates. In comparison, given the higher costs of reproduction for women, they are more selective than men in whom they choose as sexual partners and tend to desire longer-term relationships.

Parental investment theory also makes predictions regarding the traits men and women should find attractive in each other. If men tend to prefer short-term sexual opportunities to maximize their reproductive success, then they face the problem of identifying which women are fertile. Certain physical cues are associated with fertility, and it has been found that men are more attracted to women that possess these physical traits. For example, women with a waist-to-hip ratio around .70 (where the waist is 70 percent the size of the hips, producing a curvy appearance) and women with more feminine facial features (e.g., larger eyes, smaller chin) have been found to possess high amounts of estrogen and thus are relatively more fertile. Men are also more attracted to young women, perhaps because women's fertility continually declines through their adult years. By contrast, if women tend to prefer long-term relationships so that their high parental investment can be offset by investments from their mate, then they face the problem of identifying mates that have the ability to accumulate status and resources that can then be shared with themselves and their offspring. Research shows that women are attracted to men with good financial prospects, men who have social status, and men that are more ambitious. Women are also more attracted to men who are older than themselves, because older men have had more opportunity to turn their ambition into actual status and resources.

Once a relationship is formed, people face the problem of maintaining the relationship. David M. Buss (2000) has suggested that for humans jealousy was an important adaptation for maintaining relationships because people who became upset when they were in danger of losing their partner would have experienced greater reproductive success than those who did not. He also suggested that women and men should differ in the types of cues that activate their jealousy. Whereas a woman can be confident that she is in fact the mother of her children, because of internal fertilization, a man cannot be certain that he is the father. Paternity uncertainty should therefore have made men more sensitive to cues of sexual infidelity of their partners and wary of rivals that are friendly or flirtatious with their partners to ensure that their partner's children are also their own children. For ancestral women, securing the resources to raise highly dependent offspring was a challenge. The ability to raise offspring to reproductive age would be severely compromised if paternal investment were to be directed elsewhere, and therefore women should be sensitive to cues indicating emotional infidelity of their partners.

ALTRUISM AND AGGRESSION

Two behaviors that have also received much attention from sociobiologists are altruism and aggression. When presenting his theory of evolution by natural selection in 1859, Charles Darwin commented that his theory was not able to explain why individuals helped others, particularly when these altruistic behaviors limited the reproductive success of the helper. In 1964 William D. Hamilton addressed this problem with his theory of kin selection. He stated that because individuals share a portion of their genes with genetically related individuals, providing assistance to kin can therefore further one's own reproductive success. Helping behaviors should thus be observed to be directed mainly to genetically related individuals. Kin selection theory, although supported by research, could not account for why individuals were observed to provide assistance to unrelated individuals. Trivers addressed this problem in 1971 by proposing his theory of reciprocal altruism, hypothesizing that an individual will help an unrelated individual when the former expects to be the benefactor of assistance from the latter in the near future. Indeed, help is directed to unrelated individuals with the expectation that these acts of kindness will be repaid.

Aggressive behaviors may also have evolved because of the adaptive benefits they bestowed on the aggressor. According to Mark Schaller and colleagues' intergroup vigilance theory (2003), it was adaptive for human ancestors to develop a fear of strangers and of individuals who were diseased. One consequence of fear is that it can motivate aggressive behaviors to defend against perceived threats. The ancestors of contemporary humans lived in small groups and relied on each other for survival, and the presence of individuals from another unknown group could have aroused fear because of the possible threat of intruders to one's survival. People who did not fear strangers from other groups may have been more vulnerable to attack, whereas people who did fear intruders and acted to defend themselves and their group would have been more likely to survive. This tendency to respond aggressively to strangers may no longer be adaptive, however, given that humans now live in very large groups that are very diverse. Over evolutionary history people may also have developed a fear of others who were sick or diseased, given that the illness may be contracted and put one's life at risk. Stigmatizing those who were ill and removing them from the group may have been one way to avoid illness given that early humans did not have access to modern-day medicine.

TESTING SOCIOBIOLOGICAL THEORIES

Sociobiological theories are tested in many different ways. Laboratory experiments have been used to test cause-and-effect relationships between variables by manipulating the context study participants are exposed to and then measuring participants' responses. Survey studies that ask people to answer questions about their own personalities or about their likes and dislikes have been used a great deal to study, for example, the mate preferences of men and women all over the world. Field studies have been used to observe the natural behaviors of individuals as they interact in small or large groups. Archaeological records have been used to discover the types of tools human ancestors used to hunt game or to study the evolution of brain size. In addition, public records recording the behaviors of citizens of various countries over hundreds of years exist, and these records have been used to test sociobiological hypotheses regarding homicide (Daly and Wilson 1988) and the effects of birth order on behavior (Sulloway 1996).

Sociobiology is still considered a controversial field by many. Sociobiologists study current social behavior and then make conclusions about what life must have been like for humans living thousands of years ago. Because what happened in the distant past can never truly be known, opponents of sociobiology suggest that researching current behaviors does not provide insights on the evolutionary origins of these behaviors. Sociobiology has also been blamed for justifying negative social behaviors such as male violence against women and intergroup violence. Stated differently, suggesting that social behaviors evolved because they were adaptive implies that these behaviors are natural and acceptable. Although explaining why behaviors exist does not necessarily justify the existence of the behavior, many sociobiologists have not always made the effort to differentiate explanation from justification.

SEE ALSO *Darwin, Charles; Evolutionary Psychology; Nature vs. Nurture; Spencer, Herbert*

BIBLIOGRAPHY

Buss, David M. 2000. *The Dangerous Passion: Why Jealousy Is as Necessary as Love and Sex.* New York: Free Press.

Daly, Martin, and Margo Wilson. 1988. *Homicide.* Hawthorne, NY: Aldine de Gruyter.

Darwin, Charles. 1859. *On the Origin of Species by Means of Natural Selection; or, The Preservation of Favoured Races in the Struggle for Life.* London: Murray.

Hamilton, William D. 1964. The Genetical Evolution of Social Behaviour I and II. *Journal of Theoretical Biology* 7 (1): 1–16 and 17–52.

Schaller, Mark, Justin H. Park, and Jason Faulkner. 2003. Prehistoric Dangers and Contemporary Prejudices. *European Review of Social Psychology* 14 (4): 105–137.

Sulloway, Frank J. 1996. *Born to Rebel: Birth Order, Family Dynamics, and Creative Lives.* New York: Pantheon.

Trivers, Robert L. 1971. The Evolution of Reciprocal Altruism. *Quarterly Review of Biology* 46 (1): 35–57.

Trivers, Robert L. 1972. Parental Investment and Sexual Selection. In *Sexual Selection and the Descent of Man, 1871–1971*, ed. Bernard Campbell, 136–179. Chicago: Aldine.

Wilson, Edward O. 1975. *Sociobiology: The New Synthesis.* Cambridge, MA: Harvard University Press, Belknap Press.

Lorne Campbell

SOCIOECONOMIC STATUS

As social scientists in the twentieth century became more aware of and interested in social stratification and social class as a basis for understanding large areas of human behavior, interest grew in finding direct and useful ways of measuring socioeconomic status when conducting empirical research. Socioeconomic status had been taken into account in early American sociology, and seems to have been conceived as an indicator of social class itself. During the 1920s, the highly influential Chicago school of sociology had developed several creative research techniques in relation to the ecological theories of urban structure and process. Most of their research was carried out in the Chicago area and used a residential approach to social characteristics of the urban population of the Chicago area. This research was predicated on the assumption that physical distance was correlated with social distance, and that people from different ethnic groups and social classes live in different areas or zones of the city. By implication, a person's social class location was at least indirectly indicated by the area of residence, or zone of the city. This approach was part of a larger ecological orientation to the study of urban communities and posited a close correspondence between the utilization of physical space and the overall urban structure, with tendencies to place the social structure on a broad theoretical map of the city. Social stratification was regarded by these scholars as an ancillary aspect of social structure.

As a measure of socioeconomic status, the residential approach had severe limitations. Type of residence is an imperfect indicator of social-class position, as is residential location. Comparison across cities with different areal patterns of distribution of social and economic activities, including residential patterns, would also be difficult.

Interest on the part of social scientists in social class qua class itself grew during the economic depression of the 1930s. A social anthropologist, William Lloyd Warner (1898–1970), studied a northern East Coast community in the United States and used a *reputational* method applied to individuals. Warner and his research staff employed extensive observations in this small community where most adults had knowledge of the reputations of others residing in the community. These investigators relied extensively on the judgments and relative rankings of the status of community members by others in the small community. The application of the reputational method to Yankee City, the pseudonym accorded to the community, resulted in the designating of six social classes on the basis of reputational rankings of status.

The reputational approach to socioeconomic status applied by Warner has been found to have several problems. As a methodology, it is confined to quite small communities, a serious limitation during this last century of accelerated urbanization. This approach does not enable facile comparisons across communities and hence is limited in contributing to discussions of a national class structure. Also, as other social scientists studied other North American communities and found different numbers of social classes or strata in the other communities, questions were raised regarding reliability. The numbers of classes found in other studies ranged from two to as many as eleven or more, indicating serious problems in comparability. These various difficulties in using the reputational method for studying socioeconomic status pointed toward the need for measures with greater simplicity and precision that could be applied to larger communities, or the nation or a national sample, than was possible with the reputational method.

DEVELOPMENT OF MEASURES OF SOCIAL CLASS AND SOCIOECONOMIC STATUS

The first large-scale study of the stratification of an entire city was carried out by Robert S. Lynd (1892–1970) and Helen Lynd (1896–1982) during the 1920s and published in 1929. *Middletown*, the title of their resulting book, was also a pseudonym for a city of 35,000 people in Indiana. Their research method involved the detached observation techniques of social anthropology. *Middletown* was to be the first of two books on the social class structure and its consequences for the life of the citizens of this middle-sized city in Indiana.

The research by the Lynds made an important contribution to the study of socioeconomic status due to the simple, direct measures they used to indicate the social class position of the residents of the city of Middletown. To measure social class itself, the basic distinction the Lynds used was between people who work with *people* in selling and promoting consumer goods, ideas, or services, on the one hand, and people who work with *things*, often using tools in making products or performing services. The first category of occupations was referred to as the *business class*; the second broad category was designated as the *working class*. In Middletown, there were twice as many people in the working class as in the business class. The Lynds found that membership in one class in contrast to the other had large consequences in regard to many areas of life, including whom one married, opportunity for and likelihood of attending a college or university, club memberships, access to bank credit, recreational patterns, and even whether one owned an automobile and, if so, what sort of car was driven.

The Lynds found in their second study of the same city that by the middle 1930s they needed a more complex set of distinctions, and so they used six categories of people in their analysis of social class. These were reported in 1937 in *Middletown in Transition*. The observation of greater complexity in the class structure of Middletown was significant and seems to have revealed subtleties in social stratification that would influence others to follow in later research on social stratification.

Only a short time later the U.S. Bureau of the Census attempted a classification of occupations that reflects the recognition of growing complexity in the way people in the United States earn their living. The classification scheme developed by Alba Edwards (1872–1947) for the U.S. Census moved away from the Lynds' original classification between businesspeople and workers and attempted to designate greater distinctions within categories of business owners, managers, and various categories of workers.

The classification of occupations developed by Edwards in 1943 had the following major categories:

1. Professional, technical, and kindred workers

2. Managers and administrators

3. Sales workers

4. Clerical workers

5. Craftsmen

6. Operatives

7. Laborers, except farmers

8. Farmworkers

The Edwards scale did represent an attempt at the development of a scale of occupations by a ranking method that correlates with income, education, and prestige. Later research in sociology and economics showed that these correlates existed, in a general sort of way. Nonetheless, earnings overlapped considerably across such categories as professionals and managers, with managers outearning professionals, though the latter is a higher category; also the classification of skilled craftsmen contained many who earned more than clerical and sales workers. The categories are actually quite heterogeneous and cover a large number of occupations that are not very similar within a category, as for example, laboratory technicians, nurses, and public educators who are classified with physicians and lawyers, within the highest broad category of professional, technical, and kindred workers.

Edwards had attempted to develop a classification of occupations within the existing census categories, and his effort sought to separate occupations that clustered by similarity of work, educational requirements, and income. The heterogeneity within his major categories prevented him from fully achieving his goal of a national occupational system of categories of jobs based on occupations recorded by the Bureau of Census.

During the late 1950s, August B. Hollingshead (1907–1980) and Frederick Redlich (1910–2004) conducted a major study of social class and its linkages to mental illness. They used a combination of the Edwards classification scheme combined with reported educational levels of respondents that progressed from grade school through graduate education. They also utilized a series of measures of the urban ecology of the community studied. Hollingshead and Redlich not only uncovered clear relationships between social class position and mental health status, but also contributed a measure of socioeconomic status, now sometimes referred to in handbooks on social measurement as the *Hollingshead two-factor index of social position*. The main features of occupational type and educational achievement were retained and the measures of residence and neighborhood used in the original project were dropped to make it a two-factor index.

The first attempt to do research on the national ranking of the prestige of particular occupations resulted in significant advances in 1947. This research was conducted on ninety occupations, with each receiving an estimate of its prestige rather than being categorized into a set of similar occupations represented as a class of one sort or another. This research on occupational prestige was carried out on a national sample by Cecil C. North (1878–1961) and Paul K. Hatt (1914–1953) through the National Opinion Research Center.

A national and representative sample of the entire adult population for the United States was interviewed. This first effort to create a scale of occupational prestige at the national level included 2,920 persons.

Each person was asked to select one of six alternative statements representing their opinion of the "general standing" of a job. The alternatives were:

1. Excellent standing

2. Good standing

3. Average standing

4. Somewhat below-average standing

5. Poor standing

6. Do not know where to place that one

A list of ninety occupations was read to each respondent, with opinions recorded. There was a low proportion of "don't know" responses. Numerical weights were given by assigning a score of 100 for "excellent" and 20 for "poor," and then averaging answers to develop a composite score. The highest-ranking scores ranged from 96 for U.S. Supreme Court Justice and 93 for physicians and state governors, down to a low of 34 for street sweeper and 33 for shoe shiner. In general, professional and managerial occupations ranked the highest and unskilled manual laboring occupations the lowest, with many office and sales positions, as well as more highly skilled blue-collar occupations, in the middle and lower-middle levels.

The respondents were asked the main reason they had ranked the occupations as they did, and income was the most commonly given reason, followed by service to humanity and education. None of these reasons was given by more than 18 percent of the sample, indicating no broad uniformity in bases for rankings.

This scale has become known as the *North-Hatt scale*. The scale was replicated in 1963 with a national sample of 651 adults and showed strong consistency in the prestige ratings of the occupations used in the original North-Hatt scale sixteen years earlier. These scales then began to be widely used in empirical research on social stratification.

It remained for the demographer-sociologist Otis D. Duncan (1921–2004) to expand the original scale with its ninety occupations to a more complete listing. By a weighting of income levels and education of people in various occupations, Duncan was able to construct a list of 425 occupations with composite rankings known as the *Duncan socioeconomic index*. This index was published in a larger work titled *Occupations and Social Status* (1961) by Albert J. Reiss (1922–2006), Otis Duncan, Paul Hatt, and Cecil North.

The question arises as to the benefits and advantages of the various measures of occupational prestige utilized in scales that attempt to measure socioeconomic status. In answer, it can be said that occupation is utilized by large sectors of the public in modern developed societies as an indicator of social position, and hence has some significant meaning in regard to general social status and class position. Second, occupation is clearly an imperfect indicator but nonetheless correlated to some degree with other dimensions of social stratification, such as educational level and income. It is probable that these three dimensions—occupational prestige, education, and estimated income—are utilized in a simplified manner by adult members of modern societies in placing individuals in day-to-day social interaction. A third advantage is that occupation, as scaled in measures of socioeconomic status, can be ascertained directly and without great difficulty. Connected to this third advantage is the inarguable degree of objectivity in the determination of occupation. A fourth advantage of scales that indicate occupational prestige is their ease in use in comparative and international research. This is in stark contrast to the familiarity required with community standards in the studies of status rankings and stratification in smaller cities and towns. Finally, the use of occupational rankings as a socioeconomic index can and has been successfully applied in research on national levels of stratification, as well as in research on smaller communities.

In summary, measures of socioeconomic status that are based on occupation are to be seen most strongly as a methodological index of social stratification with the limitations that an index entails. As will be discussed below, this is greatly preferred over the widespread tendency to utilize occupational rankings as a synonym, or single indicator, of social class. Some scholars have used the scores on socioeconomic status measures as an alternative to making a theoretical statement about their own position on the nature of social classes, with the effect of limiting the degree of investigation of the character and impact of social classes in social life.

There is another methodological limitation in the use of socioeconomic scales. They are widely used in correlation and regression analysis and treated as interval and ratio scales of measurement. These statistical applications utilize the arithmetic operations of addition, subtraction, multiplication, and even division. The assumption of equal-appearing intervals between the score values of the prestige ratings is a dubious assumption, as is that of an absolute zero point on the scale. No occupation has been scaled with zero prestige. The effect is the violation of some of the basic assumptions of parametric statistics used in the research on stratification.

The interest that social scientists have shown in measures of socioeconomic status is considerable, and scholars

in the social sciences and neighboring disciplines have been willing to borrow these measurement scales and use them in correlation analysis with a range of variables in their fields. Perhaps this popularity of the concept of socioeconomic status, and its measurement, is a product of the interest in "status" and "status attainment" in American studies of social stratification. These concepts are most consonant with North American beliefs in personal achievement and recognizable social location or position in a community, and even ideals regarding democratic consensus. Status in popular imagery is contained within the reality of individual influence and control. An emphasis on status and status aspirations is linked with occupation, and features personal achievement and success rather than family heritage, the importance and accident of birth, much less the influence of aristocratic advantage or the more distant, structural, and superindividual effects of "class." Status achievement and status "attainment" can also be analyzed with facility through the use of occupational rating scales that seem to quantify the prestige of occupations and their relative social standing.

The updating of the North-Hatt scale sixteen years later in 1963 by Robert Hodge, Paul Siegel, and Peter Rossi demonstrated longer-range similarity in patterns of prestige evaluations. This consistency—with a few notable exceptional occupations such as nuclear physicist, recognized by only around half of the sample in 1947 in contrast to 90 percent in 1963—was so strong that the expanded lists, along with the Duncan socioeconomic index, established the reliability of these measures. Overall, these studies have demonstrated that large sectors of the American public agree on the prestige ranking of occupations in the United States and that most of these rankings are similar across a large number of industrial societies of the world. The effect was that one or another scale for the measure of socioeconomic status has frequently been used in the interim in sociological and social-psychological research.

THEORIES OF SOCIAL CLASS AND THEIR IMPLICATIONS FOR SOCIOECONOMIC STATUS

As seen above, scholars who study socioeconomic status have conceived the inequality of socially stratified orders in complex societies as consisting of ranked statuses, with the ranks ordered on the basis of shared evaluations of the importance of the various positional ranks. An assumption of shared values is made in the approach. There is also an assumption of continuous gradations in socioeconomic status positions. Sharp breaks between status gradations are not envisioned, nor is there necessarily an individual consciousness of membership in the various status levels, nor group interactions based on status levels, nor interacting groups based on prestige of position, nor demarked social classes that possess distinctive boundaries and objectively measured social characteristics.

In the mid-nineteenth century, an earlier tradition in social theory developed. This tradition emphasized the reality of social classes as the primary dimension of social stratification. These ideas have European antecedents and are seen most clearly in the scholarly writings as well as political polemics of Karl Marx (1818–1883), a social thinker of German origin. Born to a generation following Marx, another German scholar, Max Weber (1864–1920), offered strong criticism of Marx, but refined certain aspects of this overall approach, which carried a much greater emphasis on conflict, power, and social change in human social life. Since approximately the middle of the twentieth century, American sociologists such as C. Wright Mills (1916–1962) have also been developing conceptual approaches and theoretically informed research projects that analyze the role of power and conflict in social life.

This research continues to the present. To these conflict theorists, social stratification and social classes are among the most important aspects of society and social life, with enormous consequences for society as well as for the individual. This group of thinkers is likely to retain Max Weber's emphasis on social class as economic behavior with consequences for the life chances of individuals. These life chances include the likelihood of experiencing such important matters as living out the first year of life, marrying within a social stratum, attending a college or university, and engaging in certain forms of political activities.

In summary, scholars using these approaches that analyze conflict and power in social life view social classes as real, and as having boundaries. Social classes in this view also have strong consequences for individual members. The relations between classes are an important aspect of social processes in complex societies, and the various social classes and their relations are significant components of social organization, particularly in advanced, industrial societies. Persons may or may not be conscious of membership in a class, and may be confused regarding their status, but the consequences of class are real, nonetheless. In this view, class membership under some conditions can lead to heightened consciousness and organized political activity.

From the standpoint of the conflict approach, the emphasis on socioeconomic status in stratification research has taken the political fangs away from the concept of social class. In their place, the study of socioeconomic status has created an image of individuals who compete for occupations and occupational status in open markets, and through their individualistic actions pursue higher status, with the prestige of these statuses based on shared evaluation of the social import of occupations with their allied skills and contributions to the social life of the society. In much of the earlier American research on socioeconomic status, classes are nominalistic classifications, or exist in name rather than by being distinguishable through definable boundaries. Status gradations are seen as continuous, without sharp breaks—perhaps resembling a ladder—rather than as broken into class components with consequences for action in the politics of redistribution. Research that favors the analysis of socioeconomic status as a continuous line in a status hierarchy is likely to utilize concepts from structure-functional analysis and to emphasize order and integration in the stratification structures of societies. This integration of stratified orders is likely to be viewed as permeating various institutional spheres, such as the family, religion, education, and economy, and to contribute to the stability of the social order.

In conclusion, social scientists whose research and theoretical orientation have convinced them that social classes are real social entities that involve inequality on significant social goods assert that there are severe limitations with the typical use of measures of socioeconomic status. In their view, the research that applies these latter measures of inequality does not grapple with the reality of social classes within the social structure or their consequences for the life chances of individuals. The research that utilizes measures of socioeconomic status is also likely to overlook power in social life and the possibilities for political action that are implied in the historical usage of social classes in analyzing important aspects of social organization.

SEE ALSO *Blau, Peter M.; Blue Collar and White Collar; Class; Duncan, Otis Dudley; Education, Unequal; Hierarchy; Lynd, Robert and Helen; Marx, Karl; Middle Class; Occupational Status; Social Status; Social Theory; Stratification; Weber, Max; Working Class*

BIBLIOGRAPHY

Edwards, Alba M., and U.S. Bureau of the Census. 1943. *Sixteenth Census of the United States: 1940. Population: Comparative Occupational Statistics, 1870 to 1940.* Washington, DC: U.S. Government Printing Office.

Gilbert, Dennis, and Joseph A. Kahl. 1982. *The American Class Structure: A New Synthesis.* Homewood, IL: Dorsey.

Hodge, Robert, Paul Siegel, and Peter Rossi. 1966. Occupational Prestige in the United States. In *Class, Status, and Power: Social Stratification in Comparative Perspective*, ed. Reinhardt Bendix and Seymour Martin Lipset, 322–334. 2nd ed. New York: Free Press.

Hodge, Robert, Donald Treiman, and Peter Rossi. 1966. A Comparative Study of Occupational Prestige. In *Class, Status, and Power: Social Stratification in Comparative Perspective*, ed. Reinhardt Bendix and Seymour Martin Lipset, 309–321. 2nd ed. New York: Free Press.

Hollingshead, August B., and Fredrick C. Redlich. 1958. *Social Class and Mental Illness: A Community Study*. New York: Wiley.

Kerbo, Harold R. 2006. *Social Stratification and Inequality: Class Conflict in Historical, Comparative, and Global Perspective*. 6th ed. New York: McGraw-Hill.

Krauss, Irving. 1976. *Stratification, Class, and Conflict*. New York: Free Press.

Landry, Bart. 2007. *Race, Gender, and Class: Theory and Methods of Analysis*. Upper Saddle River, NJ: Pearson Prentice-Hall.

Lynd, Robert, and Helen Lynd. 1929. *Middletown: A Study in Contemporary American Culture*. New York: Harcourt.

Lynd, Robert, and Helen Lynd. 1937. *Middletown in Transition: A Study in Cultural Conflicts*. New York: Harcourt.

Miller, Delbert. 1977. *Handbook of Research Design and Social Measurement*. 3rd ed. New York: McKay.

Mills, C. Wright. 1956. *The Power Elite*. New York: Oxford University Press.

Nakao, Keiko, and Judith Treas. 1994. Updating Occupational Prestige and Socioeconomic Scores: How the New Measures Measure Up. *Sociological Methodology* 24: 1–72.

North, Cecil C., and Paul K. Hatt. 1947. Jobs and Occupations: A Popular Evaluation. *Opinion News* 9: 3–31.

Reissman, Leonard. 1959. *Class in American Society*. Glencoe, IL: Free Press.

Treiman, Donald J. 1977. *Occupational Prestige in Comparative Perspective*. New York: Academic Press.

Weber, Max. 1947. *The Theory of Social and Economic Organization*. Trans. Talcott Parsons. New York: Free Press.

Kenneth N. Eslinger

SOCIOGRAM

SEE *Sociometry.*

SOCIOLOGY

Commonly accepted definitions of sociology agree that it is the scientific or systematic study of human society. The focus is on understanding and explaining, and ranges from the individual in social interaction to groups to societies and global social processes. Unique to sociology is its emphasis upon the reciprocal relationship between individuals and societies as they influence and shape each other.

Methods of discovery range from quantitative methodologies patterned after those of natural science with the goals of explanation and prediction to strategies for social reform and service to qualitative methodologies that focus on interpretation and understanding rather than prediction.

HISTORICAL DEVELOPMENT AND THE FOUNDATION THEORIES OF SOCIOLOGY

As a discipline, sociology arose early in the nineteenth century in response to rapid social change. Major transformations in the eighteenth and nineteenth centuries, such as rapid industrialization resulting in a large, anonymous workforce with workers spending most of their time away from families and traditions; large-scale urbanization throughout Europe and the industrializing world; and a political revolution of new ideas (individual rights and democracy), directed a spotlight on the nature of societies and social change.

The French social thinker Auguste Comte (1798–1857) first coined the term *sociology* to describe a new way of thinking about societies as systems governed by principles of organization and change. Most agree that Émile Durkheim (1858–1917), the French sociologist, made the largest contribution to the emergence of sociology as a social scientific discipline. Both empirical research—collecting and quantifying social data—and abstract conceptions of society were major elements of Durkheim's research. Durkheim's work had a major, early impact on the discipline, both quantitatively and qualitatively.

In the nineteenth and twentieth centuries two more of the giants in sociological thought emerged in mainstream German sociology: Max Weber (1864–1920) and Georg Simmel (1858–1918). Additionally, Karl Marx (1818–1883), while on the edge of sociology, had a major impact on German sociology and on the discipline as a whole. Marx was concerned with the oppressiveness that resulted from industrialization and the capitalist system rather than the disorder to which other social thinkers were reacting. Advocating revolution as the only means to end the inequality between the controlling bourgeoisie class and the exploited proletariat class created by the new industrialized society, Marx produced much of his work while in exile from his native Germany (Marx and Engels [1848] 1967). His writing provides a continuous strand of sociological theory, heavily influential in Europe and, at times, in the United States. The importance of Marx's work in shaping early sociology also lies in how German sociology developed in opposition to Marxist theory (Ritzer 2000).

Weber's concern with ideas and systems of ideas (particularly religious ideas) and their effect on a capitalist economic system—specifically with Protestantism as a belief system that encouraged its members to embrace change—contrasts with Marx's reflection of the economy in ideas. Simmel's influence on sociology, unlike that of Marx and Weber, was through his studies of small-scale social phenomena. Focusing on forms of social interaction and types of actors who interact, his work was most influential on early sociologists at the University of Chicago.

In response to the poverty of immigrants and African Americans in the urban United States, projects of social reform and settlement house movements provided solutions. Much of this work was based in Chicago, where early social reformers and social thinkers combined to conduct field research and organize the first major sociology department at the University of Chicago. The sociology department, founded by Albion Small (who also founded the first sociology journal in the United States, the *American Journal of Sociology*, in 1895) dominated the discipline for fifty years. American students of sociology had easy access to Simmel's ideas, which fit with the micro, symbolic interactionist perspective, through his followers (and, in some cases, translators) Small and Robert Park.

During the early years of sociology in the United States, theoretical influences of the period were combined with empirical research and the social reform projects and service conducted in the Chicago area. Trained as a social worker, Jane Addams spoke out about the inhumane treatment of immigrants who were entering the United States at increasingly higher rates. She founded Hull House in Chicago to provide assistance to immigrant families and gathered a community of sociologists and politicians to discuss and act on urban problems. W. E. B. Du Bois, an African American sociologist at Atlanta University, studied similar social problems for the black community in the United States and wrote and spoke out against racial inequality.

SYMBOLIC INTERACTIONISM

Symbolic interactionism, the dominant perspective championed by the philosopher George Herbert Mead (1863–1931) and others influenced by Simmel at the Chicago school, was the first foundation theory in American sociology. Although the symbolic interactionist perspective emphasizes the reciprocal relationship between the individual and society, its critics complain that it overlooks the widespread effects of culture and important sociological factors such as race, class, and gender.

In the 1930s, as the influence of the Chicago school lessened, state universities throughout the midwestern United States began to incorporate sociology departments into their curriculum, with a strong focus on rural sociology. In the 1940s the emphasis in sociology shifted away from the type of descriptive research done at Chicago to sociological theory and empirical inquiry, with the rise of

influence from departments at Columbia, Harvard, and other Ivy League universities. European theorists such as Durkheim and Weber were translated and (re)introduced, and their work inspired large growth in sociological theory, particularly structural functionalism, the dominant theory in American sociology until the 1960s.

STRUCTURAL FUNCTIONALISM

Another foundation theory within sociology, the structural functional paradigm provides a view of society as a complex system of parts working together to promote both solidarity and stability for society as a whole. This perspective owes much to Comte and his concern for social integration during the rapid social change of the period. While Comte advocated social reform, in Britain the social philosopher Herbert Spencer (1820–1903) rejected social reform as intervention in the natural process of the evolution of society. Applying the principle of "the survival of the fittest" to the adaptation of societies rather than of organisms, Spencer's ideas initially gained a large following throughout England and the United States.

Functionalists, following Durkheim, emphasized the study of social order and how social reforms could provide remedies for social disorder. Social structures (relatively stable patterns of social behavior) function together to preserve society. In the United States, Talcott Parsons (1902–1979) at Harvard was the primary proponent of the structural functionalism theory that dominated American sociology until the 1960s. A student of Parsons's, Robert K. Merton (1910–2003) distinguished between manifest and latent functions of social structures, while allowing that there are also societal social dysfunctions for some. The influence of structural functionalism has declined since the 1960s with criticism for its focus on stability and static structures, its inability to deal with social change, and its failure to acknowledge how inequalities based on social class, race and ethnicity, and gender may lead to tension and conflict.

Following World War II the strong influence of sociological theory championed by Parsons and others concerned with the prestige of the discipline continued. Quantitative data methods were seen as the best way of making the discipline more professional and increasing prestige. Demography and survey research became more important with the availability of governmental funds for financing large research projects. Major advances in quantitative research eventually led to a variety of formal analyses for survey data, including multivariate statistics, path analysis, multiple regression, and complex causal models. In the late 1950s, however, traditional sociology came under attack for its preoccupation with theory and empiricism. The 1960s also brought challenges from field researchers and reformers to focus more on social problems.

SOCIAL CONFLICT THEORY

Social conflict theory is, in many ways, a reaction to the structural functionalist perspective. The social inequality pervasive in society and ignored by structural functionalists is seen as a source of conflict and change. Conflict theory examines how society is stratified along class, race and ethnicity, gender, and age categories, and how these categories are linked to the unequal distribution of resources. Patterns of social interaction are inherent with benefits for some and deprivations for others. The goal for conflict theory is to understand the conflict between the advantaged and the disadvantaged while also taking action to reduce inequality. The perspective is certainly influenced by Marx, although critics complain that it does not have a firm enough grounding in Marxism, which was well developed in European sociology but lacked support and understanding in the United States. Critics of the social conflict perspective also complain that its pursuit of political goals shows a lack of scientific objectivity—although this theory had significant influence on contemporary theories, such as feminist theory, which emphasize the importance of political goals.

Sociology since the 1960s has expanded its emphasis to focus more on questions of race and ethnicity and gender. There has also been an incorporation of professional fields such as criminology, industrial relations, and evaluation research. In the 1990s and 2000s a variety of new areas and topics achieved prominence in American sociology: economic sociology; nongovernmental organizations having to do with justice, human rights, the arts, and the environment; immigration and ethnic identities; inequality; the growth and influence of science and technology; and social capital as resources for social mobility, citizenship, and community participation.

MICROSOCIOLOGY AND MACROSOCIOLOGY

Micro and *macro* refer to the level of analysis or the area of theoretical concern. Microsociology is the study of group dynamics and interaction, whereas macrosociology focuses on large-scale social systems and institutional arrangements. One controversy about the level of analysis was often phrased as a discussion of whether phenomena could be reduced to individual level properties or whether, instead, phenomena must be viewed in terms of their "emergent" properties that do not coincide with simply aggregating the individual level. While some formulations still allude to this controversy, it is common for researchers to attempt linkages between the micro and macro by viewing the effects of one on the other.

Macrosociology At the macro level sociologists ask, what are the broad patterns of interaction that shape society as a whole, and how does this influence take place? The most common institutions, found in most societies and most often studied by sociologists, are the following five:

The family, which meets the needs of societal replenishment and the care and socialization of children. At the macrolevel, sociologists ask how the definition of family is changing and how that affects the larger society.

Education, which meets the need for the transmission of culture and social and job skills. Sociologists ask how the educational system varies across cultures and nations, how it both mirrors and perpetuates the inequality in society.

Religion, a third institution, which meets the need for explanations of the unknown. Sociologists are concerned with why religions take various forms and how religious activity affects society.

The economy, which organizes the distribution of goods and services and is a focus for sociology because it determines who—individuals, organizations, nations—gets what—resources and access to resources in nations and globally.

Politics (or "the polity," or government), which is also a participant in the distribution of power as well as the maintenance of order. Sociology looks at how the world's political systems vary, who has power and why, and whether there is a global political system.

Both within and outside the context of social institutions, sociologists explore why stratification (systems of ranking into power and prestige hierarchies) exists and how it determines individual societal outcomes. How do social class divisions (based on economic position in society) affect culture, opportunities, and social mobility? What is poverty and who are the poor? Why does inequality exist and how might it be overcome?

A current trend in sociological thought has to do with the process of globalization. Rapid changes in communication and transportation have transformed perceptions of time and space so that the world of personal experience is a global one. Sociologists ask how economic change has taken place, what is a global economy, and what are the implications of globalization? How is economic globalization connected to political development? As political boundaries change, how are cultural boundaries affected? How do local cultures conflict with an emerging global culture and what is the place of women and people of color in that relationship?

Microsociology Many different areas are investigated within microsociology from different perspectives using different methodologies. Microsociology can be broadly conceptualized as considering issues related to self and identity, status and power, cooperation and competition, exchange, legitimation, and justice.

Fundamental to most areas within microsociology is the insight that individuals define themselves, based in large part on how others see and interact with them. Because interaction is central to the self, different identities are developed and projected. Research in the general area of identity and self includes both qualitative and quantitative investigations of topics such as role taking, role making, altercasting, identity disruptions or deflections, and self-referent behavior.

Much of microsociology is related to the general area of group dynamics. This area had early ties with psychology, which fashioned much of its approach including the acceptance and use of experiments as a research tool. Status and power have been consistently important areas of work within microsociology. One of the most important insights from this line of research is that status is relative to the group; that is, while people might possess the same characteristic from one setting to another, these characteristics might have very different salience in different settings.

Other group-dynamics research included a wide range of studies that could be characterized as examining cooperation and competition. While many of these examined dyads and interaction between one group and another, others examined social dilemmas—settings in which there is some degree of conflict between individual and group interests. Once resources and incentives are under consideration, exchange becomes central. Exchange formulations, some more akin to economics and others more akin to psychology, developed and took on a distinctly sociological focus by examining how the type of exchange affected both the behavior and emotion of the exchange participants. The allocation of different resources is studied within exchange formulations, and the resulting assessments, behavior, and feelings of fairness are the focus of justice and equity formulations. Related to assessment of justice is the degree of acceptance of particular institutional arrangements or legitimation.

Ethnomethodology, or method of the people, is a type of microsociology that focuses upon the everyday practices in which people engage. This field differs from most other microsociologies by eschewing the use of abstraction to summarize observations.

CHALLENGES TO THE SOCIOLOGICAL PARADIGM

Reacting against the dominant paradigm that seemed to take a male, Western European, heterosexual model of the actor as representative of all actors, various critiques developed within sociology. These critiques are extremely varied both in their focus and methodology, but perhaps the most well known were feminist critiques. Although there had been early sociological analysis of the subordination of women (Ward 1883), most of the feminist analyses of sex and gender coincided with what is usually called the second wave of feminism, dating from the 1960s. During this period there was also increased attention to race and ethnicity.

Many of the sociological feminist writings emphasized the subordination of women and the institutionalization of patriarchy. Some of this work questioned the sex and gender association and sexual categorizations as well. One branch of this developed into "queer theory," a critique of heterosexual assumptions and power.

For the most part, feminist and other critical approaches did not question the fundamental approaches to the study of sociological phenomena. Rather, the feminist literature emphasized substantive issues that centered on societal power differentials that lead to a wide variety of life experiences that constrain almost every aspect of women's lives. Another literature emphasized how "taken for granted" assumptions of gender and sex affected what observers saw and how they interpreted it. However, there was another group of feminists who challenged traditional epistemologies and argued that who the observer was determined what could be known. This is a radical claim because it violates a traditionally accepted tenet of most sciences that intersubjectivity can be obtained: that different people can be taught to see what others can see.

Postmodernism Sometimes closely aligned with feminist critiques are postmodern critiques. These critiques emerged in the late 1970s and into the 1980s. Postmodernism is a set of sensitizing concepts and ideas rather than a well-developed and agreed-upon set of premises. These concepts challenge traditional views associated with the Enlightenment. In particular, the concepts of objectivity, the transparency of language, and the separation between science and politics are questioned. Postmodern critique has been important across most of the social sciences and the humanities, alerting sociologists to how the political becomes enmeshed in the way questions are asked and subsequently answered. Along with this is attention to grand "narratives," or ways of telling particular types of stories. From this perspective, science is one type of narrative and does not necessarily have a status different from other types of narratives such as folklore. The emphasis is upon how scientists come to believe what they believe. Some particularly radical versions of postmodernism suggest that empirical reality has little effect upon the development and testing of theories.

THE ROLE OF SOCIOLOGISTS

There is a continuing debate within sociology about the proper role of sociologists. This debate echoes questions that have always been associated with sociology: Are sociologists scientists? Are sociologists advocates and reformers? Are sociologists scholars who practice a social science, whose methodology differs from that of the natural sciences?

Because sociologists vary in their orientation, their perceived and expressed views also vary. There are some who steadfastly claim that sociologists should not become involved in political agendas or arguments lest they jeopardize their dedication and reputation for being oriented toward the truth rather than toward advocacy. There are others who argue that the subject matter of sociology dictates that sociologists become involved in providing information that reflects upon different policy initiatives. This approach separates advocacy for a particular position from provision of information. Still others argue that sociologists should be advocates for particular policies, given sociological evidence. An example of such advocacy was the American Sociological Association's filing of a brief to the U.S. Supreme Court on behalf of the University of Michigan Law School and the Student Intervenors in *Grutter v. Bollinger* (2003). In this case, the Association argued that sociological research clearly and consistently documented the pervasiveness of race in life experience such that universities cannot adequately assess candidates or their potential without considering it.

Decisions about the role of sociologists are frequently contested among sociologists themselves—a clear indication that perspectives, methods, and approaches vary considerably. However, because these contestations are often in public sociological forums, it is also a demonstration of the tolerance, or at least acceptance, of the variability within the discipline.

SEE ALSO *Groups; Methodology; Norms; Parsons, Talcott; Social Science; Social Theory*

BIBLIOGRAPHY

Berger, Peter L. 1963. *Invitation to Sociology: A Humanistic Perspective.* New York: Doubleday.

Buroway, Michael. 2004. To Advance, Sociology Must Not Retreat. *Chronicle of Higher Education* 50 (49): B24.

Calhoun, Craig, and Troy Duster. 2005. Sociology's Visions and Divisions. *Chronicle of Higher Education* 51 (49): B7.

Durkheim, Émile. [1895] 1958. *The Rules of Sociological Method.* 8th ed. Ed. George E. G. Catlin. Glencoe, IL: Free Press.

Lawler, Edward J., Cecilia Ridgeway, and Barry Markovsky. 1993. Structural Social Psychology and Micro-Macro Problem. *Sociological Theory* 11: 268–290.

Marx, Karl, and Friedrich Engels. [1848] 1967. *Manifesto of the Communist Party.* New York: International Publishers.

Mills, C. Wright. 1959. *The Sociological Imagination.* New York: Oxford University Press.

Ritzer, George. 2000. *Classical Sociological Theory.* 3rd ed. Boston: McGraw-Hill.

Ward, Lester. 1883. *Dynamic Sociology.* New York: Appleton.

Kathy J. Kuipers
Jane Sell

SOCIOLOGY, AFRICAN

The defining basis of African sociology is that it takes African *ontological standpoints* as its point of departure, not just the description or analysis of the African conditions. As the systematic study of sociational life and dynamics, sociology can neither be restricted to the study of societies created in the wake of the Industrial Revolution nor accommodate the Enlightenment's spatial division of labor between sociology and anthropology—with the latter as the study of nonindustrial societies. Similarly sociological analysis predates nineteenth-century Europe.

AFRICAN SOCIOLOGY IN ANTIQUITY

'Adb al-Rahmān Ibn Khaldūn's three-volume *Kitab Al-'Ibar* is a major sociology work on African antiquity (Dhaouadi 1990, Alatas 2006). In the first volume, *Muqaddimah* (1967 [1378]), Ibn Khaldūn set out the framework for adjudicating between competing data sources; the volume was self-consciously sociological. He outlined his new "sciences" of human organization and society 452 years before the first volume of Auguste Comte's six-volume *The Course of Positive Philosophy* (1830) was published. Ibn Khaldūn also discussed the concept of *asabiyyah* (group feeling), or the normative basis of group cohesion, how it decomposes and is reconstituted, and the ways it manifests at different levels of social organization and among different groups. This was 515 years before Émile Durkheim's *The Division of Labour in Society* (1893) was published.

TWENTIETH-CENTURY AFRICAN SOCIOLOGY

In contemporary Africa, sociology is perhaps the social science discipline that has benefited most from the "nationalist" project, both as a state-building project and as an intellectual endeavor. Sociology benefited from the state-building project as the number of universities and student enrollment grew exponentially. As an intellectual project, sociology flourished in the wake of the rebellion against anthropology and its "epistemology of alterity" (Mafeje 1997). In a series of articles published between 1967 and 1971, Bernard Magubane (1971, 2000) led the charge against social anthropology and its alter ego *Sociology in Africa*. Magubane's works involved the articulation of African ontological standpoints in the face of Eurocentric discourses of "othering." While most of the early academic African sociologists were trained as anthropologists, Omafume Onoge's rejection of the feasibility of being "a native anthropologist" (Onoge 1977) reflected a wider revolt. African sociology, he argued, must break with the alterity and negation endemic in "applied anthropology." Archie Mafeje's "The Ideology of 'Tribalism'" (1971) was a partial and situational rejection of the concept of "tribe" and a substantive rejection of "tribalism" as a viable concept for explaining political relationship in Africa. The paper was part of a wider rebellion against alterity.

In many ways Amílcar Cabral prefigured the concerns expressed by Magubane and others. Cabral's "Brief Analysis of the Social Structure in Guinea" ([1964] 1970) and "The Weapon of Theory" ([1966] 1979) are exemplary sociological analyses and products of field methods. The former served as the source codes for "The Weapon of Theory," which set an important departure from the dominant Marxist discourse of the time; it derived from a specific African ontological standpoint. If for Karl Marx and Friedrich Engels the history of humankind is the history of class struggle, Cabral argued that "the true motive force of history is the mode of production." The mantra of class struggle not only runs against the grain of observed historical patterns, it produces "for some human groups in our countries … the sad position of being people without history … [and negates] the inalienable right of every people to have its own history" (Cabral 1979, p. 125).

FROM REVOLT TO AFFIRMATION

Beyond revolt, sociology also involved the affirmation of African ontological standpoints. N. A. Fadipe ([1939] 1970), Cabral, Magubane, and Mafeje reflect such affirmation. Here Mafeje's *The Theory and Ethnography of African Social Formations* (1991) signaled an epistemic shift. The concept of "*tributary modes of production*," originally developed by Samir Amin (Mafeje 1991, p. iv), was the organizing framework for Mafeje's study of the interlacustrine kingdoms of the Great Lake region. The idea of "tributary modes of production" was meant to capture what was "outside the purview of European history" and needed to "be understood in their own terms" (Mafeje 1991, p. iii). What Mafeje produced was a concept of tributary relations that transcended several dimensions of the contents that Amin gave it.

Ruth First's *The Barrel of a Gun* (1972 [1970]) was an important development in political sociology; it was such a nuanced deployment of the category of class in explaining coup d'état on the continent that it fundamentally altered the debate. This was against the dominant Africanist explanation that gave primacy to ethnicity or "tribalism." Peter Ekeh's "Colonialism and the Two Publics in Africa" (1975) represented a similarly important deployment of grounded scholarship and a sociological mind-set in making sense of contrasting behaviors of the "political elite" in the realm of the state, on the one hand, and the "primordial public" of familial domain, on the other. In spite of the sociological contents of Ekeh's analysis, it has taken an essentialist form in the hands of several Africanists.

A major development in African sociology since 1980 is the effort to use endogenous ontological narratives as source codes for sociology. A major strand was pioneered by Akínsolá Akìwowo; another was inspired by what Oyèrónké Oyěwùmí called the African "world-sense" (Oyěwùmí 1997, p. 3). Akìwowo's works (1983, 1986, 1988a, 1988b, 1999) involved distilling sociological concepts from the *Ifá* literary corpus (a system of life commentaries, discourses, and divination among the Yoruba). Jìmí O. Adésínà (2002, 2006) extended the insights from Akìwowo's works, arguing that *Ifá* texts and the wider Yoruba ontological narratives offer distinct epistemic insights: Ti'bi-Ti're logic, the "mutual self-embeddedness of seemingly contradictory things" (Adésínà 2006, p.13). The implications for sociology are conceptual and methodological. These involve a sociological orientation to sociational life that embraces the coexistence of "opposites" and the open-endedness of outcome in social interaction or between contending social forces, nuanced discourse, and embracing senses, reason, and inspiration in sociological research.

In the early twenty-first century the most exciting area of sociological work is in the field of African gender scholarship. Much of these derive works from using African "world-sense" in sociological inquiry. The works of Ifi Amadiume (1987) and Oyěwùmí (1997, 2003, 2005) represent distinct sociological insights and allow for epistemic ruptures from the dominant North American and European feminist scholarship. As Oyěwùmí noted, "Gender categories are [not] universal or timeless … [or] present in every society at all times" (Oyěwùmí 1997, p. xi). The inscription of gender ordering in the anatomical body or the coincidence of anatomical maleness and anatomical femaleness does not reflect the experience historically or even contemporarily in the two contexts in which they worked. Igbo and Yoruba languages are gender neutral, and their social structures privilege age seniority over gender difference. Seniority within a consanguine relationship is the primary marker of social position.

Amadiume and Oyěwùmí demonstrated across the spectrum of social, occupational, political, and economic ordering in both contexts that "biology [did not and does not] determine social position" (Oyěwùmí 1997, p. 17). Both have inspired other African scholars to explore other cultural contexts. Beyond scholarship, these works are valuable for women's rights struggles. Much of the androcentric power plays and diminution of women that is often claimed in the name of "tradition" is not traditional.

SEE ALSO *African Studies; Sociology, Third World*

BIBLIOGRAPHY

Adésínà, Jìmí O. 2002. Sociology and Yoruba Studies: Epistemic Intervention, or Doing Sociology in the "Vernacular." *African Sociological Review* 6 (1): 91–114.

Adésínà, Jìmí O. 2006. Sociology, Endogeneity, and the Challenge of Transformation: An Inaugural Lecture Delivered on Wednesday, 16 August 2006, Rhodes University, Grahamstown, South Africa.

Akìwowo, Akínsolá. 1983. *Àjobí and Àjogbé: Variations on the Theme of Sociation.* Inaugural Lectures series no. 46. Ile-Ife, Nigeria: University of Ife Press.

Akìwowo, Akínsolá. 1986. Contributions to the Sociology of Knowledge from an African Oral Poetry. *International Sociology* 1: 343–358.

Akìwowo, Akínsolá. 1988a. Indigenization of the Social Sciences and Emancipation of Thought. Valedictory Lecture, 18 August. Obafemi Awolowo University, Ile-Ife, Nigeria.

Akìwowo, Akínsolá. 1988b. Universalism and Indigenisation in Sociological Theory: Introduction. *International Sociology* 3: 155–160.

Akìwowo, Akínsolá. 1999. Indigenous Sociologies: Extending the Scope of the Argument. *International Sociology* 14: 115–138.

Alatas, Farid Sayed. 2006. A Khadunian Exemplar for a Historical Sociology for the South. *Current Sociology* 54 (3): 397–411.

Amadiume, Ifi. 1987. *Male Daughters, Female Husbands: Gender and Sex in an African Society.* London: Zed Books.

Cabral, Amílcar. 1970. Brief Analysis of the Social Structure in Guinea. In *Revolution in Guinea: Selected Texts.* New York: Monthly Review.

Cabral, Amílcar. 1979. The Weapon of Theory: Presuppositions and Objectives of National Liberation in Relation to Social Structure. In *Unity and Struggle: Speeches and Writings.* Trans. Michael Wolfers, 119–137. New York: Monthly Review.

Dhaouadi, Mahmoud. 1990. Ibn Khaldun: The Founding Father of Eastern Sociology. *International Sociology* 5 (3): 319–335.

Ekeh, Peter P. 1975. Colonialism and the Two Publics in Africa: A Theoretical Statement. *Comparative Studies in Society and History* 17 (1): 91–112.

Fadipe, N. A. 1970. *The Sociology of the Yoruba,* ed. and with an introduction by Francis Olu Okediji and Oladejo O. Okediji. Ibadan, Nigeria: Ibadan University Press. (Orig. pub. 1939.)

First, Ruth. [1970] 1972. *The Barrel of a Gun: The Politics of Coup D'état in Africa.* Harmondsworth, U.K.: Penguin Books.

Ibn Khaldūn, 'Adb al-Rahmān. [1378] 1967. *The Muqaddimah: An Introduction to History.* Trans. Franz Rosenthal. London: Routledge and Kegan Paul.

Mafeje, Archie. 1977. Neocolonialism, State Capitalism, or Revolution. In *African Social Studies: A Radical Reader,* eds. Peter C. W. Gutkind and Peter Waterman, 412–422. London: Heinemann. (Orig. pub. 1973.)

Mafeje, Archie. 1991. *The Theory and Ethnography of African Social Formations: The Case of the Interlacustrine Kingdoms.* London: Codesria.

Mafeje, Archie. 1997. Who Are the Makers and Objects of Anthropology? A Critical Comment on Sally Falk Moore's *Anthropology and Africa. African Sociological Review* 1 (1): 1–15.

Magubane, Bernard. 1971. A Critical Look at the Indices Used in the Study of Social Change in Colonial Africa. *Current Anthropology* 12 (4–5): 419–445.

Magubane, Bernard. 2000. *African Sociology: Towards a Critical Perspective; The Collected Essays of Bernard Makhosezwe Magubane.* Trenton, NJ: Africa World.

Onoge, Omafume. 1977. Revolutionary Imperatives in African Sociology. In *African Social Studies: A Radical Reader,* eds. Peter C. W. Gutkind and Peter Waterman, 32–43. London: Heinemann. (Orig. pub. 1971.)

Oyěwùmí, Oyèrónké. 1997. *The Invention of Women: Making an African Sense of Western Gender Discourse.* Minneapolis: University of Minnesota Press.

Oyěwùmí, Oyèrónké, ed. 2003. *African Women and Feminism.* Trenton, NJ: Africa World.

Oyěwùmí, Oyèrónké, ed. 2005. *African Gender Studies: A Reader.* New York: Palgrave Macmillan.

Jìmí O. Adésínà

SOCIOLOGY, AMERICAN

American sociology is generally viewed through the prism of accomplishments made by native-born white males at predominately white institutions in theory, methodology, and various substantive areas of research. The history of American sociology often begins by noting that William Graham Sumner (1840–1910), during the 1872 to 1873 academic year, taught the first sociology course in this nation, Principles of Sociology (Bernard 1948). Further investigation into the history of the discipline highlights Arthur B. Woodford, who, in 1885 at Indiana University, became the first faculty member in the United States to have the word *sociology* in his official title (Himes 1949). While the first named department of sociology was established at the University of Kansas in 1889, it is generally accepted that American sociology began in earnest upon the emergence of the Chicago school of sociology, the moniker bestowed on scholars led by Robert Park (1864–1944) and Ernest W. Burgess (1886–1966), who were engaged in sociological activity at the University of Chicago between 1915 and 1930. Parallel with the origin of the sociology department at the University of Chicago in 1892 was the strengthening of the social gospel movement in the United States. The social gospel movement placed the salvation and uplift of American society above the salvation of one's individual soul. While proponents of the social gospel were interested in ameliorating urban problems, early American sociologists were interested in studying the demographic transition from rural to urban society through scientific inquiry and practical sociology, as practiced at Hull House in Chicago by Jane Addams (1860–1935) and by the antilynching activity of Ida B. Wells-Barnett (1862-1931). It was a common interest in issues such as the expanding urban population that led a group of like-minded sociologists to organize their own professional association.

The American Sociological Society (now called the American Sociological Association) was established in 1905 with Lester F. Ward (1841–1913) as its first president. Seeking to separate itself from closely related disciplines, men such as E. A. Ross, Albion Small (1854–1926), and C. W. A. Veditz (1872–1926) spearheaded the founding of this organization. While the accomplishments of early Chicago sociologists such as Park and Burgess and notable early American sociologists such as Ward, Small, Sumner, Ross, and Franklin H. Giddins are laudable as they helped define this emerging field during its infancy in the United States, few are aware that there existed during this era a parallel world of unacknowledged sociologists whose contributions to the discipline were equally, if not more, significant than those traditionally revered as the fathers of the American brand of sociology.

The teaching of sociology at black institutions began in 1894 at Morgan State University. It is provident that the emergence of this discipline in America coincided with the birth of black colleges that, in many respects, were borne from black Americans' attempts to improve their condition in this nation. According to L. L. Bernard, "Sociology [in America] was first accepted by the smaller institutions of the South and by the Negro colleges. The reasons for the Negro interest is, I think, sufficiently evident in the fact that a minority group was trying honestly to understand the social situation in which it found itself" (1948, p. 14). Ultimately, black American scholars viewed sociology as a tool with which to challenge their second-class citizenship through the establishment of research programs designed to formulate strategies to ameliorate the social, economic, and physical conditions uncovered through objective scientific research. Foremost among the institutions that established research programs on the

"Negro problem" were Tuskegee University, Howard University, Fisk University, and Atlanta University.

Tuskegee University established the Department of Records and Research, under the direction of Monroe N. Work between 1904 and 1945, for the purpose of conducting research on black Americans. Foremost among Work's accomplishments as the director of this program was the publication of the *Negro Yearbook*. This pamphlet periodically detailed the horrific and gruesome practice of lynching and other forms of violence against black Americans and was instrumental in the eventual demise of the barbaric practice. At Howard University, where Kelly Miller (1863–1939) taught the institution's first sociology course in 1895, the leadership of E. Franklin Frazier (1894–1964) during the 1930s was the driving force behind the "Howard school of thought." This concept refers to the school's "transitional [theory] that broke away from the dominant biological/genetic [racial theory] paradigm" (Henry 1995, p. 49) that was influential in introducing a multiculturalist perspective on race relations. Inquiry into the substantive area of race was also undertaken at Fisk University during the United States's Jim Crow era. Under the direction of Charles S. Johnson (1893–1956), the Race Relations Department was established to develop effective strategies by which relations between blacks and whites could be strengthened. It was at the annual institutes held at Fisk that, for one of the first times in the South, black and white Americans were able to intelligibly discuss the "Negro problem" in a safe environment, where action plans directed at bettering relations between blacks and whites were developed and implemented. While the research programs established at Tuskegee, Howard, and Fisk deserve increased attention from contemporary sociologists analyzing significant contributions to the discipline by early American sociologists, to a growing number of scholars Atlanta University stands alone as the most significant and important research center, regardless of race, during the early years of American sociology. In 1895 Atlanta University initiated a program of research, directed by W. E. B. Du Bois between 1897 and 1914, into the social, economic, and physical condition of black Americans. According to Earl Wright II (2002), the Atlanta Sociological Laboratory, the name bestowed on the group of scholars engaged in sociological activity at Atlanta University between 1895 and 1924, rightfully deserves the distinction of the first American school of sociology and birthplace of urban sociological inquiry, given that the establishment of the Atlanta school and its institutionalized program of urban sociological inquiry predates the Chicago school by almost twenty years.

In addition to serving as a resource in the struggle for human rights in the United States, black colleges were often the destination, and salvation, for many Jewish scholars forced into exile upon Adolf Hitler's ascension to power in Germany in the early 1930s. Scapegoated for

Germany's problems, Jewish sociologists such as Ernst Borinski (Tougaloo College), John Herz (Howard University), Viktor Lowenfeld (Hampton Institute), Ernst Manasse (North Carolina Central University), Fritz Pappenheim (Talladega College), and Donald Rasmussen (Talladega College) obtained positions at black colleges where their experience as minorities was an educational asset in their professional and personal interactions with black college students, faculty, and the community (Cunnigen 2003).

The history of sociology has traditionally minimized the contributions of people of color, women, gays and lesbians, and other minorities. Consequently, it is of manifest importance that contemporary and future sociologists utilize alternative theoretical frames to support the recognition and canonization of marginalized scholars. Repudiation and revision of the traditional means of canonizing sociologists will result in the overdue and deserved recognition of the contributions of scholars who, by virtue of their race, sex or gender, or sexual preference, existed as "outsiders within" their own profession.

SEE ALSO *Chicago School; Du Bois, W. E. B.; Sociology*

BIBLIOGRAPHY

Bernard, L. L. 1948. Sociological Trends in the South. *Social Forces* 27 (1): 12–19.

Cunnigen, Donald. 2003. The Legacy of Ernst Borinski: The Production of an African-American Sociological Tradition. *Teaching Sociology* 31: 397–411.

Henry, Charles P. 1995. Abram Harris, E. Franklin Frazier, and Ralph Bunche: The Howard School of Thought on the Problem of Race. *National Political Science Review* 5: 36–56.

Himes, Sandy J. 1949. Development and Status of Sociology in Negro Colleges. *Journal of Educational Sociology* 23 (1): 17–32.

Wright, Earl, II. 2002. Using the Master's Tools: Atlanta University and American Sociology, 1896–1924. *Sociological Spectrum* 22 (1): 15–39.

Earl Wright II

SOCIOLOGY, ECONOMIC

Economic sociology (ES) forms a specific sociological subfield. As with sociology—its genus—itself a multiparadigm discipline, there is some disagreement about what exactly falls under ES's rubric. To counter this difficulty ES has been defined broadly as "the sociological perspective applied to economic phenomena" (Smelser and Swedberg 2005, p. 3).

While both ES and economics study the economy in its multiple expressions, they are at variance with each other. At the risk of oversimplification, the starting point for economics is the isolated rational economic actor; whereas for ES, actors always operate in social, thus relational, contexts and do so reflexively.

EARLIER PERSPECTIVES

The sociological look upon economic phenomena has marked sociology from its outset, so it is meaningful to distinguish ES into *old* and *new* segments. Old ES refers largely to the relevant parts in the work of sociology's founding fathers, for example, Karl Marx, Émile Durkheim, Max Weber, and Georg Simmel. Indeed, Marx was concerned with the social designation of the commodity and with commodity fetishism. He also analyzed capitalism's origins as well as *capital* as a social relation. Durkheim was directly interested in this field, which he—along with Weber—named as such. He was particularly concerned with the development of the division of labor while he criticized economists for their tendency to construct an exclusive economic world, which was arbitrary and one-sided because the social dimensions were excluded or neglected, whereas he linked anomie to modern economic activity. For his part, Weber delved at length in the sociological study of economic institutions and of processes pointing out that economic action is a special form of social action. Weber advocated considering both the meaning with which actors imbue their economic action (e.g., in his *Protestant Ethic and the Spirit of Capitalism* [1904–1905]) as well as the social dimension of economic phenomena. By contrast Simmel's work is not systematically concerned with ES and is only dotted with references of an ES concern, such as analyses of interest, competition, and interlinkages between money and modernity.

Sociological interest in the economy subsided during the 1920s, although authors such as Joseph A. Schumpeter, Talcott Parsons, Neil Smelser, and Karl Polanyi offered contributions to the discussion. Since the 1960s, the attempts of some economists to extend economic interpretations into social phenomena—an approach called *economic imperialism*—challenged the established division of labor between economics and sociology. This provoked sociologists' response, which culminated in the reemergence of ES. The wider frames of the new ES, as Jens Beckert (1996) pointed out, are delineated by two parameters: It aims towards a sociological understanding of economic processes and structures, and critiques established economic types of analysis. In the meantime, increasingly, mainstream economics has come to accept a role for the social dimension, although conceptualized quite differently than it is in ES.

CONTEMPORARY PERSPECTIVES

Mark Granovetter first discussed the new ES in "Economic Action and Social Structure" (1985). Granovetter, a key figure in ES, has pointed out that all economic action and phenomena are embedded in concrete networks of social relations, social structures, normative arrangements, and institutions that constrain and channel them in particular ways. Unlike the view of Karl Polanyi, for Granovetter these actions and phenomena are more thoroughly embedded in modern societies than in premodern ones. The concept of *social embeddedness*, which is identified with ES, despite some attempts to define it narrowly, remains a general concept.

Granovetter's own work on how people obtain a job at the local level was an early application of the social embeddedness idea. He argues that getting a job, or accessing the labor market, is intrinsically a social process linked to the job seeker's social ties in specific social milieus, which are formulated and distributed under the overdetermining impact of social class. This thesis, known as the *strength-of-weak-ties thesis*, has found corroboration in a wide range of social contexts in the United States and elsewhere, for instance in Greece and Russia. Recent U.S. research with respect to other social divisions, such as gender, race, and ethnicity, on matters pertaining to employment and work have identified the prevalence of continuities in the transmittance of social inequalities rather than of discontinuities, which highlights the multifaceted social dimension in labor markets.

Another key concept in ES is that of the *social construction* of economic phenomena, which draws from the theory of constructivism advanced by Peter Berger and Thomas Luckmann in 1966. Social construction refers to the fact that economic arrangements, institutions, and regulations do not have an a priori independent existence. Instead, they are formulated as a result of human social interaction and purposeful intervention that take place in a specific social context. Once, however, an economic structure comes into being it may assume an objectivity that constrains and impacts upon economic action and practices.

Thematically, research in ES has expanded to include analyses at the micro-, mezzo-, and macro-levels of firms, markets, consumption, entrepreneurship, business groups, money, migration, networks, trust, development, formal/informal work, varieties of capitalism, forms of capital, other economic institutions, the role of culture, and other areas, with most interesting results. Such research has contributed to the deciphering of aspects of the economy, and some of the most attractive examples of ES's fruition are to be found in the work of, among others, Viviana Zelizer on the shifting meaning of money (1994), Richard Swedberg on Weber's ES (1998), and Neil Fligstein on contemporary market societies (2001).

While the expansion of empirical research continues, ES's theoretical production is currently not keeping up with expectations and needs to advance. Accordingly, researchers such as Swedberg suggest that elaborations on the sociological concept of *interest* and on an *interest-based concept of institutions* may provide new vistas for ES.

SEE ALSO *Sociology*

BIBLIOGRAPHY

Beckert, Jens. 1996. What is Sociological about Economic Sociology? Uncertainty and the Embeddedness of Economic Action. *Theory and Society* 25: 803–840.

Berger, Peter L. and Thomas Luckmann. 1966. *The Social Construction of Reality: A Treatise in the Sociology of Knowledge*. Garden City, NY: Anchor Books.

Biggart, Nicole Woolsey, ed. 2002. *Readings in Economic Sociology*. Malden, MA: Blackwell.

Fligstein, Neil. 2001. *The Architecture of Markets: An Economic Sociology of Twenty-First Century Capitalist Societies*. Princeton, NJ: Princeton University Press.

Granovetter, Mark. 1973. The Strength of Weak Ties. *American Journal of Sociology* 78: 1360–1380.

Granovetter, Mark. 1983. The Strength of Weak Ties: A Network Theory Revisited. *Sociological Theory* 1: 201–233.

Granovetter, Mark. 1985. Economic Action and Social Structure: The Problem of Embeddedness. *American Journal of Sociology* 91 (3): 481–510.

Granovetter, Mark, and Richard Swedberg, eds. 2001. *The Sociology of Economic Life*. 2nd ed. Boulder, CO: Westview Press.

Guillén, Mauro F., Randall Collins, Paula England, and Marshall Meyer, eds. 2002. *The New Economic Sociology: Developments in an Emerging Field*. New York: Russell Sage Foundation.

Koniordos, Sokratis M. 2005. Informal Support Networks in the Making of Small Independent Businesses: Beyond "Strong" and "Weak" Ties? In *Networks, Trust and Social Capital: Theoretical and Empirical Investigations from Europe*, ed. Sokratis M. Koniordos, 167–185. Burlington, VT: Ashgate.

Mouw, Ted. 2000. Job Relocation and the Racial Gap in Unemployment in Detroit and Chicago, 1980 to 1990. *American Sociological Review* 65 (5): 730–53.

Mouw, Ted. 2003. Social Capital and Finding a Job: Do Contacts Matter? *American Sociological Review* 68 (6): 868–898.

Pager, Devah, and Lincoln Quillian. 2005. Walking the Talk? What Employers Say Versus What They Do. *American Sociological Review* 70 (3): 355–380.

Parsons, Talcott, and Neil J. Smelser. 1956. *Economy and Society: A Study in the Integration of Economic and Social Theory*. Glencoe, IL: Free Press.

Polanyi, Karl. 1957. *The Great Transformation*. Boston: Beacon Press.

Schumpeter, Joseph A. 1994. *Capitalism, Socialism, and Democracy*. London: Routledge.

Smelser, Neil J., and Richard Swedberg, eds. 2005. *The Handbook of Economic Sociology*, 2nd ed. Princeton, NJ: Princeton University Press and New York: Russell Sage Foundation.

Swedberg, Richard. 1998. *Max Weber and the Idea of Economic Sociology*. Princeton, NJ: Princeton University Press.

Swedberg, Richard. 2003. *Principles of Economic Sociology*. Princeton, NJ: Princeton University Press.

Swedberg, Richard. 2004. What Has Been Accomplished in New Economic Sociology and Where Is It Heading? *European Journal of Sociology* 45 (3): 317–330.

Swedberg, Richard. 2006. The Toolkit of Economic Sociology, Working Paper No. 22. Center for the Study of Economy and Society Working Papers Series, Cornell University. http://www.economyandsociety.org/publications/wp22_swedberg_toolkit04.pdf.

Tomaskovic-Devey, Donald, and Sheryl Skaggs. 2002. Sex Segregation, Labor Process Organization, and Gender Earnings Inequality. *American Journal of Sociology* 108: 102–128.

Tomaskovic-Devey, Donald, Catherine Zimmer, Kevin Stainback, et al. 2006. Documenting Desegregation: Segregation in American Workplaces by Race, Ethnicity, and Sex, 1966–2003. *American Sociological Review* 71 (4): 565–588.

Trigilia, Carlo. 2002. *Economic Sociology: State, Market and Society in Modern Capitalism*, trans. Nicola Owtram. Oxford: Blackwell.

Weber, Max. 1978. *Economy and Society: An Outline of Interpretive Sociology*, trans. Ephraim Fischoff et al. 2 vols. Berkeley: University of California Press.

Weber, Max. 1999. *Protestant Ethic and the Spirit of Capitalism*, intro. by Anthony Gidens; trans. Talcott Parsons. London: Routledge. (Orig. pub. 1904–1905.)

Yakoubovitch, Valery. 2005. Weak Ties, Information, and Influence: How Workers Find Jobs in a Local Russian Labor Market. *American Sociological Review* 70 (3): 408–421.

Zelizer, Viviana A. 1994. *The Social Meaning of Money*. New York: Basic Books.

Sokratis M. Koniordos

SOCIOLOGY, EUROPEAN

European sociological thought can be traced to three major sources: the Enlightenment, or Age of Reason, of the eighteenth century; the Industrial Revolution; and the romantic period's counterreaction to these ideological, social, and political changes. Although there are important prefigurations of sociology (for example in the thought of Montesquieu, Marquis de Condorcet, Adam Smith, and others), the roots of modern sociology lie in the work of Auguste Comte (1798–1857), who coined the term *sociology*, Karl Marx (1818–1883), Émile Durkheim (1858–1917), and Max Weber (1864–1920). The last three are conventionally represented as the founding fathers of the discipline.

The great question posed by these thinkers is that of understanding the history and consequences of the seismic changes associated with the origins of modern capitalism (Marx and Weber), industrialization and individualization (Comte and Durkheim), and the new social order of modernity (Weber). For Marx the central focus is upon the global effects of the capitalist mode of production with its new classes and class conflict, the alienating impact of new forms of factory production, and the rise of the working class movement. For Weber, the concern shifts to understanding the ethical and religious roots of rational conduct and institutions in Europe and North America, comparative analysis of earlier European social structures and non-European civilizations, and characteristic features of modern society (the modern state and rational administration, modern capitalism, democratic politics, bureaucracy, and so on). With Durkheim the central problem is the changing basis of social solidarity (from *mechanical* to *organic* solidarity) and the corrosive impact of individualism upon traditional social orders.

Sociology adopted two related perspectives, one focusing upon the structure and dialectics of social relations (the European paradigm) and the other emphasizing the evolution of whole societies along social Darwinian principles. The latter is best represented by early American sociology, especially in the writings of William Graham Sumner (1840–1910), Lester Frank Ward (1841–1913), and Franklin H. Giddings (1855–1931). The guiding source is not Marx or Durkheim but the English evolutionist and individualistic thinker Herbert Spencer (1820–1903). Evolutionism informed by individualism and native pragmatism provided the framework for speculations about social organization, institutional adaptation, and change. However, the European tradition was not totally ignored. It entered into the texture of American sociology through the work of Albion Woodbury Small (1854–1926), the founder of the first American department of sociology at the University of Chicago in 1892 and influential editor of the *American Journal of Sociology* (from 1895). Through Small's teaching American students gained access to the conflict tradition of Georg Simmel (1858–1918). Small also helped shape the Chicago School of W. I. Thomas (1863–1947), Robert Ezra Park (1864–1944), and Ernest Burgess (1886–1966). This is the context in which American sociology discovered its unique philosophical voice in the *symbolic interactionist* philosophy of George Herbert Mead (1863–1931).

After Durkheim's death, Marcel Mauss (1872–1950) and Maurice Halbwachs (1877–1945) continued his legacy. This would prove decisive in shaping the structural anthropology of Claude Lévi-Strauss. In Germany, Marxism regressed to a dogmatic evolutionism in the form of Second International Marxism (best represented by the Soviet theorist Nikolai Bukharin [1888–1938]) but was reinvigorated by the Frankfurt School (Theodor Adorno [1903–1969], Walter Benjamin [1982–1940], Max Horkheimer [1895–1973], and others). Weber's legacy was more diffuse, transformed into the traditions of conflict theory (later represented by such thinkers as Lewis Coser [1913–], Ralf Dahrendorf [1929–], and John Rex [1925–]), action theory, phenomenological thought (through Alfred Schutz [1932–1998]), and figurational sociology (Norbert Elias [1897–1990]).

Post–World War II sociology marks a decisive shift to the American context both in the volume and quality of empirical research (associated with the Chicago School of ethnography, the Columbia School of Robert Merton [1910–2003], Paul Lazarsfeld [1901–1976], Samuel Stouffer [1900–1960], and others) and the emergence of the most original synthesis of European action theory in the work of Talcott Parsons (1902–1979). Parsons's model of social action theory in *The Structure of Social Action* (1937) was later elaborated into a rather rigid form of structural functionalism and toward the end of his life into a general systems model of societal evolution. American empiricism and Parsonian sociology are often described as the orthodox consensus of post–World War II sociology.

The breakdown of the functionalist consensus came in myriad forms: rejection of Parsonian conservatism (C. Wright Mills [1916–1962] and Alvin Gouldner [1920–1980]), the behaviorist alternative formulated by George Homans (1910–1989), the exchange theory of Peter Blau (1918–2002), symbolic interactionism (represented by Herbert Blumer [1900-1987] and Erving Goffman [1922-1982]), phenomenological and interpretive sociology (Alfred Schutz [1899–1959], Aaron Cicourel [1928–], and Harold Garfinkel [1917–]), and the resurgence of interest in conflict sociology (Randall Collins [1941–]), European critical theory, and reflexive sociology (Alvin Goulder, Alan Blum, Peter McHugh, and others). This is the period of the *theory wars* characterizing the late 1960s and 1970s. The result was the demise of structural functionalism as the sole framework for sociological thought and research and the emergence of alternative perspectives from within the European tradition. The most prominent of these are the *structuration* theories of Anthony Giddens (1938–) and Pierre Bourdieu (1930–2002) (essentially trying to overcome the separation of *action* and *structure* in sociological explanation), the reformulation of critical theory as a paradigm of communica-

tive action (in the work of Jürgen Habermas [1929–]), the globalization and world-system perspective associated with Immanuel Wallerstein (1930–) and Manuel Castells (1942–), the revival of reflexive sociology (for example in reflexive approaches to science, ethnomethodology, and reflexive modernization theory), and the appearance of *postmodern* and *poststructuralist* discourses (associated with the names of Michel Foucault [1926–1984], Jean Baudrillard [1929–], Jean-François Lyotard [1924–1998], and Jacques Derrida [1930–2004]). In the twenty-first century ideological differences between European and American social thought are less entrenched, and the future promises new dialogues with the classical thinkers and new forms of thinking in response to the postmodernization of the global economy.

SEE ALSO *Blau, Peter M.; Blumer, Herbert; Bourdieu, Pierre; Chicago School; Comte, Auguste; Condorcet, Marquis de; Derrida, Jacques; Durkheim, Émile; Empiricism; Ethnomethodology; Foucault, Michel; Giddens, Anthony; Goffman, Erving; Habermas, Jürgen; Lévi-Strauss, Claude; Marx, Karl; Marx, Karl: Impact on Sociology; Mead, George Herbert; Mills, C. Wright; Smith, Adam; Sociology, Parsonian; Spencer, Herbert; Wallerstein, Immanuel; Weber, Max*

BIBLIOGRAPHY

Parsons, Talcott. 1937. *The Structure of Social Action; A Study in Social Theory with Special Reference to a Group of Recent European Writers.* New York: McGraw Hill.

Barry Sandywell

SOCIOLOGY, FEMINIST

Sociology can be understood as a field that focuses on the interaction of individuals within society, examining the diversity of men's and women's lives and the fundamental structures of power, inequality, and opportunity that shape their experiences. Numerous feminist theories have entered sociological discourse through textbooks, scholarly articles, and at conferences. However, as Judith Stacey and Barrie Thorne (1985) conclude in their far-reaching critique of the discipline, sociology, unlike history and anthropology, has not undergone the conceptual transformation necessary for a feminist revolution. Similarly, Joan Acker's 1989 article argues that the extensive knowledge and critiques of recent feminist scholarship "neither have been integrated into, nor have they transformed the old, 'general' theories of society" (Acker 1989, p. 65). Although feminist work challenges theories based on a normative male subject, mainstream sociological research often does little more than add women and stir into existing frameworks.

Feminist studies, which seeks to interpret women's position and identity in society, is inherently fused with sociological questions surrounding social structure, culture, and economic stratification. Feminist scholars within sociology, like their counterparts in other disciplines, have asked how gender is constructed, how it is organized in social institutions, and how social change is possible. It has been argued that gender differences are not natural or biological but learned from infancy. Gender differences are maintained by key social institutions such as education, marriage, popular culture, news media, religion, government, and law. The concept of patriarchy, the systematic organization of male supremacy, is one that many feminist theorists find useful. This concept does not refer simply to a collection of individuals but a system whose core value is control and domination. Everyone is involved and implicated in this system, but each can choose how he or she participates. This emphasis on a wider system is crucial. Without it, one's thinking and discussion are reduced to the personal level, resulting in accusations, defensiveness, and hurt feelings.

Sociology's own male bias and Western foundation structures academic scholarship and theory within a male interpretation. From its inception, the discipline was conceptualized and articulated by men with interpretations of social issues and phenomenon grounded in their own experiential backgrounds. The epistemological issues that feminist researchers address when applying research methodologies are rooted in ideas and methods influenced by male hegemony over academic and scientific discourse. These issues encompass, but are not limited to, examinations of the multiple dimensions and processes that generate women's social standing, as undertaken by Niara Sudarkasa (1973), Rae Blumberg (1984), and Susan Tiano (1987). Such examinations allow for the understanding that women may have autonomy but little power, economic resources but limited autonomy, or power as members of kin groups but no access to economic resources independent of kin ties. Without an awareness of such multidimensionality in classic stratification models, inequalities seem reducible to natural differences between men and women.

Much of the work of liberal, socialist Marxist, and radical feminist theories and some of the paradigms developed, such as the *woman as other*, *woman as victim*, *woman as private property*, and *woman for exchange* are consistently found in sociological works. Gender inequalities play a significant role in the triangle of sociological stratification—race, class, and gender—in addition to the stratification among feminist theorists themselves. For example, debates within the women's movement have highlighted some of the original notions of feminism as supporting a white, middle-class ideology that negated women of color and those with lower economic positions. The effect of this stratification among feminist theorists themselves has had an impact on feminist sociology's role in the twenty-first century, rendering it difficult to address feminist issues for women all over the world and bringing forth the field's own Western female bias.

The feminist movement, from its inception, has often been critiqued by African American women and other nonwhite women, such as Willa Hemmons (1980), Vivian Gordon (1987), and Rebecca Walker (1995), as being racist and exclusive. "Contemporary feminist theory, however," as Delores P. Aldridge notes, "attempts to embrace multiculturalism, which mandates curricular attention to the experiences, historical and contemporary, of women and men of color, lesbians and gay men of all racial and ethnic groups, and women with diverse sexual, racial, and ethnic identities" (2005, p. 405). Nonetheless, feminist theory continues to face challenges as it attempts to explain the realities of these various groups of color. Many nonwhite women are calling for new theories with new names such as Africana womanist theory, Latina feminist theory, and Chicana feminist theory.

SEE ALSO *Epistemology; Feminism; Feminism, Second Wave; Gender; Gender Gap; Identity; Inequality, Gender; Intersectionality; Multiculturalism; Patriarchy; Racism; Sexuality; Sociology; Stratification; Women's Liberation; Women's Movement; Women's Studies*

BIBLIOGRAPHY

Acker, Joan. 1989. Making Gender Visible. In *Feminism and Sociological Theory*, ed. Ruth A. Wallace, 65–81. Newbury Park, CA: Sage.

Aldridge, Delores P. 2005. African American Women Since the Second World War: Perspectives on Gender and Race. In *A Companion to African American History*, ed. Alton Hornsby Jr., 395–411. Malden, MA: Blackwell.

Blumberg, Rae L. 1984. A General Theory of Gender Stratification. *Sociological Theory* 2: 23–101.

Gordon, Vivian V. 1987. *Black Women, Feminism and Black Liberation: Which Way?* Chicago: Third World Press.

Hemmons, Willa M. 1980. Black Women and the Women's Liberation Movement. In *The Black Woman*, ed. La Frances Rodgers-Rose, 285–299. Beverly Hills, CA: Sage.

Pateman, Carole. 1988. *The Sexual Contract*. Cambridge, U.K.: Polity Press.

Smith, Dorothy E. 1990. *The Conceptual Practices of Power: A Feminist Sociology of Knowledge*. Boston: Northeastern University Press.

Stacey, Judith, and Barrie Thorne. 1985. The Missing Feminist Revolution in Sociology. *Social Problems* 32 (4): 301–316.

Sudarkasa, Niara. 1973. *Where Women Work: A Study of Yoruba Women in the Marketplace and in the Home.* Ann Arbor: University of Michigan Press.

Tiano, Susan. 1987. Gender, Work and World Capitalism: Third World Women's Role in Development. In *Analyzing Gender: A Handbook of Social Science Research*, eds. Beth B. Hess and Myra Marx Ferree, 216–243. Newbury Park, CA: Sage.

Walker, Rebecca, ed. 1995. *To Be Real: Telling the Truth and Changing the Face of Feminism.* New York: Anchor Books.

Wallace, Ruth, ed. 1989. *Feminism and Sociological Theory.* Newbury Park, CA: Sage.

Delores P. Aldridge

SOCIOLOGY, INSTITUTIONAL ANALYSIS IN

Institutional analysis addresses the processes by which social structures—including both normative and behavioral elements—are established, become stable, and undergo change over time. It addresses the fundamental issues of social order and shared meaning. The normative elements include schemas, values, norms, and rules; the behavioral elements include activities, routines, interactions, and the use of resources. More so than the other social sciences, sociology has from its origins to the present time steadfastly placed the examination of institutional structures and processes at the center of its scholarly agenda.

Although attention from sociologists has been steady, the ways in which institutions are viewed and explained have varied substantially among scholars and over time. Leading classical European scholars reflect, and were no doubt partly responsible for, this diversity. Karl Marx argued that materialist structures gave rise to ideologies justifying their legitimacy—in effect, that behavioral systems determined normative frameworks. By contrast, both Max Weber and Émile Durkheim insisted that normative (symbolic) elements played an independent role in the structuring of social orders. Durkheim, particularly in his later work, stressed the important role that shared cognitive frames and belief systems—"collective representations"—played in the stability and meaning of social life. And Weber stressed the importance of "interpretation"—the employment of shared meanings by the social actor that mediate between the actor and the materialist conditions confronted.

Scholars such as Herbert Spencer and William Graham Sumner treated institutions as providing the specialized "organs" of societies, performing distinctive functions. The rules and relations defining appropriate behavior were observed to vary across political, economic, religious, and kinship sectors, and thus to give rise to diverse institutional complexes. This vision of functionally specialized subsystems organized around distinctive norms and values provided the basis for much of the research agenda for sociologists throughout the twentieth century, culminating in the theoretical codification of Talcott Parsons (1951), with his view of societal sectors differentiated by distinctive "pattern variables" (value dichotomies, such as universalism/particularism and ascription/achievement). While most sociologists pursued this macro-orientation, a few, such as Charles Horton Cooley and George Herbert Mead, emphasized the microfoundations of institutions, arguing that it is in the minds of individuals that connections between symbols and actions take place.

In the latter part of the twentieth century, two developments have been of special significance. First, the insights of Cooley and Mead were revived and reformulated by phenomenological scholars, especially Alfred Schutz and Peter Berger and Thomas Luckmann (1967). They stress the extent to which (1) social reality is a social construction; and (2) the relative importance of shared cognitive conceptions (ideas, schema) rather than normative commitments (emphasized by Parsons among others) in the establishment and preservation of social order. Meyer and Rowan (1977) applied these ideas to help account for the similarities observed in the structures of both nation-states and formal organizations. The second important development is the theoretical work of Anthony Giddens (1984), who asserts the value of privileging social processes over social structure—"structuration" versus structure. He emphasizes the "duality" of social structure, which operates both as social context—providing the framework within which all social action takes place—and as social outcome: a product that incorporates earlier understandings and practices, but also modifications introduced by present users.

DiMaggio and Powell (1983) applied these insights to analyze the structuration of *organizational fields*—collections of dissimilar organizations engaged in interrelated activities in some specialized social arena (e.g., automobile production or delivery of mental health services). DiMaggio (1991) first examined the often contentious processes by which such fields come into existence, select appropriate logics and forms, and begin to operate as a taken-for-granted part of the social world. These twin emphases on cognitive systems influencing structuration processes have been pursued productively in the past two decades by scholars examining the emergence and dominance of organizations as actors in modern societal structures and their coevolution within specialized organizational fields (Scott 2001).

SEE ALSO *Social Structure; State, The*

BIBLIOGRAPHY

Berger, Peter L., and Thomas Luckmann. 1967. *The Social Construction of Reality*. New York: Doubleday Anchor.

DiMaggio, Paul J. 1991. Constructing an Organizational Field as a Professional Project: U.S. Art Museums, 1920–1930. In *The New Institutionalism in Organizational Analysis*, eds. Walter W. Powell and Paul J. DiMaggio, 267–292. Chicago: University of Chicago Press.

DiMaggio, Paul J., and Walter W. Powell. 1983. The Iron Cage Revisited: Institutional Isomorphism and Collective Rationality in Organizational Fields. *American Sociological Review* 48 (2): 147–160.

Giddens, Anthony. 1984. *The Constitution of Society: Outline of the Theory of Structuration*. Berkeley: University of California Press.

Meyer, John W., and Brian Rowan. 1977. Institutionalized Organizations: Formal Structure as Myth and Ceremony. *American Journal of Sociology* 83: 340–363.

Parson, Talcott. 1951. *The Social System*. New York: Free Press.

Scott, W. Richard. 2001. *Institutions and Organizations*. 2nd ed. Thousand Oaks, CA: Sage.

W. Richard Scott

SOCIOLOGY, KNOWLEDGE IN

The nature of knowledge has been a central problem of philosophy at least since Greco-Roman times. Plato (427–347 BCE), for example, in *Theætetus* adopted a scientific approach to knowledge and cognition. Centuries later, the philosophers of the French and Scottish Enlightenment recognized that all social differences had social origins and were thus the result of factors subject to human control.

In general, however, philosophers have attempted rather to demonstrate that a sociology of knowledge is neither possible nor desirable. Immanuel Kant (1724–1804) thus argued that while there cannot be perception without conception, the constitutive components of cognition are a priori. Similarly, empiricists of various persuasions have maintained that scientific knowledge in particular is warranted by direct experience unaffected by social conditions. At most, the philosophies concede that extra-theoretical factors influence the genesis of ideas but not the structure or the validity of thought (context of discovery). Otherwise, quite different epistemologies—for example, that of Karl Popper (1902–1994)—have shared a rejection of the possibility of a sociological analysis of knowledge, particularly scientific knowledge, and warned against any relativism, not only in science but also for

society, that was seen as associated with the modern sociology of knowledge.

The modern sociology of knowledge, by contrast, investigates the interconnections between categories of thought, knowledge claims, and social reality—that is, the *Seinsverbundenheit* (existential connectedness) of thought described by Karl Mannheim (1893–1947). Karl Marx (1818–1883) was a significant precursor of the field, with his theory that, at least under certain historical conditions, economic realities ultimately determine the ideological "superstructure" by way of various socioeconomic processes. Émile Durkheim (1858–1917), too, is an important pioneer of the sociology of knowledge, even though he failed to develop a general model of the classificatory process. He argued, especially in *The Elementary Forms of the Religious Life* (1912) and *Primitive Classification* (1903, written with Marcel Mauss [1872–1950]), that the basic categories that order perception and experience (space, time, causality, and direction) derive from the social structure, at least in simpler societies. Durkheim, Mauss, and also Lucien Lévy-Bruhl (1857–1939) examined the forms of logical classification of "primitive" societies and concluded that the basic categories of cognition have social origins. However, they were not prepared to extend this kind of analysis to modern societies.

The sociology of knowledge owes its decisive development to the work of Max Scheler (1874–1928), Alfred Weber (1868–1958) (the *freischwebende Intelligenz* or "free-floating intelligentsia"), and especially Mannheim in the 1920s. It may be seen as the symptomatic intellectual expression of an age of crisis, and the recognition of its own rootedness in social structure and determination by social factors is perhaps its most characteristic trait. The mood of the German historical and social sciences during the period in which the sociology of knowledge developed in Germany may be described as one of "tragic consciousness." Georg Simmel's (1858–1918) view of the "tragedy of culture," as well as Max Weber's (1864–1920) assertion that an inescapable process of rationalization leads to the disenchantment of the world and to new forms of bondage, are symptomatic expressions of a period in which historians, philosophers, and especially social scientists argued intensely about the issues raised by historicism, relativism, philosophical skepticism, and the pervasive distrust in *Geist*.

It was during this period that the sociology of knowledge emerged as an analysis of the regularities of those social processes and structures that pertain to intellectual life and to modes of knowing (Scheler) and as a theory of the existential connectedness of thought (Mannheim). Both orientations distance themselves from the Marxist critique of ideology, which sees ideologies as mystifying representations of social reality and as disguises of the interests of powerful groups in society. The sociology of knowledge, by contrast, is concerned with intellectual and spiritual structures as inevitably differently formed in different social and historical settings (Mannheim).

Scheler first introduced the term *Wissenssoziologie* (sociology of knowledge) in the early 1920s, and in *Problems of a Sociology of Knowledge* (1926) he provided the first systematic introduction. Scheler extended the Marxist notion of substructure by identifying different "real factors" (*Realfaktoren*), which, he believed, condition thought in different historical periods and in various social and cultural systems in specific ways. These "real factors" have sometimes been regarded as institutionalized instinctual forces, and as representing an ahistorical concept of superstructure. Scheler's insistence on the existence of a realm of eternal values and ideas limits the usefulness of his notion of real factors for the explanation of social and cultural change.

Mannheim provided the most elaborate and ambitious programmatic foundation for a sociological analysis of cognition. Like Scheler, Mannheim extended the concept of substructure, suggesting that biological factors, psychological elements, and spiritual phenomena might take the place of primary economic relations in the substructure, but (just like the dominant theory of science) he did not think that scientific and technical knowledge could be subjected to sociological analysis. He conducted research into the social conditions associated with different forms of knowledge, and some of his studies are still considered first-rate examples of the kind of analysis that the sociology of knowledge is capable of. In addition to *Ideology and Utopia* (1929), these include Mannheim's studies of competition as a cultural form, of conservative thought, of the problem of generations, and of economic ambition.

Mannheim believed that the sociology of knowledge was destined to play a major role in intellectual and political life—particularly in an age of crisis, dissolution, and conflict—by examining sociologically the conditions that give rise to competing ideas, political philosophies, ideologies, and diverse cultural products. He persistently pursued the idea that the sociology of knowledge is somehow central to any strategy for creating a rapprochement between politics and reason, and this pursuit connects his various essays in the sociology of knowledge. But Mannheim's conception of the specific ways in which such a sociology might affect the state of political knowledge fluctuated and changed. There are three main versions: (1) sociology of knowledge as a pedagogical but also political mode of encountering and acting on the forces making up the political world; (2) sociology of knowledge as an instrument of enlightenment related to the dual process of

rationalization and individuation identified by Max Weber and comparable to psychoanalysis, acting to set men and women free for rational and responsible choices by liberating them from subservience to hidden forces they cannot control; and (3) sociology of knowledge as a weapon against prevalent myths and as a method for eliminating bias from social science, so that it can master the fundamental public problems of the time and guide appropriate political conduct.

The sociology of knowledge has recently experienced a reorientation in the direction of an analysis of everyday life and of natural scientific and technical knowledge. Peter Berger and Thomas Luckmann's *The Social Construction of Reality* (1966), written in the tradition of Alfred Schutz's (1899–1959) phenomenology and Arnold Gehlen's (1904–1976) philosophical anthropology, represents a clear departure from the preoccupation of the classical sociology of knowledge with issues of epistemology, methodology, or ideologies. Everything that is regarded as knowledge in society is now accepted as a legitimate subject matter for sociological investigations.

Inspired by developments in the history and epistemology of science—by, for example, Thomas Kuhn (1922–1996)—the sociology of knowledge in the 1970s turned in the direction of empirical analyses of the social construction of scientific facts, frequently by way of ethnographic studies of laboratory life. Such research on the "manufacture" of natural-scientific knowledge has led to a reassessment of traditional assumptions about the unique rationality of scientific knowledge. Seen through the lens of the "strong program" of the sociology of knowledge, scientific knowledge and everyday knowledge are in fact extraordinarily similar. In general, the cognitive turn in the sociology of knowledge has had little impact on science or the so-called division between the two cultures (C. P. Snow [1905–1980]) in the scientific community. Moreover, the sociology of scientific knowledge has been criticized from within the field of science and technology studies as reductionist, as overemphasizing the role of controversies in science, and as stressing a universe of inquiry that is void of nonhuman entities (e.g., instruments, measuring devices, laboratories).

The sociology of scientific knowledge also has encountered a strong reproach from philosophers of science and scientists who attempt to overcome doubts and skepticism engendered by a sociological analysis of science by placing knowledge on a firm, uncontested foundation, even outside the realm of sociohistorical experience. The dispute about the apparent attack by sociology on the validity and objectivity of scientific knowledge culminated in the 1990s in the so-called science wars. Sociologists were accused of favoring a stance of anything goes. In the end, the social nature of science and its role in society remain essentially contested.

SEE ALSO *Durkheim, Émile; Epistemology; Kant, Immanuel; Lukacs, Georg; Mannheim, Karl; Philosophy of Science; Relativism; Sociology*

BIBLIOGRAPHY

Berger, Peter, and Thomas Luckmann. 1967. *The Social Construction of Reality: A Treatise in the Sociology of Knowledge.* New York: Doubleday.

Mannheim, Karl. [1929] 1936. *Ideology and Utopia: An Introduction to the Sociology of Knowledge.* Trans. Louis Wirth and Edward Shils. London: Routledge and Kegan Paul.

Meja, Volker, and Nico Stehr, eds. 1990. *Knowledge and Politics: The Sociology of Knowledge Dispute.* London: Routledge and Kegan Paul.

Meja, Volker, and Nico Stehr, eds. 2005. *Society and Knowledge: Contemporary Perspectives in the Sociology of Knowledge and Science.* 2nd ed. New Brunswick, NJ: Transaction.

Merton, Robert K. 1945. The Sociology of Knowledge. In *Twentieth Century Sociology,* eds. Georges Gurvitch and Wilbert E. Moore. New York: Philosophical Library.

Scheler, Max. [1924] 1960. *Die Wissensformen und die Gesellschaft.* Bern, Switzerland: Francke.

Nico Stehr

SOCIOLOGY, LATIN AMERICAN

Sociology did not gain a foothold in Latin America until after World War II when Latin American universities opened sociology departments. Latin American sociology has, in general, a number of features that make it distinct from U.S. or European sociology. First, Latin American sociologists have been concerned with understanding issues of poverty and inequality. In general, they have been less concerned with value-neutral research than with research that is concerned with analyzing and improving the quality of life for the poor. As the Brazilian sociologist Fernando Henrique Cardoso stated, "The intellectuals in Latin America are important because they are the voices of those who cannot speak for themselves" (Kahl 1988, p. 179).

The scholar Alejandro Portes pointed out that in contrast to North American or European sociologists, Latin American sociologists are frequently marginalized, having little access to government and/or private institutions that fund research in wealthier nations. He also noted that the intellectual and political commitments of Latin American sociologists mean that they are frequently the first academics to suffer under authoritarian regimes. For exam-ple, sociology was outlawed in Cuba following Fidel Castro's revolution in 1959 and in Chile following the military coup d'etat of 1973. In the 1980s and 1990s, sociology made a strong comeback in Latin America in sync with its return to democracy.

DEPENDENCY THEORY

Latin American sociologists are probably best known for dependency theory, a school of loosely Marxist thought that arose in the 1960s and 1970s as a critical response to modernization theory. In the 1950s and 1960s, modern-ization theory was the dominant approach to questions of third world development. It was the policy prescribed by the United Nations and informed by the work of U.S.-based academics. In essence, modernization theory argued that underdeveloped countries, such as those in Latin America, could develop along lines similar to the United States and other developed countries in Europe. Raúl Prebisch, an influential Argentine economist, noted that the policy prescriptions of the modernization theorists were flawed because underdeveloped countries were exporting raw materials (agricultural products and miner-als) with declining rates of profit while they imported fin-ished goods from advanced countries that were more expensive every year.

Drawing on the work of Prebisch, but also Gino Germani, an economist based in Argentina, Latin American sociologists began developing dependency theory as a critical response to modernization theory. Dependency scholars argued that the underdevelopment of the third world was generated by the expansion of capitalism in advanced countries. That is, first world development occurred at the expense of the third world. Thus, underde-veloped countries could not follow the path of advanced countries because they lacked another set of countries to exploit; in addition, they could not compete with the more advanced economies and firms of the first world.

There were two schools of thought in dependency the-ory. The first, associated with the work of Andre Gunder Frank (but also Celso Furtado and Theotonio dos Santos), is considered the radical version of dependency theory. These scholars emphasized that third world economies were bound to stagnate because first world firms repatriated profits gained in the third world. Thus, third world coun-tries would never benefit from opening their countries to multinational corporations. Consequently, they recom-mended either socialist revolution or autarky; that is, de-linking from the global economy as the best means to promote national development. Critics of dependency the-ory have been quick to point out that this strategy, seen in cases such as Cuba and North Korea, has failed.

A second strand of dependency theory, associated with the work of Cardoso and Enzo Falleto, suggests a much less radical view. These scholars argued that external constraints (competition in a global capitalist market) and internal factors (such as class relations and political alliances) explain the trajectory of individual third world countries. They argued that "associated dependent development" was possible; that is, that less developed countries could have simultaneously participated in the global economy and improved the lives of their citizens. In essence, national leaders enjoyed more room to maneuver than the radical dependency scholars allowed.

VARIANTS OF DEPENDENCY THEORY

In addition to the aforementioned scholars, the work of the Mexican Pablo González Casanova should be discussed. His widely read book *Democracy in Mexico* (1970) offers a complex portrait of the ruling PRI party (Party of the Institutional Revolution) in Mexico. González Casanova acknowledged the advances made by the PRI (including land reform and a booming economy). However, he pointed out that a growing number of people, especially the indigenous, were left out of the PRI's benefits. González Casanova noted that the indigenous were experiencing what he called "internal colonialism," which acknowledges that they had traded one set of colonial powers (the Spanish) for a new one (the Creole-Spanish descendants who ruled Mexico after the War of Independence). González Casanova offered a critique of the PRI, calling for a democratic opening from within the party so that more Mexicans could benefit from its legacy.

Dependency theory played an important role in Latin American intellectual life, influencing the thought of activists in the liberation theology movement and in the United States among scholars of third world development. Dependency theory faced criticisms on the one hand from Marxists, such as the scholar Robert Brenner, who in the late 1970s underscored that dependency theorists betrayed an implicit intellectual tie, not to the German political philosopher Karl Marx but to the Scottish economist Adam Smith. Mainstream scholars criticized dependency theory because it failed to explain the trajectory of a number of newly industrialized countries (such as Hong Kong, Singapore, South Korea, and Taiwan). That, in combination with the eclipse of the Soviet Union in 1989, suggested dependency theory was doomed for the dustbin of history. In fact, a parting shot was provided by Cardoso himself, who was elected president of Brazil from 1995 to 2003 and implemented policies that differed greatly from the positions he outlined earlier in his academic career.

While the more radical variants of dependency theory have been abandoned, in the 2000s the theory is somewhat influential among scholars of development, much to the chagrin of its critics. As Portes noted in his reflection on sociology in Latin America in 2004, radical dependency theory was easily rebutted by the course of history; however, radical neoliberal development policies should also be criticized for their poor results, including increasing levels of inequality and the immiseration of the working class.

SEE ALSO *Sociology*

BIBLIOGRAPHY

Brenner, Robert. 1977. The Origins of Capitalist Development: A Critique of Neo-Smithian Marxism. *New Left Review* 104 (July–August): 25–92.

Cardoso, Fernando Henrique, and Enzo Falletto. 1979. *Dependency and Development in Latin America*. Trans. Marjory Mattingly Urquidi. Berkeley: University of California Press.

González Casanova, Pablo. 1970. *Democracy in Mexico*. Trans. Danielle Salti. New York: Oxford University Press.

Kahl, Joseph. 1988. *Three Latin American Sociologists: Gino Germani, Pablo González Casanova, Fernando Henrique Cardoso*. New Brunswick, NJ: Transaction.

Portes, Alejandro. 2004. La sociologia en el continente: convergencias preteritas y una nueva agenda de alcance medio. *Revista Mexicana de Sociología* 66 (3): 1–37.

Robert Sean Mackin

SOCIOLOGY, MACRO-

Macro-sociology is an approach to the scientific study of social life that focuses upon the large-scale social patterns of human behavior. Societies are considered as totalities, with a particular emphasis on major institutions of social life, such as the economy, the political system, the family unit, and systems of religious belief. Macro-sociology is typically concerned with the systematic examination of the major similarities and differences among societies, in particular the nature and scope of the changes that societies undergo.

Methodologically this tends to mean that macro-sociological studies focus upon a single society in a single given historical period, adopting large-scale surveys as a way of gathering data. However, many macro-sociologists have an abiding concern with how such social systems are interlinked across the world and in particular how single societies change over time. Historical-comparative methods are thus frequently used in analyzing how social systems within a given society, for example, the United States, have changed and developed throughout the nation's history.

Macro-sociology is often regarded as standing in opposition to micro-sociology. Micro-sociology typically investigates the patterns of thought and behavior that occur in relatively small-scale social groups, with a particular emphasis on different styles and codes of verbal and nonverbal communication. Micro-sociologists analyze the ways face-to-face interaction is managed and maintained and how this helps develop shared understandings within social groups. However, in the early twenty-first century this distinction is increasingly called into question as the micro-foundations of macro-sociology are made explicit (Alexander et al. 1987; Sanderson 1995). Nevertheless, macro-sociological approaches continue to play a part in international social science research, and two of the most prominent approaches are structural functionalism and conflict theory.

Structural functionalism sees societies as complex social systems of interrelated and interdependent parts that shape and influence each other. These different parts of the social system are interrelated by a commitment to the norms, values, and beliefs that integrate the entire system, which structural functionalists believe tends toward a state of equilibrium. As such, disturbances to any one part of society will require adjustments elsewhere in order for balance to be restored and for the system to avoid disintegration. Each interrelated part of the social system exists therefore precisely because it has a vital function to perform in helping to maintain the equilibrium of the system as a whole.

Conflict theory stands in opposition to structural functionalism by typically rejecting the idea that societies tend toward a state of equilibrium. This is based upon the belief that societies do not share a basic consensus over norms, values, and beliefs that operate in everyone's best interest. Rather, conflict theorists point to the various ways different individuals and social groups have competing and antagonistic interests and concerns and emphasize that these basic oppositions shape the organization of social life.

In the early twenty-first century macro-sociology is less influential in international social science than it once was. Nevertheless, it continues to provide an important foundation for approaching the study of human social life, especially in contemporary sociological theory.

SEE ALSO *Conflict; Critical Theory; Functionalism; Sociology; Sociology, Micro-; Sociology, Parsonian; Structuralism*

BIBLIOGRAPHY

Alexander, Jeffrey C., Bernhard Giesen, Richard Münch, and Neil J. Smelser, eds. 1987. *The Macro-Micro Link.* Berkeley: University of California Press.

Sanderson, Stephen K. 1995. *Macrosociology: An Introduction to Human Societies.* 3rd ed. New York: HarperCollins.

Mark Davis

SOCIOLOGY, MICRO-

The study of group dynamics and interaction is often termed microsociology. There are many different areas investigated within microsociology, and there are different perspectives and methodologies. The area can be broadly conceptualized as considering issues related to self and identity, status and power, cooperation and competition, exchange, legitimation, and justice.

The self is one of the most important concepts in microsociology, particularly in the general perspective of symbolic interaction. The self, as distinct from the psychological conceptualization of the personality, is fluid and adaptive to context. So the roles that an individual must fulfill might require him or her to be very structured in one context and very flexible and adaptive in another context. From the symbolic interaction perspective, individuals learn to define themselves in large part based upon how others see and interact with them. In this way individuals are constantly assessing and projecting different identities to themselves and others. This makes interaction fundamental to self-identity. Research within this area has focused on both qualitative and quantitative investigations of such topics as role taking, altercasting, identity disruptions or deflections, and self-referent behavior.

Group interactions themselves or types of encounters with others constitute other aspects of microsociology. Cooperation and competition were some of the earliest topics in microsociology, and they have endured in their importance. Early studies of group cohesion and identity were featured in Émile Durkheim's study of suicide, for example. More recent developments in the area examine differing incentive structures that lead toward or against cooperation. Much of this work has focused on social dilemmas, settings in which there is a conflict between individual short-term incentives and overall group incentives. Such dilemmas range from those found in dyadic relationships to larger groups such as those involved in collective movements.

Sometimes implicated in the level of cooperation and conflict or competition are characteristics of the individuals or of their positions within the group. Status is usually defined as a position in a social network, and the investigation of the development, maintenance, and diminishment of status has been pivotal in examining how groups organize and how resources are allocated. Commonly examined aspects of status are diffuse status characteristics such as ethnicity or sex and specific status characteristics such as accounting ability or ability to score soccer goals. Allocation of different resources is studied within exchange formulations, and the resulting assessments, behavior, and feelings of fairness are the focus of justice and equity formulations. Related to assessment of justice is the degree of acceptance of particular institutional arrangements or legitimation.

Microsociology incorporates many types of research methods, including case studies, documentary–historical studies, ethnomethodology, participant observation studies, surveys, and experiments. A particularly promising trend in research is the examination of the interrelationships between micro and macro phenomena. These developments do not begin with the assumption that either the micro or the macro *cause* the other; rather, they investigate how the different levels affect and are affected by each other.

SEE ALSO *Durkheim, Émile; Groups; Interactionism, Symbolic; Sociology*

BIBLIOGRAPHY

Coleman, James R. 1986. Social Theory, Social Research, and a Theory of Action. *American Journal of Sociology* 91: 1309–1335.

Lawler, Edward J., Cecilia Ridgeway, and Barry Markovsky. 1993. Structural Social Psychology and Micro-Macro Problem. *Sociological Theory* 11: 268–290.

Lovaglia, Michael J., Elizabeth A. Mannix, Charles D. Samuelson, Jane Sell, and Rick K. Wilson. 2005. Conflict, Power and Status in Groups. In *Theories of Small Groups: Interdisciplinary Perspectives*, eds. Marshall Scott Poole and Andrea B. Hollingshead, 139–184. Thousand Oaks, CA: Sage.

Jane Sell

SOCIOLOGY, OBJECTIVITY IN

SEE *Social Science, Value Free.*